Business Studies

AS Level

Third Edition

D1581678

Dave Hall • Rob Jones • Carlo Raffo

Edited by
Ian Chambers and Dave Gray

Acknowledgements

Dedication

To Elaine, Holly, Caitlin, Amanda Jane, Mandy, Sandra, Georgina, Rebecca, Jan, Natalie and Holly Anne for all their love and support in the writing of this book.

Cover design by Caroline Waring-Collins, illustration provided by Getty Images.

Graphics by Caroline Waring-Collins, Tim Button, Anneli Jameson and Rob Gittins.

Photography by Andrew Allen and Dave Gray.

Typing by Ingrid Hamer.

Proof reading by Mike Kidson, Heather Doyle and Tony Barnes.

Acknowledgements

The publishers would like to thank the following for the use of photographs and copyright material. Other copyright material is acknowledged at source. Agency central p 333, Corel pp 156,253,431,493, Digital Stock p 449, DigitalVision pp 6(b),230(tr),266,268,279,384(t),402,433, EasyJet p 341, Greenshop p 495, LocalLiberty.com p 10, Monster.co.uk p 336, PhotoArtistry p 17, Photodisc pp 26,44,66,99,105,129,135,136,138(tl),157,223,234,259,273,285,289,299,308, 330(tl,br), 354, 373(l), 383,384(bl),392,395,409,410(b),441,461,472, Pilkington Glass p 392, Renault p 459, Reg Vardy p 33, Retread Manufacturers Association p 495, Rex Features pp 19,314, Richer Sounds p 397, Stockbyte pp 6(t),11,21,49,67,101,138,175,203,206,225, 230(tl,b), 238,243,251,256,328,30(tr),342,360,370,373(r),390,410(t),413,450(br),491, The Associated Press pp 75,86,148,149,434, TopFoto pp 2(l),93,313,366, Vision Express p 336.

Office for National Statistics material is Crown Copyright, reproduced here with the permission of Her Majesty's Stationery Office.

Every effort has been made to locate the copyright owners of material used in this book. Any omissions brought to the notice of the publisher are regretted and will be credited in subsequent printings.

British Library Cataloguing in Publication Data

A catalogue record for this book is available from the British Library.

ISBN 1-902796-84-5

Causeway Press Limited

PO Box 13, Ormskirk, Lancs, L39 5HP

Contribution © Dave Hall, Rob Jones, Carlo Raffo, Ian Chambers, Dave Gray

1st impression, 2000 (reprinted twice)

3rd impression, 2004

Typesetting by Caroline Waring-Collins, Waring Collins Ltd.

Printed and bound by Legoprint, Italy.

Contents

Preface

Business Studies does not provide a step-by-step guide to how to be 'good at business'. There is no simple set of rules that can be applied at all times which will always be successful. However, by being analytical, rigorous and critical it may be possible to develop skills and approaches which can be useful, at certain times and in certain situations, when making business decisions. It is possible that different approaches will be used by different people in business and there may be disagreement as to which approach to take.

Business Studies is integrated and different areas of business are interdependent. There are links, for example, between:
- what is being produced and the funds available to pay for it (production and finance);
- the selling of the product and ethical considerations (marketing and ethics);
- the type of business and many aspects of its operation.

Being aware of these aspects of business will help us to understand how and why business decisions are made, and how they affect a variety of people, both within and outside the business. The aim of **Business Studies AS Level (Third Edition)** is to help those studying Business to understand business decisions and to be analytical, rigorous and critical in their business thinking. A number of features are included in the book which we believe will help this task.

Comprehensive course coverage The book contains material which should meet the demands of a wide range of courses. These include AS/A Level, Higher Grade, GCE in Applied Business, higher education and professional courses. The book is organised into 71 units across six sections:
- objectives, strategy and the business environment;
- marketing;
- accounting and finance;
- people in organisations;
- operations management;
- external influences.

In addition there are two units on study skills and assessment at the end. There is a development in the units contained in each section which reflects progress throughout a course and the requirements of different courses.

Guidance is given on exactly how the book can be used for specific courses in **Business Studies Teachers' Guide (Third Edition)**. To allow flexibility in course construction and teaching **Business Studies (Third Edition)** is available. It is a complete course book for A Level Business Studies and includes AS Level and A2 Level units. **Business Studies A2 Level (Third Edition)** is also available. It is designed for purchasers of **Business Studies AS Level (Third Edition)** and contains the A2 Level units in a separate book.

Flexible unit structure The unit structure allows the lecturer or teacher greater freedom to devise the course. Business Studies teachers and lecturers often teach different aspects of the course in different orders. So, whilst there is a logical order to the book, it has been written on the assumption that teachers or lecturers and students will piece the units together to suit their own teaching and learning needs and the requirements of the course being taught.

Cross referencing has been used in many of the units. This helps the teacher, lecturer or student to follow the course as they want. It will also be useful for modular courses and courses where Business Studies is only one part of the total course. The units in the book which relate to specific aspects of business, such as marketing or accounting, can be used in specialist courses or provide a short course in that area. Cross referencing also helps to stress the integrated nature of Business Studies and the interdependence and possible conflict that may exist in many areas.

Accessibility The book has been written in a clear and logical style which should make it accessible to all readers. Each unit is divided into short, easily manageable sections.

A workbook The text is interspersed with a large number of questions. The questions which appear as part of the units mostly refer to preceding information. Answers in most cases are expected to be relatively short. Questions are based on a variety of case studies, data, articles, photographs, etc. They should allow the student and teacher/lecturer to assess whether the information has been understood. Shorter 'knowledge' questions provide a means of revising each unit. A longer case study appears at the end of each unit. It draws on information contained in the whole unit and answers are expected to reflect this. The questions asked reflect the type which are set in examinations. They help students to develop knowledge, application, analysis and evaluation - the criteria used in examinations to assess responses.

Business Studies Teachers' Guide (Third Edition) provides suggested answers and mark schemes for the activities and questions that appear in this book.

Use of business examples, case studies and data Modern technology has allowed much of the book to proceed from manuscript to book form in a very short period. This has meant that we have been able to use the latest statistics and business examples available. Materials used have been chosen to demonstrate appropriate arguments and theories. They should, therefore, allow students to answer questions which require knowledge of what has happened 'in recent years' or 'over the past decade', as well as questions which deal with current debates.

Study skills and assessment The last two units in the book provide guidance on how to study and the methods of assessment used in Business Studies. They are presented in the form of a manual and are designed to be used at various stages throughout the course.

Key terms Many units contain a key terms section. Each section defines new concepts, which appear in capitals in the text of the unit. Taken together, they provide a comprehensive dictionary of business terms.

Presentation Great care has been taken with how the book has been presented. It is hoped that the layout of the book, the use of colour and the use of diagrams will help learning.

We would like to thank the following for their efforts in the preparation of the three editions of this book: Richard Dunill, for keeping the debate sharp and yet accessible; Ingrid Hamer for her long hours of typing; Nigel Lewis; Michael J. Forshaw and Chris Sawyer for bringing a 'real' accountant's view to the book; all staff and students at Bolton Sixth Form College, King George V College, Loreto College, and Manchester University School of Education; Diane Wallace and Steve Robertson for working on the early development of the book; Alain Anderton for sharing his style ideas.

Dave Hall   Rob Jones   Carlo Raffo
Ian Chambers   Dave Gray

1 Business Activity

What is business activity?

In 2003, Kelly Watson and her daughter Ruth opened a cafe in Coventry. Both had previous experience in catering. Kelly had spent the last seven years working in a school canteen, whilst Ruth had been employed by McDonald's when she was a sixth form student. Kelly invested £9,000 to help fund the setting up of the business. They called the cafe 'The Cathedral', due to its location near to the city's famous landmark. They planned to target the student market and cathedral visitors. Before trading began they had to:

- obtain a £3,000 bank loan;
- obtain a five year lease on a suitable property;
- line the kitchen with aluminium panels to conform with health and safety regulations;
- obtain a fire certificate;
- decorate the cafe area;
- buy furniture and kitchen equipment;
- find suppliers of fresh food;
- advertise the cafe in the local university.

Kelly and Ruth had different roles to play in the business. Kelly was responsible for dealing with suppliers and preparing the food. Ruth ran the cafe area. This involved waiting on tables, taking money and socialising with the customers.

Ruth and Kelly worked very long hours. The cafe opened from 8.00 am to 7.00 pm, every day of the week except Sunday. However, it was worth it because the business became successful. The Cathedral developed a reputation for good value food and a great atmosphere. After six months they were able to employ two university students to help during busy periods.

The above case illustrates many features of business activity.

- Business activity produces an **output** – a good or service. A cafe service is being provided by Kelly and Ruth.
- Goods and services are **consumed**. Cafe customers consume the service provided by Kelly and Ruth.
- **Resources** are used up. Money, food and drinks, furniture, staff, gas and electricity are just a few of the resources used by Kelly and Ruth.
- A number of business **functions** may be carried out. Administration (the paper work), managing staff (human resources) and decisions about marketing, finance and production are some examples.
- Businesses can be affected by **external factors**. The government's commitment to increasing the numbers of students in higher education may have boosted the number of students in Coventry.

Figure 1.1 shows a diagram which illustrates the nature of business activity. All types of business may be represented by this diagram - a building society, a window cleaner, a multinational chemical company, a shoe manufacturer or the BBC.

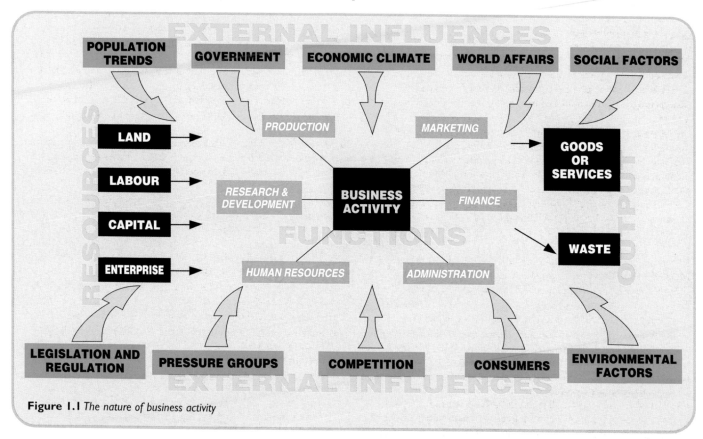

Figure 1.1 *The nature of business activity*

Business resources

Businesses use resources or FACTORS OF PRODUCTION in business activity. These are usually divided into four groups.

Land Land is not just a 'plot of land' where business premises might be located. It also includes natural resources, such as coal, diamonds, forests, rivers and fertile soil. The owners of land receive **rent** from those who use it.

Business activity uses both **renewable** and **non-renewable** resources. Renewable resources are those like fish, forests and water which nature replaces. Examples of non-renewable land resources are mineral deposits like coal and diamonds, which once used are never replaced. There has been concern in recent years about the rate at which renewable resources are being used. For example, overfishing in the North Sea has led to claims by the International Council for the Exploration of the Sea that cod stocks are now so low that fishing should stop until they recover. The number of young cod in the North Sea in early 2003 was the lowest in 20 years.

Labour Labour is the workforce of business. Manual workers, skilled workers and management are all members of the workforce. They are paid **wages** or **salaries** for their services. The quality of individual workers will vary considerably. Each worker is unique, possessing a different set of characteristics, skills, knowledge, intelligence and emotions.

It is possible to improve the quality of **human resources** through training and education. Human resources become more productive if money is invested by business or government in training and education.

Capital Capital is sometimes described as the **artificial** resource because it is made by labour. Capital refers to the tools, machinery and equipment which businesses use. For example, JCB makes mechanical diggers which are used by the construction industry. Capital also refers to the money which the owners use to set up a business (☞ unit 32). Owners of capital receive **interest** if others borrow it.

Enterprise Enterprise has a special role in business activity. The **entrepreneur** or businessperson develops a business idea and then hires and organises the other three factors of production to carry out the activity. Entrepreneurs also take risks because they will often use some personal money to help set up the business. If the business does not succeed the entrepreneur may lose some or all of that money. If the business is successful, any money left over will belong to the entrepreneur. This is called **profit**.

IKEA manufactures and supplies a wide range of furniture and household goods. It also provides office furniture for the home and office accessories. The company, based in Sweden, sells many of its products in flat-packs, which are assembled by customers who buy them.

(a) Suggest examples of land, labour and capital that IKEA may be using.
(b) Using IKEA's products as an example, distinguish between consumer goods and capital goods.

Question 1

Business functions

Figure 1.1 showed that business activity involves a number of functions. A business is a SYSTEM - it has parts that work together to achieve an objective. The functions are all parts of the system. A business is also part of other systems such as the economic and political systems (☞ unit 9). What functions does a business carry out?

● **Production** involves changing natural resources into a product or the supply of a service. Most business resources are used up in the production process. Examples of production can be seen on a building site where houses are constructed, in a dental surgery where dental treatment is given and in a coal mine where coal is extracted.

● **Marketing** has become very important in recent years due to an increase in competition in business. It is concerned with identifying consumer needs and satisfying them. Examples of marketing activities are market research, advertising, packaging, promotion, distribution and pricing.

● The **finance** department is responsible for the control of money in a business. It has a number of important duties. This includes recording transactions, producing documents to illustrate the performance of the business and its financial position and controlling the flow of money in the business.

● Dealing with enquiries, communicating messages and producing documents for the workforce are all examples of **administrative** tasks.

● The **human resources** function involves the management of people. The personnel department looks after the welfare of the workforce, and is responsible for such things as recruitment, selection, training, appraisal, health and safety, equal opportunities, payment systems and worker disputes.

● **Research and development (R&D)** involves technical research, for example, research into a new medicine or a new production technique. R&D can be very expensive. Consequently, many businesses do not have a R&D department but rely on adapting new products and new technology developed by other companies.

In a large business these functions should be easy to identify. However, a self-employed window cleaner will also carry out these functions.

● Production - cleaning windows.
● Marketing - distributing business cards to potential customers.
● Administration - dealing with enquiries from potential customers and recording their personal details in preparation for a first visit.
● Human resources management - recruiting and supervising part time helpers during busy periods.
● Finance - keeping records of all financial transactions.

Business activity is highly **integrated**. For example, production is heavily influenced by marketing activities. If marketing is effective and more of the product is sold, then more will have to be produced. Also, the finance department, for example, will carefully watch the amount of money used by other departments.

What does business activity produce?

All business activity results in the production of a good or a service. CONSUMER GOODS are those which are sold to the general public. They fall into two categories.

● **Durable goods** such as cookers, televisions, books, cars and furniture can be used repeatedly for a long period of time.

● **Non-durable goods** such as food, confectionery, newspapers and shoe polish are used very soon after they are purchased. Some of these goods are called **fast moving consumer goods**, such as soap, crisps and cornflakes.

CAPITAL GOODS are those goods purchased by businesses and used to produce other goods. Tools, equipment and machinery are examples of capital goods.

The supply of **services** has grown in recent years. Banking, insurance, hairdressing, car valeting and gardening are examples of this type of business activity.

Business activity also results in the production of waste materials. Most waste is useless and some waste, like radioactive nuclear waste, is very dangerous and expensive to dispose of. Some production techniques result in **by-products** which can be sold. For example, the brewing process generates yeast which is used by the producers of Marmite.

External factors

Business activity is affected by a number of external forces, some of which are shown in the diagram in Figure 1.1. These are beyond the control of the individual business. In some cases they constrain a firm's decisions and may prevent its growth and development.

● **The government** has a great deal of influence over business activity. In most countries the government will be in favour of business development. A **legal framework**, where all individuals abide by the law and offenders are punished, will help this. A country also needs an **infrastructure** including roads, railways, telecommunications, schools and hospitals. Some of these items may be provided by the state (☞ unit 7). Government policy can also influence business. For example, profits and many goods and services which businesses produce are taxed.

● The **economic climate** can have an impact on business activity. For example, over the period 1993-2003 the UK economy was relatively stable. Interest rates and price increases were relatively low, whilst unemployment fell steadily. These stable economic conditions allowed business activity to flourish. During this time the best performing economy in the EU was the UK's.

● **World events** can influence business activity. The attack on

---

Research 'stunted by our culture of protest'
Public opposition against high-technology and biotechnology companies has grown so strong that investors are no longer willing to support start-up companies involved in genetically modified products or those working on animals. This warning came after a survey by Grant Thornton, the business advisers. A spokesperson for the survey said that it was desperately trying to raise money in the UK for genetic modification or anything involving animals. Companies can't get enough funds and many of them are selling out to US companies. Huntingdon Life Sciences, an animal research laboratory, was forced to move its HQ to the US after intimidation by protesters.

Flights cancelled because of strike in France
In May 2003 travellers flying between Britain and France faced disruption to their journeys as a result of a strike by French air traffic controllers. British Airways, BMI, Ryanair, EasyJet and Aer Lingus were forced to cancel most of their flights to France. Passengers were promised refunds or free flights at a future date.

Source: adapted from the *Financial Times*, 27.5.2003.

(a) What is meant by the term 'external factors'?
(b) Identify the effects that they might have had in the above cases.

the Twin Towers in New York in 2001 and the military action against Iraq in 2003 affected a number of industries. There was a fall in the number of passengers travelling by air in many countries. This affected the aviation industry. There was also a fall in the number of holidaymakers which affected the tourist industry. It often takes many years for businesses to recover from such events. In some cases they may fail to survive and go bankrupt.

● Some individuals form **pressure groups** (☞ unit 70). For example, Transport 2000 is a pressure group that promotes ways of reducing the environmental and social impact of transport. It aims to reduce the use of cars and encourages individuals to use public transport, walk and cycle. If Transport 2000 is influential, the car industry is likely to be adversely affected.

● **Consumers' tastes** change. In recent years there has been an increase in demand for garden products. Gardens and gardening have been popularised by a number of television programmes on gardening. There has also been a rise in demand for vegetarian and vegan foodstuffs. Increasing numbers of people are opting for non-meat diets.

● Changes in **population** can affect the demand for products and the supply of workers. For example, the ageing of the population in the UK has meant increasing numbers of people aged 60 or over still looking for work. It has also given opportunities to businesses with products aimed at

this age groups, such as Saga holidays.

● Most businesses face **competition** from other firms. Rivals' activities often have an influence on their operations. Following the introduction of the National Lottery in the UK a number of firms in the gaming industry, such as Littlewoods the pools company and Ladbrokes the betting shop chain, suffered reductions in turnover.

● **Social factors** may influence business activity from time to time. For example, the roles of women in society have changed considerably in recent years. This has meant that more women have become involved in business management and business ownership. Some businesses have also been prepared to offer creche facilities as women have returned to work.

● **Environmental factors** have had a major effect on businesses in recent years. Some now use recycled materials in their manufacturing processes to reduce costs. Certain businesses have tried to manufacture products which are environmentally friendly in order to boost sales.

● **Legislation** and **regulation** may influence business activity. This may be in the form of government imposed laws, EU regulations, independent bodies set up by government to regulate industry or industry self-regulation.

Satisfying needs and wants

The success of a business activity depends on many factors. The most important is to supply a product that consumers want to buy. Businesses must satisfy consumers' NEEDS and WANTS to be successful. People's needs are limited. They include things which are needed to survive, such as food, warmth, shelter and security. Humans also have psychological and emotional needs such as recognition and love. Wants, however are infinite. People constantly aim for a better quality of life, which might include better housing, better health care, better education, longer holidays, and more friends. Unit 9 deals with the way in which an economy attempts to satisfy people's needs.

Markets

The **goods** and **services** produced by businesses are sold in MARKETS. A market exists when buyers and sellers communicate in order to exchange goods and services. In some cases buyers and sellers might meet at an agreed place to carry out the exchange. For example, many villages and towns have regular open air markets where buyers and sellers exchange goods and services. Also, buying and selling can be carried out over the telephone. For example, the First Direct banking facility allows customers to conduct nearly all of their banking business over the telephone. Buying and selling can also take place in shopping centres, in newspapers and magazines, through mail order, and more recently, through television and the Internet.

The goods and services of most businesses are bought by CUSTOMERS and used by CONSUMERS to satisfy their wants and needs. A business may be interested in some of the following markets.

- Consumer goods markets - where products like food, cosmetics and magazines are sold in large quantities.
- Markets for services - these are varied and could include services for individuals, such as banking, or services for industry, such as cleaning.
- Capital goods markets - where items used by other businesses are bought and sold, such as machinery.
- Labour markets - where people are hired for their services.
- The housing market - where people buy and sell properties.
- Money markets - where people and institutions borrow and lend money, such as commercial banks.
- Commodity markets - where raw materials such as copper and coffee are bought, mainly by business.

Specialisation

One feature of modern businesses is SPECIALISATION. This is the production of a limited range of goods by an individual, firm, region or country. Specialisation can take place between firms. For example, McDonald's provides a limited range of fast foods, Ford manufactures cars, Heinz processes food products and MFI manufactures and sells

Optos Retinal was set up by Douglas Anderson in Dunfermline in 1992. It produces retinal scanning machines. The business idea came to Douglas when he witnessed the shortcomings of eye-imaging tools after taking his young son for an eye examination. The examination process was distressing, requiring the patient to sit still for long periods with uncomfortable coloured eye drops. Anderson already owned an industrial design business and promptly instructed his design team to come up with a solution. The result was the Optomap Exam. This is a machine that uses two low-powered lasers to scan the retina at the back of the eye. It takes just a quarter of a second and does not use coloured eye drops. The images generated by the machine can be displayed instantly and sent by email to eye specialists for analysis.

So far, 630 of the machines have been installed and more than a million patients in Britain and America have benefited from the Optomap Exam. The machines are expensive, costing £70,000 each. However, Optos gives them to hospitals and surgeries and charges £25 each time they are used. In 2002 Optos was the fastest growing technology company in the country. Sales grew from £209,000 in 2000 to £3.7 million in 2002.

Source: adapted from *The Sunday Times*, 28.9.2003.

(a) Using the case as an example, explain what is meant by specialisation.
(b) Explain how Optos might benefit from specialisation.

furniture products. Examples of regional specialisation might be Kidderminster, which specialises in carpet production, Stoke-on-Trent, which produces pottery and Kent, which is one of the country's main hop growers. Different countries also specialise. For example, it could be argued that Scotland specialises in the distilling of whisky, Saudi Arabia in oil extraction and South Africa in the supply of gold.

Specialisation within a firm is an important part of production. Departments specialise in different activities, such as marketing, purchasing, personnel and finance. People specialise in different tasks and skills. This is called the DIVISION OF LABOUR and allows people to concentrate on the task or skill at which they are best. In business, production is divided amongst workers, who each concentrate on a limited range of tasks. For example, the building of a house involves an architect to draw up the plans, a bricklayer to build the structure, a joiner to undertake woodwork, a roofer to lay the tiles etc. It is argued that the division of labour raises the productivity and efficiency of business and the economy. There is a number of reasons for this.

- Workers can concentrate on the tasks that they do best, leaving other tasks to more specialist workers.
- People's skills are improved by carrying out tasks over a long period of time. It is also possible to develop a brand new skill.
- Time is saved because workers are not constantly changing tasks, moving from one area to another or collecting new tools.
- The organisation of production becomes easier and more effective.

Specialisation, however, does have disadvantages.

- Work can become tedious and boring. This can result in poor worker motivation with the likelihood of a higher rate of absenteeism and increased staff turnover.
- Problems can also occur when one stage of production depends on another stage. If one stage breaks down, production might be halted.
- Over-specialisation can pose problems when there is a change in demand. If people are only competent in one skill they may have to retrain, causing delays in production. Some are not able to retrain and become unemployed.

The importance of money

MONEY is anything which is generally accepted as a means of exchange. It is essential for the smooth exchange of goods and services in markets and helps specialisation.

Without money goods have to be exchanged using a BARTER SYSTEM. This involves swapping goods directly, which is inefficient. It is necessary for the wants of individuals to be perfectly matched. Searching for the perfect match in a barter deal can be very time consuming. It is also difficult to value different goods without money. In addition, giving change can be a problem when the values of the goods being exchanged do not match exactly. Money also has a number of other functions. It:

● allows individuals to save some of their income and buy goods and services at a later date;

● enables all goods and services to be valued in common units, for example, a house which costs £60,000 is worth exactly 10 times more than a car which is valued at £6,000;

● allows payments to be deferred, ie goods can be bought and payment made at a later date.

There is no single definition of the money supply. No financial asset has all the characteristics or fulfils all the functions of money perfectly. In the UK, two measures tend to be used by the government. M0 is a 'narrow' measure. It includes notes and coins in circulation, cash in banks' tills and cash held for operational reasons at the Bank of England. M4 is a 'broad' measure. It includes M0 plus a wider range of financial assets. These include money held in bank accounts by the private sector and building society deposits. Cheques, debit cards and credit cards are not money. They are a means of transferring money from one account to another.

Classification of business activity

Business activity is often classed by the type of production that takes place.

PRIMARY PRODUCTION includes activity which takes the natural resources from the earth, ie the extraction of raw materials and the growing of food. Mining, fishing, farming and forestry are examples of primary business activity. SECONDARY PRODUCTION involves manufacturing, processing and construction which transform raw materials into goods. Car production, distilling, baking, shipbuilding and office construction are examples of secondary sector activity. TERTIARY PRODUCTION includes the provision of services. Hairdressing, distribution, security, banking, theatre and tourism are all examples of business activity in this area. Other methods of classifying business include by:

● size (☞ unit 56);
● geographical area;
● sector (☞ units 6 and 7);
● ownership (☞ unit 6).

What are the trends in business activity?

Business activity does not follow a constant pattern. Different industries grow and decline over time. In the UK some major changes have occurred in the structure of the economy. Before the Industrial Revolution most of the UK's resources were used for primary production. This included industries such as agriculture and mining. During the nineteenth century, secondary production expanded rapidly. The Industrial Revolution resulted in a growing quantity of resources being employed in manufacturing.

Figure 1.2 shows the numbers of males and females employed in manufacturing and services between 1978 and 2000.

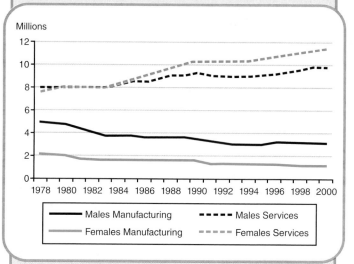

Figure 1.2 *Employment in manufacturing and services by gender*

Source: adapted from Office for National Statistics.

(a) What evidence is there in the graph to suggest that de-industrialisation has continued throughout the period shown?

(b) Explain two possible reasons why retail services may have grown sharply in recent years.

Question 4

Over the last fifty years tertiary production has grown at the expense of secondary production. The decline in manufacturing is often called DE-INDUSTRIALISATION. The process of de-industrialisation has resulted in the decline of some once prosperous industries, such as shipbuilding, textiles, steel and engineering. Certain reasons have been put forward to explain the decline including:

● changes in consumer demand;
● a lack of competitiveness amongst UK manufacturers;
● increasing competition from overseas manufacturers;
● a lack of investment in manufacturing;
● trade union restrictive practices;
● unhelpful government policy.

In contrast, service industries now account for over 70 per cent of the UK's national incoome. Financial services, personal services, household services and the leisure industry are just some growth areas. For example, in the late 1990s and early 2000s the profile of the football industry was raised significantly. A number of clubs floated on the stock exchange and the amount of money flowing into the industry rose. Indeed, in 2003 a Russian billionaire took over Chelsea FC and injected millions of his own money into the club. Media interest increased, attendances at matches in the Premier League were high and commercial activities began to flourish.

The overall trend in business activity suggests a growth in services at the expense of primary and secondary production. Care needs to be taken when identifying trends from figures. For example, output in one particular service industry may be growing but employment figures may be falling. This could be because businesses in the industry are replacing workers with technology or are reorganising to reduce the workforce. However, employment figures do show clearly the changing patterns of business activity.

key terms

Barter system - a system of exchange which involves the swapping of goods between individuals.

Capital goods - goods used to produce other goods, such as tools, equipment and machinery.

Consumers - individuals who use or 'consume' goods and services to satisfy their needs and wants.

Consumer goods - goods produced for general use by the public. They can be durable and non-durable.

Customers - individuals who buy goods and services supplied by businesses.

De-industrialisation - the decline in manufacturing.

Division of labour - specialisation in specific tasks or skills by individuals.

Factors of production - resources used by business to produce goods and services.

Markets - anywhere that buyers and sellers communicate to exchange goods and services.

Money - any substance which is generally accepted as a means of exchange.

Needs - human requirements which must be satisfied for survival.

Primary production - activities which involve the extraction of raw materials from the earth and the growing of food.

Secondary production - activities such as manufacturing which transform raw materials into finished goods.

Specialisation - in business, the production of a limited range of goods.

System - parts that work together to achieve an objective; a system can be a communications system, a business, an economic or a political system.

Tertiary production - activities which involve the provision of services.

Wants - human desires which are unlimited.

Knowledge ...Knowledge...Knowledge...Knowledge...Knowledge...Know

1. What are the 4 factors of production?
2. What is the financial reward paid to each factor of production?
3. Why is capital said to be an artificial resource?
4. Describe 6 functions involved in business activity.
5. Why is business activity highly integrated?
6. Explain the difference between needs and wants.
7. What is the difference between capital and consumer goods?
8. What is meant by specialisation in business?
9. State:
   (a) 3 advantages of specialisation;
   (b) 3 disadvantages of specialisation.
10. Briefly describe the role of money in business.
11. List 10 business activities in your local town. State which of these are examples of:
    (a) primary production;
    (b) secondary production;
    (c) tertiary production.
12. What are the possible causes of de-industrialisation?

Case study Eurocars

Sisters Gina and Toni Wilson grew up in a family that had been in the car trade for almost a century. From an early age they worked in vehicle rental, spare parts and car sales at their father's garage. After seeing the vehicle import business grow from 17,800 units in 1998 to 141,000 two years later, Gina decided to 'get a piece of the action'. She rented an office, employed one person and began importing cars from mainland Europe. Eurocars was born. After one year Gina took on her sister as sales director and appointed Stephen Hunt as managing director. Stephen was an expert at finding new cars at low prices.

The venture proved to be an immediate success. Indeed, the company expanded from their premises in Epsom, Surrey, where they had 25 cars on the forecourt, to an additional site in Cheam where they had 150 new cars and vans. They also had another 400 cars in stock in Britain and a further 1,000 in stock in mainland Europe.

The company concentrates on 'bread and butter' models rather than specialist or prestige cars. Customers are attracted by the low prices. They can save around £2,500 on the list price when buying from Eurocars. They are also reassured when they see that the cars are actually in stock. Eurocars used to sell cars to both dealers and individuals. However, they are now concentrating more on the retail trade because margins are higher.

The business is benefiting from a change in the law designed to increase competition in the sale of new cars. However, manufacturers are still trying to protect their own dealer outlets and do their best to thwart discounters such as Eurocars. For example, continental dealers often find it difficult to provide right-hand-drive UK-specification cars. 'Convertibles, for example, will be mysteriously delayed until after the summer is over', says Toni. Another problem faced by Eurocars is the amount of administration required when importing the cars. There are registration laws to deal with and payments for the cars have to be made in Euros. Also, Eurocars is vulnerable to tactical promotions used by the manufacturers' own dealers. For example, when a manufacturer announces a '£1,000 cash back' offer on a new car, it immediately affects Eurocars' business.

Source: adapted from *The Sunday Times*.

(a) Is the business activity of Eurocars in the primary, secondary or tertiary sector? Explain your answer. (4 marks)

(b) Suggest examples of land, labour and capital that might be used by Eurocars. (6 marks)

(c) Explain:
   (i) the type of market that Eurocars is operating in;
   (ii) the types of customer it serves. (12 marks)

(d) To what extent is Eurocars affected by external factors? (18 marks)

2 Starting a Business

Setting up in business

What do ICI, Virgin, Starbucks, your nearest newsagent and the local window cleaner all have in common? At some time in the past, these businesses have been set up by their owners. Many, though not all, began as small operations. They are often started by entrepreneurs (☞ unit 3) working in a small shop or factory, or from home. Alan Sugar, the businessman behind Amstrad, started by convincing customers they really were buying the last television he had left in his flat. The Body Shop began as one retail outlet opened in Brighton by Anita Roddick, having previously sold her own cosmetics. According to Barclays Bank, 342,000 starts-up took place in 2001. This was down 15 per cent on the previous year, although slightly higher than in 1997-98.

There are certain steps involved in setting up a business. They are shown in Figure 2.1 and explained in this unit. They include deciding whether to set up in business, coming up with an idea, considering its success, planning the business, getting advice and finance, and then setting up and running the business.

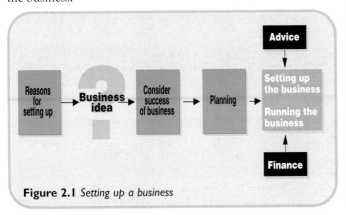

Figure 2.1 Setting up a business

Implications

What faces a person setting up their own business? He or she will come up against many problems and challenges. The way in which the entrepreneur works will probably be different to that of an employee. Take an example of a chef who has decided to 'go it alone' and open a cafe specialising in crepes and pancakes. At first, the chef would be uncertain about whether there is demand for this type of meal. Arguably this risk never goes away, but it is likely to be far greater at first until regular customers visit the cafe. The earnings of the chef are also likely to vary, depending on sales. Working for an employer, he would have earned a regular wage or salary.

The responsibility for the business would fall onto the owner. This means problems, from the non-delivery of ingredients to the placing of local adverts, will fall onto the chef. Even if employees are hired, the responsibility falls onto the owner. Many business people find that great personal commitment is needed. They must also be able to come up with new ideas and 'keep going' even if things get tough. This means the person must be single minded and self-sufficient.

Organisation of time is very important. He must decide what is to be done and place tasks in order of priority. He must also decide if the task can be done by someone else, ie what to **delegate.** Many people who set up in business talk about the lack of time to get things done. Working from 6am until midnight every night of the week is likely in the early stages. This places great stress on their personal and social life and their family and friends.

Entrepreneurs must also consider the skills they have and whether they are enough. Working for an employer may demand skill as a chef. This technical skill will be important to the cafe. However, the chef will also need management skills. These range from making sure that correct materials and equipment are available to having effective stock control. As workers are hired, the entrepreneur must develop personnel skills to control, motivate and organise the workforce. The owner will also need to sell himself and the company, a skill that is unlikely to be part of his role as an employee. Most people find that their technical skills are much greater than their managerial skills. It is often this lack of managerial skills which leads to problems. If a skill is needed which the entrepreneur does not have, he can:

- retrain, although there may be little time to attend a course and available courses are not always designed for specific needs;
- hire full time employees with the necessary skills;
- employ a specialist, such as an accountant, designer or market research agency, ideally for 'one off' tasks so that they do not become a full time cost;
- find a partner or take over another business. This is dealt with later.

Reasons for setting up

Why do people set up in business?
- Independence. Some people prefer to make their own decisions and take responsibility rather than being told what to do.
- To increase rewards. People setting up their own business often believe that they will earn more than if they were working for an employer.
- As a result of redundancy. Some businesses start when an employee is made redundant and decides to use her skills in her own venture. **Redundancy payments** can be used to fund the business.
- Commitment to a product. A business may be set up to sell a new invention or because of commitment to a product. For example, James Dyson took five years and 5,127 prototypes before creating a working model of the best selling vacuum cleaner. 10 years later, after rejection by many companies, he produced the product under his own name.

- Sometimes people extend their hobbies into a business. A stamp collector may set up a small stall at local markets, for example.
- To satisfy creative needs. A worker on a production line packing biscuits may be artistic. Setting up a business to paint portraits may allow the individual to satisfy these needs.
- A person may want to work in a particular job, but can't find employment. Someone who has trained as a hairdresser or joiner may find that setting up their own business is the only alternative to being unemployed.
- An employee may be dissatisfied with their job. Setting up in business is one alternative to looking for a job with another firm.

Getting a business idea

Anyone setting up a business must first have a business idea before they can begin. It might be a specialist shop selling items for a dolls house, a door to door hairdressing service or a company producing computers. The ideas for a business can come from many places.

- It might be an idea based on the existing skills the entrepreneur learned when doing another job.
- It might be an idea from a colleague at work or someone else in business.
- It might be an adaptation of an existing product where the entrepreneur thinks that they can do better.
- It might be a 'gap in the market' found by an entrepreneur that no other business is doing at the moment. For example, they might find that they need a product at home, but can't buy exactly what they need.
- It might be based on **market research** (☞ unit 12). It is unlikely that a new entrepreneur will have the finance to carry out detailed market research. However, simple research such as observation of customers entering a shop or a questionnaire given to a sample (☞ unit 12) of potential buyers might be possible.

The chances of success

Many businesses that are set up fail within a few years. The Department for Trade and Industry has estimated that a quarter of all business start-ups fail within the first eighteen months and 35 per cent fail after five years. If a business is going to be a success, the entrepreneur must consider a number of factors. Any one of these factors may be important. The Showering family made fine cider at a good profit in Somerset. When they produced a high quality drink from pears, in a champagne-like bottle, and called it Babycham, they became millionaires.

Take an example of someone aiming to produce and sell training shoes. There is a number of questions that may help to make this idea into a success.

The basic business idea What business is the person entering and what will be sold? It may be better to sell 'high quality and performance sports shoes' rather than just 'trainers'. Who are the customers? It may be possible to target an audience, such as 25-35 year olds in a certain income bracket. How is the product used? The shoes could be designed to be hard wearing for sports, or with fashion in mind.

Philip Barthelemy runs a web-based Internet site, LocalLiberty.com, which allows members to exchange their DVDs and video games on a face to face and legal basis. Philip was sitting in a friend's flat one wet New Years Day, looking at his DVD collection. There were over 50 DVDs, most of which had been played only once or twice. His friend had all these DVDs, but could not make use of them. So Philip thought 'why not make use of this capital?'

People are increasingly building up DVD and video games collections. Most are played only a few times and not used again. They could be exchanged with others, so that people can then spend their money on different items. This gives them more choice. Philip argues that it also allows people to meet new acquaintances and make new friends.

Philip stopped work in his job at the end of 2002 to concentrate on his business. He estimates that he works on average 60 hours a week, which is closer to 80 at peak periods. He argues 'you have to organise your day differently' and 'get out of the comfort zone'.

Philip mainly works from home to keep costs down at the start. At the moment it's just him in the business. But this could change in future. He outsources all his main key tasks.

This wasn't Philip's first business idea. But it is the first he has been comfortable with. The business needed an initial investment to start it and funding to research the idea And it would need extra funding until money comes in regularly.

Philip also realises that he will have to be flexible to squeeze down costs as much as possible at the beginning. Philip suggests that companies like Napster and eBay had inspired him. They had been successful companies that had set up for Internet trading. It is likely that much of the work he puts in at the beginning will not be remunerated. But this is only to be expected, Philip believes.

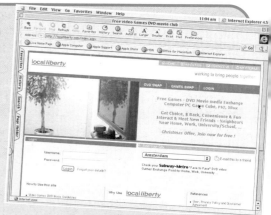

Source: adapted from startups.co.uk.

(a) Identify the ways in which Philip got ideas for his business.
(b) Explain the implications for Philip of starting his own business.

Question 1

Finding out about the market How many products exist already? Customers may prefer other types of shoes for fashion wear or a different type of design. What are the strengths and weaknesses of the competition? It may be possible to find a gap in the market, such as trainers that can be used for hiking, water sports or with a special design feature, such as a cut away back with flexible material.

It may possible to find out about the market using market research techniques (☞ unit 12). This might be through:

● desk or secondary research to find information already gathered for another purpose. An example could be looking at a Mintel report on a particular market;

● field or primary research to gather material for a specific reason which is not collected elsewhere. An example might be a questionnaire given to possible customers.

Small or new businesses may have a restricted budget. They might only be able to carry out a small survey of their own or have limited funds to hire a market research company.

Marketing and promotion What price can be charged? It may be possible to undercut competitors' prices or sell initially at less than unit cost (☞ unit 19) until the product begins to sell well. Can the business compete in some other way, such as advertising? American advertisers argue that every product has a **unique selling point** or **proposition** (USP) (☞ unit 15). The business could identify this and promote it. For example, the trainers may be 'comfortable, but robust'. How will the product be sold? The producer may sell through a retailer, representative or direct to the public, for example.

Small or new businesses might have a limited budget to spend on marketing and promotion. They might decide to find relatively cheaper ways of promoting products, such as:

● advertising in local magazines and newspapers, adding their names to trade directories, sending out leaflets by direct mail, offering discounts at first to build loyalty, and setting up an Internet website;

rather than more expensive methods such as:

● advertising on television, using national magazines or publications with glossy advertisements, making use of large national advertising agencies or advertising abroad.

People What are the main skills needed to run the business? What skills are needed to manufacture the product? The sports shoe manufacturer may need the skills of a designer or perhaps a sports scientist before production can begin. How workers can be attracted and retained in the business must also be considered. How much do you know about legislation regarding employment? The entrepreneur will have to take into account the health and safety of employees, for example.

Finance How much money is needed to start up? The business person will need to work out the costs of setting up, eg rent and rates, wages, machinery, sales and distribution costs and professional fees. How much is available to invest? The business person may have savings or insurance policies which can be

Monoli spent a number years working in the insurance industry. Then she decided to act on her friends' advice and set up a restaurant in London. Friends were always telling her that she should cook for a living. They were particularly impressed with the unusual desserts and cakes which she served.

Monoli did a food hygiene and a licence trader's course when she decided to set up. Most of the funding came from herself and a non-active business partner. She attributed her success to 'common sense along with creativity in the kitchen'. However, she also argues that years of dealing with customer claims has also given her a great insight into meeting consumer needs and the single most important thing is 'the personal touch - being flexible and accommodating'. She also argues that when starting your own business you need 'an unshakeable belief in what you're aiming to do and 100 per cent commitment'. This is shown in the 80-90 hour week which she works.

The business is doing very well at the moment. There's a two week waiting list for a table on Thursdays, Fridays and Saturdays. The business offers an early evening theatre menu at reduced prices, which has proved very popular.

Customers have asked Monoli if she is going to set up another branch of the restaurant. She is considering this for the future and has asked her business partner if he wants to put more money into the business. She feels that it might take a long time before another restaurant is profitable. And can she find people with the flair to make her desserts in exactly the style of her current restaurant?

Source: adapted in part from startups.co.uk.

(a) Examine the factors that might influence the success of this business.

Question 2

used. According to HSBC only 50 per cent of businesses borrow from a bank. Many people use redundancy cheques or sell their house to raise finance. Over and above the initial investment, how much more will be required before cash flows into the business? The sports shoe manufacturer may have orders but no cash flowing in until goods are sold. In the meantime, bills must still be paid. Often an overdraft is negotiated with the bank to see the business through this period. What other sources of finance can be used? According to the Bank of England trade credit is twice as important as bank loans as a source of finance. If the entrepreneur approaches a third party to fund start up costs, control may be lost.

The product or service offered Is the product or service ready for sale? If not, how far has it been developed? It is unlikely that the sports shoe manufacturer will find a backer for the business if the idea has not yet been developed. Is the product idea safe? It may be possible to protect the idea by PATENT or COPYRIGHT before production takes place. A patent aims to protect the inventor of a new product or process. A business may apply to the Patent Office to obtain a patent. It allows a business to design, produce and sell an invention for a number of years free from competition. During this period, the invention cannot be copied by competitors.

Is production cost effective? The manufacturer may want to consider the way the shoe is produced, the location of production, how production is organised and the materials used. Each of these will affect the cost and speed of production.

Risk, timescale and cost What are the main risks involved in the venture? How can they be reduced? The producer may try the product on a small scale basis before trading or work part time while still employed to reduce risk.

Planning

Although there are examples of businesses that just 'set up and prosper', these are limited. Most firms must plan carefully what they aim to achieve and how to do it. Answering the question 'what might make a business successful?' will help a business to produce a BUSINESS PLAN. This is a statement that outlines the way that the business will achieve its aims and objectives (☞ unit 4).

An established business may produce a business plan to show how it will obtain the funds to pay back a loan for a new piece of machinery. For a business starting up, a business plan is vital. It can be used to:

● give a clear idea of its direction and operation;
● show a bank or other institution its likely position and its ability to pay back a loan;
● identify problems that may occur to allow the business to deal with them before they can become a problem;
● highlight its strengths and weaknesses.

What is included in a business plan? Table 2.1 shows the details that might appear in the plan of a business aiming to produce and sell specialist cycle equipment.

Getting advice

There is a variety of organisations that provide help and advice for new businesses. They range from those set up by government or private organisations to individuals with

---

Look at Figure 2.2 which shows part of a business plan of a small business selling signed and numbered limited edition artists' etchings, greetings cards and picture frames.
Figure 2.2

c Major competitors - their prices, strengths and weaknesses:
Major competition is from 'Anystore' which has a well-known prints department, but this helps more often than not, as customers are drawn to the area and the small print gallery is cheaper.
Other competition is from all of the other shops selling gift items, but again they draw custom into the area.
Strengths of the small print gallery are:
Something for everyone at any price level. Once it is bought people cannot tell how much it costs.
Numbered handmade prints are exclusive and special, and possibly an investment for the future.
Weaknesses of the competition are that they are more expensive and less flexible. Jewellers, for instance have nothing under £18.00.

Source: *The Business Start-up Guide,* NatWest Bank.

(a) Explain how competition can:
  (i) help;
  (ii) harm;
  the business.
(b) If an entrepreneur was applying for a loan, why might a bank manager be interested in this information?

Question 3

Table 2.1

Features	What is included	Examples
The business	Name and address of the business What the business aims to achieve Type of organisation	Cross-Hatchard Partnership
The product or service	What is being produced What quantities will be produced The proposed price	Specialist cycles Average price £300
The market	Results of research or testing The size of the market If the market is growing or not Who will buy the product Competition and their strengths and weaknesses Methods of promotion and advertising	Growing demand for mountain cycles, racing cycles etc. Advertising in trade journals.
Personnel	Who is involved in the business What experience and skills people have	Former Raleigh workers
Buying and production	Likely costs of production Who the main suppliers are What benefits suppliers have	Production costs £30,000
Premises and equipment	The type of premises Location of premises and cost Age, style and value of machinery Replacement cost of machinery How to cope with expansion	Produced on industrial estate site
Profit	Likely profit based on: * turnover (price x sales) * costs Break even point. This is the quantity sold where turnover is equal to costs	Total costs = £55,000 At £300 need to sell 183 to break even
Cash flow	When cash will come in When cash will go out If payments will be cash or credit Difference between cash in and cash out each month	Payment by cash and credit
Finance	How much cash owners will put in How much will have to be borrowed What money is needed for How much borrowing will cost What assets can be used as security How long borrowing will be for and when it will be paid back	£5,000 put in by each of the partners

certain skills. Advice may be in the form of:
- a telephone number, email or Internet site of a specialist who can help;
- a detailed discussion or interview on the best way to set up or run a business;
- telephone numbers, addresses or Internet sites of organisations providing funds;
- training videos or seminars;
- specialist information on markets and types of business. Where can an entrepreneur obtain help?

Individuals It may be possible to get advice from people who have started their own business and have been through the process of setting up. They may be able to point out what they did right or wrong and how they might do things differently. Advice about specific skills needed for running a business might come from:
- an accountant - who can give advice on accounts, book-keeping, taxation;
- a solicitor - who can give advice on the legal requirements of the business;
- an insurance adviser - who can give advice on how to protect and cover such things as equipment and employees.

Banks All of the main commercial banks provide advice for potential business people. This ranges from information about sources of finance to helping to draw up a business plan. An adviser can help to find out whether the business is entitled to a government or EU grant. Many banks produce folders or publications with details and guidance on setting up in business. Some also run Internet websites giving advice on how to set up.

Government advice The Department of Trade and Industry's (DTI) Small Business Service runs a number of initiatives aimed at helping businesses set up and small businesses that are operating. Examples include:
- Business Bridge, which provides forums where owner managers can meet and discuss problems;
- Young Enterprise, which runs business education programmes for young people;
- The Ethnic Minority Business Forum, which advises ministers on helping ethnic minority businesses;
- The Farm Business Advice Service, which offers free advice to help farm businesses grow;
- The Small Business Research Initiative, which encourages smaller businesses to participate in government research contracts;
- Enterprise Areas, which provide the focus for policies and actions to develop enterprise in deprived communities;
- a document *Tendering for Government Contracts*, which advises small businesses on finding and bidding for public sector work;
- a network of Local Business Partnerships around the country, which enables businesses and local authorities to

work together to streamline regulations.

A government Small Firms Minister is responsible for promoting small business in Parliament. Government is also responsible for the provision of UK and EU funding to businesses. This is covered in the next section.

Business Links The DTI also manages the network of Business Links throughout the UK. Local Business Links in areas of the UK provide support, advice and guidance on a wide range of areas for businesses aiming to start up. These include advice on:
- how to set up a business and prepare a business plan;
- getting government funds and other finance;
- tax;
- employment requirements;
- legislation;
- managing the business, including sales, IT, importing and exporting, and financial control.

Enterprise agencies These were created by government specifically to help small and growing businesses. There is a network of local agencies throughout the UK. Most offer free advice on how to set up and run a business, training courses, contacts and information on potential investors.

Chambers of Commerce The British Chambers of Commerce are made up of local Chambers of Commerce. These are local, independent, non-profit making organisations funded by subscriptions from members which are businesses. Help given to small and growing businesses include training, information, networking with other businesses and help with suppliers of pensions, healthcare and legal protection.

The Prince's Trust The Prince's Trust offers support for 18-30 year olds who want to improve their career and prospects. It can provide training and advice or help in the form of a volunteer mentor to young people starting up in business. Sometimes it also provides funds, such as low interest loans or test marketing grants.

Shell LiveWire This is a scheme run by Shell to encourage people aged 16-30 to develop their business. It offers grants and advice. It also runs a competition, 'Young Business Start Up Awards', which gives £10,000 to the best business start up each year.

Business clubs The National Association of Business Clubs and Societies has clubs throughout the UK. They are made up from businesses in the local area, although there are many clubs that are not part of the Association which still offer help. Clubs can be based on one business area or a local area. Sometimes speakers, such as Inland Revenue inspectors, will be invited to talk at meetings about tax or grants. A list of members is available and businesses who are members provide help and advice to each other. A certain amount of inter-trading also takes place. This helps new businesses to make contacts and removes some of the risk when first trading.

Federation of Small Businesses This represents the interests of small businesses in the UK. It offers discounted schemes for insurance, medical care, financial services, Internet design and banking to its members.

Trade Associations Examples include The Wool Marketing Board, The Association of British Travel Agents and The Booksellers' Association. They provide information about certain types of business or industry.

Internet websites Many of the organisations mentioned above have websites which provide advice and guidance on starting a new business or running an existing business. Other organisations which provide help on the Internet include newbusiness.co.uk and virginbiz.net.

Finance

Where do new businesses find the finance that is needed to buy materials, pay wages etc? Funds can come from a number of sources.

- Personal savings or past earnings. A person aiming to set up a business in the future may have saved for some years or a redundant employee can use payments made when they became unemployed.
- Funds from partners or investors. A partnership can obtain finance from all partners, even if some are not actively involved in the business. Limited companies can raise large amounts of finance. Investors buy a 'share' of the company by purchasing shares. This is then used to finance business activity and the shareholders are paid with a dividend as a reward.
- It is possible to buy machinery and equipment and pay for it at a later date or over a period of time. Businesses may allow components or materials to be bought on CREDIT SALE or HIRE PURCHASE, where the goods are used and the cost is paid over time, plus interest. Businesses often sell goods and are paid at a later date (30, 60 or 90 days). This is known as trade credit.
- A business may decide to lease or hire equipment from a hire company. A small construction firm, for example, may hire scaffolding for a large building rather than buy their own which they might not use all the time.
- Banks or other financial institutions. Banks offer loan and overdraft facilities and charge interest. Services such as business accounts, insurance and salary payments are also available. They may be free for a time if the business remains in credit. Banks often ask for security against a loan. This can be any assets owned by the business or perhaps the house of the owner. Banks also need convincing that the loan is secure. They will ask for a

business plan, references or proof of trading in the past. Loans can be in many forms. Some allow only the interest to be paid off in the first one or two years. It may also be possible to use a mortgage to buy premises.

- Help from organisations. Businesses starting up have been able to obtain funds from various organisations, as explained in the previous section.
- Government funds. Government funds are available for businesses locating in particular areas of the country. The government also runs a **small firms loan guarantee scheme**. This allows small firms starting up or which do not have a track record to borrow. Banks lend the money and government guarantees part of the loan. Loans guaranteed are from £5,000-£100,000 for new businesses and up to £250,000 for businesses over two years old. In 2002 the average loan was £60,000.
- EU funds. A variety of funds is available from the European Union, particularly for businesses setting up in areas with

---

Omar Samaha thought his experience in the restaurant trade as head waiter would be of great help when he set up his own business, Fresco. However, he underestimated the problems of obtaining finance. He scraped together some of his own money to take over the lease on a cafe in Westbourne Grove. But his bank would not offer him any money at first without any personal assets. So Omar put together a business plan and eventually the bank was persuaded to loan him £3,000. He was also able to obtain an overdraft of £3,000 when the bank turned down a further loan a short time after starting up.

A year later Fresco was doing well. Omar wanted to open a restaurant to capture evening trade in the way that Fresco did in the day. His partner put in £25,000, but banks were reluctant to lend him the other £25,000 he needed for the venture. They were unwilling to use the lease on Fresco as security because it was for less than 25 years. Omar pointed out that the banks seemed to focus only on his first six months when making a decision about loans, rather than the more impressive figures that the business achieved later. To secure the loan, Omar would have to remortgage his personal property with the bank. But changing lenders would cost him £5,000. The deal fell through and Omar had to pay £1,000 in solicitors' fees.

But this failed to dampen his enthusiasm for the idea of a new restaurant. The property boom meant that his flat had appreciated in value. Omar was able to remortgage and borrow on the strength of this. His latest venture is the Fresco Juice Bar in Whiteleys Shopping Centre, London. Having a successful business plan and years of profitable accounts is likely to make it far easier to obtain funds.

Source: adapted from startups.co.uk.

(a) Identify the sources of finance mentioned above.
(b) Explain the problems that the business faced with each source of finance.

Question 4

problems. Grants are available in areas such as job creation, investment, energy conservation, new buildings, research into new markets and innovation.

● Business angels (☞ unit 33). The European Business Angels Network estimates there are around 125,000 investors in the UK, with an investment pool of around 3,000 million euros. Investment in businesses varies between 25,000 euros and 250,000 euros.

● Venture capitalists (☞ unit 33). These are organisations which provide funds for small and medium sized businesses with potential.

● Certain industries can sometimes offer funds for businesses. Examples have included British Coal Enterprise giving low-interest loans to firms thinking of locating in coal mining areas and similar offers from the British steel industry.

How to set up

A business person must decide what form the new business will take. What alternatives are available?

Setting up a new business alone Perhaps the simplest way of starting a business is to set up alone. There are certain advantages and problems of being a sole trader (☞ unit 6). There are few legal requirements and trading can begin straight away. However, the owner will have to take all the responsibility and bear all costs.

Setting up with others One way of avoiding the problems of a sole trader is to set up with others. A partnership would allow the business person to share the load of running the business and to raise more finance, without the demands of becoming a limited company. It is, of course, possible to start business as a limited company. This may be likely if a business is to be run as a family concern (a private limited company), or if a great deal of finances was needed because of the scale of the operation (a public limited company). Limited companies are dealt with in unit 6.

Buying a business A potential business person may be able to buy an existing business. There are many examples of this. An electrician made redundant from a large public limited company may 'buy out' a local retailer selling electrical goods who wants to retire. Managers, shareholders or directors may wish to leave one company and buy out the interests of another. In some cases the managers of a company may try to buy the business from the shareholders because they feel the company can be run better. This is an example of a management buy-out. It is also possible for a worker buy out to take place, where workers buy out the shareholders of a business.

Buying a franchise A business could set up as part of a franchise (☞ unit 6). Franchises are designed to allow new businesses with little experience and limited finance to set

up. The new business (the franchisee) buys the rights to use the name and sell the product of a well established business (the franchisor) for a fee. This reduces the risk for the new business. It also allows the new business to get help and guidance when it first operates.

Licensing This is similar to franchising. It is where a business sells the rights to use its copyright or patent on a product to another business. It may allow a business to produce its product. For example, Dyson earned 5 per cent for allowing USA producers to manufacture its vacuum cleaners under the names Fantom, Fury and Lightning. A business may also allow others to use its company name and logo. Coca-Cola does this in many countries worldwide, for example. This allows a business to earn revenue, without any any extra cost. A problem might be if the license is given to a poor producer or poor selling product which could affect the reputation of the business selling the licence.

Running a business

When a business is set up, there are legal and operational tasks that must be carried out.

Keeping records All transactions which take place must be recorded. This includes all sales of goods or services, the purchase of all materials, equipment and the payment of all bills for heating, lighting, wages, transport etc. This information can be used to show how well the business is performing. There are also certain records that some businesses must keep by law. For example, a company must produce a profit and loss account (☞ unit 31).

The use of documents When goods and services are bought and sold, a number of documents are used. They provide evidence and records of the transactions that have taken place. Some documents that might be used include:

● an invoice - a document sent with goods sold on trade credit, informing the purchaser that payment is due on a certain date;

● a cash receipt - a proof of purchase given when something is paid for in cash;

● a credit note - a document issued to a purchaser when they have overpaid, allowing 'credit' on future payments;

● proof of delivery - proof that items have been delivered and received at a certain destination.

If a business person employs workers, they will be given a contract of employment (☞ unit 48). This shows the terms under which the employee is hired and with which they must conform. Employees also need to be provided with wages or salary slips, showing their total earnings and any deductions.

The larger the business becomes, the more documents it is likely to use. Examples of documents that may be used internally include memos from, say, the production manager to the marketing manager, or agendas for meetings to discuss a new promotional campaign.

Tax and insurance Part of any revenue earned by a business must be paid to the government.

- Taxation. Profits made by a business are liable for tax. Government policy (☞ unit 65) has tried to reduce the corporation tax and income tax paid by businesses in the last decade to encourage growth and development. Businesses can claim allowances, which will reduce the amount of tax paid.
- Value Added Tax (VAT). Businesses must pay VAT on any goods they sell. Usually, they add this on to the price of a good or service. Some products in the UK are exempt from VAT, including children's clothing, food and books. A business will have VAT placed onto the cost of materials, components and other items they buy.
- National Insurance contributions. Employers must make NATIONAL INSURANCE CONTRIBUTIONS to the government and must also remove employees' contributions from their wages.
- Businesses will pay business rates to the local authority. This is a tax on the percentage value of any building owned by the business.
- Insurance. It is sensible for an entrepreneur to insure against damages and theft. If production ceases for any reason, this could be a major problem for a new business. Revenue will not be earned and there may be cash flow problems (☞ unit 35) or the business may not be able to afford the immediate cost of repairing or replacing a piece of machinery. Some insurance is required by law. All businesses must have public liability, in case a customer or visitor to the premises is injured and makes a claim.

key terms

Business plan - a statement made by a business, outlining the way it will attempt to achieve its objectives.

Copyright - the ownership of material such as books and films which is protected by law from re-use without permission.

Hire purchase/credit sale - methods used to buy goods now and pay off the balance over a period of time. In the case of the former, the goods only belong to the buyer when the final payment is made.

National Insurance contributions - payments made by employees and employers to the government as a form of insurance premium.

Patent - a licence which prevents the copying of an idea.

Knowledge

1. Give 6 reasons why people set up in business.
2. Briefly explain the likely changes an employee may find in their work if they become a business owner.
3. Where might a business idea come from?
4. What questions about:
   (a) the market;
   (b) finance;
   might a business person ask when starting a business?
5. How might a small business use a business plan?
6. List 6 aspects of a business plan.
7. What help and finance might:
   (a) Business Link;
   (b) The Department of Trade and Industry;
   (c) a commercial bank;
   provide for a small business?
8. Why might a business club be particularly useful for a small new business?
9. Why might a business need to use documents?

Case study PhotoArtistry

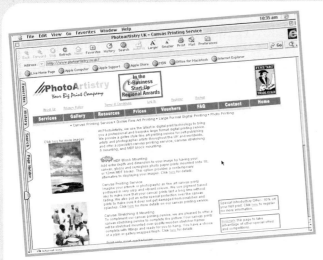

Anne Herbert was asked by other artists so many times to print their work on her large format digital printer that she decided to set up a fine art printing business. She says fine art was 'more of a hobby at first that developed into a business'. The idea of flexibility and financial freedom, however, was appealing. Anne has been inspired by women of courage such as Anita Roddick. She is an avid reader of the business pages in Sunday magazines, particularly 'how people made it' stories. It wasn't Anne's first business idea. She had worked as a jewellery designer and wanted to design costume jewellery. But she did not have the money to start the business.

After taking a BA in fine art Anne bought a printer to print her own work costing £10,000. She was working for a computer security firm and decided to set up a website to see if other artists would be interested in having their own work printed. This would help her to pay for the printer. 95 per cent of orders were taken online. The website was also used to establish leads. A free print offer was given to attract customers to the service. The website cost £1,500 to set up. All the initial spending was self-funded. She has also bought other equipment, such as a machine to laminate prints, and computers to help the printing process as the business has grown and made profit.

So why does Anne think there is a market for her work? She argues that the 'market found her'. She initially only offered a large printing service. Then people asked her to print on canvas and stretch prints onto frames, so she added those services. But she still has to do the practical business stuff, such as registering the

business and registering for VAT. She also has to work a 60-70 hour week, like many people starting and running their own business. Anne does a lot of the work herself. She has an accountant and a friend with marketing experience who works full time. Anne admits she knows little about things such as payroll, but is willing to learn.

Research has also been important. Anne says that she needed to know her market and her main competitors. She was looking to differentiate her products and give a unique USP. Computer packages are used to work out break-even points, costs and quantities required of the services offered. This helps to determine prices.

Anne spent time talking to friends before starting the business and to a person from Business Link, who has acted as a sort of mentor. Business Link was useful in helping her to write her business plan. It has never been used to apply for a bank loan, but has been used as a guide for the business. She took an MBA course at the Open University which gave her grounding in basic business principles. She is also aware of courses run by the Inland Revenue.

Apart from the website, other promotion is in the form of glossy brochures printed. A small stand was also taken at an NEC exhibition in Birmingham. But most of the promotion Anne suggests is by word of mouth.

Anne initially worked from home and ran the business as well as holding down a full time job. She was made redundant in May 2003. And she decided her home was getting too small to handle large canvas printing. She now works in an office/warehouse space of 1,500 square feet which is 10 minutes from where she lives.

Source: adapted from startups.co.uk.

(a) **Using examples from the cases, explain what is meant by the terms:**
   (i) **Business Link;**
   (ii) **USP. (6 marks)**
(b) **Identify the ways in which PhotoArtistry has obtained:**
   (i) **finance;**
   (ii) **advice. (6 marks)**
(c) **Explain the reasons why Anne Herbert set up her business. (8 marks)**
(d) **Examine the factors that are likely to affect the success of the business. (10 marks)**
(e) **Evaluate how successful the business might be in the future. (10 marks)**

3 Business Stakeholders

Who is involved in business activity?

Various groups of people have an interest in business. Such groups are referred to as STAKEHOLDERS. The interest each stakeholder has in a business will vary according to the nature of their 'stake'. Figure 3.1 shows possible stakeholders that can be identified in business activity. They include:

- owners or shareholders;
- managers;
- employees;
- customers;
- government;
- suppliers;
- the community.

It could be argued that owners, managers and employees are internal stakeholders as members of the business organisation. The remainder could be seen as external stakeholders because they are not part of the business. However, there are likely to be exceptions to this. For example, some members of the community may be employees or shareholders.

Some stakeholders may have more than one interest in the business. An employee might also be a shareholder. Managers will be employees of the business. A customer might be a member of the local community.

Stakeholders in business will usually benefit from their involvement with the organisation. Employees will earn money which they can spend on goods and services. Customers will consume the goods and services supplied by the business and the government will collect tax from the organisation.

Owners

A business is the property of its owner or owners. The owner of a van can use it to earn income by hiring it out. The owner of jewellery can wait for its value to increase and then sell it. It is possible for the owners of a business to do these things as well.

Not all owners are the same. The owner of a small business, such as a small retail outlet selling watches, may be the only person in the business. The owner would make all of the decisions, possibly use personal finance to start the firm and carry out all tasks, such as selling, ordering stock and recording transactions. In very large companies there can be thousands of joint owners. They all own **shares** (☞ units 6 and 33) in the company. This entitles them to a share in the profit, known as a DIVIDEND and a vote each year to elect the DIRECTORS of the company. Examples of shareholders might be David Whelan, the Chairman of JJB Sports plc, who it was reported owned nearly 40 per cent of its shares in 2003, or the people all over the UK who own shares in ICI or BT. The involvement of shareholders in the business will depend, perhaps, on their position in the business and the amount of money invested in it. Figure 3.2 shows a summary of the different types of business owner.

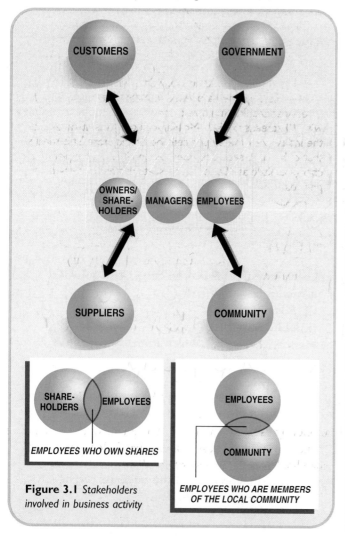

Figure 3.1 *Stakeholders involved in business activity*

EMPLOYEES WHO OWN SHARES

EMPLOYEES WHO ARE MEMBERS OF THE LOCAL COMMUNITY

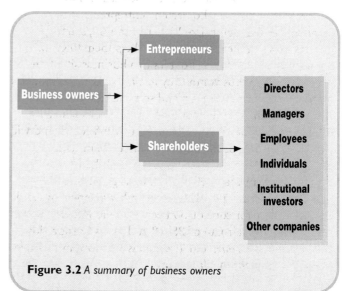

Figure 3.2 *A summary of business owners*

The entrepreneur

Unit 1 showed that **enterprise** was a **factor of production.** Arguably, it is the most important. Without an entrepreneur to organise the land, labour and capital, business activity would not take place. What is an entrepreneur? People who have this role usually perform three functions in business.

Innovation Business activity usually begins with the entrepreneur having a business idea. The entrepreneur could be said to be innovative. He or she is forming a new business where one did not exist before. When Anita Roddick opened the first Body Shop in March 1976 in Brighton, she created a new business idea of her own. This was to sell toiletries and cosmetics with conservation, the environment and animal rights in mind. Even when ideas are copied or adapted, it could be argued that the entrepreneur is being innovative. The creation of a business producing a vacuum cleaner which does not use dust bags by James Dyson may be said to be innovative. The British inventor Trevor Baylis was arguably innovative in creating a clockwork radio which could be wound up to work, rather than using electricity.

Organisation Land, labour and capital are hired by the entrepreneur and organised to produce goods or services. Decisions about the location of the premises, the method of production, product design, prices and wages are often made by the entrepreneur. If the business grows, it is likely that some of these tasks may be passed down to others.

Risk taking Setting up a business is risky. Money has to be paid out in advance to buy materials, business premises, equipment and pay wages. The entrepreneur may use some personal money to meet these costs. There is no guarantee that the final product or service will be sold. If goods are unsold then the entrepreneur will have to suffer this loss. It is not possible to insure against **unquantifiable** risks such as these, so the entrepreneur bears all the costs of failure.

The type of people who become entrepreneurs is extremely varied. Some, like Richard Branson, start businesses when they are young and help them to grow. Some people extend their hobbies to a business situation, some leave their jobs voluntarily to start a business, some use redundancy money to set up and some inherit businesses.

Entrepreneurs often tend to be associated with small firms. This is because the entrepreneur will face risk and will control all aspects of the business activity. Many small businesses do become large businesses and thus the role of the entrepreneur may well change. In large business organisations many people bear the risk, are innovative and are responsible for control. Someone such as Rupert Murdoch, the Chairman of BSkyB and News Corporation which owns *The Times* and *The Sun*, is arguably an example of an entrepreneur in a large company.

In November 2002, Stelios Haji-Ioannou stepped down as chairman of easyJet, the company that came from nowhere to become Europe's biggest discount airline in five years. Richard Branson paid tribute to him, saying 'Millions of people who could not afford to travel before are now travelling and he has done it with great style and panache'.

Mr Haji-Ioannou, son of a Greek millionaire, set up easyJet at Luton Airport in 1995. He leased two Boeing 737s and offered flights to Edinburgh for £29. In November 2002 easyJet was valued at more than £1 billion, reporting profits of £71.6 million for the year. Mr Haji-Ioannou said that he was standing down to devote more time to his other ventures. He announced plans to create new 'easy' companies, including a 'no-frills' cinema chain and a minibus service between London and other major cities in England. These new businesses are on top of the easy car-hire business and the Internet café business already up and running.

The new chairman at easyJet is Sir Colin Chandler, someone with a more traditional business background. Mr Haji-Ioannou reverted to his 'serial entrepreneur' roots. The qualities needed to run a big public company and get a company off the ground are very different.

The first easyCinema opened in Milton Keynes in May 2003. It replaces the first multiplex cinema, the Point, which opened with 10 screens in 1985. Mr Haji-Iaonnou was attracted to the industry by the 20 per cent occupancy rate. This means that only 1 in 5 seats are ever sold in cinemas. He planned to charge as little as 20p for some seats during the very quiet periods.

Source: adapted from *The Guardian* 26.11.2002 and 16.5.2003.

(a) Explain why Stelios Haji-Ioannou is an entrepreneur.
(b) Suggest why Stelios Haji-Ioannou stepped down as chairman from the successful easyJet company that he created.

Type of shareholder

Certain types of business do not have shareholders, such as sole traders and partnerships. Limited companies can raise money by issuing shares (☞ unit 6). Shareholders become the 'joint owners' of the business. The shareholder or group of shareholders with the majority of shares, ie 51 per cent, will be the majority shareholder in the business. Examples of these shareholders are shown in Figure 3.2.

Directors Directors are elected by the shareholders each year and are responsible for running the business. They do not have to hold shares in the companies they run, but generally they do. Some directors have quite large shareholdings, sometimes large enough to exert control, such as in a family business. Some businesses have **worker directors**. In Germany and in some UK companies worker directors are workers that are co-opted onto the board of directors to represent the views of the workforce. The term can also sometimes be used to describe workers in a business owned largely by employees with shares, that also run the business.

Managers Managers are usually appointed by directors and are actively involved in running the business. Some managers own shares in their companies, but they do not have to. Sometimes they are allowed to buy shares or are given shares as a bonus. It is argued that if managers own shares in the company it might motivate them to perform well in their jobs. This is because if they perform well, profits may be higher and higher dividends can then be paid to shareholders like themselves.

Employees An increasing number of employees now own shares in companies. In the twenty years before 2000, shares in privatised industries (☞ unit 7) were made available to the workforce and the public as previously state owned industries became part of the private sector. In 2000, over 90 out of the FTSE 100 companies offered share as you earn schemes (☞ unit 42). Companies have also offered shares to employees as bonuses. Sainsbury's is an example of one company which has done this. It is unlikely that employees will own enough shares to have any control in the running of the business. However, it may motivate (☞ unit 41) workers to take an interest in the company.

Individuals It is possible for individuals to own shares in companies. Any member of the public is allowed to buy shares in any **public limited company** (☞ unit 6). One common way of buying them is through a **stockbroker.** Individuals may buy shares because they want to earn dividends. Buying shares is an alternative to other methods of saving, for example putting money in a building society account. Such people play no role in running the business. Also, they rarely have any control since they own only a small fraction of the total number of shares. If individuals are not happy with the performance of the company they may sell their shares. Or sometimes people buy shares, hoping to sell them at a higher price and make a profit.

Institutional investors These are financial institutions (☞ unit 33) such as insurance companies, pension funds and unit trusts who buy shares to earn income. They buy and sell very large numbers of shares, but rarely participate in the running of the companies. Their aim is to hold those shares which they think will generate the most return. In some cases they may exert control, since they own such large blocks of shares.

Other companies Some businesses hold shares to earn income, some to control other companies and some to build up stakes in other companies with a view to taking them over in the future.

Managers

Businesses of all sizes employ managers. A MANAGER may be defined as an individual who is accountable for more work than he or she could undertake alone. In a small business the owner is likely to be responsible for all managerial tasks. When a business grows the responsibility for some decision making is often **delegated** (☞ unit 43) to others since it is not possible for one person to carry the whole burden.

There is a number of common functions of managers in business.

Organising and decision making Businesses are often divided into departments. A smaller business may have production, marketing, finance and administration departments. The owners may appoint one manager to control each department. Managers will have responsibility for all activities and employees in the department. For example, they may help to recruit employees, make decisions about how the department should be run and ensure that department objectives are met. Employees in the department will look to the manager for leadership, to solve problems, to communicate information to them, settle disputes, motivate them and represent the department at meetings.

Planning and control Managers are also likely to contribute to the overall planning of company activities along with the owner and other managers. They also have a controlling role in the business. This may involve control of finance, equipment, time and people, for example. In larger businesses, managers become more specialist and concentrate on a narrower aspect of management.

Accountability Managers are accountable to the owners. If the production department does not achieve a satisfactory level of output, the manager may have to 'shoulder the blame'. This might mean a loss of a bonus payment.

Entrepreneurial role Although managers may not risk their own money, they might risk their job. A manager might make a decision to install some revolutionary new machinery. This could be successful and the manager might be promoted. However, if the machinery is unsuccessful, leading to heavy losses, the manager may be sacked. In carrying out this task, the manager is innovating and risk taking.

Employees

The role of employees in business tends to be to follow the instructions of employers. Employees are hired by businesses to help business activity. A business needs people with a range of skills and knowledge. Many provide a training programme for new employees to familiarise them with the firm's policies and working practices. Employees will be more productive if they are taught good working practices from the time they start at a new company. Note that managers of the business are usually employees.

Employees normally sign **contracts of employment** (☞ unit 48) agreeing to follow all reasonable instructions related to their job. In return for their time and effort they receive a payment, ie a **wage** or **salary**. The amount workers are paid depends on a wide range of factors such as age, experience, qualifications, the type of industry, the nature of the job (full time or part time) and the level of skill required.

The role of employees in business has begun to change in recent years.

● They have had to cope with the introduction of new technology.
● They have been encouraged by some companies to participate more in problem solving and decision making, perhaps in teams.
● They have become more flexible and have adapted to the introduction of new working practices. For example, many employees are trained in a number of tasks and are expected to be able to change from one job to another.
● Increased emphasis has been placed on training and learning new skills. For example, departmental managers have been encouraged to develop personnel skills.

Customers

Customers are not 'members' of businesses, but they are vital to their survival. Customers buy the goods and services that businesses supply. Most customers are consumers who use or 'consume' products. Spending by customers generates income for businesses. Customers may be individuals, but could also be other businesses. For example, The Sage Group plc manufactures computer software for accounting systems. Most of its customers are other businesses.

It is important for businesses to understand the needs of their customers. Customers dictate the pattern of business activity, as firms will only produce goods and services which customers will buy. Businesses that produce unwanted goods or services may struggle and fail. The Concorde supersonic jets were taken out of service in 2003 because they were not commercially viable. There was insufficient demand for the service at the price needed to charge to cover the costs and make a profit.

Customers and consumers have many different relationships with businesses.

● Contact between businesses and customers takes place when goods or services are bought. This can vary. When services are bought there is usually a personal contact between the two groups, as there would be when a client makes an appointment to see a solicitor. In the case of water supply, the contact for many customers is limited, ie through the post when the quarterly bill arrives.
● Businesses need to communicate with consumers to find out what they want. **Market research** (☞ unit 12) helps a business to collect information about its potential customers.
● As well as collecting information from consumers, businesses also pass on information about the nature of products, the price charged, how products work and where they might be bought. **Advertising** (☞ unit 21) is often used to do this.
● Consumers are more aware today about products that are available, prices, channels of complaint and product performance. Consumers have more income than ever before, and much greater expectations of products. Businesses must take these expectations into account when

---

AStar Ltd is an insurance broker selling car, home, health and holiday insurance. Most of the policies are sold over the telephone, but a growing on-line business is beginning to contribute to the company's profit. Most of the company's shares are owned by the four directors. However, the company issues free shares to employees in relation to the amount of profit made each year. Last year the company made £2.5 million profit and 40 employees received 5,000 x 50p shares each.

(a) Explain one possible reason why AStar gives shares to its employees.
(b) To what extent can employees influence decision making at AStar?

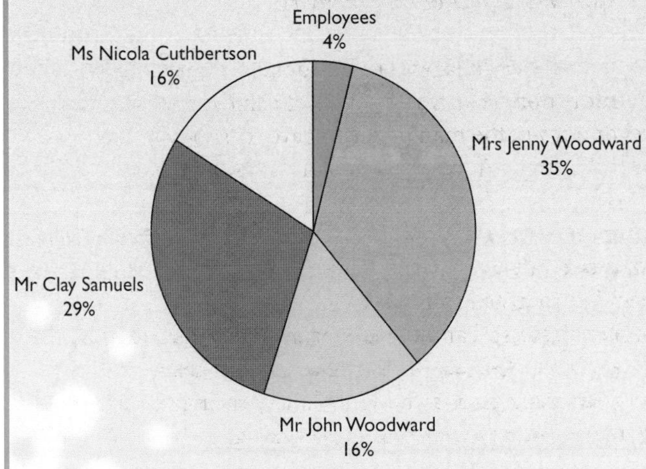

Figure 3.2 *Shareholding at AStar Ltd*

Employees 4%
Ms Nicola Cuthbertson 16%
Mrs Jenny Woodward 35%
Mr Clay Samuels 29%
Mr John Woodward 16%

Question 2

designing, manufacturing and marketing products. For example, 35 years ago a radio in a new car would have been an 'extra'. Today, a complete 'sound system' in a car is virtually a necessity.

● Businesses operate in a world where consumers have increasing rights and protection. This is dealt with in unit 71.

Because of increased consumer expectations and awareness, improved consumer rights and fiercer competition in business, the vast majority of companies work hard at promoting good customer relations. Indeed, more and more businesses are happy to give consumers a lot more than their strict legal rights. Most stores will accept returned goods and reimburse customers without too much investigation. Free after sales service is common and sales staff receive a lot more 'customer care' training.

Suppliers

Suppliers are businesses that provide resources which allow other businesses to produce goods and services. Resources might include raw materials, components, equipment, energy and services. It is important for good relations to exist between businesses and suppliers because they rely heavily on each other. Generally, businesses require suppliers to provide good quality resources at reasonable prices. They also need suppliers to be reliable and flexible. In return suppliers want businesses to provide a constant flow of profitable orders and to pay on time.

The relationship between suppliers and producers has become more important in recent years. The main reason for this is that modern production techniques often require businesses to cooperate. A business can only operate just-in-time manufacturing (☞ unit 55), for example, if suppliers are prepared to deliver quickly and at short notice.

Government

The government can influence business in a number of ways. A certain amount of legislation is aimed at business in order to protect stakeholders. Health and safety regulations are designed to protect employees in the workplace. Environmental legislation aims to protect the community and the environment from business activity. For example, the landfill tax on the disposal of waste was intended to encourage greater recycling.

The government can also affect businesses through its economic policies. An increase in interest rates, for example will raise the cost of borrowing for business (☞ unit 65) . In addition, some government activity attempts to help business. The Private Finance Initiative encourages private businesses to build roads and hospitals, which they operate. More direct help may come from European Union funds to set up in a particular area.

The government will want businesses to flourish because they provide jobs and generate wealth. If businesses are successful the government will also benefit. Tax revenues will rise, providing the government with extra funds.

Community

Many communities have a major stake in local businesses. A business is likely to provide employment and training for local people. Certain businesses, particularly small ones, draw most of their customers from the local area. Indeed, in some remote areas residents may rely almost entirely upon the goods and services supplied by local firms such as shops. Some businesses even become involved in community life. They might sponsor local social or sporting events or help raise money for local charities.

Unfortunately the existence of business in local communities can also have drawbacks. Some businesses, particularly manufacturers located in residential areas, might create noise, congestion and air pollution. Their factories may be unsightly. As a result the local community might try to exert pressure on the owners to reduce the costs borne by the community or to relocate.

Interdependence

There is a significant degree of interdependence within business. In large firms the owners are dependent upon the skill and ability of the management team. If managers perform well then the business is likely to make more profit which will benefit the owner. Managers rely on business owners for their jobs and to support their decisions.

Managers and other employees are also dependent upon each other. Employees rely on the **leadership** of management in order to do their jobs. Management depends on workers to produce output according to their instructions. Management will be accountable to the owners of the business if workers are inefficient.

Businesses are dependent on consumers. Business activity would not take place if consumers did not buy goods or services. However, consumers can only purchase these goods and services if they have income. They may earn this income from employment in business. Thus, business owners are dependent upon consumers for their income, and consumers, in their role as employees and managers, are dependent upon business owners for their income.

Objectives and conflict

Conflict can occur in business when STAKEHOLDER OBJECTIVES are different. Each type of stakeholder is likely to have a set of goals which they want to achieve. It could be argued that:

● shareholders want regular, secure and high returns and a say in the goals of the business (☞ unit 4);

● managers want responsibility, high rewards and a lack of interference in their actions;

● employees want high earnings, an interesting job and secure employment;

● customers want quality products at low prices and a good service;

● suppliers want secure, regular and profitable orders;

- government wants to achieve a large number of goals including growth in the economy and low inflation;
- the local community wants thriving local businesses which do not cause problems.

Conflict can exist between many different groups of stakeholders.

Employees and owners What might lead to conflict between the employees and the owners of a business?

- Levels of pay. In most businesses, rates of pay are negotiated every year. Bargaining takes place between employees and owners or managers. The two sides may disagree on new wage levels. This might be, for example, because workers want more than the owners or managers are prepared to pay.
- Working conditions. Conflict may arise if, for example, the working environment is too cold for employees to do their jobs.
- Changing practices. In recent years a number of new working practices have been introduced in business. Disputes may occur when employees are asked to perform new tasks or change the way they undertake existing tasks. Employees often feel that they are being asked to do more work when practices change.
- Redundancy. When employees are faced with the threat of losing their jobs, quite naturally they react. Workers are often angry when their jobs are lost due to reorganisation, for example.

Owners and managers In some businesses the management team may become powerful and influential. When this happens they may pursue their own interests rather than those of the owners. This might involve paying themselves high salaries or organising their time to suit their own needs, whilst achieving satisfactory levels of profit rather than high levels of profit. This would go against the interests of owners, who benefit more from higher profits. Such conflict may result in some owners selling their shares. This is often referred to as a **divorce of ownership and control** (☞ unit 6).

It is in everyone's interests to settle conflict as quickly as possible. Conflict can lead to lower levels of output and loss of profits for the owners. Managers and other employees may suffer from poor motivation, a lack of job security and loss of wages.

Customers and business What might lead to conflict between consumers and business?

- Price. Owners may wish to maximise their profit which might involve charging the highest possible price. However, consumers want to buy goods as cheaply as possible. If competition exists in the market (☞ unit 62) consumers will generally benefit. However, if there is a lack of competition, consumers may not have a choice except to go without.
- Quality. Consumers may be dissatisfied with the quality of the products they have bought. If consumers return goods

then businesses lose income, so disagreements often occur as to whether a firm should accept returned goods.

- Delivery time. Customers are often keen to receive the goods which they have ordered as quickly as possible. A dispute would occur if, for example, a business cannot deliver a wedding dress promised for the day of a wedding.
- After sales service. Consumers may be upset by poor after sales service. For example, if a person buys a hi-fi system and finds that it does not work, a dispute might emerge if the business refused to investigate the problem.

Suppliers, managers and owners 'New' production methods have led to a closer relationship between suppliers and managers. However, conflict does still exist. Some suppliers, particularly small firms supplying larger businesses, have criticised their customers' managers or owners for taking too long to pay for products. Late payment can cause severe hardship for smaller suppliers.

Similarly, late delivery by suppliers can cause problems for managers and owners of businesses which are customers. Late supply can delay production and may lead to lost orders and profit.

Owners and the community Conflict can arise between owners and the community when the quality of life enjoyed by local residents is threatened by business activity. The most likely causes of conflict are businesses disturbing the local community or polluting the nearby environment. An example of such conflict was the opposition of residents in South

---

In early 2003 Richard Lapthorne, former finance director of British Aerospace (now BAE Systems), was appointed chairman of Cable and Wireless (C & W). C & W is a global supplier of Internet data and voice solutions to businesses. The company which used to run the Mercury network in the UK, providing the only competition to BT in the 1980s, was once valued at £35 billion. On 21.9.2003 it was valued at just £2.961 billion. It has suffered the problems of other hi-tech companies - chronic overcapacity and falling prices for services that too many firms are offering to an insufficient number of customers.

In May 2003, the company announced plans to shed half the staff at the company's London headquarters. The cuts, to be accompanied by several hundred job losses across the group, were part of a plan to reduce overheads as the company struggled to reduce 'cash burn' across the group. One official involved in the plan said: 'It's part of the bigger overhaul. Terms of redundancy are being worked out – this will do nothing for morale'. Shares in C & W rose 4 $\frac{1}{2}$ p to 102 $\frac{3}{4}$ p after the job cuts were announced.

Source: adapted from the *Financial Times*, 30.5.2003.

(a) Explain the possible conflicts that might arise amongst the various C & W stakeholders as a result of the cost cutting exercise.

Question 3

Manchester to the construction of a new runway at Manchester Airport. They argued that noise pollution resulting from extra traffic would be intolerable.

An increasing amount of business activity is located away from residential areas. Popular sites on the edges of towns have developed. Industrial parks have been set up and some businesses have chosen to operate on greenfield sites. This trend would help to reduce conflict between business owners and local communities.

Why might businesses take a stakeholder approach?

Traditionally, large business organisations have been run to further the interests of shareholders. This involves maximising shareholder value, which usually also involves raising the share price. This is called the SHAREHOLDER CONCEPT and often means that the interests of other stakeholders are ignored. In recent years some businesses have realised the benefits from meeting the needs of a wider range of

Companies like to be trusted. Enormous effort is made by businesses through public relations, reward schemes and other measures to boost public confidence. They want to persuade us that they are good 'corporate citizens.' It makes sense because it makes money. Trusting customers become loyal customers, who in turn are more likely to keep on buying as well as purchasing new products and services in the future. However, UK company law requires public limited companies (companies owned by shareholders) to prioritise the interests of shareholders. The owners must come first.

In 2003, a survey was carried out to explore the feelings of customers in the mortgage market. The survey was conducted by Jonathan Michie, the Sainsbury Professor of Management, Birkbeck, University of London. An extract from the findings is shown below.

'A sample of responses from first time buyers who had not yet chosen a mortgage provider.
● 78% agreed with the statement: "I like the fact that building societies have no shareholders".
● 55% agreed with the statement: "I am more likely to trust a building society than a bank".
● 66% agreed with: "In the future I am more likely to deal with a building society".
A sample of responses from customers of mutual and co-operative organisations (mutual and co-operative organisations do not have shareholders, they are owned by their members).
● Faced with the statement: "The Co-op is trustworthy", 37% agreed "slightly" and 58% agreed "strongly".
● 86% agreed with the statement: "The Co-operative acts more in members' interests because it is answerable to us and not to big City investors".
● 75% agreed with the statement: "As the Co-op board of directors is elected by local members, my interests will be more honestly represented".'

Source: adapted from *The Guardian*, 24.6.2003.

FIXED RATES					
Lender	Rate	Fixed period	Deposit	Fee	Redemption penalty
Britannia	3.64%	2 years	5%	£299	Yes
Cheshire	4.34%	3 years	20%	£295	Yes
Coventry	4.39%	5 years	5%	£299	Yes
DISCOUNT/ TRACKERS					
Lender	Rate	Discount period	Deposit	Fee	Redemption penalty
Newcastle	3.03%	2 years	10%	£345	Yes
Abbey	3.30%	2 years	5%	£299	Yes
Nottingham	3.28%	3 years	5%	£299	Yes
Skipton	2.99%	5 years	5%	£395	Yes
CAPPED RATES					
Lender	Rate	Capped period	Deposit	Fee	Redemption penalty
Kent Reliance	4.48%	3 years	5%	£295	Yes
Marsden	4.89%	5 years	25%	£345	Yes

Table 3.1 *Mortgage deals*
Source: adapted from *London and Country Mortgages*.

Table 3.1 shows mortgage deals available on 28.9.2003. They were all offered by mutual organisations except for one, Abbey.

(a) Using information from the article, explain what is meant by the 'stakeholder concept'.
(b) What evidence is there in the article to suggest that companies which do not have shareholders look after their members better?

Question 4

stakeholders.

This has led to the rise of the STAKEHOLDER CONCEPT. Some businesses now take into account the needs of employees, customers, suppliers and the local community as well as shareholders when making important business decisions. The benefits of this approach might include the following.

● If the needs of employees are taken into account they may be better motivated, more productive, more loyal, more flexible and less likely to leave. Companies that focus too much on shareholder needs might find it difficult to recruit high quality staff.

● If businesses have a higher regard for the local community they might win their support. For example, if the local community is consulted when expansion plans are announced, there may be less resistance to the construction of new buildings. Having regard for the local community is also likely to improve the image of the company.

● Looking after suppliers can generate significant benefits. For example, if suppliers are paid more promptly they may become more flexible.

● If the needs of customers are satisfied more effectively there is likely to be an increase in business. For example, if firms deal with complaints in a friendly and supportive manner, customers are more likely to return and 'spread the good word'.

Knowledge

1. Describe the interest that each internal stakeholder has in a business.
2. List 3 functions of an entrepreneur.
3. Why are entrepreneurs often associated with small businesses?
4. List 5 possible groups of shareholders.
5. Briefly explain 4 roles of management.
6. 'The role of employees in business is changing.' Explain this statement using an example.
7. Briefly explain 3 ways in which businesses and consumers are related.
8. Why are owners, managers and employees interdependent?
9. Explain one source of conflict between:
   (a) owners and managers; (b) managers and employees; (c) businesses and consumers.
10. Why might businesses adopt the stakeholder concept?

Case study The Highland Bus Company

The Highland Bus Company provides bus services to a wide geographical area in the Scottish Highlands. It is owned by a small group of London-based shareholders and run by a management team from the company's headquarters in Inverness. The company was first formed in 1988 when James McGregor and his two brothers set up an express bus service between Inverness and Fort William. The company prospered and then began to grow quickly when the brothers started to acquire a number of other small bus companies throughout the Scottish Highlands.

Much of the McGregors' success was down to the control of costs. The brothers ran a very efficient operation. They ensured that every vehicle bought by the company was on the road earning fares. They also priced their services aggressively. For example, when competing for passengers on new routes they often charged half the fare of competitors. This resulted in a lot of the small operators either selling out to the McGregor brothers or just disappearing from the roads.

Once the competition was eliminated it was not uncommon to see prices rise by about 15-20 per cent above those charged by the original operators. However, since the services were reliable and more frequent than before, passengers didn't seem to complain very much. In addition, passenger traffic rose due to a sustained and effective marketing campaign. The Highland Bus Company, as it became named in 1992, used leaflets, local newspaper adverts and local radio stations to publicise its services. By 1999, the Highland Bus Company served 90 per cent of all bus routes north of Glasgow and Edinburgh.

In 2002 the brothers, who were all in their fifties, decided to step back from the company. They did consider selling out to a national passenger carrier such as Stagecoach. However, they felt that the price they would get in the current stock market climate would not reflect accurately the true value of the

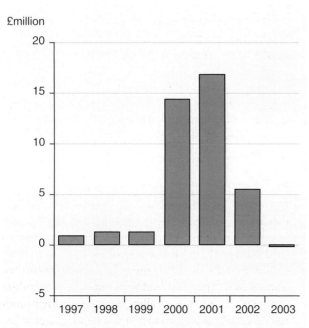

£million

Figure 3.4 *Highland Bus Company, profit 1997-2003*

company. Instead they appointed Gillian French, from a national coach company. She was installed as chief executive and given an attractive salary package. In addition to her annual salary she was to get 5 per cent of the company's profit after tax. This was a huge incentive to grow the company and keep it profitable.

In pursuit of growth Gillian looked at the possibility of running special excursions from Glasgow and Edinburgh to all parts of the Highlands and Islands. This proved to be an unfortunate ploy. Such journeys were already subject to overcapacity. An investment

in new buses, staff and marketing was a financial disaster. In an effort to recoup some of the losses Gillian embarked on a severe cost-cutting strategy throughout the organisation. She contracted out bus-cleaning, maintenance and payroll and cut administration staff to the bone. She also raised prices in the belief that customers would continue to use the services because they had no choice. Then, when passengers fell, she started to axe marginal routes. This led to more redundancies and attracted some unwanted media attention.

A group of people from Glen More, a small village in Sutherland, formed a protest group after their two-hourly bus service to Ullapool was reduced to a daily service. Further controversy arose when Gillian began delaying payments to suppliers in an effort to improve the company's cash flow. This led to one of the suppliers going out of business.

In early 2004 Gillian was sacked and James McGregor returned to the business to clear up the mess.

(a) **Using examples from the case explain the terms:**
   (i) **shareholder;**
   (ii) **stakeholder. (6 marks)**
(b) **Describe Gillian's role as a manager in the business. (8 marks)**
(c) **Explain the effects of Gillian's appointment on stakeholders in the case. (12 marks)**
(d) **To what extent might the stakeholder approach to running a company be beneficial to shareholders? (14 marks)**

Corporate aims

The CORPORATE AIMS of a business are its overall purpose. This is what the business is trying to achieve in the long term. It is likely that different types of businesses will have different aims. For example, a small plumbing business might have different aims from the Coca-Coca organisation. Aims are likely to be different at different times. A business might have a number of aims, not just the obvious one of making a profit, although not all organisations might suggest that they have this aim.

Business objectives

All businesses have OBJECTIVES. These are the **goals** of the business. They are the outcomes or targets that the business wants to gain in order to achieve its aims. The objectives of a business can be derived from its aims. For example, a business supplying recycled wood for buildings might aim to be the most important supplier of the service in an area and the first name that everyone thinks of when buying these products. The objective might be to be supplying 40 per cent of all recycled wood in the area within the next three years.

It is important for a business to have well defined objectives. These will help the business to be clear about what it wants to achieve. The performance of the business could be assessed by how effectively it achieves its objectives. For example, a business might have the objective of increasing sales by 20 per cent over three years. If it had increased sales by only 5 per cent then it might conclude that it has been unsuccessful.

It is often argued that businesses must set objectives which are SMART. This means that they should be:
- specific - stating exactly what is trying to be achieved;
- measurable - able to be measured to decide if they have been achieved;
- agreed - have the approval and understanding of everyone involved;
- realistic - able to be achieved by the business taking into account its resources, competition, markets etc;
- time specific - state a time by which they should be achieved.

Survival

From time to time all businesses, regardless of their size and status, will consider survival important.

Early stages of trading Most firms begin on a small scale, establish themselves and then grow. The owners of a new firm will probably be happy to see the firm survive in its first few months (or even years) of trading. Firms may encounter a number of problems when they first begin trading including:

- a lack of experience;
- a lack of resources;
- competition from established firms;
- unforeseen problems such as unexpected costs;
- limited recognition by customers.

Also, in the early stages decision makers might make mistakes. As a result of this uncertainty the most important business objective might be to survive in the initial stages of trading, such as the first three years.

When trading becomes difficult During a recession (☞ unit 64), for example, a business could face falling demand, bad debts and low confidence. In the UK recession of 1990-92 many well known companies ceased trading. In 1992 around 73,000 businesses collapsed. Improved trading conditions reduced this figure to around 40,000 in 1998. Individual businesses or industries may face difficulties due to competition from rivals, falling demand for their products or the effects of poor decisions. Arguably the objective of Apple, the computer manufacturer, in allowing Microsoft, a rival, to take a stake in its operation in 1997 was to protect the company during a difficult period.

Threat of takeover Firms sometimes become targets for other firms to take over. When this happens the survival of the firm in its existing form may be the main objective. One way to achieve this is to persuade the owners (the shareholders) not to sell shares to the person or company bidding for them.

In the long term it is unlikely that survival would remain the only objective, except perhaps for small businesses. Business owners tend to be ambitious and so pursue other objectives.

Profit

It is often argued that the main objective of private sector businesses (☞ unit 6) is to make a profit. It is suggested that some businesses try to PROFIT MAXIMISE. This is achieved where the difference between the total revenue earned by the business from selling its products and the total costs of those products is the greatest. The manufacturer in Table 4.1 would produce 3,000 units as this is the output where its profit is

Table 4.1 *Profit maximising position*

			£000
Output	Total costs	Total revenue	Profit
2,000	10	20	10
3,000	15	30	15
4,000	30	35	5

highest.

It may be reasonable to assume that firms aim for as much profit as possible. In practice a business is more likely to have a satisfactory level of profit as an objective. This is known as SATISFICING. Why is this likely to be a more reasonable objective?

Objectives of small firms Owners of small firms may not want to expand their output to a point where their profits are maximised. This may be because:

● it involves employing more workers, making more decisions and working longer hours;
● they may want to keep their turnover below the VAT threshold, avoiding the need to charge their customers VAT and filling in VAT returns;
● they are happy with a satisfactory profit level and their current lifestyle.

Information In practice it may be difficult to identify precisely the level of output that will maximise profits. For a business to do this it must be able to measure all of its costs at every possible level of production. It must also be able to estimate accurately the prices it can charge and predict the likely demand at these prices.

Other objectives A business might sacrifice short term profit maximisation for long term profits. This might explain why a firm lowers its price initially to build a market share and then increases price when competitors have left the market. It might also account for firms operating in the short term at a loss. In this case, the owners may be optimistic that in the future sales will pick up.

Growth

Many businesses pursue growth as their main objective. Business people argue that firms must grow in order to survive. Failure to grow might result in a loss of competitiveness, a

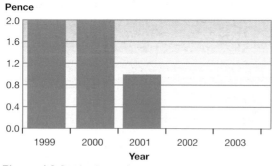

Figure 4.1 *Profit/loss before tax*

Figure 4.2 *Dividends per share*

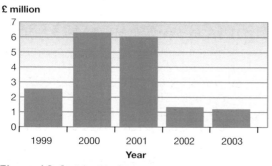

Figure 4.3 *Capial expenditure*
Source: adapted from Walker Greenbank plc, *Annual Report and Accounts, 2003.*

Walker Greenbank plc is an international group of companies which design, manufacture, market and distribute wallcoverings, furnishing fabrics and associated products for the consumer market.

Part of quote from the Chairman

'The decline in the market has been unprecedented and it is difficult to predict when it is going to stabilise. We believe the cost savings made this year will protect the group through this difficult period and if any upturn materialises the group will see a significant improvement in results. The focus will remain on cash generation, debt reduction and disposal of non-core assets ...'.

Table 4.2 *Performance details 2003*

● Operating loss of £3.8m (£6.5m in 2002)
● Loss after taxation of £7.4m (£6.6m in 2002)
● Disposal of TWIL for £0.9m in January 2003
● £2.3 million cash generated from operating activities and debt reduced by £0.6m, the first net cash inflow since 1999
● Further cost savings in the year and headcount reduced by 10%

(a) What evidence is there to suggest that Walker Greenbank's main business objective in recent years may have been survival?

decline in demand and eventual closure. If a firm is able to grow and dominate the market, in the future it may be able to enjoy some monopoly power and raise its price. By growing, a firm can diversify and reduce the risk of business enterprise. It can sell to alternative markets and introduce new products. If one market or product fails it will have a range of others to fall back on. Firms can exploit economies of scale if they grow large enough. This will enable them to be more efficient and enjoy lower costs. Motives for growth are dealt with in unit 56.

A number of people involved in business activity might benefit from growth.
- Employees may find their jobs will be more secure (although this might not always be the case if growth involves purchasing more machinery).
- Managers and directors will tend to have more power and status. For example, a director of a large oul business is likely to enjoy more power and recognition than the director of a small manufacturer.
- The salaries of directors and the chairperson are often linked to the size of the firm.
- The owners of companies might have mixed feelings about growth. On the one hand, growth often means that current profits have to be invested to fund the expansion. However, growth might generate much higher profits in the future, which will benefit the owners.

Increasing shareholder value

Many public limited companies (☞ unit 6) aim to increase SHAREHOLDER VALUE. This means they run the business in a way that will result in an increase in share price and an increase in dividends. Shareholders benefit when the share price goes up because when they sell their shares they may make a capital gain (a profit on the sale). However, shareholder value is closely linked to other business objectives. The share price will go up if there is an increase in demand for the shares, ie more investors want to buy them. An increase in demand will result if the company is expected to grow and become more profitable. Therefore, by growing the company and making more profit, shareholder value will increase.

Legislation requires companies to publish a measure of shareholder value in their annual reports. Figure 4.6 shows Silentnight Holdings total share holder return and the FTSE 350 index over the last five years. Silentnight plc is the market leader in two sectors of the domestic furniture market - beds and assembled cabinet furniture. TSR is total shareholder return, which represents share price growth and dividends reinvested. This is compared with the performance of the FTSE 350 which is an index of share prices for the top 350 companies in the UK. The graph shows that Silentnight has underperformed over the period.

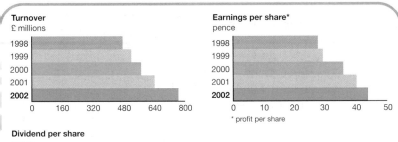

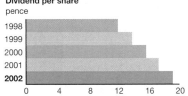

Figure 4.4 *Turnover, earnings per share and dividend per share*

Fresh prepared foods market forecast 2002-2006

Figure 4.5 *Predicted market growth*

Geest produces and markets fresh prepared foods and market-fresh produce. It has a constantly changing product portfolio and at any point in time sells around 2,000 different products. Examples include ready meals, salads, pizzas, prepared vegetables and stir frys, prepared fruit, dips, pasta and bread products, pasta sauces, soups and desserts. In 2002 around 600 new products were launched.

Source: adapted from Geest, *Annual Reports and Accounts 2002*.

Our vision
To become the best fresh prepared food and produce company wherever we operate.
We shall achieve this by excelling in service, quality, value and innovation to the delight of our customers.
We will grow in any geographical market where customer partnership and consumer demand can be developed.

(a) What evidence is there to suggest that growth is one of the objectives of Geest?
(b) Examine the possible effects of Geest's business objective on (i) shareholders and (ii) employees.

Figure 4.6 *Silentnight's TSR vs the FTSE 350 index*
Source: adapted from Silentnight, *Annual Report and Accounts, 2003.*

Managerial objectives

Sometimes the managers of a business are able to pursue their own objectives. For this to happen there must be some divorce of ownership and control. In other words the owners of the company do not necessarily control the day to day running of it. This may be possible when there is a very large number of joint owners as in a public limited company. Each owner has such a small part of the firm that he or she is able to exert little control over its running. As a result management take control and run the company according to their own objectives. These vary depending on individual managers. Some common examples might be to:

● maximise personal salary;
● maximise their departmental budgets;
● improve their status and recognition;
● maximise the number of employees in their charge;
● maximise their leisure time;
● delegate as much as work as possible;
● maximise fringe benefits, such as expense accounts for entertaining or company cars.

If managers are seen by owners to be abusing their power they are likely to be fired. To protect their positions managers often pacify owners by ensuring that the business generates enough profit to keep them satisfied. Profit may also be important to managers if their salaries are linked to profit levels.

Sales revenue maximisation

SALES REVENUE MAXIMISATION is where businesses try to gain the highest possible sales revenue. This objective will be favoured by those employees whose salaries are linked to sales. Managers and sales staff are examples of staff paid according to the sales revenue which they generate. Sales revenue maximisation is not the same as profit maximisation. In Table 4.1, the business maximised profits at an output of 3,000 units. Producing 4,000 units would have maximised sales revenue (£35,000).

Geoffrey Horrocks is the chief executive of Arnold Carrington Associates, a family civil engineering business specialising in the construction of tower blocks. He has been with the company for 7 years and guided it from a position of insecurity in the late 1990s to one of growing prosperity. The company now employs 18 people and Geoffrey's role has changed significantly. Initially he was very much involved on the engineering side, but now he deals with clients and new business. Geoffrey has delegated a great deal of responsibility to his assistant and other members of the management team. He has seen his own salary rise from £12,500 in 1997 to £110,000 in 2004. Geoffrey is a valued member of the company, but the owners, who retired to Sardinia in 2000, have lost touch with the day to day running of the business. In addition, the Carrington family are extremely wealthy and the profit from this business represents less than 5 per cent of their annual income.

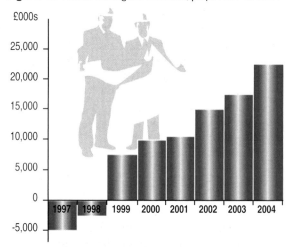

Figure 4.7 *Arnold Carrington Associates, profit 1997 to 2004*

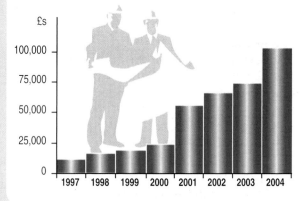

Figure 4.8 *Geoffrey Horrocks, annual salary 1997 to 2004*

(a) Explain how it is possible for management to pursue its own objectives in this business.
(b) Examine the factors that might lead to a change in the objectives of this company.

Image, reputation and social responsibility

In recent years businesses have started to appreciate how important their image is. Many have also seen the benefit of showing responsibility to a wider range of stakeholders, such as customers, employees and suppliers. Why has this happened?

- Legislation has been passed which favours consumers.
- There have been changes in social attitudes.
- Competitive pressure has forced businesses to take into account the needs of others.

Customers Companies with household names such as Heinz, Coca-Cola, Kellogg's, Ford, Cadbury's and Sainsbury's would not wish the general public to think badly of them. Some companies have made serious efforts in recent years to improve their image. For example, Skoda, the car manufacturer, has in the past had an image as a producer of 'budget', or 'unfashionable' cars. It has tried to shake off this image by exploiting its new owner's name, VW.

Faced with competition, firms are likely to lose sales if they don't take into account the needs of customers. Increasingly, firms are giving free after sales service, replacing unwanted goods without question and training their staff to deal with the public.

Employees Government and EU legislation and employee representative groups have influenced how businesses treat employees. A number of laws have been passed to protect workers (☞ units 50 and 51). An example of legislation which affects workers is the **Disability Discrimination Act, 1996.** This is designed to reduce discrimination by businesses against disabled workers.

One effect of legislation is that it protects companies with high standards of responsibility from those competitors who have little regard for health and safety at work. Unscrupulous firms will not be able to lower costs by neglecting health and safety because they will have to keep within the law.

Trade unions have argued for the rights of the workforce for many years. They have aimed to improve social facilities, wages and working conditions.

Suppliers Some firms have benefited from good relations with suppliers of raw materials and components. One example is in manufacturing, where companies are adopting **Just-in-time** manufacturing (☞ unit 55). This means that firms only produce when they have an order and stocks of raw materials and components are delivered to the factory only when they are needed. Reliable and efficient suppliers are needed by firms if they order stocks 'at the last minute'. Maintaining good relations with suppliers is likely to help this process. Examples of good relations might be prompt payment to suppliers or regular meetings to discuss each other's needs.

Behavioural theories

BEHAVIOURAL THEORIES assume that business objectives are not determined by owners and managers alone. They suggest that other stakeholders, such as the government, consumers and pressure groups, may affect the firm's objectives. The objective a company has will depend on the power of these groups to influence decisions. It is argued that groups inside and outside the business have certain minimum goals.

- The owners will require a certain level of profit to retain their interest in the business.
- Workers will demand a minimum level of pay and acceptable working conditions if they are to be retained in employment.
- Suppliers will want regular contracts, reasonable lead times and prompt payment.
- Managers will insist on enough resources to carry out their tasks (this might include an appropriate expense allowance, for example).
- The government will require the company to obey laws and pay taxes.
- Customers will demand quality products at reasonable prices.
- Pressure groups, such as environmentalists, will try to protect their interests, eg avoiding pollution.

In practice, the group with the most influence will achieve its objectives. In the 1990s animal rights pressure groups, such as Lynx, persuaded customers to buy fewer fur products. Some businesses saw sales reduced as a result and others switched to the manufacture of synthetic fur clothing. Managers and owners of large businesses sometimes pursue a policy of delayering or downsizing - reducing the number of tiers in the business hierarchy (☞ unit 40). They are convinced that such measures will make their businesses more efficient and reduce costs. This results in many employees losing their jobs.

The influence of a group may change over time or if the organisation of a business changes. For example, increased legislation might give employees more influence over

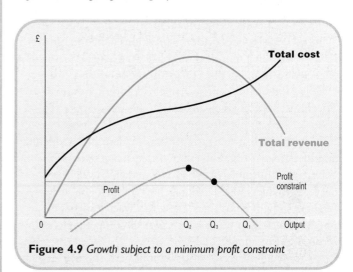

Figure 4.9 *Growth subject to a minimum profit constraint*

holidays and hours worked. A management buy out is likely to give managers more say in the business.

Sometimes groups will compromise. Figure 4.9 illustrates the total costs, total revenue and profit of a business. If it is dominated by the directors, they might have growth as an objective. This would be achieved at output level Q_1, where output is pushed to the limit before the firm makes a loss. However, the owners may prefer the business to produce a level of output Q_2 where profits are greatest. A compromise might be at Q_3, where a minimum level of profit is made for the owners, but output is high enough for some growth.

Business operations

Businesses sometimes set objectives for the operation of the organisation. For example, a business might decide that it needs to **diversify** its product range. A company might be operating with a small, relatively specific type of products. If there was a decline in demand for these products, if there was a sudden increase in competition or if the products became out of date due to changes in technology, the business might fail. Diversification is one way in which a business can protect itself against declines in certain markets. This is sometimes the reason why businesses merge with others in different markets, known as lateral integration.

A business might also decide to change the **focus** of its organisation. It might, for example, decide to focus on its main areas rather than operating in a number of areas. This is often the reason why businesses divest themselves of, or sell parts of, their organisation to concentrate on their core activities.

Objectives in the public sector

As a result of government policy in the last two decades of the twentieth century, public sector organisations (☞ unit 7) changed their objectives. Historically, the main objective of public sector businesses was to supply a public service. For example, previously state owned organisations, such as British Rail and British Gas, had to supply services in isolated regions which were unprofitable. Profit was not really a motive for public sector organisations. Many made losses.

In the 1990s public sector organisations aimed to offer their services in a more 'business like' way. The government expected them to operate efficiently and produce a cost effective and quality service. Some had fairly substantial 'surpluses', part of which are paid to the Treasury. Public sector organisations adopted many private sector business techniques, such as marketing, business planning, budgeting and investment appraisal. For example, many schools, colleges and hospital trusts actively marketed their services. Service providers were encouraged to compete for customers. Examples might be colleges trying to attract students to obtain government funds or NHS trusts competing to sell services to fund holding GPs.

For some public sector organisations performance targets

were set to ensure that a 'good' standard of service was supplied. For example, hospitals aimed to reduce waiting lists for beds and operations. Councils had their budgets cut to ensure that waste was minimised. Sixth form colleges were instructed to improve efficiency in the delivery of their education services. The performance rates of many public sector organisations are widely published. National league tables are compiled for crime and detection rates, exam results and truancy rates. Such tables are designed to introduce an element of competition in the public sector and inform the public of performance.

What determines business objectives?

There is a number of factors that can influence the choice of objective.

The size and status of the business Many small businesses might be prepared to achieve only a satisfactory level of profit or survival in difficult times rather than expand or make a large profit. Large companies might be more concerned about growth and perhaps market domination. A business that is starting up is likely to be more concerned with survival. Later, when it has become established, other objectives such as growth may be more important.

The power of stakeholders As explained earlier, behavioural theorists argue that the stakeholder group which dominates the business is likely to have the most influence over objectives. Shareholders are likely to be more concerned about profit. Outside stakeholders might be more concerned with social objectives, such as the impact of production on the environment.

Ownership The ownership of the organisation can influence objectives. Sole traders might have different objectives from larger public limited companies or they could be the same. For example, a single owner might want to make as much profit as possible, just like the many owners of a plc. However, a plc might be very concerned about image, particularly before a share issue, whereas a sole trader may see this as a fairly unimportant objective. Whether the business is part of the public or private sector is also likely to be an influence. Public sector organisations, whilst increasingly becoming aware of the need to be efficient and make surpluses, might be more concerned about their impact on the public and society than some private organisations.

Long and short term objectives Long term and short term objectives might differ. In the long run business must make a profit to survive. In the short run, however, a business might be prepared simply to break-even, particularly if trading conditions are difficult. There are other reasons why firms might sacrifice profit in the short run. For example, firms entering a new and expanding market might take time to become established and might accept losses initially. Also, businesses seeking to invest in expensive projects that will lead to greater profit at a later date might sacrifice short term profit. For example, British Biotechnology plc, the pharmaceuticals company started in 1986, had still not made a profit by 2003. Many mobile phone companies accepted large initial expenses or losses to set up in the market, hoping to make profit only after a number of years.

External and internal pressures Pressures from outside business can affect objectives. **New legislation** may force a business to change its behaviour and take into account the effect of its activities on the environment or employees. The landfill tax, for example, might have encouraged greater recycling. Changes in employee legislation could increase costs and change profit objectives. **Changing market trends** can also influence objectives. Increasing demand for products may encourage a business to grow and expand into new areas of production.

Internal pressures might also play a part. For example, the appointment of a new chairperson might completely alter the goals of the organisation. A change in production techniques or a delayering of management might also affect objectives.

Risk Pursuing some objectives might be more risky than others. For example, trying to achieve growth by entering new and unknown markets could be very risky for a business. Some businesses are happy to take risks because the potential rewards outweigh the costs involved. Others are risk averse. It might be argued by some that the move by Morrisons in 2003 to take over Safeway was risky because the company has little experience in integrating with such a large organisation.

Corporate and business culture The values and norms of behaviour developed by a business over time, its corporate culture (☞ unit 5), are likely to influence its objectives. For example, a business that has a caring corporate culture is likely to have different objectives from one with a competitive culture.

Mission statements

Businesses are increasingly producing MISSION STATEMENTS. These include descriptions of the overall aims of the business. They tend to be aimed at stakeholders in the business. So they are often found printed in the Annual Report and Accounts of public limited companies. They include information for all stakeholders, including employees shareholders and also customers. They usually express the aims of the business in 'qualitative terms', such as emphasising the desire to be the 'best in the business' or to become the 'best in the field'. They also tend to include the values and principles of the business and perhaps its corporate culture (☞ unit 5).

Sometimes mission statements are brief. They might be a

line or two stating the main priority of the business. This will help people to identify and remember the main purpose of the business. Or they might be a short statement or a page which can be displayed in places such as reception areas. They can then be viewed by staff, customers and suppliers, showing what the business is trying to achieve. They can also be placed on company websites. Sometimes businesses produce detailed mission statements. They might include a variety of features about the aims of the business, including its main purpose and how it might evaluate success. In some cases it might even include details of the objectives of the business as well, stating targets or outcomes.

An example of a mission statement is in Figure 4.10, which shows the mission statement of Reg Vardy plc, a distributor of new and used cars.

How useful are mission statements?

It could be argued that it is important for all businesses to have a mission statement. They:
● help the business to focus;

'Our purpose is to meet the needs of the motoring public'

Enthusiasm and commitment are the distinctive characteristics of Reg Vardy, a company which has grown from one garage in a North Eastern mining town into one of the country's leading quoted motor groups.

Our company enjoys an extraordinary level of loyalty and dedication amongst its management and staff, now totalling almost 5,000. Together we are working to build Reg Vardy into a national force within the retail motor industry.

Whilst aiming to continue the Group's dramatic growth, we will all recognise the challenge of maintaining and improving standards of customer satisfaction. We are determined that, as we strive for commercial success, our Company motto 'In Pursuit of Excellence' will not be compromised.

Figure 4.10 *Mission statement of Reg Vardy*
Source: adapted from Reg Vardy plc, *Annual Reports and Accounts, 2003*.

Our mission
to make a sustainable contribution to the progress of mobility for vehicles and people

Our values
respect customers, employees, shareholders, protect the environment and follow transparent corporate reporting practices

- *Leader on the world tyre market, Michelin is in pole position on all tyre mobility related service markets*
  The Group's development is based on innovation and quality. It is acknowledged by professionals as the leader, ahead of the field in the most challenging technical segments. The Group is developing a portfolio of brands complementary to the Michelin brand, able to meet the requirements of all its customers: drivers, retailers, transport professionals and vehicle manufacturers.

- *To contribute to the progress of mobility is the essence of the Group's strategy*
  In the future there will be many more vehicles but they will be safer, have greater driver/vehicle interaction and be more environmentally-friendly. This evolution in quality offers more opportunities for growth for Michelin, which intends to:

- remain a global player
- develop profitable, targeted, high added value growth
- optimise technology, innovation, marketing and service in all its areas of expertise.

- **The Group's objectives in the medium term**
  Michelin is determined to constantly improve its ability to anticipate and react to any obstacles so that it can overcome them better. The Group's medium term objectives are to:

  - balance its sales by increasing volumes in regions with high potential growth

  - exceed the market's growth by at least 2% in volume terms on the segments and zones which are priority targets

  - regularly achieve results that surpass the cost of capital employed by optimizing the allocation of assets, improving industrial flexibility, regularly achieving free cash-flow and aiming for an operating margin of 10% on average over the cycle from 2005 onwards.

Source: adapted from Michelin, *Annual Report and Accounts 2002.*

(a) Identify the objectives of the business from information included after its mission statement.

(b) Comment on the extent to which the objectives are SMART.

Question 4

- provide a plan for the future for a business;
- make clear to all stakeholders what the business is trying to achieve.

However, it has been suggested that mission statements are little more than a publicity stunt. Indeed, there is evidence to suggest that many of the statements are predictable and bland. The vast majority of organisations have mission statements and most of them contain common themes such as:

- 'our aim is to maximise shareholder value';
- 'we will focus on customer needs';
- 'we aim to become the premier supplier of ...' ;
- 'in pursuit of excellence'.

Whether or not a mission statement actually affects the way a business operates is debatable. How many staff can remember the company's mission statement, for example? Even if a company is committed to its mission statement, it may have difficulties implementing the policies and measures needed to achieve its aims. This is particularly the case where companies operate in very diverse markets.

A further problem is that the aims and objectives of the business are not always easy to distinguish from the mission statement. Sometimes businesses state that their main aim is to expand the business through acquisition and organic growth. By placing outcomes in the statement it could be argued that these are then more specific and achievable goals or objectives. Also businesses may not make a distinction between aims and objectives deliberately in order to hide what they are trying to achieve. For example, a business might state that its aim is to be more environmentally friendly and benefit the environment. But this might be a useful tool for increasing profit, which could be shown in its more measurable objectives. So the main aim of the business might be different from that stated.

key terms

Corporate aims - the overall purpose of a business.

Behavioural theories - theories which state that business objectives are determined jointly by groups of interested parties.

Mission statement - a brief summary of a firm's aims and objectives.

Objectives - the goals or outcomes a business wants to achieve.

Profit maximisation - producing a level of output which generates the most profit for a business.

Sales revenue maximisation - producing a level of output where sales revenue is greatest.

Satisficing - generating sufficient profit to satisfy the owners, not necessarily at an output which gives greatest profit.

Shareholder value - the benefit to shareholders of a rising share price and rising dividends.

SMART (objectives) - goals which are specific, measurable, agreed, realistic and time specific.

Knowledge...Knowledge...Knowledge...Knowledge...Knowledge...Knowledge...Know

1. Under what circumstances might survival be an important objective?
2. Why might a successful business still not survive in its existing form?
3. What is the difference between short term and long term profit maximisation?
4. Why might a business pursue growth as an objective?
5. Which stakeholders involved in the business are likely to want business growth? Explain why.
6. List 5 examples of managerial objectives.
7. Who would favour sales revenue maximisation in an organisation?
8. Why has the importance of image and social responsibility as a business objective grown?
9. What factors determine business objectives?
10. What might be the objectives of public sector business organisations?
11. What is included in a mission statement?

Case study Northern Foods

Northern Foods is a leading UK food producer. The company serves most of the leading retailers in the UK and operates in the eight core product areas.

1. Recipe dishes such as pasta meals and snacks, Indian, Chinese and other international dishes.
2. Chilled savoury products such as pies, pasties quiches and scotch eggs.
3. Speciality bread such as rolls, baps, muffins, scones, baguettes and croissants.
4. Bread-based snacks such as fresh chilled sandwiches, filed rolls and pizzas.
5. Cakes and puddings.
6. Fresh chilled dairy products such as desserts, yogurts, fromage frais and cottage cheese.
7. Biscuits under the name of Fox's, the UK's largest manufacturer of premium quality biscuits.
8. Frozen foods such as pizzas under the name of Goodfellas and Dalepack grillsteaks and burgers.

In addition to creating value for shareholders Northern also recognises the needs of other stakeholders such as employees, customers, suppliers, the community and the wider environment.

Employees

Northern is committed to improving the welfare of its workforce. Many of its operations have received awards for health and safety performance. For example, Pennine Foods, Walter Hollands and Palethorpes each received a gold award from the Royal Society for the Prevention of Accidents. Northern is also committed to the development of its staff. For example, the company provides a flexible, modular training programme with business benefits accruing from work-related projects which form part of the curriculum. The Northern Foods Manufacturing Management Postgraduate Certificate is accredited by Sheffield Hallam University.

Suppliers

In recent years Northern has consolidated its supply base. It claims to have a long history of trading fairly and responsibly throughout the supply chain. The company is currently working towards monitoring the ethical standards of its suppliers through a system of co-operation and collaboration.

The community

Northern supports communities near to their operating units through donations, employee secondments and employee fundraising. Donations are made through the Northern Foods Social Responsibility Committee and site-based local charity committees. For example, £266,000 of cash donations were made in 2003. Beneficiaries included Oxfam, Samaritans, Sobriety Project Yorkshire, Farm Africa and the Citizen's Advice Bureau Grimsby. Northern also offers graduate trainee managers the chance to carry out a two week assignment with a local community organisation.

The environment

Northern manages its impact on the environment by reducing emissions and making better use of resources. For example, the company met its target for energy efficiency improvement in line with the Climate Change Levy Agreement. Most of its sites beat the 2% reduction in energy consumption target and a computer programme to monitor energy consumption in their factories was developed. Also, the company's Gunstones Bakery won an award (Acorn Level 5) following an external audit for the development of an environmental management system.

Chief executive's statement

'Our aim remains the creation of shareholder value as the most effective added value food manufacturer addressing the UK retail market.'

Source: adapted from Northern Foods, *Annual Report and Accounts, 2003.*

(a) What is meant by social responsibility as a business objective? (6 marks)

(b)(i) Calculate, as a percentage of turnover, the amount of money that Northern Foods donated to charities in 2003. (2 marks)

(ii) To what extent, in your view, is Northern committed to the local community? (8 marks)

(c) Explain the factors which might affect the degree to which Northern Foods is socially responsible. (12 marks)

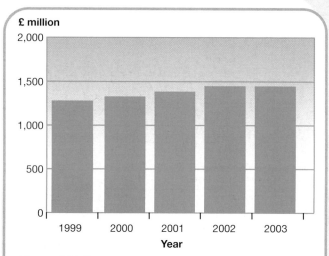

Figure 4.11 *Turnover*

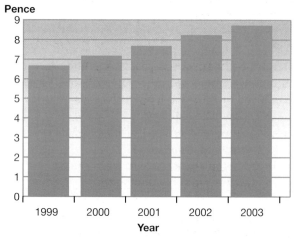

Figure 4.12 *Dividend per share*

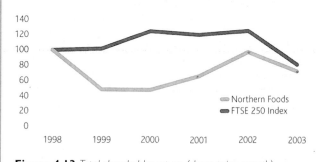

Figure 4.13 *Total shareholder return (share price growth)*

(d) Which business objectives are the most important to Northern Foods in your view? (12 marks)

5 Business Planning and Strategy

What is strategy?

Unit 4 looked at the different objectives that businesses might have. Once a business has clarified its objectives it needs to plan how to achieve them and decide on the most suitable strategies to use. A company's STRATEGY is the pattern of decisions and actions that are taken to achieve its aims and objectives. For example, in August 2003 Telling Golden Miller Group plc floated on the Alternative Investment Market (AIM). The business is a London based bus and coach operator. The placing on the AIM raised £2 million for the business, which was to be used to fund acquisitions of businesses and new depots. Since the flotation, the company has bought Crystal Coaches in Dartford, which increased the bus routes operated by the Group from 13 to 17. In January 2004 Tesco raised £773 million by a share placing on the stock exchange to fund expansion.

Planning and strategy

Most businesses will plan a strategy carefully. Business PLANNING involves deciding what is to be done, setting objectives and developing policies to achieve them. Some plans and strategies will be short term. These will focus on short term objectives such as surviving a recession. Others are long term and will be introduced to achieve long term objectives such as market domination.

There is a number of stages involved in the planning process. These include:
- identifying objectives;
- analysing the position of the business;
- deciding on a suitable strategy;
- implementing the strategy and evaluating its effectiveness.

Identifying objectives

The first stage in the process is identifying the particular objectives the business wants to achieve. This is important because without clear objectives a business may begin to under-perform. At worst it could be taken over or collapse. It is possible to categorise the objectives of a business.

Strategic objectives These are objectives that concern the general direction and overall policy of the business. They are far reaching and can influence the performance of the organisation. They will also be long-term objectives and carry a degree of risk. An example might be the merger of two of the world's largest pharmaceutical companies, Glaxo Wellcome and SmithKline Beecham in 2000 to form GlaxoSmithKline.

Tactical objectives These are less far reaching than strategic objectives. They are tactical because they are calculated and the likelihood of achieving them is more predictable. Tactical

---

Bovis Homes, the house builder, which serves the lower/middle income market with average house prices of £190,800, announced it was in a position for another year of progress in January 2004. The improvement was put down to a wider spread of sites and the continued strength of the market. Previously Bovis had concentrated its sites in the South East, South West and the Midlands, but it had recently expanded into the North of England. It suggested that sales were ahead of average and prices 10 per cent higher than forecast. Analysts predicted profits of £118 million for the business, an improvement on the record £104.7 million in 2002.

De Vere Group is a Warrington based organisation with three core activities:
- 21 up market De Vere Hotels, including the flagship Belfry Hotel at the golf course;
- Village Leisure - a chain of mid-market hotels;
- Greens, a stand alone health and fitness club.

In January 2004 it announced plans to sell two of its mid-priced hotels and two of its De Vere hotels. It argued they 'no longer fitted the company profile'. The business had carried out a three month review aimed at improving returns.

In January 2004 Boots the Chemist was expected to announce plans to cut 1,000 of the 3,000 jobs at its head office as part of a shake up in the business. The move was part of a 'Getting in Shape' programme by the company. The Boots group hoped that this new strategy would make £100 million cost savings by 2005-2006.

Source: adapted from Manchester Online.

(a) Describe the changes in strategies at the three businesses.
(b) Explain possible objectives the businesses may have had in changing their strategies.

Question 1

objectives may be set in order to achieve strategic objectives. For example, if a business has set an objective to become a global operator in six years, establishing a foothold in Europe within one year may be a tactical objective.

Operational objectives These are lower level objectives and will be short term. They will carry little risk, require less planning and can be achieved fairly quickly. For example, completing a customer order by the end of the day might be an operational objective.

Methods of analysis

Once a business has identified an objective, the next stage in planning its strategy is to consider its current position. A thorough analysis of its circumstances will provide the business with a variety of information that can be used to develop suitable strategies. Two methods that a business might use are SWOT analysis and PEST-G analysis.

SWOT analysis

The purpose of SWOT ANALYSIS is to conduct a general and quick examination of a business's current position so that it can identify preferred and likely directions in future. SWOT analysis involves looking at the internal strengths and weaknesses of a business and the external opportunities and threats.

Strengths These are things that the business and its staff do which:
- they are effective at;
- they are well known for;
- make money;
- generate business and reputation;
- lead to confidence in the market;
- cause customers to come back for repeat business;
- cause other businesses to try to learn from them.

Weaknesses These are the things that the business does badly, that it is ineffective at or that it has a poor reputation for. It also includes the factors that cause losses, hardships, disputes, grievances and complaints for a business.

Opportunities These are the directions that the business could profitably take in future because of its strengths or because of the elimination of its weaknesses. This involves a consideration of the business environment from the widest and most creative possible standpoints.

Threats Threats to a business arise from the activities of competitors and from failing to take opportunities or to build on successes. Threats also come from complacency, a lack of rigour, and from falling profits, perhaps due to rising costs.

The analysis is often carried out as a discussion exercise. It is an effective way of gathering and categorising information, illustrating particular matters and generating interest in the

business and its activities quickly. The result of such an exercise may provide a basis on which a more detailed analysis can be conducted. SWOT analysis is often used as a method by which marketing departments can plan their marketing strategy (☞ unit 25).

Pest-G analysis

PEST-G ANALYSIS examines the external environment and the global factors that may affect a business. It can provide a quick and visual representation of the external pressures facing a business, and their possible constraints on strategy. It is usually divided into five external influences on a business - political, economic, social, technological and green.

Political This is concerned with how political developments, regionally, nationally and internationally might affect a business's strategy. It might include a consideration of legislation, such as consumer laws, regulation, such as control of water companies, political pressures and the government's view of certain activities. In 2006 UK companies faced the prospect of having to comply with new UK legislation and EU regulations about age discrimination, for example.

Economic This might involve the analysis of a variety of economic factors and their effects on business. They might include:
- consumer activity - confidence, spending patterns, willingness to spend;
- economic variables - inflation, unemployment, trade, growth;
- government policy - fiscal, monetary, supply side, exchange rate;
- fixed and variable costs of the business;
- the effect of changes in product and labour markets.
For example, in a recession (☞ unit 64) demand for many products and services tends to fall. Businesses may also need to analyse the possible effects on their plans of government policy designed to lift the economy out of the recession.

Social What COMPETITVE ADVANTAGE might a business gain by social changes taking place outside of the business? For example, after the year 2000 the UK had a falling birth rate, an increase in life expectancy and an ageing population. This has led to the development of products, particularly private pensions, private medical schemes, sheltered housing developments and 'third age' holidays, aimed at the older age group. Pressure groups can also affect businesses (☞ unit 70). The anti-smoking lobby, for example, has led to smoke free areas in restaurants, in hotels, and on aircraft.

Technological Businesses operate in a world of rapid technological change (☞ unit 60). Organisations need to regularly review the impact of new technologies upon their activities. Products can become obsolete quickly. Production methods can become out of date. Communication may become inefficient as ICT develops. New markets may open.

For example, some music companies have considered sales via the Internet. The strategy towards R&D is vital in industries where technological change is rapid.

Green Environmental or 'green' factors can influence the decisions of a business. Environmental factors might include legislation to control pollution or consumers' views about the ingredients of products. Taking into account environmental considerations may raise costs, but might also generate greater sales.

Types of business strategy

When a business has completed the analysis stage it must decide upon a suitable strategy to achieve its objectives. Strategies can take a number of forms.

Functional strategies Functional strategies are designed to improve the efficiency of a business. They focus on one area, such as production, marketing, product development or financial control. However, they should not be implemented in isolation. Cooperation between departments is essential if the strategy is to be effective. Examples of functional strategies might include:

- lean production (☞ unit 55) methods to reduce waste and lower production costs;
- improving staff skills with training;
- matching consumers' needs better, through improved market research techniques.

Business level strategies These are plans a company uses to gain a competitve advantage over its rivals. They are sometimes called **generic strategies** because all businesses can use them. They often involve exploiting a particular strength that a business has. Examples of generic strategies might include:

- cost leadership, where a business aims to be the lowest cost producer in the market so that its prices can be lower;
- consolidation in a market, perhaps by developing a more effective marketing strategy;
- diversification, where a business aims to produce a wider range of goods or services.

Corporate strategies These are aimed at the long term position of the business. They are designed to develop the overall shape and nature of the organisation. For example, they might involve:

- organic growth, where a business expands through internal development by opening 10 new stores per year;
- joining together formally with another company to form a larger organisation;
- buying other companies to grow quickly.

Global strategies These involve the development of a business outside national boundaries. For example:

- setting up production plants in countries where costs are lower;

- setting up operations in other countries to avoid tariffs;
- transferring skills or products to another country because competitors in those countries lack them.

Implementation and evaluation

Once a business has identified its strategies they need to be implemented. The organisational and management systems needed to carry out the strategies have to be put into place. This might involve adapting existing systems or designing new ones. Businesses also need to maintain control while strategies are being implemented, ensuring that managers keep within their budgets, for example.

Finally, a business needs to assess whether the new strategies have been successful. To do this it must measure performance against targets that have been set. Information generated in the evaluation process may be used to adjust strategies if necessary.

Corporate culture

CORPORATE CULTURE is a set of values and beliefs that are shared by people and groups in the organisation. A simple way of explaining corporate culture might be to say that it is the 'way that things are done in business', eg the McDonald's way. For example, at Microsoft, the computer company, staff work long hours, dress casually and communicate by e-mail. These are the norms of behaviour.

Business leaders are able to create a corporate culture to help achieve the corporate objectives and strategy of the company. For example, some businesses encourage staff to solve their own problems and take risks. This will help the business to be more creative, which might make the company more innovative and give it a competitive advantage.

It is important to ensure that all staff working in an organisation understand its culture. If a positive corporate culture has been fostered by an organisation, new staff need to be trained when they are inducted (☞ unit 49). The culture must also be reinforced in everyday work situations.

There are certain benefits to a business of establishing a strong corporate culture.

- It provides a sense of identity for employees. They feel part of the business. This may allow workers to be flexible when the company needs to change or is having difficulties.
- Workers identify with other employees. This may help with aspects of the business such as team work.
- It increases the commitment of employees to the company. This may prevent problems such as high labour turnover or industrial relations problems.
- It motivates workers in their jobs. This may lead to increased productivity.
- It allows employees to understand what is going on around them. It also enables them to interpret the meaning of different organisational activities. This can prevent misunderstanding in operations or instructions

passed to them.

● It helps to reinforce the values of the organisation and senior management.

● It serves as a control device for management with which to shape employee behaviour. This can help when setting company strategy.

Marsden Wafers was in a bad way when it was bought by Alistair Marsden (no relation). The company is a wafer biscuit manufacturer in Wigan. It was purchased with help from five investors, including venture capitalists and the HSBC bank. The company had to change its name to Rivington Foods as creditors would not lend because of the previous bad reputation.

Marsden realised the value of an image to sell products. So he bought the rights to use the Pink Panther cartoon character in advertising. He needed to obtain a licence from owners MGM for this. Turnover grew from just under £1 million to £7.5 million in 2003 over an eight year period. The business sells to all the main supermarket chains, from Aldi to Tesco.

The business has perhaps found it difficult to sell into Europe. 'They are all chocolate and no biscuit' says Marsden. But this is perhaps being over critical, as the company has recently exported to markets in Kuwait and the Middle East. Not all products are winners. A wafer bar with pink chocolate did not sell because parents thought it contained 'nasties'.

The UK spends nearly £2 billion on biscuits each year and the total consumption of cakes and biscuits remains fairly constant. However, developments in production and packaging technology have meant that biscuit products now have a far longer shelf life. This makes them better for exporting overseas and selling on shelves in shops.

Rivington also has a range of gluten free wafers, endorsed by the Coeliac Society. They have taken advantage of the increased awareness of intolerance to gluten products and other ingredients which affect allergies and also a general trend in society for more health conscious products.

As a smaller manufacturer, Rivington will also be helped by product endorsement. For example, it has a range endorsed by celebrity chef Ainsley Harriot.

Source: adapted from *en*, February 2003.

(a) Analyse the situation of Rivington Foods using PEST-G factors.

Question 2

key terms

Competitive advantage - the advantage that a business has over rivals. It can be gained in a number of ways.

Corporate culture - the values, beliefs and norms that are shared by people and groups in an organisation.

PEST-G analysis - an analysis of the political, economic, social, technological and green factors affecting a business.

Planning - the process of deciding, in advance, what is to be done and how it is to be done.

Strategy - the pattern of decisions and actions that are taken by the business to achieve its objectives.

SWOT analysis - an analysis of the internal strengths and weaknesses and the external threats and opportunities facing a business.

Case study Greene King

Beer drinking in the UK is in decline. Overall sales have fallen by 9 per cent over the last decade. Wine is more appealing to women in particular, and is predicted to overtake the beer maket within the next few years. Cask ale is in even more trouble, with a 7 per cent fall in 2002 alone.

But some companies are still in there and fighting. Greene King Brewing Company sees the decline in tastes for ales as a chance to push up its market share. Its brands include IPA, Abbot Ale, Ruddles County and Old Speckled Hen. It now has a 15.4 per cent market share.

Rooney Anand was appointed managing director in 2001. He found a traditional British brewing company - conservative, hierarchical, loyal to products and ingrained habits. 'We had good beer, good brands and strong customer relationships' he said and that 'what people lacked in external focus they made up for in passion: they'd bleed Greene King'. But the focus on production lacked urgency and looking at the outside world. Buying other companies was the way to grow, rather than internally. There was little communication across functions and no feel of 'one company'.

Anand changed it round by refocussing on underused assets rather than radical cuts in jobs and changes. The company was passionate about its beer, but then why was quality so variable? Improvements have been made in many areas including labs. Greene King upgraded and gained ISO 9001 quality status across the whole company. It also began training people to taste in every department. So far 500 have been trained. No batch leaves without tasting at every part in the process. Everyone is responsible for quality. People now understand what the product is and there is greater consistency. Publicans and their staff who sell the beer are also given training and advice on storage and handling - a revolutionary improvement.

Another effort is in strengthening the brands. Too often the brands have been left unchanged. Efforts therefore need to be made to open the brands up to wider audiences, without putting off core buyers. As the figures show, there is no inevitability to the

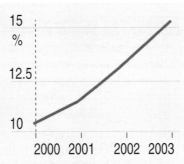

Figure 5.1 *Greene King market share of cask ale*
Source: adapted from Greene King estimates.

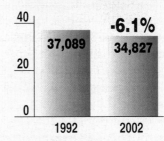

Figure 5.2 *Beer market sales*
Source: adapted from Industry estimates.

Figure 5.3 *Cask ale sales*
Source: adapted from Greene King estimates.

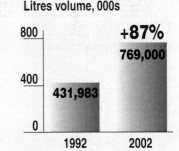

Figure 5.4 *Wine market sales*
Source: adapted from ACNielson.

decline in real-ale if it is handled correctly.

The company is keen to stress that not everything is perfect. Its a competitive world and keeping up is a marathon. However, Greene King argues that with honest products and good people there's little a firm can't do.

Source: adapted from *The Observer*, 26.10.2003.

(a) (i) **Describe the corporate culture at Greene King before the changes were made. (6 marks)**

(ii) **Suggest two problems that this might have had for the business. (6 marks)**

(b) **'Greene King changed corporate strategy.' Explain this statement using examples from the article. (8 marks)**

(c) **Explain how social factors might affect the sales of beer and wine. (8 marks)**

(d) **Evaluate the operation of Greene King using SWOT analysis. (12 marks)**

What is a business organisation?

Businesses are often referred to as organisations. An ORGANISATION is a body that is set up to meet needs. For example, the St. John's Ambulance organisation was originally set up by volunteers to train the public in life saving measures.

Business organisations satisfy needs by providing people with goods and services. All organisations will:

- try to achieve objectives (☞ unit 4);
- use resources;
- need to be directed;
- have to be accountable;
- have to meet legal requirements;
- have a formal structure (☞ unit 40).

Private sector business organisations

Unit 1 showed the different methods of classifying business. One of these methods was by sector. The PRIVATE SECTOR includes all those businesses which are set up by individuals or groups of individuals. Most business activity is undertaken in the private sector. The types of business in the private sector can vary considerably. Some are small retailers with a single owner. Others are large multinational companies, such as Exxon Mobil and Cadbury Schweppes. Businesses will vary according to the legal form they take and their ownership.

- Unincorporated businesses. These are businesses where there is no legal difference between the owners and the business. Everything is carried out in the name of the owner or owners. These firms tend to be small, owned either by one person or a few partners.
- Incorporated businesses. An incorporated body is one

which has a separate legal identity from its owners. In other words, the business can be sued, can be taken over and can be liquidated.

Figure 6.1 shows the different types of business organisation in the private sector, their legal status and their ownership. These are examined in the rest of this unit.

The sole trader

The simplest and most common form of private sector business is a SOLE TRADER or SOLE PROPRIETOR. This type of business is owned by just one person. The owner runs the business and may employ any number of people to help.

Sole traders can be found in different types of production. In the primary sector many farmers and fishermen operate like this. In the secondary sector there are small scale manufacturers, builders and construction firms. The tertiary sector probably contains the largest number of sole traders. They supply a wide range of services, such as hairdressing, retailing, restaurants, gardening and other household services. Many sole traders exist in retailing and construction where a very large number of shops and small construction companies are each owned by one person. Although there are many more sole traders than any other type of business, the amount they contribute to total output in the UK is relatively small.

Setting up as a sole trader is straightforward. There are no legal formalities needed. However, sole traders or self-employed dealers do have some legal responsibilities once they become established. In addition, some types of business need to obtain special permission before trading.

- Once turnover reaches a certain level sole traders must register for VAT.
- They must pay income tax and National Insurance contributions.

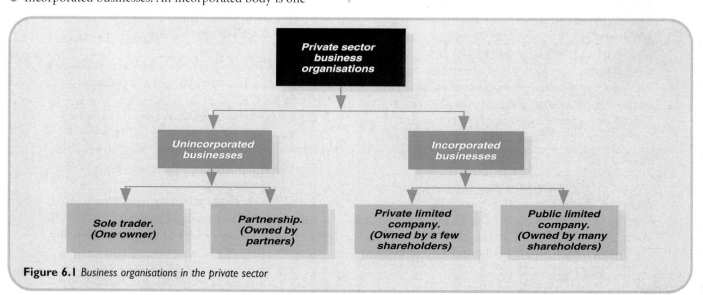

Figure 6.1 *Business organisations in the private sector*

- Some types of business activity need a licence, such as the sale of alcohol or supplying a taxi service or public transport.
- Sometimes planning permission is needed in certain locations. For example, a person may have to apply to the local authority for planning permission to run a fish and chip shop in premises which had not been used for this activity before.
- Sole traders must comply with legislation aimed at business practice. For example, legally they must provide healthy and safe working conditions for their employees (☞ unit 51).

Advantages of sole traders

- The lack of legal restrictions. The sole trader will not face a lengthy setting up period or incur expensive administration costs.
- Any profit made after tax is kept by the owner.
- The owner is in complete control and is free to make decisions without interference. For many sole traders independence is one of the main reasons why they choose to set up in business.
- The owner has flexibility to choose the hours of work he or she wants and to take holidays. Customers may also benefit. Sole traders can take individual customers' needs into account, stocking a particular brand of a good or making changes to a standard design, for example.

- Because of their small size, sole traders can offer a personal service to their customers. Some people prefer to deal directly with the owner and are prepared to pay a higher price for doing so.
- Such businesses may be entitled to government support.

Disadvantages of sole traders

- Sole traders have UNLIMITED LIABILITY. This means that if the business has debts, the owner is personally liable. A sole trader may be forced to sell personal possessions or use personal savings to meet these debts.
- The money used to set up the business is often the owner's savings. It may also come from a bank loan. Sole traders may find it difficult to raise money. They tend to be small and lack sufficient **collateral**, such as property or land, on which to raise finance. This means money for expansion must come from profits or savings.
- Although independence is an advantage, it can also be a disadvantage. A sole trader might prefer to share decision making, for example. Many sole traders work very long hours, without holidays, and may have to learn new skills.
- In cases where the owner is the only person in the business, illness can stop business activity taking place. For example, if a sole trader is a mobile hairdresser, illness will lead to a loss of income in the short term, and even a loss of customers in the long term.
- Because sole traders are unincorporated businesses, the

Elaine Thomas took over the running of her parent's fish & chip shop in Newport in 1998 when they retired. She had always wanted to run the business herself because she had ideas on how it could grow. More than half of the current business was generated during lunch times. In the week customers came in from local businesses to buy their lunch. Summer lunch times were particularly busy. In the evenings her father had always closed the shop at 8.30 pm. He wasn't interested in the 11-12.00 pm 'drunks trade' as he called it. There were two pubs within 200 yards of the shop and it seemed like a missed opportunity to Elaine. Within two weeks of taking over the business she made the following changes.

- Opening hours were extended until 12.00 midnight.
- A delivery service to local businesses was offered if they placed telephone orders over £10 (this was intended to help boost winter lunchtime trade).
- The menu was extended, offering a much wider range of fast-foods such as pizzas, home-made pies and fresh sandwiches.
- A cheaper fish supplier was used.
- Two part-time staff were hired to help share the extra work load.

The changes seemed to pay off. Over the next four years sales grew by 15 per cent per annum. Elaine was delighted and as a result became even more ambitious. She decided to open a fish restaurant. She took out a £7,000 bank loan and refurbished an empty room at the back of the shop. This was when things started to go wrong. She did not get planning permission for the restaurant and was forced to borrow another £3,000 from

her parents to pay for legal costs. The opening of the restaurant was delayed and when it was finally opened the number of diners was disappointing. Elaine spent more money advertising the restaurant, but this didn't seem to make much difference. Then, the business had a number of other setbacks. One of the nearby pubs started to sell lunch time food

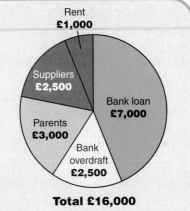

Figure 6.2 *Business debts of Elaine Thomas*

and two local businesses that were customers relocated to Cardiff. Lunch time trade fell by two-thirds as a result. Also, one of Elaine's employees badly burned her hand in the chip fryer. Elaine was underinsured and had to pay the employee compensation from the business. Elaine started to lose enthusiasm and by 2003 she was forced into bankruptcy. She owed a total of £16,000 and after selling the assets of the business she was left with only £2,500.

(a) What features of a sole trader does this case show?
(b) Using this case as an example, explain what is meant by unlimited liability.

Question 1

owner can be sued by customers in the event of a dispute.
- The business may rely on the ability and drive of one person. If that person loses interest or dies then the business will cease.

Partnerships

A PARTNERSHIP is defined in **The Partnership Act, 1890** as the 'relation which subsists between persons carrying on business with common view to profit'. Put simply, a partnership has more than one owner. The 'joint' owners will share responsibility for running the business and also share the profits. Partnerships are often found in the professions, such as accountants, doctors, estate agents, solicitors and veterinary surgeons. After sole traders, partnerships are the most common type of business organisation. It is usual for partners to specialise. A firm of chartered accountants with five partners might find that each partner specialises in one aspect of finance, such as tax law, investments or VAT returns.

There are no legal formalities to complete when a partnership is formed. However, partners may draw up a DEED OF PARTNERSHIP. This is a legal document which states partners' rights in the event of a dispute. It covers issues such as:
- how much capital each partner will contribute;
- how profits (and losses) will be shared amongst the partners;
- the procedure for ending the partnership;
- how much control each partner has;
- rules for taking on new partners.

If no deed of partnership is drawn up the arrangements between partners will be subject to the Partnership Act. For example, if there was a dispute regarding the share of profits, the Act states that profits are shared equally amongst the partners.

Advantages of partnerships
- There are no legal formalities to complete when setting up the business.
- Each partner can specialise. This may improve the running of the business, as partners can carry out the tasks they do best.
- Since there is more than one owner, more finance can be raised than if the firm was a sole trader.
- Partners can share the workload. They will be able to cover each other for holidays and illness. They can also exchange ideas and opinions when making key decisions. Also, the success of the business will not depend upon the ability of one person, as is the case with a sole trader.
- Since this type of business tends to be larger than the sole trader, it is in a stronger position to raise more money from outside the business.

Disadvantages of partnerships
- The individual partners have unlimited liability. Under the Partnership Act, each partner is equally liable for debts.

- Profits have to be shared amongst more owners.
- Partners may disagree. For example, they might differ in their views on whether to hire a new employee or about the amount of profit to retain for investment.
- The size of a partnership is limited to a maximum of 20 partners. This limits the amount of money that can be introduced from owners.
- The partnership ends when one of the partners dies. The partnership must be wound up so that the partner's family can retrieve money invested in the business. It is normal for the remaining partners to form a new partnership quickly afterwards.
- Any decision made by one partner on behalf of the company is legally binding on all other partners. For example, if one partner agreed to buy four new company cars for the business, all partners must honour this.
- Partnerships have unincorporated status, so partners can be sued by customers.

Limited partnerships The **Limited Partnerships Act 1907** allows a business to become a LIMITED PARTNERSHIP, although this is rare. This is where some partners provide capital but take no part in the management of the business. Such a partner will have LIMITED LIABILITY - the partner can only lose the original amount of money invested. She can not be made to sell personal possessions to meet any other

Doctors Wilkinson, Pritchard, Poonwalla and Sykes operate their medical centre as a partnership. The practice also employs three medical secretaries, three receptionists and two nurses. When the business was formed in 2001 it was decided that a Deed of Partnership was not needed. Each partner contributed £15,000 towards the setting up of the practice. Much of this money was spent converting an old Victorian house into a suitable practice.

Unfortunately, after two years, Dr Sykes decided to leave the practice. He did not share the same views as the other members of the partnership when it came to the prescribing of new drugs and treatments. This proved to be a problem. The business did not have enough money to pay off Dr Sykes and return the original capital contribution. The existing partnership had to be wound up and there was a difficult period when the partners couldn't agree how much profit Dr Sykes was entitled to as a result of leaving so suddenly.

(a) What are the advantages of drawing up a Deed of Partnership?
(b) In what way does the case illustrate the disadvantages of operating as a partnership?

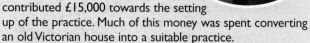

Question 2

business debts. This type of partner is called a **sleeping partner**. Even with a limited partnership there must always be at least one partner with **unlimited liability**. The Act also allows this type of partnership to have more than 20 partners.

The **Limited Liability Partnership Act, 2000** allows the setting up of a LIMITED LIABILITY PARTNERSHIP. All partners in this type of partnership have limited liability. To set up as a limited liability partnership, the business has to agree to comply with a number of regulations, such as filing annual reports with the Registrar of Companies.

Companies

There are many examples of LIMITED COMPANIES in the UK. They range from Garrick Engineering, a small family business, to British Airways which has many thousands of shareholders. One feature is that they all have a separate legal identity from their owners. This means that they can own assets, form contracts, employ people, sue and be sued in their own right. Another feature is that the owners all have **limited liability**. If a limited company has debts, the owners can only lose the money they have invested in the firm. They cannot be forced to use their own money, like sole traders and partners, to pay business debts.

The **capital** of a limited company is divided into **shares**. Each member or **shareholder** (☞ unit 3) owns a number of these shares. They are the joint owners of the company and can vote and take a share of the profit. Those with more shares will have more control and can take more profit.

Limited companies are run by **directors** who are appointed by the shareholders. The board of directors, headed by a **chairperson**, is accountable to shareholders and should run the company as the shareholders wish. If the company's performance does not to live up to shareholders' expectations, directors can be 'voted out' at an **Annual General Meeting (AGM)**.

Whereas sole traders and partnerships pay income tax on profits, companies pay corporation tax.

Forming a limited company

How do shareholders set up a limited company? Limited companies must produce two documents - the **Memorandum of Association** and **Articles of Association**. The Memorandum sets out the constitution and gives details about the company. The **Companies Act 1985** states that the following details must be included.
- The name of the company.
- The name and address of the company's registered office.
- The objectives of the company, and the scope of its activities.
- The liability of its members.
- The amount of capital to be raised and the number of shares to be issued.

A limited company must have a minimum of two members, but there is no upper limit.

The Articles of Association deal with the internal running

of the company. They include details such as:
- the rights of shareholders depending on the type of share they hold;
- the procedures for appointing directors and the scope of their powers;
- the length of time directors should serve before re-election;
- the timing and frequency of company meetings;
- the arrangements for auditing company accounts.

These two documents, along with a statement indicating the names of the directors, will be sent to the Registrar of Companies. If they are acceptable, the company's application will be successful. It will be awarded a **Certificate of Incorporation** which allows it to trade. The registrar keeps these documents on file and they can be inspected at any time by the general public for a fee. A limited company must also submit a copy of its annual accounts to the Registrar each year. Finally, the shareholders have a legal right to attend the AGM and should be told of the date and venue in writing well in advance.

Private limited companies

Private limited companies are one type of limited company. They tend to be relatively smaller businesses, although certain well known companies, such as Reebok and Littlewoods, are private limited companies. Their business name ends in Limited or Ltd. Shares can only be transferred 'privately' and all shareholders must agree on the transfer. They cannot be advertised for general sale. Private limited companies are often family businesses owned by members of the family or close friends. The directors of these firms tend to be shareholders and are involved in the running of the business. Many manufacturing firms are private limited companies rather than sole traders or partnerships.

Advantages
- Shareholders have limited liability. As a result more people are prepared to risk their money than in, say, a partnership.
- More capital can be raised as there is no limit on the number of shareholders.
- Control of the company cannot be lost to outsiders. Shares can only be sold to new members if all shareholders agree.
- The business will continue even if one of the owners dies. In this case shares will be transferred to another owner.

Disadvantages
- Profits have to be shared out amongst a much larger number of members.
- There is a legal procedure to set up the business. This takes time and also costs money.
- Firms are not allowed to sell shares to the public. This restricts the amount of capital that can be raised.
- Financial information filed with the Registrar can be

inspected by any member of the public. Competitors could use this to their advantage.

- If one shareholder decides to sell shares it may take time to find a buyer.

Porterhouse Property Management Ltd was incorporated in November 2003 as a private limited company. The registered office of the company is 27 Market Street, Kendal, Cumbria. The main aim of Porterhouse Property, as set out in clause 4 of its Memorandum of Association, are to act as a property services company and enter into financial transactions of all kinds.

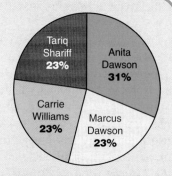

Figure 6.3 *Porterhouse Property Management Ltd - shareholders*

The chairperson, Anita Dawson, hopes to expand the company rapidly. Porterhouse currently manage about 200 country cottages in the Lake District. However, Anita wants to start buying properties and expects to use bank loans and mortgages to fund the purchases. The company is owned by four shareholders and employs eight staff.

(a) Explain the main purpose of the Memorandum of Association for Porterhouse Property Management Ltd.
(b) Discuss the possible advantages to Porterhouse Property Management Ltd of forming a private limited company.

Question 3

Public limited companies

The second type of limited company tends to be larger and is called a **public limited company**. This company name ends in plc. There are around 1.2 million registered limited companies in the UK, but only around 1 per cent of them are public limited companies. However, they contribute far more to national output and employ far more people than private limited companies. The shares of these companies can be bought and sold by the public on the stock exchange (☞ unit 33).

To become a public limited company, a Memorandum of Association, Articles of Association and a **Statutory Declaration** must be provided. This is a document which states that the requirements of all the Company Acts have been met. When the company has been issued with a **Certificate of Incorporation**, it is common to publish a **Prospectus**. This is a document which advertises the company to potential investors and invites them to buy shares before a FLOTATION. An example of a company that has been floated on the stock exchange is Egg, the online bank. Egg was floated by Prudential in 2000. It was suggested that Tussauds, Europe's

biggest attractions business, responsible for the running of Madame Tussauds waxworks, the London Eye and Alton Towers, would be floated in early 2004. The majority owner, Charterhouse Development Capital, was aiming to sell it for around £900 million.

'Going public' is expensive. This is because:

- the company needs lawyers to ensure that the prospectus is 'legally' correct;
- a large number of 'glossy' publications have to be made available;
- the company may use a financial institution to process share applications;
- the share issue has to be **underwritten** (which means that the company must insure against the possibility of some shares remaining unsold) and a fee is paid to an underwriter who must buy any unsold shares;
- the company will have advertising and administrative expenses;
- it must have a minimum of £50,000 share capital.

A public limited company cannot begin trading until it has completed these tasks and has received at least a 25 per cent payment for the value of shares. It will then receive a Trading Certificate and can begin operating, and the shares will be quoted on the Stock Exchange or the Alternative Investment Market (AIM) (☞ unit 33).

The stock exchange is a market where second hand shares are bought and sold. A full stock exchange listing means that the company must comply with the rules and regulations laid down by the stock exchange. Many of these rules are to protect shareholders from fraud. The AIM is designed for companies which want to avoid some of the high costs of a full listing. However, shareholders with shares quoted on the AIM do not have the same protection as those with 'fully' quoted shares.

Advantages

Some of the advantages are the same as those of private limited companies. For example, all members have limited liability, the firm continues to trade if one of the owners dies and more power is enjoyed due to their larger size. Others are as follows.

- Huge amounts of money can be raised from the sale of shares to the public.
- Production costs may be lower as firms may gain economies of scale (☞ unit 56).
- Because of their size, plcs can often dominate the market.
- It becomes easier to raise finance as financial institutions are more willing to lend to plcs.

Disadvantages

- The setting up costs can be very expensive - running into millions of pounds in some cases.
- Since anyone can buy their shares, it is possible for an outside interest to take control of the company.
- All of the company's accounts can be inspected by members of the public. Competitors may be able to use some of this information to their advantage. They have to publish more information than private limited companies.

- Because of their size they are not able to deal with their customers at a personal level.
- The way they operate is controlled by various Company Acts which aim to protect shareholders.
- There may be a divorce of ownership and control (☞ unit 3) which might lead to the interests of the owners being ignored to some extent.
- It is argued that many of these companies are inflexible due to their size. For example, they find change difficult to cope with.

Some public limited companies are very large indeed. They have millions of shareholders and a wide variety of business interests situated all over the world. They are known as **multinationals** which means that they have production plants in a number of different countries. For example, Kellogg's is an American based multinational company with a production plant and head office situated in Battle Creek, USA. Kellogg's has also had factories in Manchester, Wrexham, Bremen, Barcelona and Brescia near Milan.

Exiting the stock market

Sometimes a business operating as a public limited company is taken back into private ownership. This may be called 'exiting the stock market'. Why does it happen?

- The people responsible for running the business might no longer be willing to tolerate interference from the external shareholders. For example, shareholders such as financial institutions may demand higher dividends when the senior managers would prefer to reinvest profits to generate more growth.
- Sometimes businesses lose favour with the stock market. This may happen when city analysts publish unhelpful or negative reports about companies failing to reach profit targets for example. Such publicity often has the effect of lowering the share price very sharply.
- A business currently operating as a plc may be bought outright by a private individual. For example, Philip Green, bought Bhs, the high street clothes retailer, from Storehouse in 2000. He also bought Arcadia in 2002 for a reported £770 million. Both of these companies were part of a plc organisation until purchased.

Holding companies

Some public limited companies operate as HOLDING COMPANIES. This means that they are not only a company in their own right, but also have enough shares in numerous other public limited companies to exert control. This type of company tends to have a very diversified range of business activities. For example, in the UK the TTP Group plc is a holding company for a number of technology businesses. These include TTP LabTech, which supplies products to the healthcare and pharmaceutical sectors and Acumen Bioscience which develops and provides screening instruments for the drug discovery industry.

The main advantage of this type of company is that it tends to have a diverse range of business activities. This helps protect it when one of its markets fails. Also, because it is so large, it can often gain financial economies of scale. The main disadvantage is that the holding company may see the businesses it owns only as a financial asset. It may have no long term interest in the businesses or its development.

Consumer co-operatives

The UK Co-operative Movement grew from the activities of 28 workers in Rochdale, Lancashire. In 1844 they set up a retail co-operative society - The Rochdale Equitable Pioneers Society. With capital of just £28 they bought food from wholesalers and opened a shop, selling 'wholesome food at reasonable prices'. The surplus (or profit) made was returned to members of the society in the form of a 'dividend'. The dividend was in proportion to how much each member had spent. The principles of the society were:

- voluntary and open membership;
- democratic ownership - one member, one vote;
- the surplus allocated according to spending (the dividend);
- educational facilities for members and workers.

The principles of the modern co-operative movement are similar. CONSUMER CO-OPERATIVES are usually organised on a regional basis, such as The West Midlands Co-op Society or the Southern Co-op. Co-operatives are owned and controlled by their members. Members can purchase shares which entitle them to a vote at Annual General Meetings. The members elect a board of directors to make overall business decisions and appoint managers to run day to day business. Co-operatives are run in the interests of their members. Members can put themselves forward to be elected to the board of directors and become involved in a range of different activities, such as help for local community groups. Any surplus made by the co-operative is distributed to members as a dividend. Shares are not sold on the stock exchange, which limits the amount of money that can be raised.

The world's largest consumer co-operative is The Co-operative Retail Group. This was set up in 2000 by the joining of two organisations:

- The Co-operative Retail Society (CRS) in Manchester, the largest co-operative retailer at the time;
- The Co-operative Wholesale Society (CWS), which acted as a manufacturer and wholesaler of 'own brand' products for co-operative retailers.

Consumer co-operatives often have a number of different activities.

- **Food retail activities.** Perhaps the most familiar activity of co-operatives is the co-operative retail food store. Co-operative retail stores have faced fierce competition from supermarkets in recent years. They have responded by offering convenience stores which stay open later and may be sited in rural locations, such as Chelmsford (Altogether Fresher and Food Centres shops run by Chelmsford Star Co-op) or Coventry, Warwickshire and Leicestershire (Lateshops run by the Heart of England Co-op). Some are now starting to offer on-line shopping.

- **Other retail activities**. These include department stores (such as Derrys run by The Plymouth and South West Co-op), furniture shops, electrical goods shops and off licences. Shoefayre is a consumer co-operative that specialises in selling footwear.
- **Financial services**. Co-operative Financial Services (CFS) is part of The Co-operative Retail Group. It owns and runs the Co-operative Bank, whose aim is to deal only in ethical transactions, and the Co-operative Insurance Society (CIS).
- **Travel**. The UK's largest independent travel agent is Travelcare, run by The Co-operative Retail Group. Many other consumer co-operatives also offer travel services.
- **Funeral**. Funeral services are offered by some co-operatives. Examples include the Lincoln Co-operative Funeral Services and The West Midlands Co-operative Funeral Services.
- **Farming**. The Co-operative Group runs Farmcare, a farm management business. It farms around 85,000 acres in 23 locations in the UK, mostly for landowners. It grows arable crops, fruit and vegetables and has 3,000 dairy cows.

Worker co-operatives

Another form of co-operation in the UK with common ownership is a WORKER CO-OPERATIVE. This is where a business is jointly owned by its employees. A worker co-operative is an example of a producer co-operative - where people work together to produce a good or service. Examples might be a wine growing co-operative or a co-operative of farmers producing milk.

In a worker co-operative employees are likely to:
- contribute to production;
- be involved in decision making;
- share in the profit (usually on an equal basis);
- provide some capital when buying a share in the business.

In 2000 there were over 1,000 worker co-operatives in the UK. Examples ranged from Alpha Communications Ltd, a multimedia design company, to Edinburgh Bicycle Cooperative, a cycle retailer. One advantage of a worker co-operative is that all employees, as owners of the business, are likely to be motivated. Conflict will also tend to be reduced as the objectives of shareholders and employees will be the same. Worker co-operatives can involve the local community, either by giving donations to local bodies or even having them as members of the co-operative.

Building and friendly societies

Most building societies and friendly societies in the UK are MUTUAL ORGANISATIONS. They are owned by their customers, or members as they are known, rather than shareholders. Profits go straight back to members in the form of better and cheaper products. Friendly societies began in the 18th and 19th centuries to support the working classes. Today friendly societies offer a wide range of 'affordable' financial services. These include savings schemes, insurance plans and protection against the loss of income or death. They also provide benefits such as free legal aid, sheltered housing or educational grants to help young people through university. These extra benefits are distributed free of charge, paid for by trading surpluses. The government gives friendly societies special tax treatment, which reduces the amount of tax that members pay.

Building societies used to specialise in mortgages and savings accounts. Savers and borrowers got better interest rates than those offered by banks. This was possible because building societies were non-profit making. In the 1980s building societies began to diversify and compete with banks. In the late 1990s a number of building societies, such as Halifax, Alliance and Leicester, and Northern Rock, became public limited companies. The main reason for this was because mutual organisations are restricted by law from raising large amounts of capital which might be used to invest in new business ventures. This **demutualisation** process involved societies giving members 'windfall' payments, usually in the form of shares, to compensate them for their loss of membership.

Charities

Charities are organisations with very specialised aims. They exist to raise money for 'good' causes and draw attention to the needs of disadvantaged groups in society. For example, Age Concern is a charity which raises money on behalf of senior citizens. They also raise awareness and pass comment on issues, such as cold weather payments, which relate to the elderly. Other examples of national charities include Cancer Research Campaign, British Red Cross, Save the Children Fund and Mencap.

Charities rely on donations for their revenue. They also organise fund raising events such as fetes, jumble sales, sponsored activities and raffles. A number of charities run business ventures. For example, Oxfam has a chain of charity shops which sells second hand goods donated by the public.

Charities are generally run according to business principles. They aim to minimise costs, market themselves and employ staff. Most staff are volunteers, but some of the larger charities employ professionals. In the larger charities a lot of administration is necessary to deal with huge quantities of correspondence and handle charity funds. Provided charities are registered, they are not required to pay tax. In addition, businesses can offset any charitable donations they make against tax. This helps charities when raising funds.

Franchises

If a person wants independence, but is better at carrying out or improving someone else's ideas than their own, franchising might be the ideal solution. Franchising has grown steadily. It was estimated that annual turnover of franchises in the UK was around £7 billion in 2000. There were around 550 business format franchises in 2000. Over 90 per cent of

Holly Watson is a sole trader. She runs a financial services business in London. She rented an office in Fulham and has enjoyed a great deal of success since setting up in 1991. In 1997 the Inland Revenue introduced self assessment for taxpayers. Holly believed that a lot of new business could be generated as a result. She initially wanted to attract new clients by offering a competitive self-assessment tax service. She then planned to develop further business with these clients by offering a wider range of financial services, such as personal investment plans and private pensions advice.

To carry out her plans Holly needed to:
- recruit staff experienced in income tax and self-assessment;
- go on a training course to improve her knowledge of the tax system;
- move into larger premises to accommodate the new staff and to build a reception area for clients. The reception area was a drafty corridor which was not in keeping with the image of a forward looking financial services company;
- invest in advertising and promotion to attract new clients.

After a meeting with her bank manager, Holly was faced with a problem. She needed to raise £75,000 to carry out her plans. The bank, however, would not lend her any of the money as Holly was unable to offer any collateral against a loan. The bank also felt that she may have difficulty repaying such a large amount given the current position of the business. It suggested that she invite new owners to contribute some capital to the business.

(a) Describe the possible alternative business organisations that may allow Holly to raise extra funds.
(b) Suggest one type of business organisation that may be suitable for Holly's business and explain the advantages and disadvantages of your recommendation.

franchisees reported that they were trading profitably.

There are many examples of franchises in the UK. They include names such as Wimpy, Dyno-rod, Body Shop and Holiday Inn. What types of FRANCHISE exist?

- Dealer franchises. These are used by petrol companies, breweries and vehicle and computer producers. The companies (the franchisors) agree that other businesses (the franchisees) can sell their products. A written agreement between the two will cover areas such as the back up service of the franchisor, maintaining the image of the franchisor, sales targets, stock levels and the 'territory' of the franchisee. For example, Ford Motor Company has not allowed dealers more than 5 dealerships or advertising outside the allocated 'area'. Ford does not charge a fee. It earns revenue by a mark up on sales to the dealer.
- Brand franchising. This is designed to allow an inexperienced franchisee to set up from scratch. It is used by businesses such as Wimpy and McDonald's. The franchisor will already have a reputation for a product or service. It 'sells' the rights of these branded products to the franchisee. The intention is that a consumer will know they are buying the same product whether in London or Edinburgh. It is important that franchisees are monitored to make sure that the standard is maintained. To buy the franchise a business will pay an initial fee, sometimes a deposit, and then an ongoing fee which is often a percentage of turnover (a royalty of, say, 10 per cent). Often publicity, marketing and support services are carried out by the franchisor.

The benefits to the franchisor might be:
- using the specialist skills of a franchisee (as in the case of Ford dealers' retailing skills);
- the market is increased without expanding the firm;
- a fairly reliable amount of revenue (because royalties are based on turnover not profits, money is guaranteed even if a loss is made by the franchisee);
- risks and uncertainty are shared.

The advantages to franchisees might be:
- the franchisor might advertise and promote the product nationally;
- they are selling a recognised product so the chance of failure is reduced;
- services such as training and administration may be carried out by the franchisor.

Franchising is not without its problems. The royalty must be paid even if a loss is made. Also franchisees may be simply 'branch managers', rather than running their own businesses, because of restrictions in the agreement. The franchisor has the power to withdraw the agreement and in some cases, prevent the franchisee from using the premises in future.

Factors affecting the choice of organisation

Age Many businesses change their legal status as they become older. Most businesses when they start out are relatively small and operate as sole traders. Over time, as needs change, a sole trader may take on a partner and form a partnership. Alternatively, a sole trader may invite new owners to participate in the business, issue shares and form a private limited company. Public limited companies are often formed from established private limited companies that have been trading for many years.

The need for finance A change in legal status may be forced on a business. Often small businesses want to grow but do not have the funds. Additional finance can only be raised if the business changes status. Furthermore, many private limited companies 'go public' because they need to raise large amounts for expansion.

Size The size of a business operation is likely to affect its legal status. A great number of small businesses are usually sole traders or partnerships. Public limited companies tend to be large organisations with thousands of employees and a turnover of millions or billions of pounds. It could be argued that a very large business could only be run if it were a limited company. For example, certain types of business activity, such as oil processing and chemicals manufacture, require large scale production methods and could not be managed effectively as sole traders or partnerships.

Limited liability Owners can protect their own personal financial position if the business is a limited company. Sole traders and partners have unlimited liability. They may, therefore, be placed in a position where they have to use their own money to meet business debts. Some partnerships dealing with customers' money, such as solicitors, have to have unlimited liability in order to retain the confidence of their clients.

Degree of control Owners may consider retaining control of their business to be important. This is why many owners choose to remain as sole traders. Once new partners or shareholders become a part of the business the degree of control starts to diminish because it is shared with the new owners. It is possible to keep some control of a limited company by holding the majority of shares. However, even if one person holds 51 per cent of shares in a limited company, the wishes of the other 49 per cent cannot be ignored.

The nature of the business The type of business activity may influence the choice of legal status. For example, household services such as plumbing, decorating and gardening tend to be provided by sole traders. Professional services such as accountancy, legal advice and surveying are usually offered by partnerships. Relatively small manufacturing and family businesses tend to be private limited companies. Large manufacturers and producers of consumer durables, such as cookers, computers and cars, are usually plcs. The reason that these activities choose a particular type of legal status is because of the benefits they gain as a result. However, there are many exceptions to these general examples.

key terms

Consumer co-operative - a business organisation which is run and owned jointly by the members, who have equal voting rights.

Deed of Partnership - a binding legal document which states the formal rights of partners.

Flotation - the process of a company 'going public'.

Franchise - an agreement where a business (the franchisor) sells the rights to other businesses (the franchisees) allowing them to sell products or use the company name.

Holding company - a public limited company which owns enough shares in a number of other companies to exert control over them.

Limited company - a business organisation which has a separate legal entity from those of its owners.

Limited liability - where a business owner is only liable for the original amount of money invested in the business.

Limited Liability partnership - a partnership where all partners have limited liability.

Limited partnership - a partnership where some members contribute capital and enjoy a share of profit, but do not participate in the running of the business. At least one partner must have unlimited liability.

Mutual organisation - businesses owned by members who are customers, rather than shareholders.

Organisation - a body set up to meet a need.

Partnership - a business organisation which is usually owned by between 2-20 people.

Private sector - businesses that are owned by individuals or groups of individuals.

Sole trader or sole proprietor - a business organisation which has a single owner.

Unlimited liability - where the owner of a business is personally liable for all business debts.

Worker co-operative - a business organisation owned by employees who contribute to production and share in profit.

Knowledge

1. What is the difference between a corporate body and an unincorporated body?
2. State 3 advantages and 3 disadvantages of being a sole trader.
3. What is the advantage of a deed of partnership?
4. State 3 advantages and 3 disadvantages of partnerships.
5. What is meant by a sleeping partner?
6. What is the role of directors in limited companies?
7. What is the difference between the Memorandum of Association and the Articles of Association?
8. What is a Certificate of Incorporation?
9. Describe the advantages and disadvantages of private limited companies.
10. What are the main legal differences between private and public limited companies?
11. Describe the advantages and disadvantages of plcs.
12. How is a company prospectus used?
13. State an advantage and a disadvantage of a holding company.
14. State 3 features of a consumer co-operative.
15. State 3 benefits of a franchise for (a) the franchisor and the (b) the franchisee.

Case study James Hull Associates

James Hull owns Britain's largest private specialist dental business. His practice, which trades under the name of James Hull Associates, offers patients hi-tech clinical treatments, but also pampers them with soothing music and ceiling televisions in the dental surgery. James Hull has just appointed Numis Securities as a broker to look into floating the company, possibly before the end of 2003. The business is expected to be valued at between £55-£70 million and would result in Hull, who will retain 59 per cent of the business, becoming a multi-millionaire. Hull hopes to raise £20 million from the flotation.

The dental market is worth £3.25 billion a year and is said to be growing. Hull operates at the specialist end of the market. NHS dentist charges are around £80 per hour. This compares with up to £180 per hour in a private practice. However, specialists like James Hull, who may have spent a further five years training, can charge between £350 and £450 an hour. Mr Hull who started out doing mainly NHS work in 1988, currently runs 34 practices in which 85 per cent of the work is private with about 54 per cent specialist.

As part of his growth strategy James Hull bought the private practice element of the Eastman International Centre for Excellence in Dentistry, one of the most modern dentistry set-ups in the country it specialises in implants, gum and root canal work. Patients have been known to spend up to £95,000 on this type of treatment. He also announced the acquisition of two other specialist practices in October 2003. It is this specialist work that distinguishes James Hull's business from his quoted rivals, such as Oasis or Integrated Dental Holdings. The higher fees result in higher margins and faster growth for the company. Also, last year 500,000 implants were done in Germany compared to just 44,000 in the UK. Hull thinks the opportunities are huge. This will also make the flotation attractive to the City. However, dental groups have not performed that well on the stock market. The share price of Oasis is only $23\frac{1}{4}$ p. This is only about one third of its £73 million revenues. Another company, Integrated Dental Holdings (IDH), trading under the name of Whitecross, has seen its shares fall to 39p over the past year and trades at just over 10 per cent of forecast revenues of £70 million.

James Hull thinks his company will be more successful than his rivals. He says 'Although we're in the same sector, we're in a very different marketplace. People routinely pay between £5,000 and £100,000 for specialist dental treatment. We're not a "drill and fill" company'. Analysts in this sector also add that Oasis and IDH took on a lot of debt to fund their growth and are paying the price. Crucially, gross profit margins at James Hull Associates are 45 per cent compared with 39 per cent and 40 per cent of his rivals.

Source: adapted from *The Business*, 5/6.10.2003.

(a) (i) **James Hull is planning a flotation for his company. What does this mean? (6 marks)**

   (ii) **Describe the procedure that the company will have to follow before it can operate as a plc. (6 marks)**

(b) **Explain the advantages and disadvantages to James Hull Associates of operating as a public limited company. (12 marks)**

(c) **Explain how much control James Hull will have over the business after the flotation. (8 marks)**

(d) **Using evidence from the article, discuss the extent to which the flotation of the company is likely to be successful. (18 marks)**

Public sector organisations

The PUBLIC SECTOR is made up of organisations which are owned or controlled by central or local government or public corporations. They are funded by the government and in some cases from their own trading 'surplus' or profit. The amount of business activity in the public sector has decreased over the last 25 years as a result of government policy. Some public sector businesses have been transferred from the public to the private sector. However, the public sector still has an important role to play in certain areas of business activity.

Which goods and services does the public sector provide?

It has been argued that certain PUBLIC GOODS and MERIT GOODS need to be provided by public sector organisations. Public goods have two features.

- **Non-rivalry** - consumption of the good by one individual does not reduce the amount available for others.
- **Non-excludability** - it is impossible to exclude others from benefiting from their use.

Take the example of street lighting. If one person uses the light to see her way across the street, this does not 'use up' light for someone who wants to look at his watch. Also, it is impossible to stop using the light shining across the street. This means that it would be unlikely that people would pay directly for street lighting. If you paid £1 for light to cross the street, someone else could use it for free! If people will not pay, then businesses cannot make a profit and would not provide the service. Other examples of public goods may include the judiciary, policing and defence, although in some countries private policing does exist. These public goods are provided free at the point of use. They are paid for from taxation and government borrowing.

Some argue that certain merit goods should be provided by the public sector. Examples include education, health and libraries. These are services which people think should be provided in greater quantities. It is argued that if the individual is left to decide whether or not to pay for these goods, some would choose not to or may not be able to. For example, people may choose not to take out insurance policies to cover for unexpected illness. If they became ill they would not be able to pay for treatment. As a result it is argued that the state should provide this service and pay for it from taxation. The provision of merit goods is said to raise society's standard of living.

Government/publicly owned organisations

Government or publicly owned organisations may take a number of forms.

Public corporations PUBLIC CORPORATIONS are organisations set up by law to run services or industries on behalf of the government. Each corporation is run by a chairperson and board appointed by a government minister. The board is responsible for the day to day running of the corporation, but is accountable to the minister. The minister has the right to approve investment and to issue directions to the organisation in relation to matters which affect the public interest.

The **BBC (British Broadcasting Corporation)** is an example of a public corporation. It was given a royal charter to provide 'broadcasting services as public services'. It is run by a board of directors nominated by the Prime Minister, which is politically independent, although the government might try to influence its operations informally. The BBC is financed mainly though licence fees paid by television owners. However, as increasing amount of money is being raised from the sale and production of programmes for other TV companies, such as overseas businesses.

The Post Office Postal services in the UK have been provided by the public sector for many years. However, there has been a number of changes in the structure of the organisation during that time. In March 2001 the Post Office became a plc, but one wholly owned by the UK government. The change was brought about by the Postal Services Act 2000. It aimed to

(a) Is the example in the photograph above a public or a merit good? Explain your answer.
(b) Explain why either the private sector or the public sector may provide such a facility.

Question 1

create a commercially focused company with a more strategic relationship with the government. In November 2002 the name of the company was changed from Consignia to the Royal Mail Group plc. In the UK the business operates under three brands - Royal Mail, Post OfficeTM and Parcelforce Worldwide.

- **Royal Mail** provides postal services. The company has a statutory duty to provide a letter delivery service to every one of the 27 million addresses in the UK, at a uniform price, whatever the distance travelled. It must also carry out at least one daily collection from all letterboxes. Despite the increasing use of email and other electronic messaging and the continuing use of faxes, the volume of mail delivered by Royal Mail each day is 82 million items and growing.
- **Post OfficeTM** consists of a retail network with more than 14,400 branches, the combined UK total of the four major building societies and six banks. Only 500 branches are owned by Post Office Ltd, the operator of the branches. The rest are owned by the people who run the branches, including franchisees and subpostmasters and mistresses. The retail network offers more than 170 products, including financial services, travel services, government information and retail products such as greetings cards and stationery. Post OfficeTM claims that 94 per cent of people in the UK live within one mile of a post office branch, with 28 million people paying a visit at least once a week.
- **Parcelforce Worldwide** provides a time-guaranteed and next day parcel delivery service. It has the world's largest delivery network, covering more than 99.6 per cent of the world's population and reaching 239 different countries.

Network Rail In 1996 British Rail, the former nationalised rail industry, was broken up and sold off in parts. The largest part was Railtrack, the rail infrastructure which included the railway lines, stations, bridges, signals and property. Passenger transport services on the railway lines were provided by private train operators such as Virgin, Stagecoach and North Western. These businesses bid for operator's licenses from the government and paid Railtrack for using the network.

In 2002, after Railtrack was declared bankrupt, ownership was transferred to the not-for-profit company Network Rail. Network Rail is run by 100 'members' drawn from train operators, unions, passengers' groups and the public. There is perhaps some dispute about its legal status. The Office for National Statistics (ONS) classified Network Rail as a private corporation since its spending on track maintenance is not included on the national accounts. However, since the government is guaranteeing Network Rail's debt, the company cannot really 'go bust'. The strategic rail authority (SRA), the supervisory QUANGO accountable to the Department of Transport, controls Network Rail. In 2004 the government announced plans for a revamped organisation, with Network Rail running tracks and the SRA dealing with rail operations.

The Bank of England

The Bank of England is a former privately owned business that was taken into public ownership in 1946. It has a special role in the monetary system. In 1997 it was given powers by the government to decide what the level of interest rates should be in the UK. It is headed by a governor, who is accountable to the Chancellor of the Exchequer.

One business organisation that remains in the public sector, for the time being, is the Tote, the state betting operation. However, the government plans to sell this soon for around £200 million. The Tote, which has a chain of 400 high street betting shops as well as on-course outlets, turned over £500 million in the last financial year. At the end of 2003 it was expected to announce record-breaking profits. Peter Jones, the Tote chairman, wants to double its outlets to over 1,000 to give proper national coverage and spread overheads over a wider base. Currently the Tote only has 5 per cent of the betting market. The growth is expected to be funded by partnering with private equity firms or rivals.

The new operator of the Tote will be offered a seven-year licence to run the business. This means that it is extremely likely that the pooled betting business will be sold to the racing industry. At the moment the Tote is not owned by any defined entity, so it would have to be renationalised before being sold. The legislation governing the sale is likely to prohibit the company being sold in its entirety after privatisation. Bookies such as Ladbrokes, Coral and William Hill are keen to bid separately for the shops. However, Labour MPs in particular would be outraged if the Tote went to the private sector as this would break a manifesto commitment. An industry alliance known as the Racecourse Trust is expected to take on the Tote, with profits being ploughed back into the industry. The government was under pressure from the Office of Fair Trading to scrap the Tote's monopoly on pooled betting, but will avoid out-and-out privatisation.

Source: adapted from *The Observer*, 23.11.03, *The Guardian*, 24.11.2003.

(a) Using this case as an example explain the difference between a public sector business and a private sector business.
(b) Why do you think the government does not want to transfer ownership of the Tote entirely to the private sector?

Question 2

Local authority services

Some services in the UK are supplied by local authorities.
- Education. Local authorities are responsible for distributing most of the money allocated by the government to primary and secondary schools in the UK. However, some schools which have had problems have been taken out of local authority control and funded by central government.
- Recreation. Sports halls, libraries, swimming pools and parks are all examples of recreation services provided by local government.
- Housing. This includes the provision of council housing,

amenities for the homeless, sheltered accommodation and house renovation. The importance of this provision has diminished because of the purchase of council houses by tenants.

- Environment and conservation. Refuse collection, litter clearance, pest control, street cleaning and beach maintenance are examples of these services. However, an increasing number of councils is employing private sector businesses to carry out these services, such as Onyx Environmental Group plc.
- Communications. The provision of essential services to isolated towns and villages is one responsibility under this heading. Others include road maintenance and traffic control.
- Protection. This involves the provision of fire and police services, local justice, and consumer protection. Local authorities also employ trading standards officers and environmental health officers to investigate business practice and premises.
- Social services. Local government is also responsible for providing services such as community care, social workers and children's homes.

Most of the funding for the above services comes from central government grants. However, there is some scope for independent funding. For example, local authorities raise revenue from the council tax. Charges are also made for the supply of services like swimming pools and football pitches.

There are reasons why such services are provided by local rather than central government. First, it is argued that the local community is best served by those who are most sympathetic to its needs. Thus, local authorities should have the knowledge to evaluate those needs and supply the appropriate services. Second, central government is made up of large departments which often have communication problems. The decentralisation of many services should help to improve communication between the providers of services and the public. Finally, local councillors are accountable to the local electorate. If their policies are unpopular in the local community it is unlikely that they will be re-elected.

Central government departments

Central government departments supply some important services. These departments are also used to implement government policy.

- **The Treasury** is responsible for the government's economic strategy. It has many aims, including maintaining a stable economy with low inflation and sound public finances, promoting UK economic prospects and a fair and efficient tax and benefit system, ensuring a fair, competitive and efficient market in financial services which is in the public interest, improving the quality and the cost effectiveness of public services and achieving regularity and accountability in public finance.
- **The Ministry of Defence** is responsible for the provision and maintenance of the armed forces in the UK and in other parts of the world.
- **The Department for Work and Pensions** has a number of functions. It is responsible for providing benefits for those in need and other payments including child benefit, disability allowance, income support and housing benefit. It assesses benefit claims and allocates payments. It also provides help, support and benefits for people who are out of work, looking for work, returning to work or looking to start their own business.
- **The Department for Trade and Industry** aims to promote enterprise, innovation and increased productivity for business. It also provides information on all kinds of employment-related issues for employees. And it aims to develop a fairer and more prosperous economy for consumers, including consumer protection and market control.
- **The Department of Health** is responsible for the National Health Service (NHS) in the UK. It provides guidance and leadership for a variety of NHS organisations including regional health authorities, NHS trusts and Care Trusts. These organisations help to deliver local health care in the UK, such as hospitals, surgeries and health centres.
- **The Department for Education and Skills** (DfES) helps to shape government policies on education and learning and to implement these policies. These include policies designed to improve primary, secondary, tertiary, higher and adult education.
- **The Department for Environment, Food and Rural Affairs** (Defra) operates in a number of areas. For example, it seeks to limit global environmental threats, such as global warming, and safeguard people from the effects of poor air quality or toxic chemicals. It has the power to penalise those who break environmental legislation. It also aims to ensure animal health and welfare and clean and healthy water supplies, to help the food industry grow, and to protect the UK from harmful and illegal food imports.
- **The Department for Transport** implements the government's transport policy. It aims to oversee the delivery of a reliable and safe transport system which does not harm the environment. This includes areas such as road building, traffic safety and congestion, national railways, the operation of the London Underground, aviation, shipping and ports.
- **The Department for International Development** (DFID) works to promote sustainable development and eliminate world poverty.

Much of the work carried out by central and local government departments also benefits businesses in the private sector. For example, the Department for Transport gives contracts to large construction companies like Wimpey and Costain, to build roads and motorways.

QUANGOs

Some activities carried out by the government are said to be politically non-controversial. These are controlled by QUANGOs (quasi autonomous non-governmental organisations). They tend to be specialised bodies providing services which central and local government does not have the resources or the expertise to carry out. QUANGOs receive funding from and are accountable to different government departments, depending on their area of specialism. Some examples include research councils, such as the Apple and Pear Research Council, forums, such as the Zoo Forum, advisory committees, such as the Advisory Committee for Business and the Environment, tribunals and funding councils. Well known QUANGOs in 2003 included Investors in People and the Higher Education Funding Council.

It has been suggested that there are over 5,000 QUANGOS in the UK. The government defines QUANGOs more narrowly only as non-departmental government bodies (NDGBs) and suggests that there are just over 1,000 in the UK, responsible for around £23 billion.

Some QUANGOs are quite powerful. For example the Millennium Commission had the responsibility for handling funds for projects designed to celebrate the new millennium. The National Rivers Authority is responsible for the upkeep of waterways in the UK and allocating funds to clean them up.

However, in recent years they have received a certain amount of criticism. It is argued that they are not entirely non-political and can be influenced by government to achieve its objectives. It has also been suggested that members appointed by government may be biased towards its stance on certain issues. The efficiency of their operations has also been criticised.

Executive agencies

Executive agencies have become well established since their introduction in 1985. They are responsible for the supply of services previously provided by government departments. Examples include:
- the collection of government data - The Office for National Statistics;
- the processing of passport applications - The Passport and Records Agency;
- the administering of written driving tests - The Driver and Vehicle Licensing Agency;
- the operation of state pensions - The Pensions Service;
- the granting of patents - The Patents Office.

These have been separated from the policy making bodies which used to deliver them.

Executive agencies are headed by chief executives who are accountable to a government minister. Many of these leaders are recruited from the private sector. They are encouraged to introduce business principles when delivering services. The general policy of the government departments remains the responsibility of the permanent secretaries and senior civil servants.

Since the introduction of executive agencies the efficiency of services has improved considerably. For example, it now takes 7 days on average to process a passport application, compared with as much as 30 days at times in the past. Also, many benefit payments are now much cheaper to administer.

Privatisation

PRIVATISATION is the transfer of public sector resources to the private sector. It was an important feature of government policy in the 1980s and 1990s, as shown in Table 7.1. It is still seen by some as a means of improving efficiency and further privatisation is always a possibility. Privatisation has taken a number of forms.

The sale of nationalised industries NATIONALISED INDUSTRIES played an important role in the UK before 1980. They included organisations such as British Rail, British Airways, British Steel and British Telecom. These were public sector organisations which, it was argued, should be owned and controlled by the state for a number of reasons.
- To supply services which were unprofitable, such as railways in isolated areas.
- To avoid the wasteful duplication of resources where a NATURAL MONOPOLY existed.
- To control strategic industries such as energy and transport.
- To prevent exploitation by monopoly suppliers.
- To save jobs when closure threatened.

These businesses were sold off to private buyers. They became private sector businesses, owned by private shareholders.

The sale of parts of nationalised industries Some nationalised industries were broken up by parts being sold off. The Jaguar car company, which was part of the then state-owned British Leyland, was sold for £297 million. Sealink, a part of British Rail, was sold for £40 million.

Deregulation This involves lifting restrictions that prevent private sector competition. The deregulation of the communications market has allowed Mercury and cable companies to compete with British Telecom. Deregulation has also allowed bus services to be run by private sector businesses.

Contracting out Many government and local authority services have been 'contracted out' to private sector businesses. This is where contractors are given a chance to bid for services previously supplied by the public sector. Examples include the provision of school meals, hospital cleaning and refuse collection. For example, Wolds Remand Centre, run by the Group 4 security company, was Britain's first privately run prison service. In the early 1990s local authorities were forced into compulsory competitive tendering (CCT). Private businesses **had** to be asked to quote on contracts for services, bidding against council services. The contract was awarded to the most efficient, least cost service. In 2000 the Labour government replaced this. Tendering would not be compulsory and contracts would be

Table 7.1 *Sale of state owned companies to the private sector since 1979*

Date begun

1979	British Petroleum	1986	British Gas
	ICL	1987	British Airways
	Ferranti		Rolls Royce
	Fairey		Leyland Bus
1981	British Aerospace		Leyland Truck
	British Sugar		Royal Ordnance
	Cable and Wireless		British Airport
	Amersham International		Authority
1982	National Freight Corporation	1988	British Steel
	Britoil		British Leyland
1983	Associated British Ports	1989	British Water Authorities
	British Rail Hotels	1990	Electricity Area Boards
1984	British Gas Onshore Oil	1991	Electricity Generation
	Enterprise Oil	1994	British Coal
	Sealink Ferries	1995	British Rail
	Jaguar Cars	1996	British Energy
	British Telecom		Railtrack
	British Technology Group	2001	Nats (air traffic control)

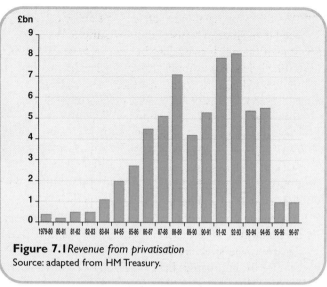

Figure 7.1 *Revenue from privatisation*
Source: adapted from HM Treasury.

awarded for 'best value' - based also on effectiveness and quality as well as efficiency.

The sale of land and property Under the **1980 Housing Act**, tenants of local authorities and New Town Development Corporations were given the right to buy their own homes. Tenants were given generous discounts, up to 60 per cent of the market value of the house, if they agreed to buy. During the 1980s, for example, about 1.5 million houses were sold. The sale of land and properties has raised almost as much money as the sale of nationalised industries.

The reasons for privatisation

During the 1980s and 1990s governments transferred a great deal of business activity from the public sector to the private sector. Different reasons have been put forward for this.
- The sale of state assets generates a great deal of income for the government. Figure 7.1 shows the revenue raised by privatisation between 1979 and 1997.
- Nationalised industries were inefficient. They lacked the incentive to make a profit, since their main aim was arguably to provide a public service. As a result their costs tended to be high and they often made losses. Also, many believed that they were overstaffed. Supporters of privatisation argued that if they were in the private sector, they would be forced to cut costs, improve their service and return a profit for the shareholders.
- As a result of deregulation, some organisations would be forced to improve their service and charge competitive prices. For example, in many areas, private firms began to compete for passengers on bus and train routes. Electricity and gas prices and telephone charges have also been reduced, arguably as a result of competition. Consumers would benefit from this and should also have greater choice. In addition, it is argued that there would be more

incentive to innovate in the private sector.
- Once these organisations had been sold to the private sector there would be little political interference. They would be free to determine their own investment levels, prices and growth rates. In the past government interference has affected the performance of nationalised industries.
- Privatisation would increase share ownership. It was argued that this would lead to a 'share owning democracy' in which more people would have a 'stake' in the success of the economy. For example, if you bought shares in BT, you would be a part owner of the company and get a dividend each year. Workers were encouraged to buy shares in their companies so that they would be rewarded for their own hard work and success.
- Privatisation should improve accountability. The losses made by many of these nationalised industries were put down to the fact that they were operating a public service. In the private sector these industries would be accountable to shareholders and consumers. Shareholders would expect a return on their investment and consumers would expect a quality service at a fair price. For example, if shareholders were not happy with the dividends paid, they could sell their shares.

Impact of privatisation on business

How have businesses changed after transferring to the private sector?
- Achieving a surplus or profit has become a more important objective. For example, the profits of BT increased from around £1,000 million in 1984, when the company was first privatised, to around £3,000 million in 1996, to nearly £3,200 million in 1998. In recent years, however, profits have fallen due to competition and poor acquisitions.
- In some cases prices have changed. In a number of cases they have fallen. Most analysts would agree that charges

made for some telephone services, gas and electricity have fallen since privatisation, for example.

● Some of the newly privatised businesses have cut back on staffing levels. For example, the Rail, Maritime and Transport Union suggested that there were 20,000 to 30,000 job losses as a result of rail privatisation. British Energy shed a quarter of its workforce before privatisation.

● Many companies increased investment following privatisation. For example, BT increased investment between 1994 and 1998 from £2,171 million to £3,030 million. Many of the water companies raised investment levels to fund new sewerage systems and purification plants. Immediately after privatisation investment rose by about £1,000 million in the water industry. However, more recently some figures suggest that investment levels are falling.

● Some of the companies have begun to offer new services and diversify. For example, North West Water offers a Leakline service which promises to repair any leaks on a customer's property provided they are outside the house.

● There has been a number of mergers and takeovers involving newly privatised companies. For example, Hanson bought Eastern Electricity and an American railway company bought the British Rail freight service. North West Water and Norweb joined together to form United Utilities and Scottish Power bought Manweb.

Arguments against privatisation

Arguments against privatisation have been put forward on both political and economic grounds. Most of the criticisms below are from the consumer's point of view.

● Privatisation has been expensive. In particular, the amount of money spent advertising each sale has been criticised. The money spent on expensive TV advertising was at the taxpayer's expense.

● It has been argued that privatisation has not led to greater competition. In some cases public monopolies with no competition have become private monopolies. These companies have been able to exploit their position. This has been a criticism levelled at gas and electricity companies. Also Railtrack managed to pay shareholders significant dividends, arguably at the expense of essential investment.

● Nationalised industries were sold off too cheaply. In nearly all cases the share issue has been over-subscribed. This shows that more people want to buy shares than there are shares available. When dealing begins on the stock market share prices have often risen sharply. This suggests that the government could have set the share prices much higher and raised more revenue. For example, there was an £11 billion rise in the value of electricity companies between privatisation in 1990 and 1996.

● Natural monopolies have been sold off. Some argue that they should remain under government control to prevent a duplication of resources.

● Once part of the private sector, any parts of the business which make a loss will be closed down. This appears to have happened in public transport. Some bus services or trains on non-profitable routes have been cut or stopped completely since deregulation.

In July 2001 Nats, the air traffic control system, was partly privatised. The organisation, which employs 5,200 people and has an annual turnover of over £500 million, is now owned by an Airline consortium (BA, Bmi, Virgin Atlantic, Britannia, Monarch, EasyJet and Airtours), the employees and the government. The main motive for the privatisation of Nats was to raise money. Air traffic is increasing by about 5 per cent a year and by 2010 traffic is expected to have risen by 43 per cent. When Nats was privatised it was working very close to its capacity. Investment was desperately needed to cope with the rise in traffic and the government felt that the private sector should fund this investment. The government also hoped to spend some of the sale proceeds on the development of public transport projects.

Unfortunately, just months after the part-privatisation, Nats began to experience financial difficulties. As a result of the terrorist attack on the New York World Trade Centre on September 11th 2001, Nats warned that revenue would fall by £230 million up to 2005 compared with previous forecasts. Transatlantic flights, which account for 44 per cent of revenues, fell by 14 per cent year-on-year in the final quarter of 2001. Overall, flights were 4 per cent lower and 11 per cent below Nats' own forecast of a year ago. The government was forced to put up to £30 million of taxpayers' money into an emergency package worked out with the banks who threatened to foreclose on loans to Nats. Banks also feared that if the government had not provided funds Nats would have gone bankrupt.

The part-privatisation of Nats was supposed to end the government's funding of the organisation. Before it went ahead the civil aviation authority (CAA), the industry regulator, warned that the part-privatisation of Nats could run into trouble in the event of a deep recession because of its suspect financial structure. Its fears have been well founded since the events of September 11th. Also many MPs, the unions and a significant number of the general public opposed the idea on safety grounds. A former transport spokesperson said part-privatisation was a crazy idea and the Liberal democrats said the government should have created a not-for-profits company that could have borrowed from the government through government-backed bonds.

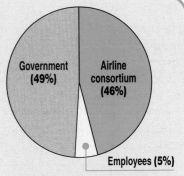

Figure 7.2 *Ownership structure of Nats after part-privatisation*
Source: adapted from *The Guardian,* 19.2.2002.

(a) Using Nats as an example, argue the case for and against privatisation.

Question 3

- Share ownership arguably has not increased. Many who bought shares sold them very quickly after. In addition, a significant number of new shareowners only own very small shareholdings in just one company.
- Many of the nationalised industries are important for the development of the nation. To put them in private hands might jeopardise their existence. For example, one of the reasons why British Steel was nationalised was to save it from possible closure. If business conditions change for the worse a private company may not guarantee supply. Also, since the shares are widely available, it is possible for overseas buyers to take control of strategic UK firms.

Regulation of privatised industries

One criticism of privatisation was that dominant industries, which were previously state owned, now operated as private sector businesses. They may be able to exploit their position by increasing their prices or reducing services. Because of this they must be controlled. Control of private sector firms is nothing new. The Competition Commission was set up to monitor firms which might act against the public's interest. It investigates cases where large dominant firms or firms merging might act to exploit their position.

Because privatisation created some private monopolies, the government set up specialist 'watchdog' agencies to protect the public. Regulatory bodies were set up to monitor and control the activities of public utilities such as gas and electricity, the organisation known as Ofgem, and the telecommunications industry, the organisation known as Ofcom (☞ unit 71).

Private Finance Initiative (PFI) and Public Private Partnerships (PPP)

The PRIVATE FINANCE INITIATIVE (PFI) was introduced in 1992, but did not really take off until the end of the 1990s. PFI is one of a range of initiatives which fall under the Public Private Partnerships (PPP) umbrella. These involve the private sector in the operation of public services. The PFI is the most frequently used. Under a PFI scheme, a capital project such as a school, hospital or housing estate has to be designed, built, financed and managed by a private consortium, under contracts that typically last for 30 years. The private consortium will be paid regularly from government funds according to its performance during that time period. If the consortium misses performance targets it will be paid less. One example of an area where PFI has been used extensively by the government is in the construction of hospitals. The government had approved 15 acute hospital PFI schemes in England by 2003. Figure 7.3 shows the schemes and their capital value.

The main advantages of PFI include the following.

- The government does not have to fund expensive one-off

Figure 7.3 *Planned PFI hospital schemes and their capital value*
Source: adapted from www.centre.public.org.uk.

payments to build large-scale projects that may involve unpopular tax increases.
- The risk involved in funding large-scale projects is transferred to the private sector. For example, if a construction company goes out of business before a project is completed the government does not have to meet any extra costs that might accrue, they are borne by the private consortium.
- Since the government is not funding the cost of projects the amount spent does not cause public borrowing to rise.

PFI does have its critics. For example, trade unions in the public sector often describe PFI as creeping privatisation of public services. Some possible disadvantages of PFI may include the following.

- As with any other forms of hire purchase the cost of the asset over a long period of time is greater than the capital cost. In particular the government can borrow money more cheaply than the private sector.
- There is a question mark over how much risk is genuinely transferred to the private sector given the government's record of bailing out private companies managing troubled public services.
- Concern has been expressed about the true cost of PFI. Public sector accountants claim that hospitals and schools would be cheaper to build using traditional methods of funding. The national audit office described the value for money test used to justify PFI projects as 'pseudo-scientific mumbo jumbo'.
- There is the worry that once private firms get involved in providing public services, the quality of provision falls as profit is pursued.
- Evidence suggests that PFI may be politically unpopular. In an election a government minister in the safe Labour seat of Wyre Forest was defeated by an independent candidate who stood as a protest against a new PFI hospital.

It may be another 20 years or more, when the first PFI contracts have been completed, before the real cost of PFI can be judged. However, the Institute of Public Policy Research, which argued that there should be no restriction on the private provision of public service, has since expressed its doubts.

Although John Prescott, the deputy Prime Minister, ruled out the wholesale privatisation of the London Underground in 1998, there has been private involvement in the provision of tube services. Under the controversial PPP, infrastructure companies maintain tracks, tunnels, stations and trains while London Underground (LU) still manages the day-to-day operation of the network and holds overall responsibility for safety. In April 2003, less than a week after the introduction of PPP, the controversy was fuelled by an incident at the Tottenham Court Road station on the Central Line.

The incident highlighted the critics' fears that safety could be at risk due to squabbles over the division of responsibilities. The network's two infrastructure maintenance companies and London Underground blamed each other for a fire alert which closed the Central Line one day in April. The problem arose when privately run Tube Lines carried out an overnight 'deep clean' of the station. This included cleaning the station's platform even though the line itself is maintained by rival infrastructure firm BCV, which was taken over by rival consortium Metronet a day later. While cleaning, dust was dislodged from the walls of the tunnel. The dust stuck to glue on the tracks which was left by contractors sticking up advertising posters on behalf of the PPP's third partner, publicly owned London Underground. The next day, when trains started running, the dust smouldered and set off fire alarms which forced the closure of a section of the Central Line for two hours during the morning rush.

Whoever was responsible for the delay could face big penalties. Under the PPP scheme, companies are fined if they exceed targets for delays. Fines can amount to £9 per passenger hour. More than 100,000 people were using the line during the morning rush meaning that a company could incur a six figure penalty for the two hour shutdown.

Tube Lines said that they clean the platform but had no responsibility for the track, BCV has responsibility for the track. However, BCV say it was LU's contractor's fault (a company called Viacom) for spilling the glue. A LU spokesman said that blame had not been attributed but also that Viacom had been spoken to. Insiders at LU said that BCV should have cleaned the glue from the line. However, BCV was still in public ownership the day of the incident. A spokesperson for RMT rail union said 'you'd better get used to it – this is the recipe for the future. The only people who are going to be kept happy by this arrangement is their lordships when it all spills into the courtroom'. 'This kind of thing was inevitable – we've been shouting it from the rooftops that this was going to happen'.

Source: adapted from *The Guardian*, 11.10.2003.

(a) Using this case as an example explain (i) what is meant by PPP (ii) how efficiency is guaranteed under PPP schemes.
(b) Analyse the possible disadvantages of PPP in this case.

Question 4

key terms

Merit goods - goods which are underprovided by private sector businesses.

Nationalised industries - public corporations previously part of the private sector which were taken into state ownership.

Natural monopoly - a situation where production costs will be lower if one firm is allowed to exist on its own in the industry, due to the existence of huge economies of scale.

Privatisation - the transfer of public sector resources to the private sector.

Private Finance Initiative (PFI) - a scheme where private businesses build hospitals and schools, for example, funded by government.

Public corporations - organisations set up by law to run services on behalf of government.

Public goods - goods where consumption by one person does not reduce the amount available to others and, once provided, all individuals will benefit.

Public sector - business organisations which are owned or controlled by central or local government, or public corporations.

QUANGOs - Quasi Autonomous Non-Governmental Organisations.

Knowledge ...Knowledge...Knowledge...Knowledge...Knowledge...Know

1. What is meant by a public corporation?
2. What is meant by non-rivalry and non-excludability when describing public goods?
3. Why are certain merit goods provided by the public sector?
4. Why do local authorities provide some public sector services?
5. How are local authority services funded?
6. Describe the responsibilities of 3 government departments.
7. Explain the difference between deregulation and contracting out as methods of privatisation.
8. What are the disadvantages of privatisation?
9. What is the function of Ofgem and Ofcom?
10. State 3 advantages and 3 disadvantages of PFI.

Case study Network Rail

When Railtrack, the owner and keeper of Britain's rail network, went bust in 2002 travellers were probably glad to see the back of an organisation associated with delays, cancellations and accidents. One of the biggest criticisms of Railtrack was that, despite consistently missing operational targets, losing money and relying on subsidies, it still managed to find the cash needed to pay shareholders. Indeed, around £700 million was paid in dividends over its six-year stewardship of the network. Railtrack was criticised for a lack of investment and spending too much time talking up the share price. In October 2002 ownership of the company was transferred to the not-for-profit company Network Rail.

Despite being taken back into public ownership, the rail industry is still regulated by a government watchdog. Tom Winsor is the rail regulator. He was appointed by the government to investigate whether Network Rail really needs the £30 billion, over the next five years, it has asked for. Winsor says that his consultants have calculated that 30 per cent of the sum asked for is the cost of inefficiency. Some examples of this are explained below.

- A maintenance contract had included a clause saying workers would be paid from the moment they arrived at the site. This led to a situation where they used motorbikes to arrive quickly at work, while their tools followed behind in slower vans.
- Network Rail allows some contractors, who are paid on a cost-plus basis, to advise Network Rail on what work needs to be done. This is rather like asking builders what work needs doing on the house, letting them name the price and then paying a percentage profit on top.
- Some parts which should last for years are being replaced after only a few months. Allegedly, this is due to unscrupulous contractors or incompetence. For example, when ballast has to be renewed, contractors have renewed all the track and sleepers as well, even though they are a long way from being worn out.
- Poor planning when the network is shut down for maintenance work (known as 'possession' of the track) often results in wasted time. For example, during many six hour possessions productive work is only undertaken for two hours. It is also common for possessions to be cancelled at the last minute, sometimes after staff have arrived on site. Network Rail revealed that a quarter of possessions were badly managed with maintenance staff working only 30 per cent or 40 per cent of the allocated time.
- One of the main problems is the contracts that Network Rail have inherited from Railtrack. Nearly £5 billion of the company's £6 billion budget is spent through contractors. Around 2,000 contractors and subcontractors were involved in maintenance and

other work, each of them, and their suppliers, taking a slice of profit. It was also argued that £1 in every £8 spent went on the management of these contracts.
- A breakdown in trust has resulted in the employment of hundreds of people to check each other's work. This mistrust has also led to disagreements about who is to blame for delays and who should pay the fines.
- Problems have arisen because Network Rail does not have a complete record of all its assets. Originally, British Rail had a lot of information about its assets but it was not organised in a systematic way. When Railtrack took over the network in 1996, large numbers of staff left the industry. Unfortunately a great deal of knowledge went with them. On the one hand information contained in the heads of engineers was lost when they left, and on the other, huge quantities of written records were destroyed. Railtrack therefore lost a vital resources − asset knowledge.

Inefficiency was not the only problem detected. Teams went through all the spending plans for track, signals, bridges, tunnels, machinery, telecommunications and property. In one case less than half the work was considered fully justified. There is also a large body of work which is either exaggerated or which Winsor and his experts cannot assess due to a lack of information.

The potential cuts in the budget are enormous. Savings between £1.4 billion and £1.7 billion could be possible in the first two years. The West Coast Mainline upgrade could be further delayed, saving up to £1 billion. Winsor reckons that in five year's time cuts of up to £2 billion a year could be made. If his recommendations are accepted by the government, Network Rail will be forced to shave £7 billion off its spending plans for the period 2004-2009. However, the company would still need £22.5 billion, £1.5 billion more than the government has budgeted for.

Source: adapted from *The Observer*, 27.6.2003.

(a) **Suggest two possible reasons why the rail industry was privatised in 1996. (4 marks)**
(b) **Explain why Railtrack was taken back into public ownership. (6 marks)**
(c) **Analyse the reasons why a government watchdog is still needed to oversee the operations of a publicly owned business organisation. (12 marks)**
(d) **Evaluate the extent to which (i) passengers and (ii) taxpayers might benefit from the work of the rail industry regulator. (18 marks)**

How are businesses organised?

All businesses need to organise their activities. Running a business involves planning, decision making, co-ordination and communication. In order to simplify these complex tasks it is helpful to organise the business into a number of clearly defined sections. For example, a business selling books to customers by mail order from a warehouse may be organised into a number of departments.

- Buying and marketing. This department purchases books from publishers. It also deals with advertising and handles the production of the mail order catalogue.
- Warehousing/dispatch. This department stores books delivered to the warehouse and deals with requests for books from the orders department. It is then responsible for putting together customers' orders and checking, wrapping, addressing and transporting parcels.
- Orders. This department receives orders from customers and informs the warehouse. It also processes all the paperwork involved in the buying and selling of books.
- Administration and finance. This department deals with payments and receipts of cash. It also handles all the personnel work, including staff wages.

This type of STRUCTURE is simple but effective. Staff in each department will understand their role. They will also know what other departments are doing in relation to their own. Small businesses may feel that they do not need to organise themselves in this way. However, as businesses grow, so does the need for organisation (☞ unit 40). Without this, the efficiency of a business could suffer. Communications may break down, mistakes might be made and staff may become confused about their roles.

The mail order business described here is organised by **function**. This is explained in the next section. There are other methods of organising a business which may be more suitable in certain situations. Large businesses often combine different methods of organisation to gain the benefits of each.

Organisation by function

One of the most common methods of organising a business is by function. This is where a business is divided into different sections or departments according to the operation undertaken. Typical functional departments in many larger businesses include production, marketing, finance and personnel. There is a number of advantages for a business in organising itself in this way.

- Specialisation. It allows each department to focus on just one business area. Specialist staff can be employed in each department. For example, the finance department may employ management and financial accountants and credit controllers. Specialisation should help to improve efficiency (☞ unit 59).

- Accountability. Each department is likely to have a manager who will be responsible for allocating departmental resources, employing staff and achieving departmental goals. The manager will be accountable to a senior executive and will be under pressure to perform. This method of organisation also allows a business to organise itself into cost or profit centres (☞ unit 28). For example, if a business decides to make one department into a cost centre, it may have to keep its costs within a limit. This will help accountability.
- Clarity. Organisation by function helps staff to understand their role and position in the business structure. For example, staff are likely to be trained in their department, will be familiar with their superiors and will know where to seek help and support.

This method of organisation will also have some drawbacks.

- Communication and co-ordination problems. When businesses are divided by function they often operate as self-contained units. Communication between departments may be limited, resulting in a lack of information sharing and some unnecessary duplication. Senior management may struggle with co-ordination if departments pursue their own objectives rather than those of the whole company. Individual departments may also be reluctant to work with other departments on projects.
- Inertia. Individual departments may become 'set in their ways' over time. They may try to resist change and prefer to

Wycombe Holdings designs and manufactures hand made furniture for retailers. However, it has recently developed an Internet shopping service where members of the public can buy furniture directly from the factory online. The company is organised into departments as shown in Figure 8.1.

Figure 8.1 *Wycombe Holdings, organisational structure*

(a) Analyse the advantages to Wycombe Holdings of using the above method of organisation.

continue their current practices.

● Bureaucracy. Organisations may become too bureaucratic. For example, there may be a large increase in paperwork if every communication from one department to another has to be made via memo or if transactions between departments require written confirmation. E-mail and company **intranets** (☞ unit 52) may solve this problem to some extent. However, time may still be wasted responding to requests.

● Suitability. Very large companies with a diversified product range could find this method of organisation unsuitable. For example, when an organisation grows there will be more departments and more layers of management. In this case senior management may find it increasingly difficult to influence what is happening lower down.

Organisation by product or activity

When a business produces a wide range of different goods or services it could find that organisation by function is not effective. Different products may need different approaches to production and marketing. For example, a multinational group may operate a supermarket chain, a property company and a construction business. It is possible that each of these businesses may have different approaches to marketing which take into account the needs of their markets. It is also

possible that different staff with different skills will be needed.

Large diversified companies often organise their business by grouping together different functional staff who are involved in the production of the same product lines or activities.

This method of organisation is often seen as 'a business within a business' and has a number of advantages.

● Each division is able to focus on the needs of a particular market segment. Thus, customers should find that their needs are satisfied more effectively.

● Each division is likely to operate as a profit centre. This will help to measure the performance of each division and allow comparisons in the business. Poor performing sections can be identified and action taken.

● Healthy competition may take place between each division. This could improve the overall performance of the organisation.

● There may be scope for reorganisation. Organisation by product provides some flexibility for the future. Loss making divisions can be closed down. Divisions supplying similar markets can be merged. Businesses that are bought by the company can be absorbed more easily. Divestment (selling) of parts of the business should also be easier.

● Co-operation may improve. Because each division is pursuing the same goal, eg profit, it is possible to share expertise and ancillary services. For example, the Burton Group, in the above illustration, might use the same

---

Arriva is a large public transport provider with a turnover that exceeded £2 billion in 2002. Its profit before tax for the year was £102.1 million. The company employs around 30,000 staff which is a 50 per cent increase since 1998. One of the

company's main objectives is growth which it hopes to achieve through acquisitions, better service delivery, innovation and marketing. The organisation of Arriva is shown in Figure 8.2.

Figure 8.2 *Arriva, organisational structure*

ARRIVA

| UK Bus | UK Trains | International | Vehicle Rental | Bus and Ccoach |

In the UK, Arriva is one of the largest bus operators with a fleet of over 6,000 vehicles serving customers in the North East, North West and South East of England, London, Yorkshire, the Midlands, Wales and Scotland.

Arriva operates two rail franchises in the UK. Arriva Trains Northern provides urban and inter-city passenger rail services across the North of England.

Arriva is one of the largest private sector providers of passenger transport in mainland Europe with some 5,000 vehicles operating in Denmark, Sweden, the Netherlands, Spain, Italy and Portugal. An extensive range of services includes trains, buses, commuter coaches and water buses.

Arriva Vehicle Rental has over 11,000 vehicles available for rent from 42 locations across the UK.

Arriva Bus and Coach distributes both new and good quality used buses and coaches for operations throughout the UK. It has the exclusive rights to import DAF bus and coach chassis and products.

Source: adapted from Arriva, *Annual Report and Accounts 2002*.

(a) Using information in Figure 8.2, explain how Arriva has organised its operations.
(b) Suggest reasons to explain why the business may be organised in this way.

Question 2

transport fleet to serve all of its branches.

Disadvantages of organisation by product include the following.

● There may be a duplication of functions in different departments. For example, an accountant may be employed in each division. It may be more cost effective to employ a small team of specialist accountants for the whole organisation.

● Competition between divisions may become counter-productive. This is likely to occur when divisions compete for the organisation's resources. A division which fails to obtain resources may become poorly motivated.

● Senior management might lose control over each individual division. For example, a decision by a junior manager in one division to extend credit to customers for longer than company policy allows might go unnoticed.

Organisation by area

Some businesses prefer to organise their activities on a geographical or regional basis. This is particularly the case if a business has a large number of very similar operations which are widely dispersed either nationally or globally. Many chainstores or multiples (☞ unit 23), for example, have this method of organisation. They tend to have a large number of stores which operate in a very similar or sometimes identical way. For example, they might sell the same products, use the same procedures and look very similar. The stores are then grouped together in regions and will be accountable to a regional or area manager. Multinational businesses operating in many different countries may also organise themselves into regions of the world, such as Europe, North America and the Far East. The advantages of organising a business geographically include the following.

● Local needs. Sometimes the needs of customers, employees and the community vary in different geographical regions. If a business is organised regionally then it should be able to serve the needs of local people more easily. This is particularly the case for multinational companies. For example, the needs of Middle Eastern customers may be different from those of North American customers.

● Improved communications. Operating on a regional basis should improve communications. For example, a regional manager may be able to more easily inform local shops of a decision than all retail outlets. To some extent this benefit is not as important today as information and communication technology allows fast and easy

---

Hanson is a large multinational company with a turnover of over £4 billion. In 2002 the company made a pre-tax profit of £433.3 million and employed nearly 30,000 staff around the world. Its core products are summarised below. Figure 8.3 shows the organisation structure of the Hanson Group.

● **Aggregates** (crushed rock, sand and gravel). Hanson is the largest producer of aggregates in the world. It produces 215 million tonnes of aggregates every year from more than 400 quarries in the UK, North America, Australia and Asia Pacific.

● **Concrete products**, such as drainage pipes for water systems and sewers and other precast concrete products such as manholes, box culverts, bridge components, retaining walls and concrete blocks and floors.

● **Bricks**. In 2002 the company made more than two billion bricks at over 35 plants in the UK, the USA and Canada.

● **Ready-mixed concrete**. Concrete is one of the world's most versatile and durable construction materials. Hanson is the third largest producer of ready-mixed concrete producing 30 million cubic metres every year from more than 800 sites in 13 different countries.

Source: adapted from Hanson, *Annual Report and Accounts*, 2002, 2003.

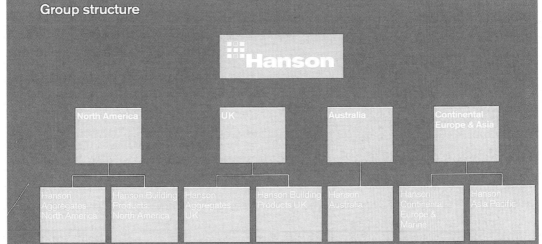

Figure 8.3 *The group structure of Hanson*

(a) Explain how Hanson is organised.
(b) Analyse the advantages of this type of organisation for the business.

Question 3

communication around the world.

● Competition. It may be possible to encourage healthy internal competition between different regions in the organisation. For example, prizes or bonuses are sometimes awarded to those regions with the highest sales or profits. In addition, regions are often used as training grounds for senior management.

Some disadvantages of regional organisation include the following.

● Duplication of resources. As with some other methods of organisation, it may not be cost effective for each region to provide certain specialist services, such as accountancy and research and development.

● Conflict. It is possible that local managers may begin to introduce their own policies. They might argue that their local situation requires a different approach from that of the business. This might lead to conflict with senior management as they see their authority being undermined.

Organisation by customer

This method is similar to organising a business by product. It involves grouping together employees who deal with a specific customer or group. This method is particularly useful where the needs of distinct customer groups are different. For example, an advertising agency might organise itself according to customer. Senior staff may be given the accounts of the most important customers. This method of organisation has a number of advantages.

● Customer needs. The needs of different customers will be served more effectively by a department focused on one particular service. Also, customers might prefer to do business with a company that is sensitive to specific customer needs.

● Market segmentation. A business may divide its market into different market segments. The advantages of market segmentation are discussed in unit 13.

However, there may also be some difficulties.

● Customer definition. It is not always possible to clearly define a particular customer group. For example, students at university may be taking a modular course, which involves more than one faculty. This may cause problems for students if different faculties operate in different ways.

● Inefficiency. It is possible that some departments are too small because they do not have enough customers. In this case costs per customer could be high. This may affect the profitability of the whole organisation.

● Control and co-ordination. As with other methods of organisation where the company is split into discrete divisions, there may be problems of control and co-ordination. Communication between departments may be limited, individual departments may pursue their own goals and senior management may find it difficult to control the organisation.

Unilever is a multinational company, which manufactures food and home and personal care products. Some of its well known brands include Knorr soups and snacks, Magnum and Cornetto ice creams, Lipton teas, Findus frozen food meals, Dove soap and OMO washing detergent. Figure 8.4 provides two pieces of analysis of sales.

Figure 8.4 *Turnover of Unilever by category, 2002*

Source: adapted from Unilever, *Annual Report and Accounts, 2002.*

(a) What two methods of organisation are suggested by Figure 8.4? Explain your answer.
(b) Analyse the possible reasons why the business might have organised itself using two methods.

Organisation by process

The production of some products or services requires a series of processes. Departments could be established to take responsibility for each process. For example, a clothing company manufacturing children's clothes may be divided into departments. Each department operates in its own workshop in the factory.

● The first stage in the production process may be design. This department would be responsible for designing new clothes and producing computerised patterns for the cutting department.

● In the cutting department fabrics are cut to size by computer operated machines. The cut fabrics are then taken to the sewing department. Here the separate pieces of fabric are sewn together to form clothes.

● The finishing department is responsible for adding seams,

frills, buttons, zips and other accessories.

● The last process in the sequence is dispatch. This department is responsible for packing the clothes and preparing the products for distribution to retailers.

Organisation by process is very similar to organisation by function and has similar benefits. Teams of staff in each department may be more focused. The company may enjoy the advantages of specialisation. There is likely to be regular communication between each stage in the production process. Management will be able to monitor clearly the performance of each department. The main disadvantage of organisation by process is a lack of flexibility. It may be difficult to switch staff from one process to another. This may be because they are not trained to work in other departments or because they do not wish to transfer. In addition, departments will have to operate at the same pace. For example, if the cutting department slows down, resources in the sewing department may lay idle. Communications problems may also arise.

key terms

Structure of a business - the way in which a business is organised.

Knowledge

1. What is meant by organisation by function?
2. Why might a business be organised in more than one way?
3. State 2 advantages and 2 disadvantages of a functional organisational structure.
4. Describe the advantages of a company organising itself by product.
5. When is regional organisation likely to be an appropriate method of organisation for a business?
6. Why might solicitors organise themselves according to customer group?
7. What is meant by organisation by process?
8. Suggest 2 types of business that may organise themselves by process.

Case study StarCars

StarCars was formed in 1994 by Ernie Anderson. He started by purchasing a Porsche 911 and hiring it out in his home town of Oxford. Demand for the car was unbelievable. By 1996 he had bought another Porsche, a Ferrari and an Aston Martin and was beginning to develop a profitable business. By 1999 he had five car hire centres - a head office and centre in Oxford, centres in Reading and Watford, and two others in London. The business was organised as shown in Figure 8.5.

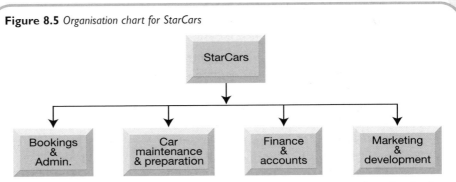

Figure 8.5 *Organisation chart for StarCars*

● **Bookings & Admin**. Each centre had one full time and two part-time staff handling bookings and administration. They dealt with customers when they booked cars, picked them up and dropped them off.
● **Car maintenance and preparation**. A 'mobile' mechanic was based at Oxford, but dealt with maintenance work on all of the cars. In each centre one person cleaned the cars and prepared them for customers before they were picked up.
● **Finance and accounts**. Two people were employed at Oxford to process wages, deal with staff problems, record business transactions, produce accounts and carry out purchasing.
● **Marketing and business development**. This section was set up in 1998 when the business started to expand. Ernie played an important role, but also hired two other staff to help him. This part of the business bought the cars. It was time consuming because the cars were expensive and required research, comprehensive knowledge, sound negotiation skills and careful judgment. The role of one of the staff was to advertise the business and find suitable sites for new centres.

Figure 8.6 StarCar centres in 2004

By 2004 StarCars had another fourteen centres, as shown on Figure 8.6. But some serious problems had arisen.

● There were communication problems. Staff in other centres often found it difficult to sort out wage queries with Oxford. Also, when a centre had a problem, such as a customer dispute, it was difficult to settle because noone seemed to have any authority. Ernie, who made all the key decisions, was often unavailable.

● Because of the distances involved, the mobile mechanic found it impossible to maintain cars all over the country. The mechanic was overworked, even though eventually an assistant was employed.

● Ernie worried about the accountability of each centre. Although he trusted the majority of his staff, he felt that there was not enough incentive for each centre to maximise performance.

● Because of the geographical distance between centres, staff felt isolated. There was often a lack of

leadership and some staff became demotivated. Staff turnover had also risen, particularly in the centres away from the South East.

Ernie felt that the solution was to organise the company geographically. Looking at Figure 8.6, he thought that the company could be divided into six areas. It would be necessary to appoint a manager responsible for each region and delegate a lot more responsibility. Regional managers would make daily visits to each centre in the region, recruit staff, and attend a management meeting with Ernie every two weeks in Birmingham. Managers could take decisions on behalf of their region without consulting Ernie.

Ernie decided to outsource all car maintenance to another business and to allow managers to buy cars for their region based on regional demand. However, managers would have to be carefully trained in this task. Ernie also decided to pay managers a low basic salary, but offer an incentive package based on the amount of time cars were hired out. If cars were hired out 80 per cent of the time an annual bonus of £10,000 would be paid. If this rose to 95 per cent a further £17,000 would be paid. Ernie expected all managers to reach the first target and the company would make a reasonable profit based on this performance. However, the second target was likely to be more of a challenge.

(a) **Explain why you think Ernie organised StarCars by function initially. (6 marks)**

(b) **Draw the new organisational chart suggested by Ernie, based on geographical location in Figure 8.6. (8 marks)**

(c) **Explain why organisation by product might be inappropriate for StarCars. (6 marks)**

(d) **Explain why accountability is likely to improve after the reorganisation. (12 marks)**

(e) **To what extent will the new organisation structure help overcome the problems StarCars is experiencing? (18 marks)**

Business and the Economic System

The basic economic problem

Unit 1 showed that business activity involved satisfying consumers' **needs** and **wants**. Businesses aim to satisfy these wants and needs by producing goods and services. When food is produced or a bus service is provided **resources** (land, labour, capital and enterprise) are used up. These resources are scarce relative to needs and wants. In other words, there are not enough resources to satisfy all consumers' needs and wants. This is known as the BASIC ECONOMIC PROBLEM. This means businesses, individuals and the government must make **choices** when allocating scarce resources between different uses. For example, a printer may have to choose whether to buy a new printing press to improve quality or some new computer

software to improve administrative efficiency.

Economics is the study of how resources are allocated in situations where they have different uses. The choices faced by decision makers can be placed in order of preference. For example, a business may be considering three investment options but can only afford one. The decision makers might decide that the order is:

1. a new computer system;
2. a fleet of cars for the sales force;
3. a warehouse extension.

The business will allocate resources to the purchase of the new computer system. The other two options are **foregone** or given up. The benefit lost from the next best alternative is called the OPPORTUNITY COST of the choice. In this example it would be the benefit lost by not having a fleet of new cars.

The function of an economy

What is an economy? An ECONOMY is a system which attempts to solve the basic economic problem. In the national economy the resources in a country are changed by business activity into goods and services which are bought by individuals. In a household economy the family budget is spent on a range of goods and services. Local and international economies also act in the same way, but at different levels. The function of an economy is to allocate scarce resources amongst unlimited wants. The basic economic problem is often broken down into three questions.

- **What should be produced?** In developed economies the number of goods and services produced from resources is immense. The economic system must decide which resources will be used to produce which products. For example, what proportion of resources should be used to produce food, housing, cars, cigarettes, cosmetics or computers? Should resources be used for military purposes? Should resources be used to generate wealth for the future? In less developed countries the decision about what to produce may be simpler. This is because the choices available are limited. For example, a very poor African village might be faced with the decision whether to produce wheat or maize. However, this is still a question about resource allocation and what to produce.
- **How should it be produced?** The way in which goods and services are produced can vary. Decisions have to be made about such things as where production will take place, the method of production and the materials and labour that will be used.
- **For whom should it be produced?** An economy has to determine how the final goods and services will be allocated amongst competing groups. For example, how much should go to students, should the unemployed receive a share of output, should Ethiopia receive a proportion of total UK output, should managers get more

---

Michael Shears runs a restaurant in London. It has only been open six months and although it has made a good start, the business is experiencing cash flow problems. Michael incurred some unexpected costs when converting the building into an attractive restaurant location. Consequently all the start-up capital was used up. However, he has managed to borrow a further £2,000 to continue the development of the business, but she cannot afford to fund all of the anticipated expenditure. Michael has identified four urgent items of expenditure:

- invest in a local radio advert to boost 'off-peak' business;
- develop and furnish a bar area where diners can wait comfortably for a table;
- completely upgrade the restaurant crockery. Michael bought the first set second hand and it does not reflect the quality of the food;
- invest in some top quality wine. The current stock does not compliment the quality of the food.

Ideally Michael would like to meet all of the above expenditure. However, he can only afford one in the list.

(a) Explain how the above example illustrates the concept of opportunity cost.
(b) Michael places the above list in the following order of preference.
   1. Develop and furnish a bar area.
   2. Invest in a local radio advert.
   3. Invest in some top quality wine,
   4. Completely upgrade the restaurant crockery.
   What is the opportunity cost in this example?

Question 1

than workers?

How the above questions are answered will depend on the type of **economic system**. It is usual to explain how resources are allocated in three types of economy - the free market economy, the planned economy and the mixed economy. The way business activity is organised will be different in each of these systems.

The organisation of production in different economic systems is also influenced by the **political system**. For example, in countries where there are free democracies, a significant proportion of goods and services are produced by independent businesses. On the other hand, in those few remaining countries which are dominated by the state, usually **communist** systems, the government plays the most important role in the production of goods and services.

Market economies

In MARKET ECONOMIES (also known as CAPITALIST ECONOMIES or FREE ENTERPRISE ECONOMIES) resources are allocated through markets (☞ unit 1).

The role of government in a free market system is limited. Its main functions are:

● to pass laws which protect the rights of businesses and consumers and punish offenders;
● to issue money and make sure that the monetary system (☞ unit 1) operates so that markets work efficiently;
● to provide certain essential products and services that would not be provided for everyone by firms, such as policing, national defence and the judiciary;
● to prevent firms from dominating the market and to restrict the power of trade unions. These activities would restrict competition and affect the workings of the market.

What to produce This decision is often made by consumers. Businesses will only produce goods if consumers will buy them and so firms must identify consumers' needs and respond to them. Firms which produce unwanted products are likely to fail.

Resources will be used to produce those goods and services which are profitable for businesses. If consumers buy more of a particular product, prices will tend to rise (☞ unit 61). Rising prices will attract firms into that industry as they see the chance of profit. For example, in recent years, new firms have set up supplying accommodation for the elderly, to exploit rising demand as the population ages in the UK.

As demand for out of date and unwanted products falls their prices will also fall. Firms will leave these industries due to a fall in profit. They will sell unwanted resources like land, buildings and equipment and make labour redundant. These resources will be used by other businesses. For example, many textile mills have closed down due to a lack of demand. Some of the buildings have been bought by other businesses and converted into furniture stores or health centres.

How to produce In market economies businesses decide this.

Businesses aim to make a profit. They will choose production methods which reduce their costs. Competition in business forces firms to keep costs and prices low. Consumers will prefer to buy their goods from firms which offer lower prices, although other things such as quality will also influence them.

How are goods and services allocated? Firms produce goods and services which consumers purchase with money. The amount of money consumers have to spend depends on their income and wealth. In market economies individuals own the factors of production. For example, workers earn wages from selling their labour. Owners of capital receive interest, owners of businesses receive profits and the owners of land receive rent. All of these can be spent on goods and services. Those individuals with the most money can buy the most products.

In practice there are no pure market economies in the world. However, some countries such as the USA and Japan have economies which possess many of the characteristics of market economies.

Implications of market economies

The working of a free market economy can affect business and consumers in many ways.

● Resources are allocated automatically by the forces of demand and supply (☞ unit 61). For example, if more people decide to buy a product, the business will expand output, hire more factors of production and earn more revenue.
● Resources are not wasted in the production of unwanted goods.
● There should be a wider choice of goods and services.
● Individuals are free to set up in business and to choose how to spend their income.
● Competition should lead to lower costs and improve quality as firms try to impress consumers. Innovation might also be more widespread as firms try to develop new products to offer more choice and new production techniques to lower costs.
● There is often an unequal DISTRIBUTION OF INCOME. Groups that cannot be involved in economic activity, such as the old or the ill, may have little or no income. Owners of profitable businesses can build up great wealth.
● MARKET IMPERFECTIONS often occur. For example, a large firm may dominate an industry by driving out competition. The large company can then force up prices and exploit consumers.
● Some goods are not provided by private firms. These include defence, but also services where they may not make a profit.
● A lot of time and money is wasted when businesses collapse. For example, a failed construction company may own partly completed buildings which can become derelict if buyers cannot be found.

In March 2002 ITV Digital went into administration. The demise of the company was bad news for the parent companies, Carlton and Granada, the Football League, subscribers, suppliers and the government. The ambition of Carlton and Granada was to build a pay TV operation capable of competing with BSkyB. They hoped that the purchase of the rights to broadcast live Nationwide football would be the kingpin of the operation.

ITV Digital disintegrated after two years of false starts, poor management and £800 million investment. After one of the worst recessions in advertising spending in memory, Carlton and Granada decided it could not tolerate the venture's massive losses. However, the cost of cutting loose from ITV Digital would be expensive, with long term repercussions. In the short term, bills of £50-£120 million could be incurred, even before any potential legal action from the Football League.

The body that represents lower league teams threatened to sue Carlton and Granada for up to £500 million in lost broadcasting and sponsorship revenues if they reneged on the three-year broadcasting deal. It was the league's refusal to renegotiate the deal that finally tipped ITV Digital over the edge. However, it was unlikely that the 72 clubs relying on the income from the deal will get anything like the money they were owed. Indeed, around 30 clubs could themselves have been on the brink of collapse. Suppliers, such as BT, set top box manufacturers and content providers could also be in trouble. They could also threaten multimillion pound law suits to recover money owed. ITV Digital's 1.3 million subscribers felt confused and angry.

The biggest losers in all of this could be the government. It was hoping to switch off the analogue television signal between 2006-2010. It would then be free to auction off the spare analogue spectrum to raise money for public expenditure. This is similar to the sale of third generation mobile phone licences. With the collapse of ITV Digital, it appeared that the government would have problems meeting the 2006-2010 target, especially taking into account the fact that Britain's cable companies, NTL and Telewest which have 1.8 million subscribers between them, were also having financial problems.

Sources: adapted from *The Guardian*, 28.3.2002 and *The Observer*, 31.3.2002.

(a) In what ways does this case illustrate some of the problems associated with market economies?
(b) How is BSkyB and the BBC likely be affected by the demise of ITV Digital?

Question 2

- Resources are often very slow to move from one use to another. For example, some workers may refuse to move from one area to another if a firm closes down, resulting in underused resources and unemployment.
- Consumers may lack the information to make choices when buying products. The range of products, their quality and their prices change so frequently that consumers find it difficult to keep up to date. Also, some firms use marketing techniques to influence consumer choice.
- In order to keep costs low, firms may choose to pollute the environment. For example, they might discharge poisonous substances into rivers.

Planned economies

In PLANNED or COMMAND ECONOMIES, government has a vital role. It plans, organises and co-ordinates the whole production process. This is unlike a market economy, where planning and organising is carried out by firms. Another difference is that resources in planned economies belong to the state. Individuals are not permitted to own property, land and other non-labour means of production.

What to produce This decision is made by government planners. They decide the type and mix of goods and services to be produced. Planners make assumptions about consumers' needs. For example, they decide how many cars, how much milk, how many shirts and how much meat should be produced. Planners then tell producers, such as farms and factories, exactly what to produce.

How to produce Government also tells producers how to produce. **Input-output analysis** is often used to make plans. For example, with a given level of technology, the state may know the land, labour, tractors and fertiliser (inputs) needed to make 1 million tonnes of wheat (the output). If an area needs 20 million tonnes, it is possible to work out the inputs needed. A complex table is drawn up which helps planners calculate the resources needed to meet the various output targets. Plans are often for 5, 10 or 15 years.

How are goods and services allocated? Goods and services are distributed to consumers through state outlets. People purchase goods and services with money they earn. Prices are set by the planners and cannot change without state instruction. Sometimes there are restrictions on the amount of particular goods and services which can be bought by any one individual, cars for example. Some goods and services, like education and health care, are provided free by the state.

Implications of planned economies

How does a planned economy affect the businesses and consumers that operate in it?
- There tends to be a more equal distribution of wealth and income. The state provides a minimum level of payment to all individuals. In addition, people are not allowed to own property, so wealth cannot be accumulated through private ownership.
- Resources are not duplicated. There is no competition in

the supply of a service like public transport, whereas in a market economy several buses might drive along the same road competing for the same passengers.

● Production is for need rather than profit. Planners decide what is needed and what is produced. Resources are not wasted through businesses producing unwanted goods.

● Long term plans can be made taking into account a range of future needs, such as population changes and the environment.

● Many resources are used up in the planning process. Vast bureaucracies, employing large numbers of people, are needed to supervise, co-ordinate and carry out plans.

● People tend to be poorly motivated. As there is no profit, there is no incentive to motivate entrepreneurs.

● Planners encourage the production of standardised goods with little variety and choice for consumers.

● Planners often get things wrong. This can lead to shortages of some goods and services and surpluses of others. Also, planners' choices are not necessarily those of individuals. For example, many command economies produce large quantities of military goods.

● Shortages of goods often result in long queues outside state shops. This often leads to black markets. Goods and services are sold unofficially by individuals well above the state imposed prices. It is argued that this leads to bribery and corruption.

● The standard of living is often poor compared with countries which use other types of economic system.

Many of the former communist countries, such as Russia, Poland and the Czech Republic, reformed their economic and political systems after 1989. They changed from planned economies to mixed economies, with a greater freedom of markets. This led to problems, as described later in this unit. In 2004 examples of planned economies might include North Korea, Cuba and Vietnam. They have many of the characteristics listed here. However, some have introduced limited private ownership and free markets to help solve some of the problems of state run systems.

Mixed economies

In reality, no country has an economy which is entirely planned or free market. Most economic systems in the world have elements of each system.

They are known as MIXED ECONOMIES. In mixed economies some resources are allocated by the government and the rest by the market system. All Western European countries have mixed economies. The public sector (☞ unit 7) in mixed economies is responsible for the supply of some public goods and merit goods. Decisions regarding resource allocation in the public sector are made by central or local government. In the private sector production decisions

North Korea is one of the world's most centrally planned and isolated economies. More than 90 per cent of the economy is socialised, agricultural land is collectivised, and the state-owned industry produces 95 per cent of manufactured goods. State control of economic affairs is unusually tight because of the small size of the population, its homogeneity and the strict rule of the leadership.

Output of the extractive industries includes coal, iron ore, magnesite, graphite, copper, zinc, lead and precious metals. Manufacturing is centred on heavy industry, including military industry, with light industry lagging far behind. Despite the use of improved seed varieties, expansion of irrigation, and the heavy use of fertilisers, North Korea has not yet become self-sufficient in food production. A shortage of arable lands, several years of poor harvests, and a cumbersome distribution system have resulted in chronic food shortages. Huge international food aid has prevented mass starvation since 1995-96, but the population remains a victim of prolonged malnutrition and deteriorating living conditions. Large amounts of military spending eat up resources needed for investment and private consumption.

The collapse of communism in the former Soviet Union and Eastern Europe in 1989-91 has disrupted important technological links. North Korea remains far behind South Korea in economic development and living standards. In November 2003, the international credit ratings agency Standard & Poor's (S&P) warned that it was simply a matter of time before the North Korean economy totally

Table 9.1 *Data for North Korea*

Population:	22.5m (est. 2003)
Climate:	Temperate with rainfall concentrated in the summer
Land use:	Arable 14%, permanent crops 2.5%, other 83.5%
Natural resources:	Coal, lead, tungsten, zinc, graphite, magnesite, iron ore, copper, gold, pyrit, salt, fluorspur and hydropower
Birth rate:	17.6 per 1,000 (est. 2003)
Death rate:	6.93 per 1,000 (est. 2003)
Literacy rate:	99%

disintegrates. A spokesperson for S&P said 'The economic model of North Korea is not sustainable'. 'We think the political leadership in North Korea does not have the capacity to undertake reforms that, say, China, began in 1979 or Vietnam began in 1986.'

Source: adapted from www.theodora.comnomy.

(a) What evidence is there in the case to suggest that North Korea is a planned economy?
(b) Analyse the drawbacks of planned economies using examples from the case.

are made by firms in response to the demands of consumers.

In the public sector, public goods and merit goods are usually provided free when used and are paid for by taxes. Examples might be roads and street lighting. In mixed economies the state usually provides a minimum standard of living for those unable to work. In the UK the state provides benefits as workers look for work and certain sickness benefits. In the public sector the state will own a significant proportion of production factors and service provision.

In the private sector individuals are allowed to own the means of production. Businesses are set up by individuals to supply a wide variety of goods and services. Competition exists between these firms. As a result, there will tend to be choice and variety. One of the roles of the government is to ensure that there is fair competition in the private sector. All private sector goods and services are allocated as in the market system described earlier.

What should be the 'degree of mixing' in this type of economy? The government will decide how much business activity there will be in the private sector and how much in the public sector. Some countries, like Sweden, allow the government to play a greater role in the supply of goods and services than others, like the UK. For example, in Sweden the government spends around 60 per cent of national income, whilst in the UK the government spends around 40 per cent. In countries where the government plays an important economic role, social provision will tend to be greater, taxes higher and the distribution of wealth and income more equal. In countries where the private sector plays the most important economic role, social provision will tend to be lower with fewer free goods and services at the point of sale. Also, taxes will be lower and the distribution of wealth and income less equal. For example, in the last two decades, income tax rates have fallen in the UK and fewer services have been supplied by the state. The distribution of income has changed in favour of the 'wealthy' during this time.

Problems of changing systems

In the late 1980s and the 1990s major changes took place in a number of Eastern European countries. The former communist regimes were overthrown and replaced by some form of democracy. In most cases, the new governments wished to introduce market economies to replace the older planned systems which were thought to be inefficient. Although each country has had different experiences, there are some common features which all countries changing to a market system have faced. Many problems have arisen as a result of these changes. Businesses in these countries have had to change how they operate to cope with new demands.

Inflation Most countries have experienced inflation - a rise in the general price level. Under a planned system prices were set by the state and, in theory, inflation did not exist. However, following liberalisation of their markets former planned economies experienced high inflation rates. In countries such as Armenia, Russia and Georgia inflation rates were more than 1,000 per cent in the early 1990s. In 2003 Hungary has forecast to have an inflation rate of only 5 per cent. Inflation affects the functions of money (☞ unit 66). In some countries businesses have reverted to bartering for resources, exchanging their products for other goods or services. Alternatively, they have exchanged their goods for currencies with stable values, such as the dollar.

Establishing the system A change to a market economy will not take place overnight. The institutions in Western economies which help the market system to work will take time to develop and operate in the former planned economies. Businesses may have problems raising finance due to a lack of institutions able to loan money. In many countries there is no stock market where shares in a company can be sold to raise finance. Other problems may result from the previous inefficiencies of planned systems. Transport, communications and markets for buying and selling goods are not yet ready for the level of business activity that will take place under a market system. This can result in late deliveries, a lack of information and a restriction in selling opportunities.

Competition Businesses in former planned economies now face competition from both within the country and from abroad. Some countries have suffered from cheap foreign goods being sold in their economy. Prices of home produced goods and services are likely to be higher than before. Previously the state had kept the prices of resources low so that the prices of final goods were also low. Removal of these controls would mean having to increase prices to make a profit.

Unemployment In a planned system unemployment should not exist. The state provides work for all individuals and makes sure that they have minimum living standards. In 2003 unemployment in Estonia, for example, was forecast to be greater than 10 per cent.

Running the business The new entrepreneurs in former planned economies will be the managers and employees of ex-state run firms. These people have no experience of how to operate in a market system. They face the prospect of making a profit or going out of business, unheard of under a planned system. Also, businesses are not used to operating under a system where profit and earnings motivate people to work. Many would still suffer from the lack of initiative associated with the planned system. Finally, the ability to organise, run and motivate business activity in these countries may not exist, and many people require training, often from Western firms or training agencies.

It has been argued that those countries with the most recent history of a market system have adjusted best to the transition. Before the Second World War, Hungary, Poland,

Slovenia and the Czech and Slovak Republics all had market systems. Countries that were part of the former USSR, with communist systems, have not performed as well. In 1996, for example, economic growth in the Slovak Republic was 7 per cent compared to -4.9 per cent in Russia. Growth did achieve positive figures by 2000, although Russia experienced further problems in the years that followed.

Transfer of ownership One major problem facing all economies changing from a planned to a market system is the transfer of ownership. Previously all resources and businesses were state owned. Farms, factories and shops now have to be passed on to employees and managers. In the former East Germany all state firms were placed in the hands of an agency (the Treuhand) which sold them off. In the former USSR, people were given vouchers which entitled them to a share of a company.

Many Eastern European countries are undertaking a huge privatisation process. In some cases privatisation experts from the UK and other western economies are recruited to advise on the transfer of assets from the public to the private sector.

After regaining independence in 1991, Lithuania attempted to recover from the command economy of the former Soviet Union. The country faced major problems, such as huge inflation (mainly due to considerably increased costs of raw materials and other resources from Russia) and falling GDP caused by the change in economic style and loss of previous economic relations. Domestic and foreign investment also fell in line with economic performance in the early 1990s. It was hard for the Lithuanian government to subsidise the big inefficient manufacturers without the involvement of the Soviet Union. Thus, drastic measures of privatisation had to be taken, changing the balance between government investment and private sector investment.

Almost 50 per cent of state property has been privatised and trade is diversifying, with a gradual shift away from the former Soviet Union to Western markets. Lithuania implemented the privatisation process more rapidly than any other Central or Eastern European country. The programme was introduced in 1991 and by 1995 eighty five per cent of a total of 8,214 companies had been privatised. Investment vouchers were chosen as the basis for privatisation. These were issued by the government and could be used for the purchase of property. 24 per cent of the vouchers have been used by Lithuanians to purchase their own apartments or houses and 66 per cent for the privatisation of state enterprises.

The process of privatisation is the backbone of the Lithuanian transformation process. It has had a significant impact on the general economic development of the country, the creation of a competitive business environment, and the development of a system of corporate governance and securities market. The privatisation of Lithuania's electricity distribution and generation companies, the state alcohol monopoly, and Lithuanian Airlines and Railways are all pencilled in for the next few years.

Source: adapted from www.nationmaster.com and www2.omnitel.net.

(a) Explain the role played by privatisation in Lithuania when changing from a planned to a more market orientated economy.
(b) Examine the problems faced by Lithuania when changing from a planned to a more market orientated economy.

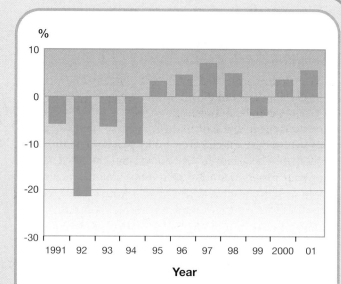

Figure 9.1 *Growth in GDP (%), Lithuania*

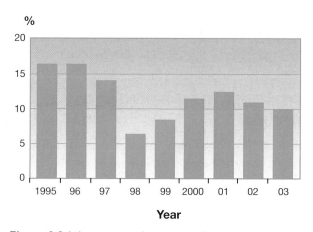

Figure 9.2 *Lithuania unemployment rate (average annual)*

key terms

Basic economic problem - how scarce resources with different uses are allocated to satisfy wants.

Distribution of income - the amount of income and wealth different groups have in a particular country.

Economy - a system which attempts to solve the basic economic problem.

Market economy or capitalist economy or free enterprise economy - an economic system which allows the market mechanism to allocate resources.

Market imperfection - any factor which hinders the free operation of markets, such as where one firm dominates resulting in exploitation.

Mixed economy - an economic system which allows both the state and the market mechanism to allocate resources.

Opportunity cost - the benefit of the next best option foregone when making a choice between a number of alternatives.

Planned economy or command economy - an economic system in which the state is responsible for resource allocation.

Knowledge ...Knowledge...Knowledge...Knowledge...Knowledge...Know

1. Why do businesses, individuals and government need to make choices about the resources they use?
2. Give 2 examples of opportunity cost.
3. What is the function of an economy?
4. What are the 3 questions an economy aims to answer?
5. Describe the benefits of market economies for:
   (a) businesses; (b) consumers.
6. Describe the problems of planned economies for:
   (a) firms; (b) consumers.
7. What determines the degree of 'mix' in a mixed economy?
8. 'A free market system in former planned economies will take time to work.' Give 3 examples which support this statement.

Case study China

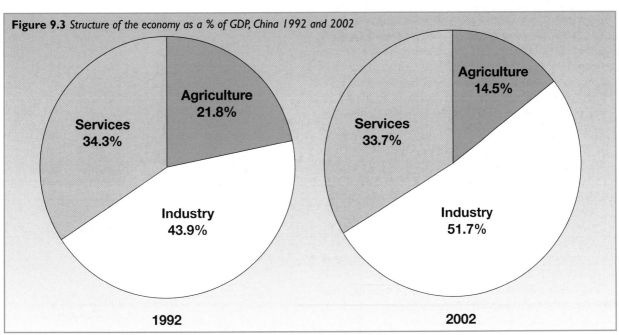

Figure 9.3 *Structure of the economy as a % of GDP, China 1992 and 2002*

1992

Services 34.3%
Agriculture 21.8%
Industry 43.9%

2002

Agriculture 14.5%
Services 33.7%
Industry 51.7%

Source: adapted from World Bank.

China, the world's fastest growing economy, is on course to overtake Britain in two years or so. National output is moving forward so fast that the country is in danger of overheating. The economy surged 9.1 per cent in the July-September period as domestic firms increased investment and foreign manufacturers such as Ford and Sony once again poured money into a country that has become the workshop of the world. According to government officials, the amount of economic activity in China soared to £570 billion in the first nine months of the year. This put China on course to achieve a growth rate of 8.5 per cent for 2003, the fastest in more than five years. If the country can maintain this pace it will overtake Britain and France to become the world's fourth biggest economy well before the end of 2005.

Business leaders are already hailing China as the powerhouse for growth in Asia, a role once held by Japan. With neighbouring nations increasing sales of raw materials to factories in China, imports jumped by 40.5 per cent in the first nine months of the year.

Many of those factories are foreign-owned as multinational firms rush to exploit China's abundant cheap labour. The latest is Ford, which announced plans yesterday for a new $1.5 billion (£900 million) plant in Chongching. 'China is really the engine that drives the entire region' Ford's chief executive officer, William Clay Ford, told reporters. 'We do expect to expand aggressively in China.' Japanese manufacturers are also pumping cash into their neighbour's economy. Sony, the world's second-biggest consumer electronics maker, revealed it has invested $8 billion in China and forecast that the country would become its second biggest market, behind only the US, within five years.

Although tens of millions of rural Chinese people scratch out a living well below the poverty line, the average disposable income in towns and cities which are home to two-fifths of China's 1.3 billion people rose 9 per cent to (£460) in the first nine months of this year. The government boasted that its measures had created 6.25 million jobs in the first nine months of the year, leaving an urban unemployment rate of 4.2 per cent. Much of the new work was created through construction projects in cities including Shanghai, as well as huge public infrastructure undertakings such as the Three Gorges dam, the world's biggest engineering project.

However, the risks for the Chinese economy are growing along with its size. A flood of spending on property and construction has raised fears of overheating and highlighted the problems of overlending by Chinese banks. With credit easy to acquire, fixed-asset investment rose 30.5 per cent in the first nine months of this year. Such is the risk of overheating that economists now believe the government is downplaying the pace of growth. GDP figures have long been criticised as unreliable, though usually for being exaggerated rather than too modest.

Source: adapted from *The Guardian*, 18.10.2003.

Investors on Wall Street were yesterday clamouring to take a stake in the explosive growth of the Chinese economy when one of the nation's biggest insurers floated on the New York stock exchange. Shares in China Life gained 34 per cent in value to $25 before falling back in line with the market. The US has a complicated relationship with China. American manufacturers in particular are critical of trade agreements that have opened their domestic market to a flood of cheap imports. Wall Street, however, is clearly embarking on a love affair with the world's most populous nation. The Chinese economy is growing at more than 8 per cent a year as its middle class expands and develops an appetite for consumer goods.

Several Chinese companies have floated on the NYSE recently. Last week, Shanghai-based hotel and air ticket company Ctrip.com International enjoyed the highest debut in New York for three years when its share price soared by as much as 108 per cent on its first day. Another Chinese insurer, PICC Property and Casualty, last month had a 50 per cent gain on the first day of trading.

Source: adapted from *The Guardian*, 18.12.2003

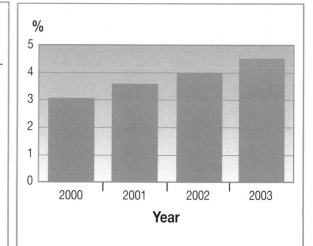

Figure 9.4 *Chinese unemployment rates (%)*
Source: adapted from World Bank, 29.8.2003.

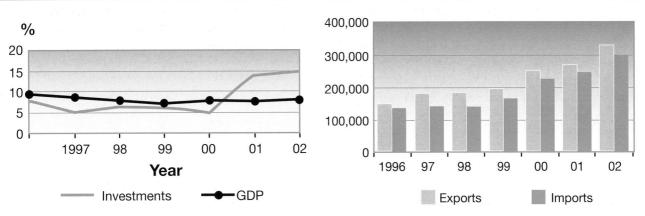

Figure 9.5 *Growth of investment and GDP in China*

Figure 9.6 *Export and import levels in China (US$m)*

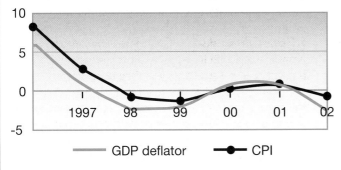

Figure 9.7 *Inflation in China (%)*

Source: adapted from World Bank, 29.8.2003.

(a) **Using examples from the case outline two problems that countries face when changing their economic system. (4 marks)**

(b) **What sort of businesses would you expect to develop in the future in China? Explain your answer. (6 marks)**

(c) **What evidence is there in the case to suggest that the Chinese economy has become more open? (12 marks)**

(d) **Evaluate the advantages and disadvantages to a UK manufacturer of locating a plant in China. (18 marks)**

Why do businesses collect data?

Information is a valuable resource in business. Businesses collect large amounts of information or DATA about their own organisations. They may also employ companies, such as Reuters, which specialises in the collection and sale of information. Examples of data that a business might collect include:

● costs of production;
● share prices and exchange rates;
● company reports;
● weekly or monthly sales figures;
● business news, for example about a potential takeover;
● market research findings.

Data are collected by businesses for a number of reasons. Most importantly perhaps, data are required in the decision making process. Managers, employees and others involved in business activity need up to date and accurate data to help them make effective decisions. For example, a business choosing from a number of investment opportunities would require the latest information on the costs and expected return of each project.

Data are required to monitor the progress of a business. Business performance could be gauged by looking at the growth or decline in turnover or profit. Changes in productivity rates can be calculated if a business has data on its inputs and output.

All businesses keep records which contain a wide range of **qualitative** (about nature or characteristics) and **quantitative** (involving measurement) data. These records contain information that is important to the business. Such records might include monthly sales figures, staff files, customer files and market reports. It is important that records are regularly updated so that they are correct when required by the business. Businesses make use of **backdata,** such as sales in previous years, to forecast what might happen in future.

Data are also used to help control a business. Financial data on payments and receipts are used to control cash flow (☞ unit 35). A financial controller, for example, might delay payment to a supplier until money is received from customers in order to avoid a cash flow problem.

Why do businesses present data?

Once data has been collected it can be stored, retrieved and presented. The volume of data collected by businesses is enormous and it is important to avoid making mistakes. The development of information and communication technology (☞ units 52 and 60) in recent years has made the handling of data far easier and less prone to error. Data can be stored on computer memory or a disk, 'called up' on a computer screen, manipulated and presented in a variety of styles. Businesses may make use of graphs, charts, tables and other pictorial methods of communicating data. Presenting data in this way:

● can be more concise and easier to understand than written information;
● can take less time to interpret;
● can identify trends clearly;
● may be effective in creating an impact or an image;
● can be used to impress a potential client.

The method of presentation a business chooses will depend on the type of data collected, who and what it is required for and how it is likely to be used. Data can be presented 'internally' and 'externally'. Examples of data presented to those inside a business might be:

● the sales department presenting a breakdown of regional sales

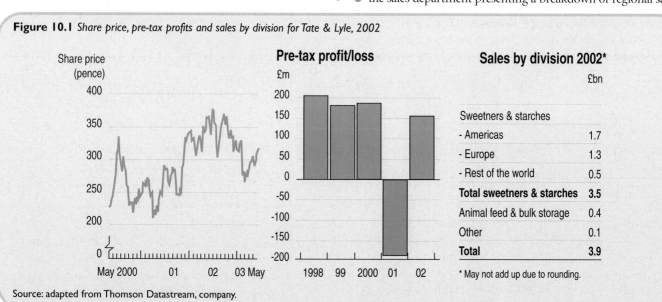

Figure 10.1 *Share price, pre-tax profits and sales by division for Tate & Lyle, 2002*

Sales by division 2002*	£bn
Sweeteners & starches	
- Americas	1.7
- Europe	1.3
- Rest of the world	0.5
Total sweeteners & starches	**3.5**
Animal feed & bulk storage	0.4
Other	0.1
Total	**3.9**

* May not add up due to rounding.

Source: adapted from Thomson Datastream, company.

figures to senior management to illustrate the popularity of products in an area or the effectiveness of promotion;

- the production manager presenting the accounts department with weekly time sheets to allow the calculation of wages and costs;
- the research and development department providing an analysis of monthly expenditure to enable budgets to be calculated;
- the personnel manager providing an analysis of staff turnover to illustrate possible problems or improvements in human resource management;
- the market research department providing research data to allow products to be designed to fit consumers' needs.

Examples of data presented to those outside the business could be:

- the accounts department providing Customs and Excise with VAT details to claim back tax on sales which are exempt from VAT;
- the publication of an Annual Report and Accounts to illustrate a company's progress over the last year to stakeholders;
- the presentation of a new market range by the marketing department to a potential customer.

Figure 10.1 shows some business data for Tate & Lyle, the sweeteners and starches producer. The data shows that the share price has fluctuated but risen over the period. Pre-tax profits have fallen between 1998 and 2002, with a huge loss being made in 2001. In 2002, the largest sales were those in the Americas division, £1.7 billion, and total sales for the year were £3.9 billion.

Bar charts

A BAR CHART is one of the simplest and most common means of presenting data. Numerical information is represented by 'bars' or 'blocks' which can be drawn horizontally or vertically. The length of the bars shows the relative importance of the data. Table 10.1 shows data on the profit made by Ragwear plc, a manufacturer, over the last six years. They are presented as a bar graph in Figure 10.2.

Table 10.1 *Profit for Ragwear plc over a six year period*

	Yr1	Yr2	Yr3	Yr4	Yr5	Yr6 £m
Profit	2.1	2.9	3.8	4.1	3.2	4.9

The main advantage of using a bar chart is that it shows results very clearly. At a glance the reader can get a general feel of the information and identify any trends or changes over the time period. Figure 10.2 shows that profit has continued to increase over the period apart from a 'dip' in year 5. This might indicate to the firm that trading conditions in year 5 were unfavourable or that the firm's performance was

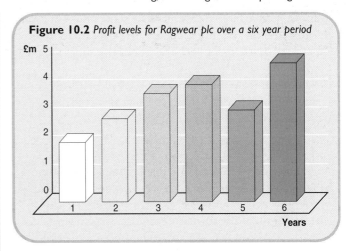

Figure 10.2 *Profit levels for Ragwear plc over a six year period*

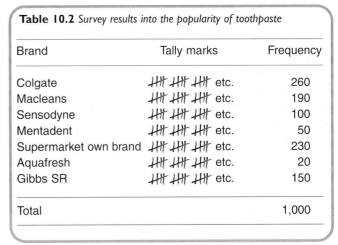

Table 10.2 *Survey results into the popularity of toothpaste*

Brand	Tally marks	Frequency
Colgate	|||| |||| |||| etc.	260
Macleans	|||| |||| |||| etc.	190
Sensodyne	|||| |||| |||| etc.	100
Mentadent	|||| |||| |||| etc.	50
Supermarket own brand	|||| |||| |||| etc.	230
Aquafresh	|||| |||| |||| etc.	20
Gibbs SR	|||| |||| |||| etc.	150
Total		1,000

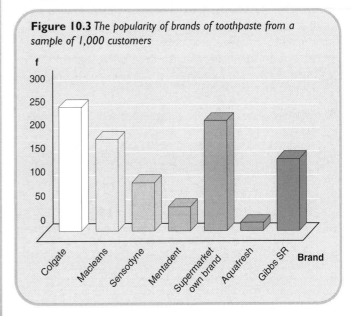

Figure 10.3 *The popularity of brands of toothpaste from a sample of 1,000 customers*

relatively poor. Bar charts are more attractive than tables and may allow the reader to interpret the data more quickly.

The bars in Figure 10.2 are drawn vertically. They could also, however, be drawn horizontally. They are also three dimensional, but they could have been two dimensional.

It is possible to produce a bar chart from collected data, such as from market research. This data may be collected in a

tally chart as in Table 10.2, which shows the results of research into the brands of toothpaste bought by a sample of supermarket customers. The total number of times each item occurs is known as the **frequency** (f). So, for example, the most popular from the survey is Colgate and the least popular is Aquafresh. Figure 10.3 shows the data from Table 10.2 as a bar chart.

Component bar charts

A COMPONENT BAR CHART allows more information to be presented to the reader. Each bar is divided into a number of components. For example, the data in Table 10.3 shows the cost structures of five furniture manufacturers in a particular year. The total cost is broken down into labour, materials and overheads.

Table 10.3 *Cost structures of five furniture manufacturers and overheads*

£000

	Oakwell	Stretton	Bradford	Jones	Campsfield
Labour	50	36	70	45	90
Materials	18	25	48	23	50
Overheads	10	10	19	9	25

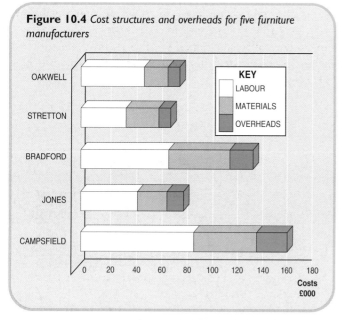

Figure 10.4 *Cost structures and overheads for five furniture manufacturers*

The data in the table are presented as a component bar chart in Figure 10.4. One advantage this chart has compared to the simple bar chart is that total costs can be seen easily. There is no need to add up the individual costs. It is also easier to make instant comparisons. For example, labour costs are the greatest proportion of total cost at Oakwell. This might suggest to a firm that Oakwell uses a more labour intensive production technique than the others. Also, labour costs at Oakwell are higher than at Stretton, but not as high as

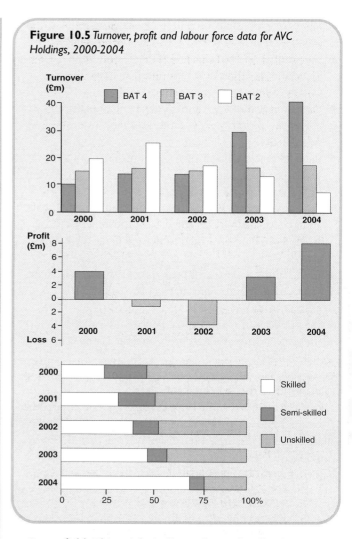

Figure 10.5 *Turnover, profit and labour force data for AVC Holdings, 2000-2004*

at Campsfield. This might indicate that Oakwell is less efficient than Stretton and a much smaller business than Campsfield.

Figure 10.5 shows three other styles of bar chart, illustrating data for AVC Holdings. This is a company that produces three types of machine tool, code named BAT 4, BAT 3 and BAT 2.

- The top chart is a **parallel** bar chart. It shows the turnover contributed by each of the company's three products. Over the time period the turnover for BAT 4 has increased from £10 million to £40 million. Sales of BAT 3 have remained fairly steady at around £15 million each year. The turnover from BAT 2 has declined from £20 million to £7 million. This type of graph is similar to a component bar chart. The advantage is that it is easier to compare changes between the components, although it is more difficult to compare totals.

- The middle chart is a **gain and loss** bar chart. It shows the profitability of the company over the time period. The performance of AVC Holdings worsened in the first three years and then improved. The profit in 2004 was £8 million. This type of chart distinguishes very clearly between positive and negative values.

- The bottom chart is a **percentage component** bar chart. It shows the breakdown of the workforce in terms of their skill with each section represented as a percentage of the workforce. In 2000 nearly 25 per cent of the workforce were skilled. In 2004 this had risen to around 70 per cent. The chart also shows that the numbers of semi-skilled workers had fallen as a percentage of the total. This might indicate that the firm had introduced new technology, leading to unskilled staff being replaced with skilled staff. One disadvantage of this presentation is that changes in the total size of the workforce are not shown.

UK Coal is Britain's largest producer of coal. The group employs over 7,000 people and has more than 20 deep and surface mine sites that produce around 20 million tonnes of coal a year. Table 10.4 shows the profit before tax, dividend per share and cash flow before financing and dividends between 1999 and 2002.

Table 10.4 *Profit before tax, dividend per share and cash flow before financing and dividends between 1999 and 2002 for UK Coal*

	1999	2000	2001	2002
Profit/loss before tax (£000)	(130,029)	17,761	(26,484)	(83,111)
Dividend per share (p)	7.5	10	10	10
Cash flow before financing and dividends (£000)	25,203	52,758	75,895	(25,183)

Source: adapted from UK Coal, *Annual Report and Accounts, 2002.*

(a) (i) Construct appropriate bar charts to present the data in the table.
(ii) Explain briefly what the bar charts show.
(b) Discuss whether you think the use of bar charts in (a) is an effective way of presenting the data.

Question 1

Figure 10.6 *A pictograph for GPA Group showing orders for aircraft in March 1999 for each year to 2007*

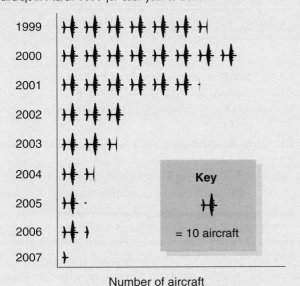

Number of aircraft

A pictograph or pictogram

A PICTOGRAPH or PICTOGRAM is another form of chart. It presents data in a similar way to bar charts. The difference is that data are represented by pictorial symbols rather than bars. Figure 10.6 shows an example of the orders which GPA Group has received for its aircraft over a nine year time period. The pictograph shows a general decline in orders. This might indicate that there is a general decline in the market or that customers are delaying future orders. One problem with a pictograph is that it is not always easy to 'divide' the symbols exactly. This makes it difficult to read precise quantities from the graph. For example, in Figure 10.6, in 2001 the number of orders is more than 60, but the last symbol is a fraction of an aircraft which makes it difficult to determine the exact size of orders placed in that year. The main advantage of this method is that the graphs tend to be more eyecatching. Such a method might be used in business presentations to attract clients or in reports to the public.

Pie charts

In a PIE CHART, the total amount of data collected is represented by a circle. This is divided into a number of segments. Each segment represents the size of a particular part relative to the total. To draw a pie chart it is necessary to perform some simple calculations. Table 10.5 shows the details of monthly output at five European plants for a multinational brick producer. The 360 degrees in a circle have to be divided between the various parts which make up the total output of 50,000 tonnes. To calculate the number of degrees each segment will contain, a business would use the following formula:

$$\frac{\text{Value of the part}}{\text{Total}} \times 360°$$

Table 10.5 *Monthly brick output at five European plants*

	Bedford	Brescia	Lyon	Bonn	Gijon	Total
Output (tonnes)	10,000	8,000	5,000	15,000	12,000	50,000

Thus, the size of the segment which represents the monthly brick output in Bedford is:

$$= \frac{10,000}{50,000} \times 360°$$

$$= 0.2 \times 360°$$

$$= 72°$$

Using the same method it can be shown that the size of the other segments representing output at the other plants will be: Brescia 58°; Lyon 36°; Bonn 108°; Gijon 86°. The number of degrees in each segment added together make 360°. A pie chart can now be drawn using a protractor or a spreadsheet or DTP software package on a computer. The pie chart is shown in Figure 10.7. Bonn makes the largest contribution to monthly output with Gijon second. The company might use this information to compare with monthly production targets.

Pie charts are useful because readers get an immediate impression of the relative importance of the various parts. They can also be used to make comparisons over different time periods. There are however, drawbacks with pie charts.

● They do not always allow precise comparisons to be made between the segments.

● If a total consists of a very large number of components, it may be difficult to identify the relative importance of each segment.

● It is difficult to show changes in the size of the total pie. For example, if the total rises over time it is possible to make the 'pie' bigger. However, the exact size of the increase is often difficult to determine because it involves comparing the areas of circles.

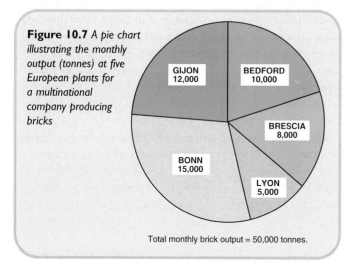

Figure 10.7 *A pie chart illustrating the monthly output (tonnes) at five European plants for a multinational company producing bricks*

GIJON 12,000
BEDFORD 10,000
BRESCIA 8,000
BONN 15,000
LYON 5,000

Total monthly brick output = 50,000 tonnes.

Histograms

Table 10.7 illustrates some data collected by market researchers on behalf of a cinema chain. It concerns the age profile of a sample of cinema goers on a Saturday. The chart shows the number of viewers in the sample that falls into various age ranges (known as **classes**). The total number of times each item occurs in each class is known as the frequency (f). So the total number of viewers in the 10-19 age range is 290. This type of data is usually shown as a HISTOGRAM as in Figure 10.8. A histogram looks similar to a bar chart, but there are some differences.

● In a histogram it is the **area** of the bars which represents the frequency. In a bar chart it is the length or height of the bars. For example, in Figure 10.8, all the columns have the same width except for the last one where the age range covers two decades and not one. This means that the frequency in the figure is not 200 as shown in the table, but 100 (200÷2 = 100). This is because in the table 200 viewers fall into the age range 60 - 79, whereas the histogram shows

Aston Villa FC is a Premier League football club. In the last financial year, 2003, its turnover was £45.4 million. Aston Villa's revenue is generated from six main sources. Table 10.6 shows the revenue from each source for 2002 and 2003.

Table 10.6 *Aston Villa revenue and its sources for 2002 and 2003*

	£ million	
	2003	**2002**
Match receipts	9.7	10.2
Broadcasting	17.0	15.5
Merit awards	2.5	5.7
Merchandising	3.7	3.8
Catering	4.4	4.1
Other commercial income	8.1	7.4

Source: adapted from Aston Villa, *Annual Report and Accounts, 2003*.

(a) Construct two pie charts to show the sources of revenue for Aston Villa FC in 2002 and 2003.

(b) Discuss the advantages and disadvantages to the business of presenting the data in this way.

Question 2

Table 10.7 *The age profile of cinema goers on a Saturday*

Age range	Frequency
0-9	180
10-19	290
20-29	500
30-39	400
40-49	350
50-59	280
60-79	200
Total	2,200

100 viewers in the age range 60 - 69 and 100 in the range 70 - 79. However, the area of the last bar coincides with the data in the table, ie it is equal to 200. The total area represented by all columns is equal to the sample size of 2,200.

● Bar charts and histograms can be used for **discrete data** - data which only occur as whole numbers, such as the number of people employed in a store. Histograms are most useful when recording **continuous data** - data which occur over a range of values, such as weight or age.

● Histograms tend to be used for grouped data, for example the number of people between the ages of 0 and 9.

The histogram in Figure 10.8 shows that the most frequently occurring age range of viewers is 20 - 29. The information might be used by the cinema chain to help plan a marketing strategy. It is possible to show the information in Table 10.7 by plotting a curve called a frequency polygon. It is drawn using the histogram and involves joining all the mid-points at the top of the 'bars' with straight lines. The frequency polygon for the data in Table 10.7 is shown in Figure 10.8. Arguably, the visual pattern of the data is shown more clearly by the frequency polygon.

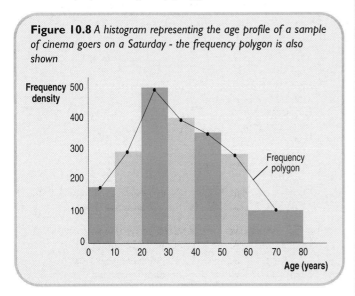

Figure 10.8 *A histogram representing the age profile of a sample of cinema goers on a Saturday - the frequency polygon is also shown*

Tables

Tables are used to present many forms of data. They may be used:

- if data are qualitative rather than quantitative;
- where a wide range of variables needs to be expressed at the same time;
- where the numbers themselves are at the centre of attention;
- when it is necessary to perform calculations on the basis of the information.

Some would argue that the use of tables should be avoided if possible. However, a poorly or inaccurately drawn graph would be less effective than a neatly presented table. Table 10.8 provides a list of the world's most powerful computers. It shows clearly where the world's largest computers are located

in order of size. It also shows the name of the company that manufactures the computer, the power of each computer and the country of location. This is a good example of a table being used to show a variety of qualitative and quantitative data (☞ unit 12).

Line graphs

LINE GRAPHS are probably the most common type of graph used by a business. A line graph shows the relationship between two variables. The values of one variable are shown on the vertical axis and the values of the other variable are placed on the horizontal axis. The two variables must be related in some way. The values of the variables can be joined by straight lines or a smooth curve. If **time** is one of the variables being analysed it should always be plotted on the horizontal axis. Output is usually plotted on the horizontal axis. The main advantage of this type of graph is the way in which a reader can get an immediate picture of the relationship between the two variables. Also, it is possible to take measurements from a line graph when analysing data. It is much more difficult to do this when reading figures from a table. Quite often more than one line is shown on a line graph so that comparisons can be made. **Economic data** is often presented on a line graph. A line graph showing interest rates over the recent period may influence a business's decision to invest, for example.

Cumulative frequency curves

When collecting data and recording it in a table, it is possible to show CUMULATIVE FREQUENCY. This is the total frequency up to a particular item or class boundary. It is calculated by adding the number of entries in a class to the total in the next class - a 'running total'. Table 10.9 shows the weights of cereal packages coming off a production line in a particular time period.

The cumulative frequencies in the table can be plotted on a graph. The graph is called an **ogive** and is shown in Figure 10.10. It can be seen, for example, that 270 packages weigh below 201.5 grams.

Table 10.8 *The World's top 10 most powerful computers*

Position	Company	Location	Country	Year	Rmax (Gigaflops)*
1	NEC	Earth Simulator Center	Japan	2002	35860
2	HP	Los Alamos National Laboratory	USA	2002	7727
3	HP	Los Alamos National Laboratory	USA	2002	7727
4	IBM	Lawrence Livermore National Laboratory	USA	2000	7226
5	Linux	Network Lawrence Livermore National Laboratory	USA	2002	5694
6	HP	Pittsburgh Supercomputing Center	USA	2001	4463
7	HP	Commissariat a l'Energie Atomique	France	2001	3980
8	HPTi	Forecast Systems Laboratory	USA	2002	3337
9	IBM	HPCx	UK	2002	3241
10	IBM	National Center for Atmospheric Research	USA	2002	3164

* Floating point operations per second

Source: adapted from Top 500 Supercomputers website.

Table 10.9 *Cumulative frequency of package weights*

Weights falling within these ranges (grams)	Frequency	Cumulative frequency
198-199	30	30
199-200	50	80 (30 + 50)
200-201	150	230 (30 + 50 + 150)
201-202	70	300 (30 + 50 + 150 + 70)
202-203	40	340 (30 + 50 + 150 + 70 + 40)
203-204	5	345 (30 + 50 + 150 + 70 + 40 + 5)

Kingfisher, which owns B&Q, Brico Depot, Castorama and Screwfix, operates around 550 stores in seven countries across Europe and Asia. In September 2003 the group suggested that hot weather across Europe would impact on sales for the year. However, Kingfisher reported that its total sales in the 13 weeks up to November 1 grew 8.2 per cent, including a rise of 2.7 per cent on a like-for-like basis. Following the news release in November the share price rallied 2 per cent.

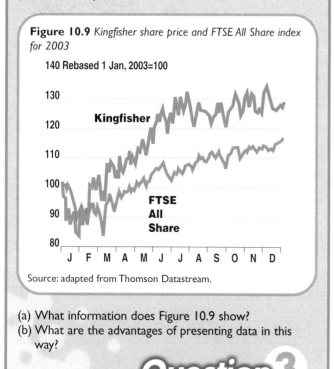

Figure 10.9 *Kingfisher share price and FTSE All Share index for 2003*

140 Rebased 1 Jan, 2003=100

Source: adapted from Thomson Datastream.

(a) What information does Figure 10.9 show?
(b) What are the advantages of presenting data in this way?

Question 3

A Lorenz curve

A LORENZ CURVE is a special type of line graph. It is a cumulative frequency curve which can be used to show the difference between actual distribution and an equal distribution. Figure 10.11 is a Lorenz curve which illustrates the way in which business is distributed between different hotels in a town. What does the curve show? If business was shared equally between all hotels then the line would be a straight 45° line. So, for example, 30 per cent of the town's hotels would get 30 per cent of all business, measured here as

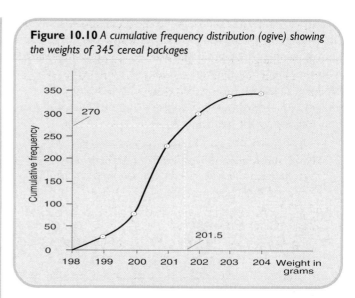

Figure 10.10 *A cumulative frequency distribution (ogive) showing the weights of 345 cereal packages*

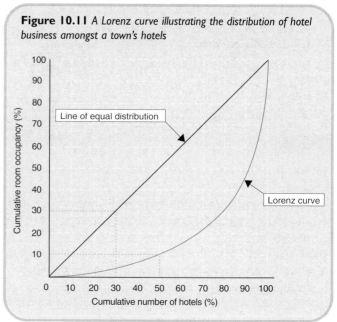

Figure 10.11 *A Lorenz curve illustrating the distribution of hotel business amongst a town's hotels*

the number of rooms occupied. The Lorenz curve shows the actual distribution of business amongst the town's hotels. For example, 50 per cent of the town's hotels have only 10 per cent of the total hotel business. This obviously indicates a very unequal distribution of business amongst the town's hotels. The further the Lorenz curve is drawn away from the 45° line the more unequal the actual distribution will be. A business might use this to analyse market share. The Lorenz curve is often used to show the distribution of wealth in a particular country.

Bias in presentation

Just as bias can affect the collection of data it can also affect its presentation. When presenting profit figures to shareholders or sales figures to customers, managers will want to show the business in the best light. There is a danger that figures may be distorted in the way they are presented, in order to make performance look better than it was.

There are two main ways in which bias can occur.

- The method of presentation could exaggerate the actual rate of change shown by the data. This can be done by cutting and expanding one axis of a graph. Darrel Huff, an American statistician, called this a 'Gee-Whiz' graph. Figure 10.12 shows the same data presented in two different ways. In graph (b) the profit axis has been cut and extended. This gives a far better impression of the growth in profit than in graph (a). Similar bias can be introduced into bar charts, pie charts and pictographs.

- A business could leave out figures that do not fit into the 'picture' it wants to portray. For example, in a presentation to customers a firm may show its sales figures have been rising over the past five years, but omit to show that the total market has been increasing at a faster rate. This, in fact, means that the market share of the business has been falling.

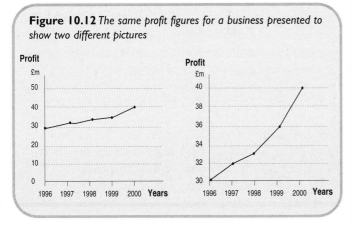

Figure 10.12 *The same profit figures for a business presented to show two different pictures*

Spreadsheets

Some types of numerical data can be presented effectively using a SPREADSHEET. A spreadsheet allows the user to enter, store and present data in a grid on a computer screen. Just as a word processor is able to manipulate text, spreadsheets can do the same with numerical data. Table 10.10 shows that the grid is made up of a number of 'cells' or blank boxes. These cells are arranged in rows (information across the spreadsheet) and columns (information down the spreadsheet). Each blank cell is able to carry information which will fall into one of three categories.

- Numerical data - these are the numbers entered by the user which will be manipulated by the program.
- Text - this refers to the words used in the spreadsheet, often headings.
- Formulae - these are the instructions given by the user which tell the computer to manipulate the numerical data, for example, add a column of entries to give a total.

An example of a spreadsheet is illustrated in Table 10.10. It contains data relating to a firm's production costs. Each column (from B to G) shows the costs of various items each month. Each row shows particular costs over the entire period. For example, row 2 shows the labour costs each

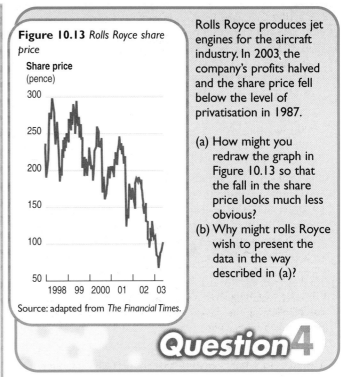

Figure 10.13 *Rolls Royce share price*

Source: adapted from *The Financial Times.*

Rolls Royce produces jet engines for the aircraft industry. In 2003, the company's profits halved and the share price fell below the level of privatisation in 1987.

(a) How might you redraw the graph in Figure 10.13 so that the fall in the share price looks much less obvious?
(b) Why might rolls Royce wish to present the data in the way described in (a)?

Question 4

Table 10.10 *An example of a spreadsheet which contains cost data*

	A	B	C	D	E	F	G
1		Jan	Feb	March	April	May	June
2	Labour	200	210	230	210	200	230
3	Materials	100	100	110	130	100	110
4	Fuel	35	35	35	30	30	20
5	Overheads	25	25	30	30	35	35
6	Total costs	360	370	405	400	365	395

The formulae for total costs in row 6 is shown below.

6	Total costs =SUM(B2..B5) =SUM(C2..C5) =SUM(D2..D5) =SUM(E2..E5) =SUM(F2..F5) =SUM(G2..G5)

month. Row 6 shows the total cost each month. The total cost is automatically calculated by the program.

In this case the formula for cell B6 would be B2 + B3 + B4 + B5 or = SUM (B2..B5). If the business changed any of the entries, the totals in row 6 would change automatically.

Some spreadsheets are much larger than the screen itself with up to 250 columns and 8,000 rows. The screen can only show part of the spreadsheet. Scrolling is used to solve this problem. This enables the user to scan over the entire spreadsheet until the section they need is shown on the screen. The advantages of spreadsheets are listed below.

- Numerical data is recorded and shown in a clear and ordered way.
- Editing allows figures, text and formulae to be changed easily to correct mistakes or make changes in the data.
- It is easy to copy an entry or series of entries from one part of the spreadsheet to another. This is particularly useful when one figure has to be entered at the same point in every

column.

- The user can add, subtract, multiply and divide the figures entered on the spreadsheet.
- A spreadsheet can calculate the effect of entry changes easily. This is sometimes referred to as the 'what if' facility, eg what would happen to cell X (total costs) if the entry in cell A (labour costs) increased by 10 per cent? The answer can be found very quickly.
- Some spreadsheet programs allow graphs and diagrams to be drawn from figures in the spreadsheet.

One problem with spreadsheets is in printing the results. Some simple spreadsheets will tend to print everything being used. This can be time consuming and wasteful. Other programs allow the user to print specific rows, columns or cells. Some spreadsheets permit the sheet to be printed sideways to allow for a wide sheet to be printed. A further complication is what should be printed out for some of the cells, eg for a particular cell, should it be the result of a formula or the formula itself?

Databases

A DATABASE is really an electronic filing system. It allows a great deal of data to be stored. Every business which uses computers will compile and use databases. The information is set up so that it can be updated and recalled when needed. Table 10.11 shows part of a database of a finance company which gives details about their clients. The collection of common data is called a file. A file consists of a set of related records. In the database pictured in Table 10.11 all the information on Jane Brown, for example, is a record. The information on each record is listed under headings known as fields, eg name, address, age, occupation, income each year. A good database will have the the following facilities.

- 'User-definable' record format, allowing the user to enter any chosen field on the record.
- File searching facility for finding specified information from a file, eg identifying all clients with an income over £24,000 in the above file. It is usually possible to search on more than one criterion, eg all females with an income over £24,000.
- File sorting facility for rearranging data in another order, eg arranging the file in Table 10.11 in ascending order of income.
- Calculations on fields within records for inclusion in reports.

In the world of business and commerce there is actually a market for information held on databases. It is possible to buy banks of information from market researchers who have compiled databases over the years. Names and addresses of potential customers would be information well worth purchasing if it were legally available. The storage of personal data on computer is subject to the **Data Protection Act** (☞ unit 51). Any company or institution wishing to store personal data on a computer system must register with the Data Protection Office. Individuals have a right under the Act to request details of information held on them.

Table 10.11 *An extract from a simple database*

Surname	First name	Address	Town	Age	Occupation	Income p.a.
Adams	John	14 Stanley St	Bristol	39	Bricklayer	£15,000
Appaswamy	Krishen	2 Virginia St	Cardiff	23	Welder	£25,000
Atkins	Robert	25 Liverpool Rd	Cardiff	42	Teacher	£21,000
Biddle	Ron	34 Bedford Rd	Bath	58	Civil servant	£40,000
Brown	Jane	111 Bold St	Newport	25	Solicitor	£22,000

key terms

Bar chart - a chart where numerical information is represented by blocks or bars.

Component bar chart - a chart where each bar is divided into a number of sections to illustrate the components of a total.

Cumulative frequency - the total frequency up to a particular item or class boundary.

Data - a collection of information.

Database - an organised collection of data stored electronically with instant access, searching and sorting facilities.

Histogram - a chart which measures continuous data on the horizontal axis and class frequencies on the vertical axis.

Line graph - a line which shows the relationship between two variables.

Lorenz curve - a type of cumulative frequency curve which shows the disparity between equal distribution and actual distribution.

Pictograph or pictogram - a chart where numerical data is represented by pictorial symbols.

Pie chart - a chart which consists of a circle where the data components are represented by the segments.

Spreadsheet - a method of storing data in cells in such a way that a change in one of the entries will automatically change any appropriate totals.

Knowledge

1. Why is it important for a business to present data clearly, accurately and attractively?
2. What are the main advantages of using bar charts?
3. What is the main disadvantage of using pictographs?
4. State 3 types of data that component bar charts can be used to illustrate.
5. What is the difference between a histogram and a bar chart?
6. Why are pie charts a popular method of data presentation?

7. What is the main disadvantage of using tables to present data?
8. State 2 ways in which bias may be shown when presenting data.
9. State the 3 types of information which a cell in a spreadsheet can carry.
10. What are the main advantages of spreadsheets?
11. What are the advantages of databases for firms?

Case study Euro Disney

Euro Disney operates two theme parks with over forty attractions, seven hotels, two conference centres, a Disney Village and a golf course. The complex is located near Paris in France and has a number of attractions.

● Adventureland aims to create an atmosphere able to fulfil the dreams of archaeologists or explorers. It contains scenes of impenetrable African jungles to an exotic South Seas island, to the magical trails and treasures of the Orient. Adventureland brings to life the universe of ancient legends, action movies and Disney adventure films.

● Main Street USA is the reconstruction of a typical small town in America in the last century, such as Missouri where Walt Disney grew up. In this historic setting guests can enjoy a meal and shop in an

atmosphere reminiscent of America's golden age between 1890 and 1910.

● Discoveryland is where visitors can catch a glimpse of tomorrow as imagined by European visionaries of the past. This starts with a trip through time in the company of Jules Verne, Leonardo de Vinci and HG Wells.

● Spectacular rides include Space Mountain, Peter Pan's flight, Indiana Jones and the Temple of Peril, Star Tours and Big Thunder.

Euro Disney has become a very popular tourist attraction since it was opened. Indeed, according to the company, 89 per cent of guests intend to recommend the destination.

Source: all information adapted from Euro Disney, *Financial Report*, 2002.

Financial overview 2002 ①

In 2002 the company opened a second theme park, Walt Disney's Studios Park. Since this attraction opened record attendances, occupancies and per guest selling were achieved, despite the weak tourism environment. Annual

revenue from all sections of the business rose by 7 per cent. However, a loss of 33.1 million euros was made. This was due to the exceptional pre-opening expenditure associated with Walt Disney's Studio Park, such as staff training and advertising.

②

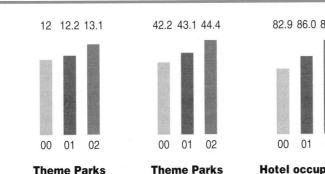
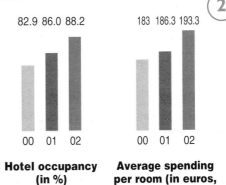

12 12.2 13.1	42.2 43.1 44.4	82.9 86.0 88.2	183 186.3 193.3
00 01 02	00 01 02	00 01 02	00 01 02
Theme Parks attendance (millions of guests)	**Theme Parks average spending per guest (in euros excluding VAT)**	**Hotel occupancy (in %)**	**Average spending per room (in euros, including VAT)**

③

Breakdown of visitors by transportation

56.1% Car
14.6% Coach
12.6% Plane
12.5% Train
4.2% Railway

④

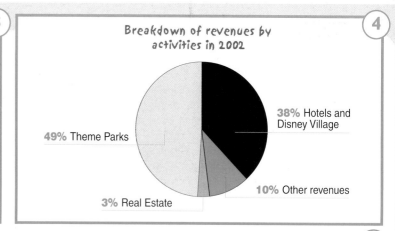

Breakdown of revenues by activities in 2002

49% Theme Parks
38% Hotels and Disney Village
10% Other revenues
3% Real Estate

⑤

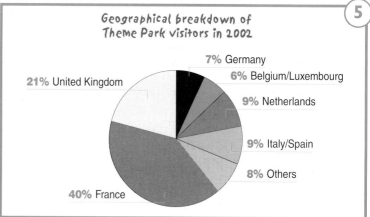

Geographical breakdown of Theme Park visitors in 2002

7% Germany
6% Belgium/Luxembourg
9% Netherlands
9% Italy/Spain
8% Others
40% France
21% United Kingdom

⑥

Revenues of the Group were generated from the following sources:

(Euros in millions)	Year ended September 30		Variation	
	2002	2001	Amount	Percent
Theme Parks	526.0	476.4	49.6	10.4%
Hotels and Disney Village	411.7	386.5	25.2	6.5%
Other	111.0	105.1	5.9	5.6%
Resort segment	*1 048.7*	*968.0*	*80.7*	*8.3%*
Real Estate Development Segment	27.3	37.2	(9.9)	(26.6)%
Total revenues	**1 076.0**	**1 005.2**	**70.8**	**7.0%**

⑦

Evolution of the share price
(Base 100 as of October 2001)

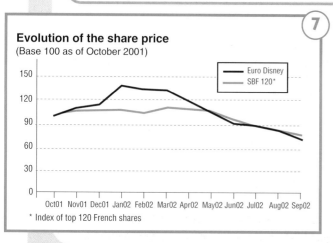

— Euro Disney
— SBF 120*

150
120
90
60
30
0

Oct01 Nov01 Dec01 Jan02 Feb02 Mar02 Apr02 May02 Jun02 Jul02 Aug02 Sep02

* Index of top 120 French shares

(a) **Describe the geographical breakdown of theme park visitors. (4 marks)**

(b) **Present the information contained in Box 3 using an alternative method. Explain why the method you have selected may be more effective. (8 marks)**

(c) **The information in Box 4 and Box 6 is similar. Explain which you think is more informative. (8 marks)**

(d) (i) **Explain what the data in Box 7 shows.**
   (ii) **How might the graph in Box 7 be presented to show the information in a better light? (8 marks)**

(e) **Evaluate the performance of Euro Disney in 2002. (12 marks)**

Marketing - a possible definition

A market is any set of arrangements that allows buyers and sellers to exchange goods and services (☞ unit 1). It can be anything from a street market in a small town to a large market involving internationally traded goods. But what is meant by the term MARKETING? Some definitions which suggest that marketing is the same as advertising or selling are incorrect. Selling is, in fact, just one of many marketing functions. One definition, from the Institute of Marketing, is that:

'Marketing is the management process involved in identifying, anticipating and satisfying consumer requirements profitably.'

There are some features of business marketing behaviour that may have led to this definition.

● Consumers are of vital importance. A product has a far greater chance of being a success if it satisfies consumers' needs. Marketing must be aimed at finding out what these needs are and making sure that products meet them. Market research (☞ unit 12) is often used by businesses for this purpose. Managers, however, also place stress on having a 'feel' for the market. This could be very important in a market with changing trends, such as fashion clothing or home decoration products.

● Marketing is a process. It does not have a start and an end, but is ongoing all the time. Businesses must be prepared to respond to changes that take place. This is shown in Figure 11.1. For example, a business marketing its own range of office furniture would be unwise to decide on a strategy and then not take into account consumers' reactions. If the firm sold modern designs, but sales were poor, it might consider designs for offices that wanted a traditional look.

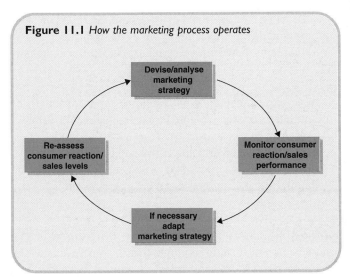

Figure 11.1 *How the marketing process operates*

● Marketing involves building relationships with customers. Profitable businesses are often built upon good customer relations. This might involve dealing with customer complaints in a careful and considered manner, for example. Customers, as a result, are likely to develop a favourable view of the business. They also continue to buy its products over a long period of time. RELATIONSHIP MARKETING is now used by some businesses, such as Tesco. This is an approach to marketing which stresses the importance of developing relationships with customers which last longer than the short term.

● Marketing is a business philosophy. It is not just a series of activities, such as advertising or selling, but more a 'way of thinking' about how to satisfy consumers' needs. A business selling good quality products, cheaply, may be unsuccessful in its marketing if it has dirty, badly organised or poorly lit facilities. Retailers such as IKEA and Asda have large 'superstores' with restaurants and play areas for children. They could be said to cater for all their consumers' shopping needs.

● Marketing affects all aspects of a business. A production department would not continue making a product that does not satisfy the needs of the consumers at whom it is aimed. In the same way, pricing decisions cannot be made without knowing how much consumers are prepared to pay.

● Marketing is not just about selling. Selling is only one part of the marketing process. Before selling their products, many businesses carry out a range of activities which take into account consumer preferences. These include market research, the testing of products on consumers and the design of products.

● Marketing and advertising are not the same. Advertising is just one of a number of tactics used by marketing departments. Other marketing methods include promotions, such as free gifts and competitions.

● Many businesses regard profit making as their main objective (☞ unit 4). Firms in competitive markets must make a profit in the long run to survive. Marketing must therefore satisfy consumers' wants **profitably**. Even when profit is not the main objective, marketing has a vital role to play. Charities, such as Oxfam and many public sector organisations such as colleges and hospitals, adapt and change the marketing of their services to satisfy their consumers' needs.

The rise in the importance of marketing

It is only in the last sixty years in the UK that marketing has begun to assume such an important role in business. What factors may have led to this?

Economic growth Economic growth (☞ unit 69) in the UK has led to an increase in the REAL DISPOSABLE INCOME of many consumers. This has resulted in a growth in demand for products and services and for a far wider range of choice. In response, businesses have developed an array of products and services which are available to the consumer. We need only think of goods that were not available twenty years ago, such as DVDs and laptop computers. Services, such as credit cards and Internet purchasing, have also been developed in response to consumers' needs.

Fashion There have been considerable changes in fashion and in the tastes and lifestyles of many consumers. For example, large numbers of people today buy products for sports which were new or were mostly ignored just a few years ago. These include mountain biking, snowboarding and hang gliding.

Technology Rapid technological change has taken place in recent years and continues to do so. Firms constantly invent, design and launch new and advanced products onto the market. One example is the electronics industry. During the 1980s and 1990s, Sony was able to launch a range of products that were not previously feasible in technical terms. These included the DVD player, the digital camcorder and mini disc players.

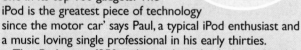

The iPod is a music player that has the capacity to store 10,000 tunes downloaded from, amongst others, the iTunes music store. 'It's the coolest thing to come out of California since the Beach Boys' according to *Stuff* magazine which listed it number one in its top 100 gadgets. 'The iPod is the greatest piece of technology since the motor car' says Paul, a typical iPod enthusiast and a music loving single professional in his early thirties.

   The iPod costs £350 and its makers, Apple, have already sold two million since it was launched two years ago. Not all, however, are so taken with the iPod and stand by their Discmans and CDs. 'I hate the idea of the iPod,' says music writer Caroline Sullivan. 'Why would anyone want to carry around 10,000 songs?' Apple have no such doubts and are planning to launch the iPod mini, capable of holding about 1,000 songs. This will be offered at a substantially lower price than the standard iPod. Apple's aim is to go after other makers of digital music players and capture a larger share of the market for players holding 100 or so songs.

Source: adapted from *The Guardian*, 2.1.2004 and 7.1.2004.

(a) What factors might have influenced Apple to launch its iPod range?

Competition The number of products competing for the consumer's attention is constantly increasing. There has been increased competition from foreign products in UK markets and a greater availability of foreign services. Competition is nothing new, but the scale of it is. Japanese and US businesses, with efficient production methods and sophisticated marketing, have been successful in UK markets. More open trade in European Union countries has also created more competition for UK firms.

Effects on business

How have the factors in the last section affected the marketing of businesses?

Economic growth Businesses are now aware of the growth in demand and the wide variety of tastes of consumers. Successful marketing is essential if businesses are going to gain their share of a growing market and increase their turnover and profit. Larger markets can pose a problem. The investment needed to launch a product onto a large market is enormous. Marketing must make sure that such products will succeed or the business can face large losses.

Fashion Tastes and fashions in today's markets are changing faster than ever before. Marketing must anticipate and respond to these changes. Toy manufacturers, for example, try to be aware of the next 'craze'. Marketing has become more important as firms have realised that consumers' tastes may be influenced. There is a variety of techniques that can be used to achieve this (☞ units 16-23).

Technology Businesses must respond to changes in technology. A firm's products can become obsolete very quickly unless it is able to respond to such changes. Marketing and production departments now work closely together to anticipate new opportunities that arise. Marketing must also provide consumers with technical details about products. It is unlikely that consumers will know all the uses of new products which have previously been unavailable. Technology has influenced the marketing methods that businesses use. Examples of technical marketing media now used by firms include advertisements on websites, electronic billboards and satellite TV.

Competition Competition, both at home and from abroad, has meant that successful marketing is vital to maintain a firm's market share. UK businesses have also had to respond to the sophisticated marketing techniques of foreign companies. This has meant that the expenditure on marketing by many UK firms has risen as a share of total spending in the last few decades.

   The British motorcycle industry serves as a warning to those firms which fail to respond. British companies such as Triumph and BSA had dominated the market for motor cycles in the UK ever since the 1930s. When the Japanese company Honda launched its 50 cc moped in the UK, British companies did not see this as a threat. Their lack of response allowed Honda and other firms, such as Yamaha and Kawasaki, to almost completely take over the market for motorcycles in the UK. By the 1980s, the British motorcycle industry had effectively collapsed.

Product orientation

Many businesses in the past, and some today, could be described as PRODUCT ORIENTATED. This means that the business focuses on the production process and the product itself.

In the past, many businesses producing consumer goods were product orientated. When radios and televisions were first produced in the UK, it was their novelty and the technical 'wonder' of the product that sold them. There were few companies to compete against each other, and there was a growing domestic market. There were also few overseas competitors. The product sold itself.

Some industries today are still said to be product orientated. The machine-tool industry has to produce a final product which exactly matches a technical specification. However, because of increased competition such firms are being forced to take consumers' needs into account. The technical specification to which a machine-tool business produces might be influenced by what customers want, for example.

The Concorde aircraft project has often been described as being product orientated. The main question was whether the aircraft was technically possible. Whether or not it could be produced at a price which would attract companies was less important. The developers assumed that a supersonic aircraft would 'sell itself'. In fact the only airlines which did buy it were British Airways and Air France, largely because of the involvement of the British and French governments in its development. For other airlines the price was too high and the number of passengers Concorde could carry was too low. Several airports, most especially New York, had indicated that they might ban supersonic aircraft because of noise. Although the project was thought to be a technological success, its failure to take into account the needs of the market meant that it was not a commercial success. In 2003 Concorde flights were discontinued.

Product orientated businesses thus place their emphasis on developing a technically sound product, producing that product and then selling it. Contact with the consumer comes largely at this final stage.

There will always be a place for product orientation. A great deal of pure research, with no regard to consumers' needs, still takes place in industry.

Market orientation

A MARKET ORIENTATED business is one which

Sales of Slim Fast, bought by Unilever for £1.4 billion, were hit in 2003. Some suggested this was a result of the surge in interest in the Atkins Diet. But the company expected the fall to be short term and not affect 'longer term growth based on the size and growth of the market' of Slim Fast. Unilever argued that the current fad for Atkins may not continue and that it was also launching a range of new products such as pastas and pizzas to rekindle demand for its product range.

Unilever has a five year 'path to growth programme', with targets for sales. It aims to focus on products that will earn the highest margins. So it sold some brands, focused on its main brands such as Dove and Liptons, and bought others, including Slim Fast and Ben & Jerry's luxury ice cream. Sales rose initially, but stalled in 2003, and growth of leading brands was expected to be below 3 per cent. Some of its prestige products were affected as well as Slim Fast. These included Calvin Klein perfume, mainly affected by the fall in tourism. The company argued that this business along with its US laundry operation would have to perform or be ditched.

When the path to growth plan ends Unilever aims to announce a new strategy focusing on emerging markets. It will also attempt to take into account three consumer trends - convenience, indulgence and health and wellness. Slim Fast nicely fits into these three categories.

Source: adapted from The Observer, 2003.

(a) Identify the factors that are likely to affect the marketing of Unilever's product range.
(b) Assess how these factors might affect Unilever's marketing.

Question 2

continually identifies, reviews and analyses consumers' needs. It is led by the market.

Henry Ford was one of the first industrialists to adopt a market orientated approach. When producing the Model T, he did not just design a car, produce it as cheaply as possible, and then try to sell it to the public. Instead, in advance of production, he identified the price at which he believed he could sell large numbers of Model Ts. His starting point was the market and the Model T became one of the first 'mass-market' products. This illustrates the market orientated approach - consumers are central to a firm's decision making.

Sony is one of many modern businesses that has taken a market orientated approach. The Sony Walkman is an example of a product developed in response to the wishes of consumers.

A market orientated business will have several advantages over one which is product orientated.

● It can respond more quickly to changes in the market because of its use of market information.
● It will be in a stronger position to meet the challenge of new competition entering the market.
● It will be more able to anticipate market changes.
● It will be more confident that the launch of a new product will be a success.

What effect will taking a market orientated approach have on a business? It must:

● consult the consumer continuously (market research);
● design the product according to the wishes of the consumer;
● produce the product in the quantities that consumers want to buy;
● distribute the product according to the buying habits and delivery requirements of the consumer;
● set the price of the product at a level that the consumer is prepared to pay.

The business must produce the right product at the right price and in the right place, and it must let the consumer know that it is available. This is known as the **marketing mix** (☞ unit 16). We will consider each aspect of the mix in more detail in subsequent units. Here it is enough to say that it involves the product, price, promotion and place.

It would be wrong to assume that the adoption of a market orientated approach will always be successful. Many well-researched products have been failures. Coloroll was a business which started in the wallpaper market and expanded into home textiles and soft furnishings. Its attempt to enter the DIY burglar alarm market, however, was a failure. The company's reputation and design skills had little value in that section of the DIY market compared with other companies, whose reputations were based on home security or electronics.

Influences on product and market orientation

Whether a business places emphasis on the product or on the market will depend on a number of factors.

The nature of the product Where a firm operates in an industry at the edge of new innovation, such as bio-technology, pharmaceuticals or electronics, it must innovate to survive. Although a firm may try to anticipate consumer demand, research is often 'pure' research, ie the researcher does not have a specific end product in mind.

Policy decisions A business will have certain objectives. Where these are set in terms of technical quality or safety, the emphasis is likely to be on production. Where objectives are

in terms of market share or turnover, the emphasis is likely to be on marketing.

The views of those in control An accountant or a managing director may place emphasis on factors such as cash flow and profit forecasts, a production engineer may give technical quality control and research a high priority and a marketing person may be particularly concerned with market research and consumer relations.

The nature and size of the market If production costs are very high, then a company is likely to be market orientated. Only by being so can a company ensure it meets consumers' needs and avoid unsold goods and possible losses.

The degree of competition A company faced with a lack of competition may devote resources to research with little concern about a loss of market share. Businesses in competitive markets are likely to spend more on marketing for fear of losing their share of the market.

In 2002 McDonald's established an alliance with General Mills and Dannon to co-brand children's foods to be sold at McDonald's restaurants. The products would include Dannon Danimals low fat yogurt drinks and General Mills's Go-gurt and Fruit Roll-ups. They will be offered as healthier alternatives to Happy Meals which have often been criticised by consumer groups.

Source: adapted from www.nacsoline.com.

Cinea is a business co-founded by Robert Schumann. Previously he had developed the DivxDVD system to prevent pirated videos. But support for the project was pulled by Circuit City. So in 1999 he formed Cinea with a group of former Divx engineers. In 2002 it began to develop a system that would stop videoing of movies off theatre screens and prevent pirated movies. The company suggested that it will 'modify the timing and modulation of the light used to create the displayed image on screens so that frame-based capture by recording devices will be distorted'. It expected to have a working prototype in two years. The development comes at a time when technology is creating digital movies that are far sharper than before. Pirated films often appear after initial screenings, made by people who smuggle cameras into cinemas.

Source: adapted from news.zdnet.co.uk.

(a) Explain whether these business are likely to be more product or market orientated using examples from the articles.
(b) Suggest the factors that are likely to have influenced the extent to which they are more product or market orientated.

Question 3

Asset-based marketing

It has been suggested that in recent years companies have been taking an asset-led approach to marketing. ASSET-BASED or ASSET-LED MARKETING is where a business develops those goods or services that make the best use of its **major strengths** or assets. This means concentrating on what the business is 'good at', although this approach would still take into account the needs of the market. For instance, many businesses have attempted to produce 'new' products that are related to successful existing products. An example might be the development of ice cream versions of best selling chocolate bars, such as the Mars Bar and Bounty. The use of this approach has certain implications for a business. It must:

● identify the main competences and strengths of the business;
● aim to produce those products that make the best use of its resources.

Marketing – a different view

Some commentators reject the basic idea behind marketing, that it is concerned with meeting consumer needs. One of the issues is the extent to which businesses respond to consumer needs as opposed to creating them. Many would argue that businesses actively work to create the need to consume more, rather than just responding to what consumers want and need. They suggest that consumer needs in general would be better met if businesses encouraged them to spend less rather than more. So whilst marketing may make sense for individual businesses and their relationships with individual

consumers it does not necessarily work at a wider level. One consequence of this so-called pressure on consumers is individuals spending beyond their means. This has led to many people taking on more debt than they can manage. Another consequence is more rapid use of the world's resources and the creation of higher levels of environmental damage (☞ unit 70).

key terms

Asset-based (asset-led) marketing - where a business develops and markets products based on its main strengths.
Marketing - the management process involved in identifying, anticipating and satisfying consumer requirements profitably.
Market orientation - an approach to business which places the requirements of consumers at the centre of the decision making process.
Product orientation - an approach to business which places the main focus of attention upon the production process and the product itself.
Real disposable income - the income with which consumers are left after taxes (other than VAT) have been deducted and any state benefits added on. Any changes in the rate of inflation are also taken into account.
Relationship marketing - an approach to marketing which seeks to strengthen a business's relationships with its customers.

Knowledge...Knowledge...Knowledge...Knowledge...Knowledge...Know

1. What is meant by the term marketing?
2. Distinguish between marketing and advertising.
3. Why is marketing described as a process?
4. How can marketing techniques be employed by non-profit making organisations?
5. What factors have made marketing so important in today's

business environment?
6. Why might product orientation still be important today?
7. What are the main advantages of a market orientated approach?
8. Why might a market orientated approach be unsuccessful?

Case study KMI and soft drinks

King of Shaves

Legend has it that King of Shaves was born when Will King mixed some of his girlfriend's oils with his shaving gel in an attempt to prevent him getting a rash when shaving. He found that non-foaming oils gave him a smoother shave. So he commissioned and bought a formula for £250. This remains the same in today's product, nine years later. You might well have some of the company's other products, Ted Baker fragrances, Fish 'Unisexy' hair products or Speedo toiletries somewhere in your bathroom.

The business, KMI (Knowledge and Merchandising Inc. Ltd), is a multimillion pound company. It is second only to Gillette in the UK in its markets. Its aim is to reach a turnover of £63 million by 2005. KMI would like to be the world's biggest shaving software brand, but says 'We've still got to get 90 per cent of men in the UK to shave first, let alone 100 per cent in the world'. The quest for world domination is underway, with Canada, Mexico, Argentina and larger European countries targeted for launch. Inroads have already been made in New Zealand, Australia and Ireland and there is an office in New York. But KMI does not intend to open offices in other countries, preferring distribution and licensing agreements with locals who know the marketplace.

The owners of the business, Will King and Herbie Dayal, although not experts in chemistry, go by the maxim of knowing what they like. Every product idea of the business has come form the office. Once they have an idea, they brief a selection of labs. KMI uses development laboratories in New York, Paris and Japan. But it assembles products in the UK as long as it makes commercial sense.

Source: adapted from *Growing Business*, September 2002.

The soft drinks market

The soft drinks market has grown in virtually every category in the world over the last few years. Changing lifestyles, needs and expectations of children, youths, adults and families are all responsible for this growth. 'Consumers' lives are becoming increasingly busy and fast paced, spawning an on-the-go culture. This has created a strong demand for refreshment in a variety of out-of-home locations, thus driving soft drinks, which are more accessible and convenient than ... hot drinks' argues Datamonitor's *Innovations in Soft Drinks* Report. Crystal drinks in the UK launched Crystal Premium in 2003, a 100 per cent pure orange juice in a single serve bottle with a sports cap, convenient for drinking on the hoof. In Germany, Nestlé has launched its iced coffee Nescafé range in slimline cans for portability.

The success of bottled water reflects the demand for lighter and healthier beverages, the need to avoid dehydration and the desire for trusted sources of clean water to drink. Sports drinks have increased demand as a result of young people's desires for cool, alternative mainstream brands. Coca-Cola launched Burn in Spain in 2003, an energy drink to ensure sustained energy. Energy and sports drinks are likely to see a 47 per cent increase in sales between 2002 and 2007 argued the Report.

Source: adapted from www.foodproductiondaily.com.

(a) (i) **State whether the businesses above are likely to be more product or market orientated. (2 marks)**

(ii) **Describe their approach to marketing, using examples from the articles. (8 marks)**

(b) **Explain the possible advantages and disadvantages to these businesses of the approach they are taking. (10 marks)**

(c) **Examine the factors which have determined their approach to marketing. (10 marks)**

(d) **Discuss how each business might take an asset-based approach in future. (10 marks)**

What is market research?

Unit 1 explained that business activity will only be successful if the output produced can satisfy people's wants and needs. Information about the things people want will help businesses to decide what to produce. This information is often found by MARKET RESEARCH.

Market research can be defined as the collection, collation and analysis of data relating to the marketing and consumption of goods and services. For example, a business might gather information about the likely consumers of a new product and use the data to help in its decision making process. The data gathered by this research might include:

- whether or not consumers would want such a product;
- what type of promotion will be effective;
- the functions or facilities it should have;
- what style, shape, colour or form it should take;
- the price people would be prepared to pay for it;
- where people would wish to purchase it;
- information about consumers themselves - their age, their likes, attitudes, interests and lifestyles;
- what consumers buy at present.

Some, mainly smaller or local, businesses have just a few customers who are well known to them. For these businesses, information about their markets can be relatively easy to find. This may be through personal and social contact with their customers. Such businesses, however, must be careful that they do not misread their customers' views and actions.

Other businesses have a more distant relationship with their customers. This may be because they have a large number of customers, operate in a range of different markets or market their products in international as well as national markets. For these businesses market information may be less easy to come by. Such businesses often find that in order to gather marketing information they need to use complex and sophisticated marketing research methods.

The terms **market research** and **marketing research** are usually used interchangeably in business books and in the media. This is the approach taken in this book. Some have suggested a distinction between the two terms. Market research, they argue, is about researching consumers' preferences and tastes. Marketing research is a wider term, which also includes the analysis of marketing strategies, for example the effect of promotions such as advertising.

The uses of market research

A market is anywhere that buyers and sellers come together to exchange goods and services (☞ unit 1). Markets are in a constant state of change. As a result a business is likely to use market research on a regular basis for a number of reasons.

- Descriptive reasons. A business may wish to identify what is happening in its market. For example, a brewery may

In January 2004 it was revealed that Radio 1 had lost nearly half a million listeners in three months. The youth-orientated station attracted 9.4 million listeners in the last three months of 2003. This was nearly 500,000 down on listeners for the period June to September in the same year. They were also nearly a million lower than the same period in 2002.

Radio 1 was confident that recent changes made to programmes, including the introduction of 'shock-jock' Chris Moyles to the breakfast show, would lead to an improvement. A spokesperson said 'These figures are obviously something we are not happy about. But we have made recent changes, like moving Chris Moyles to the breakfast show. As with any DJ it will take a while for him to settle in. It will be a couple of quarters before we see any changes.'

At the same time Radio 2 picked up an extra 700,000 listeners and for the first time the number of hours listened to Radio 2 is twice that of Radio 1. Other programmes also added listeners. These included Radio 5 Live and Radio 3, although Radio 4's audience fell. Commercial stations such as Classic FM and Virgin expected a fall in listeners. Classic FM fell by 250,000 to 6.2 million and Virgin 185,000 to 2 million.

Source: adapted from *The Daily Mail*, 30.1.2004.

(a) Explain, using examples from the article, how radio stations might use audience figures for:
(i) descriptive reasons;
(ii) predictive reasons;
(iii) explanatory reasons.
(b) Suggest how a radio station makes use of market research for exploratory reasons.

Question 1

want to find trends in its sales of various types of beer over a certain period, or to find out the types of customers who are buying a particular beer.

- Predictive reasons. A business may wish to predict what is likely to happen in the future. For example, a travel company will want to discover possible changes in the types of holiday that people might want to take over the next 2-5 years. This will place it in a better position to design new holiday packages that will sell.
- Explanatory reasons. A business may want to explain a variety of matters related to its marketing. This may include sales in a particular part of the country. A bus company, for example, might wish to research why there has been a fall in the number of passengers on a specific

route.

● Exploratory reasons. This is concerned with a business investigating new possibilities in a market. For example, a soft drinks manufacturer could trial a new canned drink in a small geographical area to test customer reaction before committing itself to marketing the product nationally.

Once a business has decided how it wishes to use market research data, the next stage is to identify the **aspects** or **areas** that it wants to concentrate on. Table 12.1 shows the different areas that could be researched and some possible elements that might be considered in each.

Table 12.1 *The scope of market research*

Area of research	Possible elements to be considered
The market	Identifying market trends Discovering the potential size of the market Identifying market segments Building up a profile of potential/actual consumers Forecasting sales levels
Competition	Analysing the strengths and weaknesses of competitors Identifying relative market shares Identifying trends in competitors' sales Finding information on competitors' prices
Promotion	Analysing the effectiveness of promotional materials Deciding upon choice of media for promotions
The product	Testing different product alternatives Identifying consumer wants Developing new product ideas Assessing consumer reaction to a newly launched product
Distributing the product	Identifying suitable retail outlets Exploring attitudes of distributors towards products
Pricing the product	Discovering the value consumers place on the product Identifying the sensitivity of the demand for the product to changes in its price

Desk or secondary research

Desk or secondary research involves the use of SECONDARY DATA. This is information which **already exists** in some form. It may be existing business documents or other publications. Some secondary data may be available from within a business. This may include the following.

● Existing market research reports.
● Sales figures. The more sophisticated these are the better. For example, sales figures which have been broken down according to **market segments** (☞ unit 13) can be particularly useful.
● Reports from members of the sales force resulting from direct contact with customers.
● Annual Report and Accounts published by businesses.
● Businesses increasingly make use of company **intranets** to provide up to date information (☞ unit 52). These are restricted to company employees. But some information

may be available on the Internet on company websites.

● Stock movements. These can often provide the most up-to-date information on patterns of demand in the market. This is because they are often recorded instantly, as opposed to sales figures, which tend to be collected at a later date.

Secondary data will also be available from sources outside the business. Individuals or other organisations will have collected data for their own reasons. A business might be able to use this for its own market research.

● Information from competitors. This may be, for example, in the form of promotional materials, product specifications or price lists.
● Government publications. There are many government publications which businesses can use. These range from general statistical publications such as *Social Trends*, the *Census of Population* and the *Annual Abstract of Statistics* through to specialist publications, such as *Business Monitor*.
● Data from customer services on complaints which have been received about a product.
● The European Union. The EU now provides a wide range of secondary data which can be highly valuable to businesses operating within EU countries. Such publications include *European Economy* and *Panorama of EU Industry* which are published by Eurostat (the Statistical Office of the European Union).
● International publications. There is a huge amount of information about overseas marketing published each year by organisations such as the World Bank and the International Monetary Fund.
● Commercial publications. A number of organisations exist to gather data about particular markets. This information is often highly detailed and specialised. Mintel, Dun and Bradstreet and Verdict are examples of such organisations.
● Retail audits. The widespread use of Epos (electronic point of sale) has meant that it is now much easier to collect detailed and up to the minute data on sales in retail outlets such as supermarkets and other retail chains. Retail audits provide manageable data by monitoring and recording sales in a sample of retail outlets. Businesses find these audits especially helpful because of the way in which they provide a continuous monitoring of their performance in the market. A well known example is data on the best selling records or CDs which make up weekly music charts. This information is collected from retail outlets in the UK.
● General publications. A business may use a range of publications widely available to members of the public for their market research. These include newspaper and magazine articles and publications such as the *Yellow Pages*.
● Increasingly businesses make use of the Internet to search for secondary data outside of their own organisation. Many of the sources of secondary information above including, for example, government publications, can now be found on the Internet.

The main advantage of secondary information collected

business can use.

Questionnaires Personal interviews, telephone interviews and postal surveys (see below) all involve the use of questionnaires.

There are certain features that a business must consider when designing a questionnaire. If it is poorly designed it may not obtain the results the business is looking for.

● The balance between closed and open questions. **Closed** questions, such as 'How many products have you bought in the last month', only allow the interviewee a limited range of responses. **Open** questions, however, allow interviewees considerable scope in the responses which they are able to offer. Open questions allow certain issues to be investigated in great detail, but they do require a high degree of expertise in the interviewer. For example, an open question might be 'Suggest how the product could be improved'.

● The clarity of questions. The questions used must be clear and unambiguous so that they do not confuse or mislead the interviewee. 'Technical' language should be avoided if possible.

● The use of leading questions. Leading questions are those which encourage a particular answer. For example, a market research agency investigating the soft drinks market should avoid the question: 'Do you think that Diet Pepsi is better than Diet Coke?' A better question would be: 'Which brand of diet cola do you prefer - Pepsi or Coke?'

Personal interviews This involves an interviewer obtaining information from one person face-to-face. The interviewer rather than the interviewee fills out the responses to questions on a questionnaire, which contains mainly 'open' questions.

The main advantage of interviews is that they allow the chance for interviewees to give detailed responses to questions which concern them. Long or difficult questions can also be explained by the interviewer and the percentage of responses that can be used is likely to be high. If needed, there is time and scope for answers to be followed up in more detail. Interviews, however, can be time consuming and tend to rely on the skill of the interviewer. For example, a poorly trained interviewer asking questions on a product she did not like may influence the responses of the interviewees by appearing negative.

Telephone interviews This method allows the interview to be held over the telephone. It has the advantage of being cheaper than personal interviewing and allows a wide geographical area to be covered. However, it is often distrusted by the public and it is only possible to ask short questions.

Postal surveys This involves the use of questionnaires sent to consumers through the post. It is a relatively cheap method of conducting field research. It also has the advantage that

---

Stephanie and Tahira are considering setting up a bridal shop selling gowns and other wedding accessories in their home town of Bolton (population approximately 260,000). Before doing so they have decided to research the market. The latest edition of *Social Trends* tells them that each year there are 252,000 first marriages. They calculate, with the UK's present population of 59 million, that this means one first marriage for every 230 people.

(a) Why is the information which Stephanie and Tahira are using known as secondary data?
(b) Explain how Stephanie and Tahira might use the information to predict likely sales. Suggest possible problems with using the data to predict demand.

Question 2

externally is that it has already been collected and is often available at little or no cost. However, it is not always in a form the firm would want. This is because it has been collected for another purpose. Consequently, secondary information needs to be adapted before it can be used in particular market research projects.

Field or primary research

Field or primary research involves collecting PRIMARY DATA. This is information which does not already exist. In other words, it has to be collected by the researcher. Field research can either be carried out by a firm itself or by a market research agency.

The main advantage of primary data is that the firm which initially collects it will be the only organisation with access to it. Primary information can therefore be used to gain marketing advantages over rival firms. For example, a package holiday firm might discover through its field research that the use of a particular airline is a major attraction for its customers. This information can then be used to win a share of the market from rival firms by using it as a feature in promotional materials. The main disadvantage of primary information is that it can be very expensive to collect. This is because field research, if it is to generate accurate and useful findings, requires specialist researchers and is time consuming.

Most primary information is gathered by asking consumers questions or by observing their behaviour. The most accurate way to do this would be to question or observe all consumers of a particular product (known as the **population**). However, in all but a few instances this would be either impractical to carry out or expensive. It is usual to carry out a survey of a **sample** of people who are thought to be representative of the total market. Methods of choosing samples are dealt with later in this unit.

Methods of field research

There is a number of different field research methods a

there is no interviewer bias and a wide geographical area can easily be covered. Unfortunately, the response rate to postal questionnaires can be poor and responses can take as long as six weeks. In addition, questions must be short, so detailed questioning may not be possible. Questionnaires must also be well designed and easy to understand if they are to work.

Observation Observation is often used by retail firms 'watching' consumers in their stores. Observers look out for the amount of time consumers spend making decisions and how readily they notice a particular display. Its advantage is that a tremendous number of consumers can be surveyed in a relatively short space of time. However, observation alone can leave many questions unanswered. For example, it may reveal that a particular display at a supermarket is unpopular, but provide no clues as to why this is the case.

IT-based research Advances in IT have led to the development of new ways in which businesses can carry out field research.

- Businesses are increasingly making use of Internet surveys, where customers can provide data onto a business websites. Email surveys are also gaining popularity.
- Retail audits consist of information collected by retailers about consumers, usually at the point at which a purchase is made. Epos (electronic point of sale) data can be used, for example, to analyse patterns and trends in sales. Data gathered from retail audits is also valuable for identifying the types of consumers purchasing particular products.
- In the UK many shopping centres have devices installed which record where customers shop. Certain recorders have been developed which 'count' the number of customers entering a shop and some even differentiate between adults, children and pushchairs. The technology provides information which allows shops to see which areas of the centre attract most shoppers. It can also be used to compare shopping centres.
- Interactive methods can also be used to gather information. Consumers may be able to express their views via Internet websites or digital television. Information can be collected when orders are placed directly via the Internet or digital television link.
- Spending patterns may be analysed from the use of credit cards and store loyalty cards. Loyalty cards allow customers to obtain a certain amount of benefits and discounts with each purchase they make within a shop or supermarket.

Focus groups This involves a group of customers being brought together on one or a number of occasions. They are asked to answer and discuss questions prepared by market researchers. The groups contain a range of individuals who are thought to be representative of the customers of the business or a particular segment of customers. Because they only involve a small number of customers, focus groups are a relatively cheap and easy way of gathering marketing research

Vegran is a company that has developed a healthy lunch bar made from carob and oats. Initially, it has decided to sell the bar in the South West for a trial period, before launching the product throughout the country. Before this, however, it wants to collect views of consumers on the taste and appearance of the bar. It is particularly interested to find out whether consumers would notice a difference in taste between chocolate and carob and their views on the bar's size and packaging.

Vegran is only a small company with a limited budget for its marketing projects.

(a) What potential advantages might test marketing have for Vegran?
(b) How useful might:
   (i) postal surveys;
   (ii) consumer panels;
   (iii) personal interviews;
   (iv) Internet surveys;
   be to the business?

Question 3

information. A problem is that the views of a fairly small number of customers may not reflect the views of the market or the market segment in which the business is interested.

Consumer panels This involves a group of consumers being consulted on their reactions to a product over a period of time. Consumer panels are widely used by TV companies to judge the reaction of viewers to new and existing programmes. Their main advantage is that they can be used to consider how consumer reaction changes over time. Firms can then build up a picture of consumer trends. Their disadvantage is that it is both difficult and expensive to choose and keep a panel available for research over a long period.

Test marketing Test marketing involves selling a product in a restricted section of the market in order to assess consumer reaction to it. Test marketing usually takes place by making a product available within a particular geographical area. For example, before the Wispa chocolate bar was marketed nationally, it was test marketed in the North East of England.

Sampling methods

Carrying out a survey of every single potential consumer (known as the POPULATION) of a firm's product would be impractical, time-consuming and costly. Businesses still, however, need to collect enough primary data to have a clear idea of the views of consumers. This can be done by taking a SAMPLE of the population. This sample group should be made up of consumers that are representative of all potential buyers of the product.

There is a number of ways in which a sample can be chosen.

Random sampling This method gives each member of a group an equal chance of being chosen. In other words, the sample is selected at random, rather like picking numbers out of a hat. Today computers can be used to produce a random list of numbers which are then used as the basis for selecting a sample. Its main advantage is that bias cannot be introduced when choosing the sample. However, it assumes that all members of the group are the same (homogeneous), which is not always the case. A small sample chosen in this way may not have the characteristics of the population, so a very large sample would have to be taken to make sure it was representative. It would be very costly and time consuming for firms to draw up a list of the whole population and then contact and interview them.

One method sometimes used to reduce the time taken to locate a random sample is to choose every tenth or twentieth name on a list. This is known as systematic sampling. It is, however, less random.

Stratified random sampling This method of random sampling is often preferred by researchers as it makes the sample more representative of the whole group. The sample is divided into segments or strata based on previous knowledge about how the population is divided up. For example, a business may be interested in how employment status affected the demand for a food product. It might divide the population up into different income groups, such as higher managerial and professional occupations, small employers and 'own account' workers etc. A random sample could then be chosen from each of these groups making sure that there were the same proportions of the sample in each category as in the population as a whole. So if the population had 10 per cent upper class males, so would the sample.

Quota sampling This sampling method involves the population being segmented into a number of groups which share specific characteristics. These may be based on the age and sex of the population. Interviewers are then given targets for the number of people out of each segment who they must interview. For example, an interviewer may be asked to interview 10 males between the ages of 18 and 25, or 15 females between the ages of 45 and 60. Once the target is reached, no more people are interviewed from that group. The advantage of this sampling method is that it can be cheaper to operate than many of the others. It is also useful where the proportions of different groups within the population are known. However, results from quota sampling are not statistically representative of the population and are not randomly chosen. They must therefore be treated with caution.

Cluster sampling This involves separating the population into 'clusters', usually in different geographical areas. A random sample is then taken from the clusters, which are assumed to be representative of the population. This method is often used when survey results need to be found quickly, such as opinion polls.

Multi-stage sampling This involves selecting one sample from another sample. So, for example, a market researcher might choose a county at random and then a district of that county may be selected. Similarly, a street within a city may be chosen and then a particular household within a street.

Snowballing This is a highly specialised method of sampling. It involves starting the process of sampling with one individual or group and then using these contacts to develop more, hence the 'snowball' effect. This is only used when other sampling methods are not possible, due to the fact that samples built up by snowballing cannot be representative. Businesses operating in highly secretive markets such as the arms trade may use this method of sampling. Similarly, firms engaged in producing highly specialised and expensive one off products for a very limited range of customers may need to rely upon snowballing when engaged in marketing research. Examples might include firms engaged in the nuclear and power generating industries.

Sample results

A business will be interested in the **range** of results it gets from the surveys it carries out. In particular, it will want to know the **significance** of any sample result. It can use **standard deviations** to find out how confident it can be about a particular sample. For example, a business might look at market research information about the possible sales of a new product. It might expect that the average sales per week will be 1,000 and the standard deviation from the average will be 100. The business can use CONFIDENCE LEVELS to analyse the data.

- It will be 68 per cent confident that sales will be plus or minus one standard deviation from the average. So it is 68 per cent confident that sales will be between 900 (1,000 - 100) and 1,100 (1,000 + 100) a week.
- It will be 96 per cent confident that sales will be plus or minus 2 standard deviations from the average - between 800 (1,000 - [2 x 100]) and 1,200 (1,000 + [2 x 100]) a week.
- It will be nearly 100 per cent confident, ie certain, that sales will be plus or minus 3 standard deviations from the average - between 700 (1,000 - [3 x 100]) and 1,300 (1,000 + [3 x 100]) a week.

These figures assume that the survey is carried out without bias and that the results resemble a normal distribution. Standard deviations can then be used to tell a business what the expected range of outcomes from a particular population will be.

The benefits of market research

An aid to decision making Perhaps the main benefit of market research is that it allows a business to make more informed decisions. This is especially important in fast changing markets. Businesses operating in such markets constantly need to adjust their marketing activities.

Reducing risk Whilst the reliability of market research information cannot be guaranteed, it does reduce risk for a business. Without market research, a business might spend large sums developing and launching a new product which could prove to be unsuccessful. Businesses are less likely to waste resources on failed activities if careful marketing research is carried out.

Providing a link with the outside world Without market research businesses may operate in a vacuum. They would have little or no way of finding out the views of their actual and potential customers. They would also find it difficult to identify future trends in their existing markets and the markets in which they plan to operate in future.

The size of markets As markets become ever larger and as new markets open up, market research becomes ever more important. In international and global markets it is impossible for businesses to operate without precise information about the needs of their customers. This is because of the huge number of customers and the large differences in their tastes.

Public relations Carrying out market research may be good for the image of a business. Consumers may feel that their views are being considered. They may also think that the business is concerned that its customers are happy. This may lead to 'corporate' brand loyalty.

The problems of market research

If market research was totally dependable, businesses could use marketing research when introducing or changing products and then be completely confident as to how consumers would respond to them. This would mean that all new products launched onto the market, which had been researched in advance, would be a success. Similarly, no products would flop because businesses would receive advance warning from their research and take any necessary measures.

In reality, things can be different. It has been estimated that 90 per cent of all products fail after they have been initially launched. Some of this, no doubt, can be put down to a lack of, or inadequate, market research. However, a number of businesses that have conducted extensive research

amongst consumers before committing a product to the market place have launched products which have failed. Given estimates which suggest that the minimum cost of launching a new product nationally is £1 million, this is a risky business.

Famous examples of thoroughly researched products which have turned out to be flops include the Sinclair C5, a cheap vehicle with more stability than a moped and lower costs than a car. In research, consumers enthused over this vehicle. In reality, it was almost impossible to sell. Similarly, when Coca-Cola launched 'New Coke' with a new formula flavour onto the market, research suggested it would be a huge success. In practice, 'New Coke' was quickly withdrawn from the shops.

Businesses want to be sure that the data they collect is reliable. One way of checking the **reliability** of data is to pose the question, 'If this information was collected again would the same or broadly similar results be obtained?' Businesses acting upon research data need to be sure that they can depend upon it. There is a great deal of debate amongst researchers about the reliability of different research methods. Reliability is a problem for both primary and secondary research data.

Primary data There is a number of reasons why 'field' research does not always provide reliable information to businesses.
- Human behaviour. Much marketing research depends upon the responses of consumers who participate in the collection of primary data. Whilst the responses of consumers may be honest and truthful at the time, it does not mean that they will necessarily respond in the same manner in future. This is because all human behaviour, including the act of consuming and purchasing goods, is to some extent unpredictable.
- Sampling and bias. As noted earlier in this unit, when undertaking marketing research it is usual to base the research upon a sample of the total population. This is because it would be impossible and costly to include every person when dealing with a large population. It is possible, however, that results from the sample may be different from those that would have been obtained if the whole population had been questioned. This is known as a **sampling discrepancy**. The greater the sampling discrepancy, the less reliable will be the data obtained.

Sampling discrepancies are caused by **statistical bias**. One reason why a sample may be not representative of the whole population is because it is not large enough. A very small sample may be different from the whole population. Another problem is that some methods of sampling are likely to introduce a higher degree of statistical bias than others. Random sampling introduces little or no bias into the sample because each member of the population has an equal chance of being selected. On the other hand, there is likely to be a high degree of bias with snowballing as the sample selected is unlikely to be representative of the population as a whole.

● Other forms of bias. It is not only the process of sampling which can introduce bias into market research. As mentioned earlier in the unit, questionnaires need to be carefully constructed to avoid the problem of encouraging particular responses from consumers through the use of leading questions. Similarly, the behaviour of interviewers can affect the outcome of interviews.

Secondary data Businesses must also be careful when using secondary data. Secondary data has often been collected for a purpose other than that for which it is being used. For example, businesses may use a government publication to estimate the size of markets in which they might wish to operate. However, these market sizes may not always accurately match the product market being researched.

Another problem is that much secondary data, including government publications and internal business publications, are out of date almost as soon as they are in print. In fast changing markets, in particular this can reduce the reliability of such data.

Quantitative and qualitative research

Data collected through desk and field research can be either quantitative or qualitative in nature. QUALITATIVE RESEARCH involves the collection of data about attitudes, beliefs and intentions. Focus groups and interviews are common methods used to collect qualitative data. An example of qualitative research could be face to face interviews with 100 purchasers of new Land Rover Discoveries to find out why they prefer this product to similar four wheel drives sold by other car manufacturers. The information collected through qualitative research is usually regarded as being open to a high degree of interpretation. This means that there are often disagreements within businesses about the significance and importance of qualitative research data.

QUANTITATIVE RESEARCH involves the collection of data that can be measured. In practice this usually means the collection of statistical data such as sales figures and market share. Surveys and the use of government publications are common methods of collecting quantitative research data. An example of quantitative research would be a survey of four wheel drive owners in West Derbyshire to establish their places of residence, ages, occupations, incomes and gender. The information collected through quantitative research is usually regarded as being open to less interpretation than that collected through qualitative research.

The overwhelming majority of children see their family holiday as an opportunity to spend more quality time with their parents, according to a survey carried out by a holiday company. The survey which questioned 500 children between the ages of five and 14, revealed that 95 per cent of children said spending precious time with the grown-ups was the most important factor in a holiday. Eight out of 10 said their parents were a lot less 'grumpy' on holiday than at home. Preferences did differ with age, with children in the five to 10 age group preferring to stay in hotels with kids' clubs, while most 11 to 14 year olds prefer villas with communal pools for making friends.

Source: adapted from *The Observer*, 20.7.2003.

(a) Would you describe the market research in the article as:
   (i) desk or field research;
   (ii) quantitative or qualitative research?
   Explain your answer.
(b) Taking into account your answer to (a)(ii), suggest what other data a travel company might be interested in and why.

Question 4

Knowledge

1. Why is market research important to businesses?
2. Explain the difference between:
   (a) descriptive research;
   (b) predictive research;
   (c) explanatory research.
3. State 5 areas that market research could concentrate on.
4. What is meant by desk research?
5. What is meant by field research?
6. Why might field research be of benefit to a business?
7. In what circumstances might:
   (a) postal surveys;
   (b) questionnaires;
   (c) observation;
   be useful?
8. What is meant by sampling?
9. Why might a stratified random sample be preferred to a random sample?
10. Suggest 3 benefits of market research to a business.
11. Why might sampling result in statistical bias?
12. What is the difference between qualitative and quantitative market research?

key terms

Confidence level - a statistical calculation which allows a business to gauge the extent of its confidence in the results of research.

Market or marketing research - the collection, collation and analysis of data relating to the marketing and consumption of goods and services.

Population - the total number of consumers in a given group.

Primary data - information which does not already exist and is collected through the use of field research.

Qualitative research - the collection of data about attitudes, beliefs and intentions.

Quantitative research - the collection of data that can be quantified.

Sample - a group of consumers selected from the population.

Secondary data - data which is already in existence. It is normally used for a purpose other than that for which it was collected.

Case study *Supermarket Shoppers*

In 2000 Opinion Research Corporation (ORC) International carried out a market research survey for the Competition Commission into the characteristics of shoppers in the UK. The survey asked 982 nationally representative consumers who were solely or jointly responsible for the household's spending on groceries about their shopping habits. Twenty per cent of the respondents were male and eighty per cent were female.

The questions were asked during in-home 40 minute interviews. Interviewing was conducted over weekdays and weekends and at different times of the day in order to encounter a spread of different types of consumers, including both workers and non-workers. Recruitment was random, in that every 'nth' door would be 'knocked on' to further ensure that a range of consumer types were interviewed. Information on a wide variety of demographic and socio-economic characteristics was also collected, enabling responses to be analysed by socio-economic group, household income and household expenditure.

Figures 12.1-12.3 and Table 12.2 show some of the results of questions asked in the survey.

Source: adapted from www.competition-commission.org.uk.

(a) Is the research carried out primary or secondary research? Explain your answer. (4 marks)

(b) Identify and describe the type of sampling carried out in the survey. (6 marks)

(c) Explain the possible advantages of the method of research used. (10 marks)

(d) Examine how the results of the survey may be useful to supermarkets. (10 marks)

(e) Discuss the extent to which the survey is likely to be reliable. (10 marks)

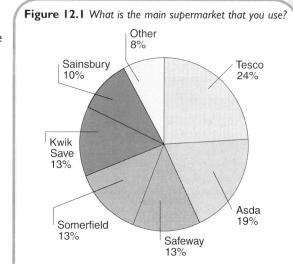

Figure 12.1 *What is the main supermarket that you use?*

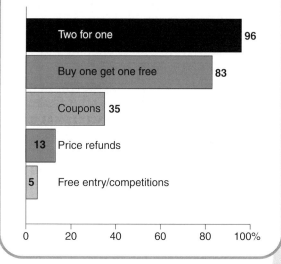

Figure 12.2 *What promotions do you look out for?*

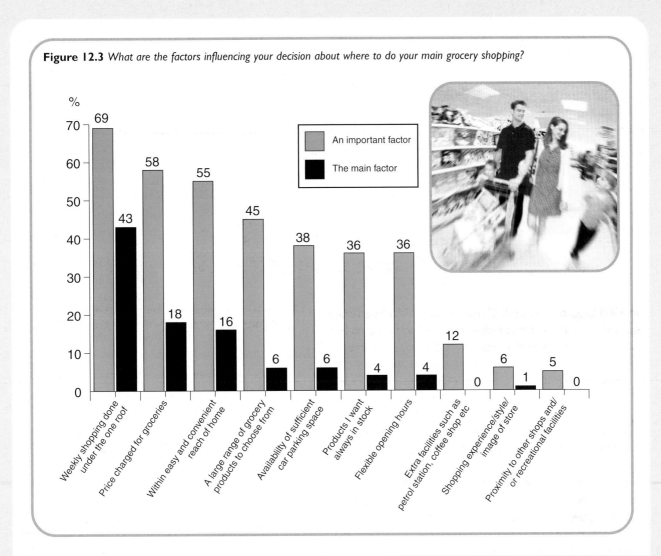

Figure 12.3 *What are the factors influencing your decision about where to do your main grocery shopping?*

Table 12.2 *How often do you carry out your main grocery shopping?*

%

	Income				Socio-economic group		
	Total	Less than £10,000	£10,000 - £17,000	More than £17,000	Total	ABC1	C2DE
More than once a week	16	20	13	14	16	16	16
Weekly	70	65	74	71	70	69	70
Fortnightly	7	8	6	8	7	7	7
Monthly or less	7	7	7	7	7	8	7

13 Market Segmentation

Market segments

Unit 12 showed the different market research methods that a business might use. Market research provides a wide variety of information about the people who may be interested in buying a business's products. For example, it might tell a business that a new chocolate bar will mainly be bought by people aged 16-25. It might indicate that older people have bought more of a magazine than younger people in the last year.

Producers may use this information to identify people with similar needs. Breaking down a market into sub-groups with similar characteristics is known as MARKET SEGMENTATION. A business can then target these groups and develop products and services for each of them.

Threshers, the off-licence chain, has in the past made use of such information. Each branch stocked goods which were suitable to the population of the area that they were serving. Branches in towns such as Eastbourne or Cheltenham, for example, had products geared towards the 'older' customer. They were, therefore, more likely to promote whisky and sherry than lager and vodka.

Segmentation by age

Many businesses pay attention to the age of their customers. Of particular interest is the segment that includes the over 60s as this segment is growing as a proportion of the total population. The marketing of financial services for older people has become popular in recent years. So has a number of other products and service areas, ranging from specialist holidays to the development of retirement housing.

Camelot is going to take the National Lottery into nightclubs and bars to encourage more under 25s to participate. In an attempt to inject some interest for younger players, Camelot is to introduce a game in clubs and bars where anyone with a lottery ticket will have their name put into a hat. A draw will take place at midnight and the lucky winner gets a free limousine ride home. Diane Thompson, Chief Executive of Camelot, said 'We know that a key customer group who we traditionally fail to engage with are the under 25s - the 'night owl' crowd. So we intend to take the brand right into their bars and clubs.'

Source: adapted from *The Guardian*, 20.9.2001.

(a) What evidence is there in the article that Camelot is breaking the market down into segments?
(b) Explain why targeting this market might be successful for Camelot.

Question 1

Segmentation by gender

Manufacturers may target either males or females. Some car producers, for example, have targeted women in their promotional campaigns for smaller hatchbacks. Manufacturers of perfumes and related products have realised the growing market for personal care products amongst men. Major brand names such as Armani and Yves Saint Laurent, as well as sports companies, have produced a range of products geared towards males. Mobile phone manufacturers target a growing number of females buying the latest 'technological gadgets', by designing accessories to suit their requirements.

Segmentation by level of education or occupation

Sometimes a business can segment its market based on how far the consumer has progressed through the education system. The market is usually divided into those who have or have not studied at higher education level. An example might be a magazine aimed at those with certain qualifications. Magazines are also sometimes geared towards particular occupations such as farming. Others are geared towards a type of employee, such as a manager or outworker.

Segmentation by social class

Markets are often divided by social class. Table 13.1 shows two measures of social class used in the UK. For the 2001 population census, the Registrar General divided social class into eight areas. Classes are based on employment status and conditions. This division is usually used in government reports and surveys. The Institute of Practitioners in Advertising (IPA) divides social class into six categories. These are used to decide which group to target for promoting a product. Because of regular changes in the pay and status of different occupations, these categories are revised from time to time. For example, the Registrar General's classification previously had only five classes.

Research often breaks these categories down even further. For example, AB, C1, C2, D and E are sometimes used to highlight the difference between levels of management, and skilled and unskilled manual workers. The media often refers to ABC1s. It is suggested that some businesses are particularly interested in people who might fall into this category as they tend to have higher incomes and levels of spending. Table 13.2 shows information from a study about the attitudes of people in the ABC1 group to financial services. This could be used by banks, insurance or pension companies to decide which customers to target.

Segmentation by income

Although linked to some extent to 'social classes' described

Table 13.1 *Segmentation by social class*

Registrar General's classification

Class 1 Higher managerial and professional occupations
      1.1 Employers in large organisations
          (eg corporate managers)
      1.2 Higher professionals (eg doctors or
          barristers)
Class 2 Lower managerial and professional occupations
      (eg journalists, actors, nurses).
Class 3 Intermediate occupations
      (eg secretary, driving instructor).
Class 4 Small employers and own account workers
      (eg publican, taxi driver).
Class 5 Lower supervisory, craft and related occupations
      (eg plumber, butcher, train driver).
Class 6 Semi-routine occupations
      (eg shop assistant, traffic warden).
Class 7 Routine occupations
      (eg waiter, road sweeper).
Class 8 Never worked/long-term unemployed.

IPA classification

A - Higher managerial, administrative or professional.
B - Middle management, administrative or professional.
C1 - Supervisory or clerical, junior management.
C2 - Skilled manual workers.
D - Semi and unskilled manual workers.
E - State pensioners, casual or lowest paid workers,
      unemployed.

Table 13.2 *Financial Services and ABC1s*

- More than one-third of ABs and more than three in ten C1s borrow more than they save. Those with children are nearly twice as likely as those without to owe more than they have saved.
- ABs and C2s find saving easier than C1s, Ds and Es.
- Just over two-thirds of ABs, and almost two-thirds of C1s, expect to fund their children out of savings and investments.
- Around one-third of ABs and one-fifth of C1s have bought savings plans, investments or insurance over the telephone. Only three ABs and two C1s in 100 have bought them over the Internet.
- Only one AB in eight, and one C1 in 16, sets aside more than £200 a month to save for a retirement pension, in addition to National Insurance contributions.
- Almost one in five ABs, and nearly one in four C1s, puts less than £50 a month into a pension.
- ABs are less worried than other social groups about the accessibility of bank or building society branches, and so are less worried about branch closures.

Source: adapted from www.researchmarkets.com.

above, income groups can be different. For example, a self-employed skilled manual worker, such as an electrician, may receive the same income as a middle manager. However, because of his or her occupations the two people will be in different social classes.

Segmentation by religion

Businesses may divide markets by religious groups. Food producers, for example, may specialise in producing Kosher food for Jewish people. Digital television has seen the growth of American style Christian television channels in the UK.

Segmentation by ethnic grouping

Markets can sometimes be segmented by country of origin or ethnic grouping. Radio stations have been geared towards African-Caribbean groups. Some products, such as clothing or hair accessories, are also geared towards this grouping.

Segmentation by family characteristics

The features of entire families may be used to segment the market. Examples of these segments include 'young singles, married with no children' (if both partners have jobs they are sometimes referred to as 'DINKIES' - double income, no kids) and 'older singles'.

Segmentation by political voting preference

Newspapers are an example of a product that is geared towards people who are likely to vote for a particular political party. *The Guardian*, for example, is arguably aimed at Labour or Liberal Democrat voters, whereas *The Daily Telegraph* has traditionally been geared towards Conservative voters.

Segmentation by geographical region

This might include considering the region of a country that consumers live in and the nature of the region, eg rural, urban, semi-rural or suburban. It may also consider the type of house, road or area of a city that people live in. This method can be especially useful in large or highly culturally diverse markets, where buying patterns are influenced by region. Businesses selling into the EU are likely to break this area down into more manageable segments. Many large businesses selling into global markets have different products for different countries or areas. For example, Nestlé has sold refrigerated profiteroles in France and a fortified drink called Milo with a malted taste in Japan. The Maggi and Crosse & Blackwell soups are adapted to suit different tastes, by varying the ingredients from one country to another.

Segmentation by personality and lifestyle

Consumers are sometimes classified according to their psychological characteristics. So, for example, sports products may be aimed at those who are interested in 'extreme' sports such as skiboarding. Chocolate manufacturers have identified two categories of chocolate eaters. 'Depressive' chocolate lovers eat chocolate to unwind predominantly during the evening. 'Energetic' chocolate eaters eat chocolate as a fast food and live life at a fast pace. People's attitude to life may also be used to segment the market. Some pension funds are geared towards those who only want investments in 'ethical' businesses. Clothes may be geared at those who are interested in 'retro' fashions from earlier decades.

Segmentation by purchases

This segments consumers according to their behaviour when purchasing a product. So, for example, consumers may be categorised according to the quantity and frequency of their purchases. One example of this is British Airways, which established an 'Executive Club' to encourage and develop the custom of regular business travellers.

Uses of market segmentation

Why might a business attempt to identify different market segments?

- The main reason is that it would hope that the information would allow it to sell more products overall and perhaps increase its profit.
- It would hope to be able to gain greater knowledge about its customers so that it could vary its products to suit their needs better.
- It might be able to target particular groups with particular products.
- It would hope to prevent products being promoted to the wrong people which would waste resources and possibly lead to losses.

One of the most commonly targeted groups for advertisers are ABC1s. In the past commercial radio was not seen as a useful way of reaching such audiences. However, recently there has been a growth in the number of 'medium' ABC1s which are part of the listenership. During a typical week, 65 per cent of ABC1s tune in or listen to commercial radio. Over a month its reach rises to 83 per cent. ABC1s tend to listen for extended periods of time, around 12 hours a week. They also have high loyalty levels to their favourite stations. On average they tune in to 2.6 different stations a week. Even younger ABC1s, who might be more experimental, tend to stay loyal to one or two stations. This information is particularly useful for advertisers using a mixed media to promote products. ABC1s often avoid TV advertising.

Main listening periods tend to take place in the morning. On a typical week 61 per cent of ABC1 adults tune into commercial radio. 19 per cent listen on Saturdays and 15 per cent on Sundays. Around a fifth of time listened to commercial radio by ABC1s is in the car. Most is at breakfast and when going home.

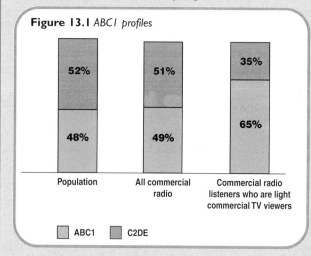

Figure 13.1 *ABC1 profiles*

Source: adapted from www.rab.co.uk.

(a) Examine the reasons why commercial radio might be a useful promotional medium for businesses aiming at ABC1s.
(b) Suggest how a business might appeal to ABC1s most effectively using this medium.

Question 2

Like Coca-Cola, Vimto has a secret recipe based on blackcurrant, raspberry and grape extracts. To generations of northerners it's the taste of their sweet youth. For those who are from the South of England or older than eight, the name Vimto might sound rather like an industrial kitchen cleaner. But it is, in fact, a sweet, fruit cordial that's big with kids and even bigger in the North.

Nichols, the Merseyside based family business that makes Vimto, is launching a campaign with the aim of making it as widely drunk in the South as it is in the North, and as popular in pubs and clubs as it is in playgroups and creches. Vimto is a strong brand selling £210 million in 30 countries. In the North West, men between 17 and 34 are 30 per cent more likely to drink Vimto than any other soft drink. Their aim is to make it more cosmopolitan, appealing, amongst others, to 17 to 34 year old women.

Source: adapted from *The Guardian*, 29.8.2003.

(a) In what two ways has the market for Vimto been segmented?
(b) How might market segmentation assist Nichols in efforts to increase sales of Vimto?

Question 3

● It might hope to market a wider range of differentiated products.

In many cases a business might employ a variety of the segmentation methods explained above. So, for example, a manufacturer of luxury apartments may be interested in segments that included single men or women with no children, in the 30-40 age range, with high incomes that fall into social class AB.

Research into why businesses are successful has shown why market segmentation is so important. One survey, for example, revealed that Japanese businesses paid far more attention to market segmentation than British businesses. A number of the UK businesses surveyed did not see their markets as made up of segments. They felt that anyone in the market could be a customer and that there was little real purpose in 'breaking down the market'. As a result, such businesses were pushed into low quality, low price segments. The Japanese businesses, however, had been able to successfully target more up-market segments.

key terms

Market segmentation - breaking down a market into sub-groups which share similar characteristics.

Knowledge ... Knowledge ... Knowle...

1 What is meant by a market segment?
2 Explain the difference between segmenting by age and by gender.
3 What are meant by social classes when discussing market segments?
4 Explain how markets can be segmented by types of purchase.
5 What might be the advantages to a business of segmenting the market?

Table 13.3 *Participation in selected sports by young people (aged 6-16) outside lessons by gender, 2002, per cent*

	Males	Females
		%
Football	57	18
Cycling	53	45
Swimming, diving, lifesaving	48	55
Tennis	25	20
Roller skating and blading, skateboarding	25	22
Cricket	22	5
Walking lasting more than 1 hour, hiking	21	23
Athletics	13	13
Cross country, jogging, road running	12	10
Aerobics, keep fit	5	19

Source: adapted from *Social Trends*, Office for National Statistics.

Figure 13.2 *Participation in sport or physical activity by age, 2000-01, per cent*

United Kingdom
Percentages

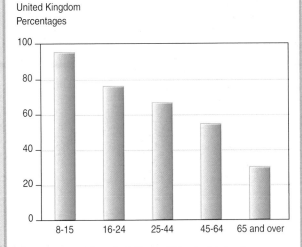

Source: adapted from *Social Trends*, Office for National Statistics.

(a) Using information from the data above, advise a manufacturer of sports leisurewear on the market segments it might target and the type of clothing it might produce.

Question 4

Case study The market for trainers

When your trainers wear out what should you buy? Or should you just change them because they look wrong? What are people in the street wearing?

Richard Wharton is buying director of Offspring, a trainer shop where you don't have to pretend that trainers are about sport. He can tell what someone will buy as soon as they walk in. A woman who looks like she would rather be in Prada might be steered towards a pair of white Converse Jack Purcells or Puma Mostros. If she's 'more of a council house girl' perhaps some Adidas Superstars or Puma Sprints. The customer wearing the new parka and split denims will head for Nike Dunks, Converse or Dunlop Green Flash. At JD Sport the Nike Air Max 90 are attractive to 'gangsta rap kind of people, though actually most of them live at home with their parents'.

Nike, started in 1972, has built its business on the assumption that hi-tech trainers would always be 'cool'. The strategy has helped it become a company that does $10 billion of business every year worldwide. It sells almost half of all the sneakers in the USA. However, current fashions are for simpler, cleaner, old-school looks. This trend is driven in the UK mainly by Puma, Adidas, Converse and Reebok. In the UK Nike has been less dominant, with about 18.5 per cent of the market. Adidas and Reebok, reflecting their European heritage, have been relatively stronger with 13.5 per cent and 13 per cent. Puma is likely to be much more significant now the company has seen a resurgence in the past eight years. It has even opened a flashy shop in Carnaby Street.

Adidas is well placed to capitalise on the trend for heritage shoes. Teenagers who would have bought skater brands such as Vans, DCs or even more obscure labels now say these are only worn by eight year olds and skaters. Teens and twentysomethings have moved on to retro shoes with slim soles and simple lines.

Nike, which benefited from a very twentieth-century love of sport, fashion and technology, finds itself associated with the hi-tech trainer at the moment it may have become unfashionable. Nike is fighting back though. The Nike Rift, a split-toed shoe developed for the African Rift Valley runners who ran barefoot but needed shoes for the Olympics, was very fashionable last year. In 2003 Nike launched the Shox XT. Its foam cylinders are supposed to work like shock absorbers, pushing your foot forwards every time your heel hits the ground.

Source: adapted from *The Guardian*, 10.1.2003.

Table 13.4 *Who wears what?*

Age	What they are wearing
Aged 14-18	<ul><li>Hard-wearing Vans Maverick - come in bold designs.</li><li>Prada Sport - eye-catching silver and blue.</li><li>Gola Harriers - popular with teenage girls because they come in bright colours.</li></ul>
Aged 19-25	<ul><li>Nike Dunks - hi-tech skate shoes based on an Eighties design.</li><li>Converse John Varvatos - a designer update to the classic Converse high top trainer.</li><li>DKNY Leanores - an elegant brown and cream shoe for young women.</li></ul>
Aged 26-35	<ul><li>Adidas Yohji Y3 - achingly hip footwear.</li><li>Paul Smith's Target - red retro design.</li><li>Puma Sprint - white and pale blue running shoes for women that are too smart for the gym.</li></ul>
Aged 36+	<ul><li>Reebok Classic - functional trainers for ageing lads who now value comfort over style.</li><li>New Balance Novo - the cute, colourful range originally marketed to US.</li></ul>

(a) **Using examples, identify the different market segmentation methods in the market for trainers. (6 marks)**

(b) **Choose one method of segmentation and describe the characteristics of trainers that might appeal to different market segments. (6 marks)**

(c) **Explain why trainer manufacturers might want to sell to different market segments. (8 marks)**

(d) **Examine how methods of market segmentation for trainers might be used successfully by manufacturers of sports clothing. (10 marks)**

(e) **Discuss the extent to which selling to different market segments is likely to be a successful marketing strategy for trainers manufacturers. (10 marks)**

What is a market?

A market is anywhere that buyers and sellers communicate to exchange goods or services (☞ unit 1). They can range from street markets, to markets for cars in many countries around the world, to goods and services bought over the Internet. Markets might be classified in a number of ways depending on their characteristics.

Geographically Markets might be **local, national** or **international**. A market held every Saturday in a small town is an example of a local market, as products are sold in the local area. National markets in the UK might be newspapers sold around the UK such as *The Guardian* or *The Financial Times*. Some products are sold in many countries in international markets, such as Coca-Cola and Pepsi, whereas some are sold just in areas such as Europe or Asia.

Buyer Goods such as ice cream and services such as DVD rental are bought by consumers in **consumer** markets. But sometimes products, such as machinery, are bought from a business by another business in **industrial** or **producer** markets.

Industry Markets might be classified according to whether they involve **primary industry**, such as oil extraction or fishing, **secondary industry** involving manufacturing, or **tertiary industry** involving services. Sometimes markets are classified according to individual industries or products. So, for example, the motor car industry and the computer industry make up different markets within the manufacturing sector.

Size Markets might be mass markets, where products are sold to many people in many countries who have similar needs, such as washing up liquid. Or they might be niche markets for specialist products sold to consumers with particular tastes and needs, such as the market for vegan food products.

Products are likely to fit into different categories. For example, a computer business such as Apple is a manufacturer in secondary industry, selling computer products in international markets, to both businesses and consumers. A tanning salon might sell niche market sunbed and beautician tertiary services, in local markets to consumers.

Market size

The size of a market can be estimated or calculated by the total sales of all businesses in the market. Market size is usually estimated in a number of ways.

- **Value.** This is the total amount spent by customers buying products. For example, it was estimated that fast food products in the UK accounted for sales worth £7.8 billion in 2002. This included branded fast food chains and independent outlets selling hot or cold eat-in food without table service, or takeaway food.

- **Volume.** This is the physical quantity of products which are produced and sold. For example, global crude steel production was nearly one billion tonnes in 2003, the highest ever. The UK produced around 12 million tonnes. Some estimates of volume are based on the number or percentage of users, subscribers or viewers. This is often the case in markets for services, such as the number of mobile phone users, the number of television viewers or the percentage of households with digital television.

Different markets are likely to differ in size. For example, recreational product markets can have different sizes. Sales of fitness equipment totalled £250 million in 2002 in the UK. In comparison, in the UK computer and video games market, sales of leisure software products in 2003 were £1.26 billion.

The market for all types of drinks in the UK was £41.39 billion in 1999. This accounted for 7.4 per cent of all consumer spending in the UK. Spending on drinks used to be around 10 per cent of all consumer spending. The fall indicated the downward pressure on prices in the drinks market even though the UK consumed a wider range of drinks products than before. The total drinks market was predicted to grow by 11 per cent over the next five years, around half the level of the period.

Source: adapted from www.theaccountants.co.uk.

(a) What was the estimated size of the UK drinks market (i) in 1999 and (ii) five years later?
(b) What might the information for the period up to 1999 indicate about changes in:
  (i) the size of the UK drinks market by volume;
  (ii) the size of the UK drinks market by value?

Question 1

Market growth

Markets can grow either rapidly or slowly, or they might contract and get smaller. Take the example of the market for recreational products. Sales of fitness equipment totalled £250 million in 2002. There had been high rates of growth for the previous two years. But it was suggested that sales growth would slow down as the market reached maturity (☞ unit 17).

However, sales of computer and video games in the UK had risen to £1.26 billion in 2003, an increase of 7.1 per cent over the previous year. In fact, sales of these products had been rising steadily for 20 years. It was predicted that this trend would continue.

On the other hand the market for handheld organisers was predicted to decline for the second straight year in 2003. Sales were predicted to fall from 12.4 million units worldwide to 11.35 million units in 2003, an 8.4 per cent decline. It was suggested that the fall was due to the rise in ownership of 'converged' mobile phones which combine organisers with phone call facilities.

What factors are likely to influence whether a market gets bigger or becomes smaller and the rate of growth or decline?

- Economic changes. An increase in income, for example, can affect different markets. Rising incomes might help the growth of the luxury car market or the market for high class restaurants. Rising incomes in countries in eastern Europe might increase the growth of products exported to these countries.
- Social changes. Changes in society can lead to a growth or decline in markets. The decline in the number of marriages and the growth in the number of lone parent families has perhaps led to a growth in the market for child care and other child support services, and for housing.
- Technological changes. Changes in technology can cause a rapid growth in certain markets and decline in others. The DVD market has expanded rapidly in recent years, perhaps at the expense of the video market. It has been suggested that MP3 players and downloading technology have led to a decline in the CD market.
- Demographic changes. Changes in the age structure of the population can affect markets. The ageing of the UK population has led to a growth in products aimed at people aged over 50, such as holidays and mobility aids.
- Changes in legislation. The privatisation of the telecommunications market, for example, has led to a growth in a variety of communication markets, including mobile phones.

Market share

MARKET SHARE or market penetration is the term used to describe the proportion of a particular market that is held by a business, a product, a brand (☞ unit 20) or a number of businesses or products. Market share is shown as a percentage. The market share of a business can be calculated as:

$$\frac{\text{Sales of the business}}{\text{Total sales in the market}} \times 100$$

Why might the measurement of market share be important? It might indicate a business that is a **market leader**. This could influence other companies to follow the

ELSPA, the Entertainment and Leisure Software Publishers Association, announced on 8 January 2004 that the UK computer games market was still buoyant and growing. UK sales of leisure software products reached an all time high in 2003 of £1.26 billion. This was an increase of 7.1 per cent over the previous year. Roger Bennett, ELSPA director general, said 'The UK video games industry sales have been on the rise for the last 20 years' and that 2004 would see the 'dynamic trend continue'.

He commented that 2003 'had provided substantial evidence of the way video games have been integrated into mainstream entertainment culture' and that the industry would 'garner new audiences from every demographic and age group.' Christmas was a particularly strong selling period, with a record 15 titles achieving platinum status of 300,000 units sold. FIFA 2004, produced by Electronic Arts, achieved double platinum status.

The presence of three 'next generation consoles' - PS2, Xbox and GameCube - helped to increase software sales. Sales of older generation consoles and games were still strong as well.

Source: adapted from www.planetgamecube.com.

(a) Describe the changes in the size of the market for video games over the period in the article.
(b) Explain the factors which may have influenced changes in the size of the market.

Question 2

leader or influence the leader to maintain its position. It might influence the strategy (☞ unit 5) or objectives (☞ unit 4) of a business. A business that has a small market share may set a target of increasing its share by 5 per cent over a period of time. It may also be an indication of the success or failure of a business or its strategy.

Figure 14.1 shows the market shares of supermarkets in the UK in September 2003. It shows for example, that the market leader was Tesco and that three quarters of the market sales were accounted for by the 'big five' supermarket chains. However, care must be taken when interpreting the market share of businesses.

- The share of the market can be measured in different ways. Market share is calculated as the sales of a business as a percentage of total market sales. Sales can be calculated in a number of ways. They might be the **value** of sales, such as £100 million a year. Or they might be calculated by the **number** or **volume** of sales, for example, 6 million products sold each year or 10 million visitors to attractions owned by a theme park company.

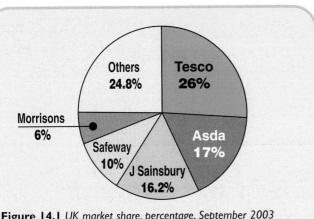

Figure 14.1 *UK market share, percentage, September 2003*
Source: adapted from www.guardian.co.uk.

● The market and the time period chosen can affect the results. Figure 14.2 shows the market shares of mobile phone handset producers in the UK. In 2002 Nokia clearly had the majority of sales in this market. However, Figure 14.3 suggests that in 2000 in the world market Nokia's dominance was not as great. In 2004 Safeway was taken over by Morrisons, giving the new business a market share similar to J Sainsbury in Figure 14.1.

● The type of product and business included might also affect the results. The results in Figure 14.2 might be different if the market had included all telephones and not just hand held telephones. This would then have included land line telephone businesses. Take another example. In 2000 it was reported that Scottish and Newcastle plc had over 50 per cent of the beer market. However, in the UK drinks market, beer made up only 40 per cent of drinks spending. So the market share of the UK drinks market of Scottish and Newcastle plc would be less than 50 per cent because the drinks market would include the sales of other drinks manufacturers such as Coca-Cola (carbonated soft drinks) and Tetley GB Ltd (tea).

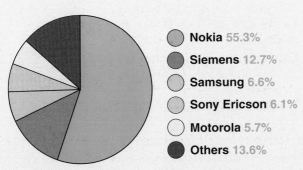

Figure 14.2 *UK mobile phone market shares, 2002*
Source: adapted from GFK.

Nokia 55.3%
Siemens 12.7%
Samsung 6.6%
Sony Ericson 6.1%
Motorola 5.7%
Others 13.6%

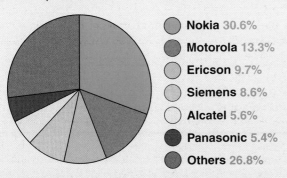

Figure 14.3 *Worldwide mobile phone market shares, 2000*
Source: adapted from news,bbc.co.uk

Nokia 30.6%
Motorola 13.3%
Ericson 9.7%
Siemens 8.6%
Alcatel 5.6%
Panasonic 5.4%
Others 26.8%

The Internet broadband market in the UK is shown in Tables 14.1 and 14.2. Broadband services can be provided by cables or Asymmetric Digital Subscriber Line (ADSL), which uses existing copper telephone lines. Internet Service Providers (ISPs) are companies that provide broadband Internet services using one of these methods.

Source: adapted from www.endersanalysis.com.

Table 14.1 *Broadband connections, December 2001 and August 2002*

	Total 2001	Market share 2001	Total 2002	Market share 2002
Cable	196,000	59%	352,000	52%
ADSL	136,000	41%	330,000	48%
Total	332,000	100%	682,000	100%

Table 14.2 *ISP broadband connections, August 2002*

	Total	Market share
Cable	**352,000**	**52%**
NTL	160,000	23%
Telewest	192,000	28%
ADSL	**330,000**	**48%**
BT	190,000	28%
Freeserve	7,500	1%
Others	135,000	20%

Source: adapted from company reports, oftel.

(a) Describe the changes in market share that took place between 2001 and 2002.
(b) Analyse the market share of BT in the provision of Internet services in August 2002.

Question 3

key terms

Market share - the proportion of total sales in a particular market for which one or more businesses or brands are responsible. It is expressed as a percentage and can be calculated by value or volume.

1. State 4 ways in which markets can be classified.
2. Explain 2 ways in which the size of a market can be calculated.
3. What is meant by a market that is (a) growing and (b) declining?
4. Give 4 factors that might influence market growth.
5. What is the formula used to calculate market share?
6. Give 3 examples of the problems of measuring market share.

Case study — The market for national newspapers in the UK

Table 14.3 shows the market for national newspapers in the UK in December 2003. The 'circulation ice age' as it has been called threatens the existence of many British newspapers. Advertising revenue is down in many businesses and sales of newspapers continue to fall. There seems to be no loyalty left amongst audiences who drift from one free CD offer here to a royal exclusive there. And people also have other things to read, not just newspapers. Where are the newspaper readers of tomorrow? They are probably playing the latest computer game on PS2.

But two newspapers are trying to buck these trends. *The Independent* launched a 'tabloid' edition on 30 September 2003. Initially this worked and readers responded. But it now faces stiffer competition after the launch of a similar tabloid by *The Times* on 26 November 2003. Sales of *The Times* were believed to have risen by 20,000 copies a day as a result.

Some commentators on *The Independent* say that its appearance and design is much cleaner than existing tabloids. There are no double page spreads and the use of pictures is more visually appealing. Where are the buyers for this new version coming from? Probably not from other newspapers in any great numbers. But there might be an audience among the young commuter classes who have yet to settle into the habit of reading a particular paper, or in fact any paper, on a regular basis. If this is the case then the rise might be short lived rather than continuous and difficult to sustain over a long period.

What if every newspaper launched a tabloid alternative? Would the retail trade have enough space to stock them? Would it increase the cost to stock them, as *The Independent* now faces, adding greatly to distribution costs?

Source: adapted from *The Guardian*, 10.10.2003, 5.12.2003.

(a) **Describe the features of the market for daily newspapers in the UK. (6 marks)**
(b) **(i) Calculate the size of the market in December 2002 and December 2003. (4 marks)**
     (ii) Calculate and describe the change in the size of the market between December 2002 and December 2003. (4 marks)
(c) **From Table 14.3, assess the changes in the market share of *The Sun* and *The Independent* over the period December 2002 to December 2003. (8 marks)**
(d) **Examine the factors that may affect:**
     (i) the size of the market in future; (8 marks)
     (ii) the market share of *The Times*. (10 marks)

Table 14.3 *National daily newspaper circulation, December 2003*

Title	Dec 2003	Dec 2002
The Sun	3,276,454	3,447,108
Daily Mirror	1,900,155	2,031,596
Daily Star	828,825	819,203
Daily Record	484,894	522,388
Daily Mail	2,299,043	2,327,732
Daily Express	851,199	916,055
Daily Telegraph	888,613	923,815
Times	594,134	619,682
Financial Times	425,387	440,036
Guardian	359,273	378,516
Independent	205,303	181,933

Source: adapted from Audit Bureau of Circulations.

Marketing objectives and tactics

MARKETING OBJECTIVES are the **goals** that a business is trying to achieve through its marketing. A business might have a number of marketing objectives.

Growth A business might want to increase sales, revenue, profit and market share (☞ unit 14) through marketing. It might be able to increase its revenue by selling more products. Or it might be able to charge a higher price. Both should lead to higher profits. So might launching new products. Businesses aiming to grow often attempt to create a **competitive advantage** over their rivals (☞ unit 5). Marketing can help a business to do this. Examples of businesses that have grown rapidly as a result of marketing include the low cost flight companies EasyJet and Ryanair.

Maintaining sales and market share A business may attempt to prevent losses and declining sales, and maintain market share, through its marketing. There are reasons why a business might do this.
- When a new product is launched. New products often require marketing and promotion to break into the market and for sales to take off.
- To develop over the long term. Some products have very long life cycles (☞ unit 17) such as the Mini motor car and Heinz Beans. They have sold continuously over many years as a result of marketing extension strategies designed to maintain sales. Extension strategies are often used in the mature stage of the product life cycle to prevent a decline in sales.

Product differentiation It is possible to **differentiate** products from those of competitors by changing the marketing mix (☞ unit 16), such as charging a lower or higher price, changing the packaging, design and ingredients of the product, advertising and other forms of promotion, or selling the product in different types of retailer. Examples might be the change in the name and advertising of the sweets Opal Fruits to Starburst or the setting up of a website by BA to sell flights through the Internet.

Product introduction and innovation The marketing objective of a business might be to launch new products onto the market. Market research could have indicated that this product would be successful. Some businesses introduce products regularly, such as new versions of computer software and games. Car producers regularly introduce newer versions of cars to replace older models. For example, the Ford Mondeo replaced the Sierra and the Ford Focus replaced the Escort. Some products, however, are genuinely new and innovative. It might be that new technology has created a new product or research has found a new medicine, for example.

Consumer knowledge and satisfaction Consumers need to know what products are available from businesses. They also need to be happy about the products they buy. Businesses which have satisfied consumers are more likely to gain brand loyalty (☞ unit 20).

A company's marketing objectives will be influenced by the corporate aims and objectives of the business (☞ unit 4). For example, the aim of a DVD and video rental chain might be to become the most well known name in the UK. Its objective might be to increase sales turnover by 20 per cent over 2 years to achieve this. So its marketing objectives could be to spend an extra £1 million on promotion to teenagers in magazines and product 'tie-ins' to make them more aware of the service.

There is a relationship between the different marketing objectives. For example, in the early 1990s Adidas found its market share under threat in the European sports shoe market. This was a partly as a result of a successful

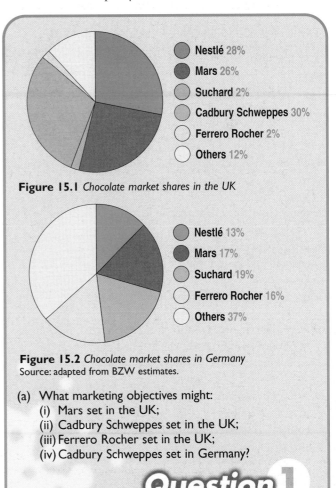

Figure 15.1 *Chocolate market shares in the UK*

- Nestlé 28%
- Mars 26%
- Suchard 2%
- Cadbury Schweppes 30%
- Ferrero Rocher 2%
- Others 12%

Figure 15.2 *Chocolate market shares in Germany*
Source: adapted from BZW estimates.

- Nestlé 13%
- Mars 17%
- Suchard 19%
- Ferrero Rocher 16%
- Others 37%

(a) What marketing objectives might:
(i) Mars set in the UK;
(ii) Cadbury Schweppes set in the UK;
(iii) Ferrero Rocher set in the UK;
(iv) Cadbury Schweppes set in Germany?

Question 1

promotional campaign by Nike. Adidas attempted to regain market share by its own marketing campaign, with the objective of differentiating its product. It promoted its trainers as having 'street credibility'. After the year 2000, Adidas launched a number of product ranges with a 'retro' 1970s look in an attempt to increase sales and win market share.

There is also a relationship between the marketing objectives of a business and its MARKETING TACTICS. Marketing tactics are short term, small scale methods a business might use to achieve its marketing objectives. For example, a furniture business with the objective of increasing sales revenue after Christmas might have a 30 day offer where customers can choose a free chair with any three seater sofa they buy.

Constraints on marketing objectives

It is argued that the marketing objectives a business sets should be SMART in the same way as the overall objectives of the business (☞ unit 4). They should be **specific**, stating exactly what is trying to be achieved, able to be **measured** to decide if they have been achieved, which usually involves setting **targets**, **agreed** by everyone involved, **realistic** and able to be achieved within the constraints of the business and **time specific**, stating exactly when they should be achieved.

There is a number of constraints that could affect the marketing objectives set by a business. They can be internal and external.

Internal These include the following.
- Finance. It may be difficult to launch new products, for example, if a business lacks funds.
- Organisation. A business which does not have a specialised marketing department might have a different marketing strategy from to one which does. A business operating in many countries might market differently from one in a local or national market.
- The product. A product with a poor image is unlikely to generate increases in sales.
- Price. Some consumers might expect to see a high price for 'luxury' products or they might feel that they are lacking in quality and buy other products instead.
- Place. The channels of distribution can affect marketing. For example, selling over the Internet might be a way of differentiating a service or increasing sales.

External These include the following, sometimes called PEST-G factors (☞ unit 24).
- Political factors. Legislation might restrict the type of advertising used for a product in an attempt to differentiate it from those of rivals.
- The economy. Increases in consumer spending, falls in interest rates (☞ unit 65) and low inflation (☞ unit 66) can all improve the chances of a business increasing its

sales and profit. An increase in the number of new businesses may reduce the market share of a company that is dominant.
- Social factors. Changes in tastes can affect spending by consumers. Fashionable products can often increase sales rapidly.
- Technology. New products may be created as technology develops. The Internet has also helped to increase consumer awareness of products.
- Green or environmental factors. These can often restrict the type of product that a business produces, such as the development of businesses selling managed wood as an alternative to other wood or plastic products.

These factors are often found by carrying out a

In 2004 Kodak announced it would cease production of traditional 35 mm cameras in the US and Europe at the end of the year. Sales in America fell below 8 million in 2003, a 20 per cent fall since 2002. The decision was based largely on the runaway success of digital cameras. Sales of film for traditional cameras had fallen by £2 billion in two years.

Kodak was betting its future on digital photography, printing and health imaging. The President of Kodak's digital and film imaging systems said 'We will focus our film investments on opportunities that provide faster and attractive returns'. But Kodak did not intend to halt production of traditional cameras totally. There were plans to expand manufacturing in Asia, Latin America and Eastern Europe where demand was still growing. It would also continue to produce disposable 35 mm cameras.

Kodak also announced plans to cease production of its Advanced Photo System cameras, launched in 1996, which gave wide shot capability. Demand had failed to live up to expectations.

Digital cameras are now outselling traditional cameras. Previously they had been more expensive, produced poorer quality pictures and needed large amounts of battery power. However, the quality of digital cameras sold for less than £200 has now improved greatly. Statistics show that only 14 per cent of pictures taken on digital cameras are printed. The rest are downloaded, emailed or deleted.

Supporters of traditional cameras argue that their photographs are still superior to those of digital cameras, particularly in the depth of colour.

Source: adapted from the *Daily Mail*, 14.1.2004.

(a) Carry out a marketing audit of Kodak to identify the (i) internal factors and (b) external factors affecting its marketing objectives.

MARKETING AUDIT. This is an analysis of the internal organisation and procedures of the business and the external factors which affect its marketing decisions. It will also help to identify the strengths, weaknesses, opportunities and threats faced by the business, called SWOT analysis (☞ unit 24).

Changing objectives into strategy

Figure 15.3 shows the stages involved in developing marketing strategies from marketing objectives.

● The first three stages involved in the process help the business to set its **marketing objectives**. It is important that the marketing objectives fit in with the overall corporate aims and objectives of the organisation to prevent conflict. A marketing audit and SWOT analysis will help to decide achievable and feasible marketing objectives.
● The business can then decide what **marketing strategies** to use to achieve its marketing objectives. Some of the marketing strategies that a business might use are explained in the rest of this unit.
● The business will then carry out it marketing strategies.
● Having carried out its marketing strategies, a business must evaluate how effective they have been. This review will affect future corporate aims and objectives, marketing objectives and marketing strategies set by the business.
  The process of using marketing planning and marketing strategies is explained in detail in units 24 and 25.

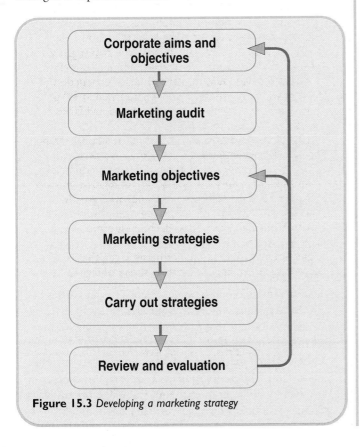

Figure 15.3 *Developing a marketing strategy*

Marketing strategies

MARKETING STRATEGIES are the approaches taken by a business to help it achieve its objectives. A business can have a number of different strategies.

Competitive strategies These are strategies which allow a business to compete more effectively with competitors. A business might try to differentiate its products from those of rivals. Or it might attempt to target a particular market segment. Or it might try to be the lowest cost organisation in the market.

Growth strategies These are strategies which try to increase sales. The Ansoff Matrix is a useful model to analyse these strategies (☞ unit 25). There are four strategies a business might use.

● **Market penetration or expansion** involves expanding sales of existing products in existing markets. A business would hope to increase the brand loyalty of its existing customers and persuade people buying other products to change. Examples of penetration might be the growth of Nokia phones or Tesco supermarket becoming the market leaders in the UK in their markets.
● **Product development** is the introduction of new products to existing markets. An example might be the introduction of a tabloid version of *The Times* and *The Independent* newspapers.
● **Market development** is where a business markets existing products in new markets. A business might decide to market a product to a new **segment** of the market (☞ unit 13), such as a different age group, type of user or country. An example might be the introduction in the UK of the Spanish retail clothes chain Zara.
● **Entry into new markets** involves new products developed for new markets. A business might decide to market a new product aimed specifically at a new market. They are likely to be genuinely new products, such as the introduction of MP3 players or DVD machines.

Market positioning MARKETING POSITIONING takes into account the views and perceptions that consumers have about products. To make a choice from a vast number of products, consumers categorise products according to a range of factors, such as quality, status or value for money. These categories define the products' position.

  Businesses know that consumers position products in relation to those of competitors. There can be a 'pecking order' or 'product ladder'. Products might be **market leaders**. They are usually the main selling product and decisions on prices and promotion are often followed by other products, known as **market followers**.

  Businesses use various methods to place their products in the desired position in consumers' eyes. For example, in the food and drinks market a business might stress products':

- benefits, such as the warmth of 'Ready Break' breakfast cereal or the low fat and low calories of 'Special K';
- UNIQUE SELLING POINT or PROPOSITION, such as the minerals and herbs in Purdey's drinks which are designed to give energy;
- attributes, such as Flora Pro-active and Benecol which emphasise reductions in cholesterol. Attributes are also important for technical products, such as mobile phones or computers, where consumers need information about such factors as memory to make a decision;
- origin, for example in the beer market Castlemaine emphasises it is from Australia while Boddingtons stresses it is from Manchester;
- luxury, such as Thorntons chocolates.

As markets and consumers' tastes change a business may try to REPOSITION its product. This can involve changing the image of the product, its features or its target market. For example, Lucozade was changed from a drink which people took when they were ill to one used by sports people.

In January 2004 Wall's announced it was to launch 'diet' versions of its top selling ice cream brands, such as Magnum and Carte d'Or. This was in response to the decision by many parents to ban their children from eating ice cream, following a number of recent surveys showing the relationship between eating fatty foods and obesity. It was argued that over a third of youngsters aged 2-15 were overweight and one in six were clinically obese.

Ice cream was facing an image crisis and in danger of being placed in the same category as other perceived junk foods such as burgers, fries and crisps. The diet versions of Magnum would cut the fat content from 17 per cent to 11.7 per cent and Carte d'Or from 5 per cent to less than 2.5 per cent.

The chairman of Unilever Ice Cream and Frozen Food, the makers of Wall's Magnums and Carte d'Or said 'One of the great myths is that you can't sell diet ice cream. We are going to debunk that. About 20 per cent of our total ice cream portfolio will be changed in a significant way.' He also added 'We will get a competitive advantage' and that 'We are moving to a higher unsaturated fat profile. We want to be beyond reproach.'

Source: adapted from *The Daily Mail*, 22.1 2004.

(a) Explain Wall's strategy using (a) the Ansoff Matrix and (b) market positioning.
(b) Examine the reasons why the business might be following these marketing strategies.

Market mapping

A useful method for analysing the position of a product in relation to other products in the market is market mapping. PERCEPTUAL or MARKET MAPS show the position of a variety of products in a market based on the **perceptions of customers** rather than businesses. The information used to position products within a map may be found by market research.

Perceptual maps show two attributes of products. Figure 15.4 shows a perceptual map of men's clothes shops drawn from a survey of customers in Merseyside and Lancashire. It shows shops which people perceive have large numbers of younger customers and charge lower prices, such as Top Shop, shops which customers feel have more highly priced adult men's clothes, such as Ted Baker, and shops with moderately priced clothes aimed at older customers, such as Greenwoods.

The business can then use this to decide where to position its own products. For example, a new business might decide to aim at younger customers. Or a business might reposition itself, for example, charging higher prices and changing its products to appeal to more older customers.

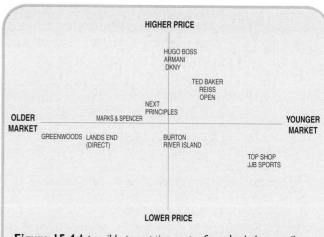

Figure 15.4 *A possible perception map of men's clothes retailers* Source: independent survey.

Targeting the market

Sometimes businesses try to market products to all consumers. At other times they might choose particular groups to concentrate on, their TARGET MARKETS. What strategies might a business use in each case?

- **Undifferentiated marketing** is where a business aims its products at most sections of the market. It is likely to be suited to products that cannot be differentiated to suit sections of the market.
- **Differentiated marketing** is where different products are marketed to different groups of people or the same product by different means. For example, some banks have financial services which vary for teenagers, students,

businesses and retired couples or online, telephone and branch banking.

- **Concentrated marketing** is where a business focuses on a certain section of the market. An example might be a product that is available only to certain people, such as an under 26 European student rail pass.

Some businesses are trying to move away from undifferentiated marketing strategies to better target consumer needs. Milk, for example, has in the past been mainly marketed in an undifferentiated way. There was little choice other than pasteurised or sterilised. Today milk is differentiated according to fat level, such as full fat, semi-skimmed or skimmed, or by source, such as cows milk, goats milk or soya.

A business might make use of CONSUMER PROFILES to target the market. This is information which tells a business about consumers of a particular product and their characteristics. It might include where they live, how old they are, whether they are male or female, how much they earn or their lifestyle. For example, in the UK 50 per cent of cinema goers are age 15-24. Cinemas might target this age group when deciding which films to show.

Identifying the target market can be more complicated. Sometimes the buyer might not be the main influence on the choice of product. An increasing example of this is the effect of PESTER POWER. This is where children constantly 'nag' to persuade their parents to purchase products. They might be the latest brand of clothing that is worn by their friends at school, buying Sky television and its many channels or a fast food burger meal when shopping. It has been suggested by some researchers in the UK that pester power results in a

purchase in around two-thirds of cases.

Mass vs niche marketing

MASS MARKETING is similar to undifferentiated marketing. A business will offer almost the same products to all consumers and promote them in almost the same way. Examples of products that might be mass marketed include Coca-Cola and Microsoft computer software.

Mass marketing has a number of features and benefits. Products are usually sold to large number of consumers. They may also be marketed in many different countries, known as **global marketing**. This means that businesses can manufacture large quantities and the average costs can be reduced as the business gains economies of scale (☞ unit 56).

However, there can be problems. It is often expensive to set up production facilities to provide mass marketed products. Such products also face competition in parts of the market from producers who might be more effective by targeting market segments. So mass marketing does not necessarily guarantee profitable products.

NICHE MARKETING involves a business aiming a product at a particular, often tiny, segment of a market. It is the opposite of mass marketing, which involves products being aimed at whole markets rather than particular parts of them. Tie Rack and Classic FM are both examples of attempts to exploit niche markets.

Why do firms attempt this type of marketing?
- Small firms are often able to sell to niche markets which have been either overlooked or ignored by other firms. In this way, they are able to avoid competition in the short run at least.
- By targeting specific market segments, firms can focus on the needs of consumers in these segments. This can allow them to gain an advantage over firms targeting a wider market.

There is, however, a number of problems with niche marketing. These include the following.
- Firms which manage successfully to exploit a niche market often attract competition. Niche markets, by their very nature, are small and are often unable to sustain two or more competing firms. Large businesses joining the market may benefit from economies of scale which small firms are unable to achieve.
- Many small firms involved in niche marketing have just one product aimed at one small market. This does not allow a business to spread its risks in the way that a business producing many goods might be able to.
- Because niche markets contain small numbers of consumers, they tend to be faced by bigger and more frequent swings in consumer spending than larger markets. This may mean a rapid decline in sales following an equally rapid growth in sales.

Kids are a major driving force in decisions to buy. And it's not just toys. They voice demanding opinions in everything including computers, television sets, vehicles and holiday destinations. More than 30 per cent of parents surveyed by Cartoon Network and global research body NFO among 3,218 kids aged aged 7-14 said that their children would accompany them to go and buy electronic and non-electronic durables. The survey also showed that pester power had increased in areas like toothpaste, toothbrushes and hair shampoo. Important features that influence children include appealing advertisements and free gifts. Musical adverts and star studded adverts have had a heavy influence on them too. Their main television favourites are cartoons, sports programmes and movies.

Source: adapted from www.chenaibest.com.

(a) Explain how consumer profiles might be useful to businesses selling computers and television sets using examples from the article.
(b) How might the information in the article affect the choice of target market of these businesses?

key terms

Consumer profiles - statistical information about consumers of a particular product and their characteristics

Marketing audit - an analysis of the internal organisation and procedures of the business and the external factors which affect its marketing decisions.

Marketing objectives - goals that a business attempts to achieve through its marketing.

Marketing positioning - the view consumers have about factors such as the quality, value for money and image of the product relative to those of competitors.

Marketing strategies - the goals that a business is trying to achieve through its marketing.

Marketing tactics - the short term, small scale methods a business can use to achieve its marketing objectives.

Mass marketing - the marketing of a product to all possible consumers in the same way.

Niche marketing - the marketing of products to a particular, small segment of the market.

Unique selling point or proposition - the aspects of a product that make it unique to others.

Repositioning - an attempt to change the views of consumers about a product relative to its competitors.

Perceptual or market maps - diagrams showing two characteristics of a product in relation to those of other products in the market.

Pester power - the constant requesting by one group of another to buy products. It often applies to children 'nagging' parents to make purchases.

Target market - the consumers which businesses choose to concentrate their selling efforts on.

Knowledge  ...Knowledge...Knowledge...Knowledge...Knowledge...Know

1. Identify 5 marketing objectives.
2. What else must marketing objectives fit in with?
3. Explain the difference between an internal and external marketing audit.
4. State 3 types of marketing strategy.
5. What is meant by (a) PEST-G factors and (b) SMART marketing objectives?
6. Identify the 4 types of strategy used in the Ansoff Matrix.
7. What does a perception map tell a business about its products?
8. Explain the difference between differentiated and undifferentiated marketing.
9. Explain the difference between mass and niche marketing.
10. Why might a business concentrate on a niche market?

Case study Recovery Kitchens Ltd

Recovery Kitchens Ltd is owned and run by Elle Jeffers and Arturo Vasques. The business manufactures kitchens using recycled and reclaimed wood. It sells mainly to two types of customer - those who are concerned about the environment and want to see wood recycled rather than destroyed, and those who want a genuinely 'old' looking and aged kitchen to fit in with the style of their house. The business operates from a workshop in the North West of England which has enough space for its current needs but little room for expansion.

The kitchens do not come cheap. There is a tremendous amount of work involved in reclaiming old wood and making it suitable for production. Sources of wood have to be found. The wood has to

be sanded, prepared and recut. Sometimes wood that has been bought turns out not to be suitable.

The business has been operating for about three years and now has a strong loyalty from customers who want this type of product. They tell their friends, who also buy kitchens. And sales have started to pick up in other areas of the country, particularly East Anglia, where the style of kitchen suits a great deal of older housing which is relatively cheaper than nearer to London.

Recovery Kitchens Ltd has been thinking of making some changes. It is concerned about its long term position. It is facing competition from some local businesses that offer cheaper pine products which can look very similar to reclaimed wood kitchens or more

expensive 'Shaker - type' kitchens which have a simple style and traditional feel.. And it feels that it can take the idea of the environmental image of the business further by making kitchens from managed wood. This is wood where the supplier guarantees to replant trees for all those cut down. Recovery Kitchens Ltd can then use this in its promotion to further enhance its green image and offer something a little different to customers wanting kitchens for older properties. It is also considering whether it should reduce its price a little. It has asked local people for their views on the prices charged by some kitchen manufacturers and their knowledge of the company name. This produced the perceptual map in Figure 15.5.

The business is concerned about whether it will have the finance to buy the managed wood. It might have to borrow, and interest rates look set to rise.

Source: adapted from independent research.

(a) **What are the target markets of the business? (4 marks)**
(b) **Explain the internal and external factors that might affect the business. (12 marks)**
(c) **Explain why the business might be said to be operating in a niche market. (8 marks)**
(d) **Examine the possible objectives of the business in moving to managed wood kitchens. (12 marks)**
(e) **Discuss whether the business should follow its new strategy and sell managed wood kitchens. (14 marks)**

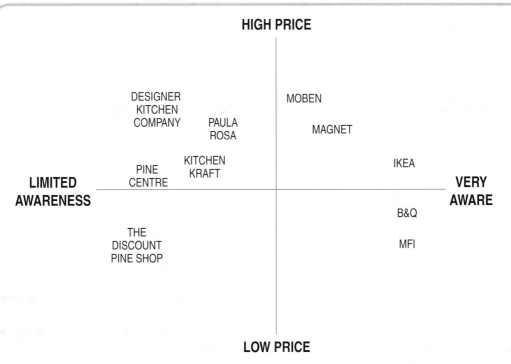

Figure 15.5 *Perceptual map of kitchen manufacturers from customers in the North West*

The Marketing Mix

In order to achieve its marketing objectives (☞ unit 15), as well as the overall objectives of the company, a business must consider its MARKETING MIX. The marketing mix refers to those elements of a firm's marketing strategy which are designed to meet the needs of its customers. There are four parts to the marketing mix - product, price, promotion and place. These are often known as the four 'Ps', as illustrated in Figure 16.1. To meet consumers' needs, businesses must produce the right product, at the right price, make it available at the right place, and let consumers know about it through promotion.

Product Businesses must make sure that their products are meeting the needs of their customers. This means paying close attention to a number of the features of the product.

● How consumers will use the product. A furniture manufacturer, for example, would market different products for home use than it would for office use. Products created for the office would need to be sturdy, able to withstand regular use and be long lasting. Products created for the home would need to stress features such as the quality of the fabric, design and the level of comfort.

● The appearance of the product. This is likely to involve a consideration of such things as colour. Food manufacturers, for example, go to great lengths to ensure that their products have an appealing colour. In some cases this means adding artificial colourings to alter the appearance. There are many other factors to be taken into account during the product's design. These include shape, taste and size. Deodorant manufacturers and toilet cleaning fluid producers amongst others might also consider aroma.

● Financial factors. There is little point in a firm producing a product which meets the needs of consumers if it cannot be produced at the right cost. All things being equal, a good produced at high cost is likely to be sold for a high price. Unless consumers are convinced that a product is value for money, they are unlikely to purchase it. They might take into consideration factors such as the quality of the product or **after sales service**.

Figure 16.1 Elements of the marketing mix

```
                    MARKETING
                       MIX
         ┌────────────┼────────────┬────────────┐
      PRODUCT       PRICE        PLACE       PROMOTION
     Appearance   Cost based    Retailers    Advertising
      Function   Competitor based Wholesalers Sales promotion
        Cost    Consumer based  Distribution Personal selling
```

In 2001 JJB, the sports and fitness wear retailer was pumping up sales. David Whelan, the Chairman of JJB, said sales had been supported by special, selective offers and advertising campaigns. JJB's product policy is to stock the main brands such as Nike, Reebok and Adidas alongside a selection of secondary brands like Patrick and Lotto. Mr Whelan said 'JJB believes that it will maintain its current market leading position by this product policy and by regular, selective promotions.' The company is also closing small high street stores in favour of large out-of-town stores. In 2001 it had 232 superstores.

In 2003 it sold its TJ Hughes department stores which sold discounted clothing. The business aimed to concentrate on its core activities, selling sports clothing and equipment. It also aimed to further open large superstores. A spokesperson said 'Our two-storey sites which have a health club on the ground floor and a superstore above it have been very successful. We will look to expand this concept in the future. We have about 13 of these stores across the M62 corridor from Hull to Southport and there is a lot of scope for growth'.

Source: adapted from *The Guardian*, 6.7.2001 and www.manchesteronline.co.uk.

(a) Identify elements of the marketing mix from the article.
(b) Explain how these elements might help JJB to gain a competitive advantage over its rivals.

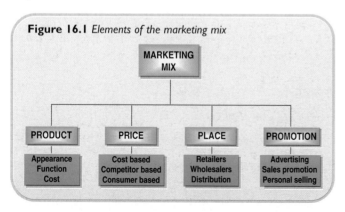

Question 1

● The product's life cycle (☞ unit 17). After a period of time the sales of all products rise and then later start to fall. A business must decide whether to allow the product to decline and cease its production or to try to revive it in some way.

● A product's unique selling proposition (☞ unit 15). This is the aspect or feature of the product that may differentiate it from its rivals. It may help a business to gain a **competitive advantage** (☞ unit 5) over competitors.

● Market position (☞ unit 15). This is the view that consumers have of a product compared to that of its competitors. For example, a product might be seen as 'up market' or alternatively 'low cost' by buyers.

Price The pricing policy that a business chooses is often a reflection of the market at which it is aiming. Prices will not always be set at the level which will maximise sales or short run profits. For example, a business may charge a high price because it is aiming to sell to consumers who regard the product as exclusive rather than because production costs are high. The way in which the customers influence the pricing policy of a business is dealt with in unit 19. However, factors such as production costs can also influence pricing (☞ unit 27).

Promotion There is a number of promotional methods a business can use including above the line promotions, such as TV advertising, and below the line promotions such as personal selling (☞ units 21 and 22). A business will choose a promotion method it feels is likely to be most effective in the market in which it operates. For example, methods such as '10 per cent off your next purchase' are used with 'fast moving consumer goods', such as canned food and packets of biscuits. National television advertising will only be used for products with a high sales turnover and a wide appeal.

Place This refers to the means by which the product will be distributed to the consumer (☞ unit 23). The product must get to the right place, at the right time. This means making decisions about the way in which the product will be physically distributed, ie by air, sea, rail or road. It also means taking into account how the product is sold. This may be by direct mail from the manufacturer or through retail outlets such as supermarkets.

When considering the marketing mix of services, the 4Ps are sometimes argued to be 7Ps. The importance of the following is also stressed.
- The **people** involved in providing the service.
- The **process** - the mechanisms, activities and procedures involved in delivering the service, such as delivery time of a meal.
- **Physical evidence**, such as the appearance of the environment in which the service is provided.

Choice of marketing mix

Each business must decide upon its own marketing mix. It is important that the right **balance** between price, product, promotion and place is achieved. It could be argued that as businesses become more market orientated all elements are important. However, at times businesses may stress one or more elements of the mix. The mix a business chooses will depend upon certain factors.
- The type of product it is selling. For example, a business marketing highly technical products is likely to emphasise its products' qualities rather than giving a free good as a promotion. However, a business marketing a product very similar to that of its competitors may wish to emphasise a lower price or use some method of promotion.
- The market they are selling to. Businesses selling consumer goods aimed at the mass market are likely to emphasise the promotional and price aspects of their marketing mix. Firms selling machinery or industrial goods are likely to stress the product itself.
- The degree of competition it faces. A business operating in a competitive market, with many close rivals, is likely to

stress the importance of price in its marketing mix. In less competitive markets price might not be seen as being so important.
- The marketing mix of competitors. Businesses cannot afford to ignore the mix chosen by competitors. For example, confectionery manufacturers lay particular emphasis upon the availability of their products in a wide range of retail outlets. These include petrol stations, newsagents, off-licences and DIY stores. The emphasis here is on place. Any business wishing to compete in this market would, therefore, be unable to overlook the importance of place in this marketing mix.
- The position of a business within an industry. Businesses that are leaders within their industries tend to have a greater degree of freedom over the particular marketing mix which they choose. Such businesses include Nike and Coca-Cola. Other businesses are in less strong positions, but may operate in industries with strong market leaders. Where this occurs the relatively weaker businesses often choose to 'mimic' the marketing mix of the dominant business.

Three decades after the launch of the VW Golf it was given the 'nerd treatment' in adverts in an attempt to revive sales. The message is keep buying the iconic car that changed the world. Analysts pointed to a range of problems that led to a near 60 per cent fall in fourth quarter profit of the business. But the major worry seemed to be the prospect of its core model flopping. One expert said 'I think the advertising has backfired. What they are saying is really "we don't need to change". In today's market that is going to cause problems'. Another argues 'the seeds were planted a few years back, around 1999/2000' and suggested that the problem was the poor products launched at the time. All models apart from two showed falling sales in January. These included the Beetle (down 6.4 per cent), the Passat (down 19 per cent) and the Polo (down 40 per cent).

Another problem seems to stems from the price. In the past VW may have had the brand loyalty to charge a higher Mercedes-like premium price in its market segment. But no more. Given the weak market in Europe and the cut-throat competition, particularly from the USA, the Golf was too expensive. You could get a car for 15,220 euros. But there was no radio, air conditioning or other features now considered as standard. If added, the price came to 17,100 euros, compared to 15,200 for the GM Astra. On the first of February 2004 VW threw in air conditioning free and sales rose from 350 to 650 a day. The market has also been more innovative with the development of small people movers. VW in contrast has been conservative, with few innovations.

Source: adapted from *The Observer*, 22.2.2004.

(a) Using examples from the article, suggest the factors that might influence the marketing mix of the VW Golf.
(b) Examine changes that VW might need to make to its marketing mix given the difficulties it faces.

Question 2

The marketing mix and the scope of business activity

A wide range of organisations is engaged in marketing activities. Marketing is not confined to well known businesses, such as BMW and PepsiCo, operating in a national and international environment. It is also used by smaller firms operating in local markets. However, the size of a business and the extent to which it operates in the private or public sector can affect its marketing mix.

Non-profit making organisations There has been a huge increase in the marketing activities in which non-profit organisations such as schools and colleges, charities and hospitals engage. One of the reasons for this is that non-profit organisations in the public sector (☞ unit 7) increasingly need to compete with other similar businesses for their customers (who are still usually called patients, students, clients or other appropriate terms by these organisations). The funding of such organisations is now usually linked to their ability to attract 'customers'. For example, if a college student chooses to attend College A to study for a course, rather than College B, College A will receive funding for this student and College B will not. This provides an incentive for public sector organisations to attract students. Not surprisingly they have employed marketing strategies and techniques to help them meet consumer needs and gain an advantage over rival organisations.

For many non-profit organisations, particularly those in the public sector, price may be less important as a component of the marketing mix than for other businesses. There are two reasons for this. First, such organisations often do not receive any money directly from their customers. For example, colleges and hospitals receive their money through funding organisations set up by the government. Second, the price which their customers are charged is often set by the government and is, therefore, out of the control of individual organisations.

For charities, pricing is also likely to be a less important element of the marketing mix. This is because they do not have a priced product in the sense that many other businesses do. Instead they rely on donations from individuals and groups.

Small businesses For many small businesses, particularly sole proprietors, sophisticated marketing strategies are beyond their means. They often have so much work keeping their businesses ticking over on a day to day basis, they do not get the chance to think strategically about their marketing. Certain elements of the marketing mix may be out of the control of small business owners. For example, a survey by Barclays Bank found that 60 per cent of small businesses depend upon word of mouth to promote themselves. In addition, many small businesses do not have the opportunity to alter the way in which their goods or services are distributed. Thus, the importance of place in the marketing mix may be less.

Businesses operating in industrial markets Such firms have other businesses as their consumers. For example, the manufacturers of fork lift trucks do not market their products for use in consumers' homes. Instead, they are aimed at businesses who are interested in buying these products, such as warehouses. The differences between consumer and industrial markets mean that the marketing mix for businesses operating in these two areas may vary a great deal. Whereas the marketing mix for many mass market consumer goods often places emphasis upon advertising campaigns in the media, industrial marketing tends to rely upon personal contacts and the role of personal selling (☞ unit 22). International shows or fairs are important events, where producers can make contact with industrial customers.

Consumer markets Many marketing theories and concepts have been developed to explain the behaviour of consumer markets, especially those for high sales, mass market goods.

In 2003 Jenny Bodey set up the smallest of small businesses in a single shop. It was a wedding shop in Bootle, Liverpool, called The Bridal Lounge. By Christmas 2003 and January 2004 she had experienced record days of sales. Perhaps this was her choice of business. The profit margins on products in this market are very high. Dresses that are bought for £119 can be sold for £449 and still remain competitive. In the first year sales were predicted to be £56,000 but turned out to be nearer £80,000. She could now easily look at opening a second shop within a couple of years, although she needs to be careful because the area where her current shop is sited has very low overheads.

Jenny also has some advice for others looking to start up. She says budding entrepreneurs should not be too keen to offer discounts and promotions. 'I was giving people £100 of accessories with certain deals, but I've halved that. People don't expect a deal to be so generous. She also says 'I did quite a lot of advertising from regional based wedding magazines to wedding brochures and the local press. If I had a stall at a wedding fair I would take an advert in the brochure as everyone who visited my stall would take the brochure away with them.'

Source: adapted from *en*, February, 2004.

(a) Suggest reasons why the marketing mix of this business has been successful.

Question 3

key terms

Marketing mix - the elements of a business's marketing that are designed to meet the needs of its customers. The four elements are often called the 4 'Ps' - price, product, promotion and place.

Most businesses operating within such markets tend to focus upon all aspects of the marketing mix, paying a great deal of attention to every element.

International marketing Businesses engaged in international marketing will often vary their marketing mix from one country or region of the world to another. Product names, product specifications, prices, distribution networks and promotional campaigns may all be different. For example, car and paper prices are often lower in Europe than in the UK.

Knowledge ...owledge...Knowledge...Knowledge...Knowledge...Know

1. Identify the 4 elements of the marketing mix.
2. What features of a business's product are important in the marketing mix?
3. Explain the difference between price and place in the marketing mix.
4. State 4 factors that influence a business's choice of

   marketing mix.
5. 'The size of a business is likely to affect its marketing mix.' Explain this statement.
6. Why might advertising be less important to a supplier of industrial equipment than personal contact with customers?

Case study Cinemas and the Internet

UK cinema chains are dramatically stepping up their efforts to reach movie goers. They are building up highly sophisticated databases so that they can immediately alert customers when their favourite film actor is next going to appear on the screen. Targeting specific movie audiences is one of the chief preoccupations of the major cinema chains, who are desperate to foster customer loyalty. Recognising the surge of interest in Bollywood movies, Warner Village Cinemas has created a dedicated Bollywood mini website. 'Bollywood is quite a thing at the moment and the Asian market needs to be catered for,' says Sarah Kelly, director of marketing and sales for Warner Village.

Online ticket sales are booming. In 2001 Warner Village Cinemas sold 1.5 million tickets on the net in the UK and the figures are continuing to climb in line with the current boom in cinema attendances. 'It's 200 per cent up. Consumers want convenience and it's our role to make it as convenient as possible for them to book tickets with us' Kelly says.

New media is increasingly becoming a crucial part of the marketing mix. For the release of Spider Man, Warner Village Cinemas offered a free downloadable superhero screen saver and a competition to win tickets to the premiere. For another summer smash, Stuart Little 2, kids were encouraged to download vouchers that they could take to the cinema to claim a model of the plane flown by the mouse star.

Like Warner Village Cinemas, the Odeon chain has seen a huge surge in online cinema bookings and is equally enthusiastic about the potential of new media

and its ability to personalise communications. 'The web is a great source of information and it allows us to speak very effectively to different audience segments' says Luke Vetere, head of marketing for Odeon UK.

Some commentators argue that mobile technology will become increasingly important. This could mean film trailers being sent direct to mobiles with a link to a ticket buying service. This might involve, for example, receiving a picture of Tom Cruise and the times when you can see his latest film.

Regular movie goers should prepare themselves for a virtual avalanche of Tinseltown and Bollywood new media marketing. It will be coming soon, as they say, to a computer, mobile phone and TV screen near you.

Source: adapted from *The Guardian*, 12.8.2002.

(a) **Identify elements of Warner Village Cinemas' marketing mix using examples from the article. (8 marks)**
(b) **Explain the factors that may have influenced Warner Village Cinemas' marketing mix. (10 marks)**
(c) **Explain why cinema chains might be placing so much emphasis upon new media as part of their marketing mix. (10 marks)**
(d) **To what extent do you think new media marketing techniques as described in the article would be useful to:**
   (i) **small businesses;**
   (ii) **colleges seeking to target school leavers? (12 marks)**

The product life cycle

A business aiming to achieve its marketing objectives
(☞ unit 15) must be aware of the PRODUCT LIFE CYCLE.
The product life cycle shows the different stages that a
product passes through and the sales that can be expected at
each stage. Most products pass through six stages -
development, introduction, growth, maturity, saturation and
decline. These are illustrated in Figure 17.1.

Development During the development stage the product is
being designed. Suitable ideas must be investigated,
developed and tested. If an idea is considered worth
pursuing then a **prototype** or model of the product might be
produced. A decision will then be made whether or not to
launch the product. A large number of new products never
progress beyond this stage. This is because management is
often reluctant to take risks associated with new products.

 During the development stage it is likely that the business
will spend to develop the product. As there will be no sales at
this stage the business will initially be making a 'loss' on the
product.

Introduction This stage is when the product is new on the
market and sales are often slow. Costs are incurred when the
product is launched. It may be necessary to build a new
production line or plant, and the firm will have to meet
promotion and distribution costs. Therefore, it is likely that
the product will still not be profitable.

 The length of this stage will vary according to the product.
With brand new technical products, eg washing machines,
compact disc players and personal computers, the
introduction stage can be quite long. It takes time for
consumers to become confident that such products 'work'. At
first the price of such products may be quite high. On the
other hand, a product can be an instant hit resulting in very
rapid sales growth. Fashion products and some FAST

MOVING CONSUMER GOODS may enjoy this type of
start to their life.

Growth Once the product is established and consumers are
aware of it, sales begin to grow rapidly. The product then
becomes profitable. If it is a new product and there is a rapid
growth in sales, competitors may launch their own version.
This can lead to a slowdown of the rise in sales.

Maturity At some stage the growth in sales will level off. The
product has become established with a stable market share at
this point. Sales will have peaked and competitors will have
entered the market to take advantage of profits.

Saturation As more firms enter the market it will become
saturated. Some businesses will be forced out of the market,
as there are too many firms competing for consumers.
During the maturity and saturation stages of the product life
cycle many businesses use extension strategies to extend the
life of their products. These are discussed below.

Decline For the majority of products, sales will eventually
decline. This is usually due to changing consumer tastes, new
technology or the introduction of new products.

Different product life cycles

Many products have a limited life span. Their product life
cycles will look similar to that shown in Figure 17.1. For
some products there is a very short period between
introduction and decline. They are sometimes called 'fads'.
The slope of the product life cycle in the introduction and
growth period will be very steep and the decline very sharp.
Examples of such products might be Rubik cubes in the
1980s and children's toys, such as the Micropets in 2003.
Once consumers lose interest in a product and sales fall, a
business may withdraw it from the market. It may be
replaced with another new product. Sometimes poor selling
products are withdrawn in case they damage the image of the
company.

 However, businesses must take care not to withdraw a
product too early. Over time certain products have become
popular again. For example skateboards which were popular
in the 1980s regained popularity in the mid-1990s and the
early twenty first century.

 Some businesses still enjoy profits from products which
were launched many years ago. The Oxo cube was launched
in 1910, Kellogg's Cornflakes were launched in 1906 and
Theakston's Old Peculier, a strong ale, was launched in the
eighteenth century. These products still sell well today in a
form fairly similar to their original.

 Because of the high cost of investment, car producers often
set product life cycles of 10 years for their models. For many

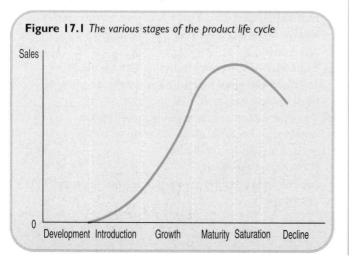

Figure 17.1 *The various stages of the product life cycle*

products life cycles are getting shorter, especially in areas like electronics. In the computer industry, some models and software have become obsolete within a very short period as new versions appear which are more technically advanced. For example, in 1995 Microsoft launched its operating software Windows 95. It was later replaced by Windows 98, Windows 2000 and Windows XP.

Extension strategies

It is clear from the product life cycle that the sales of products decline, although at different rates. Firms can attempt to extend the life of a product by using EXTENSION STRATEGIES. They may decide to use one or more of the following techniques.

● Finding new uses for the product. Video tape which had previously been used for video recorders attached to televisions was adapted to be used with portable camcorders.

● Finding new markets for existing products. During the last ten years there has been a boom in the sales of sports clothing. This was largely due to a significant increase in the use of sports clothing as fashionwear.

● Developing a wider product range. Lucozade was originally sold as a product to those recovering from an illness. By extending the product range to include a 'Sports' version, a huge increase in sales has been achieved. Lego constantly develops new versions of a product that started out as a plastic set of building blocks.

● Gearing the product towards specific target markets. Mobile phone companies have packages geared to the needs of 18-21 year olds. Banks have accounts for teenagers under 17 which provide cheque books and cash dispenser cards but not cheque guarantee cards.

● Changing the appearance, format or packaging. Coca-Cola is available in traditional sized cans, in glass or plastic bottles, or in mini sized cans. Swatch constantly redesigns its entire range of watches as a means of stimulating consumer interest.

● Encouraging people to use the product more frequently. Manufacturers of what were previously known as 'breakfast cereals' have used promotional campaigns to encourage the use of their products at different times throughout the day.

● Changing the ingredients or components. Many microwave food products are available as 'weight watchers' or 'low fat' meals, as well as more traditional meals. Many cars are now equipped with CD players and air conditioning as standard.

The effect that an extension strategy can have on the product life cycle is shown in Figure 17.4. As the market becomes saturated and sales begin to fall, the decline in sales is delayed by the use of an extension strategy.

It would be sensible for a business to try to extend the life of a mature product **before** sales start to decline. Firms that can predict falling sales from **market forecasts** may attempt to use extension strategies before the decline takes place, ie in the maturity stage.

The product life cycle and capacity

Capacity utilisation is the extent to which a business uses the

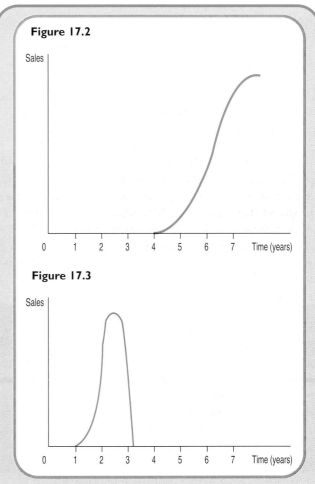

Figure 17.2

Sales | Time (years)

Figure 17.3

Sales | Time (years)

(a) Examine Figures 17.2 and 17.3. For each of these, name a product which you think might have a similar product life cycle.
(b) Why do some products have a very long life cycle (greater than 50 years)?
(c) Sketch the current product life cycle of three of the following products:
  (i)   A compact disc by a leading performance artist/group (you will need to specify the name of the CD);
  (ii) ice cream Mars Bars;
  (iii) Coca-Cola;
  (iv) Hovis bread;
  (v)   Rice Krispie bars;
  (vi) Finding Nemo DVD;
  (vii) the Ford Focus;
  (viii) a football strip of a Premier League team (you will need to specify the team).

Question 1

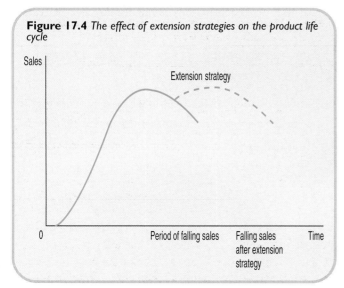

Figure 17.4 *The effect of extension strategies on the product life cycle*

capacity that it has to produce a particular product (☞ unit 59). It is the relationship between what a business actually produces and what it is capable of producing. A business working at full capacity that is unable to produce any more of a product will be at maximum capacity utilisation. A business that can still produce more with its existing technology and machinery is likely to be working at less than full capacity.

The product life cycle is linked to capacity utilisation.

- At launch sales of a product are likely to be limited. So a business will have spare capacity.
- When a product is at its growth stage a business will often be expanding its production and using up spare capacity to meet the rising demand for the product.
- When a product is in its maturity stage a business may be operating at full capacity. If sales continue to grow it must decide whether to invest to expand capacity.
- In the decline stage the capacity that a business has to produce a product will often be underutilised. This is because sales and therefore production may be cut back.

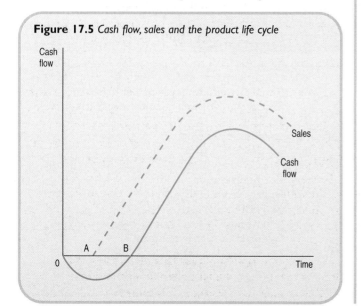

Figure 17.5 *Cash flow, sales and the product life cycle*

One of the main reasons why businesses seek to extend the life cycles of products is so that they can continue to operate at nearer to full capacity. Products with long maturity stages allow businesses to operate at or near full capacity for a number of years and can be highly profitable.

The product life cycle and cash flow

Figure 17.5 shows the cash flow of a business over a product life cycle.

- Before product launch a business will spend to develop the product and yet no money is coming into the business from sales. So cash flow is likely to be negative.

Breaking up is hard to do. Has the UK fallen out of love with the KitKat? It was launched as Rowntree's Chocolate Crisp in 1935 and renamed KitKat in 1937. The following year it was the company's most popular product. It first became a national favourite in the war years of the 1940s when the government endorsed it as a healthy, cheap food.

Ever since it has been the most popular chocolate bar in the UK. It was one of the main reasons behind the takeover of Rowntree by Nestlé in 1989. It maintained its supremacy even faced with competition from Nestlé's own Smarties and Black Magic. According to the KitKat website, 47 bars are eaten every second in the UK.

However, in 2003 sales fell by 5 per cent from nearly £123 million in 2002 to £116 million by the end of 2003. 'Saying the business is in crisis is extreme' argued a consumer brands analyst. 'But maintaining its position in the UK confectionery market is going to be a challenge. It's a cut-throat market.' UK consumers eat £4 billion worth of chocolate a year. But analysts believe that saturation point has almost been reached.

Information resources statistics now suggest that KitKat has been overtaken by its rivals Dairy Milk and the Mars Bar. Consumers may also be looking to healthier brands in future. So how will the company react. To some extent it already has with the launch of KitKat Chunky in 1999 and KitKat Orange. And in future it is considering launching lemon cheesecake KitKat, already a hit in Japan and Germany, as well as a curry flavoured version.

Source: adapted from *The Independent*, 15.2.2004.

(a) Using information from the article, draw and label the product life cycle for KitKat.
(b) Identify significant periods in the product life cycle of KitKat using examples from the article.
(c) Discuss how changes made in the future might affect the product life cycle of KitKat.

Question 2

- At launch, at point A, a product begins to sell. Cash flowing out of a business is still likely to be greater than cash flowing in, so cash flow will be negative. Sales have yet to take off and a business might be spending on promoting the product.
- In the growth period, eventually revenue from the product will be greater than spending (point B) and so cash flow becomes positive. This is because sales will be increasing and average costs may be falling as output increases (☞ unit 56).
- In the maturity stage cash flow will be at its highest. The product will be earning its greatest revenue.
- In the decline stage, sales will fall and so cash flow will decline.

Uses of the product life cycle

Why might a business be interested in analysing the product life cycle of its existing products or anticipating the life cycle of new products?

- It will illustrate the broad trends in revenue that a product might earn for the business.
- It will identify points at which businesses may need to consider launching new products, as older ones are in decline.
- It will identify points at which extension strategies may need to be introduced.
- It may help a business to identify when and where spending is required, eg on research and development at the start, on marketing at the introduction and when extension strategies are required.
- It may help to identify points at which a business should no longer sell a product.
- It will help a business to manage its product portfolio - its mix of products. This is discussed in the next section.
- It will give an indication of the profitability of products at each stage in its cycle.
- It will allow a business to plan different styles of marketing that a product might need over its life cycle.

The product mix

Product life cycle analysis shows businesses that sales of products eventually decline. It is possible to delay this decline using extension strategies.

A well organised business will attempt to phase out old products and introduce new ones. This is known as managing the PRODUCT MIX (or PRODUCT PORTFOLIO). With a constant launch of new products, a business can make sure a 'vacuum' is not created as products reach the end of their life.

Figure 17.6 shows how a business can manage its product mix. Say that a business over a particular time period aims to launch three products. By organising their launch at regular intervals, there is never a gap in the market. As one

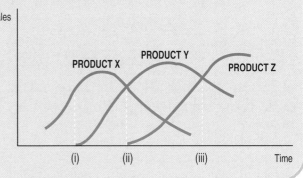

Figure 17.6 *Launching products successively (as older products decline, new products are launched onto the market)*

product is declining, another is growing and further launches are planned. At point (i), as sales of product X are growing, product Y has just been launched. This means that at point (ii), when sales of product X have started to decline, sales of product Y are growing and product Z has just been launched.

This simple example shows a 'snapshot' of three products only. In practice, a business may have many products. It would hope that existing products remain in 'maturity' for a long period. The profit from these mature products would be used to 'subsidise' the launch of new products. New products would be costly at first, and would make no profit for the business.

Examples of businesses that have successfully managed their product mix are sweet manufacturers. Companies such as Nestle produce a wide range of products, including KitKat, Milky Bar and Yorkie, and constantly look to launch new products.

The product mix includes **product lines**. These are groups of products which are closely related to each other. One example is the launch of a range of products associated with a new film. Product lines in this area include anything from T-shirts and mugs to books and CDs for films such as Shrek, Finding Nemo and Lord of the Rings. One of the most successful product lines of all time has been the Mickey Mouse merchandise of the Walt Disney Company.

Managing the product mix

One problem for firms in planning their product mix is that it is very difficult in practice to tell what stage of the life cycle a product is at. Also, there is no standard lifetime for products. For example, young people's fashion clothing has life cycles which can be predicted with some certainty. Others are less reliable. Who, for example, could have predicted the lengthy life cycles of products such as Heinz baked beans and the VW Beetle, or the short life of products such as the Sinclair C5 - a sort of 'mini-car' introduced in the 1980s.

A useful technique for allowing firms to analyse their product mix is the **Product Portfolio Matrix** developed by the Boston Consulting Group. It is sometimes called the

Table 24.1 *The Product Portfolio Mix (Boston Matrix)*

		MARKET GROWTH	
		High	Low
MARKET SHARE	High	STAR	CASH COW
	Low	PROBLEM CHILD	DOG

Boston Matrix. This matrix places products into four categories.

- 'Star' products are those with a large share of a high growth market.
- 'Problem children' might have future potential as they are in growth markets, but their sales are not particularly good.
- 'Cash cows' are those which are able to generate funds, possibly to support other products. They are mature products with a stable market share.
- 'Dogs' are products that may be in decline.

These are shown in Table 17.1.

Businesses must ensure that their product mix does not contain too many items within each category. Naturally, firms do not want lots of 'Dogs', but they should also avoid having too many 'Stars' and 'Problem children'. Products on the left hand side of the table are in the early stages of the product life cycle and are in growing markets, but the cost of developing and promoting them will not yet have been recovered. This will drain the firm's resources. Balancing these with 'Cash cows' will mean the revenue from the 'Cash cows' can be used to support products in a growing market. The development cost of 'Cash cows' is likely to have already been recovered and promotional costs should be low relative to sales.

This does not mean though that firms would want lots of 'Cash cows' and few 'Problem children' and 'Stars'. This is because many of the 'Stars' and perhaps some 'Problem children' might become the 'Cash cows' of the future.

The Boston Matrix has not been without its critics. They argue that the matrix can cause businesses to focus too much upon pursuing increases in market share as opposed to, for example, attempting to consolidate market share or improve other aspects of the performance of a product. It is also suggested that the model fails to take account of the way in which products within a business can support one another.

New product development

Planning the product mix requires the continual development and launch of new products. New products are needed to replace products coming to the end of their life cycle and to keep up with changes in the market. This is called **new product development**.

In some industries the need to plan ahead is very important. In the chemical industry, development work is

Lokotronics is a company producing a range of electrical goods. Table 17.2 shows the sales from just four of its products over the period 1996 to 2004.

Table 17.2

Sales (000)

Year	Product A	Product B	Product C	Product D	All products
1996	2	8	-	-	
1997	4	10	-	-	
1998	8	6	9	-	
1999	12	3	15	-	
2000	18	1	18	2	
2001	20	-	16	6	
2002	22	-	11	15	
2003	22	-	10	20	
2004	21	-	8	25	

(a) From the sales figures, describe the product life cycles of:
  (i) Product A;
  (ii) Product B.
(b) Calculate the total sales of all products in each year.
(c) Comment on the management of the product mix over the period.

Question 3

done on products which might not reach the market for over ten years. In the motor industry many cars take over five years to develop.

New products normally pass through five stages when they are being developed.

Generating ideas The first stage is when firms generate ideas. Ideas for new products come from a variety of sources.

- Identifying gaps in the market, perhaps through market research. An example of this has been the development of vegetarian microwave dishes by food producers.
- Scientific research. Firms such as ICI devote huge amounts to research and development expenditure. As a result they have developed products ranging from 'non-drip paint' to bio-degradable plastics.
- Creative ideas or 'brainstorming'. Products such as the jet engine have come about as a result of this.
- Analysing other products. When developing new products many businesses will analyse products manufactured by competitors. They aim to include, adapt or improve upon the best features of these products in their own designs. Some businesses adapt their own successful products to make new products.

Analysis The second stage is the analysis of those ideas generated in the first stage. There are a number of questions a firm might ask. Most importantly, it must find out if the

Table 17.3

Stage	Number of ideas	Pass rate
Generation of ideas	40	1 in 5
Business analysis	8	1 in 2
Development	4	1 in 2
Test marketing	2	1 in 2
Commercialisation and launch	1	1 in 1

product is marketable - if enough consumers wish to buy it to allow the firm to make a profit. Businesses must also decide if the product fits in with the company's objectives, if it is legal and if the technology is available to produce it.

Development The third stage is the actual development of the product. This may involve technical development in the laboratory or the production of a prototype. Such work will be carried out by the **research and development** department. An important part of this process is the actual design of the product. Some preliminary testing may be carried out to find out whether or not the product actually meets consumers' needs.

Test marketing Stage four involves the TEST MARKETING of a product. Test marketing occurs when a new product is tested on a small, representative section of the total market. The test market area should share characteristics which are similar to those found in the market as a whole. The benefit of test marketing is the high degree of reliability of results gained. It is carried out because of the high cost and risk of launching a product in a large, usually national, market. Test marketing can itself be costly, but not as expensive as a national launch which fails. One problem is that it allows competitors to see the new product and gives them the chance to take counter-action before a national launch.

Commercialisation and launch The final stage is the launch and commercialisation. Here any problems found during test marketing must be solved. The firm will then decide on the 'marketing package' it will use to give the product launch

the greatest chance of success.

At each of the five stages, many ideas are rejected. This means that very few ideas generated in the first stage will actually end up as a product launched onto the market. In Figure 17.7 and Table 17.3, an example is shown where 40 ideas were put forward for a new product. In this company the majority of ideas do not get beyond the first stage. The pass rate at this stage is only 1 in 5, with 4 out of 5 ideas being rejected. After that, the number of ideas which survive from one stage to the next increases as the pass rate falls from 1 in 5 ideas to 1 in 2. At the end of the process, only 1 out of a total of 40 ideas has survived to be launched onto the market.

Constraints on new product development

There is a wide range of **constraints** on businesses. These will restrict the number of new products developed.

Availability of finance and resources In highly competitive markets businesses find that their profit margins are squeezed. This means that financial and human resources are often not available to develop new products. An example of this is in the market for budget fashion clothing. Businesses in this market tend to copy products developed for designer labels.

Cost Even when businesses have resources, the cost of developing new products may be prohibitive. The development of products in the electronics market can cost millions of pounds. As technological boundaries have been

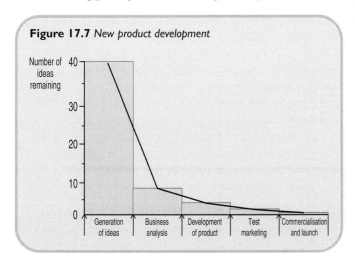

Figure 17.7 *New product development*

In 2000 LG Electronics introduced its famous Internet fridge. For £8,000 owners could check their email, surf the web and watch TV all on the LCD screen on the front of their fridge. LG is still very proud of the product. 'We are constantly looking at ways of developing products in this area,' said Andrew Mullen, LG's New Product Development Manager.

Mr Mullen promises that in future the fridge will be able to connect to a security camera so owners can see who is knocking at their door. LG is also working on variations of the fridge, though it could be some time before they come to market. Mr Mullen does believe, though, that within a decade Internet access and entertainment facilities will be a staple on all fridges other than really cheap models.

Source: adapted from *The Guardian*, 26.7.2003.

(a) To what extent is this product a result of new product development?
(b) Identify the constraints which may have restricted the development of the LG Internet fridge.

pushed forward, the cost of even modest new product development has risen sharply. Also, in many markets products have increasingly shorter life spans. This means that less time is available to recover development costs.

Market constraints There is little point in a business developing a new product unless consumers are prepared to purchase it at a price which can cover development and production costs. Many so-called 'tremendous ideas' for new products have been abandoned. This is because firms believe they cannot find a profitable market for the product. In addition, consumers can be resistant to change. This is often because of the time and effort consumers need to spend in getting to know how new products 'work'. There is also evidence that consumers are resistant to new products which represent a radical departure from existing products. New versions of existing products are sometimes more popular with consumers than totally new ideas for this reason.

Legal constraints Firms cannot develop whatever new products they wish. Legislation must be taken into account. For example, a pharmaceutical company wishing to develop a new product must be sure that it adheres to health legislation.

Technology The development of technology can affect the type of product or service provided. 100 years ago computers did not exist. Today they are sold in a variety of ways to different businesses. Internet cafes have also been set up which allow consumers to pay for time on the Internet. Technology may also affect manufacturing processes. Developing a new material for use in clothing which it is not possible to produce in the quantities required is unlikely to be successful.

key terms

Extension strategies - methods used to extend the life of a product.
Fast moving consumer goods - products with high levels of sales which are sold within a short period of time, such as soap powder or tinned foods.
Product life cycle - this shows the different stages in the life of a product and the sales that can be expected at each stage.
Product mix (product portfolio) - the particular mix of products which a firm is marketing.
Test marketing - testing a product out on a small section of a market prior to its full launch.

Knowledge

1. Briefly describe the various stages in the product life cycle.
2. Why might a product have a 'steep' life cycle?
3. How can a firm extend the life of its products?
4. Explain how a business can prevent a 'vacuum' in its product mix.
5. What is meant by a product line?
6. What is meant by the Product Portfolio Matrix?
7. How can the Product Portfolio Matrix help a business to manage its product mix?
8. What is meant by new product development?
9. State 2 ways in which a business can generate new product ideas.
10. What is meant by the 'pass rate' of new products?

Case study Murphy Drinks Ltd

Murphy Drinks Ltd had been producing powdered chocolate drinks for over thirty years. The company was set up as the market for vending machines producing hot drinks had just begun to mushroom in the 1960s. Its first product, 'Murphy's Vending Chocolate', came onto the market in 1963.

Its success in gaining a 35 per cent share of the market for vended chocolate drinks in under five years acted as the foundation stone for the future actions of the company. Ever since 1968, the percentage market share held by Murphy's vending chocolate had never fallen below this 35 per cent mark and, at times, had risen as high as 42 per cent. Sales generated by this

product were in excess of £160,000 in the financial year ending in 2003.

The success of the vending chocolate gave Murphys the confidence to develop a new product in 1969 called 'Catering Chocolate'. This was aimed at the hotel, canteen and restaurant market. Although 'Catering Chocolate' was successful in gaining a 20 per cent share of its market, the cost of developing it made Murphys cautious about attempting to launch any further products. In total, almost £15,000 was spent over a two year period in the process leading up to the product being marketed to hotels, restaurants and canteens throughout the country.

It wasn't for another eighteen years that Murphys attempted to launch a new product. This time, in response to changing tastes in the hot drinks market, it developed a low calorie chocolate drink called 'Lifestyle'. This low calorie drink was sold in sachets and distributed mainly through the larger supermarket chains. Despite its past successes, Murphys initially found it difficult to establish a firm footing for this product. However, the last two years, 2002 and 2003, had witnessed a substantial growth in the sales of 'Lifestyle' as consumer and retailer resistance to it was broken down by a series of promotional campaigns. Sales revenue in 2003 amounted to over £100,000.

Encouraged by the success of 'Lifestyle' in the retail sector, Murphys had made the decision in 2003 to launch a product line which it had been developing for a number of years. This was a range of flavoured chocolate drinks called 'Hi-lifes'. There was a high degree of initial interest from consumers in this product range, but it was too early - only six months after the launch - to evaluate its likely success.

Murphys also wanted to develop a new chocolate drink (called Bliss) and had a number of ideas which needed to be considered. However, members of the board of directors were split on this issue. Some were keen to go ahead with the new product development programme for two main reasons: first, out of concern about the falling sales of 'Catering Chocolate' and second, because they felt that now was the time to capitalise upon their recent success with 'Lifestyle'. Other members of the Board were much more cautious. Not only were they concerned about

Table 17.4 *Cost of developing a new chocolate drink (Bliss)*

	Cost per idea	No. of ideas	Pass rate
Generation of ideas	£50	40	1 in 5
Analysis of ideas	£500	8	1 in 2
Development	£8,000	4	1 in 2
Test marketing	£13,000	2	1 in 2
Launch and commercialisation	£35,000	1	1 in 1

upsetting their present product mix, but there were worries about the cost of developing this product.

Table 17.4 shows the different stages involved in the development of this new product and the cost at each stage.

(a) **At what stage of the life cycle were each of Murphy's products in 2003? Explain your answer. (6 marks)**

(b) **From the figures given in the table, calculate the total cost to Murphys of developing the new chocolate drink, Bliss. (6 marks)**

(c) **Other than cost, what might prevent Murphys from developing a new product? (8 marks)**

(d) **Examine the possible extension strategies that Murphys might use for Catering Chocolate. (10 marks)**

(e) **Evaluate the extent to which Murphy's existing product mix is well managed. (10 marks)**

Price and demand

Businesses operate in markets where they produce and sell, or **supply**, products that consumers want and are able to buy, or DEMAND. The interaction of supply and demand can determine the price of a product (☞ unit 61). This unit considers the factors affecting the demand for an individual business's products and the way in which these factors can influence the price that the business might charge.

The demand curve of a business

Businesses need to understand how the demand for a product can affect the price that they can charge for it. This relationship can be shown by a demand schedule and a demand curve. For most products the relationship between demand and price is inverse. As the price goes up, the quantity demanded goes down. As the price goes down, the quantity demanded goes up. So, for product A shown in Figure 18.1, a rise in price from OP to OP_1 (£20 to £40) will lead to a fall in the quantity demanded from OQ to OQ_1 (£5,000 to £3,000).

Some products have a demand curve which looks different to that shown in Figure 18.1. 'Prestige' perfumes are designed to appeal to wealthy consumers. A low price might put off

Table 18.1 *The demand schedule for Product A*

Price (£)	Quantity demanded
10	6,000
20	5,000
30	4,000
40	3,000
50	2,000

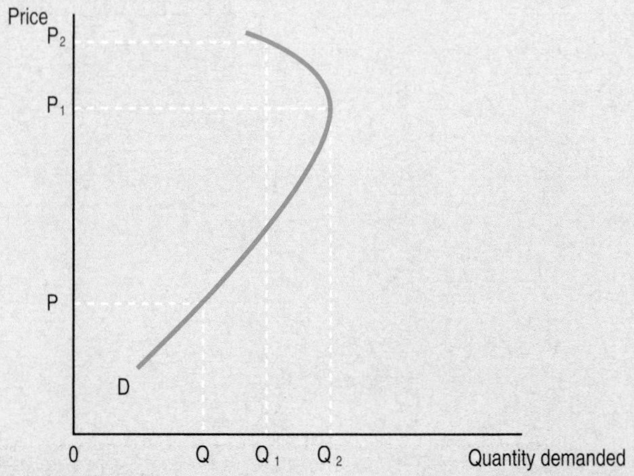

Table 18.2 shows the demand schedules for three products manufactured by different businesses.

Table 18.2 *The demand schedule for products A, B and C*

Price (£)	Quantity demanded(A)	Quantity demanded(B)	Quantity demanded(C)
5	50,000	10,000	40,000
10	30,000	15,000	30,000
15	20,000	25,000	25,000
30	10,000	16,000	20,000

(a) Draw the demand curve for each product.
(b) Identify the types of product which might have a demand curve like product B.

Question 1

consumers of such a product, given the association made between a higher price and high quality. This means that the quantity demanded over lower price ranges may increase as price rises for such a product. This would create an entirely different demand curve. Figure 18.2 shows the demand curve for such a product. An increase in price from OP to OP_1 causes the quantity demanded for this perfume to increase from OQ to OQ_2. However, an increase in price from OP_1 to OP_2 causes the quantity demanded to fall from OQ_2 to OQ_1. In this part of the curve a more normal relationship between demand and price exists. An increase in price leads to a fall in the quantity demanded. Speculative goods are also said to have upward sloping demand curves. As prices rise people buy more of them, hoping to sell them for a profit at a later date.

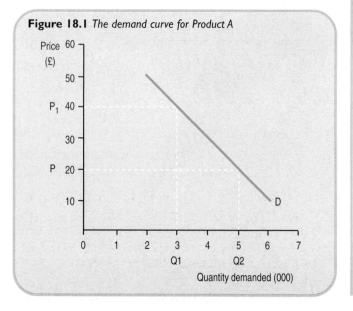

Figure 18.1 *The demand curve for Product A*

Figure 18.2 *The demand curve for a prestige perfume*

Other factors influencing the demand for a business's products

Other than price there is a range of factors affecting the demand for an individual business's products. A change in any of these factors can cause a shift in the whole demand curve (as opposed to a change in price which causes a movement along the demand curve). Figure 18.3 shows an increase in the demand for a product by the demand curve moving outwards from D to D_1. A decrease in the demand for the product is shown by the demand curve shifting inwards, from D to D_2. What factors might lead to a change in demand and how will this affect a particular business?

- The consumers at which the product is aimed may experience an increase in income. The business may be able to sell more of the product at a given price (OQ -OQ_1) or charge a higher price (OP - OP_1). If incomes fall, the demand curve shifts inwards and the quantity demanded may fall (OQ - OQ_2) or the price may fall (OP - OP_2). An example may be increased demand for Bosch dishwashers as incomes increase.
- The price of a rival's goods may change. If a rival's price goes up, customers may be more willing to buy more of this product. If a rival's prices fall customers may reduce demand for this product. An example may be a fall in demand for one newspaper as another cuts its price.
- The price of a complementary product may fall. For example, if the price of DVD players falls, people may buy more of these and so the demand for DVDs themselves could increase. A rise in the price of a complementary product may lead to a fall in demand for the related product.
- Changes in tastes and fashion. There has been a change in the type of food products that have become popular in recent years. Examples include organic foods bought from supermarkets, flavoured and specialist coffees from shops such as Starbucks, and cholesterol reducing spreads such as Flora Proactive and Benecol.
- Marketing campaigns. Asda, for example, has pursued a low pricing marketing campaign and is often found to have the lowest supermarket prices in studies. It has supported this with the 'Asda price' adverts on television showing people saving money.
- Changes in population. A large shopping mall such as the Trafford Centre in Manchester is likely to find an increase in demand if offices and housing are drawn close to its location.
- Government legislation and regulation can affect demand. Local pubs and breweries, for example, may find a fall in demand as a result of a reduction in the legal alcohol limit for drinking and driving.

How businesses use demand curves

Demand curves are useful tools to businesses in terms of analysing and planning their marketing activities. In particular they enable businesses to:
- calculate revenue to be earned for any given price change;
- predict the likely reaction of consumers to price changes;
- predict the likely impact upon revenue of price changes.

Calculating revenue

One of the reasons why businesses are interested in their demand curve is because it enables them to calculate revenue that may be earned for a particular price that is charged. Revenue can be calculated using using a simple formula:

$$\text{Price} \times \text{quantity demanded} = \text{total revenue}$$

Table 18.3 reproduces Table 18.1 showing the revenue that a business will earn for product A at different prices, given its demand schedule.

Price (£)	Quantity demanded (Q)	Total revenue (P x Q)
10	6,000	60,000
20	5,000	100,000
30	4,000	120,000
40	3,000	120,000
50	2,000	100,000

Table 18.3 *The demand schedule for Product A*

So, for example, the revenue of the business at a price of £30 would be £30 x 4,000 = £120,000. If the price were to change to £20 the revenue would be £20 x 5,000 = £100,000. Thus we can see that a change in price from £30 to £20 has led to a fall in revenue from £120,000 to £100,000, a fall of £20,000.

This process can help a business to identify the point on

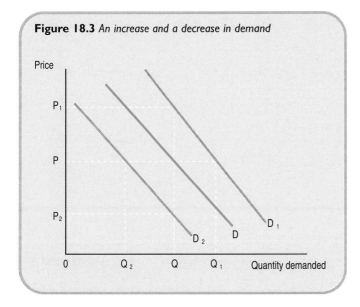

Figure 18.3 *An increase and a decrease in demand*

Table 18.4 *The demand schedule for Product A*

Price	Quantity demanded	Total revenue	Quantity demanded (+2,000)	Total revenue
(£)	(Q)	(P x Q)	(Q)	(P x Q)
10	6,000	60,000	8,000	80,000
20	5,000	100,000	7,000	140,000
30	4,000	120,000	6,000	180,000
40	3,000	120,000	5,000	200,000
50	2,000	100,000	4,000	200,000

the demand curve and the price at which revenue is maximised. This can be seen from Table 18.3. At prices below £30 the business actually increases the revenue by raising its price. At prices above £40 revenue falls as prices are increased. The business earns most revenue between £30 and £40.

It is also possible to show the effect of changes in demand on revenue. Table 18.4 shows the effect on Product A's revenue of an increase in demand of 2,000 at each price level.

Price sensitivity

All businesses are likely to be concerned about the sensitivity of the demand for their products to price changes. In other words, they will want to predict what will happen to the quantity demanded of their product if there is a change in price. The sensitivity of quantity demanded to changes in price is known as the PRICE ELASTICITY OF DEMAND (PED). It can be calculated using the following formula:

$$PED = \frac{\text{Percentage change in quantity demanded}}{\text{Percentage change in price}}$$

or

$$\frac{\text{Change in quantity demanded}}{\text{Original quantity demanded}} \div \frac{\text{change in price}}{\text{original price}}$$

Inelastic demand A business selling its product in a particular market may face the demand schedule and demand curve in Table 18.6 and Figure 18.4. If the price is raised from £5 to £6 (a 20 per cent change), the quantity demanded falls from 10,000 to 9,000 units (a 10 per cent change). This is shown in Figure 18.5. The price elasticity of demand is:

$$PED = \frac{-10\%}{20\%} = (-)0.5$$

or $$PED = \frac{-1,000}{10,000} \div \frac{1}{5} = \frac{-1}{10} \times \frac{5}{1} = \frac{-1}{2} \text{ or } (-)0.5$$

It is usual to ignore the minus sign, so that a figure that is less than 1 but greater than 0 tells the business that demand for the product is **price inelastic**. This means that the percentage change in quantity demanded is less than the

---

A stationery shop selling fibre tipped pens has estimated the following demand schedule for its products.

Table 18.5 *The demand schedule for fibre tipped pens*

Price (£)	Quantity demanded
2	800
3	600
4	500
5	400
6	350
7	300
8	260
9	225
10	200

(a) Calculate the change in total revenue for fibre tipped pens of:
 (i) an increase in price from £2 to £3;
 (ii) an increase in price from £7 to £10;
 (iii) a decrease in price from £5 to £3.
(b) Explain why the business might be reluctant to raise prices above £7 per pen.

Question2

Table 18.6 *A demand schedule*

Price £	Quantity demanded (units)	Total revenue £
4	11,000	44,000
5	10,000	50,000
6	9,000	54,000

Figure 18.4 *The effect of a change in price on quantity demanded*

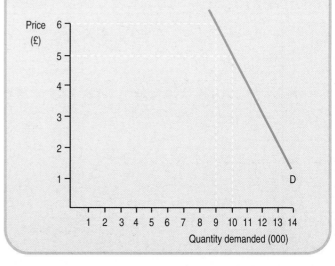

percentage change in price. In other words, consumers do not change the quantity of a good they demand proportionally more than any change in price.

What effect will a change in price have on a business's total revenue? Table 18.6 and Figure 18.4 show that a rise in price from £5 to £6 will increase revenue from £50,000 to £54,000. This is because the rise in price is proportionally greater than the fall in the quantity demanded. A business which raises its price will hope that demand for the product is price inelastic.

A reduction in price from £5 to £4 will result in a fall in revenue from £50,000 to £44,000, even though the quantity demanded has increased from 10,000 to 11,000 units.

Elastic demand A business operating in a different market may face the demand schedule in Table 18.7. An increase in price from £20 to £24 (a 20 per cent change) results in a fall in quantity demanded from 10,000 units to 6,000 units (a 40 per cent change). Price elasticity of demand is therefore:

$$PED = \frac{-40\%}{20\%} = (-)2$$

$$\text{or} \quad PED = \frac{-4,000}{10,000} \div \frac{4}{20} = \frac{-1}{10} \times \frac{5}{4} = \frac{-1}{10} \text{ or } (-)2$$

As this figure is greater than 1, the business can conclude

Table 18.7 *A demand schedule*

Price £	Quantity demanded (units)	Total revenue £
16	14,000	224,000
20	10,000	200,000
24	6,000	144,000

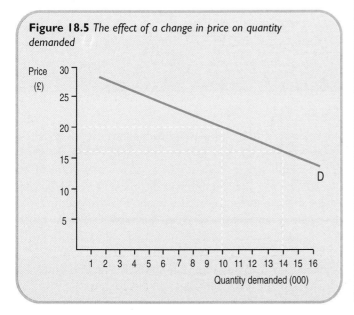

Figure 18.5 *The effect of a change in price on quantity demanded*

Kaldor Ltd manufactures reproduction juke boxes which play CDs. Jukeboxes that play old 45 records can cost around £1,000 or a great deal more. Large jukeboxes in pubs can cost thousands of pounds as well. But Kaldor had seen other 'reproduction' jukeboxes that did not cost as much and were far smaller. It decided to manufacture smaller jukeboxes that stand on a table. They sold for £200 and hold three CDs at a time. The jukeboxes have been selling well and so the business raised the price to £240. As a result sales fell from 800 to 600 per month. Kaldor is now questioning the decision to raise the price.

(a) Calculate the price elasticity of demand for Kaldor's jukeboxes.
(b) Explain whether or not the decision to raise the price was a good choice by the business.

Question 3

that demand for its product is relatively **price elastic**. This means that the percentage change in quantity demanded is greater than the percentage change in price. When demand is price elastic, consumers react to changes in price by changing the quantity they demand by a greater proportion.

Table 18.7 and Figure 18.5 show that if the business reduces its price from £20 to £16, quantity demanded will increase from 10,000 to 14,000 and total revenue will increase from £200,000 to £224,000. This is because the increase in quantity demanded is proportionally greater than the fall in price. If a business is aiming to cut its price, it will hope demand for the product will be price elastic. An increase in price from £20 to £24 will lead to a fall in revenue from £200,000 to £144,000.

Factors affecting price elasticity of demand

There are two main factors which are thought to affect the price elasticity of demand.

- The number of substitutes for a product. A product with a wide range of substitutes is likely to be highly sensitive to price changes and relatively price elastic. This is because the more substitutes there are for a particular product, the more easy it is for consumers to purchase another product when price changes occur. For example, most types of fish are likely to be relatively price elastic. This is because if the price of one type of fish goes up, consumers can easily swap to another type of fish.

- Time. The longer the period of time, the more price elastic the demand for a product is likely to be. The more time consumers are given, the more able and willing they are to adjust their buying habits. Take, for example, a rise in the price of gas. Over a short period of time, it would be difficult for consumers to buy less gas. Ownership of a gas cooker and gas central heating systems means in the short term that it is difficult to use other types of power. However, over a longer period of time it may be possible for consumers to switch to oil or electricity.

Income elasticity of demand

INCOME ELASTICITY OF DEMAND is a measure of the sensitivity of demand to changes in income. It can be calculated using the formula:

$$\frac{\text{Percentage change in quantity demanded}}{\text{Percentage change in income}}$$

Businesses will want to know the income elasticity of demand for their products. This will help them to judge the effect of a change in their consumers' income on the demand for their products.

- If a rise in income leads to a relatively greater rise in quantity demanded then income elasticity of demand is positive and greater than one.
- If a rise in income leads to a relatively smaller rise in quantity demanded then income elasticity is positive but less than one.
- If a rise in income leads to no change in quantity demanded then income elasticity of demand is zero.
- If a rise in income leads to a fall in quantity demanded then income elasticity of demand is negative.

Advertising elasticity of demand

ADVERTISING ELASTICITY OF DEMAND is a measure of the responsiveness of demand to changes in advertising expenditure. It is measured by the following formula:

$$\frac{\text{Percentage change in quantity demanded}}{\text{Percentage change in advertising expenditure}}$$

Businesses need to be able to measure the effectiveness of their advertising campaigns. One way of doing this is to consider the impact on consumer demand of spending on advertising. This can provide businesses with valuable data which can enable them to judge how far consumers are influenced by advertising campaigns. It also allows businesses to evaluate the relative success of advertising campaigns. If the percentage increase in quantity demanded is a great deal larger than the percentage increase in advertising spending, then advertising elasticity of demand is strong and positive. This may tell a business that advertising is effective in influencing consumers.

Cross elasticity of demand

The CROSS ELASTICITY OF DEMAND shows the response of quantity demanded of one good to a change in the price of another. It allows a business to gauge how demand for its products will react if the price of either rival's products or complementary goods change. It can be calculated using the formula:

$$\frac{\text{Percentage change in quantity demanded of good X}}{\text{Percentage change in price of good Y}}$$

- Goods which are substitutes and compete with each other have a positive cross elasticity. An increase in the price of one newspaper (good Y) should lead to a fall in demand for this product and an increase in demand for another newspaper (good X). Both changes are positive. A fall in the price of good Y will lead to a fall in the demand for good X. Two negatives cancel out to make a positive.
- Goods which are complements to each other have a negative cross elasticity. An increase in the price of an electrical product (good Y) should lead to a fall in demand for this product and a fall in demand for batteries (good X). One change is positive, the other is negative.

Limitations of demand curves

It is often very difficult for an individual business to develop its own demand curve. This is because many businesses do not have sufficient information to construct their individual demand curves. They do not have the market research data to enable them to assess the likely demand for their products over a given range of prices. Often this is because of the high cost of collecting such market information. Such businesses tend to develop a PERCEIVED DEMAND curve. This is a demand curve based upon the 'feel' which managers and owners have for their market. It will involve rough estimations of the likely impact upon demand of upwards or downwards changes in prices.

Some larger businesses with access to detailed market information are in a much better position to develop demand curves which can assist them in making more informed decisions about their prices. However, even for such businesses the demand curve may be of limited value. This is because the demand curve can only provide information about the likely response of consumers to a change in the price of a particular product at a given point in time. In fast changing markets such information may quickly go out of date and will be of limited value unless it is regularly updated.

key terms

Advertising elasticity of demand - the responsiveness of demand to a change in advertising expenditure.
Cross elasticity of demand - the responsiveness of the demand of one product to a change in the price of another.
Demand - the quantity of a product purchased at any price.
Income elasticity of demand - the responsiveness of demand to a change in income.
Price elasticity of demand - the responsiveness of demand to a change in price.
Perceived demand - the demand which the managers and owners of a business believe exists for their products in a particular market.

Knowledge

1. What does the demand curve of a business show?
2. What might the demand curve for a product judged on quality rather than price look like?
3. What are the factors affecting the demand for a product?
4. How is price elasticity of demand calculated?
5. What is the difference between inelastic and elastic demand?
6. What effect will a change in price have on the revenue of a firm facing inelastic demand for its product?
7. State 2 factors affecting the price elasticity of demand for a product.
8. Why might a business be interested in its advertising elasticity of demand?
9. Suggest a limitation when using a demand curve for a business.

IceStyle is a manufacturer of skiing products, including skis, snowboards and skiboards, outdoor clothing and skiing accessories. Recently it has found that the price of skiing holidays for its customers has risen by 4 per cent due to the level of the exchange rate. This resulted in a 6 per cent fall in sales last year. In an attempt to battle against the fall in demand, the business launched a high profile marketing campaign designed to promote skiwear as leisure clothing. It particularly targeted the 'youth' market, attempting to stress a link between extreme sports and fashion. So far a 10 per cent increase in advertising expenditure has resulted in a 2 per cent increase in sales.

(a) Using the figures above calculate the:
   (i) cross elasticity of demand;
   (ii) advertising elasticity of demand.
(b) In each case, what do the results tell IceStyle about the demand for its product?

Case study Bodyline

Bodyline is a small firm based in the West Midlands which manufactures womens' swimwear. Its products are distributed through four main types of outlet - mail-order catalogues, department stores, womens' clothing chains and independent retailers.

The business was set up in early 2003. The two women, Elaine and Penny, who started up the firm had originally been friends at University. One had studied for a degree in Art and Design, the other in Business Studies.

Their main product was to be a swimsuit, the Californian, which had been designed in a wide range of dazzling colours. Their marketing strategy had been to aim for the bottom end of the market, offering a cheap, but fashionable garment which would be within the reach of a wide number of consumers' pockets. Marketing research into the demand for the Californian showed that sales at different prices were likely to be as in Table 18.8.

Elaine and Penny found that they were able to sell all of their production at a price of £18. They sold Californians at this price for six months and made a fair profit. The market was fairly stable at this time and few sudden changes were expected in the near future. Penny felt that by reducing the price a little they would be able to capture more of the market. Elaine was not so sure and the two debated the decision over the next six months without taking any action.

By early 2004 a number of rival businesses developed similar product lines using bright colours, having seen the initial success of Bodyline in the market. As Elaine had commented, one of the worst things about the new products was that 'the Californian designs no longer stood out in the shops and are the same as other products now available'. In what had seemed like a short period of time to these two entrepreneurs, their niche in the market had all

but disappeared.

After their initial success many of the new businesses had attempted to undercut Bodyline's prices. The effect on the demand curve for the Californian is shown in Table 18.9.

(a) What is the relationship between price and demand for Californians shown in Table 18.8? Use examples in your answer. (6 marks)

(b) Calculate the elasticity of demand for Californians for a reduction in price from:
  (i) £18 to £16;
  (ii) £16 to £14.
  (6 marks)

(c) Explain whether demand for Californians is elastic or inelastic and how this would affect price and demand. (6 marks)

(d) Using Table 18.9, explain the idea of cross elasticity of demand for Californians. (10 marks)

(e) Assess whether you think Penny was right to suggest a reduction in price using your answer to (b) and total revenue calculations. (12 marks)

Table 18.8 *Demand curve for Californians*

Price	Quantity of Californians
£14	18,000
£16	14,000
£18	10,000
£20	6,000

Table 18.9 *Effect of a change in competitors' prices on the demand for Californians*

Price of other products	Quantity of Californians
£14	16,200
£12	12,600
£10	9,000
£8	5,400

Pricing strategies

The extent to which a business can influence its price will depend upon the degree of competition that it faces. A fruit and vegetable stall on a local market could be faced with several other stalls close by, as well as local supermarkets. It will need to set prices that are in line with its immediate competitors. Otherwise the consumers can easily choose to buy elsewhere. In contrast Virgin and GNER are the only train operators on many of the mainline routes in the UK and face much less direct competition than the market stall. The effects of the degree of competition that a business faces is explained in unit 62.

When a business does have the scope to set its price there is a number of PRICING STRATEGIES it might choose. When launching **new products** it might choose one of the following strategies.

- Penetrating the market. A business may set its price deliberately low in order to gain a footing in the market. This could also be used when a business is launching an existing product into a new market, for example.
- Skimming or creaming. If a business realises that its product has a unique selling point (☞ unit 15) it may be in a position to charge a high price for a limited time in order to take advantage of the newness of the product. This is known a skimming or creaming the market. New generation mobile phones which can take and send pictures are priced much higher than 'traditional' phones as mobile phone companies skim this new market.

When a business is looking at pricing strategies for **existing products** it might choose from the following strategies.

- Price taking. In very competitive markets a business might decide to follow closely another firm's price increases or reductions. The retail market for 'white goods' such as fridges and freezers is an example.
- Price leadership. In some markets, often controlled by a small number of large companies, there is an accepted price leader. They will decide first to increase or lower prices, knowing that other companies will soon follow. The pricing of petrol is an example.
- Destroying competition or capturing the market. Some firms may seek to capture the market through aggressive price cutting. EasyJet and Ryanair have pursued this policy to gain increased market shares of the air travel market.
- Price discrimination. A business may be in a position to discriminate by charging different prices for the same product to different groups of consumers. For example renting a caravan on a holiday park for two weeks in the school holidays will often cost twice as much as renting the same caravan in June or September.

Pricing tactics

Once a company has decided upon its overall pricing strategy, it can also use price as a tactical promotional tool. This will usually involve temporary changes in prices to attract customers to specific products for a period. These PRICING TACTICS may include the following.

- Special promotional offers, such as buy one, get one free. Waterstone's has offered three paperback books for the price of two and Morrisons two pizzas for £5.
- Loss leaders. A business may deliberately lower the price of a popular product in order to attract customers into the store to buy the product and hopefully other products.
- Discounts on normal prices. This might be for a period of time, such as just before Christmas, for regular customers, such as special offers for loyalty card holders, or for people who buy larger quantities, for example schools getting discounts on supplies of pens, paper and stationery.
- Introductory offers. This is where the price a customer pays for the first purchase is lower than for subsequent purchases. For example, Broadband has been offered by service providers at £5.50 per month for the first three months and then £15.50 per month after three months.

Factors affecting pricing decisions

What factors influence the price a business sets for its product?

Objectives The pricing strategy chosen by a business is likely to reflect the extent to which it wants to maximise profits or sales. A business seeking to maximise short term profits may use more aggressive and perhaps risky pricing strategies.

The marketing mix The price chosen by a business must complement the other aspects of the marketing mix (☞ unit 16). This means that the price must fit in with the nature of the product itself and the way in which it is being promoted and distributed to consumers. For example, a low quality product being sold in retail outlets at the bottom end of the market is likely to be sold at a fairly low price.

Costs A business which cannot generate enough revenue over time to cover its costs will not survive. In the long run, a business must charge a price which earns enough revenue to cover its total cost of production (fixed and variable) at any level of output. This means that businesses must take account all of their costs when setting price. In the short run, however, it is unlikely that a business would expect to cover the fixed costs of its factory or machinery (☞ unit 27). Providing its price is high enough to generate revenue that covers its variable costs, the firm will stay in business.

The price of each product in a market will be influenced by a variety of factors. For some products, the ability of a business to set its price is limited. For others, there will be more scope for a business to set the price it wants to charge.

(a) What factors do you think have influenced the price of the products in the photographs?

Question 1

Revenue below this will cause the firm to cease production. As a result businesses may have greater flexibility in the short term when making pricing decisions.

Competition Competition can affect pricing decisions (☞ unit 62). For a market trader, the price of her goods is largely determined by prices on nearby stalls selling similar goods. Such a trader will have little room for manoeuvre compared to a business which faces less competition.

Consumer perceptions and expectations Businesses must pay attention to what consumers think a product is worth. A product priced above what consumers consider its value to be may generate low sales because of doubts about its **value for money**. A product priced too low may also generate low sales. This is because consumers often suspect that such products have something wrong with them or that they are of inferior quality. For example, a business marketing high fashion clothing would be careful to ensure that its products were priced higher than those offered to the mass market.

Businesses have the opportunity to influence consumer perceptions through aspects of the marketing mix, such as advertising. By improving the view consumers have of the product, businesses can give themselves more scope when setting prices. In some cases firms actually encourage consumers to think of their products as expensive. For example, Thorntons chocolates have been marketed as a quality confectionery item.

Market segment Businesses that produce a range of products are likely to have some aimed at particular market segments (☞ unit 13). This is true, for example, of all major car manufacturers. They are, therefore, likely to charge different prices for each segment. However, the price which they charge to one segment of the market will affect the prices charged to other segments. A product competing in the top end of the market will need to have a different price from one aimed at the middle or bottom end of the market.

Legal constraints The price of a number of products is affected by **taxation**. This raises the price above the level that might have been set by manufacturers. Products affected greatly by taxation include cigarettes, alcoholic drinks and petrol. There is also a number of products which are offered to consumers below the price that producers would normally charge. Such products are **subsidised** by the government. An example might be low priced travel on public transport for young people and pensioners. The price of products such as water and gas are determined by regulatory bodies (☞ unit 71).

Cost based pricing

All businesses are influenced by their costs when determining prices with costs acting as a 'bottom line' when choosing a price. But some use COST-BASED PRICING as their strategy for price setting. Businesses using cost-based pricing are those where the influence of cost is more important than other factors such as market conditions or competitors' pricing. The local garage repair business or domestic repair services like electricians and plumbers are likely to take a cost-based approach.

There is a number of methods that businesses use to set their prices which are based upon particular costs.

Cost plus pricing This involves setting a price by calculating the average cost (☞ unit 27) of producing goods and adding a MARK-UP for profit. If a business produces 10,000 goods costing £50,000, the average cost would be £5.00. A mark up of 20 per cent would mean goods would cost an extra £1.00 and the price would be £6.00 per product. Retailers often use

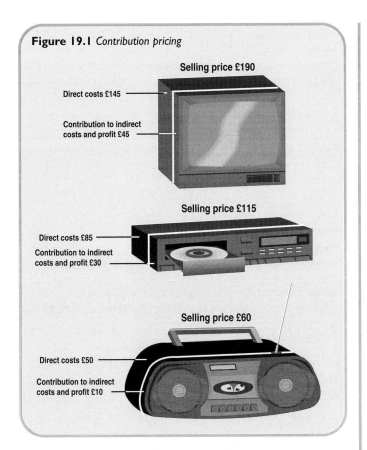

Figure 19.1 *Contribution pricing*

Selling price £190
Direct costs £145
Contribution to indirect costs and profit £45

Selling price £115
Direct costs £85
Contribution to indirect costs and profit £30

Selling price £60
Direct costs £50
Contribution to indirect costs and profit £10

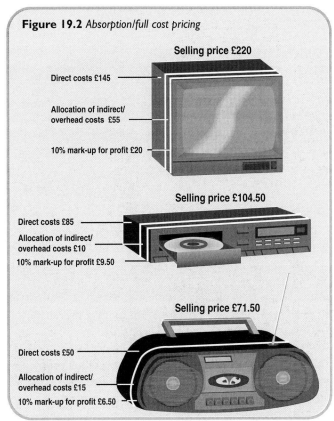

Figure 19.2 *Absorption/full cost pricing*

Selling price £220
Direct costs £145
Allocation of indirect/overhead costs £55
10% mark-up for profit £20

Selling price £104.50
Direct costs £85
Allocation of indirect/overhead costs £10
10% mark-up for profit £9.50

Selling price £71.50
Direct costs £50
Allocation of indirect/overhead costs £15
10% mark-up for profit £6.50

this method of pricing. Say that a department store buys a colour TV from wholesalers for £200 and its mark-up to allow for a profit is 100 per cent. The retail price to consumers will be £400.

The attractiveness of cost plus pricing is that it is a quick and simple way of setting a selling price. It also ensures that sales revenue will cover total costs and generate profit. A criticism, however, is that a fixed mark-up does not allow a business to take market needs into account when setting prices. In addition, no attempt is made to allocate indirect costs to particular products. This means they do not reflect the resources being allocated by the business to that particular product or product range.

Contribution pricing This method takes into account that different products within a company might need to be priced using different criteria. For each product, a price is set in relation to the **direct costs** of producing that product and any **contribution** (☞ unit 29) that the business wants that product to make towards covering its **indirect cost** and towards profit. Thus for a manufacturer of electrical goods, some prices might be as set out as in Figure 19.1.

No one product will be **expected** to account for all the indirect costs of the business. Each product's selling price would make some contribution to meeting indirect costs. If the producer expected to sell 100 items of each product and had to cover indirect costs of £6,500 and generate profit of £2,000 (£8,500) then:

Product A   £45×100 = £4,500   contribution
Product B   £30×100 = £3,000   contribution
Product C   £10×100 = £1,000   contribution

£8,500

This allows businesses more flexibility than the cost plus approach. Successful products can be priced to make a large contribution. Less successful products or new products can be priced more competitively, as they need only to make a lower contribution to overheads and profits. Indeed, new products might even be making a negative contribution, ie their price does not even cover the **marginal cost** of production. Demand factors as well as cost factors are now being taken into account.

Absorption cost/full cost pricing A business may attempt to take into account the indirect costs that can be attributable to a particular product in deciding on a price. This is known as **absorption** or **full cost pricing**. In its simplest form an arbitrary method is used to allocate indirect costs to each product, for example, a percentage of total sales or total direct costs. The electrical goods manufacturer might charge the prices in Figure 19.2. A mark-up is then added for profit.

A more sophisticated method of allocation can also be used. Using this method to allocate indirect costs, each element of the cost will be treated separately. This means the

Figure 19.3

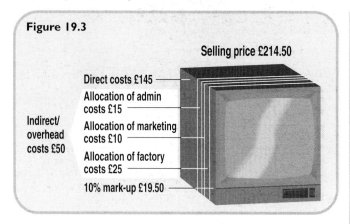

Selling price £214.50

Direct costs £145

Allocation of admin costs £15

Allocation of marketing costs £10

Indirect/overhead costs £50

Allocation of factory costs £25

10% mark-up £19.50

selling price of a product will absorb elements of each overhead cost.

As we can see from Figures 19.2 and 19.3 the price of the TV is different according to the method used. A different costing formula will lead to a different final price. Under the arbitrary method a larger allocation of indirect/overhead costs was made to the television's final price.

Target pricing This is sometimes known as **target profit pricing**. It involves businesses setting prices that will earn them a particular level of profit, which has been clearly targeted. When setting a target price (or profit) businesses make use of break-even analysis (☞ unit 30). Figure 19.4 shows the break-even chart for a small business producing leather briefcases. It is based upon a selling price of £90, fixed costs of £30,000 and variable costs of £30 per briefcase. In order to break-even the business must produce and sell 500 briefcases. If, however, it wishes to target a profit of £30,000 then it must produce and sell 1,000 briefcases. Using break-even analysis in this way businesses can target a particular level of profit for their product.

We know from unit 18 that the price which is charged for a product affects the demand for a product. The precise relationship between demand and price is measured by price

Figure 19.4 *A break-even chart for a briefcase manufacturer*

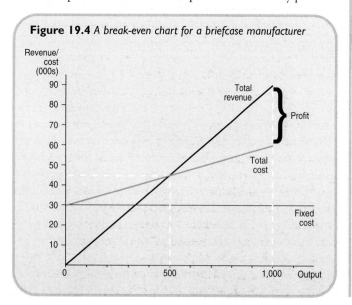

Table 19.1 *Profits and break-even at different price levels for a briefcase manufacturer*

Price	Estimated demand at given price	Total revenue	Total costs (Fixed costs = £30,000 variable costs = £30)	Break-even point	Profit
(£)		(£)	(£)		(£)
80	1,100	88,000	63,000	600	25,000
90	1,000	90,000	60,000	500	30,000
100	800	80,000	54,000	429	26,000

Patel and Co has been manufacturing aluminium ladders since the business was set up in 2000. Its sales up to now have been based upon two products, a 10 metre and a 15 metre folding ladder. The business has adopted a cost plus method of pricing for each ladder, as illustrated in Table 19.2.

Table 19.2

10 metre ladder	Average cost per unit £92	20% mark-up to cover profit £18.40	Selling price to trade £110.40
15 metre ladder	Average cost per unit £125	20% mark-up to cover profit £25.00	Selling price to trade £150.00

Because of the success of these two products and pressure from competition, the company has developed a new product, a ladder which would allow people to gain constant access to their lofts, but which will be permanently attached to the loft entrance. With a third product, the company's accountant felt that a contribution pricing approach should now be used to price each of their products. He set out some initial calculations of their likely prices, as in Table 19.3.

Table 19.3

	Direct costs per unit	Contribution to indirect cost and profit	Price
10 metre ladder	£80	£35	£115
15 metre ladder	£105	£40	£145
Loft ladder	£185	£5	£190

The pricing for the loft ladder was set at a level which was in line with the price of competitors, which was £190.00.
(a) Identify the benefits to the company of using a contribution pricing approach compared to a cost plus approach for their ladders.
(b) Is the loft ladder a viable product for the company to produce given the figures produced by the accountant? Explain your answer.

Question 2

elasticity of demand. Thus the briefcase manufacturer may wish to estimate the demand for its briefcases at various price levels. It can then choose a price and associated sales which will enable it to make the profit that it wants. This is shown in Table 19.1. Table 19.1 shows that the business would not benefit at present from either lowering or raising its price from £90.

Problems of cost based pricing

Cost based pricing does have a number of problems. It is a product and cost orientated approach which does not refer to consumers' wishes or flexibility. Contribution pricing does, however, allow more flexibility than cost plus pricing for a particular marketing strategy. Full or absorption cost pricing may result in prices being set too high or too low in relation to consumers' wishes or competitors' prices. They are also inflexible in response to market changes, as these would not necessarily be reflected in the costs of a company. The more sophisticated the costing method used when pricing, the more accurate is the allocation of costs to a product, but the further the price might be from what the market will bear.

Market orientated pricing

MARKET ORIENTATED PRICING methods are those which are based upon an analysis of the conditions in the market at which a product is aimed. As such, they are much better suited to market orientated businesses.

Penetration pricing This is used by businesses seeking to gain a foothold in a market, either with new products or with established products being placed in new markets. It involves pricing a product at a low level so that retailers and consumers are encouraged to purchase the product in large quantities.

There are two main reasons why businesses use penetration pricing.
● Consumers are encouraged to develop the habit of buying the product, so that when prices eventually begin to rise they will continue to purchase it.
● Retailers and wholesalers are likely to purchase large quantities of the product. This should mean that they will not buy from other suppliers until they have sold most of their stock. Businesses can thus gain a significant slice of the market.

Penetration pricing, because of its high cost, is often used by large firms operating in mass markets, such as those selling biscuits, sweets, washing powder and canned drinks. It is also a policy used by new businesses or established businesses in other areas to break into a new market. It is not a policy that is suitable for products with short life cycles. There is usually not enough time to recover the cost of lost revenue from the initially low price. One exception to this is new CD singles. They are sometimes launched at a lower price in the first few weeks of release before being raised to their full price.

Market skimming Market skimming involves charging a high price for a new product for a limited period. The aim is to gain as much profit as possible for a new product while it remains unique in the market. It usually means selling a product to the most profitable segment of the market before it is sold to a wider market at a lower price.

There are two reasons why businesses adopt market skimming. They may try to maximise revenue before competitors come into the market with a similar product. Often new techniques or designs mean that entirely new products, or new versions of a product can be offered. Examples include new fashions in clothes, new childrens' toys and new inventions. When first launched, a basic digital watch could cost as much as £50 or £60. Now they often sell for as little as a few pounds. Market skimming can also be used to generate revenue in a short period of time so that further investment in the product can be made. Companies in the electronics and pharmaceutical industries often use skimming for this reason.

Customer value pricing This involves charging the price that consumers are prepared to pay. Products which have prestige names attached to them, such as Rolex, may be able to command a higher price because of the status of these names. Products for one-off events, such as music festivals or sports finals, may be given a high price because they are unique.

Loss leaders LOSS LEADERS are products priced at very low levels in order to attract customers. The price of a loss leader is set lower than the average total cost of producing the product. The company selling the product makes a 'loss' on each product sold. Businesses use this pricing technique because they expect the losses made on the loss leader to be more than compensated for by extra profits on other products. It is often used by larger supermarkets which sell everyday products such as baked-beans, bananas and corn flakes for very low prices. They aim to attract more customers into their stores, drawn in by the low prices. The 'captive' customers will then buy more highly priced and profitable items.

Psychological pricing Many businesses seek to take account of the psychological effect of their prices upon consumers. This is known as psychological pricing. A common example is the use of prices just a little lower than a round figure, such as £199.99 rather than £200, or £29.99 rather than £30. Businesses using these slightly lower prices believe that they will influence the consumers' decision as to whether or not to purchase. Such slightly lower prices also suggest that consumers will be looking for value for money. For this reason, the producers of high status products such as prestige cars or designer clothing tend to avoid such prices. Instead, they often choose prices which psychologically match their consumers expectations of higher quality. So, for example, a price of £100 may be charged for a designer shirt rather than £99.99.

Table 19.4 shows the range of prices being offered by various retailers for a FujiFine Pix Digital Camera.
(a) Describe the type of pricing strategies in this market.
(b) Compare strategies that may be being adopted by Simple Computers with Cameras2U.com.

Table 19.4

Retailer	Price
Cameras2U.com	£84.99
Simply Computers	£149.00
Digital Camera Company	£109.00
CPixMania	£86.00
Ebuyer	£82.24
Argos	£99.99

Source: adapted from kelkoo.co.uk.

Price discrimination Price discrimination occurs when a firm offers the same product at different prices when consumers can be kept separate. An example is BT's policy of charging different prices to business and residential users at different times of the day and the weekend. This allows BT to take into account the differences in cost which exists at peak and off peak times. So, for example, calls may be charged at a higher rate on Monday to Friday, 8am-6pm, than at weekends.

This price discrimination is **time based**. The price you pay for a phone call is based upon the time of day or the day of the week when you use the service. Other businesses which use this policy are rail companies (cheaper off peak travel), and holiday firms which charge higher prices for their product during school holidays.

Price discrimination can also be **market based**. This involves offering different market segments the same product at different prices. An example of this is students being given discounts on coach and bus travel.

Discounts and sales These tend to support the pricing strategies used by businesses. They often mean a reduction in the standard price for particular groups of consumers. A very common form of discount is the seasonal 'sales' of retailers. The aim is to encourage purchasers at times when sales might otherwise be low and to clear out of date and out of fashion stock. Discounts may also be given to those customers who buy in bulk or in large quantities.

Competition based pricing

With COMPETITION BASED PRICING it is the prices charged by competitors which are the major influence on a producer's price. It is used mostly by businesses which face fierce and direct competition. As a rule, the more competitive the market and the more homogeneous the products competing in that market, the greater the pressure for competition based pricing. Markets similar to the model of oligopoly (☞ unit 62) will often use this form of pricing. For example, soap powder producers tend to be influenced by the price of competitors' products.

Going rate pricing This occurs in markets where businesses are reluctant to set off a price war by lowering their prices and are concerned about a fall off in revenue if prices are raised. They examine competitors' prices and choose a price broadly in line with them. It also occurs when one dominant business establishes a position of **price leadership** within a market. Other firms will follow suit when the price leader changes its prices. This type of policy can be seen when a petrol company changes the price of a gallon of petrol or when banks and building societies change interest rates.

Companies which operate in markets where going rate pricing occurs will often be frustrated by their inability to control their prices more closely. A strategy often used in such circumstances is to establish a strong **brand** identity for your product and to differentiate it from others on the market (☞ unit 20). This would be through unique design features or quality of service. An oil company's decision to upgrade all of its service stations is an example of an attempt to achieve this. A strong brand identity and unique product features allow firms much greater scope for choosing their own price levels.

Destroyer pricing The aim of destroyer pricing is to eliminate opposition. It involves cutting prices, sometimes greatly, for a period of time long enough for your rivals to go out of business. It could be argued that the offering of low price airline tickets by Ryanair and EasyJet in the 1990s was designed to drive out competition from the national European airline carriers and force some of them out of business. Some, like BA and KLM, responded by setting up their own low-price carriers and cutting prices. Others, like Sabena and SwissAir, did go out of business.

Closed bid pricing This method of pricing occurs when firms have to TENDER a bid for work which they are going to carry out. This is common practice for firms dealing with the government or local authorities. For example, if a new road is to be built firms will be invited to put in a bid to win a contract for the work. Firms will clearly need to pay very close attention to the price at which they expect their competitors to bid. Sometimes, when a number of firms bid for a contract, those with the highest prices are likely to be rejected. Another example of this type of pricing are the bids that the government organises for the National Lottery. In 2004 Camelot had won both the rounds of bidding against rival companies, including Richard Branson's Virgin group.

key terms

Competition based pricing - methods of pricing based upon the prices charged by competitors.

Cost based pricing - methods of pricing products which are based upon costs.

Loss leaders - products with prices set deliberately below average total cost to attract customers who will then buy other, more profitable, products.

Market orientated pricing - methods of pricing based upon the pricing conditions in the market at which a product is aimed.

Mark-up - that part of a price which seeks to provide a business with profit as opposed to covering its costs. It is used in cost plus pricing.

Pricing strategies - the pricing policies or methods of pricing adopted by businesses.

Tender - a bid to secure a contract for work.

Pricing tactics – ways of using price as a promotional tool usually over a short period of time.

Knowledge...Knowledge...Knowledge

1. State 5 pricing strategies a business might use.
2. Identify 4 different pricing tactics that a business might use.
3. What are the main factors affecting a firm's pricing decisions?
4. Explain the difference between cost plus pricing and contribution pricing.
5. State one advantage and one disadvantage of cost plus and contribution pricing for a firm.
6. What is meant by absorption cost pricing?
7. Why might a firm use penetration pricing?
8. What is market skimming?
9. What types of firm might use market skimming as a pricing strategy?
10. Why might a business sell a product as a loss leader?
11. What is meant by psychological pricing?
12. What is meant by price discrimination?
13. Under what circumstances might a firm use competition based pricing?
14. Explain the terms:
    (a) going rate pricing;
    (b) destroyer pricing;
    (c) closed bid pricing.
15. Give 2 examples of tendering.

Case study Anatomy of a Budget Flight

On today's 10.45 EasyJet Flight from Luton to Nice, a popular route in August, some people will have paid only £20 for their seats. A flight of nearly 700 miles for less than the price of 2 CDs. Yet the airline still makes a profit. How does it do it?

Others on the flight, the late bookers, may have paid closer to £140 for the same flight. But this still represents a revolution in travel. The average price for all EasyJet flights is £48.70. In the days before no-frills airlines, a passenger would pay over £200 for a seat to Nice, however early they booked.

Low fares still equate to very healthy profits

Table 19.5 *The cost of a single EasyJet flight*

Ground handling charges (baggage, check-ins etc)	£542
Airport charges	£817
Credit card charges (for on-line bookings)	£101
Administration (contribution to head office costs)	£728
Fuel	£614
Navigation (for air traffic control)	£420
Advertising	£215
Cost of the aircraft	£676
Tax on profits	£251
Crew salaries and training	£643
Maintenance and servicing	£584
Total outgoings	**£5,591**
Ticket sales	**£6,136**
Profit	**£545**

for the low-cost airlines. Ryanair is the only European carrier to make profits in each of the past 13 years. For EasyJet, every time a flight takes off the company receives on average £6,136 in fares and makes £545 in profit. This represents good business when it caries twenty million passengers on 156,000 flights in a year. Its profit margin of 8.9 per cent is well above that of Tesco, which makes just 3.6p in the pound profit.

Table 19.5 shows how the £6,136 and £545 are accounted for.

There is a broad philosophy behind behind the low-cost airline game which was set out 30 years ago by Herb Kelleher who founded SouthWest Airlines in Texas, the world's first budget airline. His philosophy had 4 rules.

- Rule 1 – Only fly one type of plane. This makes maintenance and repairs easier. Southwest, EasyJet and Ryanair all uses the Boeing 737.
- Rule 2 – Drive down cost every year. EasyJet seek to reduce costs by 8 -10 per cent each year by reaping economies of scale. It demands better terms from suppliers and uses the Internet to cut out travel agent fees.
- Rule 3 – Turn around your aircraft as quickly as possible. A sit anywhere policy for passengers makes loading quicker. A single plane should make 8 flights a day and only spends 30 minutes standing still on the tarmac at each end.
- Rule 4 – Don't try to sell anything except seats. Price is the best form of loyalty. Avoid loyalty schemes, AirMiles or duty frees.

Source: adapted from *The Guardian*, 20.8.2003.

(a) **Using examples from the article, explain what is meant by:**
   (i) price discrimination;
   (ii) full cost pricing. **(6 marks)**
(b) **Using Table 19.5, explain the method of costing that might be used by EasyJet to determine the price of its flights. (6 marks)**

(c) **Explain, using examples, how Herb Kelleher's 4 rules might influence the pricing strategy of low-cost airlines. (8 marks)**
(d) **Examine how a business such as BA might respond to the strategies used by competitors such as Ryanair and EasyJet. (10 marks)**
(e) **Evaluate the effectiveness of EasyJet's pricing strategies. (10 marks)**

20 Brands

What is a brand?

A BRAND is a name, term, sign, symbol, design or any other **feature** that allows consumers to identify the goods and services of a business and to differentiate them from those of competitors. So a recognised brand might be:

● the use of the 'Mc' **name** by McDonald's in its products such as the Egg McMuffin or Chicken McNugget;
● the Nike 'swoosh' **logo**;
● the three stripes **design** on Adidas sports products;
● the use of the **colour** orange in promotions by the Orange communications company or B&Q;
● the **slogan** 'You've been Tangoed' with the Tango drink;
● the **'tune'** which accompanies references to the Intel Pentium Processor fitted into computers in radio and television adverts.

A brand might be one product, a family or range of products or the actual business itself. So, for example, a Nestlé KitKat is an individual product produced by Nestlé. KitKat Chunky and KitKat Kubes are also part of the KitKat family. Nestlé is the name of the company which produces KitKats, other confectionery products such as Milky Bar and Smarties, and foods such as breakfast cereals.

BRAND NAMES are the parts of the brand that can be spoken, such as the name of the product, ie Heinz Baked Beans or a Barbie doll. A BRAND MARK is the design or symbol used in the brand, such as the apple used on Apple Macintosh computers. It is possible to protect the use of a

TRADEMARK by copyright (☞ unit 2). A company might use its TRADE NAME as a brand, such as Virgin, Disney or Starbucks. In some cases the company name might be as well known as its products or even more well known. Sony would be known to many people, as might its Sony Walkman, but many other products in its organisation might not.

Table 20.1 shows the most valuable brands in 2002.

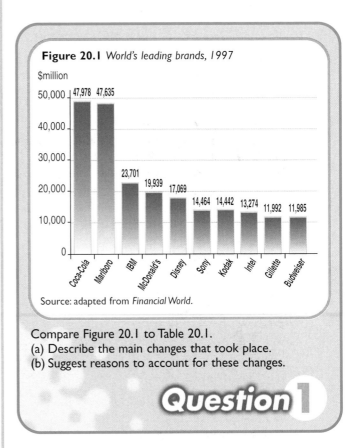

Figure 20.1 *World's leading brands, 1997*

Source: adapted from *Financial World*.

Compare Figure 20.1 to Table 20.1.
(a) Describe the main changes that took place.
(b) Suggest reasons to account for these changes.

Question 1

Brand equity

Well known brands are important to a business. It is argued that brands **add value** to a product. A business will hope that its products:

● will be known by large amounts of consumers - they will have **brand awareness or recognition**;
● will be bought rather than those of others - they will have **brand preference**;
● will be bought by customers over and over again - they will have **brand loyalty**.

Products that have these compared to other products are likely to have BRAND EQUITY. They are important assets that are worth something to businesses which have them (☞ unit 34). They will generate high revenue, promotion and repeat purchases. Sometimes they can be sold for a high value. For example, when Nestlé bought Rowntree for $2.5

Table 20.1 *Most valuable brands by value, 2002*

Rank	Brand name	Brand value ($ million)	Parent company
1	COCA-COLA	69,637	Coca-Cola Company
2	MICROSOFT	64,091	Microsoft Corp.
3	IBM	51,188	IBM Corp.
4	GE	41,311	General Electric Company
5	INTEL	30,861	Intel Corp.
6	NOKIA	29,970	Nokia Corp.
7	DISNEY	29,256	Walt Disney Company
8	MCDONALD'S	26,375	McDonald's Corp.
9	MARLBORO	24,151	Philip Morris Companies
10	MERCEDES	21,010	DaimlerChrysler AG
11	FORD	20,403	Ford Motor Company
12	TOYOTA	19,448	Toyota Motor Corp.
13	CITIBANK	18,066	Citigroup Inc.
14	HEWLETT-PACKARD	16,776	Hewlett Packard
15	AMERICAN EXPRESS	16,287	American Express
16	CISCO SYSTEMS	16,222	Cisco Systems Inc.
17	AT&T	16,059	AT&T Corp.
18	HONDA	15,064	Honda Motor Company
19	GILLETTE COMPANY	14,959	Gillette Company
20	BMW	14,425	Bayerische Motoren Werke

Source: adapted from *Business Week*, Interbrand.

billion in 1988 it acquired a number of brands including Kit Kat and After Eight.

It could be argued that the value of brands can only be measured accurately when they are sold. Legislation in the UK states that the value of 'goodwill' for brands is only shown on the accounts of businesses when it is bought (☞ unit 34).

Developing a brand

There is a number of important features in developing and maintaining a successful brand for a business.

Being the first or filling a gap It is suggested that successful brands are often the first in the market. This might mean being the first products to reach target customers or to use new technology. It might also mean taking advantage of a gap in the market or new developments. Examples may include financial services sold over the Internet or organic or environmentally friendly food brands.

Choosing the right brand name It is important to choose an effective brand name. It should be:
- easy to pronounce and spell, especially if operating in international markets, for example Lego;
- short and to the point so it is easy to remember, for example Nike;
- indicate something about the benefits of the product or its uses, for example Flora Pro-active;
- help the customer to identify when buying, for example J-17 (just seventeen) magazine;
- distinctive, for example Virgin;
- different to others, so that it can be registered as a trademark.

Finding a USP Brands which are successful have a unique selling point or proposition (USP) (☞ unit 15). This is what makes them different from other products and what makes people want to buy them. The USP can be in many forms. For example, a Mercedes car might have an **attribute**, such as 'well built'. The Mercedes might have a **benefit** to the customer, such as not breaking down because it is reliable. A Rolex watch might have a **value** for customers, such as 'prestige'. A pair of Vans trainers might appeal to teenagers' **personality** by having 'street credibility'.

Positioning the brand A brand must be positioned in the right place in the market for it to be successful (☞ unit 15). A business, for example, might sell a 'high quality' brand. It is more likely to be successful if the target market is people with high incomes looking for a superior product than those looking for a bargain. The marketing mix of the business is an important to positioning the brand. So, for example, high quality jewellery is likely to be:
- a **product** manufactured from high quality materials and design;

- sold for a **premium price**;
- **promoted** in a way that reflects the status of the product;
- sold in **places** that reflect the product's features, such as high quality jewellery stores.

Brand protection Brands must be protected by the use of trademarks and copyright. Brands are bought because of the features that customers perceive them to have. However, if cheap, counterfeit copies flood the market, brands may loose their credibility. Also, if all products were able to copy the designer logo of a well known brand, then it would loose its effectiveness.

Liverpool nut company, Trigon, was looking to rebrand in association with the business magazine *en* and MAT:designers. Three designs were shortlisted.
- MCN Food Company Limited. Trigon food product are mainly nuts. But it was important that any brand did not restrict future development of products. So an abbreviation of the warning on some nuts products - may contain nuts - seemed perfect. This was used as a logo which gave a strong corporate identity. There was also an element of humour which could be exploited in promotion.
- Lightly Salted Food Company. To add value, the word food rather than snacks was incorporated into the name. However, it was important to include a clue to Trigon's original business. So a description of the flavour was used - 'lightly salted'. Animals eating nuts were to be used on stationery to create a sense of humour.
- Elephant - The Big Snack Company. An elephant is a large likeable animal that is identified with nuts. It gave an abstract solution. The design and logo to be used looks like something that had been developed over the years on snack packets. This gave a sense of history to the design and the company.

Source: adapted from *en*, 2003.

(a) Why is meant by rebranding?
(b) What factors have influenced the new brand of the business?
(c) Which new brand do you think the business might choose? Explain your answer.

Question 2

Types of brand

Brands can come in a number of forms.

Manufacturer brands MANUFACTURER BRANDS are brands created by the producers of goods and services. The goods or services bear the producers name. Examples might be Kellogg's corn flakes, Gillette razors or IBM computers. The manufacturers are involved in the production, distribution, promotion and pricing decisions of these products.

Own label brands OWN LABEL or DISTRIBUTOR or PRIVATE BRANDS are products which are manufactured for wholesalers or retailers by other businesses. But the wholesalers and retailers sell the products under their own name. Examples of products containing the retailers name include Tesco beans or Marks & Spencer food. Sometimes the retailer will create its own brand name, for example, George clothes sold at Asda. These products allow a retailer to buy from the cheapest manufacturer, reducing its cost. It will hope to promote its own products effectively to shoppers in its outlets.

Generic brands Some GENERIC BRANDS are products that only contain the name of the actual **product category** rather than the company or product name. Examples might be aluminium foil, carrots or aspirin. These products are usually sold at lower prices than branded products. They tend to account for a small percentage of all sales.

Branding strategies

Individual branding A business may attempt to brand individual products with individual brand names. An example might be the large number of washing powder brands sold by Procter & Gamble and Unilever including Daz, Bold, Tide, Dreft, Omo, Radion, Surf, Persil and Ariel. The main advantage of this is that individual brands can be developed for market segments. Also, failure by one brand will not have an adverse effect on another.

Family branding This is where a business has a brand name which includes a number of different products. It can sometimes mean including the company name which then becomes a CORPORATE BRAND. So for example, Heinz baked beans, spaghetti and soups are all foods manufactured by the company. The advantage of this strategy is that marketing campaigns can be spread across a range of products and a business can gain marketing economies of scale (☞ unit 56). Also, a customer might have bought one product and, as a result of confidence in the brand name, might buy other products.

Combination branding This is a middle way between the two previous branding strategies. It involves an emphasis being placed upon the family, corporate and individual brand name. This is a strategy which has been used to good effect by Cadbury Schweppes. It has a range of products such as Wispa, Milk Tray, Flake and Dairy Milk. All of these brands have a strong identity. However, the limelight is always shared with the name Cadbury's, so that for consumers the two brand names appear to naturally go together.

Brand extensions or stretching BRAND EXTENSIONS are when an existing brand name is used for a new brand in a similar market. Examples of this might include Coca-Cola producing Diet Coke or Cola-Cola with lemon or 'light

versions' of beers. BRAND STRETCHING is when an existing brand name is taken into unrelated markets. An example might be the Virgin brand name which has been used on a variety of businesses operations, including music shops, trains, financial services, and travel and holidays. The advantage of this strategy is that new products may find it easier to become established.

Reasons for branding

There is a number of reasons why businesses use branding.
- To create brand loyalty. Consumers often have a high degree of loyalty to popular, well established, brands. In many markets it can be very difficult for firms to compete unless they have a strong brand identity.
- To differentiate the product. Especially in markets where products are fairly similar, it is important for a firm that its own products can be clearly distinguished from others. A clear brand identity can help to achieve this.
- To gain flexibility when making pricing decisions. The greater the loyalty of consumers to a particular brand, the more room for manoeuvre a firm will have in its pricing decisions. A survey by Business Marketing Services found that consumers were reluctant to switch from well known brands in the hotel, car hire, computer and transatlantic flights markets. For example, in the car hire market pricing discounts of over 20 per cent were required to persuade consumers to switch from Hertz or Avis to one of the lesser known companies.

'Whyte and Mackay is a global spirits company with significant core brands, namely Whyte and Mackay Scotch Whisky, The Dalmore Single Highland Malt, Isle of Jura Malt Whisky, Glayva Liqueur and Vladivar Vodka. The company is also the world's leading supplier of own label, private label and branded Scotch Whisky.'

'With four malt distilleries and the only grain distillery in the Highlands of Scotland, Whyte and Mackay distils, blends, bottles and packages Scotch whisky and other spirits for many markets and customers around the world.'

'Hibernian Football Club today announced it had secured a sponsorship agreement with Whyte and Mackay, one of the UK's leading blended whiskies, worth £1 million over the next five years.'

Source: www.whyteandmackay.co.uk.

(a) Using examples, distinguish between manufacturer brands and own label brands.
(b) Suggest branding strategies that Whyte and Mackay might make use of.

Question 3

● To help recognition. A product with a strong brand identity is likely to be instantly recognised by most consumers. This may mean consumers trust the product and are therefore more willing to buy it. Some brand names are used to describe whole classes of products, such as Sellotape and Hoover.

● To develop a brand image. It is argued that customers respond to brand images with which they identify. Some consumers respond to brands that allow them to pursue multiple goals. Volvo, for example, stresses that its cars not only protect but allow the user to escape to remote places. Consumers also react to brands that offer 'extreme consumption experiences' such as Haagen-Dazs ice cream or Starbucks coffee.

Problems with branding

Branding might not always be a successful strategy for some businesses for a number of reasons.

● As explained earlier, some products are generic. This can make it difficult to establish an effective brand.

● Not all markets are suited to brands. It has been suggested, for example, that people buy wine based on the name of the grape or the region where wine is produced rather than the brand name.

● It can be expensive to promote and maintain a brand. Establishing a successful brand in a competitive market can be very costly. Small business may not be able to afford this.

Luxury car maker Mercedes Benz has topped the 'bling - bling' rap charts. The charts are named after the rap term for showy jewellery or any kind of expensive flashy style. The Mercedes Benz brand name was used in rap songs more than any other products. It had 112 name checks in songs in 2003, more than double its nearest rival. Most mentions were from rapper Fifty Cent, who mentioned it four times. He also named checked 31 different products in his songs.

A spokesperson for *American Bandstand* said 'Hip-hop has always been about defining status. And aligning yourself with brands in lyrics are the best short cuts - especially if you want to be understood by a global audience.'

Table 20.2 *Products plugged by hip-hop artists in US Billboard magazine chart*

Position	Product	Number of mentions
1.	Mercedes	112
2.	Lexus	48
3.	Gucci	47
4.	Cadillac	46
5.	Burberry	42
6.	Prada	39
7.	Cristal champagne	37
8.	Hennessy	35
9.	Lamborghini	34
10.	Chevrolet	33

Source: adapted from American Bandstand.

(a) Examine how the use of branding in this way might benefit a business.

key terms

Brand - a name, term, sign, symbol, design or any other feature that allows consumers to identify the goods and services and differentiate them from those of competitors.

Brand equity - the value of the brand to the business.

Brand extensions - when the brand name is used for new products in related markets.

Brand mark - the design or symbol used in the brand.

Brand name - the parts of the brand that can be spoken, such as the name of the product.

Brand stretching - when the brand name is used for new products in unrelated markets.

Corporate brand - when the name of the business is used as the brand name.

Generic brands - products that only contain the name of the product category rather than the company or product name.

Manufacturer brands - brands created by the producers of goods and services.

Own label or distributor brands - products which are manufactured for wholesalers or retailers by other businesses.

Trademark - the sign, symbol or other feature of a business that can be protected by copyright.

Trade name - the registered name of the business, which can sometimes be used as a brand name.

Knowledge...Knowledge...Knowledge...Knowledge...Knowledge...Knowledge...Know

1. Identify 5 features that a brand might have.
2. How might a brand have equity or worth to a business?
3. When might a business be able to measure the value of its brands?
4. Suggest 5 features of an effective brand name.
5. Why is brand protection important?
6. State 3 types of brand.
7. Suggest 4 types of brand strategy.
8. State 5 benefits of branding to a business.
9. State 3 situations where branding may not be effective.

Case study McDonald's-Disney alliance grows

In 2001 the ten year alliance between McDonald's and Disney was reaching its mid-point. It was suggested that McDonald's was aiming to 'spice up' its promotional campaign, while preparing for its food service debut at the new Disney California Adventure theme park in Anaheim, California. Part of the spicing up by McDonald's was the launch of a family promotion tied to the popular 'Who wants to be a millionaire' programme which is shown on Disney's ABC television channel.

Jack Greenberg, McDonald's chairman and chief executive, said 'We have moved way beyond doing only movie promotions with Happy Meal toys.' He suggested that in addition to joint marketing and opening food service venues on Disney properties, the partnership was working to create in-store entertainment for children using computer software. For example, Disney was developing software for the chain of McMagination playstation kiosks aimed at kids in McDonald's drive through outlets. These would 'accentuate the drive though experience'.

McDonald's was also expected to introduce a 'House of Mouse' Happy Meal promotion which would feature Mickey Mouse, as well as several other Disney characters. It was the first time that Mickey Mouse had been introduced into McDonald's restaurants.

Four of the Top Ten Happy Meals at McDonald's have tie ins with Disney. Analysts suggest that the alliance is generally favourable and had a positive impact on sales. However, they noted that McDonald's may be dependent on the success of Disney movies.

McDonald's was also scheduled to launch a 'Burger Invasion' restaurant in Disney's California Adventure. This was a 5,000 square foot restaurant shaped like a giant burger. It has an 8 foot revolving sign with golden arches, as well as a menu featuring items such as Happy meals, double cheeseburgers, Big Macs and french fries. It was described as 'the most extensively branded facility' inside a Disney park. The new facility would also include a fingerboard toy exclusive to the new location.

Source: adapted from *Nations Restaurant News*, 22.1.2001.

(a) Using examples from the article, identify features of the McDonald's brand. (8 marks)

(b) Explain why McDonald's might be involved in an alliance with Disney. (10 marks)

(c) Examine the branding strategies used by McDonald's and Disney. (10 marks)

(d) Discuss the extent to which branding is likely to be successful for McDonald's and Disney. (12 marks)

21 Promotion Above the Line

What is promotion?

PROMOTION is the attempt to draw attention to a product or business in order to gain new customers or to retain existing ones. Different methods of promotion are shown in Figure 21.1.

Businesses often refer to promotion **above the line** and **below the line**. Above the line promotion is through independent media, such as television or newspapers. These allow a business to reach a wide audience easily. Most advertising is carried out 'above the line'. Some advertising, however, is carried out by methods over which a firm has direct control, such as direct mailing. These and other direct methods of promotion (known as below the line promotion) are dealt with in unit 22. This unit looks at how businesses advertise their products through different media.

The objectives of promotion

A business must be clear about exactly what it is trying to achieve through its promotion. The main aim of any promotion is to obtain and retain customers. However, there is a number of other objectives, some or all of which any successful campaign must fulfil.

- To make consumers aware or increase awareness of a product.
- To reach a target audience which might be geographically dispersed.
- To remind consumers about the product. This can encourage existing consumers to re-purchase the product and may attract new consumers.
- To show a product is better than that of a competitor. This may encourage consumers to switch purchases from another product.
- To develop or improve the image of a business rather than a product. Much **corporate advertising** is carried out with this in mind, and is dealt with later in this unit.
- To reassure consumers after the product has been

purchased. This builds up confidence in the product and may encourage more to be bought at a later date.
- To support an existing product. Such promotions may be used to remind consumers that a reliable and well thought of product is still available.

Businesses sometimes consider their promotion using **models**. For example, AIDA is a method used to consider advertising. It suggests that effective advertising will raise Awareness (A) and encourage Interest (I), Desire (D) and Action (A), so that consumers buy the products. The DAGMAR (Defining Advertising Goals for Measured Advertising Results) model is also used to measure the effect of advertising. A business can measure how far the group that is targeted has progressed along the scale below.

Unawareness...Awareness...Comprehension...Conviction...Action

Types of advertising

Advertising has achieved a central place in business activity across the world as firms have begun to face global as well as national competition. In the UK it has been estimated that between 1 and 2 per cent of national income is spent on advertising.

Advertising is often placed into different categories. INFORMATIVE ADVERTISING is designed to increase consumer awareness of a product. Examples include the classified advertisements in local newspapers, new share offers, grants available to small firms and entries in the *Yellow Pages*. New products may be launched with informative advertising campaigns to make consumers aware of their presence. It is usually argued that this type of advertising helps consumers to make a rational choice as to what to buy.

PERSUASIVE ADVERTISING tries to convince consumers to purchase a product, often by stressing that it is more desirable than others. It is argued that this type of advertising distorts consumer buying, pushing them to buy products which they would otherwise not have bought. In reality, almost all advertising is persuasive to some extent. Very few major campaigns aim to be entirely informative.

REASSURING ADVERTISING is aimed at existing customers. It tries to persuade them that their purchase was correct and that they should continue to buy the product. Banks and building societies often use this method to assure customers that their investments are safe.

Types of advertising media

There is a wide range of ADVERTISING MEDIA that firms can choose from in order to make consumers aware of their products.

Television Because of its many advantages, television

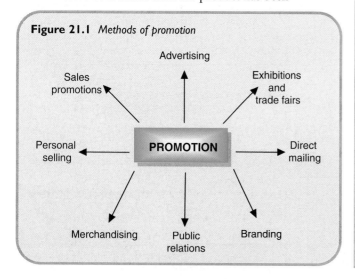
Figure 21.1 *Methods of promotion*
Advertising — Sales promotions — Exhibitions and trade fairs — Personal selling — PROMOTION — Direct mailing — Merchandising — Public relations — Branding

advertising is often used by businesses marketing consumer goods to a mass market. The fast changing trends in television were likely to provide opportunities for television advertising after the year 2000. 99 per cent of males and females watch television in the UK. The growth of cable, satellite and digital television may attract companies to advertise on television. By 2004 half of UK households had access to some form of digital television. Businesses may be particularly attracted to advertise on digital television as packages on Sky, for example, may be subscribed to by higher earning and spending groups.

Newspapers and magazines Newspapers and magazines are an important medium for the advertising of mass market products. It has been estimated that there were 39 million readers of a national newspaper each week in 2002 and that four out of five adults read a national newspaper. Newspapers and magazines can also be useful for targeting a particular audience or market segment (☞ unit 13). For example, businesses selling riding equipment might advertise in *Horse and Hound* or a business selling musical equipment might advertise in *Total Guitar*. Newspaper advertising can also be useful for smaller businesses. It was estimated in 2004 that 40 million adults weekly read a local newspaper.

Cinema Cinema attendances fell from a high of around 1.4 billion in 1951 to reach a low of 53 million in 1984. The 1990s, however, saw a revival in attendances, partly as a result of the better facilities offered by large multiplex cinemas. By 2003 attendances had improved to 167 million. As a result, advertisers began to pay greater attention to this medium. Firms such as Wrangler have even produced advertisements principally designed for use on large cinema screens. Of all the advertising media available to a business, the cinema has the greatest potential for having a strong impact on its audience.

Radio In recent years there has been a growth in the number of independent radio stations in the UK. These include local stations, such as Capital in London and Key 103 in Manchester, national stations such as Virgin and Talk Radio and specialist stations such as Smooth FM and Classic FM. For advertisers this has meant an increase in both the number and type of radio stations on which they can advertise.

There has been an increase in the number of people listening to radio. This trend may be likely to continue with the development of digital radio and Internet radio stations. Both large companies such as Cunard and Kleenex Tissues, as well as smaller businesses, have found radio effective in reaching target customers.

Posters or billboards Posters appear in a variety of locations and tend to carry short messages. This is because motorists and pedestrians usually only have a few seconds to consider them. An effective poster is likely to be large, attention grabbing and placed in a site where it is highly visible to large numbers of

people. The development of electronic screens containing 'posters' with rotating advertisements is a development in this area which may attract businesses.

The Internet Figure 21.1 shows the dramatic increase in the importance of the Internet as an advertising medium in the UK. By 2003, 48 per cent of households (11.9 million) could

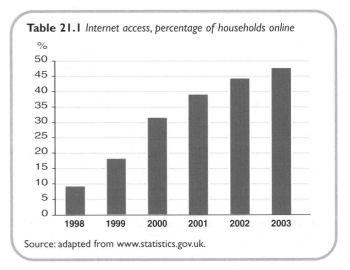

Table 21.1 *Internet access, percentage of households online*

Source: adapted from www.statistics.gov.uk.

Online supermarket shopping was slammed by customers for being slow and frustrating in a survey by *The Grocer* magazine in 2004. The survey asked supermarkets to deliver 33 items. Not one store was able to deliver all thirty three and one store even sent out-of-date sausages.

Net users, particularly first timers, criticised supermarket websites as being difficult to navigate. Some take too far too long to log on and there were often problems working out exactly where products which customers were looking for were located on the site.

Of the six supermarkets tested, Sainsbury's and Asda were amongst the most efficient, delivering 32 of the 33 items requested. One customer argued 'I was so disappointed by online shopping ... it could be a lot clearer', another that ' I spent too long trying to guess which department items would be in' and one even said 'I would not consider using the service again'. Logging on time varied from ten seconds in one case to ten minutes in another.

The deputy editor of *The Grocer* said 'Time and again we hear that navigating a supermarket Internet site is an issue, even for those with fast Internet connections'. Some good news was that there was said to be improved choice on websites. Tesco is the market leader for online shopping with nearly a nationwide coverage and products of £12.2 million. Asda plans to cover 40 per cent of the UK from August.

Source: adapted from *The Daily Mirror*, 20.4.2004.

(a) Examine the advantages and disadvantages to supermarkets of using the Internet to advertise to customers.

Question 1

Table 21.1 *Advertising media*

Medium	Advantages	Disadvantages
Television	• Creative advertisements can attract attention and have a great impact. • Advertisements can demonstrate the product in use. • Can reach a vast audience. • Increased scope for targeting the audience, eg digital television. • The message can be reinforced by continuous advertisements.	• Relatively expensive initial cost. • The message is short lived. • Consumers may not watch commercials. • Technical information is difficult to explain. • There may be a delay between seeing the advert and visiting the shops.
National newspaper	• National coverage. • Reader can refer back. • Relatively cheap. • Detail of the product can be provided.	• No movement or sound. • Usually limited to black and white. • Individual adverts may be lost amongst large quantities of other advertisements.
Regional newspaper	• Good for regional campaigns and test marketing. • Can be linked to local conditions.	• Cost per reader higher than national newspapers. • Reproduction, layout etc. may be poor.
Magazines	• Colour advertisements possible. • Targeting possible with specialist magazines. • Advertising can be linked to features. • Magazines may be referred to at a later date.	• A long time exists between advertisements being placed and magazine being printed. • Competitors' products are also being advertised. • No movement or sound.
Cinema	• Colour, sound and movement can be used. • Advertisements can be highly localised. • A 'captive' audience for advertisements. • Great impact on the consumer. • Age groups can be targeted.	• Limited audience. • Message is short lived. • Message may only be seen once.
Radio	• Enables use of sound. • Most consumer groups covered. • Minority programmes can target audiences. • Produced cheaply. • Younger audience targeted.	• Not visual. • No copy of material. • Interruptions to music may prove irritating. • May not capture the audience's attention.
Posters and billboards	• National campaigns possible. • Most groups covered. • May encourage impulse buying through location close to shops. • Seen repeatedly. • Excellent for short, sharp messages, eg, election 'promises'.	• Limited amount of information. • Difficult to measure effectiveness. • Weather and graffiti can ruin the poster.
Internet	• Relatively cheap and easy to set up. • Number of 'hits' can be monitored. • Can be targeted. • Can be easily changed.	• Limited audience. • Possible technical problems of connection, viewing, ordering, maintaining.

access the Internet from home, an increase from just 9 per cent in 1998. As a result, businesses have shown a growing interest in advertising via websites on the Internet. One major advantage is that websites can be accessed by consumers all over the world, giving companies a worldwide market. Many companies now have their own websites to advertise products and some even allow customers to purchase online using credit cards. By 2003 over half of UK Internet users were using websites to buy goods and services.

The advantages and disadvantages of different advertising media are shown in Table 21.1.

Choice of advertising media

How do firms decide which medium will be most suitable for their product? There is a number of factors that advertisers may take into account.

Cost Small firms will be mainly concerned with what media they can afford. Larger firms will need to consider the cost effectiveness of each of the different media. For example, although television is the most expensive medium, it reaches huge numbers of consumers. This means the cost per sale from a television advertisement may be relatively low. The Internet is a relatively low cost method of advertising.

The audience reached Given that many products are aimed at certain segments, it makes sense for firms to place their advertisement in a medium which the target audience is likely to see or hear. Firms must aim to reduce **wastage** in their advertising. 'Wastage' means advertising to those other than the target audience. Clearly a certain amount of wastage will occur with most TV advertising, whilst very little will occur when advertising in, say, specialist magazines. Advertising on the Internet can be targeted, but the audience may be limited.

The advertising of competitors A major TV advertising campaign by one firm may, for example, be followed by a counter campaign from its competitors.

The impact Firms will aim to make the greatest impact when advertising. Different products will require different media to do this. For example, some products such as sports equipment will benefit from being shown in action to have the most impact on an audience. Television and cinema are the obvious choice of media in such cases.

The law There are legal restrictions in the UK which mean that some products cannot be advertised in particular media. This is discussed in detail later in this unit. One example of this is the ban on advertising tobacco on TV in the UK.

The marketing mix The advertising campaign should be integrated with other types of below the line promotion (☞ unit 22). For example, sponsorship of a sports event and an advertisement for the product on the sports pages of a newspaper may be effective.

The presentation and recording of information If an advertisement is designed to be visual, with little written information, then posters on billboards or magazine articles can be effective. Magazine advertisements can also include a lot of text, usually in small print. Advertising on television will also be useful for visual images and has the advantage that words can be spoken at the same time. A short radio advert can provide a certain amount of spoken information, although it will be difficult for the listener to remember everything. Advertising on the Internet allows large amounts of information to be downloaded free of charge.

Controls on advertising

Consumers sometimes complain that advertisements either mislead or exploit. For this reason, there is regulation, legislation and codes of practice to protect the consumer.

Legislation and regulation The **Trades Descriptions Act, 1968** states that products must correspond to the claims made for them in advertisements. It is, therefore, illegal to include ingredients on a label which are not present or make unproven claims about the effects of, say, weight loss products. Descriptions of services provided by firms must

In 2004 it was reported that readership of regional newspapers rose to 40 million adults every week. This was a year-on-year increase for the industry as a whole of 1.8 per cent. Readership of paid-for weekly newspapers grew by 15 per cent over the past 10 years. The weekly paid-for sector represented 80 per cent of all regional titles.

Kevin Beatty, managing director of Northcliffe Newspapers and chairman of the Newspaper Society's Marketing Committee, said 'Local and regional newspapers are in excellent health: readership is on the increase and major new advertisers are coming into the medium because of its closeness to communities and its proven effectiveness. All mainstream media are battling to maintain audience share; the fact that once again nearly half of all local and regional titles have grown circulation reflects the strong and enduring affinity this industry retains with its customers.'

Source: adapted from www.newspapersoc.org.uk, 26.2.2004.

(a) Examine the factors which may influence businesses to advertise in regional and local newspapers.
(b) Assess which types of business are most likely to use this form of media.

Question 2

also be accurate. The Act prevents businesses from misleading the consumer about 'sales'.

The **Competition Commission** has powers to investigate anti-competitive behaviour by firms (☞ unit 71). Such anti-competitive behaviour may be in the form of high levels of spending on advertising, for example. This raises costs within an industry and could act as a barrier to prevent other firms from entering the market.

The **Office of Communications** (Ofcom) regulates the communications industry (☞ unit 71). It took over the roles of the Broadcasting Standards Commission, the Independent Television Commission, the Radio Authority and the Radiocommunications Agency which monitored advertising on radio and television.

Independent bodies The main independent body which regulates and controls advertising in the UK is the **Advertising Standards Authority (ASA)**. It is an independent body responsible for making sure that advertisements conform to the **British Code of Advertising, Sales Promotion and Direct Marketing** (The CAP Code). This states that advertisements should be:
● legal, decent, honest and truthful;

- prepared with a sense of responsibility to consumers and to society;
- in line with the principles of fair competition generally accepted in business.

Over 10,000 advertisements are referred to the ASA each year. In 2002, 13 per cent of advertisements complained about were found to breach the Code. In 2004 the ASA upheld a claim against an advertisement which stated 'Complete Brush Wash System from Alpine Cleaning Services ... The only mobile brush wash machine available with built in pressure washer!' The complainants, who possessed a similar machine, challenged the claim.

If the ASA finds that an advertisement breaches the Code, it may ask the business involved to withdraw the advertisement. Although it has no legal power to force a business to withdraw an advertisement, the ASA can put pressure on a business to do so by:
- publishing its findings;
- withdrawing privileges associated with ASA membership;
- asking media to refuse to carry future advertisements.

In the example of the car wash system above, the ASA worked with the company to amend the wording on the advertisement.

The ASA can also refer the business to the Office of Fair Trading (☞ unit 71), which has the power to seek an injunction to prevent further advertisements. Businesses often make use of the ASA's service which allows advertisements to be checked before they are shown, to make sure they comply with the Code.

Around 30 million press advertisements are published in the UK each year. ASA research shows that the majority are legal, decent, honest and truthful. Compliance with the CAP Code achieves levels of 96 per cent for press advertisements, 99 per cent for posters and 91 per cent for direct marketing.

Pressure groups Certain pressure groups (☞ unit 70) seek to influence advertising. FOREST, for example, is a pressure group which aims to defend the rights of tobacco firms to advertise. The British Medical Association (BMA) and Action on Smoking and Health (ASH) take the opposite view. Women's groups have sought to influence firms to produce advertisements which are not sexist. Pressure groups campaigning for better safety on roads have sought to persuade car and tyre manufacturers to produce advertisements showing less aggressive driving.

Advertising and society

Advertising has the potential to affect the lives of many people. This is because, for most, regular exposure to advertising is almost unavoidable. How might advertising affect individuals?
- It adds to the cost of marketing products. This money could have been spent on improving products or price reductions. It is likely that consumers will pay more of any advertising costs than firms.

- It is argued that advertising encourages people to buy products which they might not otherwise have purchased. This may, perhaps, lead to a society where people are judged according to how much they consume rather than their value as human beings.

In 2001 the ASA ruled on an objection to a poster for a computer company. It contained a picture of an iBook laptop computer with an image of a skateboarder. The objection was that the image shown on the iBook screen in the poster misrepresented and exaggerated the quality of the screen images on the iBook.

The advertisers argued that the poster did not misrepresent the images on an iBook screen. They demonstrated still and moving images on an iBook and explained that the screen image had to be converted before being placed onto the poster to be printed. Because the poster image had been enlarged, the printed image on the poster was not as well-defined as the iBook screen image. The ASA acknowledged that, for technical reasons, it was impossible to transfer the screen image directly onto a poster. It ruled that the image shown on the iBook screen in the poster did not misrepresent the screen images available on the iBook and that the poster was not misleading.

In 2002 the ASA ruled on a poster and leaflet for an Internet car trader. It stated 'Would you buy a used car from this man?' and claimed 'Now you can. AA Buyacar ...'. A footnote stated 'Please note that the AA will act as an appointed intermediary for the purchase of your vehicle from our reputable supplier. Your contract for the purchase of the vehicle will be with the supplier.' The objections were that the advertisements misleadingly implied customers could buy from the AA and that the footnote on the poster was illegible at normal viewing distance.

In both cases the complaints were upheld. In the first case, the ASA ruled that the advertisement implied that cars could be bought direct from the AA. It concluded that the headline claim was misleading and advised the advertisers not to repeat the claim and to reword it with help from the Committee of Advertising Practice (CAP) Copy Advice team.

In the second case the ASA considered that the footnote in the leaflet was legible, but it was too small on the poster to be read by a sighted person, with normal vision, viewing for a reasonable length of time, at a reasonable distance. It asked the advertisers to ensure that footnotes on posters were legible in future and advised them to seek help from the CAP Copy Advice team.

Source: adapted from www.asa.org.uk.

(a) Explain why the advertising in the above cases might have been investigated by the ASA.
(b) Suggest how the decisions by the ASA might affect how the businesses approach advertising in future.

- Environmentalists are concerned about high levels of consumption and the role of advertising in encouraging this. They doubt whether the earth's resources can sustain current levels. There is a growing trend amongst consumers to look at the type of goods they buy and also how much they consume, as they become more aware of long term problems.
- Advertising can encourage people to buy products which are regarded as being damaging to society.
- Advertisements often encourage behaviour which might be to the detriment of society as a whole. An example is the fast 'macho' driving often seen in advertisements for cars and related products.

In its defence, the advertising industry would point to a number of arguments to justify its role.
- Advertisements offer a choice to consumers which allows them to make more informed consumption decisions.
- Advertisements give valuable information to consumers which might otherwise be difficult to come by.
- Advertisers respond to and reflect the needs, wishes and attitudes of consumers; they do not 'create' them.
- Advertising earns revenue for television and radio and allows newspapers and magazines to be sold at lower prices.
- The advertising industry employs large numbers of people. They are employed directly, through advertising agencies, and indirectly through jobs that may result from a successfully advertised product.

Corporate advertising

CORPORATE ADVERTISING is concerned with promoting a company as a whole, rather than individual products. An example of corporate advertising can be seen in the detergent market. Companies such as Unilever and Nestlé have their name on branded packets. The amount spent on corporate advertising has doubled in recent years and this trend is expected to continue.

Companies ranging from ICI to Benetton to BP have jumped on this bandwagon.

There are two reasons why companies need to sell themselves now more than ever. First, companies must now be seen to be responsible good 'citizens'. This means communicating. Second, there is growing pressure for the company to become a **brand** (☞ unit 20). Companies need to ensure that their corporate image is positive.

Corporate advertising often makes use of **slogans, brand names** or **catchlines**. Nestlé, for example, identifies its name on products. So, for example, all KitKats have the name Nestlé clearly marked on their covers. Even more dramatically, the Chambourcy brand of yoghurt was renamed Nestlé. Nestlé uses the corporate slogan 'Good food, Good life' to build up its reputation as a company which can be trusted to provide quality food and improve life. In a similar way, Vodafone, by sponsoring Ferrari's Formula 1 racing team, is attempting to build a successful brand image by encouraging customers to associate its product with another successful product.

Corporate advertising allows a company to advertise its whole philosophy. Corporate messages are aimed at a variety of different, yet connected, audiences. These include employees, local groups, the trade, government, the media, financial institutions and the 'general public', as well as consumers themselves. There are problems, however. The corporate values of one company may not be different to those of another, so that target audiences may not be able to distinguish between the messages of different firms. Also, less may be spent on advertising individual brands, as a business uses resources to promote the whole company.

BASF Corporation is the world's leading chemical company, producing high-performance products, such as chemicals, plastics, performance products and agricultural products. In 2002 it had sales of $34 billion and more than 89,000 employees throughout the world. 'Helping make products better' is its slogan and 'We don't make a lot of the products you buy. We make a lot of the products you buy better' is its corporate statement. This has made the BASF corporate advertising campaign the most recognised of any corporate campaign from the North American chemical industry. The business does not make many finished products. Virtually all of the 6,000-plus products made by the company are ingredients that enhance the finished products consumers buy. Its television advertising campaign features many of these products with comments. They include:
- a picture of a tennis player, focussed in on the shoe, with the phrase 'we don't make the tennis shoe we make it grip better';
- a picture of a band in a recording studio with the phrase 'we don't make the studio, we make it quieter';
- a picture of a man on a beach with the phrase 'we don't make sun screen, we make it stronger'.
- a picture of a car being filled with petrol with the phrase 'we don't make the fuel, we make it burn cleaner'.

In 2004 the company introduced a new innovative ultraviolet light (UV) absorber that will help sunscreen and cosmetic manufacturers. ' ... Uvinul A Plus offers reliable protection against UVA rays that penetrate deeper into the skin over long periods without the need for additional stabilisation' said Alyson Emanuel, Director, Cosmetic Ingredients for BASF in North America.

Source: adapted from www.basf.com.

(a) Identify features of corporate advertising by the company.
(b) Explain why such a business might use corporate advertising.

key terms

Advertising media - the various means by which advertisements can be communicated to the public.
Corporate advertising - advertising which is meant to promote a whole company rather than a particular product or product line.
Informative advertising - advertising which primarily seeks to provide consumers with information about a product.

Persuasive advertising - advertising which seeks to influence and persuade consumers to buy a product.
Promotion - an attempt to retain and obtain customers by drawing attention to a firm or its products.
Reassuring advertising - a method used to assure consumers about their purchases and encourage them to make repeat purchases.

Knowledge ...Knowledge...Knowledge...Knowledge...Knowledge...Knowledge...Know

1. What is above the line promotion?
2. Why might advertising be both above and below the line promotion?
3. What are the objectives of promotion?
4. What choices of advertising media do firms have?
5. What criteria might firms use in order to decide upon their choice of advertising media?

6. What is the role of an advertising agency?
7. What is the role of the ASA?
8. Why might an advertisement be banned under the Trades Descriptions Act?
9. State 3 arguments for and 3 arguments against advertising.
10. What is the objective of corporate advertising?

Case study Conrack and Eco-Store

Conrack

Conrack Ltd is a private limited company which specialises in manufacturing products from 'managed' wood. Managed wood is wood which when cut down for timber is replaced by planting a new tree. Its policy is only to purchase wood from suppliers that guarantee to conform with these requirements.

The business has been successful in selling to customers who are interested in preserving the environment. They are attracted by the idea that the products they buy do not use up the earth's resources, which are preserved for future generations. Conrack's slogan is 'What we use, we replace'. Products include kitchen and dining tables. It also manufactures housing 'parts', such as window ledges and doors, from managed wood, as well as conservatories and garden outhouses.

In 2004 the business had a manufacturing factory just outside Manchester and two retail outlets in the area north of Manchester. Its turnover was £800,000 and it had a promotion budget of around £15,000 per annum. It had concentrated mainly on local

advertising in the region. The managing director, Kim Barnett, argued that small scale but thought provoking advertisements might be particularly influential in attracting interest in the company's products.

Eco-Store

The Eco-Store is a company with a national chain of stores in the UK. The shops are based on 'old style' American stores. Food is sold loose from barrels and sacks to remove the need for packaging and waste. Liquids and drinks are filled into bottles or containers rather than being sold in plastic or glass bottles. Environmentally friendly goods are also sold. These include products made from recycled plastic and wood and recycled paper. The company has seen rapid growth in the 1990s and early twenty first century. By 2004 it had a turnover of £200 million. It had decided to review its marketing strategy. It particularly wished to develop a caring image for the company. It hoped in its advertisements to stress the 'homely nature' of the stores and products. It felt that this would attract families to shop at its stores.

Table 21.2

Advertisement in local newspaper per week -
  £51 per issue (based on a business card sized advertisement of 5 cm x 2 cm)

Advertisement on local radio
  Fixed costs - £500-£1,000
  Cost per minute - £100-£200

Leaflets
  Single colour
    Fixed costs - £125
    Cost per thousand - £50
  Full colour
    Fixed costs - £200
    Cost per thousand - £200

Internet website
  £1,000 per year

Poster on a fleet of buses for a month - £300

Insert into *Yellow Pages* per annum
  1.5 cm box - £154
  3 cm box - £272
  4.5 cm box - £367

Advertising in a specialist magazine (per issue)
  1/4 page black and white £400
  Full page 2 colour £1,300
  Full page full colour £1,700

Advertising in a national newspaper -
  £20,000 per quarter page advert

Television advertising - £50,000 per 30 seconds, plus fixed costs.

(a) **Identify the possible objectives of the two businesses. (6 marks)**
(b) **How might Eco-Store be able to make use of corporate advertising? (6 marks)**
(c) **Explain, using examples, how the methods of promotion might be made:**
    (i) persuasive;
    (ii) informative;
    (iii) reassuring;
    for customers of the businesses. (6 marks)
(d) **Examine the factors which might affect the choice of medium of each business. (10 marks)**
(e) **Select appropriate media which the business might use. Justify your choices for each business. (12 marks)**

What is promotion?

Promotion below the line refers to those promotional methods which do not depend upon media such as newspapers and TV. Instead, it takes place by methods over which firms have some degree of control. These include direct mail advertising, exhibitions and trade fairs, sales promotions, merchandising, packaging, personal selling and public relations. A business, such as Hilton Hotels, might promote its hotels by using a combination of promotions, for example public relations and sales promotions.

Below the line promotion allows a business to aim its marketing at consumers it knows are interested in the product. Above the line advertising in newspapers means that the promotion is seen by most of the readers, even though some will not be interested. With below the line promotions, firms are usually aiming their message at consumers who are either known to them or who have been chosen in advance. For example, direct mail advertisers will pick exactly which consumers they wish to send their mail to, rather than going for blanket coverage. Businesses promoting through exhibitions, such as the Boat Show, can be certain that the majority of those attending will be interested in the products on show.

There may be problems that result from below the line promotions.
- As with advertising, they are expensive and their outcome is difficult to predict.
- They are often 'one off' events, which have an impact for a limited period.
- Some types of promotion, such as direct mail and personal selling, are disliked by consumers.

Direct mailing

Direct mailing involves sending information about a product or product range through the post. The consumer can usually buy the product by placing an order by post or telephone. Although sometimes unpopular with the public, direct mail is a fast growing area of promotion. It has proved very effective for firms trying to reach a target audience. Some companies use direct e-mailing, where consumers or businesses receive product information through their e-mail inbox. Systems, however, exist for unwanted e-mails to be blocked as this method of selling has proved unpopular for some people.

Direct mail is one means of **direct marketing** (☞ unit 23), which is often seen as part of a firm's distribution network.

Exhibitions and trade fairs

Exhibitions and trade fairs are used by firms to promote their products. They are visited by both industrial and ordinary consumers. Examples of better known fairs and exhibitions include the Motor Show, the Boat Show and the Ideal Homes

Anna Lever runs a shop which sells imported comics from the USA and Europe. She stocks well known comics by Marvel and DC, such as X-men and Batman, and also a small line of European comics. Anna also sells comics by independent publishers in the UK. The market for comic sales in the UK tends to be a niche market, selling to specialist collectors, teenagers, students and children, and older people who Anna argues 'want to recapture their youth, by reading the stories they read when they were children and teenagers.'

There is a small number of chains selling comics in the UK, such as Forbidden Planet, but many other independent shops. The nearest competitor for Anna's shop is over 50 miles away. Anna often tries local mailing in the area. General mailing to all people tends to be waste of time, so she must carefully target her audience. She also keeps clients regularly updated via e-mails. Most regular customers are happy to receive information about the latest issues although some newer customers have objected to this 'spam'.

Every month Anna makes the trip to the nearest city and puts up a stall in the comic mart on Sundays. She tends to see the same faces there all the time, and can build up contacts. There may also be people coming to 'have a look' on their day off and some have become regular clients. She has also occasionally taken a stand at the large fair held at the NEC in Birmingham a few times a year. She finds the trip is tiring, takes a lot of time out of her week and does not always pay for itself.

Source: adapted from company information.

(a) Why might it be important for Anna's business to use a trade fair as part of its promotional mix?
(b) Assess whether a trade fair might be more successful than direct mail advertising in promoting and selling comics.

Exhibition. Why do businesses find them useful?

● They give the chance to show how a product actually works. This is important in the case of bulky or complex technical products. The marketing of industrial and agricultural machinery is often done through trade fairs.

● Consumer reaction to a product can be tested before it is released onto the market.

● Some trade fairs and exhibitions are held overseas. They can form a part of a firm's international marketing strategy.

● A fair or exhibition may attract press coverage. New products may be launched to take advantage of this. The Motor Show is widely used for this purpose.

● They allow customers to discuss a product with members of the management team. It is not unusual for the managing directors of a business to attend a trade fair. For industrial consumers, in particular, this can be a valuable point of contact.

● Technical and sales staff are available to answer questions and discuss the product.

Sales promotions

Sales promotions are the incentives offered to consumers to encourage them to buy goods and services. They are used to give a short term 'boost' to the sales of a product. This is different to building up brand recognition and loyalty, which may be a longer term aim. There is a variety of sales promotions that a business can use.

● Coupons and loyalty cards. These involve either providing money off or refunds on specific purchases or allowing savings to be made over time for being a loyal customer. The Boots Advantage loyalty card, first launched in 1997, had 15 million customers by 2004.

● Competitions. Prizes are sometimes offered for competitions. To enter, consumers must first buy the product. Tabloid newspapers often use this type of promotion. They try to attract customers through large cash prizes in their 'bingo' competitions.

● Product endorsements. These are widely used by a range of manufacturers, where well known personalities are paid to use products. For example, sports products companies will sign up teams and successful sports personalities to promote their products. The competition between sports companies has often been reflected by the teams they supply - Real Madrid has worn Adidas while Manchester United and Barcelona have worn Nike.

● Product placing. This involves a firm paying for product brands to be placed on the sets of films and TV programmes. Car manufacturers are often eager to see their vehicles driven by Hollywood stars in popular movies.

● Free offers. A free 'gift' may be given with the product. An example of might be music magazines, which regularly offer readers free CDs of featured artists.

● Special credit terms. This has been increasingly used by firms. It includes offers such as interest free credit and 'buy now pay later' schemes.

Why have these methods become popular?

● Sales promotions can be used as a method to break into a new market or introduce a new product into an existing market. They can also be used as a means of extending the **product life cycle** of an existing product (☞ unit 17).

● They are a means of encouraging consumers to sample a good or service which they might not have bought otherwise. Once the initial good has been purchased it is likely that further goods will be bought. Many magazines offer free gifts ranging from CD Roms to make-up in their first issues hoping that their consumers will continue to buy.

● Customers feel 'rewarded' for their custom. They may, as a result, develop a loyalty to a particular product or business.

● Customers identify products or businesses with things that they like or are attracted to. A customer is therefore more likely to purchase a product.

● Sales promotions provide businesses with feedback on the impact of their marketing expenditure, for example, through the number of coupons returned or the amount spent on loyalty cards.

Sales promotions are not without problems. The free flight offer of Hoover in 1992 is one example. It offered two free flights to the US with the purchase of products worth over £200. The company misjudged the number of people taking advantage of the offer. This meant extreme pressure on the company to produce the goods consumers were demanding. Also many consumers did not receive the holidays on dates or at times they wished. By 1993 there were so many complaints that Maytag, Hoover's US parent company, had to intervene

---

Evidence of product placement abounds in Hollywood movies. In Charlie's Angels a mobile handset rings and the action cuts to a shot of a Nokia phone. In Mission Impossible 2 Tom Cruise can be seen donning a well known brand of sunglasses. In the last Austin Powers movie Mike Myers said 'Hey!Hey!Hey! Get your hands off my Hiney baby!' seconds before a bottle of Heineken beer appeared in the shot. The marketing agency involved in the Heineken placement estimated a sales increase of 15 per cent and greatly increased product recognition amongst 21 to 29 year olds.

Nearly all Hollywood studios today have a department devoted to product placement and it is part of the everyday business of making movies. In many cases cash does not change hands. Often a company such as mobile phone maker or an airline will agree to provide their good or service free in exchange for a prominent placement.

Source: adapted from news.bbc.co.uk/1/hi/entertainment.

(a) Identify the benefits of using product placement as a method of sales promotion from the article.
(b) What might be the disadvantages of this method of promotion?

to make sure flights or compensation were provided. It was estimated that the cost of dealing with these problems was £21.1 million.

Branding

A brand is a name, term, sign, symbol, design or any other feature that allows consumers to identify the goods and services of a business and to differentiate them from those of competitors. So a recognised brand might be a brand name such as Tesco or Virgin, a logo such as the Ellesse logo on sports wear or another feature such as the use of the colour orange in B&Q stores. The use of brands as a means of promotion is covered in detail in unit 20.

Merchandising

MERCHANDISING is an attempt to influence consumers at the POINT OF SALE. The point of sale is anywhere that a consumer buys a product. It may be, for example, a supermarket, a department store, a bank or a petrol station. Consumers are intended to buy based on 'what they see' rather than from a sales assistant. The aim of merchandising is to encourage sales of a product and therefore to speed up the rate at which stocks are turned over (☞ unit 57).

There is a number of different features of merchandising.

- Display material. A good display should attract attention, enhance certain aspects of a product and encourage the 'right frame of mind' to make a purchase. Department stores lay great stress on window displays. Banks make sure that the services which they offer, such as insurance and loan facilities, are well displayed in their branches.
- The layout of products at the point of sale. Many retail outlets, such as supermarkets, design the layout of their stores very carefully. Their aim is to encourage consumers to follow particular routes around a store. Retail outlets often place popular items at the back or sides of a store. Consumers, on their way to these, are encouraged to walk past other items which they might buy. Another tactic is to place related products next to each other, so consumers buy both.
- Stocks. A firm must make sure that stock levels are maintained and shelves are quickly restocked. Shelf space is usually allocated according to the amount of a product which a business expects to sell. For example, a supermarket will give more space to products on special offer.
- Appropriate lighting and the creation of desirable 'smells'. Generally lighting is kept soft where browsing is encouraged and bright where there is a need to suggest cleanliness as, for example, at a cosmetics counter. Smells are used to encourage the right atmosphere. Bread smells are often wafted into supermarkets and food retailers.

Packaging

A product's packaging is important in its overall marketing. This is because consumers often link the quality and design of a product's packaging with the quality of the product itself. Unsuitable packaging may affect sales.

What factors should firms consider when deciding upon how to package their product?

- Weight and shape. These can affect the cost of distributing a product. For example, bulky packaging may mean high distribution costs.
- Protection. Products must not be damaged in transit or in storage. They must also be protected against light, dust and heat.
- Convenience. The packaging must be easy to handle by the consumer and distributors.
- Design. The design of the packaging should be eye catching and help the consumer to distinguish it from others. It should also fit in with the overall marketing of the product and project the brand image. Colour is likely to be important here.
- Information. It is likely that the package will contain information required by the consumer. For technical products, the packaging will need to include information about how the product should be used. For food products, there are legal requirements about the information that must be on the package, such as details of the ingredients contained.
- Environmental factors. Manufacturers are facing increasing pressure to cut down on the amount and type of packaging placed around products. Consumers and pressure groups (☞ unit 70) stress the wastefulness of this and its impact upon the environment. The response of some manufacturers to this pressure has been to use recyclable materials.

Personal selling

Personal selling occurs when a company's sales team promotes a product through personal contact. This can be done over the

Domino's Pizza has 230 stores across the UK and Ireland and over 7,000 stores worldwide. It was the first pizza delivery company in the world to offer online pizza ordering. Dominoes is estimated to have a 20 per cent share of the UK pizza and delivery market.

Domino's heat wave delivery bags are specially designed to keep the pizzas oven-hot during delivery. They contain a patented disc that is preheated as well as being specially lined. The inner material of the bag is made of Thinsulate insulation, which eliminates unwanted moisture and keeps the pizza hot and crisp.

The pizza is contained in a corrugated pizza box. This design keeps moisture from weakening the box, while preventing cheese from sticking to the top during delivery. The packaging also shows the company's logo. It has been suggested that more than 80 per cent of the pizza's box is made from recycled paper.

Source: adapted from www.dominos.com and www.dominos.co.uk.

(a) What factors might be important to the business in deciding the packaging for its take-away pizzas?

Question 3

telephone, by setting up meetings, in retail outlets, or by 'knocking on doors'. In general, the more highly priced, technically complex or individual the product, the greater the need for personal selling. Most firms supplying industrial markets rely upon personal selling in the form of **sales representatives**.

The main advantage of personal selling over other methods is that individuals can be given personal attention. Most forms of promotion tend to deliver a 'standard message' to a 'typical' consumer. With personal selling the individual consumer's needs can be dealt with and the product shaped to meet these needs.

There are certain purposes which personal selling can serve.
- Creating awareness of and interest in a product.
- Explaining the functions and technical aspects of a product.
- Obtaining orders and, in some cases, making deliveries.
- Encouraging product trials and test marketing.
- Providing rapid and detailed feedback from the consumer to the producer via the sales representative.

One disadvantage with personal selling is that it can be expensive. The cost of maintaining a team of sales representatives can be very high. Another problem is the dislike of 'callers' by consumers. There are also legal and ethical issues about the way products are sold that need to be considered.

Public relations

PUBLIC RELATIONS is an organisation's attempt to communicate with groups that form its 'public'. Such groups may include the government, shareholders, employees and customers. The aim of such communications is to increase sales by improving the image of the firm and its products. This can be done directly by the business itself through a public relations activity. On the other hand a television programme or a newspaper could be used.

Consumers appear to attach great importance to messages conveyed through public relations. Take the example of a new restaurant which has just opened. It would expect to promote a positive image of itself through its own promotional materials. Such communications may, therefore, be taken 'with a pinch of salt' by consumers. However, a good write-up in a newspaper or restaurant guide is likely to be taken much more seriously by consumers.

Businesses often use **press conferences** to attract publicity. These might involve inviting journalists to a company presentation, where they are given information. The business may take the opportunity to launch a new or updated product. Sometimes, businesses provide free products for conference members to try out. Conferences may also be used for presentations to trade customers.

Businesses also make use of **press releases**. These are written accounts of events or activities which may be considered newsworthy. For example, new multi-million pound contracts gained by firms such as British Aerospace are announced on TV news bulletins. Such news stories usually originate from press releases issued by businesses themselves.

Because of the importance of maintaining good relations with the media, a business may appoint a **publicity manager**. As well as promoting favourable press stories, publicity managers must respond to criticisms and try to ensure that there are no unfavourable press notices.

Other than conferences what other public relations activities may firms use?
- Donations to charities etc. These can range from a small contribution to a college mini bus appeal to a large

Virgin is a company noted for its effective marketing. In November 2003, Virgin Blue, the group's budget airline announced the details of its share flotation. Sir Richard Branson said at a press conference in Brisbane 'We believe the future is bright for Virgin Blue and, as such, we plan to maintain a significant stake in Virgin Blue as part of our global airline strategy'.

In 2004 the Virgin website contained the following press release.

'VIRGIN MOBILE BACKS YOUNG DRIVING TALENT WITH SPONSORSHIP OF BRITISH FORMULA BMW TEAM'
Virgin Mobile, the UK's fastest growing mobile network, is delighted to confirm its sponsorship of the British Formula BMW team set up by Barwell Motorsport, in a bid to establish one of the most high-profile young driver support schemes in British motorsport – The Virgin Mobile Scholarship.'

Source: adapted from www.virgin.com and www.smh.com.au.

E-top up time!

Love Pay As You Go, but sick of messing around with vouchers? Then we may have the answer to your prayers!

It's called E-top up!

(a) Identify the promotional methods used by the Virgin Group in the article.
(b) Explain how such methods might benefit the business.

Question 4

donation to Comic Relief's 'Red Nose Day' or the 'Children in Need' appeal . Whilst some make payments anonymously, others take advantage of the opportunity for a good public relations event. The approach of a firm to such an event is likely to be determined by its particular ethical stance (☞ unit 70).

● Sponsorship. This is popular in the sporting world. Examples have included the links between Coca-Cola and the Olympic Games, McDonald's and the World Cup, and Nike and Tiger Woods. Other types of sponsorship take place in the arts world with ballet, opera and theatre being sponsored by businesses. Firms such as ICI and BP choose to sponsor educational programmes.

● Company visits. Jaguar Cars and Warburtons Bakeries have allowed members of the public to visit their manufacturing and research plants as part of their public relations activities.

key terms

Merchandising – a promotion specifically at the point of sale of a product.
Point of sale promotion - a promotion at any point where a consumer buys a product.
Public relations - an organisation's attempts to communicate with interested parties.

Knowledge

1. What is below the line promotion?
2. What is direct mailing?
3. Why do businesses promote their products at trade fairs and exhibitions?
4. Identify 4 different types of sales promotions.
5. Where is merchandising likely to take place?
6. Which aspects of their merchandising should businesses pay attention to?
7. What factors do businesses need to consider when packaging their products?
8. What is the main advantage of personal selling?
9. What is public relations?
10. Under what circumstances might public relations activities be most effective?

Case study *The Card Up Their Sleeve*

According to market researchers, around 85 per cent of households have at least one loyalty card. The use of loyalty cards began in the British supermarket retail market, one of the most competitive in the world. Merlin Stone, business researcher for IBM, states 'Grocery retailing in the UK is a classic oligopoly with the top three or four firms accounting for 60 per cent of the market'. In such a fierce climate there's a constant search for smart weapons to gain an edge.

The loyalty scheme began with the Tesco Clubcard in 1995. One year later Clubcard holders were spending 28 per cent more at Tesco and 16 per cent less at Sainsbury's. Sainsbury's retaliated with the Reward card and other retailers including Boots and WH Smiths developed similar schemes. In September 2002 a new 'consortium' loyalty card - Nectar - was introduced, with members including Sainsbury's, BP, Debenhams and Barclaycard. By February 2004, with the help of a £50 million advertising campaign, Nectar had 11 million UK households signed up.

There is no catch or con to loyalty reward schemes. Tesco gives customers a point worth a penny for every pound spent. Card holders receive Clubcard vouchers which they can spend instore or redeem against special offers such as hotel tokens or free bowling or cinema tickets. Boots gives the most generous rates - 4 points (worth 4p) per pound spent and the Boots Advantage card now has 15 million members. Running such schemes will cost the companies substantial sums. So where is their return?

Retailers who launch loyalty schemes experience between 1 and 4 per cent increase in sales. But in addition to the increased sales, the cards have given retailers ways of analysing their shoppers. Every swipe of the card sends customer spending information into a databank profile of their purchase history, along with the information customers give when they sign up for the card. This allows retailers to find out about the customers' habits, lifestyle and preferences. For example a mother or father of teenage children may spend up to £150 per week in a supermarket. The retailer will analyse this expenditure for a period of months and identify those areas where the family could be tempted to increase their purchases. The family may only buy one type of cereal and so the retailer might give an incentive of extra loyalty points on a different, but high-profit, cereal. Tesco, for example, sends loyalty letters with special offers to 10 million Clubcard homes four times a year.

A proportion of shoppers do not want to play the loyalty game. For them, a more important consideration in deciding where to shop is price. Asda, which does not run a loyalty scheme, has just come top of the *Grocer* magazine's Lowest Priced Shopping Basket for the sixth year running. In 2003 the store's market share rose from 15.5 per cent to 16.3 per cent and was challenging hard for the number two slot in the supermarket pecking order.

Source: adapted from *The Guardian*, 19.7.2003.

(a) **Why were loyalty cards were first introduced into the grocery retail sector in the UK? (6 marks)**

(c) **Explain why Sainsbury's, BP, Debenhams and Barclaycard might have launched a 'consortium' loyalty card. (6 marks)**

(d) **Analyse how loyalty cards would help retailers like Tesco to improve the impact of their other sales promotion methods. (8 marks)**

(d) **Assess the benefits and costs of loyalty card schemes for:**
   (i) **consumers:**
   (ii) **retailers. (10 marks)**

(e) **Evaluate Asda's decision not to introduce a loyalty card. (10 marks)**

23 Place - Distributing the Product

Channels of distribution

Distribution is about one of the 4 'Ps' of the marketing mix (☞ unit 16) - place. A business must get the product to the right place, at the right time. A product which is effectively priced and promoted may not be a success unless the consumer is able to purchase it easily.

A CHANNEL OF DISTRIBUTION is the route taken by a product as it passes from the producer to the consumer. Figure 23.1 shows some of the most popular channels of distribution that are open to a business. A producer can sell its products:

- directly to the consumer (channel 1);
- through a retail outlet (channels 2, 4, 6, 7);
- through a wholesaler (channels 3, 4, 7);
- using an agent (channels 5, 6, 7).

Sometimes the channel of distribution can be straightforward. Take the example of a village bakery. The bread and cakes are baked in the same place as they are sold. Consumers buy direct from the producer (channel 1 in Figure 23.1). Other examples include the sale of 'home' produced local computer software, the sale of farm products 'on site', or the sale of music or data which is downloaded from the Internet.

However, some businesses manufacture their goods and provide their services from large, central units in order to benefit from **economies of scale** (☞ unit 56). Their consumers may be located over a wide geographical area. Having a distribution channel similar to that of the village baker could mean disaster. It is likely, in this case, that more complex methods of distributing the product are needed. This may involve the use of INTERMEDIARIES - wholesalers, retailers or agents.

Intermediaries

What intermediaries are involved in the distribution of products?

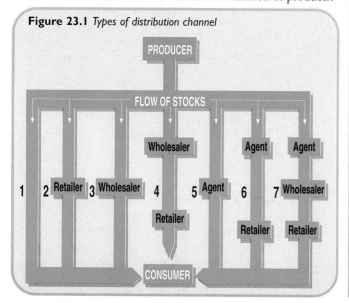
Figure 23.1 *Types of distribution channel*

Wholesalers These often act as links between producers and retailers. Their main task is to buy in bulk from manufacturers and to break this down into smaller quantities which can then be handled by retailers. Examples in the UK include Makro and Costco. Channel 4 in Figure 23.1 has traditionally been the most common method of distribution because of the benefits for the businesses involved. Wholesalers can benefit **manufacturers** in a number of ways.

- They have well established distribution networks and are likely to have strong links with retailers.
- By breaking the manufacturers' products down into smaller batches and taking care of distribution problems, they free the manufacturer to concentrate upon production.
- For multi-product firms, they can help to solve distribution problems, especially when wide geographical areas are involved. Figure 23.2 shows how wholesalers are able to help a firm producing six products distributed over a wide area. By using a wholesaler, the manufacturer is able to deliver all six products to one site. Imagine the difficulties if the manufacturer had to deliver every one of the products to each of the retailers.
- They can bear the cost of storage or warehousing.
- They provide a source of market research information, for example, by asking retailers how their stock is selling in different areas.

Wholesalers also help **retailers**. They offer a choice of products from a variety of manufacturers and provide a 'local' service, often delivering products. Wholesalers sometimes sell direct to the public (channel 3). An example might be a kitchenware wholesaler holding a one week sale for members of the public in order to clear out old stock.

Despite the benefits wholesalers offer, they are not without their problems. Some wholesalers may not promote the products as a business might want, which might harm the firm's marketing efforts. By using a wholesaler the business is passing on the responsibility for marketing - possibly a risky venture. The wholesaler is also likely to take some of the profit.

Retailers Because of the problems of wholesalers, a number of manufacturers prefer to deal with retailers directly, by setting up their own distribution networks. Many of the larger retail outlets, such as Sainsbury's and Marks & Spencer, have dealt directly with the manufacturer. This is shown as channel 2 in Figure 23.1. Retailers are an important part of distribution, particularly to manufacturers selling to consumer markets. Retailing is dealt with in more detail later in this unit.

Agents and brokers The usual role of agents is to negotiate sales on behalf of a seller. A ticket agency, for example, will sell tickets to consumers for a range of events, such as concerts and plays. The ticket agency does not usually take

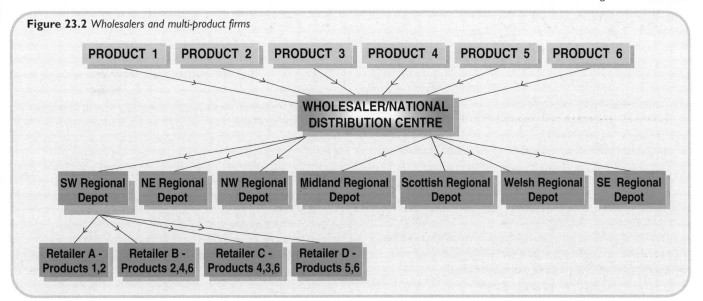

Figure 23.2 *Wholesalers and multi-product firms*

ownership of the tickets it offers. Instead it takes a **commission** (☞ unit 42) on those which it does sell and returns the rest.

Most travel agencies operate in this way. They earn commission on those holidays which they sell, but never actually buy 'blocks' of holidays. The agents are the link between those providing a good or service and those wishing to buy them (channel 5 in Figure 23.1).

Agents are often used by firms wishing to break into a foreign market. They are helpful to businesses which are unsure about the trading practices and legal requirements in foreign countries. They help to take the risk out of trading abroad. People and organisations which are involved in the buying and selling of commodities, such as copper, tin, coffee or sugar, in international markets are known as brokers. After being bought these commodities are broken down and sold on to firms for processing or to be used in manufacturing.

The choice of distribution channel

How does a producer decide which channel of distribution will get the product to the right place at the right time? An efficient channel of distribution will allow a business to make products available to consumers quickly, when required, and at a minimum distribution cost to the firm itself. Large firms often choose different channels for different products.

There are many factors that can influence a business's decision.

The product The nature of the product itself will influence the type of distribution channel chosen.

● Perishable or fragile goods, such as fresh fruit, require direct channels of distribution, so that the time spent handling the product is reduced.
● Technically complex goods also need a direct link between the producer and the consumer. This is so that any problems which arise from installation or use can be

quickly dealt with, without the need to go through an intermediary. Firms installing computers operate in this way to maintain close links with consumers.
● Goods or services which are tailor made tend to have more direct channels, so that the consumer's needs can be passed

Many supermarkets now sell organic and wholefood products grown by farmers. Such competition has made it increasingly difficult for independent health food shops. But rather than simply stoking up at the next supermarket visit, consumers are now clubbing together, forming buying groups to make even bigger savings buying direct from wholefood wholesalers. Priya Hallam, a member of a buying group in Ashbourne, Derbyshire, said 'Some friends told us how much they were saving each year. By cross referencing the items we always brought with the equivalent from our local wholesaler, we worked out we would save over a thousand pounds a year. That's before the cost of petrol to travel to our local Sainsbury's.'

Forming a buying group, for those living in remote rural areas, may be the only way to get products to the door. Highland Wholefoods in Scotland, for example, serves many groups who live miles from a suitable wholefood retailer.

The motivation for setting up buying groups varies. Saving time and money is the main reason, with wholesale prices being around 25 per cent cheaper on organic items. But Tess Rigby who runs the Ashbourne buying group says 'It's helped me to become vegan, because I no longer have to drive round lots of different shops to get what I want.'

Source: adapted from *The Observer*, 10.8.2003.

(a) Describe how the channels of distribution have changed in the article.
(b) Explain the possible (i) benefits and (ii) problems for customers of the new channel of distribution.

Question **1**

to the producer.

● Goods which are heavy or are packaged in non-standard shapes are likely to require a direct channel of distribution. If handling is difficult, the cost of distribution is likely to be high. A producer will want to minimise the charges for the handling of such products.

● Convenience goods, such as canned drinks and food, need to be widely available through retailers. Firms that are unwilling to sell to a wide range of retailers are likely to find rival brands on shop shelves.

● Producers wishing to sell large quantities of low valued goods are likely to use a wholesaler. They will not want to keep stocks of low valued goods if they are receiving orders for more highly priced goods. Selling through wholesalers will mean they can sell low valued products in bulk, as quickly as possible.

● Products that do not require physical delivery, such as data or other forms of computer file, can use direct methods. However, they might also be available through intermediaries such as retailers for those without the technology to use the Internet in this way.

The market

● Large and dispersed markets may require intermediaries. Smaller, local markets can often use a system where consumers buy directly. This is also true of the size of an order, where smaller orders can be sent by a more direct channel of distribution.

● The market segment (☞ unit 13) at which the product is aimed may influence the retail outlet at which the product is made available. For example, products aimed at travelling business people may be sold near to railway stations. Consumer goods are often sold via a retailer or directly to the consumer, whereas industrial products may pass through an agent or wholesaler. International sales may also need to be made through an agent.

● The time period within which consumers expect a response to orders is sometimes an influence. A business may be forced to find the most direct means of distribution or lose an urgent order to a rival.

Legal restrictions Legislation may influence the channel that can be used for particular products. Certain drugs, for example, can only be sold by pharmacists through a prescription. Only those with special gaming licences are able to operate casinos.

The company Larger companies are often able to set up their own distribution networks. They have the resources to set up warehouses, build and operate distribution sites and purchase transport. They are also often able to take advantage of **economies of scale** (☞ unit 56). For example, a large firm may be able to purchase a fleet of lorries. Manufacturers may open up their own retail outlets, but this will only be effective if the value of the product is high, a wide range of goods or services are sold or large quantities are sold. An alternative is for a

producer to develop links with retailers.

Smaller firms are far less likely to be able to set up their own distribution system. They would tend to use intermediaries, such as wholesalers.

KFM Ltd manufactures interactive whiteboard software. Increasingly, interactive whiteboards are being used in education for teaching and in business for conferences and presentations. KFM started as a small operation selling direct to customers from an industrial estate in Milton Keynes. It would place adverts in specialist magazines and often tailor products to the specific needs of customers.

Recently the business has expanded and now wants to sell more standardised products in greater quantities. KFM has been approached by a retail chain which wants to stock its product range in stores under the 'business and education' section. The retailer feels that the growing market in interactive whiteboards means that more customers will be looking for this type of software. KFM has also been looking to expand in the USA. It is interested in adapting its products for the US market. However, it is aware that legislation might affect its product specification and also that it lacks knowledge about the US market. It has considered a number of alternatives - using an agent to find a retail chain to stock the products, selling to a warehouse business or licensing the product to a US manufacturer.

(a) Examine the factors that might affect KFM's channel of distribution:
   (i)   as a small operation;
   (ii) as it expands in the UK;
   (iii) as it expands abroad.
(b) Which channel of distribution would you advise KFM to use? Explain your answer.

Physical distribution

Physical distribution is the movement of products from one place to another. It is an important part of the marketing process for two main reasons.

● Failure to deliver a product in the right quantities, at the right place and at the right time can damage an effective marketing effort.

● The cost of physical distribution can be high - in some cases higher than the cost of actually producing the product.

Two aspects of physical distribution are important to a business - holding stocks and transporting products.

Holding stocks Ideally a business would be able to guarantee every customer the product they wanted, whenever they wanted it. To do this a firm would have to hold huge amounts of stock. Holding excessive amounts of stock is very costly. Holding very low stock levels, however, could mean turning down orders.

The solution is for a business to assess the level of stocks needed to maintain an agreed level of customer service. This often means holding enough stock to satisfy regular orders, but not enough to deal with sudden changes in demand. This will depend on the market in which the product is selling.

Transporting products This is concerned with how goods can be physically delivered to markets. Firms need to consider the relative costs and speed of transporting their goods by road, rail, sea or air. For example, aeroplanes are faster than ships when transporting exports from the UK. However, firms must decide whether this advantage outweighs the costs which result from using this mode of transport. There are times when the nature of a product dictates the transport. For example, an Orkney Islands based firm which sells freshly caught lobsters to Paris restaurants has little choice but to fly this product to France.

When transporting goods, firms must also consider possible damage to or deterioration of goods. Packaging may help to reduce damage and deterioration, for example, if vacuum packs are used.

Retailing

Retailers are responsible for the sale of products to the final consumer. It is unlikely that products bought by a consumer from a retailer will be sold again, in the way that wholesalers distribute to many different retailers. Second hand exchanges are perhaps the only exception to this.

Retailers have a major role to play in the distribution of most products. This is because they have the ability to reach huge numbers of consumers, in different markets, over a wide area. Retailers, therefore, can influence manufacturers, insisting on high standards of product quality and delivery times.

Marks & Spencer, for example, is particularly concerned about the quality of products supplied to it. It has an advantage over some retailers because the products which it stocks are OWN BRANDS (☞ unit 20) and because of its size and influence in the retail sector. Smaller retailers may have little influence over manufacturers. This is because the success of such retailers in attracting customers is often dependent upon whether or not they stock brands which are currently in demand.

Retailers can be grouped according to their characteristics.

Multiple shop organisations These are businesses with perhaps ten or more establishments, or a group of specialist shops dealing in a particular group of products. Examples include Oddbins, the wine merchants, and Carphone Warehouse, the mobile phone retailer. For consumers, multiple shops have two benefits. They usually offer a wide choice of products in their specialist area. Also, they have often developed an established image, so consumers will be familiar with the level of service, value for money and quality which they can expect.

Supermarkets These sell mainly foodstuffs in premises with a minimum of 400 square metres of floor space. Many buy direct from manufacturers rather than through wholesalers and sell products which are fast moving, ie with a short SHELF LIFE, in large volumes. The majority of supermarkets are part of chains, such as Sainsbury's, Tesco, and Asda. There is an growing trend for supermarkets to provide 'own-brand' goods. There has also been a growth of supermarkets stressing lower prices and selling less well known brands. Examples include Aldi and Netto.

Superstores or hypermarkets These are huge stores which tend to be found on the outskirts of towns and cities. Their advantage is the ability to offer a range of products under one roof. Many of the multiple organisations mentioned above now have superstores in out of town locations. Examples include PC World, Comet and Marks & Spencer.

Department stores Large department stores are found in some city centres, selling a vast variety of different goods on many floors. Famous department stores include Harrods in London and Macy's in New York. Business such as Debenhams and Selfridges also run department stores. They tend to sell more highly priced and luxury goods. However, the high cost of running such stores has forced their closure some cases. Increasingly there is a trend for some stores to towards lease or rent space within the store to businesses selling branded goods (☞ unit 20), such as clothing.

Retail co-operatives Retail co-operatives (☞ unit 6) differ from other types of retail organisation in terms of their ownership and the way in which profits are distributed. They are owned by 'members' rather than shareholders and profits are distributed to customers in the form of a dividend rather than being given to shareholders. Retail co-operatives have faced extreme competition from large superstores and hypermarkets. They have attempted to compete by setting up their own superstores and concentrating on convenience stores with late night opening hours, geared to the needs of the local community. Parts of the Co-operative organisation, such as the travel business and the funeral service operation, continue to thrive.

Independent retailers The smaller local shop, often owned by a sole trader, is still important for selling many types of products, eg newspapers and tobacco. These rely heavily on the supply of nationally known or branded goods through a wholesaler or a manufacturer's agent. Groups of independent retailers might also join together in order to benefit from the bulk purchasing of stock or joint advertising. These are sometimes known as **voluntary chains**. They are an attempt by independent retailers to match the strengths of large chains.

Direct marketing

DIRECT MARKETING is sometimes thought to be the same

as direct mailing (☞ unit 22). In fact, direct mailing is just one type of direct marketing. Direct marketing occurs when sales are made without intermediaries being involved. For consumers, this means being able to make purchases from their own homes.

Direct marketing is perhaps the fastest growing means of distribution and is expected to continue into the future. There is a number of reasons for this. Changing work patterns and technology mean that many now find it easier to shop from home. The increased range of products available, and their specialised nature, mean that certain products cannot be purchased from 'usual' outlets such as shops. Also, the increased use of credit cards makes buying in this way easy and direct.

Direct marketing also has advantages for firms. There are no intermediaries to take part of the profits. The producer is able to control its own marketing and also has a chance to reach consumers, who might not otherwise have bought from shops.

Direct marketing can be achieved through a variety of methods.

The Internet Shopping via the Internet is rapidly increasing in popularity as more people have a computer at home and make use of fast broadband connection. Customers are often able to search for company websites, browse the products available and their prices, and then place the order online. They are often able to pay with their credit card by entering financial details onto a website order form, which is then processed. Depending on the products for sale, the customer will either:
● have products delivered to their home after the order is processed;
● be allowed to download products such as information or music to their computer;
● be allowed access to information on screen on a website.
  Using the Internet for shopping has major advantages for both customers and businesses.
● Orders can be placed at any time that customers have access to the computer, at any time of day or night.
● Customers do not have to travel. They can view a large range of products from their computer and pay for them online.
● It is possible to buy products from other countries and use services such as 'PayPal' to pay in other currencies.
  However, not all people have access to, or knowledge about, the Internet. Orders might experience technical problems and people can not test or handle the products in a similar way to viewing in a catalogue. Also, people may resent the spam (junk mail on computer) that often results from buying online.

Direct mail This involves posting promotional materials to homes and workplaces. Consumers then place an order and products are sent to the buyer's address. At present, the average British adult receives five items of direct mail each month. This is just half the average in Europe, and one-tenth of what floods through the average US letterbox.

There is a number of benefits of direct mail for businesses and consumers.
● Personalised communications with the potential purchaser's name on a letter can improve sales.
● Groups of consumers or **market segments** can be targeted.
● Detailed information can be provided.
● Groups of consumers who are widely dispersed can easily be reached.
  Despite its benefits, it is unpopular in some quarters and also suffers from a number of disadvantages.
● Consumers do not like the personalised nature of direct mail and the amount sent to their home address.
● The databases with potential consumers' names and addresses on them quickly go out of date, so that a large amount of mail goes to the wrong people.
● It is felt to be a 'waste of paper' which uses up a valuable resource - wood.
  For many businesses, such as Readers Digest, direct mailing has been very successful. In addition, many charities such as Oxfam and Greenpeace are able to raise large sums in this way.

Direct response advertisements These are advertisements placed in newspapers and magazines, and on the TV and

---

In 2000 Great Universal Stores (GUS), the UK's biggest home shopping group, cut 800 jobs when it merged its struggling mail order business with the Argos catalogue shop to try to reverse falling profits. GUS faced a 5.7 per cent drop in annual pre-tax profit to £379.6 million. The biggest fall occurred in the British mail order business, where pre-tax profit fell by £85 million to £21 million.

The company argued that a substantial fall in clothing sales at its mail order business, with catalogues such as Kays and Great Universal, was caused by competition from discount retailers. The merged business was expected to save costs of £80 million over a three year period, partly by combining buying and delivery systems. GUS's chief executive said 'We think we can lower the risk by combining it with Argos.'

Argos's pre-tax profits rose from £117 million to £137.4 million. In the present financial year the company said Argos reported sales growth of 18 per cent in April and May. UK mail order sales dropped 7 per cent in the same months because of a continued lack of demand for clothing. The company announced a rollout of its Argos Additions catalogue at all its stores by 2001 and believed it could become a business worth £300 million.

Source: adapted from *The Guardian*, 9.6.2000.

(a) What examples of direct marketing and retailing are suggested in the article?
(b) Contrast the advantages of these types of distribution from the consumers point of view.

Question 3

The music industry faces a huge task in combating illegal downloading of music from the Internet. Record companies have long argued that 'free' downloading or sharing music, which the customer does not pay for, has reduced record sales. However, a study by Harvard and the University of North Carolina suggests that file-sharing may help music sales. It concluded that file-sharing had no effect on the sale of popular CDs in the second half of 2002. It even suggested that for the top 25 albums, with sales of more than 600,000 copies, there was a positive effect - 150 downloads were said to increase sales by one copy.

People are prepared to pay for downloading music. Napster is the former illegal online download site which now sells legal downloads paid for by customers. Its figures show that the biggest purchasers of downloads to burn on to CDs via its on-demand service are the same people who pay $10 a month to listen to as much music as they like via its streaming service.

Some feel that the music industry should turn the current challenges facing it to its advantage. Paul Myers, CEO at Wippit which has signed deals to distribute music from EMI, believes the music business should be thinking long term and says 'This message would be much more powerful if it was also backed up by a campaign encouraging legal downloads. A TV commercial for the new Outkast CD or a personal message to a P2P user could contain the message "If you're going to download it, download it legally from Wippit".'

People outside the US are also showing interest in legal downloads. This is backed by figures from Peter Gabriel's OD2, Europe's largest digital music distribution service. It showed that over a million digital downloads were bought via its retail partners across Europe. This bodes well for the arrival of Apple's iTunes and the new Napster in the UK.

How long will the music industry still be about selling CDs? 'Five years from now we'll still be selling CDs, but I think a substantial part of our business will be digital sales' said one commentator.

Source: adapted from *The Guardian*, 5.4. 2004.

(a) Describe how music is sold to customers using examples from the article.
(b) Examine the factors that might affect the distribution and sales of music.
(c) Discuss whether 'Five years from now we'll still be selling CDs, but a substantial part of the business will be digital sales'.

Question 4

radio. Consumers are encouraged to fill in a coupon or make a telephone call in order to purchase a product. There should be enough information in the advertisement to allow people to make a decision.

Direct response broadcasting is the selling of products through TV commercials, often in late night slots. Records, CDs and telephones have been sold in this way. There are now TV channels devoted entirely to direct response advertising, such as QVC on Sky Television. The introduction of digital television has increased this type of marketing. Consumers with digital television are linked to a telephone line which allows interactive television and the direct ordering of products.

Personal selling This can be a useful form of direct marketing. It is dealt with in unit 22.

Telephone selling This involves ringing people up at their home or workplace and trying to sell a good or service. The advantage is that the seller can deal personally with a consumer. However, it is felt to be intrusive by many consumers. It has often been used as a means of marketing financial services, such as insurance, and advertising space on products such as calendars.

Mail order catalogues This involves a range of products being included in a catalogue which people can read through at home. Orders can usually be placed by telephone or in writing. It has been seen recently as an outdated means of marketing, but innovations such as the Next Directory with 24 hour delivery have breathed new life into it.

Trends in retailing and direct marketing

Retailing is a fast changing sector of the UK economy. Today's retail scene is very different from that which existed 30 years ago. Changes in direct marketing have also greatly affected the way in which goods and services are purchased by customers. What are the changes that have taken place?

Shopping centres A number of American-type shopping 'malls' have been built in the UK. These include the MetroCentre in Gateshead, The Mall near Bristol and the Trafford Centre in Manchester. They contain a wide range of retail outlets, cafes and restaurants and other services, such as theatre booking. They are designed to provide all the shopping facilities that customers need in one place. They promote shopping as a leisure activity and a 'day out for the family'. They are often found away from city areas because of their size.

Retail parks There has been a growth of out-of-town retail 'parks', such as Kinnaird Park near Edinburgh and Fosse Park South near Leicester. They are usually sited on the edges of urban developments as a result of a lack of building land and relatively high rents in city and town areas. Retail parks often contain superstores of high street chains, supermarkets or hypermarkets and restaurant chains. The extent to which they will benefit customers depends on a variety of factors. Those able to travel may benefit from a wider choice of products in a particular superstore. Another benefit is the ease of parking. However, if there is a limited number of retailers, customers may be unable to compare prices as they might in the 'high street' or city centre. Those without transport may face increased prices at local shops as retailers attempt to cover their costs. Retail parks are sometimes criticised for leading to traffic congestion and also for a decline in town centre retailing.

Call centres These are usually large offices with staff sitting at telephones who deal with customers. They are mainly used to sell insurance, airline tickets and hotel rooms. They also act as information centres for providers of rail or telephone services. In 1998 there were 3,500 call centres in the UK employing 400,000 people. However, after the year 2000 there was an increasing trend for businesses, such as BT, to site their call centres in low labour cost countries such as India.

Changes in technology Many developments in retailing have resulted from new technology. For example, bar codes on products are a common feature in most retail outlets. They recognise the cost of products, allowing them to be quickly totalled. Some supermarkets have facilities for customers to 'read' prices as they shop around the supermarket, which saves time at checkouts. Increasingly electronic point of sale (Epos) data is used to gauge consumer tastes, so that trends can be identified and particular groups targeted. Tesco, for example, has used the information from loyalty cards to select wine buyers for 'cheese and wine tasting evenings'. Bar codes can also be used to update stock levels. Many retailers use in-store cameras to record when and where consumers are tempted to pause and consider whether to buy a product. Cameras are also used for in-store security.

The growth of 'online shopping' As explained earlier, there is an increasing trend for online shopping via websites on the Internet. Many businesses, including supermarkets such as Tesco, have their own sites. Barnes and Noble has fought with Amazon to be the world's largest bookseller by expanding its sales online.

Discount stores Discount stores are chains of shops under one name which specialise in selling cheaper products. They are often aimed at customers looking for value for money. However, many customers may find a particular product sold cheaper than in other retail chains. They also encourage impulse buying, as people are motivated to buy a product at a low price which otherwise they might not have bought. Examples of discount chains include The Works, which specialises in stationery and books, and Poundland, which sells products for £1.

Variable opening hours There has been a growing trend for longer opening hours to fit in with patterns of work and leisure. Some 'convenience stores' attract customers by staying open until 11pm at night. Flexible opening hours were previously an advantage of small businesses. However, some supermarkets also remain open until late on certain days and others have all night shopping. Increasingly, city centre retailers are opening on Sunday.

Diversifying Increasingly retailers are offering a wider variety of products and services. The traditional products for sale at one type of retailer are changing as they are faced with growing competition. Many garages, for example, now sell food and magazines. Some even offer microwave cooking facilities. Financial services are also becoming available in places where they were unlikely to be sold previously. Pensions are available from Marks & Spencer and some supermarkets offer banking facilities and pharmacies. Supermarkets are also diversifying by selling non-food products such as clothing and electrical goods.

The relative decline of independents In the last 50 years the number of independent grocers in the UK has been cut by over two-thirds. This has largely been due to the increasing growth of supermarket and hypermarket chains selling food.

Reductions in costs Businesses have increasingly been looking for ways to reduce distribution costs. This has led to businesses wishing to supply in larger quantities to retailers in order to achieve economies of scale (☞ unit 56). Retailers can also benefit from lower costs by buying in bulk. The larger retail chains are in a stronger position to do this. This has, to some extent, accounted for the decline in the independent retailer. Remaining open for longer hours may also reduce a business's average total costs (☞ unit 27). This is because the fixed costs of the business, such as the retail outlet, are being spread over a greater output. Even though variable costs may increase, average total costs may fall.

Second hand shops There have been second hand shops in the UK for many years, including second hand car dealerships. Charity shop chains, such as Age Concern and Scope, have gained a high profile in town centres in certain parts of the UK. It is likely, however, that this will always be a small part of the total retail market.

Knowledge...Knowledge...Knowled

1. Why is distribution so important to a firm's marketing mix?
2. What is a channel of distribution?
3. List the 5 types of organisation which can be involved in a channel of distribution.
4. What is the main role of an intermediary?
5. Explain the difference between a wholesaler and a retailer.
6. Why do manufacturers use wholesalers?
7. What is the difference between an agent and a broker?
8. What factors might influence the choice of distribution channel?
9. What is the difference between direct mailing and direct marketing?
10. Why might a business be reluctant to use direct mailing?
11. Explain 4 trends in retailing and their effect on business.

key terms

Channel of distribution - the route taken by a product as it passes from producer to consumer.
Direct marketing - a method of distributing products directly to consumers, without the use of intermediaries such as wholesalers and retailers.
Intermediaries - firms which act as a link between producers and consumers in a channel of distribution.
Own brands - products which have the brand name of their retailer on them.
Shelf life - the average length of time it takes for a product to be sold, once it has been displayed by a retailer.

Case study Tesco

When it comes to shopping, Tesco is one of the most well know names in the UK. In 2003 it had group sales of £28,613 million, an 11.5 per cent increase over the previous year. Its pre-tax profits were £1,361 million, up by 13.3 per cent. Table 23.1 shows the number of stores the business has in a variety of countries and its potential new stores in future.

Table 23.1 *Tesco stores*

Number of stores	Sales area	New stores opened inc. acquisitions in 2002/03	Planned openings in 2003/04	Country
1,982	21.8m sq ft	1,265	59	United Kingdom
77	1.7m sq ft	1	6	Republic of Ireland
53	2.5m sq ft	5	5	Hungary
66	3.4m sq ft	20	5	Poland
17	1.6m sq ft	2	4	Czech Republic
17	1.4m sq ft	4	4	Slovakia
52	4.8m sq ft	17	6	Thailand
21	2.1m sq ft	7	8	South Korea
3	0.3m sq ft	1	1	Taiwan
3	0.3m sq ft	3	1	Malaysia
2,291	39.9m sq ft	1,325	99	

'Our strategy of building a profitable international business of scale, both in Europe and Asia continues to make excellent progress. In a six-year period we have built up a substantial chain of hypermarkets. Our overseas operation now accounts for almost half of Group space.'

Source: adapted from Tesco plc, *Annual Review and Summary Financial Statement, 2003*, Financial highlights, Our markets, Chief Executive's review.

Innovation is part of our every day job for customers. This year we have introduced over 5,000 new food products, increased our Finest brand to nearly 1,100 products and introduced 500 Grab & Go counters in our stores.

Source: adapted from Tesco PLC, *Annual Review and Summary Financial Statement, 2003*, Chief Executive's review.

Tesco.com is the largest e-grocer and most profitable e-retail business in the world. This year our turnover reached £447 million. Each week in the UK we deliver over 110,000 orders. We have 65 per cent share of the UK internet grocery market.

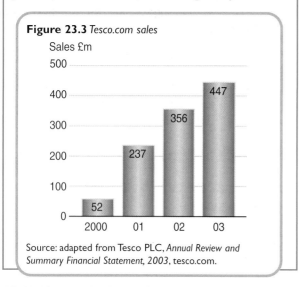

Figure 23.3 *Tesco.com sales*

Sales £m

2000: 52
01: 237
02: 356
03: 447

Source: adapted from Tesco PLC, *Annual Review and Summary Financial Statement, 2003*, tesco.com.

We acquired T&S Stores, a leading convenience retailer. This acquisition increases our share of the convenience market from one to five per cent. We will convert 450 T&S stores to our Express format over the next three to four years bringing the Tesco range and offer to many more customers in neighbourhood locations.

Source: adapted from Tesco PLC, *Annual Review and Summary Financial Statement, 2003*, Chief Executive's review.

Half our new space in the UK this year has been for non-food. This, along with improved capability has seen our non-food market share grow to 5 per cent. This year we have achieved a 16 per cent share of chart music sales, introduced our Finest brand to non-food, and extended the Value brand. We have gained share on Health and Beauty extending our volume market leading position. Cherokee, our exclusive clothing range is available in over 300 stores. Cherokee, Florence & Fred and the Value clothing brands have gone from strength to strength.

Source: adapted from Tesco PLC, *Annual Review and Summary Financial Statement, 2003*, Chief Executive's review.

In April 1997, Tesco and GXS developed the Trading Information Exchange (TIE). Via a web, suppliers can view daily electronic point-of-sale (EPOS) data. This allows them to respond more quickly to variations in customer demand and to ensure that optimum stock is available on Tesco shelves at all times. A spokesperson for Procter & Gamble, for example, reported that the system allowed it to spot that a product had sold 8,000 units in two days instead of the expected 10,000 a week. The stock of the product was instantly replenished, which avoided disappointing customers.

Source: adapted from www.gxs.com/downloads/cs_tesco2.

(a) **Describe the channel of distribution at Tesco using an example. (4 marks)**

(b) **What retail category might Tesco fall into? Explain your answer. (4 marks)**

(c) **Explain how Tesco is making use of:**
   (i) **new technology;**
   (ii) **direct marketing. (8 marks)**

(d) **Examine how the use of technology might affect:**
   (i) **Tesco;**
   (ii) **its suppliers**
   (iii) **customers. (12 marks)**

(e) **Assess the factors which may influence how Tesco operates in future. (12 marks)**

24 Marketing Planning

Marketing planning

To help make marketing decisions a business must plan effectively. MARKETING PLANNING is the process by which future marketing activities are systematically planned. Not all businesses have a marketing plan. Some smaller businesses, for example, may make marketing decisions on a short term basis or in response to changing conditions. However, we will see later that planning has a number of benefits for all businesses.

A business's MARKETING PLAN is influenced by the **strategic plans** of the business and the overall corporate aims. A large public limited company such as Unilever, Nestlé, Unigate or the Rank Group will have an overall plan for the business and the aims and objectives that it wishes to achieve. Companies within the business will then develop marketing plans for their businesses and for individual products which fit in with the overall strategic plan. For example, the Rank Group will have an overall corporate strategy. This will influence the plans of its divisions. Detailed marketing plans may be drawn up for Mecca Bingo outlets in its gaming division and its Hard Rock Cafe operations. A manufacturer such as Unilever will have corporate objectives, but detailed marketing plans will be drawn up by Liptons Teas, which is part of Unilever, and even for individual products such as Flora.

The marketing plan

The marketing plan is concerned with a number of questions.

Where is the business at present? A business can only plan where it is going if it knows where it is starting from. Finding out where a business is at the moment involves a **marketing audit**. This analyses the **internal** and **external** factors which affect a business's performance. Most businesses analyse their current position by using SWOT analysis (☞ unit 5), which identifies the business's strengths, weaknesses, opportunities and threats. Table 24.1 shows a possible SWOT analysis for a manufacturer of soft drinks. The business will have some control over internal factors. External factors are out of the control of a business. These include political, economic, social, technological and green (PEST-G) factors outlined later in this unit.

Where does the business wish to be in future? This involves the business setting **objectives** to be achieved. The objectives provide goals and targets for the business to aim at. They may include such goals as a growth in sales or gaining a certain market share in future.

Table 24.1 SWOT analysis of a soft drinks manufacturer

STRENGTHS (the strong points of the business)

- Current products are market leaders in some countries in terms of sales and market share.
- Brand loyalty to products and to the corporate identity.
- Effective promotion.
- Flexibility in production methods.
- Excellent distribution network.
- Constant R&D leading to new ideas.

WEAKNESSES (the problems it has at present)

- Age of the life cycle of certain products.
- Restricted product range could cause problems if sales suddenly fall.

OPPORTUNITIES (that may arise in future)

- Expansion into newer markets such as sports drinks, low calorie drinks and drinks with new flavours.
- Expansion into new geographical areas such as Eastern Europe.
- Development of a global brand and possible global marketing.
- Possible growing demand for soft beverages.
- Legislation on drink driving may encourage growth of soft drink sales.

THREATS (that may arise and should be avoided/prevented if possible)

- Growing competition from supermarket own brands.
- Increasing competition from competitors bringing out new products.
- Competition from alcoholic beverages and non-alcoholic beers and lagers.
- Legislation on ingredients could force changes in production.

How will a business achieve its objectives? A business must decide how to get where it wants to go. It will have **marketing strategies** (☞ unit 25) which it will use to achieve its objectives. For example, if it wishes to increase its market share at the expense of a market leader then it may use market challenger strategies. Marketing strategies can be expressed in terms of the marketing mix (☞ unit 16). So a company wishing to gain a 10 per cent increase in market share must make sure that it has the the right product, at the right price, with an effective promotion and distribution policy.

Factors influencing the market plan

A marketing audit should identify the internal and external factors which affect a business. There is a number of possible factors that may fall into each category.

Internal factors

- The marketing mix. Of great importance to the internal audit will be an examination of the effectiveness of the marketing mix. This will include an analysis of each element of the marketing mix. For example, projections regarding the life span and future profitability of each of the firm's products may be carried out. It should also include an analysis of how well the elements of the marketing mix fit together, for example, the extent to which distribution channels are compatible with the promotions may be considered.
- People. A huge range of people will be involved in devising and implementing marketing plans. The objectives of these people will determine the targets set in the plan. Also the skills and abilities of those people working for a firm will determine whether targets can be met.
- Finance. Firms can set themselves ambitious marketing goals. However, unless finance is available to fund plans, such goals are unlikely to be achieved.
- Production processes. Any marketing plan must take into account whether the firm can produce the product. There is little point in planning to increase market share unless enough of the product can be produced to achieve this. Similarly, a firm cannot plan to launch a new product if it cannot manufacture it.

External factors
An analysis of the external influences on a business usually involves a consideration of PEST-G factors. These are the political, economic, social, technological and environmental factors which affect a business's performance.

- Political. There is an increasing amount of legislation and regulation that may affect the marketing plans of a business. It can vary from controls on the ingredients of products to restrictions on price changes of the privatised utilities, such as water and gas. Much of the new legislation affecting the UK is from the European Union.
- Economic. A wide range of economic factors may affect a business's marketing plans. A buoyant economy, for example, may lead to increased demand for products, higher incomes and the possibility of price increases. Growing unemployment may lead to a fall in future levels of demand. Marketing plans should also take into account the pricing, promotion, distribution and product policies of rival businesses.
- Social. Changes in society can have consequences for marketing planning. The decline of the so-called nuclear family and the changing role of women may influence how a business promotes its products. The ageing of the population may influence the types of products which are developed and the channels of distribution used to deliver products to customers.
- Technological. Changes in technology can affect marketing plans in a variety of ways. It may make it possible for businesses to manufacture products that were previously

---

Knightsbridge is perhaps the last place you would expect a food fight. But in 2003 America's hottest fast food brand, Krispy Kreme, arrived in Britain. Dubbed the 'fast food of the future', the company opened its first fast food shop in Harrods' food hall. It might sound like an unlikely competitor for Britain's afternoon tea brigade, especially in the Atkins society of today. But the company can't make enough of its calorie-laden snacks in the US. Profits have doubled every year for the past three years. Competition to run franchised stores in the US is so strong that rights to new sites are traded like shares. In 2003 *Fortune* magazine branded Krispy Kreme as the hottest food business in America.

The British may never have tried a Krispy Kreme doughnut. But most people have seen the red, green and white logo on US programmes shown in the UK. The doughnut is Homer Simpson's favourite. Sex and the City has an over-eating boyfriend who loves them. And snacks feature in major films, such as Bruce Almighty. They are also the thing to be seen eating at weddings and parties. Even Madonna has been photographed eating them.

There's more to the product than a sweet taste. Marketing plays an important role. Doughnuts are baked freshly every minute in glass ovens in the front of shops. Customers can see them as they walk past a store. Harrods is having a hole cut in the window to encourage customers to walk through and buy. And sales staff play a part as well. They give any customer not buying a doughnut a free one within sixty seconds.

This is also the right time to move into Europe. When things are bad people comfort themselves with sugar. During the recent economic downturn the only fast food firms that have grown are doughnut chains. These include Krispy Kreme and its competitor Dunkin Doughnuts, owned by British drinks business Allied Domecq.

But can Britain be tempted away from biscuits and cakes? Thirty new stores will be opened in the UK in the next year. Don Henshall, head of the UK operation, says 'In Britain the doughnut is a market without a market brand. Krispy Kreme wants to be that brand. It's a big shift to get your head around, but look what has happened in the coffee market. Ten years ago Britons all drank awful instant coffee - now look how the choice has grown.'

Source: adapted from *The Observer*, 28.9.2003.

(a) Identify:
  (i) where Krispy Kreme is in the UK market at present;
  (ii) where the business wants to be in future.
(b) Explain any strengths, weaknesses, opportunities and threats for Krispy Kreme in the UK market.

Question 1

thought to be too costly. It may also lead to greater obsolescence and shorter product life cycles. New technological developments such as interactive television and the Internet may change the promotional methods that a business uses.

● Green factors. Environmental factors are playing an increasing role in the operation of businesses (☞ unit 70). Legislation on pollution and emissions might influence production. The expectations of consumers about packaging and ingredients might affect marketing. Pressure groups (☞ unit 70) can affect decisions. Taking into account the effects of operations on the environment can increase business costs, but may also increase sales.

Businesses should be careful to consider how each of the above factors affects consumers and their buying behaviour. Changes in external factors can cause changes in the wants and needs of consumers. An effective plan should anticipate these changes as well as any other issues affecting consumers' needs.

The benefits of marketing planning

● The main benefit of marketing planning is that it ensures a business takes time to reflect upon its marketing activities. In today's competitive environment it is not enough for businesses to carry on doing what they have done successfully in the past. They must constantly evaluate and develop their marketing policies. The marketing plan allows them to do this and can be seen as a means of ensuring the survival of the business.

● The marketing plan **co-ordinates** the various aspects of marketing. It takes a holistic view of a business's marketing activities. This should lead to better co-ordination and integration of the different elements of marketing. It should also allow all employees and all areas of the business to be aware of marketing objectives, helping to ensure that they 'pull in the same direction'.

● The marketing plan makes sure that human and financial resources are used where they are most needed. It will also make sure resources will not be wasted on unprofitable activities.

● Businesses will set marketing objectives and targets in their marketing plan. Management, as a result, will have a clear set of criteria against which they can evaluate the success of products.

● Marketing plans may encourage greater employee motivation. Employees are likely to be more prepared for changes in company policy and in the climate of trading. They should therefore be able to act in a more confident and informed manner. They are also likely to feel more secure in the knowledge that the business has planned for the future.

● A marketing plan should make banks feel more confident about offering loans to a firm. Shareholders may also be more confident about buying shares in a business.

Problems with marketing planning

For many businesses the main problem with marketing plans lies in their confusion as to what marketing actually is. Marketing plans often concentrate upon issues such as product development or increasing sales, but ignore customers' needs. Satisfying consumers' needs should be at the forefront of any marketing plan. A plan which centres around the expected success of a new advertising campaign, for example, is unlikely to be successful unless consumers' needs are satisfied. British Airways, Dunlop, and Woolworths are all businesses which have won awards for advertising campaigns in the past. It is arguable whether these campaigns directly led to any improvement in sales.

Paul Rossington had just been appointed Marketing Manager of SBC plc, a firm which had forty years' experience of supplying a range of instrumentation and components to the aircraft industry.

Paul had decided that his first act would be to involve a range of managers in drawing up a marketing plan. To this end, he called a meeting requesting the presence of all senior managers within the firm.

At the meeting, he began with a short presentation outlining the advantages to SBC plc of marketing planning. He then invited comments from all those assembled. The sales manager chipped in with the first comment; 'It's about time we started advertising more heavily in trade journals and stopped turning out products with the wrong specifications'. The production manager came next; 'I don't know why you dragged me up here to this meeting. You concentrate on the marketing and I'll get on with the production side. So long as you keep me informed of developments we'll be happy down in production.'

Paul was beginning to feel uncomfortable, but it wasn't until the senior accountant's remark that he really felt worried about having accepted this new post. 'I suggest you go away and write this plan and then call another meeting when you're in a position to discuss it with us', she had said.

(a) What advantages of marketing planning would you have advised Paul to mention in his brief presentation?
(b) From the comments made at the meeting, explain any problems which you think SBC plc will have with marketing planning.

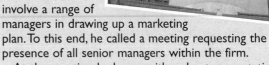

Question 2

Many businesses in the UK are organised into personnel, finance, production, and marketing departments. The success of the marketing plan will depend upon each of these areas being prepared to put aside their own goals to satisfy consumers' needs. This can be difficult, especially in a large business, where loyalty to the department can override more important goals. One suggested way of solving this problem is for businesses to be organised around customer groups rather than 'functions'.

Marketing plans often include too much information for them to be useful to managers. In order to overcome this problem, plans should be brief and concentrate upon key factors.

There is a danger that a business may embrace the planning ethos too eagerly. This may lead to the establishment of planning departments which become isolated from those responsible for carrying the plans out. This can have the effect of further divorcing marketing plans from the needs of customers.

Marketing plans often fail to **prioritise** objectives. Plans may include as many as 100 objectives. This means that it becomes difficult to decide whether objectives are being met.

Overall, it is important that a business's marketing plan is geared up to the particular set of circumstances in which it operates. This means a marketing plan which is sensitive to prevailing market conditions, the nature of the markets in which the business is operating and the customers at which the business's products are aimed.

Evaluating marketing plans

It is essential that businesses evaluate the success of their marketing plans. This will provide them with information on which to base future plans. Businesses also need to know whether or not planned activities were carried out in the manner which was planned.

The evaluation of marketing plans can take place both during the period of time in which the plan is being carried out and at the end of the time period (often one year) that the plan covers. Evaluation which takes place during the period of implementation may allow managers and directors to better control marketing activities.

It is important that marketing plans are evaluated against clear, measurable criteria. To do this, clear performance targets must be agreed and set during the process of marketing planning. Such performance targets are often time specific. This means that they are expected to be achieved by a certain date during the implementation of the plan. For example, a plan may require a 5 per cent growth in market share by the end of the first six months. A business may use a number of methods to evaluate a marketing plan.

Sales analysis This is an analysis of either the volume or the value of sales. If a business achieves a sales target then it may consider its marketing plan to be successful. This method is the most commonly used to evaluate marketing plans. Sales

Figure 24.1 shows the results of research by Tim Ambler and Flora Kokkinaki of the London Business School. They carried out a survey of 531 finance officers and marketers who were asked: 'What measures does your company use to track marketing ... performance?' From the results 5 main categories, shown in Figure 24.1, were identified. The figure indicates how frequently senior management used these measures according to marketers and finance officers.

Figure 24.1 *Importance of measures of marketing effectiveness for senior management (average)*

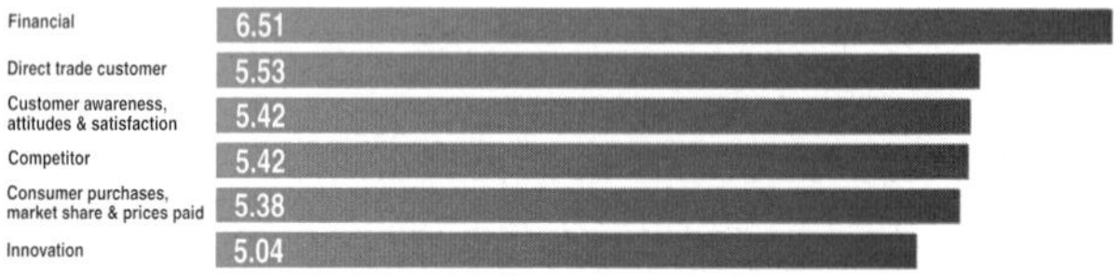

Financial	6.51
Direct trade customer	5.53
Customer awareness, attitudes & satisfaction	5.42
Competitor	5.42
Consumer purchases, market share & prices paid	5.38
Innovation	5.04

531 senior marketers and finance officers were asked to rate the importance that senior management attaches to different measures of market effectiveness in a 7 point scale.

Source: adapted from LBS.

(a) Explain what is likely to be included in 'Financial' measures of marketing effectiveness.
(b) Why are senior managers likely to regard this as the most important measure of marketing effectiveness?
(c) Suggest reasons why other measures of marketing effectiveness may be more important in certain instances.

Question 3

analysis is especially valuable to a business as it can be linked to a whole range of variables such as:
- sales by region;
- sales by product;
- sales by customer types;
- sales via different distribution channels.

The problem with using sales analysis in isolation is that it may not be related to what is taking place in the wider market. For example, a business may be experiencing high sales growth and so consider its marketing plan successful. However, it may be operating in a growing market in which competitors are experiencing even higher sales growth.

Market share analysis This method examines a business's sales in terms of market share. It enables performance in relation to competitors to be more accurately guaged. For example, if a business meets its target of an increase in market share of 5 per cent over a year then it may consider its marketing planning to be successful. Together, sales analysis and market share analysis are a powerful tool for evaluating marketing planning.

Marketing profitability analysis Profitability is concerned with the relationship between profits and costs. In the context of marketing planning, profitability analysis is calculated by subtracting the marketing costs of a product from the revenue gained from the product:

MARKETING PROFIT = sales revenue of a product
(quantity sold x price) - marketing costs (marketing research,
advertising, distribution, promotion etc.)

Thus a product with high revenue and relatively low marketing costs will be highly profitable. In contrast a product with low sales revenue and relatively high marketing costs will be less profitable.

The main benefit of calculating marketing profitability is that it can highlight some of the most and least profitable markets. Take the example of a business seeking to increase sales of a particular product by moving into two new markets A and B. In market A, an increase in sales of 10 per cent can be achieved with additional marketing costs of 5 per cent. In market B an increase in sales of 45 per cent can be achieved with additional marketing costs of 5 per cent. This business may wish to focus upon the more profitable market B.

The problem with calculating marketing profitability is that it is often difficult to calculate the marketing costs of particular products. For example, many promotional activities, such as trade fairs and corporate advertising, cannot be easily apportioned to individual products in businesses with a range of products.

Satisfaction surveys Many businesses undertake analysis of their customer satisfaction surveys. These are detailed surveys designed to identify the reactions of customers to their products. They use this data to assess the extent to which marketing plans are leading to increases or decreases in customer satisfaction.

Number of enquiries generated Many businesses pay very careful attention to the numbers of enquiries generated in particular aspects of their business. For example, financial service businesses monitor and evaluate the enquiries generated by direct mailshots as a means of evaluating the success of such promotions.

key terms

Marketing planning - the process by which marketing activities are identified and decided upon.
Marketing plan - a detailed account of the company's marketing at present, what it wants it to be in future and how it intends to change it.

Knowledge ... Knowledge ... Knowledge

1. How is a marketing plan affected by a business's strategic plan?
2. State 3 aspects of the marketing plan.
3. What does SWOT analysis show?
4. State 3 internal and 3 external factors that may be taken into account when carrying out a SWOT analysis.
5. State 3 benefits of marketing planning.
6. State 3 problems of marketing planning.
7. Suggest 4 ways in which a business might evaluate its marketing plan.

Case study The XBox, 2001-2004

2001

Microsoft launched its XBox video game console in 2001. It planned to spend $500 million on the launch of the new product, including spending on marketing, advertising and support to retailers and software makers. Prior to the launch, the senior vice president of the company's games division said 'We have to build demand for this to be successful.' The new product, which would include DVD drive and Internet access, was part of the plans of the business to move beyond the PC market. Microsoft also planned to tap into the market for devices that combine television and the Internet, and to offer online gaming.

Microsoft was developing 30 video games inhouse and approving many games from other software developers. It was suggested that the XBox would have three times the performance of Sony's PlayStation 2 (PS2). By the time the XBox was released Sony's PS2 and Sega's Dreamcast would already have been on the market for a year.

Source: adapted from news.com.

2002

One down three to go. In February 2002 Sega announced that it would cease production of the Sega Dreamcast games console and quit the hardware business. Instead it decided to produce games for other games consoles. The three left remaining were Sony's PS2, Microsoft's XBox and Nintendo's GameCube. In 2002 there were 30 million PS2 consoles worldwide (as well as 90 million old PS1 consoles). Contrast that to the 4 million XBoxes worldwide.

   The Internet gaming market is growing. It has been estimated that it would be a $20 billion industry by 2005. In 2002 Sony's PS2 and Microsoft's XBox were planned to be linked to the Internet for interactive gaming. However, unlike the XBox the PS2 would require additional equipment to be bought. Previously people could play games through their PCs on the Internet. But now they could take advantage of the stunning graphics of games consoles.

Source: adapted from www.ciol.com, abcnews.go.com.

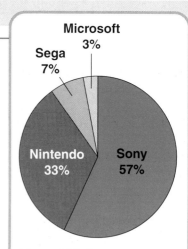

Figure 24.2 *Games consoles market share estimates, February 2002*
Source: adapted from market research firm, NPD.

2003

Between August 2002-03 Microsoft's XBox was the only gaming console to show positive market share growth in the US. It was suggested that sales increased 6 per cent in the US, giving it a 27 per cent market share. In comparison sales of Sony's PS2 fell to 36 per cent and Nintendo's GameCube fell to 22 per cent. In May 2003 the price of the XBox was cut in the US from $199 to $179 in response to a similar cut in the price of Sony's PS2. XBox sales have been fuelled by the success of its almost 400 software games, including Star Wars games. XBox Live, Microsoft's online gaming service, had over half a million subscribers.

   In October 2003 Nintendo reduced the price of its GameCube to $99 in the US. Within 35 days it was suggested that it had doubled its market share in the US from 19 to 37 per cent as a result, becoming a strong second in the market.

Source: adapted from xcox.the maingroup.com and www.forbes.com.www.lawrence.com.

2004

In 2004 Sony announced that it had shipped over 50 million consoles since the launch of PS2 in 2000. This compared to nine million sales worldwide of Microsoft's XBox. This gave XBox 15 per cent of the global market, a long way from Sony's estimated 70 per cent global market share. The majority of XBoxes are in the US (6 million), with 2.2 million in Europe. Microsoft admits it is weak in Asia, where it has struggled to make an impact in Japan in particular.

   Analysts suggested that Microsoft loses $100 on every XBox it sells. Yet the company has strong relationships with retailers and it has acquired game developers RARE and Bungie to produce games exclusive to XBox.

   Microsoft is pinning many of its hopes on the broadband market. It is particularly concentrating its marketing on areas of the world where broadband penetration is high, such as South Korea. This gives great possibilities when XBox live is launched in these countries.

Source: asia.cnet.com,and www.forbes.com.

Trends and forecasts

It is suggested that the video games console market has a cyclical trend in its pattern of sales. Levels in 2003 were expected to fall worldwide compared to 2002 by more than 2 million units. Although shipments of Microsoft XBox and Nintendo GameCube were expected to rise, this was not enough to offset the expected fall in Sony PS2. Price cutting was also likely to reduce revenues by £2 billion. However, the three companies were expected to introduce new versions of their games consoles by 2005, generating an upward trend. It was estimated that by the end of 2003 the Sony PS2 was the market leader, followed by the Microsoft XBox and then the Nintendo GameCube.

Source: adapted from www.instat.com.

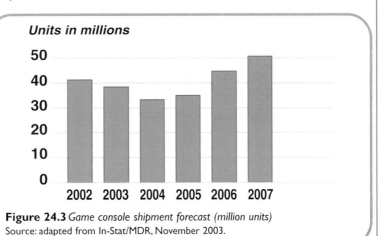

Figure 24.3 *Game console shipment forecast (million units)*
Source: adapted from In-Stat/MDR, November 2003.

(a) **Using examples from the information, describe the benefits of marketing planning for businesses in the game consoles market. (6 marks).**

(b) **Explain the external and internal factors affecting businesses in the game consoles market. (10 marks)**

(c) **Carry out a SWOT analysis of X-Box's position in the market. (12 marks)**

(d) **Evaluate the success of marketing planning by Microsoft for X-Box. (12 marks)**

Marketing analysis and strategy

It is important for a business to understand the needs of its customers. An understanding of customers' needs helps a business to determine how to price, promote and place a product. For example, information gained from market research by a company may indicate that the most likely buyers of a new product will be females, over the age of 25, who are professionals. Finding out about the needs of this group should allow the company to decide how to target the market and the best marketing mix for those consumers being targeted. The business may decide to promote the product in colour supplements of quality newspapers, to use high quality paper in the product and to charge a relatively high price.

Such strategies tend to be functional (☞ unit 5). However, many businesses have to make marketing decisions which include wider and longer term marketing issues. These include matters such as how a business can gain a competitive advantage (☞ unit 5), in which markets a business should operate and where a business wishes to be in future years. These **marketing strategies** can affect the entire business.

Marketing decision making

The decisions taken by businesses about their marketing strategy can be based on a number of factors. Sometimes the strategy a business chooses might be based on 'hunches'. These may be qualitative factors that are not quantifiable. This is often the case in smaller businesses, where one person or just a few people make the decisions. For example, a partner in a design business might decide to promote the design of websites at the expense of its film service because she 'feels' that the business will gain more customers this way and increase turnover and profit. Or a sole trader manufacturing specialist fashion clothes might have a 'gut feeling' that a certain style will be making a comeback.

A more rigourous approach, often used by larger businesses, is where:
● assumptions are made and objectives are set;
● information is gathered;
● a hypothesis or theory is put forward;
● this is tested using quantifiable data;
● then it is reviewed.
This approach is similar to the testing of theories used in subjects like science. In business, a multinational company aiming for growth, based on market research information could hypothesise that the market for sales in China will grow greatly during the next five years. It could test market products in China to verify its ideas. The business might then decide to target its products and marketing at the Chinese market as a result. This approach is sometimes referred to as the **marketing model**.

It is often suggested that such an approach reduces the risk that decision will be incorrect and strategies will fail. However, this does not mean that gut feeling decisions cannot be effective, but they may be more risky. Large businesses might not be prepared to take this type of risk. Small businesses might not want to either. But the may have no choice if they do not have the time or resources to carry out detailed decision making techniques.

Factors influencing a business's marketing strategy

There is a number of factors that may influence a business's marketing strategy.

The objectives of the business The marketing strategy that a business uses must reflect the objectives of the business as a whole. Marketing strategies must therefore be consistent with the wider corporate objectives of the organisation (☞ unit 4). For example, a business which is aiming to reduce the number of countries into which it operates should not develop international marketing strategies which go against this wider, corporate strategy (☞ unit 5). However, marketing strategies are not always secondary to corporate objectives. In some businesses, marketing information and strategies often have a strong influence upon corporate objectives and strategy. A growing market amongst ethical customers, for example, may persuade the business to deal only with those businesses that conform to certain ethical principles.

The strategies of competitor businesses As shall be seen later in this unit, many businesses take account of the strategies of their competitors when setting their own marketing strategies. For example, if a competitor promotes all of its company products on the internet successfully, other businesses may follow.

The structure of the market Marketing strategies will be influenced by the level of competition and the degree of change within different markets. In less competitive markets, with relatively little change, for example, businesses may find that their strategies require only minor adjustments from one period to another. In more competitive and dynamic markets businesses may find that marketing strategies require far reaching changes on an annual basis. For example, a manufacturer of active wear clothing aimed at 16-24 year olds may need to constantly monitor changes in tastes.

The attitudes of key decision makers within businesses Marketing strategies are likely to be influenced by the attitudes of decision makers towards matters such as the desirability of risk and change. Such attitudes are influenced by the environment within which a business operates, but also by the views of managers and directors and the culture of the business itself (☞ unit 5). For example, new managers aiming to alter the 'direction' of a business may decide to change the entire distribution network to mail order and sell off its retail outlets because this has worked successfully in other businesses.

The size of the business Larger businesses are likely to be strongly influenced by one or more of the above factors when making decisions about their marketing strategies. Smaller and medium sized businesses, however, often find strategic decision making more challenging. This is because the owners and managers of such businesses are often so immersed in the operational side of their work that they take few opportunities to adopt a strategic outlook. As a result, marketing strategy may be influenced by 'intuition' and responses to daily pressures.

The strengths of the business **Asset-based or asset-led marketing** (☞ unit 11) is where a business develops those products that make the best use of its 'core competences'. These are the major strengths of the firm. It produces goods or services that make the best use of its resources. Many businesses see brand loyalty or goodwill as a major **intangible asset**.

The marketing strategy adopted by such businesses will therefore attempt to develop products that can be associated with the brand names of its successful products. Many food manufacturers have followed this marketing strategy in recent years. Examples have included ice cream Mars Bars and Kit Kat Chunky. One of the most successful companies in the world, the Walt Disney Company, has perhaps followed this strategy into a number of areas. The launch by IKEA of a new range of furniture or a construction company moving into house renovation might be other examples. Examples in the service industry might include travel companies buying cottages to let for holidays or buying ships to sell cruise holidays.

Competitive marketing strategies

Many businesses are finding that the markets in which they operate are increasingly competitive. Two factors might explain this. First, the increasing internationalisation of trade means that many markets that were dominated by domestic business are now open to foreign competition. Businesses operating within the EU experienced increases in competition after the creation of the single European market. Second, government attempts throughout the world to release market forces have led to many markets being privatised and liberalised. This has often led to greater competition.

These changes have led businesses to pay careful attention to their competitors when creating marketing strategies.

Businesses often carry out COMPETITOR ANALYSIS. This provides businesses with a variety of information about their rivals. Businesses can then use this information to develop suitable COMPETITIVE MARKETING STRATEGIES. Competitive strategies allow businesses to compete most effectively with their rivals and to maximise their competitive advantage.

Competitor analysis

Competitor analysis allows a business to develop a knowledge and understanding of its competitors' behaviour before deciding on a suitable strategy. There is a number of aspects to competitor analysis.

In 2004 Levi went back to the drawing board with its classic Levi 501 jeans. They were recut in a bid to attract a new generation of wearers. Too many young people were put off by 'middle aged men' such as Top Gear presenter Jeremy Clarkson, who continued to wear jeans. The company planned to spend £10 million on the new jeans aimed at the under 25s rather than over 40s. The jeans would retail at £50 a pair and would resemble the original denim work trousers designed and marketed by Levi Strauss in 1873. A TV campaign would support the launch. The company suggested that the 501s on general sale in the UK were very eighties and nineties and had begun to look dated. Levi had faced competition from a wide variety of jeans manufacturers. These included own brand jeans from shops such as Gap, 'designer' jeans from Firetrap, Armani and Ted Baker, as well as traditional jeans manufacturers such as Wrangler.

In the USA everybody's heard of Levi jeans, but not enough people were buying them. Instant brand recognition is not enough. It had some success in wooing women, particularly its new low waist jeans for young women. People knew that Levis made good quality jeans, but wanted more than a box fit. Research has shown that its image perception is improving, but it needs to react more quickly to fast changing trends in the fashion scene.

Source: adapted from *The Daily Mail*, 30.1.2004 and www.mercurynews.com.

(a) Identify the factors that may have contributed to the changes in marketing strategy by Levis.
(b) To what extent do you think that Levis might make use of its assets in its new strategy?

Identifying competitors This would appear to be a straightforward task for a business. For example, a cinema complex in Bristol may consider that its competitors are other cinemas in the same city. However, this would be based upon the assumption that the Bristol cinema defines its competitors as other businesses offering the same or similar products. Further analysis of a cinema's competitors might reveal that cinema complexes are competing not only with other such complexes, but also with a range of other leisure based businesses, such as bowling alleys, football clubs and sports centres. Businesses can define their competitors in three main ways.

● Other businesses providing the same or a similar product. For example, P&O, the business which operates cross Channel ferries, might identify Brittany Ferries and Sea France as its competitors. This is because all these competitor companies also offer cross Channel ferries. Some businesses may wish to take this aspect of competitor analysis further by identifying those businesses providing the same or a similar product to the same market segment. Here P&O would analyse the market segments using Brittany Ferries and Sea France.

● Other businesses with products which provide the same service. In this case P&O might regard its competitors as Hoverspeed, which operates Seacats and hovercrafts across the Channel and Le Shuttle which, like cross Channel ferries transports passengers and vehicles between Folkestone and Calais. A wider interpretation of this category would include Eurostar, the train service which uses the Channel Tunnel to transport passengers from Britain to continental Europe and airline companies offering flights from London to cities such as Paris and Brussels.

● Other businesses seeking to satisfy the same or a similar customer need. Here P&O may see themselves as competing with other travel businesses competing for holiday spending money.

Michael Porter developed a model which identified five 'forces' of competition which affect a business (☞ unit 62). These include new market entrants competing with established businesses, competition from substitute products, competition from the rivalry of established firms, the bargaining power of consumers and the bargaining power of suppliers. Porter supports the view suggested above, that an analysis of competition should not be restricted to businesses producing the same or a similar product. He extends his view of competition not only to businesses competing for the same customers, but also to businesses competing for suppliers and to future competitors entering markets.

On October 23 2003 Capital Radio was knocked off its perch as the No.1 London radio station for the first time in 30 years. It was replaced by Chrysalis-owned Heart. Other stations in the Capital group fared better. London alternative music station Xfm, for example, added listeners and market share. Outside London, Century FM recorded its best ever listening figures.

(a) Using the methods of identifying competitors in the text above, describe the possible competitors to Capital Radio.

(b) Using the data in the tables, examine the possible objectives of:
(i) Capital Radio; (ii) Heart; (iii) Xfm.

Table 25.1 *London commercial radio stations' share of listeners, three months to September 14, 2003*

Position	Station	Share
1	Heart	7.2%
2	Capital 95.8	7.0%
3	Classic	5.2%
4	Magic	5.0%
5	Kiss	4.1%
6	Virgin	3.4%
7	LBC	2.4%
8	Capital Gold	2.3%
9	Xfm	2.1%

Source: adapted from Rajar.

Table 25.2 *All London radio stations' share of listeners, three months to September 14, 2003*

Position	Station	Share
1	BBC Radio 4	15.8%
2	BBC Radio 2	10.0%
3	Heart	7.2%
4	Capital	7.0%
5	Classic	5.2%
6	Magic	5.0%
7	BBC Radio 1	4.5%
8	BBC Radio 5	4.4%
9	Kiss	4.1%
10	Virgin	3.4%
11	LBC	2.4%
12	Capital Gold	2.3%
13	Xfm	2.1%
14	Jazz	2.0%
15	BBC Radio 3	1.7%
16	BBC London	1.1%

Source: adapted from Guardian Unlimited, 23.9.2003.

Table 25.3 *Time spent on selected free time activities, 2001-02*

	Hours and minutes per day	
	Males (weekday)	Females (weekday)
TV, video and radio	2;02	1:39
Socialising	0:32	0:44
Games and hobbies	0:18	0:09
Reading	0:15	0:16
Sports and exercise	0:11	0:09
Attending entertainment and cultural events	0:03	0:05

Source: adapted from *Social Trends, 2004*, Office for National Statistics.

Question2

Examining competitors' strengths and weaknesses Here a business will wish to examine a whole range of elements of competitors' businesses, from the specifications and technical aspects of competitors' products, through to relationships with suppliers and customers. Especially important in this type of competitor analysis is the identification of **critical success factors**. These are the factors which may give a competitor an edge in the market and allow it stand out from others. For example, the critical success of a business could be identified as the quality of its product or the after sales service provided to customers.

The main problem associated with examining customers' strengths and weaknesses is the difficulty of obtaining data. In general there is a need to rely upon secondary data and the experiences of customers, suppliers and others associated with the competitor business.

Identifying competitors' objectives and strategies It is important that not too much emphasis is placed upon the assumption that competitors will be attempting to maximise their profits. Some businesses attempt to satisfice rather than to maximise profits. Other businesses have objectives which do not directly relate to increased profits even if, in the longer term, the aim is to create additional profits. Such objectives include entering new markets, improving cash flow and leading a market technologically. Again, businesses will need to rely heavily upon secondary data when undertaking competitor analysis in this area.

Competitive strategies - cost leadership, differentiation and focus

It is suggested that there are three main competitive marketing strategies.

Cost leadership The aim of following a cost leadership strategy is to gain a cost advantage over competitors. This cost advantage can then be passed on to consumers in the form of lower prices. Businesses can gain a cost advantage by having higher levels of productivity and more efficient supplier and distribution networks. Amstrad is an example of a business which has pursued this strategy. It provides electrical goods cheaper than those of competitors. The main problem with cost leadership is that it focuses upon costs of production and lower prices rather than the needs of customers. This may create certain problems. For example, consumers might not always wish to purchase the lowest price product as it may have been perceived as being of lower quality.

Differentiation This strategy is where a business offers consumers something different from that which is offered by its competitors, in order to gain an 'edge' over them. The difference can be in terms of something real, such as a

technical difference in the product itself, or perceived, such as a strong brand identity developed through a promotional campaign. In the latter case, consumers must actually believe the perceived difference. Guinness, for example, has been differentiated both in terms of its smooth consistency and taste, and through a campaign which promotes it as an 'intelligent' drink.

Focus Businesses adopting focus strategies concentrate upon particular market segments rather than the market as a whole. They attempt to meet effectively the needs of a clearly defined group of consumers. By following this strategy, a business seeks to gain a competitive advantage over other businesses which spread their efforts over a wider range of consumers. For example, there is a small but thriving market for hand made, made to measure suits.

Competitive strategies - market positioning

Another set of alternative competitive marketing strategies is based upon the 'position' which a business wishes to occupy in relation to other businesses operating in the same market.

Market leader strategies In many markets there is one business which is generally recognised as the MARKET LEADER. Market leaders tend to have the largest share of a particular market. Market leaders may also be businesses which lead the market in terms of price changes and promotional spending. An example of a market leader might be Microsoft in the software market. There is a number of strategies which market leaders can adopt to improve or maintain their market leadership.

- Expanding the total market. As holders of the largest market share, market leaders stand most to gain by expanding the market. Expanding the market can be achieved by attracting new product users, promoting new uses for the product or encouraging greater product usage. For example, breakfast cereal manufacturers have tried to get consumers to eat cereal at different times of the day.
- Expanding market share. Market leaders may use the range of elements in the marketing mix to expand their current market share at the expense of competitors'. For example, Microsoft increased its share of the computer software market by establishing its product as the standard PC operating system.
- Defending current market share. The aim here is to prevent competitors from increasing their market share at the expense of the market leader. Most market leaders take the view that defending market share can best be achieved by continually improving the way in which they meet consumer needs. Often this is achieved with the use of complex and sophisticated marketing strategies. For example, some commentators have seen the development by Nestlé of a range of brands in the instant coffee market not only as an example of meeting new needs, but also as a

sophisticated form of defence. The development of the Alta Rica, Cap Colombie and Blend 37 brands can be seen as a defence of Nescafé and Gold Blend from competitors seeking to damage Nestlé's share of this market by gaining a foothold in smaller segments.

Market challenger strategies MARKET CHALLENGERS are those businesses with a substantial share of the market. However, they hold second, third or lower positions in the market in relation to the market leader. Not all businesses with lower market shares than the leader are market challengers. To be defined as market challengers businesses must be in a strong enough position to challenge the leader and be willing to adopt strategies to win more market share. There are three main types of strategies which market challengers can adopt.

- Direct attacks on the market leader. Here the market challenger must be prepared to directly compete in terms of the market leaders' strengths and also to match its marketing mix. To do this the market challenger must be able to match the resources of the market leader and to respond to retaliatory actions by the market leader. Such retaliatory action often takes the form of price cutting and aggressive promotion and distribution campaigns.
- Indirect attacks on the market leader. Because of the problems involved in mounting a direct attack upon a market leader, many market followers choose to adopt less confrontational strategies. One of the most common is to identify areas in which the market leader is less strong and to develop products designed to address these weaknesses. For example, businesses have attempted to compete with crisp manufacturers Walkers by offering exotic snack foods such as popadums and Chinese rice crackers.
- Attacking firms other than the market leader. This allows a business to increase its market share by attacking relatively weaker businesses. For example, many of the larger brewing businesses have increased their market share in this way in the UK by taking over smaller breweries.

Market follower strategies Many businesses occupying lower positions in a market do not wish to challenge the market leader. Challenges on a market leader often lead to retaliatory action and cause expensive battles which often hurt challengers more than they do leaders. For this reason many businesses choose to follow the strategy of market leaders. There are three main types of MARKET FOLLOWERS.

- Those who imitate market leaders. Own brand products in supermarkets fall into this category, as do canned drinks such as Virgin Cola. In more extreme cases imitation may lead to cloning. This occurs when one business seeks to copy the market leaders' products without originating anything itself.
- Innovative businesses. Such businesses lack the resources to challenge market leaders. They tend to willingly follow moves made by market leaders so that they do not change

the structure of the market.
- Businesses not capable of challenging market leaders which are content to satisfice. It is not unusual to find such businesses in the take away food market. These businesses have little competitive advantage. They tend to be vulnerable to changes in the market and may fail as a consequence.

Market niche strategies Market niches are very small segments of the market. They are sometimes described as segments within segments. The majority of businesses which operate in niche markets tend to be small and medium sized. However, some larger businesses have divisions specialising in market niches. Niches can be based upon geographical location, specific product differentiation, customer group or product type. Examples of businesses adopting market niche strategies include Tie Rack, Reuters and TVR, the sports car manufacturers.

Travel giants, such as Thomas Cook and JMC, slashed their prices of Spanish holidays by an average £150 in 2004. This was almost unheard of. But it was in response to the growing impact made by cut price airlines. It was seen as a deliberate attempt to win back custom from the low cost airlines.

It was the first time that the major companies felt that they had to cut the cost of ordinary family holidays to popular destinations. Two adults travelling to Majorca with Thomas Cook would save £120. Five adults going to Gran Canaria with JMC would save £210. Cosmos introduced a 'two kids free' deal to seven family resorts.

Bookings for holidays in popular resorts such as Spain had been sluggish. However, resorts outside the eurozone, such as in the eastern Mediterranean, were doing well.

Source: adapted from *The Daily Mail*, 26.1.2004.

(a) Analyse the competitive strategies and market positions of the businesses in the travel industry using examples from the data.

Marketing strategies for growth

Many businesses operate in or intend to move into markets where business growth is both desirable and possible. Businesses operating in such markets will tend to emphasise growth in their corporate and marketing objectives. Growth may be in the form of increased sales revenue or turnover, greater profits, increased capital or more land and employees. There is a range of marketing strategies that growth orientated businesses can adopt. Growth orientated marketing strategies are not suited to all businesses, however. In shrinking markets, for example, a business may wish to maintain previous sales levels or just survive rather than aim for growth.

The ANSOFF MATRIX is a useful tool for businesses aiming for growth. The Ansoff Matrix shown in Figure 25.1 illustrates both existing and new products within existing and new markets. Four possible marketing strategies to achieve growth are revealed by the Matrix.

		PRODUCT	
		Existing	New
MARKET	Existing	Market penetration	Product development
	New	Market development	Diversification

Figure 25.1 *The Ansoff Matrix*

Market penetration As suggested by the Ansoff Matrix, the purpose of market penetration is to achieve growth in existing markets with existing products. There is a number of ways in which businesses can achieve this.
- Increasing the brand loyalty of customers so that they use substitute brands less frequently. Well known brands such as Kellogg's Corn Flakes make use of this strategy.
- Encouraging consumers to use the product more regularly. An example might be encouraging people to drink canned drinks at breakfast.
- Encouraging consumers to use more of the product. An example might be a crisp manufacturer producing maxi sized crisp packets rather than standard sized crisp packets.

Product development This is concerned with marketing new or modified products in existing markets. The development of the Ford Focus, intended to act as a replacement for the Ford Escort, is an example of product development. Confectionery manufacturers such as Cadbury and Nestlé regularly use this strategy in order to stimulate sales growth.

Market development This involves the marketing of existing products in new markets. For example, the Halifax has extended its banking activities to the Spanish market and Harvey Nichols, a retail outlet previously limited to London, has opened a branch in Leeds and Manchester.

Diversification This occurs when new products are developed for new markets. Diversification allows a business to move away from reliance upon existing markets and products. This allows a business to spread risk and increase safety. If one product faces difficulties or fails, a successful product in another market may prevent the business overall facing problems. However, diversification will take a business outside its area of expertise. This might mean that its performance in new markets is relatively poor compared to more experienced operators. The move by Mercedes Benz into the market for small, high volume cars and the move by Virgin into financial services and the air passenger business are perhaps examples of this marketing strategy.

Marketing strategy issues

Social marketing SOCIAL MARKETING was first analysed by Kotler and Zaman in 1971. It was defined as 'the design, implantation and control of programs to influence the acceptability of social ideas involving considerations of product planning, pricing. Communication, distribution and market research'. In the late 1990s it was agreed by many researchers that it involved the use of marketing techniques to bring about changes in behaviour that benefit society. So social marketing makes use of the tools of commercial marketing, such as market research, segmentation, branding and the use of the marketing mix.

Examples of social marketing might include a reduction in tooth decay by improved dental hygiene, an improvement in people's health by changing their diet, a reduction in disease by improved medication or an improvement in the water system by the use of fluoride.

Social marketing is not the same as businesses being socially responsible (☞ unit 70). This tends to be businesses that consider the effect on the environment etc, but are ultimately judged on profit for shareholders. Social marketing is different because its success is judged on the benefit to society rather than commercial goals. Nor is it the same as ethical businesses that are concerned about fair and socially acceptable business practices (☞ unit 70).

However, some profit orientated businesses do engage in social marketing. Procter & Gamble, for example, contributed to a major social marketing drugs prevention initiative in the North East of England.

Green marketing Today the world faces a 'green' problem - the need to make the environment sustainable and yet still develop. This provides a number of challenges for marketing. GREEN MARKETING has been defined as 'the management process responsible for identifying, anticipating and satisfying customers and society in a profitable and sustainable way'. It involves using resources in a way that is sustainable, so they can be replenished or replaced in future. It also involves producing pollution and waste which can be absorbed into the environmental system.

The adoption of green marketing policies can have implications for marketing strategy. Businesses must try to identify 'green consumers' through market research. Businesses will only be able to satisfy their needs if they can find out the concerns of these consumers. Products and packaging must be environmentally friendly. They must be designed for re-use or recycling. Promotion may need to change. Advertising must be chosen to present a green image. Discounts may need to be given to persuade people to change to more environmentally friendly products. Sponsorship must be carefully chosen. Pricing might also be affected. Sometimes consumers might pay a slightly higher prices for free range products, for example. Distribution channels must be chosen which reduce pollution and congestion.

It has been suggested that effective green marketing will be successful if businesses have marketing strategies which follow the 7 Cs.

- Customer orientated, taking into account the views of customers about the environment.
- Commercially viable, so that products will meet consumer needs but still make a profit.
- Credible to customers, but also to other stakeholders, such as shareholders or government.
- Consistent with marketing and other business aims and objectives.
- Clear and not hidden in technical jargon.
- Co-ordinated with other business strategies.
- Communicated effectively, both internally to employees and others in the business and externally, to consumers and other stakeholders outside the business.

The impact on businesses of adapting more environmentally policies is explained in unit 70.

Internet marketing The growth of the Internet (☞ unit 52) has led many businesses to consider the use of INTERNET MARKETING STRATEGIES. These are the marketing approaches used by a business selling products over the Internet. They may be similar to those used by businesses using other methods of distribution (☞ unit 23). However, there are some specific factors relating to marketing via the Internet that a business might need to consider when deciding on an Internet marketing strategy.

- Targeting the market. The target market might be regarded as restricted or larger. For example, the target market might be only people using the Internet. So a business selling an online magazine to older people in a particular area of the country might have a smaller target market than usual. However, a magazine about a topic that appeals to all people, no matter what age, region or country they come from might gain a larger market from the Internet because it is a worldwide web.
- Market research. It may be possible to gain research

information about the market from the Internet. For example, some businesses download cookies and spyware onto computers to find out information about users of websites. There is software available to prevent this, so information may be restricted.

- The website. The main point of contact with the company on the Internet is the website. Image management is important. A well designed website that operates efficiently will present a good image. People like pictures, but text is more important. Users must be able to find their way around the website easily.
- Promotion. There is a variety of forms of promotion that businesses can use for their website on the Internet. They can buy advertising on other sites. They can make sure their site is included on search engines. They can also use bulletin board systems (BBSs). A BBS is like a storage facility that allows people to send and receive messages through their computers, as well as send and receive files. They can be used to gather information about a topic or to buy and sell products. Many businesses use BBSs to send electronic mail to distributors and to talk to business prospects. Mail order business, banks and travel agents often make use of BBSs.
- The nature of the product for sale can influence the website. Some products are sold online or can be downloaded, such as subscriptions to sites or written information. Others sell products which are sent to customers.
- Methods of payment. Businesses must decide how customer will pay for products. Some allow purchasers of products to pay online using credit cards. Businesses must be aware and comply with legislation about privacy of financial information. And they must comply with data protection legislation (☞ unit 51) regarding information they keep about customers.
- Coordination. Internet marketing must be coordinated with other forms of marketing. For example, it is often useful to include the website address with other forms of publicity such as leaflets or advertisements.

Buzz marketing BUZZ MARKETING is where businesses attempt to generate a positive image or 'buzz' about products through non-traditional marketing methods. It is a form of 'stealth' strategy. It usually involves businesses using word of mouth to promote a product. A business might employ groups to talk about products in appropriate places, for example software games in Internet cafes. People who are thought to be 'trend setters' might be employed to ride around in vehicles, eat food in public or wear clothing. For example, DaimlerChrysler generated pre-launch promotion for its PT Cruiser in the USA by placing cars in rental fleets around the trendy Miami Beach area.

The advantage of this type of marketing is that it can be a cheap and effective method for a narrow range of products, which have a target market and which people care about. It may also be useful for younger target audiences who have yet to develop brand loyalties. However, it is argued that it might be less effective for products that people have less interest in, such as washing powder. It might also lose its effectiveness if all businesses are attempting to generate a buzz for their products.

key terms

The Ansoff Matrix - a model which identifies growth strategies for businesses based on an analysis of their products and their markets.

Buzz marketing - a strategy which uses word of mouth and peer group approval to market products.

Competitor analysis - identifying the strengths and weaknesses of competitors and their products.

Competitive marketing strategies - marketing strategies directly based upon particular approaches to dealing with competitors.

Green marketing - a strategy which takes into account the effects of marketing on the environment.

Internet marketing strategies - the use of the worldwide web to market and sell products.

Market challengers - businesses which are in a position to threaten the market leader.

Market follower - a business which mimics or copies the strategies of the dominant businesses or businesses in the market.

Market leader - a business which makes decisions which tend to be followed by other businesses in the market.

Social marketing - a strategy where the success of marketing is evaluated on the extent to which society benefits.

A successful buzz campaign hinges on finding the right messages carriers. Ford was aware of the importance of this to its strategy when replacing the well loved Escort with the Ford Focus. The idea was to position the Focus as a hip, young person's car and help it win the war against competitors such as the market leading Honda Civic.

Ford looked for its style gurus in the New York youth marketing boutique Fusion Five. It was able to identify 120 influential buyers in five markets - New York, Miami, Los Angeles, Chicago and San Francisco. Each of the 120 people were given a Focus to drive for 6 months. They kept a record of where they went and what they did.

So did it work? Well certainly for Joe Regner, a 21 year old operations manager in Miami. He spotted a yellow Focus parked near the hip hop station WEDR and stopped to check it out. The Focus had been loaned to a DJ at the station, Jill Tracey. Joe ordered his and persuaded his girlfriend to switch from buying a Honda Civic. Ford sold over 200,000 cars in its first full year.

The person who ignites the buzz depends on the product. ConAgra Foods' Hebrew National Unit searched 12 US cities for 250 PTA presidents, Hispanic community leaders and Jewish mothers to serve on 'mom squads'. They drive around in yellow vehicles with a Hebrew National logo, hosting backyard hot dog barbecues and passing out discount coupons. The company vice chair of marketing said that even a loved American food like hot dogs can benefit from 'viral marketing'.

Source: adapted from www.businessweek.com.

(a) Explain why this strategy might be known as viral marketing.
(b) Examine the factors that might lead to the success of this type of marketing.

Question 4

Knowledge ...Knowledge...Knowledge...Knowledge...Knowledge...Know

1. What is meant by a strategic marketing decision?
2. What factors will affect a business's marketing strategy?
3. State the 3 aspects of competitor analysis.
4. How might a business define its competitors?
5. What are the 5 forces of competition according to Porter?
6. What is meant by a critical success factor?
7. Explain the difference between a cost leadership and a differentiation strategy.
8. Suggest 3 ways in which a market leader might protect its market position.
9. Suggest 3 ways in which a market challenger might improve its market position.
10. What 4 methods of growth strategy are suggested by the Ansoff Matrix?
11. How might a business gain greater penetration in an existing market with an existing product?
12. State 5 ways in which Internet marketing might affect the marketing strategy of a business.

Case study Coca-Cola

Table 25.4 *Coca-Cola Company, key financial information, 2002*

Sales	$19,564m
One year growth in sales	2.6%
Net income	$3,050m
One year growth in net income	23.2%
Employees	56,000
One year employee growth	47.4%

Source: adapted from www.hoovers.com.

Sales and net income

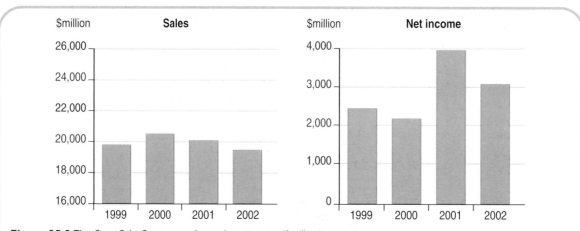

Figure 25.2 *The Coca-Cola Company, sales and net income ($million)*
Source: adapted from www.hoovers.com.

Problems or not?

Coca-Cola is the world's leading soft drinks company and regarded by many as the best known brand in the world. So why in 2000 did observers suggest there may be problems? Between 1997 and 2000 it had three different chief executives and it slipped from 3rd to 15th in the US ranking of most admired companies published by business magazine *Fortune*. In 1999, despite no evidence of contamination, the product was banned in France, Luxembourg, Belgium and the Netherlands. It was also investigated by the European Commission for acting as a monopolist and the share price fell from £50 in 1998

to £30. It faced growing competition from many sources, including cappuccino chains and energy drinks. A UK agent for drinks manufacturers suggested that parents in the UK preferred children to drink Sunny Delight. It may also have suffered from its own dominance. Some people regarded large conglomerates with suspicion. And their large centralised structure made it difficult to respond quickly to marketing challenges.

Source: adapted from *The Guardian*, 2.10.2000.

Diversification

Coca-Cola has been diversifying. In Japan it sells tea for example. In 2001 it planned to launch five new brands in the UK. These included Fanta Icy lemon, a still drink for teenagers called Alive and a sport energy drink called PowerAde.

In the UK Coca-Cola owns Malvern Water. In 2004 it planned to increase its presence in the bottled water market by launching the Dasani brand backed by a £7 million advertising campaign. It believed this would double its share of the UK bottled water market worth £800 million. The perceived benefits of drinking bottled water instead of tap water had led to a surge in this market. It is largely dominated in Europe by Danone and Nestlé which together account for around a third of all sales. However, the product was withdrawn quickly after chemicals were detected and plans to relaunch it were postponed.

In 2002 the company launched Vanilla Coke. The product followed on from a DIY trend in the USA where people would add a shot of vanilla to their coke drink to make it sweeter. It was predicted that the product would be as successful as previous versions such as the lemon flavoured diet coke launched in 2001 and cherry coke launched in the 1980s, but avoid the problems of New Coke which changed the taste of coke original in 1985 but was hastily withdrawn due to poor response.

Source: adapted from *The Guardian*, 2.10.2000 and 18.4.2004,enjoyment.independent.co.uk and www.euromonitor.com.

Marketing

Coca-Cola has changed its marketing to take advantage of new advertising initiatives. In Britain it used the Coke Auction. People collect tokens from coke bottles and cans and then use them to bid on the Internet for goods and services. A student won £6,000 towards fees and living expenses. Another winner had lunch with Kevin Keegan.

In 2001 it planned to spend £25 million on viral or buzz advertising. This was used for the Energy drink Burn launched by the company in October 2000. There is no large advertising campaign behind Burn. It was just stocked in trendy London bars and customers talked it up by word of mouth. Coca-Cola argued that customers in this niche market would have rejected a large advertising campaign.

The company also planned to involve trendy advertising agencies such as Soul and Mother in its promotion in the UK. And in 2002 it doubled its advertising expenditure to over £50 million in the UK, including sponsoring Team England in the World Cup.

Source: adapted from *The Guardian*, 8.2.2001 and www.euromonitor.com.

UK market share

In 2001 Coca-Cola maintained its share of the UK soft drinks market at 19.7 per cent. Fruit and vegetable juice showed strong growth. One hundred per cent juice grew by 6.5 per cent in 2002. Britains were increasingly prepared to pay a premium for concentrated juice, including smoothies.

Source: adapted from *The Guardian*, 8.2.2001 and www.euromonitor.com.

(a) **Identify the competitors of Coca-Cola. (6 marks)**
(b) **Explain the position of Coca-Cola in relation to its competitors. (6 marks)**
(c) **Explain the different marketing strategies used by (i) Coca-Cola and (ii) other businesses in the soft drinks market. (14 marks)**
(d) **Examine reasons why these businesses may have used such strategies. (12 marks)**
(e) **Discuss the extent to which Coca-Cola's marketing strategies have been successful. (12 marks)**

US market share

In the USA Coca-Cola had 44.3 per cent of the US soft drinks market in 2002. It saw its market share drop in 2001 by 0.5 per cent, but gain 0.6 per cent in 2002. Pepsi, its nearest rival, had 31.4 per cent market share.

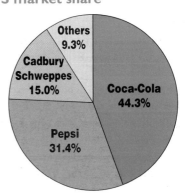

Figure 25.3 *Market share of the US soft drinks market*

Source: adapted from *The Guardian*, 10.1.2003 and www.findarticles.com.

What are accounts?

All businesses produce ACCOUNTS. These are statements that provide financial information about a business. The statements might include information about the revenue, costs and profit that a business records during the year. Or information about debts, capital and assets of a business might be listed. A statement might also show the flows of cash into and out of the business during the year. Table 26.1 shows a simplified profit and loss account for J Conrad, a sole trader who is a manufacturer of leather shoes.

Table 26.1 *Simple profit statement for Conrad Ltd 2003*

J Conrad
Profit and loss account 2003

	£	£
Sales revenue		201,511
Cost of sales		125,870
Gross profit		**75, 641**
Wages	18,300	
Rent	20,000	
Heat & Light	5,900	
Other overhead costs	25,320	
		69,520
Net profit		**6,121**

What does the account shoes?
- That £201,511 was generated from the sale of shoes during the year.
- A total of £125,870 was paid for costs of sales, including materials and other production costs.
- The profit after the costs of sales are deducted is £75,641.
- Other costs included £20,000 for rent and £5,900 in heat and light. The total of these overhead costs during the year were £69,520.
- The net profit made during the year was £6,121. This is calculated by subtracting all costs, £125,870 and £69,520 (ie £195,390) from the sales revenue of £201,511.

ACCOUNTING is a process that involves recording, classifying and summarising business transactions. In a small business the owner might record business transactions and then pay an accountant to produce the final accounts from those records. A very large business might employ BOOKKEEPERS to record and classify transactions and a team of accountants to produce accounts and other financial information.

Businesses produce accounts because they are legally obliged. For example, a sole trader will need information from accounts to help complete a self-assessment declaration for the Inland Revenue. This is used to calculate how much income tax the sole trader must pay. Larger companies need to produce accounts to provide information for external users such as shareholders and creditors. Accounts may also be used internally. For example, they might be used by managers to assess the performance of the business. The use of accounts made by all stakeholders (☞ unit 3) is discussed in the next section.

Who uses accounts? – internal needs

The main users of financial information are likely to be **management**. Up to date and accurate financial data will help to improve the running of the business. It can also be used for a number of other activities.
- Recording. The values of all of a company's resources and lists of its transactions can be recorded by hand or on computer. The records can then be used to show company **assets**, **liabilities** and **capital**, for example. Here it is enough to say that assets are the resources of the business, such as equipment, liabilities are amounts of money owed by the business, such as a bank loan, and capital is the money introduced into the business by the owners.
- Analysis and evaluation. It is possible to evaluate the performance of the company, make comparisons with competitors and keep a record of the firm's progress over a period of time.
- Control. Financial information helps the control of money flowing in and out of the business. This becomes more important as the firm grows and the amounts of money used increase.

Employees are another group of people who might need financial information. During wage bargaining, information about the profitability, liquidity and financial prospects of the business could be used to decide if management can meet a particular wage demand.

The **owners** (internal or external, or both) will have a vested interest in the company's financial position. They will naturally assess its performance. For example, shareholders will decide whether any dividend is satisfactory or not. On the other hand, a sole trader might look at the annual profit and decide whether or not they could earn more from another activity.

Owners might also use accounts in a **business plan** (☞ unit 2). For example, if a group of entrepreneurs are planning to set up a new business, they might produce a business plan when applying for a bank loan. In that plan the bank might want to see some **projected accounts**. These are accounts based on financial information such as costs and revenue, that the owners plan to achieve in a future trading period.

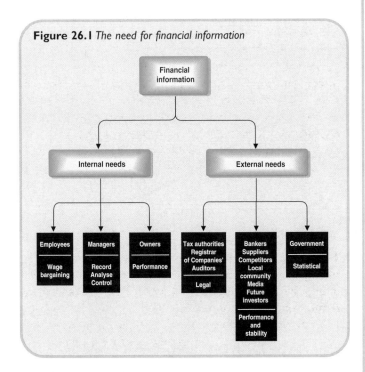

Figure 26.1 *The need for financial information*

Who uses accounts? – external needs

Certain external parties, from time to time, need financial information about a company. Companies are legally obliged to provide information to the following institutions.

- Tax authorities. The Inland Revenue may require proof of income when assessing the tax liabilities of businesses and business owners. Accounts can be used to provide confirmation of income. Customs and Excise may require access to business accounts when calculating VAT and excise duties owed by businesses. The Department for Social Security may require accounts to check whether a business has paid enough National Insurance contributions.

- Auditors. Every year the accounts of limited companies have to be checked by an independent firm of accountants and registered auditors. The process of checking the authenticity of accounts is called AUDITING, explained in the next section.

- Registrar of Companies. All limited companies have to register with the Registrar of Companies when they are formed. One of the conditions of registration is that they submit a copy of their final accounts every year. Copies of these accounts are made available to the general public on demand.

A number of external groups are interested in the performance and financial stability of businesses.

- Bankers. When deciding whether to lend money to a

business, bank managers will want to base their decisions on a range of up-to-date information. Financial information, such as accounts, provide managers with an insight about whether a business is capable of meeting loan and interest payments. Existing businesses will probably have to submit accounts from several years trading. New businesses may have to provide projected accounts.

- Suppliers. Many businesses buy goods and services using **trade credit** (☞ unit 33). However, before a supplier allows a new customer to buy on credit a **credit search** may be undertaken. This involves analysing a range of information relating to the financial circumstances of the business. Accounts may provide suppliers with some useful information regarding the ability to pay for goods bought on credit.

- Competitors. The accounts of limited companies are available for public scrutiny. Therefore competitors may wish to analyse them in order to make comparisons. For example, a supermarket chain may look at its competitor's accounts to see whether their turnover and profit has grown as fast. Also, if a competitor is contemplating an aggressive takeover it can use the information to help make a decision.

- Local community. Sometimes people might show an interest in a business that is located in their community. For example, the local community might use accounts to see if the company has any expansion plans that might create jobs in the area. Quite often the well-being of local businesses is vital for the prosperity of local economies.

- The media. Business and commerce is often the subject of newspaper, TV and radio reports. There are specialists that focus on business information. For example, *The Financial Times* is a newspaper devoted almost entirely to business and financial reports. Also, Working Lunch on BBC, provides daily updates on company news and financial markets. Company accounts give valuable information to journalists and producers when writing their reports and making programmes. Some sections of the media provide information services on personal finance. Company accounts might be used to help give audiences and readers advice on buying shares for example.

- Investors and financial analysts. The accounts of public limited companies are produced mainly to inform shareholders about the progress and performance of the company. However, accounts are also used by potential investors and financial analysts. They might be used to help make decisions when purchasing shares in different companies. For example, pension funds and insurance companies employ financial analysts to manage the money collected from pension contributions and insurance premiums. A lot of this money is invested in shares and analysts will use accounts to help them decide which companies to invest in.

- Government. The government may have an interest in a company's financial information. The Office for National

Tomkins is a world-class global engineering and manufacturing group. Its three core activities include Industrial Automotive, Air Systems Components and Construction Products. In 2002 the following financial information was published in its Annual Reports and Accounts.
● Operating profit was £182.6 million. Excluding the impact of acquisitions, disposals and currency translation. This represents an increase of 6.8 per cent.
● Operating margins rose by 8.7 per cent.
● Strong net cash position of £157.6 million.
● Second interim dividend declared of 3.4p per share.
The following table of information was also extracted from the published accounts.

Table 26.2 *Tomkins turnover, profit before tax, ordinary dividends, share price and enterprise value*

£million

	2002	2001	2000	1999
Turnover	3,373.8	4,105.5	5,640.4	5,359.3
Profit before tax	272.5	299.3	478.6	496.8
Enterprise value	2,651.0	1,994.7	3,406.0	3,772.8
Ordinary dividends	12.00p	12.00p	17.45p	15.15p

(a) Explain how (i) the media and (ii) potential investors might use the financial information in the case.
(b) If you were an investor would you invest in this company? Explain your answer.

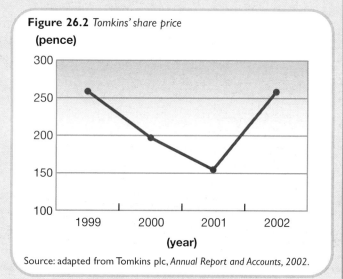

Figure 26.2 *Tomkins' share price*

Source: adapted from Tomkins plc, *Annual Report and Accounts, 2002*.

Question 1

Statistics gathers a wide range of business and financial information which it makes available to the public. Some of the data will be extracted from company accounts. It is usually summarised and published in journals such as the *Annual Abstract of Statistics*. This information is used by the government to monitor the progress of the economy and help evaluate the success of its economic policies. It might also be used by students, for example, when doing research.

Who produces accounts?

Accountants are responsible for supplying and using financial information. They are employed by businesses specialising in accountancy, or by large firms which have their own financial departments. Accountancy specialists sell their services to small and medium sized firms as well as self-employed individuals. They use the transactions recorded by these groups to produce final accounts. They may also advise clients on various financial matters such as taxation and investment.

Another function of these specialists is auditing. Businesses which produce their own final accounts must by law have them checked for authenticity by an independent firm of accountants. This audit is performed annually.

Accountants also carry out internal audits of businesses. These are audits which check that internal procedures are being carried out correctly. For example, a business may audit its pension fund arrangements to prevent misuse of funds.

There are two branches of accounting - FINANCIAL ACCOUNTING and MANAGEMENT ACCOUNTING.

The role of financial accountants is to make sure that a company's accounts are a 'true and fair' record of its transactions. They supervise the book-keeping process, which involves recording the value of every single business transaction. From time to time they summarise these records and convert them into statements which may be used by those parties described earlier in the unit.

Financial accountants are concerned with the past. They need to know about accounting techniques, company law, auditing requirements and taxation law. The ability to work under quite severe time pressure with a variety of personnel, at all levels in the business, is also important.

Management accountants are more concerned with the future. They do need knowledge of accounting concepts and methods, but they also require training in economics and management science. Such accountants are involved in decision making and problem solving in the business. They are responsible for producing cost and financial data, interpreting financial statements and preparing forecasts and budgets. They act as 'information servants' to the management team, but also help in planning and control.

A subsidiary of management accounting is cost accounting. Cost accountants carry out detailed costing projects. This involves working out the cost of particular business activities, such as calculating the cost of opening a new store, launching a new product or changing working practices.

Business statements

At the end of a trading year all businesses produce final

Finance Director
Highways Agency

Six Figure Base + Package

London

The Highways Agency is an Executive Agency of the Department for Transport (DfT) responsible for operating, maintaining and improving the strategic road network in England on behalf of the Secretary of State for Transport. With annual programme expenditure of £5bn and assets valued at £60bn, the delivery of the ten year plan for transport, major PFI contracts and a complex set of accounts this is a fascinating and challenging post.

Reporting to the newly appointed Chief Executive and working closely with key stakeholders, you will:
- Provide financial leadership through enhanced reporting and quality management information.
- Advise the Chief Executive and the Board on investment, business and governance issues for the Agency.
- Manage complex Agency accounts.
- Contribute to the strategic planning of the Agency.

You will need to be able to demonstrate:
- Qualified accountant with at least 10 years PQE in a major and complex organisation.
- A track record of leadership, achievement and delivery at senior level.
- Experience in a relevant commercial environment, or a public sector setting.
- The ability to manage, motivate, develop a team and to contribute strategically.

The post will be offered as a three-year fixed term appointment with the possibility of renewal or permanency with an attractive final salary pension.

The Highways Agency welcomes applications from all people and communities we serve.

Please request an information pack by e-mail or telephone quoting reference NAO/5961ST. Closing date 30th January 2004.

Odgers Ray & Berndtson, Freepost 27 LON20748, London W1E 1ED • Tel: 0870 240 3087
e-mail: nfp.response@odgers.com • www.odgers.com

Figure 26.3 *A job advertisement*
Source: Highways Agency.

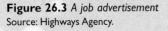

(a) What evidence is there in the advert to suggest that the Highways Agency is trying to recruit a management accountant?

accounts. A profit and loss account and a balance sheet (☞ units 31 and 32) generally form the basis of these accounts, although public limited companies publish a full annual report which contains a wider range of financial statements and reports.

Balance sheet A balance sheet provides information about the company's funds and how they are used in the business. It lists the assets, liabilities and capital of the business and, to some extent, shows the wealth of the company. A balance sheet describes the financial position of a business at a particular point in time.

Profit and loss account The profit and loss account provides a summary of the year's trading activities, stating the revenue from sales (the turnover), business costs, profit/loss and how the profit is used.

Cash flow statement Certain companies are required to produce cash flow statements in their accounts. A cash flow statement shows the flows of cash into and out of a business in a trading year.

Notes to the accounts The balance sheet and profit and loss account show summarised information. 'Notes to the accounts' are a more detailed analysis of some entries in these statements.

Directors' report This statement, written by the directors, is required by law. It contains information which might not be shown in other financial statements, such as the number of employees, changes of personnel on the board of directors and any special circumstances arising.

Chairperson's statement One of the chairperson's roles is to communicate with the shareholders. This can be done by making a statement in the annual report. The chairperson discusses the company's general performance and comments on events during the trading year which might be of interest to the shareholders. Future prospects are also discussed and shareholders are encouraged to remain loyal to the company.

Auditor's report Auditors must make a brief report to confirm that the accounts give a 'true and fair view' of the firm's financial position, assuming, of course, that they do!

Statistics Companies often include tables and graphs in their annual report. They can be used to illustrate trends and comparisons. They might show turnover, profit, dividends or earnings per share, for example.

The use of IT in accounts

Many businesses now use information technology (IT) in their accounts department. A number of companies, such as Sage, provide fully integrated software packages which handle the whole accounting function. Such packages are very sophisticated and, provided details of all transactions are entered into the system, they are capable of numerous tasks. These might include:
- keeping records of transactions with all customers showing up to date balances on all accounts;
- keeping records of transactions with all suppliers showing up to date balances on all accounts;
- producing daily, weekly, monthly or annual sales figures;
- producing an aged debtors list;
- producing an aged creditors list;
- producing trial balances;
- producing profit and loss accounts;
- producing balance sheets;
- calculating staff wages and producing wages slips;
- producing stock details.

Advantages of computerised systems

There are certain advantages to a business in having computerised accounting systems.
- Speed. Large numbers of transactions can be processed much more quickly in computerised than in manual systems.

- Capacity. Some businesses conduct billions of transactions each year. If records of these transactions were stored in manual systems a huge quantity of resources would be required. In addition, access to information stored in a computer is very easy. From the billions of transactions that might be recorded, an operator can instantly call up details of one single transaction.
- Efficiency. Because large volumes of data can be processed quickly, computer systems require a smaller workforce than manual systems. Therefore the cost of collecting and recording transactions can be reduced.
- Data handling. Information can be input and accessed from different locations around the country or the world. For example, a supermarket chain might have several hundred branches in the UK, each with twenty or more checkouts. The sales information from all of these sources eventually goes to one central processing unit where it is sorted and stored in the appropriate accounts. Information from every store can be retrieved and monitored from head office. **Electronic data exchange** may be used to transmit information in this way.
- User friendly. The design of accounting programmes means that staff do not need a detailed knowledge of bookkeeping and accounts to be able to input and retrieve data. Consequently, training costs could be lower and a business might employ non-specialist staff in the accounts department to keep labour costs down.
- Accuracy. Computerised systems are more accurate than manual systems when processing data. Partly this is because computers do not become distracted or tired when performing large numbers of routine operations.
- Security. By using a system of passwords, it is possible to restrict access. This prevents the unauthorised use of sensitive information. Intranets (☞ unit 52), which allow one computer to communicate with another like the larger Internet, may be also used by larger businesses. However, with intranets the communication is confined to computers within a business, therefore, outsiders are prevented access.

Disadvantages of computerised systems

The widespread use of computerised accounting systems suggest that the benefits outweigh the drawbacks. However, there are certain disadvantages.

- Cost. The cost of purchasing and then upgrading computer hardware and software can be expensive. Staff training costs can also be high. It is sometimes necessary to employ specialist IT staff to monitor the system. This adds to the cost.
- Technical problems. There is a wide range of computer systems and it is not always easy for a business to choose the most appropriate package. If an incorrect choice is made the mistake may be costly. Problems often arise when a new computer system is installed. It might not run smoothly because of 'bugs' in the system. Other difficulties arise if a 'virus' is downloaded from the Internet or via an email, or if inexperienced staff cause the system to crash. When this occurs, it can lead to problems and delays to staff, customers and suppliers.
- Industrial relations. The use of computerised systems may cause industrial relations problems. If staff see technology as a threat to their jobs or status, they might not cooperate with management when systems are installed This can result in delays and friction between managers and employees.
- Security. Although security can be increased by the use of passwords, employees or outsiders might be able to 'hack' into the system. This unauthorised access might be used by a disgruntled employee to sabotage the business, or by a competitor who hopes to gain an advantage.
- Operator error. Computer systems are only effective if data is inputted correctly. If inaccurate data is entered, the reports that are generated will also be inaccurate, misleading and of little use. This problem is sometimes described as 'GIGO', ie garbage in, garbage out.

Social auditing

Unit 70 discusses the growing importance of social responsibility in business. In an effort to become better corporate citizens some businesses carry out a SOCIAL AUDIT. This is a way of measuring and reporting on an company's social and ethical performance. It is a move away from the traditional method of evaluating performance which measures accounting information such as revenue, profit or dividends. Businesses that undertake social audits are accountable to a wider range of stakeholders and are also committed to following the audits recommendations. Social accounting may look at the firm's impact on the environment, the workforce, suppliers or the wider community.

Social accounting might use the following process.
- Identify the stakeholders (☞ unit 3) who are affected by its activities. These could be employees, suppliers, customers or local communities.
- Select a range of indicators that can be used to measure social performance. For example, to assess the impact a firm has on the environment it might measure factory emissions, water usage, fuel usage, waste generation or the use of recycled materials. Some businesses set targets which they hope to achieve.
- Gather information and report on the company's performance. This is an ongoing process and involves monitoring the indicators selected in the previous stage. Both quantitative and qualitative data may be gathered.
- Arrange for a social audit to be carried out. This might be done internally by assessing whether performance targets have been met from the previous year. Alternatively a business might employ an independent social auditing consultant. This acts as a safeguard against misleading information and can protect the interests of stakeholders.

Critics argue that social accounting is just a public relations exercise and a means of improving its corporate image. However, companies that have adopted social accounting, such as BP, Shell, the Coop and Body Shop, would probably say that it helps them to satisfy the needs of a wider range of stakeholders. It makes them aware of the impact the business has on society.

Knowledge ...owledge...Knowledge...Knowledge...Knowledge...Know

1. Why is it important for managers to have access to information?
2. Which users have a legal right of access to accounts?
3. State the internal users of accounts.
4. How might the media use accounts?
5. Explain the importance of accounts to shareholders and potential investors.
6. What might be the role of a management accountant in business?
7. State 5 advantages and 5 disadvantages of using IT in accounts.
8. Explain the significance of the term GIGO when using computers in accounts?
9. Explain how a business might undertake a social audit.
10. List the financial statements that might appear in the Annual Report and Accounts of a public limited company.

Balfour Beatty's business is in the creation and care of essential assets. It serves the international markets for rail, road and utility systems, buildings and complex structures. Over recent years the company has recognised that its social and ethical performance has come under increasing scrutiny. In response to this Balfour Beatty now publishes a comprehensive Safety, Environment and Social report. It covers four key areas - sustainable development, safety and health, environment and social. The report is audited by csr network Ltd, an independent specialist in the field of corporate social reporting. Figure 26.4 shows environmental data about various businesses that make up the Balfour Beatty group, such as Heery.

(a) Explain how the data shown in Figure 26.4 might be used by Balfour Beatty.
(b) Why is it important that Balfour Beatty's social report is audited?

Figure 26.4 *Balfour Beatty environmental data*

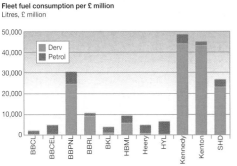

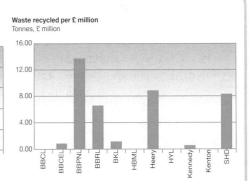

Source: adapted from Balfour Beatty, *Safety, Environment and Social Report,* 2002.

Question 3

key terms

Accounts − financial statements that provide information about a firm's financial circumstances.

Accounting − the process of recording, classifying, and summarising business transactions with the aim of providing useful financial information for a range of users.

Auditing − an accounting procedure which checks thoroughly the authenticity of a company's accounts.

Bookkeepers − people involved in the recording and classifying of business transactions.

Financial accounting − the preparation of company accounts from business records.

Management accounting − the preparation of financial statements, reports and data for use by managers.

Social auditing − collecting information and reporting back on the impact of the business on society and the environment.

Case study Scottish & Newcastle

Scottish & Newcastle is a major international brewing group. Some of its famous brands include Fosters, John Smith's, Kronenbourg, Youngers Tartan and Newcastle Brown Ale. It operates breweries in at least fourteen different countries in Europe and Asia and exports to more than sixty countries worldwide.

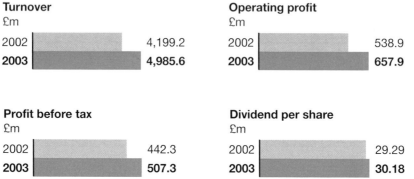

Figure 26.5 *Turnover, operating profit, profit before tax and dividend per share*

Turnover
£m

2002	4,199.2
2003	**4,985.6**

Operating profit
£m

2002	538.9
2003	**657.9**

Profit before tax
£m

2002	442.3
2003	**507.3**

Dividend per share
£m

2002	29.29
2003	**30.18**

Figure 26.6 *Extracts from chairman's statement*

Performance

Our businesses continued to focus on developing strong market positions and S&N's key brands continued to gain value and share across their markets.

Group turnover increased by 18.7% to £4,985.6m and operating profit rose to £657.9m including the first time contributions from Hartwall, BBH and Mythos Breweries. Operating profit also benefitted from a reduction in royalty payments to Danone following the acquisition of Danone's remaining interests in Brasseries Kronenbourg and Alken Maes, but has been impacted by incremental costs in the UK supply chain.

Our Managed Retail business continued to outperform its competitors in like for like sales, cost efficiency and return on investment with operating profits up 6.5% in a very competitive market.

Your directors are pleased to recommend a final dividend of 20.0p, an increase of 3.0%.

Figure 26.7 *Turnover by business and region, top five brands' share of branded volumes and volume growth of top five brands*

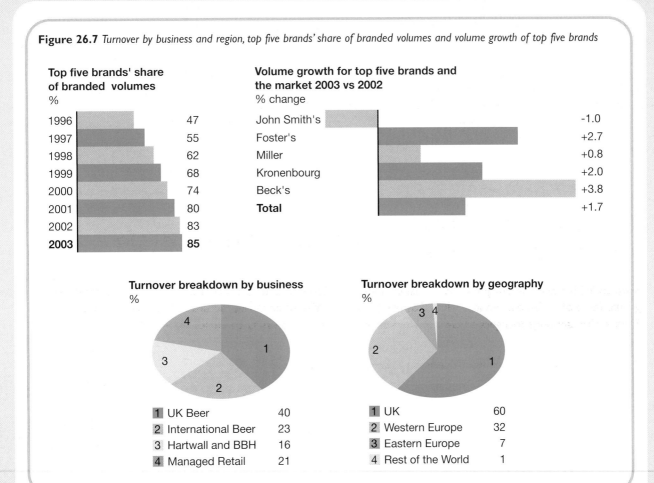

Top five brands' share of branded volumes
%

1996	47
1997	55
1998	62
1999	68
2000	74
2001	80
2002	83
2003	**85**

Volume growth for top five brands and the market 2003 vs 2002
% change

John Smith's	-1.0
Foster's	+2.7
Miller	+0.8
Kronenbourg	+2.0
Beck's	+3.8
Total	+1.7

Turnover breakdown by business
%

1	UK Beer	40
2	International Beer	23
3	Hartwall and BBH	16
4	Managed Retail	21

Turnover breakdown by geography
%

1	UK	60
2	Western Europe	32
3	Eastern Europe	7
4	Rest of the World	1

Figure 26.8 *Extract from Corporate Social Responsibility Report*

Being a good neighbour

We are very aware of our responsibilities to the communities in which we operate, especially in countries whose cultures and infrastructures are very different to our own.

The CSR report contains several examples of work we have undertaken within the supply chain in order to influence the social and environmental performance of our suppliers, to share our knowledge and to support the development of their businesses.

We also undertake many activities to support our local communities. These range from funding the building of a new fire station in Portugal to a mentoring scheme for small businesses in Belgium.

Source: adapted from Scottish & Newcastle, *Annual Report and Accounts, 2003.*

(a) (i) **Identify four users that might be particularly interested in the financial information in Figure 26.5. (4 marks)**
(ii) **Explain what their interest might be. (8 marks)**
(b) **Describe the function of the chairman's statement in Figure 26.6. (6 marks)**

(c) **Analyse the reasons why competitors might be interested in the information in Figure 26.7. (10 marks)**
(d) **On the basis of the evidence provided, discuss which stakeholders are the most influential in the business. (12 marks)**

The costs of production

A business needs accurate and reliable cost information to make decisions. A firm that is aiming to expand production to meet rising demand must know how much that extra production will cost. Without this information it will have no way of knowing whether or not it will make a profit. You will be familiar with your own costs. These are the expenses you have, such as travel costs to school or college. Similarly, businesses have expenses. These might include wages, raw materials, insurance and rent.

Economists usually think of costs as **opportunity costs** (☞ unit 9). The opportunity cost is the value that could have been earned if a resource was employed in its next best use. For example, if a business spends £40,000 on an advertising campaign, the opportunity cost might be the interest earned from depositing the money in a bank account. A business is concerned, however, with ACCOUNTING COSTS. An accounting cost is the value of a resource used up in production. This is shown in the business accounts as an asset or an expense. For example, if a firm buys some fuel costing £5,500, this is shown as an expense in the accounts.

It is also important to understand how a firm's costs change in the SHORT RUN and the LONG RUN.

- The short run is the period of time when at least one factor of production (☞ unit 1) is **fixed**. For example, in the short run, a firm might want to expand production in its factory. It can acquire more labour and buy more raw materials, but it has a fixed amount of space in the factory and a limited number of machines.
- In the long run, all factors can vary. The firm can buy another factory and add to the number of machines. This will increase **capacity** (the maximum amount that can be produced ☞ unit 59) and begin another short run period.

Fixed costs

Costs which stay the same at all levels of output in the short run are called FIXED COSTS. Examples might be rent, insurance, heating bills, depreciation (☞ unit 38) and business rates, as well as **capital costs** such as factories and machinery. These costs remain the same whether a business produces nothing or is working at full capacity. For example, rent must still be paid even if a factory is shut for a two week holiday period when nothing is produced. It is worth noting that 'fixed' here means costs do not change as a result of a change in **output** in the short run. But they may increase due to, say, inflation. Figure 27.1 shows what happens to fixed costs as a firm increases production. The line on the graph is horizontal which shows that fixed costs are £400,000 no matter how much is produced.

What happens over a longer period? Figure 27.2 illustrates 'stepped' fixed costs. If a firm is at full capacity, but needs to

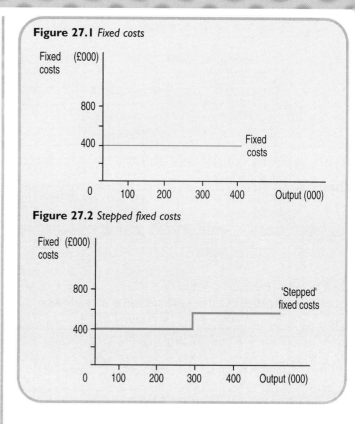

Figure 27.1 *Fixed costs*

Figure 27.2 *Stepped fixed costs*

raise production, it might decide to invest in more equipment. The new machines raise overall fixed costs as well as capacity. The rise in fixed costs is shown by a 'step' in the graph. This illustrates how fixed costs can change in the long run.

Variable and semi variable costs

Costs of production which increase directly as output rises are called VARIABLE COSTS. For example, a baker will require more flour if more loaves are to be produced. Raw materials are just one example of variable costs. Others might include fuel, packaging and wages. If the firm does not produce anything then variable costs will be zero.

Figure 27.3 shows a firm's variable costs. Assume that the firm buying new machinery in Figure 27.1 produces dolls and that variable costs are £2 per doll. If the firm produces 100,000 dolls it will have variable costs of £200,000 (£2 x 100,000). Producing 500,000 dolls it will incur variable costs of £1,000,000 (£2 x 500,000). Joining these points together shows the firm's variable costs at any level of output. As output increases, so do variable costs. Notice that the graph is **linear**. This means that it is a straight line.

Some production costs do not fit neatly into our definitions of fixed and variable costs. This is because they are not entirely fixed or variable costs. Labour is a good example. If a firm employs a member of staff on a permanent basis, no

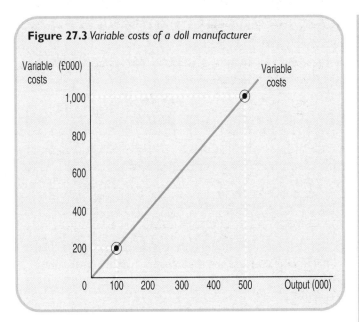

Figure 27.3 *Variable costs of a doll manufacturer*

matter what level of output, then this is a fixed cost. If this member of staff is asked to work overtime at nights and weekends to cope with extra production levels, then the extra cost is variable. Such labour costs are said to be SEMI-VARIABLE COSTS. Another example could be the cost of telephone charges. This often consists of a fixed or 'standing charge' plus an extra rate which varies according to the number of calls made.

Total costs

If fixed and variable costs are added together they show the TOTAL COST of a business. The total cost of production is the cost of producing any given level of output. As output increases total costs will rise. This is shown in Figure 27.4, which again shows the production of dolls. We can say:

Total cost (TC) = fixed cost (FC) + variable cost (VC)

The business has fixed costs of £400,000 and variable costs of £2 per doll. When output is 0 total costs are £400,000. When output has risen to 300,000 dolls, total costs are £1,000,000, made up of fixed costs of £400,000 and variable costs of £600,000 (£2 x 300,000). This information is summarised in Table 27.1. Figure 27.4 shows the way that total costs increase as output increases. Notice that as output increases fixed costs become a smaller proportion of total costs.

Table 27.1 *Summary of cost information for the doll manufacturer*

			£000
Output (units)	Fixed cost	Variable cost	Total cost
0	400	0	400
300	400	600	1,000

Jimmy Draper has run his own building firm for 25 years in Worcester. When he first set up he concentrated on repair and maintenance work and employed just one other person. However, he became more ambitious and eventually took on extensions and loft conversions. Seven years ago he built his first complete house. He made a handsome profit on the construction and also benefited from rapidly rising house prices. He now employs 12 staff and keeps 15 sub-contractors busy.

(a) Look at the photograph. State two examples of
(ii) fixed costs and (ii) variable costs.
(b) Jimmy owns a builder's yard and office on a local industrial estate. What semi-variable costs might be incurred in the office? Explain your answer.

Question 1

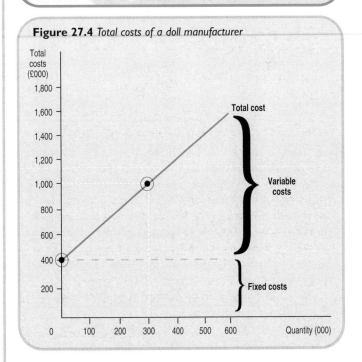

Figure 27.4 *Total costs of a doll manufacturer*

Direct and indirect costs

Costs can also be divided into direct and indirect costs. DIRECT COSTS are costs which can be identified with a particular product or process. Examples of direct costs are raw materials, packaging, and direct labour. INDIRECT

COSTS or OVERHEADS result from the whole business. It is not possible to associate these costs directly with particular products or processes. Examples are rent, insurance, the salaries of office staff and audit fees. Indirect costs are usually fixed costs and direct costs variable costs, although in theory both direct and indirect costs can be fixed or variable.

Average and marginal costs

The AVERAGE COST is the cost per unit of production, also known as the UNIT COST. To calculate average cost the total cost of production should be divided by the number of units produced.

$$\text{Average cost} = \frac{\text{Total cost}}{\text{output}} \quad \text{or} \quad \frac{\text{Fixed cost + variable cost}}{\text{output}}$$

It is also possible to calculate **average fixed costs**:

$$\text{Average fixed cost} = \frac{\text{Total fixed cost}}{\text{output}}$$

and **average variable costs**:

$$\text{Average variable cost} = \frac{\text{Total variable cost}}{\text{output}}$$

Take the earlier example of the doll manufacturer with fixed costs of £400,000 and variable costs of £2 per unit. If output was 100,000 units:

$$\text{Average fixed cost} = \frac{£400,000}{100,000} = £4$$

$$\text{Average variable cost} = \frac{£2 \times 100,000}{100,000} = £2$$

$$\text{Average total cost} = \frac{£400,000 + (£2 \times 100,000)}{100,000}$$

$$= \frac{£600,000}{100,000} = £6$$

MARGINAL COST is the cost of increasing total output by one more unit. It can be calculated by:

$$\text{Marginal cost} = \frac{\text{change in total cost}}{\text{change in output}}$$

For example, if the total cost of manufacturing 100,000 dolls is £600,000 and the total cost of producing 100,001 dolls is £600,002, then the marginal cost of producing the last unit is:

$$\text{Marginal cost} = \frac{£600,002 - £600,000}{100,001 - 100,000} = \frac{£2}{1} = £2$$

The relationship between average and marginal cost and their uses for the businesses are discussed in unit 52.

The problems of classifying costs

There is a number of possible ways in which costs can be classified.
- By type. This involves analysing business costs and deciding whether they are **direct or indirect**.
- By behaviour. Economists favour this method. They classify costs according to the effect that a change in the level of output has on a particular cost. **Fixed, variable,**

Stella Parker and Fiona Dobson recently set up a business partnership. They rented a small kiosk in a Luton shopping mall to make and sell mini-pizzas to shoppers, shop workers and nearby office staff. They got the idea from similar kiosks they had seen on holiday in Lloret de Mar, Spain. They decided to make their own pizza bases on the premises and use fresh ingredients for the toppings. They thought the aroma of baking pizzas and the display of freshly chopped vegetables would attract customers. The oven that they leased allowed mini-pizzas to be produced in batches of 10.

The costs incurred by the business are shown below.

Fixed costs

Rent for kiosk	£140 per week
Lease on oven	£50 per week
Other fixed costs	£10 per week

Variable costs

Bases	£5.50 per batch
Toppings	£3.50 per batch
Other variable costs	£1.00 per batch

Table 27.2 *Cost schedule for Stella's and Fiona's mini-pizza business*

Batches	0	10	20	30	40	50	60	70	80	90	100
Total fixed costs	200	200	200	200	200	200	200	200	200	200	200
Bases	0	55									
Toppings	0	35									
Other variable costs	0	10									
Total variable costs											
Total costs											

(a) Complete Table 27.2 and plot the graphs for fixed costs, variable costs and total costs (use a range of output from 0 to 100 batches).

(b) Show the effect on your graph of an increase in fixed costs to £300.

(c) Explain why the oven lease and pizza toppings are both examples of direct costs.

Question 2

semi-variable, **average and marginal costs** all fall into this category.

● By function. It is possible to classify costs according to the business function they are associated with. For example, costs could be listed as **production, selling, administrative or personnel**.

● By nature of resource. This involves classifying costs according to the resources which were acquired by a business, for example, **materials, labour or expenses**.

● By **product, job, customer or contract** A multi-product manufacturer, such as Heinz for example, might classify costs according to the product line (beans, soups, puddings) they are associated with. Solicitors might classify costs by identifying them with particular clients.

The classification of costs is not always straightforward. In some cases the same business cost can be classified in several ways. For example, the earnings of a full time administrative assistant may be classified as a fixed cost, if they do not vary with output, and an indirect cost, if they are not associated with a particular product. The costs of a worker earning piece rates might be a direct cost if they can be associated with a particular product and a variable cost if they rise as the output of the worker increases.

Another problem relating to costs concerns the allocation of indirect costs. When calculating the cost of producing particular products it is necessary to allocate indirect costs to each of the different products a business manufactures. In practice this may be difficult.

The way in which costs are classified will depend on the purposes for which the classification is being undertaken and the views of the management team.

Long run costs

Most of the costs discussed so far in this unit have been short run costs, ie the time period where at least one factor of production is fixed. In the long run, all factors of production are likely to be variable.

Total revenue

The amount of money which a firm receives from selling its product can be referred to as TOTAL REVENUE. Total revenue is calculated by multiplying the number of units sold by the price of each unit:

Total revenue = quantity sold x price

For example, if the doll producer mentioned earlier sells 300,000 dolls at a price of £5 each:

Total revenue = 300,000 x £5 = £1,500,000

Figure 27.5 shows what happens to total revenue as output rises. Notice that the graph is **linear**.

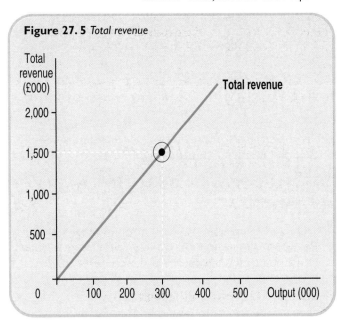

Figure 27.5 *Total revenue*

Profit and loss

One of the main reasons why firms calculate their costs and revenue is to enable them to work out their **profit** or **loss.** Profit is the difference between revenue and costs.

Profit = total revenue - total costs

For example, if the doll manufacturer in the earlier example produces and sells 300,000 dolls, they sell for £5, fixed costs are £400,000 and variable costs are £2 per unit, then:

Thompson & Son makes standard golf trolleys which it sells to pro-shops at golf clubs. The trolleys are hired out by the pro-shops to players. Last year Thompson & Son made and sold 5,000 trolleys. Figure 27.6 shows the costs and profit made by the business last year.

(a) What was the value of total revenue for Thompson & Son last year ? Explain your answer.
(b) Calculate (i) the price charged for the trolleys and (ii) the average cost per trolley.

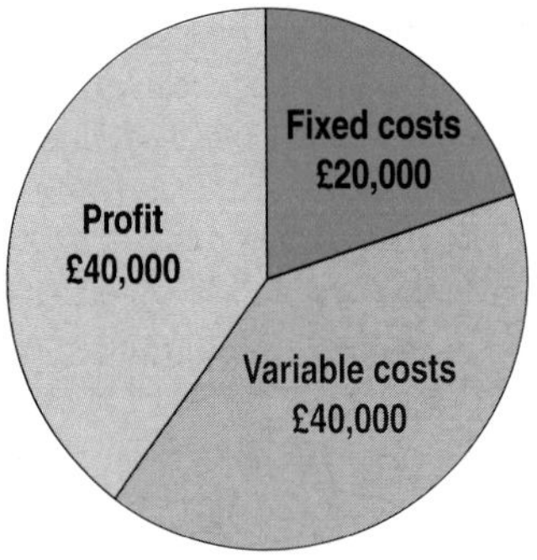

Figure 27.6 *The uses of total revenue of Thompson & Son*

Question 3

Profit = £5 × 300,000 - (£400,000 + [£2 × 300,000])

= £1,500,000 - (£400,000 + [£600,000])

= £1,500,000 - £1,000,000

= £500,000

It is possible to calculate the profit for a business at any level of output using this method.

Using profits and the quality of profits

How does a business use, or utilise, any profit that it makes?

● Part of any profit may be taken by sole traders or partners, or distributed to shareholders as dividends (☞ unit 6). Large public limited companies have thousands of shareholders. Paying a dividend is one way of encouraging people to buy shares so businesses can raise finance.

● The remaining, undistributed, profit is retained within the business. Retained profit can then be used for investment and future growth. For example, a business might invest in new machinery or produce innovative new products. It is unlikely that all profit will be invested. So some will be retained in case of emergencies or to safeguard the business in future if trading conditions get worse.

On the other hand, losses will result in the reduction of any retained profit for previous years. It is also likely that a business making losses would not pay a dividend.

The **quality** of the profit made by a business is sometimes said to be important. It may be possible for a business to make a short term profit by raising its price or cutting its costs. Or a business can sell machinery to raise revenue. These one-off activities may increase revenue or reduce costs. However, higher prices might reduce sales. Selling machinery might reduce output. So profit might not recur. It is argued, therefore, that profits that are earned earned year after year are likely to be of higher quality for a business then one-off profits.

Knowledge

1. What is the difference between opportunity costs and accounting costs?
2. How do you account for a 'stepped' fixed cost function?
3. Why are some costs said to be semi-variable?
4. What happens to variable costs as a proportion of total costs when output rises?
5. Explain the difference between direct and indirect costs.
6. How is:
   (a) average fixed cost;
   (b) average variable cost;
   calculated?
7. How is total revenue calculated?
8. What information is required to calculate a firm's profit?
9. What problems might there be when clarifying costs?

key terms

Accounting cost - the value of an economic resource used up in production.

Average cost or unit cost - the cost of producing one unit, calculated by dividing the total cost by output.

Direct cost - a cost which can be clearly identified with a particular unit of output.

Fixed cost - a cost which does not change as a result of a change in output in the short run.

Indirect cost or overhead - a cost which cannot be identified with a particular unit of output. It is incurred by the whole organisation or department.

Long run - the time period where all factors of production are variable.

Marginal cost - the cost of increasing output by one more unit.

Semi-variable cost - a cost which consists of both fixed and variable elements.

Short run - the time period where at least one factor of production is fixed.

Total cost - the entire cost of producing a given level of output.

Total revenue - the amount of money the business receives from selling output.

Variable cost - a cost which rises as output rises.

Case study *Customer Services Training (CST)*

Handa Bakila left her job as head of customer services for an international airline to set up Customer Services Training. She is based in Dorchester and provides specialised training courses for staff in the retail sector. Her courses usually last for one day and tend to focus on dealing with face-to-face customer complaints. However, Handa is flexible and happy to tailor the subject of courses to the needs of clients. In 2002 she charged £600 for a day's course which she set up in a local hotel near to the client's premises. She takes a maximum of 40 trainees and includes refreshments and lunch time meals in the price.

In 2002 CST put on 200 courses and made a reasonable profit. However, Handa felt that her effort was worth a greater financial reward. In 2003 she decided to advertise her services more aggressively in London. Handa would be able to charge more and the amount of time spent travelling would be reduced. She spent £3,000 on a special promotion and decided to raise the price of the training courses from £600 per day to £800 per day. Handa felt that this was justified because of the higher variable costs associated with arranging courses in London. In 2003 the number of courses arranged by CST fell to 150.

(a) Using examples from the case explain the difference between fixed and variable costs. (8 marks)

(b) In 2002, what was the marginal cost of the 200th course? Explain your answer. (4 marks)

(c) Calculate the profit made by CST in (i) 2002 and (ii) 2003. (14 marks)

(d) To what extent did Handa's decision to raise price from £600 to £800 achieve her objective? (14 marks)

Table 27.3 *Financial information for CST 2002 and 2003*

	£	
	2002	**2003**
Car lease per annum	5,000	5,000
Insurance per annum	1,000	1,200
Other fixed costs per annum	2,000	2,800
Special promotion	0	3,000
Room hire fees per course	150	200
Refreshment costs per course	150	180
Training materials per course	50	50
Other variable costs per course	50	70
Price per course	600	800

Collecting cost data

A business incurs costs at all stages of production. It will have to pay for resources bought from outside the business, such as raw materials or components. It will have labour, electricity and other costs involved in producing products from these materials. Cost data can be used in a variety of ways. For example, a builder might gather cost data to determine how much it has cost to build an extension for a customer. Unless the builder knows exactly how much the extension has cost to build, it will be very difficult to set a price that will make enough profit. Cost data might also be used to evaluate the performance of different departments in the business. Departments that keep costs low are likely to have performed well.

Cost centres

One way of collecting and using cost data effectively is to divide the business into COST CENTRES. A cost centre is an individual part of the business where costs are incurred and can be recorded easily. For example, Canning Insurance has four types of insurance which it offers customers - Car Insurance, House Insurance, Holiday Insurance and Life Assurance. Each of these operates as a cost centre. The total costs incurred by the business during 2003 was £5.6 million. The costs incurred by each cost centre were:
- Car Insurance £1.2 million;
- House Insurance £2.0 million;
- Holiday Insurance £0.9 million;
- Life Assurance £1.5 million.

Canning Insurance might conclude from this information that the Holiday Insurance has the best control over its costs. However, other factors will have to be taken into account, such as the size of each department.

How can a business be divided into cost centres? There is a number of ways and the method chosen by a business will depend on its circumstances.
- **By product.** Canning Insurance, in the example above, uses this method. It means that costs are measured for each of the products of a business. So each product is a cost centre.
- **By department.** Many businesses are divided into departments such as marketing, production, accounts and human resources. Each department can be treated as a cost centre.
- **By geographical location.** A business which has operations all over the country or world might use this method. For example, a supermarket chain with stores all over the UK may treat each one as a cost centre.
- **By employee.** In some businesses it is appropriate to measure the costs incurred by individual members of staff. For example, a salesperson could be treated as a cost centre and examples of costs might be wages, National Insurance contributions, motor expenses, overnight accommodation expenses and entertaining expenses.
- **By machine.** It is possible to use a machine, such as a vehicle, as a cost centre by recording all its costs. These might be leasing charges and payments for fuel, motor tax, insurance and maintenance.

Profit centres

A PROFIT CENTRE is very similar to a cost centre. The difference is that in addition to recording costs at each centre, revenues are also recorded. This allows a business to calculate how much profit each centre makes. The use of profit centres makes it much easier to compare the performance of each different part of the business. For example, a supermarket chain can identify the most profitable stores in the country by comparing the profit each centre makes. Profit centres can only be used effectively if an activity generates revenue. For example, since a research and development department does not generate any revenue directly, it is unlikely to be used as a profit centre. A business can be divided into profit centres in the same way as it would be into cost centres, provided the centre generates revenue.

Advantages of using cost and profit centres

There are certain advantages to a business of using cost and profit centres.

Improving accountability Although it is important to measure the performance of the whole business, it is also helpful to monitor the progress of different products, regions or departments, for example. Cost and profit centres can be used to hold individual parts of the business accountable. Without cost and profit centres an inefficient department might not be identified and held accountable for its poor performance.

Helping decision making To make decisions about different parts of the business managers need financial information about those different parts. Cost and profit centres help provide this information. For example, if managers are trying to decide which product to discontinue, to make way for a new product, it can use information gathered from profit centres. Managers are likely to stop supplying the least profitable product.

Improving motivation The performance of cost and profit centres is likely to depend on the quality of work done by the people employed in them. It is possible to motivate staff in centres by offering them incentives to achieve goals or targets. For example, a clothes chain might give bonus payments to staff working in stores if they achieve monthly profit targets. This should help to motivate them to produce their best work. It is also common to delegate control of cost and profit centres to middle managers. Managers may be better motivated if they are offered promotion, for example, when targets are met.

Tracing problems If part of the business is suffering it may be possible to trace a specific problem if cost or profit centres are used. For example, if one of the stores in a supermarket chain is suffering from a high labour turnover, its recruitment and training costs will be high. Labour productivity may also be lower. This will restrict the performance of the store and will show up as higher costs if it were operating as a cost centre. This may not come to light so easily if the costs of the entire business were recorded together.

Problems of cost and profit centres

Dividing a business into cost and profit centres might also lead to problems.

Conflict If a business is divided into individual parts, conflict between those parts may arise. Staff are likely to be more interested in the performance of their own centre than the performance of the whole business. This might lead to competition for resources and a reluctance to share valuable information. The performance of the whole business might suffer as a result.

Cost allocation Not all costs are incurred directly by a particular cost centre. Some costs are incurred by the business as a whole. For example, a chain store might spend £2 million on a national advertising campaign. How should this cost be allocated between cost or profit centres? One way might be to divide the cost equally between all the stores. But this might not be fair because a very large store may get more benefit from the campaign than a smaller store. This suggests that the larger store should bear more of the campaign's cost. In practice, the allocation of such costs between centres is difficult. When costs are not allocated fairly the performance of a particular centre can be distorted.

Factors outside the business It is common for the performance of a business to be affected by external factors such as the state of the economy, competition, the weather or pressure groups. However, it is possible that the performance of each individual cost or profit centre is not affected to the same extent. For example, a UK fast food chain might

experience intense competition in the south west, therefore the performance of centres operating in that region will be hit. This might have a demotivating effect on staff in those centres.

Wasting resources Operating cost or profit centres may result in the business as a whole wasting money. If all centres are responsible for performing the same tasks there may be some duplication of resources. For example, it may be more cost effective if the purchasing of resources for each department in a business is done centrally. Resources may also be wasted gathering financial information from each centre. It is possible that the costs of operating cost or profit centres may not be outweighed by the benefits.

Staff pressure Some of the staff given the responsibility of running a cost or profit centre may not have the skills to do so. This might create pressure and demotivate staff. This is more likely to happen if responsibility is delegated too far down the hierarchical structure.

Knowledge

1. State 2 reasons why it might be important to gather cost information.
2. Explain how it is possible to use a product as a cost centre.
3. State 3 other ways of choosing a cost centre.
4. Explain the difference between a cost centre and a profit centre.
5. Explain why it might not be possible to operate a maintenance department in a business as a profit centre.
6. Explain 4 advantages of using cost and profit centres.
7. What problems might be encountered when using cost and profit centres?

key terms

Cost centre - an individual part of a business where costs can be identified and recorded easily.
Profit centre - an individual part of the business where costs and revenue can be identified and recorded easily.

Case study MacSports

Irene MacDonald owns MacSports, a small chain of sports shops in Scotland. The business consists of six stores located around some of the larger Scottish towns and cities. They sell sports equipment, sportswear and an increasing amount of sports energy products.

Irene divided the business into profit centres when she opened the third shop. She wanted to know exactly how each shop performed so that she could monitor the performance of the individual parts of the business and reward the staff in the best performing shops. Each shop had a manager and was paid a bonus of 5 per cent of profit each year. Also, staff in the best performing shop each year were given a free weekend holiday in New York or Paris. In 2003 the best performing shop was Glasgow East. This is shown in Table 28.1, which includes Irene's directors salary.

After analysing the data, Irene was concerned about the performance of the Inverness shop, managed by Andy. Shortly after the publication of the data she made a special visit to the store. She made a few brief notes which are shown in the memo below.

(a) **Using examples from the case explain the term profit centre. (6 marks)**

(b) **Describe the allocation of the director's salary between profit centres. (6 marks)**

(c) **Explain how MacSports uses profit centres to motivate its staff. (8 marks)**

(d) **Examine the reasons why conflict might arise between MacSports' profit centres. (10 marks)**

(e) **To what extent can Andy be blamed for the poor performance of the Inverness shop? (10 marks)**

- Too much sports equipment, not enough sportswear
- Scruffy part-time staff
- Poorly displayed stock — especially in the window

But Andy, the manager, says:
- Road works in the high street have disrupted pedestrian traffic for 7 months
- Part-time staff have been very unreliable

Table 28.1 *MacSports, revenues, costs and profit 2003*

	Glasgow East	Glasgow West	Aberdeen	Edinburgh	Inverness	Dundee
Revenue	165,001	128,990	99,210	111,999	54,008	83,000
Costs						
Wages	46,000	36,000	30,000	32,000	27,000	28,000
Stock	61,009	49,330	37,009	54,000	26,000	21,000
Heat & light	3,000	3,540	2,100	2,900	1,990	2,001
Director's salary	10,000	10,000	10,000	10,000	10,000	10,000
Other costs	8,600	6,003	5,400	6,500	4,500	3,000
Total costs	128,609	104,873	84,509	105,400	69,490	64,001
Profit/loss	**36,392**	**24,117**	**14,701**	**6,599**	**-15,482**	**18,999**

29 Contribution

What is contribution?

Craig Eckert sells second hand cars. His last sale was £400 for a Golf GTI. He bought the Golf at a car auction for £220. The difference between what he paid for the car and the price he sold it for is £180 (£400 - £220). This difference is called the CONTRIBUTION. It is not profit because Craig has fixed costs to pay such as rent, insurance and administration expenses.

Contribution is the difference between selling price and variable costs. In this case the selling price was £400 and the variable cost was £220. The £180 will **contribute** to the **total fixed costs** of the business and the **profit**.

Contribution per unit and total contribution

A business might calculate the contribution on the sale of a single unit, or the sale of a larger quantity, such as a whole year's output.

Unit contribution In the above example the unit contribution was calculated. It was the contribution on the sale of one unit, a single car. The formula for calculating the unit contribution is:

Contribution per unit = selling price - variable cost

Total contribution When more than one unit is sold the total contribution can be calculated. For example, a textile company receives an order for 1,000 pairs of trousers. The variable costs are £7.50 a pair and they will be sold for £9.00 a pair. The total contribution made by the order is:

Total contribution = total revenue - total variable cost
= (£9.00 × 1,000) - (£7.50 × 1,000)
= £9,000 - £7,500
= £1,500

The £1,500 in this example will contribute to the textile company's fixed costs and profit. The total contribution can also be calculated by multiplying the unit contribution by the number of units sold.

Total contribution = unit contribution × number of units sold
= (£9.00 - £7.50) × 1,000
= £1.50 × 1,000
= £1,500

Contribution and profit

Contribution can be used to calculate profit. Take the example again of Craig Eckert the car salesperson. He wants to

---

Myriem Sriti designs and makes duvet covers using high quality fabrics. She set up a business from home converting a spare room into a small workshop in 2001. Most of her orders came from recommendations, but she does place an advert in the local newspaper every month. She charged her last customer £140 for a king size duvet cover. The variable costs for the order, which included the cost of fabric, thread, lace and buttons, came to £87.

(a) Calculate the contribution per unit made by the last order.
(b) The business received an order from a local retailer for 20 duvet covers. They were sold for £90 each and the variable costs were £63 each. Calculate the total contribution made by this order.

Question 1

calculate the profit his business makes in January. Table 29.1 shows the variable cost and selling price of cars in January 2004. The fixed costs of the business in the same month are also shown in Table 29.2

Table 29.1 *Variable costs and price of cars sold by Craig Eckert - January 2004*

(£)

Description	Variable cost	Selling price	Contribution
Nissan Micra	410	490	80
VW Polo	900	1,200	300
Fiat Tipo	560	620	60
Volvo 740 SE	460	580	120
Seat Ibiza	320	370	50
Astra Auto	1,100	1,350	250
Nissan Primera	1,250	1,520	270
BMW 318i	1,900	2,500	600
Escort Estate	200	250	50
Golf GTI	220	400	180
Total	**7,320**	**9,280**	**1,960**

Table 29.2 *Monthly fixed costs of the business*

Description	£
Office rent	300
Insurance	20
Telephone	50
Administration expenses	50
Total	**420**

The total contribution from car sales in January was £1,960. This is calculated by subtracting the total variable costs, ie the cost of purchasing the cars, from the total revenue (£9,280 -

£7,320). Total revenue is the amount of money received from the sale of the 10 cars during January. The profit for January 2004 is:

    Profit = total contribution - fixed costs
          = £1,960 - £420
          = £1,540

So the business made £1,540 profit in January 2004.

In unit 27 profit was calculated by subtracting total costs from total revenue. If this method is used here, the profit made by Craig Eckert's business in January is:

    Profit = total revenue - total cost
          = total revenue - (fixed cost + variable cost)
          = £9,280 - (£420 + £7,320)
          = £9,280 - £7,740
          = £1,540

The answer is the same as before, £1,540. However, the contribution method can often be quicker than the method explained in unit 27 because there is slightly less calculation.

Fixed costs, variable costs, contribution and profit

The relationship between fixed costs, variable costs, profit and contribution is shown in Figure 29.1. The pie charts show information from Craig Eckert's business in January 2004. Figure 29.1 shows how the total revenue of £9,280 is divided between the variable cost (£7,320) and contribution (£1,960). The second chart shows how total revenue is divided between variable cost (£7,320), fixed costs (£420) and profit (£1,540). Note that the value of contribution (£1,960) is equal to the value of fixed cost (£420) and profit (£1,540) added together.

Contribution costing

How can a business make use of contribution calculations? Calculating the contribution to fixed costs and profit that a product makes might help a business in decision making. This is known as **contribution costing**. For example, say that a design business has limited time and resources. It has been approached by two clients who want a new corporate logo and image designing this week. The prices and variable costs and contribution are shown below.

● Design 1 - Price £3,000, variable costs £2,500, contribution per unit £500 (£3,000 - £2,500)
● Design 2 - Price £3,000, variable costs £800, contribution per unit £2,200 (£3,000 - £800)

So the business might choose the second design as it contributes more to fixed costs and profit.

Other uses of contribution

A business might use contribution in a number of other ways.

● Contribution can be used to calculate the **break-even point**. This is the level of output where total cost and total

Mandy Weston runs an automatic car wash near Junction 1 on the M27 in Hampshire. She charges £4 for each wash. In the last week of February the business washed 480 cars.

Mandy rents a giant washing machine for £600 per week and pays students a total of £300 per week to help run the business. Other fixed costs, such as insurance and advertising, amount to £100 per week. Variable costs, such as water, detergent and electricity, are £1.50 a wash.

(a) Calculate the total contribution for the last week in February.
(b) Calculate the profit made by Mandy's business in the last week of February using two methods.

Question2

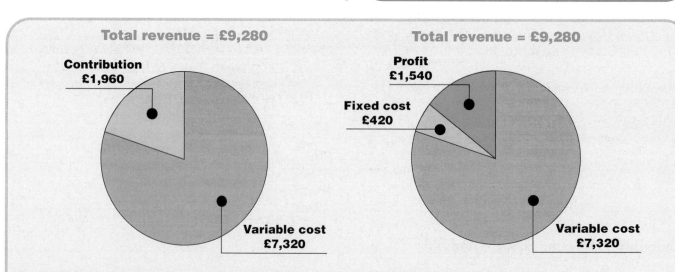

Figure 29.1 *The relationship between variable costs, contribution, fixed costs and profit for Craig Eckert's business - January 2004*

revenue are exactly the same. This is explained in unit 41.
- Some businesses price their products in relation to the variable costs incurred. This is called **contribution pricing** and is explained in unit 19.
- Sometimes a business has to make a **special order decision**. Contribution is used to help a business decide whether to accept an order from a customer below the normal listed price.

key terms

Contribution – the amount of money left over after variable costs have been subtracted from revenue. The money contributes towards fixed costs and profit.

Knowledge ...Knowledge...Knowledge...Knowledge...Knowledge...Know

1. A product sells for £10 and the variable costs are £8.50. What is the contribution per unit?
2. A clothes retailer buys 240 jumpers for £27. The jumpers are sold for £39 each. What is the total contribution made by the jumpers?
3. What is the formula for calculating profit using contribution?
4. If total contribution is £120,000 and fixed costs are £96,000, what is profit?
5. If total variable costs are £450,000 and contribution is £225,000, what is total revenue?
6. State 3 ways in which contribution can be used by a business to help make decisions.

Case study Kumas Kitchens

Stanley and Nita Kumas run a food business in Oxford. They rent a mobile kitchen unit for £300 a month and sell kebabs to late night revellers in Oxford City centre. They sell four different kebab products and a selection of fizzy drinks. Details of costs, prices and sales for June 2004 are shown in Tables 29.3 and 29.4.

In July 2004 Nita suggested that they try to sell oven ready fries. The mobile kitchen unit had an oven which was rarely used and it wouldn't be too much trouble to sell another product. They both agreed and fries were introduced in August. They sold for £1.00 per portion and the variable costs were 60p. In that month 130 portions were sold. Unfortunately the quality of the fries was unstable because the oven could not retain a constant heat. Also people were often kept waiting for the fries. This resulted in complaints from customers and some suggested that they might take their business away.

Table 29.4 *Monthly fixed costs (£)*

Rental charges	300
Insurance	65
Fuel	30
Charitable donation	25
Other fixed costs	20

(a) **State three possible examples of variable costs incurred by Stanley and Nita's business. (3 marks)**
(b) **Using the Lamb Kebab as an example, explain the difference between unit contribution and total contribution. (6 marks)**
(c) **Calculate the total contribution made by each of the products sold in June 2004. (10 marks)**
(d) **Calculate the profit made by the business in June 2004. (6 marks)**
(e) **Calculate the total contribution made by the oven ready fries in August and discuss whether Stanley and Nita should continue to sell them. (10 marks)**

Table 29.3 *Costs, price and sales of products sold by Stanley and Nita's business in June 2004*

(£)

	Lamb Kebab	Chicken Kebab	Special Kebab	Felafel Kebab	Fizzy Drinks
Price	2.20	2.00	2.50	1.70	1.00
Variable costs	1.20	0.90	1.30	0.40	0.30
June sales	550	620	290	160	280

Breaking even

Businesses often like to know how much they need to produce or sell to BREAK-EVEN. If a business has information about fixed costs and variable costs and knows what price it is going to charge, it can calculate how many units it needs to sell to cover all of its costs. The level of sales or output where **total costs** are exactly the same as **total revenue** is called the BREAK-EVEN POINT. For example, if a business produces 100 units at a total cost of £5,000, and sells them for £50 each, total revenue will also be £5,000 (£50 x 100). The business will break-even at this level of output. It makes neither a profit nor a loss. Firms may use break-even analysis to:

- calculate in advance the level of sales needed to break-even;
- see how changes in output affect profit;
- see how changes in price affect the break-even point and profit;
- see how changes in costs affect the break-even point and profit.

Calculating the break-even point using contribution

It is possible to calculate the break-even point if a firm knows the value of its fixed costs, variable costs and the price it will charge. Take an example of a small producer, Joseph Cadwallader, who makes wrought iron park benches in his foundry. His fixed costs (FC) are £60,000 and variable costs (VC) £40 per bench. He sells the benches to local authorities across the country for £100 each.

The simplest way to calculate the break-even point is to use **contribution** (☞ unit 29). Contribution is the amount of money left over after the variable cost per unit is taken away from the selling price. For Joseph's park benches, the contribution is:

Contribution = selling price - variable cost
Contribution = £100 - £40
Contribution = £60

To calculate the number of benches Joseph needs to sell to break-even, the following formula can be used:

$$\text{Break-even point} = \frac{\text{Fixed costs}}{\text{Contribution}}$$

$$= \frac{£60,000}{£60}$$

= 1,000 benches

Joseph Cadwallader's business will break-even when 1,000 park benches are sold.

Calculating the break-even point using total revenue and total cost

Another way of calculating the break-even point is to use the total cost and total revenue equations. In the case of Joseph Cadwallader:

Total cost = fixed cost + variable cost
or TC = £60,000 + £40Q
and Total revenue = price x quantity sold
or TR = £100Q

where Q is the quantity produced and sold, ie the number of park benches. A firm will break-even where total cost is equal to total revenue. Therefore we can write:

TC = TR
£60,000 + £40Q = £100Q

To find Q we can calculate:

60,000 = 100Q - 40Q
60,000 = 60Q
$\frac{60,000}{60}$ = Q
1,000 = Q

It is possible to check whether this answer is correct by calculating total cost and total revenue when 1,000 benches are produced. If the answers are the same, the break-even quantity is correct.

TC = £60,000 + (£40 x 1,000) = £60,000 + £40,000 = £100,000
TR = £100 x 1,000 = £100,000

Both TC and TR are equal to £100,000, so the break-even quantity is 1,000 benches. This also confirms that the answer using the contribution method was correct.

Profit and loss

Total cost and total revenue equations can be used to calculate the amount of profit or loss the firm will make at particular levels of output. At any level of output below the break-even point the firm will make a loss. Output produced above the break-even level will make a profit. Thus, if the bench manufacturer were to produce 1,200 benches, profit would be:

$$Profit = TR - TC$$
$$= (£100 \times 1,200) - (£60,000 + [£40 \times 1,200])$$
$$= £120,000 - (£60,000 + £48,000)$$
$$= £120,000 - £108,000$$
$$Profit = £12,000$$

Break-even charts

The use of graphs is often helpful in break-even analysis. It is possible to identify the break-even point by plotting the total cost and total revenue equations on a graph (☞ unit 27). This graph is called a BREAK-EVEN CHART. Figure 30.1 shows the break-even chart for Joseph Cadwallader's business. Output is measured on the horizontal axis and revenue, costs and profit are measured on the vertical axis. What does the break-even chart show?

AutoCafe Ltd manufactures automatic coffee machines in a small factory based in Swansea. They are sold directly to offices, factories and other employers for £500 each. AutoCafe's annual fixed costs are £250,000. The variable costs incurred when making a single machine are shown in Figure 30.2.

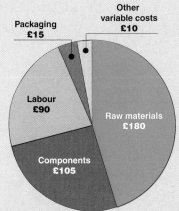

Figure 30.2 The variable costs incurred by AutoCafe Ltd when making one coffee machine

(a) Show the formulae for (i) total cost and (ii) total revenue.
(b) Calculate how many coffee machines AutoCafe Ltd needs to produce in a year to break-even.
(c) Calculate how much profit would be made if AutoCafe Ltd produced 4,000 coffee machines in a year.

Question 2

• The value of total cost over a range of output. For example, when Joseph produces 1,500 benches total costs are £120,000.

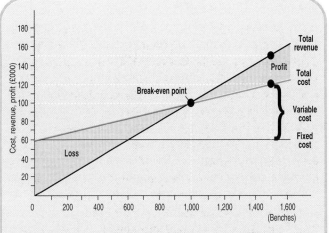

Figure 30.1 Break-even chart for Joseph Cadwallader

Graham Jones produces beer trays which he sells to cafés and local authorities. He has recently secured two new contracts and is about to step up production in his small factory. This has increased his fixed costs quite significantly. In order to see the effect the increase in costs would have on the profitability of his business over a range of output he drew up a break-even chart.

Figure 30.3 Break-even chart for Graham Jones

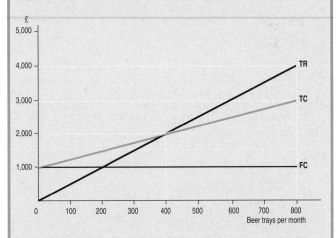

(a) Using the break-even chart shown in Figure 30.3 state:
    (i) the number of beer trays needed to break-even;
    (ii) total revenue and total cost at this level of output;
    (iii) the price charged for the beer trays;
    (iv) the value of fixed cost per month;
    (v) the value of variable cost per tray.
(b) Graham expects to produce and sell 800 beer trays per month. State:
    (i) the amount of profit made at this level of output;
    (ii) total variable cost.

Question 3

- The value of total revenue over a range of output. For example, when Joseph produces 1,500 benches total revenue is £150,000.
- Some break-even charts show the level of fixed costs over a range of output. For example, the fixed costs for Joseph's business are £60,000.
- The level of output needed to break-even. The break-even point is where total costs equal total revenue of £100,000. This is when 1,000 benches are produced.
- At levels of output below the break-even point, losses are made. This is because total costs exceed total revenue.
- At levels of output above the break-even point, a profit is made. This profit gets larger as output rises.
- The relationship between fixed costs and variable costs as output rises. At low levels of output fixed costs represent a large proportion of total costs. As output rises, fixed costs become a smaller proportion of total costs.
- The profit at a particular level of output. If Joseph produces 1,500 benches, profit is shown by the vertical gap between the total cost and total revenue equations. It is £30,000.

The margin of safety

What if a business is producing a level of output above the break-even point? It might be useful to know by how much sales could fall before a loss is made. This is called the MARGIN OF SAFETY. It refers to the range of output over which a profit can be made. The margin of safety can be identified on the break-even chart by measuring the distance between the break-even level of output and the current (profitable) level output. For example, Figure 30.4 shows the break-even chart for Joseph Cadwallader. If Joseph produces 1,200 benches the margin of safety is 200 benches. This means that output can fall by 200 before a loss is made. If Joseph sells 1,200 benches the chart shows that total revenue is £120,000, total cost is £108,000 and profit is £12,000.

Businesses prefer to operate with a large margin of safety. This means that if sales drop they still might make some profit. With a small margin of safety there is a risk that the business is more likely to make losses if sales fall.

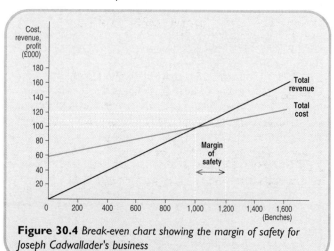

Figure 30.4 *Break-even chart showing the margin of safety for Joseph Cadwallader's business*

Advantage of break-even analysis

The break-even chart is an easy visual means of analysing the firm's financial position at different levels of output. Business decision makers can see at a glance the amount of profit or loss that will be made at different levels of production. The chart can also be used to show the effect on the break-even point, the level of profit and the margin of safety of changes in costs or price.

Changes in price Figure 30.5 shows the effect of a 10 per cent increase in price for Joseph Cadwallader. This causes the total revenue function to shift from TR_1 to TR_2 indicating that total sales revenue has increased at all levels of output. The higher price means that the business will break-even at a lower level of output, ie 857 benches. It will also mean higher levels of profit (or lower losses) at every level of output. The margin of safety will also increase assuming an output of 1,200 benches is produced. (This is not shown in Figure 30.5.)

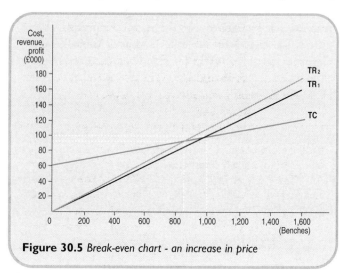

Figure 30.5 *Break-even chart - an increase in price*

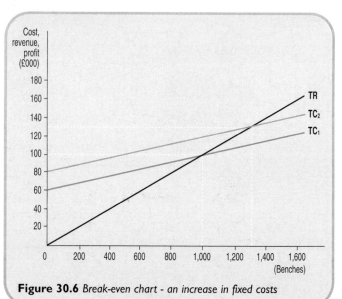

Figure 30.6 *Break-even chart - an increase in fixed costs*

Increases in fixed costs Figure 30.6 shows the effect of an increase in fixed costs of £20,000 for Joseph Cadwallader. The total cost function makes a parallel shift upwards from TC_1 to TC_2. This occurs because a rise in fixed costs causes total cost to increase by the same amount at every level of output. As a result the break-even level of output rises to 1,333 benches. At all levels of output profit falls (or losses rise). There is no longer a margin of safety if 1,200 benches are produced. Joseph's business will make a loss at this output.

Increase in variable costs An increase in variable costs will increase the gradient of the total cost function. This is illustrated in Figure 30.7 by a shift from TC_1 to TC_2. The break-even level of output for Joseph Cadwallader rises to 1,200 benches when variable costs rise by £10. At an output of 1,200 there is no margin of safety as the firm breaks-even.

Limitations to break-even analysis

Break-even analysis as an aid to business decision making does have some limitations. It is often regarded as too simplistic, and many of its assumptions are unrealistic.

- It assumes that all output is sold and no stocks are held. Many businesses hold stocks of finished goods to cope with changes in demand. There are also times when firms cannot sell what they produce and choose to stockpile their output to avoid laying off staff.
- The break-even chart is drawn for a given set of conditions. It cannot cope with a sudden increase in wages and prices or changes in technology.
- The effectiveness of break-even analysis depends on the quality and accuracy of the data used to construct cost and revenue functions. If the data is poor and inaccurate, the conclusions drawn on the basis of the data are flawed. For example, if fixed costs are underestimated, the level of output required to break-even will be higher than suggested by the break-even chart.

- Throughout the analysis it has been assumed that the total cost and total revenue functions are linear. This may not always be the case.
- Many businesses produce more than one single product. It is likely that each product will have different variable costs and different prices. The problem is how to allocate the fixed costs of the multi-product business to each individual product. There is a number of ways, but none is perfect. Therefore, if the fixed costs incurred by each product is inaccurate, break-even analysis is less useful.
- Some fixed costs are stepped. For example, a manufacturer, in order to increase output, may need to acquire more capacity. This may result in rent increases and thus fixed costs will rise sharply. Under these circumstances it is difficult to use break-even analysis.

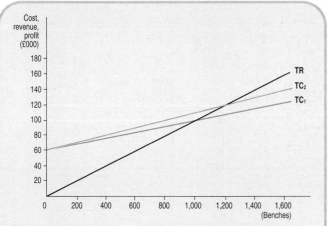

Figure 30.7 *Break-even chart - an increase in variable costs*

Knowledge...Knowledge...Knowledge...

1. How can break-even analysis be used?
2. How can the contribution be used to calculate the break-even level of output?
3. How can the break-even level of output calculation be checked?
4. State 5 things which a break-even chart can show.
5. What effect will a price increase have on the margin of safety?
6. What effect will a fall in fixed costs have on the margin of safety?
7. What effect will a fall in variable costs have on the break-even level of output?
8. State 3 limitations of break-even analysis.

Case study *Jeffers Garden Designs*

During a long hot summer Marion Jeffers noticed that the garden furniture she bought the last year had faded badly. She decided she could do better. So she set up in business making her own furniture designs and selling them to garden centres and retailers in Wiltshire. She drew up a business plan, which included a schedule of her costs and a break-even chart. These are shown in Table 30.1 and Figure 30.8. Marion aimed to break-even in the first year. She knew that covering her fixed and variable costs would be a challenge. However, Marion felt she could charge £200 for a furniture set which included folding wooden chairs, a table and umbrella. She could also avoid renting or buying premises by converting an unused barn on her land into a workshop.

Table 30.1 *Marion Jeffers' fixed and variable costs*

Fixed costs	£
Machinery	2,600
Tools & equipment	2,200
Van	2,100
Barn conversion costs	2,300
Other fixed costs	800
Total	**10,000**

Variable costs	£
Labour	60
Wood	20
Canvass	10
Metal fittings and screws	5
Other variable costs	5
Total	**100**

(a) **Using the example in the case explain what is meant by break-even. (5 marks)**

(b) **Marion's business plan also included a table to show how much profit/loss she would make at different levels of output. This is shown in Table 30.2, but it is incomplete. Using the break-even chart in Figure 30.8 complete Table 30.2. (7 marks)**

Table 30.2

No. of sets	40	80	100	120	160
Total revenue					
Total cost					
Profit/loss					

(c) (i) **In the first year of trading Marion produced and sold 140 garden sets. State the margin of safety and explain what it means. (6 marks)**

    (ii) **Calculate the profit at this level of output. (2 marks)**

(d) **In the second year the fixed costs for the business fell to £6,000.**

    (i) **Calculate how many garden sets the business would need to produce and sell to break-even in the second year of trading (assume that price and variable costs remain the same). (8 marks)**

    (ii) **In the second year Marion's business produced and sold 120 garden sets. Calculate the profit made by the business. (6 marks)**

(e) **Discuss the problems Marion may have encountered when using break-even analysis. (8 marks)**

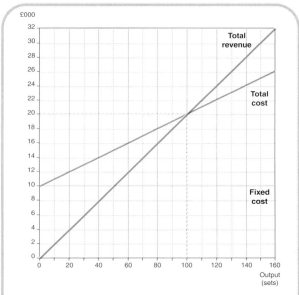

Figure 30.8 *Break-even chart for Marion Jeffers' business*

The nature of profit

Profit is the driving force in most businesses. There are few, if any, which attach no importance to making profit, the exceptions perhaps being charities. Even state run industries, whose major objective has been to provide a comprehensive service (☞ unit 7), have pursued profits in recent years.

Profit has a number of functions. The prospect of making profit motivates people to set up in business. Without profit there would be little incentive for individuals to commit their time and personal resources to business activity. Economists often refer to **normal profit**. This is the minimum reward an entrepreneur must receive in order to maintain interest in the business. If the business does not earn this amount of profit the owner will pull out and pursue other opportunities.

Profit also helps resource allocation in market economies (☞ unit 9). Businesses that make profits are able to purchase more raw materials and labour in order to expand production. Investors are attracted to those businesses that are likely to give the greatest financial reward. Economists call this abnormal profit - the amount by which total profit is greater than normal profit.

The amount of profit that a business makes is a measure of how well it is performing. Those firms that supply quality products which are efficiently produced and sold at prices which are attractive to consumers will tend to be more profitable. However, there are other factors which affect the performance of a business, such as the competition a business faces (☞ unit 62). From an accountant's point of view, profit is the amount of money left over in a particular trading period when all business expenses have been met. Profit can then be:

● retained;
● used to pay tax;
● distributed to the owners of the company.

Gabrielle Fisher terminated her contract with a large fabric manufacturer and set off on a tour of Malaysia and the Phillipines. On return, and inspired by her trip to the Far East, Gabrielle set up in business designing fabrics based on Oriental patterns. She had given the venture a great deal of thought. Gabrielle was highly regarded in the industry and could command a £30,000+ salary as a fabric designer. She felt that unless she could clear £25,000 after all business expenses had been met, the venture would not be worth her while.

(a) What is the value of normal profit for Gabrielle?
(b) Why might she accept a lower return than her previous salary?
(c) If Gabrielle cleared £40,000 in her first trading year what would be the value of abnormal profit?

Question 1

If expenses exceed sales revenue in a trading period then there will be a loss. It is the accountant's definition of profit which we will be referring to in this unit.

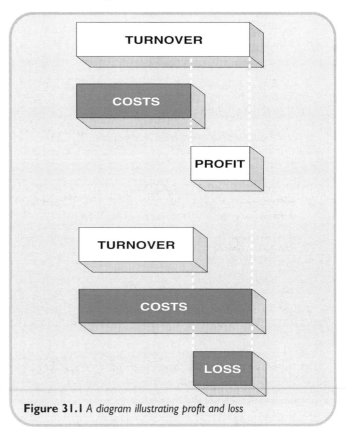

Figure 31.1 *A diagram illustrating profit and loss*

Measuring profit

At the end of the trading year most owners like to see how well their company has performed. One initial indication of performance is the amount of profit (or loss) that the business has made during that year. Figure 31.1 illustrates how profit (and loss) is measured. It is the difference between turnover and business costs. Businesses measure their profit by compiling a **profit and loss account**. This is a summary of all business transactions and shows the flow of expenditure and income in a trading period. A profit and loss account for the year ending 31 January 2004 is shown in Table 31.1 (over the page). It shows the business transactions for Virginian Carpets Ltd, a carpet wholesaler which specialises in Moroccan carpets. It is divided into three sections: the TRADING ACCOUNT; the PROFIT AND LOSS ACCOUNT; the PROFIT AND LOSS APPROPRIATION ACCOUNT.

The trading account

The trading account shows the revenue earned from selling products (the turnover) and the cost of those sales. Subtracting one from the other gives GROSS PROFIT. In Table 31.1, Virginian Carpets Ltd made a gross profit of

Table 31.1 *The profit and loss account for Virginian Carpets Ltd for the period ending 31.1.2004*

VIRGINIAN CARPETS LTD
Profit and loss account for the
year ended 31 January 2004

		£
(less)	Turnover	900,000
	Cost of sales	500,000
	Gross profit	400,000
(less)	Expenses	300,000
	Operating profit	100,000
(plus)	Non-operating income	20,000
	Profit on ordinary activities before interest	120,000
(plus)	Interest receivable	5,000
(less)	Interest payable	15,000
	Profit on ordinary activities before taxation/ Net profit	110,000
(less)	Corporation tax	27,500
	Profit after tax	82,500
(less)	Dividends	40,000
	Retained profit for the period	42,500

£400,000 in the year ending 31.1.04.

The **turnover** or **sales revenue** figure shows the income from selling goods or services. For the year ending 31.1.04, Virginian Carpets Ltd had a turnover of £900,000. According to the **realisation concept** a sale is made only when goods are delivered to customers. This is important because profit must be **included** in the same trading period as sales. Goods which have been manufactured but not sold to customers are **excluded** and goods which have been sold and payment not received are **included**. The final turnover figure may have to be adjusted for a number of reasons.

● Businesses must exclude indirect taxes such as VAT from the turnover figure. VAT is added to the sale price of goods. It is paid by consumers to businesses, which then hand it over to the government. Including VAT would overstate a firm's turnover.

● Sales of goods which are returned because they are faulty or unwanted must be removed from the turnover figure. Turnover will be overstated if their value were included.

● Errors often occur on invoices - documents which tell the purchaser how much is owed for the goods that are purchased. If there is an error which overstates the value of a sale, an adjustment must be made to turnover. Businesses usually send a credit note to cover the exact amount that the purchaser has been 'overcharged'.

● Sometimes a customer who has bought goods on credit is unable to pay for them. The turnover figure is usually left unchanged. However, businesses do record the value of an unpaid sale as a business expense in the profit and loss

account as a bad debt.

The second figure listed in the trading account is the **cost of sales**. This refers to all costs of production. It will include direct costs such as raw materials, the wages of labour and other indirect costs or OVERHEADS associated with production (known as production overheads) such as fuel and rent.

It is often necessary to adjust the cost of raw materials for changes in stock. The cost of sales for Virginian Carpets Ltd in Table 31.1 is £500,000. This is mainly the cost of buying carpets for resale from Morocco. However, it is likely that during the trading year some of the carpets sold were bought in previous trading years and held in stock. Also, some of the carpets bought during the trading year will remain unsold and so the cost of sales must be adjusted.

In Table 31.2, at the beginning of the trading year, Virginian

Table 31.2 *Cost of sales adjusted for stock*

	£
Opening stock 1.2.03	80,000
Purchases during the year	600,000
	680,000
less Closing stock 31.1.04	180,000
Cost of sales	500,000

Kemp Ltd is an engineering company. It produces metal products for toolmakers in the motor car industry. The company has tried to improve its efficiency recently by reducing the amounts of stock it holds. Money tied up in stock is unproductive. The trading account for Kemp Ltd is shown in Table 31.3

Table 31.3 *Trading account for Kemp Ltd, year ending 31.3.04*

Kemp Ltd
Trading account year ending 31.3.04

	£	£
Turnover		1,340,000
Cost of sales		
Purchases	450,000	
Plus Opening stock	98,000	
	548,000	
Less Closing stock	76,000	
		472,000
Gross profit		***

(a) (i) Calculate the value of gross profit, indicated by *** in the trading account.
   (ii) How might the gross profit change if a customer fails to pay for £35,500 for goods bought on credit?
(b) To what extent has Kemp Ltd been successful in reducing its holding of stock during the year?

Question 2

Carpets had £80,000 worth of carpets in stock. During the trading year £600,000 worth of new carpets were imported from Morocco. At the very end of the trading year the stock of carpets unsold was valued at £180,000. Therefore the cost of sales was £500,000. Only purchases of goods for resale are included in 'cost of sales' figures. Expenditure, such as stationery, that is not for resale is not included.

The gross profit of £400,000 in Table 31.1 is found by subtracting the cost of sales from the turnover.

The profit and loss account

The profit and loss account is an extension of the trading account. In practice, there is no indication of where the trading account ends and the profit and loss account begins. However, once a business has calculated its **gross profit** it can then calculate how much profit (or loss) it has made by adding any extra income it has earned and subtracting its expenses and tax. In Table 31.1 the **profit after tax** earned by Virginian Carpets Ltd for the year ended 31 January 2004 was £82,500.

The first item to be subtracted from the gross profit figure is **expenses**. Expenses are those overheads or indirect costs that are not involved in production of goods and services. They include advertising and promotion, wages of the administration staff and depreciation. Table 31.4 gives a breakdown of the expenses incurred by Virginian Carpets Ltd during the trading year. They reflect the type of costs associated with companies. The breakdown of these figures is normally shown in the notes to the accounts or a separate Trading and Profit and Loss Account.

Subtracting expenses from gross profit gives a figure for OPERATING PROFIT. Operating profit is often regarded by businesses as the key indicator of trading performance. It is generally defined as the profit made by a company as a result of its ordinary trading activities.

Table 31.4 *Operating (administrative) expenses of Virginian Carpets Ltd*

Expenses	£	£
Wages and salaries (admin.)	110,000	
Rent and rates	40,000	
Heating and lighting	30,000	
Advertising	15,000	
Motor expenses	24,000	
Telephone	8,000	
Printing and stationery	13,000	
Insurance	9,000	
Accountancy fees	4,000	
Provision for bad debts	12,000	
Depreciation	35,000	
		300,000

The company will then add any **non-operating income** to its operating profit. Non-operating income is income which is not earned from the direct trading of the company. This could include dividends from shares held in other companies or rent from property that is let out.

The next stage is to add or subtract **interest**. Interest is received by a business from deposits in financial institutions and is paid out on borrowings. If any interest is receivable it is added. If any interest is paid out it is subtracted.

When this final adjustment has been made the resulting figure is the **profit on ordinary activities before tax** (sometimes known as NET PROFIT) - £110,000. In the notes to the accounts there are often further details of expenses incurred during the year. For example, by law, the notes must show the directors' rewards, ie salaries, the auditor's fee, depreciation of fixed assets, donations and the number of employees receiving payments.

The final entry in the profit and loss account is the profit after taxation, £82,500. All limited companies have to pay corporation tax on profits over a certain amount to the government. The amount paid by Virginian Carpets Ltd is £27,500.

The profit and loss appropriation account

The final section in the profit and loss account is the **appropriation account**. This shows how the company profit or loss is distributed. Any profit made by a company is distributed in a number of ways. In Table 31.1, the profit of Virginian Carpets Ltd is distributed as follows:
- £27,500 is paid to the Inland Revenue for corporation tax;
- £40,000 is paid to shareholders in the form of a dividend;
- £42,500 is retained by the business for the year (2004) for internal use in future periods. The business is also likely to have profit from previous years. If, for example, it had £127,500 retained profit from previous periods then it would have £127,500 plus £42,500 or £170,000 profit to **carry forward** to future years.

Most companies retain a proportion of profit for investment or as a precaution. The amount paid out in dividends is determined by the board of directors and approved by the shareholders at the Annual General Meeting. Although the business is not legally obliged to pay dividends, shareholders may be dissatisfied if they are not paid.

The relationship between the balance sheet and the profit and loss account

Some of the information contained in the profit and loss account is transferred to the balance sheet.
- The **retained profit in the business** is placed in **reserves** on the liabilities side of the balance sheet. Retained profit belongs to the shareholders until it is used to fund some venture in the future. If a loss is made, the retained profit figure in the balance sheet will be reduced.

Matalan made a name for itself as a discount retailer, selling clothes to lower income consumers from fairly basic retail stores. However, since 2001 Matalan has adopted a new marketing strategy. It has been changing its image, partly due to greater competition from other discount stores such as Primark. The company is improving the appearance of its stores and extending its product line with the aim of attracting more middle-class shoppers. The 2003 profit and loss account for Matalan is shown in Table 31.5.

(a) What is the value of:
   (i) operating profit in 2003;
   (ii) turnover in 2002;
   (iii) dividends in 2003;

Table 31.5 *Profit and loss account for Matalan plc, 2003*

	2003 £m	2002 £m
Turnover	**1,021.5**	?
Cost of sales	855.3	710.4
Gross profit	**166.2**	137.0
Administrative expenses	47.9	29.1
Operating profit	**?**	107.9
Net interest payable	0.9	0.3
Profit on ordinary activities before taxation	**117.4**	107.6
Taxation	30.7	33.5
Profit on ordinary activities after taxation	**86.7**	74.1
Dividends	?	29.3
Profit retained for the period	**53.4**	44.8

Source: adapted from Matalan plc, *Annual Report and Financial Statements, 2003.*

(b) (i) Calculate the percentage change in turnover and profit after tax between 2002 and 2003.
   (ii) Briefly explain to what extent Matalan's new marketing strategy is proving to be a success.

Question 3

- The **taxation** payable and the **proposed** dividend are shown in the **current liabilities**. Tax is owed to the Inland Revenue and dividends are eventually paid to the shareholders.
- The **depreciation** figure from operating expenses has an effect on the **fixed assets** section of the balance sheet. The value of fixed assets is reduced each year by the amount shown as depreciation in the profit and loss account.

Public limited company accounts

Public limited companies have similar accounts to those of private limited companies, such as Virginian Carpets. They must also publish their accounts by law. This allows the public to see the financial position and performance of the company and decide if buying its shares is worthwhile. Existing shareholders can also gauge the company's performance.

It is likely that the published profit and loss account of a large public limited company will be slightly different from that of a private company.

- Accounts often show the **earnings per share** in the appropriation account. This is calculated by dividing the profit after tax by the total number of issued shares. For example, if a company's net profit after tax is £1.6 million

and 5 million shares have been issued:

$$\text{Earnings per share} = \frac{\text{Net profit after tax}}{\text{No. of shares issued}}$$

$$= \frac{£1.6m}{5m}$$

$$= 32p$$

The earnings per share gives an indication of a company's performance.

- Plcs usually pay dividends twice a year. About half way through the financial year a company might pay an **interim dividend**, usually less than half the total dividend. At the end of the financial year the **final dividend** is paid.
- From time to time business may make a 'one-off' transaction. An example of an **exceptional item** might be a very large bad debt which is deducted as normal in the profit and loss account, but disclosed separately in the notes. In recent years some of the commercial banks have had to make such entries after incurring bad debts from

Table 31.6 *The profit and loss account of Joanna Cullen, a sole trader*

JOANNA CULLEN
Trading and profit and loss account for the year ended 31.5.04

2003 £		2004 £	£
130,000	Turnover		150,000
25,000	Opening stock	30,000	
65,000	Purchases	70,000	
90,000		100,000	
30,000	*less* Closing stock at selling price	35,000	
60,000			65,000
70,000	Gross profit		85,000
	less:		
1,000	Casual labour	2,000	
2,500	Motor expenses	3,000	
800	Telephone	1,000	
2,500	Printing, stationery and advertising	3,000	
1,300	Electricity	1,500	
8,000	Rent and rates	9,000	
400	Insurance	500	
2,500	Bank interest and charges	2,500	
2,000	Depreciation - car	2,000	
900	Depreciation - fixtures and fittings	900	
21,900			
			25,400
48,100	Net profit		59,600

Third World countries. An example of an **extraordinary item** might be the cost of management restructuring. Generally they arise from events outside the normal business activities and are not expected to occur again. The expenditure would normally be listed in the profit and loss account, below the line showing profit after tax.

- In the profit and loss appropriation account of a public limited company, the retained profit figure is sometimes called **transfer to reserves**.

- **Net interest** may sometimes be shown. This is difference between interest paid and any interest received. For example, if a business paid £2.6 million interest during the year and also received £0.2 million interest, **net interest payable** would be £2.4 million (£2.6 million - £0.2 million). If a business paid £2.6 million interest and received £3.0 million interest, **net interest receivable** would be £0.4 million.

- Limited companies often produce **consolidated accounts**. This happens when a business group is made up of several different companies or divisions. Each company is likely to retain a separate legal identity and produce its own accounts. However, the group is also obliged to produce accounts for the whole organisation. These consolidated

accounts are produced by adding together the results of all the individual companies.

Sole trader accounts

Table 31.6 shows the trading and profit and loss account for Joanna Cullen, a retailer selling computers. The differences and similarities between the profit and loss account of a sole trader and a limited company can be illustrated from Table 31.6. The profit and loss account of a sole trader normally shows how the year's purchases are adjusted for stock by including opening and closing stocks. In addition, a more detailed list of expenses is included. This allows a comparison with the previous year. A profit and loss appropriation account is not included since there is only one owner and all profit is transferred to the capital account in the balance sheet.

The uses of profit and loss accounts

- Business owners are keen to see how much profit they have made at the end of the trading year. The size of the profit may be a guide to the performance of the business. A comparison is also possible because a profit and loss account will show the previous year's figures. It is possible to calculate the gross profit margin and net profit margin from the profit and loss account. The ratio of gross profit to sales turnover is known as the GROSS PROFIT MARGIN. It can be calculated by:

$$\frac{\text{Gross profit}}{\text{Turnover}} \times 100$$

The gross profit margin of Virginian Carpets in 2004 would have been:

Clair Dunnil runs a camera and photography accessories shop in Torquay. In recent years the profit made by the business has declined. Clair has had to reduce prices to compete with large discount stores and internet retailers. In 2002 the business made a loss of £4,300. However, in 2003 trade picked up as she started to stock more digital camera equipment. Clair was particularly pleased with the December sales when 25 per cent of the annual turnover was generated. In 2004 she hopes to raise prices again.

Table 31.7 *Trading account for Claire Dunnil, year ending 31.1.04*

Clair Dunnil
Profit and loss account year ended 31.1.04

	£	£
Sales		145,000
Cost of sales		
Add Opening stock	10,000	
Purchases	75,000	
	85,000	
Less Closing stock	19,000	
		66,000
Gross profit		**79,000**
Expenses		
Wages	26,000	
Leasing	16,000	
Insurance	2,000	
Advertising	5,000	
Other expenses	10,000	
Depreciation	6,000	
		65,000
Net profit		**14,000**

(a) Why do you think that more detail is shown in a sole trader's profit and loss account compared with that of a limited company?
(b) How might you account for the change in the value of stock during the year?

Question 4

$$\frac{£400,000}{£900,000} \times 100 = 44.44\%$$

A rise in the gross profit margin may be because turnover has increased relative to costs of sales. A fall may be because costs of sales have risen relative to turnover. Gross profit does not take into account the general overheads of the business. So a business may be more interested in the ratio of net profit to turnover or the NET PROFIT MARGIN. This can be calculated by:

$$\frac{\text{Net profit}}{\text{Turnover}} \times 100$$

The net profit margin of Virginian Carpets in 1999 would have been:

$$\frac{£110,000}{£900,000} \times 100 = 12.22\%$$

- A profit and loss account can be used to see how well a business has controlled its overheads. If the gross profit is far larger than the net profit, this would suggest that the company's overheads are quite high. However, if there is little difference between the two this could suggest that a business has controlled its overheads.
- A business can use the profit and loss account to help measure its growth. A guide to a business's growth may be the value of turnover compared with the previous year's. If the turnover is significantly larger than the previous year's, this could suggest that the business has grown.
- The earnings per share is also shown on the profit and loss account for limited companies. This shows shareholders in a limited company how much each share has earned over the year. However, this is not necessarily the amount of money which they will receive from the company. This is the dividends per share.

Limitations of profit and loss accounts

- Business accounts cannot be used to show what is going to happen in the future. The profit and loss account uses historical information. The account shows what has happened in the past. However, it may be possible to identify future trends by looking at the accounts for a longer time period, say, four or five years. The cash flow forecast statement and other budgets may be helpful in predicting future business performance. These are discussed in units 35 and 36.
- Stakeholders who are interested in the accounts must be aware that it is possible to disguise or manipulate financial information in the accounts. For example, a business may attempt to hide its profits to reduce tax or to deter a potential takeover. Alternatively, a business may try to show a greater profit to satisfy shareholders.

key terms

Gross profit - turnover less cost of sales.
Gross profit margin - expresses operating profit before tax and interest (gross profit) as a percentage of turnover.
Net profit - profit on ordinary activities before taxation.
Net profit margin - shows the ability of a business to control overheads and expresses net profit before tax as a percentage of turnover.
Operating profit - the profit made by a business as a result of its ordinary trading activities.
Overheads - indirect business expenses which are not

chargeable to a particular part of work or production, eg heating, lighting or wages.
Profit and loss account - shows net profit after tax by subtracting business expenses and taxation from operating profit.
Profit and loss appropriation account - shows how the profit after tax is distributed between shareholders and the business.
Trading account - shows operating profit by subtracting the cost of sales from turnover.

Knowledge ...Knowledge...Knowledge...Knowledge...Knowledge...Knowledge...Know

1. What is meant by profit from an accountant's point of view?
2. What is likely to happen to a business if normal profit is not made?
3. Distinguish between gross and operating profit.
4. What adjustments might need to be made to turnover during the year?
5. Why is it necessary to adjust purchases for changes in stock levels?
6. What is meant by non-operating income?
7. How might a limited company appropriate its profits?
8. How are earnings per share calculated?

9. What is the difference between the interim and the final dividend?
10. What is the difference between an extraordinary item and an exceptional item?
11. How might the profit and loss account of a sole trader be different from that of a limited company?
12. How might the profit and loss account be used by a business?
13. How might a business calculate its: (a) gross profit ratio; (b) net profit ratio?
14. 'A business may disguise its accounts.' Why might this be a problem for a business attempting a takeover?

Case study Dana Petroleum

Dana Petroleum is a British independent oil and gas exploration company. Around 90 per cent of its oil and gas production is undertaken in Europe. Figure 42.2 shows North Sea sites, although the company also has exploratory and production projects in Africa, the Far East and Russia. 2002 was a good year for Dana with both production and reserves reaching record highs. The company more than doubled its number of producing fields, delivering strong revenue growth and a more balanced portfolio of exploration, development and production. During 2002:

- turnover increased 45 per cent to £38.6 million and net profit was up 22 per cent to £6.8 million;
- average production rose 41 per cent, Otter and

Caledonia fields were brought onstream and proven and probable oil and gas reserves increased 10 per cent to a record 116 million barrels;
- three further oil and gas discoveries were made offshore UK and Ghana;
- new acreage and extension licenses were granted in UK, Ghana, Mauritania and Australia;
- search costs remained low and ahead of target of $2 per barrel;
- a number of acquisitions and divestments (the purchase and sale of business assets) were made and new deals set up to strengthen the company's position.

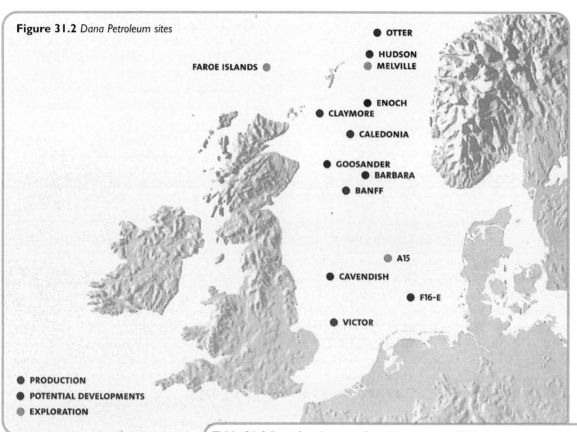

Figure 31.2 *Dana Petroleum sites*

OTTER
HUDSON
MELVILLE
FAROE ISLANDS
ENOCH
CLAYMORE
CALEDONIA
GOOSANDER
BARBARA
BANFF
A15
CAVENDISH
F16-E
VICTOR

● PRODUCTION
● POTENTIAL DEVELOPMENTS
● EXPLORATION

(a) Identify four possible examples of administration costs for Dana Petroleum. (4 marks)
(b) In 2002, according to the profit and loss account, earnings per share were 0.62p. Explain what this means and how it could have been calculated. (8 marks)
(c) Using the case as an example, explain whether the business had net interest payable or receivable. (8 marks)
(d) Calculate the (i) gross profit and (ii) net profit margins for 2001 and 2002. (8 marks)
(e) Using the answers in (d), and any other information in the case, evaluate the company's performance in 2002. (12 marks)

Table 31.8 *Dana Petroleum, profit and loss account, 2002*

Dana Petroleum plc
Profit and loss account year ended 31.12.02

	2002 £000	2001 £000
Turnover	**38,588**	26,639
Cost of sales - continuing operations	26,606	16,839
Gross profit	**11,982**	9,800
Administrative expenses	2,663	1,596
Operating profit	**9,319**	8,204
Group share of loss of associated company	54	58
Profit on ordinary activities before Interest	**9,265**	8,146
Interest receivable	677	866
Interest payable and similar charges	1,711	1,345
Profit on ordinary activities before taxation	**8,231**	7,667
Taxation	1,266	1,234
Profit on ordinary activities after taxation	**6,965**	6,433
Minority interest	155	850
Profit for the financial year	**6,810**	5,583
Earnings per share	**0.62p**	0.59p

Source: adapted from Dana Petroleum plc, *Annual Report and Accounts, 2002.*

Introduction to the balance sheet

What does a BALANCE SHEET show? It is like a photograph of the financial position of a business at a particular point in time. The balance sheet contains information about the **assets** of a business, its **liabilities** and its **capital**.

- ASSETS are the resources that a business owns and uses. Assets are usually divided into current assets and fixed assets. Current assets are used up in production, such as stocks of raw materials. They can also be money owed to a business by debtors. Fixed assets, such as machinery, are used again and again over a period of time.
- LIABILITIES are the debts of the business, ie what it **owes** to other businesses, individuals and institutions. Liabilities are a **source** of funds for a business. They might be short term, such as an overdraft, or long term, such as a mortgage or a long term bank loan.
- CAPITAL is the money introduced by the owners of the business, for example when they buy shares. It is another source of funds and can be used to purchase assets.

In all balance sheets the value of assets (what a business uses or owns) will equal the value of liabilities and capital (what the business owes). Why? Any increase in total assets must be funded by an equal increase in capital or liabilities. A business wanting to buy extra machinery (an asset) may need to obtain a bank loan (a liability), for example. Alternatively, a reduction in credit from suppliers (a liability) may mean a reduction in stocks that can be bought (an asset). So:

$$\text{Assets} = \text{capital} + \text{liabilities}$$

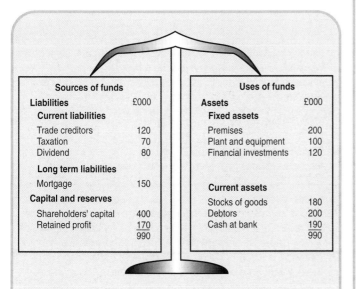

Sources of funds		Uses of funds	
Liabilities	£000	**Assets**	£000
Current liabilities		**Fixed assets**	
Trade creditors	120	Premises	200
Taxation	70	Plant and equipment	100
Dividend	80	Financial investments	120
Long term liabilities			
Mortgage	150	**Current assets**	
Capital and reserves		Stocks of goods	180
Shareholders' capital	400	Debtors	200
Retained profit	170	Cash at bank	190
	990		990

Figure 32.1 *The assets, liabilities and capital of a private limited company*

This is shown in Figure 32.1. The diagram shows the types of asset and liability that might appear on the balance sheet of a private limited company. There are differences in the assets and liabilities shown in the balance sheets of sole traders and limited companies. This is explained later in this unit.

In March 2003 Kathy Smith, a qualified and experienced nurse, set up HomeCare. The business provides care services to elderly patients who live on their own. Most of her clients are private but she also does some work for the health service. Kathy used £10,000 of her own money to set up the business. The following information is also known about the business.

- It has a long term bank loan of £5,000.
- HomeCare owns a specialised vehicle with a wheelchair lift valued at £13,200.
- There is £1,670 cash in the business bank account.
- HomeCare owes £300 to a local newspaper for an advert it placed.
- HomeCare is owed £250 by one of its clients.
- Kathy has some cash in hand that belongs to the business.

(a) Which of the above items are HomeCare's assets?
(b) Use the equation 'Assets = capital + liabilities' to calculate the value of cash in hand.

Question 1

Table 32.1

BREAKOUT LTD
Balance sheet as at 31 August 2004

	£000	£000
Fixed assets		
Premises	1,200	
Fixtures and fittings	1,100	
Equipment	700	
		3,000
Current assets		
Stocks	800	
Debtors	500	
Cash at bank	400	
	1,700	
Current liabilities		
Trade creditors	200	
Other liabilities	300	
Dividends	200	
	700	
Net current assets		
(working capital)		1,000
Total assets less		
current liabilities		4,000
Creditors: amounts		
falling due after one year		
Mortgage	1,100	
Bank loan	200	
		1,300
Net assets		**2,700**
Capital and reserves		
Ordinary share capital		
(2,000,000 shares at £1)	2,000	
Retained profit	700	
		2,700

FIXED ASSETS are assets with a life span of more than one year. They might include the buildings, musical and lighting equipment, drinks equipment behind the bar, tables and seats.

CURRENT ASSETS are assets that are likely to be changed into cash within one year. They might include cash deposited at the bank and stocks of goods, such as cigarettes and drinks. They might also include customers or businesses that owe money to Breakout Ltd - the debtors of the business.

CURRENT LIABILITIES are debts that have to be repaid within 12 months. They might include money owed to suppliers of drinks or food, telephone and electricity bills - the creditors of Breakout Ltd. They may also include corporation tax payable to the Inland Revenue for profit earned in the past or dividends owing to shareholders. Bank overdrafts are also a current liability.

*The value of NET CURRENT ASSETS or **working capital** can be found by:*
Current assets - current liabilities
Calculating working capital is important for a business. The working capital a firm has indicates whether or not it can afford to pay its day to day bills.

*The value of **total assets less current liabilities** can be found by:*
(Fixed assets + current assets) - current liabilities

The debts that a business owes which are payable to creditors after 12 months are LONG TERM LIABILITIES. They might include a mortgage which has been taken out to purchase buildings. They could also include any long term loans used to buy equipment, for example.

The value of NET ASSETS can be found by:
(Total assets less current liabilities) - long term liabilities

*The **capital and reserves** figure is equal to the value of net assets. The total of capital and reserves is sometimes called **capital employed** or **shareholders' funds**. Capital and reserves are a liability for the business - money that it owes. Shareholders' funds include the money that is put into the business by people purchasing shares. It is the value of shares when first sold rather than the current market value. Retained profit is profit that the business has made in previous years. It is money which is owed to the owners. However, it has been retained in the business to buy equipment or to help cash flow rather than distributing it as a dividend.*

Table 32.2 *Information from a balance sheet for Barden Ltd as at 30.4.04*

	£000	£000
Fixed assets		
Factory	11,000	
Plant and machinery	5,000	
Equipment	2,500	
Financial assets	1,000	
		19,500
Current assets		
Stocks	3,000	
Work-in-progress	2,500	
Debtors	3,500	
	9,000	
Current liabilities		
Trade creditors	3,500	
Other liabilities	2,500	
	6,000	
Net current assets		****
Total assets less current liabilities		****
Creditors falling due after more than one year	6,000	
Net assets		****
Capital and reserves		
Share capital	9,000	
Other reserves	2,000	
Retained profit	5,500	
		****

Barden Ltd manufactures components for forklift trucks. It is located in Bristol and serves a major manufacturer of forklift trucks in Cardiff. Table 32.2 shows information that may be contained in the balance sheet for Barden Ltd as at 30.4.04.
(a) Suggest two examples of:
  (i) other current liabilities;
  (ii) creditors falling due after more than one year;
  that the business might have.
(b) Explain why:
  (i) the value of debtors is shown as an asset;
  (ii) the value of trade creditors is shown as a liability.
(c) From the information in Table 32.2, calculate the value of:
  (i) net current assets;
  (ii) total assets less current liabilities;
  (iii) net assets;
  (iv) capital and reserves.

Presenting the balance sheet

Table 32.1 shows the balance sheet of Breakout Ltd. It is a business that owns a small chain of nightclubs. It is presented here in a vertical format. Businesses now use this method when presenting their accounts, although in the past they were shown in a horizontal format similar to Figure 32.1. The balance sheet is a record of the company's assets, liabilities and capital.

One advantage of presenting the balance sheet in this format is that it is easy to see the amount of **working capital** (current assets - current liabilities) that a business has. This is important because the working capital shows whether a business is able to pay its day to day bills (☞ unit 37). The net assets (total assets - current liabilities - long term liabilities) of a business are also clearly shown.

The balance sheets of public limited companies

Table 32.3 shows the balance sheet of a public limited company, Crestfell plc. It is a major manufacturer of food products. A number of new balance sheet items are included

compared to those of a private limited company. They reflect the type of transactions of a public limited company.
● **Investments** might be shares held by Crestfell in another company. Investments can be fixed or current assets.
● **Tangible fixed assets** could be factories and equipment.
● **Intangible assets** might be the value of the company's good name with customers (goodwill, ☞ unit 34).
● The value of **provision for liabilities and charges** would include a variety of charges such as reorganisation costs, post retirement benefit payments and deferred taxation.
● **Called up share capital** might include different types of shareholders' funds, including ordinary and preference share capital.
● **Revaluation** sometimes appears under capital and reserves to balance an increase in the value of fixed assets. A business may buy a building for £100,000. Later it may be worth £160,000. This £160,000 would be included in the tangible assets figure. However only £100,000 would appear under capital and reserves as this was the original amount spent. Capital and reserves have to be revalued by £60,000 so that assets still equal liabilities plus capital and reserves.

Table 32.3 *The balance sheet of Crestfell plc, 31 August 2004*

Crestfell plc
Balance sheet as at 31 August 2004

	2004 (£m)	2003 (£m)
Fixed assets		
Tangible assets	920	780
Intangible assets	150	140
Investments	20	10
	1,090	930
Current assets		
Stocks	220	210
Debtors	410	390
Cash at bank	70	40
	700	640
Creditors (amounts falling due in one year)	(550)	(500)
Net current assets (working capital)	150	140
Total assets less current liabilities	1,240	1,070
Creditors (amounts falling due after more than one year)	(350)	(240)
Provision for liabilities and charges	(70)	(70)
Net assets	**820**	**760**
Capital and reserves		
Called up share capital	110	100
Revaluation	130	130
Retained profit	580	530
	820	**760**

Figures in brackets show values to be subtracted.

Company law requires both **private and public** limited companies to show both this year's and last year's figures in published accounts. This allows comparisons to be made. When the balance sheets for Crestfell plc as at 31 August 2003 and 2004 are compared, most of the figures have changed.

Depreciation and the balance sheet

In accounting, it is recognised that the cost of a fixed asset is gradually consumed as it wears out. The measure of **consumption** or any other reduction in the useful economic life of a fixed asset is known as DEPRECIATION.

Table 32.4 *Notes to the accounts of Crestfell plc showing depreciation of tangible fixed assets, 2004*

Tangible assets

	Land & buildings £m	Plant, machinery & vehicles £m	Fixtures & fittings £m	Total £m
Cost	380	950	70	1,400
Depreciation & amortisation	50	400	30	480
Net book value	330	550	40	920

Accountants must make an allowance for this when showing the value of assets. They estimate the amount by which asset values depreciate. They then deduct depreciation from the value of assets before placing the value on the balance sheet. The term AMORTISATION is used for the changing value of fixed assets with a limited life, such as a lease or an intangible asset. For example, a business may pay to lease a building. The lease has a value. When the lease runs out after, say, 10 years, it has no value.

Details about depreciation are shown in the **notes to the accounts**. An example of these notes is shown in Table 32.4. Unit 38 shows how depreciation can be calculated.

Sole trader balance sheets

Earlier it was mentioned that sole trader balance sheets will be different to those of limited companies. Take the example of Joanna Cullen, a sole trader running a retail outlet that sells computers. Her balance sheet is shown in Table 32.5. There is a number of differences between a sole trader and a limited company balance sheet.

- The sole trader has a capital account rather than a 'capital and reserves' section. Sole traders are set up with the personal capital introduced into the business by the owner. Joanna Cullen introduced a further £4,500 into the business during 2004, according to the balance sheet in Table 32.5.
- It is likely that a sole trader will need to withdraw money from the business for personal reasons during the year. This is subtracted from the capital account and is shown as DRAWINGS in the balance sheet. The balance on the capital account is the amount owed to the owner. This is equal to the assets of the company.
- A limited company has many sources of capital and reserves. However, all companies will show shareholders' funds (often listed as capital and reserves), which will not be in a sole trader's balance sheet.
- The shareholders of a limited company are paid a dividend. This appears in the figure for current liabilities. As sole traders do not have shareholders no such figure will be included in their accounts.

Table 32.5 *Balance sheet for Joanna Cullen as at 31 May 2004*

JOANNA CULLEN
Balance sheet as at 31 May 2004

2003 £		2004 £	£
	Fixed assets		
10,000	Car		8,000
7,900	Fixtures and fittings		7,000
17,900			15,000
	Current assets		
30,000	Stocks	35,000	
4,000	Debtors and prepayments	5,000	
3,000	Bank account	4,000	
1,000	Cash in hand	1,000	
38,000		45,000	
	(*less*) Current liabilities		
20,000	Creditors and accrued charges	25,000	
18,000	Working capital		20,000
35,900	**NET ASSETS**		35,000
	(FINANCED BY)		
30,000	**Opening capital**		35,900
-	Capital introduced		4,500
48,100	(*add*) Net profit		59,600
78,100			100,000
42,200	(*less*) Drawings		65,000
35,900			35,000

The use of balance sheets

The balance sheet has a number of uses for a business.

- In general, it provides a summary and valuation of all business assets, capital and liabilities.
- The balance sheet can be used to analyse the **asset structure** of a business. It can show how the money raised by the business has been spent on different types of asset. The balance sheet for Crestfell plc in Table 32.3 shows that £1,090 million was spent on fixed assets in 2004. Current assets, however, accounted for only £700 million.
- The balance sheet can also be used to analyse the **capital structure** of a business. A business can raise funds from many different sources, such as shareholders' capital, retained profit and long term and short term sources.
- Looking at the value of **working capital** (☞ unit 37) can

Seafood City is cash and carry, owned by Malcolm Partridge a sole trader. It sells a wide range of fresh and frozen fish and seafood. It serves retailers, hotels, restaurants, and increasingly members of the public who are prepared to exceed the £50 minimum spending limit. The balance sheet for Seafood City is shown in Table 32.6.

Table 32.6 *Balance sheet for Seafood City, 2003*

Seafood City
Balance sheet as at 31.12.03

	£	£
Fixed assets		
Fixtures and fittings		129,300
Vehicle		23,100
		152,400
Current assets		
Stocks	131,210	
Debtors	31,390	
Cash at bank and in hand	10,070	
	172,670	
Less Current liabilities		
Trade creditors	45,790	
Loan	12,000	
	57,790	
Working capital		***
NET ASSETS		267,280
FINANCED BY:		
Opening capital		***
Add Net profit		110,010
		300,030
Less Drawings		32,750
CAPITAL EMPLOYED		267,280

(a) (i) Calculate the value of working capital for Seafood City.
  (ii) Explain why the working capital is an important item in the balance sheet.
(b) (i) What is the value of opening capital for Seafood City?
  (ii) What will be the value of opening capital for Seafood City in the next financial year?

indicate whether a firm is able to pay its everyday expenses or is likely to have problems. The value of working capital is the difference between current assets and current liabilities. It shows the money left over after all current liabilities have been paid that can be used to settle the day to day debts of the business. In the 2004 balance sheet for

Crestfell plc the value of working capital was £150 million.
- A balance sheet may provide a guide to a firm's value. Generally, the value of the business is represented by the value of all assets less any money owed to outside agents such as banks or suppliers. The value of Crestfell plc in 2004 was £820 million.

Limitations of balance sheets

There are also limitations to balance sheets.
- The value of many assets listed in the balance sheet may not reflect the amount of money the business would receive if it were sold. For example, fixed assets are listed at cost less an allowance for depreciation (☞ unit 38). However, the depreciation allowance is estimated by accountants. If estimates are inaccurate, the value of assets will also be inaccurate .

- Many balance sheets do not include intangible assets (☞ unit 34). Assets such as goodwill, brand names and the skills of the workforce may be excluded because they are difficult to value or could change suddenly. If such assets are excluded, the value of the business may be understated.
- A balance sheet is a static statement. Many of the values for assets, capital and liabilities listed in the statement are only valid for the day the balance sheet was published. After another day's trading, many of the figures will have changed. This can restrict its usefulness.
- It could be argued that a balance sheet lacks detail. Many of the figures are totals and are not broken down. For example, the value of tangible assets for Crestfell plc in 2004 was £920 million. This figure gives no information about the nature of these assets.

key terms

Amortisation – used to refer to depreciation in the context of leases and intangible assets. In the USA amortisation is taken to mean the same as depreciation.
Assets - resources used or owned by the business in production.
Balance sheet - a summary at a point in time of business assets, liabilities and capital.
Capital - a source of funds provided by the owners of the business used to buy assets.
Current assets - assets likely to be changed into cash within a year.
Current liabilities - debts that have to be repaid within a year.
Depreciation – the measure of wearing out, consumption or

other reduction in the useful economic life of a fixed asset.
Drawings - money withdrawn by a sole trader from the business for personal use.
Fixed assets - assets with a life span of more than one year.
Liabilities - the debts of the business which provide a source of funds.
Long term liabilities - debts that are payable after 12 months.
Net assets - the value of total assets minus current liabilities minus long term liabilities. The value is equal to capital and reserves on the balance sheet.
Net current assets - current assets minus current liabilities. Also known as working capital.

Knowledge

1. What is a balance sheet?
2. Why is a balance sheet a static business document?
3. Why must the value of assets on a balance sheet be equal to the value of liabilities plus capital?
4. What is the difference between fixed and current assets?
5. State 3 examples of the fixed assets that a business might have.
6. State 3 examples of the current assets that a business might have.
7. Why is the balance sheet shown in a vertical format?
8. What is the difference between tangible and intangible fixed assets?
9. What is the difference between current and long term liabilities?
10. State 3 current liabilities that a business might have.
11. Why is revaluation of assets sometimes included under capital and reserves?
12. How does depreciation affect the balance sheet?
13. State 3 items that might appear on the balance sheet of a public limited company but not a sole trader.
14. Suggest 3 uses of balance sheets for a business.
15. Suggest 3 limitations of balance sheets.

Case study Pubs 'n' Bars plc

Pubs 'n' Bars plc owns and operates a group of community pubs located mostly in the south of England. The company was listed on the alternative investment market (AIM) in 1999 and since then it has grown from owing 51 to 64 public houses. 43 of the pubs are run by managers with the remainder being operated by tenants on three year leases. The tenants are tied to the company's nominated beer supplier. Most of the pubs are 'locals', each with its own character and attracting customers from the immediate area. Managers are encouraged to take an entrepreneurial approach to running the pubs by introducing new sources of income, such as food and accommodation.

A strategic change was also made to the running of the company. This involved switching those pubs where the provision of food was an important source of income from managed houses to tenancies. This change affected six of the group's pubs. It was felt that such businesses were run more effectively when run by 'owner operators'. This did prove to be the case. Table 32.7 shows the balance sheet for Pubs 'n' Bars plc for 2002. Table 32.8 shows an analysis of current liabilities.

Source: adapted from Pubs'n'Bars, *Annual Report and Accounts, 2002.*

(a) Describe the main tangible assets that Pubs 'n' Bars is likely to own. (4 marks)

(b) Describe what has happened to working capital over the two years. (4 marks)

Table 32.7 *Pubs 'n' Bars plc balance sheet as at 31st December*

	2002 £	2001 £
Fixed assets		
Tangible assets	23,515,713	21,413,377
Intangible assets	1,666,483	1,731,267
	25,182,196	23,144,644
Current Assets		
Stocks	552,299	623,517
Debtors	2,609,391	1,456,145
Cash at bank and in hand	39,833	52,112
	3,201,523	2,131,774
Creditors: Amounts falling due within one year	(3,090,974)	(5,302,988)
Net Current Assets/ (Liabilities)	110,549	(3,171,214)
Total Assets less Current Liabilities	25,292,745	19,973,430
Creditors: Amounts falling due after more than one year	(11,569,149)	(9,290,099)
Provisions for Liabilities and Charges	(227,426)	(230,411)
Net Assets	13,496,170	10,452,920
Capital and Reserves		
Called up share capital - equity interests	4,287,442	4,287,442
Share premium account	4,522,209	4,522,209
Revaluation reserve	2,866,802	559,712
Profit and loss account	1,819,717	1,083,557
Shareholders' Funds	13,496,170	10,452,920

Table 32.8 *An analysis of current liabilities for Pubs 'n' Bars, 2002*

Creditors: Amounts falling due within one year

	2002 £	2001 £
Bank loans and overdrafts	642,597	3,262,282
Trade creditors	760,433	642,075
Amounts owed to group undertakings	-	-
Corporation tax	338,812	273,086
Social security and other taxes	301,092	341,480
Other creditors	228,991	68,256
Obligations under finance leases	337,110	285,860
Accurals and deferred income	246,130	215,577
Proposed dividends	235,809	214,372
	3,090,974	5,302,988

(c) (i) Explain, using examples from the case, what is meant by 'Creditors: Amounts falling due within one year'. (6 marks)

(ii) How might Pubs 'n' Bars be affected by the change in this amount? Explain your answer. (6 marks)

(d) Analyse what has happened to the value of Pubs 'n' Bars over the two years. (10 marks)

(e) Discuss how useful the balance sheet is to Pubs 'n' Bars plc. (10 marks)

33 Sources of Finance

The need for funds

Firms need money to get started, ie to buy equipment, raw materials and obtain premises. Once this initial expenditure has been met, the business can get under way. If successful, it will earn money from sales. However, business is a continuous activity and money flowing in will be used to buy more raw materials and settle other trading debts.

If the owner wants to expand, extra money will be needed over and above that from sales. Expansion may mean larger premises, more equipment and extra workers. Throughout the life of a business there will almost certainly be times when money has to be raised from outside.

The items of expenditure above fall into two categories - CAPITAL EXPENDITURE or REVENUE EXPENDITURE. Capital expenditure is spending on items which may be used over and over again. A company vehicle, a cutting machine and a new factory all fall into this category. Capital expenditure will be shown in a firm's balance sheet because it includes the purchase of fixed assets (☞ unit 32). It also includes the maintenance and repair of buildings and machines.

Revenue expenditure refers to payments for goods and services which have either already been consumed or will be very soon. Wages, raw materials and fuel are all examples. It also includes the maintenance and repair of buildings and machines. Revenue expenditure will be shown in a firm's profit and loss account (☞ unit 31) because it represents business costs or expenses.

Internal sources of finance

Figure 44.1 shows how sources of finance are either internal or external. Internal sources can only be used when a business is established because money cannot be taken out of a business until revenue has been generated by trading activities. Although most of this unit focuses on external sources of finance, internal sources are very important. This is because internal sources are cheap. A business does not have to pay interest, for example, if it uses its own money to fund activities. There are three important internal sources of finance.

- **Profit**. Retained profit (☞ unit 31) is profit after tax that has not been returned to the owners. It is the single most important source of finance for a business. Around 65 per cent of all business funding comes from retained profit. It is the cheapest source of finance, with no financial charges such as interest, dividends and administration. However, there is an opportunity cost. If retained profit is used by the business it cannot be returned to the owners. This may lead to conflict if the shareholders of a public limited company, for example, see that dividend payments have been frozen because the directors have used the profit in

the business.
- **Working capital**. It may be possible to 'squeeze' working capital to provide extra finance for the business. One way of doing this is to operate a 'tighter' credit policy. For example, a business might reduce the trade credit period, so that money is received from customers more quickly. Or a business might collect long-standing debts by applying more pressure to customers. Both these options might result in a loss of orders and damage customer relations. Another approach is to reduce stock holding. Money tied up in stocks is unproductive. If a business can reduce stock, money is released and can be used for more productive activities. But having too little stock can be a problem. For

(a) Look at the photographs. State which transactions to buy these items are revenue expenditure and which are capital expenditure.
(b) Why might expenditure on equipment need to be repeated?
(c) Explain why it might be easier to cut capital expenditure rather than revenue expenditure.

Building materials

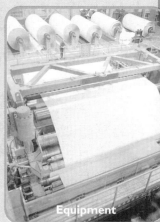
Equipment

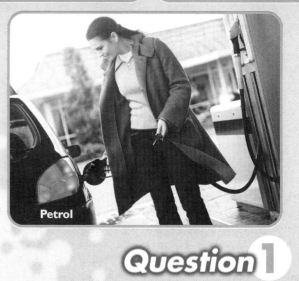
Petrol

Question 1

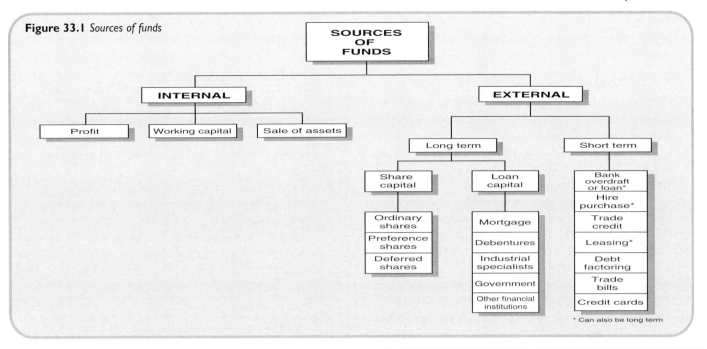

Figure 33.1 *Sources of funds*

example, a business might find it difficult to cope with a surge in demand if stocks are too low.

● **Sale of assets.** An established business may be able to sell some unwanted assets to raise finance. For example, machinery, land and buildings that are no longer required could be sold off. Large companies can sell parts of their organisation to raise finance. For example, in 2003 Scottish & Newcastle put its £2.4 billion pub estate up for sale. It wanted to sell the 1,540 pub estate to focus on brewing. Another option is to raise money through a SALE AND LEASEBACK. This involves selling an asset, such as property or machinery, that the business still wants to use. The sale is made to a specialist company that leases the asset back to the seller. This is an increasingly popular source of finance.

External long term sources of finance

External long term capital can be in the form of share capital or loan capital.

Share capital For a limited company SHARE CAPITAL is likely to be the most important source of finance. The sale of shares can raise very large amounts of money. ISSUED SHARE CAPITAL is the money raised from the sale of shares. AUTHORISED SHARE CAPITAL is the maximum amount shareholders want to raise. Share capital is often referred to as PERMANENT CAPITAL. This is because it is not normally **redeemed**, ie it is not repaid by the business. Once the share has been sold, the buyer is entitled to a share in the profit of the company, ie a **dividend** (☞ unit 3). Dividends are not always declared. Sometimes a business makes a loss or needs to retain profit to help fund future business activities. A shareholder can make a CAPITAL GAIN by selling the share at a higher price

Table 33.1 *Summary and explanation of the ways in which new shares can be made available to investors on the stock exchange*

INITIAL PUBLIC OFFERING (IPO)	
Public issue	Potential investors might apply to an ISSUING HOUSE, such as a merchant bank, after reading the company prospectus. This is an expensive method, but suits big issues.
Offer for sale	Shares are issued to an issuing house, which then sells them at a fixed price. This is also expensive but suits small issues.
Sale by tender	The company states a minimum price which it will accept from investors and then allocates shares to the highest bidders.
PLACING	
Private placing	Unquoted companies (who do not sell on the Stock Exchange) or those with small share sales approach issuing houses to place the shares privately with investors.
Stock exchange placing	Less popular issues can be placed by the stock exchange with institutional investors, for example. This is relatively inexpensive.
AN INTRODUCTION	Existing shareholders get permission from the Stock Exchange to sell shares by attracting new shareholders to the firm. No new capital is raised.
RIGHTS ISSUE	Existing shareholders are given the 'right' to buy new shares at a discounted price. This is cheap and simple, and creates free publicity. Issues can be based on current holdings. A 1 for 5 issue means that 1 new share is issued for every 5 currently held.
BONUS ISSUE	New shares are issued to existing shareholders to capitalise on reserves which have built up over the years. No new capital is raised and shareholders end up with more shares, but at lower prices.

than it was originally bought for. Shares are not normally sold back to the business. The shares of public limited companies are sold in a special share market called the STOCK MARKET or STOCK EXCHANGE, dealt with later in this unit. Shares in private limited companies are transferred privately (☞ unit 6). Shareholders, because they are part owners of the business, are entitled to a vote. One vote is allowed for each share owned. Voting takes place annually and shareholders vote either to re-elect the existing board of directors or replace them. Different types of shares can be issued.

- **Ordinary shares**. These are also called EQUITIES and are the most common type of share issued. They are also the riskiest type of share since there is no guaranteed dividend. The size of the dividend depends on how much profit is made and how much the directors decide to retain in the business. All ordinary shareholders have voting rights. When a share is first sold it has a nominal value shown on it - its original value. Share prices will change as they are bought and sold again and again.
- **Preference shares**. The owners of these shares receive a fixed rate of return when a dividend is declared. They carry less risk because shareholders are entitled to their dividend before the holders of ordinary shares. Preference shareholders are not strictly owners of the company. If the company is sold, their rights to dividends and capital repayments are limited to fixed amounts. Some preference shares are **cumulative**, entitling the holder to dividend arrears from years when dividends were not declared. Some are also **redeemable**, which means that they can be bought back by the company.
- **Deferred shares**. These are not used often. They are usually held by the founders of the company. Deferred shareholders only receive a dividend after the ordinary shareholders have been paid a minimum amount.

When a company issues shares there is a variety of ways in which they can be made available to potential investors as shown in Table 33.1.

Loan capital Loan capital may come from a number of sources.
- Debentures. The holder of a debenture is a creditor of the company, not an owner. This means that holders are entitled to an agreed fixed rate of return, but have no voting rights. The amount borrowed must be repaid by the expiry date.
- Mortgage. Only limited companies can raise money from the sale of shares and debentures (☞ unit 6). Smaller enterprises often need long term funding, to buy premises for example. They may choose to take out a mortgage. A mortgage is usually a long term loan, from, say, a bank or other financial institution. The lender must use land or property as security on the loan.
- Industrial loan specialists. A number of organisations provide funds especially for business and commercial uses. These specialists tend to cater for businesses which have difficulty in raising funds from conventional sources. In recent years there has been a significant growth in the number of VENTURE CAPITALISTS. These provide funds for small and medium sized companies that appear to have some potential, but are considered too risky by other investors. Venture capitalists often use their own funds, but also attract money from financial institutions and '**Business Angels**'.

Business Angels are individuals who invest between £10,000 and £100,000, often in exchange for an equity stake.

A typical Angel might make one or two investments in a three year period, either individually or together with a small group of friends, relatives or business associates. Most investments are in start-ups or early stage expansions. There are several reasons why people become Business Angels. Many like the excitement of the gamble involved, or being part of a new or developing business. Others are attracted by the tax relief offered by the government. Some are looking for investment opportunities for their unused income, such as retired business people.

- Government assistance. Both central and local government have been involved in providing finance for business. Business start up schemes (☞ unit 2) can provide a small amount of income for those starting new businesses for a limited period of time, providing they meet certain criteria. Financial help is usually selective. Smaller businesses tend to benefit, as do those setting up in regions which suffer

---

The following letter was sent to a financial advisor.

Dear Sir

I want to start my own business. I believe there is a niche in the bar market on the south coast of England. What is the best way of raising £60,000? This would allow me to rent premises. But I would prefer to buy because I think renting is wasted money. It is likely that this would cost nearer £200,000.

Advisor's reply

Buying freehold will not only save the 'wasted' rent but also provide an asset which the financier can use as security. You may therefore find more success going for this option.

You should speak to your local banks and get them to look at your proposal and business plan. The government's Small Firm Loan Guarantee Scheme is aimed at people like you – those looking for start-up capital but with little security. The government acts as guarantor of 75 per cent of the loan up to a limit of £100,000 for start-ups. But the lending is done by banks and they must like the project and believe that it will succeed.

You will therefore need to raise additional capital to get the £200,000 required. One idea is to use a business angel. To find such a backer you could speak to the National Business Angels Network. It may also be worth checking your local Business Link to see if you are eligible for any grants.

(a) Why might the Small Firm Loan Guarantee Scheme be suitable for the entrepreneur in the above example?
(b) Discuss the advantages to the entrepreneur of raising money from a business angel.

Question 2

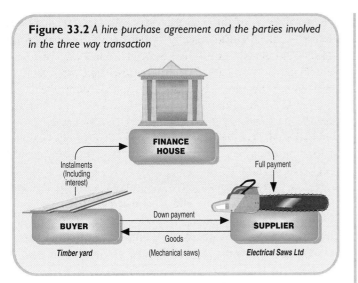

Figure 33.2 *A hire purchase agreement and the parties involved in the three way transaction*

from heavy unemployment.

● Other financial institutions. Banks, for example might under certain conditions give a business a long term loan which will be repaid over a number of years. The bank may require some form of collateral on the loan, and a business may need to present a business plan (☞ unit 2) to secure the loan.

External short term sources of finance

Bank overdraft This is probably the most important source of finance for a very large number of businesses. Bank overdrafts are flexible. The amount by which a business goes overdrawn depends on its needs at the time. Interest is only paid by the business when its account is overdrawn.

Bank loan A loan requires a rigid agreement between the borrower and the bank. The amount borrowed must be repaid over a clearly stated time period, in regular instalments. Most bank loans are short or medium term. Banks dislike long term lending because of their need for security and liquidity. Sometimes, banks change persistent overdrafts into loans, so that firms are forced to repay at regular intervals.

Hire purchase This is often used by small businesses to buy plant and machinery. Sometimes, a hire purchase agreement requires a down payment by the borrower, who agrees to repay the remainder in instalments over a period of time. FINANCE HOUSES specialise in providing funds for such agreements. Figure 33.2 illustrates the working of an agreement and the parties involved. The buyer may place a down payment on a machine with the supplier and receives delivery. The finance house pays the supplier the amount outstanding and collects instalments (including interest) from the buyer. The goods bought do not legally belong to the buyer until the very last instalment has been paid to the finance house.

If the buyer falls behind with the repayments the finance

house can legally repossess the item. Finance houses are less selective than banks when granting loans. Hence their interest rates are higher. They add a servicing charge for paying in instalments which also leads to higher rates. Hire purchase agreements can sometimes be for longer periods.

Trade credit It is common for businesses to buy raw materials, components and fuel and pay for them at a later date, usually within 30-90 days. Paying for goods and services using trade credit seems to be an interest free way of raising finance. It is particularly profitable during periods of inflation. However, many companies encourage early payment by offering discounts. The cost of goods is often higher if the firm does not pay early. Delaying the payment of bills can also result in poor business relations with suppliers.

Leasing A LEASE is a contract in which a business acquires the use of resources such as, property, machinery or equipment, in return for regular payments. In this type of finance, the ownership never passes to the business that is using the resource. With a **finance lease**, the arrangement is often for three years or longer and, at the end of the period, the business is given the option of then buying the resource. In accounting, the payments are treated as capital expenditure. With an **operating lease**, the arrangement is generally for a shorter period of time, and the payments are treated as revenue expenditure.

There are some advantages of leasing.
● No large sums of money are needed to buy the use of equipment.
● Maintenance and repair costs are not the responsibility of the user.
● Hire companies can offer the most up to date equipment.
● Leasing is useful when equipment is only required occasionally.

Jo Li runs a mini-market in Gloucester. He sells a wide range of groceries, confectionery, newspapers, greetings cards, stationery and a small range of hardware products. He also rents out videos and allows his daughter space in the store to sell freshly made pizzas. The business is successful but Jo Li works very hard. The store is open from 7.00 am to 10.30 pm seven days a week. He has recently obtained a licence to sell alcohol. He spent £6,000 of retained profit extending the premises so that extra shelving could be fitted to develop the sale of beers, wines and spirits. Jo Li now needs to stock the new section at an estimated cost of £3,000.

(a) What are the advantages to Jo Li of using retained profit to extend the premises?
(b) Discuss whether Jo Li should use a bank overdraft or trade credit to buy the stock for the new section of the mini-market.

Question 3

- A leasing agreement is generally easier for a new company to obtain than other forms of loan finance. This is because the assets remain the property of the leasing company.

However:

- over a long period of time leasing is more expensive than the outright purchase of plant and machinery;
- loans cannot be secured on assets which are leased.

Debt factoring When companies sell their products they send invoices stating the amount due. The invoice provides evidence of the sale and the money owed to the company. Debt factoring involves a specialist company (the factor) providing finance against these unpaid invoices. A common arrangement is for a factor to pay 80 per cent of the value of invoices when they are issued. The balance of 20 per cent is paid by the factor when the customer settles the bill. An administrative and service fee will be charged.

Trade bills This is not a common source of finance, but can play an important role, particularly in overseas trade and commodity markets. The purchaser of traded goods may sign a **bill of exchange** agreeing to pay for the goods at a specified later date. Ninety days is a common period. The seller of the

goods will hold the bill until payment is due. However, the holder can sell it at a discount before the maturity date to a specialist financial institution. There is a well developed market for these bills and all holders will receive payment at the end of the period from the debtor.

Credit cards Businesses of all sizes have uses for cards. They can be used by executives to meet expenses such as hotel bills, petrol and meals when travelling on company business. They might also be used to purchase materials from suppliers who accept credit cards. Credit cards are popular because they are convenient, flexible, secure and avoid interest charges if monthly accounts are settled within the credit period. However, they tend to have a credit limit. This may make them unsuitable for certain purchases.

Capital and money markets

Businesses have to look to external sources for their finance. **Financial intermediaries** are the institutions responsible for matching the needs of **savers**, who want to loan funds, with those of **investors**, who need funds. These groups do not naturally communicate with each other. Intermediaries provide the link between them.

A number of financial institutions hold funds for savers, paying them interest. In addition, they make finance available to investors who, in turn, are charged interest. Some deal in capital, ie permanent and long term finance, while others deal in money, ie short term loans and bills of exchange. They offer a variety of commercial and financially related services.

The stock market The capital market is dominated by the London Stock Exchange, which deals in second hand shares. The main function of a stock exchange is to provide a market where the owners of shares can sell them. If this market did not exist, selling shares would be difficult because buyers and sellers could not easily communicate with each other. Savers would be less inclined to buy shares and so companies would find it more difficult to raise finance by the issue of shares.

A stock exchange enables mergers and takeovers to take place smoothly. If the price of a company's shares begins to fall due to poor profitability, a predator may enter the market and begin to build up a stake in that company. Once the stake is large enough a predator can exert control over the company.

A stock exchange also provides a means of protection for shareholders. Companies which have a stock exchange listing have to obey a number of Stock Exchange rules and regulations, which are designed to safeguard shareholders from fraud.

Finally, it is also argued that the general movement in share prices reflects the health of the economy. However, there are times when share price movements could be very misleading. For example, they fell very sharply in 2003 just before the Iraq war when the UK economy was quite stable.

Insurance companies, pension funds, investment trusts,

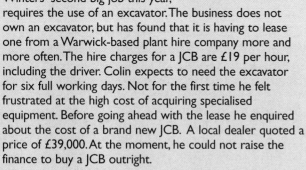

Winters, a small building contractor, has just won a contract to build an extension to a local factory. The contract is worth £78,000 and is expected to take two months. Colin Winter, the owner, employs two other staff and operates from a small builder's yard in Leamington Spa. The contract, Winters' second big job this year, requires the use of an excavator. The business does not own an excavator, but has found that it is having to lease one from a Warwick-based plant hire company more and more often. The hire charges for a JCB are £19 per hour, including the driver. Colin expects to need the excavator for six full working days. Not for the first time he felt frustrated at the high cost of acquiring specialised equipment. Before going ahead with the lease he enquired about the cost of a brand new JCB. A local dealer quoted a price of £39,000. At the moment, he could not raise the finance to buy a JCB outright.

(a) Explain the advantages to the business of using a lease to fund the acquisition of the excavator.
(b) Calculate the cost of leasing the excavator. State any assumptions you feel are necessary.
(c) Suggest how Colin might fund the purchase of a new excavator.
(d) What factors might encourage the business to buy an excavator outright?

Question 4

unit trusts and issuing houses (merchant banks) are some of the institutions which trade in shares.

Banks and other financial institutions The money market is dominated by the major commercial banks, such as the NatWest or the HSBC. They allow payments to be made through the cheque system and deal in short term loans. Savings banks and finance corporations also deal in short term funds. Building societies also provide a source of finance. They have tended to specialise in long term loans for the purchase of land and property.

At the heart of this highly complex market system is the **Bank of England**. This plays a role in controlling the amount of money loaned and interest rates (☞ unit 65).

In recent years many of the above institutions have changed in nature. Due to competition, changes in legislation and mergers there has been a great deal of diversification. In particular, there is now little real difference between the role of a building society and that of a bank.

The Alternative Investment Market and OFEX In June 1995 the Alternative Investment Market was established. Its purpose was to give small, young and growing companies the chance to raise capital and trade their shares more widely, without the cost of a full stock market listing. In order to join the market, a nominated adviser must be appointed, such as a stockbroker, banker or lawyer. The adviser must supervise the admission procedure and be responsible for ensuring that the company complies with AIM regulations. The admission procedure takes three months. The cost of a listing is about £100,000. Another market called OFEX was set up by J.P. Jenkins, the specialist market-maker in small company shares. It is not regulated by the stock exchange, but only stock exchange member firms can deal directly on OFEX. OFEX offers a market place in the shares of unlisted companies that have no interest in joining AIM. Two of Britain's biggest private companies, Weetabix and National Parking Corporation, both feature on OFEX. Also, OFEX acts as a 'feeder' to AIM because flotation and other costs are less at the initial stages.

The choice of the source of finance

A number of factors are important when choosing between alternative sources of finance.

Cost Businesses obviously prefer sources which are less expensive, both in terms of interest payments and administration costs. For example, share issues can carry high administration costs while the interest payments on bank overdrafts tend to be relatively low.

Use of funds When a company undertakes heavy capital expenditure, it is usually funded by a long term source of finance. For example, the building of a new plant may be financed by a share issue or a mortgage. Revenue expenditure

tends to be financed by short term sources. For example, the purchase of a large amount of raw materials may be funded by trade credit or a bank overdraft.

Status and size Sole traders, which tend to be small, are limited in their choices of finance. For example, long term sources may be mortgages and perhaps the introduction of some personal capital. Public and private limited companies can usually obtain finance from many different sources. In addition, due to their size and added security, they can often demand lower interest rates from lenders. There are significant economies of scale (☞ unit 56) in raising finance.

Financial situation The financial situation of businesses is constantly changing. When a business is in a poor financial situation, it finds that lenders are more reluctant to offer finance. At the same time, the cost of borrowing rises. Financial institutions are more willing to lend to secure businesses which have **collateral** (assets which provide security for loans). Third World Countries which are desperate to borrow money to fund development are forced to pay very high rates indeed.

Gearing GEARING is the relationship between the loan capital and share capital of a business. A company is said to be **high geared** if it has a large proportion of loan capital to share capital. A **low geared** company has a relatively small amount of loan capital. For example, two companies may each have total capital of £45 million. If the first has loan capital of £40 million and share capital of only £5 million it is high geared. The other company may have share capital of £30 million and loan capital of £15 million. It is relatively low geared.

The gearing of a company might influence its finance. If a business is high geared, it may be reluctant to raise even more finance by borrowing. It may choose to issue more shares instead, rather than increasing the interest to be paid on loans.

There are several ways of measuring gearing. One way is to look at the relationship between loans and equity.

$$\text{Gearing ratio} = \frac{\text{Loans}}{\text{Equity}} \times 100$$

Table 33.2 *Advantages and disadvantages of being high geared and low geared*

	Advantages	Disadvantages
Low geared	The burden of loan repayments is reduced. The need for regular interest payments is reduced. Volatile interest rates are less of a threat.	Dividend payments have to be met indefinitely. Ownership of the company will be diluted. Dividends are paid after tax.
High geared	The interest on loans can be offset against tax. Ownership is not diluted. Once loans have been repaid the company's debt is much reduced.	Interest payments must be met. Interest rates can change, which causes uncertainty. Loans must be repaid and may be a burden, increasing the risk of insolvency.

If the ratio is less than 50 per cent the company is said to be low geared. This means that the majority of a business capital is likely to be raised from shareholders. Table 33.2 shows the advantages and disadvantages of being low or high geared.

Capital structure

The CAPITAL STRUCTURE of a business refers to the different sources of funds a business has used. Capital structures can vary considerably depending on the type of business. For example:

- sole traders will not have any share capital in their capital structure;
- firms which have funded expansion by reinvesting profits may not show any long term loan capital in their capital structure;
- debt laden companies may have large amounts of loan capital in their capital structure.

Sources of finance and the balance sheet

Unit 32 showed how a balance sheet is produced. The liabilities 'side' shows the debts of the company, ie the money owed to others. It is made up of:

- capital – money introduced by the owners of the company;
- other liabilities – money owed to people and institutions other than the owners, such as a bank.

It was also stated that these are the sources of funds used by the business, for example to buy assets. The liabilities side is divided into three sections – capital and reserves, long term liabilities and current liabilities.

Capital and reserves Capital is the amount of money owed by the business to the owners. If all the company's assets were sold and the liabilities paid off, any money remaining would belong to the owners. Initially, capital represents the amount of money used to start a business.

During the life of a business the amount of capital changes. It will increase if the owners introduce money or if profits are retained. If the owners withdraw money from the firm or a loss is made then the capital of the business will fall. Because of this, capital is known as an **accumulated fund**. Capital is not physical in nature, and the term is used differently by business personnel and economists. To the accountant, capital is the difference between assets and liabilities.

$$\text{Capital} = \text{total assets} - \text{total liabilities}$$

If there is negative capital, where liabilities are greater than assets, then the firm is said to be INSOLVENT. In this situation it is illegal for the firm to continue trading. **Working capital** or circulating capital, is the amount of money a business needs to fund day to day trading. This could be payment of wages and energy costs or the purchase of components. Unit 37 shows how a business calculates it

working capital. Here we can say:

$$\text{Working capital} = \text{current assets} - \text{current liabilities}$$

In the case of sole trader or a partnership, capital might be introduced from personal savings or a loan. For a public limited company, the main source of capital is from the sale of **ordinary shares**, ie share capital. The total value of **issued share capital** is shown in the **shareholders' funds**. This is the money raised from the sale of shares. It is calculated by multiplying the number of shares sold by the price at which they were originally sold, ie the nominal value. In the notes to the accounts the **authorised share capital** will be stated. This is the maximum amount of share capital that shareholders want the company to raise. The authorised share capital is often larger than the issued share capital, but never smaller, as companies keep their options open to issue more shares later. For tax reasons preference shares are much less popular in today's business.

Reserves are shareholders' funds which have been built up over the life of the company. Three kinds are shown in the balance sheet.

- Share premiums. If a company issues shares, and the price they charge is higher than the nominal value, the share premium will be the difference. For example, if a 25p share is issued at 40p, the share premium is 15p. Dividends cannot be declared by the business as a result of such premiums.
- Revaluations. At times, particularly during periods of high inflation, some of the company's assets increase in value. If the values are updated on the asset side of the balance sheet then it is necessary to make an equal adjustment on the liabilities side. The entry is recorded under the heading of revaluation. It is a reserve because the benefit of any increase in asset values will be enjoyed by the owners of the company.
- Retained profits. The directors always retain a part of the company's profits as a precaution or to finance new business activities. When profits are not paid as dividends they are retained in reserve.

Long term liabilities Long term loans over a year must be repaid by the company and are called long term liabilities. The most common listed in company balance sheets are debentures and mortgages.

Current liabilities Current liabilities are those short term financial debts which must be repaid within one year.

- Trade creditors. This is when goods are purchased from suppliers and paid for at a later date. Another current liability which is very similar is an accrued charge. Certain expenses occur from day to day, but are only invoiced periodically. For example, most firms use electricity every day but are billed only four times a year. If at the end of a trading year a bill has not been received, accountants will estimate the charge for the electricity used and record it in

the balance sheet as an accrued charge.
- Bank loans and overdrafts. Loans which are repayable within twelve months are classed as current liabilities. In addition, even if bank overdrafts last for more than a year, because they are repayable 'on demand' they are shown as current liabilities.
- Taxation. Most firms pay tax at the latest possible date. When a company has been notified by the Inland Revenue,

the amount owed to them is shown in the balance sheet as a current liability.
- Dividends payable. Once a dividend has been declared it has to be approved at the Annual General Meeting by the shareholders. It is assumed that the proposed dividend will be approved and because it will be paid shortly after it is listed as a current liability.

Knowledge

1. Why do businesses need to raise finance?
2. State the internal sources of finance.
3. What is the difference between ordinary, preference and deferred shares?
4. State the advantages to a business of a bank overdraft compared with a bank loan.
5. What is the difference between a finance lease and an operating lease?
6. What is the function of financial intermediaries?
7. Describe the functions of a stock exchange.
8. What factors affect the choice of source of finance?
9. 'Capital structures can vary depending on the type of business.' Explain this statement with an example.

key terms

Authorised share capital - the maximum amount which can be legally raised.
Capital expenditure - spending on business resources which can be used repeatedly over a period of time.
Capital structure - the way in which funds are raised by a business.
Capital gain - the profit made by selling a share for more than it was bought for.
Equities - another name for an ordinary share.
Finance houses - a specialist institutions which provide funds for hire purchase agreements.
Gearing - the relationship between funds raised from loans and from issuing shares.
Insolvency - where a company does not have enough assets to meet its liabilities. An inability to meet debts.
Issuing house - any institution which deals with the sale of new shares.
Issued share capital - amount of current share capital

arising from the sale of shares.
Lease - a contract to acquire the use of resources such as property or equipment.
Permanent capital - share capital which is never repaid by the company.
Revenue expenditure - spending on business resources which have already been consumed or will be very shortly.
Sale and leaseback - the practice of selling assets, such as property or machinery, and leasing them back from the buyer.
Share capital - money introduced into the business through the sale of shares.
Stock market - a special share market, usually where second hand shares can be traded.
Venture capitalists - providers of funds for small or medium sized companies that may be considered too risky by other investors.

Case study *Karr Associates*

Karr Associates organises trips, visits and events for companies that want to entertain clients. Clients would be taken to see high profile sporting events, such as race meetings and international cricket, football and rugby matches. Karr Associates was also getting an increasing number of inquiries for hospitality at Premier League football stadiums. By 2004 the business was well established. But Seth Karr, the founder, felt that he needed a website and brochures to promote the business to more lucrative clients. Seth estimated that the total cost would be £15,000, mainly because he would have to outsource the jobs to specialists. He would need to meet the cost of:

● someone to write the brochure;
● an IT expert to design and run the website;
● a photographer to take high quality photographs at some of the events that he organised;
● a printer to produce the brochure;
● a mailing company to distribute the brochure to potential clients.

In addition to this promotion, Seth felt that the company's office should reflect the quality shown in the brochure. He could hardly negotiate deals for glamorous corporate hospitality in his current office above a carpet shop. Seth found a number of possible new offices, but they were far more expensive than he anticipated. Also, most landlords wanted tenants to sign fairly long term lease agreements with a six month payment up front. To meet this payment and furnish the office would cost £20,000.

Seth knew that the finance for this new approach would have to come from outside the business. All the retained profits had been used up. Karr Associates didn't really own anything to sell. Seth had accounts to show that the business was profitable, but had very little collateral. After a meeting with his accountant Seth looked again at his finance options.
1. A mortgage, using his own apartment as security.
2. An unsecured bank loan.
3. Set up a limited company and sell shares to members of the family.
4. Attract a business angel to invest in the company.

Apart from the unsecured bank loan, which Seth favoured, all the options had their disadvantages. He decided to go for an unsecured bank loan on the grounds that the business was very profitable, very

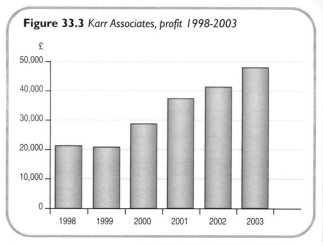

Figure 33.3 *Karr Associates, profit 1998-2003*

low geared and was capable of repayment within four years. He spent two weeks writing a detailed business plan, arranged a meeting with the bank manager, and hoped that his powers of

persuasion would do the trick. Figure 33.3 shows the profit made by Karr Associates in the last five years.

(a) Explain what is meant by an unsecured bank loan. (4 marks)

(b) Calculate the monthly payments Karr Associates would have to make to the bank if the unsecured loan was granted at a rate of 8 per cent a year, over 4 years. Include both the interest and the capital sum of £35,000. (6 marks)

(c) Discuss the factors that might have led Seth and his accountant to arrive at the finance options listed above. (10 marks)

(d) Analyse the disadvantages of using (i) a mortgage secured on the apartment (ii) a business angel to raise the £35,000. (10 marks)

(e) Discuss whether or not the bank manager is likely to grant Karr Associates an unsecured loan. (10 marks)

Assets and the balance sheet

Assets are the **resources** used by business. A company will **use** the funds it earns to purchase assets which add value to a company. Most assets are physical in nature and are used in production. However, there are some, such as goodwill, which do not fall into this category, although they still add value. They are called intangible assets because they are non-physical. One of the functions of a balance sheet (☞ unit 32) is to provide a summary of all business assets and their values. Assets are usually valued at their original cost, less a deduction for depreciation. This is to take into account that they wear out over a period of time and are worth less (☞ unit 38).

Fixed assets

Resources with a life span of more than one year are called **fixed assets** (☞ unit 34). Fixed assets, such as machinery, can be used again and again until they wear out. Some fixed assets like land and property do not depreciate, although they have to be repaired. In the balance sheet, fixed assets are divided into **tangible**, **intangible** and **financial** assets. Each of these are dealt with in detail in the following sections.

Tangible assets

TANGIBLE ASSETS are physical assets that can be touched. The most long term or the least **liquid** of these assets (the most difficult to turn into cash) appear at the top of the list of fixed assets on the balance sheet. For a farmer or a small manufacturing company these are likely to be the most important and largest fixed assets, if owned.

Land and property can either be **freehold** or **leasehold**. Freehold property is owned outright by the business. It is valued on the balance sheet at its original cost, less depreciation. In the past, inflation has resulted in soaring property prices. Accountants have advised many companies to revalue their land and property so that the accounts reflect more accurately a 'true and fair view' of the company. When assets are revalued in this way on the assets side of the balance sheet, an equivalent entry must be made on the liabilities side in reserves to balance the accounts.

Leasehold land and property is rented from an owner and is a company asset. Any capital amount paid for the lease appears separately as 'leasehold property'. This amount is **written off** (☞ unit 38) over the period of the lease. This means the value of the lease is reduced by an amount each year as it depreciates.

Fixed assets which are not land or property are referred to as plant, machinery and equipment. Again, they are valued at cost less depreciation. Large companies often have vast amounts of these assets. The balance sheet will, in this case, not list separate assets, but give only a total.

Intangible assets

Some fixed assets are not tangible, but are still valuable, income-generating resources. These are INTANGIBLE ASSETS.

Goodwill Over many years of trading companies build up goodwill. They may have gained a good reputation, which means that customers will use their services or purchase their products. If the company is to be sold in the future, some value needs to be placed on this goodwill and included in the purchase price. From an accountant's point of view, goodwill is equal to the amount by which the purchase price of a business exceeds the **net assets** (total assets - total liabilities).

Take the example of Amanda Storey, a young, newly qualified accountant, who decides to set up in business. She considers renting an office, advertising her services in the local press and distributing business cards. However, she is approached by Geoff Horrocks, an accountant who is considering retirement. Clearly it would pay Amanda to buy Geoff's list of established clients. The agreed price would represent goodwill.

According to accounting convention the value of **purchased** goodwill should be shown on the balance sheet and then depreciated (or amortised) over its expected useful economic life. The reason for this is that goodwill eventually wears off unless there is new investment to maintain or improve customer relations. In the case of businesses that have not been sold, the value of goodwill is omitted from the balance sheet. Therefore any goodwill, or other intangible assets shown on the balance sheet, means that they have been purchased.

Patents, copyrights and trademarks If a company or an individual invents and develops a unique product, a patent can be obtained from the patent office. This is a licence which prevents other firms from copying the product. Patents have been granted in the past for products as diverse as cats eyes in 1935 and Polaroid cameras in 1946.

Copyright prevents the re-use of published works, such as books, plays, films and music without the author's consent. Michael Jackson allegedly paid £48 million for a back catalogue of 250 Beatles' songs, out-bidding former Beatle Paul McCartney. Substantial fees are paid to copyright owners of music used in TV advertisements. Occasionally, certain magazines will allow a part of their publication to be used free of charge. Trademarks generally signify a manufacturer's name. The right to sell another company's products may have to be registered if they carry a trademark and a fee may be charged.

Research and development Normally research and development (R&D) costs are classified as revenue expenditure (☞ unit 33). However, if a project is expected to earn a substantial income in the future, its costs may be recorded as capital expenditure and included as an intangible asset in the balance sheet. The costs are written off over the period when income is generated.

Brand names Many companies enjoy successful brand names. Recently, some of these companies have debated the inclusion of these intangible assets in the balance sheet because they generate income for a lengthy period of time in some cases. This means that the amount a successful brand name is estimated to be worth should be included as an intangible asset on the balance sheet, so that the true value of a company's assets is made clear.

When an intangible asset is written off it is described as **amortisation** rather than depreciation.

Financial assets

These are often called **investments** in the balance sheet. They usually refer to shares held in other companies. If the shareholding in a particular company is more than 50 per cent then that company is classified as a **subsidiary**. If the holding is between 20 per cent and 50 per cent then the company is described as an **associated company**. Finally, any holdings of less than 20 per cent are called **trade investments**.

There is a number of motives for holding shares in other companies. These are shown in Figure 34.1. Some companies hold shares to earn income. **Holding companies** (☞ unit 6) such as Kingfisher, for example, specialise in buying and controlling other companies. In some cases, businesses are bought, broken up, and parts sold at a profit. This activity has

been described as **asset stripping**.

Another motive for holding shares is to diversify in order to reduce risk. Companies also buy firms in the same line of business to exploit economies of scale, ie horizontal integration (☞ unit 56). They may also seek to buy out their suppliers or distribution networks, ie vertical integration.

Finally, other financial investments might include government bonds or deposits of foreign currency. All financial assets are listed at cost in the balance sheet.

Current assets

Short term assets which can be changed into cash within one year are called **current assets** (☞ unit 32). There is a number of common current assets.

Stocks Most businesses hold stocks of finished goods. Stocks are classed as current assets because the business would hope to sell them within twelve months. The quantity of stocks held by a company will depend on the nature of the company.

Work-in-progress is also classified as stock. It represents

Reg Vardy operates 78 new car dealerships of which 17 represent specialist makes and models. The remaining dealerships operate as franchises. The company also has a contract hire business, Vardy Contract Motoring. In 2003 Reg Vardy's profit before tax rose 19 per cent to £38.8 million. Of this, £3.95 million was achieved from the sale of property and receipts of goodwill on the disposal of businesses. During 2003 the total market for new cars in the UK was expected to be 2.45 million, possibly the largest on record. However, due to over-supply in the market, prices have been depressed. Nevertheless Reg Vardy has performed well and expected to do even better in 2004.

Source: adapted from Reg Vardy, *Annual Report & Accounts, 2003*.

Table 34.1 *An extract from Reg Vardy balance sheet, 2003*

	2003 £000	2002 £000
Fixed assets		
Intangible assets (goodwill)	1,324	1,278
Tangible assets	154,788	162,024
Investments	3,155	3,155
	159,267	166,457

(a) Give four possible examples of tangible assets that Reg Vardy might own.
(b) Some of Reg Vardy's profit has been generated from goodwill. Explain what is meant by goodwill and how this has arisen.

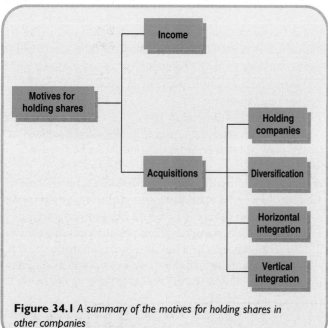

Figure 34.1 *A summary of the motives for holding shares in other companies*

Question 1

partly finished goods, eg half built properties. We also include stocks of raw materials and components in current assets. The business would expect to change them into finished goods which would then be sold, hopefully within a year.

Debtors In some lines of business, when a sale is made, it is common to receive payment at a later date. Any amounts owing by these customers at the end of the financial year are listed as **debtors** in the balance sheet. In order to speed up the payment of bills some firms offer cash discounts. In addition, debt factors offer a debt collecting service.

Related to debtors is another current asset - **prepayments**. A prepayment is a sum, such as insurance, rent or uniform business rate, which is paid in advance. At the end of the financial year any service which has been paid for but not fully consumed is listed in the balance sheet as a prepayment.

Cash at bank Most businesses deposit their takings in a bank. From the bank account various business expenses are paid for. If the bank balance is positive at the end of the trading year the amount will be shown as a current asset in the balance sheet.

Cash in hand Many businesses have cash on their premises. This is often called **petty cash**. Cash is used to pay for small or unexpected transactions, eg the purchase of toilet paper.

Together, cash at bank and cash in hand represent the firm's most **liquid resources**. Businesses need to hold just the right amount of cash. Too much cash means business opportunities are being wasted as the money could be invested in other assets. Too little cash may prevent the business from making urgent purchases. Cash management is dealt with in more detail in unit 35.

Investments Some investments held by businesses may be short term. They may include shares in other companies, bonds or deposit accounts. If it is possible to convert these investments into cash within 12 months they are listed as investments under current assets.

Liquidity

Liquidity (☞ unit 37) refers to the speed or ease with which assets can be converted into cash without suffering any capital loss. For example, a house is an illiquid asset. It could be sold for cash for, say, £100, but the owner would be likely to lose money. In the balance sheet the least liquid assets (fixed assets) are listed at the top and the most liquid (current assets) are placed at the bottom.

Fixed assets like land and buildings tend to be very illiquid. It can sometimes take a long time to sell such assets. Possibly the most illiquid of all assets is a highly specialised item of machinery, ie a machine which has been especially made for a company. This type of capital good will prove very difficult to sell since demand will be limited.

Some fixed assets may be much easier to sell and are

therefore more liquid. Vehicles, non-specialised machinery like a cement mixer or a JCB, and standard tools and equipment, which have a variety of uses, are all examples.

The least liquid of the current assets is stock. Stocks of finished goods are expected to be sold, but business fortunes change and sales can never be guaranteed. The liquidity of raw material stocks can vary. Non-specialised materials like coal will be more liquid than specialised components since they are easier to sell. Debtors are more liquid than stocks because goods have been sold and the business is legally entitled to payment. However, money has not yet been

---

Bellway plc is a construction company with 14 regional house building divisions. In 2002 the company sold 6,044 homes across all 14 divisions. Despite the total home production in the UK falling to its lowest level for 54 years, Bellway has, since 1992, trebled the number of homes sold and quadrupled its market share. It was one of the first companies to embrace the trend towards inner city living. This has resulted in apartment schemes being developed in every division, representing 35 per cent of the total homes sold. Profit before tax rose from £101.5 million to £125.3 million in 2002.

Source: adapted from Bellway, *Annual Report & Accounts, 2002.*

Table 34.2 *Current assets and an analysis of stocks for Bellway, 2002*

	2002 £000	2001 £000
Current assets		
Stocks	737,262	644,421
Debtors	21,522	21,491
Cash at bank and in hand	73,381	4,059

	2002 £000	2001 £000
Work in progress and stocks	736,009	639,572
Grants	(3,348)	(8,483)
Payments on account	(19,548)	(9,387)
	713,113	621,702
Showhomes	17,723	14,483
Part exchange properties	6,426	8,236
	737,262	644,421

(a) Using this case as an example, explain what is meant by work-in-progress and why it is classified as a current asset.
(b) Calculate the percentage change in the value of stocks between 2001 and 2002 and suggest a reason for the change.

Question 2

Aled Thomas owns a sheep farm in Gwent. The farm has been in the family for 112 years. It consists of 2,000 acres of hill farmland, a large five bedroomed farmhouse, some outbuildings, one tractor and other tools and equipment. The farm has struggled to generate cash in recent years so Aled started to run a bed and breakfast operation in 2001. This has helped to improve the liquidity of the business.

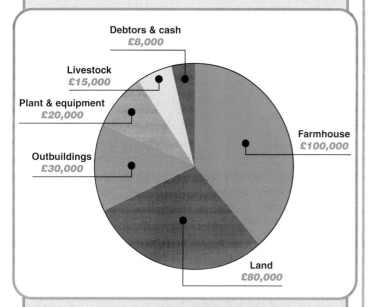

Figure 34.2 *Asset structure of Aled Thomas's farm*

(a) Farmers are sometimes described as 'asset rich and cash poor'. Using examples from the case, explain what you think this means.

(b) How do you think the bed and breakfast operation improved the liquidity of the business?

Question 3

received so it cannot be spent. In addition, there are times when firms cannot pay and so the debt has to be written off (known as bad debts).

Cash at the bank and cash in hand are obviously the most liquid assets of all.

Asset structure

The ASSET STRUCTURE of a business refers to the amount of capital employed in each category of asset. Asset structures will vary according to the nature of the industry in which a business is competing. Manufacturing companies will tend to have a large amount of capital tied up in plant, machinery and equipment. Construction firms will have a significant amount of work-in-progress. Businesses which face seasonal demand may hold large stocks of finished goods at particular times of the year. In the retail trade, public houses and restaurants will have very few debtors, or even none.

A profit maximising company will want to purchase those assets which yield the greatest return. Fixed assets are the productive assets of a business, so firms will want to invest as much of their capital as possible in these. However, some capital must be kept in current assets to fund day to day expenditure. It is not possible to conduct business activity without current assets. Some firms may exist with very little capital employed in fixed assets. Retailers often have a large proportion of current assets if they rent premises (stock in particular).

Company law and the balance sheet

According to the **1948** and the **1967 Companies Acts** the following information should be included in the balance sheet.

- The authorised and issued share capital.
- The amount of share premium.
- The amount of reserves.
- Details of debentures, mortgages, long term loans, short term loans, overdrafts, trade creditors, proposed dividends, taxation due and amounts due to subsidiaries.
- The separation of fixed and current assets.
- The method of valuation of fixed assets.
- The aggregate amounts provided for depreciation of fixed assets.
- Values of trade investments and shares in subsidiaries and any amounts due from subsidiaries.
- Details of current assets.
- The corresponding figures for the end of the previous year should be given.

These legal requirements are attempts to make company accounts standard and help protect the interests of shareholders. Much of the legislation is designed to clarify certain financial information so that the readers of accounts are not misled. The legislation does not place any unnecessary financial or administrative burden on the company and does not affect its decision making.

Westwood Frozen Foods plc is a frozen food wholesaler. It has a large depot just outside London and distributes frozen food to small and medium sized retailers, hotels and other businesses in the catering industry. The company also owns Seafood Ltd, a subsidiary which supplies a wide range of frozen sea food. Table 34.3 shows some financial information about the assets and liabilities which would be included in the company's balance sheet for the year ending 31.5.2003.

Table 34.3 *Assets and liabilities of Westwood Frozen Foods plc*

	(£000)
Cash at bank and in hand	40
Share capital	4,400
Warehouse	2,500
Taxation	2,410
Other reserves	1,250
Debentures	2,000
Debtors	9,480
Stock	6,410
Trade creditors	8,120
Bank overdraft	6,480
Retained profit	5,920
Equipment	5,810
Vehicles	3,240
Investments	3,100

(a) Identify the (i) fixed assets and (ii) current assets.
(b) Draw pie charts to show: (i) the relative values of fixed assets; (ii) the relative values of current assets; (iii) the relative values of fixed to current assets; (iv) the relative values of assets to each other.
(c) Explain why this type of business may have such an asset structure.

Question 4

key terms

Asset structure - the proportion of capital employed in each type of asset.

Intangible assets - non-physical business assets.
Tangible assets - assets which are physical in nature.

Knowledge ...Knowledge...Knowledge...Knowledge...Knowledge...Know

1. What is the difference between tangible and intangible assets?
2. How is it possible to calculate the value of goodwill?
3. Distinguish between a subsidiary, an associated company and a trade investment.
4. What is meant by asset stripping?
5. What is the difference between debtors and prepayments?
6. What is the difference between a liquid and an illiquid asset?
7. Why is a specialised machine an illiquid asset?
8. What is the main determinant of a firm's asset structure?

Case study Oxford Biomedica and Air

Oxford BioMedica

Oxford BioMedica specialises in the development of novel therapeutics for the treatment of cancer, neurodegenerative diseases and other disorders. During 2002 the company progressed from being a research-orientated company to a mid-stage product development company, with successful trials being completed for its products TroVax and MetXia.

In 2002 the biotechnology industry continued to suffer from the general downturn in the market, with many companies running short of liquid resources. Oxford BioMedica saw its share price fall along with many others in the industry.

However, through careful management the company was able to extend the cash life of the business by almost a year and bring its products closer to the market. Oxford BioMedica plans to use partners in the pharmaceuticals industry to produce and market its products.

In 2002 the company's turnover was just £173,000. It made a loss for the year of £11.66 million. This is typical of companies in this industry which research for long periods and may not sell products until they are trialled and developed. Figure 34.3 shows the asset structure of the business.

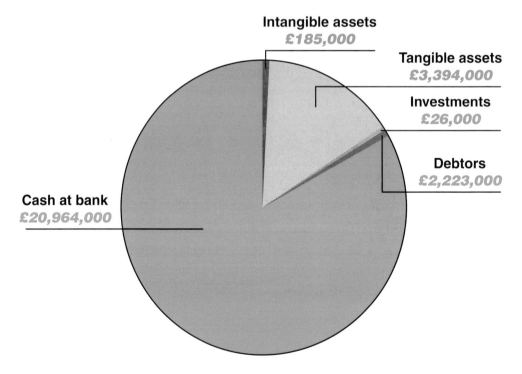

Figure 34.3 *Asset structure, 2002*
Source: adapted from Oxford BioMedica, *Annual Report and Accounts*, 2002.

Air music & media group plc

Air music & media group plc was founded in 1995, when Air music & media began trading with USA and European customers. The group set up two record labels through its subsidiary, Going For A Song Ltd, between 1997 and 2000 and has access to around 100,000 music tracks.

Air's core activities are the development and acquisition of music copyrights, the licensing of third party music copyrights and the exploitation of those rights through the production and sale of budget priced audio compact discs and cassettes. In 2002, sales were mainly to music wholesalers or distributors.

Air's products cover a broad spectrum of music genres. Collectively the products could be referred to as middle of the road or easy listening. Most of the products comprise music by well known artists or compilations such as 50s, 60s, 70s and 80s music and rock 'n' roll, country, jazz, blues, ambient, new age and world music. The products retail at below £5 in the UK. This is significantly different to chart or fashion-led music products, which typically retail at £15. In 2002 Air turned over £4.374 million and made a profit after tax of £522,859. Figure 34.4 shows the asset structure of the group in 2002.

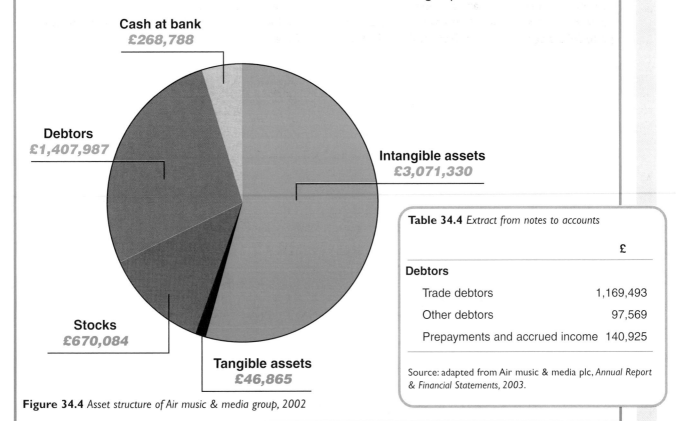

Cash at bank £268,788

Debtors £1,407,987

Intangible assets £3,071,330

Stocks £670,084

Tangible assets £46,865

Table 34.4 *Extract from notes to accounts*

	£
Debtors	
Trade debtors	1,169,493
Other debtors	97,569
Prepayments and accrued income	140,925

Source: adapted from Air music & media plc, *Annual Report & Financial Statements, 2003.*

Figure 34.4 *Asset structure of Air music & media group, 2002*

(a) **An analysis of Air's debtors is shown in Table 34.4. Explain the difference between trade debtors and prepayments for the company. (6 marks)**

(b) **The investments for Oxford BioMedica are shares in subsidiaries. Explain what this means. (6 marks)**

(c) **Calculate the proportion of total assets which are current assets for each company. (8 marks)**

(d) **Assess the liquidity of each company. (8 marks)**

(e) **Account for the differences in the asset structures of Air and Oxford BioMedica. (12 marks)**

35 Cash Flow

The importance of cash

Cash is the most LIQUID of all business assets. A business's cash is the notes and coins it keeps on the premises and any money it has in the bank, for example. Cash is part of, but not the same as, working capital (☞ unit 37). Working capital contains other assets, such as money owed by debtors, which are not immediately available if a business needs to pay bills, for example.

Why is cash so important to a business? Without cash, it would cease to exist. There is a number of reasons why firms fail. The most common tend to be:

- lack of sales;
- inadequate profit margins;
- poor choice of location;
- reliance on too small a customer base;
- poor management of working capital;
- poor cash flow.

According to a Confederation of British Industry (CBI) survey, 21 per cent of business failures are due to poor cash flow or a lack of working capital. Even when trading conditions are good, businesses can fail. Many of these businesses may offer good products for which there was

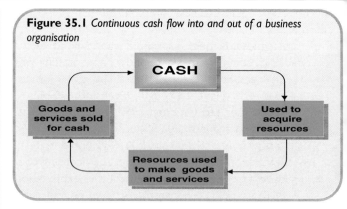

Figure 35.1 *Continuous cash flow into and out of a business organisation*

some demand. They have the potential to be profitable and yet still went into RECEIVERSHIP. Probably the most likely cause of this is that they ran out of cash.

The role of cash in a business is shown in Figure 35.1 which shows a simple CASH FLOW CYCLE. This is the continuous movement of cash into and out of a business. Initially, cash is used to buy or hire resources. These resources are converted into goods or services which are then sold to customers in exchange for cash. Some of the money from sales will be used to finance further production. In a successful business, this flow of cash is endless. If this flow of cash ceases at some stage

Table 35.1 *Cash flow forecast statement for Fishman's Ltd*

(£000s)

	Jan	Feb	Mar	Apr	May	Jun	Jul	Aug	Sep	Oct	Nov	Dec
Receipts												
Cash sales	451	360	399	410	490	464	452	340	450	390	480	680
Capital introduced									300			
Total receipts	451	360	399	410	490	464	452	340	750	390	480	680
Payments												
Goods for resale	150	180	150	180	150	180	150	180	150	180	220	250
Leasing charges	20	20	20	20	20	20	20	20	20	20	20	20
Motor expenses	40	40	40	40	40	40	40	40	40	40	40	40
Wages	100	100	100	100	100	100	100	105	105	105	125	125
VAT			126			189			187			198
Loan repayments	35	35	35	35	35	35	35	35	35	35	35	35
Telephone		11			12			12			14	
Miscellaneous	20	20	20	20	20	20	20	20	20	20	20	20
Total payments	365	406	491	395	377	584	365	412	557	400	474	688
Net cash flow	86	(46)	(92)	15	113	(120)	87	(72)	193	(10)	6	(8)
Opening balance	11	97	51	(41)	(26)	87	(33)	54	(18)	175	165	171
Closing balance	97	51	(41)	(26)	87	(33)	54	(18)	175	165	171	163

Brackets show minus figures.

then the business will be unlikely to continue.

Controlling cash flow

It is important that a business continually monitors and controls its cash flow. It must ensure that it has enough cash for its immediate spending. However, it should avoid holding too much cash because cash is an unproductive asset. Holding cash means that the business might lose out on the profit from investing the cash. A business will have more effective control over its cash flow if it:

- keeps up to date business records;
- always plans ahead, for example by producing accurate cash flow forecasts;
- operates an efficient credit control system which prevents slow or late payment.

The need to keep up to date records of business transactions is very important. The quality of decision making is better if accurate information is available when choosing between different courses of action. Problems can arise if decisions are based on inadequate or inaccurate information. For example, say a business fails to record that a £20,000 payment has been made to a supplier. A manager may go ahead with the purchase of a new machine costing £30,000 believing that the firm's cash position is better than it actually is. The business may not have enough money in the bank to cover a cheque given in payment.

Advances in information technology have enabled businesses to keep more up to date records and access information very quickly. However, mistakes can still occur if computer operators fail to input information correctly. Methods of improving cash flow are dealt with in unit 48, which considers how a business might improve its liquidity.

Cash flow forecasting

Most businesses produce a regular CASH FLOW FORECAST. This lists all the likely receipts (**cash inflows**) and payments (**cash outflows**) over a future period of time. All the entries in the forecast are estimated because they have not occurred yet. The forecast shows the planned cash flow of the business month by month. Table 35.1 shows a twelve month cash flow forecast statement for Fishman's Ltd, a grocery wholesaler located in Ipswich.

What is predicted to happen to cash flow at Fishman's over the twelve month period?

January The company will have an opening cash balance of £11,000 in January. In January receipts are expected to be £451,000 and payments £365,000. This means that an extra £86,000 (£451,000 - £365,000) will be added in this month - a positive net cash flow. The closing balance should be £97,000 (£11,000 +£86,000).

February In February expected payments (£406,000) are

The **receipts** of the business are the monthly inflows of cash. For Fishman's, cash sales result from the sale of groceries to local retailers and other customers. The sales figures are probably based on the previous year's. In September the owners have introduced £300,000 of fresh capital to the business. The total amount of cash a business expects to receive each month is shown as total receipts. Some businesses sell goods on credit. If this is the case, the figures in the statement should show cash actually received in that month and not the value of goods sold.

Payments are the outflows from the business. Some payments are for the same regular amounts, such as leasing charges (£20,000) and loan repayments (£35,000). Other payments vary, such as purchases of goods for resale. Some payments such as telephone charges are made on a quarterly basis. It is also possible for payments to be annual such as accountancy fees. These do not appear for Fishman's, perhaps because they employ their own accountant. The total amount of cash a business expects to pay out each month is shown as total payments. If a business buys goods on credit, cash payments made to suppliers are included when they occur and not the value of goods received in a particular month.

Net cash flow for a month is found by subtracting total payments from total receipts. If receipts are greater than payments, net cash flow is positive. If payments are greater than receipts, net cash flow is negative - shown by brackets around a figure.

- The **opening balance** in January will be the value of December's closing balance in the previous year.
- The **closing balance** for a month is found by adding or subtracting the net cash flow for the month from the opening balance.
- The closing balance of one month becomes the opening balance of the next month. It can be positive or negative figure.

greater than expected receipts (£360,000). This means that there will be a negative net cash flow of £46,000 in February. However, the opening balance of £97,000 will cover this and the business will not have a cash flow problem. It ends the month with a positive closing balance of £51,000 (£97,000 - £46,000).

March In March payments again will be greater than receipts, giving a negative net cash flow of £92,000. However, this is now greater than the opening balance of £51,000. This means that the business faces a negative closing balance of £41,000 and will have a cash flow problem. It would have to find some way to finance this, perhaps by borrowing from a bank.

March to May The business will have cash flow problems in March and April, when it faces negative closing balances, even though in April receipts are greater than payments (a positive net cash flow). In May, however, the negative opening balance of £26,000 is outweighed by the positive net cash flow of £113,000. The business will have a positive closing balance of £87,000 and no cash flow problem.

June to December In June and August, but not July, the business would have cash flow problems. From September onwards, when there will be positive closing balances every month, there appear to be no cash flow problems. This is because the owners plan to introduce £300,000 into the business in September.

Why do businesses prepare cash flow forecasts?

Businesses draw up cash flow forecast statements to help control and monitor cash flow in the business. There are certain advantages in using statements to control cash flow.

Identifying the timing of cash shortages and surpluses
A forecast can help to identify in advance when a business might wish to borrow cash. At the bottom of the statement the monthly closing balances are shown clearly. This will help the reader to identify when a bank overdraft will be needed. For example, Table 35.1 showed that Fishman's would need to borrow money in March, April, June and August. In addition, if a large cash surplus is identified in a particular month, this might provide an opportunity to buy some new equipment, for example. A business should try to avoid being overdrawn at the bank because interest is charged. If certain payments can be delayed until cash is available, this will avoid unnecessary borrowing.

Supporting applications for funding When trying to raise finance, lenders often insist that businesses support their applications with documents showing business performance, outlook and solvency. A cash flow forecast will help to indicate the future outlook for the business. It is also common practice to produce a cash flow forecast statement in the planning stages of setting up a business.

Ella Sankey owns a launderette business in London. She leases premises and employs two local people on part time contracts. There are 14 washing machines, 6 dryers and 2 computers offering Internet services. The launderette is open from 7.00 am to 11.00 pm, but is only staffed between 10.00 am and 5.00 pm. Ella manages the business from home and can be contacted by mobile phone if there are problems. Her main task is to empty the machines each day and bank the cash. Revenue has fallen by 25 per cent in the last 18 months. The business lost student trade when washing machines were installed in the halls of residence. Ella has produced a six monthly cash flow forecast to monitor the cash position of the business, as shown in Table 35.2.

(a) Explain how Ella Sankey would calculate:
    (i) total payments in July;
    (ii) net cash flow in July;
    (iii) the closing balance in July;
    (iv) the opening balance in August.
(b) Explain what is happening to the cash position of Ella's launderette business and suggest reasons why she might be worried about the future.

Table 35.2 *Cash flow forecast for Ella Sankey's business, July-December 2003*

						(£)
	July	Aug	Sept	Oct	Nov	Dec
Receipts						
Cash	3,464	3,556	3,647	3,588	3,612	3,541
Sale of old machines			450			
Capital introduced			2,500			
Total receipts	3,464	3,556	6,597	3,588	3,612	3,541
Payments						
Lease on premises	1,000	1,000	1,000	1,000	1,000	1,000
Wages	1,200	1,200	1,200	1,200	1,200	2,000
Electricity		986			1,098	
New machines			3,000			
Water			430			510
Other expenses	150	150	150	150	150	150
Drawings	1,000	1,000	1,000	1,000	1,000	1,000
Total payments	3,350	4,336	6,780	3,350	4,448	4,660
Net cash flow	114	(780)	(183)	238	(836)	(1,119)
Opening balance	1,004	1,118	338	155	393	(443)
Closing balance	1,118	338	155	393	(443)	(1,562)

Enhancing the planning process Careful planning in business has become more important in recent years. This helps to clarify aims and improve performance. Producing a cash flow forecast is a key part of the planning process because it is a document concerned with the future.

Monitoring cash flow During and at the end of the financial year a business should make comparisons between the predicted figures in the cash flow forecast and those which actually occur. By doing this it can find out where problems have occurred. It could then try to identify possible reasons for any significant differences between the two sets of figures. For example, it might be that an overpayment was made. Constant monitoring in this way should allow a business to control its cash flow effectively.

Improving forecasts

Cash flow forecasts may not be helpful if they are inaccurate. Very inaccurate forecasts could lead to businesses getting into trouble and running out of cash. How can a business improve the accuracy of its cash flow forecasts?

Accurate data A cash flow forecast is based on anticipated flows of cash into and out of the business. Some of these flows will be known for certain. For example, a business usually knows what some of its overheads will be next year,

such as rent, rates and insurance. Other costs such as wages may have been negotiated for the next year. Variable costs such as raw materials are may be more difficult to predict. This is because output might fluctuate unexpectedly or suppliers may change their prices.

Generally, cash outflows are easier to predict than cash inflows. Most of the cash coming into the business is from sales. It can sometimes be difficult to estimate what sales will be exactly in future. Some businesses have advanced orders, such firms in the holiday industry, which will help to improve accuracy. Others do market research, whilst many rely on projections based on the previous year's figures. When cash inflows and outflows are unknown it is better to overestimate costs and underestimate revenues. New businesses have particular problems when producing forecasts. This is because they have no past data on which to base projections. They also tend to underestimate costs and over estimate revenues.

Biased forecasts Businesses sometimes manipulate cash flow forecasts. For example, a business may overestimate cash inflows to improve the strength of the business on paper. It might do this if it was borrowing money from a bank. A manager may overestimate costs and underestimate sales so that credit can be taken when the real figures are better. If forecasts are biased they are not likely to be accurate.

Kieran Venkat runs an off-licence in the Manchester suburb of Rusholme. He has recently extended his premises into the property next door and is looking to acquire a wider range of stock. The cost of the extension has completely exhausted the business of its cash reserves and Kieran needs to borrow some money to buy stock. He needs to borrow £5,000 for nine months. In order to support his application for a bank loan he drew up the nine month cash flow forecast shown in Table 35.3. The forecast assumes that the loan has been granted and repayments are included.

(a) Calculate the following figures for Kieran's cash flow forecast.
   (i) Cash sales and total receipts for October.
   (ii) Total payments for August.
   (iii) Closing balance for November.
   (iv) Opening balance for January.
(b) As well as supporting his application for a bank loan, how else might this cash flow forecast help Kieran in running his business?

Table 35.3 *Cash flow forecast statement for Kieran Venkat*

(£)

	Jul	Aug	Sep	Oct	Nov	Dec	Jan	Feb	Mar
Receipts									
Cash sales	3,800	4,000	5,000	?	6,000	9,000	7,000	3,000	3,500
Bank loan	5,000								
Total receipts	8,800	4,000	5,000	?	6,000	9,000	7,000	3,000	3,500
Payments									
Stock	7,000	3,000	3,400	3,400	4,000	6,100	4,800	2,000	2,400
Loan repayments	620	620	620	620	620	620	620	620	620
Casual labour	200	200	200	200	200	400	200	200	200
Miscellaneous costs	100	100	100	100	100	100	100	100	100
Drawings	500	500	500	500	500	500	500	500	500
Insurance				450					
Advertising	370								
Telephone			170			200			210
Total payments	8,790	?	4,990	5,270	5,420	7,920	6,220	3,420	4,030
Net cash flow	10	(420)	10	(270)	580	1,080	780	(420)	(530)
Opening balance	(90)	(80)	(500)	(490)	(760)	(180)	?	1,680	1,260
Closing balance	(80)	(500)	(490)	(760)	?	900	1,680	1,260	730

(c) On the basis of this cash flow forecast alone, discuss whether a bank would grant Kieran a loan.

 Question 2

Table 35.4 *Thorntons, cash flow statement*

	2002 £000	2001 £000
Cash inflow from operating activities	21,160	21,117
Returns on investments and servicing of finance	(3,489)	(4,155)
Taxation	507	902
Capital expenditure and financial investment	(2,754)	(1,587)
Equity dividends paid	(4,486)	(4,492)
Cash inflow before use of liquid resources and financing	10,938	11,785
Management of liquid resources	(2,292)	264
Financing - issue of shares	1	-
- decrease in debt	(10,752)	(10,716)
(Decrease)/increase in cash in the period	(2,105)	1,333

Source: adapted from Thorntons plc, *Annual Report and Accounts.*

Table 35.5 *Thorntons, net cash inflow from operating activities*

	2002 £000	2001 £000
Operating profit	10,410	10,148
Loss on disposal of fixed assets	405	73
Depreciation charges	13,373	13,117
Amortisation charges	113	-
Non-cash movements in provisions	(443)	(584)
Operating cash flows before working capital improvements	23,858	22,754
Cash flow relating to previous years provisions	(33)	(107)
(Increase)/decrease in stocks	(853)	3,781
Increase in debtors	(1,674)	(1,413)
Decrease in creditors	(138)	(3,898)
Net cash flow from operating activities	21,160	21,117

Source: adapted from Thorntons plc, *Annual Report and Accounts.*

Coping with external factors Cash flow forecasts could be improved if business managers could predict future events such as changes in interest rates, the weather and the behaviour of competitors. One way to allow for unforeseen events is to have **contingency funds** built into the cash flow forecast. For example, a business may make a monthly allowance for unexpected costs, including it as a cash outflow. Another approach could be to make regular adjustments to cash flow forecasts during the trading period. If forecasts are updated regularly, predictions may be more accurate. It is also possible to produce a series of forecasts. For example, a business might produce three, a 'worst case', a 'best case' and one in the 'middle'. This could show the business what is likely to happen to its cash position in different situations.

Cash flow statements

The management of funds is easier if there is documented information on business performance. The balance sheet (☞ unit 32) shows the assets and liabilities of a business at a point in time. The profit and loss account shows how the year's profit is distributed. In 1991, the Accounting Standards Board (ASB) published its first Financial Report Standard, FRS 1 'Cash flow Statements'. The new standard required companies to publish a CASH FLOW STATEMENT in the annual accounts. Note that this is **not** the same as a cash flow forecast. Cash flow statements may include receipts and payments from the previous two years. These may not be disclosed elsewhere in published financial statements. Another advantage is that a cash flow statement must be shown in a standardised presentation. This allows a comparison between different companies.

FRS 1 requires cash flows to be disclosed under standard headings. These are:
● operating activities;
● returns on investments and servicing of finance;
● taxation;
● investing activities;
● financing;
in that order.

Table 35.4 shows a cash flow statement for Thorntons plc, the confectionery company. The entries in the cash flow statement are explained as follows.
● In 2002 the net cash inflow from operating activities was £21.16 million. The way in which the business generated this profit is shown in Table 35.5.
● From this £3.489 million is subtracted. This is the difference between interest received from money invested and interest paid on loans. In 2002 Thorntons made a net payment of interest.
● During the year Thorntons received a corporation tax repayment from the Inland Revenue equal to £507,000.
● In 2002 Thorntons spent £2.754 million on capital expenditure, such as tangible assets.
● £4.486 million was paid to shareholders in the form of dividends.
● The net cash inflow before the use of liquid resources and financing was £10.938 million.
● In 2002 £2.292 million cash was placed in a deposit account.
● A very small amount of capital was raised through the issue of shares, just £1,000.

Look at Table 35.4 and 35.5.
(a) What happened to Thorntons' net cash position in 2001?
(b) Explain why these statements might be useful to Thorntons.

Question3

- £10.752 million was used to repay much of Thorntons debt.
- The total net cash outflow for Thorntons in 2002 was £2.105 million.

Criticisms of cash flow statements

The inclusion of cash flow statements helps to clarify the cash position of a business. However, there are some criticisms of cash flow statements.

- In practice, little new information is shown in the statements. The law encourages disclosure but does not enforce it.
- Small limited companies are not bound to publish a cash flow statement because they are owner managed. However, medium sized firms are. This seems to lack a little logic since most medium sized firms are also owner managed.
- Cash flow statements are based on historical information. It is argued that cash flow statements based on future predictions are more useful.

The difference between cash and profit

It is important for businesses to recognise the difference between cash and profit. At the end of a trading year it is unlikely that the value of profit will be the same as the cash balance. Differences between cash and profit can arise for a number of reasons.

- During the trading year a business might sell £200,000 worth of goods with total costs of £160,000. Its profit would be £40,000. However, if some goods had been sold on credit, payment by certain customers may not yet have been received. If £12,000 was still owing, the amount of cash the business had would be £28,000 (£40,000-£12,000). Thus, profit is greater than cash.
- A business may receive cash at the beginning of the trading year from sales made in the previous year. This would increase the cash balance, but not affect profit. In addition, the business may buy resources from suppliers and not pay for them until the next trading year. As a result its trading costs will not be the same as cash paid out.
- Sometimes the owners might introduce more cash into the business. This will increase the cash balance, but have no effect on the profit made. This is because the introduction of capital is not treated as business revenue in the profit and loss account. The effect will be the same if a business borrows money from a bank.
- Purchases of fixed assets will reduce cash balances, but have no effect on the profit a company makes. This is because the purchase of assets is not treated as a business cost in the profit and loss account.
- Sales of fixed assets will increase cash balances but have no effect on profit unless a profit or loss is made on disposal

Table 35.6 *Cash flow forecast statement for Jeanwear Ltd, July to December*

(£)

	Jul	Aug	Sep	Oct	Nov	Dec
Receipts						
Cash sales	40,000	50,000	50,000	70,000	90,000	90,000
Bank loan						30,000
Total cash receipts	40,000	50,000	50,000	70,000	90,000	120,000
Payments						
Cost of sales	18,000	30,000	30,000	40,000	60,000	60,000
Wages	8,000	8,000	8,000	10,000	10,000	8,000
Overheads	10,000	18,000	10,000	15,000	20,000	15,000
Computer system						50,000
Total payments	36,000	56,000	48,000	65,000	90,000	133,000
Net cash flow	4,000	(6,000)	2,000	5,000	-	(13,000)
Opening balance	12,000	16,000	10,000	12,000	17,000	17,000
Closing balance	16,000	10,000	12,000	17,000	17,000	4,000

Table 35.7 *Profit per month Jeanwear Ltd*

	Jul	Aug	Sep	Oct	Nov	Dec
Profit*	4,000	(6,000)	2,000	5,000	0	7,000

* Cash sales - operating costs (cost of sales + wages + overheads)

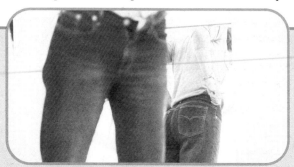

Jeanwear Ltd produces denim products for the mail order market. It advertises products in weekend newspaper supplements. It has enjoyed some success in recent years. However, the directors believe that profits could be raised if it could cut costs. At the beginning of 2004 it was decided that a new computer system would be installed. This was expected to reduce administrative overheads and the monthly wage bill. Table 35.6 shows a cash flow forecast statement and profits for the six month trading period starting in July 2004. It was anticipated that the computer system will be bought and installed in December. Part of the cost would be met by a bank loan.

(a) What is the difference between the profit made by the business over the period and the closing cash balance?
(b) Suggest two reasons why there may have been this difference.
(c) Explain the effects on the (i) cash flow and (ii) profit of the business if the computer system had not been bought.

Question 4

of the asset. This is because the cash from the sale of a fixed asset is not included in business turnover.

- The amount of cash at the end of the year will be different from profit because at the beginning of the year the cash balance is unlikely to be zero. If, at the beginning of the year, the cash balance for a business is £23,000, then the amount of cash a business has at the end of the year will exceed profit by £23,000.

It is possible for a business to trade for many years without making a profit. For example, British Biotech, a pharmaceuticals company, traded between 1985-98 without ever making a profit. The company survived because it was able to generate cash. Extra cash was introduced by shareholders on several occasions since 1985. In 1998 the company lost £44.8 million. However, the cash in the bank was £132.8 million. Shareholders may be happy to contribute more capital if they think that a company has a lot of potential. However, it is possible for a profitable business to collapse if it runs out of cash. This is likely to happen if a business has to meet some substantial unexpected expenditure or if a bad debt occurs.

Knowledge

1. Explain the operation of the cash flow cycle.
2. Why is it important that a business:
   (i) does not hold too much cash;
   (ii) holds sufficient cash?
3. Briefly explain what a cash flow forecast includes.
4. How does a cash flow forecast indicate whether a business faces cash flow problems in future?
5. Explain why a business prepares a cash flow forecast.
6. What are the advantages of businesses preparing cash flow statements?
7. How is it possible for a profitable business to collapse?

key terms

Cash flow cycle - the continuous movement of cash in and out of a business.
Cash flow forecast - a prediction of all expected receipts and expenses of a business over a future time period which shows the expected cash balance at the end of each month.

Cash flow statement - a financial statement which shows sources and uses of cash in a trading period.
Liquid asset - an asset which is easily changed into cash.
Receivership - the liquidation (selling) of a firm's assets by an independent body following its collapse.

Case study *Westview Caravans*

Betty and Bob Hawkins own a small caravan site in Devon. They bought the business in 2000 when they retired. They preferred to spend their £200,000 life savings on a small business rather than invest it in other ways. They felt that running the business would not only generate a steady annual income but also occupy their time. The business consisted of a dwelling house on a cliff top and eight four-berth caravans.

In the first two years the business did well, as projected by the previous owners. However, in 2002 a storm during Autumn damaged four of the eight caravans. About the same time Bob was ill for a few weeks and wasn't able to carry out repairs. The couple had little spare cash and couldn't really afford to pay a contractor to carry out the necessary work.

Betty and Bob sit down to think about their cash flow for 2003. The site is closed from November to March, so there is no revenue in these months. They decide to repair two of the caravans in March. However, they will have to replace the other two in July using a bank loan. They are reluctant to take out a loan, but they are worried that operating with only six caravans will reduce their revenue.

Before approaching the bank, Betty and Bob draw up a cash flow forecast. They look at the bank statements of the business from previous years and produce Table 35.8 showing the expected revenue from letting the caravans and expected overheads for 2003. The following financial information is also available.

- £250 interest is expected to be received in April.
- Betty and Bob include the £8,000 bank loan in July which they hope the bank will give them.
- Betty and Bob take £1,100 every month from the business for their own use.
- £500 ground rent and £400 rates are payable each month.
- Water rates are expected to be £560 in April and £680 in October.
- Repairs are expected to be £450 in March.
- The new caravans will cost £10,000 in July.
- The opening balance is £5,200 in January.

Table 35.8 *Estimated letting revenue and other overhead costs, 2003*

(£)

	JAN	FEB	MAR	APR	MAY	JUN	JUL	AUG	SEP	OCT	NOV	DEC
Letting revenue	0	0	0	1,200	1,800	2,000	4,100	5,400	3,200	1,000	0	0
Other overheads	0	0	0	200	200	300	300	300	200	100	0	0

(a) **Explain why a cash flow forecast might be helpful to Betty and Bob when applying for a bank loan. (4 marks)**

(b) **Produce a cash flow forecast for Betty and Bob's caravan business for 2003. (12 marks)**

(c) (i) **Calculate the expected profit for 2003. (6 marks)**

(ii) **Using examples, explain why the expected cash position at the end of the trading year is different to the expected profit. (8 marks)**

(d) **Discuss whether you think the bank will give Betty and Bob a loan for the new caravans. (10 marks)**

What is budgeting?

As businesses expand the need for control grows and becomes more difficult. A small business can be run informally. The owner is the manager, who will know everyone, be aware of what is going on and will make all decisions. In larger firms work and responsibility are delegated, which makes informal control impractical. To improve control, budgeting has been developed. This forces managers to be accountable for their decisions.

A BUDGET is a plan which is agreed in advance. It must be a plan and not a forecast - a forecast is a prediction of what might happen in the future, whereas a budget is a planned outcome which the firm hopes to achieve. A budget will show the money needed for spending and how this might be financed. Budgets are based on the objectives of businesses. They force managers to think ahead and improve co-ordination. Most budgets are set for twelve months to coincide with the accounting period, but there are exceptions. Research and Development budgets, for example, may cover several years.

Information contained in a budget may include revenue, sales, expenses, profit, personnel, cash and capital expenditure. In fact, budgets can include any business variable (known as a budget factor) which can be given a value.

One very well known budget is 'The Budget'. The Chancellor of the Exchequer prepares a budget for a particular period. It will take into account the government's spending plans and how these plans will be financed by taxes and other sources of funds.

Approaches to budgeting

Budgets can be divided into different categories. Objectives budgets and flexible budgets take different approaches to planning.

- **Objectives budgets** are based on finding the best way of achieving particular objectives (☞ unit 4). They contain information on how a business will achieve these objectives. For example, a sales budget might show how a sales target will be met.
- **Flexible budgets** are designed to change as business changes. Changes in business conditions may result in very different outcomes than those budgeted for. A flexible budget takes these into account. For example, the sales budget may be altered if there is sudden increase in demand resulting in much higher sales levels.

A business will also set budgets over the long term and short term.

- **Capital budgets** plan the capital structure and the liquidity of a business over a long period of time. They are concerned with equity, liabilities, fixed and current assets and year-end cash balances.

- **Operating budgets** plan the day to day use of resources. They are concerned with materials, labour, overheads, sales and cash. There are three important operating budgets. The **profit budget** estimates the annual business costs, the year's turnover and the expected profit for the year. The **cash budget** simply plans the receipts and payments. It shows a firm its cash balance at specified times in the budget period. The **budgeted balance sheet** incorporates the budgeted profit and loss account and the closing balance in the cash budget. It also takes into account planned changes in assets and liabilities.

The preparation of budgets

The way in which a budget might be prepared is shown in Figure 36.1. It is a step by step process. The first step is to decide upon a budget period and state the objectives which are to be achieved. The budget period may vary according to the type of budget, but one month or one year is usual. Often the objectives will be set at board level. Targets for performance, market share, quality (provided it can be quantified) and productivity are all examples.

John Chandler is marketing manager at Wicksons, a chain of 54 shoe shops. Most of the marketing budget is used for adverts in magazines and promotions in stores. The business also has a stand at the Milan Shoe Exhibition, where it has the chance to develop contacts and research future styles. One of John's responsibilities is to produce cost budgets for his department. The cost budget for the second six months of 2003 is shown in Table 36.1.

Table 36.1 Cost budget for Wicksons marketing department, 2003

(£)

	JUL	AUG	SEP	OCT	NOV	DEC
Wages & salaries	4,300	4,300	4,300	4,300	4,300	4,300
Office expenses	500	500	450	450	450	400
Advertising expenses	2,000	10,000	2,000	2,000	10,000	2,000
Promotion expenses	2,500	2,200	3,800	1,700	1,600	2,500
Milan Shoe Exhibition					12,000	
Other overheads	500	500	500	500	700	500

(a) How much does the Wicksons' marketing department plan to spend in the second half of 2003?
(b) Explain how the preparation of this budget might help Wicksons.

Question 1

The next stage involves obtaining information upon which the budget can be based. Some information can be obtained from previous results. Historic information can be useful, although some budgetary techniques ignore the past and make a fresh start. Forecasts are another source of information. These are estimates of likely future outcomes. Some business variables are easier to forecast than others. It is fairly easy to predict future costs, but difficult to estimate future sales. This is because sales levels are subject to so many external factors.

It is then possible to prepare two important budgets - the sales budget and the production budget. These budgets are related and affect all other budgets. For example, sales targets can only be met if there is productive capacity. Also, a firm would be unlikely to continue production if it could not sell its products. The sales budget will contain monthly sales estimates, expressed in terms of quantities per product, perhaps, and the price charged. From the sales budget, and with knowledge of stock levels, the production budget can be determined. This will show the required raw materials, labour hours and machine hours. At this stage the business should know whether or not it has the capacity to meet the sales targets. If it is not possible, then it may be necessary to adjust the sales budget.

Subsidiary operating budgets can be drawn up next. These will be detailed budgets prepared by various departments. Budgets are often broken down, so that each person in the hierarchy (☞ unit 40) can be given some responsibility for a section of the budget.

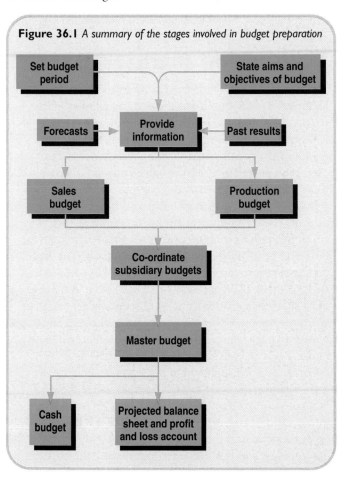

Figure 36.1 *A summary of the stages involved in budget preparation*

The master budget is a summary statement. It shows the estimated income, anticipated expenditure, and, thus, the budgeted profit for the period. The cash budget can also be prepared when all other budgets are complete. This budget is particularly useful since it shows the monthly flows of cash into and out of the business. It will help to show whether future cash flow problems might occur.

The final step is to prepare the projected balance sheet. This shows the financial position that will result from the firm's budgets.

Problems of preparing budgets

Business may sometimes find that there are problems when preparing budgets.

Using planned figures Problems tend to arise because figures in budgets are not actual figures. The figures are plans, which could be based on historical data, forecasts or human judgment. A business might simply take historic data and add an arbitrary percentage to arrive at the budgeted value. The most important data in the preparation of nearly all budgets is sales data. If sales data are inaccurate, many of the firm's budgets will be inexact. The accuracy of sales data might be improved if market research is used (☞ unit 12). However, it may be difficult to estimate sales of new products for a future period.

Collecting information The preparation of budgets is a managerial process. It requires a great deal of co-ordination. This is because different parts of the organisation provide information for budgets. Some businesses appoint a budget officer. This person is responsible for collecting data and opinions, keeping managers to the budget timetable and carrying out budgetary administration.

Time Preparing budgets can be time consuming and use up resources. The whole process can also be held up. This is because many of the major budgets, such as the master budget, cannot be prepared until other smaller budgets have been produced. A delay in approving budgets is also likely to cause problems. If budgets are prepared after the start of the time period in which they will be used, their value is reduced. To avoid delay, a business must prepare a careful timetable for their approval and stick to it.

Conflict The preparation of budgets may lead to conflict between departments or members of staff. For example, a business may only have limited funds. The marketing department may want to promote a product but new machinery may be needed in the R&D department.

Preparing a sales revenue budget

A sales revenue budget will show the planned revenue for a period of time. Emerald Artwork produces four products,

AD23, AD24, AE12 and AE13. They sell for £12, £20, £25 and £30 respectively. The planned sales levels for a four month period in 2004 are shown in Table 36.2.

Table 36.2 *Planned sales figures for Emerald Artwork*

	FEB	MAR	APR	MAY
AD23	100	100	100	100
AD24	50	80	80	100
AE12	40	50	40	50
AE13	30	30	50	50

The sales revenue budget is prepared by showing the planned revenue in each month. This is calculated by multiplying the predicted sales levels by the prices. The sales revenue budget is shown in Table 36.3.

Table 36.3 *A sales revenue budget for Emerald Artwork*

	FEB	MAR	APR	MAY
AD23	£1,200 (£12x100)	£1,200 (£12x100)	£1,200 (£12x100)	£1,200 (£12x100)
AD24	£1,000 (£20x50)	£1,600 (£20x80)	£1,600 (£20x80)	£2,000 (£20x100)
AE12	£1,000 (£25x40)	£1,250 (£25x50)	£1,000 (£25x40)	£1,250 (£25x50)
AE13	£900 (£30x30)	£900 (£30x30)	£1,500 (£30x50)	£1,500 (£30x50)
Total	£4,100	£4,950	£5,300	£5,950

A production budget

Once Emerald Artwork has produced a sales budget, it is possible to calculate its production budget. The example in Table 36.4 assumes stock levels stay the same throughout the

Table 36.4 *A production budget for Emerald Artwork covering production of all 4 products*

	FEB	MAR	APR	MAY
Cost of materials (£3 per unit)	£660 (£3x220)	£780 (£3x260)	£810 (£3x270)	£900 (£3x300)
Direct labour costs (£4 per unit)	£880 (£4x220)	£1,040 (£4x260)	£1,080 (£4x270)	£1,200 (£4x300)
Indirect labour costs (£2 per unit)	£440 (£2x220)	£520 (£2x260)	£540 (£2x270)	£600 (£2x300)
Overheads (10% of direct & indirect costs)	£1,320x10% = £132	£1,560x10% = £156	£1,620x10% = £162	£1,800x10% = £180
Total	£2,112	£2,496	£2,592	£2,880

The Mansfield Motor Centre is a large motor business based on the outskirts of Mansfield. The business employs 32 staff and made a profit of £5.8 million in 2002. Table 36.5 shows a six month sales revenue budget for 2003.

Table 36.5 *Six month sales revenue budget for the Mansfield Motor Centre, 2003*

(£000)

	JAN	FEB	MAR	APR	MAY	JUN	TOTAL
Repairs and servicing	458	456	786	876	776	765	4,117
MOTs	110	98	97	89	103	130	627
Motor car sales	1,445	1,256	1,329	1,876	2,228	2,667	10,801
Parts and accessories sales	786	978	678	834	1,021	1,200	5,497
Total	**2,799**	**2,788**	**2,890**	**3,675**	**4,128**	**4,762**	**21,042**

(a) Explain how the sales revenue budget for Mansfield Motor Centre has been calculated.
(b) Suggest where the information in the above budget might have come from.

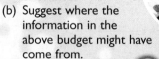

4 month period. The figures are based on expected sales in Table 36.2.

Zero-based budgeting

The financial information used in most budgets is based on **historical** data. For example, the cost of materials in this year's production budget may be based on last year's figure, with perhaps an allowance for inflation. Production and manufacturing costs, such as labour, raw materials and overheads, are relatively easy to value and tend to be controlled using methods such as standard costing.

However, in some areas of business it is not so easy to quantify costs. Examples might be certain marketing, administration or computer services costs. Where costs are unable to be justified then no money is allocated in the budget for those costs. This is known as ZERO-BASED BUDGETING (ZBB) or ZERO BUDGETING. A manager must show that a particular item of spending generates an adequate amount of benefit in relation to the general objectives of the business for money to be allocated in a budget.

This approach is different to the common practice of extrapolating from past costs. It encourages the regular evaluation of costs and helps to minimise unnecessary purchases. The concept of **opportunity cost** is linked to ZBB. Opportunity cost is the cost of the next best alternative. When choices are made, businesses try to minimise the opportunity

Questcorp plc is a large provider of security systems in the UK. It specialises in systems which protect business premises in rural locations. The financial controller of Questcorp has suggested that expenditure in some departments could be better controlled if the company used zero-based budgeting. The expenditure for four departments is shown in Table 36.6.

Table 36.6 *Expenditure in four key departments for Questcorp plc*
£

	2000	2001	2002	2003	2004
Marketing	120,000	140,000	178,000	219,000	270,000
R&D	250,000	321,000	377,000	679,000	900,000
Production	300,000	400,000	560,000	780,000	980,000
Admin.	45,000	50,000	54,000	79,000	93,000

(a) How might the R&D budget holder justify spending in the department?
(b) Why might zero-based budgeting be a problem for the marketing department launching a new product?
(c) To what extent might Questcorp benefit from zero-based budgeting?

Question 3

cost. ZBB also involves a cautious approach to spending, so that costs are minimised. Both include an element of 'value for money'.

The main advantages of ZBB are that:
- the allocation of resources should be improved;
- a questioning attitude is developed which will help to reduce unnecessary costs and eliminate inefficient practices;
- staff motivation might improve because evaluation skills are practised and a greater knowledge of the firm's operations might develop;
- it encourages managers to look for alternatives.
ZBB also has some disadvantages.
- It is time consuming because the budgeting process involves the collection and analysis of quite detailed information so that spending decisions can be made.
- Skilful decision making is required. Such skills may not be available in the organisation. In addition, decisions may be influenced by subjective opinions.
- It threatens the status quo. This might adversely affect motivation.
- Managers may not be prepared to justify spending on certain costs. Money, therefore, may not be allocated to spending which could benefit the business.
To deal with these possible problems, a business might give each department a 'base' budget of, say, 50 per cent. Departments could then be invited to bid for increased

expenditure on a ZBB basis.

The benefits of budgets

- Budgets provide a means of controlling income and expenditure. They regulate the spending of money and draw attention to losses, waste and inefficiency.
- They act as a 'review' for a business, allowing time for corrective action.
- Budgets can emphasise and clarify the responsibilities of executives.
- They enable management to delegate responsibility without losing control, because subordinates are expected to meet budget targets which are known in advance by senior management.
- Budgets help ensure that capital is usefully employed by checking that the capital employed is consistent with the planned level of activity.
- They help the co-ordination of the business and improve communication between departments.
- Budgets provide clear targets which can be understood by personnel lower down in the organisational structure (☞ unit 40). They should also help to focus on costs.

The drawbacks of budgets

- Budgets might lead to resentment from some of the firm's personnel, particularly if they are not involved in the preparation. This could result in poor motivation and targets being missed.
- If budgets are too inflexible then it is possible that the business could suffer. For example, a member of the sales team may be prevented from finalising an overseas contract because the overseas travel budget is spent.
- If the actual business results are very different from the budgeted ones then the budget can lose its importance.

Variances

A VARIANCE in budgeting is the difference between the figure that the business has budgeted for and the actual figure. Variances are usually calculated at the end of the budget period, as that is when the actual figure will be known. They can be **favourable** (F) or **adverse** (A).

Favourable variances occur when the actual figures are 'better' than the budgeted figures.
- If the sales revenue for a month was budgeted at £25,000, but turned out to be £29,000, there would be a £4,000 favourable variance (£29,000-£25,000).
- If cost were planned to be £20,000 and turned out to be £18,000, this would also be a favourable variance of £2,000, as actual costs are lower than planned.

Adverse variances are when the actual figures are worse than the budgeted figures. Actual sales revenues may be lower than planned, or actual costs may be higher than planned.

Managers will examine variances and try to identify reasons why they have occurred. By doing this they might be able to improve the performance of the business in the future.

key terms

Budget - a quantitative economic plan prepared and agreed in advance.
Variance - the difference between the actual value and the planned value in a budget.
Zero based budgeting or zero budgeting - a system of budgeting where no money is allocated for costs or spending unless they can be justified by the fund holder (they are given a zero value).

Knowledge ...Knowledge...Knowle

1. How might a budget improve managerial accountability?
2. What is the difference between objectives budgets and flexible budgets?
3. State examples of 3 types of budget.
4. Suggest 3 problems when preparing a budget.
5. Describe the benefits of budgets.
6. Describe the drawbacks of budgets.
7. What does an adverse variance tell a business?
8. What might cause a sales variance?
9. Why might a business use zero-based budgeting?

Hammond Gardening Services Ltd is owned by Mike Hammond. He employs one other person and provides garden maintenance services in Surrey. He has two main sources of revenue - maintenance contracts with schools and hospitals and work from private households. Mike advertises his services regularly in local newspapers and enjoyed an increase in business in 2003 due to the warm summer. Table 36.7 shows revenues and costs for Hammond Gardening Services in 2003.

Table 36.7 *Hammond Gardening Services, costs and revenue, 2003*

	Budget	Actual	Variance
Revenue			
Maintenance contracts	35,600	36,100	500F
Private households	36,400	38,980	2,580F
Total revenue	**72,000**	**75,080**	**3,080F**
Costs			
Wages	12,000	13,050	1,050A
Motor expenses	2,400	2,800	400A
Materials	1,200	1,450	250A
Advertising	650	350	300F
Other overheads	1,800	1,970	170A
Total costs	**18,050**	**19,620**	**1,570A**
Profit	**53,950**	**55,460**	*******

(a) Using information in the case, explain what is meant by (i) a favourable and (ii) an adverse variance.
(b) Calculate the profits variance for the business in 2003 and explain reasons why it is favourable.

Case study Maison JP et Chateau JP

Jean Paul Delmoureaux owns two restaurants in London. The business is well established and under strict financial control. Jean Paul, who trained as a chef in some of the world's top hotels, set up the business in 1996 when he opened Maison JP in Hampstead. Serving high quality French cuisine, the restaurant quickly grew in popularity, attracting diners from all over London. In 1999 he opened Chateau JP in Notting Hill. Both restaurants are aimed at diners who are willing to pay a little more for meals and the prices

reflect this. However, costs are high due to the expensive locations, highly paid staff and the high quality fresh ingredients. To keep the high costs under control Jean Paul has always used budgets. Every six months Jean Paul meets with each restaurant manager to agree a budget. Annual budgets were used, but Jean Paul found that they lacked accuracy. Tables 36.8 and 36.9 show the costs and revenue for the restaurants in the first six months of 2004.

Managers used to complain about preparing the

budgets. They argued that it was too time-consuming when they would be better employed running the restaurants. Jean Paul responded by offering managers financial rewards related to the budgets. Managers are now given 30 per cent of any favourable variance on the six-monthly budgets.

Table 36.8 *Maison JP, costs and revenues*

(£)

	JAN	FEB	MAR	APR	MAY	JUN	TOTAL
Budgeted revenue	51,000	53,000	56,000	62,000	65,000	70,000	357,000
Budgeted costs	41,900	42,900	45,200	47,100	48,500	50,500	276,100
Budgeted profit	9,100	10,100	10,800	14,900	16,500	19,500	80,900

(£)

	JAN	FEB	MAR	APR	MAY	JUN	TOTAL
Actual revenue	50,230	53,700	56,400	62,500	71,000	72,100	365,930
Actual costs	42,150	42,650	45,200	47,300	50,750	49,200	277,250
Actual profit	8,080	11,050	11,200	15,200	20,250	22,900	88,680

Table 36.9 *Chateau JP, costs and revenues*

(£)

	JAN	FEB	MAR	APR	MAY	JUN	TOTAL
Budgeted revenue	55,000	56,000	61,000	68,000	73,000	76,000	389,000
Budgeted costs	44,800	44,700	45,200	48,100	50,300	53,800	286,900
Budgeted profit	10,200	11,300	15,800	19,900	22,700	22,200	102,100

(£)

	JAN	FEB	MAR	APR	MAY	JUN	TOTAL
Actual revenue	56,400	59,300	64,200	71,300	71,000	77,100	399,300
Actual costs	43,350	43,150	44,600	47,100	50,800	52,200	281,200
Actual profit	13,050	16,150	19,600	24,200	20,200	24,900	118,100

(a) **Where might the information contained in the budgets have come from? (6 marks)**

(b) **Calculate the following variances for both restaurants for the six month period: (i) total revenue; (ii) total costs; (iii) profit. (6 marks)**

(c) **Which restaurant manager has produced the most accurate budget? Explain your answer. (6 marks)**

(d) **Analyse the advantages to Jean Paul Delmoureaux of using budgets in his business. (10 marks)**

(e) **Jean Paul Delmoureaux is suspicious about the variance for Chateau JP. He suspects that the manager might have deliberately overestimated costs in the budget so that the bonus will be larger. To what extent might this be true? (12 marks)**

37 Working Capital

What is working capital?

WORKING CAPITAL (sometimes called circulating capital) is the amount of money needed to pay for the day to day trading of a business. A business needs working capital to pay expenses such as wages, electricity and gas charges, and to buy components to make products. The working capital of a business is the amount left over after all current debts have been paid. It is:

● the relatively liquid assets of a business that can easily be turned into cash (cash itself, stocks, the money owing from debtors who have bought goods or services);

minus

● the money owed by a business which needs to be paid in the short term (to the bank, to creditors who have supplied goods or services, to government in the form of tax or shareholders' dividends payable within the year).

In the balance sheet of a company (☞ unit 32) working capital is calculated by subtracting current liabilities from current assets:

Working capital = current assets - current liabilities

Working capital problems

Provided that current assets are twice the size of current liabilities, working capital is usually large enough for most businesses to avoid problems. However, if the value of current assets is less than one and a half times the size of current liabilities, a business may be short of working capital. It might then have problems meeting its immediate debts. Some businesses, such as supermarkets and retailers, can operate if their working capital is smaller than this. These businesses have a very quick turnover of goods and sales are usually for cash which prevents possible problems developing.

Cash is only part of working capital. It is possible for a business to have adequate working capital because its current assets are three times the size of its current liabilities. However, over a very short period of time it may have insufficient cash to pay its bills. It will therefore have a cash flow problem (☞ unit 35).

The working capital cycle

Managing working capital in a business is crucial. In many types of business, particularly manufacturing, delays or **time lags** exist between different stages of business activity. For example, there is a lag between buying materials and components and changing them into finished goods ready for sale. Similarly, there may be a delay between finishing the goods and the goods being sold to a customer. The WORKING CAPITAL CYCLE, shown in Figure 37.1, helps to illustrate the intervals between payments made by a business and the receipt of cash. The cycle shows the movement of cash and other liquid resources into and out of a business. Time lags can occur at a number of stages in the working capital cycle.

Lag 1 Businesses usually purchase resources such as raw materials, components, fuel and other services from suppliers on credit. This means that a business can obtain resources without having to pay for them immediately. There might be a lag of up to 90 days before payment to suppliers has to be

Table 37.1 *Merchant Retail Group's current assets and current liabilities, 2002 and 2003*

	2003 £000s	2002 £000s
Current assets		
Stocks	16,949	15,107
Debtors	8,142	8,479
Investments	426	0
Cash at bank and in hand	952	541
	26,469	**24,127**
Current liabilities		
Loans and overdrafts	10,939	18,414
Trade creditors	8,561	6,290
Corporation tax	3,853	3,326
Other taxes and social security	1,514	1,548
Other creditors	1,059	846
Accruals and deferred income	2,782	2,983
Proposed dividends	2,178	1,638
	30,886	**35,045**

Source: adapted from Merchant Retail Group, *Annual Report and Accounts, 2003.*

Merchant Retail Group is a specialist perfumery retailer and department stores group. The Group has three main businesses The Perfume Shop, Joplings and A. de Gruchy.
● The Perfume Shop has 86 branches situated in prime shopping locations. It sells a wide range of branded perfumes at value for money prices.
● Joplings is a department store division located in the north east of England. It operates four stores including the landmark department store in Sunderland and a ten acre retail park at Hexham.
● A. de Gruchy, located in St Helier, is the leading department store on Jersey.

(a) Calculate the working capital for the Merchant Retail Group in 2003 and 2002.
(b) Comment on:
(i) the amount of working capital in 2003;
(ii) the change in working capital from 2002 to 2003.

Question 1

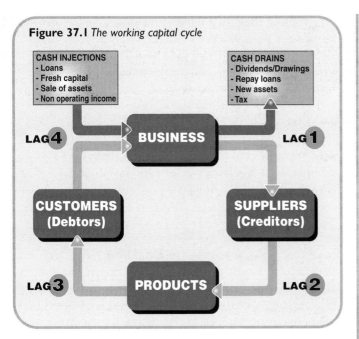

Figure 37.1 The working capital cycle

CASH INJECTIONS
- Loans
- Fresh capital
- Sale of assets
- Non operating income

CASH DRAINS
- Dividends/Drawings
- Repay loans
- New assets
- Tax

LAG 4 BUSINESS LAG 1

CUSTOMERS (Debtors) SUPPLIERS (Creditors)

LAG 3 PRODUCTS LAG 2

made. The length of the lag depends on suppliers' conditions. When a business is first set up, trade credit may not be granted until that business has proved to be creditworthy.

Lag 2 The next lag may occur as resources are turned into products using fixed assets, such as equipment. Work-in-progress (partially finished goods) is created and other costs are incurred, such as wages. The production process can take a long time depending on the nature of business activity. For example, for a cereal farmer this time lag could be about nine months. This would be the time it takes for corn seeds to be planted, grow into plants and eventually ripen so that the corn can be harvested. Alternatively, a furniture manufacturer might take about four to six weeks to make two armchairs and a settee for a customer.

Lag 3 Even when production is complete, a time lag can exist. Businesses may store their finished goods before they are sold to customers. This can be expensive. There may be warehousing costs and opportunity costs. However, storage enables a business to cope with unexpected increases in demand and allows continuous production. In recent years many businesses have adopted just-in-time (☞ unit 55) manufacturing methods. Goods are only produced to order. This minimises stock holdings and reduces this time lag. When goods are distributed to customers further costs result, such as transport and handling costs.

Lag 4 A fourth time lag occurs when goods have finally been sold to customers. It is common business practice to allow customers to pay their bills over 30-90 days. However, depending on the nature of the business activity, this time lag can vary. For example, in many areas of retailing, goods are sold for cash only and this time lag is eliminated. Once cash has been collected from customers much of it is used to keep the process going, for example buying more materials and paying wages.

Williams & Son

Williams & Son is a small property development company in Bradford. It buys plots of land or derelict properties and then builds houses or small apartment blocks. The business aims to complete one or two developments each year. Williams & Son incurs legal costs and pays architects fees before any building can begin. Most of the materials used by Williams & Son are bought on 60 days' credit from local builder's suppliers. Sometimes the new properties are not sold until after they have been completed. The business employs two other workers.

Tina's Taxi Service

Tina McKenna leases two minibuses and operates an airport taxi service in Gloucester and Cheltenham. She employs two drivers and also drives herself. The 24 hour service is successful, but competition is tightening in the area. Drivers are paid 25 per cent of their fares and get to keep their tips. They are paid weekly. All journeys are booked through Tina and drivers are instructed to accept only cash when collecting fares. In addition to the drivers' wages the main variable cost is diesel. Tina has an account with a local garage and is given 30 days credit.

(a) Analyse the differences in the working capital cycles of the two businesses above.

Question 2

Figure 37.1 also shows that a business can enjoy injections of cash from sources other than the sale of products. Loans, the sale of assets and new capital are common examples. However, at the same time there will be cash drains from the business. Cash will leak from the cycle to pay dividends or drawings, to pay tax, to repay loans and to purchase new fixed assets.

Managing working capital

The length of time lags can be crucial when managing the working capital cycle. Business managers must attempt to prolong the first time lag by delaying payments to suppliers. However, this requires careful judgment because a business would not want to damage relations with valuable suppliers. Also, if payments are delayed for too long this could cause hardship for suppliers and eventually contribute to their downfall. Managers would ideally want to reduce:
- production time;
- the storage time of finished goods before they are dispatched to customers, by reducing stock holdings or encouraging just-in-time manufacturing, for example;
- the time it takes for customers to settle their bills, by monitoring and checking late payments or offering discount for early settlement, for example.

Liquidity and profibility

Businesses that have difficulty controlling their cash flow and working capital are often said to have LIQUIDITY PROBLEMS. Liquid assets (☞ unit 34) are those assets that

Oldbury Metal Fittings Ltd makes a wide range of metal brackets, hinges, handles and other small metal products for manufacturers in the West Midlands area. All of its products are made to order and are sold on 120 day credit terms. Most of its suppliers offer 60 day credit terms. Products are manufactured in batches of around 500 - 1,000. An order takes no more than two days to complete. On the 12.6.2004 the managing director of the company received a memo from the company accountant.

OLDBURY METAL FITTINGS LTD MEMO

To: MD   **From:** Patricia   **Date:** 12.6.2004.

I think we should meet urgently to discuss the company's working capital. Once again the timing of payments and receipts is causing problems.

(a) Describe the nature and length of the four time lags in the working capital cycle for Oldbury Metal Fittings.
(b) Suggest why the problem in the memo has probably arisen.
(c) Explain two possible measures which might help to overcome the problem.

Question 3

are easily changed into cash. They either do not have enough cash to pay immediate debts or cannot convert their liquid assets into cash quickly enough. It is possible for businesses to calculate whether they have sufficient working capital using a ratio such as the **current ratio**. This is calculated by:

$$\text{Current ratio} = \frac{\text{Current assets}}{\text{Current liabilities}}$$

If a typical business has a current ratio of between 1.5:1 and 2:1 then it should not experience these problems.

A business could use the **acid test ratio** as a measure of liquidity. This method excludes stock from current assets as stock is not a very liquid asset.

$$\text{Acid test ratio} = \frac{\text{Current assets - stocks}}{\text{Current liabilities}}$$

If the acid test ratio is equal to 1, or very close to 1, this would suggest that the business has sufficient working capital.

Sources of liquidity problems

LIQUIDITY crises in a business often result from a number of errors in the control of working capital.

Overtrading Young and rapidly growing businesses are particularly prone to OVERTRADING. Overtrading occurs when a business is attempting to fund a large volume of production with inadequate working capital. Established companies trying to expand can also face this problem.

Investing too much in fixed assets In the initial stages of a business, funds are limited. Spending large amounts quickly on equipment, vehicles and other capital items drains resources. It may be better to lease some of these fixed assets, leaving sufficient cash funds.

Stockpiling Holding stocks of raw materials and finished goods is expensive. Money tied up in stocks is unproductive. Stocks may become obsolete. In addition, stocks of raw materials in particular cannot be easily changed into cash without making a loss. Stock control is an important feature of managing working capital. Firms should not buy in bulk if discounts are not enough to compensate for the extra cost of holding stocks.

Allowing too much credit A great deal of business is done on credit. One of the dangers is that firms allow their customers too long for payment. This means that the firm is waiting for money and may actually be forced to borrow during this period. Failure to control debtors may also lead to bad debts. Taking early action is the key to the effective control of debtors. At the same time businesses must maintain good relations with customers. Small firms are particularly vulnerable if they are owed money by much larger companies. Powerful businesses are often accused of endangering smaller companies by delaying payments to them.

Taking too much credit Taking more credit might appear to help a firm's cash position since payments are delayed. However there are some drawbacks. Taking too much credit might result in higher prices, lost discounts, difficulties in obtaining future supplies and a bad name in the trade. At worst, credit might be withdrawn.

Overborrowing Businesses may borrow to finance growth. As more loans are taken out interest costs rise. Overborrowing not only threatens a firm's cash position, but also the overall control of the business. It is important to fund growth in a balanced way, by raising some capital from share issues. A well publicised example was the overborrowing by Robert Maxwell from the employees' pension fund of Maxwell Communications.

Underestimating inflation Businesses often fail to take inflation into account. Inflation raises costs, which can cause cash shortages. This is often the case if higher costs, such as wages or raw materials, cannot be passed on in higher prices. Inflationary periods are often accompanied by higher interest rates which place further pressure on liquid resources.

Inflation is also a problem because it is difficult to predict future rates. Although it can be built into plans, firms often underestimate it.

Unforeseen expenditure Businesses are subject to unpredictable external forces. They must make a financial provision for any unforeseen expenditure. Equipment breakdowns, tax demands, strikes and bad debts are common examples of this type of emergency expense.

Unexpected changes in demand Although most businesses try to sustain demand for their products, there may be times when it falls unexpectedly. Unpredicted changes in fashion could lead to a fall in demand. This could lead to a lack of sales and cash flowing into a company. Travel companies in the UK have faced this problem in the past. Companies have to 'buy' holidays before they are sold. External factors, including a recession, may have led to many of these holidays remaining unsold as consumers changed their holiday buying patterns. Firms may also have lost revenue if holidays were discounted in an attempt to sell them.

Seasonal factors Sometimes trade fluctuates for seasonal reasons. In the agriculture industry, cereal farmers have a large cash inflow when their harvest is sold. For much of the year, though, they have to pay expenses without any cash flowing in. This situation requires careful management indeed, although it is possible to predict these changes.

Poor financial management Inexperience in managing cash or a poor understanding of the working capital cycle may lead to liquidity problems for a business.

Resolving a liquidity crisis

Liquidity problems can be prevented by keeping a tight control on working capital. Inevitably though, there will be occasions when firms run short of liquid resources. When this does happen the firm's main aim will be survival rather than profit. The following measures might be used to obtain liquid resources.
- Stimulate sales for cash, offering large discounts if necessary.
- Sell off stocks of raw materials - below cost if necessary.
- Sell off any fixed assets which may not be vital for operations.
- Sell off fixed assets and lease them back.
- Mount a rigorous drive on overdue accounts.
- Sell debts to a factoring company.
- Only make essential purchases.
- Extend credit with selected suppliers.
- Reduce personal drawings from the business.
- Negotiate additional short term loans.

In all cases, action must be taken quickly. If the firm survives the liquidity crisis, it is important to identify the causes and make sure it does not happen again.

Newsplayer, the online broadcaster is facing a cash crisis after revealing it has just over £100,000 left in the bank, and its directors are not being paid while new funds are raised. The company, which owns 1,000 hours of ITN and Reuters news material, made pre-tax losses of £2.4 million for the six months to April 30. Turnover from its range of video-on-demand services, including Newsplayer.com, and its licensing agreements with other sites has also slumped to £113,505 compared with £350,526 for the previous six months. With just £100,252 left in the bank, the directors of the company said they would take payment in the form of shares until new funds could be raised.

Having recently signed agreements with NTL to provide two channels to its broadband service and with EMI to provide digital download services, the company's chief executive remained confident that Newsplayer would pull through its current cash flow problems.

It is attempting a £700,000 share placement to pay for the acquisition of US partner Global Media Services and fund ongoing operations. Having transferred all its technology resources to the US, the company said it would save more than £500,000 a year and had reduced its costs to less than £900,000 a year. 'In addition to the content and distribution deals we have signed during the period, the first half of the year has seen a focus on increasing efficiency and reducing costs,' the chief executive added.

The company said it remained confident it would break even before the end of the year, but the group's forecast relies on increasing the number of deals to boost revenues. It has suffered from the slow roll-out of the high speed broadband connections required to view video footage over the Internet and last year said it was switching its focus to the more developed markets in the US and Asia.

Source: adapted from *The Guardian*, 30.7.2003

(a) Explain why Newsplayer may have experienced cash flow and liquidity problems.
(b) Explain how the business may overcome these problems.

Credit control

Most businesses have some sort of CREDIT CONTROL system, so that money owing can be collected quickly and easily. A 'tight' or 'easy' credit policy may be adopted. Tight credit terms may be used to improve liquidity, reduce the risk of bad debts, exploit a sellers market, or maintain slender profit margins. Easy credit terms may be designed to clear old stocks, enter a new market or perhaps help a regular customer with financial difficulties.

The company accountant and the sales manager often work closely with the credit controller, since credit policy

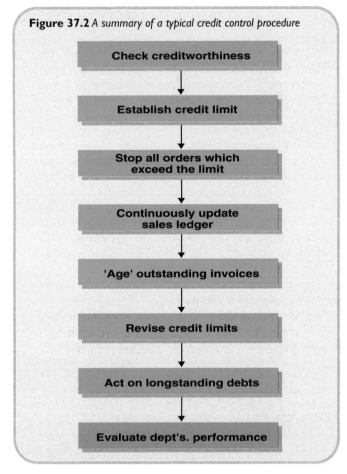

Figure 37.2 *A summary of a typical credit control procedure*

- Check creditworthiness
- Establish credit limit
- Stop all orders which exceed the limit
- Continuously update sales ledger
- 'Age' outstanding invoices
- Revise credit limits
- Act on longstanding debts
- Evaluate dept's. performance

will affect the financial position of the firm and sales. Between them they set targets for the credit control department such as the value of bad debts or the length of time it takes to collect debts.

Firms have procedures to help credit control. Figure 37.2 shows an example. Many firms will not do business with a new customer until their creditworthiness has been checked. This can be done by asking for references from a supplier, a banker's reference, or a credit rating agency's report. From this information the credit controller can set a credit limit based on the risk involved.

When an order exceeds the credit limit, the credit controller should investigate. The result may be a stop being placed on the order, a request to the customer to pay any outstanding debt, or simply allowing the order to go ahead.

Credit control records, which show customer orders and payments, must be up to date. Every month outstanding invoices must be 'aged', to identify customers who owe money over 30, 60 and 90 days.

If there are persistent debts, the credit controller must take action. A statement of the account should be sent, followed by a second one with a letter. Next a telephone call to the debtor should be followed by a personal visit. Finally, as a last resort, it may be necessary to take legal action to recover the debt.

Some firms use an independent **debt factor** (☞ unit 33) to assist in credit control. There has been quite a growth in this

type of business in recent years. A factor is a business that will provide finance to a business against its debts for a fee. It often pays a certain amount to the business 'up front' and the remainder as debts are collected.

Late Payment of Commercial Debts

Small businesses complain that larger organisations use their power to exploit smaller firms by making them wait before payment is made. This can create severe cash flow problems for small businesses, particularly when the large firm is the only customer of the small firm. The government recognised the problem and introduced the **Late Payment of Commercial Debts (Interest) Act 1998** to give small firms help. The Act financially penalises late payers. It gives businesses a right to charge interest on unpaid commercial debts. Interest can run from three points, depending on how a contract is drafted.
- An agreed date.
- A fixed occurrence (ie delivery of the goods).
- Thirty days from (i) the day after the supplier has performed its duties, eg delivery, or (ii) 30 days after the buyer has received notice the supplier is claiming a sum due (for example receipt of an invoice).

Interest can be claimed at the rate of 8 per cent above the official dealing rate of the Bank of England. So if this was 4 per cent, interest on the debt can be lawfully charged at 12 per cent. Compensation can also be claimed. This is claimed as a fixed sum as well as accruing interest as follows:
- if the debt is less than £1,000 - £40;
- if the debt is £1,000 but less than £10,000 - £70;
- if the debt is more than £10,000 - £100.

Only time will tell whether this Act will be effective. Its critics say that the worst thing a business can do when a customer can't or won't pay is ask for even more money.

Knowledge...Knowledge...Knowle

1. How is the value of working capital calculated?
2. At what point does a business have sufficient working capital to avoid a problem?
3. State 4 time lags that exist in the working capital cycle.
4. State 2 ways in which time lags can be reduced.
5. What is meant by a liquidity problem?
6. What does the current ratio show?
7. State 5 causes of a liquidity crisis.
8. What could a business do with its stocks of raw materials to help in a liquidity crisis?
9. What steps should a credit controller take to deal with persistent debts?
10. How might a business prevent a debt problem before it gives credit to a customer?

key terms

Credit control - the process of monitoring and collecting the money owed to a business.

Liquidity - the ease with which an asset can be changed into cash.

Liquidity problems - difficulties that arise because of the lack of assets that can easily be converted into cash to make immediate payments.

Overtrading - a situation where a business attempts to raise production without increasing the size of its working capital.

Working capital - the funds left over to meet day to day expenses after current debts have been paid. It is calculated by current assets minus current liabilities.

Working capital cycle - the flow of liquid resources into and out of a business.

Case study Emerson Engineering Ltd

Emerson Engineering Ltd makes a range of components in a modern factory in Sheffield. It employs 43 staff. About 80 per cent of its output is sold to two manufacturers in the UK. The company is efficient, ambitious and reasonably profitable. In recent years it has grown by taking over some smaller competitors in the north.

In 2003 Emerson's sales director gave a presentation at an industrial exhibition in Munich. As a result the company received a number of inquiries from foreign producers. Eventually one of the larger companies placed a sizeable order. To meet these orders Emerson had to step up production. This involved recruiting 4 more staff, purchasing a new machine, buying more materials and components and paying overtime to employees.

However, the expansion began to escalate following a visit to the factory by some French delegates. Two days after their visit another large order was received. Emerson was now beginning to feel stretched. It needed to recruit more staff and buy even more resources. Emerson's cash had run out and the company was dangerously close to exceeding its overdraft limit. Indeed, it would have to exceed this limit at the end of the month to pay wages, which again included large overtime payments.

One of the problems was the credit terms agreed with the foreign customers. They were offered 90 days credit and so far none of the work for these orders had been delivered. The credit period did not start until the goods had been delivered. To add to this was the usual problem of exacting payment from its regular two customers. Whilst they provided Emerson with a reliable stream of profitable orders, they nearly always seemed to delay payment to well

beyond the agreed credit period.

Two days before the foreign orders were due to be delivered on 23.5.2003, an emergency board meeting was held to discuss the cash flow problem. During the meeting three possible solutions were discussed.

- Sale and lease back of machinery to Henderson Associates, a specialist sale and lease back company.
- Sell debts to a debt factoring company.
- An unsecured short term bank loan.

Table 37.2 shows the value Emerson's current assets and current liabilities the day of the emergency board meeting and 12 months ago. Figure 37.3 shows the company's monthly cash position in the previous trading period.

Table 37.2 *Current assets and current liabilities for Emerson Engineering Ltd, 23.5.2003*

	2003 £000s	2002 £000s
Current assets		
Stocks of raw materials and components	1,229	1,001
Work-in-progress	3,445	1,765
Debtors	2,189	1,778
Cash at bank	0	1,239
	6,863	**5,783**
Current liabilities		
Trade creditors	3,112	2,311
Taxation	1,299	1,365
Other creditors	2,100	1,765
Bank overdraft	2,460	0
	8,971	**5,441**

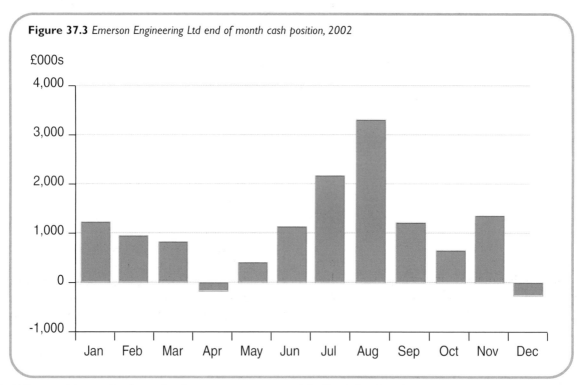

Figure 37.3 *Emerson Engineering Ltd end of month cash position, 2002*

(a) **What evidence is there in the case to suggest that Emerson is overtrading? (6 marks)**

(b) **(i) Calculate the value of working capital for Emerson in 2002 and 2003. (6 marks)**

(ii) Do the answers in (i) confirm that Emerson has a cash flow problem? Explain your answer. (6 marks)

(c) **Explain the disadvantages to Emerson of using (i) sale and lease back (ii) debt factoring to resolve the cash crisis. (10 marks)**

(d) **Discuss whether you think Emerson is in danger of going out of business. (12 marks)**

38 Depreciation and the Valuation of Assets

How are assets valued?

One of the problems in financial accounting is how to place a value on assets. Accountants value assets at **historical cost**, ie the cost of the asset when it is first purchased.

There are reasons why assets should be valued in this way. Business transactions are entered into records as they occur. For example, if a firm buys a vehicle for £15,000 and pays cash, two entries will be made in the records. Also, accountants would argue that historical cost can be checked. It is based on actual costs and is better than methods which involve estimates. Other methods of valuation, such as those which take into account inflation, are also used. As yet, though, a suitable replacement has not been found.

One problem with historical cost accounting is how to put a value on fixed assets like property. In recent years there have been times when the values of land and buildings have risen sharply - as much as 30 or 40 per cent in one year. Unless the accounts are amended, they will not reflect the true value of the business. It is common now to revalue assets such as property every few years. Inflation distorts the value of assets and any other value which is measured in money terms.

This unit considers the valuation of two sets of assets - fixed assets, such as machinery, and current assets, such as stock. The valuation of these assets causes particular problems for accountants.

Valuing fixed assets - the use of depreciation

Fixed assets are used again and again over a long period of time. For example, a milling machine might be used for many years to produce metal components. A motor business would expect automated production lines to run for many years.

Figure 38.1 *A summary of the factors which might cause depreciation*

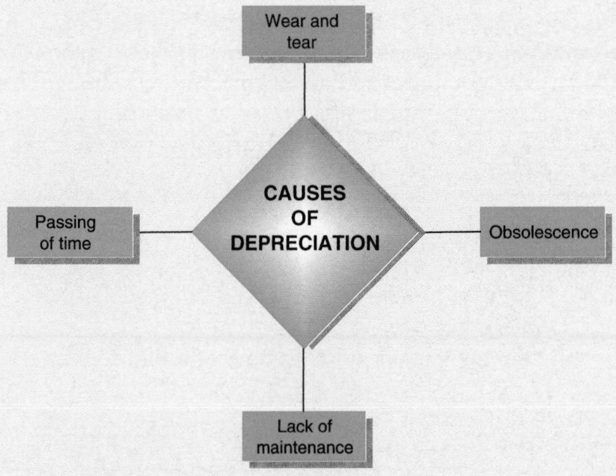

```
              Wear and
                tear
                 |
Passing      CAUSES
of time  —   OF      —  Obsolescence
           DEPRECIATION
                 |
              Lack of
            maintenance
```

During their operation fixed assets are consumed and its value is 'used up'. This measure of consumption or any other reduction in the useful economic life of a fixed asset is known as depreciation (☞ unit 32).

Why might fixed assets depreciate?

- Machinery, tools and equipment all suffer wear and tear when they are used. They deteriorate, which can sometimes affect their operation or effectiveness. Eventually they will have to be replaced.
- Changing technology can often make assets OBSOLETE. Although a machine may still work, it may not be used because a new machine is more efficient.
- Capital goods which are hardly used or poorly maintained may depreciate quickly. The life of machinery can be prolonged if it is 'looked after'.
- The passing of time can also lead to depreciation. For example, if an asset is leased, the 'buyer' can use the asset for a period of time. As the expiry date gets close, the lease becomes worth less and less.

Depreciation and the accounts

Each year accountants must work out how much depreciation to allow for each fixed asset. This can then be used in the balance sheet and the profit and loss account.

The balance sheet (☞ unit 32) will show the NET BOOK VALUE of assets. This is their original value minus depreciation. So if a piece of machinery is bought for £10,000 and depreciates by £3,000 in the first year, its book value would be £7,000. The book value falls each year as more depreciation is deducted.

Depreciation is shown in the profit and loss account under expenses (☞ unit 31). This indicates that part of the original value is 'used up' each year (known as revenue expenditure (☞ unit 33). Eventually the entire value of the asset will appear as expenses, when the asset depreciates fully. This process of reducing the original value by the amount of depreciation is known as WRITING OFF.

There are good reasons why a firm should allow for depreciation each year in its accounts.

- If it does not, the accounts will be inaccurate. If the original value of assets was placed on the balance sheet this would overstate the value. The value of assets falls each year as they depreciate.
- Fixed assets generate profit for many years. It seems logical to write off the value of the asset over this whole period, rather than when it is first bought. This matches the benefit from the asset more closely with its cost.
- A sensible firm will know that assets must be replaced in future and allow for this. Even though depreciation appears as an expense on the profit and loss account, it is actually a

PROVISION. Expenses involve paying out money. In the case of depreciation, no money is paid out. A business simply recognises that assets have to be replaced and 'provides' for this by placing a value in the accounts.

Calculating depreciation - the straight line method

The STRAIGHT LINE METHOD is the most common method used by business to work out depreciation. It assumes that the net cost of an asset should be written off in equal amounts over its life. The accountant needs to know the cost of the asset, its estimated residual value, ie its 'scrap' value after the business has finished with it, and its expected life in years. The formula used is:

$$\text{Depreciation allowance (each time period)} = \frac{\text{Original cost - residual value}}{\text{Expected life (years)}}$$

Assume a delivery van costs £28,000 to buy and has an expected life of 4 years. The residual value is estimated at £4,000.

Table 38.1 *A summary of the annual depreciation allowance and book value of the delivery van using the straight line method*

Year	Depreciation allowance (each year) £	Net book value £
1	6,000	22,000
2	6,000	16,000
3	6,000	10,000
4	6,000	4,000

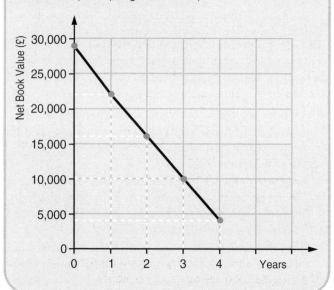

Figure 38.2 *A graph illustrating the book value of the delivery van over its lifetime (straight line method)*

$$\text{Depreciation allowance} = \frac{\text{£28,000 - £4,000}}{\text{4 years}}$$

$$= \frac{\text{£24,000}}{4}$$

$$= \text{£6,000}$$

When calculating depreciation it is helpful to draw up a table to show how an asset is written off over its lifetime. Table 38.1 shows the depreciation allowance charged to the profit and loss account each year, and the net book value which is listed in the balance sheet. We can illustrate this on a graph as shown in Figure 38.2. These are some advantages to using this method.

● It is simple. Little calculation is needed and the same amount is subtracted from the book value each year.
● It is useful for assets like a lease, where the life of the asset and the residual value is known precisely.

Calculating depreciation - the reducing balance method

The REDUCING or DECLINING BALANCE METHOD assumes that the depreciation charge in the early years of an

Edwards Ltd produces plank and strip boards for wooden flooring and skirting boards for the building industry. The business operates from a small factory in Nottingham. In 2003 a new computerised sawing machine was bought for £39,000. Kerry Edwards, the owner of the business, expects the new machine to last for 6 years when it will have a residual value of £3,000.

(a) Calculate the annual depreciation allowance using the straight line method.
(b) (i) Draw up a table to show how the machine is written of over its life.
     (ii) What is the net book value at the end of year 4?

Question 1

Table 38.2 *A summary of the annual depreciation allowance and book value of the vehicle using the reducing balance method*

Year	Depreciation allowance (each year) £	Net book value £
1	11,200 (28,000 x 40%)	16,800
2	6,720 (16,800 x 40%)	10,080
3	4,032 (10,080 x 40%)	6,048
4	2,419 (6,048 x 40%)	3,629

asset's life should be higher than in the later years. To do this, the asset must be written off by the same percentage rate each year. This means the annual charge falls.

Assume a vehicle is bought for £28,000 and has a life of four years. Table 38.2 shows how the vehicle can be written off using the reducing balance method. A 40 per cent charge will be made each year and the firm expects a **residual value** of £3,629.

Table 38.2 shows the depreciation allowance in the profit and loss account in each of the four years. It also shows the book value which would be listed in the balance sheet. Notice that the depreciation allowance falls every year. This is shown in Figure 38.3. What if the business expected the residual value to be £4,000? The depreciation charge for this can be calculated using the formula:

$$\text{Depreciation rate} = \left[1 - \sqrt[n]{\frac{\text{Residual value}}{\text{Cost}}} \right] \times 100$$

Where n = estimated life of the asset, ie 4 years, so:

$$\text{Depreciation rate} = \left[1 - \sqrt[4]{\frac{4,000}{28,000}} \right] \times 100 = 38.52\%$$

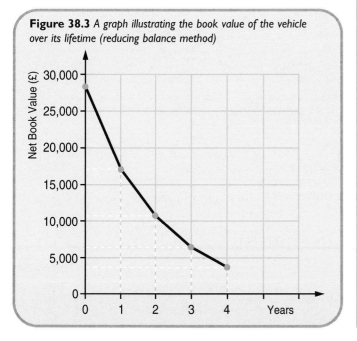

Figure 38.3 *A graph illustrating the book value of the vehicle over its lifetime (reducing balance method)*

There are some advantages to using the reducing balance method.

- It takes into account that some assets, machinery for example, lose far more value in the first year than they do in the fifth year, say. So the book value reflects more accurately the real value of the asset in the balance sheet.
- For many assets, maintenance and repair costs grow as the asset ages. Using the declining balance method results in a more equal total expense each year for fixed assets related costs. For example, at the end of year 1 the depreciation charge for a machine might be £4,500 with only a £500 maintenance charge. In year 5 the depreciation charge might have been £1,500 and repairs and maintenance may have been £3,000. Although the two totals are not the same (£5,000 and £4,500), as the depreciation charges fall the maintenance and repair costs rise.

William Marshall owns an arable farm in Suffolk. He farms 6,000 acres and employs 4 staff. In the summer of 2004 William decided that he was no longer prepared to lease a combine harvester to harvest his cereal crops. He purchased a brand new combine harvester for £75,000. With good care and maintenance he hoped to keep the machine for 5 years. (After five years a residual value of £5,832 was estimated.)
(a) Draw up a table to show the annual depreciation allowance and the book value at the end of each year. Use the reducing balance method and write off 40 per cent each year.
(b) Draw a line graph to show the annual book value at the end of each year.
(c) Explain why the reducing balance method of depreciation might be more suitable for an asset like a combine harvester.

Question 2

Other methods of calculating depreciation

The **sum-of-the-years' digits method** assumes that fixed assets depreciate quicker in the early years. The calculation is based on the sum-of-the-years' digits, given the expected life of an asset, less the residual value. For an asset which has an expected life of 4 years the sum-of-the-years' is 10, ie 4+3+2+1 = 10. The depreciation charge for the first year will be $^4/10$ of the original cost, the second year it will be $^3/10$ of the original cost and so on.

Assuming a cost of £28,000, a life span of 4 years and a residual value of £4,000, the **net value** of the asset is £24,000 (£28,000 - £4,000). We can draw up a table to show the annual depreciation charge and the book value each year (Table 38.3).

Table 38.3 shows that the depreciation allowance falls in a similar way to the reducing balance method.

Table 38.3 *A summary of the annual depreciation allowance and book value of the asset above, using the sum-of-the-years' digits method*

Year	Depreciation allowance (each year)	Net book value
	£	£
1	9,600 (24,000 x 4/10)	18,400
2	7,200 (24,000 x 3/10)	11,200
3	4,800 (24,000 x 2/10)	6,400
4	2,400 (24,000 x 1/10)	4,000

Another method called the **usage method** (or **machine hour method**) takes into account that some assets wear out more rapidly the more they are used. Thus, depreciation is based on the number of hours a machine, for example, is used during the accounting period. It is not a method that is often used by firms.

The disposal of assets

The book value of assets rarely reflects their precise value. So if an asset is sold, a business usually makes a profit or a loss. This is likely if the asset is sold before the end of its expected life. For example, if a machine is bought for £100,000 with an expected life of 10 years and residual value of £15,000, the depreciation allowance each year will be £8,500 (using the straight line method). If the firm decides to sell the machine at the end of year 7 and receives £44,000, it earns a profit of £3,500 because the book value at the end of year 7 is £40,500. A firm must show this in the accounts. It is common practice to deal with profit or loss on disposal by adjusting that year's depreciation charge. If a profit is made, the depreciation charge will be reduced by the amount of the profit. If a loss is made, the depreciation charge will be increased by the amount of the loss. If the profit or loss is very large then it will be treated as an exceptional item in the accounts (☞ unit 31).

Venetta Gains runs a design business in Cheltenham. Due to the rapid growth in her business in areas such as fabric design, she has decided to buy a new computer. She spent £5,000 on a system which would include a software design package. Venetta planned to use the computer for 8 years, by which time it would have a scrap value of £200.
(a) Calculate the annual depreciation allowance using the straight line method and draw up a table to show the book value at the end of each year.
(b) At the end of the third year Venetta was forced to upgrade her system because it had become outdated. Venetta sold her old system for £1,000. Calculate the profit or loss on disposal.
(c) Comment on the size of the profit/loss.

Question 3

Valuing current assets - stock valuation

When accounts are produced, a firm must calculate the quantity and value of the stocks which it is holding. The value of **stocks** at the beginning and the end of the trading year, ie the **opening stock** and the **closing stock**, will affect the gross profit for the year. This is because the cost of sales in the trading account is adjusted for changes in stock. If, for example, the closing stock is overvalued, then the cost of sales will be lower and the gross profit higher. This is shown in Tables 38.4 and 38.5. In Table 38.4 the closing stock is £11,300, the cost of sales (adjusted for stock) is £57,400 and gross profit is £40,500.

In Table 38.5 the closing stock is now valued at £14,100 instead of £11,300, so the cost of sales (adjusted for stock) is lower at £54,600 and the gross profit higher at £43,300.

A **stock take** can be used to find out how much stock is held. This involves making a list of all raw materials, finished goods and work-in-progress. Stock valuation is more difficult. The 'prudence' concept in accounting does not allow selling prices to be used because profit is only recognised when a sale has been made. So stocks are valued at historic cost or net realisable value, whichever is the lowest. Normally stocks would be valued at cost. But there are circumstances when net realisable value is lower. If goods are damaged in

Table 38.4

	£	£
Turnover		97,900
Opening stock	12,300	
Cost of sales	56,400	
	68,700	
Less closing stock	11,300	
		57,400
Gross profit		40,500

Table 38.5

	£	£
Turnover		97,900
Opening stock	12,300	
Cost of sales	56 400	
	68,700	
Less closing stock	14,100	
		54,600
Gross profit		43,300

Table 38.6 *A record of stock transactions showing how a closing stock figure is calculated using the FIFO method of stock valuation*

Date	Stock received and price	Stock issued and price	Stock valuation	
			Goods in stock	Total £
01.6.04	100 @ £5		(100 @ £5 = £500)	500
04.6.04	200 @ £6		(100 @ £5 = £500) (200 @ £6 = £1,200)	1,700
25.6.04		100 @ £5	(200 @ £6 = £1,200)	1,200
02.7.04		100 @ £6	(100 @ £6 = £600)	600
12.7.04	200 @ £6.50		(100 @ £6 = £600) (200 @ £6.50 = £1,300)	1,900
23.7.04		100 @ £6	(200 @ £6.50 = £1,300)	1,300
24.7.04		100 @ £6.50	(100 @ £6.50 = £650)	650

stock, they may sell for a lot less than they cost to produce. Also, some products face severe changes in market conditions. Clothes tend to fall in value when fashions change, and may need discounts to sell them.

What happens to stock valuation when the cost of stock changes over time? Say a business buys some goods at the start of the year, but finds that half way through their cost of replacement has gone up. How are they valued? Three methods can be used.

- FIFO (first in first out).
- LIFO (last in first out).
- Average cost.

First in first out

The FIRST IN FIRST OUT method assumes that stock for production is issued in the order in which it was delivered. Thus, stocks that are bought first are used up first. Any unused stocks at the end of the trading year will be those most recently bought. This ensures that stocks issued for production are priced at the cost of earlier stocks, while any remaining stock is

valued much closer to the replacement cost. Assuming that the opening stock is zero, consider the following stock transactions in Table 38.6.

On 1.6.04 a business receives 100 units of stock at £5, which means it has £500 of goods in stock. On 4.6.04, an extra 200 units at £6 (£1,200) are added, making a total of £1,700. On 25.6.04, 100 units are issued from stock for production. As it is first in first out, the goods are taken from the 1.6.04 stock, priced at £5 - the first stock to be received. This means £500 is removed from stock leaving 200 units valued at £6 (£1,200) left in stock.

By using the FIFO method, the value of stocks after all the transactions is £650.

Last in first out

The LAST IN FIRST OUT method assumes that the most recent deliveries are issued before existing stock. In this case, any unused stocks are valued at the older and probably lower purchase price. Table 38.7 shows how the previous transactions are adjusted for a LIFO stock valuation. On

Table 38.7 *A record of stock transactions showing how the closing stock figure is calculated using the LIFO method of stock valuation*

Date	Stock received and price	Stock issued and price	Stock valuation	
			Goods in stock	Total
				£
01.6.04	100 @ £5		(100 @ £5 = £500)	500
04.6.04	200 @ £6		(100 @ £5 = £500) (200 @ £6 = £1,200)	1,700
25.6.04		100 @ £6	(100 @ £5 = £500) (100 @ £6 = £600)	1,100
02.7.04		100 @ £6	(100 @ £5 = £500)	500
12.7.04	200 @ £6.50		(100 @ £5 = £500) (200 @ £6.50 = £1,300)	1,800
23.7.04		100 @ £6.50	(100 @ £5 = £500) (100 @ £6.50 = £650)	1,150
24.7.04		100 @ £6.50	(100 @ £5 = £500)	500

1.6.04, 100 units of stock are received at £5, meaning £500 of goods are in stock. On 4.6.04 an extra 200 units of stock valued at £6 are added (£1,200) - a total of £1,700. When 100 units of stock are issued on 25.6.04 they are taken from the most recent (last) stock received, priced at £6. So £600 of stock is removed. This leaves 100 units at £5 and 100 units at £6 in stock - a total of £1,100.

This time the value of stocks remaining after the transactions is £500. If the value of stocks is rising, the LIFO method gives a lower finishing stock than the FIFO method.

Average cost

This method involves recalculating the average cost (AVCO) of stock every time a new delivery arrives. Each unit is assumed to have been purchased at the **average price** of all components. In practice the average cost of each unit is a weighted average and is calculated using the following formula:

$$\frac{\text{Existing stock value + value of latest purchase}}{\text{Number of units then in stock}}$$

Using the same stock transactions as before we can find the closing stock by drawing up Table 38.8. This time the weighted average cost method is used.

When the AVCO method is used the value of stock following the transactions is £622. This stock figure lies closer to the FIFO method of stock valuation. It is often used when stock prices do not change a great deal. In practice it is the FIFO and average cost methods which are most commonly used by firms. Indeed , the LIFO method does not conform to the accounting standard SSAP, nor is it acceptable for tax purposes with the Inland Revenue. Once a method has been chosen it should conform with the 'consistency' convention and not change. This is also true for calculating depreciation.

During a trading period the following stock transactions were recorded for a company:
01.7.03 50 units were bought @ £2 per unit.
03.8.03 100 units were bought @ £2.20 per unit.
19.8.03 100 units were issued.
23.9.03 200 units were bought @ £2.30 per unit.
25.9.03 150 units were issued.
(a) Assuming that the opening stock was zero, calculate the value of closing stock using the:
    (i) FIFO method; (ii) LIFO method; (iii) AVCO method. Present your answers in tables using a spreadsheet.
(b) If the stock listed in the transactions above was perishable, which of the three methods is most suitable for the physical issuing of stock? Explain why.
(c) Why do you think that the LIFO method is the least favoured by firms?

Question 4

Knowledge

1. Why are assets valued at historical cost in the accounts?
2. Explain why assets fall in value.
3. Why is it necessary to provide for depreciation?
4. What are the main differences between the straight line and reducing balance methods of calculating depreciation?
5. What is meant by opening stock and closing stock?
6. Explain the difference between the LIFO and FIFO methods of stock valuation.
7. Why is stock not valued at its selling price?

Table 38.8 *A record of stock transactions showing how the closing stock is calculated using the weighted average cost method of stock valuation*

Date	Receipts	Issues	Weighted average cost £	Stock valuation	Total £
01.6.04	100 @ £5		5.00	(100 @ £5 = £500)	500
04.6.04	200 @ £6		5.67	(300 @ £5.67 = £1,701)	1,701
25.6.04		100	5.67	(200 @ £5.67 = £1,134)	1,134
02.7.04		100	5.67	(100 @ £5.67 = £567)	567
12.7.04	200 @ £6.50		6.22	(300 @ £6.22 = £1,866)	1,866
23.7.04		100	6.22	(200 @ £6.22 = £1,244)	1,244
24.7.04		100	6.22	(100 @ £6.22 = £622)	622

key terms

First in first out (FIFO) - a method of stock valuation which involves issuing stock in the order in which it is delivered, so that the remaining stock is valued closer to its replacement cost.

Last in first out (LIFO) - a method of stock valuation which involves issuing more recent deliveries first, so that closing stock is valued at the older and possibly lower purchase price.

Obsolete - an asset that is no longer of any use to a business.

Net book value - the historical cost of an asset less depreciation accumulated each year.

Provision (in relation to depreciation) - an allowance made in the accounts for depreciation.

Reducing or declining balance method - a method used to calculate the annual depreciation allowance which involves writing off the same percentage rate each year.

Straight line method - a method used to calculate the annual depreciation allowance by subtracting the estimated scrap value from the cost and dividing the result by the expected life of the asset.

Writing off - the process of reducing the value of an asset by the amount of depreciation.

Case study Loch Ness Water Ski School

In 2003 Danny McLintock set up a business teaching people how to water ski on Loch Ness. This is something Danny had been thinking about for several years. He was a keen water skier and wanted to combine business with pleasure. He had also been saving hard to fund the venture. The business is based in Fort Augustus and most of his customers are tourists with a taste for the outdoor life. Danny uses notices and brochures to advertise his water skiing services in local hotels, pubs and youth hostels.

He purchased a second hand power boat and a variety of equipment including wet suits and water skis. Danny also bought a second hand Land Rover. This would be needed to tow the boat and launch it safely from the slipway at Fort Augustus. The

business was more successful than Danny dared to imagine. Due to the warm summer in 2003 there were plenty of tourists willing to enjoy the experience. Danny was also contacted by local youth groups and some schools and offered them group discounts for lessons. Some information about Danny's fixed assets is shown in Table 38.9.

(a) **Why should the business allow for depreciation in its accounts? (6 marks)**

(b) **Calculate the total depreciation allowance for Danny's business in 2003 using (i) the straight line method and (ii) the reducing balance method (write off 30 per cent each year). (14 marks)**

(c) **Explain why the profit made by Danny's business will be higher if the straight line method is used. (6 marks)**

(d) (i) **At the end of the year Danny realises that the boat needs to be replaced with a more powerful one. Calculate the profit or loss on disposal if the old boat is sold for £2,200. (6 marks)**

   (ii) **Discuss what has most likely caused the power boat to depreciate in this case. (8 marks)**

(e) **Danny is unsure about which method of depreciation to use in the accounts. Discuss the advantages and disadvantages of each and recommend which method he should use. (10 marks)**

Table 38.9 *The fixed assets of Danny McLintock's business*

	Cost	Expected life	Residual value
Power boat	£4,500	4 years	£500
Land Rover	£2,500	5 years	£500
Equipment	£1,000	6 years	£100

The nature of investment

Investment refers to the purchase of capital goods. Capital goods are used in the production of other goods, directly or indirectly. For example, a building contractor who buys a cement mixer, some scaffolding, a lorry and five shovels has invested. These goods will be used directly in production. If the contractor buys a computer, a filing cabinet and a photocopier for the firm's office, this is indirect investment. Although these items will not be used in production the business would not run as efficiently without them.

Investment might also refer to expenditure by a business which is likely to yield a return in the future. For example, a business might spend £20 million on research and development into a new product or invest £10 million in a promotion campaign. In each case, money is being spent on projects now in the hope that a greater amount of money will be generated in the future as a result of that expenditure.

Investment can be **autonomous** or **induced**. Autonomous investment is when a firm buys capital goods to replace ones which have worn out. Any new investment by the firm resulting from rising sales or expansion is induced investment.

Types of investment

Investment can be placed into various categories.

- Capital goods. This includes the purchase of a whole variety of mechanical and technical equipment. Vans, lathes, computers, robots, tools, vehicles and information technology are examples.
- Construction. This includes spending on new buildings that are bought or constructed by the firm. Factories, shops, warehouses, workshops and offices are examples.
- Stocks. This is a less obvious item of investment, since it does not fit neatly into the earlier definition. However, because stocks of finished goods and work-in-progress (☞ unit 57) will earn income in the future when they are sold, they are classed as investment.
- Public sector investment. Central and local government fund about twenty five per cent of all investment in the economy. Examples of public sector investment include the building of schools, motorways, hospitals and expenditure on goods like buses, dustcarts and equipment for the civil service. The factors which influence the level of public sector investment are often very different from those which affect private sector investment. This is dealt with later in this unit.

Risk in investment

The decision to invest by business is the most difficult it has to make because of the risk involved. There is often a number of alternative choices. A firm buying a new fleet of cars for its sales staff has to decide which model of car will suit the

company best of all. There may also be a considerable choice of projects. For example, a firm may need to choose whether investment in a new packaging machine which increases efficiency would be more profitable than a new computer system.

If all cost and revenue data upon which a decision would be based was accurate, there would not be a problem. However, revenue information in particular comes from predictions. It may be based on forecasts of future demand and conditions in the economy. Even costs, which are perhaps easier to predict, can vary.

Most investment decisions are uncertain because they are

In March 2002, ITV Digital, the world's most expensive digital terrestrial TV company, went into administration. It was hoped that the purchase of the rights to broadcast live Nationwide football would be the kingpin of the operation. However, after an investment of £800 million and one of the worst recessions in advertising spending in memory, Carlton and Granada decided they could not tolerate the massive losses. The cost of cutting loose from ITV Digital would be expensive and could have long term repercussions. In the short term, bills of £50-£120 million could be incurred. This was before any potential legal action from the Football League.

The body that represents lower league teams threatened to sue Carlton and Granada for up to £500 million in lost broadcasting and sponsorship revenues if they reneged on a three-year broadcasting deal. It was the league's refusal to renegotiate the deal that finally tipped ITV Digital over the edge. However, it was unlikely that the 72 clubs relying on income from the deal would get anything like the money they were owed. Indeed, around 30 clubs could themselves be on the brink of collapse. Suppliers such as BT, set top box manufacturers and content providers could be left in the lurch. They could also threaten multimillion pound law suits to recover money owed. Meanwhile ITV Digital's 1.3 million subscribers were left feeling betrayed, confused and angry.

The biggest losers in all of this could be the government. It was hoping to switch off the analogue television signal between 2006-10. The government is keen to drive forward the population's commitment to digital TV. It would then be free to auction off the spare analogue spectrum to raise money for public expenditure. This is similar to the sale of third generation mobile phone licences.

Sources: adapted from *The Guardian*, 28.3.2002 and *The Observer*, 31.3.2002.

(a) Using this case as an example, explain why investment is risky.
(b) Describe briefly the effects of the failed investment on the (i) private sector and (ii) public sector.

Question 1

long term decisions, where resources are committed for a period of time. Investment projects have failed both in the private sector and the public sector. For example, in the private sector, independent TV production company, the Television Corporation, had to write off £13 million on Californian subsidiary Pacifica in 2003. The company was still reeling from a failed bid to set up a Formula One version of power boating. The company had already written off £2.6 million, including £400,000 in the previous year. In the public sector, the government spent a lot of money on equipment which was used in the development of the Concorde aircraft. This also proved to be commercially unsuccessful. Concorde services were stopped in 2004.

Investment is also said to be risky because it is often funded with borrowed money. This means that the return on any investment project must also cover the cost of borrowing. Also, if the investment project fails the company may be left with a heavy debt burden and possibly without the means to repay it. The Channel Tunnel project experienced such problems in the late 1990s. Around £5 billion was owed to several hundred banks following the construction of the tunnel link. Although the company was covering its operating costs, it has ceased interest payments to the banks. It was suggested that it was unlikely ever to be able to repay the original £5 billion borrowed. This was still the case in 2004.

The factors affecting private sector investment

Figure 39.1 shows the factors which might affect private sector investment decisions.

Motives To begin with, firms must have a reason to invest.
● All firms have to replace worn out equipment.

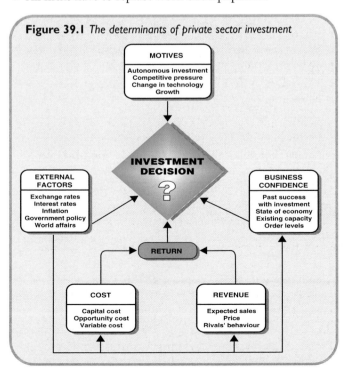

Figure 39.1 *The determinants of private sector investment*

● To be competitive on costs, price and quality, firms may have to invest or risk losing customers to their rivals. For example, most building societies invested in the refurbishment of their branches in the 1990s. Once one society improved its branch most others copied.
● The availability of new technology (☞ unit 60) may persuade firms to invest. When technology becomes available, firms are often keen to use it if they can afford to.
● Firms may wish to grow, to be more profitable or to increase their market influence. Growth involves investment in more plant, equipment and other productive assets.

Return If firms have a reason to invest, they must then decide whether it is worthwhile. One influence on this is the return on the investment. The return on an investment project can be found by subtracting the cost of the project from the expected revenue. There are three major costs. Capital costs might be the cost of a new factory. Opportunity costs (☞ unit 9) are the foregone alternatives the investment funds might have been used for, eg higher dividends to shareholders. Direct variable costs include the running costs of the project, eg labour or fuel costs.

Calculating the expected revenue is not easy. Expected sales are hard to predict with accuracy because many factors affect them. Market research (☞ unit 12) can only predict sales to some extent. Sales can also be influenced by the price set by the business in the future and by rivals' behaviour. Both of these factors are unpredictable.

Business confidence Entrepreneurs and managers will be either optimistic or pessimistic about the future of their businesses. Confidence may be influenced by a range of factors. These include whether or not previous investment has been a success, the state of the economy, the existing level of capacity and future order levels. A pessimistic business person may be less likely to invest than an optimistic one.

External factors External influences can be direct or indirect. For example, high interest rates may directly affect the cost of investment. If money is borrowed the business will pay back more. This can indirectly affect confidence. Inflation could affect costs, revenue and confidence. World affairs, such as problems in the Middle East in 2003, or rising exchange rates, may make investment abroad seem less attractive.

The factors affecting public sector investment

What factors influence investment by central government and local authorities?
● Investment in new schools, roads and hospitals, for example, will be influenced by national and local needs. As the demands of the population grow, more of these facilities will be needed.
● Political factors may also influence the quantity and type of

investment. In the recent past, the government has aimed to reduce public investment in order to reduce the size of the public sector in general. It has also reduced it in specific areas, such as on defence.

● The availability of government funds and the opportunity cost of investment spending. If revenue from taxes is falling, there may be fewer investment funds. If the opportunity costs of investment projects are high, then they may be cancelled. The state of the economy will be important. For example, falling unemployment in the late 1990s and early twenty first century reduced government spending on unemployment benefit. This perhaps meant that extra funds were available for spending on health or education.

Investment appraisal and net cash flows

INVESTMENT APPRAISAL describes how a private sector business might objectively evaluate an investment project to determine whether or not it is likely to be profitable. It also allows businesses to make comparisons between different investment projects. There is a number of quantitative methods that a business might use when evaluating projects. However, they all involve comparing the **capital cost** of the project with the NET CASH FLOW.

● The capital cost is the amount of money spent when setting up a new venture.
● The net cash flow is the amount of money the business expects to receive each year over the life of the investment project, less the estimated running costs.

Consider a haulage company that invests in a new lorry. Table 39.1 shows the capital cost, the estimated revenue, the estimated running costs and the net cash flow each year over the life of the lorry. The lorry is expected to last for 5 years. The capital cost is the £80,000 paid to the vehicle supplier. The lorry is purchased in year 0, ie 'now'. The net cash flow by the end of year 1 is £19,000. This is found by subtracting the estimated running costs, such as fuel, drivers wages and insurance, from the estimated revenue generated by the lorry from carrying goods (£56,000 - £37,000). In this example the business would compare the capital cost of £80,000 with the total net cash flow of £87,000 (£19,000 + £21,000 + £22,000 + £15,000 + £10,000), when evaluating the investment. It may use one of the appraisal methods discussed in this unit.

Payback period

The PAYBACK PERIOD refers to the amount of time it takes

Table 39.1 *Capital cost and net cash flow from an investment (£)*

	Year 0	Year 1	Year 2	Year 3	Year 4	Year 5
Capital cost	80,000	0	0	0	0	0
Estimated revenue	0	56,000	60,000	62,000	58,000	55,000
Estimated running costs	0	37,000	39,000	40,000	43,000	45,000
Net cash flow	-80,000	19,000	21,000	22,000	15,000	10,000

for a project to recover or pay back the initial outlay. For example, an engineer may invest £500,000 in new cutting machinery and estimate that it will lead to a net cash flow (after operating costs) over the next five years, as in Table 39.2.

Table 39.2 *Expected net cash flow from some new cutting machinery*

						£000
	Yr 0	Yr 1	Yr 2	Yr 3	Yr 4	Yr 5
Net cash flow	(500)	100	125	125	150	150
Cumulative net cash flow	(500)	(400)	(275)	(150)	0	150

Here the payback period is four years. If we add together the net cash flows from the project in the first four years it amounts to £500,000 (ie 100 + 125 + 125 + 150).

The payback period can also be found by calculating the **cumulative net cash flow**. This is the cash flow each year taking into account revenue and operating costs (net cash flow) and the initial cost of the machine. When the machine is first bought, in year 0, there is negative cash flow of minus £500,000, the cost of the machine. Next year the revenue minus operating costs are £100,000. So the cumulative net cash flow is -£500,000 + £100,000 = -£400,000. In year 4 it is zero, so all costs have been covered.

When using this method to choose between projects, the project with the shortest payback will be chosen. Assume a business is appraising three investment projects, all of which cost £70,000. The net cash flow expected from each project is shown in Table 39.3.

Table 39.3 *Expected net cash flow from three investment projects*

							(£000)
	Year 1	Year 2	Year 3	Year 4	Year 5	Year 6	Total
A	10	10	20	20	30	40	130
B	20	20	20	20	20	20	120
C	30	30	20	10	10	10	110

In this example project C would be chosen because it has the shortest payback time, ie 2 years and 6 months. How is this calculated? In years 1 and 2 the net cash flow is £30,000 + £30,000 = £60,000. To pay for an investment of £70,000 the remaining £10,000 (£70,000 - £60,000) comes from year three's net cash flow. This is £20,000, which is more. So the number of months in year 3 it takes to pay the £10,000 can be calculated as:

$$\frac{\text{amount required}}{\text{net cash flow in year}} \times 12 = \frac{£10,000}{£20,000} \times 12 = 6 \text{ months}$$

Project A's payback stretches into the fifth year and project B's into the fourth.

Note that **total cash flow** is not taken into account in this method. In fact project C has the lowest total return over the six years.

Advantages
● This method is useful when technology changes rapidly, such as in the agriculture industry. New farm machinery is designed and introduced into the market regularly. It is important to recover the cost of investment before a new machine is designed.
● It is simple to use.
● Firms might adopt this method if they have cash flow problems. This is because the project chosen will 'payback' the investment more quickly than others.

Disadvantages
● Cash earned after the 'payback' is not taken into account in the decision to invest.
● The method ignores the profitability of the project, since the criterion used is the speed of repayment.

Natalie and Liam Mead run a 4,600 acre arable farm in Steeple Aston, Oxfordshire. They grow barley and wheat and have enjoyed rising profitability in the last 5 years despite EU instructions to set aside some of their land each season. Natalie believes that a lot of their success is down to their investment strategy. They invest regularly in up-to-date agricultural technology and use the payback method when evaluating alternative projects. In 2004 they were considering four purchases:
● new state-of-the-art bailer at a cost of £20,000;
● replacing one of the tractors at a cost of £60,000;
● five new corn trailers at a cost of £3,000 each;
● four new storage silos at a total cost of £40,000.
The expected net cash flow from each of the above investments is shown in Table 39.4.

Table 39.4 *Expected net cash flow from investments made by Natalie and Liam Mead*

(£000s)

Year	1	2	3	4	5	6	7	8	9	10	Total
Bailer	4	4	4	4	4	4	4	4	4	4	40
Tractor	10	10	10	10	10	10	10	8	8	8	94
Trailers	2	2	2	2	2	2	2	2	2	2	20
Silos	10	10	10	6	6	6	4	4	2	2	60

(a) What particular external factors might influence Natalie and Liam's investment decisions in future years?
(b) Calculate, to the nearest month, the payback period for each purchase.
(c) If Natalie and Liam decide to make just one purchase, which should be undertaken according to this method of appraisal?

Question 2

Average or accounting rate of return

The AVERAGE RATE OF RETURN or ACCOUNTING RATE OF RETURN (ARR) method measures the net return each year as a percentage of the capital cost of the investment.

$$\text{Average rate of return (\%)} = \frac{\text{Net return (profit) per annum}}{\text{Capital outlay (cost)}} \times 100$$

For example, the capital cost and expected net cash flow from three investment projects are shown in Table 39.5.
A business would first calculate the profit from each project by subtracting the total net cash flow of the project from its capital cost, ie £70,000 - £50,000 = £20,000 for project X. The next step is to calculate the profit per annum by dividing the profit by the number of years the project runs for, ie £20,000 ÷ 5 = £4,000 for X. Finally, the ARR is calculated by using the above formula, ie

$$\text{ARR (Project X)} = \frac{£4,000}{£50,000} \times 100$$
$$= 8\%$$

Table 39.5 *The capital costs and net cash flow from three investment projects*

	Project X	Project Y	Project Z
Captal cost	£50,000	£40,000	£90,000
Return Yr 1	£10,000	£10,000	£20,000
Yr 2	£10,000	£10,000	£20,000
Yr 3	£15,000	£10,000	£30,000
Yr 4	£15,000	£15,000	£30,000
Yr 5	£20,000	£15,000	£30,000
Total net cash flows	£70,000	£60,000	£130,000

The results for all three projects are shown in Table 39.6. Project Y would be chosen because it gives a higher ARR (10 per cent) than the other two.
The advantage of this method is that it shows clearly the profitability of an investment project. Not only does it allow a range of projects to be compared, the overall rate of return can be compared to other uses for investment funds. In the example in Table 50.6, if a company can gain 12 per cent by placing its funds in a bank account, it might choose to postpone the investment project until interest rates fall. It is also easier to identify the **opportunity cost** of investment.
However, the method does not take into account the effects of time on the value of money. The above example assumes that, for project X, £10,000 of income for the firm in two years' time is the same as £10,000 in one year's time. Some allowance

Table 39.6 *The average rate of return calculated for three investment projects*

	Project X	Project Y	Project Z
Capital cost	£50,000	£40,000	£90,000
Total net profit (ncf - capital cost)	£20,000	£20,000	£40,000
Net profit p.a. (profit ÷ 5)	£4,000	£4,000	£8,000
ARR	8%	10%	8.9%

must be made for the time span over which the income from an investment project is received for it to be most useful.

Discounted cash flow or net present value

This method of appraisal has certain advantages. It deals with the problems of **interest rates** and **time**. The return on an investment project is always in the future, usually over a period of several years. Money earned or paid in the future is worth less today. Why?

What if £100 is placed in a bank account when the rate of interest is 10 per cent? At the end of the year it will be worth £110 (£100 + £100 x 10 per cent) or (£100 x 1.1). At the end of two years it will be worth £121 (£110 + £110 x 10 per cent) or (£110 x 1.1). This shows that money grows over time if it is deposited or lent with interest. Table 39.8 shows how the value of £100 grows over a 10 year period if left in a bank account when the rate of compound interest is 10 per cent.

Put another way, a fixed sum paid in the future is worth less than a fixed sum paid today. Why? The £100 could have been placed in a bank account for 3 years and could have grown to £133. So a fixed sum of £100 received in 3 years time will be far less than £100 today. The value today of a

Table 39.8 *The value of £100 over a 10 year period if left in a bank account when the compound rate of interest is 10 per cent (rounded to the nearest pound).*

Year	Value of £100 at compound rate of interest of 10 per cent
0	£100
1	£110
2	£121
3	£133
4	£146
5	£161
6	£177
7	£195
8	£214
9	£236
10	£259

Scotmart is a small supermarket chain based in the north of Scotland. It has stores in Sutherland, Caithness, Inverness, Moray, Nairn, Cromarty and Perth. Scotmart is now considering a substantial investment programme to consolidate its position in the Scottish grocery market. The following investment projects are under consideration:
● acquiring Aberdeen Provisions, a small regional supermarket chain, for £30 million;
● building some brand new stores in Ullapool, Wick, Helmsdale and Elgin at a cost of £40 million;
● diversifying into DIY supplies in its current stores at a cost of £25 million.
The expected net cash flow from the three investment projects is shown in Table 39.7.

Table 39.7 *Expected net cash flow from investment projects of Scotmart*

(£ million)

Year	1	2	3	4	5	6	7	8	9	10	Total
Acquisition	0	0	5	5	5	8	8	8	12	12	63
New stores	4	5	6	6	8	8	9	9	12	12	79
Diversify	5	5	5	5	5	5	5	5	5	5	50

(a) Calculate the average rate of return for each project.
(b) Which project should Scotmart invest in according to this method of investment appraisal?
(c) What might be the opportunity cost of the investment chosen in your answer to (b)?

Question 3

sum of money available in future is called the PRESENT VALUE. What is the present value of £100 in 3 years? This can be found by the formula:

$$\text{Present value} = \cfrac{A}{\cfrac{(1 + r)^n}{100}}$$

where A = amount of money, r = rate of interest and n = number of years. The present value of £100 received in three years time is (assuming a 10 per cent interest rate):

$$\text{Present value} = \cfrac{£100}{\cfrac{(1 + 10)^3}{100}} = \frac{£100}{(1.1)^3} = \frac{£100}{1.331} = £75.13$$

This shows the £100 received in 3 years time is worth less than £100 today. How much less depends on two things.
● Interest rates. If interest rates rise to 20 per cent then present value would be:

$$\frac{£100}{(1+\frac{20}{100})^3} = £57.78$$

- The length of time. If £100 was received in 25 years time the present value would be:

$$\frac{£100}{(1+\frac{10}{100})^{25}} = £9.23$$

DISCOUNTED CASH FLOW takes into account that interest rates affect the present value of future income. It shows that the future cash flow is discounted by the rate of interest.

How can this be used to decide whether investment should take place? Assume an investment project costs £100,000 and yields an expected net cash flow over a 3 year period - year 1, £30,000; year 2, £40,000; year 3, £50,000. The rate of interest remains at 10 per cent over the time period. The present value of the future income stream using the technique described above will be:

$$\text{Present value} = \frac{£30,000}{(1+0.1)^1} + \frac{£40,000}{(1+0.1)^2} + \frac{£50,000}{(1+0.1)^3}$$

$$\text{Present value} = \frac{£30,000}{(1.1)^1} + \frac{£40,000}{(1.1)^2} + \frac{£50,000}{(1.1)^3}$$

$$\text{Present value} = \frac{£30,000}{1.1} + \frac{£40,000}{1.21} + \frac{£50,000}{1.331}$$

Present value = £27,272 + £33,057 + £37,565 = £97,894

The above investment project is not viable since the present value of the net cash flow (£97,894) is less than the cost (£100,000). The NET PRESENT VALUE (NPV) of the project which shows the return on the investment less the cost is:

NPV = Present value of return - cost

= £97,894 - £100,000 = - £2,106

Before the DCF procedure was applied, the total income would have been £120,000 (£30,000 + £40,000 + £50,000). A decision maker may have thought the project profitable without the use of DCF. It is sometimes mistakenly thought that DCF is used to take the effects of inflation into account. In fact it is used to take into account the effect of **interest rates**.

Alternative calculations

Sometimes it may not be necessary to use the DCF formula. Information is sometimes available which makes the DCF procedure much easier. We may be **given** the present value of

Table 39.9 *Present value of £1 receivable at the end of 6 years at 5 per cent*

After	0yr	1 yr	2 yrs	3 yrs	4 yrs	5 yrs	6 yrs
Present value of £1	£1.00	£0.95	£0.90	£0.86	£0.82	£0.78	£0.75

£1 at the end of a number of years at a particular rate of interest. For example, Table 39.9 shows the present value of £1 receivable at the end of 6 years if the interest rate is 5 per cent. Note that the values are rounded off to two decimal places.

Again assume that an investment project costing £100,000 yields an expected net cash flow stream over a three year period of £30,000 (year 1), £40,000 (year 2) and £50,000 (year 3). The present value of an income stream can be calculated using information from Table 39.9.

Present value of income in yr 1 = 30,000 x £0.95 = £28,500
Present value of income in yr 2 = 40,000 x £0.90 = £36,000
Present value of income in yr 3 = 50,000 x £0.86 = £43,000
Total present value of all income = £107,500

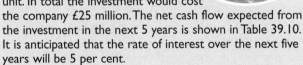

The Tyneside Oil Company, located in Newcastle, processes oil in its large and highly automated refinery. It is now considering the development of its own distribution arm. A distribution operation would involve the purchase of several oil tankers, the acquisition of some adjacent land and a purpose built loading unit. In total the investment would cost the company £25 million. The net cash flow expected from the investment in the next 5 years is shown in Table 39.10. It is anticipated that the rate of interest over the next five years will be 5 per cent.

Table 39.10 *Expected net cash flow from the oil company's investment*

Year	1	2	3	4	5	Total
	£4m	£4m	£8m	£8m	£8m	£32m

(a) Calculate the present value of the future net cash flow from the investment project.
(b) Calculate the net present value and state whether the business should go ahead with the investment.
(c) How might the answer to (b) be different if the interest rate was 10 per cent throughout the 5 year period? Show the calculations of the present value of future income and the net present value in your answer.

Question 4

This investment project is viable because the present value of the return (£107,500) is greater than the cost (£100,000). The NPV is £7,500.

Internal rate of return

This technique also makes use of discounted cash flow. To decide on the INTERNAL RATE OF RETURN (IRR) a firm must find the rate of return (x) where the net present value is zero. This internal rate of return is then compared with the market rate of interest to determine whether the investment should take place. Assume an investment project costs £10,000 and yields a one year return only of £13,000. The market rate of interest is 14 per cent. To calculate the IRR (x):

$$\text{Cost} = \frac{A}{(1+x)^1}$$

$$10,000 = \frac{13,000}{(1+x)^1}$$

$$(1+x) = \frac{13,000}{10,000}$$

$$1+x = 1.3$$

$$x = 1.3 - 1$$

$$= 0.3 \text{ or } 30\%$$

Since the IRR (x) of 30 per cent is greater than the market rate of interest (14 per cent) the firm should invest in the project. When this is applied to projects over a longer period the calculation becomes more complex. However, the method remains the same.

An alternative approach is to use trial and error. This means choosing a discount rate, calculating the net present value (NPV) and seeing whether it equals zero. If it does not then another rate must be chosen. This process is continued until the correct rate is found. For example, assume that an

Table 39.11 *The NPV of an investment project at three different discount rates*

(£)

Year	Net cash flow	Present value of income at:		
		10%	7.5%	5%
1	5,000	4,545	4,651	4,762
2	5,000	4,132	4,325	4,555
3	10,000	7,513	8,045	8,643
4	20,000	13,661	14,970	16,447
5	20,000	12,442	13,828	15,661
Total	60,000	42,273	45,919	50,048
NPV		-7,727	-4,081	48

investment project costs £50,000 and earns a five year return.

Table 39.11 shows the actual return and the present value of the return over the five year period at different discount rates. If a 10 per cent discount rate is used the NPV is less than zero, ie -£7,727. Also, if a 7.5 per cent discount rate is used the NPV is less than zero, ie -£4,081. If a 5 per cent rate is used the NPV is as near to zero as is needed, ie just £48. Thus, 5 per cent is the internal rate of return. Figure 39.2 shows the relationship between the discount rate and the NPV. As the discount rate increases the NPV falls. The IRR is shown on the discount rate axis where NPV is zero.

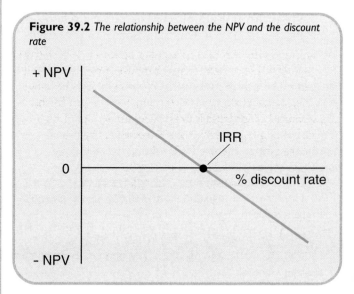

Figure 39.2 *The relationship between the NPV and the discount rate*

Other factors influencing investment decisions

In addition to the factors which might influence investment decisions already outlined in this unit, a number of other factors might be considered.

Human relations Some investment projects can have a huge impact on the staff in an organisation. For example, investment in plant automation might lead to mass redundancies. A business might decide to postpone plans to automate their plant if it thought the damage to human relations in the organisation would be too severe.

Ethical considerations Along with many other business decisions, managers are taking more of an ethical stance when choosing courses of action. For example, a chemicals producer might decide to build a new plant in a location which does not minimise financial costs but does reduce environmental damage. Such a decision might help to enhance the image of a company.

Corporate strategy Many businesses have long term corporate objectives (☞ unit 4) which are laid down in their corporate strategy. Such long term objectives might influence short term investment decisions. For example, a business operating a chain of theme pubs might be considering some repairs to a fire damaged pub. Repairs might be postponed because the pub in question was due for complete refurbishment in the next financial year.

Availability of funding A large number of investment projects fail to get started because businesses are unable to raise the necessary money to fund the project. A significant proportion of these will be small businesses which have difficulty in

persuading investors and lenders to provide funding.

Current cash flow A firm's cash flow position (☞ unit 35) may influence investment decisions. Investment projects are a notorious drain on a firm's resources. Businesses often underestimate the cost of investment and struggle to fund their usual activities because money is being directed to the new project. Consequently, if a business has a poor cash flow position it might postpone or cancel investment projects to avoid cash flow problems.

key terms

Average rate of return or accounting rate of return (ARR) - a method of investment appraisal which measures the net return per annum as a percentage of the initial spending.
Discounted cash flow (DCF) - a method of investment appraisal which takes interest rates into account by calculating the present value of future income.
Internal rate of return (IRR) - the rate of return at which the net present value is zero.
Investment appraisal - the evaluation of an investment project to determine whether or not it is likely to be worthwhile.

Net cash flow - the earnings, income or revenue from an investment, less the operating costs.
Net present value (NPV) - the present value of future income from an investment project, less the cost.
Present value - the value today of a sum of money available in the future.
Payback period - the amount of time it takes to recover the cost of an investment project.

Knowledge

1. What is meant by the term investment?
2. Explain the difference between autonomous and induced investment.
3. State the 4 types of investment.
4. Why is the investment decision risky?
5. State the factors that might influence (a) private sector and (b) public investment?
6. What is the function of investment appraisal in business?
7. Explain briefly how a business would appraise investment using the payback period.
8. What are the advantages and disadvantages of the payback method?
9. What does the average or accounting rate of return method of investment appraisal aim to measure?
10. Why is the discounted cash flow/NPV method of appraisal used in business?
11. Suggest how environmental considerations may affect an investment decision.

Case study Parkinson & Co

Parkinson & Co is a food processing company. It has a large factory in Reading and produces a range of canned food products such as soups, vegetables, fruits, processed meats and beans. The business is keen to expand but is unable to increase capacity at its current site. It is considering the construction of a new factory and operating from twin sites. Since an increasing amount of its produce is sold in Europe, sites are being considered in Lyon, France and Valencia, Spain.

The Lyon Site

The main advantage of this site is that distribution costs and delivery times would be minimised. Parkinson & Co has customers in Germany, Belgium, Italy and Austria, and Lyon is more central than Valencia. However, labour costs are likely to be higher and French workers are represented by strong trade unions. Working practices in Lyon are much less flexible than those in the UK and any effort by Parkinson & Co to introduce untraditional working practices might be met with some resistance. Another problem is that planning permission may be more difficult to obtain in Lyon.

The Valencia Site

Although the Valencia site is further away from most customers than the proposed Lyon site, it is a much cheaper option. The cost of land is lower in this part of Spain and planning permission is more readily granted for commercial developments. Wage rates are lower and there is a more plentiful supply of labour since unemployment is higher here. It is thought that industrial relations might be better as well. However, another problem is the level of congestion on the roads around this part of Spain. This could affect delivery times.

The capital costs and estimated net cash flows from the two factories over a six year period are shown in Table 39.12.

(a) Using this case as an example, explain the difference between induced and autonomous investment. (4 marks)

(b) For each of the two sites calculate the:
  (i) payback period (to the nearest month); (4 marks)
  (ii) average rate of return; (6 marks)
  (iii) net present value. (8 marks)

(c) On purely financial grounds, which site is the most financially viable? Explain your answer. (4 marks)

(d) Discuss the advantages and disadvantages to Parkinson & Co of using the methods of investment appraisal in (b). (10 marks)

(e) Using all the available information, discuss which site you think Parkinson & Co should select. (14 marks)

Table 39.12 *Capital cost and estimated net cash flows from the two factories*

	Year 0	Year 1	Year 2	Year 3	Year 4	Year 5	Year 6
The Lyon site							
Capital cost	8.2m						
Estimated net cash flow		2.3m	2.6m	2.7m	3.0m	3.3m	3.4m
The Valencia site							
Capital cost	6.1m						
Estimated net cash flow		2.2m	2.5m	2.7m	2.9m	3.2m	3.2m

Table 39.13 *Present value of £1 receivable at the end of 6 years at 5%*

After	Year 0	Year 1	Year 2	Year 3	Year 4	Year 5	Year 6
Present value of £1	£1.00	£0.95	£0.90	£0.86	£0.82	£0.78	£0.75

Human resources

Unit 1 explained that different resources or factors of production are involved in business activity. The HUMAN RESOURCES of the business are the people employed by the business. In a small business, such as a window cleaning service, the owner might be the only human resource. He or she will carry out most, if not all, tasks. In a large multinational company there are likely to be thousands of workers. Some will be manual workers. Some will be skilled workers or administration staff. There will also be managers and directors. The organisation of these human resources is vital if a business is to be successful.

The formal organisation of a business

There are several types of business organisation, including sole traders, partnerships, limited companies and public sector organisations (☞ units 6 and 7). However, each will have its own internal structure - the way in which human resources are organised. This is known as the FORMAL ORGANISATION of the business. It takes into account such things as:
● the relationships between individuals;
● who is in charge;
● who has authority to make decisions;
● who carries out decisions;
● how information is communicated.

Different businesses tend to have different objectives (☞ unit 4). There will also be differences in relationships, how they are managed and how decisions are made. Because these activities can be arranged in various ways, businesses tend to have different BUSINESS STRUCTURES. There are, however, likely to be some similarities. For example, many large companies are controlled by a few directors, are divided into departments with managers, section heads and have many workers in each department.

One method of organising a business is where managers put people together to work effectively based on their skills and abilities. The structure is 'built up' or it '**develops**' as a result of the employees of the business. In contrast a structure could be **created** first, with all appropriate job positions outlined, and then people employed to fill them. It has been suggested that the entrepreneur Richard Branson worked out a complete organisation structure for his Virgin Atlantic airline before setting up the company and then recruited the 102 people needed to fill all the positions.

Organisation charts

Many firms produce ORGANISATION CHARTS. These illustrate the structure of the business. Figure 40.1 shows a 'traditional' type of chart. It is a chart for an engineering firm, Able Engineering. Different types of businesses are likely to have different charts. The chart in Figure 40.1 may be simpler than one drawn for a large public limited company, although the style will be similar. It may be more involved, however, than a chart for a partnership.

Why do businesses draw such charts?
● To spot communication problems. An organisation chart indicates how employees are linked to other employees in the business. If information is not received, the business can find where the communication breakdown has occurred by tracing the communication chain along the chart.
● Organisation charts help individuals see their position in a

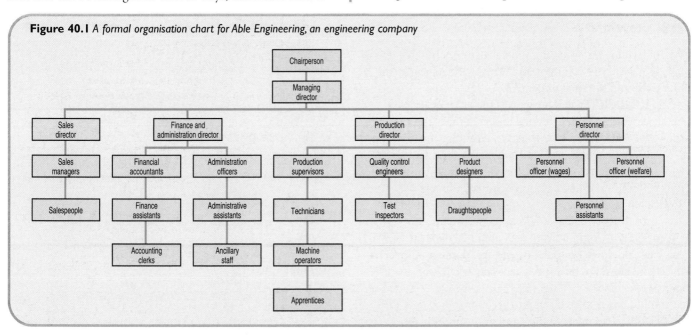

Figure 40.1 *A formal organisation chart for Able Engineering, an engineering company*

business. This can help them appreciate their responsibilities, who has authority over them and who they are accountable to.
- Organisation charts allow firms to pinpoint areas where specialists are needed. For example, in Figure 40.1 Able Engineering recognises it needs designers and draughtspeople as part of the production 'team'.
- Organisation charts show how different sections of the firm relate to each other. For example, the chart for Able Engineering shows the relationship between salespeople and technicians. They are both at the same level in the hierarchy, but work in different departments and are responsible to different managers.

Simply producing an organisation chart is of limited use to a business. The business will only achieve its objectives if it understands the relationships between employees and other parts of the business.

Ainscough Engineering Ltd produces ground support equipment for the aviation industry. The company has a traditional organisational structure. The managing director is responsible to the chairperson and has a sales director, finance director, personnel director and production director accountable to her. On the production side of the business, there are a works manager, technicians, test engineers and machine operators. In addition, the company employs a number of personnel assistants, financial and administrative staff, and salespeople.

(a) Draw an organisation chart from the information about Ainscough Engineering Ltd.
(b) Briefly explain two ways in which the business might use the chart.

Question 1

Chain of command and span of control

When deciding on its organisation structure, a business must take into account two important factors - the management **hierarchy** and the **span of control**.

The HIERARCHY in a business is the order or levels of management in a firm, from the lowest to the highest rank. It shows the CHAIN OF COMMAND within the organisation - the way authority is organised. Orders pass down the levels and information passes up. Businesses must also consider the number of links or levels in the chain of command. R. Townsend, in his book *Up the Organisation*, estimated that each extra level of management in the hierarchy reduced the effectiveness of communication by about 25 per cent. No rules are laid down on the most effective number of links in the chain. However, businesses generally try to keep chains as short as possible.

Another factor to be taken into account is the SPAN OF CONTROL. This refers to the number of subordinates

working under a superior or manager. In other words, if one production manager has ten subordinates his span of control is ten. Henri Fayol (☞ unit 44) argued that the span of control should be between three and six because:
- there should be tight managerial control from the top of the business;
- there are physical and mental limitations to any single manager's ability to control people and activities.

A narrow span of control has the advantage for a firm of tight control and close supervision. It also allows better co-ordination of subordinates' activities. In addition, it gives managers time to think and plan without having to be burdened with too many day to day problems. A narrow span also ensures better communication with subordinates, who are sufficiently small in number to allow this to occur.

A wide span of control, however, offers greater decision making authority for subordinates and may improve job satisfaction (☞ unit 41). In addition, there are likely to be lower costs involved in supervision. Figure 40.2 shows two organisation charts. In the first (a), there is a long chain of command, but a narrow span of control. The second (b) shows a wide span, but a short chain.

Authority and responsibility

Employees in the hierarchy will have responsibility and

Figure 40.2

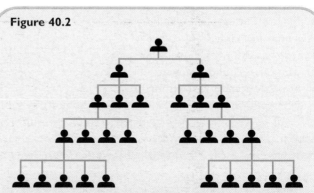

(a) A long chain of command and a narrow span of control. A production department may look like this. One manager is helped by a few assistant managers, each responsible for supervisors. These supervisors are responsible for skilled workers, who are in charge of a group of semi-skilled workers. Close supervision is needed to make sure quality is maintained. This is sometimes referred to as a tall organisational structure.

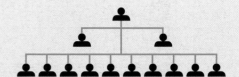

(b) A short chain of command and a wide span of control. A higher or further education department may look like this, with a 'head' of department, a few senior staff and many lecturing staff. Staff will want a degree of independence. This is sometimes referred to as a flat organisational structure.

authority. However, these terms do not mean the same thing.

RESPONSIBILITY involves being accountable or being required to justify an action. So, for example, managers who are responsible for a department may be asked to justify poor performance to the board of directors. The personnel department may be responsible for employing workers. If a new worker was unable to do a particular job, they would be asked to explain why.

AUTHORITY, on the other hand, is the ability to carry out the task. For example, it would make no sense asking an office worker to pay company debts if she did not have the authority to sign cheques. Employees at lower levels of the hierarchy have less responsibility and authority than those further up. However, it may be possible for a superior to **delegate** (pass down) authority to a subordinate, eg a manager to an office worker, but retain responsibility. Increasingly, businesses are realising the benefits of delegating both authority and responsibility.

Line, staff and functional authority

Line, staff and functional authority are terms used to describe the type of relationship that managers may have with others in the hierarchy.

Line authority Line authority is usual in a hierarchy. It shows the authority that a manager has over a subordinate. In Figure 40.1, the production director would have line authority over the designers. Communication will flow down from the superior to the subordinate in the chain of command. The advantage of this is that a manager can allocate work and control subordinates, who have a clear understanding of who is giving them instructions. The manager can also delegate authority to others if they feel this will make decision making more effective.

In large organisations, the chain of command can be very long. This means that instructions given by those at the top of the chain of command may take time before they are carried out at a lower level.

Staff authority Many larger organisations now have staff authority. Staff authority might be when a manager or department in a business has a function within another department, for example, giving specialist advice. A marketing manager may give advice to the production department based on market research into a new product. Personnel managers have responsibilities for personnel matters in all departments. Although the specialist can give advice, they have no authority to make decisions in the other department.

Functional authority Functional authority is when a specialist has the authority to make a line manager accept his or her advice. It is different from staff authority, where the specialist can only advise. For example, the finance manager may have overall authority over the budget holder in the marketing department.

Problems may occur in a business if people do not

understand where authority and responsibility rest. This means that managers must know whether their authority is line, staff or functional. Unfortunately, this can lead to friction. Line managers are sometimes thought of as 'first class citizens' and staff managers are thought of as costly 'overheads' who are not contributing anything of worth to the organisation. Also, the authority of functional managers is not accepted by line managers at times.

Delegation

Managers are increasingly being asked to carry out strategic activities that affect the whole business. This has resulted in the need to DELEGATE authority and responsibility for certain tasks to employees further down the hierarchy. Delegation can provide benefits to a business, as explained in the next section. When is delegation likely to be effective?

- Researchers such as Spetzer (1992) have suggested that employees need to be **empowered** (☞ unit 43) in order to make effective decisions. They need to be given self-confidence and control of what they do.
- If managers only delegate when they are overloaded, subordinates may be resentful.

The Manchester Film Association is an SME in the centre of the city's 'cultural quarter'. Its main activities are video, film and multimedia production. It employs 9 full time staff. Mike joined the company 6 months ago. He recently graduated, but has little work experience. However, he has proven so far in the work that he has done for clients to be innovative. He often has ideas that no-one else has considered. Shoaib has worked for the business for 15 years. He has built up considerable production and post-production skills. Lisa had previously set up her own website design and consultancy operation. She has experience in managing projects, working to deadlines and taking responsibility for clients' requests.

The managing director of the business, Paula, has been approached by a fast growing leisure company to produce an innovative multi-media training programme on CD Rom for newly recruited employees. The company wants the programme to be interactive, but it must be ready within two months. Paula decided to ask Mike to look after the project. However, almost from the start he seemed to have problems. He did not ask for help when it would have been useful. He found it difficult to organise others and often missed deadlines he had set. After four weeks, Paula was concerned that the project would not be completed.

Source: adapted from company information.

(a) Explain why delegation may not have been effective in this case.
(b) Examine what action Paula should now take.

Question 2

- Delegation requires planning. Managers must be clear about what needs to be done. Instead of freeing time, poor delegation may take up managers' time as they try to correct problems.
- Managers must take time to explain delegated tasks clearly. Employees may waste time or make mistakes because of lack of information. Telling subordinates why the work is important helps to create shared values.
- Allow participation. It is useful to discuss the task with those to whom it has been delegated. Subordinates will then know from the start what the task will include. It also helps managers to decide if delegation is appropriate. A person may feel they do not have the skills to carry out the task.
- The employee given a delegated task should also be given the authority and responsibility to carry it out. Managers must tell others in the business that the delegated person is acting on his or her behalf. This will avoid difficulties, such as the questioning of authority.
- Managers must avoid interfering with delegated tasks.
- Delegated tasks should be given to suitable employees. It would be inappropriate to delegate a marketing task to an employee in personnel. Employees must also have the training to carry out the task.
- Provide support and resources. If an employee is delegated a task without suitable support and resources this could lead to anxiety, frustration and the task being badly done.

Research has shown that when factors like these are taken into account, delegation was four times as likely to be successful.

Centralisation and decentralisation

Centralisation and decentralisation refer to the extent to which authority is delegated in a business. If there was complete centralisation, then subordinates would have no authority at all. Complete decentralisation would mean subordinates would have all the authority to take decisions. It is unlikely that any business operates in either of these ways. Even if authority is delegated to a subordinate, it is usual for the manager to retain responsibility.

Certain functions within a business will always be centralised, because of their importance. For example, decisions about budget allocation are likely to be centralised as they affect the whole company. The decision to distribute profits is also taken only by a few.

Advantages of centralisation Why might a business centralise authority?

- Senior management have more control of the business, eg budgets.
- Procedures, such as ordering and purchasing, can be standardised throughout the organisation, leading to economies of scale and lower costs.
- Senior managers can make decisions from the point of view of the business as a whole. Subordinates would tend

to make decisions from the point of view of their department or section. This allows senior managers to maintain a balance between departments or sections. For example, if a company has only a limited amount of funds available to spend over the next few years, centralised management would be able to share the funds out between production, marketing, research and development, and fixed asset purchases in different departments etc.

- Senior managers should be more experienced and skilful in making decisions. In theory, centralised decisions by senior people should be of better quality than decentralised decisions made by others less experienced.
- In times of crisis, a business may need strong leadership by a central group of senior managers.
- Communication may improve if there are fewer decision makers.

Advantages of decentralisation or delegation Some delegation is necessary in all firms because of the limits to the amount of work senior managers can carry out. Tasks that might be delegated include staff selection, quality control, customer relations and purchasing and stock control. A greater degree of decentralisation - over and above the

---

In 2003 The Future Network plc, the international specialist magazine publisher, announced the final stages of the restructuring of its UK business, which began in February 2001. Under the reorganisation plan, Future divided its UK business into three operating divisions – games, computing and entertainment. This was to be accompanied by a reduction in fixed operating costs in the UK by approximately £4 million, through cuts in staffing levels and property overheads.

The changes to the business involved reductions in centralised support services, and in Internet and magazine teams and rationalisation of the company's property portfolio. There was also to be an important change in the way the UK business was managed, by devolving operational responsibility to the individual divisions as profit centres.

Colin Morrison, Chief Operating Officer of The Future Network, said 'This plan is important because of the substantial reduction in our fixed operating costs against a broadly unchanged magazine portfolio. But much more than that, this restructuring and decentralisation plan simplifies our business, and will improve our focus, agility and control. We will now be more streamlined and much better placed to take advantage of our market-leading positions in the important UK market.

Source: adapted from www.thefuturenetwork.plc.uk.

(a) Describe the organisational changes at The Future Network plc.
(b) Examine the possible benefits and disadvantages for the business of these changes.

Question 3

minimum which is essential - has a number of advantages.

- It empowers and motivates workers (☞ unit 43).
- It reduces the stress and burdens of senior management. It also frees time for managers to concentrate on more important tasks.
- It provides subordinates with greater job satisfaction by giving them more say in decision-making, which affects their work (☞ unit 41 on McGregor's Theory Y).
- Subordinates may have a better knowledge of 'local' conditions affecting their area of work. This should allow them to make more informed, well-judged choices. For example, salespeople may have more detailed knowledge of their customers and be able to advise them on purchases.
- Delegation should allow greater flexibility and a quicker response to changes. If problems do not have to be referred to senior managers, decision-making will be quicker. Since decisions are quicker, they are easier to change in the light of unforeseen circumstances which may arise.
- By allowing delegated authority, management at middle and junior levels are groomed to take over higher positions. They are given the experience of decision making when carrying out delegated tasks. Delegation is therefore important for management development.

Different forms of business structure

Despite the variety of formal business organisation that exists, there are four main types of structure most often found.

The entrepreneurial structure In this type of business structure, all decisions are made centrally. There are few collective decisions and a great reliance on 'key' workers. It is often found in businesses where decisions have to be made quickly, such as newspaper editing.

Most small businesses also have this type of structure, as illustrated in Figure 40.3(a). These businesses rely on the expertise of one or two people to make decisions. Decision making is efficient up to a point because:

- decisions can be made quickly;
- subordinates understand to whom they are accountable;
- little consultation is required.

However, as the business grows, this structure can cause inefficiency as too much of a load is placed on those making decisions.

The bureaucratic, pyramid or hierachical structure This is the traditional hierachical structure for most medium sized and large businesses and perhaps the most well known. It is illustrated in Figure 40.3(b). Decision making is shared throughout the business. Employees are each given a role and procedures are laid down which determine their behaviour at work.

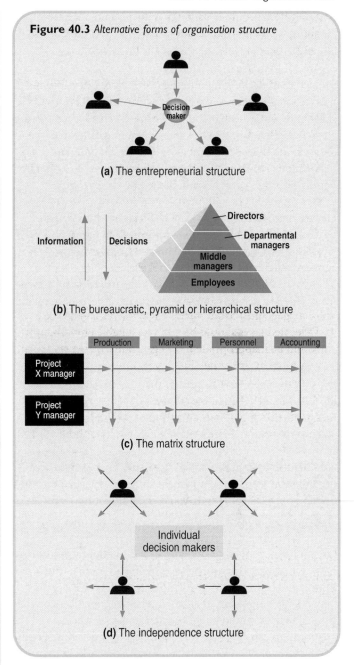

Figure 40.3 *Alternative forms of organisation structure*

(a) The entrepreneurial structure

(b) The bureaucratic, pyramid or hierarchical structure

(c) The matrix structure

(d) The independence structure

Specialisation of tasks (☞ unit 1) is possible. This means that a departmental structure, with finance, personnel, production and marketing employees, can be set up. Specialisation may allow the business to enjoy economies of scale. Recently, this type of structure has been criticised for its inability to change and meet new demands.

The matrix structure This emphasises getting people with particular specialist skills together into project teams, as illustrated in Figure 40.3(c). Individuals within the team have their own responsibility. The matrix structure was developed to overcome some of the problems with the entrepreneurial and bureaucratic structures. **Matrix management** involves the co-ordinating and support of specialist teams within a matrix structure.

Managers often argue that this is the best way of organising people, because it is based on the expertise and skills of employees and gives scope for people lower down the organisation to use their talents effectively. For example, a project manager looking into the possibility of developing a new product may draw on the expertise of employees with skills in design, research and development, marketing, costing etc. A college running a course for unemployed people may draw on the skills of a number of lecturers in different departments. In this way, a matrix structure can also operate within a business that has a bureaucratic structure. The matrix model fits in with managers who have a Theory Y view of employees (☞ unit 41). It is suggested that this structure improves flexibility and motivation of employees. It has recently lost favour because it often needs expensive support systems, such as extra secretarial and office staff. There may also be problems with co-odinating a team drawn from different departments and the speed of decision making.

The independence structure This emphasises the individual and is almost a 'non-organisation'. The other three methods put together the contributions of a number of people so that the sum of their efforts is greater than the parts. All efforts are co-ordinated so that the business benefits. The independence structure is a method of providing a support system. Barristers' chambers and doctor's clinics have worked in this way. It is attractive to independent people who are confident of their ability to be successful. This form of organisation tends to be unsuitable for most types of business because of the lack of control and co-ordination.

Informal business structure

Organisation charts show the formal organisation of a business. However many relationships between employees in business are informal. The INFORMAL BUSINESS STRUCTURE is the network of relationships that develop between members on the basis of their common interests and friendships. These relationships can affect the way a business operates. Krackhardt and Hanson (1993) in a study of informal networks in the banking industry found three types of relationship.
- Advice networks - who depends on who to solve problems and provide information.
- Trust networks - which employees share potential information and back each other up in times of crisis.
- Communication networks - which employees regularly talk to each other on work related matters.

They recommended that businesses use informal structures to solve problems. For example, a study showed that a bank's task force group was unable to find ways of improving the bank's performance. The leader of the task force held a central position in the 'advice network'. Employees relied on her for technical advice. However, she only had one 'trust link' with a colleague. Management did not want to label the group as a failure or embarrass a valued employee by dismissing her as team leader. Instead, it redesigned the task force in line with the informal organisation of the business by adding a person in the trust network to share responsibility for group leadership.

Factors influencing organisational structures

There is a number of factors which might influence the organisation and the structure of a business.
- Size. As a business grows, it is likely to move away from an entrepreneurial structure towards one where authority is passed to other employees. A large firm will also tend to have a longer chain of command, with more levels in the hierarchy.
- Views of the owners or leadership styles. If owners wish to retain control in the business, they will want a narrow span of control. Owners or managers who wish to motivate or encourage employees may delegate decision making.
- Business objectives. If the business decides to expand rapidly, perhaps by merger, it is likely to find that its span of control gets wider. An example might be a business setting up an operation in a foreign country or deciding to sell into a foreign market.
- External factors. Changes in external factors can often influence business organisation. In periods of recession or rising costs, a business may be forced to reduce its chain of command to cut costs. Similarly, in a period of economic growth (☞ unit 69), a firm may employ extra managers as specialists to gain economies of scale.
- Changes in technology. The introduction of new technology can change the structure of a business. For example, a new system of production may remove the need for quality controllers, or an information technology system could reduce the role of administration.
- The informal structure. If the informal structure does not complement and support the formal structure, this may lead to problems.
- Corporate culture (☞ unit 5). The norms of behaviour in a business might influence its organisational structure. For example, a business that has developed with a team based approach to decision making, a casual dress code and a management that are very approachable might find it difficult to change suddenly to a structure with layers of hierarchy and formal decision making processes. Charles Handy in *Understanding Organisations* (1976) identified four cultures which reflect the organisation structures in Figure 40.3. The **power** culture is structure (a) with one powerful decision maker. The **role** culture is structure (b) where everyone in the hierarchy has a clear role. The **task** culture is structure (c) based on a team approach. The **person** culture is structure (d).

Recent trends

Some businesses over the last ten years have changed their organisations to make them into flatter structures. This is process is called **delayering**. It has often meant taking out layers of middle management, which will affect the hierarchy, span of control and chain of command. Businesses have also changed their organisation in other ways.

● A study by Cressey and Jones suggested that banks have moved from traditional, bureaucratic, stratified structures, with narrow job tasks, into profit centred, performance orientated businesses that empower employees to take responsibility.

● According to Paul Iles there is a much greater emphasis on multi-skilled teams and delayered organisations in manufacturing. This has led to greater financial flexibility,

employee autonomy, self-monitoring and devolved decision making.

● Du Gay suggested that a number of factors have led to changes in the retail sector. Increased globalisation and competition have meant businesses must be able to respond more quickly. As a result they have reduced the number of layers in their hierarchy. Also businesses need to be more aware of consumers' needs. As a result they have restructured into flatter, team based organisations to allow employees to see that the way they work should be more helpful for the way they would consume.

Figure 40.4 *Wesley Hains' organisational structure*

Laura   Mitchell

WESLEY HAINS

Kieran   Ella

Wesley Hains runs a card design business in Cardiff. He employs four staff - Laura, Mitchell, Kieran and Ella. Laura manages the office in Cardiff dealing with telephone and e-mail enquiries, visitors, administration and a small amount of marketing. Mitchell, Kieran and Ella are

card designers and all work from home in various parts of the country. Mitchell lives and works in a small croft in Glen Cona in North West Scotland. The designers are all linked by computer to the main Cardiff office. This ensures good communications. For example, design briefs are sent direct by Wesley using e-mail and design copy is transmitted direct to Wesley's terminal when designs are completed. Some specialisation takes place amongst the designers. Mitchell designs birthday cards, Kieran designs postcards and Ella works on specialist projects. Wesley is occupied with customers, ensuring that design briefs are satisfied by his designers and looking for new business. He spends three days a week out of the office.

(a) What type of organisational structure does the business have at present?
(b) In September, Wesley secured a contract with an American card manufacturer. Wesley had to recruit four more designers as a result. He decided to employ a full-time salesperson to sell designs in the US. He also bought a small printing business in Newport to print and supply cards as well as designing them. Explain why Wesley might decide to change the organisational structure of his business.

Question 4

---

key terms

Authority - the right to command a situation, a task or an activity.
Business structure - the way in which a business is organised.
Chain of command - the way authority and power are passed down in a business.
Delegation - authority (and sometimes responsibility) passed down from superior to subordinate.
Formal organisation - the relationships between employees and the organisational structure determined by the business, as shown in an organisation chart.

Hierarchy - the order or levels of management of a business, from the lowest to the highest.
Human resources - the employees of a business.
Informal business structure - the relationships between employees that are based on the common interests of employees.
Organisation chart - a diagram which illustrates the structure of an organisation.
Responsibility - the duty to complete a task.
Span of control - the number of subordinates working under a superior.

Knowledge

1. What are the features of the internal structure of a business?
2. How might an organisation chart be used in a firm's induction programme?
3. Draw a simple organisation chart showing:
   (a) a partnership with two partners and 6 employees;
   (b) a large company with a board of directors, six departments, and two more levels in the hierarchy.
4. What is meant by a 'wide span of control'?
5. What problems might a 'wide span of control' have for a business?
6. Explain the difference between line, staff and functional authority.
7. Why might businesses have line, staff and functional authority?
8. Give three situations where centralised decision making may be useful for a business.
9. What factors influence effective delegation?
10. Why is empowerment important when tasks are delegated?
11. State 4 advantages of delegation.
12. What problems might a matrix structure cause for a business?
13. What type of business might be organised with:
    (a) an entrepreneurial structure;
    (b) an independence structure?
14. Why is it important for businesses to understand their informal business structures?

Case study AGF Irish Life and Granada

AGF Irish Life

AGF Irish Life is the largest commercial general insurer in Ireland. It has an income of over £250 million and 800 staff. In 2000 it faced a volatile domestic market for insurance. And there was an added threat from European insurers interested in international business. So it turned a threat into an opportunity under the banner Project 2000.

The company delayered and it changed its traditional if somewhat static departmental structure (including sales, underwriting, claims etc.) into dynamic teams, each responsible for the total needs of a targeted group of brokers. The customer benefited by having the same people dealing with all their needs. Employees were also empowered and became mulitskilled in the process. A 30 per cent improvement in turnaround time for enquiries was found as a result of the new system. Another feature was that tasks could be carried out concurrently.

Source: adapted from www.topcall.com.

Granada

In 2001 Granada made 100 staff redundant as part of a sweeping reorganisation involving a delayering of the management structure. The company argued 'We do not need a second layer of people to second guess the management at ITV.' It was also suggested that the organisation would be streamlined. The old complicated structure would be replaced by a simpler, two-pronged organisation. One part, Granada Content, would deal with production while the other, Granada Platforms, would deal with broadcasting. Granada Content would also handle the company's online and broadband activities.

Source: adapted from *The Guardian*, 13.6.2001.

(a) Identify the changes in the organisational structures at the two businesses. (6 marks)
(b) What factors have influenced the changes in organisational structures? (10 marks)
(c) Explain how the changes might affect:
   (i) employees at the businesses;
   (ii) management at the businesses;
   (iii) clients of the business. (12 marks)
(d) Assess to what extent the changes will benefit the businesses. (12 marks)

The satisfaction of needs

If asked, most people who work would probably say they do so to earn money to buy goods and services. However, this is not the only **need** that is satisfied by working.

A list of people's needs that may be satisfied from work might be very long indeed. It could include, for example, the need for variety in the workplace, which may be satisfied by an interesting job. Employees may also need to feel appreciated for the work they do, which could be reflected in the prestige attached to their job.

Individuals are not the same. Therefore, it is likely that lists made by any two people of their needs and how they can be satisfied will be very different. There are some reasons for working that could apply to everyone, such as the need to earn money. However, some reasons have more importance for particular individuals than others. One employee may need to work with friendly colleagues, whereas another might be happy working on his own.

Why is it important for a business to find out what satisfies the needs of its employees? It is argued that if an individual's needs are not satisfied, then that worker will not be MOTIVATED to work. Businesses have found that even if employees are satisfied with pay and conditions at work, they also complain that their employer does not do a good job in motivating them. This applies to all levels, from the shopfloor to the boardroom. It appears in many companies that employers are not getting the full potential from their employees because they are not satisfying all of their employees' needs. Figure 41.1 shows one example of how a business might make decisions, having first identified an employee's needs.

It is important for a business to motivate its employees. In the short run a lack of motivation may lead to reduced effort and lack of commitment. If employees are watched closely, fear of wage cuts or redundancy may force them to maintain their effort even though they are not motivated. This is **negative motivation**. In the long term, a lack of motivation may result in high levels of absenteeism, industrial disputes and falling productivity and profit for a business. So it is argued that well motivated employees will be productive which should lead to greater efficiency and profits for a business.

Maslow's hierarchy of needs

The first comprehensive attempt to classify needs was by **Abraham Maslow** in 1954. Maslow's theory consisted of two parts. The first concerned classification of needs. The second concerned how these classes are related to each other.

Maslow suggested that 'classes' of needs could be placed into a **hierarchy**. The hierarchy is normally presented as a 'pyramid', with each level consisting of a certain class of needs. This is shown in Figure 41.2.

The classes of needs were:
● physiological needs, eg wages high enough to meet weekly bills, good working conditions;
● safety needs, eg job security, safe working conditions;
● love and belonging, eg working with colleagues that support you at work, teamwork, communicating;
● esteem needs, eg being given recognition for doing a job well;
● self-actualisation, eg being promoted and given more responsibility, scope to develop and introduce new ideas and take on challenging new job assignments.

Figure 41.2 can also be used to show the relationship between the different classes. Maslow argued that needs at the bottom of the pyramid are basic needs. They are concerned with survival. These needs must be satisfied before a person can move to the next level. For example, people are likely to be more concerned with basic needs, such as food, than anything else. At work an employee is unlikely to be concerned about acceptance from colleagues if he has not eaten for six hours.

Once each level is satisfied, the needs at this level become less important. The exception is the top level of SELF-ACTUALISATION. This is the need to fulfil your potential.

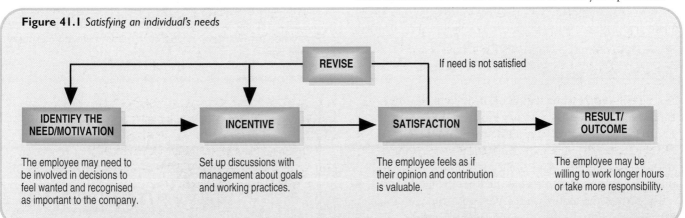

Figure 41.1 *Satisfying an individual's needs*

REVISE — If need is not satisfied

IDENTIFY THE NEED/MOTIVATION → INCENTIVE → SATISFACTION → RESULT/OUTCOME

The employee may need to be involved in decisions to feel wanted and recognised as important to the company.

Set up discussions with management about goals and working practices.

The employee feels as if their opinion and contribution is valuable.

The employee may be willing to work longer hours or take more responsibility.

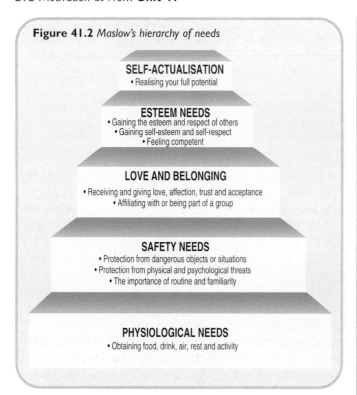

Figure 41.2 *Maslow's hierarchy of needs*

SELF-ACTUALISATION
• Realising your full potential

ESTEEM NEEDS
• Gaining the esteem and respect of others
• Gaining self-esteem and self-respect
• Feeling competent

LOVE AND BELONGING
• Receiving and giving love, affection, trust and acceptance
• Affiliating with or being part of a group

SAFETY NEEDS
• Protection from dangerous objects or situations
• Protection from physical and psychological threats
• The importance of routine and familiarity

PHYSIOLOGICAL NEEDS
• Obtaining food, drink, air, rest and activity

Maslow argued that although everyone is capable of this, in practice very few reach this level.

Each level of needs is dependent on the levels below. Say an employee has been motivated at work by the opportunity to take responsibility, but finds he may lose his job. The whole system collapses, as the need to feed and provide for himself and his dependants again becomes the most important need.

Maslow's ideas have great appeal for business. The message is clear - find out which level each individual is at and decide on suitable rewards.

Unfortunately the theory has problems when used in practice. Some levels do not appear to exist for certain individuals, while some rewards appear to fit into more than one class. Money, for example, needs to be used to purchase 'essentials' such as food, but it can also be seen as a status symbol or an indicator of personal worth.

There is also a problem in deciding when a level has actually been 'satisfied'. There will always be exceptions to the rules Maslow outlined. A well motivated designer may spend many hours on a creative design despite lack of sleep or food.

Taylor's Scientific Management

Research into the factors that motivate individuals had been carried out long before Maslow's 'hierarchy' of needs. **Frederick W. Taylor** set out a theory of SCIENTIFIC MANAGEMENT in his book *The Principles of Scientific Management* in 1911. Many of the ideas of today's 'scientific management school' come from the work of Taylor.

The turn of the century in the USA was a time of rapid expansion. Compared to today, the organisation of work on

the shop floor was left much more in the hands of workers and foremen. Workers often brought their own tools and decisions about the speed of machines were left to operators. There were few training programmes to teach workers their jobs and skills were gained simply by watching more experienced colleagues. Decisions about selection, rest periods and layoffs were frequently made by foremen.

Taylor suggested that such arrangements were haphazard and inefficient. Management did not understand the shop floor and allowed wasteful work practices to continue. Workers, on the other hand, left to their own devices, would

---

In 2003 an administrative, secretarial and support staff survey from London recruitment consultant Gordon Yates examined what has the greatest impact on job satisfaction. 70 per cent gave 'a good boss' the highest rating with 'interesting work' also highly placed. Only 35 per cent put 'salary level' in the top position. Despite being paid more money, PAs were more dissatisfied than ever. In 2003, 41 per cent were less satisfied with their work and 20 per cent were undecided whether to remain in their current career. Much of this dissatisfaction is rooted in the uncertain economic climate and the resultant redundancies, budget cutbacks and higher workloads. But the greatest impact on job satisfaction comes from human elements of the job - a good boss, interesting work, pleasant colleagues and a positive working atmosphere. Secretarial and support staff still appear to be valued lowly, despite having pivotal roles in offices. 'I'm not recognised as a valued member of the team,' said one secretary. Other comments included 'I'm not challenged enough', 'It's boring work' and 'I don't get enough variety'.

A survey by Lloyds TSB and campaign group Working Families found one in five employees think they work for 'the boss from hell'. Another concern was finding sufficiently stimulating work. Working for many people seems to make the job less interesting. 'Because I work for so many people, I cannot really do PA things and am rather turning into a glorified typist,' said one secretary. A quarter of today's support staff are graduates who tend to seek increasing challenges, responsibility and advancement in the role.

When asked 'What do you like best about working as a secretary or in a support role?' responses included 'Being the lynchpin, being and feeling productive.' There is a particularly strong impression that this group takes pleasure in the fact that they are encouraged to utilise their skills of organising and supporting others. 'I can organise people well and find it rewarding when I have made their job/day easier' says one.

Source: adapted from *The Guardian*, 19.1 2004.

(a) Using Maslow's hierarchy of needs, explain the factors that are likely to influence the motivation of secretarial and support staff in the surveys.
(b) Using Maslow's hierarchy of needs, explain why being paid more money may not necessarily motivate such staff.

Question 1

Table 41.1 *Taylor's method, designed to find the 'best way' to carry out a task at work*

- Pick a dozen skilled workers.
- Observe them at work and note down the elements and sequences adopted in their tasks.
- Time each element with a stop watch.
- Eliminate any factors which appear to add nothing to the completion of the task.
- Choose the quickest method discovered and fit them in their sequence.
- Teach the worker this sequence; do not allow any change from the set procedure.
- Include time for rest and the result will be the 'quickest and best' method for the task. Because it is the best way, all workers selected to perform the task must adopt it and meet the time allowed.
- Supervise workers to ensure that these methods are carried out during the working day.

do as little as possible. 'Soldiering' would also take place (working more slowly together so that management did not realise workers' potential) and workers would carry out tasks in ways they were used to rather than the most efficient way. Taylor's scientific principles were designed to reduce inefficiency of workers and managers. This was to be achieved by 'objective laws' that management and workers could agree on, reducing conflict between them. Neither party could argue against a system of work that was based on 'science'. Taylor believed his principles would create a partnership between manager and worker, based on an understanding of how jobs should be done and how workers are motivated.

Taylor's approach How did Taylor discover what the 'best way' was of carrying out a task? Table 41.1 shows an illustration of Taylor's method.

Taylor had a very simple view of what motivated people at work - money. He felt that workers should receive a 'fair day's pay for a fair day's work', and pay should be linked to output through piece rates (☞ unit 42). A worker who did not produce a 'fair day's work' would face a loss of earnings; exceeding the target would lead to a bonus.

In 1899 Taylor's methods were used at the Bethlehem Steel Works in the USA, where they were responsible for raising pig-iron production by almost 400 per cent per man per day. Taylor found the 'best way to do each job' and designed incentives to motivate workers.

Taylor's message for business is simple - allow workers to work and managers to manage based on scientific principles of work study. Many firms today still attempt to use Taylor's principles. In the 1990s, the Bishop of Salford, when shown around a Littlewoods store, was told by the store manager that what he was looking for from potential Littlewoods workers was 'strong backs and nimble fingers'. This may not have been the official approach from Littlewoods, but it was seen locally as the use of Taylor's ideas.

Problems with Taylor's approach There is a number of problems with Taylor's ideas. The notion of a 'quickest and best way' for all workers does not take into account individual differences. There is no guarantee that the 'best way' will suit everyone.

Taylor also viewed people at work more as machines, with financial needs, than as humans in a social setting. There is no doubt that money is an important motivator. Taylor overlooked that people also work for reasons other than money. A survey in the early 1980s (Warr, 1982) asked a large sample of British people if they would continue to work if it were not financially necessary to do so. Nearly 70 per cent of men and 65 per cent of women said they would. This suggests there may be other needs that must be met at work, which Taylor ignored, but were recognised in Maslow's ideas which came later.

Human relations

Taylor's scientific management ideas may have seemed appealing at first glance to business. Some tried to introduce his ideas in the 1920s and 1930s, which led to industrial unrest. Others found that financial incentives did motivate workers, and still do today. However, what was becoming clear was that there were other factors which may affect workers' motivation.

The Hawthorne studies Many of the ideas which are today known as the 'human relations school' grew out of experiments between 1927 and 1932 at the Hawthorne Plant of the Western Electric company in Chicago. Initially these were based on 'scientific management' - the belief that

Anmac Ltd is a small expanding high-tech company. It employs approximately 25 workers in two factories, one at Chester and one at Stafford. The employers organise work on a fairly informal basis. Workers work at their own pace, which often results in a variable level of output. Recently orders for their advanced micro-electronic circuit boards have increased rapidly. The firm has decided that, to cope with the orders, increased production is needed. Two suggestions have been put forward.

- Encourage the workers to work overtime at the Chester plant.
- Redeploy some of the workers from Chester to Stafford where there is a shortfall of workers.

The workers at the Chester plant are mainly married women in their twenties, many with young, school aged children and husbands who also work.

(a) Explain how Taylor's scientific management principles might be used to solve the problems faced by Anmac Ltd.
(b) What problems might Anmac Ltd find in using such principles?

Question 2

workers' productivity was affected by work conditions, the skills of workers and financial incentives. Over the five year period, changes were made in incentive schemes, rest periods, hours of work, lighting and heating and the effect on workers' productivity was measured. One example was a group of six women assembling telephone relays. It was found that whatever changes were made, including a return to the original conditions, output rose. This came to be known as the HAWTHORNE EFFECT.

The study concluded that changes in conditions and financial rewards had little or no effect on productivity. Increases in output were mainly due to the greater cohesion and communication which workers in groups developed as they interacted and were motivated to work together. Workers were also motivated by the interest shown in their work by the researchers. This result was confirmed by further investigations in the Bank Wiring Observation where fourteen men with different tasks were studied.

The work of **Elton Mayo** (and Roethlisberger and Dickson) in the 1930s, who reported on the Hawthorne Studies, has led to what is known today as the human relations school. A business aiming to maximise productivity must make sure that the 'personal satisfactions' of workers are met for workers to be motivated. Management must also work and communicate with informal work groups, making sure that their goals fit in with the goals of the business. One way to do this is to allow such groups to be part of decision making. Workers are likely to be more committed to tasks that they have had some say in.

There are examples of these ideas being used in business today. The Volvo plant in Uddevalla, opened in 1989, was designed to allow workers to work in teams of 8-10. Each team built a complete car and made decisions about production. Volvo found that absenteeism rates at Uddevalla averaged 8 per cent, compared to 25 per cent in their Gothenburg plant which used a production line system. Other examples have been:

- Honda's plant in Swindon where 'teamwork' has been emphasised - there were no workers or directors, only 'associates';
- McDonald's picnics, parties and McBingo for their employees where they were made to feel part of the company;
- Mary Kay's seminars in the USA, which were presented like the American Academy awards for company employees.

Problems There is a number of criticisms of the human relations school.

- It assumes workers and management share the same goals. This idea of workplace 'consensus' may not always exist. For example, in the 1980s Rover tried to introduce a programme called 'Working with Pride'. It was an attempt to raise quality by gaining employee commitment. This would be achieved by greater communication with

employees. The programme was not accepted throughout the company. As one manager stated: 'We've tried the face-to-face communications approach. It works to a degree, but we are not too good at the supervisory level ... enthusiasm for the Working with Pride programme is proportionate to the level in the hierarchy. For supervisors it's often just seen as a gimmick ...'.

- It is assumed that communication between workers and management will break down 'barriers'. It could be argued, however, that the knowledge of directors' salaries or redundancies may lead to even more 'barriers' and unrest.
- It is biased towards management. Workers are manipulated into being productive by managers. It may also be seen as a way of reducing trade union power.

Table 41.2 *The effect of introducing a piece rate system into clothes manufacture*

Group	Number in group	Action taken to introduce system	Resignations within 40 days of introduction	Change in output
A	100	Group told the changes will take place next week	17%	-2%
B	150	Management introduces changes with the help of group to suit their needs	0%	+10%
C	200	Group told the changes will take place next week	7%	0%
D	50	Management explains the need for change to group	2%	+2%
E	100	Management explains the need for change and discusses this with the group	0%	+5%

Table 41.2 shows the results of a survey carried out in Bryant and Gillie, a manufacturer of children's clothing. The company introduced a piece rate system of work - a system where employees are paid according to the number or quantity of items they produce. Five groups were involved in the new system. Different actions were taken to introduce the system to each group. The table shows the effect on labour turnover and output of these actions.

(a) To what extent do the results support the human relations explanation of workers' motivation?
(b) Using the results of the survey in Table 41.2, advise the management on the likely action needed to motivate workers when changing work practices.

Question 3

Theory X and Theory Y

In 1960 **Douglas McGregor** published *The Human Side of Enterprise*. It was an attempt to apply the implications of Maslow and the work of Taylor and Mayo to business. In it, he gives different reasons why people work. He coined the terms Theory X and Theory Y to describe these differences. Table 41.3 shows the main ideas of the two theories.

Theory X assumes that people are lazy. If this is accepted, then the only way to get people to work is by using strict control. This control can take one of two forms. One method is to use coercion - the threat of punishment if rules are broken or targets not achieved. This is often known as the 'stick' approach. The problem with threats is that they are only effective if the person being threatened believes that they will be carried out. Modern employment laws and company wide agreements, have made this difficult for managers. For this reason, a 'carrot' approach may be more suitable. People have to be persuaded to carry out tasks by promises or rewards. In many ways this theory is similar to Taylor's view of people at work as shown earlier in this unit.

Theory Y, on the other hand, assumes that most people are motivated by those things at the top of Maslow's hierarchy. In other words, people are responsible, committed and enjoy having control over work. Most people, given the opportunity, will get involved in work, and contribute towards the solution of a problem that may arise. This theory is similar in some ways to the **human relations school**.

Business managers tend to say that their own assumptions are closer to Theory Y than to Theory X. But tests on management training courses tend to show that their attitudes are closer to Theory X than they might like to admit. In addition, many managers suggest that, while they

---

Table 41.3 *Theory X and Theory Y*

Theory X	Theory Y
• Workers are motivated by money	• Workers have many different needs which motivate them
• Workers are lazy and dislike work	• Workers can enjoy work
• Workers are selfish, ignore the needs of organisations, avoid responsibility and lack ambition	• If motivated, workers can organise themselves and take responsibility
• Workers need to be controlled and directed by management	• Management should create a situation where workers can show creativity and apply their job knowledge

---

In the heatwave of 2003, 510 staff at Volkswagen were invited to cool down with ice cream or watermelon by the business. This casual treat reflects the approach of the business and its total reward package. The head of HR says 'We are a service business ... so all our value added has to be through our people. This means that they have to be as motivated as possible.' This is not to suggest that the formal stuff is not important. The company is in the top 25 per cent of payers, offering good earnings, pension schemes and maternity benefits. So although people are driven by cash benefits, the business suggests that this is not enough. 'Younger recruits in particular now ask about sabbatical, flexible working and green policies. We have to be able to provide them with a genuine and credible answer.'

The change in attitude to the workforce began about 5 years ago. Ideas about bundling cash and non-cash motivator together came from the USA. Their introduction has been driven by a number of factors. Shortages of skilled staff have led to employers' attempts to maximise their attractiveness. Economic downturns also led employers to stress the benefits of flexible working, training and career progression.

Source: adapted from *People Management*, 29.1.2004.

(a) Using examples from the article, explain whether Volkswagen is taking a Theory X or Theory Y approach to motivation.
(b) Explain how taking such an approach might affect Volkswagen.

Question 4

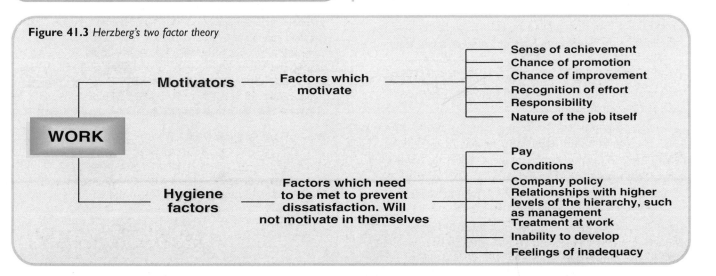

Figure 41.3 *Herzberg's two factor theory*

WORK

Motivators — Factors which motivate —
- Sense of achievement
- Chance of promotion
- Chance of improvement
- Recognition of effort
- Responsibility
- Nature of the job itself

Hygiene factors — Factors which need to be met to prevent dissatisfaction. Will not motivate in themselves —
- Pay
- Conditions
- Company policy
- Relationships with higher levels of the hierarchy, such as management
- Treatment at work
- Inability to develop
- Feelings of inadequacy

themselves are like Theory Y, workers are closer to Theory X. This theory has been used by managers to organise employees in business.

In practice, it could be argued that most firms behave according to Theory X, especially where shopfloor workers are concerned. The emphasis is on the use of money and control to encourage workers to behave in the 'correct way'. The same organisations might behave according to the assumptions of Theory Y when dealing with management. A representative of a banker's union wrote in the *Independent on Sunday*, 'The lower down the ladder you are, the less control you have over your work environment. Managers can do as they please, stretch their legs whenever they want. Clerical workers, if they are working in a data-processing centre, for example doing entries for cheques or credit cards, are disciplined if they don't complete a given number of key strokes in an hour or a day. Half the time they don't know what they are doing. They don't see any end product. More and more work has been downgraded.'

Herzberg's two-factor theory

In 1966 **Fredrick Herzberg** attempted to find out what motivated people at work. He asked a group of professional engineers and accountants to describe incidents in their jobs which gave them strong feelings of satisfaction or dissatisfaction. He then asked them to describe the causes in each case.

Results Herzberg divided the causes into two **categories** or **factors**. These are shown in Figure 41.3.
- MOTIVATORS. These are the factors which give workers **job satisfaction**, such as recognition for their effort. Increasing these motivators is needed to give job satisfaction. This, it could be argued, will make workers more productive. A business that rewards its workforce for, say, achieving a target is likely to motivate them to be more productive. However, this is not guaranteed, as other factors can also affect productivity.
- HYGIENE FACTORS. These are factors that can lead to workers being **dissatisfied**, such as pay or conditions. Improving hygiene factors should remove dissatisfaction. For example, better canteen facilities may make workers less dissatisfied about their environment. An improvement in hygiene factors alone is not likely to **motivate** an individual. But if they are not met, there could be a fall in productivity.

There is some similarity between Herzberg's and Maslow's ideas. They both point to needs that have to be satisfied for the employee to be motivated. Herzberg argues that only the higher levels of Maslow's hierarchy motivate workers.

Herzberg's ideas are often linked with **job enrichment** (☞ unit 43). This is where workers have their jobs 'expanded', so that they can experience more of the production process. This allows the workers to be more involved and motivated, and have a greater sense of achievement. Herzberg used his ideas in the development of clerical work. He selected a group of workers in a large corporation. Performance and job attitudes were low. Herzberg redesigned these jobs so that they were given more responsibility and recognition.

Problems Herzberg's theory does seem to have some merits. Improving pay or conditions, for example, may remove dissatisfaction at first. Often, however, these things become taken for granted. It is likely that better conditions will be asked for in following years. Evidence of this can be seen in wage claims which aim to be above the rate of inflation in some businesses every year. Job enrichment may also be expensive for many firms. In addition, it is likely that any benefits from job improvements will not be seen for a long time and that businesses will not be able to continue with

---

'To have a really happy workforce, you've got to do more than pass out party hats and serve birthday cake.' Over the years, I've tried a lot of things to make work fun, such as playing rock music, group lunches and sports after work. But after a while people get tired of it. Beyond the money, people expect more and more out of their work today. They want to contribute, learn, grow and feel that they are part of a successful enterprise that is making a difference in the world. Try to take into account the following.
- Today's workers at all levels want to know why they are doing something. Don't just say, 'Drop everything you're doing and rush this shipment out. Take time to explain why.
- Today's workers want to work hard and have pride in their work, but they need appreciation and recognition for their contribution. Be generous with compliments.
- Today's workers want input and accessibility to their managers, but many shy away from giving input unless you make it easy for them. Small group meetings where you ask for suggestions are a good way to get people involved.
- Today's workers want to feel that their work is making a difference. Explain why their work matters. Tell them success stories about people who use your products and post press clippings on the bulletin board.

Recently the person who runs our website left for another job. The manager of this area wanted to get a qualified candidate from the outside. But I want our company to go out of our way to retain people. So we divided the job among several people, giving them all a great chance to grow and learn something new. Another manager told me that when I'm in a good mood it helps boost up everyone else, but when I'm not, it darkens people's days.

Source: adapted from Streetwise Small Business Start-Up.

(a) Explain the (i) factors which motivate employees (ii) hygiene factors which are needed to prevent dissatisfaction using examples from the business in the article.

Question 5

such a policy in periods of recession.

Surveys that have tried to reproduce Herzberg's results have often failed. This may have been because different groups of workers have been examined and different techniques used. Also, there is a problem in relying too much on what people say they find satisfying or dissatisfying at work as this is subjective. For example, if things go wrong at work individuals have a tendency to blame it on others or factors outside of their control. On the other hand if individuals feel happy and satisfied when they are at work then they tend to see it as their own doing.

McClelland's managerial needs

David McClelland suggested that what motivates people is that they learn in early childhood that certain types of behaviour lead to 'gratification'. They develop needs based on this behaviour. For example, a girl may have a great need to achieve, encouraged by parents who help her to be successful at school. When she becomes employed, she will behave in a similar way. There are, McClelland argues, three basic needs - achievement, affiliation, power.

● The need for achievement. This is one of the keys to a company's success. People who have high achievement needs often become successful entrepreneurs (☞ unit 2). Such people like to take responsibility and risks, and want quick feedback on how they have performed. They like to set their own goals and standards and achieve these on their own. However, it is also likely that people with a need to achieve will not work well in groups.

● The need for affiliation. McClelland found that some successful people in business did not, as he expected, score high on the need to achieve. In large firms, managers' goals can often by achieved by working with others, rather than by their own efforts. Such managers have a need to relate to others and will try to gain the acceptance of their superiors and work colleagues.

● The need for power. Some individuals with high achievement and affiliation needs still had problems in influencing or controlling others, McClelland found. To be successful there was often a need to get people to work together. McClelland called this the power motive. He recognised that although the need for power is often seen as undesirable (where one person dominated others) it can also be seen in a positive light. It might reflect the ability of an individual to persuade, influence or lead people. Research suggests that people with a need for power tend to be in higher and more influential positions in business.

According to McClelland, a business needs to know how these three needs affect an individual. For example, a person that has high affiliation needs may not make a good marketing manager. Such a person would, based on the theory, constantly look for acceptance and support for all decisions. It is likely that this job would need someone who was far more self-motivated.

Vroom/Lawler and Porter

The theories of motivation that have been dealt with so far assume that people try to meet goals and so satisfy their needs. Vroom's and Lawler and Porter's theories state that this relationship is not so simple. First, each individual will have different goals. Second, people only act to achieve their goals if they feel there is a chance of success. Third, the value of the goal to the individual will also affect that person's motivation.

These theories might affect the way a business designs its pay and benefit systems and also the design of tasks and jobs to enable people to satisfy their needs. They take into account that people have different needs, and that some may want autonomy and responsibility at work, whereas others may not.

Criticisms of motivation theories

At first sight it would appear that a business interested in increasing its employees' motivation at work has a fairly simple task. The theories in this unit are divided into two groups. The scientific management/Theory X group argues that workers are lazy, need controlling and are only interested in monetary rewards. The human relations school/Theory Y/Vroom group argues workers have many needs that might be achieved if they have more control and responsibility. A business, it seems, only needs to identify which view is effective and use the findings to motivate its workforce.

In practice it is difficult to conclude whether either one of these broad perspectives is 'right or wrong'. Any one view may be right or wrong depending on the circumstances. If the business is geared towards hierarchy and authority, and work is routine and monotonous, people may choose to do such work in return for cash. For example, in 1969 Goldthorpe and Lockwood in their famous study, The Affluent Worker, found that workers on a Vauxhall car assembly line saw work as a means to earn high wages. This would allow workers to enjoy life outside work more. Wedderburn and Crompton's study in 1972 of a large chemical plant in North East England found much the same thing. Their results showed that the level of pay, job security and good welfare benefits were far more important to workers than job interest. In such cases, individuals regard monetary rewards as being more important than such factors as responsibility.

However, at other times, job interest and involvement may outweigh financial rewards. This may be true, for instance, in worker buyouts, when employees are prepared to accept lower financial rewards to maintain job security and have a say in the running of the business.

It is also argued that many motivation theories were developed in earlier times, when work conditions were different. Work methods did not need the advanced levels of technological knowledge and problem solving skills that they do today. These skills now require higher levels of education and a change in the relationship between management and the shop floor.

Maccoby (1988) suggested that motivation theories which are too concerned with giving promotion and control to the individual employee may be misdirected. He argued that individuals can be given extra responsibilities in a variety of ways, such as dealing with more customers, teaching other employees, solving problems and making deals. This type of employee does not need as much management, since she is more likely to manage herself or to work as part of a team with shared management. The word **empowerment** (☞ unit 43) is often used to describe this view of motivation. Team empowerment is used to describe teams that are given discretion to make unsupervised decisions.

What conclusion can be drawn from these points?

- Employees are likely to have different priorities at different times and in different circumstances.
- Employees aiming to increase their wage or salary are not likely to show much interest in job satisfaction (at that time).
- When employees are not involved in pay bargaining then they are likely to be interested in the quality of working life and job satisfaction.
- A business cannot generalise about what motivates people.

It must try to understand the views workers may have at any one time, before deciding how best to motivate them.
- Employees in modern organisations are likely to be more skilled in team working, problem solving and the use of information technology. Motivation theories have to take this into account to be useful to a business.

key terms

Hawthorne effect - the idea that workers are motivated by recognition given to them as a group.

Hygiene factors - those things that can lead to workers being dissatisfied.

Motivated - being encouraged to do something.

Motivators - those things that can lead to workers being satisfied.

Self-actualisation - a level on Maslow's hierarchy where an employee realises his or her full potential.

Scientific management - a theory that suggests that there is a 'best' way to perform work tasks.

Knowledge

1. Why is it important for business to satisfy workers?
2. Name 5 needs in Maslow's hierarchy that an individual might have at work.
3. What are the aims of Taylor's scientific management theory?
4. According to Taylor, how are people motivated?
5. What is meant by the human relations school of thought?
6. What, according to the human relations school, is the main motivator at work?
7. Explain the difference between Theory X and Theory Y.
8. How is Theory X like Taylor's view of scientific management?
9. According to Herzberg's theory, what factors are likely to:
   (a) increase job satisfaction;
   (b) reduce dissatisfaction at work?
10. What general conclusions can a business draw from the criticisms of motivation theory?

Case study Mendelsons

Lee Worsnip has worked as an assistant in the financial analysis department of Mendelsons Insurance for two years. He is 24 years of age and joined Mendelsons from college with good exam results. Lee also obtained some extra qualifications by taking night school courses. He started as junior clerk, and quickly moved to a more senior post, which paid a better salary. However, he has been in this post for a while now.

Lee's aim was to use the job as a stepping stone to one of the sales teams. The business was pleased that Lee looked on the job in this way, as it is in favour of encouraging people to get on. However, it is difficult to get onto one of the sales teams, particularly when the company has placed so much emphasis on its graduate recruitment. This may be one of the things that seems to be bothering Lee. Recently the Unit Trust team hired a graduate trainee instead of Lee, although he did accept that the new recruit had an advantage as she was a qualified actuary.

Until a few months ago, Lee had been an above average employee. He was always cheerful, enthusiastic and willing, and picked things up quickly. Lee used to make an excellent contribution to regular weekly meetings. And he was prepared to do one-off projects, always seeming to be able to squeeze in the extra work. He was also quite prepared to work late.

Lately, however, he seems to lack motivation. He has missed some meetings and taken days off. He complained that other members of the meetings had more senior posts and felt they did not listen to his views. He said 'I shouldn't be treated simply as some Theory X worker who gets their pay and goes home.'

The other day, Lee refused to take on a low level task. He suggested that he was fed up doing routine work and not leaving the office every day until 8 o'clock. Lee also argued that he was never allowed to make decisions and his work was always checked, as if he wasn't trusted. In the end some of these tasks had to be given to other members of staff, increasing their work load. Lee's absences has put additional pressure on the team.

Lee has also started being offhand. He was

overheard several times being rude to people who asked him for information or help. Last week, at a team meeting about new procedures, Lee suggested that they had been drawn up in secret behind his back.

(a) What is meant by the terms:
  (i) lack of motivation;
  (ii) Theory X worker? (6 marks)
(b) Explain the problems that (i) Lee and (ii) the business might have as a result of a lack of motivation. (10 marks)
(c) Using a motivation theory, examine reasons why Lee may lack motivation. (12 marks)
(d) Suggest ways in which the business might improve Lee's motivation. (12 marks)

Financial and non-financial rewards

Unit 41 outlined theories which have tried to explain the factors that motivate people at work. Some of these theories stress that money is the most important factor. The scientific/Theory X approach, in particular, argues that workers respond to **financial rewards**. It is argued that such rewards are necessary to motivate a reluctant workforce. Employees see work as a means to an end. As a result they are far more likely to be interested in monetary rewards.

In contrast, the human relations/Theory Y view argues that workers are motivated by a variety of factors. An employee working in a car assembly plant, for example, may be highly motivated by working as part of a team. Poor pay may lead to employees being dissatisfied, which can make other **non-financial rewards** less effective in motivating them.

The next two units examine how these theories can be used. This unit looks at how a business might use financial rewards and incentives.

Payment schemes

How are employees rewarded for the work they do? There is a number of methods that may be used.

Time rates TIME RATES are used when workers are rewarded for the amount of time they spend at work. Employees are paid in the form of weekly **wages** or monthly **salaries**. For many workers in the UK, pay is fixed in relation to a standard working week. Workers who work longer than this may be paid **overtime**, perhaps at a higher rate. In addition, holidays with pay are included for most British industries. Examples of time rates are the £22,000 a year paid to a teacher or the £5.00 per hour paid to a cleaner in, say, Newcastle.

Time rates are a simple way of calculating pay for a business. They are useful when a business wants to employ workers to do specialist or difficult tasks that should not be rushed. Employees can ensure that work is of a high quality without worrying about the time they take.

Time rates are also useful when working out the pay of service sector employees or people working in groups. In these cases it is very difficult for a business to work out the exact value of the employee's output. An example might be doctors, where it is virtually impossible to calculate the value of work. From an employee's point of view, time rates guarantee income.

Annualised hours Many employers have found that payment based on a fixed working week can be inflexible. For example, half the year employees may be idle after 3pm every day, but are still paid for a 'full day's' work. The other half of the year they may work into the evening and be paid overtime. To cater for fluctuations in demand some employers pay staff on the basis of a certain number of hours to be worked in a year. These are known as ANNUALISED HOURS CONTRACTS.

For annualised hours contracts, the number of hours to be worked each year is fixed. However, the daily, weekly or monthly hours are flexible. So employees may have a longer working day at peak times and work less when demand is slack. An employee's pay is calculated on the basis of an average working week, for example 35 hours, which is paid regardless of the actual number of hours the employee works.

There are certain advantages. An employee has a guaranteed income each week. Employers often see this as a way of avoiding overtime, reducing costs, increasing flexibility and improving efficiency. One water company found that its service engineers would leave a job part completed in order to get back to their depot by 5pm, even if the job only required a further hour's work. When the company introduced annualised hours contracts the engineers had to complete any job they had started, even if it meant working beyond 5pm. The advantage for the water company was much greater customer satisfaction and efficiency, as service engineers did not have to make two round trips to a job. The engineers were able to negotiate a higher basic pay. They also benefited from a more flexible shift system, which meant they could increase their number of rest days.

Piece rates A system of PIECE RATES is the easiest way for a business to make sure that employees are paid for the amount of work they do. Employees are paid an agreed rate for every item produced. For this reason it is known as a PAYMENT BY RESULTS system. It is often used in the textile industry. Piece rates are arguably an INCENTIVE to workers. The more they produce, the more they earn.

From a business's point of view, this system links pay to output. However, there is a number of problems. Employees have no basic pay to fall back on if machinery fails or if the quality of the goods produced is unacceptable. Trade unions, in particular, have campaigned against this method of payment as it often results in low pay and low living standards. There have also been disputes in the past about what 'rate' should be paid. Some firms may feel that the method encourages workers to sacrifice quality in favour of higher rewards.

Because of the problems of lack of basic pay, most firms use a system where pay is made up of two elements. There is a fixed or basic pay, calculated on the time worked and a variable element, often when a **target** has been reached. It is argued that this extra element motivates workers to increase productivity, while the time element gives security. Incentive schemes are dealt with later in this unit.

Commission In some businesses COMMISSION makes up the total earnings of the workers. This is true of some insurance salespeople and some telesales employees. Commission, like piece rates, is a reward for the quantity (or value) of work. Employees are paid a percentage of the value of each good or service that is sold. It could be argued that it suffers from the same problems and gives the same incentive as a piece rate system. The benefit to the employer is that it can indicate the level of business 'won' rather than just output achieved. Earnings surveys have shown that the numbers of people receiving commission is falling. The proportion of people's total earnings made up of commission is also declining.

Fees Fees are payments made to people for 'one-off' tasks. Tasks tend to be geared towards the needs of the client, rather than a standard service or product. The amount paid will depend on a variety of factors. These might include the time taken to finish the task or the difficulty of the task. Often fees are paid to people providing services, such as solicitors, performers etc.

Fringe benefits FRINGE BENEFITS are payments other than wages or salaries. They include things like private medical insurance, profit-related bonus schemes, a company car, subsidised meals, transport allowances, loan or mortgage facilities etc. Fringe benefits have grown in importance. This is especially the case in the executive, management and professional area. From an employer's view, providing benefits rather than pay may actually be cheaper as they do not need to pay National Insurance contributions. An employee might also prefer to receive benefits such as private medical insurance, that avoids waiting for treatment, rather than pay. Despite their attraction, fringe benefits can cause status problems. Also, benefits such as a company car may be liable for tax, although some benefits avoid tax such as certain company pension schemes.

Table 42.1 shows some of the fringe benefits that have been offered by companies in the UK.

Employer objectives for pay

There is a number of objectives employers will have when paying their workforce.

Motivation It has been argued that workers are motivated by money (☞ unit 41). This may be a rather simple view of workers' behaviour. Yet it is clear from the way that employers use money incentives that they believe employees react to the prospect of increasing their earnings. For example, many firms are attempting to link pay with performance because they believe that employees care about pay.

Employers must give consideration to any system they use. For example, if payments are made when targets are achieved, these targets must be realistic. Payment systems are often negotiated between **groups**, such as company representatives and trade unions.

Table 42.1 *Fringe benefits*

Company	Function	Fringe benefit
Dyson Appliances	Vacuum cleaner manufacturer	Dyson cleaner at reduced rate for new employees
Text 100	PR Agency	2 'Duvet days' (unscheduled holidays) a year
Air Products	Industrial gas supplier	Free exercise classes and subsidised gym and yoga classes, free annual medical checks
Saatchi & Saatchi	Advertising agency	Company pub - 'The Pregnant Man'
Virgin Group	Travel, entertainment, media, retail and financial services	24 hour parties
Body Shop	Cosmetics manufacturer and retailer	£100 a year to 'buy' a training course in new skill of their choice
Tesco	Food retailer	SAYE tax free share option scheme

The Directors Remuneration Report Regulations, introduced in 2002, were an attempt to increase the transparency of perks given to executives in plcs. This would be particularly useful for shareholders reading annual reports, concerned about their investment and the relationship between the earnings of executives and their rewards. Several firms had already reported perks given to executives before the regulations came into force, including a free monthly ration of 400 cigarettes given to British American Tobacco directors and various benefits to company chief executives such as:
● a £20,000 relocation allowance paid by BT;
● free dental benefits for life paid by HSBC;
● £230,000 annual rent paid by Reuters.
The value of such perks are unlikely to eat too much into the bottom line profits of companies at the moment. But it was suggested that they should be ignored by shareholders at their peril, as UK perks were modest compared to those of US executives.

Source: adapted from *The Observer*, 27.4.2003.

(a) Explain the effects that the legislation might have on the different stakeholders mentioned in the article.

Question 1

Cost Employers are interested in the profitability or cost-effectiveness of their business. Any system that is used by the business must, therefore, attempt to keep the cost of labour as low as possible in relation to the market wage in that industry. This should enable the firm to increase its profits.

Prestige Managers often argue that it is a 'good thing' to be a good payer. Whether high pay rates earn an employer the reputation of being a good employer is arguable. What seems much more likely is that the low-paying employer will have the reputation of being a poor one in the eyes of employees.

Recruitment and labour turnover Payment rates must be competitive enough to ensure the right number of qualified and experienced employees stay within the business. This will prevent a high level of **labour turnover** (☞ unit 45). This is also true of vacant posts. A business must pay rates which encourage the right quality and quantity of applicants.

Control Certain methods of payment will reduce costs and make the control of labour easier. These are examined later in this unit.

Employee objectives for pay

Employees will have their own objectives for the payment they receive.

Purchasing power A worker's standard of living is determined by the level of weekly or monthly earnings. The **purchasing power** of those earnings is affected by the rate of inflation (☞ unit 66). Obviously, in periods of high inflation workers are likely to seek higher wages as the purchasing power of their earnings falls. Those whose earnings fall behind the rate of inflation will face a decline in their purchasing power.

Fair pay Employees often have strong feelings about the level of payment that is 'fair' for a job. The employee who feels underpaid may be dissatisfied and might look for another job, be careless, or be absent a great deal. Those who feel overpaid may simply feel dishonest, or may try to justify their pay by looking busy.

Relativities Employees may be concerned about how their earnings compare with those of others. 'How much do I get relative to ... ' is an important factor for a worker. Workers with a high level of skill, or who have trained for a long period, will want to maintain high wages relative to less 'skilled' groups. **Flat rate** pay increases, such as £10 a week for the whole workforce, would erode differences. A 5 per cent increase would maintain the differences.

Recognition Most people like their contribution to be recognised. Their pay gives them reassurance that what they are doing is valued.

Composition Employees often take into account the way their earnings are made up. It is argued that younger employees tend to be more interested in high direct earnings rather than indirect benefits like pensions. Incentive payments are likely to interest employees who want to increase their pay. Married women and men are generally less interested in overtime payments, for example, and regard other factors more highly.

Incentive schemes

The pay that employees receive often reflects the nature of the job. However, some payment systems try to relate pay to the performance or commitment that an employee makes to the business, known as **incentive schemes**. Businesses attempt to induce high commitment and performance from employees with high pay in order to gain the maximum output.

Incentive schemes for manual and non-manual employees
Incentive payments have been widely used in the management of manual workers in the past. Increasingly, incentives are being paid to workers not directly involved in production. Schemes are now being used for administrative workers and in service industries. For example, a business may set sales targets for its departments. Employees in those departments can then be rewarded with a BONUS once targets are reached. Sales representatives in many companies are set targets each month and are paid bonuses if they reach them.
Bonus payments come in many forms. One method is a bonus paid per extra output above a target as in the piece rate system. However, one-off payments are often used by businesses to motivate workers. Bonuses can be paid at certain times of the year in a lump sum (often at Christmas). They can also be built into the monthly salary of some workers, such as staff working in certain hospitals.

Although the bonus may be paid for reaching a target, it may also be for other things. Rewards for punctuality or attendance are sometimes used. Some businesses reward their 'best' salesperson with a bonus. One unusual example of this is Richer Sounds, the hi-fi retail outlet, where workers in a retail outlet that performed best over a period were rewarded with the use of a Rolls Royce for a month!

The problem with regular bonuses is that they are often seen as part of the employee's basic pay. As a result, they may no longer act as a motivator.

Productivity agreements are also a form of bonus payment, where rewards are paid providing workers achieve a certain level of 'productivity'. They are usually agreed between employees' groups and management to 'smooth over' the introduction of new machinery or new techniques that workers need to learn.

Incentive schemes fall into three categories.
● Individual schemes. Individual employees may be rewarded for exceeding a target. The benefit of this scheme is that it rewards individual effort and hence employees are more likely to be motivated by this approach.
● Group incentives. In some situations, like assembly lines,

the need is to increase group output rather than individual output. Where one worker relies on the output of others, group incentives may also have benefits. They can, however, put great pressure on all group members to be productive. It can also be difficult for a new recruit to become part of the group, as existing members may feel they will have to compensate for his inexperience.

● Factory-wide schemes. Employees are given a share of a 'pool' bonus provided the plant has reached certain output targets. The benefit to management is that incentives are related to the final output rather than sections of the plant. Furthermore, in theory at least, employees are more likely to identify with the company as a whole.

The difficulty with this type of scheme is that there is no incentive to work harder, as there is no direct link between individual effort and reward. Some employees that work hard may have their rewards reduced by others who do not - the same problem as group incentives.

Incentive schemes for managers and directors In the 1990s there has been a large increase in the use of incentive schemes for managers and directors. These have usually been

One of the biggest changes that to
Spencer after the year 2000 wa
performance element and a c
around five years. Last year w
living increase for managers. V
available in 2001 into a perfo
spokesperson. A senior bonus
apply to the top 50 or 60 exec
around 1,000 managers. This is p
  Staff are also eligible to a sales re
been a major influence on performance local
managers have been given greater discretion over
awarding bonuses. For example, six staff at Purdsey who
were short of their target with a day left set up a gift shop
in Yorkshire Water's head office to make up the difference
and meet the target. This is indicative of the improvement
in motivation and morale. A new bonus scheme based on
attendance has reduced absenteeism significantly. For
example, the absenteeism rate fell from 4.5 per cent to
1 per cent in the M&S food hall at the MetroCentre in
Gateshead.

Source: adapted from *People Management*, 10.1.2002.

(a) Describe the (i) employee incentives and
    (ii) management incentives mentioned in the article.
(b) Examine the possible objectives of the incentive
    schemes.

linked to how well the company has performed, often following restructuring, delayering or the privatisation of companies such as the public utilities (☞ unit 7). Share ownership schemes are often used to motivate managers.

There is evidence to suggest that management perform better if they 'own' part of a business, for example after an internal buyout. However, other research indicates that incentive schemes may not necessarily be the most important motivator at work for many managers. The Ashridge Management Index is a indicator of managers' attitudes based on a survey of 500 middle and senior managers. When asked what motivates them, 61 per cent of managers placed challenging work first. Other high-scoring motivators included 'letting people run their own show' and 'seeing the impact of decisions on the business'. These factors, along with high basic salary (35 per cent), topped the motivation league table.

Types of incentive scheme

Incentive schemes can take many forms. **Individual output schemes** relate pay to the performance of individual employees.

Piece rate schemes We have already seen that piece rates can be an incentive. Producing more will earn the worker more. Each unit, over and above a target, is rewarded with a bonus or commission payment. In the past there have often been disputes about the rate that should be paid for each unit produced. Businesses have tried to solve this by using individual time-saving schemes - the incentive is paid for time saved when carrying out a task. Using Taylor's work study methods (☞ unit 41) a work study engineer calculates the **standard time** that an employee should take to complete a task. The employee then receives incentive payments if the task is completed in a shorter time. If it is not possible to work due to shortage of materials or some other reason, the time involved is not counted. Such schemes, however, mean employees still suffer from variable payments. Despite these problems this type of incentive can be used when carrying out short, manual tasks where output can vary.

Performance related pay PERFORMANCE RELATED PAY (PRP) schemes link the annual salary of an employee to their performance in the job. PRP schemes have spread rapidly in recent years and now form an important part of white collar pay in the public and private sector. Nearly all the major banks, building societies and insurance companies now use performance systems. A number of large manufacturers, such as Cadbury's and Nissan, have introduced schemes (at times extending them to the shop floor) as well as public sector industries, such as the civil service, NHS and local government.

The shift towards PRP can be seen as part of a more general movement towards 'pay flexibility' in British industry.

● Organisations have sought to tie pay increases to measures of business performance, not just through PRP schemes

304 Motivation in Practice - Financial Rewards **Unit 42**

but through other mechanisms, such as profit sharing.

● There has been a move away from national, industry-wide pay agreements to local, plant-wide agreements. This has given managers greater discretion in the way they match rewards to particular business units.

● There is a new focus on the individual employee and rewards which reflect her performance and circumstances, which has meant that collective methods of pay determination have become less important.

PRP schemes come in many forms, but the majority have some common features.

● Individual performance is reviewed, usually over a year. This may take the form of comparing performance against agreed objectives.

● At the end of the review the worker will be placed in a 'performance category'. The 'excellent' performer, for instance, may have exceeded all his agreed targets and produced work of a high standard. The category the worker falls into will determine the size of payment or whether payment is made at all.

● The performance payment can vary. Sometimes there may be a small cash bonus or the award of increments on a pay scale. In others, the entire salary and progression through scales can depend on the results of the performance review. This kind of 'merit only' scheme means a 'poor' performer will be punished, as they will not receive extra pay.

There are problems with PRP. It is based on individual achievement, so the better a person does the more that person is paid. However, there may be disputes about how performance is to be measured and whether a person has achieved enough to be rewarded. Also, the system is not likely to work if people do not react to the possibility of rewards by working harder.

The following example of two sales consultants highlights some practical problems. Jane and Ruth are sales consultants for an insurance company and both had set targets for a six month period. Ruth met her target comfortably and received the agreed bonus of £5,500 for reaching on-target earnings. Jane failed to reach her agreed target because her sales manager left the company and poached three of Jane's best customers just before they signed agreements with Jane. Jane's bonus was therefore reduced to only £2,500 for a lower level of sales. Jane had no control over this, but felt she had worked just as hard as Ruth and therefore deserved a similar bonus.

Research also shows that many organisations may be out of tune with their employees, placing too much emphasis on incentives. The effectiveness of performance related pay, in particular, is called into question. Ashridge researchers describe it as 'the biggest mismatch between what organisations are seen to be relying on to motivate managers and what actually motivates them'. Research by ACAS also suggests that PRP schemes tend to demotivate rather than motivate staff.

Commission As explained earlier, commission is where employees are often rewarded for the amount of orders they bring in to a business, for example salespeople. The more business they gain, the more they are paid.

Collective output schemes relate pay to the performance of a group or other unit of the business.

Measured daywork The idea of measured daywork may provide the answer to the problems of piece rate schemes. Instead of employees receiving a variable extra amount of pay depending on their output, they are paid a fixed sum as long as an agreed level of output is maintained. This should provide stable earnings and a stable output, instead of 'as much as you can, when you can, if you can'.

The first major agreement based on the principles of measured daywork was the National Power Loading Agreement in coal mining in 1966. London Docks and British Leyland both reverted to more traditional 'payment by result' methods in the late 70s. Although productivity gains may not have been great, most surveys found that measured daywork improved industrial relations and that less expenditure was spent on dealing with grievances. Furthermore, measured daywork seemed to give management a greater control over such payment schemes. In practice, the need for flexibility in reward schemes has meant that measured daywork is rarely used as an incentive scheme today.

Profit sharing Profit sharing takes place in business organisations such as partnerships (☞ unit 6). Profits are either shared equally or as agreed in any partnership deed of agreement drawn up by the business. Partners or employees of business have an incentive to be as productive as possible. The more profit the business makes, the more they earn.

Profit related pay Profit related pay involves employees being paid a cash 'bonus' as a proportion of the annual profits of the company. In previous years a certain amount of profit related pay has been exempt from taxation. However, this was no longer to be the case after the year 2000. Profit related pay has a number of problems for employees. It is not linked to individual performance and rewards can fluctuate from year to year depending on the performance of the business.

Share ownership Businesses may offer the possibility of purchasing shares in the company as an incentive. This is sometimes reserved for managers. In large businesses wider share ownership amongst all employees may be encouraged. There is a number of different employee share schemes. **Savings-related** share option schemes, for example, allow an employee to save each month over, say, five years. They can then take up an option to purchase a number of shares at a value stated when the shares are offered - the option price. The advantage of buying shares to employees is that they feel part of the company and are rewarded with **dividends**

(☞ unit 3) if the company performs well.

In the 1990s evidence suggested that share ownership was slowly spreading among growing businesses. Out of 63 companies floated on the Stock Exchange in 1996, 39 operated all employee share schemes. However, 52 companies had Inland Revenue approved executive share schemes. Even more had non-approved schemes for top executives. A UK index of quoted employee-owned companies showed that share prices had outperformed those of conventionally owned rivals over the past few years. The index tracked 30 companies where more than 10 per cent of shares were held by or for employees. The index rose threefold since January 1992, outstripping the FT-SE All Share index by 89 per cent. A survey of EU companies suggested there was a growing trend towards share ownership schemes in the twenty first century.

Incentive schemes can also relate to the **input of employees**.

Merit pay This bases pay upon the behaviour of employees, such as flexibility, co-operation and punctuality. Employees demonstrating these traits may be rewarded more highly than others.

Skills-based pay Here employees are rewarded according to the physical and mental capabilities. So, for example, an employee demonstrating a wider range of skills may earn

higher rewards.

Problems with incentive schemes

There is a number of problems that financial incentives schemes have.

● Operating problems. For incentives to work, production needs to have a smooth flow of raw materials, equipment and storage space, and consumer demand must also be fairly stable. These conditions cannot be guaranteed for long. If raw materials did not arrive or ran out, for example, the worker may not achieve a target and receive no bonus for reasons beyond his control. If this happens the employee is unlikely to be motivated by the scheme, and may negotiate for a larger proportion of earnings to be paid as guaranteed 'basic' pay.

● Fluctuating earnings. A scheme that is linked to output must result in fluctuating earnings. This might be due to changes in demand, the output of the worker or machinery problems. As in the case above, the worker is likely to press for the guaranteed part of pay to be increased, or store output in the 'good times' to prevent problems in the 'bad'. Alternatively, workers may try to 'slow down' productive workers so that benefits are shared out as equally as possible.

● Quality. The need to increase output to gain rewards can affect quality. There is an incentive for workers to do things as quickly as possible and this can lead to mistakes. Workers filling jars with marmalade may break the jars if they work too quickly. This means the jar is lost and the marmalade as well, for fear of splinters. For some businesses, such as food processing, chemicals or drug production, errors could be disastrous.

● Changes in payment. Because of the difficulties above, employers constantly modify their incentive schemes. Improved schemes should stop workers manipulating the system and may give renewed motivation to some workers. However, constant changes mean that employees do not always understand exactly how to gain rewards.

● Quality of working life. Incentive schemes which use payment by results require a certain type of job design (☞ unit 43). This often means tight control by management, routine and repetition. Theory X (☞ unit 41) argues that production will only be efficient if workers know exactly what to do in any situation and their activities are tightly controlled by management. The result of this is that boredom and staleness may set in and the worker's 'standard of life' at work may be low.

● Jealousy. Individual workers may be jealous of the rewards earned by their colleagues. This can lead to problems in relationships and a possible lack of motivation. Increasingly, businesses are using group or plant-wide incentives to solve this.

Table 42.2 *Extent of incentive schemes (% of organisations offering incentives)*

		%
Scheme	Management employees	Non-management employees
IPRP*	40	25
Team-based pay	8	8
Skill/competency pay	6	11
Profit-related pay	35	34
Employee share ownership	17	15

* Individual performance related pay.

Source: adapted from Institute of Personnel Development (IPD).

A survey of 5,000 businesses by the IPD suggested that a variety of different incentive schemes were used by UK businesses. Some were more popular than others. Also, some were used more for manual than non-manual employees.

(a) Suggest reasons to account for the use of incentive schemes shown in Table 42.2.

Question 3

- For incentives to work effectively it must be possible to measure performance. For example, a business must be able to measure the number of components made by a worker if she is paid a bonus after 20,000 are made a month.
- Problems may take place if the rewards are based on the performance of a team, but some workers are more productive then others in the team.

Given these problems, why are financial incentive schemes still used by many firms? Managers may find a use for a certain incentive scheme. For example, a scheme can be used to overcome resistance to change. A business introducing new technology, such as computers, may offer an incentive for staff to retrain or spend extra time becoming familiar with the new system. Employees often see benefits in such systems of payment. They may feel that they are gaining some control over their own actions in the workplace, being able to work at their own pace if they so wish. Furthermore, many businesses believe that incentive schemes ought to work as it is logical to assume that employees work harder if they are offered financial rewards.

Are incentives effective?

How effective are incentive schemes according to research?

- Pearce and others (1985) research into merit pay amongst managers in US Social Security Administration found little effect on organisational performance. The Institute of Personnel Development (1999) suggested that managers view merit pay as having only a modest effect on employee commitment. In a study, 53 per cent said that there had been 'no change' in such commitment.
- Gerhard and Milkovich (1992) found the use of bonuses for managers had a positive effect on the rate of return on capital employed in business.
- Kruse and Weitzman (1990) found that profit sharing had a positive effect on productivity and company performance, although whether schemes led to improved performance or whether such performance allows business run such schemes is debatable.

The Department for Education insisted that teachers' pay must be linked to performance as part of its plans to modernise public sector services and that teachers could not expect an above-inflation pay increase in 2004. The department was also considering giving individual schools more power to set pay rates for their staff. A spokesperson said 'The government is strongly of the view that the priority for this year is not a general increase in pay above the rate of inflation, but instead action to promote workforce reform and tackle workload issues.'

In 2002, the government introduced a performance-related bonus scheme to boost teachers' pay and help retain staff. Experienced teachers, who had taught for six years, could apply for a one-off bonus of £2,000. Almost all teachers who applied for the performance pay got it. But a study by the Institute of Education in London found little evidence that payments had improved results or attracted more people into teaching. It suggested that it was difficult to determine the impact of any one teacher on a pupil's progress. 'A pupil may have private tuition, help at home, or any number of external influences. So we may never know objectively whether performance-related pay has positive effects on pupil learning outcomes' said Professor Dalton, co-author. He argued that 'market theories do not necessarily work in the public sector. A bricklayer may lay more bricks if paid a bonus, but this does not apply to teachers, who are highly motivated professionals already working to maximum capacity.' The research even suggested that bonus payments could be counterproductive because teachers were used to working together instead of competing with each other.

The researchers said it is a 'difficult if not impossible task' to devise a performance related pay system for teachers that makes them work harder and more productively, does not need expensive monitoring, encourages teamwork and discourages teaching to the test.

Source: adapted from the *Daily Telegraph*, *The Independent*, 2002.

(a) Evaluate the possible effectiveness of performance related pay for teachers.

Question 4

key terms

Annualised hours contracts - a payment system based on a fixed number of hours to be worked each year, but a flexible number of hours each day, week or month.
Bonus - usually an extra payment made in recognition of the contribution a worker has made to the company.
Commission - a payment system where employees are paid a percentage of the value of each good or service that is sold.
Fringe benefits - payments made to employees instead of salaries or wages.

Incentive - a reward given to employees to encourage them to work harder.
Payment by results - payment methods that reward workers for the quantity and quality of work they produce .
Performance related pay - management's attempts to increase worker productivity by linking pay with performance.
Piece rates - a payment system where employees are paid an agreed rate for every item produced.
Time rates - a payment system that rewards workers for the amount of time they spend at work.

1. What is the difference between financial and non-financial rewards?
2. What are the problems for employees of using a piece rate system?
3. Why might a piece rate system be used as an incentive?
4. Give 3 examples of the use of commission.
5. State 4 objectives that employees may have for pay.
6. State 4 objectives a business might have for a system of payment.
7. What is the difference between an individual and a factory-wide incentive scheme?
8. Why might a group incentive scheme discourage some workers rather than encourage them?
9. Describe how a measured daywork system operates.
10. What is meant by profit sharing?
11. Briefly explain 4 problems with incentive schemes.

Case study Incentives for Value Added Resellers

Value Added Resellers (VARs) are businesses which take a manufacturer's product and add their own value before selling it. For example, a VAR might take an operating system, add its own specialist software for, say, architects, and then sell the bundle to architect businesses. Manufacturers offer VARs a number of incentives to sell their products.

'The best incentive is money in the pocket' said one VAR. Most incentive schemes are based on money and commissions. Other means are used, but do they work? 'Freebies' such as day trips and air miles are commonly on offer. But in the day-to-day slog of running a business, motivation to take advantage of such benefits can be hard to muster. 'We don't really bother with these schemes' said one VAR. 'They create more administration than they're worth. 'Luxury rewards are still available as part of wider packages. For example, the top performing VAR for SolidWorks, was invited to Hawaii.

Opinions on whether rewards for individuals are effective will depend on to whom you speak. There will always be salespeople who thrive on beating the competition and who want to gain recognition for doing so. Peter Dickin, marketing manager at Delcam, feels that a more inclusive approach is required. 'Incentives targeted just at salespeople neglect the contribution of others, which can be demotivating. We tend to favour schemes that foster team building.'

Incentive schemes that reward a group of high-performing VARs have to be carefully structured to create a level playing field to give companies of different sizes and locations a chance. Clearly this is not always being achieved. One disgruntled VAR said 'I have never, ever been incentivised by any scheme I have worked with in the past. Overpaid VAR managers justify their own existence, even so far as coming up with jollies that they had no prior interest in, such as driving racing cars and sailing around the Leeward Isles.'

Schemes based mainly on the volume of sales can have negative implications for all parties. 'The aims of the incentives that we work to are not those that suit our long-term business goals, nor the needs of our customers,' said one VAR. 'They are generally incentives to motivate short-term business.'

The opportunity to gain marketing funds is another regular element of incentive schemes, particularly where a business wants to make inroads into a particular market. IBM, for example, offers a special marketing fund to companies who join its Top Contributor Programme and commit themselves to selling $100,000 of software to the SME (small and medium sized business) market.

As free trips and luxury gifts are used less, terms such as 'active business management' have crept into the language of incentives. 'We don't incentivise on volume' explains John Mitchell, Manager of Indirect Channels, Europe, PLM Solutions. 'We incentivise VARs to invest in their business and improve the quality of their service to our customers.'

Many VARs are dubious about whether the incentives on offer actually made them do anything differently. Not offering incentives doesn't go down well either. One VAR said "Our own main vendor doesn't offer any incentive schemes (or even buy drinks at the bar at sales events). So we will have to do our best focusing upon making money for ourselves.'

Source: adapted from retailsystemseller.com.

(a) **What is meant by the terms:**
 (i) **luxury rewards;**
 (ii) **incentivise on volume? (6 marks)**
(b) **Describe the different payment and incentive schemes in the article. (10 marks)**
(c) **Examine the advantages and disadvantages to such schemes for VARs. (12 marks)**
(d) **Assess which incentives are likely to be most motivating to VARs selling products such as computers for manufacturers to small businesses. (12 marks)**

The need for non-financial rewards

Financial rewards have often been used in the past by firms in an attempt to motivate employees to improve productivity. However, increasingly businesses have realised that:

● the chance to earn more money may not be an effective motivator;
● financial incentive schemes are difficult to operate;
● individual reward schemes may no longer be effective as production has become organised into group tasks;
● other factors may be more important in motivating employees.

If other factors are more important than pay in motivating workers, it is important for firms to identify them. Only then can a business make sure its workforce is motivated. Figure 43.1 shows some of the factors that employees might consider important in their work environment. Many of these have been identified by the theories of Mayo and McGregor (☞ unit 41). A business may consider introducing non-financial incentives to help employees satisfy these needs.

Job design and redesign

The dissatisfaction with financial incentive schemes reached its peak in the 1960s and 1970s. In response the 'Quality of Working Life Movement' began to develop ideas which were based around the 'human relations school', as first outlined by the Hawthorne studies (☞ unit 41). It was argued that workers were likely to be motivated by non-monetary factors and that jobs needed to be DESIGNED or REDESIGNED to take these factors into account. Five principles were put

Investing in the skills of people makes smart business sense according to Ben Reed of IPBartenders. If you don't the good people leave and the poor ones stay. 'On the Continent barpeople are regarded as professionals' says Reed. 'They are held in high esteem' and that is not always the case in the UK. Work is often treated as casual and staff are treated accordingly. Staff should be encouraged to develop skills and take pride in their work. Recognition of a job well done is a key factor in developing satisfaction.

Happy, successful staff need to be empowered and inspired. This goes beyond telling staff what to do and how to do it. They need to know why and they need to have the skills to make informed customer decisions. Many skills are required to serve the customer what they want, including a knowledge of customer choice, how to mix drinks and the popularity of certain brands. Staff with a knowledge of wines are far more able to influence customer choice. They also need to be aware of legislation regarding drinking age and how to cope with tricky situations.

It is also important for them to have the right equipment and materials. Making sure that the work areas is sensibly organised and uncluttered will help. And workers will also respond to co-operation and team work. Team incentives can be very useful. Remember, if staff don't enjoy working in the bar, customers won't enjoy drinking in it.

Source: adapted from *The Publican*, 27.10.2003.

(a) Suggest ways in which a business might motivate its bar staff other then paying higher wages.
(b) Explain how this will affect:
   (i)   employees;
   (ii) customers;
   (iii) the business.

Question 1

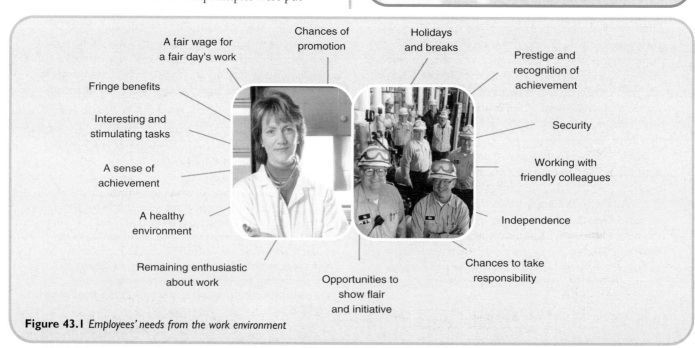

Figure 43.1 *Employees' needs from the work environment*

A fair wage for a fair day's work

Chances of promotion

Holidays and breaks

Prestige and recognition of achievement

Fringe benefits

Interesting and stimulating tasks

Security

A sense of achievement

Working with friendly colleagues

A healthy environment

Independence

Remaining enthusiastic about work

Opportunities to show flair and initiative

Chances to take responsibility

forward which any incentive scheme needed to consider.

- The principle of closure. A job must include all tasks necessary to complete a product or process. This should ensure that work is meaningful for employees and that workers feel a sense of achievement.
- Control and monitoring of tasks. Jobs should be designed so that an army of inspectors is not needed. The worker, or the team, should take responsibility for quality.
- Task variety. There should be an increase in the range of tasks that a worker carries out. This should allow job rotation to occur and keep the workers interested in their work.
- Self-regulation. Employees should have control of the speed at which they work and some choice over work methods and sequence.
- Interaction and co-operation. The job structure should allow some social interaction and the chance for an employee to work in a group.

Various methods were devised to try and put these principles into practice. They included job enrichment, job enlargement, job rotation, quality control circles and employee participation in groups. These are examined later in this unit.

One likely result of poor job design is that employees will not achieve their full potential. This means that the firm's output may suffer as a result. For example, an architect who is constantly having her work checked for accuracy is unlikely to be as productive as possible, due to constant interruptions. Another problem with jobs which do not meet workers' needs is that they are likely to lead to poor motivation, absenteeism and a lack of quality in work.

Job enlargement

JOB ENLARGEMENT involves giving an employee more work to do of a similar nature. For example, instead of an employee putting wheels onto a bicycle he could be allowed to put the entire product together. It is argued that this variety prevents boredom with one repetitive task and encourages employees' satisfaction in their work, as they are completing the entire process.

Critics of this method argue that it is simply giving a worker 'more of the same'. It is often called the problem of **horizontal loading** - instead of turning five screws the worker turns ten! In many businesses today such tasks are carried out more effectively by machines, where repetitive tasks can be completed quickly and efficiently without strain, boredom or dissatisfaction. It could even be argued that allowing employees to complete the entire process will reduce efficiency. This is because the fall in productivity from carrying out many tasks more than offsets any productivity gains from increased worker satisfaction.

Job enlargement is more efficient if workers are organised in groups. Each worker can be trained to do all jobs in the group and **job rotation** can take place. This is discussed in the next section.

Job rotation

JOB ROTATION involves an employee changing jobs or tasks from time to time. This could mean, for example, a move to a different part of the production line to carry out a different task. Alternatively, an employee may be moved from the personnel to the marketing department where they have skills which are common to both. From an employee's point of view this should reduce boredom and enable a variety of skills and experience to be gained. An employer might also benefit from a more widely trained workforce.

Although job rotation may motivate a worker, it is possible that any gains in productivity may be offset by a fall in output as workers learn new jobs and take time to 'settle in'. Worker motivation is not guaranteed if the employee is simply switched from one boring job to another. In fact some workers do not like the uncertainty that job changes lead to and may become dissatisfied. Although used by firms such as Volkswagen in the past, where employees carried out a variety of production tasks, job rotation has been less popular in the last decade.

Team working

The Swedish car firm Volvo is a well quoted example of a company that has effectively introduced 'teamwork'. In both its plants at Kalmar and Uddevalla, it set up production in teams of 8-10 highly skilled workers. The teams decided

---

METALLURGIST ROLLED PRODUCTS

NEWPORT

If you believe that you have the skills, qualifications and personal qualities required to meet the challenge of this role, please write with a full CV and current salary details to Mike Salthouse, Personnel Department, Alcan Rolled Products UK, Castle Works, Rogerstone, Newport, Gwent NP1 9YA.

Based in Newport and part of the Alcan Aluminium Group, Alcan Rolled Products UK is the country's leading producer of aluminium sheet and coil.

As a Metallurgist, you will work within Product and Rolling Process Development. You must have the ability to work closely with production teams and have a thorough knowledge of metallurgy.

Of degree calibre (in a relevant discipline), you must have at least five years' experience of working in a similar role. You ideally have a background in Process Control or Development in hot or cold rolling and possess some Quality Assurance experience. With the ability to communicate effectively at all levels and to work as an active team member, you have the personal influence required to effect change.

Alcan is an equal opportunity company and operates a no smoking policy.

Figure 43.2

(a) Identify elements of the five principles of job design in the post being advertised in Figure 43.2.
(b) Discuss the extent to which job redesign, job enlargement or job rotation is likely to be needed for the person appointed.

Question 2

between themselves how work was to be distributed and how to solve problems that arise. It is arguable whether these practices led to an increase in productivity, but the company firmly believed that this method of organisation was better than an assembly line system. A similar system has been used at Honda UK. TEAM WORKING has a number of benefits.

● Productivity may be greater because of pooled talents.
● People can specialise and draw on the skills and knowledge of others in the team.
● Increasingly businesses are finding that the abilities of teams are needed to solve difficult business problems.
● Responsibility is shared. People may be more prepared to take risks.
● Ideas may be created by brainstorming.
● It allows flexible working.

However, in practice team work does not always produce the desired results. Part of the problem may lie in the way teams are organised. Members may fail to work well together for several reasons, from lack of a sense of humour to clashing goals. Studies of teams in the US have shown a number of problems with team work.

● Too much emphasis on harmony. Teams probably work best when there is room for disagreement. Papering over differences sometimes leads to vague or bland recommendations.
● Too much discord. Tension can destroy team effectiveness.
● Poor preparation. It is important that team members prepare for meetings by focusing on the facts. Members should have a detailed knowledge of the issues at hand and all work with the same information.
● Too much emphasis on individualism. For example, teams failed to deliver results at Apple Computers in the 1980s because of the emphasis the company placed on individualism.
● A feeling of powerlessness. To work well, teams must be able to influence decisions.
● The failure of senior management to work well together. This creates problems because team members may walk into meetings with different priorities.
● Meeting-itis. Teams should not try to do everything together. Too many meetings waste the team's time.
● Seeing teams as the solution for all problems. Some tasks are better accomplished by individuals, rather than groups.

Job enrichment

The idea of JOB ENRICHMENT came from Hertzberg's two factor theory (☞ unit 41). Whereas job enlargement expands the job 'horizontally', job enrichment attempts to give employees greater responsibility by 'vertically' extending their role in the production process. An employee, for example, may be given responsibility for:
● planning a task;
● quality control;
● work supervision;
● ordering materials;

● maintenance.

Job enrichment gives employees a 'challenge', which will develop their 'unused' skills and encourage them to be more productive. The aim is to make workers feel they have been rewarded for their contribution to the company. Employees will also be provided with varied tasks, which may possibly lead to future promotion.

It is not, however, without problems. Workers who feel that they are unable to carry out the 'extra work', or who consider that they are forced into it, may not respond to incentives. In addition, it is unlikely that all workers will react the same to job enrichment. Trade unions sometimes argue that such practices are an attempt to reduce the labour force, and disputes about the payment for extra responsibilities may arise. In practice, job enrichment has been found to be most successful in administrative and technical positions.

Multiskilling

MULTISKILLING is a term used to describe the process of enhancing the skills of employees. It is argued that giving

A major reorganisation at Granada's Meridian subsidiary was expected to result in changes in the operations of employees. Granada agreed to a £6 million investment in Meridian's new headquarters, on the Solent Business Park near the M27, outside Fareham. The new broadcasting centre will be kitted out with the latest production technology, allowing journalists and producers to move from tape-based to a less labour intensive desktop editing system. As a result, Meridian said it expected more multi-skilling, with journalists getting more involved in filming and production. But redundancies are anticipated among editors, camera operators and graphics staff. However, the business also expected to cut jobs, including studio and post production staff, as well as 'backroom' departments such as admin, IT, finance, personnel and sales.

Source: adapted from *The Guardian*, 20.11.2003.

In 2000 it was suggested that in the near future you could order a bespoke home from Wimpey. It would be built in a factory, taken to a site and then put up in a couple of days. Increasingly people with higher incomes were demanding homes that could be changed to suit their specifications. This new way of building homes, in clean, efficient factories instead of dirty, untidy building sites, would attract a new breed of young worker. They would be flexible employees, able to change from one manufacturing task to another, and from manufacturing to building, rather than traditional inflexible workers in old craft skills.

Source: adapted from *The Guardian*, 23.2 2000.

(a) Examine the factors which have led to the need for workers to be multi-skilled in these businesses.
(b) Explain how multi-skilling might affect the stakeholders in these businesses.

Question 3

individuals the skills and responsibilities to deal with a greater variety of issues will allow a business to respond more quickly and effectively to problems. So for example, a receptionist might have been trained to pass on calls to other people in a business. Multiskilling this job could mean that the receptionist now deals with more straightforward enquiries himself. This would result in a quicker response to the customer's enquiry. It would also free up time for other people to work on more demanding activities.

Certain motivation theories suggest that giving individuals more skills and responsibilities can improve their work performance (☞ unit 41). A criticism of multiskilling is that individuals are only given more skills so that they are expected to work harder without any extra pay. Problems may also result if workers are not trained adequately for their new roles.

Quality control circles

QUALITY CONTROL CIRCLES are small groups of workers (about 5-20) in the same area of production who meet regularly to study and solve production problems. In addition, such groups are intended to motivate and involve workers on the shopfloor. Unlike job enlargement and job enrichment, they allow the workforce directly to improve the nature of the work they are doing.

Quality control circles are becoming popular in Britain. They started in America, where it was felt workers could be motivated by being involved in decision making. The idea gained in popularity in Japan and was taken up by Western businesses. Examples of their use can be found in Japanese companies setting up plants in the UK in the 1990s. Honda at Swindon has had 52 teams of six people looking at improvements that can be made in areas allocated to the groups, for example, safety.

Quality control circles are only likely to work if they have the support of both management and employees. Businesses have to want worker participation and involvement in decision making, and set up a structure that supports this. Workers and their representatives also need to support the scheme. Employees must feel that their views within the circle are valued and must make a contribution to decisions.

Empowerment

Unit 40 explained that decisions that were delegated would be more successful if employees were empowered. EMPOWERMENT of employees involves a number of aspects.
- Recognising that employees are capable of doing more than they have in the past.
- Making employees feel trusted, so that they can carry out their jobs without constant checking.
- Giving employees control of decision making.
- Giving employees self confidence.
- Recognising employees' achievements.
- Developing a work environment where employees are

motivated and interested in their work.

Many businesses now recognise the need to empower employees. There is a number of advantages of this for a business and for employees.
- Employees may feel more motivated. This should improve productivity and benefit the business in the long term, for example by reducing absenteeism.
- Employees may find less stress in their work, which could reduce illness and absenteeism.
- Decisions may be made by those most suited to make them.
- There may be greater employee skills and personal development.
- Businesses may be able to streamline their organisations and delegate decision making.

However, empowerment is sometimes criticised as simply a means of cutting costs and removing layers from the business. Passing decision making down the hierarchy might allow a company to make managers redundant. Employees are given more work to do, but for the same pay. Some businesses argue that they want to empower workers, but in practice they are unable or unwilling to do this. For example, a manager may feel insecure about subordinates making decisions that might affect his position in the business. Feeling that they may 'make the wrong decision' might lead to constant interruptions which are counter-productive. A further problem is the cost involved to the business, such as the cost of training employees or changing the workplace.

The problems of job redesign

A business may decide to redesign jobs to increase workers' motivation. The actual process of redesigning existing jobs is often difficult to carry out in practice for a number of reasons.
- Employees' reactions. Employees may be familiar with the old approach to doing a job and may resent new changes. They might not want the extra duties that result from job redesign.
- Employers' views and costs. Job redesign may be expensive. New methods often require extra training. In addition, redesigned jobs might lead employees to claim extra pay for new responsibilities. There is no guarantee that the redesign of jobs will increase productivity in the long term.
- Technology. The introduction of new machinery can make job redesign more difficult. Certain jobs have had to be redesigned almost totally as new technology has changed production processes. In some cases employees have had to learn totally new skills, such as when newspaper page design on computer screens replaced old methods of cutting and pasting type onto pages. At other times skills may be made redundant. When Morgan cars produced their front panels in the late 1980s with machinery instead of their usual 'handmade' techniques, workers were arguably turned from skilled panel makers to non-skilled machine operators.

● Effects on output and productivity. Redesigned jobs need to be evaluated to gauge whether they have actually motivated the workforce to increase output.

Employee involvement schemes in practice

The non-financial methods so far in this unit are examples of EMPLOYEE INVOLVEMENT SCHEMES. They can be categorised according to how involved employees are. For example, in teamworking employees are encouraged to extend the range and type of tasks undertaken at work. Employees are less involved perhaps through quality circles. This is an example of an upward problem solving scheme, designed to tap into employee knowledge and opinion. However, studies seem to indicate that downward communication schemes are more popular. They are designed to inform and educate employees and include informal and formal communication (☞ unit 52). The level of active employee involvement here tends to be minimal.

Surveys have shown that employee involvement schemes have been increasingly used by UK businesses over the last 20 years. But they have had problems. Sometimes they contradict each other and they are rarely part of a human resource strategy. Managers often lack the enthusiasm and commitment and many employers have not given enough time and resources to training supervisors to run them.

Goal setting and management by objectives

Goal setting is part of a more general theory of **management by objectives** (MBO). MBO was put forward by Peter Drucker in 1954 and is covered in unit 44. It suggests that a business should define objectives or targets for an individual to achieve and revise those targets after assessing the performance of the worker.

In 1984 Ed Locke wrote *Goal Setting: A motivational technique that works*. According to Locke, the idea that in order to improve job performance you need to motivate workers by making jobs more satisfying is wrong. He argued that satisfaction comes from achieving specific **goals**. In addition, the harder these goals are, the greater the effort and satisfaction. His message was for businesses to set specific goals that people can achieve and that have been negotiated. 'Do your best', he argued, is not specific. Employees must also have feedback on the progress they are making and then they will perform. The assumption behind the theory is that people will do what they say they will do, and then will strive hard to do it.

Organisation behaviour modification

Businesses have used the theory of organisation behaviour modification (OBMod) with management by objectives when motivating employees. OBMod assumes that workers'

behaviour is determined by the consequences of their actions. For example, a worker who receives a reward as a result of increasing productivity is likely to work harder. Similarly, workers try to avoid behaving in ways that produce no reward or lead to punishment.

OBMod is based on the work of psychologists such as Thorndike and Skinner, who argue that since we cannot observe people's attitudes we should observe their behaviour. Managers should therefore observe how employees' behaviour is affected by the consequences of their actions. These consequences can be broken down into four categories.
● The employee receives something he likes.
● Something the employee dislikes is taken away.
● Something the employee likes is taken away.
● Something the employee dislikes is given.

The first two categories are known as **reinforcers**, as they lead to an increase in the behaviour that precedes them. If a junior manager gives a good presentation and receives praise (something he likes), then the behaviour that resulted in praise (the good presentation) will be reinforced. This is an example of **positive reinforcement**. If something the employee dislikes is taken away, this is called **negative reinforcement**.

The other two categories are kinds of **punishment**. They tend to reduce the behaviour that precedes them. For example, if a worker is constantly late and is fined (something he dislikes), he may try to reduce the number of times he is late.

Examples of positive reinforcement include:
● employees in Xerox's personnel department being given 'X certificates' to pass to others in the company that they felt deserved reward. Each certificate was redeemable for $25;
● passengers being given coupons on American Airlines which they can pass on to staff who they feel deserve recognition;
● an American factory in Mexico where 15 per cent of the workforce arrived late. Management decided to reward good timekeeping by paying workers two pesos (16 cents at the time) a day extra if they started work early. Lateness fell from 15 per cent to 2 per cent, at little extra cost to the company.

Employee Assistance programmes

Employee Assistance Programmes (EAPs) started in America in the 1940s. They began to appear in the UK in the 1990s. These schemes have been developed to help staff cope with difficulties, such as the loss of someone close or the effects of unemployment on the household. In addition, they are sometimes used to help with dealing with personal internal conflicts inside a business. An EAP usually consists of confidential telephone counselling on an issue for employees and their families, paid for by employers. Employers are aware that life for individual employees is becoming more demanding. They recognise that if they want to motivate employees, they need to provide support services that cater for their more general needs. Sometimes such services are provided directly by employers, but it is more common to use a third-party supplier. Staff can then be assured of privacy and neutrality. Some two million employees in Britain are covered by these schemes. 75 per cent of them

receive the service from a consultancy.

Achieving a work-life balance

Recently there has been a stress on the need for employers to deal with the work-life balance of employees. Life is becoming faster and more complex, but without the support of communities or extended families. It is suggested that unless employers are sympathetic and supportive of employees' external needs, there could be an increase in health related absences such as stress. This could affect the operation and efficiency of the business.

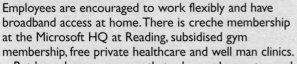

Is Microsoft the best business to work for in the world? Its employees seem to think so. The IT sector is very competitive. So giving financial rewards such as stock options have had to be redesigned. How do you keep the best and brightest when they feel that they have had a pay cut? Microsoft has won accolades for its work-life balance. Employees are encouraged to work flexibly and have broadband access at home. There is creche membership at the Microsoft HQ at Reading, subsidised gym membership, free private healthcare and well man clinics.

But how does a company that asks employees to work such long hours win awards for work-life balance? It's more than just about balancing day to day life. It's about choice. Workers are empowered to make choices about when they work and what they do, and they are listened to. An attempt to take away fuel cards from employees and get them to pay on their own cards was scrapped within half an hour after negative feedback. Openness is a recurrent theme, as is trust. Employees can work where and when they want to as long as they keep the schedule up to date.

Source: adapted from *People Management*, 12.6.2003.

(a) Explain why employees might be motivated at Microsoft.
(b) Examine the possible problems of such an approach for the business.

Question 4

key terms

Employee involvement schemes - systems used to motivate employees through their participation in decision making of the business.
Empowerment - to give official authority to employees to make decisions and control their own activities.
Job design (redesign) - changing the tasks and activities of a job, perhaps in an attempt to motivate workers.
Job enlargement - giving an employee more work to do of a similar nature.
Job enrichment - an attempt to give employees greater responsibility and recognition by 'vertically' extending their role in the production process.
Job rotation - the changing of jobs or tasks from time to time.
Multiskilling - the processes of enhancing the skills of employees.
Teamworking - Employees working in small groups with a common aim.
Quality control circles - small groups of workers in the same area of production which meet regularly to study and solve all types of production problems.

Knowledge ...Knowledge...Knowledge...Knowledge...Knowledge...Knowledge...Kno

1. State 5 possible non-financial rewards that may be an incentive for individuals.
2. What principles would a 'good' job have according to the 'Quality of Working Life Movement'?
3. State 4 methods of job redesign.
4. 'Job enlargement is simply a method of horizontal loading.' Explain this statement.
5. Under what circumstances might job rotation not lead to an increase in productivity?
6. Suggest 4 problems of working in teams.

7. Why is job enrichment said to extend an employee's role in the firm vertically?
8. What are the advantages to an employee of quality control circles?
9. State 3 features of empowerment.
10. Show, using an example, how positive reinforcement can motivate a worker.
11. Why might a business have an Employee Assistance Programme?
12. What is meant by achieving a work-life balance?

Case study BMW's New Oxford Way

each shift has a 45 minute team talk so that workers can discuss problems and air suggestions and ideas. These ideas have led to changes in practices. For example, a worker in one area of production suggested recycling screws that were being thrown out further down the production line. This led to an increase in supply of 1 million screws. Another suggestion to use rubber instead of foam strips saved thousands of pounds.

The scheme also lets managers and directors work on the production line. So workers and employers work side by side, which has reduced the gulf between them. A manager said 'Wings is saying "here is the empowerment to go and do things".'

Three years on workers appear to have seized the opportunities. 'There is more enthusiasm ... the conversations are no longer negative ... people are better informed and more open ...' said a manager. And the business itself has seen tangible benefits. BMW has implemented over 8,000 staff ideas and production targets in 2002 were exceeded by more than 60 per cent. Changes contributed to savings of more than £6.3 million over a 12 month period.

Source: adapted from *People Management*, 6.11.2003.

BMW is known by many car buyers for its high quality products. When it sold The Rover Group in 2000 it retained the Mini brand. But it knew that the overhaul of the Mini would also require changing practices at its production plant at Cowley in Oxford. The £230 million refit of its Oxford plant by BMW corresponded with the launch of a major change programme - The New Oxford Way.

The central element of the programme was Wings (Working in Groups). It involves hundreds of self-steered teams of between 8 -15 people across manufacturing areas. They were given the power to tackle production problems themselves, when before they would have had to call in other departments. Tasks are also rotated within groups to prevent boredom on the production line.

The focus in the groups is on initiative and self-management rather than being management led. Employees receive external training and coaching in working as part of a team. Heike Schneeweis, HR Director at BMW, said that the setting up of Wings created a turnaround in working practice and behaviour. She argued that the teams 'diminished the power of the traditional hierarchical structure and gave more responsibility to working teams.'

The day to day duties of one member in each team has been halved so that they can concentrate on developing team members and the way teams operate. Every fortnight,

(a) **Suggest examples of:**
   (i) **job rotation;**
   (ii) **job redesign;**
   (iii) **multiskilling;**
   (iv) **job enrichment;**
   which have taken place at BMW. (8 marks)
(b) **What view of motivation is management likely to take about workers at BMW? (8 marks)**
(c) **Explain the benefits of team working at BMW for:**
   (i) **employees;**
   (ii) **the business itself. (12 marks)**
(d) **Discuss to what extent empowerment is necessary for the success of the Wings system. (12 marks)**

What is management?

Unit 3 explained that managers are an important group involved in business activity. It is difficult to define exactly what is meant by 'management'. However, many agree that managers are responsible for 'getting things done' - usually through other people. The term manager may refer to a number of different people within a business. Some job titles include the word manager, such as personnel manager or managing director. Other job holders may also be managers, even though their titles do not say it.

It could be argued that managers:

- act on behalf of the owners - in a company, senior management are accountable to the shareholders;
- set objectives for the organisation, for example, they may decide that a long term objective is to have a greater market share than all of the company's competitors;
- make sure that a business achieves its objectives, by managing others;
- ensure that corporate values (the values of the organisation) are maintained in dealings with other businesses, customers, employees and the general public.

The functions of management

Henri Fayol, the French management theorist, listed a number of **functions** or **elements** of management.

Planning This involves setting objectives and also the strategies, policies, programmes and procedures for achieving them. Planning might be done by line managers who will be responsible for performance. However, advice on planning may also come from staff management who might have expertise in that area, even if they have no line authority. For example, a production manager may carry out workforce planning (☞ unit 45) in the production department, but use the skills of the personnel manager in planning recruitment for vacancies that may arise.

Organising Managers set tasks which need to be performed if the business is to achieve its objectives. Jobs need to be organised within sections or departments and authority needs to be **delegated** so that jobs are carried out. For example, the goal of a manufacturing company may be to produce quality goods that will be delivered to customers on time. The tasks, such as manufacturing, packaging, administration, etc. that are part of producing and distributing the goods, need to be organised to achieve this goal.

Commanding This involves giving instructions to subordinates to carry out tasks. The manager has the authority to make decisions and the responsibility to see tasks are carried out.

Sibelius produces the number one selling system for writing music on computers. It was started by two brothers - Ben and Jonathan Finn. In 2001 Jeremy Silver joined and spent his first three months developing a three year plan. Perhaps as a result, in 2002 he was appointed chief executive and amalgamated the London and Cambridge offices of the business in London. He realised he had to tread carefully, saying 'You have to be sensitive because you can't come into a business that has been in operation for nine years and make radical transformations overnight.' Having gained the confidence of the owners, Jeremy had to win over the staff. He felt that he needed to be seen to make changes which would benefit both staff and the owners.

The relocation he had pushed for went a long way to solving the communication problems that existed between the two sites, along with changes in internal communication systems. He said 'When I started here I spent time with everybody individually. I did that very systematically, fixing slots with every member of staff. There is an all company meeting every Monday at 10am and we have an open door policy which ensures that people can just walk into your office and talk to you.' Bringing the US office in line has been a little more tricky. The staff there are not used to communicating so much with head office. But he hopes to solve this problem by spending more time in the US. The business has also started pension and health care schemes to tell employees 'We believe in you'.

Source: adapted from *People Management*, 7.8.2003.

(a) Explain the functions of management that Jeremy Silver might have carried out at Sibelius.
(b) Examine the possible benefits for the business.

Question 1

Co-ordinating This is the bringing together of the activities of people within the business. Individuals and groups will have their own goals, which may be different to those of the business and each other. Management must make sure that there is a common approach, so that the company's goals are achieved.

Controlling Managers measure and correct the activities of individuals and groups, to make sure that their performance fits in with plans.

Management by objectives

Peter Drucker worked in the 1940s and 1950s as a business adviser to a number of US firms. He is credited with the idea of MANAGEMENT BY OBJECTIVES (MBO) from his book *The Practice of Management* (1955). Drucker grouped the operations of management into five categories.

- Setting objectives (☞ unit 4) for the organisation. Managers decide what the objectives of the business should be. These objectives are then organised into targets.

Managers inform others of these targets.

- Organising the work. The work to be done in the organisation must be divided into manageable activities and jobs. The jobs must be integrated into the formal organisational structure (☞ unit 40) and people must be selected to do the jobs (☞ unit 47).

- Motivating employees (☞ unit 41) and communicating information (☞ unit 52) to enable employees to carry out their tasks.

- Job measurement. It is the task of management to establish objectives or yardsticks of performance for every person in the organisation. They must also analyse actual performance and compare it with the yardstick that has been set. Finally, they should communicate the findings and explain their significance to others in the business.

- Developing people. The manager should bring out the talent in people.

Drucker's MBO approach suggests that employees and employers need to work to shared objectives based on the **mission statement** and corporate aims of the business (☞ unit 4). If they didn't, different sections of a business might work differently. For example, the marketing department may want to develop and launch a new product that might need additional production capability. At the same time the production department may be looking to save costs by closing down parts of the manufacturing plant.

Drucker argued that businesses need to:
- set out their clear objectives;
- make plans that would enable those objectives to be realised;
- implement those plans;
- monitor and evaluate whether the objectives had been achieved.

Objectives must be SMART - specific, measurable, agreed, realistic and time specific (☞ unit 4).

Businesses that make use of MBO must take into account that employees can be involved in many different functions and levels. Once corporate objectives have been set by senior managers, managers within functional areas must plan exactly how they can be achieved. This will mean setting objectives for groups and individuals further down the hierarchy. This process can be used by a business to appraise the performance of employees against objectives (☞ unit 4). A business can then reward employees with bonuses or other methods for achieving objectives. This should help to motivate workers, as long as the objectives to be achieved are clear and understood by employees.

Advantages and disadvantages of MBO

There are some advantages with management by objectives.
- Employees can be motivated to perform at improved levels once clear objectives have agreed between them and their line managers.
- Because employees and managers know their objectives

they will work to a single purpose.
- Objectives and plans can be co-ordinated throughout the organisation. This means that different business functions should not pull in different directions and frustrate each others' work
- MBO helps senior managers to have a much clearer system of controlling the direction and performance of the business.

Although there a many potential advantages to MBO, there may be problems.

- MBO may be unresponsive to changing conditions. The time involved in setting the mission statement, corporate objectives and other objectives might result in a dated plan and implementation process. As a result managers may not be responding to new challenges because they are following a plan developed some time ago.

- MBO assumes that all people in a business have the same goals and concerns. However, there is evidence that people have different approaches to work. A young enthusiastic manager developed through a company's graduate training programme may have an optimistic and go getting approach to work. A long standing employee who sees work as being a means to enjoying other things in life and who has been passed over for promotion may be more cynical about the objectives set by management.

- In the 1990s Drucker himself suggested that MBO only works if you know the objectives clearly. But he also suggested that many businesses may not.

Kaplin Price is a furniture manufacturer. It is increasingly facing stiff competition from abroad, but is not certain how best to react to this. Should it expand rapidly? Or should it rationalise to some extent? What would happen if it differentiated its products in some way from those of its competitors? Unless it makes a decision soon, it might find that its costs have escalated and it may be forced to shut down.

It has also experienced difficulties with its internal organisation. Last year it attempted to launch a new range of products with the intention of expanding its market share. It was not clear exactly what share it wanted to achieve, just that it wanted sales to grow. It set in place an incentive system for its sales representatives. Those that reached a certain target of sales would receive a bonus. However, it did not explain to the reps exactly what the target would be. This meant that they lacked motivation and whether they should be paid the bonus or not was decided by managers with a 'gut feeling' about individuals if there had been improved sales from the whole team.

(a) Using examples, examine ways in which adopting an MBO approach might solve the difficulties faced by Kaplin Price.

Question 2

Being a manager

In contrast with Fayol or Drucker, **Charles Handy** argued that any definition of a manager is likely to be so broad it will have little or no meaning. Instead he outlined what is likely to be involved in 'being a manager'.

The manager as a general practitioner Handy made an analogy between managing and staying 'healthy'. If there are 'health problems' in business, the manager needs to identify the symptoms. These could include low productivity, high labour turnover or industrial relations problems. Once the symptoms have been identified, the manager needs to find the cause of trouble and develop a strategy for 'better health'. Strategies for health might include changing people, through hiring and firing, reassignments, training, pay increases or counselling. A manager might also restructure work through job redesign, job enrichment (☞ unit 43) and a redefinition of roles. Systems can also be improved. These can include communication systems, reward systems, information and reporting systems budgets and other decision making systems, eg stock control.

Managerial dilemmas Handy argued that managers face dilemmas. One of the reasons sometimes given for why managers are paid more than workers is because of the dilemmas they face.
● The dilemma of cultures. When managers are promoted or move to other parts of the business, they have to behave in ways which are suitable for the new position. For example, at the senior management level, managers may deal more with long term strategy and delegate lower level tasks to middle management more often. If a promoted manager maintains a 'culture' that she is used to, which may mean taking responsibility for all tasks, she may not be effective in her new position.
● The trust-control dilemma. Managers may want to control the work for which they are responsible. However, they may have to delegate work to subordinates, trusting them to do the work properly. The greater the trust a manager has in subordinates, the less control she retains for herself. Retaining control could mean a lack of trust.
● The commando leader's dilemma. In many firms, junior managers often want to work in project teams, with a clear task or objective. This can mean working 'outside' the normal bureaucratic structure of a larger organisation. Unfortunately, there can be too many project groups (or 'commando groups') for the good of the business. The manager must decide how many project groups she should create to satisfy the needs of her subordinates and how much bureaucratic structure to retain.

The manager as a person Management has developed into a profession and managers expect to be rewarded for their professional skills. Managers must, therefore, continue to develop these skills and sell them to the highest bidder.

Managerial roles

Henry Mintzberg suggested that, as well as carrying out certain functions, the manager also fulfils certain roles in a firm. He identified three types of role which a manager must play.
● Interpersonal roles. These arise from the manager's formal authority. Managers have a **figurehead** role. For example, a large part of a chief executive's time is spent representing the company at dinners, conferences etc. They also have a **leader** role. This involves hiring, firing and training staff, motivating employees etc. Thirdly, they have a **liaison** role. Some managers spend up to half their time meeting with other managers. They do this because they need to know what is happening in other departments. Senior managers spend a great deal of time with people outside the business. Mintzberg says that these contacts build up an informal information system, and are a means of extending influence both within and outside the business.
● Information roles. Managers act as channels of information from one department to another. They are in a position to do this because of their contacts.
● Decision making roles. The manager's formal authority and access to information means that no one else is in a better position to take decisions about a department's work.
   Through extensive research and observation of what managers actually do, Mintzberg drew certain conclusions about the work of managers.
● The idea that a manager is a 'systematic' planner is a myth. Planning is often carried out on a day-to-day basis, in between more urgent tasks.
● Another myth is that a manager has no regular or routine duties, as these have been delegated to others. Mintzberg found that managers perform a number of routine duties, particularly 'ceremonial' tasks.
● Mintzberg's research showed that managers prefer verbal communication rather than a formal system of communication (☞ unit 52). Information passed by word of mouth in an informal way is likely to be more up to date and easier to grasp.

Leadership

The ability to lead within organisations is of growing interest to businesses. This has resulted from the need to lead companies through change, brought about by an increase in competition and changes in technology and economic conditions.

   Earlier in this unit it was shown that a manager might have a leadership **role**. To be a good leader in business it has been suggested that a manager must know what direction needs to be taken by the business and plan how to achieve this. Leaders will also be able to persuade others that the decisions that they have taken are the correct ones.

   Leaders are often thought to be charismatic people who have 'something about them' that makes them stand out from others. It has been argued that there are certain personality traits that are common to leaders. However, studies have failed to prove this is the case.

In order to identify 'leadership', studies have shifted to examine what leaders, and in particular managers, do - that is, what behaviour is associated with leadership. This is dealt with in the next sections.

The qualities of leadership

One approach to finding out what makes good leaders is to identify the qualities that they should have. A number of **characteristics** have been suggested.

- Effective leaders have a positive self image, backed up with a genuine ability and realistic aspirations. This is shown in the confidence they have. An example in UK industry might be Richard Branson, in his various pioneering business activities. Leaders also appreciate their own strengths and weaknesses. It is argued that many managers fail to lead because they often get bogged down in short term activity.

- Leaders need to be able to get to the 'core' of a problem and have the vision and commitment to suggest radical solutions. Sir John Harvey-Jones took ICI to £1 billion profit by stirring up what had become a 'sleeping giant'. Many awkward questions were raised about the validity of the way things were done, and the changes led to new and more profitable businesses on a worldwide scale for the firm.

- Studies of leaders in business suggest that they are expert in a particular field and well read in everything else. They tend to be 'out of the ordinary', intelligent, and articulate. Examples might be Anita Roddick, the founder of Body Shop or Bill Gates, the founder of Microsoft.

- Leaders are often creative and innovative. They tend to seek new ideas to problems, make sure that important things are done and try to improve standards. One example might have been the restructuring of BHS by David Dworkin. He reorganised the business so that stock did not remain on the shelves until it sold at full price. The price of slow selling stock was cut immediately to get rid of it and new stock brought in.

- Leaders often have the ability to sense change and can respond to it. A leader, for example, may be able to predict a decline of sales in an important product or the likelihood of a new production technique being available in the future.

One of the key leadership issues after the year 2000 is likely to be how to deal with international markets and globalisation. Leaders may face challenges such as:

- international recruitment to overcome domestic staff shortages;
- cross-border mergers, acquisitions and joint ventures;
- the opening of new markets in Eastern Europe, South East Asia and China;
- European social policy directives, affecting business in member countries;
- developments in information and communications technology.

Chris Mallard is business unit manager for one of Timkin Desford's two steel businesses which make components for the automotive industry. He inherited a business in pain, with a lack of investment, worried owners and an industry with problems. The workforce seemed to have been living in the shadow of closure forever.

Mallard had to achieve a 40 per cent reduction in costs in 18 months for the business to survive. One solution was to change the manufacturing process. It would involve redesigning processes, setting tasks and using appropriate controls. But he felt that this was just the traditional way of doing things. So forced himself to look at the problems of the business though fresh eyes. 'The real task was gaining trust and changing people's mindsets' he said. As a result he developed a plan called 'constant communication'. It relied on people talking, arguing, questioning and reflecting, and then talking some more. It was uncomfortable and not what people expected. He also took a higher profile and had to keep reminding himself that disagreement doesn't have to mean conflict.

Eventually people got used to the system. They developed faith in the proposals and the results were that targets were met ahead of schedule and there was a rejuvenated workforce. He said 'It was tough and I felt I was constantly going against the flow' but that it could not have been done any other way.

Source: adapted from *People Management*, 28.6.2001.

(a) Examine the leadership characteristics shown at Timkin Desford.

Question 3

Leadership styles

Another approach is to examine different styles of leadership. There is a number of styles that managers might adopt in the work setting.

Autocratic An AUTOCRATIC leadership style is one where the manager sets objectives, allocates tasks, and insists on obedience. Therefore the group become dependent on him or her. The result of this style is that members of the group are often dissatisfied with the leader. This results in little cohesion, the need for high levels of supervision, and poor levels of motivation amongst employees.

Autocratic leadership may be needed in certain circumstances. For example, in the armed forces there may be a need to move troops quickly and for orders to be obeyed instantly.

Democratic A DEMOCRATIC leadership style encourages

participation in decision making. Democratic leadership styles can be persuasive or consultative.

● Persuasive. This is where a leader has already made a decision, but takes the time to persuade others that it is a good idea. For example, the owner of a business may decide to employ outside staff for certain jobs and persuade existing staff that this may ease their work load.

● Consultative. This is where a leader consults others about their views before making a decision. The decision will take into account these views. For example, the views of the marketing department about whether to launch a new range of products may be considered.

Democratic leadership styles need good communication skills. The leaders must be able to explain ideas clearly to employees and understand feedback they receive (☞ unit 52). It may mean, however, that decisions take a long time to be reached as lengthy consultation can take place.

It has been suggested that a democratic style of leadership may be more effective in business for a number of reasons.

● There has been increased public participation in social and political life. Democratic management reflects this trend.

● Increasing income and educational standards means that people now expect greater freedom and a better quality of working life.

● Research suggests that this style is generally more effective. Managers are able to 'tap into' the ideas of people with knowledge and experience. This can lead to better decisions being made.

● People involved in the decision making process are likely to be more committed and motivated, to accept decisions reached with their help, to trust managers who make the decisions and to volunteer new and creative ideas.

Paternalistic PATERNALISTIC leaders are similar to autocratic leaders. They make all the decisions and expect subordinates to obey these decisions. However, whereas an autocratic leader may be uninterested in the well being of subordinates, a paternalistic leader places a great deal of importance on their welfare. In the past there have been number of paternalistic leaders, such as Joseph Rowntree and George Cadbury. Examples of their concern for employees included the building of new houses which they could rent at low rates. As with autocratic leaders, paternalistic leaders do not give subordinates control over decision making.

Laissez- faire A LAISSEZ-FAIRE type of leadership style allows employees to carry out activities freely within broad limits. The result is a relaxed atmosphere, but one where there are few guidelines and directions. This can sometimes result in poor productivity and lack of motivation as employees have little incentive to work hard.

Team-based leadership

The growth of flatter and matrix style structures,

empowerment, job redesign and team working has affected the type of leadership that managers might use in a business. Managers are more likely today to organise and co-ordinate the workings of a variety of employees at different levels, in different functions and with different skills. In a sense they have become **team-based leaders**.

Traditional approaches to leadership and management that are linked to authority, status and power are likely to be of limited use to team based leaders. Team leaders are less likely to be individuals who give orders and have a clear understanding of exactly how a task is to be done than people who:

● have the the ability to bring together the right blend of workers to allow business problems to be solved and action implemented;

● can motivate staff in the team to problem solve and accomplish a task;

● know and understand corporate objectives;

● know what resources are available to implement actions to achieve objectives;

● evaluate a team and decide if the task has been carried out.

Team-based leadership often happens in businesses where the idea and use of a hierarchy is less relevant. This may happen, for example, in a SINGLE STATUS organisation

---

John Timpson is chief executive of the 320 strong chain of key cutting and shoe repair outlets. The business has doubled its sales to £48 million and tripled profits to £3.5 million over the past six years. He believes the business he runs now is on far better shape than ever.

This might in part be due to his somewhat unconventional management style. He is a keen advocate of upside-down management. He works hard to make sure that stores remain the focus of the business, constantly visiting and encouraging staff to take responsibility for their own outlets. 'It's the only way you can run this business,' he says. 'Don't you get fed up when you go into a shop and they say 'I can't do that or I'll have to check with the area manager.'

Timpson states 'I've put a notice up in the shops which says that the staff have got my authority to do whatever they want to give you amazing service. They can spend up to £500 without authorisation to settle complaints. There's not much I can do to help customers walking into our Dumfries or Plymouth shop right now.'

The relationship is based on trust. Despite the stores dealing primarily in cash, theft isn't an issue. Employees can write to complain without fear of reprisals. Branch staff are also consulted about any major policy changes.

Source: adapted from *en*, June 2001.

(a) Using information from the article, explain the leadership approaches at Timpson.
(b) Suggest implications for the business of these approaches.

Question 4

where every worker is treated the same. They have the same facilities, same dress codes and same terms and conditions of employment. Every worker is made to feel as if they are an important part of the organisation.

Factors affecting leadership styles and approaches

The type of leadership style adopted by managers will depend on various factors.

- The task. A certain task may be the result of an emergency, which might need immediate response from a person in authority. The speed of decision needed and action taken may require an authoritarian or autocratic style of leadership.
- The tradition of the organisation. A business may develop its own culture which is the result of the interactions of all employees at different levels. This can result in one type of leadership style, because of a pattern of behaviour that has developed in the organisation. For example, in the public sector (☞ unit 7) leadership is often democratic because of the need to consult with politicians etc.
- The type of labour force. A more highly skilled workforce might be most productive when their opinions are sought. Democratic leadership styles may be more appropriate in this case.
- The group size. Democratic leadership styles can lead to confusion the greater the size of the group.
- The leader's personality. The personality of one manager may be different to another manager and certain leadership styles might suit one but not the other. For example, an aggressive, competitive personality may be more suited to an authoritarian leadership style.
- Group personality. Some people prefer to be directed rather than contribute, either because of lack of interest, previous experience, or because they believe that the manager is paid to take decisions and shoulder responsibility. If this is the case, then an autocratic leadership style is more likely to lead to effective decision making.
- Time. The time available to complete a task might influence the leadership style adopted. For example, if a project has to be finished quickly, there may be no time for discussion and an autocratic style may be adopted.

Why do leaders adopt different styles?

A number of theories have been put forward to explain the most appropriate leadership style when dealing with certain situations or groups at work.

Fiedler In 1976, F. Fiedler argued that 'it is easier to change someone's role or power, or to modify the job he has to do, than to change his leadership style'. From his 800 studies he found that it is difficult for people to change leadership styles - an 'autocrat' will always lead in autocratic style whereas a

leader that encourages involvement will tend to be 'democratic'. Different leadership styles may also be effective depending on the situation. He concluded that, as leaders are unable to adapt their style to a situation, effectiveness can only be achieved by changing the manager to 'fit' the situation or by altering the situation to fit the manager.

In business it is often difficult to change the situation. Fiedler suggested that a business should attempt what he called **leadership match** - to choose a leader to fit the situation. Leaders can be either **task orientated** or **relationship orientated**. So, for example, a business that faced declining sales might need a very task orientated manager to pull the business around, even if the tradition of the firm might be for a more democratic style of leadership.

Hersey and Blanchard P. Hersey and K.H. Blanchard argued that a leader's strategy should not only take account of the situation, but also the maturity of those who are led. They defined maturity as the ability of people to set targets which can be achieved and yet are demanding.

A leader will have **task behaviour or relationship behaviour**. Task behaviour is the extent to which the leader has to organise what a subordinate should do. Relationship behaviour describes how much support is needed and how close personal contact is. Together these will decide which of the following leadership styles will be used.

- **Delegating** leadership is where a leader allows subordinates to solve a problem. For this type of leadership style to work, subordinates need to be mature and require little support at work.
- **Participating** leadership is where a leader and subordinates work on a problem together, supporting each other. In this situation subordinates are slightly less mature than when a leader delegates and so need more support.
- **Selling** leadership is where a leader persuades others of the benefits of an idea. Workers are likely to be only moderately mature and require a great deal of support.
- **Telling** leadership is where a leader tells others what to do. Workers are fairly immature. They are told exactly what to do and little contact or support is needed.

Wright and Taylor In 1984, P. Wright and D. Taylor argued that theories which concentrate on the situation or maturity of those led ignore how skillfully leadership is carried out. They produced a checklist designed to help leaders improve the performance of subordinates. It included the following.

- What is the problem? An employee may, for example, be carrying out a task inefficiently.
- Is it serious enough to spend time on? This could depend on the cost to the business.
- What reasons may there be for the problem? How can it be solved? These are shown in Table 44.1.
- Choosing a solution and evaluating if it is the most effective one.
- Evaluation of the leader's performance.

Table 44.1

Possible reasons for performance problem	Possible solutions
Is the person fully aware of the job requirements?	Give guidance concerning expected goals and standards. Set targets.
Does the person have the ability to do the job well?	Provide formal training, on the job coaching, practice, etc.
Does the person find the task rewarding in itself?	Simplify task, reduce work load, reduce time pressures, etc.
Is good performance rewarded by others?	Reward good performance and penalise poor performance.
Does the person receive adequate feedback about performance?	Provide or arrange feedback.
Does the person have the resources and authority to do the task?	Provide staff, equipment, raw materials; delegate if necessary.
Do working conditions interfere with performance?	Improve lighting, noise, heat, layout; remove distractions etc.

This can be used to identify the most suitable leadership style in a particular situation. For example, if the problem above is caused because the employee has been left to make his own decisions and is not able to, a more autocratic leadership style may be needed. On the other hand, if the employee lacks motivation or does not have the authority to make decisions, greater discussion or delegation may be needed.

Theory X and Theory Y

The views which managers and leaders have about workers can affect management and leadership styles. If workers are seen as lazy and motivated only by money (called Theory X workers by McGregor, ☞ unit 41) they will need to be controlled and given financial incentives. Theory Y workers are likely to be motivated by many factors. Such workers may repond to a more democratic leadership style and be given more responsibility and authority.

Criticisms of a leadership approach

The media often suggests that 'heroic' leaders are vital to making a successful business. Such leaders make things happen. They are heroes because they alone have the vision, personality and capability to bring things about in the business, either by themselves or through others.

Although not denying that leaders have special qualities, it could be argued that focusing too much on leadership can create problems. For example, this approach may lead to the conclusion that a business without a heroic leader may not be able to function properly. Or it might suggest that the heroic leader is the most important thing to organisational

effectiveness. It also perhaps devalues the role and importance of other employees.

There is evidence to suggest that effective businesses are those which are more concerned with the creativity of their products and organisational structures that enable those products to be produced and sold than those that rely heavily on leadership. It could be argued that the ability to team work, delegate and manage others effectively is more important in the daily workings of creative organisations than the attributes of heroic leadership, such as vision, command and personality.

key terms

Autocratic leadership - a leadership style where the leader makes all decisions independently.
Democratic leadership - a leadership style where the leader encourages others to participate in decision making.
Laissez-faire leadership - a leadership style where employees are encouraged to make their own decisions, within limits.
Management by Objectives (MBO) - a management theory which suggests that managers set goals and communicate them to subordinates.
Paternalistic leadership - a leadership style where the leader makes decisions, but takes into account the welfare of employees.
Single status organisation - a business where all employees have equal conditions.

Knowledge

1. State 5 functions of management.
2. Briefly explain the process of management by objectives.
3. Give 3 examples of a managerial dilemma.
4. Why might a good manager not always be a good leader?
5. Briefly explain 5 qualities of leadership.
6. State 6 factors which might affect the choice of leadership style.
7. According to Fiedler's theory, why should a business attempt a leadership match?

Case study Boots Contract Manufacturing (BCM)

Boots Contract Manufacturing (BCM) is the manufacturing department of the Boots Company. The organisation is known for its strong, safe brands and traditional paternalistic leadership and management structures. In 2000 it decided to shake up its leadership style. 160 managers were taken to the exclusive resort of Chamonix in the Alps as part of a leadership development programme. The business was adamant that the change in style should be radical and genuinely change the leadership of the company. It aimed to break down functional boundaries and develop a more flexible and creative approach for the 21st century.

Source: adapted from *People Management*, 2.5.2002.

The Chamonix leadership development programme was created by training consultancy Apter. Commentators have suggested that 'Traditional structures and processes cannot keep up with the level of change that companies like Boots are going through' and that 'There's this immense sense that they're chasing the light on the horizon and its moving away from them.'

Source: adapted from *People Management*, 2.5.2002.

In 2000 BCM made 3000 staff redundant as a result of trading difficulties. The Organisation Development Manager at BCM said 'The executive knew that we were going to have to get the business back up and running again. And yes it was partly about morale. But it was also about bringing something new to the way people worked'.

Source: adapted from *People Management*, 2.5.2002.

(a) **Outline the features of the leadership style traditionally found at BCM. (8 marks)**
(b) **Examine the reasons for the change in leadership style at BCM. (12 marks)**
(c) (i) **Using examples from the information, suggest a possible leadership style that BCM might use. (8 marks)**
   (ii) **Discuss whether the benefits of this style will outweigh the costs. (12 marks)**

Part of the leadership course in the Alps involved responding to risk and changing what was thought to be possible. The company wanted leaders to take more responsibility for their actions rather than hide in a culture of permission.

Source: adapted from *People Management*, 2.5.2002.

A study by David Burnham from the Burnham Rosen Group which supports business leaders looked at the relationship between leadership style and employee morale. Figure 44.1 shows the results. It shows the extent to which employees feel that they take responsibility, they have team spirit, there is organisational clarity and are effectively rewarded under different leadership styles. These include:
- institutional leaders who see themselves as the source of power - leadership was something they do to others;
- interactive leaders who derive power from others such as the teams, groups and organisations which they lead.

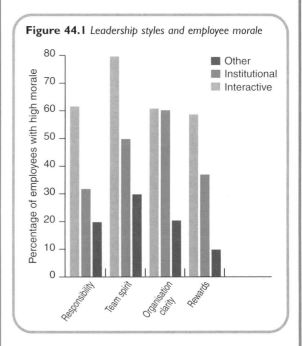

Figure 44.1 *Leadership styles and employee morale*

Source: adapted from *People Management*, 3.4.2003.

45 Workforce Planning

The work of the personnel department

Many large and medium sized businesses today have a personnel department. Its main role will be to manage the firm's HUMAN RESOURCES. These are the employees or personnel in a business that help it to achieve its objectives. They might include production workers, office staff, members of the marketing team, accountants or cleaners.

The personnel department will deal with many factors associated with employees. These include:

- human resources or workforce planning;
- recruitment and selection;
- induction and training;
- promotion and transfers;
- appraisal and termination of employment;
- discipline;
- rewards and conditions of employment;
- working conditions;
- career development and welfare;
- wage bargaining.

What is human resources planning?

HUMAN RESOURCES PLANNING or WORKFORCE PLANNING is the method by which a business forecasts how many and what type of employees it needs now and in future. It also involves matching up the right type of employees to the needs of the business. A business will work out its labour requirements, its **demand**, and make sure that an appropriate **supply** is planned. For example, a growing business, such as a call centre, might find that it needs an extra 20 telephone operators over the next year. It may, therefore, plan to recruit an extra 20 operators over the period. An engineering business that loses a large order for parts may plan to make 50 workers redundant.

The HUMAN RESOURCES or WORKFORCE PLAN is usually one of the responsibilities of the personnel or human resources department and is one part of **human resources management**. It is also linked to the plans of the organisation. For example, when two accounting businesses, Cooper & Lybrand and Price Waterhouse, planned to merge they anticipated a growing demand for accounting skills, particularly in areas such as Eastern Europe, Latin America and China, and felt that the combined firm would be better able to cope. The companies planned to take on an extra 1,000 employees a week worldwide as a result. If staff were not used in one country, they would be deployed elsewhere.

The steps that a business takes when planning its workforce are shown in Figure 45.1. So:

Change in demand for workers = workers from within the business + workers from outside the business

Planning can be **short term** or **long term**. Short term planning is aimed at the immediate needs of the business, such as filling vacancies left, say, as a result of maternity leave. Long term planning will try to plan for the future. For example, if a company was aiming to change its production techniques in the next few years, it would need to plan the number of employees, training needed and perhaps the incentives and motivation that workers would require.

Forecasting employee demand

In the future a business may need more workers, less workers

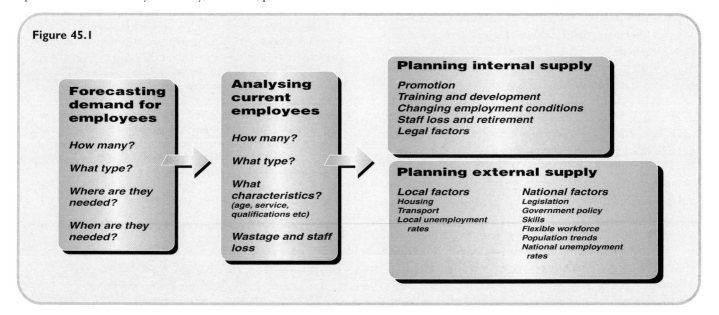

Figure 45.1

Forecasting demand for employees

How many?

What type?

Where are they needed?

When are they needed?

Analysing current employees

How many?

What type?

What characteristics? *(age, service, qualifications etc)*

Wastage and staff loss

Planning internal supply

Promotion
Training and development
Changing employment conditions
Staff loss and retirement
Legal factors

Planning external supply

Local factors
Housing
Transport
Local unemployment rates

National factors
Legislation
Government policy
Skills
Flexible workforce
Population trends
National unemployment rates

or workers with different skills. How might a business predict the workers it needs in future?

Using past information Forecasting techniques allow a business to predict what will happen in future from past figures. Figures collected from years in the past are referred to as **time series** data or **backdata**. So, for example, if a business has had a steady increase in staff of 2 per cent a year over the last five years, it might expect this to continue. However, this method is not very sophisticated. It does not take into account the development of the business that may be outlined in a business plan. It predicts the number of employees required based on previous growth or reduction figures, without considering future plans. A business, for example, may decide to install new machinery, which might reduce the number of employees it needs.

Workers' productivity A manufacturer may employ a total of 50 staff and produce 550 products a week. This means that it has an output per worker of 11 products (550÷50). If it wanted to produce an extra 55 products, it would need to employ an extra 5 staff (55÷11). If output had to be cut to 495 products, only 45 workers would be needed (495÷11). This is a rather simple way of predicting demand. It does not take into account **economies** and **diseconomies** of scale (☞ unit 56). As demand for products increases, a business may be able to raise output by using equipment more efficiently rather than hiring more workers. In addition, an increase in output will have a smaller effect on non-production workers. For example, if the amount of work doubled, support services may only need to increase by 30-50 per cent. Although more technical and production staff may be employed, this may not be matched by an increase in management and office staff.

Work study This allows a business to find the numbers of staff needed to carry out a task efficiently. For example, a business may decide to change its production methods so that all of a product was manufactured in a 'cell' rather than as parts in batches (☞ unit 54). This would mean that workers would work in teams, take responsibility for decisions and have to be multi-skilled. Careful consideration would need to be made of exactly what extra work staff would be doing and whether more or less staff would be needed. Without suitable work studies, a business may over or underestimate the actual number of staff needed to carry out future business plans.

Using business and management knowledge A business may ask experienced managers at all levels for their views on the employees needed in the future. For example, the manager of a large firm of solicitors may know that more part time staff are likely to be needed in the near future as there is a growing number of clients suing others for personal accident compensation. The manager of an advertising agency may predict that staff may be needed for the growing market in internet advertising. The manager of a hotel chain may predict that fewer staff are needed for catering as the demand for conference meals has fallen off.

Calculating staff loss Workers leave their jobs from time to time. They may retire, be promoted, be dismissed, join other businesses, leave to have children or simply resign. If a worker leaves a job then a **vacancy** exists which the business has to fill. One useful indicator of people leaving a business is the **percentage wastage rate** or the **labour turnover index.** This shows the number of employees leaving as a percentage of those who could have left. For example, if a business employing 70 staff finds that 18 left the previous year, the wastage rate or LABOUR TURNOVER is:

$$\frac{\text{Number of staff leaving per period}}{\text{Average number of staff in post during the period}} \times 100 = \frac{18}{70} = 25.7\%$$

This could be used to predict the numbers of employees that may leave in future and the need to employ new workers. Similar predictions may be made about the numbers of employees that are likely to be promoted or to retire.

Many factors might influence the demand by a business for

Ancillary staff working in public services include cleaners, laundry staff and caterers. In the late 1980s research on labour turnover in the NHS revealed an average rate of 45 per cent a year among ancillary staff. In one health authority it was 111 per cent. Privatisation has had a great effect on ancillary workers. In the early 1990s, 98 per cent of care provided by social services in England, such as meals on wheels and personal care, came from local authority in-house workforces. In 2000 just under half did.

The introduction of compulsory competitive tendering (CCT), where local authority services were bid for by private suppliers, saw a great reduction in the number of workers employed. Competition meant the cutting of labour costs and workloads had to be increased.

In 2001 the government announced a near 50 per cent increase in hospital consultants in England over the next decade. Rises in nurses, midwives, GPs and physiotherapists were also promised to help restore the credibility of the service at a time of complaints about waiting lists for consultations and treatment, ward hygiene and quality of life in hospitals. A Department of Health source said 'Increasing the number of staff in training is vital if we are to increase the capacity of the NHS and its ability to deliver faster, better care for patients when and where they need it.'

Source: adapted from *The Guardian*, 9.1.2001 and 15.2.2001.

(a) Examine how demand for staff in the NHS might be estimated.

Question 1

workers. If more products are sold, more workers may need to be employed to increase output. New equipment may require workers with different skills. Labour saving equipment might reduce the need for workers. Businesses that have a high labour turnover might need to employ new workers on a regular basis. Promotion or retirement will also create vacancies. A change in the goals of the business may increase or decrease demand for staff. A business aiming to reduce the layers in its hierarchy may demand fewer workers in future. Changes in production techniques, such as a move from assembly line production to team work or cell production, might mean that fewer or different types of workers are demanded by a business. The latest business theories can also affect demand. The move to teamwork in the 1990s in some businesses may have increased demand for 'team leaders'.

Analysing current employee supply

Once a business has decided on the number and type of employees it needs in future, its next step is to ask: 'how do we ensure that we have the right people at the right time to meet the workforce planning requirements?'

A starting point is for a business to analyse the current position of its employees. This is likely to involve calculating the number of employees working in particular jobs and identifying their category and function. It may also mean gathering information on their age, length of service, qualifications and performance results. For example, a business that wants to employ managers may look at the number of graduates on its staff. A business trying to reduce its workforce by retirement may examine the ages of its employees. Data relating to employee 'flows' through the business, staff loss and how the nature of the present staff is changing are also important. For example, a business that wants to introduce flexible work practices may take into account the number of part time staff it has or the percentage of the business that is made up of teleworkers.

From the analysis of future demand and the current workforce, a business can decide on the number and type of employees that it may plan to recruit **internally** and **externally** in future to achieve its targets (☞ unit 46). It can also decide how it might reduce its existing workforce if necessary. These are discussed in the next sections.

Planning internal employee supply

A business may plan to meet future changes in demand with workers from inside the organisation. It may also plan to reduce its workforce. Whether a business can meet its future workforce requirements from existing employees may depend on a number of factors.

Promotion A business may decide to promote employees from inside the organisation. Some businesses encourage internal promotion (☞ unit 46). The advantage of promoting existing workers is that they already know about the business's practices and culture. They may also be able to adapt more easily to a new job than an outsider. Some workers may also have been 'filling in' temporarily and have experience of the job. Promoting internally would leave a vacancy further down the hierarchy which would need to be filled. This would add costs and time to filling the vacancy.

Staff development and training A business is more likely to be able to find a suitable employee from inside the organisation if it has training and development programmes (☞ unit 49). Training may provide the skills needed to allow an employee to move to a new position. For example, many larger businesses have graduate training programmes which train employees with degrees for management positions. Businesses that have development programmes which identify how workers can improve, appraise workers' abilities and view the development of employees as important, are more likely to employ an internal candidate. If a business needs to reduce its workforce in a particular department it may consider retraining its employees and **redeploying** them to another part of the organisation.

Staff loss and retirement A workforce supply plan should also take into account staff loss and rates of retirement. High rates of labour turnover, as explained earlier, create vacancies. However, they may also lead to large numbers of skilled workers leaving a business which can affect the number of suitable internal candidates for a job. If large numbers of employees are retiring, this may lead to problems when trying to fill senior management posts which require experienced employees. A business may make use of retirement as a means of reducing the workforce if necessary. People can sometimes be encouraged to take 'early retirement', if they are given a financial incentive (☞ unit 48).

Flexibility A business may be able to change its workforce practices and conditions in order to meet its labour supply requirements. For example, a business may change the number of hours that people work in a period. Employees may be asked to work 1,950 hours in a year rather than 37.5 hours a week. This means that a business can have employees in work for longer than 37.5 hours when they are needed at peak times. If a business wants to add extra responsibility to the role of workers it may encourage teamwork or the multiskilling of workers. It may also decide to make new jobs part time or jobs that can be shared by two people in order to increase the flexibility of the business.

Legal factors If a business finds that its demand for workers is likely to fall in future it may decide to make workers redundant. There are legal conditions which affect how and when workers can be made redundant (☞ unit 48). They may also be entitled to redundancy or **severance** payments.

T Hodgson is a shop that specialises in painting and decorating materials. It employs seven full time staff. It also hires three part time staff, usually at weekends. Recently two of its older staff have retired, including its main buyer of specialist paints. It now has to appoint someone with the knowledge to buy in the latest painting materials. It has decided to promote one member of staff who has shown initiative in taking courses at night school. But it is concerned that more training may be necessary. As it has lost a 'shop floor' employee, it must also consider whether to hire more part time workers or make one of its part time workers into a full time employee.

In 2003 Sainsbury's confirmed plans to cut jobs as part of a two-year review of the company's operations. It aimed to cut over 1,000 positions in total, mainly through normal staff turnover, by March 2005. The reduction was expected to generate annual savings of about £20 million, but added 'The process is not about saving money, it is about streamlining the organisation.' Most of the redundancies were to come from the company's supply chain operation and not staff in stores. 350 jobs had already been axed, including 50 in marketing. A spokesperson said that redeployment and natural staff turnover had accounted for another 300 posts, leaving 500 jobs still to be cut. The review is part of a three-year recovery programme launched last year which was designed to make overall savings of £250 million a year.

Source: adapted from *The Guardian*, 13.6.2003.

(a) Explain the ways in which these businesses have met their human resource requirements from their current employees.
(b) Discuss the effects of these methods on:
    (i) the businesses;
    (ii) their employees.

Planning external employee supply

A business may plan to employ workers from outside the organisation. There are local and national factors that have to be taken into account by a business when planning its external employee requirements.

- The availability and price of housing in an area. Some employees may not be able to afford housing in a highly priced area such as London, for example. The availability of new housing on a nearby estate may encourage young families with children to move to an area.
- The ease and availability of public transport. Working at a factory in a remote area may prove difficult for an employee without a car. Areas with efficient rail or bus

links may prove popular for some workers. Possible restrictions or charges on cars in city areas may influence external employee supply in future.
- Competition. The closing or opening of other businesses in an area may either help or hinder external supply of labour. If businesses close there may be more skilled labour from which to choose. New businesses may reduce the availability of skilled workers. However, they are also likely to train workers, so that it may be possible to 'headhunt' required employees more easily (☞ unit 46).
- Unemployment. High rates of unemployment in an area lead to a large supply of workers who are available for work. This increases choice for a business looking to recruit from outside the organisation. High rates of national unemployment may make workers more willing to travel.
- Availability of skills. Specialist skills may be found in particular areas. For example, the area around Stafford, known as the Potteries, traditionally had skilled pottery workers. Some workers made unemployed in shipyard areas such as Tyneside were able to transfer their skills to other related industries when shipyards closed.
- The availability of flexible workers. Many businesses are taking advantage of the use of teleworkers. These are people who are employed to work at home and make use of technology such as the fax and computer to communicate with the business. They work from home which reduces business costs. Some workers are 'employed' by the business, but are not guaranteed work. They are brought in only when required, such as when demand is high. An example might be a delivery firm asking drivers to be 'on call' in case of busy periods. The availability of these workers increases the flexibility of businesses.
- Government training and subsidies. Government funded training and employment schemes subsidise businesses for taking on young workers for a period of time (☞ unit 49). This reduces their cost to a business and allows a 'trial run' of a possible employee.
- Population and demographic trends. Changes in the structure of the population can affect external recruitment (☞ unit 46). In the UK there is a growing number of older workers who are available for work. The increase in the number of women joining or returning to the workforce is also likely to affect the supply plans from outside the organisation.
- Government legislation. There are restrictions on the nature and type of advertisements that can be used when recruiting from outside the business. There are also laws which protect the pay and conditions of workers when they are employed (☞ units 50 and 51).
- Costs. The earnings of workers from outside the business might affect recruitment. Hiring workers on lower wages can reduce costs. The cost of setting up factories or offices to employ workers must also be taken into account and businesses must assess the relative costs of employees in different areas and with different skills.

Seasonal workers employed by Asda at Christmas 2003 would have benefits and job security equivalent to those of full-time colleagues. The new 'seasonal squad' would have the same status as permanent staff, but with a contract to work an annual, rather than weekly, number of hours. The new recruits would be allowed to work for as little as ten weeks of the year. The contracts would cover Christmas, Easter and the school summer holidays. Positions included greeters, porters, checkout operatives and warehouse workers. 'We recognise that people are looking for flexibility across the working year, not just the working week' said Caroline Massingham, Asda retail people director. 'If you're one of the many people that want to balance long periods of leave with a fulfilling job, the options are limited,' she also added.

Asda hoped that more over 50s would be encouraged to join its 22,357 workers in this age group. The supermarket's flexible working package includes one week's leave for new grandparents and up to two years for a career break. It said that since recruiting older workers, it has seen absence levels drop, customer service improve and labour turnover fall.

Source: adapted from *The Guardian*, 24.10.2003.

BT confirmed plans to open two new call centres in India in 2003 that would create more than 2,000 jobs. The centres would be in Delhi and Bangalore. The cost of opening call centres in India is up to 30 per cent cheaper than in the UK. The two new call centres, which will cost around £3 million to set up, will deal with operations such as telephoning people in the UK to remind them to pay their bills. Last summer, HSBC's Indian call centre employees were praised by the company for being more efficient, polite and enthusiastic than their British counterparts.

Research by recruitment business Adecco suggested British companies will create up to 100,000 call centre jobs in India by 2008. This would slash their wage costs and take advantage of a pool of skilled workers, many of them graduates. Once a call centre is set up, the wage bill makes up two-thirds of its operation costs. Indian call centre workers earn about £1,200 a year, less than a tenth of the £12,000 starting salary of an employee in Britain. But there can be problems. Businesses can have difficulties keeping a grip on everyday operations in a centre so far away from their base and there may be quality control issues.

Source: adapted from *The Guardian*, 7.3.2003.

(a) Explain why these situations are examples of planning employee supply from outside the organisation.
(b) Examine the factors that might affect the recruitment of workers from outside the organisation in these situations.

Question 3

key terms

Labour turnover - the number of people that leave a business over a period of time as a percentage of the number of people employed.

Human resources - the employees or personnel in a business which help it to achieve its goals.

Human resources plan or the workforce plan - the suggested quantity, quality and type of employees a business will require in future and how this demand is to be met.

Workforce planning or human resources planning - the process of calculating the number of employees a business needs in the short term and the long term and matching employees to the business's requirements.

Knowledge ...Knowledge...Knowledge...Knowled

1. State 5 tasks that the personnel department may carry out.
2. What are the steps a business takes when planning its workforce?
3. Explain 3 ways that a business might forecast its demand for employees.
4. Suggest 3 reasons why a business may demand more employees.
5. State 3 features of a business's current workforce that it may be interested in analysing.
6. Suggest 5 factors that might affect the possibility of recruiting employees from within the business.
7. Why is labour turnover important to a business?
8. Explain 2 ways in which a business might make itself more flexible.
9. Explain the difference between redeploying workers and retirement as a means of reducing the workforce.
10. Suggest 5 factors that might affect the external supply of workers.

Case study *Stewart and Mathers*

Stewart and Mathers is a solicitor, with offices in Lancashire and London. Its head office is situated in Skelmersdale, a 'new town' created to rehouse the overspill of people moving out of Liverpool in the 1960s as inner city housing was knocked down. Skelmersdale is situated next to the M58 and is a half an hour's drive from the cities of Manchester and Liverpool. The planners decided that:

● high private car usage must be catered for, while still encouraging public transport;
● pedestrians and traffic should be separated in the town centre and residential areas;
● industry should be concentrated in separate, but easily accessible, areas;
● open spaces should be provided, but the housing should be designed to foster a close community atmosphere;
● there must be no urban sprawl, and a clear boundary between town and country;
● the town must try and attract a balanced population structure;
● housing in Skelmersdale was to be high density, but without high rise flats;
● residential areas were to be close to the town centre where most facilities were concentrated.

After the year 2000 the business saw a steady growth in its sales of services. Table 45.1 shows figures relating to the workforce over the period. Stewart and Mathers realised that more cases were being taken out against individuals and companies for accidents which led to personal injury. This mirrored the situation in the USA. Large sums were often paid to employees injured at work, to people who had been hurt in 'road rage' attacks and for complaints against the State for injuries as a result of badly maintained roads or pavements. Most of

Table 45.1

	Sales revenue (£m)	Total employees	Employees leaving
2000	1.1	70	3
2001	1.2	72	4
2002	1.4	75	5
2003	1.6	80	5
2004	2.0	100	6

the decisions in the business were taken by the three partners, two of whom had previous experience of working in other countries. There were 10 people in the business who were 'fee earners'.

The organisation decided that it wanted to expand rapidly to take advantage of growing business in this area. It encouraged its administrative staff lower in the hierarchy to train in law qualifications or take the Institute of Law examination. This would allow them to progress to become a solicitor's assistant. It advertised widely in the local area to fill vacancies and 'headhunted' graduates of the ILEX (Institute of Legal Secretaries) courses at local colleges who had been trained in basic law skills. It would also be able to take advantage of the government's New Deal by employing young workers for a small number of posts.

However, some of its senior management positions needed to be filled quickly and so the business advertised in national magazines and quality newspapers. If necessary it was prepared to subsidise managers for a short time if they were prepared to move to the area immediately. This might mean that they have to leave property unsold in a different part of the country or leave family and work away from home for a period.

(a) **What factors could have affected the promotion of internal employees within the business to higher posts? (6 marks)**
(b) **Explain how the business may have forecast the increased need for employees after the year 2000. (10 marks)**
(c) (i) **Calculate the labour turnover of the business over the period. (4 marks)**
   (ii) **Examine the possible effects of changes in labour turnover on the business. (10 marks)**
(d) **To what extent might the business be able to recruit workers from outside the organisation for:**
   (i) **jobs at the base of the hierarchy;**
   (ii) **managerial jobs? (10 marks)**

The need for effective recruitment

This unit concentrates on the first stage in the management of human resources - recruitment. The personnel department will aim to attract the 'best' candidates for the job and then to choose the most suitable. If the wrong person is recruited, this can cause problems for a business. The person appointed may find the job boring or too difficult, which could lead to a lack of motivation and poor productivity. If the person leaves, there will be administration costs for the personnel department. The business will face the extra costs of advertising, interviewing and training. There will also be a settling in period until the new employee has learned the job.

Employing a suitable person should allow the business to get the most out of its human resoources. In addition, recruiting the best employees may give a business a competitive edge over rivals (☞ unit 5). To make sure the 'best' person is chosen, businesses must be clear about:
- what the job entails;
- what qualities are required to do the job;
- what rewards are needed to retain and motivate employees.

Recruitment is becoming more and more important in business. This is especially the case where employees need to be flexible or work autonomously, or where direct control over workers is difficult.

Job analysis

Before a business recruits new employees, the personnel department usually carries out some form of JOB ANALYSIS. Job analysis is a study of what a job entails. It contains the skills, training and tasks that are needed to carry out the job.

Job analysis can be used by firms in many ways. These include selecting employees, setting pay, disciplinary interviews, promotion and job appraisal (dealt with later in this unit). For example, if a firm was trying to choose an applicant for the post of systems analyst, it may use job analysis to find out exactly what a systems analyst does in that firm.

In order to find out about what is involved in a job, the personnel department must gather data about all the different elements in that job. It is likely that people associated with the job will have different views about what is involved.
- The occupant of the job. She will have the most detailed knowledge of what the job requires. However, she might change the information to exaggerate her own status, or leave parts of the job out because they are taken for granted.
- The job holder's superior. She will have her own view of what the job involves, but is unlikely to be fully aware of all job details.
- Subordinates and others with whom the job holder is in regular contact. They are likely to have observed the

behaviour of the job holder over a period of time. Once again, any bias or error which the observer may have must be taken into account.
- Specialist observers, such as job analysts. These can provide an independent view of the work being carried out. The major problem is that the job holder, knowing she is being observed, may adjust her behaviour.

Having collected this information, it must then be analysed. This is often done by using five categories.

Task analysis This involves the study of those tasks an employee carries out when doing their job. Any job will be made up of a variety of tasks. A task is seen as a collection of activities that result in an objective being achieved. For example, an employee may have the task of reporting on stock levels in the company.

Activity analysis This is a study of the activities which make up a task. These will include physical activities and the intellectual demands of the job. So an employee whose task is to do a stock check might need to understand how to use the computerised stock control program and understand the concept of lead time (☞ unit 57).

Skills analysis This involves a study of the skills that are needed to do the job. These could be the ability to use a computer program or the ability to work with others, for example.

Role analysis This is the information gathered from the job holder, superiors and colleagues. The duties, responsibilities and behaviour expected from the job holder are discussed to produce a role description which all involved agree upon.

Performance analysis This attempts to set the criteria that will be used when evaluating how well a job holder carries out the job. It involves identifying standards and expectations. For example, an employee may need to ensure that stock wastage is kept to a certain level. This will give a target to aim at while carrying out stock control.

Job description

Once a business has analysed what a job entails, it is important to draw up a description of the job. The JOB DESCRIPTION is a simple 'word picture' of the job. It will often contain some of the elements in Table 46.1.

The job description has a number of uses. It allows the firm to tell candidates for a job what is expected of them. It also helps personnel officers to decide on the qualities that successful candidates must have.

When candidates are appointed, the job description can be used to gauge whether the employee is doing the job

Table 46.1 *Possible job description of a design artist*

General information	Job title, such as 'designer'. Place of job within the business. Job summary, eg main tasks.
Job content information	Tasks involved, eg details of tasks. Purpose of tasks, eg develop designs for products. Methods involved, eg drawing, CAD etc. Other duties, eg part of design team. Responsibility, eg control of other staff.
Working conditions	Physical environment, eg work area. Social environment, eg holidays. Economic conditions, eg length of working day.
Performance information	Criteria for measuring performance, eg quality of designs.

'properly', by comparing their activities with the description. Disputes about the work an employee has to do can also be settled by looking at the job description.

A good example of 'tight' job descriptions are those for McDonald's employees. They are given because employees are expected to be very flexible and interchangeable in their jobs - so that when a worker comes to a job or task, they know exactly what to do. McDonald's employees have in the past been given a 385 page operations manual. It was full of details on how each task should be performed. It included instructions such as 'Cooks must turn, never flip, hamburgers... once, never two at a time ... Cashiers must make eye contact and smile at every customer'.

The job description is a means of communication (☞ unit 52). It suffers from the usual problems of misunderstanding and distortion. It is also a simplification, as it is rarely possible to include every feature of a particular job.

Person specification

Once the skills and knowledge needed to perform a particular job have been outlined in the job description, they are often reworded into a PERSON SPECIFICATION (sometimes referred to as the human specification or the job specification). This shows a profile of the type of person needed to do the job.

Such a description can then form the basis for the selection of the most suitable person to fill the job. Table 46.2 shows a possible example.

It is important that the person specification fits the 'culture' of a business (☞ unit 5). Goffee (London Business School) and Jones (Henley Management College) suggest that there are two cultures in the workplace - sociability and solidarity.

Table 46.2 *A possible person specification of a draughtsperson*

Attainments	Essential to have evidence of application and capacity for detailed work.
	Desirable to have some knowledge of technical drawing and of engineering terms.
	Must have at least 4 GCSEs grade C or above, or vocational qualification in engineering or manufacturing at equivalent level.
	Previous experience of record keeping in technical office or library is essential.
	Experience of working with engineering drawings is desirable.
General intelligence	Brisk reactions and accurate memory are needed.
Specialised aptitudes	Neat, quick and accurate at clerical work.
Interests	Practical and social.
Disposition	Self-reliant, helpful, friendly.
Circumstances	Likely to stay for at least 3 years.

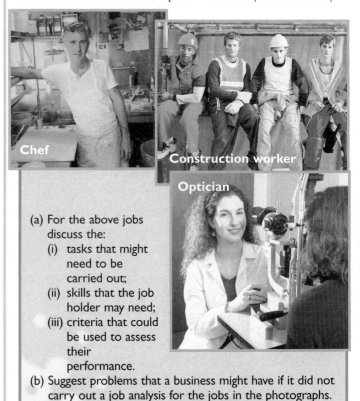

Chef

Construction worker

Optician

(a) For the above jobs discuss the:
   (i) tasks that might need to be carried out;
   (ii) skills that the job holder may need;
   (iii) criteria that could be used to assess their performance.
(b) Suggest problems that a business might have if it did not carry out a job analysis for the jobs in the photographs.

Question 1

Unit 46 Recruitment 331

The sociable workplace has a friendly atmosphere, openness and a sharing of ideas. A workplace with solidarity has mutual interests and shared goals. A business must ensure that individuals who are recruited fit the culture of the organisation or they may be an unsuitable appointment.

Job evaluation

A business can use JOB EVALUATION to compare the value of different jobs. Any job can be broken down into a number of factors. These are the skills, effort, responsibility, knowledge and tasks that the job entails. This allows the business to decide on the wages or salary for that job. If another job has greater skill or responsibility, then the business may award it a higher rate of pay.

Job evaluation has become more popular over the last decade. It has been seen by businesses as a rational way of working out why some jobs are paid more than others. It has also been used in equal pay cases (☞ unit 50). For example, if there is a dispute about equal pay, the job evaluation will help to show if employees are doing work of equal value. When using job evaluation, a business must remember certain points.

● Job evaluation is about the job and not the performance of the employee in the job.
● Experienced people decide on the value of a job. Whilst this is likely to give useful results, they are not 'perfect'.
● It allows firms to set differential rewards for jobs. This does not rule out collective bargaining (☞ unit 74) to raise these rates.
● Only pay is determined, not other earnings, such as incentives.

The most popular method of job evaluation is a points scheme. A number of factors (skill, problem solving etc.) are found which are common to all jobs. Each factor is given a weighting according to its importance. A job description is then prepared and points are allocated to each factor. The total number of points determines the value of the job, and the wages or salary to be paid.

Whilst it can be useful, job evaluation is costly for firms. Also, some jobs will still be 'underpaid' or 'overpaid', as it is a matter of human judgment.

Methods of recruitment

If vacancies do exist then the personnel department must fill them. Often firms fill vacancies by recruiting new employees - **external** recruitment. An alternative is to appoint **internally** from within the business. In the short term, particularly if funds are not available for extra workers, it may be possible to reorganise the work in order to fill the 'gaps' left by vacant positions. For example, the work could be shared out between the remaining employees.

This option might be used if the workload was felt to be too light in the department before the vacancy existed, or if the section is very 'tightly knit'. A further option is to pay existing workers overtime rates to cover the output lost by the employee who has left. Internal reorganisation is not without its problems. These include how the work should be divided and what rewards employees should receive for 'extra' work.

External recruitment to fill vacancies is likely to become increasingly difficult given the population trends in some Western developed countries. In the UK, skills shortages and demographic changes (☞ unit 63) will make recruitment from outside more difficult. Employers will either need to change their strategies to take into account the falling number of potential recruits in competitive markets, or be faced with vacant positions. This may require the use of innovative forms of recruitment, employing previously inactive workers, flexible working or job sharing. In addition, with many jobs now requiring high levels of skill, some businesses may find a shortage of appropriately qualified and experienced people.

Internal recruitment

It is argued that internal recruitment strengthens employees' commitment to the company. The personnel department of Kellogg's, for example, has stated the following courses of action in its recruitment policy handbook.

'(a) Offer the job to an existing employee, as a promotion or transfer.
(b) Advertise internally, if a suitable candidate is likely to be available internally.
(c) Advertise externally if no suitable candidate is likely to exist internally (and display notice internally to the effect that the advertisement is appearing).

Except in special cases, all vacancies should be advertised internally before external recruitment methods are used.'

There is a number of advantages to advertising jobs 'inside' the business.
● It gives employees within the company a chance to develop their career.
● There may be a shorter induction period as the employee is likely to be familiar with the company.
● Employers will know more about internal candidates' abilities. This should reduce the risk of employing the 'wrong' person.
● Internal recruitment may be quicker and less expensive than recruiting from outside the business.
However, there are also disadvantages.
● Internal advertising limits the number of applicants.
● External candidates might have been of better quality.
● Another vacancy will be created which might have to be filled.
● If, having investigated ways of filling the vacancy internally the business still does not appoint, then it must find ways to obtain candidates externally.

External recruitment

There are many ways of attracting candidates from outside the company. The choice of method often depends on the type of vacancy and the type of employee a business wants.

Each method has its own benefits and problems, although it could be argued that the overall advantages of external advertising are the opposite of the disadvantages of internal advertising, for example, there is a wider number of applicants.

Commercial employment agencies These are companies that specialise in recruiting and selection. They usually provide a shortlist of candidates for a company to interview, but can also provide temporary workers. Examples include Alfred Marks and Hays Accountancy Personnel.

The advantage of commercial agencies is that they are experienced in providing certain types of worker, such as secretaries and clerical staff. They also minimise the administration for the employer involved in recruiting staff. Their main drawback is that they tend to produce staff who only stay in a job for a short time. Another problem for the business is the cost of paying fees to the agency.

Job centres and professional recruitment agencies These are government run and private organisations which try to help people obtain work. Their main advantage is that they can find applicants easily and can quickly draw from local or national databases.

Headhunting 'Headhunting' involves executive agencies approaching individuals, who have a reputation in a field of work, with employment offers. The main advantage is that a business can directly approach someone with a known specialism. This is of particular use to employers not experienced in a specialist field. The main disadvantages are the cost, the fact that the recruit may remain on the consultant's list even after they have changed jobs, and that candidates outside the 'network' are excluded.

The Careers Service As well as providing careers guidance to young people and adults, the Careers Service also collects local job vacancies and distributes them to their clients in schools and in the local area. Their main advantage is that they can produce regular enquiries from young people who are likely to be looking no further than the local area for employment and who would be able to take up a post quickly. Their disadvantage is that they work on a local rather than a regional or national basis.

Government funded training schemes Government funded training schemes (☞ unit 49) provide training for the young, long term unemployed, lone parents and disabled in order to improve their job prospects. They include for example:
● the New Deal, which allows people to have subsidised employment and training with a business or work experience with a voluntary organisation or environmental task force;
● Modern Apprenticeships, run by businesses and training providers, where employees and apprentices sign a 'training agreement' for the period of the apprenticeship. Employees are usually given employed status and train towards a vocational qualification.
The advantage to a business of offering such a scheme is that the costs of employing workers will be reduced because of the funding from government. The business will also have a 'free trial' of a potential employee.

Visiting universities - 'the milkround' This involves companies visiting universities around the country with the aim of recruiting employees. Its main advantage is that it provides easy access to candidates of graduate standard. It is also fairly inexpensive and convenient through using the

---

The Ceramic Company is a business based just outside Stafford. It is owned by Geoff and Janet Kelsey. It employs 10 staff, some of which are part time. Its main products are clay pots manufactured for earthenware and household goods retailers. Larger pots are manufactured for garden centres in the area. The business also manufactures hand painted tiles. This is a time consuming and fairly labour intensive process, but has been a growing proportion of total sales over the last year.

As sales have expanded, particularly to areas outside the locality, Janet is spending more time away from the workshop. Janet feels that she needs to appoint one of the staff to be the manager in her absence. The person would handle the ordering of materials, coordinate work to meet deadlines and deal with full time and part time staff as well as outworkers. Both Geoff and Janet feel that it would be easier to promote someone from within the business as there may not be enough work to justify the appointment of a full time manager.

However, they are both concerned that although two possible candidates have worked for the business for eight

years, they do not have the experience of organisation. In particular, when a large order comes in, there is often a need to quickly order materials and perhaps organise part time workers to work extra hours. Of the other two possible candidates, one is part time, but has had experience of managing a garden centre in the area. The other is the youngest worker in the business, although she is keen to develop with the company. She has seen the possibility of moving into other craft areas. Recently she was interviewed for a business that specialised in interior design, but she turned down the job.

Source: adapted from company information.

(a) Explain why this is an example of an internal recruitment method.
(b) Suggest benefits to the business of recruiting in this way.
(c) Discuss which candidate the business should recruit for the new post.

university appointments service. The main drawbacks are that often the interviewees are simply enquiring about a job and that interview schedules can be very time consuming and tiring. These problems have become worse as student numbers have increased in recent years.

Advertising Apart from using the above methods, employers will often advertise their jobs to a wider audience. They may place their own adverts in the media or they may deal with an advertising agency to get help with drafting advertisements and placing them in suitable media. The agency will usually book the space in the chosen media, prepare the layout, read and correct proofs, and check that the right advertisement has appeared in the right publication, at the right time. The agency will usually be aware of the following methods of job advertising.

- Vacancy lists outside premises. This is an economical method, but it will only be seen by a few people and little information can be included.
- Advertising in the national press. This has the advantage of wider coverage. However, it can be costly and may reach people who are not interested.
- Advertising in the local press. This will be read by local people seeking employment. Evidence suggests, however, that the local press is not read by professionals.
- Advertising in the technical press. This reaches the appropriate people, but may be published infrequently.
- Television advertising. This reaches large numbers, but can be expensive.

Internet recruitment Businesses can advertise jobs on their own Internet website or they can hire space on other sites. A company website is used to provide a great deal of information and adding a section advertising jobs might be relatively low cost method of advertising, especially if many jobs are advertised. The business would also not need to pay an agency to advertise the jobs. Some sites are set up to advertise jobs in particular specialist areas, such as teaching or the NHS. However, a possible problem with this form of advertising is that it only reaches those who have access to and can use the Internet, and who can find the required website.

Producing a job advertisement

As important as choosing the most appropriate media through which to advertise a vacancy is the drafting of the advertisement. The decision on what to include in a recruitment advertisement is important because of the high cost of space and the need to attract attention. Both factors will encourage the use of the fewest number of words. Some of the information that might be included is:

- the job title;
- the name and address of the employer;
- the salary and any other remuneration;
- details of the vacancy;
- the skills and experience required for the successful candidate;
- any other benefits;

Carlotta Del Santo runs a travel business in Kent which specialises in sports holidays in Spain and the Balearic Islands. She has recently found a great increase in demand for corporate and club golfing holidays and club trips to see Spanish football matches. The business now needs to recruit two new employees. An employee who speaks fluent English and Spanish is needed to liaise with operators abroad. Another employee with experience in organising travel holidays is also required.

(a) Identify the methods of recruitment suggested in the advertisement.
(b) Examine the advantages of these methods to Carlotta's business when recruiting employees.

Question 3

- what the applicant needs to do to apply;
- where to apply and to whom.

Employee segmentation

The standard of service is increasingly important to customers buying products. Providing an excellent service means matching employees' actions to the needs of customers. So businesses are trying to answer the question 'What behaviour by employees creates greater customer satisfaction?'

One way of doing this is to segment employees into groups depending on the profile of customers. This is known as EMPLOYEE SEGMENTATION. It means that businesses must organise and recruit specific types of employees to match the profiles of their customers. So, for example, B&Q knows that its customers often want advice about products. Therefore it recruits staff with experience of DIY who can talk sympathetically to customers about its products. In call centres it has meant a change of approach to one based on relationships with customers. Employees now tailor responses to customers' needs, based on information about the customer which is shown on a computer screen. Productivity is measured not by how many calls are taken but by how many problems are resolved first time. It is argued that such an approach leads to greater customer loyalty and repeat sales for businesses.

Factors affecting recruitment

A study by Illes and Robertson (1997) of recruitment strategies identified factors which can affect recruitment and make it successful.

- The recruitment literature sent out to candidates can influence their decision about whether to apply or not. Informal sources of information, such as word of mouth and referrals, are seen as more accurate sources of information than formal advertisements. Applicants who come through such informal routes are more likely to stay with the business, reducing levels of labour turnover (☞ unit 45). This is because they have more realistic expectations when appointed.
- Businesses that want to recruit from under-represented groups, such as ethnic groups, the disabled or women, must ensure that their recruitment strategies are targeted, rather than using general recruitment procedures.
- The recruitment message affects applicants. Glossy, positive images may attract applicants, but can cause problems later if the job does not meet expectations. Job previews and work samples can lead to self-selection. Once experienced, a candidate may decide not to continue with the application. Site visits and opportunities to talk to colleagues can also help. Different messages may affect different groups. For example, flexible schedules can attract retired people.
- The behaviour of recruiters can affect applicants. For example, the presence of women recruiters and managers on site visits and interviews can create a positive impression.
- Applicants appear to respond well to recruiters who are seen as competent, informed and credible, and have interpersonal skills.
- Delays in response put off applicants as they may indicate how they will be treated if appointed.
- Applicants seem to respond more positively towards recruiters of the same gender, ethnicity, age and location.

key terms

Employee segmentation - when a business recruits types of employees who match the profiles of its customers.
Job analysis - a study of what the job entails, such as the skills, tasks and performance expected.
Job description - a simple word picture of what the job entails.
Job evaluation - a method used by businesses to compare the value of different jobs and perhaps set wages or salaries.
Person specification - a profile of the type of person needed to do a job.

The Halifax is working to recruit older professionals who have technical expertise and might be looking to wind down. Martin Freeth, a lawyer in the Halifax legal department is an example. He was recruited shortly before he turned sixty. He says 'I deal with mortgage queries from the branch network, but occasionally I speak directly to borrowers when they are upset. It's useful to have a weight of experience to calm them down because there are few situations I haven't come across'. The products that Halifax sells do appeal to older customers, but the sales operation has been wrongly seen as a 'young environment'. So the business is holding open days aimed at customers aged 45-60.

The Halifax is also looking to train school leavers. It suggests that such groups face even more prejudice, that a real plan is needed and that work experience needs to be improved as it has often missed its mark.

Another important part of recruitment is the advertising. Past adverts were seen as too dull, with people simply shown in staff uniforms. They did not portray a fun, dynamic environment in which to work. Now when a branch has a vacancy it uses a recruitment guide to select appropriate pictures with approved images. The recruitment advertisements will now include staff and models of different age, sex and race. Research has shown that 90 per cent of staff now recognise the responsibility to equal opportunities. This was only 25 per cent in 1998.

Source: adapted from *People Management*, 22.2.2001.

(a) Explain the features of recruitment at Halifax which might make it effective using examples the article.
(b) To what extent is the business using employee segmentation methods?

Knowledge

1. Why do businesses need to recruit effectively?
2. Give 2 reasons why companies carry out job analysis.
3. How is a job description useful to the personnel department?
4. What is the difference between a job description and a person specification?
5. Give 5 factors that might be on a person specification.
6. How might job evaluation be used by a business?
7. State two ways in which a business could reorganise instead of appointing internally or externally to cover a vacancy.

8. What is meant by:
   (a) internal recruitment;
   (b) external recruitment?
9. Give 3 reasons why a business might recruit internally.
10. State 5 methods of external recruitment.
11. Why might a business recruit using an advertising agency rather than a job centre?
12. What factors are important to show in a job recruitment advertisement?

Case study Online recruitment

Many retailers are going online to find extra staff at peak sales times. At Harrods the January sales staff had been carefully recruited to deal with the rush. Harrods used the Internet to attract the staff it needed. Other sites such as Monster.co.uk and inretail.co.uk have set aside special sections for seasonal staff. Richard Jenkins, recruitment manager at New Look, said the Internet was an obvious choice to find people willing to handle the tills at this time of year. He suggested that Internet recruitment represents a significant part of overall recruiting at the business and was likely to expand.

The trend is not just limited to retailers. The Tussaud's Group, which operates Alton Towers and Thorpe Park, also uses the Internet for seasonal rushes. An obvious advantage is speed. People can be recruited quickly as jobs can be posted that day. Asking the applicant to answer 'screening questions' can save time sorting through applications. But perhaps the greatest advantage is targeting. Group advertising manager at Tussaud's, Matthew Mee, says 'You can pinpoint niche populations more accurately' and that 'Internet advertising has benefits because 'an advertisement in a newspaper is hit or miss because it relies on people buying the paper that day.' Jobs are placed on websites for a month rather than just a day. Another major advantage is cost savings, particularly the savings from commission to recruitment agencies. These can sometimes be 15-30 per cent of the salary of the job.

It is possible to place one-off adverts on sites. But the real savings come from running the whole recruitment process online. This means everything from posting the job on the website or on sites run by other companies, receiving CVs by e-mail, and sending offers of jobs. The optician chain, Vision Express, is a business which has opted for an integrated online recruitment system. Heidi Farrell, resourcing manager at the company, realised that it did not have a 'standard advertising approach' and that recruitment was rather piecemeal, using a variety of different methods in an ad-hoc way. Another problem was that the company recruited from four main groups - optical professionals, managers, sales assistants and lab technicians. These groups have different interests and concerns. Finding the right way to recruit them can be difficult. The Internet approach allowed a standardised recruitment process to be set up.

Like many other businesses, Vision Express does not just use the Internet. The initial recruitment strategy uses press advertising to get things rolling. This is an effective way of launching the campaign. A recruitment advert placed in a trade paper in November had several people in the advanced stages of recruitment just two weeks later.

Some businesses have even taken things further. They are becoming so concerned about reducing time and cutting costs that they are texting applicants on mobile phones. Often the recruitment process starts with a telephone interview, so texting is a natural extension process given the new technology available. It is easy for an applicant to return a message and the loss of several days can be prevented.

However, this does not mean that the days of the recruitment advertisers are numbered. The Chairman of the Association of Online Recruiters says that traditional advertisements still have a place. But he thinks that they may become corporate branding exercises. They will set out the organisation's values and direct job seekers to the website of the business. He predicts that the website will become more like the 'hub' of recruitment activity. Others are more cautious. Many businesses are using websites simply as shop windows for jobs. But recruitment is not done online. This is because there can be technical problems with online systems. People also sometimes have difficulty understanding the process online. One suggested 'nothing substitutes for a well planned recruitment campaign and selection process by businesses who know what they are doing'.

Source: adapted from *People Management*, 26.12.2002.

(a) **Identify alternative methods to Internet recruitment suggested in the article. (4 marks)**
(b) **Explain why recruitment using the Internet is an example of an 'external' source of recruitment. (6 marks)**
(c) **Examine the (i) benefits and (ii) problems of using Internet recruitment for retail businesses looking to hire employees in rush periods such as Christmas. (10 marks)**
(d) **Compare Internet recruitment and headhunting as methods of hiring managers for retailers such as Vision Express. (10 marks)**
(e) **Discuss the extent to which Internet advertising will be the most popular method of recruitment in future and whether all businesses are likely to use Internet advertising. (10 marks)**

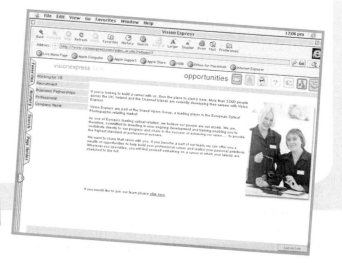

Effective selection - making the right choice

Selection is growing in importance for firms. As explained in unit 64, businesses need to recruit and then select the 'right' person for the job. If the candidate chosen is unsuitable, the business may be faced with the cost of poor performance by the employee. There will also be extra costs in selecting and training a replacement when that employee leaves.

Businesses have also realised the need for a fair and valid choice of candidate. The most suitable applicant will only be chosen if selection is based on ability, skills and knowledge, rather than race or gender, for example. **Equal opportunities** legislation has helped to make impartial selection more likely, although there are still arguments about the 'fairness' involved in selection (☞ unit 50).

Effective selection should lead to the most suitable candidate being employed, in terms of their skills and motivation, as well as reducing the cost of selection. Personnel managers play an important part in this. They help to prepare the job analysis, job description, and person specification, and decide exactly how to recruit. They also advise on the nature of application forms, how to SHORT LIST or LONG LIST from them, and how to conduct tests and interviews. Finally, they will influence how the information is evaluated and what decisions should be made about candidates.

Application

The first time that a business receives information about candidates for a job it is advertising is when they apply for the job. Applicants may have collected details about the job from the business itself or from a job centre, for example. Some jobs ask for a letter of application from the applicants in which they explain why they want the job. This is often accompanied by a CURRICULUM VITAE (CV). The CV is a list of the applicant's:

- personal details (name, address, nationality etc.);
- educational qualifications;
- hobbies and interests;
- past job experience;
- reasons why the candidate is suitable for the job (strengths);
- references or names and addresses of referees who will provide references. **References** are a confirmation of the abilities, skills and experience of the candidate.

Growing use is being made of application forms by businesses. They have a number of benefits. All applicants give details in a standard way, rather than the different approaches of letters of application. This makes sorting applications and short listing far easier. This task is often called 'pre-selection'. It involves the 'sifting out' of applicants who least fit the requirements of the person specification and job description. The application form is often used as the basis of the interview and can be a starting point for personnel records.

The application form covers the information contained in a CV above, such as personal details, education and job experience. Certain forms leave out some of the above, while others include much more. Whatever the format, the form helps applicants 'present' their case. Also, by gaining biographical information, the personnel department has a simple way of matching the applicant's qualifications, interests, past experience etc. to their person specification (☞ unit 46). This allows the firm to decide quickly which of the applicants is suitable for a job. Table 47.1 shows a checklist

---

Table 47.1

- Handwriting is often larger than type. Do the boxes/areas on the form give enough room for the applicant to complete the information?
- Forms that take too long to complete may be completed haphazardly or not at all. Is the time the form takes to complete appropriate to the information the employer needs?
- Some questions may be illegal, offensive, or not essential. Does the form ask only for information appropriate to the job?
- Word processing software makes it possible to produce separate application forms for each post advertised and to make them user friendly. One way of doing this is to use introductory paragraphs explaining why the information in each section is being sought.

Frost Frame is a small company producing double glazed windows. It has decided to expand production. In particular, it is looking for someone with skills in working with stained glass. Having placed an advertisement in the local newspaper, the company sent out application forms. The standard application form was used which had been devised for all general workshop employees. It did not ask any questions related to the applicant's specific skills. After four weeks it has received three applications and only one candidate looks worth interviewing. However, it is unclear from his answers whether he will be entirely suitable.

(a) Identify problems that Frost Frame may have had with its application form.
(b) Analyse the possible implications for the company if it decides not to interview the candidate?

Question 1

of points which can be used to help a business design an application form.

Interviews

Most people have at least one experience of being interviewed prior to employment. Few people enjoy interviews. Often this is because the interviewer appears to be more interested in finding fault than being helpful.

The personnel department is usually involved in interviewing, both in carrying them out and helping managers to adopt good interview practice. By following certain guidelines, the business hopes to employ the 'right' person for the job. It also aims to carry out the interview in a way that is fair to all candidates and well structured. These guidelines might include the following.

- The interview should allow information to be collected from candidates which can be used to predict whether they can perform the job. This can be done by comparing replies with the criteria that successful applicants should have.
- The business should give candidates full details about the job and the organisation. This will help them decide whether the job would suit them.
- The interview should be conducted so that candidates can say that they have had a fair hearing.

The interview has, however, been criticised as not always being an effective 'tool'. Some of the main criticisms are:

- interviewers often decide to accept or reject a candidate within the first three or four minutes of the interview, and then spend the rest of the time finding evidence to confirm their decision;
- interviews seldom change the initial opinion formed by the interviewer seeing the application form and the appearance of the candidate;
- interviewers place more stress on evidence that is unfavourable than on the evidence that is favourable;
- when interviewers have made up their minds very early in the interview, their behaviour betrays their decision to the candidate.

The problem with these criticisms is that they do not solve the problems, only identify them. No matter what other means of selection there may be, the interview is crucial. If it is thought to be unreliable, it should not be discarded. Businesses must simply make sure they carry it out properly.

Conducting an interview

There is a number of factors which could be taken into account when carrying out interviews. The interview should be conducted around a simple plan and be based on a number of questions against which all candidates will be assessed. It is also considered good practice to prepare a suitable place for the interview, such as a warm, quiet, ventilated room. The interviewer should also ensure that the candidates have a friendly reception and are informed of what is expected of them.

An average interview may take around 30 minutes. An interview plan organises the time to cover the important areas in assessing applicants. The plan must be flexible enough to allow the interviewer to explore areas that may come up during the interview. An example is shown in Table 47.2.

Many recruitment handbooks spell out the 'dos and don'ts' of interviewing. Some of the 'dos' that the interviewer may take into account include the following.

- Introduce yourself to the candidate.
- Adopt a suitable manner, show respect and be friendly.
- Make sure the interview is not interrupted.
- Conduct the interview at an unhurried pace.
- Have a list of questions that need to be asked.
- Encourage the candidate to talk by using 'open' questions such as:
    'Tell me about your present/last job ...'
    'What is your opinion on ...?'
    'What do you find interesting in ...?'
- Concentrate on those areas not fully covered by the application form.
- Be alert for clues in the candidate's answer, probe where necessary, and be more specific in the questioning if you are not satisfied.
- When the interview has ended, make sure the candidate has no further questions and let the candidate know when the decision will be made, eg within seven days.
- Write up your assessment notes immediately.
- Prepare for the next interview.

The interviewer will have gained a great deal of information from the interview. It will help the interviewer to have a

Table 47.2 *Organising an interview*

Organisation	Tasks	Time (minutes)
Introduction	Who are they? Who are you?	2 3
Body of interview	Begin questioning. Ask questions which probe what they have learnt from their experiences/qualifications /interests and how they would apply this to their new position.	10
	Let the candidate ask questions. Explain about the organisation.	5
	If any questions are left, clear them up.	5
	Tell the candidate what happens next, eg 'We will let you know in 10 days'.	3
Close of interview	Finish tidily.	
After the interview	Assess the candidate. Prepare for next interview.	10/15 10/15

checklist of the criteria used when assessing candidates. Table 47.3 shows two possible lists. The interviewer can make notes about candidates next to each criterion and compare the information with the person specification after the interview, to decide if the person is suitable.

Table 47.3 *Criteria used in assesing candidates*

Rodgers' 7 point plan	Munro-Fraser 5 point plan
Physical make-up	Impact on others
Attainments	Qualifications
General intelligence	Innate abilities
Specialised aptitude	Motivation
Interests	Emotional adjustment
Disposition	
Circumstances	

Testing

Businesses appear to be taking a greater interest in testing. There are strong arguments for and against the use of tests in selection. Those in favour argue that many interviews in business are unstructured and do not really allow a business to predict performance. They also point to the greater accuracy and objectivity of test data. Those against dispute this objectivity. They also argue that predictions from test results can mislead. For example, does a high test score mean high job performance and a low score mean low job performance?

There is a number of tests that are used in selection. These are often associated with different levels of staff.

- Aptitude tests measure how well a candidate can cope when faced with a business situation or problem.
- Attainment tests measure an individual's ability using skills they have already acquired. For example, a candidate for an administration post may take a word processing test.
- Intelligence tests aim to give an indication of overall 'mental' ability. A variety of questions are asked in such tests covering numeracy and literacy skills, as well as general knowledge. It is assumed that a person who scores highly will be able to retain new knowledge and to succeed at work.
- Personality tests, also known as psychometric tests, examine the **traits** or **characteristics** of employees. For example, they might indicate that a manager does not change her mind once her decision is made or that an employee is willing to experiment and adapt to change. Personality tests may allow a business to predict how hard working or motivated a employee will be or how suited she is to a job. The usefulness of such tests depends on whether the business feels that they are a suitable way of selecting employees. The business must also have qualified personnel to carry out the tests. Such tests do have problems. There is unlikely to be a standard personality profile of the 'ideal employee' to compare tests results against. The tests also rely on the individual being honest. Often, however, candidates try to pick the answer that they feel is wanted. In addition, some traits measured in the tests may not be relevant to job performance.

Selection exercises

As well as interviews and tests, more and more companies are using a variety of:

- role play exercises;
- group presentations;
- PSYCHOMETRIC TESTS, which attempt to assess a candidate's personality;

- One of eight applicants applying for a trainee position was put forward largely due to the level of maturity shown. Most candidates, all university graduates, acted their age. He got the edge by being positively different. He was calm, relaxed and self assured.
- A candidate was not put forward due to the number of times he laughed during interview. Even allowing for nerves, he did not appear serious enough.
- A candidate was too rehearsed. Each question was given the same answer, which at times was not appropriate to the question being asked.
- A candidate was rejected because of her attitude towards an aptitude test. Another candidate was rejected on his attitude towards a female interviewer, when he tried to flirt.
- A candidate was rejected when his mobile phone went off during the interview. This may not be a problem in itself, but the candidate then had a lengthy telephone call.
- A candidate was recommended for second interview and offered a job. The main attribute was the candidate's honesty. She had suffered some illness with her previous employer. The candidate gave a complete and honest account of her illness and current prognosis.
- A candidate's CV was average in presentation and detail, but the enthusiasm and spirit in the covering letter encouraged the business to interview the candidate.
- A candidate gave only a satisfactory interview. However, what stood out was his approach having received a call for interview. He contacted the interviewer thanking him for the opportunity of the interview and confirming he would be attending. He then independently approached the interviewer's secretary to make sure he had the right directions and was polite to the secretary on attending the interview.

Source: adapted from www.sfrecruitment.co.uk.

(a) Using examples from the case, advise candidates of features of a successful interview.
(b) Using examples, explain how interviews might be useful for helping a business to select the most suitable candidate for a job.

Question 2

- simulations;
- assessment centres, which attempt to evaluate a wider range of skills using a variety of techniques to help a business analyse the capabilities of candidates.

These allow candidates to demonstrate social skills and problem solving skills which they may need to use in the job. For example, a salesperson may show persuasive communication skills in a role play situation. The use of exercises has a number of benefits for a business.

- They allow more information to be gathered about a candidate than other methods of selection.
- They show how well candidates react to situations such as team working, responding to customers or meeting deadlines.
- They allow large numbers to be assessed and may save on costs.

The Skipton Building Society's Accelerate to Management Programme (ATM) is aimed at people in lower level management and supervisory jobs. In 2003, five candidates were picked out of sixteen who applied with the backing of their line manager. The selection process starts with a verbal and numerical reasoning test. Candidates are also given a OPQ 32 personality profile which assesses their drive and self-perception. Candidates who 'pass through' are then invited to a competency based interview with a panel of senior managers and HR specialists. Shortlisted candidates are then asked to give a brief verbal presentation on a specific subject. The business argues that a crucial factor in the whole selection process is a high level of motivation. The ATM programme manager says 'We look for signs of enthusiasm and understanding about what they would be taking on'.

Source: adapted from *People Management*, 24.7.2003.

(a) What evidence is there that the business short lists and long lists candidates?
(b) Identify the selection methods used by The Skipton Building Society.
(c) Suggest advantages to the business of using these methods for the selection of candidates for management jobs.

Question 3

Interviewing and technology

Businesses are increasingly making use of technology in selection.

Videoconferencing Some businesses use videoconferencing as an interviewing tool (☞ unit 52). For example, it can cost less than £1,000 for a recruiter in the UK to interview six candidates in the US by video link. Videoconferencing is not likely to replace the face-to-face interview because people still need the 'human touch'. However, it will help to save time and money. Glaxo-SmithKline, the pharmaceuticals company,

has used video-interviewing in the initial screening of candidates. It has found this to be a way of saving on travel expenses, particularly when an interview would have involved international air travel.

Telephone interviews There is a growing trend among companies to select candidates by using the telephone. Phone interviews have a number of advantages. Savings can be made on costs and managers need to spend less time away from their desks. They can also prevent discrimination due to visual appearance. However, telephone interviews are not always suited to all types of interview situation and certain candidates may not interview well over the telephone.

The Internet The use of online questionnaires on company, websites can help in the short or long listing process. For example, it may be possible to assess a candidates CV from answers given to a standard questionnaire. This will reduce costs greatly in the application stage. It might even be possible to given candidates an online tests to assess their abilities.

The future In future, businesses might even consider using technology such as webcams and the Internet for interviews. This might be used, for example, if a candidate had to be interviewed from another country.

Evaluating selection

How can a business tell if selection has been effective? It could simply decide that if it has appointed the 'right' candidate, then its aim has been achieved. However, selection will involve costs to a business. There will be expenses in sending out application forms and perhaps travelling expenses for candidates. Staff will also have to give up time to carry out the interviews.

So, for example, if ten people were interviewed for three posts, but only one applicant was suitable, selection may not have been effective. In this case the firm would have to readvertise and interview other candidates as two posts would be unfilled. The personnel department's role would be to check all stages of selection to find out where problems had arisen. For example, when short listing, a suitable candidate may have been 'left out'. At an interview a possible candidate may have been rushed, so he was not given the chance to do his best.

Research in the 1990s and after the year 2000 suggests certain factors that lead to successful selection.

- Ability tests, job knowledge tests and situational judgement tests, where candidates are tested on how they would respond to a real business problem, have been found to be very effective in predicting future job performance.
- Personality measures and employment interviews, especially when they are structured, have emerged as stronger predictors of job performance than was previously believed.

EasyJet has 80 per cent of ticket sales via the Internet. So it makes sense for it to use this in its selection process. Pilots, for example, are asked to fill in a customised, online application form. All correspondence between applicants and EasyJet is then carried out online. Successful applicants are invited to a pilot workshop or assessment centre. Unsuccessful ones are filed away to be contacted later when they may have more experience.

CVs and applications are picked up from the website and sent to the relevant manager. But they are also logged on to the HR system where they can be electronically screened to see how they match up to existing jobs and vacancies. This allows personnel to build up a database of potential recruits for the future.

The business can be very effective in screening out applicants that have little chance of selection. Pilots, for example, must have a number of flying hours. It is immediately obvious from the application form if a candidate does not have this experience. It also filters out speculative applications from 16-year olds wanting to be pilots.

The business is less convinced about the value of online testing. EasyJet uses psychometric tests for recruiting pilots, but these are still pen and paper tests. One of the problems is the lack of feedback form candidates with online testing.

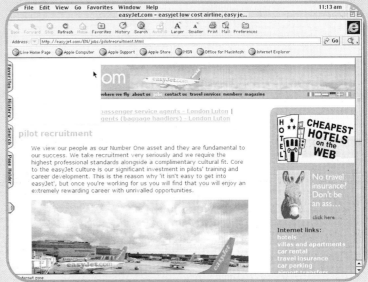

Source: adapted from recruiter.totaljobs.com.

(a) Identify the methods of selection used at EasyJet.
(b) Discuss to what extent online selection methods are useful for the business in the selection of pilots.

Question 4

key terms

Curriculum Vitae - a list of the applicant's personal details, experience and qualifications.
Long listing - reducing the number of total candidates to a manageable list, that might be reduced further.

Psychometric tests - methods of selection designed to assess a candidate's personality.
Short listing - reducing the original number of candidates to a small number to be interviewed.

Knowledge

1. Why has selection become increasingly important to businesses?
2. State 5 features covered in an application form.
3. What criteria might a personnel department take into account when designing an application form?
4. Name 4 types of tests that a personnel department might carry out when selecting applicants for a job.
5. What are the main problems with personality tests as a method of selection?
6. Explain the main problems with interviews.
7. State 5 'dos' when conducting an interview.
8. How might a business evaluate its selection procedure?
9. How might a business make use of technology when conducting an interview?
10. What is meant by a selection exercise?

Case study Breaking with tradition

Looking smart and smiling at an interview may be a thing of the past. At Inkfish Call Centre anyone given an initial interview won't even have to leave home. Why? Because they are carried out by telephone. 'It's popular with candidates who often find it a lot less daunting and more relaxing than being thrown straight into a face-to-face interview' says Ruth Ebbern-Robinson, head of HR. Telephone interviews resulted from a policy to employ a wider age group. Many of the recruiters at the business were young and so 'Telephone interviewing soon proved a good way of avoiding any kind of discrimination by young folk who can think people are over the hill at 40. It worked perfectly because if you can't see someone, you don't know how old he or she is. People who are successful in the phone interview are then invited to a selection day run by company personnel representing a wide range of ages' according to Ruth Ebbern-Robinson.

Telephone interviews also avoid discrimination on ethnic grounds and disability. There are no visual clues and research has found that there's no bias towards accent. A company spokesperson at B&Q says about telephone interviews, 'We introduced it a few years ago to provide a consistent means of recruitment and one in which we couldn't, even subliminally, prejudice certain groups such as people with disabilities'. She also says 'Candidates benefit because telephone interviews can be arranged at a mutually convenient time, and time and money is saved by cutting out travel. You don't have to think about what you're going to wear and there's a good chance you won't even need to take time off from your current job'.

Businesses may also benefit. If a job involves communicating by phone, it gives employers an insight into the employee's telephone skills. Not having to find a location also means that more candidates can be interviewed, leading to a fairer recruitment process.

However, telephone interviews do have problems.
- Research shows that interviews with multiple interviewers are most fair and valid, which is not possible over the phone.
- If the job does not require any telephone communication, there is a chance that the candidate might not be comfortable with this kind of medium.
- Not everyone can find somewhere quiet in their home or at work for a phone interview.
- Interviewees may find that telephone interviews are structured, with questions which are less open ended than those asked in a face-to-face interview.
- Interviews may be through an automated system. This

is rare, although it is becoming popular for secretarial, receptionist and other customer-facing positions.
- Interviewees may answer questions too quickly. Silences are more prominent over the phone and can seem longer than they really are.

Shell uses telephone interviews for graduates. Candidates may not live near a Shell recruitment centre or simply prefer to be interviewed by phone. Shell then invites successful candidates along to a follow-up interview in person. Angela Baron, employee resourcing adviser for the CIPD, believes this is essential. 'Telephone interviews are no substitute for more detailed interviewing' she says. 'Telephone interviews are particularly beneficial for applicants who switch careers.' 'Many companies would see from this person's CV that they have no direct experience for this role and bin it. Those that use telephone interviews, on the other hand, would have the chance to check out their generic skills and may wind up with a more suitable recruit.'

Source: adapted from *The Guardian*, 13.8.2003.

(a) Explain what is meant by (i) a CV and (ii) face-to-face interview. (4 marks)

(b) Explain why employers might use telephone interviews for employees in sales or call centres. (6 marks)

(c) Examine the ways in which a business might short list candidates for telephone interviews. (6 marks)

(d) Explain the advantages of telephone interviewing for:
(i) employees;
(ii) businesses. (8 marks)

(e) Suggest the factors that a business like B&Q might need to take into account to carry out a successful telephone interview. (8 marks)

(f) Discuss whether telephone interviews on their own are likely to lead to a successful appointment. (8 marks)

The contract of employment

Once a business has selected an employee (☞ unit 47), the successful candidate must be **appointed**. Once appointed, employees are entitled to a CONTRACT OF EMPLOYMENT. This is an agreement between the employer and the employee under which each has certain obligations. It is 'binding' to both parties in the agreement, the employer and the employee. This means that it is unlawful to break the terms and conditions in the contract without the other party agreeing.

As soon as an employee starts work, and therefore demonstrates that she accepts the terms offered by the employer, the contract comes into existence. It is sometimes a written contract, although a verbal agreement or an 'implied' agreement are also contracts of employment. The **Employment Rights Act, 1996** requires employers to give employees taken on for one month or more a **written statement** within two months of appointment. This written statement sets out the terms and conditions in the contract. Some common features shown in the written statement are:
- the names of the employer and the name of the employee;
- the date on which the employment is to begin;
- the job title;
- the terms and conditions of employment.

The duties and rights of employees and employers

Employees that are appointed by a business are covered by certain employment protection rights. Government legislation makes it a duty of employers to safeguard the rights of individuals at work. These are **individual labour laws**, as opposed to collective labour laws which affect all employees. They fall into a number of areas.

Discrimination Employees can not be discriminated against on grounds of gender, race or disability (☞ unit 50). So, for example, a business can not refuse to appoint a candidate for a job only because that person is female.

Pay Employees must be paid the same rate as other employees doing the same job, a similar job or a job with equal demands (☞ unit 50). They also have the right to itemised pay statements and not to have pay deducted for unlawful reasons.

Absences Employees have a right to maternity leave, time off for union or public duties and time off to look for training or work at times of redundancy. They also have a right to guaranteed payments during a period of lay off or medical suspension. Employees have a right to return to work after maternity leave. **The Employment Act, 2002** extended the rights of parents who worked. It gave working mothers and

working adoptive parents 26 weeks paid maternity leave and a further 26 week unpaid maternity leave. It increased maternity pay as well. Two weeks paid leave were also given to working fathers.

Dismissal Employees have the right not to be dismissed or face disciplinary action for trade union activity or on health and safety grounds. They also have a right to notice of dismissal. Employers have the right to terminate contracts of employment under certain circumstances, such as misconduct. These are discussed later in this unit.

Health and safety Employers have duties to provide a safe and healthy environment in which employees can work (☞ unit 51). In the UK the **Health and Safety at Work Act, 1974** is the main legislation protecting employees. However, many other UK and EU regulations exist and are being constantly introduced to raise standards of safety at work.

The duties of employees may be set out in the written statement of the contract of employment. For example, employees may be expected to conform to standards of behaviour and conduct at work. These may include standards of attendance, punctuality, dealings with colleagues and dress. Standards of quality and accuracy of work, speed of work and safety are also likely to be expected of employees.

Vicarious liability

In certain circumstance legislation forces business to have VICARIOUS LIABILITY. This is where a business must accept responsibility for the actions of its employees. Employers are

---

In 2003 a partner in a firm of solicitors drew up documents that were then used to commit fraud. Neither the fraudulent partner nor the firm benefited from the crime. However, the House of Lords judged that the firm was liable for the actions of its employees. This judgment was based not on the benefit to the employer because there was none, other than usual solicitors' fees, but on the wrongful act committed in the course of employment. This is what made the partnership liable. Even if the employee had acted entirely for his own benefit, the employer would still be liable. The employer would have made a decision that the employee was fit to do the job and so the risk that the employee would commit a wrongful act would lie with the employer.

Source: adapted from *People Management*, 9.10.2003.

(a) Explain why the solicitors partnership was vicariously liable in this case.
(b) Explain how this might affect (a) the business and (b) the employee.

Question 1

liable for the wrongful acts of employees providing these happen during the course of their employment and are connected with it. So, for example, a construction business may be liable if its workers cause damage to an adjoining building whilst carrying out repairs to a client's building. Businesses found to be vicariously liable might incur fines or other penalties.

Conditions of work and service

The written statement of the contract of employment will contain information about the conditions of work and service agreed by the employer and employee. Conditions may include the following.

The number of hours to be worked The statement will show the hours to be worked per week or over a period such as a year in the case of annualised hours (☞ unit 42). The number of hours must conform to legislation. For example, in 1998 the **European Union Working Time Directive** allowed workers to limit their working hours to a maximum of 48 hours per week, although workers such as junior doctors and senior executives were excluded. Details of the start and finish times may also be included, along with any meal or rest breaks. If an employee is expected to work 'shifts', this should be stated. Shift work is where an employee may work, for example, from 9am-5pm in the day for a week and then from 9pm-5am at night the following week.

The **Employment Act, 2002** introduced, for the first time, rights regarding flexible working. Mothers and fathers of children under 6 or disabled children under 18 have the right to request flexible working arrangements. Employers can only refuse the request if there is a clear business reason.

The designation of the job Workers may be employed in **full time** jobs or **part time** jobs. They may also be given a **permanent job** or a **temporary job** that only lasts for a period of time. The period of employment would usually be stated in the case of a temporary job. If a worker is expected to be based in a factory or office, this place of employment should also be mentioned. Some employees may be expected to work from home or to travel. If this is the case then arrangements that cover this such as support from the employer or travel expenses should be mentioned. These are discussed in the next section.

Pay The method of payment used to reward the employee is usually included in the written statement. She might be paid a wage or a salary. Payment may be by cheque or directly into a bank account. The rate of pay would be specified, such as £5 per hour or an annual salary of £20,000 a year. There may also be an indication of any bonuses, commission or overtime, incentive schemes and deductions from wages. Pay must conform to legislation. For example, employers are bound by the **Equal Pay Act 1970** (☞ unit 50). This states that an employee must be paid the same rate as another employee doing the same job, a similar job or a job with equal

demands.

Benefits Benefits that the employer is offering to the employee are usually included.

● The annual number of days paid **holiday** is often stated and any restrictions on when they can be taken. Statutory holidays are often stated as being taken.
● If the business runs its own **pension scheme** or offers to contribute to an individual or stakeholder pension, this may be stated along with contribution rates.
● There may be information on the length of time and the rate at which **sick pay** is available over and above any statutory rate.
● Any other benefits given by the business might also be included. Benefits can be wide ranging, from subsidised holidays to membership of leisure facilities to company cars.

Disciplinary procedures The written statement may indicate the immediate superior of the employee, who might be responsible for induction, training, supervision and discipline. In a larger business these are likely to be carried out by the personnel department. The **Employment Rights Act, 1996** states that employers must explain their disciplinary procedures. These are the rules that set standards of conduct at work. Employees must also be clearly informed of the consequences of breaking these rules, how this will be investigated and the rights of appeal against a decision. Employees that break rules could be liable for disciplinary action. This may be in the form of a verbal or written warning, suspension or even dismissal in some cases.

Notice Employees may leave a business to change jobs, to stop work totally or to have children. When employees do not intend to return they have to 'hand in their notice'. In other words they have to inform (or notify) the employer before they leave. The length of time that notice must be given by employees before they leave may be indicated in the written statement and must comply with legislation. This may be 'one week's notice' or 'one month's notice' for example. Similarly, the contract may state the length of 'notice' to be given by employers to employees before making them redundant or dismissing them. The length of notice will vary depending on the length of service.

Grievance procedures If an employee has a complaint against other staff or against their treatment at work then a business may have its own internal grievance procedure. Details of these procedures and who to contact in case of complaints may be included in the written statement. Employees should also be aware of how to contact an industrial tribunal, ACAS (the arbitration service) or a trade union in the case of a complaint. The **Employment Act, 2002** introduced minimum internal grievance procedures that businesses must have. They are designed to improve communication, so that employees can raise grievances, and to reduce the number of unfair dismissal claims.

Employee rights The rights of employees to union

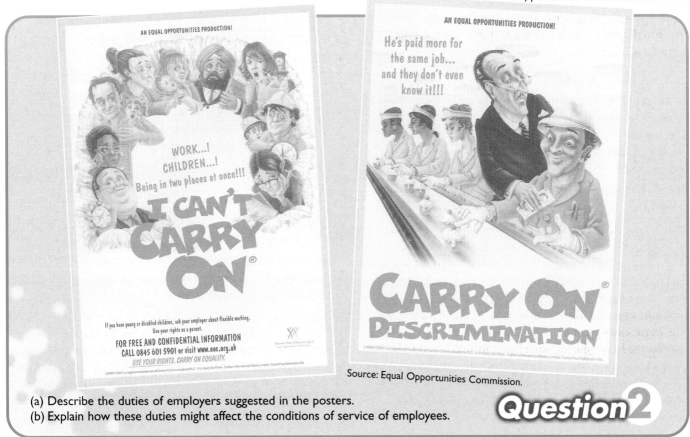

Source: Equal Opportunities Commission.

(a) Describe the duties of employers suggested in the posters.
(b) Explain how these duties might affect the conditions of service of employees.

Question 2

representation, time off and equality of treatment as explained above may be outlined in the written statement of the contract of employment. The **Employment Act, 2002** gave trade union representatives the right to time off for training so that they can carry our their duties.

Types of employment

A number of different definitions can be used to classify the way in which people are employed.

Employees and self-employment If an employer provides and controls work, supplies equipment and pays tax and National Insurance contributions for the worker, then the worker is an EMPLOYEE. An employee will work under the conditions of the contract of employment agreed with the employer. If the worker makes her own decisions about accepting work and conditions of work, and pays her own tax and National Insurance contributions, the worker is likely to be SELF-EMPLOYED. Working at home does not necessarily mean a worker is self-employed, as discussed in the section on homeworkers later in this unit. To be self-employed, a worker must be in business on her own account. Businesses sometimes 'contract out' work to self-employed people to save on the costs of extra employees. For example, buildings in city centres which are mainly glass may hire window cleaners rather than employing staff, even though regular cleaning may be needed.

Permanent and temporary employment PERMANENT

workers are employed by a business for an indefinite period of time. For example, a flour mill may employ a full time quality controller to check wheat as it arrives. He will work for the business until he leaves, either by choice, because he is forced to by the business or when he retires. TEMPORARY workers are employed for a limited period. For example, the mill may employ temporary workers for a period of six months to operate machines that 'mill' the wheat into flour.

In the UK, around 10 per cent of all workers are temporary workers. Businesses needing casual work at busy times employ temporary workers. So do farms, which employ seasonal workers as 'pickers' during the harvesting period. Shops employ retail assistants at Christmas for a fixed period. One advantage of temporary workers is that they no longer have to be employed once demand falls off. They can also be hired when required, for example to cover staff on maternity leave or for 'one-off' tasks. Costs may be lower because temporary workers do not receive the benefits of permanent workers. Some businesses use temporary jobs to try out workers who may later become permanent. One problem with temporary workers, businesses argue, is that they are less reliable than permanent staff.

The **Employment Act, 2002** introduced the right for fixed term employees not to be treated less favourably than similar permanent staff.

Full and part time employment Workers may be employed full time or part time by a business. Part time workers are defined in *Labour Market Trends* published by The Office for

National Statistics as 'people normally working for not more than 30 hours a week except where otherwise stated'. An advantage of part time workers is the flexibility they provide for a business. For example, part time workers may be employed at times of peak trade, such as in public houses at the weekend. They may be employed to allow supermarkets to stay open later in the evening.

Part time work can also benefit employees. It allows workers such as lone parents who have difficulty working full time to be employed. Students or others with low incomes can supplement their wages. The long term unemployed or people who are retraining may find it a way to 'get back to work'.

The **Part-time Workers (Prevention of Less Favourable Treatment) Directive 2000** and the **Employment Relations Act, 1999** ensure that part time workers are treated no less favourably in their terms and conditions of employment than full time colleagues. For example, the Directive states that part timers working under 30 hours a week must receive the same hourly, overtime, sickness and maternity pay, and leave and holiday entitlements as a 'comparable' full-time employee of the same employer. Equal treatment also applies to redundancies, training and access to pensions schemes. Exceptions are allowed to meet 'legitimate objectives' of employers.

Homeworkers and teleworkers A wide range of different people working in the UK might be classed as **homeworkers**. It may include for instance farmers, shop owners, representatives, telesales people, hotel owners and some computer operators. They may be employed by a business to work at home or they may be self-employed. They may be full time or part time. **Teleworker homeworkers** are people who work from their own home, or use it as base, and who could not do so without a telephone or computer. There were 2.2 million teleworkers in the UK, around 7.4 per cent of the workforce, in 2004.

For an employer, the use of homeworkers has a number of advantages. As these workers are not based at the place of employment, the cost of equipment is reduced and less space is needed. There are also fewer problems with absenteeism and transport delays, such as people arriving late to work or who are unable to get to work because of bad weather. People with children are able to work more easily, at times when they want. However, there may be communication problems if staff can not be contacted. Also, it is far more difficult to monitor and control the work of employees.

Flexible working arrangements Different types of workers can have flexible working arrangements. There are many different types of flexibility. Workers might have flexible working hours, having to work a number of hours in the day or week, but able to choose what hours to work. Or they might work a reduced number of days but longer hours each day. **Job sharing** is becoming more popular as people seek

part time work. This is where the tasks involved in a job description are divided between two people, for example. They often work at different times. Examples could be a legal secretary's job, part of which is carried out by one person from 9am to 12am and another person from 12am to 5pm, or two GPs in a doctors practice working on different days or weeks.

A growing number of businesses are taking advantage of the use of flexible arrangements. Legislation in the UK allows certain employees to request flexibility. Flexible arrangements can be beneficial for both employees and employers. Employees can choose the times they want to work to fit in with circumstances. Employers have the chance to change work patterns to fit in with production and demand.

Table 48.1 *The growth in temporary work by occupation, 1992-2000, per cent of total net increase*

Standard Occupational Classification

1. Managerial and administrative	5		
2. Professional	26	*Including:*	
		Engineers	5
		Health	3
		Teaching	14
3. Associate professional	10	*Including:*	
		Computer programmer	2
		Welfare worker	2
4. Clerical and secretarial	23		
5. Craft and related	-1		
6. Personal and protective	23	*Including:*	
		Health related	4
		Childcare related	17
7. Sales	7		
8. Operatives	7		
9. Routine manual	0		

(a) Describe the changes taking place in the table.
(b) Explain why these changes might have taken place.

Termination of contracts

Why might a contract of employment come to end? The contract may be terminated either by the employee or the employer for a number of reasons.

Changing jobs and promotion Employees may leave a business to change jobs. Their existing contract would end and they would be given a contract for their new job. As stated earlier, employees can not usually leave immediately. They often have to work out a period of 'notice', such as one week or one month. Employees who are promoted internally (☞ unit 45) are also likely to be given a new contract of employment as their terms and conditions may have changed. For example, a machine operator who was appointed to be supervisor may have different wages, benefits, deductions and leave entitlements.

Dismissal Employees may be dismissed for a number of reasons. These may be for unfair reasons, such as joining a trade union. If an employment tribunal finds that a person has been dismissed unfairly, it has the power to reinstate the employee. There are lawful reasons, however, for dismissing an employee. These may include misconduct or because an employee is incapable of doing a job. A period of notice is required, but the length will vary depending on how long the employee has worked for the business. The **Employment Relations Act, 1999** reduced the qualifying period for protection against unfair dismissal to one year.

Redundancy Another lawful method of dismissing an employee is on grounds of redundancy. This is where there is no work or insufficient work for the employee to do. The **Employment Rights Act, 1996** states that employees are entitled to redundancy or SEVERANCE payments. They also need to meet other criteria. For example, they must have a contract of employment (ie not be self-employed). Some people, such as members of the armed forces, The House of Commons and the House of Lords are not covered by the Act. Neither are people who are retiring over the age of 60/65 or who are coming to the end of a contract or an apprenticeship.

Retirement and early retirement Some people decide to leave work when they are entitled to this state pension. However, many take 'early retirement' and finish work before. They will then live on state benefits or a private pension which they can draw upon at an earlier age. Some employers that want to get rid of older workers or reduce staff numbers offer attractive 'early retirement' packages to encourage people to leave work. People do not have to leave work at these ages. Some employees are now seeing the benefit of employing older workers (☞ unit 50).

Illness Employers can dismiss employees if they are no longer able to do a job. However, employees may chose to leave a job themselves if they are too ill to continue. Some businesses provide private health cover for employees who need to finish work. Other employees would need to live on state benefits or private insurance benefits.

End of duration of contract Some temporary employees are only given a contract to work for a limited period of time. For example, contractors may hire construction workers to work on a large project, such as a shopping centre, for a period of two years. After the project finished the employees' contract would end.

Breach of contract

If either the employee or employer suffers a financial loss as a result of a BREACH OF CONTRACT by the other party, they may claim damages. For example, an employee on a fixed term contract who is asked to work an extra two weeks to finish the job, but is not paid, may claim as a result. Claims by employees and employers are normally taken to either the the county court or another civil court. An employee can take a claim to an industrial tribunal if an amount is outstanding when the contract is terminated and if it is not related to certain categories, such as patents. Industrial tribunals often settle claims quicker than courts but there is a limit to the amount they can award.

Rue du Paris is a chain of restaurants specialising in French cuisine. It expanded rapidly in the 1990s and employed increasing numbers of employees. However, the setting up of many celebrity chef restaurants and the growing number of restaurants aimed at clients wishing to spend large amounts on meals meant that by 2003 it was facing problems. Its main aim was to change its staffing levels to suit a slimmed down organisation.

The business faced a number of staffing problems. Chefs at Rue de Paris had been moving to work for competitors at higher rates of pay. After training its employees for a number of years, they took their skills elsewhere. Some of its least experienced chefs had been 'moonlighting' at other restaurants. They had hurried their cooking, leaving early to work in other establishments and in many cases they had broken the terms of their employment contracts. A few chefs were over the age of 60. They had a great deal of experience, but perhaps the company was looking to younger people with new ideas that could really move the business forward.

Some of the newer restaurants had been set up with flexible staff because the business was unsure how they would perform. Some staff had been employed on fixed term contracts, for example. Other staff had part time contracts, with flexible hours. Two restaurants in particular had been doing very poorly and the company had to decide whether to close them.

(a) Examine the ways in which the business might terminate the contracts of its employees which may help solve the problems it faces.

key terms

Breach of contract - breaking of terms agreed in the contract of employment by the employers and the employees.

Contract of employment - an agreement between an employer and an employee in which each has certain obligations.

Employee - a worker for whom an employer provides and controls work, supplies equipment and pays tax and National Insurance contributions.

Permanent employment - employment for an indefinite period of time.

Self-employed - a worker who makes his or her own decisions about accepting work and conditions of work, and pays his or her own tax and National Insurance contributions.

Severance pay - an amount payable to an employee on termination of contract.

Temporary employment - employment for a limited or finite period of time.

Vicarious liability - when employers are liable for the wrongful actions of their employees.

Knowledge ...Knowledge...Knowledge...Knowledge...Knowledge...Knowledge...Knon

1. 'A contract of employment is an agreement that is binding to both parties.' Explain this statement.
2. What is a written statement of the contract of employment?
3. State 3 rights of employees of a business.
4. State 3 duties of employees of a business.
5. Suggest 5 conditions of work that may appear on the written statement.
6. Explain 3 differences between an employee and a person who is self-employed.
7. Why might a business employ temporary workers?
8. What is meant by job sharing?
9. What are the advantages of job sharing for an employee?
10. What is meant by a homeworker?
11. Suggest 3 advantages of homeworkers for a business.
12. State 5 reasons why a contract of employment may be terminated.

Case study The growth of teleworkers

Teleworking is becoming popular for both employers and employees. The Labour Force Survey (LFS) and other market research estimates suggest that the number of teleworkers in the UK is around 2.2 - 2.4 million. This is about 7.4 - 8.6 per cent of the UK working population. The LFS defines teleworkers as 'people who do some paid or unpaid work in their own home who could not do so without using both a telephone and a computer'. This includes:

● people who work in their own home (teleworker homeworkers);
● teleworkers who work elsewhere but use home as a base;
● occasional teleworkers who spend at least one day a week working in their own home or using home as a base.

Lloyds TSB has recognised the benefits of teleworkers. A spokesperson stated 'Under the company's new Work Options scheme, employees can ask to work a variety of ways - job sharing, variable hours, teleworking, reduced hours and term-time working.' These provide staff with a means to 'balance home and work life effectively in a win-win initiative which aims to meet the aims of the business and individuals'. The initiative has been introduced not only to allow staff to work differently but to enable the business to retain skilled workers and attract new employees. The option was not just available to women, men or carers with children, but all staff, whether for study, sport or other commitments.

Source: adapted from www.royaldeaf.org.uk.

Footballfangs.com is a London based business that offers football kits, fashion clothing and fancy dress outfits for dogs. The business was set up by Tracey Davis and is run by her and her friend from home. They do not employ other full time or part time staff. The products are sold online via a website. The business also sells wholesale football shirts for dogs to Premiership and League clubs. All products are imported and sold globally. The website is updated every day and designed and managed in-house.

The business hopes to expand in future. It aims to be the market leader in the UK and Europe and take a sizeable chunk of the US market. It has thought about the possibility of using teleworkers in future to increase sales.

Source: adapted from www.the-bag-lady.co.uk.

In 2002 an agreement was signed in Brussels between major European multinational employers and trade unions on the protection of teleworkers. It was hoped that this would form the basis of future legislation. The deal covered data protection, privacy, equipment, health and safety, organisation of work, training and collective rights issues. The aim was to give teleworkers the same protection as premises-based employees. Several companies currently adopt similar proposals, including British Gas and IBM.

Source: adapted from news.zdnet.co.uk.

Table 48.2 *Teleworkers: employees and self-employed, part time and full time*

Per cent

Teleworker homeworkers	All	Men	Women
Employees	44	43	45
Self-employed	56	57	55
Full-time	52	74	34
Part-time	47	26	66

Home-based teleworkers	All	Men	Women
Employees	41	40	46
Self-employed	59	60	54
Full-time	81	88	57
Part-time	19	12	43

Occasional teleworkers	All	Men	Women
Employees	84	82	88
Self-employed	16	18	12
Full-time	90	96	78
Part-time	10	4	22

Source: adapted from *Labour Force Survey*.

Table 48.3 *Teleworkers by occupation*

Per cent

Teleworker homeworkers	All	Men	Women
Managers & senior officials	22	28	16
Professional	19	30	10
Associate professional & technical	27	31	23
Administrative & secretarial	24	5	40
Skilled trades	3	*	*
Sales and customer service	*	*	*
Other	5	*	7

Home-based teleworkers	All	Men	Women
Managers & senior officials	21	22	20
Professional	20	19	24
Associate professional & technical	24	21	34
Administrative & secretarial	3	*	9
Skilled trades	23	29	*
Sales and customer service	3	2	5
Other	6	6	6

Occasional teleworkers	All	Men	Women
Managers & senior officials	37	42	28
Professional	33	31	35
Associate professional & technical	17	15	20
Administrative & secretarial	5	*	11
Skilled trades	5	7	*
Sales and customer service	*	*	*
Other	3	3	*

Source: adapted from *Labour Force Survey*.

(a) **Identify the different types of employment using examples from the data. (4 marks)**

(b) (i) **What types of workers are most suited to telework? (4 marks)**

(ii) **Explain why these occupations are suited to telework. (6 marks)**

(c) **Outline the benefits to staff and employers at Lloyds TSB of using teleworkers. (8 marks)**

(d) **Examine how the introduction of legislation to protect teleworkers might affect teleworkers. (8 marks)**

(e) **Discuss whether Footballfangs.com should employ teleworkers in its business in future. (10 marks)**

Induction

Newly appointed employees are most likely to leave the business in the early weeks of employment. This is called the **induction crisis**. How can employers prevent this? One approach is to help the new employee settle in quickly and feel comfortable in the new job by using an INDUCTION programme. Induction programmes are not usually about a specific job the employee will be doing, but the way in which the business works. They may contain information about some or all of the following.

- The organisation - history, development, management and activity.
- Personnel policies.
- Terms of employment - including disciplinary rules and union arrangements.
- Employee benefits and services.
- Physical facilities.
- General nature of the work to be done.
- The role and work of the supervisor.
- Departmental rules and safety measures.
- The relationship of new jobs to others.

They may also contain:

- a detailed description of the employee's job;
- introduction to fellow workers;
- an explanation of the values that the business feels are important, such as good attendance;
- follow up after several weeks.

Even with these, induction is unlikely to work without careful timing and without making sure that the employee adjusts to the new social and work environment. Experiments have shown that it is possible for the time taken for induction to be halved and costs reduced by two-thirds if it is well planned. To do this, the programme must focus on the anxieties of the new employees, instead of on what it is thought they should be told.

The aims of training

Training involves employees being taught new skills or improving skills they already have. Why might a business train its employees? It is argued that a well trained workforce has certain benefits for the business.

- Well trained workers should be more productive. This will help the business to achieve its overall objectives, such as increasing profit.
- It should help to create a more flexible workforce. If a business needs to reorganise production, workers may have to be trained in new tasks.
- It will help the introduction of new technology. New machinery or production processes can be introduced more quickly if workers are trained to use them effectively.
- It should lead to increased job satisfaction for employees. Well motivated workers are more likely to be more productive.
- It should reduce accidents and injuries if employees are trained in health and safety procedures.
- It may improve the image of the company. Customers are more likely to have confidence in personnel who are confident, competent and have knowledge of products or processes. Good applicants are also more likely to be attracted if a training programme is part of the job.
- It can improve employees' chances of promotion. The business, as a result, should have qualified people in important posts.
- Training can give a business a competitive advantage over rivals (☞ unit 5). This is increasingly important in competitive markets.
- Globalisation means that businesses are increasingly

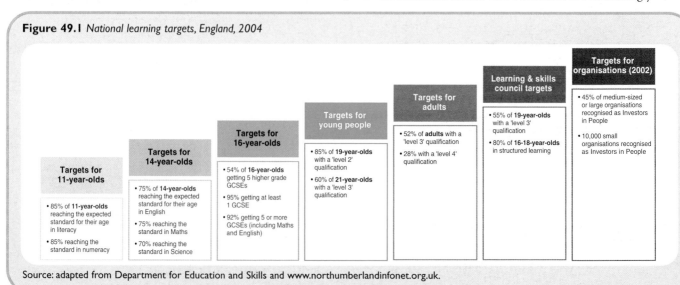

Figure 49.1 *National learning targets, England, 2004*

Targets for 11-year-olds
- 85% of **11-year-olds** reaching the expected standard for their age in literacy
- 85% reaching the standard in numeracy

Targets for 14-year-olds
- 75% of **14-year-olds** reaching the expected standard for their age in English
- 75% reaching the standard in Maths
- 70% reaching the standard in Science

Targets for 16-year-olds
- 54% of **16-year-olds** getting 5 higher grade GCSEs
- 95% getting at least 1 GCSE
- 92% getting 5 or more GCSEs (including Maths and English)

Targets for young people
- 85% of **19-year-olds** with a 'level 2' qualification
- 60% of **21-year-olds** with a 'level 3' qualification

Targets for adults
- 52% of **adults** with a 'level 3' qualification
- 28% with a 'level 4' qualification

Learning & skills council targets
- 55% of **19-year-olds** with a 'level 3' qualification
- 80% of **16-18-year-olds** in structured learning

Targets for organisations (2002)
- 45% of medium-sized or large organisations recognised as Investors in People
- 10,000 small organisations recognised as Investors in People

Source: adapted from Department for Education and Skills and www.northumberlandinfonet.org.uk.

competing in international markets. Training is important if a business wants to be able to operate in these markets.

The need for training

It could be argued that, if left to themselves, businesses would not spend enough on training. They may feel that the costs of training are too high or that they will not see enough benefits. In this case there is said to be LABOUR MARKET FAILURE. The market, in this case the labour market, is not working at its most efficient. When market failure takes place, the government often attempts to solve the problems. It could do this either by:

● providing government training courses;
● providing incentives for individuals to train or for businesses to encourage their employees to take courses.

The government sets education, training and learning targets in the UK. Figure 49.1 shows the targets in England for 2004.

A major problem with the UK supply of labour is SKILLS SHORTAGES amongst workers. This is where there is a large number of vacancies because individuals do not have the abilities, skills, experience or qualifications necessary to do the jobs which employers require. In March 2004 the Office for National Statistics published figures suggesting that the five highest ranked occupations with skills shortages were science and technology professionals and associate professionals, skilled construction and building trades, business and public service

Park Royal in west London is Europe's biggest industrial estate. There are 1,800 firms employing 40,000 people. But it demonstrates a lot that is wrong with the UK workforce. Manufacturing grew here by 11 per cent in 2002, the only place in London it expanded. But workers earn on average less than £12,000 a year. Most have only basic skills and some have none at all. A large number of recent immigrants work on the site. Many have English only as their second language. The older businesses which used to employ apprentices or train workers in a 'paternalistic way' have all moved, leaving a mass of smaller, often struggling, companies to fill the gaps.

People in the building industry also face problems. They can go to college to learn the basics of carpentry. But they can only qualify with work experience. However, many small firms won't take on unqualified workers to give them the experience they need.

Attempts to upgrade skills through training mean that people could earn more and the area might be regenerated. There is also a high degree of staff turnover. Reducing this would leave more money to pay higher wages.

Source: adapted from *People Management*, 12.6.2003.

(a) Examine the reasons why skills shortages might exist at Park Royal.
(b) Suggest how improving skills shortages might benefit businesses.

Question 1

professionals and skilled metal and electrical trades. Occupations which seemed less likely to have skills shortages included administration, sales and customer services.

Identifying the need for training

How does a business know if training is required? One method might be to use the job description (☞ unit 46) to find the skills and knowledge needed to do the job. If there is a difference between the knowledge and skills of the employee and those actually required, this may indicate a need for training.

Employees can also be asked about areas where they feel their performance is inadequate, areas where they have problems, and any 'gaps' in their knowledge and skills. This should make them more committed to training. Training needs are found at different levels within a business.

● The organisational level. A business may need to train workers if there have been changes in a company's goals or objectives, or an introduction of new processes. For example, a move to 'Just-in-time' methods of stock control (☞ unit 57) may mean that workers must be able to constantly monitor stock. Training may also be needed as a result of company surveys or changes in the law. Sometimes workers find that their jobs no longer exist, due to changes in technology or reorganisation of the business for example. As a result, it may be necessary to **retrain** these workers in the knowledge and skills needed for completely new jobs.
● The departmental level. An indication of the need for training may come from personnel statistics, such as absence levels, turnover levels, production levels and customer complaints. Any differences between departments could show that training is needed.
● The individual level. At this level information from appraisal may be useful. Managers may also request that employees receive extra training. Increasingly, however, workers are identifying their own needs and designing their own personal development plans.

Once a need for training has been identified, a business must decide what skills and approaches should be achieved at the end of the training period. They may be something as simple as 'be able to replace a tyre'. There may also be some criteria to measure how well the trainee has learnt the skill, such as 'type a letter with no more than one mistake', and details on how to perform a task, such as 'always be polite and helpful when taking telephone calls'.

Training needs may be put together as a training or staff development plan. However, the business must take into account whether it has the financial resources to carry out the plan. This will depend on its **training budget**.

The cost of training

Businesses faced with problems may see spending on training as a luxury which has to be cut. This is often the case in times of recession (☞ unit 64). For example, in the recession of 1991 in the UK the number of people receiving job-related training fell by 177,000 from the 1990 figure. Businesses often argue that training leads to increased costs, disruption, wasted time and more effort on their part. Financial costs might include the wage allowance paid to the employee, supervision costs, fees for training at a local college and equipment and travel allowances. To some extent these costs are offset by government payments for training schemes paid to the employer.

At one end of Park Royal in west London is a success story. Hazelwood Breadwinner employs 650 people making sandwiches for supermarkets, airlines and other retail outlets. Darrin Sinclair, the training manager, says 'The company does a fair amount of training' with help from the European Social Fund. But a tight budget prevents him doing as much as he would like. For instance, at £600 a head, the cost of putting people through the supervisor's exams is too much. So his 20 trainees will just get a certificate of participation.

Park Royal Partnership is a body set up by local employers to regenerate the area through improving transport, the environment, business advice and training. It has recently got together with local colleges and other umbrella organisations to break through the minefield of government funding, the shape it takes, the strings attached and the poor communication to providers.

In particular, training for adults has taken a back seat to training the unemployed and young people in the past. Furthermore, at the other end of the spectrum training and development has tended to focus on managers and professionals. Those who had skills tended to get even more. This left the low skilled in a twilight zone with few career prospects.

Source: adapted from *People Management*, 12.6.2003.

(a) Identify the barriers to training that exist using examples in the article.

On-the-job and off-the-job training

The Spring 1998 Labour Force Survey showed that nearly 3.4 million employees of working age said that they had received job-related training in the four weeks before the survey. The figure for Spring 2002 was 3.9 million. Training is sometimes divided into two types. **On-the-job training** takes place when employees are trained while they are carrying out an activity, often at their place of work. **Off-the-job training** takes place away from the job at a different location. It may, for example, involve release from the job for periods of time to attend a course at a college. Table 49.1 shows information on the relative importance of on-the-job and off-the-job training.

Table 49.1 *Employees of working age (16-64 males, 16-59 females) receiving job related training four weeks before before survey, Spring 2001, percentages of all employees of working age*

	Percentages and hours		
	Males	Females	All persons
Any job related training	14.4%	18.5%	16.4%
On-the-job only	4.7%	5.5%	5.1%
Off-the-job only	6.8%	9.5%	8.1%
Both on- and off-the-job training	2.9%	3.6%	3.2%
Average number of hours of training in the last week	14.6hrs	11.9hrs	13.1hrs

Source: adapted from *Labour Force Survey*, Office for National Statistics.

Methods of training

Business may use a variety of training methods. Some might be carried out as the job is being done. Others might take place away from the job. Sometimes training may be a combination of training whilst doing the job and away from the place of work.

Working next to another employee This is a traditional type of on-the-job training sometimes referred to as 'sitting next to Nellie'. 'Nellie', the experienced worker, shows the trainee exactly what to do. It can vary from working next to a machine operator to travelling with a salesperson. One-to-one training like this has complications for a business. Where one employee is training another, the quality of the training will depend on the ability, willingness and time available to the tutor. Such training may mean that one employee does not 'produce' themselves, while they are training the other employee. In cases where a specialist is employed to train others, this can be costly for the business.

Coaching This is where a coach will guide the trainee through the use of the equipment or a process in the same way that swimmers are trained. An example might be a technician being trained how to operate a heart monitor whilst working in a hospital.

Mentoring This involves the trainee being 'paired' with a more experienced employee. The trainee carries out the job but uses the 'tutor' to discuss problems that may occur and how best to solve them

Job rotation In some large companies this has been used for the training of 'high fliers'. The employee works in different departments for short periods - picking up skills from each. The aim is that when the person is promoted and reaches the 'top' of the business, she will have a range of experiences which can be used.

In-house courses Businesses may put on courses for their employees and staff them from their own workers. One example is induction courses, which are used to introduce new recruits to a business and help them settle in. A firm might also run a course aimed at achieving a specific goal. For example, if a new computer system was introduced into a department, employees in the section may be trained in its use on a short course. Courses may also be run by the personnel department for marketing and finance managers in the business, to help them improve staff motivation. Some businesses have their own training centres.

Another option is for a business to run its own courses away from the place of work. It could be for one day, a weekend, a week or a longer period. Courses are often for specialist reasons, such as working in teams or Total Quality Management (☞ unit 58). These courses can make use of simulations. One example is in the training of pilots, when trainee pilots can learn to fly a plane without the worry of accidents. Businesses sometimes simulate business activity during courses. Trainees are divided into teams and compete with each other, making business decisions and carrying out tasks. Other forms of simulation might include an 'in-tray exercise', where the trainee might be told they are leaving the country tomorrow and must clear an in-tray of letters and memos. Sometimes these course lead to qualifications.

Self-awareness training This is where trainees complete self-assessment questionnaires, such as a Myers-Briggs test. Questions may be asked about personal values, individual learning styles, how the individual interacts with others, personality and interests. The trainee then receives feedback from the person carrying out the questionnaire.

Traditional and Modern Apprenticeships In the past, businesses took on 'trainee' workers. They served an 'apprenticeship' over a period of time, often in a skilled trade to become a tradesperson, such as a carpenter. When they 'qualified' they were made employees of the business. Most of these schemes do not operate today. 'Modern' apprenticeships are dealt with in the next section.

Graduate training Some businesses run graduate training

programmes. These are designed for graduates with degree qualifications and are often used to train employees for senior or management positions in the business. A study in 2001 suggested that around one in four graduates are likely to receive training, one in six of those with GCSE qualifications and only one in twenty of people with no qualifications.

Vocational courses There are many different organisations that provide work related or 'vocational' training. Trainees usually work towards a vocational qualification. These are awarded by bodies such as Edexcel, OCR or AQA, or professional organisations such as ACCA (the Association of Chartered Certified Accountants) and The Institute of Personnel Management. Vocational qualifications can take many forms and can be taken in schools, colleges, universities and private training establishments. Qualifications vary from accounting to hairdressing, to leisure and tourism, to engineering, to social care, to journalism.

Self-paced/distance learning There is a number of terms for self-paced learning. These include distance learning, open learning and flexible learning. The main feature of all these approaches is that the trainee controls the pace and the timing of their own learning. Learning is often from materials provided by a tutor. There may be a meeting at the end of a certain period. The main problem with this form of training is the lack of help when the trainee finds the materials difficult.

E-learning Businesses are increasingly making use of e-learning. This is where trainees make use of multimedia to learn. It can take a number of forms. For example, a business might use software to teach all its employees simply how to use microsoft word or to create induction training for new employees. Trainees might also learn by using material which is either downloaded from or accessed via the Internet or via e-mail. For example, it might be possible to play an online simulation of a business problem to teach decision making skills. E-learning has the advantage that material can be regularly and quickly updated. It can also be cost effective as there is no need for a tutor and facilities may not need to be

IQdos has created a training system for the Crown Prosecution Service in the UK. Over 4,000 lawyers and case workers needed to be trained in the complex measures relating to vulnerable witnesses which became law in 2002. Classroom training in this detailed areas would have been expensive and time consuming. Also, people training in this area would need a great deal of preparation work before they could begin training. Classroom training would therefore have been of limited use for those who were unprepared. The IQdos system was designed for trainees to complete before a three day classroom course. This type of learning is now being used in other areas. It is particularly applicable to law training where legislation changes rapidly

and material needs to be regularly updated. However, there was always some dispute about training of 'soft' skills using multimedia. Its easy to see that right and wrong answers can be assessed. But what about training for supervisory skills of managers?

Source: adapted from *People Management*, 20.2.2003.

(a) Discuss the extent to which e-learning might be applicable for businesses in the legal profession.

hired for a course. People can also train from home or any other computer terminal and it helps distance learning However, it may lack the face to face interaction and help given by more traditional methods, unless a tutor is 'online' to answer questions.

Training initiatives

Government initiatives to encourage training take a number of forms.

Modern apprenticeships These are training schemes designed for employees to train in an apprenticeship while doing a job. The government gives financial assistance to businesses to take on young people aged 16-24 as apprentices over a period usually of between one and three years. Trainees in most cases have full time employee status and are paid a wage. Training can either take place in work or using an external training provider. Modern apprenticeships exist at two levels - advanced and foundation. Both lead to National Vocational Qualifications (NVQs), key skills qualifications and Technical Certificates. There are modern apprenticeships in a variety of industries, including agriculture, construction, health and beauty, and finance, insurance and real estate. In 2003, over 47,000 modern apprentices started advanced courses and over 115,000 started foundation courses.

New Deal This is a scheme designed to get people back into work. It is mandatory for young jobseekers aged 18-24 who are claiming Jobseeker's Allowance. It is also available for those over 25. There are also voluntary programmes, such as New Deal for Lone Parents, for people claiming benefits who want to work. Employers who employ people on the New Deal may be entitled to a subsidy and a training grant. The scheme is run through Jobcentres in the UK. In 2004 at the end of September 2003 the New Deal for Young People had nearly 90,000 participants. The New Deal 25 plus had over 58,000.

Learning and skills councils The Learning and Skills Council (LSC) is responsible for funding and planning education and training for over 16 year olds in England (☞ unit 49) There are regional councils throughout the UK. They have funds allocated by government to encourage work based training and education business links. Part of the work of LSCs involves the management of the **Entry to Employment (E2E) Programme**. This is designed to provide training for employees below vocational 'level 2'. Modern apprenticeships are also administered through the LSCs.

Work Based Learning for Adults Work Based Learning for Adults is a combination of customised training, structured work experience and guidance to help people get work. Adults can take prevocational training, recruitment training, or occupational skills training. It is available to anyone over 25 who has been out of work for six months or more. Training can lead to vocational qualifications. Adults who are training are given extra benefits, travelling allowances and short work 'tasters'. Between April 2001 and September 2003, 181,000 people had started this type of programme.

Investors in People This is a government initiative, set up in 1991, to encourage the development of skills in the workplace. It provides a training and employee relations quality standard to which employers can commit themselves. To achieve the standard, employers must meet certain criteria. These include a commitment to develop all employees, regular planning to review training, action to develop new recruits and existing staff, and evaluating investment in training. Companies that

Marc Collins was looking for a record deal. But no matter how many demos he sent off, he did not get any replies from established record companies. So he started looking for ways to make contacts. A leaflet in a Jobcentre caught his eye ' - New Deal for Musicians'. The New Deal personal adviser worked with him to find out exactly what he was interested in. After discussions, Marc started the course. Part of his training involved working in a studio which specialised in remixes. He received the same level of benefits as before, but also a top up during his training. After a few weeks, the studio was so impressed with his work that they offered him a permanent job.

Source: adapted from www.newdeal.gov.uk

Donny Patel is in his third year of an Advanced Modern Apprenticeship and is working towards NVQ Level 3. He works as a chef at a public house in Essex, where he is responsible for preparing food and designing the menus. He argues that 'as a chef you need to practise your skills every day to perfect them. The Modern Apprenticeship programme gave me the chance to work in a professional kitchen and I learn something new every day'. Donny has worked as a chef for three years and aims to run his own business. 'I've gained so much experience that one day I'd like to put it to the test and run my own cafe bar' he said.

Source: adapted from www.realworkrealpay.info.

(a) Examine the potential benefits for:
 (i) employees;
 (ii) businesses;
 of the training initiatives mentioned above.
(b) Discuss whether such initiatives might always be to the benefit of businesses.

Question4

achieve the standard can display a plaque, which is valid for a certain period.

Evaluation of training

As businesses have demanded greater value for money, it has become important to evaluate training. Evaluation is simple when the result of the training is clear to see, such as when training workers to use new technology. Where training is designed to give a certain result, such as:

- a health and safety course;
- a word processing course;
- a design course;

evaluation can be based on observed results. This may be a reduction in accidents, increased typing speed or designs with greater impact.

It is more difficult to evaluate the success of a management training course or a programme of social skills development. It is usual to use end of course questionnaires, where course members answer a number of questions. The problem is that the course will have been a break for most employees from the normal work routine. This can make the participants' view of training appear of more value than it is. Also questionnaires tend to evaluate the course and not the learning. This often means that the person attending the course is assessing the quality of the tutors and visual aids, instead of what has been learnt.

To overcome these problems a business might:

- ask participants and managers to complete a short questionnaire at the start of the course to focus their minds on what they hope to get from it;
- give out another questionnaire at the end of the course focusing on learning and what could be applied back at the job;
- give further questionnaires to review the effects of the course on performance.

This helps employees to concentrate on what has been learnt. This process may, however, be costly for the business.

Appraisal

After a period of time working in a job (and regularly after), a firm may APPRAISE the employee. This is an attempt by the business to find out the qualities, usefulness or worth of its employees.

Appraisal can be used by a business to:

- improve performance;
- provide feedback;
- increase motivation;
- identify training needs;
- identify potential for promotion;
- award salary increases;
- set out job objectives;
- provide information for human resource planning;
- assess the effectiveness of the selection process.

The problem with having all of these aims is that the person carrying out the appraisal may have conflicting roles. If appraisal is designed to help performance and to act as a basis for salary awards, the appraiser would have to be both judge and helper at the same time. This makes it difficult to be impartial. It is also difficult for the person being appraised. A worker may want to discuss problems, but is likely to be cautious about what they say in case they jeopardise any possible pay rise. One way around this is for the appraisal system to review the performance of the worker only.

Many appraisal schemes have been linked to **performance appraisal**, called **performance management**. This involves observing, measuring and developing the performance of employees. Performance can be 'measured' against criteria such as output, quality and speed.

Carrying out appraisal

Appraisal has, in the past, been seen as most suitable for employees in management and supervisory positions. Increasingly, clerical, secretarial and manual staff, with skilled or technical jobs, are also being appraised.

Who carries out the appraisal? There is a number of people that might be involved in appraising an individual. Appraisers may be referred to as **raters**. These are people who 'rate' the performance of an individual.

- Superiors. Most appraisals are carried out by the employee's superior. The advantage of this is that the supervisor usually has intimate knowledge of the tasks that a worker has been carrying out and how well they have been done.
- People 'above' the immediate superior can be involved in appraisal in two different ways. They may 'approve' the superior's appraisal of the employee. A manager further up the hierarchy may also directly carry out the appraisal. This is more likely to happen when individuals decide if a worker has the potential for promotion, for example.
- Self appraisal. This is a relatively new idea and not greatly used. Individuals do carry out self appraisal in traditional appraisal schemes, although the superior's decision officially 'counts'. The ratings that the employer has given may be changed, however, in the light of the employee's comments.
- Peer appraisal. It is sometimes argued that appraisal by peers is reliable and valid as they have a more comprehensive view of the employee's job performance. The main problem, though, is that peers may be unwilling to appraise each other. This can be seen as 'grassing'.
- Subordinates. Appraisal by subordinates is another less well used method. It is limited, as subordinates will only know certain aspects of the work of other employees.
- 360 degrees appraisal. This method gathers ratings from a combination of supervisors, peers and subordinates. Self-ratings and customer ratings may also be used. It provides feedback to individuals on how their performance is viewed by business stakeholders (☞ unit 3). It also encourages individuals to self-diagnose their strong and weak areas and identifies where training is needed. The information from 360 degrees appraisal can help a business when making personnel decisions, such as who to

choose for promotion.

Many firms have used appraisal systems only to find that they have to change or abandon them after a short time. Others 'battle' on with the system, but recognise that it is inadequate or disliked. What factors influence the success of an appraisal system?

- Purpose of the system. Effectiveness will be greater if all involved are clear about what the system is for.
- Control. It is vital that the system is controlled by senior and line management and isn't something done simply 'for the personnel department'.
- Openness and participation. The more feedback that appraisees are given about their ratings, the more likely they are to accept the process. Similarly, the more the employee is allowed to take part in the system, the greater the chance of gaining their commitment.
- Appraisal criteria. The criteria must be related to the job, be easy to use and appear fair to the worker.
- Training. Training may be needed in how to appraise and how to conduct interviews.
- Administrative efficiency. Appraisal must be carried out so that it causes as few problems as possible for both parties. It also needs to be confidential.
- Action. Appraisal needs to be supported by follow-up action. Plans that are agreed by appraiser and workers must be checked, to make sure they take place.
- Selection of raters. The choice of rater should be carefully controlled to avoid, for example, individuals nominating only 'friendly raters' to provide them with feedback.
- Anonymity of raters. Ratings should be made anonymously to encourage honest appraisal.
- Training of raters. Raters should be trained to complete rating and appraisal forms accurately.

Is training becoming more popular?

Ashton and Felstead (2003), in their review of research on training in the UK, suggested a number of reasons to explain the evidence of increased training in the UK over the last five years.

- There has been an improvement in the UK's skills base due to the investment by government to increase numbers in higher education.
- Some employers have played their part in improving skills. Companies with Investors in People and a commitment to training are now training all staff, including the unskilled. This has resulted in the general upskilling of employees in business.
- A group of businesses now state that strategic human resource management is central to business development, and that training is part of that strategy. In addition, a small group of 'leading edge' or high performance organisations use employees' skills as a source of

competitive advantage.

However, a group of UK businesses is still not committed to training. They only engage in formal training when they are forced, either by government legislation or customer requirements. For example, some manufacturing firms can only become suppliers to large retail firms when they obtain ISO 9000. Some argue, therefore, that the UK still appears to be struggling to catch up with competitors in Europe in its investment in training. They also suggest that it may be falling behind new competitors from South East Asia.

Pettersford plc is a manufacturer of plastic cartons and other containers. It has a number of plants around the UK. In 2002 it faced rising costs and falling productivity. The business had previously used annual appraisal methods. Every year employees were reviewed to discuss their performance over the year. It was often one a way communication process, with the line manager 'telling' the employee why they had done well or badly, and how they might improve next year. At the end of the appraisal, employees were asked to make their own comments. But only a short time was left for this and usually the employee could not remember issues that had arisen up to 12 months previously.

Faced with the possibility of closure, the business introduced a quarterly performance review for all its factories. It did allow this to be amended if a plant felt that it did not want four, but the business was adamant that it need to get away from the annual reviews. Another change was that each employee nominated two of their work colleagues to comment on their work. At first people were reluctant to criticise, but eventually, as people became more comfortable with the system, the business and employees found constructive criticism and praise useful. The dialogue also had to be more of a two way process, so that employees could express their own views.

The appraisal was backed up by regular meetings with managers, where suggestions at the appraisal could be introduced into the work environment. Employees gave a 'personal commitment' at their review and this was implemented with the help of the line manager and senior staff. Employees also felt that they could take more initiative, by making suggestions at appraisal meetings. Previously they had simply 'keep their heads down' hoping to get it all over quickly.

The business found that productivity rose as a result of the changes. One spokesperson said 'If you give people some recognition for their work, and listen to what they have to say in return, then it's not only the employee who benefits'.

(a) Explain the problems that existed in the old method of appraisal at Pettersford plc.
(b) Identify the methods of appraisal in the new system.
(c) Discuss the advantages and disadvantages of the new appraisal system for (i) employees and (ii) the business.

Question 5

key terms

Appraisal - evaluating the usefulness of the employee to the business.
Induction - the introduction of a new employee to the business.
Labour market failure - the inability of the market to allocate resources, in this case labour, optionally.
Skills shortages - where potential employees do not have the skills demanded by employers.

Knowledge ...Knowledge...Knowled

1. Briefly explain the purpose of induction.
2. Why is training important to a business?
3. Give 5 aims of training.
4. State 4 methods which could be used to identify training needs.
5. What is the difference between on-the-job and off-the-job training?
6. Briefly explain 3 methods of off-the-job training.
7. How can training be evaluated?
8. What is meant by performance appraisal?
9. How can appraisal help a business?
10. Who might carry out appraisal in a business?

Case study INA Bearing Company

In 2001 INA Bearing Company, a Welsh Engineering plant, embarked on a programme of change with retraining at the forefront. Low cost competition from eastern Europe had meant that the factory, which makes engine components, had cut its workforce by 500 since the early 1990s. Faced with the possibility of closure, the management decided to transform the factory into a 'production location of choice' for high tech products by boosting the skills of its remaining workforce. This required a huge amount of investment training and development to create a culture of continuous improvement.

Getting the workforce back to learning while operating around the clock was no small challenge. Time and resources were limited because manufacturing output had to be maintained. Employees had also become cynical about training initiatives in the past which had faltered. The suggestion put to employees was that 'even if this place does close' they now would have better skills and a marketable and portable qualification which would help then to be attractive elsewhere.

The business initially brought in a 5S training programme (sort, straighten, sweep, standardise, self-discipline) to improve the work environment. At the end of training, the workforce told management the areas in which they would enhance the environment. This led to improvements in productivity, quality and health and safety.

The company started an NVQ programme back in 1998, but this did not get off the ground. It was suggested that 'supervisors were left to do the assessing, but they did not have the time, commitment or will so nothing

was done'. So the programme was relaunched. All 200 operators now worked towards NVQ level two in performing manufacturing operations. A local technical college was brought in to provide supervision of the course.

Team leaders also faced problems. They were spending too much time on machines and not enough on their leadership roles. So they were trained in communication skills for team leaders, taking an NVQ level three in management.

INA is committed to employees taking charge of their own learning. It has set up a learning centre at the plant. Employees can now make use of access Learndirect courses and 100 people have signed up for them.

Source: adapted from *People Management*, 6.11.2003.

(a) **Identify the reasons why retraining was necessary at the business. (4 marks)**
(b) **Explain why the original NVQ programme could have failed. (4 marks)**
(c) **Using examples, explain the types of:**
   (i) on-the-job training;
   (ii) off-the-job training;
   (iii) e-learning;
   that might have taken place at the business. (12 marks)
(d) **Examine the advantages of training for:**
   (i) employees at the business;
   (ii) the business itself. (10 marks)
(e) **Assess possible training methods that might be effective for a business operating for 24 hours a day. (10 marks)**

50 Equal Opportunities

What are equal opportunities?

Units 46 and 47 explained the methods used to recruit and select candidates. Choosing one candidate rather than another is known as DISCRIMINATION. If a man is chosen rather than a woman, when they are both equally qualified, the business has discriminated in favour of the man and against the woman.

Some discrimination is legal and may be considered reasonable. For example, a business may choose a candidate for the post of quality controller in a meat factory because he has 10 years experience, rather than a school leaver. However, if another person with experience did not get the job because she was a woman, or from an ethnic minority, this is illegal in the UK. It could also be said to be unreasonable. The rest of the unit will use the term discrimination in this way. Discrimination occurs not only in selection, but areas such as training, promotion and wages.

EQUAL OPPORTUNITIES mean that everyone has the same chance. In other words, a candidate or employee is not discriminated against because of their sex or race. UK legislation helps to promote this. So do EU laws. These are examples of **individual labour laws** aimed at protecting individuals at work. **Collective labour laws** deal with legislation affecting employee groups such as trade unions.

Why are businesses concerned about equal opportunities? Giving everyone the same chance can affect the productivity, costs and organisation of a business.

Reasons for discrimination

There are certain groups of individuals in society and in business that are arguably discriminated against. Such groups may include:
- women;
- people from ethnic minorities;
- disabled people;
- older people.

Discrimination may occur because of **unproven** ideas or stereotypes about certain groups, such as the following examples.
- Women might not want to take too much responsibility at work because of home commitments; women who are married are less likely to want to be relocated; women with children may be less reliable than men because their main responsibility is to their children.
- Members of certain ethnic minority groups could be difficult to employ because of problems with religious holidays.
- A person in a wheelchair may be less capable than a non-disabled person.

- Older people may be less adaptable, are not interested in coping with new technology and might work more slowly.
All these and many other unproven ideas can affect the way people view these groups during recruitment and selection, and when they are employed.

Women at work

Women form a large and increasing proportion of the working population. In 1979 women accounted for around 38 per cent of all people of working age in employment. By 2003, this had risen to nearly 44 per cent. There is still evidence to suggest that women are discriminated against in the work force.
- There are differences between the earnings of men and women. In 2003 the average hourly earnings of men were £10.04 per hour. For women it was £8.21 per hour.
- Certain industries, such as construction, and certain occupations, such as managers and senior officials, still tend to have male majorities. This is shown in Figure 50.1. In the UK women hold less than one in ten of the top positions in FTSE 100 companies, the police, the judiciary and trade unions.
- Occupations in which women are mainly employed tend to be low paid. Male dominated occupations tend to be more highly paid. For example, in 2002, 75 per cent of working women were in the five lowest paid sectors. In engineering and construction, 97 per cent of modern apprentices are men, earning £115 a week. In social care, 89 per cent of apprentices are women, earning around £60 a week.
- In 2003, 57 per cent of women in employment worked full time. For men, the figure was 91 per cent.
- The rate of employment amongst women with children under five is 54 per cent compared to 72 per cent for women with no children. This perhaps suggests the problem finding jobs for women with young children.

On the other hand, it could be argued that the differences between men and women at work are getting smaller.
- There has been a growth in women's employment opportunities in recent years. The need for a more flexible workforce, equal opportunities legislation, demographic changes and the awareness of the role of women in the workforce have meant that business increasingly look to women to fill vacancies.
- Having children is perhaps less of a constraint than it used to be. Some businesses offer creche facilities or allow work at home to encourage women workers with children. Some women choose to pursue a career instead of having children or return to work after childbirth. Women are remaining in education longer or returning to study. This makes them more qualified for higher grade posts.
- The 'gender gap' in activity rates is getting smaller. The number of women in employment or seeking work rose

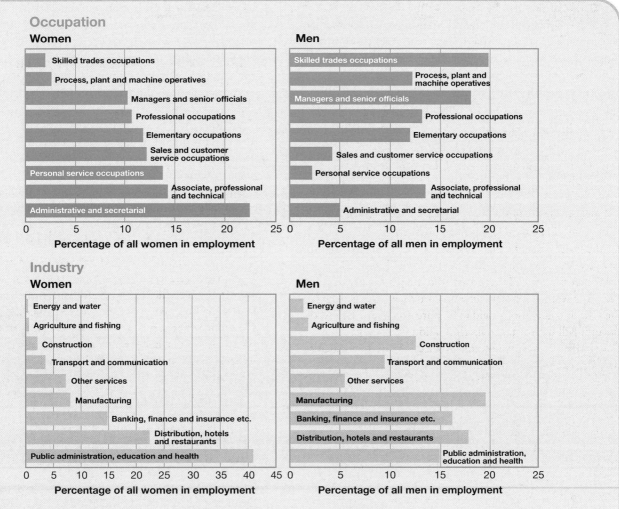

Figure 50.1 *Proportion of men and women employed by occupation and industry, UK, 2003*
Source: adapted from Labour Force Survey.

from 66 per cent to 73 per cent between 1984-2003. Over the same period it fell from 88 per cent to 84 per cent for men.

● The gender gap in employment rates is also getting smaller. In 1984, 58 per cent of women were employed compared to 77 of men. In 2003 the employment rate was 70 per cent for women and 79 per cent for men. This is shown in Figure 50.2.

Legislation and guidance

In the UK, legislation and regulations exist to promote sexual equality at work.

Equal Pay Act The **Equal Pay Act 1970** stated that an employee (whatever their gender) doing the same or 'broadly

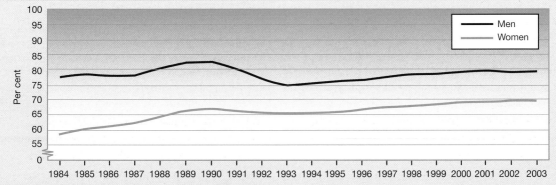

Figure 50.2 *Working age employment rate by sex, UK, 1984-2003*
Source: adapted from Labour Force Survey.

similar' work as a member of staff of the opposite sex is entitled to equal rates of pay and conditions. The Act aimed to eliminate discrimination in wages and other conditions of work, such as holidays, overtime, hours and duties. The Equal Pay Act was amended in 1983 to allow female employees to claim equal pay for work of 'equal value' to that done by a man. The 1970 Act ruled that an employee should be paid equal pay for work which is 'like work' or 'work rated as equivalent' to that of another employee. But the 1983 amendment made it possible for equal pay to be claimed for work of equal value in 'terms of the demands made on her'. Such demands could include the effort, skills and decisions made by an employee. Whether the work was of equal value or not would be determined by job evaluation (☞ unit 46).

Sex Discrimination Act The **Sex Discrimination Act 1975** made it generally unlawful to discriminate either directly or indirectly against someone on grounds of their sex or being married. Direct discrimination is where an employer treats someone less favourably than another person because of their sex. An example could be where a woman was not employed because it was felt she would not fit in because of her gender. It would also include harassment at work. Indirect discrimination is where an employment condition is applied equally to men and women, but one gender has less chance of complying with it. An example might be if an employer insists on an employee being over, say, six feet tall when it is not necessary for the job. Discrimination is unlawful in areas such as job advertisements, selection, interviews, promotion, training, dismissal and terms of employment. In 1986 the Act was updated, removing restrictions on women's hours of work. This meant that women were more able to take jobs with flexible hours or shift work.

European Union law Businesses in the UK must also comply with European Union (EU) law concerning discrimination. **Article 141 of The Treaty of Rome**, for example, states that 'men and women should receive equal pay for equal work'. The **Equal Pay Directive** explains that equal pay means 'for the same work or for work which equal value is attributed'. **The Equal Treatment Directive** deals with all aspects of employment, promotion, training, work conditions and dismissal. It states that there should be 'no discrimination on grounds of sex, either directly or indirectly, particularly with reference to marital or family status'. Other influential directives include **The Parental Leave Directive**, which allows parental leave and unpaid leave to look after sick or disabled dependants, and **The Part Time Workers Directive**, which states that part time workers should be paid on a pro-rata basis to full time workers. The **European Court of Justice (ECJ)** hears cases and passes rulings relating to sex discrimination in EU member countries.

Effects on business Legislation can have a number of implications for businesses. For example:

- advertisements must not discriminate on the basis of sex or marital status. This means that job titles should be sexless, as in 'cashier' or 'salesperson';
- there is a greater need for job analysis, job descriptions and person specifications (☞ unit 46). In particular, a person specification must not restrict the job to men or women, unless it is essential;
- interviews must be carried out in a structured way to help to limit any prejudice that an interviewer may have;
- people can not be selected for dismissal because they are male or female.

If employees feel that they have been discriminated against they can take their case to an **employment tribunal.** Under the **Employment Act 2002**, employees can use a questionnaire to request key information from their employer when they are deciding whether to bring a case. They might also take

---

Advice page

'I work next to a male colleague in my office. He is on the same scale as me and is the same age. But I have recently found out that he is being paid far more than me. I have asked my employers about this. But I was told that although the job we do is similar in terms of decisions and responsibility, we do not do exactly the same job and so I do not have a case.'

'I recently arranged with my employers to have time off work to give birth to my daughter. I agreed a date when I would return to work. However, during the time I was off work my employers say that there has been a reorganisation in the department. All the other employees have a job. But the employers said that they was looking to make some staff redundant and as I was unlikely to be able to carry out the same duties as before with a young child to look after I no longer had a job.'

'Our employers have told us that the image of the company needs to be improved. They want staff to wear specially designed woollen jackets bearing the company logo. They say that these are smart and will help to promote the company image. However, the jackets are very heavy and will be extremely uncomfortable to wear in summer. The employers have stated that all women staff must wear the jackets. But they argue that men do not need to wear the jackets, as jackets are part of suits men wear, which are smart enough.'

Source: adapted from *Labour Research*.

(a) Suggest how the female employees in these businesses might argue a case of discrimination against their employers in a tribunal.

Question 1

their claim to **court**. Businesses found to be discriminating might be ordered to put into practice measures to prevent it occurring. In some cases they may also be asked to pay compensation.

Equal Opportunities Commission Employees can request help from the **Equal Opportunities Commission (EOC)**. This is a government body which:
● works with employers toward eliminating discrimination;
● tries to promote equal opportunities;
● helps employees making complaints;
● investigates complaints of discrimination;
● issues notices preventing a business from discriminating;
● reviews the Equal Pay Act.

In 1997 the EOC drew up a statutory code of practice on equal pay. This contained descriptions of how businesses could organise their pay systems to avoid unfair discrimination. In 2003 this was updated to take into account verdicts in recent cases of discrimination at tribunals and in courts.

Ethnic minorities

There is evidence that certain ethnic groups are discriminated against, often in recruitment and selection. Figure 50.3 shows that unemployment rates of ethnic minority groups are higher than those of whites and economic activity rates and employment rates are lower.

Legislation and guidance

Race Relations Act, 1976 An awareness of the position of ethnic groups and attempts to deal with DIVERSITY ISSUES

have led to anti-discrimination legislation. The **Race Relations Act 1976** makes it generally unlawful to discriminate directly or indirectly on grounds of race. Racial grounds included colour, race, nationality or ethnic origin. Direct discrimination is where a person is treated less favourably compared to someone else on racial grounds. An example would be a person not being employed because it was felt they belonged to a racial group that might be unreliable. Indirect discrimination is where an employment condition is applied equally but a racial group has less chance of complying with it. An example would be not allowing the wearing of turbans, which would rule out Sikhs from being employed.

Under the Act an employer can not discriminate on grounds of race:
● in making arrangements for deciding who should be offered the job;
● in the terms offered;
● in refusing or deliberately omitting to offer employment.

Effects on business The implications for the employer are similar to those of the Sex Discrimination Act. Advertisements should be worded so that there is no indication that some ethnic

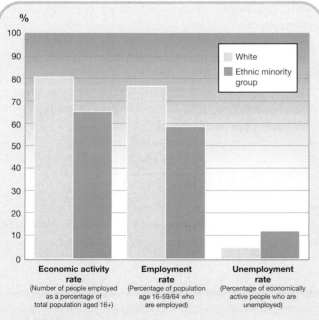

Figure 50.3 *Economic activity rates, employment rates and unemployment rates, whites and ethnic minorities, UK*
Source: adapted from Labour Force Survey.

In the 1990s targets were set for public services, such as the armed forces, the fire service and the immigration service, to employ workers from ethnic minority groups. The change in public services policy aimed to employ the same percentage of ethnic minorities as there were in the population, around 6 per cent. Nationally just 2 per cent of police officers were made up from ethnic minorities. In areas where ethnic minorities made up a higher percentage of the population, targets would be higher. For example, in parts of London they made up nearly 20 per cent of the population.

By 2003 it was suggested that nearly a third of public bodies had failed to comply with the requirement of the amended Race Relations Act. This set targets for improving race equality in services such as police forces. 1 in 10 public bodies had done nothing to comply with the law. Some organisations, however, had been successful in meeting the requirements. Examples included the London Fire Brigade, which had raised its profile amongst ethnic minorities by holding open days, events and visits in mosques and at festivals. It had also introduced mentoring to promote awareness and help employees from ethnic minorities to become integrated.

Source: adapted from *The Independent*, 30.10.2003.

(a) Explain why it could be argued that discrimination exists in public services.
(b) Explain why the changes made by the London Fire Brigade may prove successful in removing discrimination against ethnic minorities.

groups are preferred to others. Writing a job description and person specification will also be useful. The use of selection tests should be monitored. Many tests discriminate against people from minority backgrounds in the way they are designed. Also, people from some ethnic backgrounds may be at a disadvantage because the method of testing is alien to their culture.

The Act was amended in 2002. Protection was extended against racial discrimination by public authorities and public authorities, such as police forces and health trusts, were required to promote racial equality. In 2003 it was amended further to take into account the requirements of the **EU Race and Ethnic Origin Directive 2000**. For example:

- a wider definition of indirect discrimination would be used and people could make a claim against an employer even before they had been put at a disadvantage;
- people from ethnic groups had a legal right to claim against racial harassment.

Employees who feel that they have been discriminated against on grounds of race can take their case to an employment tribunal. In 2001 there were nearly 4,000 claims, a 280 per cent increase from 1997. However, the success rate at hearings was only 16 per cent compared to 65 per cent for redundancy cases and 28 per cent for sex discrimination.

Commission for Racial Equality The Commission for Racial Equality (CRE) is a publicly funded, non-government body that promotes 'fair treatment and equal opportunities for everyone regardless of race, colour, nationality or ethnic origin'. Its tasks include:

- giving information to staff who think they have been racially harassed;
- working with businesses to promote practices that ensure equal treatment;
- running campaigns to encourage organisations and people to create a just society;
- making sure all laws take into account race relations legislation.

It has the power to advise and assist people with complaints about racial abuse, conduct formal investigations and take legal action against advertisements and applications that racially discriminate.

The CRE produces a **Race Relations Code of Practice** which gives practical guidance to help employers, trade unions, employment agencies and employees understand the provisions of the **Race Relations Act**. It provides guidance on:

- types of unlawful discrimination, such as an employer demanding higher language standards than are needed for the effective performance of the job;
- selection criteria that are relevant to the job to prevent subjective and racial discrimination occurring;
- training opportunities to gain the skills required for a job.

Disabled people

There are many different ways of defining disabled people. The Labour Force Survey (adjusted) defines them as 'those

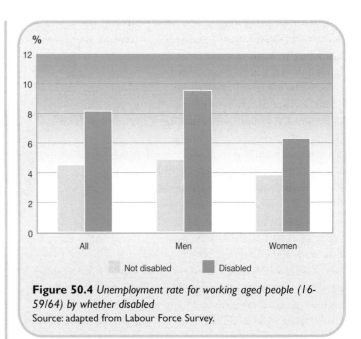

Figure 50.4 *Unemployment rate for working aged people (16-59/64) by whether disabled*
Source: adapted from Labour Force Survey.

with a long-term health problem/disability that limits the kind or amount of paid work they can do'. Figure 50.4 shows that disabled people have higher unemployment rates than non-disabled.

Legislation and guidance

Disability Discrimination Act The **Disability Discrimination Act, 1995** defines disability as 'a physical or mental impairment which has a substantial and long term (at least 12 months) adverse effect on people's ability to carry out normal day-to-day activities'. The Act makes it unlawful for a business (with 15 or more employees in 2003, although this figure may change) to discriminate against a person in:

- recruitment;
- selection or dismissal;
- the terms of employment offered;
- promotion, transfers, training or other benefits.

A business would discriminate if it treats one person **less favourably** than others for a reason relating to disability, unless the treatment is **justified**.

What is less favourable treatment? An example of discrimination might be if two people applied for a job as a translator, but a disabled person in a wheelchair did not get the job because of his disability, even though he was the better translator. Discrimination would also take place if a business asked the disabled person for a driving licence when no driving was involved in the job of translator. To avoid discrimination, a disabled person must be given the job if he is the best candidate.

When is less favourable treatment justified? There must be relevant and substantial (ie not trivial) reasons to treat people less favourably to avoid discrimination. For example, if the employer had to move to new premises just for one disabled candidate to be employed, this might be a substantial reason not to employ the worker. However, employers must make 'reasonable' adjustments for disabled workers. These are adjustments that involve relatively little cost or disruption. They might include:

- changing fixtures, fittings, furniture and equipment, such as modified telephones for people with hearing difficulties or workstations for people in wheel chairs;
- improving access to a building, such as adding a ramp for a wheelchair user;
- changing building features, such as braille in a lift to help a visually impaired employee;
- changing work conditions, such as allowing absences for treatment;
- providing extra training.

The Disability Rights Commission The Disability Rights Commission (DRC) is an independent body established by government to eliminate discrimination against disabled people. Its main roles involve:

- providing advice and information for disabled employees, including a helpline;
- supporting disabled people to gain their rights under legislation as well as legal cases;
- organising conferences, campaigns and events to change the law and business policy to protect disabled people;
- providing an independent conciliation service for disabled people.

It also produces a code of practice which outlines the rights of employees under legislation and how business can meet these requirements.

Older people

There is evidence to suggest that older people are discriminated against.

- Employment rates fall as people get older, as shown in Figure 508.5. The employment rate is the percentage of the population in a given age group in employment.
- Older workers are more likely to be working part time. This is particularly the case for people over state retirement age. For example, 91 per cent of men aged 16-64 are employed full time compared to just 35 per cent of men aged over 65. For women, 57 per cent aged 16-59 are employed full time compared to 25 per cent working part time. This might be because of choice. But it might also be because employers are less willing to take on older workers full time.
- Older people are less likely to receive training. In 2003, employees aged 16-19 were over twice as likely to have participated in job-related training than those aged 50-59/64.

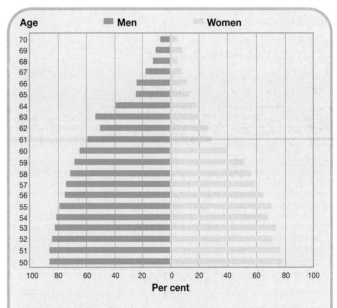

Figure 50.5 *Employment rates of people aged 50-70 by gender, UK, Spring 2003*
Source: adapted from Labour Force Survey.

Legislation and guidance

In the past, the main protection for older employees was against redundancy (☞ unit 48). For example, if they were made redundant they were often entitled to severance pay. In difficult periods, older people may be the first to be made redundant. They are sometimes persuaded to accept voluntary redundancy by taking early retirement.

There was also no specific protection against age discrimination when seeking employment and in training or promotion. However, cases taken to an employment tribunal have been won using sex or race discrimination in relation to

---

Val Miles was paralysed from the chest down after a skiing accident. She has now started to work full time again after rehabilitation. But she experienced problems at some of her interviews. In one case, she gave a presentation to the tops of the heads of two interviewers, who were so uncomfortable about making eye contact they looked down all the time. She was so ill at ease she performed badly. At other interviews she has arrived to be told 'there are only a few steps up to the front door'. She has also had to travel long distances to find there is no disabled parking. And some businesses are keen to interview a disabled candidate just so they can meet equal opportunities requirements.

Her experience working for the National Glass Centre has been far better. The interview went well. She was escorted to the lift and shown the disabled toilets. The business operates from a new purpose built building with disabled access.

Source: adapted from *People Management*, 24.1.2002.

(a) Identify discrimination that might have taken place in the article.
(b) Explain how the businesses in the article might make 'reasonable' adjustments to prevent discrimination against disabled people.

age. For example, a case by an employee against the Civil Service bar on people aged over 32 was judged to discriminate against black people, since black employees were older than white employees at the time due to adult immigration.

The EU **Employment Framework Directive** obliges all EU member states to introduce laws preventing age discrimination by 2006. There will, however, be some circumstances where discrimination will be permitted, for example where safety is an issue or to recruit younger workers when a number of employees are nearing retirement age.

Some argue that there are actually advantages to a business in employing workers 'over 40'.

- The over 40s have greater experience and better judgement in decision-making.
- The over 40s have already satisfied many of their needs for salary and status and are able to concentrate more on job responsibilities.
- The over 40s have a greater 'social intelligence' and the ability to understand and influence others.

B&Q, the chain of DIY stores, has recognised the benefits of employing older people, and has adopted a policy of hiring over 50s in its stores.

Why might businesses have equal opportunities policies?

Certain businesses operate an **equal opportunities policy**. This means that the business is committed to giving all applicants an equal chance of, say, selection, no matter what their sex, sexuality, race, age, marital status, religion or disability. The aim of such a policy is to remove discrimination in all areas of the business, including promotion, training and financial rewards, so that the culture of the organisation is not to exclude any employees whatever their race, colour, nationality or gender. Examples of employers that operate such a policy have included Ford and Kingfisher the retail group.

How will such a policy affect business?

- A business is far more likely to employ the 'best' person for the job if everyone is given an equal opportunity. The quality of applicants may also improve.
- Equal opportunities for training are likely to lead to a better qualified workforce in key positions, although the cost of training could increase.
- Workers may become better motivated if, for example, the chances of promotion are equal. They are also more likely to remain with the business, reducing staff turnover and costs.
- Production may need to be reorganised. This might include more flexible hours, job rotation or even job sharing. For example, an office job could be carried out by a mother in the morning (when children are at school) and by a male in the afternoon. A more flexible workforce may be better able to respond to change.
- There may be extra wage costs. Paying women equal wages

to men will raise the total wage bill.

- Extra facilities may be needed. This can vary from ramps for wheelchairs to children's creches.
- Recruitment, selection and training procedures may have to change.
- The image of the business or jobs in it may have to change. This could improve the image to the customer. Rank Xerox, for example, found that jobs in the business were often seen

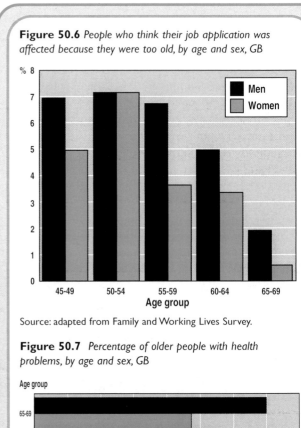

Figure 50.6 *People who think their job application was affected because they were too old, by age and sex, GB*

Source: adapted from Family and Working Lives Survey.

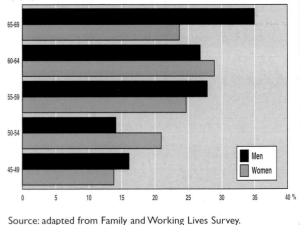

Figure 50.7 *Percentage of older people with health problems, by age and sex, GB*

Source: adapted from Family and Working Lives Survey.

(a) Describe the trends taking place in Figures 50.6 and 50.7.
(b) How might these trends explain why age discrimination takes place?

as 'men's' jobs or 'women's' jobs and tried to change this.

It is argued that POSITIVE ACTION by employers is an important part of a good equal opportunities policy. Positive action describes a range of measures that can be taken to provide equality of opportunity. Examples of positive action are training to meet the needs of racial groups and encouragement to apply for particular jobs. Positive action is only lawful if people of particular groups are **under-represented** in work.

Effective equal opportunities policies must also take into account discrimination against which there is no legislation. It is suggested that employers discriminate against candidates with regional accents in interviews. A survey of recruitment specialists found that they felt Liverpool, Manchester and Birmingham accents were negative. 'Upper class accents' led to hostility in Scotland. Discrimination also takes place against people who employers perceive as being 'fat'. One NHS Trust, for example, set a size limit when recruiting which would have ruled out any candidate over 5 feet 10 inches, weighing over 12 stone 12 pounds.

Sexual orientation

The **Employment Equality (Sexual Orientation) Regulations 2003** came into force in 2003 in the UK to comply with an EU directive. They outlaw discrimination in employment based on sexual orientation towards people of the same sex, the opposite sex or the same sex and the opposite sex. This can be:

- direct discrimination (where someone is treated less favourably than another on grounds of sexual orientation);
- indirect discrimination (where a criterion or practice places people of a particular sexual orientation at a disadvantage);
- harassment or victimisation of people of a particular sexual orientation.

There are some exemptions, for example where the employer applies a particular sexual orientation to avoid conflict with religious convictions.

key terms

Discrimination - to make a selection or choice from alternatives, such as an applicant for a job. The term is often used to mean an illegal or unreasonable selection in the context of equal opportunities.

Diversity issues - relating to the proportion of the workforce that is made up of different ethnic groups.

Equal opportunities - where everyone has the same chance. In business this can mean the same chance of selection, promotion etc.

Positive action - measures geared towards improving the employment opportunities and training of groups that are under-represented at work.

Knowledge

1. State 4 groups that are often discriminated against by businesses.
2. Why might there have been an improvement in employment opportunities for women?
3. What are the main points of:
   (a) The Equal Pay Act;
   (b) The Sex Discrimination Act;
   (c) The Race Relations Act;
   (d) The Disability Discrimination Act?
4. What effect might equal pay legislation have on wages and opportunities for women in the UK?
5. State 3 ways in which an employer might avoid discriminating against minority groups when recruiting for jobs.
6. What advantages might candidates over 40 have for a business when compared to younger applicants?

Case study Removing discrimination in banking

UK banks have been at the forefront of businesses waking up to removing racial discrimination. They are realising that unless race issues are on the agenda, businesses are limiting their 'pool of talent and target market' according to Allan Leighton, Chairperson of Race for Opportunity (RfO), a government initiative which offers advice to businesses on how to treat ethnic minorities.

Lloyds TSB focusses on the issue of race within its graduate recruitment. In 1997 it identified that only three per cent of graduates came from ethnic minorities when twelve per cent were graduating from these groups. It has worked with ethnic minority graduates and their families to show them that banking is a worthwhile career. The imagery on banking literature has been changed to include the faces of ethnic minority employees and included case studies of successful employees. It has also built links with universities with larger numbers of ethnic minority students.

By 2003 the intake from ethnic minority groups had risen to 25 per cent. In 2003 it reported a 30 per cent increase in sales in some branches where staffing was changed to reflect the ethnicity of its customers. It feels that now it does not have to do too much more because one in four applications comes from an ethnic minority candidate for every post.

Carl Gilleard, Chief Executive of the Association of Graduate Recruiters (AGR), says that the 'kind of commitment we are now seeing is leading to significant improvements not only in terms of recruitment opportunities, but also retention and progression'. However, it's one thing to get graduates from ethnic minorities in. It's another to keep them and ensure fair promotion opportunities. This can involve mentoring and networking. It might also involve training schemes geared particularly towards ethnic minorities, aimed at improving their confidence and strengths. All graduates are likely to take into account an organisation's policy on discrimination when deciding to work for them, according to Gilleard.

Barclays Bank has a specialist diversity unit which helps it recruit staff from ethnic minorities. Over the last two years its recruitment of ethnic minority employees has risen from 6.3 per cent to 8.3 per cent. The policy extends even to the top of the business. Two employees from ethnic minority groups have now been appointed to the board of the organisation. The bank focusses on four key areas - fairness in recruitment and selection, handling inappropriate behaviour, building an inclusive culture and work-life balance.

The whole process of recruitment at the bank has been reviewed. The number of universities from which graduates have been selected has been increased. Recruitment agencies used by the businesses have been briefed to encourage them to attract a diverse range of candidates. Role models amongst ethnic minorities in the bank were identified to act as inspiration to others. Also those who wanted to progress were given extensive career training.

Source: adapted from *The Independent*, 30.10.2003.

(a) Using examples from the case, explain what is meant by the phrases:
  (i) racial discrimination;
  (ii) inclusive culture. (6 marks)
(b) Explain the term positive action and examine how positive action has been taken by banking businesses. (10 marks)
(c) Examine the potential (i) benefits and (ii) costs to banking businesses of policies to reduce racial discrimination. (12 marks)
(d) Evaluate the success of banking businesses in meeting the requirements of legislation regarding racial discrimination. (12 marks)

Why is protection needed?

Why might a business protect its employees? There are certain laws protecting people in the workplace. Legislation has laid down rules about:

● health and safety;
● employment protection (dismissal, redundancy and leave of absence);
● wage protection;
● recruitment, selection and training (☞ units 46-49).
● data about employees.

This legislation provides guidelines and acts as a constraint on how a business makes decisions. In addition, from a purely practical point of view, it makes sense for a business to protect its workers. Satisfied employees are far more likely to help a business achieve its goals. A business may also feel it has a moral obligation to protect employees. As their employer, it should look after their interests in the workplace.

Health and safety at work

Providing a healthy and safe environment can mean many things. It could include some of the following.

● Providing and maintaining safety equipment and clothing.
● Maintaining workplace temperatures.
● Ensuring adequate work space.
● Ensuring adequate washing and toilet facilities.
● Guaranteeing hygienic and safe conditions.
● Providing breaks in the work timetable.
● Providing protection for the use of hazardous substances.
● Providing protection from violence, threats or bullying.
● Providing a relatively stress free environment.

It is likely that the conditions for a healthy and safe environment will vary depending on the nature of the task carried out. Ensuring the health and safety of a mine worker will require different decisions by a business from protecting an office worker. Although both must be protected from adverse effects of equipment, for example, protection is likely to be different.

Businesses must protect people outside the workplace who might be affected by activities within it, eg those living near a chemical or industrial plant. They must also protect visitors or customers to shops or premises.

Health and safety legislation

In the UK, laws to protect employees have been passed for over 100 years. There are also many regulations concerning health and safety at work which are updated from time to time as work conditions change. In addition, businesses may follow codes of practice designed to protect workers.

The Health and Safety at Work Act, 1974 The aim of the **Health and Safety at Work Act, 1974** is to raise the standard of safety and health for all individuals at work, and to protect the public whose safety may be put at risk by the activities of people at work.

Every employer is required to prepare a written statement of their general policy on health and safety. Employees must be advised of what the policy is. Management have the main responsibility for carrying out the policy. In the case of negligence, proceedings can be taken against an individual manager as well as against the business. The Act also places a duty on employees while they are at work to take reasonable care for the safety of themselves and others. The employee is legally obliged to comply with the safety rules drawn up by management. Employers or employees who fail to comply can be taken to court and fined. Part of the Act requires a business to give training, information, instruction and supervision to ensure the health and safety at work of employees.

The Act is backed up by the Health and Safety Executive (HSE) and the Health and Safety Commission (HSC), which are responsible for seeing that the Act is carried out. Health and safety inspectors are appointed to make sure the law is being carried out. They have the power to enter employers' premises, carry out examinations and investigations, take measurements, photographs and recordings, take equipment and materials and examine books and documents. The HSE/HSC have the power to issue **codes of practice** to protect people in various situations, for example:

● the protection of individuals against ionising radiation;
● the control of lead pollution at work;
● time off for training of safety representatives;
● control of substances hazardous to health (various).

The Health and Safety at Work Act is the main Act which allows new regulations to be brought in as appropriate.

UK and EU regulations There is a number of regulations relating to health and safety in the UK. Regulations are introduced to cope with new work situations. Increasingly UK regulations are influenced by European Union (EU) directives, which are agreed by member countries of the EU.

The **Working Time Regulations, 1998** were important regulations introduced into the UK as a result of an EU directive which addressed concerns over the problems caused by long work hours. They provided a number of rights for most employees including:

● a maximum working week of 48 hours a week;
● 4 weeks annual paid leave a year;
● 11 consecutive hours' rest in any 24 hour period;
● a 20 minute rest break after 6 hours' work;
● a limit of an average 8 hours' work in any 24 hours for night workers.

The regulations were amended in 2003 to include some groups that were previously excluded, such as 'non-mobile workers in road, rail and sea transport'. In 2003 the UK was the only EU country with an opt-out clause, which allowed employees to work longer than the 48 hour a week limit if they and their employer both agree.

Table 51.1 shows some examples of regulations which affect UK and EU businesses.

Table 51.1 *UK/EU health and safety regulations*

Manual Handling Operations Regulations, 1992 (Directive 90/269/EEC) Relate to the transport and handling of loads.

Workplace (Health, Safety and Welfare) Regulations, 1992 (Directive 89/654/EEC) Relate to the requirements of conditions at work, such as maintenance, ventilation, space and rest facilities.

Personal Protective Equipment at Work Regulations, 1992 (Directive 89/656/EEC) Relate to protective clothing and equipment.

Health and Safety (Display Screen Equipment) Regulations, 1992 (Directive 90/270/EEC) Relate to the use of computer screens.

Safe Use of Work Equipment, Provision and Use of Work Equipment Regulations, 1998 (Directive 89/655/EEC) Relate to the safe use of equipment and machinery.

The Management of Health and Safety at Work Regulations, 1999 (Directive 89/391/EEC) Relate to the assessment of risk and the implementation of health and safety arrangements to keep employees safe.

The Maternity and Parental Leave Regulations, 1999 (Directive 96/34/EEC) Relate to time off work for mothers and fathers when children are born.

Control of Asbestos at Work Regulations, 2002 Relate to the assessment and control of risk associated with asbestos on premises.

The Control of Substances Hazardous to Health Regulations, 2003 Relate to the handling, use and control of substances used in production which might affect the health of workers, such as nuclear fuel or chemicals.

Employment protection

Unit 48 showed that employees are entitled to a contract of employment when they are first appointed to a job. The contract of employment is an agreement between the employer and the employee on the terms and conditions under which the employee will work. An employee may be able to claim for a breach of contract by the employer. Employees are also protected by legislation against discrimination (☞ unit 50).

The **Employment Relations Act, 1999** stated that employees who have worked for an employer for a year had a right not to be unfairly dismissed. It also aimed to introduce 'family friendly policies', such as parental leave for people adopting a child, and to remove limits on awards for unfair dismissal. Certain people cannot claim unfair dismissal, such as an independent contractor or freelance agent, who are not employees.

There is a number of reasons why employees might be dismissed which may be **unfair** dismissal under the conditions of the Act (and its amendments).

- Because they were trying to become or were a member of a trade union. Alternatively, because they refused to join or make payments to a union.
- On the grounds of pregnancy, even though she was able to do the job.

New and expectant mothers
The Department of Trade and Industry has estimated that there are around 350,000 pregnant women at work in the UK. More than one in four experience a miscarriage, one in 200 babies are stillborn and 100 premature babies are born each year. In 2001, out of 1,434 potential tribunal cases involving pregnancy or maternity related discrimination, 95 per cent involved some breach of health and safety legislation.

Work related road travellers
Every year 3,5000 people are killed and 40,000 are seriously injured according to the Health and Safety Executive. Over a thousand of those killed and 13,000 of those injured involve people at work. They include drivers of heavy goods vehicles, company cars and vans, and dispatch riders who ride bikes or motorcycles.

Employers have a legal duty under The Management of Health and Safety at Work Regulations, 1999. They must assess the risk to employees and carry out measures to ensure their protection. Certain groups of workers have been identified as at risk at work.

Source: adapted from *Labour Research*, March, November, 2003.

(a) Explain why these groups might be most at risk at work.
(b) Suggest ways in which businesses could protect the groups mentioned above.

Question 1

- Making workers redundant without following the correct procedure. This is dealt with later.
- As a result of a transfer of a business, such as when one business is bought by another. However, if the business can prove it was for economic, technical or organisational reasons, it may be considered fair.
- For refusing to work on a Sunday. The **Sunday Trading Act, 1994** gives shop workers the right not to be dismissed for refusing to work on Sundays.

There are reasons why dismissal may be **fair**. The employer must have a valid reason and must act 'reasonably' when dealing with this reason.

- The employee is incapable of doing the job or is unqualified.
- 'Misconduct' of the employee, such as persistent lateness (minor) or theft (major).
- The employer is unable to employ the worker. For example, a lorry driver may no longer be employed if he has lost his driving licence.
- Any other substantial reason. For example, false

details may have been given on the job application form.

● Redundancy can take place if the employer needs to reduce the workforce. This could be because a factory has closed or there is not enough work to do. The job must have **disappeared**. In other words, it is not redundancy if another worker is hired as a replacement. Certain procedures must be followed by employers. They must consult with trade unions over any proposed redundancy. If the union feels the employer has not met requirements, it can complain to a tribunal. Employees are entitled to a period of notice, as well as a redundancy payment based on how long they have been in continuous employment.

If a worker feels that he has been unfairly dismissed, he can take his case to an **employment tribunal**. This is dealt with in the next section. For example, a tribunal may decide that an employee who resigns as a result of the employer's actions has been **constructively** dismissed. To do this the employer must have acted in a way that is a substantial breach of the employment contract. An example might be where the employer demoted a worker to a lower rank or lower paid position for no reason.

Unfair dismissal - what to do

If an employee feels that he has been unfairly dismissed, what can he do about it? It may be possible for a worker and a business to settle the dispute voluntarily. If not, the employee may decide to complain to an **employment tribunal**. Figure 51.1 shows the stages involved in this.

The complaint must be received within 3 months of the end of contract. A notice of application is sent to the employer asking if they wish to contest the case. Details of

the case are then sent to the **Advisory, Conciliation and Arbitration Service** (ACAS). Its role is to help settle the dispute before it reaches a tribunal through conciliation.

Before the complaint does reach a tribunal, there may be a pre-hearing assessment. If either party has a case that is not likely to succeed, they can be told and also informed that they may be liable for costs. The aim of this stage is to 'weed out' hopeless cases.

Once a complaint goes to a hearing at a tribunal, the employee is entitled to legal advice. After the hearing the tribunal will make a decision. If this is in favour of the employee then the tribunal can order:

● the employee to be reinstated in the same job;
● the employee to be re-engaged in another job;
● compensation to be paid.

It is possible to appeal against a tribunal's decision. This will be heard by the Employment Appeal Tribunal. An employee who disagrees with the decisions of an **employment tribunal** and an appeal tribunal may take his or her case to the European Court of Justice (ECJ). This is the highest court of appeal under EU law. If a case is upheld, then UK businesses must comply with its decision as the UK is an EU member.

Wage protection

The main legislation relating to pay in the UK is the **Wages Act, 1986**. This sets out conditions for payments to workers and deductions from wages. Wages are defined as any sum paid to the worker by the employer in connection with the job. This includes fees, bonuses, commission, sick pay, gift tokens or vouchers. Certain payments, such as redundancy payments, expenses or loans are not included.

Deductions made from wages that are covered by the Act include:

● those that must be taken or are agreed upon, such as income tax or National Insurance;
● those shown in the contract of employment;

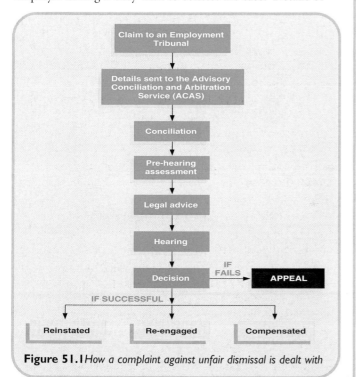

Figure 51.1 *How a complaint against unfair dismissal is dealt with*

John Smart was employed by Jones and Harcourt, a paper merchant in Oxford. The company buys paper in bulk from foreign mills and distributes it to users in the UK. Trade and paper prices began to fall and the company was looking for ways of cutting costs. John had been employed as warehouse manager to control the arrival and delivery of paper. With no prior consultation, one Monday in March, a director informed John that his services were no longer required. John was told that he was to be made redundant at the end of the week. The following week the company employed a younger man to do John's job, at a far lower salary.

(a) Comment on the fairness of John's dismissal.
(b) What advice would you give John about his next course of action?

Question 2

● those agreed by the worker in writing, such as trade union payments;

providing that these are the agreed amounts. If the employer deliberately decides not to pay part of a worker's wages, then employees can complain to a tribunal. This is a similar process to complaints about dismissal.

Wage protection is also provided through Acts which apply to other areas of employment protection. For example:

● the equal treatment of men and women is covered by the **Equal Pay Act, 1970** (☞ unit 50)
● payment during maternity or paternity leave is covered in the **Employment Act, 2002** (☞ unit 48).

The minimum wage

The **National Minimum Wage Act, 1998** introduced a minimum wage for workers in the UK. It is unlawful to pay a worker below the rate set for the minimum wage. In 2003 this was £3.80 for workers aged 18-21 and £4.50 for workers aged 22 and over (the adult rate). There was an increase to £4.10 for 18-21 years olds and £4.85 for people aged 22 and over in 2004. There was also a minimum wage for employees aged 16-17 of £3.00 an hour from 1 October 2004.

Why did the government want to introduce a minimum wage?

● To prevent poverty. It would prevent workers being paid very low wages by employers.
● To reduce inequality between the pay of men and women. Women often work in low paid full time or part time jobs.
● To benefit businesses. Greater equality and fairness should motivate employees, reduce staff turnover and improve workers' productivity.

Some businesses argue that raising the wages of low paid workers increases their costs. To pay the higher wages, a business may need to make other workers unemployed or take on fewer new workers, particularly younger workers or people just starting work.

In 2003 the minimum wage rates for employees aged 18-21 and adults aged 22 and over was raised compared to rates in 2002. Table 51.2 shows how rates have increased since its introduction into the UK in 1999. There was growing concern about the effect that this would have on younger employees, who were falling behind. Workers aged 22 and over received a 7.1 per cent increase compared to only a 5.6 per cent increase for 18-21 year olds. The argument for lower rates has been to ensure that younger people are not 'priced out of the market', although the Low Pay Commission (LPC) argue that there is 'little evidence to support that the minimum wage has had any adverse effects on employment'.

McDonald's had a minimum hourly rate of £3.75 outside London in 2001. It raised this in 2002 to £4.10 in line with the new adult hourly rate for people aged 22 and over. It made a decision, however, to set a rate for 18-21 year olds of £3.90, above the minimum wage for this age group. But it kept its 17 year olds on £3.75.

Unions have argued that pay should be related to ability rather than age. Removing age-related rates can be beneficial. For example, in the hotel and catering industries many employees are managers and supervisors before the age of 22.

Table 51.2 *The widening gap in the National Minimum Wage*

Date	Rate 22+ £	Rate 18-22 £	Difference pence
Apr 99	3.60	3.00	60
Jun 00	3.60	3.20	40
Oct 00	3.70	3.20	50
Oct 01	4.10	3.50	60
Oct 02	4.20	3.60	60
Oct 03	4.50	3.80	70
Oct 04	4.85	4.10	75

Source: adapted from *Labour Research*, May 2003.

(a) Describe the changes in the minimum wage since its introduction in the UK.
(b) Discuss whether business should pay the minimum adult wage rate to all workers, no matter what their age.

The Social Chapter

The European Union's Social Chapter is an attempt to encourage minimum wages and conditions of work in member countries. It was argued that a business may attempt to respond to falling profits or greater competition by cutting costs. This could lead to poor pay and work conditions for employees. To prevent this, member countries outlined an agreement which covered such areas as:

- a limit on hours of work;
- 'fair and reasonable' rewards;
- minimum wages;
- free collective bargaining;
- access to training;
- workers' involvement in company decision making;
- health and safety;
- union recognition;
- equal opportunities.

The UK signed up to the EU Social Chapter in 1997, with the election of a Labour government. The previous Conservative government argued that the conditions:

- restricted a business's ability to reduce wages when necessary;
- did not allow a business to be flexible when employing workers and making them redundant;
- would increase costs.

When the UK signed up, UK laws would have to be changed to comply with the conditions of the Social Chapter. For example, the number of hours to be worked by most employees must be limited to 48 hours, part time and full time workers would be given equal rights, and employees would have a right to paid holidays each year. Other changes would include the introduction of **European works councils** (EWC) in businesses, to negotiate workers' wages with employers, and the setting of a minimum wage as discussed in the previous section.

Data protection

Businesses keep large amounts of data about their employees. Even small businesses will keep basic information about the earnings of employees and deductions such as pension payments. They might even keep a record of the number of days absent from work.

Large public limited companies will have a huge amount of information about the many employees who work for the organisation. This might include numerical information such as salaries. It might also include written reports, such as an annual review of an employee's progress written by his or her manager. Their application forms are also likely to be kept on record, as well as any disciplinary procedures that have been carried out as a result of their behaviour at work.

Much of the data held by businesses about employees is sensitive, personal information. Increasingly it is being stored on computer files or disks. Businesses must make sure that this information is protected so that it is only available to

---

In 2003 Black & Decker, the tool manufacturing company, introduced software which would allow it to monitor e-mails sent by its employees. A spokesperson for the company said that it had become increasingly aware of the dangers of e-mail misuse as it raises serious issues regarding employee productivity, corporate privacy and legal liability. The software, Mailmeter, will allow the company to generate reports about the amount of e-mail traffic and the domain names of the computers sending and receiving e-mails, without reading the content of e-mails. It is often suggested that using such software helps IT departments to adhere to the law regarding employee privacy.

However, if the business does deem it necessary to analyse e-mail content for disciplinary procedures it must be aware of the data protection law. It must follow strict guidelines if any use of information that is found is to be considered lawful.

Source: adapted from *Computer Weekly*, 28.4.2003.

(a) Explain ways in which the use of the software by Black & Decker might:
  (i) help it comply with the law relating to the protection of employees;
  (ii) lead to the breaking of the law regarding the protection of employees.

Question 4

---

those with the authority to see it.

The **Data Protection Act, 1998** protects information about employees which is kept by businesses. Any business processing data about employees must comply with a number of principles. There are eight principles put in place to make sure that the information is handled properly. They say that data must be:

- fairly and lawfully processed;
- processed for limited purposes;
- adequate, relevant and not excessive;
- accurate;
- not kept for longer than is necessary;
- processed in line with employees' rights;
- secure;
- not transferred to countries without adequate protection.

Employees have the right to see information that employers keep about them under the Act. They can also request that incorrect information is removed, prevent the processing of information under certain circumstances, stop direct marketing to themselves using the information and claim compensation for misuse.

To what extent will a business protect its employees?

There are strong arguments to support the protection of

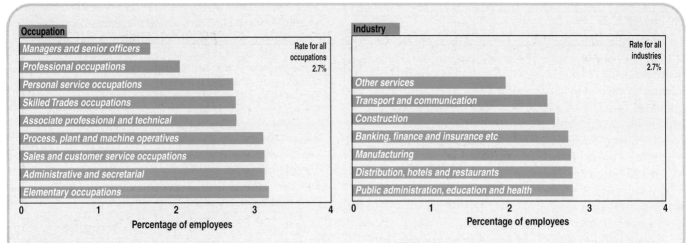

Figure 51.2 *Percentage of employees absent from work for at least one day in the reference week due to sickness or injury, by occupation and industry, UK, summer 2003, not seasonally adjusted*
Source: adapted from *Labour Force Survey.*

employees by their employers.

● Businesses that protect their employees are likely to have a healthy and motivated workforce, free from accidents, injury and illness.

● A business which breaks the law may be ordered to pay compensation and fined. Over the period 1993-2003 a TUC report stated that unions had won over £3 billion injury compensation for workers. In 2001, £305 million was paid out in injury cases for over 39,000 employees.

● The loss of employees due to lack of protection may require costly recruitment of new employees.

● The work of injured employees may need to be covered by part time employees, which is an extra cost.

● Employees off sick or injured may cause disruption, lost production, the missing of deadlines or serious delays. The Labour Force Survey estimated that 40.2 million days were lost per year due to workplace injury in 2002 compared to 23.9 million in 1998. In 2003, around 3 per cent of all employees reported at least one day's absence. The number of days lost due to sickness or illness in the UK in different

occupations and industries is shown in Figure 51.2.

● Poor work conditions may affect the productivity of employees and the business, and profits.

● Businesses that do not protect employees may get a poor reputation, which could affect the quality of future applicants.

However, some businesses still fail to protect their employees adequately. Perhaps the main reason for this is the cost involved in protection. Buying safety equipment, changing work practices to ensure safety, setting up safety courses, ensuring legislation is met, and filling in the many forms associated with ensuring safety are time consuming and costly activities. Small businesses in particular find it difficult to keep up with constant changes in safety laws and requirements. They might even decide that it is worth taking the risk that accidents will not occur or that they will not be found out breaking the law. As long as these things do not happen, they can save money by not spending to protect their workers completely.

Knowledge

1. State 5 types of health and safety dangers that may exist in business.
2. Briefly explain 3 pieces of legislation regarding health and safety at work.
3. Under what circumstances might dismissal be:
   (a) fair;
   (b) unfair?
4. What is the role of an industrial tribunal in protecting the employee at work?
5. 'An employee without a strong case for unfair dismissal may face problems if a tribunal finds against them.' Explain this statement.
6. State 2 pieces of legislation affecting the wages of employees in UK businesses.
7. What does the European Social Chapter aim to achieve?
8. Discuss 2 effects that signing the Social Chapter may have on the business of a country that signed the agreement.
9. What is meant by data protection?
10. State 3 advantages to a business of protecting its workers.

Case study   *Dangers that are clear and present*

Accidents can come in many different ways, shapes and forms at work. Take the apparently safe environment of the office. Slips, trips and falls are the single largest cause of major injuries at work. The Health and Safety Executive (HSE) suggests that the cost to employees each year of such accidents is £300 million and the overall cost to society is between £810-840 million. Trailing wires or unstable boxes of stationery left on the photocopier might not appear to be a problem. But many accidents, resulting in lost days work, are caused as a result of such apparently innocent situations.

Accidents can take many forms. Examples in the local authority offices of Westminster City Council include a woman who tripped on a box and fell onto a filing cabinet, damaging her cheekbone and the corner of her eye socket. Another female employee fell on a workstation cable and shattered her arm. Neither returned to work. And there is also the problem of constantly ringing phones causing stress and distracting employees.

The Health and Safety at Work Regulations, 1999 require employees to carry out risk assessment to assess health risks in office. But are risks being assessed? According to the HSE, only 39 per cent of organisations undertake risk assessment of workstations. There are also the risks of using chemicals, such as toner in photocopiers. And there is the issue of lifting heavy loads.

Businesses face problems if they do not look after their employees. The largest pay-out ever as compensation for injuries at work to a UNISON union member was £600,000 as a result of a disabling accident. Another member received £35,000 after lifting items that were too heavy. In most cases employees say that they would give back the money to regain their health.

But what about the risks of potentially dangerous activities such as the storage and handling of fuel? BP has ordered its drivers not to deliver fuel as a result of concerns over the safety of its employees in the past.

An investigation was launched into BP in 2000 as a result of safety breaches in the past, such as by the HSE in 2000 into

• seven major alerts in 14 months at the

Grangemouth plant, which has highly flammable chemicals, including fires, an exploding pipe and the failure of the main power cable;

• a reduction in staffing levels at a plant in Essex which resulted in the HSE ordering the business to stop operating as it believed the plant could not be shut down in an emergency;

• the shutting down of the main oil platform by the HSE in 1999 for two gas leaks.

In April 1999, the business was prosecuted after two contractors were overcome by nitrogen fumes.

BP stated that unfortunately accidents do occur. But it argued that even in attempts to cut costs, it never compromises safety. And if an accident happens the business investigates and works with authorities to make sure it never happens again.

Source: adapted from *The Observer*, 1.10.2000 and 10.12.2000.

(a) **Identify the types of risk to employees mentioned in the article. (6 marks)**

(b) **Explain how:**
(i) the Health and Safety Executive;
(ii) legislation;
may affect the organisations mentioned in the article. (8 marks)

(c) **Examine the problems which (i) employees and (ii) organisations may face as a result of accidents at work. (12 marks)**

(d) **Recommend changes which the organisations in the article might make to prevent accidents taking place. (12 marks)**

(e) **Discuss the extent to which organisations are likely to protect their employees. (12 marks)**

What is communication?

Communication is about sending and receiving information. Employees, managers and departments communicate with each other every day in business. For example, in a sole trader organisation, the owner may inform the workers verbally that an order for goods has to be sent out in the next two days. In a company, the personnel manager might send a 'memo' to all departments informing them about training courses that are available.

Good communication is vital for the efficient running of a business. A company exporting goods abroad is likely to have major problems if it fails to give the exact time of departure to its despatch department. Similarly, problems will also arise if instructions are not clear and goods are delivered to the wrong address.

Effective communication will only happen if information is sent, received and then understood. Some examples of information and methods of communicating in business might be:

- information on how to fill out expenses claims forms in a memo sent from the accounts department;
- verbal comments made by a manager to an employee informing them that continued lateness is likely to result in disciplinary action by the company;
- employment details given to a new employee on a written contract of employment (☞ unit 48);
- information on sales figures sent from the sales manager to the chief executive by e-mail or saved as a spreadsheet on computer disk;
- face-to-face negotiations between management and employee representatives over possible rewards for agreeing to changes in work practice;
- a group meeting taking place to discuss how quality could be improved in a work section;
- an order for 20 books faxed to a publisher from a bookshop;
- an advertisement for a salesperson placed on a company website on the Internet.

The communication process

Communication within business can take many forms. There are, however, some common features of all communications that take place in the workplace. Figure 52.1 shows an example.

Who sends and receives information? Information must be received and understood by the person or group to whom it was sent. Communication can take place between managers and employees, as well as between representative bodies, such as trade unions. Information is also passed to people and organisations outside the company. For example, company newspapers such as *Ford News* not only inform employees about the firm, but present a picture to the outside world of its operations.

What message is being communicated? For communication to be effective the correct **message** must be sent and received. Messages can be sent for a number of reasons.

- To provide information about the company. Management might inform the workforce about production levels achieved during the previous year. Some information is required by law, for example, the business has to tell employees about their conditions of employment.
- To give instructions, for example, to instruct market research to be carried out.
- To persuade people to change attitudes or behaviour, for example, to warn an employee who is consistently late of the likely action.

What channel is being used? Communication can be along different routes or CHANNELS in the organisation. Sometimes this can be between a manager and a subordinate (**vertical**) or between two departments (**horizontal**). As well as this **formal** type of communication, information is often passed **informally** between departments and employees. Communication can also be to other people within the organisation (**internal**) or to those outside the organisation (**external**).

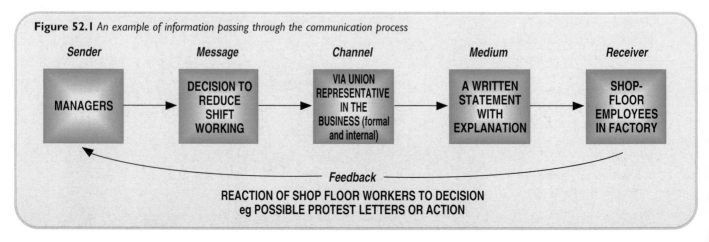

Figure 52.1 *An example of information passing through the communication process*

Sender	Message	Channel	Medium	Receiver
MANAGERS	DECISION TO REDUCE SHIFT WORKING	VIA UNION REPRESENTATIVE IN THE BUSINESS (formal and internal)	A WRITTEN STATEMENT WITH EXPLANATION	SHOP-FLOOR EMPLOYEES IN FACTORY

Feedback
REACTION OF SHOP FLOOR WORKERS TO DECISION
eg POSSIBLE PROTEST LETTERS OR ACTION

What medium is being used? Information can be communicated in a variety of ways or through different COMMUNICATION MEDIA. These vary from written methods, such as annual reports, to oral methods such as discussions, to the use of **information and communication (ICT) technology**, such as a fax machine, e-mail or the Internet.

Feedback Communication is not complete until the message is received and the receiver confirms that it is understood through feedback of some sort, for example written or verbal confirmation.

Formal/informal communication

Within a business there are both formal and informal channels of communication. Formal channels are recognised and approved by employers and employee representatives. An example of a formal channel would be a personnel department giving 'notice' to an employee about redundancy.

Informal communication channels can both help and hinder formal communications. Information that is communicated through the **grapevine** (☞ unit 40) may become distorted. This might, in extreme situations, cause industrial relations disputes. However, the grapevine can be acknowledged by management and actively approved of. Some firms issue a 'leak' along the grapevine to see what reaction it might provoke, making changes based on the reaction of employees to proposals, before issuing final instructions. Rumours, such as of a launch of a new product by a competitor, can be useful to a business.

Research has shown that effective communication requires both formal and informal channels. Formal statements can then be supported by informal explanations. A business might inform employees that it is introducing new machinery and then management may discuss this with employees and their representatives to find the best way to do it.

An insurance and risk consulting business, Marsh, carried out a survey of staff in preparation for a programme to align people behind the Marsh brand. Part of the programme involved the HR department conducting a communications survey of around 10,000 employees in eight countries. The Director of European Communications said 'We wanted to find out how people felt emotionally and intellectually about working in the organisation'. It was suggested that six years ago communications with employees was about often about simply 'pumping out newsletters'. However, the company now suggested that in a service business, where people are the brand, communication is absolutely strategic to business operations.

Source: adapted from *People Management*, 30.8.2001.

(a) Identify:
    (i) who is sending and receiving the message at Marsh;
    (ii) the message that is being sent.
(b) Explain whether the message is an internal or external communication.
(c) Explain how a formal and an informal channel might be used in this situation.

Question 1

It is also possible to make the distinction between **line** and **staff** communication (☞ unit 40). Line communication has authority behind it. Staff communication does not. An example of staff communication may be where a manager attempts to persuade a worker that it is a 'good idea' to do something.

Vertical and lateral communication

Information can be communicated downwards, upwards and laterally. These different channels of communication are shown in Figure 52.2. **Downwards** communication has, in the past, been used to tell employees about decisions that have

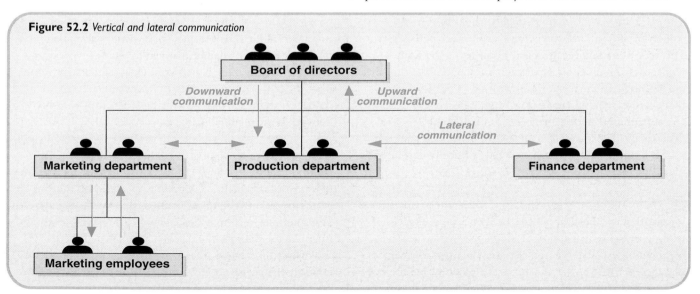

Figure 52.2 *Vertical and lateral communication*

already been made. It may be important as it:
- allows decisions by managers to be carried out by employees;
- ensures that action is consistent and co-ordinated;
- reduces costs because fewer mistakes should be made;
- should lead to greater effectiveness and profitability as a result of the above.

There is evidence, however, that the flow of information **upwards** can also help in decision making.
- It helps managers to understand employees' views and concerns.
- It helps managers to keep more in touch with employees' attitudes and values.
- It can alert managers to potential problems.
- It can provide managers with the information that they need for decision making and gives feedback on the effects of previous decisions.
- It helps employees to feel that they are participating and can encourage motivation.
- It provides feedback on the effectiveness of downwards communication and how it can be improved.

Lateral communication takes place when people at the same level within an organisation pass information. An example might be a member of the finance department telling the marketing department about funds available for a sales promotion. One problem that firms sometimes face is that departments may become hostile towards each other if they don't understand the problems that each face. The marketing department may want these funds, but this might adversely affect the firm's cash flow.

Communication networks

Communication takes place between different individuals and parts of a business and between a business and outside bodies. There are advantages and disadvantages to a business of using different types of communication NETWORK.

The circle In a circle, sections, departments etc. can communicate with only two others, as shown Figure 52.3a. This type of communication may occur between middle managers from different departments at the same level of the organisation. The main problem with this type of network is that decision making can be slow or poor because of a lack of co-ordination. If middle managers from different departments had been given the task of increasing sales and profits in the short term, they may have difficulty developing a strategy that all would agree on.

The chain The chain (Figure 52.3b) is where one person passes information to others, who then pass it on. This approach tends to be the formal approach adopted by hierarchical organisations, such as the Civil Service. The main advantage is that there is a leader/co-ordinator at the top of the hierarchy who can oversee communications downwards and upwards to

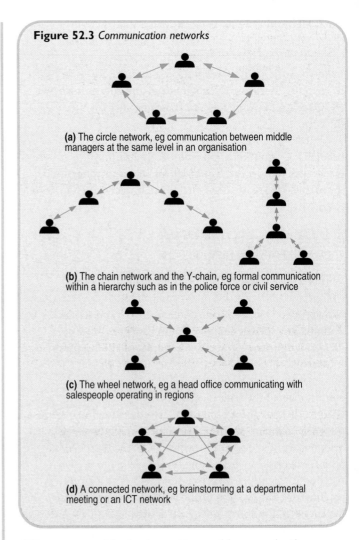

Figure 52.3 *Communication networks*

(a) The circle network, eg communication between middle managers at the same level in an organisation

(b) The chain network and the Y-chain, eg formal communication within a hierarchy such as in the police force or civil service

(c) The wheel network, eg a head office communicating with salespeople operating in regions

(d) A connected network, eg brainstorming at a departmental meeting or an ICT network

different areas of the business. One problem may be the isolation felt by those at the bottom of the network. Their motivation may be less than others if they feel at the periphery. This network does not encourage lateral communication.

The wheel In the wheel pattern (Figure 52.3c) there is a person, group or department that occupies a central position. This network is particularly good at solving problems. If, for example, the North West region of an insurance company had been asked to increase sales by central office, then the North West regional manager would be at the centre of policy initiative communicating with local managers about the best way forward. The leader in this network is the regional manager.

A connected or 'all channel' network The 'all channel' communication system (Figure 52.3d) might be used in small group workings. With its participatory style, and more open communication system, the connected network provides the best solutions to complex problems. This type of network might be used, for example, when a department needs to 'brainstorm'. Its disadvantages are that it is slow and that it tends to disintegrate under time pressure to get results when operated in a group.

Which communication network may be most suitable for the following types of message?
(a) An instruction to despatch an order by a certain date.
(b) Discussions about possible extension strategies for a mature product.
(c) A message from head office to local building societies to change mortgage interest rates.
(d) Reacting to a bomb alert in an office block.
(e) Imposing budget cuts in a local authority.
(f) Organising a retirement party.
(g) Developing a brand identity for a consumer product.
Explain your answer in each case.

Question 2

One solution to the problem of passing complex communications has been solved by the use of INFORMATION and COMMUNICATION TECHNOLOGY. A complex connected network can be set up where instructions and information are passed between many people or departments, or even parts of a business overseas.

Communication media

There is a number of methods or media that can be used to communicate information in businesses. Many of these methods can be delivered via electronic media. These are explained in the next section.

Written communication The **letter** is a flexible method which provides a written record. It is often used for communications with others outside the organisation. It can also be used internally where a confidential written record is needed, eg to urge employees against strike action, to announce a redundancy etc.

A **memorandum** is the same as a letter, but is only used for internal communications. It is sent via the internal mail system. Memoranda are useful for many sorts of message, particularly for confirming telephone conversations. Sometimes they are used instead of a telephone. One criticism often made of firms is that they have too many 'memos', when short written notes would do the same job. Some businesses send 'memos' via e-mail. This allows a person to send a message to another person's computer. The memo can then be called up and read by the person receiving it.

Reports allow a large number of people to see complex facts and arguments about issues on which they have to make a decision. A written report does not allow discussion or immediate feedback, as does a meeting, and it can be time-consuming and expensive to produce. However, it does have advantages for passing messages to groups. First, people can study the material in their own time, rather than attending a meeting. Second, time that is often wasted at meetings can be better used. Third, the report is presented in an impartial way, so conflict can be avoided.

Routine information can be communicated through the use of **forms**. A well designed form can be filled in quickly and easily. They are simple to file and information is quickly retrieved and confirmed. Examples of forms used in business include expense forms, timesheets, insurance forms, and stock request forms.

The **noticeboard** is a method which cheaply passes information to a large number of people. The drawbacks to noticeboards are that they can become untidy or irrelevant. In addition, they rely on people reading them, which does not always happen.

Larger companies often print an internal **magazine** or **newspaper** to inform employees about a variety of things. These may include staff appointments and retirements, meetings, sports and social events, results and successes, customer feedback, new products or machinery and motivating competitions, eg safety suggestions. The journal usually avoids being controversial. It may not deal with sensitive issues, such as industrial relations or pollution of the environment, and may stop short of criticising management policy or products. It is designed to improve communication and morale, and it may be seen by outsiders (especially customers) who might get a favourable impression of the business.

Face-to-face communication Face-to-face communication involves an oral message being passed between people talking to each other. Examples might be:
- a message passed between two workers about how long is left before lunch;
- an instruction given to an employee to change jobs in a job rotation scheme (☞ unit 43);
- a warning given by a health and safety officer to a worker.

Group meetings involve face-to-face communication. Meetings can take a number of forms. They may be formal meetings which are legally required, such as the Annual General Meeting of a limited company. They might also be meetings of groups within the business to discuss problems, such as collective bargaining negotiations or meetings of quality circles. Team briefings are also a common method of face-to-face communication in business. Many meetings, however, are simply informal discussions taking place to pass information between employees or managers, such as a 'chat' over lunch.

Face-to-face communication has several advantages. It:
- allows new ideas to be generated;
- allows 'on the spot' feedback, constructive criticism and an exchange of views;
- encourages co-operation;
- allows information to be spread quickly among people.

However, face-to-face communication, such as meetings, can have problems, especially if:
- the terms of reference (defining the purpose and power of the meeting) are not clear;
- the people attending are unskilled or unwilling to communicate;

- there is insufficient guidance or leadership to control the meeting;
- body language creates a barrier.

Oral communication Oral communication can take place other than in face-to-face situations in a business. The **telephone** is a common method of oral communication between individuals in remote locations or even within an organisation's premises. It provides some of the interactive advantages of face-to-face communication, while saving the time involved in travelling from one place to another. It is, however, more 'distant' and impersonal than an interview for the discussion of sensitive matters and does not provide written 'evidence'. This disadvantage can be overcome by written confirmation.

Sometimes messages can be communicated to groups of employees through a **public address system**. This might operate through loudspeakers placed at strategic points, eg in workshops or yards, where staff cannot be located or reached by telephone.

Information and communication technology

Rapid developments in technology have greatly changed the way businesses communicate with each other. It is now possible to deliver messages instantly, over great distances and to a number of people at the same time via a variety of electronic media.

The Internet The INTERNET is a vast source of information for businesses and individuals who have access to a computer. The introduction of broadband in the UK means that websites containing images and text can be quickly viewed and information can be downloaded. The Internet is useful for external communication, although it might also be useful for internal communication in certain circumstances. For example, businesses can:

- advertise jobs to employees inside and outside the business (☞ unit 46);
- allow people to view financial reports or company mission statements (☞ unit 4);
- allow customers to buy products and pay using credit card details;
- gain market research information (☞ unit 12);

as well as providing stakeholders with a large amount of information about the company.

In February 2004 it was estimated that there were 295 million active Internet users in the world, of which 20 million were in the UK. By far the largest user was the USA, with 141 million users. One major problem is the sending of online junk mail, known as spam. In 2004 it was estimated that 1.2 billion spam messages would be sent worldwide.

Intranets Information on the internet is available to the public. This makes it impossible to send confidential messages. A business INTRANET is under the control of the company using it so information sent can be controlled. For example, a company with 150 administration staff may all be linked by an intranet. They can send messages and access common information.

It is suggested that the biggest savings from the intranet will come from the distribution of standard information throughout an organisation. For example, information such as the internal phone numbers, diaries and timetables quickly become out of date. In electronic format, however, they could be revised as soon as a change occurs and made available to all staff through a 'browser'. Intranets may also be extended into 'extranets'. These could include other business stakeholders, such as customers and suppliers, as well as the staff of a business. For example, suppliers mght be able to view their stockholdings held by a company's warehouse to make sure they are provided when required.

E-mail Many businesses have e-mail addresses. They allow businesses and individuals to communicate immediately with others via word processed text or images that are contained on a computer. Information sent from one e-mail address, via a computer, modem and telephone to another address is stored by the 'server' - a computer dedicated to storage and network facilities. It stays in that address until it is picked up by the receiver. The advantage of e-mail is that long documents can be immediately sent to other people anywhere in the world without them being there.

Mobile phones Many companies and individuals now have mobile phones. These are portable telephones which can be carried around by the user. Telephone calls can be made and received from most areas, often in different countries. There are particularly useful for employees who work outside the office or factory and who move around. Urgent messages can be sent and received immediately. Companies such as Orange and Vodafone offer a variety of services, including receiving and storing messages.

Answerphones Answerphones record messages when the receiver is unable to answer the telephone. They allow important messages to be stored and received if, for example, an employee is away from her desk. They also allow messages to be sent from one company or person to another outside normal office hours. The information will be received when work starts the next day. This is particularly useful when there are time differences between countries. Some people find answer phones impersonal and may not leave a message.

Paging devices These are devices which are useful for people who work outside a business and move around a lot, such as sales representatives. They may also be used by workers in a large organisation, such as a doctor in a hospital. A 'bleeper' alerts the receiver to a message waiting for him on a prearranged telephone number.

Videoconferencing and teleconferencing Videoconferencing is a method of communication which allows individuals in different locations to interact as if they were in the same room. Individuals can see each other on monitors with the use of cameras and talk to each other via telephone lines. This is particularly useful when employees need face-to-face interaction, but work in locations that are distant from each other. It also saves the time taken to get to a central meeting place. Teleconferencing is where many people are linked together via telephone lines. Each person can talk to all others as if they were in the same location.

Lap top computers The development of portable computers means that business people can work in different locations to their office. They allow people to continue working during train journeys, for example, and to e-mail text and images to others via satellite link. They prevent working time from being wasted. They also have the advantage of immediate sending and receiving of information at a variety of locations. Some lap top computers have to be plugged into a telephone terminal to receive e-mail, which can be a problem.

Multi-media communications Businesses are now able to communicate information through a mixture of media. They combine visual images, written text and audio transmissions. This is known as multi-media. Many multi-media programmes are interactive, so that an individual can enter into dialogue with the information that is contained in the programme. The use of multi-media as a business communication tool is particularly useful in the area of training. Individual employees can interact with ideas and concepts developed in the multi-media training package at their own pace.

Electronic noticeboards Businesses are making more use of electronic noticeboards. These communicate the latest information to employees via visual display units located in public places around the business, such as in reception. Their advantage over normal noticeboards is that they can be kept up to date. The main disadvantages are that they are limited to particular locations in the business and the information may not be relevant to everyone who sees it.

Fax machines Faxes are similar to e-mail, but the information is already on paper in the form of text or images. This information is read by a fax machine, converted into audio signals, and sent down a telephone line to another fax machine. The machine then reconverts the signals into text and graphics. The advantages of fax machines are that they send messages instantly and that the receiver does not have to be there to receive the message. A disadvantage compared to e-mail is that it can take a long time to process a large document via the fax. The information also has to be printed out or written before it can be sent.

The merger of Exel (formerly the National freight Corporation) and the Ocean Group in 2000 presented a major communications challenge. Ocean was a shipping business operating across 120 countries. Excel was a rail-based distribution firm which managed supply chains for retailers and manufacturers in 6 countries.

'We realised from the start that we needed to communicate with three constituencies - investors, customers and employees' said Chris Stevens, Group HR director. A communication team was set up to ensure that messages sent to all three groups were identical. A corporate publication, *Growing Together*, a monthly cassette for managers including interviews with people around the world about the integration, regular bulletins to senior managers from the chief executive and an electronic weekly update were provided. Communications went out from the date of the merger in a disciplined way. Staff were informed at the same time as the market about changes.

The effect was new contracts worth £300 million. A survey after the changes found that 70 per cent of managers said they understood the company's goals.

Source: adapted from *People Management*, 30.8.2001.

(a) Identify the methods of communication mentioned in the article.
(b) Explain the benefits of using these methods for the business.

Question 3

Barriers to communication

We have seen that effective communication will take place if the message is received and understood by the receiver. There is a number of factors that might prevent this from happening.

The skills of the sender and receiver The ability of the sender to explain a message and the receiver to understand it are important in communication. If an order must be sent out by a certain date, but the sender simply asks for it to be sent as early as possible, communication would not have been effective. If the receiver does not understand what stocks to take the order from, incorrect goods may be sent.

Jargon A word or phrase which has a technical or specialised meaning is known as jargon. The terms understood by a certain group of people may be meaningless to those who don't have this knowledge. One example of this was in Schools of Motoring, where for many years drivers were given the instruction 'clutch in' or 'clutch out', which nearly always confused the trainee. Later the instruction was changed to 'clutch down' and 'clutch up'. Technical information about a product which is not understood by the marketing department may result in misleading advertising and poor sales.

Choice of communication channel or medium Sometimes the channel or medium chosen to send the message may not communicate the information effectively. An example of this might be where a manager attempts to pass a message to an employee, but would have been more successful if the message had gone through a representative. Another example is that safety campaigns are sometimes unsuccessful because slogans and posters are used to persuade individual employees about the importance of safe working practices rather than changes being discussed.

Perceptions and attitudes How employees perceive other people can affect how they interpret the message that is sent. Employees are more likely to have confidence in people they trust, because of past experience of their reliability. On the other hand, if an employee has learned to distrust someone, then what she says will be either ignored or treated with caution. The way employees view things can be affected by being part of a group.

Form of the message If the message is unclear or unexpected the receiver is unlikely to understand it or remember it. The rate at which we forget is considerable. We have probably forgotten half of what we hear within a few hours of hearing it, and no more than 10 per cent will remain after two or three days.

The sender of the message must make sure it:
- does not contain too much information;
- is not poorly written;
- is not presented too quickly;
- is not presented in a way that the receiver does not expect;
- conveys the information that he actually wants to communicate;
- is written in a way that the receiver will understand.

Stereotypes People can often have beliefs about others. This may result in a **stereotype** (☞ unit 50) of some people. It is possible that, if one person has a stereotype of another, this may affect how they interpret a message. So, for example, if a male manager has a certain stereotype of women being less rational and able than men, his first reaction might be to ignore a female manager's communication because he believes she does not understand the information.

Length of chain of command or distance If information is passed down by word of mouth through a number of receivers, it is possible for the message to be distorted. This may result in the wrong emphasis or wrong information being received by the individual or group at the end of the communication chain. Industrial relations problems in business have sometimes been a result of a long chain of command (☞ unit 40).

Wrong target for the message Businesses sometimes send the wrong information to the wrong person. This can result in costly delays and errors and perhaps a poor image in the eyes of the public.

In 2001 the BBC needed to 'make the place feel different'. Previously the communication team had been part of the marketing department, where the press office had been the most significant activity. But here 'everyone relied on rumour and hearing things through the grapevine'. The new system set up a separate communications team, made up of the communications and the human resources teams. The aim was to ensure that employees would be the first to hear about anything, before rumours could get started.

New intranet sites called 'The Biz' and "Extra, Extra' were created. Team briefings and a redesigned staff newspaper were also put in place. But the most important change was a change of view from the top. The chief executive had to take it seriously. The chief executive at the time Greg Dyke, had an informal style that helped.

The change in communication style was an uphill struggle. The attitude of staff was often 'This is a miserable place, but we have got to do the best we can.' So the challenge was to make the BBC an exciting and attractive place to work. Amendments were made to the operation of the staff forum, for example. It had become a 'whinge session'. This was changed so members of the executive came in to speak and discuss problems.

A survey showed that after the changes the number of people relying on the grapevine fell from 70 per cent to 48 per cent and that there was a 10 per cent decrease in the number of people finding out about internal matters through external channels.

Source: adapted from *People Management*, 30.8.2001.

(a) Explain the factors that may have created communication problems at the BBC.
(b) Suggest how the changes made might have improved communication.

Breakdown of the channel This could be due to technical problems. For example, a business may rely on its management information system on the computerised network. If this breaks down, businesses might have problems dealing with enquiries. Banks, for example, are unable to tell customers what their balances are if computer terminals are not working.

Different countries and different cultures A business may have a problem sending a message from one country to another because of time differences. This is particularly a difficulty if an urgent decision is needed. Individual country traits can sometimes affect communication. A study of North and South American business people found that they each had different 'conversation distances'. In meetings, problems developed as South American business people came towards people they were talking to, whilst North Americans retreated.

Problems with information and communication technology

Although new technologies can help communication, there are problems both with the amount of information sent and the use of the new technology.

- Information overload. Large amounts of information can be sent instantly by such media as fax, e-mail and the Internet. This may result in information overload. Individuals and organisations may not be able to fully process all of the information that is sent. As a result, effective communication may not take place.
- Introduction. Electronic media can sometimes create problems when they are first introduced. Staff need training, which is time consuming. Mistakes can be made if information is not stored, as there may be no written record. There may also need to be a change in work methods and employees may work at a slower pace as they get used to the new methods and equipment.
- Misuse of new technology. There is evidence to suggest that employees spend more time using the internet and e-mail facilities than is necessary. 'Browsing' the Internet and constantly checking e-mail for new messages can waste time. Employees may also use the technology for non-business messages.
- Confidentiality. Electronic media often send messages that can be seen be people other than the intended receiver. This can be a problem if the sender wants the message to remain confidential.
- Viruses. Computer viruses can damage information kept on computers, although it is possible to protect information by using software.

Factors affecting choice of medium

There is a number of factors that affect which medium a business will use in any situation.

- Direction of communication. Some methods may only be suitable for downward communication, such as films and posters. Other methods are useful for upwards communication only, such as suggestion schemes. Many methods are useful for both.
- Nature of the communication. The choice of communication method may depend on the nature of the message being sent. For example, a comment from a manager to a subordinate about unsatisfactory work may need to be confidential. It is important for the manager to choose a method which does this.

- Many messages are best sent by the use of more than one communication medium. Company rules, for example, might most effectively be communicated verbally on an induction course and as a written summary for employees to take away as a reminder.
- Costs. Films, videos and some tapeslides can be expensive. A business must decide whether the message could be sent just as well by other media.
- Variety. If, for example, a company tries to communicate too many messages by means of a noticeboard, then employees may stop reading it. To make sure messages are sent effectively, a variety of media should be used.
- Speed. If something needs communicating immediately then verbal or electronic communications tend to be quickest.
- Is a record needed? If it is, there is no point in verbally passing on the information. If it is communicated verbally, it may need written confirmation.
- Length of message. If the message is long, verbal communication may mean the receiver does not remember everything that has been said. If a simple yes or no answer is needed, written communication might not be suitable.
- Who will receive the message? The sender must consider how many people will receive the message. She must also take into account where the receiver will be and whether there is access to a means of communication.

Management information systems

A management information system (MIS) in a business is an ICT system that supplies information and communication services. It usually takes the form of integrated programmes and applications that deal with:

- order transactions;
- project planning;
- co-operative work support, such as networked schedules and diaries;
- personnel and customer databases;
- programmes to assist decision making, which pull together key performance indicators of the organisation.

The applications use both automated and manual procedures. In a well designed MIS, the different applications are not independent. They are interconnected subsystems that form a coherent, overall, integrated structure for information and communication services. An effective MIS system can help an organisation improve productivity. It should increase the amount and speed of information that can be communicated and also help to improve the quality and scope of management decisions.

key terms

Channel of communication - the route by which a message is communicated from sender to receiver.
Communication media - the written, oral or technological methods used to communicate a message.
Information and communication technology - the use of technology to deliver messages and data from groups, individuals or businesses to others.
Internet - the worldwide web, which allows information to be accessed and communicated by computer throughout the world.
Intranet - a means of communication available within a business, which allows information to be accessed by and communicated to all employees and owners via computer.
Network - the links that allow a message to be communicated between a number of people.

Knowledge ...Knowledge...Knowledge...Knowledge...Knowledge...Knowledge...Kno

1. Why is good communication important for a business?
2. Why might a business want feedback in the communication process?
3. Explain the difference between:
   (a) formal and informal communication;
   (b) lateral and vertical communication.
4. How might upward communication be useful to a business?
5. Give an example of a message that might be sent using the following communication networks.
   (a) The circle.
   (b) The chain.
   (c) The wheel.
   (d) A connected network.
6. State 5 methods of written communication that a business might use.
7. When might face-to-face communication be more useful than written communication?
8. What is (a) videoconferencing; (b) teleconferencing; (c) e-mail?
9. Suggest two ways in which a business may use the internet.
10. State 5 factors that might affect the choice of communication.
11. State 5 barriers to communication.

Case study Pearson's Brewery Distribution Depot

'If there's something wrong, I was usually the last person to know about it; messages from the pubs never seemed to be getting through to the right people.' This was one of the first comments Jerome Rogers heard when he took over as distribution manager of Pearson's Brewery, a medium sized business located in Essex, which served the East Anglia region.

The comment was made by one of the local planners in the large distribution depot of the brewery. Jerome was carrying out a series of interviews with his staff to find out both his own workforce's and the publicans' views about how the depot was operating.

The present system was that when the telephone rang in the office with an order any one of the 4 assistants would answer it. The load planners would then try to group orders together, but there were no regular delivery rounds. The supervisor prided himself on getting orders out quickly - he would give them out on a random basis to the delivery workers who, therefore, rarely made regular visits to one set of pubs.

Through his interviews, Jerome detected a number of problems with the system. He had previously worked in a small brewery where everyone was on first name terms and where good communications with customers was a major objective. He was surprised with the contrast between Pearson's and his old company.

Jerome felt that some way of informing all employees in the depot about its operation may help to develop a corporate culture of unity. He was also looking for ways to keep in more regular contact with head office so that he might advise them of progress and perhaps receive some help with problems.

Depot organisation

The depot's organisation was divided into 3 sections.

- In the office were 4 clerical assistants who took incoming calls from the publicans whom the brewery supplied. The publicans usually phoned in their weekly orders, but would also phone if deliveries were late or incomplete.
- Also in the office, but in a sectioned off area, were 4 load planners who worked at computer terminals, sorting and organising the delivery loads between pubs.

- In the rest of the depot there were 65 delivery employees who carried out the deliveries to the pubs. They communicated with the office via their supervisor, who collected the delivery plans at the start of the day and gave them to the employees making the deliveries.

Results from interviews

- Deliveries were often late. The delivery workers were not very motivated by the work and would 'spin out' a delivery in order to earn overtime.
- Communication between the office and the delivery workers was poor, resulting in poor relations between the two groups.
- Within the office the 2 groups appeared to work in isolation. Each did not know what the other group was doing.
- Publicans felt that there was a lack of interest in their problems. If publicans phoned in on Friday with a rush order, or to find out why a delivery had not been made, they got the impression that no one wanted to help them.
- If there was a problem it was impossible to contact the delivery employees. For example, if someone in the depot noticed stock was left behind, he or she could not contact the driver to return to make up the incomplete order.
- There was often no written record of the orders that were phoned in by the publicans.

(a) **Identify the communication problems that exist at Pearson's Brewery. (4 marks)**

(b) **Explain why these problems exist. (8 marks)**

(c) **Explain how the business might inform the workforce about possible solutions to the communication problems. (8 marks)**

(d) **Suggest possible solutions to the communication problems at the business. (10 marks)**

(d) **Assess the effects on the business of these solutions. (10 marks)**

What is production?

PRODUCTION takes place when resources, such as raw materials or components, are changed into 'products'. Land, labour, capital and enterprise - the factors of production (☞ unit 1) - are used in the production process. The use of land and a tractor to grow cabbages is an example of production in **primary industry.** An example of **secondary industry** would be the use of wood, plastic, glue, screws, labour, drilling and cutting equipment to manufacture furniture.

Today production is often referred to more generally as those activities that 'bring a product into being'. Activities which are part of **tertiary industry,** such as services, would be included in this definition. A bank might talk about providing a 'product' in the same way as a carpet manufacturer. Examples of products in a bank's product portfolio might include mortgages, current accounts, house insurance and foreign currency. Direct services from the producer to the consumer, such as car repairs or decorating, can also be regarded as production in this sense.

Features of production

Production takes place when a business takes INPUTS, carries out a PROCESS and produces an OUTPUT or product. Production by a jewellery manufacturer may include the following.

- Inputs are the raw materials and components used by a business. These may include gold, silver and precious stones.
- Processes are the methods used to convert raw materials and components into products. Processes might include designing, cutting, bending, soldering and polishing. Such processes are often performed using machines and tools. For example, metal cutters, specialist jeweller's tools, a soldering iron and a small polishing machine might be used.
- Outputs are the products or services produced when inputs are converted. They might include rings, brooches, bangles, bracelets and necklaces.

Planning and controlling production

For production to be effective, it needs to be planned and controlled.

Planning All businesses, whether small or large, need to plan production. Some large firms employ production planners for this task. A number of factors can influence the plan.

- Demand from customers. Businesses get orders from different customers, for different products, with different specifications, at different times. A business must plan which orders should go out first and which can wait.
- The design of a product might affect planning. For example, the design specifications of a product might state that certain materials must be used or certain processes, like high quality finishing, must be carried out.
- Planning must make sure that there are enough resources available. Many businesses purchase stocks (☞ unit 57) of raw materials and components and keep them until they are needed. Others order 'just in time'.

Loading This involves deciding which 'work centres' will carry out which tasks. A work centre may be an employee, a machine, a production cell or a process such as welding.

(a) Using the businesses shown in the photographs, explain what is meant by production.
(b) Explain whether the activities of the businesses are examples of primary, secondary or tertiary production.

Question 1

Sequencing Production usually involves arranging tasks and processes in a sequence. For many products the order of tasks will rarely change, such as in the production of bread. This is often the case when fairly large numbers of the same product are produced. However, when non-standard or customised products (☞ unit 54) are made, the order in which tasks and processes are arranged may need to change.

Scheduling The production schedule will show times when particular tasks and processes should start and finish. This is particularly important when large production projects are being undertaken, such as the construction of a large building. The aim of scheduling is to ensure that resources, such as workers, are not idle whilst waiting for someone else to finish a job before starting their own. **Gantt charts** can be used to help scheduling. A Gantt chart is a visual display showing how tasks might be sequenced over time. The Gantt chart in Figure 53.2 shows the tasks required to produce a batch of 1,000 brackets by an engineering company. The chart shows that:

- cutting begins on Monday and takes two days;
- bending, the longest task, begins on Tuesday. It takes three days and can begin before the entire batch has been cut;
- on Thursday welding begins before the entire batch has finished the bending process. Welding takes two days;
- painting begins on Friday even though the whole batch has not been welded and painting the whole batch takes two days;
- packing, which takes only half a day, cannot begin until Tuesday, when the whole batch has been painted.

Dispatching This involves giving instructions about the tasks to be carried out for a particular period. Instructions may be given verbally or in written form.

Progressing This is an ongoing monitoring process. It requires supervisors, teams or managers reporting on the progress of jobs. Managers or teams may have to identify problems and help solve them. They should also try to eliminate bottlenecks and encourage workers, when necessary, to speed up the job.

W.H. Brakspear & Sons has brewed beer in its Henley brewery, Oxfordshire, since 1799. The brewer markets about six brands of real ale (cask conditioned beer) including XXX Mild, Bitter, Regatta Gold and Old Ale. It owns about 300 tied houses and has used much the same brewing processes since it began.

Figure 53.1 *Production of beer in the brewery*

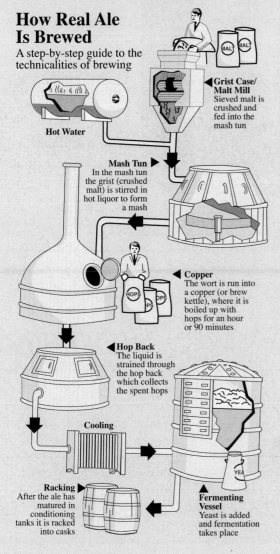

Source: adapted from the *Good Beer Guide*.

(a) State two examples of inputs used by Brakspear.
(b) Describe two planning activities Brakspear might undertake when brewing beer.

Task	M	Tu	W	Th	F	M	Tu
Cutting	■	■					
Bending		■	■	■			
Welding				■	■		
Painting					■	■	
Packing							■

Figure 53.2 *Gantt chart showing the sequence of tasks required to produce a batch of 1,000 metal brackets by an engineering company*

Added value

A business adds value to raw materials which it uses in the production process. ADDED VALUE can be found in the difference between the cost of purchasing raw materials and the price which the finished goods are sold for. In Figure 53.3 the builder will use inputs such as land, bricks, wood, tiles, frames, glass and other materials to build a house. The total cost of all the inputs is £31,000. The centre of the diagram shows the various processes required in the construction of the house. These include digging, bricklaying, roofing, tiling, plumbing, joining, painting and other tasks. As a result of these processes an output is produced. In this example the output is a house, which is sold by the builder for £89,000. The **value added** in this case is £58,000 (£89,000 - £31,000).

£58,000 is not the **profit** made by the builder. Part of the £58,000 will be used to pay the wages of employees and business overheads such as insurance, motor expenses and tax. So the profit figure will be lower than the value added figure. Value added is the difference between the price at which goods or services are sold and the cost of raw materials. Profit is the difference between the price at which goods or services are sold and all costs of production.

For services, it is sometimes more difficult to see how value is added. A supermarket will buy in a product from a producer or wholesaler. It will sell the product for a higher price to customers than it has paid for it. The difference in price is added value. The retailer is adding value because it is providing a service (making the products available in a convenient location) to the customer.

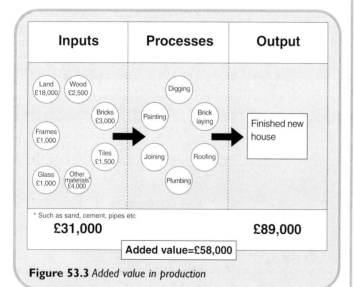

Figure 53.3 *Added value in production*

Production decisions

Businesses make a number of important production decisions. A clothing manufacturer, for example, might decide to produce a new range of casual trousers. This could involve using a new type of cloth, changing the layout of the factory, increasing the size of its warehouse, employing more

Al Brennan runs a paving business in Towcester. Most of his jobs involve paving patios or drives during the summer. He employs two workers between May and October and advertises in the local newspaper and *Yellow Pages*. His most recent job was paving a driveway for a customer in Northampton, which took three days. He charged £1,400 for the job and the costs incurred are shown in Figure 53.4.

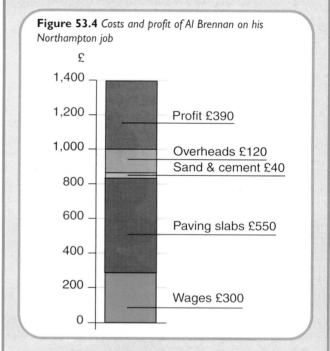

Figure 53.4 *Costs and profit of Al Brennan on his Northampton job*

(a) Describe how Al Brennan adds value in the above case.
(b) Calculate the value added by the business.

Question 3

labour and introducing a new quality control system. One production decision will often lead to other decisions having to be made. Decisions made by businesses might include some of the following.

What to produce A business must decide what product it wants to produce. The product may be a new product, that no other business has produced, or an adaptation of its own or a competitor's products. For example, 'Little Feet' are foot shaped plastic moulds which keeps two socks together in the wash. The creator, Andrea Marks, based the design on grips used to hold tea towels in kitchens. Many supermarkets now offer financial services such as savings accounts similar to those of banks.

What production method should be used Businesses choose how best to make their products. Different businesses might use different production methods, even when they make the same products. For example, TVR and Nissan both manufacture cars. TVR hand-builds its cars in a small factory in Blackpool. Its production techniques make more use of skilled workers than Nissan's and the car bodies are made from fibre glass. Nissan mass produces cars in factories around the world. It relies more on robots, computers and other machines than TVR and uses metal for the car bodies.

Where production should be located Business owners have to decide where best to locate their premises. Generally, they will find locations where costs will be lowest. Small business owners may locate near to where they live. Large multinationals may locate production in countries where the government gives them subsidies and grants.

How large the business should be Most businesses start off small and then grow. There are many advantages of growing. One is that costs are likely to fall due to economies of scale (☞ unit 56). However, some business owners are content to remain relatively small, to avoid the extra responsibilities growth brings for instance.

How to ensure quality Businesses are more likely to be successful if they can produce high quality products. Businesses have to decide how they might improve quality (☞ unit 58). This might involve using more expensive raw materials, training staff to higher levels or introducing a quality system, such as total quality management (TQM).

key terms

Input - the raw materials used in production.
Output - the goods or services resulting from production.
Process - the method used to convert inputs to final goods or services.
Production - the transformation of resources into goods or services.
Added value - the difference between the cost of raw materials and the selling price.

Knowledge...Knowledge...Knowle

1. State 3 examples of production in the (a) primary (b) secondary and (c) tertiary industries.
2. State 5 features of planning and controlling production.
3. Explain how a cereal manufacturer adds value to production.
4. 'The retailer marked up the wholesale price by 10 per cent.' Explain why this is an example of calculating value added.
5. Why is value added not the same as profit?
6. State 5 questions about production that a business may consider.

Case study Lafarge

Lafarge, which is quoted on the Paris and New York stock exchange, is one of the world's biggest producers of building materials. It owns Blue Circle, a UK based cement maker, and produces more cement than any other producer in the world. Lafarge has operations in 75 countries, employs over 75,000 worldwide and has over 250,000 shareholders.

Processes involved in cement production
- **Blasting**. Raw materials such as limestone and clay are blasted from a quarry. Due to the cost of transporting such a heavy raw material, cement works are usually located very nearby.
- **Crushing**. Large lumps of limestone pass through a crushing machine and are then transported to the plant by conveyer.
- **Raw grinding**. The raw materials then pass through a mill where they are very finely ground into what is called 'raw mix'.
- **Burning**. The raw mix is preheated before it goes into the kiln. Once inside the kiln the raw mix is burnt at 150°C by flames that reach a temperature of 2000°C. This process produces clinker which is cooled by fans as it leaves the kiln. Clinker is the basic material needed to make cement.
- **Grinding**. Additives such as gypsum are combined with the clinker before it is finally ground into cement powder.
- **Storage, packing and dispatch**. The cement is usually stored in huge silos before being dispatched in tankers or bagged.

Lafarge opened a new production line in the Kujawy cement plant, located west of Warsaw, in Poland. The production capacity now amounts to 1.6 million tonnes per year, an annual increase of 500 000 tonnes. With its state-of-the-art technological and environmental standards, Kujawy is among the most modern industrial sites of the Group. The new dry process line, which uses the most environmentally friendly technology, replaces the 3 older wet process lines. The investment in this project amounted to 90 million euros. The new line features a low consumption of fuel (decreased by 60 per cent) and power (decreased by 30 per cent). The decrease in fuel consumption has also allowed a considerable reduction in CO_2 emissions. Moreover, dust emissions are seven times lower than previously due to state-of-the-art technology.

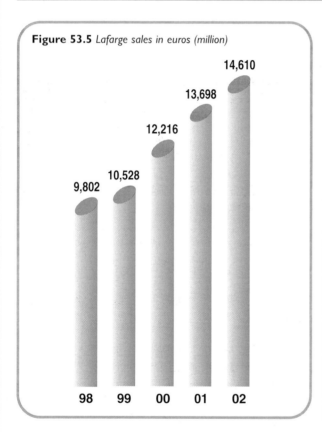

Figure 53.5 *Lafarge sales in euros (million)*

- 98: 9,802
- 99: 10,528
- 00: 12,216
- 01: 13,698
- 02: 14,610

Lafarge owns over 800 quarries worldwide and was recently refused permission by a Scottish court to quarry up to 600 million tonnes of rock from Roineabhal mountain on the Scottish island of Harris. The proposed site for the quarry was in an area of outstanding natural beauty. The quarry was opposed by most of the islanders and environmentalists said if the quarry were built it would leave a scar six times higher than the cliffs at Dover.

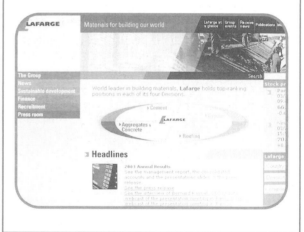

Source: adapted from Lafarge website and *The Guardian*, 10.1.2004.

(a) **Explain how Lafarge is involved in both primary and secondary production. (4 marks)**

(b) **Outline the possible role of a production planner in the manufacturing of cement at Lafarge. (6 marks)**

(c) **Using cement production as an example, explain what is meant by (i) inputs (ii) processes and (iii) outputs. (12 marks)**

(d) **Explain how Lafarge adds value when manufacturing cement. (8 marks)**

(e) **Discuss two production decisions that Lafarge may have made and how they could have affected production. (10 marks)**

Deciding how to produce

A business must decide on the most suitable method to manufacture its goods or to provide services. It is likely that products which are different will be produced differently. For example, a plastic drinks bottle may be produced using automated machinery, but a wrist watch may be assembled by hand. Products that are similar can also be produced in different ways. The Ford Motor Company and Morgan Cars both produce cars, but different processes are used. Ford builds cars using a production line and semi-skilled labour, but Morgan cars are hand built by skilled workers. There are three important decisions that businesses must make when choosing how to produce. These are shown in Figure 54.1, along with the factors which influence these decisions. In the diagram it is assumed that the firm has already decided 'what' to produce. When deciding how to produce, the objective of the firm will be to minimise the cost per unit of output, ie PRODUCTIVE EFFICIENCY.

What production method will be used? Production is sometimes divided into one of three methods. JOB PRODUCTION is where one job is completed at a time before moving on to another. An example might be a costume made for a television play set in the nineteenth century. BATCH PRODUCTION involves dividing the work into a number of different operations. An example would be bread production, where each batch goes through several different baking stages before it is completed. FLOW PRODUCTION involves work being completed continuously without stopping. The production of cars on a production line might be one example.

Some industries may combine different methods of production. For example, a large brewery may produce 'batches' of beer, but then send them to a bottling line for packaging, where flow production is used. Such combinations are particularly common in the food industry.

What factors of production will be used? Businesses are often faced with a wide choice between alternative production factors. For example, a builder planning to construct a new house must decide what building materials to buy, which tools to use, which sub-contractors to employ and whether to hire any extra labour. The builder will be faced with a choice in all of these cases. If he decides to hire a labourer, there may be hundreds or even thousands of people to choose from in the area.

How will the factors of production be combined? A third production decision concerns the way in which the available production factors should be combined. For example, should an assembly plant invest in a highly automated assembly

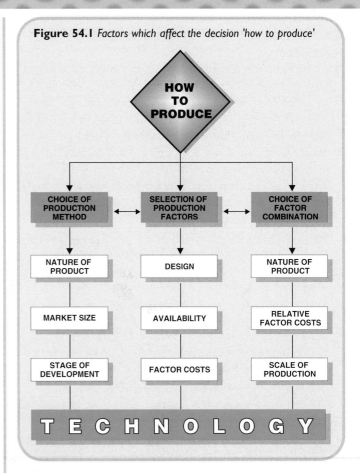

Figure 54.1 *Factors which affect the decision 'how to produce'*

operation, or employ a large semi-skilled labour force to undertake the work?

There is a relationship between the three decisions concerning how to produce. For example, if a large UK firm produced sheet glass using flow production techniques, it is likely that it would require labour with certain skills and that it may be capital intensive.

Job production

Job production involves the production of a single product at a time. It is used when orders for products are small, such as 'one-offs'. Production is organised so that one 'job' is completed at a time. There is a wide variety of goods and services which are produced or provided using this method of production. Small scale examples include the baking of a child's birthday cake, a dentist's treatment session or the construction of an extension to a house. On a large scale, examples could include the building of a ship, the construction of the Channel Tunnel or the manufacture of specialised machinery. Job production is found both in manufacturing and the service industries. Because the numbers of units produced is small, the production process tends to be labour intensive. The workforce is usually skilled craftsmen or specialists and the possibility of using labour saving machinery is limited. Many businesses adopt this method of production when they are 'starting up'.

Advantages of job production What are the benefits to businesses?

- Firms can produce unique or 'one-off' orders according to customer needs. For example, a wedding dress may be designed and produced for the individual taste of a client. It is also possible to change the specifications of a job at the last minute even if the work has actually begun.
- Workers are more likely to be motivated. The tasks employees carry out often require a variety of skills, knowledge and expertise. Their work will be more demanding and interesting. They will also see the end result of their efforts and be able to take pride in their work. Jobs may be carried out by a team of workers aiming to achieve the same objectives. This should help raise the level of job satisfaction.
- The organisation of job production is fairly simple. Because only one job is done at a time, co-ordination, communication, supervision and inspection can be regularly carried out. Also, it is easier to identify and deal with problems, such as a defective damp proof course in a house or a poorly cooked meal in a restaurant.

Gillian Windsor-Jones owns WebCare, a business that creates and manages business websites. Gillian has done an increasing number of jobs for schools and colleges in her local area. Her last job was to build a website for a college in Pershore, Worcestershire. The site contained

information about the college, such as its location and catchment area, the subjects offered, its achievements, the teaching staff and its extra curricula activities. The site has links to feeder schools and other educational agencies. It was also possible to contact the college using the web site by sending an email. The services offered by WebCare include:
- choosing and registering a web site domain name;
- selecting and configuring a web site hosting service;
- web site design, coding, and testing;
- deployment of web sites to a host;
- help promoting web sites;
- monitoring web site visitors and performance.

(a) What evidence is there in the case to suggest that WebCare uses job production?
(b Analyse the advantages of this method of production to customers of WebCare.

Disadvantages of job production There are, however, some disadvantages with job production.

- Labour costs will be high because production tends to be labour intensive. The workforce is likely to be skilled and more versatile. Such employees will be more expensive. The amount of time each employee spends on a particular job will also be long.
- Because there is a variety of work, to many specifications, the business would need a wide range of tools, machines and equipment. This can prove expensive. Also, it may not be possible to achieve economies of scale (☞ unit 81) because only one 'job' is produced at a time.
- Lead times can be lengthy. When building a house the business has to incur costs which cannot be recovered until the house is sold. Sometimes the sale of a house can take a long time.
- Selling costs may also be high. This is likely if the product is highly complex and technical. The sales team will need to be well qualified, able to cope with questions and deal with problems concerning sales and installation. Some firms employ agencies to help reduce their selling costs.

Once the demand for a firm's product rises, job production may become costly. Firms may prefer to use a method more suited to producing larger quantities. This is not always the case. Even if demand is high, each customer may require a unique order. In addition, many firms believe that the 'personal touch' they can offer in job production is important. As a result they may choose not to change to other production methods. Other production methods require some degree of product standardisation. This may result in more efficient production, but a loss of 'individuality'.

Batch production

Batch production may be used when demand for a firm's product or service is regular rather than a 'one off'. An example might be furniture where a batch of armchairs is made to a particular design. Production is divided into a number of operations. A particular operation is carried out on all products in a batch. The batch then moves to the next operation.

A baker uses batch production when baking bread. The operations in the baking process are broken down in Table 54.1.

These operations would be performed on every batch of bread. There is some standardisation because each loaf in the

Table 54.1 *Operations involved in the production of a batch of bread*

1. Blend ingredients in a mixing container until a dough is formed.
2. Knead the dough for a period of time.
3. Leave the dough to rise for a period of time.
4. Divide the dough into suitable units (loaves) for baking.
5. Bake the loaves.
6. Allow loaves to cool.

batch will be the same. However, it may be possible to vary each batch. The ingredients could be changed to produce brown bread or the style of baking tin could be changed for different shaped loaves.

A great number of products are produced using this method, particularly in manufacturing, such as the production of components and food processing. For example, in a canning plant, a firm may can several different batches of soup, each batch being a different recipe. Products can be produced in very large or very small batches depending on the level of demand. Larger production runs tend to lower the **unit** or **average cost** (☞ unit 27) of production. New technology (☞ unit 60) is increasingly being introduced to make batch production more efficient.

Advantages of batch production. What benefits will this method have for a business?

- Even though larger quantities are produced than in job production, there is still flexibility. Each batch can be changed to meet customers' wishes. It is particularly suitable for a wide range of similar products. The settings on machines can be changed according to specifications, such as different clothes sizes.
- Employees can concentrate on one operation rather than the whole task. This reduces the need for costly, skilled employees.
- Less variety of machinery would be needed than in job production because the products are standardised. Also, it is possible to use more standardised machinery.
- It often results in stocks of partly finished goods which have to be stored. This means firms can respond more quickly to an urgent order by processing a batch quickly through the final stages of production.

Disadvantages of batch production. There are also disadvantages with batch production.

- Careful planning and co-ordination are needed, or machines and workers may be idle, waiting for a whole batch to finish its previous operation. There is often a need to clean and adjust machinery before the next batch can be produced. This can mean delays. In brewing, one day of the week is used to clean equipment before the next batch begins.
- Some machinery may have to be more complex to compensate for the lower skill levels required from the labour force. This may lead to higher costs.
- The workforce may be less motivated, since they have to repeat operations on every single unit in the batch. In addition, they are unlikely to be involved with production from start to finish.
- If batches are small then unit costs will remain relatively high.
- Money will be tied up in work-in-progress (☞ unit 57) since an order cannot be dispatched until the whole batch has been finished.

WMN Algram is a medium-sized manufacturing company based in a 44,000 square foot plant on Plymouth's Language Industrial Estate. The company produces precision mould tools and thermoplastic components for the aerospace and motor industries. It is a flexible company supplying a wide range of products. However, the wide product range means that staff often have to shut down its 16 injection and vacuum forming moulding machines while they are changed over to the next order.

Some time ago, Stephen Brown, managing director, decided these 'set-up' times had to be reduced in order to make Algram more competitive. 'Our set-up and changeover process has been a real thorn in the company's side and a threat to our efficiency and competitiveness' says Mr Brown. 'A lot of time was being wasted while our machines were changed over, and the frequency meant we were incurring a significant cost penalty'.

The answer to the problem was to invite South West Manufacturing Advisory Service (SWMAS) into the factory. One of its consultants spent a week working with small group of Algram employees addressing the problem. At the end of the visit he was able to make recommendations to Algram which reduced set-up times. The average change-over time for Algram's injection moulding machines was down from 200 minutes to just 66 minutes, with the one-hour mark within reach. The time for vacuum formers was halved from 240 to 120 minutes. If this kind of improvement were spread across the whole business, direct costs would be reduced by 5 per cent and an extra 8,000 hours of capacity would be generated. It was suggested that what the team created on the shop floor at Algram was a changeover much more like a Formula 1 pit-stop.

Source: adapted from DTI web site.

(a) Which method of production do you think Algram uses? Explain your answer.
(b) Explain how the case highlights some of the problems associated with this method of production.

Question 2

Flow production

Most people will have some idea of flow production from pictures of motor car factories. Production is organised so that different operations can be carried out, one after the other, in a **continuous** sequence. Vehicles move from one operation to the next, often on a conveyer belt. The main features of flow production are:

- large quantities are produced;
- a simplified or standardised product;
- a semi-skilled workforce, specialising in one operation only;
- large amounts of machinery and equipment;
- large stocks of raw materials and components.

Flow production is used in the manufacture of products as

Food products can be manufactured in batches or using flow production techniques.

varied as newspapers, food and cement. It is sometimes called **mass production,** as it tends to be used for the production of large numbers of standard products, such as cars or breakfast cereals. Certain types of flow production are known as **continual flow production,** because products such as clothing material pass continually through a series of processes. **Repetitive flow production** is the manufacture of large numbers of the same product, such as plastic toy parts or metal cans. **Process production** is a form of flow production which is used in the oil or chemical industry. Materials pass through a plant where a series of processes are carried out in order to change the product. An example might be the refining of crude oil into petrol.

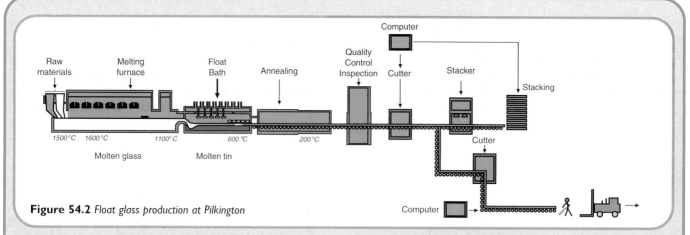

Figure 54.2 *Float glass production at Pilkington*

Pilkington Glass, the St Helens based manufacturer, produces float glass. A number of years ago the company developed a unique production method to manufacture float glass, a distortion free, flat glass with a fire polished finish. Figure 54.2 shows the different processes used in its production.
- Raw materials such as sand, soda ash, limestone, dolomite and alumina, are weighed, blended and fed continuously into the melting furnace. Recycled broken glass is also fed into the furnace to reduce waste.
- At temperatures of 1,600°C, the raw materials are melted inside the furnace. The molten glass moves through the tank, stirred by water cooled stirrers.
- The molten glass passes into the float bath and undertakes a forming process. It floats on the molten tin (because it is less dense) and spreads to form a ribbon. As it travels along inside the chamber, the glass ribbon cools to about 600°C and the imperfections are melted out.
- An annealing process is then used to cool the glass. This removes the stress from the glass so that it can be cut.
- Pilkington uses a computer-controlled automatic warehousing facility. Customers' orders are fed into the computer which works out cutting sizes and instructs the cutting heads to meet the order sizes.
- Panes are stacked automatically and can then be loaded into lorries for distribution.

The whole production process is automated, controlled and monitored by computers. The number of staff involved is minimal. For much of the time the factory floor is deserted.

There is only a maintenance team on duty. The computer room has the highest number of staff in the production area.

Source: adapted from company information.

(a) Using this case as an example, describe the features of flow production.
(b) How does this case highlight the advantages of flow production?

Question 3

Flow production relies on the use of computers. Computers send instructions to machines, control production speeds and conditions, and monitor quality. They allow large numbers of products to be produced continuously to exact standards or control continuous production which requires many processes.

Advantages of flow production Why might a business use flow production?
- Unit costs are reduced as firms gain from economies of scale (☞ unit 56).
- In many industries the process is highly automated. Production is controlled by computers. Many of the operations are performed by robots and other types of machinery. Once the production line is set up and running, products can flow off the end non stop for lengthy periods of time. This can reduce the need for labour, as only machine supervisors are needed.
- The need to stockpile finished goods is reduced. The production line can respond to short term changes in demand. For example, if demand falls the line can be shut down for a period of time. If it rises then the line can be opened.

Disadvantages of flow production What are the disadvantages of flow production?
- The set up costs are very high. An enormous investment in plant and equipment is needed. Firms must therefore be confident that demand for the product is sufficient over a period of time to make the investment pay.
- The product will be standardised. It is not possible to offer a wide product range and meet different customers' needs.
- For a number of reasons, worker motivation can be a serious problem. Most of the manual operations required on the production line will be repetitive and boring. Factories with production lines tend to be very noisy. Each worker will only be involved in a very small part of the job cycle. As a result of these problems worker morale may be low and labour turnover (☞ unit 45) and absenteeism high.
- Breakdowns can prove costly. The whole production system is interdependent. If one part of the supply or production line fails the whole system may break down.
In the 1990s flow production processes were changed in an attempt to solve some of these problems. Japanese manufacturers setting up businesses in the UK introduced methods to improve efficiency. Just in time manufacturing (☞ unit 55) for example, helped to reduce the cost of holding stocks. Some vehicle manufacturers attempted to introduce an element of job production into flow processes by **customising** products for clients. For example, a range of different cars were produced on the same production line. Cars in the same model range differed in colour, engine size, trim and interior design.

Choice of production method

The method of production chosen might depend on a number of factors.

- The nature of the product. Many products require a specific method of production. For example, in the construction industry, projects such as bridges, roads, office blocks and sewers must be produced using job production. Cereal farming involves batch production. A plot of land undergoes several processes before it 'produces' a crop.
- The size of the market. Fast moving consumer goods like soap, confectionery and canned drinks are normally produced using flow production because the market is so big. When the market is small, flow production techniques are not cost effective.
- The stage of development a business has reached. When firms are first set up, they often produce small levels of output and employ job or batch production methods. As they grow and enjoy higher sales levels they may switch to flow production.
- Technology. The current state of technology will affect all decisions concerning how to produce. As technology advances, new materials and machinery become available. Changes in technology often result in firms adopting new methods of production. For example, the development of computers and robotic welders has radically changed the way in which cars are manufactured. Also, car manufacturers are now able to produce different models on the same production line at the same time.

Choosing factors of production

A firm has to choose materials, tools, equipment, machinery and labour before production can begin. The more complex the product, the more difficult this will be. There is often a variety of materials and equipment to choose from. For example, a small manufacturer of jeans has to consider which type of cloth, cotton, stud, zip, sewing machine and labour to use. What influences the factors of production a business chooses?
- The actual design itself may specify which materials to use. For example, a new savoury snack will be made to a strict list of ingredients.
- There may be limited amounts of labour, capital or materials. A company recruiting people with a specialist skill may find that supply 'runs out'. It may then have to recruit unskilled workers and train them.
- Businesses will aim to use the cheapest factors, assuming that there is no difference in quality. If there is a difference in quality then the firm must decide which factor most suits its needs and budget. For example, when a company buys a new computer there is a wide range of models to choose from, at a range of different prices. They will have to select a model which suits their needs, and also one which they can afford.

Combining factors of production

Businesses must also decide what combination of factors of

Table 54.2 *The effect on output as more workers are employed, given a fixed amount of capital*

								(Units)
Capital	40	40	40	40	40	40	40	40
No. of workers	1	2	3	4	5	6	7	8
Total output	4	10	18	30	45	52	55	56

production they will use. The firm can adopt one of two approaches. LABOUR INTENSIVE techniques involve using a larger proportion of labour than capital. CAPITAL INTENSIVE techniques involve employing more machinery relative to labour. For example, chemical production is capital intensive with only a relatively small workforce to oversee the process. The postal service is labour intensive with a considerable amount of sorting and delivery done by hand.

The approach that is chosen depends on a number of factors.

● The nature of the product. Everyday products with high demand, like newspapers, are mass produced in huge plants using large quantities of machinery.
● The relative prices of the two factors. If labour costs are rising then it may be worth the company employing more capital instead.
● The size of the firm. As a firm grows and the scale of production increases, it tends to employ more capital relative to labour.

Combining different amounts of labour and capital can affect the **productivity** of these factors in the short run (☞ unit 27). As more units of labour are added to a fixed amount of capital, the output of the extra workers will rise at first and then fall. This is shown in Table 54.2, where the amount of capital is fixed at 40 units. For example, when the second worker is hired the total amount produced (**total**

output) rises by 6 units (10-4). When the third worker is employed, output rises by 8 units (18-10), ie a higher amount.

The amount added by each extra worker (the **marginal output**) continues to rise until the sixth worker is employed. Then output rises by a smaller amount (7 units = 52-45). This is called the **law of diminishing returns** (☞ unit 53). Output rises at first because workers are able to specialise in particular tasks, which improves the productivity of extra workers. However, there reaches a point where workers are not able to specialise any more and the productivity of the extra worker begins to fall.

key terms

Batch production - a method which involves completing one operation at a time on all units before performing the next.
Capital intensive - production methods which employ a large amount of machinery relative to labour.
Flow production - very large scale production of a standardised product, where each operation on a unit is performed continuously one after the other, usually on a production line.
Job production - a method of production which involves employing all factors to complete one unit of output at a time.
Labour intensive - production methods which rely on a large workforce relative to the amount of machinery.
Productive efficiency - production methods which minimise unit costs.

Knowledge

1. What are the 3 main decisions which have to be made regarding the method of production?
2. Under what circumstances might a business become more capital intensive?
3. State 3 types of products which may be manufactured using job production.
4. Describe the advantages and disadvantages of job production.
5. State 3 products that are generally manufactured using batch production.
6. Describe the advantages and disadvantages of batch production.
7. Describe 4 features of flow production.
8. What factors might affect the way a business chooses to combine factors of production?

Case study VegMeal

VegMeal makes a range of vegetarian soups which are sold to retailers in the UK. The business was set up by Peter Andrews. At the age of 16, he was selling hot soups from a stall that he cooked in a local market. They were popular and he was encouraged to produce the soup in larger quantities.

When he left school he rented some premises and began producing batches of soup for local retailers and other customers. He circulated information showing that he could produce up to 25 different soups. However, it became obvious that four of the soups were considerably more popular than the others. These were:

- lemon and white bean;
- spicy green pea and coriander;
- mediterranean vegetable and pasta;
- creamy parsnip.

Gradually, he cut back on the range so he could produce larger batches of the more popular soups. He knew that this would lower costs. Eventually he would only make other soups if the orders were large enough to justify cleaning the machinery and setting up production for a new variety.

For three years Peter enjoyed a steady and profitable period of growth. He was very busy and the business was operating at full capacity. Then in 2002 two things happened. He was approached by a large manufacturer in the food industry asking if he would supply them exclusively. At the same time, a national supermarket chain asked if he could supply them with several hundred thousand units per week. Peter was not keen on becoming an exclusive supplier. He felt this would cut down his options in the future and, although the financial terms of the offer were attractive, he did not want to be tied to one customer. However, the supermarket order looked very impressive, even though production would have to be stepped up greatly. This would mean some major investment and probably a switch in production methods. There was enough room in the factory to install a small production line and use flow production. Peter had been to a trade fair that year and knew that plant could be installed capable of producing several different varieties of soup. The cost of this would be huge and the changes in working practices might be a stumbling block for Peter's production staff.

After some lengthy meetings with the supermarket, Peter secured a three year supply contract. He drew up a business plan impressive enough to persuade a venture capitalist to lend £450,000 to help fund the new production line. Switching to flow production would increase capacity from 20,000 units per week to 800,000 units. Unit costs would be lowered from 42p to 23p, not including the cost of the new line.

The installation of the new line did not go exactly to plan. Some of the usual problems when switching to capital intensive production methods were encountered.

(a) Explain what is meant by the term 'capital intensive production methods'. **(6 marks)**

(b) Explain the problems that Peter might have encountered when using batch production to produce 25 different varieties of soup. **(8 marks)**

(c) Analyse the advantages to VegMeal of switching to flow production. **(12 marks)**

(d) Assess whether the problems the business might have encountered when switching production methods were likely to outweigh the advantages. **(14 marks)**

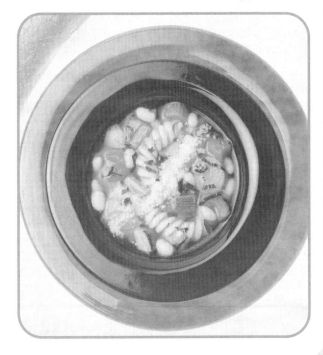

55 Lean Production

What is lean production?

LEAN PRODUCTION is an approach to production developed in Japan. Toyota, the Japanese car manufacturer, was the first company to adopt this approach. Its aim is to reduce the quantity of resources used up in production. Lean producers use less of everything, including factory space, materials, stocks, suppliers, labour, capital and time. As a result, lean production raises productivity and reduces costs. The number of defective products is reduced, lead times (☞ unit 57) are cut and reliability improves. Lean producers are also able to design new products more quickly and can offer customers a wider range of products to choose from. Lean production involves using a range of practices designed to reduce waste and to improve productivity and quality.

Kaizen (continuous improvement)

KAIZEN is perhaps the most important concept in Japanese management. It means continuous improvement. Every aspect of life, including social life, working life and home life, is constantly improved. Everyone in the business is involved. Kaizen is said to be an 'umbrella concept'. A wide range of different production techniques and working practices must be carried out for it to be effective. Figure 55.1 shows examples of the techniques, principles and practices. They should result in ongoing improvements. This approach argues that a day should not pass without some kind of improvement being made somewhere in the business.

There is a number of features of Kaizen which affect a business.

Continuous improvement Kaizen has been the main difference between the Japanese and the Western approaches to management in the past. The attempts of Western businesses to improve efficiency and quality have tended to be 'one-offs'. In Figure 55.2 the solid line illustrates the Western approach. Productivity remains the same for long periods of time, then suddenly rises. The increase is followed by another period of stability, before another rise. Increases in productivity may result from new working practices or new technology. The dotted line shows the Japanese approach. Improvements are continuous. They result from changes in production techniques which are introduced gradually.

Eliminating waste The elimination of waste (called *muda* in Japan) in business practices is an important part of Kaizen. Waste is any activity which raises costs without adding value to a product. Examples may be:

● time wasted while staff wait around before starting tasks, such as waiting for materials to arrive;
● time wasted when workers move unnecessarily in the workplace, such as walking to a central point in the factory to get tools;
● the irregular use of a machine, such as a machine which is only used once a month for a special order;
● excessive demands upon machines or workers, such as staff working overtime seven days a week which causes them to be tired and work poorly.

Firms that adopt the Kaizen approach train and reward workers to continually search for waste and to suggest how it might be eliminated.

Implementing continuous improvement It is often difficult for workers in a business to look for continuous improvement all the time. Japanese businesses tried to solve this problem by introducing the PDCA (Plan, Do, Check, Action) cycle. It is a series of activities that lead to improvement.

● Plan. Businesses must identify where improvement is needed.

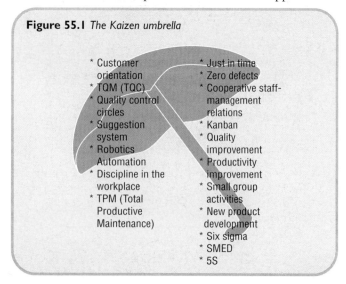

Figure 55.1 The Kaizen umbrella

* Customer orientation
* TQM (TQC)
* Quality control circles
* Suggestion system
* Robotics Automation
* Discipline in the workplace
* TPM (Total Productive Maintenance)
* Just in time
* Zero defects
* Cooperative staff-management relations
* Kanban
* Quality improvement
* Productivity improvement
* Small group activities
* New product development
* Six sigma
* SMED
* 5S

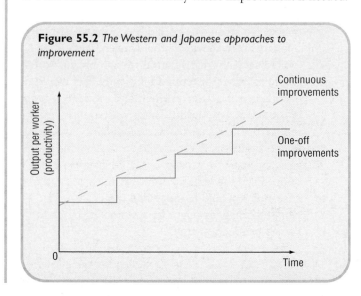

Figure 55.2 The Western and Japanese approaches to improvement

Output per worker (productivity) / Time

Continuous improvements

One-off improvements

Data must be gathered and used to develop a plan which will result in improvement.

- Do. Once the plan has been finalised it must be carried out. The plan is likely to be implemented by workers, on the production line perhaps.
- Check. The next stage in the cycle is to check whether or not there has been an improvement. This task may be carried out by inspectors.
- Action. If the plan has been successful, it must be introduced in all parts of the business.

Julian Richer is a disciple of Kaizen. He heads the hi-fi retailing chain, Richer Sounds, which he set up with just one shop in 1979. In recent years he has earned a reputation for 'wacky' but very effective management ideas. Richer places great emphasis on establishing a rapport with every new member of staff. He invites new employees to his house for three days where they 'work hard and play hard'. They undergo an intensive training course, but also enjoy tennis, badminton, snooker, swimming, dance and films.

Every Richer store offers free coffee and mints to customers and has a mirror which says 'you are looking at the most important person in this shop'. If it is raining when a customer buys a new hi-fi system they are given a free umbrella. Customers' opinions are monitored and staff bonuses are linked to customer satisfaction.

Staff are encouraged to express their ideas. They are given £5 each once a month to visit the pub together and talk about new ideas. Staff with the best customer service records are given the use of four classic cars - Jaguars and Bentleys. There are also five holiday homes which they can book free of charge. Absenteeism is between 1 and 2 per cent less than the national average. If staff are caught stealing from the store they are dismissed instantly. He has a fanatical attention for detail, working from a cardboard worksheet that lists his tasks in minute handwriting.

Richer has a policy of slow growth, arising from past mistakes when he tried to over-reach himself. His policies, plus highly competitive pricing, have earned the business a place in the *Guinness Book of Records* as the world's busiest retailer.

Source: adapted from *The Financial Times*.

(a) Identify Kaizen business techniques or practices which Julian Richer adopts at Richer Sounds. In each case explain your answer.
(b) Explain the possible benefits to Richer Sounds of the Kaizen approach.

Just-in-time manufacturing

JUST-IN-TIME (JIT) manufacturing is an important part of lean production and the kaizen approach. It was developed in the Japanese shipbuilding industry in the 1950s and 1960s. The industry recognised that a great deal of money was tied up in stocks. Traditionally, one month's supply of steel was held by a shipyard. However, as the industry became more competitive, shipbuilders insisted that steel suppliers deliver orders 'just-in-time', ie a few hours or less before the steel was needed. This reduced the need for high levels of working capital and improved the financial performance of the business. JIT was extended to every stage of production. For example, raw materials were delivered JIT to be made into parts, parts were delivered JIT to be made into goods and goods were produced and delivered JIT to be sold.

JIT was introduced in other Japanese industries, such as the car industry, and then spread to other parts of the world, such as the USA and Europe. JCB has used JIT in its Rochester plant. When JCB excavators are manufactured, every machine on the production line has already been sold. Supplies of components, such as engines from Perkins, and raw materials, such as steel plate, arrive on the day they are needed. JIT manufacturing requires high levels of organisational skills and reliable suppliers.

Table 55.1 shows the advantages and disadvantages of JIT manufacturing.

GD Mountfield is the UK's largest manufacturer of garden machinery. To improve efficiency it needed to reduce stocks, increase productivity and improve delivery performance during the peak 5 month period which accounted for 80 per cent of its sales. Also, space was needed for new products. With many key components bought from foreign suppliers, and heavily seasonal demand, the company held large stocks and used a warehouse to smooth out purchasing, assembly and sales. Even with 70 per cent of floor space allocated to storage, delivery was still inadequate at peak times.

GD Mountfield made a number of changes to the way it operated. To reduce stocks it employed a parts 'regulator', using clearly defined storage locations to give visual control of stock. This ensured that the parts coming in were matched to the number of parts used. The company also began a negotiation process with its suppliers to adopt JIT techniques and improve supplier management. As a result of the changes the company improved its product availability to wholesalers and responded more effectively to demand.

Source: adapted from Bourton Group website.

(a) Explain why GD Mountfield introduced JIT techniques.
(b) Explain why it would be important for GD Mountfield to have good relations with its suppliers when introducing JIT.

Question 1

Question 2

Table 55.1 *Advantages and disadvantages of JIT manufacturing*

Advantages

- It improves cash flow since money is not tied up in stocks.
- The system reduces waste, obsolete and damaged stock.
- More factory space is made available for productive use.
- The costs of stockholding are reduced significantly.
- Links with and the control of suppliers are improved.
- The supplier base is reduced significantly.
- More scope for integration within the factory's computer system.
- The motivation of workers is improved. They are given more responsibility and encouraged to work in teams.

Disadvantages

- A lot of faith is placed in the reliability and flexibility of suppliers.
- Increased ordering and administration costs.
- Advantages of bulk buying may be lost.
- Vulnerable to a break in supply and machinery breakdowns.
- Difficult to cope with sharp increases in demand.
- Possible loss of reputation if customers are let down by late deliveries.

The 'Kanban' system

KANBAN is a Japanese term which means signboards or cards. The Kanban system is a method used to control the transfer of materials between different stages of production. The kanban might be a solid plastic marker or coloured ping-pong ball. They might be used to:

- inform employees in the previous stage of production that a particular part must be taken from stocks and sent to a specific destination (conveyance kanbans);
- tell employees involved in a particular operation that they can begin production and add their output to stock (production kanbans);
- instruct external suppliers to send parts to a destination (vendor kanbans).

`Kanbans are used to trigger the movement or production of resources. Used properly, they will be the only means of authorising movement. Kanbans are an important part of JIT manufacturing as they prevent the build up of stock or parts in a factory.

Time-based management

TIME-BASED MANAGEMENT involves reducing the amount of time businesses take carrying out certain tasks, such as launching new products or cutting lead times in production. Time-based management is a feature of lean production because it involves eliminating a type of waste, ie time. Time in business is a valuable resource. Productivity can be improved if tasks are carried out more quickly. Time-based management has a number of effects on a business.

- Manufacturers focus on customer needs. Customers are given a wide range of products to choose from, ie different models with different specifications. The same model car can be produced according to different specifications, such as different colours, engine sizes and trims. Manufacturers

can achieve this by reducing the length of production runs. Shorter production runs will also allow a firm to cut customer lead times, so customers are not kept waiting.

- Manufacturers use other lean production methods, such as JIT and cellular manufacturing, and total quality management (☞ unit 58). These methods prevent delays on production lines, reduce stock levels and improve scheduling. This means employees are not waiting around for work to arrive.
- Machines must be versatile. They must be able to produce a variety of products and be adjusted to a range of settings. Settings must be changed quickly and easily to deal with shorter production runs.
- Manufacturers speed up the design process by carrying out a number of design tasks simultaneously. The traditional approach to design is to carry out one task after another. However, time can be saved if design tasks can be completed at the same time. Such an approach needs co-ordination and communication between each design team. This approach has been called LEAN DESIGN.

Mass producers (☞ unit 56) argue that economies of scale will only be achieved and costs cut if products are standardised and production runs are long. Producing a variety of different models will lead to shorter production runs and higher average costs. Time-based management challenges this view. It may be possible to produce smaller quantities, because costs can be reduced by time savings.

There may be certain advantages for a business using a time-based management system.

- Customers will benefit. A wider range of products will be available and there will be faster delivery times. This might result in higher sales levels for the firm.
- Lean design will result in shorter lead times. This means that resources will be used more effectively and product development will be faster. This will give the business a competitive edge in the market.
- Other lean production techniques will increase efficiency, the quality of products will be improved and waste will be minimised.
- The time spent on a range of production tasks is reduced. This helps to improve productivity and reduce unit costs. As a result manufacturers may offer their products at lower prices or enjoy higher profit margins.

However, it could be argued that some costs might rise as a result of using time-based management. The versatile machinery which this method requires may be more expensive. Staff may also need to be trained in a wider range of skills and tasks to cope with the flexibility in production. Shorter production runs may result in the loss of some economies of scale.

Empowerment

Empowerment (☞ unit 43) involves giving employees the power to make decisions in a business. The aim of empowerment is to give employees more control over their own work conditions. Workers in the past have tended to follow the instructions of managers. They were rarely required to think, make decisions, solve problems or work creatively. There was often conflict between management and workers, and little cooperation and team-spirit.

In recent years many businesses have learned that efficiency will improve if workers are given the opportunity to involve themselves in decision making. Workers will be better motivated and the business may gain from the creativity of its workers. Workers may also be more flexible and adaptable. For example, a worker may speak directly to a customer about changes in an order. For empowerment to be successful, managers must have faith in their workforce. They must also trust them and work in partnership without conflict.

Empowerment is not without difficulties. Some workers may not be able to make their own decisions and training may be required to teach them such skills. Managers may resent giving up authority. Some staff may even abuse their power to make decisions.

Teamworking

A growing number of businesses are introducing teamworking in their organisations. This involves dividing the workforce into fairly small groups. Each team will focus on a particular area of production and team members will have the same common aims. Teamworking probably works best in businesses that do not have a hierarchical structure (☞ unit 40) and which have an organisational culture which supports group work. Effective teamworking requires co-operation between workers and management, training for staff and workers being given responsibility to make decisions.

Both the business and employees might benefit from teamwork. Workers should develop relationships with colleagues and a 'team spirit' which may improve motivation and productivity. Flexibility might improve. For example, team members might be more willing to cover for an absent colleague. Teams might plan their own work schedules, share out tasks, choose their methods of work and solve their own problems. This should lead to quicker decision making and the generation of more ideas. It is also suggested that communication and labour relations may improve as a result of teamworking. However, there may be conflict between team members and managers may resent the responsibility delegated to teams. Teamwork also results to some extent in a loss of specialisation amongst workers, which is often found in flow or mass production techniques.

Cellular manufacturing

Flow production (☞ unit 54) involves mass producing a standard product on a production line. The product undergoes a series of operations in sequence on a continuous basis until a finished product rolls off the 'end of the line'.

CELLULAR MANUFACTURING or CELL PRODUCTION adopts a different approach and involves dividing the workplace into 'cells'. Each cell occupies an area on the factory floor and focuses on the production of a 'product family'. A 'product family' is a group of products which requires a sequence of similar operations. For example, the metal body part of a machine might require the operations cut, punch, fold, spot weld, dispatch. This could all be carried out in one cell. Inside a cell, machines are grouped together and a team of workers sees the production of a good from start to finish.

Take the example of a furniture manufacturer making parts for a kitchen range in a cell. The raw material, such as wood, would be brought into the cell. Tasks such as turning on a lathe or shaping by routing would be carried out at workstations. The part would then be assembled and passed on to stock. The cell may also be responsible for tasks such as designing, schedule planning, maintenance and problem solving, as well as the manufacturing tasks which are shared by the team.

The advantages of cellular manufacturing include:
- floor space is released because cells use less space than a linear production line;
- product flexibility is improved;
- lead times are cut;
- movement of resources and handling time is reduced;
- there is less work-in-progress;
- teamworking is encouraged;
- there may be a safer working environment and more efficient maintenance.

E M Solutions is based in Lisburn, County Antrim. It employs over 350 people in the design and manufacture of cabinets for the networking, storage and computer industries throughout Europe. The company is committed to continuous improvement and recently moved from traditional batch production to cellular manufacturing. This required considerable investment in CNC punching, programmable laser cutting and ancillary equipment to make the cabinets. Reorganisation into cellular manufacturing resulted in the allocation of dedicated cells to customers. The changes required major planning in terms of the allocation of equipment, personnel and staff training programmes. Each aspect of these activities was geared to the needs of customers, resulting in dedicated personnel and equipment being assigned to specific customer accounts.

Cellular manufacturing has improved the work flow and reduced work-in-progress to a minimum. It gives operators the opportunity to measure key dimensions, empowers them to control the quality of their own work and also allows the next person in the cell the opportunity to inspect the previous operation. There have been great reductions in warranty returns, scrap, and rework, and fewer customer complaints.

Source: adapted from NMP Case Studies – Edgecumbe Instruments Ltd.

(a) Using this case as an example, explain the difference between batch production and cellular production.
(b) How have E M Solution's customers benefited from the switch to cellular manufacturing?

Question 3

Six Sigma

Six Sigma is a Japanese method developed by Motorola. It takes its name from the Greek letter 'sigma' used in statistics to indicate standard deviation. It is a statistical approach designed to eliminate defects in processes. A process must not produce more than 3.4 defects per million. A Six Sigma defect is defined as anything that fails to match customer specifications.

Six Sigma involves collecting data on performance in processes and then evaluating it. Businesses can reduce variations in performance by using one of two Six Sigma approaches. DMAIC (define, measure, analyse, improve, control) is an improvement system for existing processes that result in too many defects. DMADV (define, measure, analyse, design, verify) is an improvement system used to develop new processes.

Single Minute Exchange of Dies (SMED)

Many manufacturers are under pressure to offer a wider variety of products. This has resulted in companies having to reduce the size of batches they produce. So it is important to reduce changeover or set-up time. Bottling industries can spend more than 20 per cent of production time on changeovers, for example. Single Minute Exchange of Dies (SMED) is an approach to reduce output and quality losses due to changeovers. It was developed in Japan by Shigeo Shingo and has allowed companies to reduce changeover times from hours to minutes. He developed a method to analyse the changeover process, enabling workers to find out for themselves why the changeover took so long, and how this time can be reduced. There are four key steps in SMED.

- Suppress useless operations and convert IS operations (those which must be done while the machine is stopped) into ES operations (those which can be done when the machine is running).
- Simplify fittings and tightenings.
- Work together.
- Suppress adjustments and trials.

SMED has often resulted in workers approaching changeovers with a 'pit-stop mentality'.

5S (Sort, Set, Shine, Standardise and Sustain)

5S is a Japanese approach to housekeeping in the factory. It is a method of organising, cleaning, developing and sustaining a productive work environment. What does 5S stand for?

- **Sort.** This is about getting rid of the clutter in the factory. Only items such as necessary work tools should be in the factory environment. All other items, such as excess inventory, should be removed.
- **Set in order.** The work area should be organised so that it is easy to find what is needed.
- **Shine.** This is to do with keeping the work area clean. Make it 'shine'.

- **Standardise.** Once the most effective cleaning and sorting methods have been established, they should be used as standards for the whole factory.
- **Sustain.** Mechanisms should be implemented to ensure that the standards achieved are recognised by everyone and used in the future.

This approach has helped businesses to improve efficiency because the work environment is less cluttered and more organised.

Rojee Tasha Stampings Ltd produces stamped metal components and subassemblies for automobiles. To improve productivity the company adopted a number of lean manufacturing techniques.

- SMED was introduced to cut machine set-up times. In a practical example, workers on two press machines broke down the entire changeover process into small activities in order to determine the time wasted for adjustments and readjustments. As a result of this exercise, the changeover time was reduced from 62 minutes to 13 minutes, with a similar result obtained in the case of the second press machine.
- A major concern of the company was machinery breakdown. A maintenance worker was recruited which dramatically reduced response time to machinery breakdown. A successful preventive maintenance programme was also introduced.
- Engineers were trained on error-proofing. This helped to identify ten major quality-related issues and recommendations were made for action covering various production areas.
- The company formalised its training activities. It established technical training schedules that reflected its development plan. Lean production methods such as SMED were introduced and teams were formed to solve problems. After 6 months of training, 9 machine operators became multi-skilled, ready to train new recruits.
- In conjunction with 5S activities and the application of error-proofing methods, extensive training also contributed to gains in product quality and the consequent 50 per cent cut in the volume of products returned by customers.

As a result of these and other measures the company turnover increased by 36 per cent, production space was increased by 43 per cent, machine downtime was reduced by 100 per cent, lead time was reduced by 50 per cent, changeover time for press machines was reduced by 80 per cent, worker flexibility increased by 100 per cent and staff motivation improved significantly.

Source: adapted from Ten3 web site.

(a) Using examples from the case, explain what is meant by lean production.
(b) Explain what is meant by SMED and how the method benefited the business.

Question 4

key terms

Cellular manufacturing or cell production - involves producing a 'family of products' in a small self-contained unit (a cell) within a factory.

Just-in-time manufacturing - a production technique which is highly responsive to customer orders and uses very little stock holding.

Kanban - a card which acts as a signal to move or provide resources in a factory.

Kaizen - a Japanese term which means continuous improvement.

Lean design - keeping the resources and time used in the design process to a minimum.

Lean production - an approach to operations management aimed at reducing the quantity of resources used up in production.

Time-based-management - involves setting strict time limits in which tasks must be completed.

Knowledge *...Knowledge...Knowle*

1. What are the aims of lean production?
2. What is meant by the Kaizen umbrella?
3. Explain the purpose of the PDCA cycle.
4. Describe 4 advantages of JIT manufacturing.
5. What is the purpose of the Kanban system?
6. Describe the 3 principles of time-based manufacturing.
7. What are the advantages of time-based manufacturing?
8. Give 2 advantages and 2 disadvantages of empowerment.
9. Why is teamworking a growing trend in businesses?
10. Describe how cellular manufacturing works.

Case study *Gateshead Holdings*

'The culture here when I arrived was a joke. People didn't come here to work, they came to skip work. The place was a complete mess. There were raw materials, spoilt work and finished products scattered all over the factory floor. No one could be bothered to do anything. Dragging this place into the twenty first century has been a long and painful task.'

Those were the words of Geoff Cartwright, the production manager at Gateshead Holdings. The business manufactures metal components. Geoff led a management buy-in of the company in 1999. It was sold by the family that owned it for £1. The company had lost money for five consecutive years and had got into debt. Geoff had been looking for an ailing company to buy for two years. He loved manufacturing and wanted a challenge.

The problems at the factory prior to the buy-in were largely the result of low pay, a lack of training, dated working practices and weak management. Industrial relations were also poor and there were no incentives for the workers. Consequently, the business had declined and was losing market share rapidly.

When Geoff arrived he spoke face to face with all 146 workers individually. He explained to each of them his three year plan. However, the overwhelming majority were unimpressed. They just did not believe it was possible to transform a business with a 'traditional work culture' into a modern, lean, customer-focused organisation. The changes made between 1999 and 2002 included the following.

● The factory layout was completely changed. Workers were divided into teams and each team worked in a cell concentrating on a 'family' of products. 5S was also introduced.

● The workforce was reduced by 25 through voluntary redundancies. The remaining workers were reorganised. A flat structure was introduced and all supervisory and middle management posts were eliminated.

● Workers were given multi-skill training so that they could work on any machine and do any job in their cell. They were also taught how to maintain machinery and attend to minor breakdowns. They were trained in customer service so that all staff could deal with questions. The training was also designed to empower staff so that they could solve their own problems.

● Waste in the factory was cut by using JIT and six sigma.

● A system of annualised hours was introduced and

overtime eliminated. Paid holiday was increased from four to five weeks.

● Wages were increased in stages from the statutory minimum wage in 1999 to £7.50 per hour in 2003.

● An incentive scheme was introduced which was linked to sales revenue and defects. There was also an attendance bonus scheme. Workers received a £200 bonus if they went three months without being absent. A further £1,000 was paid if staff went a whole year without a day off.

Making the changes was not easy for the management buy-in team. There was a lot of resistance, especially to the training sessions. A massive 76 per cent of the workforce had never received any training at all whilst employed at Gateshead Holdings. The first few training sessions were greeted with a negative attitude. However, after a very powerful motivational speech from Geoff, eventually the workforce started to cooperate as they began to see sense in what the business wanted to do. Geoff also won the respect of the workers because he spent a great deal of the time in the factory helping to deal with problems.

In 2003, the company made a small profit for the first time in eight years. Geoff responded to this by

Table 55.2 *Staff turnover at Gateshead Holdings, 1995 - 2003*

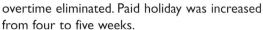

1995	1996	1997	1998	1999	2000	2001	2002	2003
35%	39%	41%	49%	34%	19%	11%	9%	6%

organising a party for staff and their friends in a special function room at St James Park, home of Newcastle United.

(a) What evidence is there to suggest that Gateshead Holdings introduced Kaizen between 1999 and 2003? (4 marks)

(b) What is the purpose of introducing 5S into the factory? (6 marks)

(c) Explain possible reasons for the changes in staff turnover between 1995 and 2003. (8 marks)

(d) Examine how waste would be reduced by introducing JIT and Six Sigma. (10 marks)

(e) Discuss the most important factors which helped Geoff and his team to transform Gateshead Holdings into a profitable company. (12 marks)

56 Business Size and Economies of Scale

Defining size

In the UK there are around four million businesses. Their sizes vary. A company like BP Amoco has operations around the world, employs thousands of people and has a turnover of billions of pounds. A self-employed joiner may operate in a small workshop, employ one other person and have sales of just a few thousand pounds. Most businesses begin on a small scale and then grow. What is the difference between a large firm and a small firm? When does a small firm become large? How might size be measured?

Turnover Sales revenue that a business earns could be used to measure size. For example, Royal Bank of Scotland, is a large business. Its turnover in 2002 was £16,815 million.

The number of employees A business with thousands of employees may be considered large. IBM, the computer manufacturer, for example, employed over 300,000 people in 2004. The term Small and Medium-sized Enterprises (SMEs) is often used when talking about relatively small firms. The EU uses the following criteria to measure firm size:
● micro firm: maximum of 9 employees;
● small firm: maximum of 49 employees;
● medium firm: maximum of 249 employees;
● large firm: 250 or more employees.

The amount of capital employed This measure is based on the amount of money invested in the business. The more money invested the larger the business. For example, in 2003 GUS had capital employed of £2,640 million. EasyNet, in comparison, had capital employed of only £21 million.

Profit Businesses which have higher profits than others may be classed as larger businesses. For example, in 2002 Unilever made a pre-tax profit of £2,499 million. Helphire, the company that helps drivers involved in accidents, on the other hand made a pre-tax profit of £5.25 million.

Market share It could be argued that a business with a 43 per

cent market share (☞ unit 14), is larger than one which has a 9 per cent market share in the same industry. Coca-Cola, for example sells over 50 per cent of all cola drinks worldwide.

Market capitalisation This is the current share price multiplied by the number of shares. Table 56.1 shows the largest 5 companies in the UK according to this measure.

According to the EU, a firm is considered to be:
● 'small' if it has a turnover of 7 million euros, a balance sheet total of not more than 5 million euros (ie capital employed), a maximum of 49 employees and is not more than 25 per cent owned by one or more companies satisfying the same criteria;
● medium-sized if it has a turnover of not more than 40 million euros, a balance sheet total of not more than 27 million euros, a maximum of 249 employees and the same 25 per cent criteria as above;
● large if it exceeds the criteria above.

Problems with measuring size

In practice, measuring the size of a business may not be easy. A

Babcock International Group plc is a support services company with four main business divisions in the UK.
● Babcock Defence Services provides a wide range of support and training services to the Royal Navy, British Army and RAF;
● Babcock Engineering Services supports the activities of customers in the defence, marine, oil & gas and supply chain service markets;
● Babcock Infrastructure Services enables customers to reduce costs on their built infrastructure portfolio;
● Babcock Naval Services operates HM Naval Base Clyde in partnership with the MoD, providing the full range of support services.

The company employs several thousand staff and had a turnover of £423.5 million in 2003 (approximately 629.6 million euros at exchange rate of £1=1.48 euros). The value of Babcock's capital employed in 2003 was £87.4 million (approximately 129.9 million euros). In March 2003 the company's share price was 90p and it had 145,580,737 shares in issue.

Source: adapted from Babcock International, *Annual Report and Accounts, 2003*.

(a) Using evidence from the case determine whether Babcock is a small, medium or large business.
(b) In March 2004, Babcock's share price was 130p and the number of shares issued was little changed. Using this as an example, explain why market capitalisation may not always be useful as a measure of business size.

Question 1

Table 56.1 *The largest 5 UK firms (market capitalisation), 2004*

Company	Market capitalisation (£bn)	Industry
1. HSBC	£96,271 million	Banking
2. BP	£95.666 million	Oil (integrated)
3. Vodafone	£91,257 million	Telecommunications
4. Glaxo SmithKline	£66,657 million	Pharmaceuticals
5. Royal Bank of Scotland	£50,518 million	Banking

Source: adapted from *The Sunday Times*, 29.2.2004.

highly automated chemical plant may only employ 45 people, but have a turnover of 50 million euros. According to the number of employees, the EU would class it as a small business. However, according to the level of turnover it could be classed as a large business.

Using the level of profit may also be misleading. A large company may have problems and make only a small profit over a period of time and yet still stay in business. One of the problems of using market capitalisation is that share prices change constantly. This means company size is fluctuating all the time. It is the size of the business relative to its particular sector in an industry that is important. Is it large enough to enjoy the benefits of size in the market? Is it too large or too small in relation to other organisational needs of the business?

Reasons for growth

In many industries it is rare for a firm to remain exactly the same size for any length of time. Most businesses start small and then grow in size. They may aim to grow for a number of reasons.

- Survival. In some industries firms will not survive if they remain small. Staying small might mean that costs are too high because the firm is too small to exploit economies of scale. In addition, small firms, even if they are profitable, may face a takeover bid from a larger firm.
- Gaining economies of scale. As firms grow in size they will begin to enjoy the benefits of ECONOMIES OF SCALE. This means that unit production costs will fall and efficiency and profits will improve. This is dealt with later in the unit.
- To increase future profitability. By growing and selling larger volumes, a firm will hope to raise profits in the future.
- Gaining market share. This can have a number of benefits. If a firm can develop a degree of monopoly power (☞ unit 61) through growth, it might be able to raise price or control part of the market. Some personnel also enjoy the status and power associated with a high market share. For example, it could be argued that Richard Branson enjoys the publicity which goes with leading a large company like Virgin.
- To reduce risk. Risk can be reduced through diversification. Branching into new markets and new products means that if one product fails success in others can keep the company going. For example, tobacco companies have diversified into breweries to guard against a fall in demand for cigarettes.

Methods of growth

There is a number of ways in which a company might grow. **Internal growth** is when a firm expands without involving other businesses. ORGANIC GROWTH means that the firm expands by selling more of its existing products. This could be achieved by selling to a wider market, either at home or abroad. It is likely that internal growth will take a long time for many businesses, but will provide a sound base for development. A quicker alternative is **external growth.**

Tesco has become the UK's largest supermarket chain and is continuing to grow. It is increasing the number of stores it operates, and extending its product range rapidly into non-food items. The company sells more DVDs than HMV, more shampoo than Boots, and its £4 jeans outsell Levis, Wrangler and Gap put together. It is developing its smaller outlets, on petrol forecourts for example, growing its online business and is also developing businesses abroad.

Table 56.2 *Tesco, financial information*

	1999	2000	2001	2002	2003
Sales	18,546	20,358	22,773	25,654	28,613
No. of stores	821	845	907	979	2,291
No. of employees	126,914	134,896	152,210	171,794	188,182
Dividend per share	4.12p	4.48p	4.98p	5.60p	6.20p

Source: adapted from Tesco, *Annual Report and Accounts, 2003.*

(a) What evidence is there to suggest that Tesco has enjoyed strong growth over the last five years?
(b) What do you think might be the main motives for Tesco's growth?

Question 2

This can be by ACQUISITION or TAKEOVER of other businesses or by MERGING with them. A takeover is when one company buys control of another. A merger usually means that two companies have agreed to join together and create a new third company. In practice these terms are often used interchangeably. In recent decades merger activity has increased greatly leading to a concentration of ownership in many industries. Mergers and takeovers are discussed in unit 89.

It had also been suggested that companies can attempt to grow in one of three ways. Companies can grow by **acquisition**. For example, AXA, the insurance business, has grown by taking over foreign firms in the US, UK and Japan. However, some companies that have attempt to grow by acquisition have become bigger but not better, and ultimately failed as a result. Examples might be Polly Peck, the food, electronics and textiles group, and Ratners, the jewellery store.

Some companies grow by **innovating** and providing new products. Examples may be Microsoft and Intel. A problem for such companies is that rivals start to copy their ideas, which may slow down growth.

Companies that grow by **robust growth** might include Coca-Cola and Procter & Gamble. They have long term

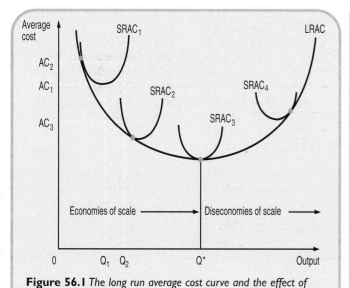

Figure 56.1 *The long run average cost curve and the effect of economies of scale*

growth as an objective, take consumers' needs into account, are prepared to invest in information technology and value the skills of their workforce.

Benefits of growth

Earlier in this unit it was argued that firms grow to achieve economies of scale. Economies of scale are the reductions in costs gained by businesses as they increase in size. Unit 38 showed that, in the long run, a firm can build another factory or purchase more machinery. This can cause the average cost of production to fall. In Figure 56.1 a firm is currently producing in a small plant and its short run costs are $SRAC_1$. When it produces an output equal to Q_1 its average cost will be AC_1. If it raises production to Q_2, average costs will rise to AC_2. The rise in average costs is a result of **diminishing returns**.

If the firm expands the scale of its operations (which it can do in the long run) the same level of output can be produced more efficiently. With a bigger plant, represented by $SRAC_2$, Q_2 can be produced at an average cost of just AC_3. Long run average costs fall due to economies of scale and will continue to do so until the firm has built a plant which minimises long run average costs. In the diagram this occurs when a plant shown by $SRAC_3$ is built. This is sometimes called the MINIMUM EFFICIENT SCALE of plant. When output reaches Q^* in this plant, long run average costs cannot be reduced any further through expansion. Indeed, if the firm continues to grow it will experience rising average costs due to DISECONOMIES OF SCALE, as in $SRAC_4$ in Figure 56.1. This is dealt with later in the unit.

Internal economies of scale

What are the different economies of scale a firm can gain? INTERNAL ECONOMIES OF SCALE are the benefits of growth that arise within the firm. They occur for a number of reasons.

Technical economies Technical economies arise because larger plants are often more efficient. The capital costs and the running costs of plants do not rise in proportion to their size. For example, the capital cost of a double decker bus will not be twice that of a single decker bus. This is because the main cost (engine and chassis) does not double when the capacity of the bus doubles. Increased size may mean a doubling of output but not cost. The average cost will therefore fall. This is sometimes called the principle of **increased dimensions.** In addition, the cost of the crew and fuel will not increase in proportion to its size.

Another technical economy is that of **indivisibility.** Many firms need a particular item of equipment or machinery, but fail to make full use of it. A small business may pay £400 for a word processor. The cost will be the same whether it is used twice a week by a part time clerical worker or every day. As the business expands, more use will be made of it and so the **average cost** of the machine will fall.

As the scale of operations expands the firm may switch to mass production techniques. Flow production (☞ unit 54), which involves breaking down the production process into a very large number of small operations, allows greater use of highly specialised machinery. This results in large improvements in efficiency as labour is replaced by capital.

Firms often employ a variety of machines which have different capacities. A slow machine may increase production time. As the firm expands and produces more output, it can employ more of the slower machines in order to match the capacity of the faster machines. This is called the **law of multiples.** It involves firms finding a balanced team of machines so that when they operate together they are all running at full capacity.

Managerial economies As the firm grows it can afford to employ specialist managers. In a small business one general manager may be responsible for finance, marketing, production and personnel. The manager may find her role demanding. If a business employs specialists in these fields, efficiency may improve and average costs fall. If specialists were employed in a small firm they would be an indivisibility.

Financial economies Large firms have advantages when they try to raise finance. They will have a wider variety of sources from which to choose. For example, sole traders cannot sell more shares to raise extra funds but large public limited companies can. Very large firms will often find it easier to persuade institutions to lend them money since they will have large assets to offer as security. Finally, large firms borrowing very large amounts of money can often gain better interest rates.

In the past the government has recognised the problems facing small firms. A number of schemes have been designed to help small firms raise funds (☞ unit 2).

Purchasing and marketing economies Large firms are likely to get better rates when buying raw materials and components in bulk. In addition, the administration costs involved do not rise in proportion to the size of the order. The cost of processing an order for 10,000 tonnes of coal does not treble when 30,000 tonnes are ordered.

A number of marketing economies exist. A large company may find it cost effective to acquire its own fleet of vans and lorries, for example. The cost to the sales force of selling 30 product lines is not double that of selling 15 lines. Again, the administration costs of selling do not rise in proportion to the size of the sale.

Risk bearing economies As a firm grows it may well diversify to reduce risk. For example, breweries have diversified into the provision of food and other forms of entertainment in their public houses. Large businesses can also reduce risk by carrying out research and development. The development of new products can help firms gain a competitive edge over smaller rivals.

External economies of scale

EXTERNAL ECONOMIES OF SCALE are the reductions in cost which any business in an industry might enjoy as the industry grows. External economies are more likely to arise if the industry is concentrated in a particular region.

Labour The concentration of firms may lead to the build up of a labour force equipped with the skills required by the industry. Training costs may be reduced if workers have gained skills at another firm in the same industry. Local schools and colleges, or even local government, may offer training courses which are aimed at the needs of the local industry.

Ancillary and commercial services An established industry, particularly if it is growing, tends to attract smaller firms trying to serve its needs. A wide range of commercial and support services can be offered. Specialist banking, insurance, marketing, waste disposal, maintenance, cleaning, components and distribution services are just some examples.

Co-operation Firms in the same industry are more likely to cooperate if they are concentrated in the same region. They might join forces to fund a research and development centre for the industry. An industry journal might be published, so that information can be shared.

Disintegration Disintegration occurs when production is broken up so that more specialisation can take place. When an

---

In 2001 Themutual.net merged with the e-mail specialist KeepAhead. Themutual, which changed from a service provider to a dot.com marketing firm to survive after the dot.com collapse, said the tie-up would enable better exploitation of a promising market in e-mail advertising. KeepAhead invites users to sign up to e-mail newsletters on a range of topics, allowing the formation of a detailed profile of users, and offering advertisers the opportunity to undertake targeted campaigns.

While revenue from banner advertising has collapsed, the e-mail advertising market has strengthened. Managing director of Themutual.net, Ben Heaton, said 'E-mail advertising clearly is an effective medium. It allows advertisers to target the people they want to, and they are willing to pay for it. They are not willing to pay for banner advertising.' The merger will allow the firms to exploit a combined database of 500,000 subscribers, and to pool assets totalling £500,000.

Source: adapted from news.bbc.co.uk.

A reason why some IT companies become dominant is obvious - economies of scale. This is important in computing, because the cost of R&D and the construction of manufacturing plants, are major parts of the price. If it costs $100 million to get a product to market and 100 million are sold, the development cost is $1 each. If you only sell a million, it's $100 each. Microsoft has exploited economies of scale to the hilt. It often launches products at less than half the price of rivals. When PC databases cost around $400-500 each, Microsoft came in with Access at a special offer price of $99. Vermeer sold its web development software, Front Page, for $695. Microsoft bought it and then relaunched it at $149.

Source: adapted from *The Guardian*, 15.2.2003.

(a) Analyse the economies of scale that might be enjoyed by the business in the cases.

Question 4

industry is concentrated in an area firms might specialise in the production of one component and then transport it to a main assembly car plant. In the West Midlands a few large car assembly plants exist whilst there are many supporting firms, such as Lucas, manufacturing components ready for assembly.

The limits to growth

There is a number of factors which might limit the growth of business. If a firm expands the scale of its operations beyond the minimum efficient scale diseconomies of scale may result, leading to rising long run average costs.

Most **internal diseconomies** are caused by the problem of managing large businesses. Communication becomes more complicated and co-ordination more difficult because a large firm is divided into departments. The control of large businesses is also demanding. Thousands of employees, billions of pounds and dozens of plants all mean added responsibility and more supervision. Morale may suffer as individual workers become a minor part of the total workforce. This can cause poor relations between management and the workforce. As shown in Figure 56.1, long run average costs start to rise once a business reaches a certain size. Technical diseconomies also arise. In the chemical industry, construction problems often mean that two smaller plants are more cost effective than one very large one. Also, if a firm employs one huge plant and a breakdown occurs, production will stop. With two smaller plants, production can continue even if one breaks down.

External diseconomies might also arise. These may occur from overcrowding in industrial areas. The price of land, labour, services and materials might rise as firms compete for a limited amount. Congestion might lead to inefficiency, as travelling workers and deliveries are delayed.
There are other constraints on the growth of firms.
- Market limitations. The market for high performance power boats is limited due to their high market price, for example. Also, unless a firm is a monopoly, growth will tend to be restricted due to the existence of competitors in the market.
- Lack of funds. Many small firms would like to grow, but are not able to attract enough investors or lenders.
- Geographical limitations. Some products are low value and bulky. High transport costs may discourage the firm from distributing to customers far away. This means it cannot grow. Bread, beer and crisps may fall into this category. However, with improved communication networks, national distributors of these products have entered the market. Also, the provision of services is often limited to local markets. For example, people are not likely to travel very far to have their hair cut.

Reasons for the survival of small firms

Despite the advantages of large scale production, many firms choose to remain small. Also, small firms sometimes have advantages over larger ones.

Personal service As a firm expands it becomes increasingly difficult to deal with individuals. Many people prefer to do business with the owner of the company directly and are prepared to pay higher prices for the privilege. For example, people may prefer to deal directly with one of the partners in an accountancy practice.

Owner's preference Some entrepreneurs may be content with the current level of profits. Some will want to avoid the added responsibilities that growth brings. Others will want to remain below the VAT threshold or will not want to risk losing control of their business.

Flexibility and efficiency Small firms are more often flexible and innovative. They may be able to react more quickly to changes in market conditions or technology. Management can make decisions quickly, without following lengthy procedures.

Lower costs In some cases small firms might have lower costs than larger producers in the same market. For example, large firms often have to pay their employees nationally agreed wage rates. A small firm may be able to pay lower wages to non-union workers.

Low barriers to entry In some types of business activity like grocery, painting and decorating, gardening services and window cleaning, the set up costs are relatively low. There is little to stop competitors setting up in business.

Small firms can be monopolists Many small firms survive because they supply a service to members of the local community which no other business does. People often use their local shop because it provides a convenient, nearby service, saving them the trouble of travelling.

The popularity of small firms in the economy

During the past twenty years there has been a growth in the number of small businesses in the UK. Self employment has also grown. What factors have led to these trends?
- Rising unemployment has had an important impact. People with redundancy payments have had the capital to set up in business. In some cases unemployed workers saw self-employment as the only means of support.
- The government and local authorities introduced a number of measures to encourage the development of small businesses. **Business start-up schemes** (☞ unit 2) provided funds for small businesses for an initial period. Tecs and Business Links provided advice on running businesses and obtaining finance. European initiatives have included loans from the European Investment Fund and finance for training from the European Social Fund.

- There have been changes in the structure of the economy The expansion of the tertiary sector has contributed to the growth in small businesses. Many services can be undertaken more effectively on a small scale.

The growth in the number of small firms has had several effects on the economy.

- Increased flexibility. Smaller firms can adapt to change more quickly because the owners, who tend to be the key decision makers, are close at hand to react to change. For example, a customer may insist that the extension to her house is finished one week before the agreed time. The business owner can put in the extra hours required and perhaps encourage employees to help out. Business owners may also react quickly when some new technology becomes available. This increased flexibility might help the UK economy win more orders from abroad.

- It could be argued that wage levels might fall as a result of more smaller firms. Employees in small businesses often negotiate their own wage rates with the owner. Since they are not in a powerful position on a one to one basis, there may be a tendency for initial wage rates and future wage increases to be relatively lower. This will help to keep business costs down.

- More casual and part time work may have been created. Small firms are often reluctant to employ full time staff because it is more expensive. For example, part time workers may not be entitled to the same level of holiday pay as full time workers. Casual and part time staff also help to improve flexibility. When a business is quiet it can lay off casual staff to reduce costs.

- Staff loyalty may have been improved. In small businesses, relationships between the owners and other staff may be quite good because they are dealing with each other at a personal level. This might improve motivation and productivity as well as staff loyalty.

- Trade union membership may have declined. In small businesses where relatively fewer workers are employed, trade union membership tends to be lower. This might have implications for the rights of workers in small businesses. It might lead to claims that in some cases, staff are being exploited by small business owners.

- Consumers might benefit from the growth in the number of small firms. More small firms often results in more competition and a wider choice in the market. For example, there has been a growth in the number of computer software producers in recent years. This has led to a variety of 'games' and programs for business and personal use.

The contribution made by SMEs (Small and Medium-sized Enterprises) in the UK is shown in Figure 56.2. There were an estimated 3.8 million businesses at the start of 2002, an increase of 1.4 per cent over the year. Almost all of these enterprises, 99.1 per cent, were small with less than 49 employees. Only 27,000 were medium-sized (50-249 employees) and 7,000 were large, with over 250 employees. At the start of 2002, SMEs accounted for more than half of the business turnover and employment in the UK. SMEs employed an estimated 22.7 million people, 43.7 per cent in small enterprises and 11.9 per cent in medium-sized enterprises. The combined turnover of the 3.8 million businesses in the UK was £2,200 billion. Small businesses accounted for 37 per cent of this and medium-sized businesses accounted for 15 per cent.

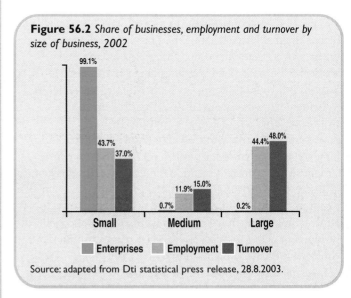

Figure 56.2 *Share of businesses, employment and turnover by size of business, 2002*

Source: adapted from Dti statistical press release, 28.8.2003.

1. How can the size of a firm be measured?
2. State 5 reasons for growth.
3. What is the difference between internal and external growth?
4. Buying firms to grow quickly can sometimes be a problem. Explain this statement.
5. What are the main sources of: (a) internal economies; (b) external economies; (c) diseconomies; of scale?
6. Explain 5 reasons why small firms survive.
7. Describe 5 limitations to growth.
8. Why has there been a growth in the number of small firms in recent years?
9. What effect will the growth in the small firms sector have on the flexibility of employers?

Case study Small Firms

Figure 56.3 *Share of employment in small businesses, less than 49 employees, by industry sector, UK 2002*

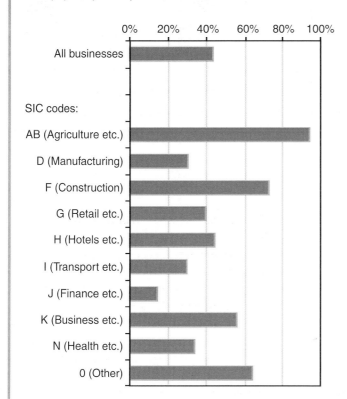

Source: adapted from Dti statistical press release, 28.8.2003.

Ganesh Kumar owns a film production company called Vision Ltd. It makes documentary programmes which it sells to television companies. The programmes are not usually made to order, so the company has to fund the writing, filming and editing of the programmes before any sales are made. In fact funding has always been a problem. Ganesh has struggled for eight years to grow the company but the same obstacle remains. Money lenders and potential investors see the business as high risk. It costs a lot to make a film and there is no guarantee that it will sell. The last production, a documentary about community life in the Scottish Highlands, was sold for £800,000 to two television broadcasters. However, Ganesh had to raise £500,000 to get it made. Most of the firm's capital comes from retained profit and a bank overdraft.

Marcham Uniforms is owned by the Marcham family and produces corporate uniforms and suits. The business was established in 1987 and has been successful under the leadership of Tom Marcham, who owns 30 per cent of the company. Four other family members share in the ownership of the business and also work in the organisation. In 2001, Tom was put under pressure buy his youngest son to expand the business. However, Tom argued that the extra work and responsibility required to grow Marcham Uniforms would not be worth the benefits. Further growth would have meant moving premises, investing in new machinery and taking on more staff in an area where unemployment was virtually nil. Tom suggested that the money the family members were making was more than adequate. He also said that the company's priority was to ensure that the present customers got the best service possible. Some extracts from the balance sheet are shown in Table 56.3.

Table 56.3 *Extracts from Marcham Uniform's balance sheet*	
Fixed assets	£220,000
Net current assets	£46,500
Mortgage	(£30,000)
Net assets	**£236,500**
Share capital	£50,000
Reserves	£186,500
Capital employed	**£236,500**

Kim Watson owns a highly specialised business in Fareham, Hampshire. It provides gourmet dinner parties prepared and served in the client's home. Kim offers a planning service where she meets the client and plans the dinner party in detail, discussing menus, for example. She buys food products, wines and spirits from very high quality suppliers and uses a collection of high quality china, cutlery, glassware and table linen. Dinner, up to eight courses, is then prepared and served by a team of highly trained staff according to the requirements of the client. Kim employs three full-time and 4 part-time staff. The dinner parties are truly special occasions and the prices charged reflect this. Kim can charge up to £200 per head excluding wines and spirits. Most parties are for between four and ten people. In 2003 the turnover for Kim's business was £350,980

(a) **Which industrial sectors have an above average number of small firms? (4 marks)**

(b) **What evidence is there to suggest that the three businesses above are SMEs? (8 marks)**

(c) **The finance sector has the smallest number of small firms. It is a sector dominated by some very large banking corporations such as HSBC and the Royal Bank of Scotland. Analyse the economies of scale they might enjoy. (12 marks)**

(d) **Explain why the three firms above might be likely to remain small. (12 marks)**

(e) **Discuss why small firms have managed to survive in such large numbers. (14 marks)**

Managing materials

Businesses purchase raw materials, semi-finished goods and components. A washing machine manufacturer, for example, may buy electric motors, circuit boards, rubber drive belts, nuts, bolts, sheet metal and a variety of metal and plastic components. These stocks of materials and components are used to produce products which are then sold to consumers and other businesses. Managing the materials is an important part of any business. Materials management involves:
● the purchasing of stocks and their delivery;
● the storing and control of stocks;
● the issue and handling of stocks;
● the disposal of surpluses;
● providing information about stocks.

Purchasing

Purchasing involves the buying of materials, components, fuel, tools, machinery, equipment, stationery and services by the business. It also includes any method that allows the firm to obtain the goods and services it needs, such as hiring.

The various stages in the purchasing process are shown in Figure 57.1. Purchasing usually begins when the purchasing department is notified of a particular need. For example, a firm's stores or a particular department may send a **requisition form** asking for more stationery.
The purchasing department will then act on this. Most purchases are repeat purchases from regular suppliers. Orders are placed with the supplier at previously agreed prices and delivery accepted under previously arranged terms. New products may need different materials and new suppliers. This will involve a period of search and negotiation, as the buyer tries to find the best deal. If there is a delay in delivery, it is the purchasing department's responsibility to find out why and speed up delivery. Once the goods have arrived the invoice is checked and then payment can be made.

In manufacturing the purchasing department works closely with the production and finance departments. Most purchasing is carried out on behalf of the production department. The finance department needs information about purchases to make payments and record the transactions.

The importance of purchasing

The importance of purchasing is likely to vary according to the nature and size of the business. In many service industries purchasing is not very important. This is because materials are only a small fraction of the total cost of the final product. For example, hairdressing involves very little purchasing, as production involves a skill and uses few materials. However, a large manufacturer requires a large amount of materials, components etc. and so the firm will employ a purchasing department made up of specialists. In order for the firm to remain competitive the department must obtain the best quality materials, at least cost, and the quickest delivery. Failure to do so may lead to increased cost. The objectives of the purchasing department are:
● to obtain the quality and quantity of goods and materials that the firm requires;
● to purchase goods and materials at the most competitive prices;
● to ensure speedy delivery;
● to arrange delivery at the appropriate site, gate or location;
● to choose reliable suppliers and maintain good relations with them.

Kevin Clarke works in the purchasing department for Compton Engineering, a company that designs, manufactures and services heating systems for office blocks and other large buildings. He has received the requisition form shown in Figure 57.2. It is for some parts for a machine that has just broken down. They have not been ordered before.

Figure 57.2 *Requisition form for Compton Engineering*

Compton Engineering - Requisition Form		
Date	Description	Quantity
23.4.04	Gear system CNC cutter - Type 211A	1
23.4.04	Switching mechanism - CNC cutter - Type 211A	1

Authorisation: *F. Gordon*   Date required: *ASAP (Urgent)*

(a) Describe the process that Kevin might follow when responding to the requisition form.
(b) What features of the process described in (a) might be particularly important in this case?

Figure 57.1 *Stages in the purchasing process*

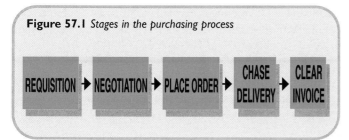

REQUISITION → NEGOTIATION → PLACE ORDER → CHASE DELIVERY → CLEAR INVOICE

Centralised and decentralised purchasing

In some businesses, **centralised purchasing** is used. This is where the purchasing for the whole business is carried out by one department. The advantage of this method is that **economies of scale** can be gained as large scale buyers enjoy lower rates and market power. Also, the same quality and standard of materials can be set throughout the business. The distribution and warehousing of supplies can also be better planned.

Decentralised purchasing may reduce the cost and burden of administration. Purchasing officers in each department may be more in touch with the needs of that department. In retailing, if purchasing is undertaken by each store manager, the needs of each store can be better catered for. The added responsibility might also motivate store managers.

Vendor rating

It is important for a business to evaluate suppliers. A poor supplier may delay production, which can be costly. The measurement of suppliers' performance is called VENDOR RATING. A business must choose **criteria** which could be used to measure the performance of a supplier.

A simple vendor rating system is shown in Table 57.1. The supplier is awarded a mark for performance based on five criteria. For example, the supplier has a good price record, scoring 18 out of a possible 20. Adding the scores gives a total vendor rating of 71/100. When deciding which supplier to chose from alternatives, a firm is likely to pick the one with the highest rating. If a business feels that some criteria are more important than others, it may give them more value using a weighting system. One problem with this system is how to judge a supplier's performance against criteria. It may be possible to use records. But sometimes evaluation may simply be the subjective opinion of a manager.

Table 57.1 *A simple vendor rating system*

Criteria	Max. score	Actual score
Quality	20	17
Price	20	18
Delivery	20	10
Communication	20	12
Flexibility	20	14
Total	100	71

Make or buy?

Another decision which a business often faces is whether to make a component itself or buy it from a supplier. There are reasons for both making a product and buying it in, as shown in Table 57.2. In recent years businesses have tried to improve their flexibility. One method of doing this is to outsource

production (☞ unit 90). This is where a business uses the services of another firm, to produce its components for example. A business that aims to outsource production will buy in components rather than make its own.

Table 57.2

Motives for making	Motives for buying
● Making is cheaper.	● Buying is cheaper.
● There are no suitable suppliers.	● To increase specialisation.
● Delivery times cannot be met by suppliers.	● Uneconomical to make small quantities.
● Quality standards cannot be met by suppliers.	● Lack of capacity.
● Spare capacity exists in the factory.	● Transfer risk to the vendor.
● To maintain secrecy.	● Avoid investment in specialist plant or labour.
● To ensure continuity of supply.	
● To retain labour during a slack period of trading.	

The nature of stocks

Businesses prefer to minimise stock holding because it is costly. In practice a variety of stocks are held, for different reasons.

- Raw materials and components. These are purchased from suppliers before production. They are stored by firms to cope with changes in production levels. Delays in production can be avoided if materials and components can be supplied from stores rather than waiting for a new delivery to arrive. Also, if a company is let down by suppliers it can use stocks to carry on production.
- Work-in-progress. These are partly finished goods. In a TV assembly plant, WORK IN PROGRESS would be TVs on the assembly line, which are only partly built.
- Finished goods. The main reason for keeping finished goods is to cope with changes in demand and stock. If there is a sudden rise in demand, a firm can meet urgent orders by supplying customers from stock holdings. This avoids the need to step up production rates quickly.

Stocks are listed as current assets (☞ unit 32) in the firm's balance sheet. Stocks are fairly liquid business resources and the firm would normally expect to convert them into cash within one year. They are also part of working capital (☞ unit 37).

Normally, at least once every year, a business will perform a **stock take**. This involves recording the amount and value of stocks which the firm is holding. The stock take is necessary to help determine the value of total purchases during the year for a firm's accounts. A physical stock take can be done manually by identifying every item of stock on the premises. Many firms have details of stock levels recorded on computer.

The cost of holding stocks

In recent years stock management has become more important for many firms. Careful control of stock levels can improve business performance. Having too much stock may mean that money is tied up unproductively, but inadequate stock can lead to delays in production and late deliveries. Efficient stock control involves finding the right balance. One of the reasons why control is so important is because the costs of holding stocks can be very high.

- There may be an **opportunity cost** (☞ unit 9) in holding stocks. Capital tied up in stocks earns no rewards. The money used to purchase stocks could have been put to other uses, such as new machinery. This might have earned the business money.
- Storage can also prove costly. Stocks of raw materials, components and finished goods occupy space in buildings. A firm may also have to pay heating, lighting and labour costs if, for example, a night watchman is employed to safeguard stores when the business is closed. Some products require very special storage conditions. Food items may need expensive refrigerated storage facilities. A firm may have to insure against fire, theft and other damages.
- Spoilage costs. The quality of some stock may deteriorate over time, for example perishable goods. In addition, if some finished goods are held too long they may become outdated and difficult to sell.
- Administrative and financial costs. These include the cost of placing and processing orders, handling costs and the costs of failing to anticipate price increases.
- Out-of-stock costs. These are the costs of lost revenue, when sales are lost because customers cannot be supplied from stocks. There may also be a loss of goodwill if customers are let down.

Intercomp is a supplier of computer hardware and software. It buys from a number of manufacturers in the US and distributes them to trade customers in the UK. It currently has £23.6 million of stock in the warehouse.

(a) Describe three stock holding costs that Intercomp might incur.
(b) Six months ago, Intercomp ran out of a best selling computer. What out-of-stock costs might have been incurred?

Question 2

Stock levels

One of the most important tasks in stock control is to maintain the right level of stocks. This involves keeping stock levels as low as possible, so that the costs of holding stocks are minimised. At the same time stocks must not be allowed to run out, so that production is halted and customers are let down. A number of factors influence stock levels.

- Demand. Sufficient stocks need to be kept to satisfy normal demand. Firms must also carry enough stock to cover growth in sales and unexpected demand. The term BUFFER STOCK is used to describe stock held for unforeseen rises in demand or breaks in supply.

The specialist plumbers' merchants division of The Wilky Group supplies bathroom fittings to UK house builders such as Laing Homes. Although Wilky deals with these large developers direct, each developer has a number of subcontracted plumbers who carry out work on their behalf. This means that Wilky has to deal with, and deliver to, many customers. This results in a huge mountain of paper and endless opportunities for mistakes. As the business has expanded in recent years, so has the number of difficulties in the warehouse, such as picking errors, stock losses and warehouse congestion. According to Albert Wilkinson, the Group's founder, 'Pick errors cost us a fortune. We have to pacify angry customers, arrange collection of the incorrect deliveries, raise all the necessary paperwork, put the items back in stock and either credit or re-deliver the right products'.

To resolve these problems Wilky installed an Enterprise Resource Planning (ERP) system. With this new stock control system, all products are scanned in as they are unloaded off the lorries and then stored in the warehouse. If a product is delivered without a barcode, the warehouse team would simply print off a customised barcode sticker on a dedicated bar coding printer located in the goods-in area. Then, when the product is picked, it is scanned again ensuring that the right item is picked and the stock records are updated automatically.

The introduction of the ERP system has been a success. According to Mr Wilkinson, 'The bar coding system has taken us into a new world, a world where our old systems could never have coped. It has turned this division of the business around and we are now making record profits every month. We have real time stock control, no bottlenecks in the warehouse operation, virtually error free picking, greatly reduced stock losses, greater visibility and above all, very, very happy customers who get exactly what they want, when they want it'.

Source: adapted from Oasis Systems website, July 2003.

(a) Analyse the benefits of the ERP system to (i) Wilky and (ii) Wilky's customers.
(b) Why is it important for a business to know exactly how much stock it has?

Question 3

- Some firms **stockpile** goods. For example, toy manufacturers build up stocks in the few months up to December ready for the Christmas period. Electricity generating stations build up stocks of coal in the summer. During the summer, demand for electricity is low so less coal is needed. At the same time, prices of coal during the summer months are lower, so savings can be made.
- The costs of stock holding. The costs of holding stock were described earlier. If stock is expensive to hold then only a small quantity will be held. Furniture retailers may keep low stock levels because the cost of stock is high and sales levels are uncertain.
- The amount of working capital available. A business that is short of working capital will not be able to purchase more stock, even if it is needed.
- The type of stock. Businesses can only hold small stocks of perishable products. The stock levels of cakes or bread will be very small. Almost the entire stock of finished goods will be sold in one day. The 'life' of stock, however, does not solely depend on its 'perishability'. Stocks can become out of date when they are replaced by new models, for example.
- LEAD TIME. This is the amount of time it takes for a stock purchase to be placed, received, inspected and made ready for use. The longer the lead time, the higher the minimum level of stock needed.
- External factors. Fear of future shortages may prompt firms to hold higher levels of raw materials in stock as a precaution.

Stock control

It is necessary to control the flow of stocks in the business. This ensures that firms hold the right amount. Several methods of stock control exist. They focus on the RE-ORDER QUANTITY (how much stock is ordered when a new order is placed) and the RE-ORDER LEVEL (the level of stock when an order is placed).

- Economic order quantity (EOQ). It is possible to calculate the level of stocks which minimises costs. This is called the **economic order quantity**. It takes into account the costs of holding stock, which rise with the amount of stock held, and the average costs of ordering stock, which fall as the size of the order is increased.
  A business must calculate the EOQ to balance these costs.
- Fixed re-order interval. Orders of various sizes are placed at fixed time intervals. This method ignores the economic order quantity, but ensures that stocks are 'topped up' on a regular basis. This method may result in fluctuating stock levels.
- Fixed re-order level. This method involves setting a fixed order level, perhaps using the EOQ. The order is then repeated at varying time intervals.
- Two bin system. This simple method involves dividing stock into two bins. When one bin is empty a new order is placed. When the order arrives it is placed into the first bin and stocks are used from the second bin. When the second

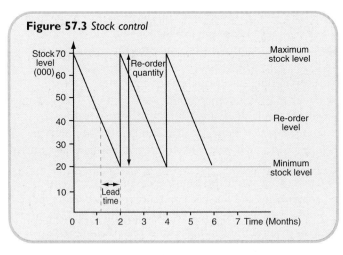

Figure 57.3 *Stock control*

bin is empty stocks are re-ordered again.

A stock control system is shown in Figure 82.3. It is assumed that:

- 50,000 units are used every two months (25,000 each month);
- the maximum stock level, above which stocks never rise, is 70,000 units;
- the minimum stock level, below which stocks should never fall, is 20,000 units, so there is a buffer against delays in delivery;

Figure 57.4 shows the usage of a component, 5000XTD, for Bromley Ltd, over a seven month period. Bromley Ltd assembles electric lawn mowers using five main components. It found a new and cheaper supplier for the 5000XTD just two months ago.

Figure 57.4 *Stocks of 5000XTDs at Bromley Ltd*

(a) Identify the (i) lead time; (ii) minimum stock level; (iii) re-order level; (iv) re-order quantity for the 5000XTD.
(b) Explain the reason for the change in the stock level after the sixth month.
(c) What might be the consequences of this change for the business?

- stock is re-ordered when it reaches a level of 40,000 units (the re-order level);
- the re-order quantity is 50,000 units - the same quantity is used up every two months;
- the lead time is just under one month. This is the time between the order being placed and the date it arrives in stock.

This is a hypothetical model which would be the ideal for a business. In practice deliveries are sometimes late, so there is a delay in stocks arriving. Firms may also need to use their buffer stocks in this case. It is likely that re-order quantities will need to be reviewed from time to time. Suppliers might offer discounts for ordering larger quantities. The quantities of stocks used in each time period are unlikely to be constant. This might be because production levels fluctuate according to demand.

Too much or too little stock

Why might having too much or too little stock be bad business practice?

Too much stock
- Storage, insurance, lighting and handling costs will all be high if too much stock is held.
- Large stock levels will occupy space in the premises. There may be more productive ways of using this space, such as improving the layout of the factory.
- The opportunity cost will be high. Money tied up in stocks could be used to buy fixed assets, for example.
- Large stock levels might result in unsold stock. If there is an unexpected change in demand, the firm may be left with stocks that it cannot sell.
- Very large stocks might result in an increase in theft by employees. They may feel the business would not miss a small amount of stock relative to the total stock.

Too little stock
- The business may not be able to cope with unexpected increases in demand if its stocks are too low. This might result in lost customers if they are let down too often.
- If deliveries are delayed the firm may run out of stock and have to halt production. This might lead to idle labour and machinery while the firm waits for delivery.
- The firm is less able to cope with unexpected shortages of materials. Again, this could result in lost production.
- A firm which holds very low stocks may have to place more orders. This will raise total ordering costs. Also, it may be unable to take advantage of discounts for bulk buying.

Computerised stock control

Stock control has been improved by the use of computers. Many businesses hold details of their entire stock on computer databases (☞ unit 10). All additions to and issues from stocks are recorded and up to date stock levels can be found instantly. Actual levels of stock should be the same as shown in the computer printout. A prudent firm will carry

out regular **stock checks** to identify differences.

Some systems are programmed to automatically order stock when the re-order level is reached. In some supermarkets, computerised checkout systems record every item of stock purchased by customers and automatically subtract items from total stock levels. The packaging on each item contains a **bar code**. When this is passed over a laser at the checkout, the sale is recorded by the system. This allows a store manager to check stock levels, total stock values and the store's takings at any time of the day. Again, the system can indicate when the re-order level is reached for any particular item of stock.

Access to stock levels is useful when manufacturers are dealing with large orders. The firm might need to find out whether there are enough materials in stock to complete the order. If this information is available, then the firm can give a more accurate delivery date.

JIT and stock rotation

In recent years many businesses have changed their approach to stock management. To reduce costs, firms have held low levels of stocks. In some cases holdings of both finished goods and raw materials have been reduced to zero. This approach to stock control is the key feature of **just-in-time manufacturing** (JIT)(☞ unit 55).

Businesses often use systems to control the flow of stocks in and out of their store areas. This flow of stock is sometimes called STOCK ROTATION. One system used to rotate stock is called **First In First Out** (FIFO). This means that those stocks which are delivered first are the first ones to be issued. This method is useful if stocks are perishable or if they are likely to become obsolete in the near future. A second method of stock rotation is called **Last-In-First-Out** (LIFO). This system involves issuing stock from the latest rather than the earliest deliveries. This method might be used if the stocks are difficult to handle and it is physically easier to issue the more recent deliveries. However, when using this method it is important that stocks are not perishable. 'Old' stock could remain in store for long periods before it is finally used.

key terms

Buffer stocks - stocks held as a precaution to cope with unforeseen demand.
Lead time - the time between the order and the delivery of goods.
Re-order level - the level of stock when new orders are placed.
Re-order quantity - the amount of stock ordered when an order is placed.
Stock rotation - the flow of stock into and out of stores.
Vendor rating - a method of measuring and evaluating the performance of suppliers.
Work-in-progress - partly finished goods.

1. What are the activities involved in materials management?
2. What is meant by purchasing in business?
3. Describe the various stages in the purchasing process.
4. What are the objectives of the purchasing department?
5. What effect can poor purchasing have on a business?
6. What are the advantages of centralised purchasing?
7. What is meant by:
   (a) components;
   (b) finished goods?
8. What are the costs of holding stocks?
9. Why are buffer stocks held by firms?
10. Why do some firms stockpile?
11. Describe the advantages of computerised stock control.

Case study *Prestwick plc*

Prestwick plc assembles bicycles in its Glasgow based-based factory. It uses batch production and supplies retailers in Scotland and the north of England. The company has been troubled by stock problems in recent months. One of the difficulties is coping with frequent changes in design. This has resulted in the company being left with stocks of parts that are rapidly going out of date. Another problem is supplier reliability. Some suppliers of bicycle components have let down Prestwick. In extreme cases, supplies of components have failed to arrive, resulting in lost production.

The business is becoming worried about its stock position. The senior management team has met and identified three possible solutions.

● Adopt a JIT approach to stock management.
● Make some of the components themselves.
● Use a computerised stock control system.

(a) Identify the (i) lead time (ii) minimum stock level (iii) re-order level (iv) re-order quantity for the gear system component in Figure 57.6. (8 marks)
(b) Explain the problems associated with holding too much stock. (10 marks)
(c) What evidence is there to suggest that Prestwick plc is carrying too much stock? (10 marks)
(d) Examine the possible reasons for the stock movement patterns for (i) gear systems and (ii) pedals in Figures 57.6 and 57.7. (12 marks)
(e) Evaluate the proposals made by the senior management team to resolve the stock problems. (12 marks)

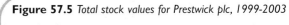

Figure 57.5 *Total stock values for Prestwick plc, 1999-2003*

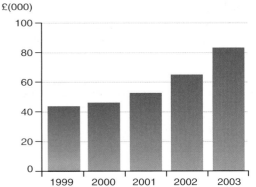

Figure 57.6 *Stock movements of gear systems - type 23X*

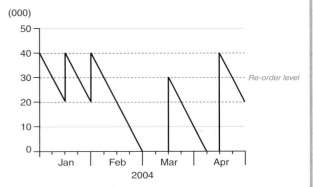

Figure 57.7 *Stock movements of pedals - type WB12*

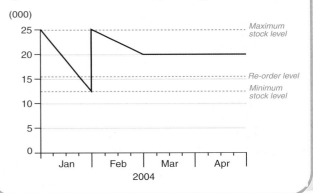

58 Quality

What is quality?

Consumers, faced with many goods or services at similar prices, are likely to consider QUALITY when making choices. Quality could be described as those features of a product or service that allow it to satisfy customers' wants. Take an example of a family buying a television. They may consider some of the following features:

- physical appearance - they may want a certain style;
- reliability and durability - will it last for 10 years?
- special features - does it have stereo sound?
- suitability - they may want a portable television;
- parts - are spare parts available?
- repairs - does the shop carry out maintenance?
- after sales service - how prompt is delivery?

They may also consider features which they perceive as important, such as:

- image - is the manufacturer's name widely recognised?
- reputation - what do other consumers think of the business or product?

The importance of quality has grown in recent years. Consumers are more aware. They get information through magazines such as *Which?* that contain reports on the quality of certain products. They also have more disposable income and higher expectations than ever before. Legislation and competition have also forced firms to improve the quality of their products.

Businesses, faced with competition, are also concerned about the quality of their:

- design - the ideas and plans for the product or service
- production processes - the methods used to manufacture the goods or provide the services.

Poor designs may lead to problems with the materials and the functions of the finished good or service. It costs time and money to redesign poor products. Clients are unlikely to use businesses with poor designs again. Problems also occur with poor quality production processes. Faulty products are costly for a business. Machinery that breaks down or constantly needs to be repaired will also be expensive. Late delivery and productivity that results from poor quality in production can harm a business's reputation.

Quality in production

Traditionally, in manufacturing, production departments have been responsible for ensuring quality. Their objectives might have been to make sure that products:

- satisfy consumers' needs;
- work under conditions they will face;
- operate in the way they should;
- can be produced cost effectively;
- can be repaired easily;
- conform to safety standards set down by legislation and independent bodies.

At Kellogg's, the cereal manufacturer, for example, samples of breakfast cereal in the past have been taken from the production line every half hour and tested. The testing took place in a food review room twice a day and was undertaken by a small group of staff. Each sample, about 50 in total, was compared with a 'perfect' Kellogg's sample and given a grade

---

Kwik-Fit, the car repair and replacement specialist, takes quality seriously. The business aims to give its customers the benefits they really want - fast service, quality products and competitive prices. According to the chairman 'We aren't interested in satisfied customers. We want delighted customers'. 'Our aim is to look after our customers and our people better than anyone else in the automotive parts repair industry'. The business argues that success is due to getting results in five key areas, called 'The Kwik-Fit System':

- identifying and responding to current and future motoring needs;
- developing specialist repair and replacement outfits;
- well-trained and highly motivated staff;
- sophisticated computer systems and management support;
- a distinctive and high-profile brand image.

Kwik-Fit's ability to identify and exploit trends in its markets is illustrated by its Child Safety Scheme which encourages the fitting of child safety seats in cars and the introduction of an interest-free credit plan.

Staff training at Kwik-Fit receives considerable investment - around £2.5 million. All service staff are trained in customer service as well as technical skills. The bold claim 'You can't get better than a Kwik-Fit fitter' is deliberately made to give staff something to live up to. It's on the overalls of all staff. 'To the public, "You can't get better than a Kwik-Fit fitter" is an advertising slogan' says the chairman. 'To us, it's a philosophy.'

Source: adapted from Bnet website.

(a) What (i) actual and (ii) perceived features might a consumer consider important when using Kwik-Fit's car repair and replacement service?

(b) What evidence is there in the case to suggest that Kwik-Fit takes quality seriously.

Question 1

between 1 and 10. 10 was perfect but between 9.8 and 7, although noticeable to the trained eye, was acceptable to the customer. Below 7 the consumer would notice the reduction in quality. The cereals were tested for appearance, texture, colour, taste etc. More sophisticated tests were carried out in a laboratory where the nutritional value of a sample, for example, was measured.

Quality control in UK organisations, in the past, often meant inspecting other people's work and the product itself after production had taken place. By today's standards this is not quality control, but a method of finding a poor quality product (or a problem) before it is sold to the consumer. Today businesses are less concerned about 'Has the job been done properly?' than 'Are we able to do the job properly?' In other words inspection is carried out during the production process. This means that problems and poor quality products can be prevented before final production. Such a preventative approach has been used by Japanese businesses and is known as TOTAL QUALITY MANAGEMENT (TQM). It is now being adopted by many companies in the UK.

Quality assurance

Businesses are increasingly taking into account the needs of customers. QUALITY ASSURANCE is a method of ensuring quality that takes into account customers' views in the production process. This can affect the business in a number of ways. For example, customers may be consulted about their views through market research (☞ unit 12) before a product is manufactured or a service provided. They may also be part of a consultation group involved at the design and manufacturing stage.

Quality assurance attempts to guarantee that quality has been maintained at all stages in the production process. The aim is to stop problems before they occur rather than finding them after they occur.

Businesses also work to quality assurance **codes of practice**. These show that a production process has been carried out to a certain standard and to the required specification. Once a business has been assessed and has achieved a certain standard, it is regularly checked by the awarding organisation to make sure standards are maintained. ISO 9000 is an international standard which businesses seek to achieve.

Product standards

Businesses also include signs and **symbols** on their products which tell a customer about the product's standards. Examples of such quality symbols include:

- safety goggles which are awarded the BSI kitemark, telling the customer that the product has been independently tested to a specific standard;
- inflatable arm bands which are awarded the CE mark, an EU award. This tells the customer that they have been tested not to deflate during use and carry a safety warning about supervision;
- the Lion Mark, awarded by the British Toy and Hobby

Association (BTHA), which shows that manufacturers have a strict code of practice on toy safety, advertising and counterfeiting.

Some businesses support such guarantees with WARRANTIES. If goods are warranted, it means that the manufacturer will undertake any work necessary arising from a defect in the product 'free of charge'. Warranties are popular with products such as cars and a wide range of electrical appliances.

Total quality management

Errors are costly for business. It is estimated that about one-third of all the effort of British business is wasted in correcting errors. There are benefits if something is done right the first time. Total quality management (TQM) is a method designed to prevent errors, such as poor quality products, from happening. The business is organised so that the manufacturing process is investigated at every stage. It is argued that the success of Japanese companies is based on their superior organisation. Every department, activity and individual is organised to take into account quality at all times. What are the features of TQM?

Quality chains Great stress is placed on the operation of QUALITY CHAINS. In any business a series of suppliers and customers exists. For example, a secretary is a supplier to a manager, who is the customer. The secretarial duties must be carried out to the satisfaction of the manager. The chain also includes customers and suppliers outside the business. The chain remains intact if the supplier satisfies the customer. It is broken if a person or item of equipment does not satisfy the needs of the customer. Failure to meet the requirements in any part of the quality chain creates problems, such as delays in the next stage of production.

Company policy and accountability There will only be improvements in quality if there is a company-wide quality policy. TQM must start from the top with the most senior executive and spread throughout the business to every employee. People must be totally committed and take a 'pride in the job'. This might be considered as an example of job enrichment (☞ unit 43). Lack of commitment, particularly at the top, causes problems. For example, if the managing director lacks commitment, employees lower down are unlikely to commit themselves. TQM stresses the role of the individual and aims to make everyone accountable for their own performance. For example, a machine operator may be accountable to a workshop supervisor for his work.

Control Consumers' needs will only be satisfied if the business has control of the factors that affect a product's quality. These may be human, administrative or technical factors. This is shown in Figure 58.1. The process is only under control if materials, equipment and tasks are used in the same way every time. Take an example of a firm making

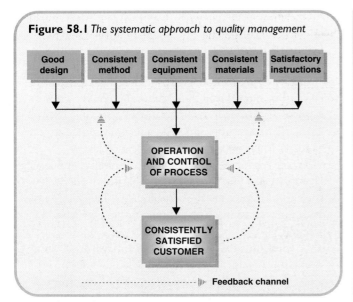

Figure 58.1 *The systematic approach to quality management*

biscuits. Only by cooking in the same way can the quality be consistent every time. These methods can be documented and used to assess operations. Regular audits must be carried out by the firm to check quality.

Information is then fed back from the customer to the 'operator' or producer, and from the operator to the supplier of inputs, such as raw materials. For example, a retailer may return a batch of vehicles to the manufacturer because the gears were faulty. The manufacturer might then identify the person responsible for fitting the gears. An investigation might reveal that the faulty gears were the responsibility of a component supplier. The supplier can then be contacted and the problem resolved. Quality audits and reviews may lead to suggestions for improvements - a different material, perhaps, or a new piece of equipment.

Monitoring the process TQM relies on monitoring the business process to find possible improvements. Methods have been developed to help achieve this. STATISTICAL PROCESS CONTROL (SPC) involves collecting data relating to the performance of a process. Data is presented in diagrams, charts and graphs (☞ unit 10). The information is then passed to all those concerned.

SPC can be used to reduce variability, which is the cause of most quality problems. Variations in products, delivery times, methods, materials, people's attitudes and staff performance often occur. For example, statistical data may show that worker attitudes may have led to variations in output late on Friday afternoon. Discussion might result in a change in the 'clocking on' and 'clocking off' times to solve the problem.

Teamwork TQM stresses that teamwork is the most effective way of solving problems. The main advantages are:
- a greater range of skills, knowledge and experience can be used to solve the problem;
- employee morale is often improved;
- problems across departments are better dealt with;

- a greater variety of problems can be tackled;
- team 'ideas' are more likely to be used than individual ones.

TQM strongly favours teamwork throughout the business. It builds trust and morale, improves communications and cooperation and develops interdependence. Many UK firms in the past have suffered due to lack of sharing of information and ideas. Such approaches have often led to division between sections of the workforce.

Consumer views Firms using TQM must be committed to their customers. They must be responsive to changes in people's needs and expectations. To do this, information must be gathered on a regular basis and there must be clear communication channels for customers to express their views. Consumers are often influential in setting quality standards. For example, holiday companies issue questionnaires to their customers on the way back from a package holiday. The information can be used to identify the strengths and weaknesses of their operations. Such information can be used to monitor and upgrade quality standards.

Zero defects Many business quality systems have a zero defect policy. This aims to ensure that every product that is manufactured is free from defects. A business that is able to guarantee zero defects in customers' orders is likely to gain a good reputation. This could lead to new clients and improved sales.

Using TQM

TQM helps companies to:
- focus clearly on the needs of customers and relationships between suppliers and customers;
- achieve quality in all aspects of business, not just product or service quality;
- critically analyse all processes to remove waste and inefficiencies:
- find improvements and develop measures of performance;
- develop a team approach to problem solving;
- develop effective procedures for communication and acknowledgement of work (☞ unit 70);
- continually review the processes to develop a strategy of constant improvement.

There are, however, some problems.
- There will be training and development costs of the new system.
- TQM will only work if there is commitment from the entire business.
- There will be a great deal of bureaucracy and documents and regular audits are needed. This may be a problem for small firms.
- Stress is placed on the process and not the product.

Poka-Yoke

Poka-Yoke (meaning 'inadvertent mistake' and 'prevent' in

Japanese) is a quality assurance technique developed by manufacturing engineer Shigeo Shingo. It aims to eliminate defects in products by preventing or correcting mistakes as early as possible. While visiting the Yamada Electric plant in Japan, Shingo was told about a problem with the assembly of a product that had a switch with two push-buttons supported by springs. Sometimes workers assembling the switch would forget to insert a spring under each push-button. The error would not be found until the product reached a customer, which was embarrassing and expensive.

Shingo suggested a solution that became the first poka-yoke technique. In the old method, workers began by taking two springs out of a large parts box and then assembling the switch. In the new approach, a small dish is placed in front of the parts box and the workers' first task is to take two springs out of the box and place them on the dish. Workers then assemble the switch. If springs remain on the dish, workers know they have forgotten to insert them. Poka-yoke techniques fall into two categories.

- A **prevention** device makes it impossible to make a mistake at all. An example is in the design of a 3.5 inch computer disk. The disk is designed to be asymmetrical, so it will not fit into the disk drive in any other way than the correct one. Prevention devices remove the need to correct a mistake, since one has not been made in the first place.
- A **detection** device warns workers when a mistake has been made, so that the problem can be corrected. The small dish used at the Yamada Electric plant was a detection device. Another example would be an alarm that sounds in a car when the seat belt is not fastened.

Quality circles

TQM stresses the importance of teamwork in a business. Many businesses have introduced quality circles (☞ unit 43) into their operations. Quality circles are small groups of staff, usually from the same work area, who meet on a regular and voluntary basis. They meet in the employer's time and attempt to solve problems and make suggestions about how to improve various aspects of the business. Issues such as pay and conditions are normally excluded. After discussions, the team will present its ideas and solutions to management. Teams are also involved in implementing and monitoring the effectiveness of solutions. In order for quality circles to be successful certain conditions must exist.

- A steering committee should be set up to oversee the whole quality circle programme.
- A senior manager should ideally chair the committee. Managers must show commitment to the principle of quality circles.
- At least one person on the committee should be accountable for the programme.
- Team leaders should be properly trained.

Costs of ensuring quality

Firms will want to monitor the costs of quality control carefully. All businesses are likely to face costs when trying to **maintain** or **improve** the quality of their products and services.

- The cost of designing and setting up a quality control system. This might include the time used to 'think through' a system and the training of staff to use it.
- The cost of monitoring the system. This could be the salary of a supervisor or the cost of an electronic sensor.
- There will be costs if products do not come up to standard. Faulty goods may have to be scrapped or reworked. Product failures might also result in claims against a company, bad publicity and a possible loss of goodwill.
- The cost of improving the actual quality. This may be the cost of new machinery or training staff in new working practices.
- If the whole quality system fails, there may be costs in setting it up again. Time may be needed to 'rethink' or adjust the system. Retraining might also be necessary.

It has been suggested that between 10-20 per cent of the revenue of a business is accounted for by quality related costs. This means that billions of pounds could be saved by UK businesses by cutting such costs. The vast majority of these costs is spent on appraisal and failure, which add very little to the quality of the product. Eliminating failure will also help to reduce appraisal and failure costs.

Although quality control systems are costly, it is argued that their benefits outweigh the costs. The actual quality of the product should be improved, so customers are more likely to purchase the product. Business costs may be cut if faults in products are identified before the product reaches the market. The costs of failure once the product has reached the market are likely to be much higher than those during manufacture.

Best practice benchmarking

BEST PRACTICE BENCHMARKING (BPB) is a technique used by some businesses to help them discover the 'best' methods of production available and then adopt them. BPB involves:

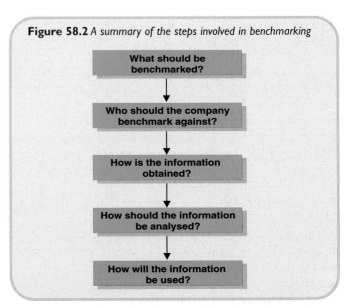

Figure 58.2 *A summary of the steps involved in benchmarking*

What should be benchmarked?

↓

Who should the company benchmark against?

↓

How is the information obtained?

↓

How should the information be analysed?

↓

How will the information be used?

- finding out what makes the difference, in the customer's eyes, between an ordinary supplier and an excellent supplier;
- setting standards for business operations based on the best practice that can be found;
- finding out how these best companies meet those standards;
- applying both competitors' standards and their own to meet the new standards and, if possible, exceed them.

Figure 58.2 illustrates the five main steps in BPB. The first step is to **identify** exactly what the company intends to benchmark. Benchmarks that are important for customer satisfaction might include consistency of product, correct invoices, shorter delivery times, shorter lead times and improved after sales service. For example, Motorola, the communications company, has benchmarked the yield and product characteristics of a range of its activities including its assembly, warehousing and purchasing performance.

The second step involves **choosing a company** to set the benchmark against. This may be done by asking customers who they feel is the best in the field. Business analysts, journalists, stockbrokers or industrialists may also be used. Rank Xerox and Centreparc, the leisure group, have used other parts of their own organisations which have developed a reputation for excellence.

In the third step, information can be **gathered** from a number of sources, such as magazines, newspapers, trade association reports, specialist databases, customers and suppliers. Companies in the same industry often share information. An example may be businesses supplying local markets, such as garden centres. The benefits of this are that the worst performers can get advice from the best and perhaps visit their premises.

The **analysis** of information is best done with quantitative techniques. For example, a firm might compare numerical data relating to delivery times.

The final stage involves **using** the information. Once standards have been found and set, they must be communicated throughout the business. Improvements must be funded, introduced and monitored. Once a company becomes the best in the field others will begin to benchmark against them. This means the company must continue to benchmark their own process.

Independent bodies and trade organisations

Certain bodies and associations exist that promote quality which are independent of government or businesses seeking to gain quality standards.

The British Standards Institution The British Standards Institution (BSI) is an independent organisation that attempts to set quality standards in industry. It performs a number of functions.

- Any business can apply to the BSI for an inspection of its

Bellingham plc supplies high quality, self-service products for worldwide financial institutions and retail markets. These include automatic teller machines, account services and interactive systems designed to provide 24-hour operation. Bellingham aims to be the 'model company' in its industry. It has been involved with benchmarking for a decade and has identified a list of key indicators for comparison with selected high profile companies. At the Basingstoke plant, desk research is carried out and directors and management are asked to nominate the most significant indicators. Further research identifies potential benchmark partners who have relevant data and who are willing to share. Bellingham believes that focusing on high profile companies is justified because they are the ones most familiar with benchmarking and tend to operate best practices. Benchmarking activities at Bellingham have focused on office equipment manufacturers and industries associated with electronics. These have sufficient common ground for discussion and the exchange of data.

Bellingham plc sees benefits in this programme coming from the 'shared knowledge' and likely 'best-in-class' performance comparisons. These will help Bellingham introduce improvement programmes and gain 'world class performance' throughout all its activities.

Table 58.1 *The top ten benchmarking indicators identified by managers and directors*

1. Product reliability
2. Out-of-box quality
3. Return on assets
4. Revenue growth
5. Levels of inventory
6. Time taken from product concept to market launch measured in months
7. Main line yield (the number of units which pass main line test expressed as a percentage of units produced)
8. Advanced development schedules vs. planned
9. Actual research and development costs vs. planned
10. Manufacturing cycle time measured in days

(a) Describe Bellingham's approach to benchmarking.
(b) What might be the benefits of benchmarking to Bellingham plc?

Question 2

---

product. Those that achieve and maintain a standard can carry the **BSI kitemark**. The kitemark tells the customer that the product has been tested to destruction, to ensure that it meets with certain safety standards. Products that carry a kitemark include some cricket helmets, kitchen units, child car safety seats, door locks, curtains, and sofa and duvet covers. This is shown in Figure 58.3.

- The BSI also issues a number of other product standards. These include BS 4224 for yachts, which shows the product conforms to standards used in yachting and ensures the tensile strength of yarns, and BS 2724, which sets performance levels for the amount of UV light through sunglasses. BS 7131 grades the pile of carpets according to quality and durability. There are four grades used in the UK - light, medium, heavy and extra heavy.

- The BSI and other independent bodies, such as Lloyds, offer BS EN ISO 9000 registration. The title reflects the European (EN) and international (ISO) recognition for this series. BS EN ISO 9001 gives quality assurance in design, development, production, installation and servicing and is suitable for businesses which have a large element of design in their operations. BS EN ISO 9002 gives quality assurance in production, installation and servicing, for businesses which produce fairly standard products with little or no design. BS EN ISO 9003 gives quality assurance in final inspection and testing. This standard is suitable for small firms or where customers can check quality themselves through inspection.

Firms seeking certification have to show that their methods and procedures meet the recognised standards and comply with requirements. They are inspected on a regular basis to make sure that standards are being maintained. BS EN ISO 9000 certification can help a business to:

- examine and improve systems, methods and procedures to lower costs;
- motivate staff and encourage them to get things right first time;
- define key roles, responsibilities and authorities;
- assure orders are consistently delivered on time;
- highlight product or design problems and develop improvements;
- record and investigate all quality failure and customer complaints and make sure that they do not reoccur;
- give a clear signal to customers that they are taking measures to improve quality;
- produce a documented system for recording and satisfying the training needs of new and existing staff regarding quality.

The British Electrotechnical Approvals Board This is a body which inspects domestic electrical equipment. Manufacturers of domestic electrical appliances will be keen for the BEAB to approve their products. Approval can serve as a recognition of quality that customers will recognise.

The Consumers Association This is the body which follows up complaints by people about faulty products or services. They also make recommendations about products and services to customers. This takes into account such things as quality, reliability and value for money. Often survey results appear in their *Which?* magazines.

The Institute of Quality Assurance (IQA) The Institute of Quality Assurance is the only professional body in the UK whose sole purpose is the promotion and advancement of quality practices. The IQA has three main objectives.

- To seek the advancement of quality management and practices and help the exchange of related information and ideas.
- To promote the education, training, qualification and development of people involved in quality assurance and the management for quality.
- To provide a range of services to members and, where appropriate, to the community at large.

The Association of British Travel Agents (ABTA) The Association of British Travel Agents is a trade association which has drawn up a code of practice for its members. The code aims to improve the trading standards of activities related to the sale of holidays. Travel agents are allowed to register with ABTA if they agree to follow their code of practice.

The Wool Marketing Board This allows manufacturers to carry the label shown in Figure 58.3 if their garments are made entirely of pure new wool. Obtaining a trademark is a way for a firm to give quality assurance to customers. If customers know that the quality of a product is guaranteed, they are more likely to buy the product. Also, there is less need to inspect the product, and returns and re-ordering are reduced.

The British Toy and Hobby Association (BTHA) developed the Lion Mark as a symbol of toy safety to be displayed on toy packaging. Toy manufacturers that want to include the Lion Mark must take out a licence with the BTHA. The manufacturer must sign a strict code of practice which sets standards relating to toy safety and advertising, as well as counterfeiting and markings on toy guns. The Lion Mark was adapted by the BTHA and the British Association of Toy Retailers (BATR) for shops. If the symbol is displayed in a shop it indicates that the retailer has agreed to a strict code of practice. They agree only to offer safe toys for sale and to ensure staff are briefed on toy safety matters such as age warnings.

A number of laws exist which protect consumers (☞ unit 71) from poor trading practices. They have tended to focus on safety aspects and consumer exploitation. However, increasingly UK laws and EU regulations are taking into account product quality. The laws are enforced by local inspectors, called **Trading Standards Officers.**

Figure 58.3 *The Kitemark and the Woolmark*

Pure new wool

KC Stadium, home to Hull City AFC and Hull FC Rugby League, is a state-of-the-art all-seater spectator arena with a capacity of 25,000. It also contains administrative offices, players' accommodation and souvenir shops together with 28 executive boxes, a restaurant overlooking the pitch, hospitality suites and a supporters bar. The stadium will also be used for other local, national and international sporting fixtures, concerts and events. Bison, the UK's leading producer of structural precast products, supplied the main contractor, Birse Construction, with 2,494 terrace units, 16,180 m² of precast prestressed flooring units, 210 m³ of staircases and 440 structural walls.

Bison is committed to customer satisfaction. All Bison manufacturing plants are members of the British Standards Institution Registered Firms Scheme for Quality Assurance to BS EN ISO 9001 for the design and manufacture of precast concrete products. Membership of the scheme ensures that all procedures and disciplines relevant to the design and manufacturing processes are subject to independent approval and periodic review by the BSI. All Bison UK factories have been assessed by the BSI and awarded Certificates of Assessed Capability under the scheme covering quality assurance for the manufacture of precast concrete products. Bison claims that as a customer you can be sure that all aspects of production, design, detailing and quality control have been independently inspected and have achieved the high level of competence and quality required by the BSI.

Also, Bison Structures Limited has been assessed by the SCQAS (Steel Construction Quality Assurance Scheme Limited) to BS EN ISO 9001. It has been registered for the design, manufacture, supply and erection of structural steelwork for retail, industrial and commercial buildings, car parks, leisure facilities and other private and public sector projects.

Source; adapted from Bison website.

(a) What role does the BSI play in Bison's quality assurance?
(b) Using examples from the case, suggest advantages to Bison of BS EN ISO 9001 registration.

1. What is meant by the quality of a product?
2. Explain the difference between actual and perceived quality.
3. Explain the difference between quality control and quality assurance.
4. State 5 implications of TQM for a business.
5. Why is teamwork so important in TQM?
6. What are the costs of ensuring quality?
7. Describe the steps in best practice benchmarking.
8. What is the role of the British Standards Institution?
9. Explain the advantage of manufacturing trademarks to a business.

key terms

Best practice benchmarking - imitating the standards of an established leader in quality and attempting to better them.
Quality - features of a product that allow it to satisfy customers' needs. It may refer to some standard of excellence.
Quality assurance - a method of working for businesses that takes into account customers' wants when standardising quality. It often involves guaranteeing that quality standards are met.
Quality chains - when employees form a series of links between customers and suppliers in business, both internally and externally.
Statistical process control - the collection of data about the performance of a particular process in a business.
Total quality management - a managerial approach which focusses on quality and aims to improve the effectiveness, flexibility, and competitiveness of the business.
Warranties - guarantees that faulty products will be repaired or replaced within a period of time.

Case study Window Care

WindowCare manufactures PVCU windows. It employs 400 people and has grown successively year on year to its present £30 million plus turnover. In 1999 it was one of the UK's fastest growing companies. WindowCare serves two mainstream markets - the residential construction industry and the replacement window and conservatory industry. The PVCU industry's reputation in this sector could have posed problems to the company's success, had WindowCare not set out to prove that its quality was genuine. Hyung Taik Lee, WindowCare's marketing manager, explained that 'we supply replacement windows and products for new buildings, and people had become very wary of PVCU. The industry has a bad reputation - it's known for cowboys and white van man, so proving your product is of good quality has always been an issue.'

Proving that its quality matched up to its claims was exactly what the company set out to do. Hyung Taik Lee says 'We decided that the only way to lose this stigma was to go for the Kitemark'. WindowCare's commitment to gaining approvals provide convincing, third party proof that its products are manufactured to the highest possible standards can be seen in its current list of successes.

- ISO 9002 registration with BSI.
- Kitemark to BS 7412 for plastic windows made from extruded hollow profiles.
- Kitemark to BS 7950/BS 7412 for enhanced security performance of casement and tilt/turn windows for domestic applications.
- Kitemark to BS 5713 for hermetically sealed flat double glazing units.

The hard work has paid off for the company. Concerns about the quality of products, particularly in new build projects, means that specifiers now demand proof that PVCU windows meet stringent standards, and the Kitemark is a recognised mark of quality and integrity. Hyung Taik Lee said 'The NHBC is trying to raise standards to such a degree that it now specifies the Kitemark for windows. We cannot sell into the new build sector without the Kitemark.'

In 2003, in order to reinforce its commitment to quality, WindowCare introduced total quality management (TQM) throughout the whole of its organisation. The company invested a huge £3 million

in a training programme. Although a minority of the directors felt that an investment of £3 million was too high, some of the benefits of introducing TQM have been impressive.

- Staff were organised into teams which improved motivation and encouraged them to solve problems for themselves.
- Defects were reduced to 0.12 per cent, with 0.1 per cent the target for next year.
- Some administrative procedures were streamlined, resulting in a complete elimination of overtime and a reduction in the hours worked by staff from 36 to 35 per week. Basic pay was not cut in line with hours worked.
- BSI inspectors have reduced their visits, resulting in huge savings and less stress.
- Improved communications have resulted from the introduction of quality chains.

(a) Define the terms (i) kitemark and (ii) zero defects. (4 marks)

(b) Describe the benefits to:
  (i) the business;
  (ii) its employees;
  of WindowCare introducing TQM in its organisation. (8 marks)

(c) Why might WindowCare be suitable for other companies to benchmark against in future? (8 marks)

(d) Examine the factors which may have influenced the introduction of quality techniques at WindowCare. (10 marks)

(e) Discuss whether WindowCare should continue to gain ISO accreditation in future. (10 marks)

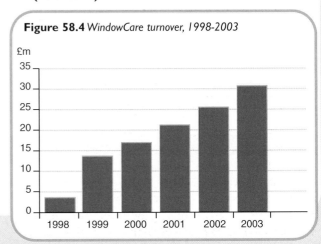

Figure 58.4 *WindowCare turnover, 1998-2003*

What is efficiency?

The objective of a business might be to be profitable (☞ unit 4). One way of doing this is to increase efficiency. EFFICIENCY is to do with how well resources, such as raw materials, labour and capital can be used to produce a product or service. Businesses often use costs as an indicator of efficiency. A manufacturer, for example, that finds its **average costs** (☞ unit 27) falling may well be improving efficiency as long as the quality of goods or services does not fall. Generally, as efficiency improves firms become more profitable. However firms may still be profitable without being efficient. This may perhaps be the case with firms that have a great deal of market power. BT, for example, operated profitably in a market free from competition for many years. This does not necessarily mean that increased profits came from being more efficient. Why might businesses want to measure efficiency?

- To improve control of the business. Information about the efficiency of different parts of a business will allow managers to find strengths and weaknesses.
- To make comparisons. The efficiency of different plants can be compared, for example. The efficiency of the business compared to one of its competitors may also be useful.
- To help negotiations. Efficiency indicators can help a business when discussing wage rates, levels of staff and working practices with trade unions, for example.

How might efficiency be measured? Lower average costs or rising profitability are only **indicators** of efficiency. It is difficult to measure efficient business practice as many factors influence it. It is possible, however, to measure the efficiency of a process or an input such as labour or capital.

Measuring efficiency

How might a business measure the efficiency of a production process or its capital or employees?

Measuring labour productivity Labour PRODUCTIVITY can be found by dividing the output over a certain period by the number of workers employed:

$$\text{Labour productivity} = \frac{\text{Output (per period)}}{\text{Number of employees (per period)}}$$

If a small market garden employs 20 pickers who pick 40,000 lettuces a day, their productivity is 2,000 lettuces per worker each day.

This ratio measures the output per employee and is a useful indication of the efficiency of the labour force. There are, however, problems when calculating the ratio. For example, which workers should be counted? Should the maintenance crew, management, and clerical staff be counted, or should the ratio concentrate on direct labour only, ie shopfloor workers? How should part time workers and the long term sick be treated? How can the ratio accommodate a multi-product plant, where an employee's efforts might contribute to the production of more than one product?

What factors may lead to an improvement in labour productivity?

- There may be a change in the amount or quality of another input. For example, tools and equipment may have been replaced by more up to date and effective ones.
- The way in which labour and shifts are organised could be improved.
- Inefficient businesses with low labour productivity may be closed.
- Some of the improvement may result from increased effort from the workforce.
- The number of workers may be cut.

Measuring capital productivity A business may be interested in the productivity of its capital. This is becoming increasingly likely as more and more firms become capital intensive. A capital productivity ratio can be calculated by dividing output by the amount of capital employed in a given time period.

$$\text{Capital productivity} = \frac{\text{Output}}{\text{Capital employed}}$$

If a factory employed 10 sewing machinists and the total number of garments sewn in a day was 900, the productivity of capital would be 90 garments per machine each day.

Again, improvements in the productivity of capital may not be the result of more efficient capital alone. For example, the performance of an engine can be improved if it is serviced regularly and used carefully.

The labour and capital productivity ratios above are 'partial factor' productivity ratios. They measure the efficiency of just one input. A firm might want to measure the efficiency of the combined inputs it uses.

$$\text{Multi-factor productivity} = \frac{\text{Output}}{\text{Labour + materials + capital + etc.}}$$

This ratio takes into account that efficiency can be influenced by the quality and effectiveness of all inputs.

Measuring value added In recent years some firms have calculated the value added by the business where:

Value added = Sales revenue - external expenditure

This is a measure of overall company performance and shows the money available for reinvestment in the business and distribution to shareholders.

In the UK productivity for the whole economy can be measured as gross value added (GVA). This is the value of gross domestic product or national income in the economy plus subsidies minus taxes. Labour productivity can then be measured as GVA per head by dividing this figure by employment. The GVA per head in 2001 in the UK, for example, was £37,340.

Assessing business efficiency is a complicated task. A whole variety of measures are required and there is no single indicator which reflects accurately the overall efficiency of a business. A range of financial ratios may also be used to help assess the performance of a business.

UK Coal is Britain's largest producer of coal. It employs around 7,000 people. In 2002, the price of coal was at historically low levels. In addition, demand from UK power stations was falling due to power generators using more gas to generate electricity. The amount of power generated by coal fell from 34 per cent in 2001 to 32 per cent in 2002. This trend was expected to continue. Table 59.1 shows profit/loss before tax, output of coal and number of employees for UK Coal in 2001 and 2002.

Source: adapted from UK Coal, *Annual Reports and Accounts, 2002.*

Table 59.1 *Profit/loss before tax, output of coal and number of employees for UK Coal in 2001 and 2002*

	2001	2002
Profit/loss (£000)	-£26,484	-£83,111
Output (millions of tonnes)	22.3	21.9
Number of employees	7,376	6,902

(a) Calculate the labour productivity for UK Coal in 2001 and 2002 and comment on the change over the two years.
(b) The number of employees shown in Table 59.1 includes administrative workers. How might this affect measurements of labour productivity?

Work study

WORK STUDY is an attempt to find the 'best' or most 'efficient' way of using labour, machines and materials. The work of F W Taylor (☞ unit 41) is said to have formed the basis of work study methods.

Work study uses two techniques - method study and work measurement. Method study involves identifying all the specific activities in a job, analysing them, and finding the best way to do the job. This could be an existing job or a new one. Method study will allow a firm to:
● identify an optimum way to carry out a task;
● improve the layout of the factory or the workplace;
● minimise effort and reduce fatigue;
● improve the effectiveness of processes;
● improve the use of labour, machines and materials;
● establish the costs of particular activities to help with accounting;
● achieve results in the least time.

Once the best work method has been found, work measurement can be used to find the effort needed to carry out a task to an acceptable standard. The results can be used to design incentive schemes and determine staffing levels.

How is work measurement carried out? One example might be a worker being observed by a work-study assessor. The assessor might watch a worker set up a cutting machine, cut 10 patterns, reset the machine for a different pattern, and cut 10 more patterns, and record the findings. The performance might be rated against a scale of, say, 0 - 100, such as the British Standard Rating Scale (where 100 is the standard performance of an average, experienced, motivated worker). It is possible for an efficient and motivated worker to exceed 100 on this scale. Work-study assessors are often disliked by employees. Some regard these time and motion officers with suspicion and feel threatened. Workers are sometimes expected to work harder in the future as a result of their observations.

Ergonomics is also an important feature in work study. Machines and the environment should be adapted so that the individual can achieve the best performance. A study of the working area might concentrate on such things as air temperature, humidity, radiation, noise levels and lighting. A study of the positioning of dials might be used when studying machines. EU legislation has laid down a set of rules relating to the use of VDUs by employees, for example.

Improving efficiency

There is a variety of methods that a business might choose which could improve efficiency. Some of the main methods are explained in the sections that follow. The aim of the business when introducing changes to improve efficiency is to increase the productivity of factors of production, reduce costs and raise profits. Increasingly businesses are adopting company-wide approaches which involve the whole business in improving efficiency.

Changes to the workforce

Improvements in efficiency can be made by making labour more productive and reducing labour costs. How can a business make labour more productive?

- Division of labour. If all the tasks involved in constructing a housing estate were carried out by one worker this would be highly inefficient. If tasks are divided between workers, this allows each worker to specialise on the job they do best, such as joinery or plastering (☞ unit 1).
- Incentives. Incentives may motivate workers to be more productive (☞ units 42 and 43). They may be in the form of a reward, such as a bonus.
- Changes in hours and payments. Employees may be asked to work shifts which allow equipment to be run for 24 hours. Flexitime systems allow staff to choose what days they wish to work within limits. Annualised hours (☞ unit 42) mean that workers can be asked to stay at home during slack periods, but work when trading picks up.
- Employing different types of workers may reduce labour costs and increase productivity. Workers who work from home, such as teleworkers who communicate with a business by e-mail or fax are often hired by business. They save on office costs. Part time workers or temporary employees may also reduce costs. Workers who job share might allow a job to be filled by two part time employees.
- Teamwork. This involves employees working closely together in teams when carrying out tasks. For example, quality circles (☞ unit 43) are groups of workers who meet to analyse and solve problems, and then pass on their findings to management. Cell production, where a product is manufactured from start to finish when operations are closely linked, is also more effective if teams carry out the work.
- Training. It is generally agreed that the efficiency of the workforce is linked to the amount and quality of education and training that it receives (☞ unit 49). Some businesses have their own training schemes, such as health and safety, graduate training programmes or Modern Apprenticeships. Some employees follow training courses leading to NVQs.
- Multi-skilling. Multi-skilling is where employees are trained in a variety of operations. It may allow a business to reduce its workforce, as more tasks are carried out by fewer workers.
- Empowerment. This involves giving workers responsibility to make their own decisions and making them feel valued (☞ unit 43). Empowered workers are likely to be better motivated and to make better decisions, which could increase productivity.
- Employees may be involved in job enlargement, job enrichment or job rotation (☞ unit 43). These methods allow individual workers to undertake more tasks than they might otherwise have carried out.

Port Talbot Engineering is a supplier of forged conrods, a car engine component. It employs 200 staff who were being offered terms and conditions (piecework, fixed shift patterns, collective bargaining etc) that were at least 20 years out of date. Recognising that the 'us and them' culture was holding back efficiency improvements and the development of the business, the company decided to implement a new partnership agreement with trade unions and staff representatives.

A consultant was employed to begin the task. The initial approach was to hold a four day workshop with union reps and staff to draft, in outline, the new agreement. The approach adopted by the workshop was to find out what both management and unions would want, given a 'clean slate'. After the workshop all employees were briefed in small groups by in-house people who had been coached in expert and structured delivery. The consultant provided materials for the briefings such as documents to show how individual employees would be affected.

A ballot was held which showed that 64 per cent of the site's workers were in favour of accepting the new proposals. This included single status issues such as grades, shift patterns, sick and holiday pay, overtime payments, and new ways of working such as flexible working and multi-skilling.

The agreement meant that the company could operate more flexibly and meet customer demand more effectively. Improved incentives for the workforce helped to raise productivity by 35 per cent. Four months after the implementation, all performance indicators were positive and all targets were met. The systems implemented at Port Talbot Engineering were also introduced in sister companies.

Source: adapted from various websites.

(a) How might some of the new practices improve flexibility at Port Talbot Engineering?
(b) Why do you think staff at Port Talbot Engineering voted in favour of the new agreement?

Question 2

Standardisation

STANDARDISATION involves using uniform resources and activities or producing a uniform product. It can be applied to tools, components, equipment, procedures and business documents.

Changing systems can be very expensive, although there are benefits. A construction firm that builds a range of flats, for example, would benefit if all were fitted with standard cupboards. Savings are made in a number of ways. Bulk purchases can be made, the same tools and procedures could be used for fitting and training time could be reduced. This is an example of internal standardisation. Standardisation can also be more general. For example, efficiency will improve if there are standard components like nuts, bolts, pipes, screws and wire or standard measurements terminology, procedures and equipment.

The creation of the Single European Market in 1992 aimed

to standardise regulations, procedures and specifications about quality, health and safety. This has benefited all businesses in EU member countries.

The main disadvantage is that the designers are constrained. They can not change production easily to suit the individual consumer. Designers may also face a more demanding job if they have to design products which must contain certain standard components and dimensions. Standardisation may also lead to inflexibility, which could result in a slower reaction to change.

Factory and office layout

The way in which a factory or office is set out can affect efficiency. The machinery and work stations should be set out so that effort and cost are minimised and output is maximised. This will be achieved if:

- the area is safe and secure;
- handling and movement are minimised;
- good visibility and accessibility is maintained;
- flexibility is maximised;
- managers are co-ordinated.

There is no standard method of factory layout because different products need different techniques. Also, different companies producing the same product might choose different methods. For example, both Guiness and Brakspears produce beer, but the layouts of their breweries are very different. Brakspears uses very traditional brewing techniques. Guiness uses more up to date methods. What are the common types of factory layout?

Process layout This system involves performing similar operations on all products in one area or at one work station. For example, the manufacture of wellington boots involves a mixing process where PVC resin and stabiliser are mixed, a moulding process which takes place on a moulding machine, a trimming operation where the boots have unwanted material cut off, and packaging ready for distribution. Each of these processes is undertaken on all boots at each work station, and work stations are located in different parts of the factory.

This type of layout is often used with batch (☞ unit 54) or cell production (☞ unit 55) because of its flexibility. Planning is needed to avoid machines being overloaded or remaining idle.

Product layout With this method, machinery and tasks are set out in the order required to make the product. The products 'flow' from one machine or task to another. Flow production techniques (☞ unit 54) use this method. It is popular because handling time is reduced and there is greater control. However, it can only be used if there is large demand for the product.

Fixed position layout This involves performing operations on the work-in-progress and then returning it to a fixed

location after each process. Alternatively, resources are taken to a site at which production occurs. An example would be the construction of a bridge.

It is not just factories which may change their layout to improve efficiency. For example, some businesses have given more thought to the way their offices should be laid out. Some favour 'open plan' offices. This is where large numbers of employees all work in the same area with no walls or partitions. This could help to improve communication and lead to a 'team spirit' in the organisation. Businesses such as supermarket chains also consider very carefully the best way to lay out their stores. One of their objectives is to ensure that parts of the store do not become congested when the store is busy.

Sheffield-based Barlow Joinery supplies custom-made interior fittings to major UK financial institutions and supermarkets. Following the acquisition of a new unit to raise capacity, Barlow employed a small working party, made up of its own staff and specialist consultants, to review efficiency in part of its operations. The focus was on the Sainsbury's cell in the unit. It was found that quality and productivity were good. However, the use of space in the production area was poor. One of the methods used to improve space utilisation was to implement a more efficient layout. The new layout involved making the following changes.

- Assembly benches, which accounted for the majority of the area's fixtures, were rearranged thereby releasing 30 per cent of the original space. Benches were also modified for greater efficiency, flexibility and safety. By building the project leader a new desk, his bench was also released for more appropriate purposes.
- Storage packs for PU frames were relocated. They were also sorted and slow moving items were sent off-site. This eliminated the safety hazard posed by driving the forklift truck through 'pedestrian' areas.
- Building a new wood storage rack in a new location to free up a prime position in the cell. The design and labelling makes it easier to see what is in stock and prevents retrieval damage.

The extra space created could either accommodate an increase of up to £300,000 in sales, or house machines from another site.

Source: adapted from Burton Group website.

(a) Explain how the new factory layout at Barlow Joinery has improved efficiency.
(b) What other benefits might Barlow Joinery enjoy as a result of the new layout?

Question 3

Quality of the production process

It may be possible to improve efficiency by introducing measures to improve the quality of the product or the production process.

- Total Quality Management (TQM) (☞ unit 58) is an approach which aims to reduce the number of errors made in a business. It also encourages staff to continually review and check their work. Fewer errors should improve efficiency because there will be less waste and less repeat work.
- Benchmarking involves a business identifying another organisation which is the very best in a particular field (☞ unit 58). For example, a business may recognise that a company has a low rate of absenteeism. It could identify the reasons why its absenteeism record is so low and adopt its methods.
- Some businesses adopt recognised quality standards in their operations (☞ unit 58), such as the BS EN ISO 9000. Once this standard has been awarded, regular checks are made to ensure standards are maintained. Such high standards will tend to pressurise businesses into being efficient.

Reorganisation of the business

Many businesses have reorganised themselves to improve efficiency. This usually involves changing the structure of the organisation.

- Delayering involves reducing the number of layers in the managerial hierarchy (☞ unit 40). By stripping out layers of management, for example, businesses may save money. There may be other benefits too if businesses empower (☞ unit 43) the rest of the workforce.
- Downsizing is where the size of the business is reduced. This could mean closing down some unprofitable operations. Downsizing usually results in cutting the size of the workforce. This could save money and improve productivity.
- Outsourcing is where a firm allows a sub-contractor to undertake some work which was done by the business. This could improve efficiency if the sub-contractor can do the work at a lower cost.
- Many businesses relocate some, or parts, of their operations to improve efficiency. The main motive for relocation is to take advantage of cheaper resources in the new locations. For example, some companies have relocated their call centres in India. Call centres are labour intensive and labour is far cheaper in India. Some manufacturers have also switched production. For example, James Dyson, the manufacturer of the Dyson Dual Cyclone vacuum cleaner, decided to switch production from the UK to Malaysia in 2002. The government in the UK also has a record for relocating its activities to save money. For example, the DVLC was relocated in Swansea a number of years ago. Businesses are also 'relocating' some of their business activities onto the Internet. For example, banks offer online banking services, which reduces staffing levels and the need for expensive high street branches.

Changes in business size

Some businesses believe that they can improve efficiency by growing. This is because larger businesses can exploit **economies of scale** (☞ unit 56). By exploiting economies of scale businesses will enjoy lower costs. Some mergers and takeovers are motivated by this objective.

Technological improvements

Investment in new technology will often improve efficiency (☞ unit 60). New machinery may be quicker, more accurate, be able to carry out more tasks, and work in more extreme conditions than older equipment or labour. Many machines are controlled by computers and can undertake very complex tasks.

- In the primary industry, technology has raised productivity dramatically. The main reason for this is because, in agriculture for example, machinery has replaced people.
- In secondary industry, robots, lasers, CNC machines and automated plants have been increasingly introduced. This has resulted in large increases in efficiency and a reduction in costs.
- Even in the tertiary sector, which tends to be labour intensive, the scope for using technology has increased. For example, a French leisure company has opened a small chain of hotels which are unstaffed for most of the day. People check in using their credit cards and make no contact at all with staff. A small team of staff visit the hotels for a short time each day to clean and service the rooms. Information and communication technology has improved the ability to communicate over large distances (☞ unit 52).

The benefits to stakeholders of improving efficiency

Improvements in efficiency can benefit a number of business stakeholders.

- Shareholders. Improved efficiency will tend to lower costs and raise profits. With greater profits shareholders may be paid higher dividends and higher share prices. Businesses will also have more profit to reinvest. This could help to protect the long term future of the business.
- Customers. If greater efficiency reduces costs businesses may offer products at lower prices. Customers might benefit if the quality of products are improved. Delivery times and customer service might also be better.
- Employees and managers. A more efficient workforce may be better motivated and enjoy more job satisfaction. They may be valued more by employers, get better training, be given opportunities to use their talents and enjoy better working relationships with managers. Employees may also benefit from higher wages and better working conditions.
- Suppliers. Suppliers may benefit from better relationships

with businesses and prompter payment. Measures such as just-in-time manufacturing rely heavily on good relationships with suppliers.
● Community. Better efficiency might reduce waste and lower social costs such as pollution.
● Government. If greater efficiency leads to higher profits, the government will gain more tax revenues.

Capacity utilisation

CAPACITY UTILISATION is about the use that a business makes from its resources. If a business is not able to increase output, it is said to be running at **full capacity**. Its capacity utilisation is 100 per cent. So if a 52 seater coach from London to Edinburgh has 52 passengers, it is operating at full capacity. If it had 32 passengers it would be operating at less than full capacity and so it would have EXCESS, SURPLUS, SPARE or UNUSED CAPACITY.

Businesses do not always operate at full capacity. It may not be possible to keep all resources and machinery fully employed all the time. However, most businesses would wish to be operating at close to full capacity, such as 90 per cent.

In some cases businesses even choose to operate at less than full capacity to be flexible. For example, they might want to have capacity to cope with increased orders from regular customers. Without this, a business might let down its customers and risk losing them.

Capacity utilisation can be measured by comparing actual or current output with the potential output at full capacity using the formula:

$$\text{Capacity utilisation} = \frac{\text{Current output}}{\text{Maximum possible output}} \times 100$$

A printing operation might be able to operate for ten hours, six days a week using shifts. If last week it only had work enough to operate for 48 hours, the capacity utilisation would be:

$$\text{Capacity utilisation} = \frac{48}{(10 \times 6)} \times 100 = 80\%$$

Another measure might be if a printing machine is capable of printing 10,000 leaflets in a time period but only prints 9,000. It has a capacity utilisation of (9,000 ÷ 10,000) x 100 = 90 per cent. In this case the machine has unused, excess, surplus or spare capacity of 10 per cent.

Costs and capacity utilisation

A business can lower its unit or average costs if it can increase its capacity utilisation. This is because some of its costs are fixed. Higher levels of capacity utilisation and higher levels of output, will make a business more efficient. Table 59.2 shows capacity utilisation output, variable cost, fixed cost, total cost

and average cost for a component manufacturer. When capacity utilisation is raised from 60 per cent to 80 per cent, for example, average cost falls from £2.42 to £2.31. This is because the fixed costs of £50,000 are spread over more units of output. This explains why firms will always be keen to raise capacity utilisation.

Table 59.2 *Capacity utilisation, output, variable cost, fixed cost, total cost and average cost for a component manufacturer*

Actual output (units)	120,000	160,000
Maximum possible output (units)	200,000	200,000
Capacity utilisation	60%	80%
Variable costs (£2 per unit)	£240,000	£320,000
Fixed costs	£50,000	£50,000
Total cost	£290,000	£370,000
Average cost	£2.42	£2.31

Improving capacity utilisation

A business will make better use of its resources if it increases its capacity utilisation. Its unit costs will be lower and profits will be higher. How can firms increase capacity utilisation?

Reduce capacity A business might decide to cut capacity. It might do this by rationalising, for example. This involves reducing excess capacity by getting rid of resources that the business can do without. There is a number of measures a business might take.
● Reducing staff by making people redundant, employing more part time and temporary staff and offering early retirement.
● Selling off unused fixed assets such as machinery, vehicles, office space, warehouses and factory space.
● Leasing capacity. Debenhams has leased unused floor space in its stores to other retailers, for example. Parts of a factory could also be leased to another manufacturer. The advantage of this is that the space may be reclaimed if demand picks up again.
● Moving to smaller premises where costs are lower.
● Mothballing some resources. This means that fixed assets, such as machinery, are left unused, but maintained, so that they can be brought back into use if necessary.

Increase sales If a business sells more of its output, it will have to produce more. Therefore capacity utilisation will rise. A business might need to spend on promotion to increase sales, for example. If these costs are not covered by the extra revenue generated, raising capacity utilisation in this way may not be viable.

Increase usage A problem that many businesses face is

dealing with peak demand. Train operators can find that capacity utilisation is close to 100 per cent during the 'rush hour', but perhaps as low as 10 per cent late at night. Such businesses would like to increase capacity utilisation during 'off-peak' hours. This might explain why discounts are offered for 'off-peak' travel.

Subcontracting A business might find that only some of its resources are under utilised. For example, there may be insufficient work for an accountant. One option would be to do without the full time accountant and hire a firm of chartered accountants to produce the accounts at the end of the financial year. A manufacturer may decide that it would be more cost effective if it used a supplier to make one of its components, rather than make it itself.

Redeployment If a business has too many resources in one part of the business, it may be possible to deploy them in another part. For example, a bank may ask some of its employees to work in another branch for a short period.

Advantages and disadvantages of working at full capacity

Working at full capacity has some benefits.
- Average costs will be minimised because fixed costs will be spread across as many units of output as possible. This will help to raise profits.
- Staff motivation might be good if workers feel secure in their jobs.
- A busy operation can improve the company's image. As a result customers might be more confident when placing orders.

However, there some drawbacks when a firm is unable to increase output any more.
- The pressure of working at full capacity all the time might put a strain on some of the resources. For example, workers might be doing too much overtime, resulting in tiredness and stress. This might cause accidents or absence. Machines may also be overworked to breaking point.
- The business might lose lucrative orders from new customers.
- There may be insufficient time for staff training and important maintenance work.

The Kings Arms Hotel, owned and run by the Parkinson family, has 20 rooms, a bar and a restaurant. It is in a good location near the coast and does particularly well in the summer. However, in the winter occupancy is not so good. In 2003, Kathy Parkinson tried a number of marketing activities to attract more custom 'out of season'. One of the main tactics used was to offer two nights for the price of one during the week in November, December and January. Table 59.3 shows occupancy during 2002 and 2003.

Table 59.3 *Occupancy at the Kings Arms Hotel 2002 and 2003*

	2002	2003
Total room nights available	7,300	7,300
Total room nights occupied	4,897	5,292

(a) Calculate the capacity utilisation of the hotel in 2002 and 2003.
(b) To what extent do you think the marketing activities helped to improve (i) capacity utilisation and (ii) profitability of the Kings Arms Hotel?

key terms

Capacity utilisation – the use that a business makes of its resources.

Efficiency - how well inputs, such as raw materials, labour or capital can be changed into outputs, such as goods or services.

Excess, surplus, spare or unused capacity – when a business has more resources than it needs to satisfy current demand.

Productivity - the ratio of outputs to inputs in a production process, such as the output of a given amount of labour or capital.

Standardisation - the use of uniform resources and activities.

Work study - a process which investigates the best possible way to use business resources.

Knowledge ...owledge...Knowledge...Knowledge...Knowledge...Knowledge...Kno

1. Why might businesses wish to measure efficiency?
2. How might (a) labour productivity and (b) capital productivity be measured?
3. What is meant by multi-factor productivity?
4. What does 'value added' measure?
5. What are the benefits of work study for a business?
6. Describe 4 methods of improving labour productivity.
7. What are the advantages and disadvantages of standardisation?

8. Explain the difference between process and product factory layout.
9. State 3 ways in which a business may be reorganised to improve efficiency.
10. State 5 benefits to a business of improving efficiency.
11. Identify the ways in which a business might improve capacity utilisation.
12. State 3 advantages and 3 disadvantages of operating at full capacity.

Case study Maritime Navigation Systems

Maritime Navigation Systems (MNS) was originally established to produce navigation systems for the Royal Navy. For 40 years the company did very well. It grew and widened its customer base into Europe. However, in 2002 the company's directors finally accepted that it would have to take measures to reduce capacity and push harder to improve productivity.

In 1998, MNS started to lose customers to foreign competitors. Unfortunately it was unable to generate business from other sources and, gradually, the company started to slide. In 2002, the business made a loss for the first time in its history. MNS reacted by employing a consultant to carry out a work study.

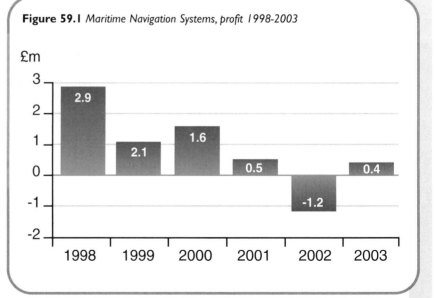

Figure 59.1 *Maritime Navigation Systems, profit 1998-2003*

The results of the study confirmed the directors' worst suspicions. Its working practices were inflexible and out of date, the company was overstaffed, some machinery was obsolete and the factory layout was inappropriate. A number of recommendations were made by the consultant.

- Move to a smaller factory.
- Reduce staffing from 89 to 60.
- Introduce teamworking, job rotation and multi-skilling.
- Invest £2.4 million in new technology.
- Change the layout of the factory.

The directors agreed that all of the recommendations should be met. In 2002, MNS moved from its large old factory in Gillingham to a smaller, but much newer site, in Rochester. It spent £250,000 on a training programme so that workers could be multi-skilled. It offered voluntary redundancy and retirement packages to 20 of the staff and reduced staffing to 69. Finally, it bought some new machinery and sold off obsolete and unwanted machinery and equipment.

The results of the 'shake-up' were encouraging. In 2003, when relocation and redundancy costs were stripped out, MNS returned to profit. There were dramatic changes in labour productivity and capital utilisation. It also appeared that worker motivation

had improved. Staff seemed to prefer teamworking and the initial fears about having to do more than one job had all but faded. Figure 59.1 shows profit for MNS between 1998 and 2002. Table 59.4 shows some production data for 2002-2003.

(a) Using this case as an example, explain what is meant by capacity utilisation. (4 marks)
(b) Calculate (i) labour productivity and (ii) capital utilisation for **MNS** in 2002 and 2003. (8 marks)
(c) Explain how the changes identified in (b) will benefit **MNS**. (8 marks)
(d) Explain what is meant by a work study and how it benefited **MNS**. (8 marks)
(e) Explain how multi-skilling and teamworking might have helped to improve labour productivity at **MNS**. (10 marks)
(f) **MNS** could have chosen other ways to increase capacity utilisation. Discuss whether it chose the best options. (12 marks)

Table 59.4 *Output, staff employed and factory capacity 2002 and 2003*

	2002	2003
Output (systems)	2,300	2,200
Staff employed	89	69
Capacity (systems)	6,000	3,000

The nature and impact of technology

One of the most significant factors affecting how businesses have operated in the twentieth century has been the impact of new TECHNOLOGY. It is easy to see its impact when we consider some of the changes that have taken place in business.

- New products, such as camcorders, compact discs, laptop computers and services such as direct purchasing from television.
- New production processes, such as robotic welding, and computer controlled cutting machines.
- New materials such as silicon chips for computer circuit boards and polystyrene for packaging.
- Changes in business operations and new skills. For example, as a result of automatic cash tills in banking, many staff have been retrained to sell financial services.

There are many ways in which technology can be defined. One approach is to say that it is 'a creative process which uses human, scientific and material resources to solve problems and generate better efficiency'. Some examples make this clear. A business that uses video conferencing to communicate with branches spread all over the country is using technology. So is a plant which uses lasers to detect faults in products as they move along the production line.

How does technological progress take place? It is usually by means of **invention** and **innovation**. Invention is the discovery of something new. Some examples include the laser beam in 1960 by Dr. Charles Townes, the micro-processor in 1971 by Marcian Hoff in the USA and the Rubik Cube in 1975 by Professor Erno Rubik in Hungary. Inventions are then developed into products. The laser beam has been used for cutting in industry, micro-surgery in hospitals and spectacular lighting shows in displays.

Inventions are sometimes made by creative people 'outside' business. For example, the ball point pen was invented by a sculptor, and the pneumatic tyre by a veterinary surgeon! Today, most research is carried out by teams of people working for a business, university or the government. The rewards to inventors can be very high indeed, if their inventions can be used commercially and patented (☞ unit 2).

In business, innovation is the commercial exploitation of an invention. An invention is not usually in a form that consumers will buy. The product must be developed to meet consumers' needs, so that it can be sold profitably by business. UK firms have, perhaps, been reluctant to do this in the past. For example, the first working computers were developed in the 1930s. Since then Japan and America have led the world in hardware production and computer research. Enormous investment is often required to innovate once a technical breakthrough has been achieved.

One aspect of new technology is that new materials are developed. The new Mercedes CLS Coupe, launched in March 2004 at the Geneva Motor Show, came with scratch-resistant, nanotechnology-based paint as standard. The new clear lacquer top coat, which provides gloss and weatherproofing properties, is the result of a four-year collaboration between Mercedes and US-based automotive coatings supplier PPG Industries. Scratch-resistant coatings already existed, but they had no elasticity. They crack when exposed to the extreme temperatures that cars must withstand. PPG's new coating, called Ceramiclear, remains elastic when heated.

Most paintwork scratches are caused by minute particles of dust or sand that become lodged in car wash brushes. After 40 wash cycles, scratches on a vehicle using Ceramiclear were about half the width and depth of those in conventional paintwork. The coating retained about 80 per cent of its gloss compared with 20 per cent with a standard clearcoat. The new paint will also protect against degradation caused by ultraviolet radiation or salt and chemicals, but not deliberate vandalism. Mercedes was able to introduce the new coating without making any changes to its production process. Eventually, the scratch-resistant paint will be applied to the entire Mercedes range.

Source: adapted from *The Engineer*, 5.3.2004.

(a) Using this case as an example, explain the difference between innovation and invention.
(b) How will Mercedes and PPG Industries benefit from collaboration on the project?

Question 1

Applications in the primary sector

Primary industry has been affected by the introduction of new technology in a number of ways. In agriculture the use of tractors, combine harvesters, lifting equipment, grain drying machines and automatic milking and feeding apparatus have helped to increase output, reduce time and waste, and improve conditions. Agrochemicals and pesticides have raised crop yields. Biological research has helped to develop plants and crops which are more resistant to disease and more attractive to consumers. Genetically modified foods are argued to have better resistance to disease. In extractive industries, such as mining, cutting, lifting and tunnelling machines have all led to increased output. There have also been improvements in safety equipment and mining conditions for workers. The extraction of oil now takes place on large oil rigs with computer controlled drilling equipment. This improves the speed and accuracy of production. In fishing, the introduction of refrigerated boats has helped to improve productivity. Forestry has benefited from cutting, lifting and haulage equipment.

One problem with the use of more efficient technology is that resources are used up more quickly. It may be possible to control this in the case of **renewable resources**, such as timber, by replanting and managed forestry. However, unless new forms of power can be developed, there are likely to be problems in future with extracting large amounts of the world's finite resources such as coal and oil. There have also been criticisms of genetically modified food and its possible effects on humans.

Applications in the secondary sector

New technology has led to major changes in manufacturing. Many factories and production lines employ complex mechanical, electrical and electronic systems. Even smaller manufacturing businesses have benefited from the introduction of new equipment and processes. Examples of new technology can be found in a number of areas.

Robots Robots are increasingly used on assembly and production lines. They have some form of arm, which moves to instructions given by a computer. Repetitive tasks, such as installing components, can be carried out many times with great accuracy. Such tasks may lead to boredom, lack of motivation, tiredness and human error if undertaken by employees. Robots may also increase the flexibility of a business. For example, in 1998 small robots, each with its own set of paint cans, were installed in the paint shop of the Volkswagen-Audi car plant in Germany. The robot could be activated at a few minutes' notice when a customer wants a colour which is not included in the current program. Using the robot means that customer demand for less popular colours can be satisfied without having to clean out the pipes of the main painting apparatus, which would be costly.

Computer aided design COMPUTER AIDED DESIGN (CAD) is now used by businesses in the design process, before a product is manufactured. Examples of products designed using CAD include vehicle bodies, plastic containers to hold milk and oil, furniture and clothing. Designing on computer allows a business to produce accurate drawings, which can be viewed in 3D and altered cheaply and quickly for a client. Designs can be accurately measured and tested on computer for faults, such as unsuitable components or dimensions, which might have caused problems during manufacture.

Computer numerically controlled machines Products can be manufactured using COMPUTER NUMERICALLY CONTROLLED (CNC) machines. Instructions are given to the CNC machine by the operator. The machine then carries out its instructions, controlled by a computer. An example might be a CNC milling machine which is used to cut out a mould of a mouse in plastic. The computer controls the cutting to produce the shape of a mould. In the textile industry computer controlled sewing, cutting and printing machines are used. Some CNC machines make use of probes and **coordinate measuring machines** (CMM). These are designed to make simple or complex measurements, check batches or components one at a time and inspect geometric or irregular shapes. CMMs are accurate to within a few microns. CNC machines can produce shapes and cut quickly and accurately. They can also carry out repetitive tasks without human error. The instructions can be changed easily to carry out different tasks. For example, JCB uses CNC machines to cut a wide range of patterns from metal plates for its mechanical diggers.

Computer aided manufacture In many factories computers are used to design products and the information is then fed

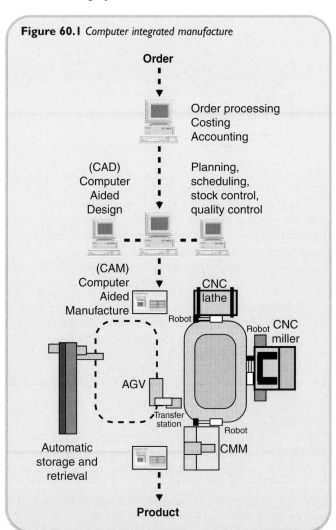

Figure 60.1 *Computer integrated manufacture*

into CNC machines. This automated operation is known as COMPUTER AIDED MANUFACTURE (CAM). For example, a manufacturer of telephones may design a new shape using a CAD software program on computer. The instructions may be taken from the CAD program and inputted into CNC machines. These machines will reproduce the shapes, guided by the information contained in the computer. Other examples of CAM include computer controlled manufacture of plastic bricks at Lego, computer controlled assembly lines at Sony and computer controlled temperatures, flow rates and ingredients for pizza production at McCain Foods. The computer controlled weaving system produced by Bonas stores designs on computer in one part of a factory and sends production information to looms in other parts of the factory. These then weave the designed fabric.

Computer integrated manufacture Some businesses have integrated the entire design and production process. Computers are used to guide and control the production of a good. Employees supervise the manufacturing part of the operation, checking that it is working effectively and repairing faults. This system is known as COMPUTER INTEGRATED MANUFACTURE (CIM). There is a number of stages in the operation. They are shown in Figure 60.1.

- Orders are received via e-mail, fax or letter and inputted into the system. Costings are carried out on computer using **spreadsheet** programs (☞ unit 10). Customers are stored on **databases**. Accounts are kept on computer and regularly updated. Orders which are received are processed and invoiced at a later date.

- The design department uses CAD packages to design the product for a client, making changes on computer. The instructions to manufacture the design are produced and fed through to the production part of the system.
- Production is planned and scheduled. Parts and materials are ordered as required by the computer, which monitors stock and automatically reorders where necessary.
- The instructions for production are passed to CNC machines which manufacture the product. CMM machines monitor the quality of the work.
- Robots are used to transfer products from one CNC machine to another.
- **Automatically guided vehicles (AGV)** take components to the machines.
- Finished products are taken to the stores or for dispatch.

Applications in tertiary industry

The supply of services has tended to be relatively more labour intensive (☞ unit 54) in the primary and secondary sectors. This is because supplying services often requires direct and personal contact with customers. However, the use of technology in the tertiary industry is becoming more widespread in a number of areas.

Government and private services There is a range of services provided by government or private alternatives. New technology used in health care and dental care has improved services considerably. Developments in new vaccines and drugs have reduced suffering and cured diseases that not long

---

The development of genetically modified (GM) foods in the agriculture industry has attracted attention in recent years. Scientists have been working to improve plants for human benefit for many decades. Some of the research and development is to do with Bt toxins (Bacillus thuringensis). These are toxins that can kill damaging insects. Three crops in particular have been subject to GM testing.

- Corn. 'Bt corn' removes the need for scouting and spraying to stop the European corn borer.
- Cotton. Cotton requires the intensive use of pesticides to combat many different pests. Most of these pests have developed resistance to the pesticides. 'Bt cotton' avoids the cost of time and money researching into new and more powerful pesticides.
- Soybeans. This is one of the two most important crops in the USA. About 60 per cent of the soybeans harvested in 1999 were GM.

The main advantages of GM crops may include the following.
- Better weed and pest control.
- Costs can be reduced because GM crops require less ground preparation before they are sown. Seeds can be drilled directly into last year's ground, which conserves soil moisture and cuts soil erosion.
- The development of higher yielding crops. This could help to reduce global starvation.

- The possible creation of foods with 'built-in' medicines and vaccines. For example, hepatitis B gene has been spliced into bananas. Researchers are also trying to create cooking oils with less saturated fat, soybean oil with high levels of Vitamin E and strawberries containing an anti-cancer chemical.
- 'Bt corn' has less mycotoxin contamination, which is often found in cattle feed. This cuts the chances of livestock being lost.

In 2003, 600 meetings took place in the UK to discuss GM crops. More than half of the people attending the meetings said that they should not be introduced under any circumstances and only 2 per cent said they would be happy to eat GM foods.

Source: adapted from www.asft.ttu.edu and http://news.bbc.co.uk.

(a) Explain the possible advantages of GM crops to (i) farmers and (ii) consumers.
(b) Why do you think pressure groups might resist the introduction of new technology into food production?

Question **2**

ago may have led to deaths. Surgeons can carry out exact operations using lasers, viewing them on television screens with the use of fibre optics. Replacement teeth can be produced for patients which exactly fit jaw shapes from materials which will last for years. Government information can now be found easily on the Internet.

Financial services Businesses selling financial services match customers with appropriate financial products. For example, client information can be fed into a computer to identify the most suitable insurance policy or savings plan. The sale of financial products such as ISAs, pensions and insurance policies is increasingly carried out on the Internet. Some banks offer online banking services. Many financial organisations now have cash dispensers outside their premises. These can be used by customers who want to take out cash with a minimum of fuss or out of normal working hours. Some banks have cash dispensers inside, and customers can enter the bank in non-business hours using 'swipe cards' to open doors. This gives extra security to customers using the facilities.

Distribution The introduction of containers has made the handling of freight quick and easy. They can be hauled onto trailers and locked in position. This prevents movement during transport and possible damage and theft. At port or rail terminals, containers can be loaded safely and quickly onto trains or ships using cranes. Refrigerated containers allow perishable goods to be transported long distances without deteriorating.

Personal services Dating agencies use computers to match couples using personal information held on databases about clients' characteristics and preferences. Agencies also make use of video technology to record messages from clients. On-line dating agencies allow people to register on the Internet.

Post and communication Technology has helped to improve the speed and efficiency of postal and packaging delivery. Many businesses have franking machines which weigh and record the required postage. Bar codes allow a free post or business service to be provided by firms. A customer can return a leaflet or envelope without charge to a business. Machines at the post office will read the bar code and bill the business providing the service. Post offices make use of video and televisions to advertise their services.

Hotels, restaurants and transport In the travel industry technology allows customers to travel without a ticket. They can book a flight over the telephone or the Internet using a credit card. The same card is then used to pick up a boarding pass from an airport machine or a check-in counter. Travellers to Australia can obtain an 'electronic visa'. Entry can be organised by giving passport details to a travel agent. These details are sent electronically to the appropriate port of

entry. Booking for hotels or theatre tickets can also be made by credit card. Meals at restaurants can be paid for by a 'swipe or switch' card. The transaction is recorded by a machine and the money is automatically transferred from the current account of the customer.

Advertising In advertising, television makes increasing use of advances in filming technology and special effects to make adverts more sophisticated and entertaining. There is also a growing selection of advertising media. For example, advertisers have used rotating messages on the 'touchlines' of sporting events and in city centres on the sides of buildings. The Internet provides worldwide advertising, but only to Internet users.

Retailing Retailing has benefited in many ways from new technology (☞ unit 23).

- The packaging of goods has changed greatly in recent years. New materials such as polystyrene and strong plastic wrap have improved the way in which goods are packaged. The materials have been lighter and stronger, have provided better protection, and have been easier to handle. Many firms have redesigned the packaging of goods to increase sales. In some cases new technology has helped. For example, Lucozade and other soft drinks have been packaged in flexible bags instead of cans and bottles.
- There has been a growth in home shopping. Computers and televisions have been linked together to enable shoppers to browse at home and then place orders by telephone or through a link (☞ unit 52). The Internet is a growing means of direct selling to customers at home.
- Payment has been made easier. Bar codes and hand held recorders allow customers to register the prices of goods as they shop. This saves time and queues at the checkout. Goods can be paid for by credit or 'swipe cards', increasing security as the customer does not have to carry cash.

Information technology

INFORMATION TECHNOLOGY (IT) is the recording and use of information by electronic means. Some of the uses of IT have already been explained in the previous sections. However, there are some common uses of IT which may apply to businesses operating in primary, secondary or tertiary industry.

- Administration. Many routine tasks can be carried out quickly by computer. These may include customer invoicing or billing. Standard letters or memos may be produced which can be easily changed if necessary. Large amounts of information about customers may be stored on databases.
- Personnel. Personnel files are now easily kept on databases. They can be regularly updated. Spreadsheets also allow calculations of salaries and deductions.
- R&D. Computer aided design can be used to research new materials or new product ideas. For example, tests may be carried out on the endurance of materials using a CAD

simulation. Recording, monitoring, regulating, forecasting and analysing data are all tasks that can be carried out more easily.

- Finance. Many firms record all financial transactions on spreadsheets. Some allow instant production of financial information such as profit and loss accounts, cash flow forecasts, budgets and financial ratios. It is also possible to make checks on outstanding payments that are due from customers so that credit control will be effective.

- Communications. Developments in information and communications technology (ICT) (☞ unit 52) means that information can be collected, stored and sent electronically in a fraction of a second. This saves money and makes sure information is passed correctly. Mobile telephones, faxes and e-mail mean that people can work from a variety of locations. Information can be sent over great distances and at any time. The Internet provides wide ranging communication opportunities, including promotion, on-line buying and e-mailing.

- Production information. Information may be stored on the terms of suppliers. Production costs may be calculated on spreadsheets. The ordering of stocks or components may be carried out by computer.

- Information and sales. Many businesses now have their own website on the Internet, providing company information. Some are using sites to provide information or to sell products to customers. A readers' survey by *Marketing Technique* about use of the Internet by businesses found 75 per cent of respondents worked for

companies with their own site. Two-thirds of respondents used the Internet to monitor competitors' activities.

Data protection

The rapid development in the use of IT has led to legislation about the collection, storage, processing and distribution of data (☞ unit 51). The **Data Protection Act, 1998** includes eight conditions with which users must comply.

- Personal data should be obtained and processed fairly and lawfully.
- Personal data can only be held for specified and lawful purposes.
- Personal data cannot be used or disclosed in any manner which is incompatible with the purpose for which it is held.
- The amount of data held should be adequate, relevant and not excessive.
- Personal data should be accurate and kept up to date.
- Personal data should not be kept for longer than is necessary.
- An individual shall be entitled to:
  (a) be informed by any data user if he or she is the subject of personal data and also have access to that data;
  (b) where appropriate, have data corrected or erased.
- Security measures must be taken by data users to prevent unlawful access, alteration, disclosure, destruction, or loss of personal data.

The **1990 Computer Misuse Act** identified certain offences relating to use of computers.

- A person causing a computer to perform a function with

The number of industries supplying online services is growing rapidly. One sector where online business activity has made a major impact is the gaming industry. Online betting exchanges, which allow individuals to bet against each other, have started to threaten some of the big operators such as Ladbrokes and William Hill. The exchanges provide technology that matches punters wanting to bet on the outcome of an event with those wanting to take their bet or 'lay' it. The exchanges make money by charging a commission (around 5 per cent) from whoever wins.

Betfair is the biggest of some 25 internet exchanges, with about 90 per cent of the market. It has 30,000 active members a week from 85 different countries and matches bets worth £50 million. Betdaq has 35,000 customers in 140 countries and has around £25 million in bets a week. It uses a different methodology from Betfair to arrive at this figure, however.

The advantages to customers of betting exchanges over traditional betting shops include:
- better prices;
- you can bet that something will lose;
- bets can be hedged by backing and laying as prices fluctuate in the run up to an event such as a horse race, football match or cricket match;
- you can keep on betting during the event;
- betting can be done in the comfort of your home and without speaking to a member of staff (although telephone

betting services have been available for a while).

On the downside, betting exchanges have attracted negative publicity. There has been evidence of suspicious betting patterns surrounding the alleged under-performance of certain jockeys and horses. One case involved a jockey with a substantial lead approaching the winning line failing to 'ride out' his horse properly. He was overtaken and the race was won by another horse. Betfair reported the suspicious betting patterns to the Jockey Club which is responsible for regulating and monitoring the industry. In addition to this, there have been alleged scandals where markets have been opened and punters, attracted by generous odds, have been trapped into betting on events where the result is already known. Betfair and Betdaq say to this, caveat emptor (let the buyer beware). Users should be wary when they see such generous odds.

Source: adapted from *The Financial Times*, 16.3.2004.

(a) Using examples from this case, explain the advantages and disadvantages to consumers of buying products and services using the Internet.

(b) What are the attractions to businesses of using the Internet to supply products and services.

intent to secure access.
- Unauthorised access to a computer with the intent to commit a further offence.
- Unauthorised and intentional modification of computer memory or storage media.

An offence is committed if access is unauthorised or if the person knows it is unauthorised. Many codes of practice state that employees may only access information held on a computer which is a relevant part of their work.

There is some legislation regarding the use of the Internet. EU legislation prevents the downloading of copyright music and allows businesses to block downloading, for example. EU legislation in 2003 made it illegal to send junk e-mail, known as spam, by businesses to individuals.

Benefits of new technology

There is a number of benefits to business of using new technology.

Increased productivity More can be produced with less and, as a result, businesses may gain higher profits. In addition, fewer of the environment's resources may be used up.

Reducing waste Introducing new technology often results in time being saved and fewer materials being used. For example, technology has created printing machines which waste less paper when printing books or magazines. How resources are used has attracted a great deal of attention in recent years. As the world's population continues to grow it will be necessary to improve resource use even further.

Improving the working environment Statistics on accidents at work show that the working environment is safer as result of new technology. Mining and manufacturing in particular have benefited. Modern equipment has made work easier and more tolerable. For example, fork lift trucks mean workers no longer need to load goods by hand. These improvements also help to remove workers' dissatisfaction.

Benefits to society Many new products have come onto the market in recent years. Personal stereo systems, video recorders, satellite and digital television, high performance cars and microwave ovens are some examples. New products mean wider consumer choice and possibly higher living standards. Other developments have helped to make our lives easier, such as automatic cash dispensers and mobile telephones.

Improvements in communications Faster means of transport (such as the jet aircraft), answerphones, e-mail, computer network links and fax machines are all examples of inventions which have helped to improve the speed of communications.

Higher incomes If firms enjoy greater profits they can afford to pay higher dividends to shareholders and higher wages to employees. Also, if efficiency is improved then products may

be sold at lower prices. As the country's income increases the government collects more tax revenue. This could be used to improve the quality of public services or alternatively to reduce the overall level of taxation or government borrowing.

Problems with new technology

The introduction of new technology can also cause problems for both business and society.

Cost Development, installation and maintenance can often prove costly. Also, businesses may have to lay off and retrain staff, leading to redundancy payments and retraining costs. If firms borrow to meet these costs, they will have to pay interest. Reorganisation may also be needed. Production may be changed from batch to flow production (☞ unit 54), job descriptions may be changed (☞ unit 46) and in some cases a larger or smaller plant may be needed.

Labour relations In the past, trade unions have resisted the introduction of some new technology because of the threat to their members' jobs. The growth of union and business partnerships after the year 2000 may have made the introduction of new technology easier.

Job skills New technology creates jobs which require new, technical skills, but replace manual jobs. These new jobs cannot be done by the existing workforce unless they can be retrained. Often, this is not possible.

Breakdowns Automated production lines are interdependent. If one part of the line breaks down the whole process may stop. There may also be teething problems. Breakdowns occur when technology is first installed. For example, it is argued that the Stock Exchange Automatic Quotation (SEAQ) share dealing system was partially to blame for the 1987 Stock Exchange crash. The system automatically triggered selling instructions, causing big falls in some share prices.

Motivation Some staff may dislike working only with machines. This may affect their motivation (☞ unit 41).

Management The management of technological change is considered very difficult. One reason is due to the rapid pace of the change. When new technology becomes available business managers have to decide whether or not to purchase it, or wait for the next important breakthrough. Deciding when to invest in new technology is very difficult. The management of the human resources leading up to the change, and during the change, requires great skill. People are often unhappy about change in their lives.

Unemployment and employment Much new technology is labour saving. Tasks once carried out by people will be done by machines. As a result people may become unemployed.

For example, in automated production lines tasks such as assembly and quality checks are done by robots and CMMs. One or two employees may act as supervisors. On the other hand technology has to be designed, manufactured, installed, programmed, operated, serviced and replaced, which may create new jobs.

IT problems Computer software can become infected by viruses. A computer virus is a programme written to deliberately damage or destroy software and files. Such viruses are very damaging. It is possible for businesses to use software to check the existence of viruses. They can then be blocked from entering the computer system if included on e-mails, for example. If a virus has entered the system, it can be removed.

Computer software has other problems which can affect a business. They may have to constantly buy the latest software to be compatible with clients or suppliers who use more modern versions. Modern machines may not run older software. New software may not be able to convert older programs. The **millennium bug** was a major problem for businesses in 1999 as certain computers might not have recognised the year 2000.

Leisure time People have gained more leisure time as a result of new technology. They need to learn how to use this extra time in a constructive way. Businesses are taking advantage of this. For example, it is argued that there is enough demand in the UK for many more golf courses.

An ageing population Medicine has benefited greatly from new technology. One effect of this is that the population of many countries is now 'ageing'. As a result the pressure has increased on those in work to support the aged. Demands on public funds will also increase and the government will have to find money for facilities which are needed for the elderly (☞ unit 63).

key terms

Computer aided design - the use of computers when designing products.
Computer aided manufacture - the use of computers in the manufacture of products.
Computer numerically controlled machines - machines which have their operations controlled by a computer program.

Computer integrated manufacture - the use of computers to control the entire production process.
Information technology - the recording and use of information by electronic means.
Technology - a creative process which uses human, scientific and material resources to solve problems and improve efficiency.

Knowledge

1. What is meant by technology?
2. What is the difference between invention and innovation?
3. State 4 areas of a business that might benefit from new technology.
4. How has new technology been used in marketing?
5. How might a business exporting products abroad make use of new technology?
6. How has information technology been incorporated in production?
7. How has business security used information technology?
8. Why was the Data Protection Act introduced?
9. In what ways has new technology benefited
   (a) business owners;
   (b) management?
10. Briefly explain problems that:
    (a) workers;
    (b) management;
    may face with the introduction of new technology.
11. How might business exploit the Internet?

Case study *Technology Companies*

Table 60.1 *Top Ten fastest growing unquoted technology companies*

Rank	Company	Business	Sales growth, 2000-02	2002 sales	In profit, 2002?	Founded
1	Optos	Retinal scanning developer	320%	£3.68m	No	1992
2	Trayport	Trading software developer	286%	£3.09m	Yes	1993
3	Investis	Website technology developer	268%	£2.08m	No	2000
4	KVS	E-mail storage manager	239%	£8.15m	No	1999
5	Irisys	Infrared sensor maker	230%	£1.38m	No	1996
6	Empower Interactive	Wireless messaging provider	221%	£1.56m	No	2000
7	Pinnacle Telecom	Telecoms services provider	186%	£2.74m	No	1998
8	Complinet Group	Compliance software developer	182%	£2.49m	No	1997
9	Pole Star	Tracking systems provider	181%	£1.19m	No	1998
10	Molecular Profiles	Pharmaceutical researcher	181%	£1.26m	Yes	1997

In recent years, the media has been writing off technology companies, while investors have been warned to avoid them. However, evidence suggests that many of these companies are now doing very well. Table 60.1 shows the top 10 in *The Sunday Times* ARM Tech Track 100 league table of fastest growing unquoted technology companies.

These companies, along with the rest of the top 100, have increased their sales by at least 100 per cent a year between 2000 and 2002. Average sales per company are forecast to rise by 36 per cent in 2003 from £6.8 million to £9.3 million. The league table, which was published for the third year by Fast Track, features a range of little known innovators – small companies behind the famous high street brands and cutting edge products. Three of the top ten companies are profiled over the page.

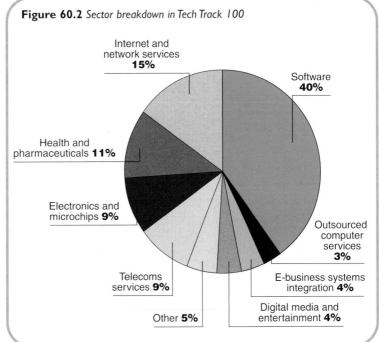

Figure 60.2 *Sector breakdown in Tech Track 100*

- Internet and network services **15%**
- Software **40%**
- Health and pharmaceuticals **11%**
- Electronics and microchips **9%**
- Telecoms services **9%**
- Other **5%**
- Digital media and entertainment **4%**
- E-business systems integration **4%**
- Outsourced computer services **3%**

Trayport

Edmund Hor bought the name Trayport for £100 and started looking for IT contract work. He had worked as a commodities and foreign exchange trader while at university, so it was no surprise when his first client was an energy broker. As a result of this work, a software application called Global Vision was developed. It was designed for online trading of energy and commodities such as coal, gas and metals. An eighth version of the software has been launched to cater for currency and credit derivatives. Trayport claims that 2,700 trading screens worldwide run its software. Its sales have grown from £207,000 in 2000 to £3.1 million in 2002, when the company reported a profit.

Empower Interactive

If you have ever played Who Wants To Be A Millionaire? on a mobile phone or sent a text message, it is likely that you have used Empower's SMS (short messaging service) technology. SMS was originally designed to send short messages between two phones. However, because of the delay in launching third generation phones, Empower is responding to the demand for more complex uses. It has high profile customers such as Orange and BT. The company managed to raise £20 million from institutional investors and sales have risen by 221 per cent to £1.6 million in 2002. The company has made significant losses since it was formed, but expected to break even in 2005.

Molecular Profiles

This company came out of Nottingham University and provides research support for the pharmaceutical and chemical industries. It investigates the level of contamination in drugs, helping manufacturers to improve their processes. It can also identify counterfeit drugs so that companies can take action against the producer. The firm's sales grew by 181 per cent a year from 2000 from £160,000 to £1.3 million in 2002. However, they are beginning to flatten out.

Source: adapted from *The Sunday Times*, 28.9.2003.

(a) **Why do you think the technology companies are described as 'innovators'? (4 marks)**
(b) **Identify the most important sector in the Tech Track 100 and suggest reasons why it dominates the technology industry at this level. (6 marks)**
(c) **Comment on the profitability of technology companies and explain two reasons for the pattern. (8 marks)**
(d) **How might these technology companies benefit (i) consumers, (ii) other businesses and (iii) the economy? (12 marks)**
(e) **Discuss possible reasons why technology companies might have been the subject of adverse publicity. (12 marks)**

Markets and the external environment

A market is any situation where buyers come into contact with sellers to exchange goods and services (☞ unit 1). The markets in which a business sells its products are part of the EXTERNAL ENVIRONMENT in which the business operates. Businesses do not operate in a vacuum. There are factors outside the business that may affect its decisions.

- The state of competition. A new competitor entering a market could lead to a reduction in the sales of existing firms.
- The labour market. The availability of low priced labour may influence the location of a business.
- Economic factors and the state of the economy. If people have more money to spend, this may encourage businesses to produce new products. If exchange rates are stable, a business may be more willing to trade on foreign markets.

Paul Merrick runs an instrument repair business. He has been successful in the local area, particularly amongst semi-professional musicians and parents wanting repairs to their children's guitars and violins. His speciality is the repair of acoustic instruments. Music retail shops can often deal with electric instruments, but may charge high prices for time consuming work on acoustic instruments.

Paul now wants to set up a workshop rather than work from home. He is likely to have to borrow money and interest rates are forecast to rise soon. The business might be eligible for a grant if Paul employs some people in the workshop, but he is unsure. He knows a few school leavers who would be keen to work for him, but they would need training. He would want to pay more than the minimum wage to motivate them, but he is aware this will raise his costs and also that there are restrictions on the length of time that employees can work. However, Paul feels that there is a growing demand, particularly in the case of cheaper instruments which tend to break more easily. And people seem to have more money to spend on leisure activities these days.

Source: adapted from company information.

(a) Using examples from the case, identify the external factors affecting the business.
(b) A friend has approached Paul. She discussed the possibility of buying guitars from the USA and selling them in this country. What external factors might Paul take into account before making a decision?

- Government objectives and government policy. If the government offers training funds, a business may be willing to employ young workers for a period. The reduction of interest rates means that businesses may borrow as they have less to pay back.
- Legislation. There might be laws that affect the product, eg controls on the ingredients that can be used in food.
- Population. The size, age and sex distribution of the population can affect demand for a product, eg an increase in the birth rate would affect firms marketing baby products.
- Social factors, eg an increase in the amount of crime directed against businesses will affect firms differently. A few, such as security firms, may benefit. Others may find that their costs increase due to, for example, higher insurance premiums.
- Political factors. A shop may change its opening hours because of the influence of a local pressure group.
- Environmental factors. Increased consumer awareness has led many firms to re-evaluate their impact upon the environment. An environmentally friendly business may spend more on waste disposal.
- Technology. The rate of change of technology may influence the type of good produced, eg the development of the microchip has made possible a whole new range of products.

One of the most important influences of markets on businesses is the way in which they help to determine prices. In all markets, buyers (often referred to as consumers) demand goods and services from sellers who supply them. It is the interaction of demand and supply within markets that determines the prices of goods or services.

Demand

Demand is the amount of a product that consumers are willing and able to purchase at any given price. Demand is concerned with what consumers are actually able to buy (what they can afford to and would buy), rather than what they would like to buy. So, for example, we could say that the demand for cars in the UK market at an average price of £9,000 might be 130,000 a year.

Table 61.1 shows a **demand schedule** for button

Table 61.1 *The demand schedule for button mushrooms*

Price per kilo (£)	Quantity demanded (000 kilos)
0.50	100
1.00	80
1.50	60
2.00	40
2.50	20

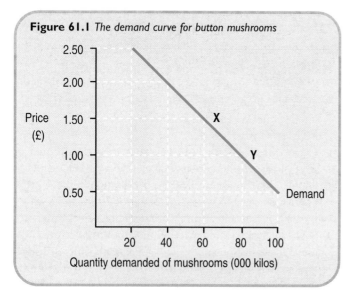

Figure 61.1 The demand curve for button mushrooms

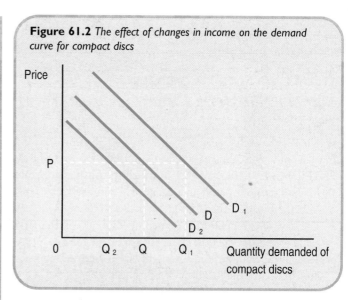

Figure 61.2 The effect of changes in income on the demand curve for compact discs

mushrooms. These figures can be used to draw a **demand curve** as in Figure 61.1. In practice, demand curves are not a straight line, but are usually drawn in this way for simplicity.

The curve shows the quantity of a good or service that will be demanded at any given price. As with nearly all such curves, it slopes downwards from left to right. This is because the quantity demanded is likely to be higher at lower prices and lower at higher prices - **ceteris paribus** (assuming no other things change). In Table 61.1 more button mushrooms are bought at a price of £0.50 than at a price of £2.50.

A change in the price of a good or service will lead to a change in the quantity demanded. This is shown on the demand curve as a movement along (up or down) the curve. In Figure 61.1, a fall in price from £1.50 to £1, for example, will result in a movement along the curve from point X to point Y.

This will result in a rise in the quantity demanded from 60,000 to 80,000 kilos. The demand curve itself has not moved from its original position. Price changes only lead to an **extension** (rise) or **contraction** (fall) in the quantity demanded.

Changes in demand

As well as price, there is a number of other factors which might affect the demand for a product. Unlike price, a change in any of these factors might cause the whole demand curve to **shift**. This might result in an increase in the demand for a good. The result is that more of a product will be demanded at any given price. Alternatively, it may result in a fall in demand, so less is demanded at any given price.

Income   It is reasonable to assume that the higher the incomes of consumers, the more they will be able to buy. When incomes in the country as a whole increase, the demand for products will increase. However, the rise in income is unlikely to be the same for everyone. Some consumers will have large increases in income. Others will find that their incomes do not increase at all. Thus, demand

for a product will only increase if the incomes of those consumers buying the product increase.

Assume that consumers of compact discs have had a rise in their income. The demand for compact discs increases as a result. This is shown in Figure 61.2 as a shift to the right of the demand curve from D to D_1. The demand for compact discs has increased at any given price level. In Figure 61.2, demand has risen from OQ to OQ_1. On the other hand, if consumers' incomes were to fall, this would cause the demand for compact discs to fall at any given price. The result of this would be a shift of the demand curve to the left from D to D_2 in Figure 61.2. Demand will have fallen from OQ to OQ_2.

The price of and demand for other goods The demand for one product often depends on the price of and demand for another. For example, the demand for one brand of tea bags can be influenced by the price of other brands. A rise in the price of one brand is likely to cause an increase in the demand for others. This is often true of products which have close **substitutes**, such as canned drinks. An increase in the price of cassette tapes may result in a shift in demand from D to D_1 in Figure 61.2. Fewer tapes would be bought if prices rose, leading perhaps to increased demand for compact discs.

Complementary goods are those which are used together. Examples include cars and petrol, and DVD players and DVDs. An increase in the price of one will affect the demand for the other. A fall in the price of compact disc players may lead to a shift in demand from D to D_1 in Figure 61.2. More players would be bought and so the quantity demanded of discs would also rise.

Changes in tastes and fashions Some products are subject to changes in tastes and fashions. Skateboards, for example, were bought in huge quantities in the 1970s. They then went out of fashion for a number of years only to come back into favour again. It is more usual for a company to stop producing products which have gone out of fashion altogether. Other products have shown more gradual changes in demand. In recent years, the demand for red meat has gradually declined as tastes have changed, often in response to health concerns. This has caused the demand curve for red meat to shift to the left. This means that at any given price, less red meat is now demanded than in previous years. The growth in CD sales over the last decade has shifted the demand curve to the right. Some have suggested that the demand curve for compact discs may shift to the left in the future as Internet access to music becomes more popular.

Changes in population As well as changes in population levels, changes in the structure of population can affect demand. The increase in the proportion of over 65s in the population of Western industrialised countries will have an effect upon the demand for a number of products. They include winter-sun holidays, sheltered housing and leisure facilities. This means that, other things staying the same, the demand curve for products associated with the old will shift to the right, with more being demanded at any given price.

Advertising Successful advertising and promotion will shift the demand curve to the right, with more being demanded at any given price. A successful advertising campaign for CDs could have this effect.

Legislation Government legislation can affect the demand for a product. For example, a law requiring all cyclists to wear helmets would lead to an increase in the demand for cycling helmets at any given price.

This section has examined the market demand for goods and services. This is a summing or totalling of the demand curves for individual businesses' products. So, for example, the market demand curve for CDs, which has been much discussed in this section, is a totalling of the individual demand curves of all the businesses which produce CDs. Unit 18 examines the demand curve for individual businesses.

Supply

SUPPLY is the amount of a product which suppliers will offer to the market at a given price. The higher the price of a particular good or service, the more that will be offered to the market. For example, the amount of button mushrooms supplied to a market in any given week may be as shown in Table 61.3.

These figures have been plotted onto a graph in Figure 61.3, which shows the supply curve for button mushrooms. The supply curve slopes up from left to right. This is because at higher prices a greater quantity will be supplied to the market and at lower prices less will be supplied.

A change in price will cause a movement either up or down the supply curve. The curve will not change its position assuming that all other factors remain the same. There is a number of other factors that may affect supply other than price. Changes in these factors will cause the whole supply curve to shift.

Costs of production A fall in the costs of production due, for

---

Table 61.2 *The demand schedule for ice cream at a local theme park*

Price (£)	Quantity demanded
0.80	2,000
0.90	1,600
1.00	1,200
1.10	800
1.20	400

Table 61.2 shows the monthly demand schedule based on the average price of ice creams at a local theme park. It has been predicted that the following changes to the market will occur:
● incomes will rise so that there will be 500 more bought at each level;
● the prices of substitute goods (ice lollies etc.) are likely to rise so that there would be another 500 bought at each price level.
(a) Draw the original demand curve from the figures in the table.
(b) Show the combined effect on the demand curve of the changes in the market.

Question 2

Table 61.3 *The supply schedule for button mushrooms*

Price per kilo (£)	Quantity supplied (000 kilos)
0.50	20
1.00	40
1.50	60
2.00	80
2.50	100

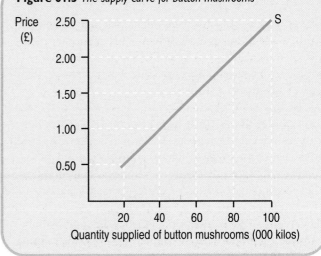

Figure 61.3 *The supply curve for button mushrooms*

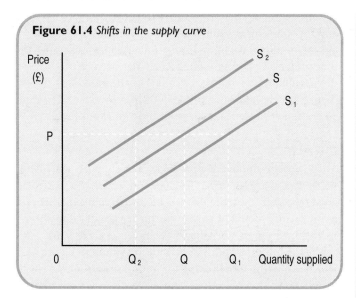

Figure 61.4 Shifts in the supply curve

example, to new technology will mean that more can be offered at the same price. This will cause the supply curve to shift to the right as shown in Figure 61.4, from S to S_1. A rise in the costs of production would cause the supply curve to shift to the left, from S to S_2. A rise in raw material costs or wage costs could lead to such a shift.

Changes in production Where it is possible to shift production from one area to another, the price of other products can influence the quantity supplied. For example, many farmers are able to produce a wide range of crops on their land. A rise in the price of broccoli, might encourage farmers not only to produce more broccoli, but less of other crops such as turnips. The broccoli price change has affected the quantity of turnips supplied to the market. So a rise in the price of broccoli would shift the supply curve for turnips to the left, in Figure 61.4 from S to S_2.

Legislation A new anti-pollution law might increase production costs causing the supply curve to shift to the left. Similarly, a tax on a product would shift the supply curve to the left.

The objectives of firms Firms might seek to increase their profit levels and their market share. This might reduce the overall level of supply as other firms are forced out of business. The result of this would be a shift of the supply curve in Figure 61.4 from S to S_2.

Expectations If businesses expect future prices to rise they may restrict current supplies. This would be shown as a shift to the left of the supply curve in Figure 61.4, from S to S_2. Similarly, if businesses expect worsening trading conditions they might reduce current supply levels in anticipation of this.

The weather The weather can influence the supply of agricultural products. For example, in the UK a late spring

frost can reduce the supply of strawberries, from say S to S_2 in Figure 61.4.

It was shown earlier in this unit that the market demand curve is a summing of individual firms' demand curves. Similarly, the market supply curve is an adding up of the supply curves of individual firms.

Price and output determination

How does the interaction of demand and supply determine the market price and output? Market prices are set where the plans of consumers are matched with those of suppliers. The point at which the demand and supply curves intersect is known as the EQUILIBRIUM PRICE. This is shown in Figure 61.5. The equilibrium price of button mushrooms is £1.50. The figure is drawn from Tables 61.1 and 61.3. At this price 60,000 mushrooms will be produced.

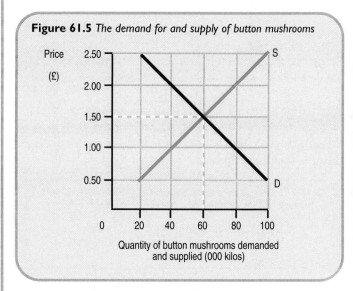

Figure 61.5 The demand for and supply of button mushrooms

Changes in demand and supply

Shifts in the demand or supply curves will cause a change in the market price.

Changes in demand Assume that there has been a rise in income which has resulted in an increase in demand. The effect of this, as shown in Figure 61.6a, is a shift in the demand curve to the right, all things remaining the same, from D to D_1. This leads to an increase in quantity demanded from OQ to OQ_1. This increase in demand raises the equilibrium price from OP to OP_1. As a result, the quantity supplied extends as well, as producers will supply more at the higher price.

If demand falls, due to lower incomes, from D to D_2, this leads to a fall in quantity demanded from OQ to OQ_2. The equilibrium price falls from OP to OP_2 and at this lower price suppliers will supply less.

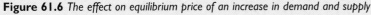

Figure 61.6 *The effect on equilibrium price of an increase in demand and supply*

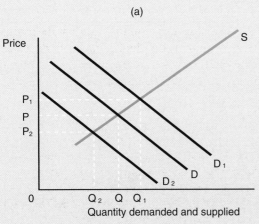

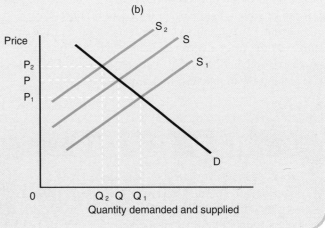

Figure 61.7 *The demand for and supply of organically grown broccoli*

(a) What is the equilibrium price of organic broccoli?
(b) Explain the effect that the following factors will have on: (i) the equilibrium price of organic broccoli; (ii) the demand for organic broccoli or the supply of organic broccoli by businesses in the market.
  ● A reduction in the average incomes of consumers purchasing organic vegetables.
  ● Improved organic farming methods leading to a reduction in the cost of producing organic broccoli.
  ● All types of organic vegetables becoming increasingly popular with greater health consciousness amongst food consumers.
  ● A fall in the price of non-organic broccoli.

Question 3

Changes in supply Figure 61.6b shows the effect on the equilibrium price of changes in supply. An increase in supply may have been as a result of lower labour costs. This shifts the supply curve from S to S_1. The equilibrium price falls from OP to OP_1 as the supply curve shifts from S to S_1. Consumers are more willing and able to buy goods at the lower price and so the quantity demanded rises as well from OQ to OQ_1.

If supply is cut, the supply curve moves to the left from S to S_2. The equilibrium price rises from OP to OP_2. Consumers are less willing to buy products at this higher price and so the quantity demanded falls from OQ to OQ_2.

Excess demand and excess supply

EXCESS DEMAND occurs when the demand for a product is greater than its supply. This can be illustrated using the demand for and supply of mushrooms shown in Figure 61.8. At a price of £0.50 per kilo, 100,000 kilos of button mushrooms are demanded, but only 20,000 kilos are supplied by businesses. This means that there is an excess demand of 80,000 kilos (100,000 - 20,000). This excess demand will result in a shortage of mushrooms, with many consumers being left disappointed.

EXCESS SUPPLY occurs when the supply of a product is greater than the demand for it. In Figure 61.8, at a price of £2.50, 100,000 kilos of button mushrooms are supplied by businesses, but only 20,000 are demanded. This means that there is an excess supply of 80,000 kilos of button mushrooms. This excess supply will result in a surplus (sometimes referred to as a glut) of button mushrooms. This

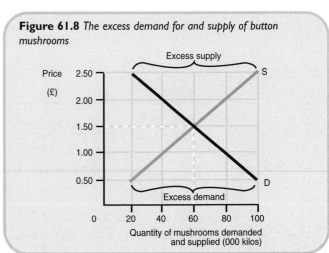

Figure 61.8 *The excess demand for and supply of button mushrooms*

will mean a huge quantity of unsold button mushrooms for businesses, with no immediate buyers.

It can be seen in Figure 61.8 that it is only at the equilibrium price, £1.50, that there is no excess demand or supply. At this price all products supplied to the market are purchased and all buyers able to afford the price of £1.50 per kilo will be able to purchase their intended quantity.

key terms

Excess demand - a situation where the quantity demanded of a product is greater than the quantity supplied at a given price.
Excess supply - a situation where the quantity supplied of a product is greater than the quantity demanded at a given price.
External environment - the factors outside a business that may influence its decisions. .
Supply - the quantity of products which suppliers make available to the market at any given price.
Equilibrium price - the price at which the quantity demanded is equal to the quantity supplied.

Table 61.4 *The demand for and supply of sunflower oil*

Price per litre (£)	Quantity demanded (Million litres)	Quantity supplied (Million litres)
0.50	800	500
0.75	700	600
1.00	600	700
1.25	500	800

(a) Draw the demand and supply diagram for sunflower oil using the figures in Table 61.4.
(b) What is the equilibrium price for sunflower oil?
(c) What will be the excess demand or excess supply of sunflower oil at the following prices?
  (i) £0.60;
  (ii) £0.90;
  (iii) £0.70;
  (iv) £1.15.

Question 4

Knowledge

1. State 6 external factors that may affect a business's decisions.
2. What happens to the amount consumers are willing and able to buy as the price of a product falls?
3. State 4 factors that cause the market demand to move to the right.
4. What happens to the amount that businesses are willing to offer to the market as price increases?
5. State 4 factors that cause the market supply curve to shift to the left.
6. What effect will a shift in demand to the left have on equilibrium price and the supply by businesses in a market?
7. What effect will a shift in supply to the right have on equilibrium price and the demand by consumers in a market?
8. What problems will excess supply cause for some businesses in a market?

Case study The price of oil

Figure 61.9 *The price of oil*

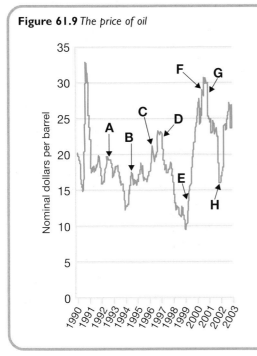

A OPEC production reaches 25.3 million barrels per day, the highest in over a decade.

B Nigerian oil workers' strike.

C Extremely cold weather in the US and Europe.

D Iraq begins exporting oil under United Nations Security Council Resolution 986.

E OPEC pledges additional production cuts for the third time since March 1998. Total pledge cuts amount to about 4.3 million barrels per day.

F USA releases 30 million barrels of oil from the Strategic Petroleum Reserve (SPR) over 30 days to bolster oil supplies, particularly heating oil in the Northeast.

G Weak world demand largely as a result of economic recession in the United States and OPEC overproduction.

H OPEC oil production cuts, unrest in Venezuela, and rising tension in the Middle East.

Figure 61.9 shows how the price of oil has fluctuated between 1990 and 2003. The price of oil on world markets is affected by many factors, as shown in the Figure.

One of the factors is the actions of OPEC, the Organisation of Petroleum Exporting Countries. This is an organisation made up of countries around the world which produce oil and sell it to businesses and other organisations in other countries. It has eleven members including Iran, Iraq, Saudi Arabia, Venezuela, Nigeria and Libya, whose economies rely heavily on income from oil exports. OPEC's primary mission is to 'achieve stable prices which are fair and reasonable for producers and consumers.'

OPEC countries meet to agree on the amount of production and supply of oil onto the world market. For example, in February 2004 OPEC agreed to stop overproducing crude at once, and then cut quotas by 1 million barrels. One problem with this is that countries do not always agree. Even when they do, some countries go back on the agreement. Another problem is that countries producing oil who are not OPEC members, such as Russia or Norway, might expand production when OPEC is trying to cut it.

Source: adapted from OPEC website and www.cbsnews.com.

(a) Who are likely to be the (i) demanders and the (ii) suppliers of oil? (6 marks)

(b) Suggest factors which are likely to affect the (i) demand for and (ii) supply of oil in world markets. (10 marks)

(c) Explain, using examples from the data, how changes in demand and supply over the period 1990-2003 have:
(i) raised the price of oil;
(ii) reduced the price of oil. (12 marks)

(d) Assess the extent to which OPEC is likely to be able to influence the world price of oil. (12 marks)

Markets and competition

Unit 61 showed how the prices of products and services can be determined by demand and supply. In market economies, the forces of demand and supply will influence prices in a wide range of different markets. These could be markets divided by geographical boundaries including:

- local markets, such as the market for houses in South London;
- regional markets, such as the market for out of town entertainment in the North West of England;
- national markets, such as the market for personal computers in the UK;
- international markets, such as foreign exchange markets.

On the other hand they could be markets differentiated by use including:

- highly specialised markets, such as the market for water polo playing equipment;
- non-specialist markets, such as the market for potatoes.

The degree of competition in a market will affect how prices are determined. Assessing the level of competition in a market is not as easy as it sounds. Two businesses operating a local bus route, for example, may seem to have little competition except each other. In fact they face competition from other forms of transport such as trains, mini buses and taxis. A new chocolate bar will face **direct** competition from other chocolate bars. But it will also face **indirect** competition from other forms of confectionery, such as crisps or sweets.

Degrees of competition

The amount of competition that exists in a market is known as the MARKET STRUCTURE. There is a number of widely recognised MODELS OF COMPETITION with different market structures. They vary according to:

- the amount of knowledge consumers have about different products;
- the ease with which firms can set up and compete within the market;
- the number of firms operating within the market;
- the extent to which rival products are different;
- the amount of control which businesses exert within their markets;
- the extent to which individual businesses can determine the price of their goods and services.

Perfect competition

The model of PERFECT COMPETITION assumes businesses produce products which are exactly the same. Consumers have 'perfect knowledge' of the market. They are aware of what is being offered by all businesses. There are no barriers to prevent firms from setting up and there is a large number of firms in competition with one another.

Businesses in such markets are known as PRICE TAKERS. Each individual firm has no influence over the price which it charges for its products. If a firm were to charge a higher price than others then no consumers would buy its products, since every product is exactly the same and they would know exactly where to go to buy an alternative. A firm that charged a price below that of others would be forced out of business.

In reality, it is not easy to identify markets which conform to the model of perfect competition. However, there are some which have many of the characteristics of a perfectly competitive market. One example in the UK could be agriculture. There are large numbers of farmers providing farm produce for the market. Farming businesses tend, generally, to be small scale and are unable to influence market price. Furthermore, it is likely that one vegetable will be much the same as another on a different farm. Information about this market is also available in trade journals.

One advantage for businesses of operating in conditions of perfect competition is that they have a strong incentive to operate efficiently. Inefficient businesses are forced out of perfectly competitive markets.

However, there are certain problems.

- Businesses only make what are known as 'normal profits'. Normal profits are relatively modest. They are only just enough to prevent new businesses being attracted to the market and existing businesses from leaving the market. Businesses operating under normal competition making

(a) Do you think the businesses producing the above products or services are competing in local, regional, national or international markets? Explain your answer.
(b) What other businesses might: (i) Abbey and (ii) McDonald's compete against?

Question 1

larger than normal profits would quickly see these profits eroded by the entrance of new businesses into the market forcing prices, and therefore profits, down.

● Businesses operating under perfect competition are not able to control their prices. This is because of the competitiveness of the markets in which they operate. Such businesses have little control over their own destinies. They are completely governed by market conditions.

It is for the above reasons that businesses prefer to operate in conditions that are less competitive than perfect competition. Wherever possible, the majority of businesses attempt to exert some control over the degree of competition in markets in which they operate.

Monopoly

MONOPOLY occurs when one business has total control over a market and is the only seller of the product. This **pure monopoly** should not be confused with a **legal monopoly**, which occurs in the UK when a firm controls 25 per cent or more of a market.

Monopolists are likely to erect barriers to prevent others from entering their market. They will also exert a strong influence on the price which they charge for their product. However, because monopolists are the only supplier of a product, it does not mean that they can charge whatever they want. If they raise the price a great deal demand will fall to some extent. Because of the influence monopolists have on their price, they are often called **price makers**.

Although there are many businesses in the UK which exert a great deal of power in the markets in which they operate, few, if any, could be described as being a pure monopoly. In the past, however, certain businesses have come close to exerting pure monopoly power. Before competitors such as Transco were able to supply gas to consumers, British Gas enjoyed a monopoly position in the gas market. It was the sole supplier of piped gas in the UK. On the other hand, it could be argued that British Gas was operating in the energy market and therefore faced competition from electricity and oil companies. One of the main reasons why British Gas no longer exerts such control over the market for gas is that the government introduced **legislation** to increase competition in markets where monopolies previously existed (☞ unit 71).

From a business's point of view monopoly has certain advantages and problems. To some extent these are the reverse of the benefits and problems of perfect competition. For example, monopolies tend to make 'abnormal' profits compared to competitive businesses. However, there may be little or no incentive for a large business to innovate if it faces a lack of competition. It may therefore be less efficient and profitable than it is capable of being, resulting in bureaucracy, inefficient management and a lower dividend for shareholders.

Monopoly, perfect competition and consumers

Businesses often attempt to restrict competition in the markets in

which they operate. This allows them to have a greater control of prices and to become more profitable. In addition, governments seek to regulate markets in order to control monopolies and protect consumers. This might suggest that competition is better for consumers than monopoly. However, under certain circumstances, consumers may benefit from monopolies.

Prices It might be expected that prices for consumers would be higher under monopolies than under perfect competition. However, monopolies can sometimes provide consumers with lower prices than businesses operating under competitive conditions. This is because the large size of many monopoly businesses allows them to gain economies of scale (☞ unit 56). Cost savings gained by operating on a large scale may allow monopolies to earn large profits. They might then set prices either lower than or the same as low profit making businesses operating under perfect competition.

Choice It could be argued that a large number of businesses competing against each other will lead to greater choice of products for customers. However, there are conditions where competition does not lead to wider choice for consumers. For

---

In January 2004 TelePassport Telecommunications, the first private telephone operator in Cyprus, pledged to reduce call rates by 15 per cent after gaining approval from the Telecommunications Regulator. Previously the only telephone company had been CyTA, a government controlled company.

TelePassport's president, Socratis Hasikos, said 'Statistics show that in 1998 CyTA made a profit of £50 million which increased to £62 million in 1999 and in 2001 reached £91 million. According to CyTA they expected to reap a profit of £107 million from the period 1998-2002, yet they earned a profit of £218 million. How can this be possible if they are not over-charging their customers? Now, they must present their costs and expenses to the Telecommunications Regulator, who has given them 15 days to do so.' He believed that CyTA delayed presenting its expenses because 'they have been paying out too much money and need to earn it back by charging more, or they have simply been ripping off customers'.

It was suggested that the entry of Cyprus into the EU would open the door to healthy competition for CyTA. Hasikos argues 'Our aim is not to attack CyTA, but to offer customers a better service at cheaper rates. Competition need not be negative, but could push CyTA into also lowering their prices.'

Source: adapted from www.xak.com.

(a) Identify and explain the type of model of competition before the entry of TelePassport Telecommunications into the market in Cyprus.
(b) Examine how (i) businesses and (ii) consumers are likely to be affected by the change in competition that is taking place in Cyprus.

Question 2

example, many believe that a wider choice of channels operated by an increasing range of television companies is not improving choice. This is because competing businesses tend to replicate the products of their competitors. In the US, consumers are faced with vast numbers of channels offering what many regard as low quality programmes.

Innovation Businesses in competitive markets have the incentive to innovate as they try to differentiate their products from those of competitors. However, the relatively large profits made by monopolies allow them to invest heavily in research and development, which could lead to innovations. Smaller businesses facing intense competition may not be able to finance this research.

Monopolistic competition

This is a market model where there is **imperfect** competition. This means that there is some restriction on competition.

MONOPOLISTIC COMPETITION exists where a large number of relatively small firms compete in an industry. There are few BARRIERS TO ENTRY, so that it is fairly easy for firms to set up and to leave these markets.

Each firm has a product that is **differentiated** from the others. This is achieved through **branding**, when a product is given an identity of its own (☞ unit 20). A business will face competition from a wide range of other firms competing in the same market with similar, but differentiated, products.

Firms operating under these conditions are not price takers, but they will only have a limited degree of control over the prices they charge. There are few markets of this kind in the UK. Two examples might be legal services and the manufacture of certain types of clothing.

Oligopoly

When there are many firms, but only a few dominate the market, OLIGOPOLY is said to exist. Examples include the markets for petrol, beer, detergents, paint and sweets. The majority of businesses in the UK operate under this type of competition.

Under oligopoly, each firm will have a differentiated product, often with a strong brand identity. Several brands may be competing in the same market. Brand loyalty amongst customers is encouraged by advertising and promotion. Firms in such markets are often said to compete in the form of non-price competition. Prices are often stable for long periods, disturbed only by short price wars.

Although brand loyalty does allow some price control, businesses often follow the price of the market leaders. This means that they tend to be interdependent.

Barriers to entry exist. If it was easy for new firms to enter the industry, they would set up and take the market share of the few large producers. Examples of barriers to entry might be:

● legal restrictions, such as patents which prevent other businesses copying products for a period of time;

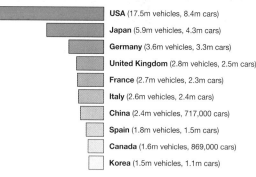

Figure 62.1 *The world's biggest automotive markets in 2001*

USA (17.5m vehicles, 8.4m cars)
Japan (5.9m vehicles, 4.3m cars)
Germany (3.6m vehicles, 3.3m cars)
United Kingdom (2.8m vehicles, 2.5m cars)
France (2.7m vehicles, 2.3m cars)
Italy (2.6m vehicles, 2.4m cars)
China (2.4m vehicles, 717,000 cars)
Spain (1.8m vehicles, 1.5m cars)
Canada (1.6m vehicles, 869,000 cars)
Korea (1.5m vehicles, 1.1m cars)

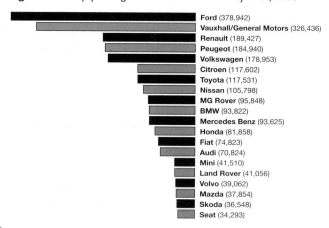

Figure 62.2 *Top passenger car brands in the UK by sales, 2003*

Ford (378,942)
Vauxhall/General Motors (326,436)
Renault (189,427)
Peugeot (184,940)
Volkswagen (178,953)
Citroen (117,602)
Toyota (117,531)
Nissan (105,798)
MG Rover (95,848)
BMW (93,822)
Mercedes Benz (93,625)
Honda (81,858)
Fiat (74,823)
Audi (70,824)
Mini (41,510)
Land Rover (41,056)
Volvo (39,062)
Mazda (37,854)
Skoda (36,548)
Seat (34,293)

Table 62.1 *The World's Top 10 automotive manufacturers, 2002*

Company	Region of origin	Global vehicle sales
General Motors	(US)	8.5m
Ford	(US)	7.0m
Toyota	(Japan)	6.2m
Volkswagen	(Europe)	5.0m
DaimlerChrysler	(US)	4.5m
PSA Peugeot-Citroen	(Europe)	3.3m
Honda	(Japan)	2.8m
Nissan	(Japan)	2.7m
Renault	(Europe)	2.4m
Fiat	(Europe)	2.1m

Source: adapted from www.mind-advertising.com.

(a) Which of the models of competition do you think best describes the motor vehicle market? Explain your answer using examples from the data.

(b) What influence might any one of the top twenty car manufacturers be likely to have on the price of cars in the UK market?

Question 3

- high start up costs, such as the cost of manufacturing;
- the promotion or advertising required, for example, in the tobacco or soap powder industries;
- arrangements between businesses, for example in the 1990s newsagents could not stock ice creams by other producers in certain manufacturers' freezers (known as freezer exclusivity);
- collusion between businesses in cartels, which act together to prevent new entrants.

Table 62.2 *A summary of the characteristics of models of competition*

	Perfect competition	Monopolistic competition	Oligopoly	Monopoly
Barriers to entry	None	Few	Many	Almost impossible for new firms to enter the market
Number of of firms	Many	Many	A few	One
Influence over price	None	Some	Strong	Very strong
Differentiated product	No	Yes	Strong brands	No competition; not necessary

Porter's five forces analysis

The models of competition outlined above provide a useful means of describing markets. It can be argued, however, that they project businesses as being largely passive, simply accepting the constraints of their market structures. Michael Porter (1980) in his book *Competitive Strategy*, suggested that in certain circumstances businesses can influence the markets in which they operate. He outlined five forces that determine the extent to which businesses are able to manage competition within their markets.

Rivalry among competitors Porter argues that competitive rivalry is the main force that affects the ability of businesses to influence markets. This includes:

- the number of competitors - the more competitors the less likely it is that a business will be able to have influence;
- their ability to differentiate products - a promotional campaign by a business to differentiate its product will increase its influence;
- the rate of growth of the market - in a fast growing market competition may be less intense and individual firms will have more scope to influence the market;
- the existence of barriers to exit - competition may be intense in markets where businesses are deterred from leaving the market. Exit barriers may include the costs of

high redundancy payments or losses as a result of having to sell machinery at reduced prices.

The threat of new entrants The number of businesses in a market may not always be a useful guide to competition in that market. This may also depend on the ability of businesses to enter the market. If it is easy for businesses to enter markets then competition is likely to be greater. This will restrict the ability of a business to influence the market. It is possible that businesses may be prevented or deterred from entering markets due to barriers to entry. For example, the need to invest heavily in new plant and machinery or to match high levels of promotional spending could deter new businesses from entering a market.

Glamour magazine is leader of the women's monthly magazine market. Its closest rival, *Cosmopolitan*, is one pound more expensive. *Glamour* is seen by many as being younger, funkier and more celebrity orientated, with stars such as Jennifer Lopez on its front cover. *InStyle* and *Company*, although experiencing sales increases, cannot match the 537, 474 sales achieved by Glamour. The older women's market is not looking quite so healthy with declining or static sales for *Good Housekeeping* and *Prima*. The so-called 'middle youth market' has *Red*, *She* and *Eve* competing for customers, while the market for more intelligent upmarket women's glossies is fought for between *Marie Claire* and *Vogue*.

Source: adapted from *The Guardian*, 13.2.2003.

(a) Using Porter's five force analysis, examine *Glamour's* ability to manage competition in the market for women's monthly magazines.

The threat of substitute products This depends upon the extent to which businesses can differentiate their products from those of competitors. A business which struggles to differentiate its products is likely to face intense competition. This is why businesses spend large sums of money attempting to make their products different or seem different from those of competitors. For example, the success of a chain of pizza restaurants may depend on its ability to appear to offer a style of pizza that others do not.

The bargaining power of customers Where customers are strong, there is likely to be more competition between producers and their influence will tend to be weaker. The factors affecting the power of consumers may be:
● the number of customers;
● whether they act together;
● their importance, for example, large supermarket chains have had great influence over food manufacturers;
● their ability to switch products;
● regularity of purchases, for example, consumers on holiday are often 'one-off' purchasers prepared to pay a higher price.

The bargaining power of suppliers Powerful suppliers can increase the costs of a business and decrease the extent to which it can control its operations. The power of suppliers is likely to depend upon the number of suppliers able to supply a business and the importance in the production process of the product being supplied. For example, if a JIT manufacturer can easily switch supplier, the producer will have greater control of the production process.

key terms

Barriers to entry - factors that might deter or prevent businesses from entering a market.
Market structure - the characteristics of a market which determine the behaviour of firms operating within it.
Model of competition - a simplified theory to explain the types of competition between businesses.
Monopolistic competition - a market structure with freedom of entry and exit, differentiated products and a large number of small firms competing.
Monopoly - a market structure in which only one firm supplies the entire output, there is no competition and barriers to entry exist.
Oligopoly - a market structure with a small number of dominant firms, producing heavily branded products with some barriers to entry.
Perfect competition - a market structure with perfect knowledge, many buyers and sellers, freedom of entry and exit and a homogeneous product.
Price taker - a firm that is unable to influence the price at which it sells its products.

Knowledge ...Knowledge...Knowledge...Knowledge...Knowledge...Know

1. Explain the difference between a local and an international market.
2. What determines the amount of discretion firms have in making their pricing decisions?
3. What is the difference between a price taker and a price maker?
4. What are the 4 models of market competition?
5. Under what conditions might a firm be unable to influence the price it sets for its product?

Case study The UK market for magazines

In 2004, the most fascinating magazine battle for years was about to take place. IPC, a part of AOL Time Warner, was about to launch its newest magazine, *Nuts*. This would be a direct competitor for *Zoo*, published by its rival Emap. IPC forecast that it would sell more than 200,000 copies a week, nearly as much as IPC's *Loaded* magazine sells in a month. The company predicted that it would be surprised if it didn't exceed this.

IPC's chief executive Sylvia Auton said that '... strategies that have served us well over the decades are not going to get us to where we want to go'. IPC is number one or two in 10 of its 16 key areas. But it perhaps lacks a 'wow' title like Emap's *Heat* or Conde Nast's *Glamour*. It does have a proud track record. *Loaded* perhaps defined the male lifestyle magazine in the 1990s. *What's on TV* defined the budget listings sector and now has sales of nearly 1.7 million over a six month period. *Loaded*, however, slipped to fifth in its area in 2003 while clubbers' magazine *Muzik* shut up after sales fell below 40,000. *Now's* top spot in the celebrity sector is also under threat. In the first half of last year its lead over *Heat* was down to just 25,000 copies.

The 'wow' title IPC is looking for could be *Nuts*. It's marginally more upmarket than its competitor *Zoo*. It concentrates more on cars and men's gadgets than its competitor. IPC also says 'It was determined not to do something derivative' and that *Nuts* is a 'blend and mix of content. It's entertaining and amusing'. IPC and Emap are clearly knocking lumps out of each other. 'It has to be a good thing for the magazine market' says IPC editorial director Mike Soutar.

And then there is Richard Desmond's celebrity title *New!* It came from nowhere to sell 340,000 copies in the first six months. Soutar says 'he's changed the ... newspaper industry and now he is trying to do the same with magazine. In a growing market you can steal market share, but if it's going to be sustainable then it has to be different from its rivals'.

Source: adapted from *The Guardian*, 9.2.2004.

Table 62.3 *Top selling IPC titles, Jan-June 2003*

What's on TV	1,689,621
Now	590,544
Chat	575,585
Woman	571,482
TV Times	529,632
Woman's Own	484,705
Woman's Weekly	465,500
Marie Claire	376,476

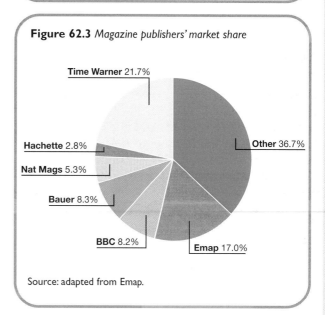

Figure 62.3 *Magazine publishers' market share*

Time Warner 21.7%
Other 36.7%
Hachette 2.8%
Nat Mags 5.3%
Bauer 8.3%
BBC 8.2%
Emap 17.0%

Source: adapted from Emap.

(a) (i) Are the magazines mentioned in the article selling into a local, national or international market? **(2 marks)**
   (ii) Suggest why they might be selling into this market. **(6 marks)**
(b) Identify the model of competition which best explains the market for magazine publishing and describe the characteristics of the market using examples. **(12 marks)**
(c) Examine how this type of competition might affect (i) businesses producing magazines and (ii) consumers of magazines. **(10 marks)**
(d) Assess the extent to which a new business might be able to enter the market in this type of competition. **(10 marks)**

The influence of population on business

People are vital to the operation of businesses. They provide organisations with labour. People also demand the goods and services that businesses produce. Changes in total population can affect businesses. A growing population is likely to place greater demand on a country's resources. Businesses are also affected by the structure of the population of the markets within which they operate. A higher proportion of people who are elderly means greater need for support. This unit considers the main trends in these DEMOGRAPHIC FACTORS and how they influence the operation of businesses.

Population size and business

In 2004 the world's population was estimated to be 6.3 billion people. Forecasts by the United Nations in 2004 cut 400 million from the estimate of the world's population in 2050. It expected 8.9 billion people on Earth in 2050, rather than the 9.3 billion forecast in 2002. This was due to the effect of falling birth rates and other factors such as illness in certain countries.

Different countries have different population sizes. Their

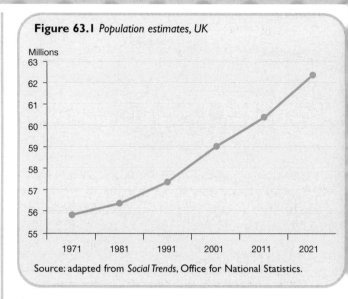

Figure 63.1 *Population estimates, UK*

Source: adapted from *Social Trends*, Office for National Statistics.

populations also grow at different rates. For example, the UK's population in 2004 was estimated to be around 59.2 million. Figure 63.1 shows predictions for population growth to the period from 1971 to 2021. The figures suggest that the population would increase by around 5.5 per cent from 2002 to 2021. Population growth in the UK was around 0.1-0.3 per cent per annum in the early twenty first century. In contrast,

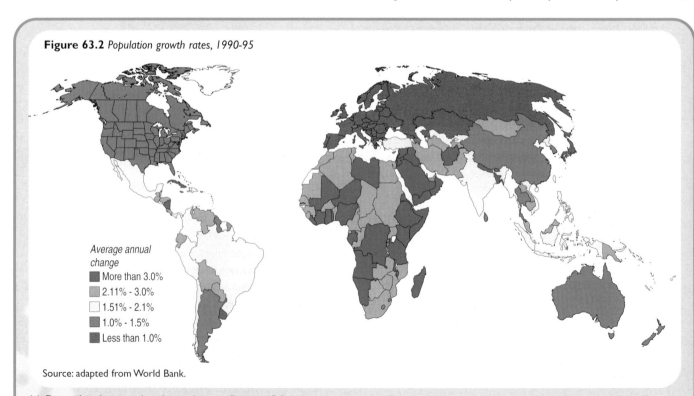

Figure 63.2 *Population growth rates, 1990-95*

Average annual change
- More than 3.0%
- 2.11% - 3.0%
- 1.51% - 2.1%
- 1.0% - 1.5%
- Less than 1.0%

Source: adapted from World Bank.

(a) Describe the trends taking place in Figure 63.2.
(b) Using this information, explain the possible benefits and problems for businesses based in (i) Africa and (ii) eastern europe.

Question 1

Somalia, with a population of 9.2 million, had an annual population growth rate of 3.2 per cent.

What effect might a growing population have on businesses?

- There is likely to be greater demand for goods and services.
- There is likely to be a larger pool of labour.
- There may be growing pressure on resources, if population growth is greater than the growth in output.

The factors affecting population growth and business

What factors might determine the growth of a country's population and how might this affect businesses? It is suggested that there are three main factors which affect population growth - births, deaths, and migration. Table 63.1 shows how these factors can affect the UK population, both in the past and in the future.

Table 63.1 *Factors affecting population changes, UK*

				Thousands
	1981-91	1991-2002	2002-11	2011-21
Population at start	56,357	57,439	59,207	60,524
Live births	757	725	681	704
Deaths	655	628	612	617
Net natural change	103	96	69	86
Net migration	43	66	100	100
Overall change	146	163	169	186

Source: adapted from *Social Trends*, Office for National Statistics.

The number of births If nothing else changes, a greater number of births will increase the population of a country. A larger number of births may affect businesses in a number of ways. This is discussed in the next section.

The number of deaths If nothing else changes, a smaller number of deaths should increase the population. Furthermore, changes in the number of years people are expected to live can affect businesses. This is also discussed in the next section.

Migration NET MIGRATION is the difference between the number of people entering a country (immigration) and the number leaving (emigration). **Positive** net migration occurs when more people enter the country than leave it. **Negative** net migration occurs when more people leave the country than enter it.

Changes in immigration and emigration might affect businesses in a country in a number of ways.

- **Immigration.** The effect of immigration on the demand for a business's products may depend upon the age and income levels of immigrants and where they settle. For example, parts of North London reflect immigration from Arab countries. A range of businesses, such as restaurants and supermarkets, have emerged to meet the needs of those settling in that area. The effects of immigration upon labour supply may depend upon the need for businesses to recruit the skills that immigrants possess. Where there are labour shortages, immigration can be a way of filling vacancies. The National Health Service, for example, has often relied upon immigrants to fill posts. Immigrants may also possess entrepreneurial skills which will help them to set up their own businesses.
- **Emigration.** This occurs when people leave a country. Large scale emigration from certain areas or by certain age groups can affect demand for businesses serving particular parts of the country or age groups. Emigration can also affect the pool of qualified workers that businesses can choose from. There are two reasons for this. First, emigrants tend to be mainly young people between the ages of 20 and 40. They are more likely to possess the energy and up-to-date skills and knowledge most in demand by businesses. Second, many emigrants from the UK are amongst the most highly skilled and able employees. They are likely to be tempted away by offers of better salaries and conditions elsewhere.

Age distribution of the population and business

POPULATION STRUCTURE is concerned with the breakdown or distribution of the population according to a variety of categories. This age distribution of the UK population looks at the numbers of people in the total population that fall into different age groups.

The birth rate, death rate and net migration from a country can all affect the age distribution of the population. Changes in these factors can affect businesses in a number of ways.

Birth rate The BIRTH RATE is measured by the number of live births per thousand of the population. The birth rate varies according to many factors. For example, in the UK in the 1970s there was a decline in the birth rate, perhaps due to better contraception and a growing number of women choosing to go out to work. The growing number of births in the 1980s may have been due to the larger number of women of child bearing age. In the late 1990s the birth rate fell. Women in their twenties were having 1.3 children on average, compared to 1.9 thirty years earlier. In the early twenty first century the birth rate in the UK, as in other developed countries, was rising slightly. This was predicted to continue to around 2021, when it would fall again.

How might a fall in the birth rate affect businesses?

- It could be argued that the fall in the birth rate in the 1970s should have led to a decline in the demand for baby products. However, increases in real incomes may have offset this, so that businesses selling baby products have continued to be successful.

● A decline in the birth rate does have consequences for the future supply of labour. Falls in the birth rate can lead to a 'demographic timebomb', with shortages of young workers available to businesses. The low number of births in the 1970s led to a smaller proportion of teenagers and people in their 20s in the 1990s. It was suggested that there could be labour shortages in the 1990s as a result. The recession in the early 1990s and falls in demand prevented this to some extent.

● Falls in the birth rate can lead to lower school numbers. This may be reflected in a fall in demand for teachers and for school materials.

An increase in the birth rate may also affect businesses. After the Second World War (1945) there was a large increase in the birth rate. These 'baby boomers' were approaching middle age in the early twenty first century. Many businesses attempted to target these groups. For example, record companies reissued music on CD that these people may have listened to when they were younger, hoping for them to buy again.

The death rate The DEATH RATE is the number of deaths per thousand of the population. The death rate in the UK and other EU nations has been declining steadily since the end of the Second World War. Combined with increases in the population as a whole in the UK, the decline in the death rate has meant steadily increasing numbers of people in older age categories. It is suggested that the number of people aged 60 and above will continue to increase in the future. The UK is said to have an **ageing population**. This means that there is a growing number of older people as a proportion of the population. What will be the effects of this ageing population?

● Changing patterns of demand. Some elderly people enjoy relatively high retirement incomes. This means that the demand for goods and services associated with the elderly is likely to increase. There could be increasing demand for leisure activities for the elderly, medical products, sheltered housing and specialist household goods. An example of a business which has benefited from this change is Saga holidays. It began by specialising in vacations for over 50s. Now it has expanded its activities into financial services.

● Effects on the labour market. Advances in medicine, better sanitation and housing and increasing affluence have all led to people living longer and healthier lives. One of the side effects of this has been an increasing pool of labour amongst those in their 50s, 60s and even 70s.

● Effects on government. An ageing population is likely to mean more demand for state provided services like hospitals and provisions such as bus passes and state

pensions. There is also likely to be a need to raise more money from those in work, for example by taxation, to pay for those who are retired. There will be a rise in the DEPENDENCY RATIO. This is the proportion of dependants or non-workers to workers.

Migration If large numbers of younger or older people are emigrating from or immigrating to a country, this can affect its age distribution. For example, the emigration of large numbers of younger people from a country will tend to leave it with an older population, as discussed in the previous section.

Gender distribution of the population and business

There is a higher proportion of women in the UK population than men. In the early twenty first century these ratios were 51.1 per cent and 48.9 per cent. This is despite the fact that more boys than girls are born in the UK. The main reason for this is that the death rate is higher for men than for women. On average, women live longer than men. This means that there are higher proportions of women in older age groupings.

Table 63.2 shows that over the age of 65, there is a greater population of women than men. The gender imbalance amongst younger age groupings is far less marked. Providing services for older, often single women may represent an increasingly important market for businesses. A change in the ratio of men to women may also affect the birth rate. Fewer women may mean fewer children are born.

Although not directly related to the gender distribution, arguably the single biggest change for businesses in this area has been the increasing number of women entering the labour market. Businesses are increasingly targeting women in their marketing of products such as cars and electrical goods. Women are also obtaining senior posts in management and becoming a relatively larger part of the workforce. Businesses have to respond to this in their recruitment and provision of facilities for women (☞ unit 50).

Table 63.2 *Population by gender and age, percentages, UK 2002*

	-16	16-24	25-34	35-44	45-54	55-64	65-74	75+	Total (m)
Males	21	12	14	15	13	11	8	6	28.9
Females	19	11	14	15	13	11	9	9	30.3

Source: adapted from *Social Trends*, Office for National Statistics.

Figure 63.3 *Economic activity rates of males and females, UK, percentages*

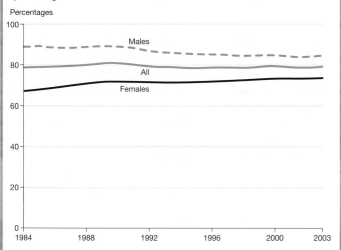

Figure 63.4 *Economic activity rates of male and females by age, UK, percentages*

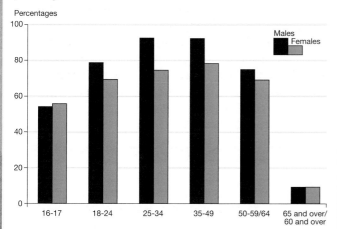

Source: adapted from *Social Trends*, Office for National Statistics.

(a) Identify the trends taking place in the data.
(b) Comment on the advert in the light of these trends.

Geographical distribution of population and business

The movement of people between countries is called migration. The location and movement of people within a country may also affect businesses. In the 1990s and after the year 2000 there were a number of trends in the UK population that could have affected businesses.

● Urban and rural location. In Great Britain, almost 90 per cent of people lived in urban areas in the 1990s. In recent years this trend has been reversed in certain parts of the country. For example, there have been noticeable declines in the population of some inner cities. The South East of England experienced the largest net percentage gain in population. In future some cities might see an increase in population as a result of inner city centre developments, such as those in Liverpool to coincide with its status as European Capital of Culture in 2008.

● Age and location. In general, younger people are more likely to live in urban areas than older people. In the 1990s 41 per cent of the population under 30 lived in urban areas, compared to 36 per cent in rural areas.

● Age and migration. Young people tend to have higher mobility than older people.

How might businesses have been affected? It is possible that businesses may react to demand by younger people in cities. For example, in Inner London house builders have responded to these changes by building houses and flats suited to the needs of younger people. Their marketing of these developments has been geared to the needs of younger buyers. The movement out from cities may encourage support businesses or entertainment to locate in semi-rural or urban fringe areas. Examples may be multiplex cinemas, shopping malls and family orientated pubs.

Other changes in the structure of the population

Households One of the most significant changes in the structure of the population has been changes in the households within which people live. Increasingly people are living in smaller units, especially one person households, and less in extended and nuclear family groups. This has been the result of increases in the number of divorces and older people living longer after their partners have died. Businesses may be able to cater for the needs of people in these groups by developing fast, microwavable food, single accommodation or singles holidays, for example.

Ethnic minority groups The age structure of ethnic minority groups may vary. For example, people from black groups other than Black African and Black Caribbean are more likely than people from the Chinese group to have been born in the UK. Certain ethnic groups have a younger age structure. 45 per cent of Bangladeshis in the UK are under the age of 16, for instance.

1. What does the population growth rate show?
2. Suggest 3 effects of a growing population on businesses.
3. State 3 factors that affect population size and growth.
4. What happens to population if net migration is negative?
5. How might immigration affect businesses?
6. State 2 factors that might cause a fall in the birth rate.

7. How might a fall in the birth rate affect a business?
8. State 2 benefits to a business of an ageing population.
9. How might a larger proportion of women than men affect population?
10. State 2 other features of the structure of population that might affect a business.

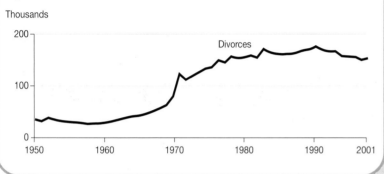

Figure 63.5 *Divorces, UK, thousands*

Table 63.3 *Households by size, UK, percentages*

	1971	1981	1991	2001	2003
One person	18	22	27	29	29
Two people	32	32	34	35	35
Three people	19	17	16	16	15
Four people	17	18	16	14	14
Five people	8	7	5	5	5
Six or more	6	4	2	2	2

Source: adapted from *Social Trends*, Office for National Statistics.

(a) Identify the trends taking place in the data.
(b) Examine how these trends might have affect businesses in the UK.

Question 3

key terms

Birth rate - the number of live births per thousand of the population.
Death rate - the number of deaths per thousand of the population.
Demographic factors - features of the size, location and distribution of the population.
Dependency ratio - the proportion of dependants or non-

workers to workers.
Net migration - the difference between the number of people entering a country (or region) and the number leaving it.
Population structure - the breakdown of the people in a country into groups based on differences in age, gender, geographical location etc.

Case study The future of the UK population

The UK population is predicted to increase more rapidly than before and peak at more than 65 million in 2051. Almost all the growth will be among older people and the working age population will start to decline within the next twenty years. This will leave the UK increasingly dependent on immigrants to maintain its economic vitality. 'Immigration is one part of ensuring the continued success of the UK economy and supporting an ageing population,' said Beverley Hughes the then Home Office Minister.

The number of people of working age is expected to rise to 37.8 million by 2011. Partly this is due to the raising of the retirement age for women to 65. By 2021 the working population will be 39.4 million, but after it will start to fall.

The total UK population is predicted to increase to 64.8 million in 2031. The number of children under 16 is projected to fall by 7.4 per cent from 2002 to 2014. The number of people of state pensionable age is projected to increase by 11.9 per cent from 2002 to 2011. These projections suggest a big change in the balance between generations. In 2002 there were about 850,000 more children than pensioners. From 2007 pensioners will be in the majority and by 2031 they will exceed the number of children by about 4 million.

Source: adapted from *The Guardian*, 2003.

(a) **Outline the main population trends in the UK from the data. (8 marks)**

(b) **Explain possible reasons to explain why these trends have occurred. (10 marks)**

(c) **Examine the effects of each of these trends on the supply of labour to businesses. (10 marks)**

(d) **Assess, in future, how businesses might change their products and services to take advantage of these trends. (12 marks)**

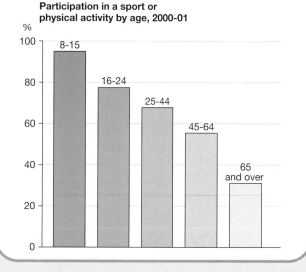

Figure 63.6 *Population data, UK*
Source: adapted from Office for National Statistics.

Interest in television programme type by age, 2002

	16-24	25-64	65 and over
News	83	94	97
Factual	69	87	84
Drama	75	80	87
Entertainment	89	76	70
Regional	50	72	85
Current affairs	57	68	79
Educational	45	61	52
Sports	51	54	53
Arts	30	33	43
Children's	41	33	17
Religious	11	19	51

The economy and government

Unit 61 explained that a number of external factors can affect businesses. One of these factors is the economy in which the businesses operate. Changes in the economy can affect how businesses make decisions. For example, a growing economy, with increased spending by consumers, may encourage a business to expand production. Governments often attempt to influence the economy in order to achieve their objectives. The activities of government can also influence businesses.

The business cycle

Economies tend to grow over a period of time. This is known as **economic growth** (☞ unit 69). Growth can be measured by changes in national income. National income is the total amount of income, output or spending in the economy. It can be measured in a number of ways, including GROSS DOMESTIC PRODUCT (GDP) and GROSS NATIONAL PRODUCT (GNP).

Output does not grow smoothly. It tends to fluctuate, going through 'ups and downs'. These short term fluctuations are known as the BUSINESS CYCLE. It is argued that all economies go through these cycles which illustrate fluctuations in the level of activity in the economy.

Figure 64.1 shows a traditional business cycle. There are four parts to the business cycle, indicated on the diagram. The broken line shows the long-term path of economic growth.

Boom In a BOOM (also called a peak) consumer spending and investment will be high. Many businesses will experience high levels of demand from people with increasing incomes. Profits should be high for most firms and wages might be rising. Output will be high and the economy will be growing

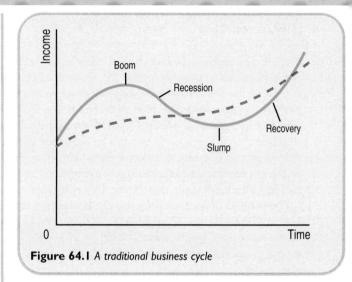

Figure 64.1 A traditional business cycle

steadily. Business and consumer confidence is also likely to be high.

Recession A RECESSION (also called a downturn, downswing or economic slowdown) is where incomes and output start to fall. Business might experience a fall in demand for their products and a decline in profit. Some might start to lay off workers.

Slump A SLUMP (also called a depression) occurs at the bottom of the cycle. Unemployment is likely to be high and confidence, spending, investment and profits low. Many firms may be forced out of business. Sometimes, when growth is taking place, but only very slowly, this is also called a recession.

Recovery A RECOVERY (also called an expansion or upswing) is where income starts to rise again after a slump. Output will begin to increase as spending and confidence

Table 64.1 *Effects of the business cycle*

	Sales	Output	Wages	Profit	Confidence	Unemployment	Spending	Prices	Imports	Start-ups/ closures	Investment/stocks
Boom	High	High	Rising fast	High	Strong	Low	Strong	Rises above average	Rise above average	Many start ups/ few closures	High
Recession	Falling	Falling	Rises slow down	Falling or losses	Weakening	Rising	Falling	Rises slow down	Falling	Start ups fall/ closures increase	Falling
Slump	Low	Low	Little or no rise	Losses	Weak	High	Weak	Rises below average, none or may fall	Low	Few start ups/ many closures	Low
Recovery	Rising	Rising	May rise	Rising	Rising	Falling	Start to rise	Start to rise	May rise	Start ups rise/ fewer closures	Start to rise

increases. Businesses will start to employ more workers as a result.

The different stages of the cycle have many different types of effect on business. These are shown in Table 64.1.

Causes of changes in the business cycle

What causes these fluctuations in the level of economic activity? A number of factors have been suggested.

Changes in investment Investment in machinery and equipment, for example, can have a major effect on the business cycle.

In a boom period spending by customers will be high and businesses will be investing and expanding output. But there is likely to be a ceiling or limit to this. Workers might not be available to hire due to high employment levels. There might be delays in meeting high demand and some investment might be unused. Eventually, businesses will cut back on investment. Interest rates might also be raised in periods of growth to prevent price rises. Higher interest rates are also likely to make businesses cut back on investment.

When investment starts to fall, this has many effects. Businesses making machines and equipment lay off workers. Wages and spending fall as a result, leading to further job losses and cuts in income and spending. Confidence in business is also likely to fall. Higher interest rates discourage borrowing, which also cuts spending and income. So falls in investment can lead to a multiplied reduction in AGGREGATE DEMAND, which brings about a recession.

On the other hand, in a slump there is likely to be a floor below which investment will no longer fall. The need to replace worn out machines and low interest rates will encourage investment. This generates jobs and spending, leading to even larger increases in income. Confidence increases and the economy then starts to recover.

Stock levels Changes in stocks can also influence the business cycle. Businesses hold stocks of materials or finished goods to respond quickly to demand from customers (☞ unit 57).

In a boom businesses will have expanded their stock to meet demand. However, if there is a slight fall in demand this might indicate to a business that it needs to hold less stock. The business will then reduce its stock levels or **destock**. This can have a major effect on other businesses. Suppliers will have fewer orders and their output may fall. They may lay off workers and spend less themselves. This will all lead to a fall in spending and output in the economy, leading to a recession.

In a slump, eventually, a business will have reduced its stock to its lowest level. It will then need to buy new stocks. Slight increases in demand may also fuel spending on increased stocks. This will help the economy to recover.

Durables Consumer durables can also affect the business

cycle. Consumer durables are products such as cars or washing machines which can be used many times and are only used up, or consumed, over a number of years. Consumers are able to delay or bring forward spending on these products.

In a recession, for example, consumers' incomes may be low. They may decide to put off buying a new car. This means that spending may fall, leading to a slump. However, eventually people will need to replace their worn out washing machines and cookers. And in a slump, interest rates are likely to be low which could encourage spending. Both of these might generate an increase in output in the economy and lead to recovery.

In a recovery period, with incomes rising, people might bring forward spending on consumer durables, helping a boom in the economy. In a boom period interest rates are likely to be high to prevent inflation. This may reduce demand, which could lead to recession.

Table 64.2 shows the government's statistics on the number of new businesses registering and deregistering for VAT. This data can be used as a guide to the number of new businesses starting up and the number of existing businesses closing down.

Table 64.2 *VAT registrations and deregistrations; United Kingdom; 1986-2001*

	Numbers registering	Numbers deregistering	Net change
1986	193,754	169,068	
1987	211,793	172,581	
1988	245,802	179,651	
1989	258,838	181,005	
1990	239,107	191,838	
1991	204,564	209,844	
1992	187,000	226,000	
1993	191,000	213,000	
1994	168,240	188,140	
1995	163,960	173,230	
1996	168,200	156,965	
1997	182,600	164,500	
1998	186,300	155,900	
1999	178,500	172,000	
2000	183,000	177,100	
2001	175,500	162,700	

Source: adapted from *Labour Market Trends*, Office for National Statistics.

(a) Complete the net change column in the table above and using the data, identify:
 (i) a boom year;
 (ii) a slump year.
(b) What evidence is there that the economy was moving out of recession in 1996? Explain your answer.
(c) Why might the number of business start-ups and closures be a good guide to the state of the economy?

Question 1

Government objectives

Businesses and consumers have an expectation that governments will try to solve economic problems. The success, or otherwise, of government policies will affect a business's external environment. For example, if a business is thinking of expanding, its decision will be affected by future inflation, which may raise the price of components needed to produce goods. Government policy which controls inflation will result in a more stable climate and will allow the businesses to expand with confidence. So if the government is able to meet its objectives, it is likely to create an environment where businesses are also successful. It is argued that governments have some common economic objectives.

Control of inflation Inflation is a rise in the general level of prices. Some are rising and some may be falling, but overall prices are increasing. Governments usually set **target rates** at which they want to keep inflation. In practice, the targets which governments set themselves often depend upon the inflation rate from previous years. In the years after 2000 in the UK, inflation targets were set at 2.5 per cent. This reflected the relatively low inflation in that period.

Governments aim to achieve an inflation rate at or below the level of their competitors. An inflation rate which is higher than those of competitors can mean higher prices for exports and a loss of sales by UK businesses to those of other countries. Inflation can also restrict a government's ability to achieve its other economic objectives. The problems that inflation can cause for business are dealt with in unit 98.

Employment Full employment occurs when all who want a job have one at a given wage rate. It is suggested that the UK came closest to achieving this between 1950 and 1970 when the rate of unemployment never reached above 4 per cent (about one million unemployed). After that unemployment rose through the 1980s and 1990s, but declined again in the early twenty first century.

The level of unemployment in an economy can be seen as an indicator of its success. A falling rate may show an economy doing well. Firms employ extra workers to produce more goods and services and new businesses set up in order to take advantage of opportunities which may occur. A rising unemployment rate, on the other hand, could indicate an economy which is in recession. Firms will be making some of their employees redundant. Others may be closing down and new ventures will be put their ideas on ice until conditions improve. Unemployed people will have less to spend and this will affect firms' revenue and profits. The effects of unemployment on business are dealt with in unit 67.

Economic growth Economic growth (☞ unit 69) is said to exist if there is a rise in economic activity. This is often measured by increases in gross domestic product (GDP). Most governments judge the overall performance of an economy by the figures for growth. Economic growth is good for most businesses. A growing economy should mean that trading conditions are favourable and that there are new business opportunities. However, there is another view that growth harms the environment and that sustaining growth in the long term may be impossible as the world's resources begin to run out.

A growth rate of 3-4 per cent per year may be considered good in Western economies. But some countries such as Malaysia, China, Vietnam and Uganda experienced average annual growth rates of between 5-10 per cent in the 1990s.

The balance of payments Governments usually attempt to achieve equilibrium or a surplus on the current account of the balance of payments (☞ unit 68). This would mean that the value of exports going out of a country is either the same as or greater than the value of imports coming into a country. At worst they would aim to prevent a long term deficit on the current account of the balance of payments. This occurs when the value of imports exceeds the value of exports. The problem with a current account deficit is that it must be financed either by borrowing from abroad or by running down savings. For one or two years this may not be a problem, but if the deficit persists then the country's debts will increase.

Government policy to prevent a balance of payments deficit can have a major effect on business and is dealt with in unit 105.

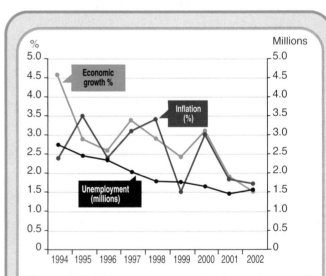

Figure 64.2 *Inflation, economic growth and unemployment, uk*
Source: adapted from *Labour Market Trends, Annual Abstract of Statistics,* ONS.

(a) Compare the relationship between:
  (i) inflation and economic growth;
  (ii) unemployment and economic growth;
  in the UK between 1994 and 2002.
(b) Discuss to what extent the government has met its objectives for inflation, unemployment and economic growth over this period.

Question2

It may be difficult for a government to achieve all of its objectives at the same time. For example, say that the government was concerned about the level of inflation. It may try to reduce spending in the economy to keep prices down. However, reduced spending may lead to fewer sales of products and some businesses may have to make workers unemployed (☞ unit 67). The government may then have to find other ways of encouraging businesses to create jobs. If unemployment continues to rise, the government may have been been successful in controlling inflation, but not in preventing rising unemployment.

On the other hand the success in meeting objectives may be relative, compared with other periods. For example, unemployment may rise from 1.1 to 1.2 million over the period of a year. It might still be argued that a government has been relatively successful in meeting its longer term objective if unemployment had been 3 million three years earlier.

Governments and business

In order to achieve their objectives and create a climate in which businesses can prosper, governments are involved in a number of activities. These activities often influence business behaviour.

Taxation In order to finance their spending on health, welfare and education governments tax individuals and businesses (☞ unit 65). In the UK, sole traders such as window cleaners pay **income tax**, a tax on their earnings. Companies also pay tax. **Corporation tax** is a tax on profits made by businesses. **Value added tax** is a tax which is a percentage of the price of the product. Businesses are affected by the amount of taxes which individual consumers pay. The levels of these taxes can be an important factor in determining how much consumers have to spend on the goods and services provided by businesses.

Spending and borrowing The levels and direction of government spending can affect businesses in a number of ways.

● Reductions or increases in payments to older people or changes in old age pensions will alter the income of older groups. Business targeting older people may benefit as a result.

● Governments may spend directly. Expenditure on road building or hospitals might lead to an increase in revenue for contractors and employment for skilled labour. Incentives for businesses to employ and train workers, such as the New Deal in the UK (☞ unit 49), might encourage businesses to employ young workers.

● The government might provide incentives for private industry to help improve the efficiency of the health service, for example.

If a government spends more than it receives it is said to have a **budget deficit**. It will then have to borrow. In the UK the

amount borrowed by government is known as the **public sector net cash requirement** (PSNCR).

Spending, taxation and borrowing are important aspects of FISCAL POLICY. This is the means by which governments attempt to control the level of total spending in the economy.

Money and interest rates Governments are concerned with the amount of money circulating in the economy. The government in the UK has given responsibility for the control of interest rates, part of MONETARY POLICY, to the Bank of England. The decisions made by the Bank of England on the level of interest rates can have a great impact upon businesses. A fall in interest rates might encourage businesses to borrow as they have less to pay back in interest.

Trading and relations with other countries Countries trade goods and services with each other. This can be affected by government action. For example, trade restrictions such as quotas or tariffs (☞ unit 68) by a government may prevent imports from businesses abroad entering the country. One of the most important relationships for the UK is that with

---

On 1 October 2002 the first toll road in the UK for 100 years was opened in Durham. Motorists were charged £2, payable to Durham County Council, to enter a small part of the city centre between 10am and 4pm from Monday and Saturday. A ticket machine is linked to an automatic barrier, which lowers when drivers pay to leave the charging area. Motorists that try to avoid the charge and are caught by security cameras are fined £30.

The area has seen a 90 per cent drop in traffic as a result - from 2,000 to 200 vehicles a day. Now there is almost a 'pedestrianisation' of the area. The County Council leader said 'It is interesting to see how how traders are learning to adjust their delivery hours and methods and to see how people who live and work in the zone are readjusting'.

However, there was criticism of the scheme from small independent traders having to pay £2 every time they make a delivery to their shops. Some can have at least 500 deliveries a year. They also argue there are fewer casual visitors.

Source: adapted from news.bbc.co.uk.

(a) Examine how the scheme might affect:
   (i)   customers;
   (ii)   local businesses in the charging area;
   (iii) suppliers from outside the area delivering to businesses within the charging area;
   (iv)   business transport that has to pass through the charging area;
   (v)   employees of businesses in the area;
   (vi)   government

Question 3

other European countries who are a part of the European Union (EU). This might affect UK businesses in a number of ways. For example, they must comply with EU laws concerning minimum wages. They also face increased competition from EU businesses as a result of the single market.

The operation of markets UK governments have attempted to carry out actions to allow markets to operate efficiently. They have used a range of policies designed to make markets more competitive. Such policies have included the opening up of services previously only carried out by local authorities to all businesses. This, for example, has led to school meals being provided by private businesses. Other examples include economic policies designed to improve the labour market and the setting up of bodies to regulate utilities, such as gas and water, where it feels that consumers need protection.

Legal framework Businesses are affected by the law. As employers they are affected by employment laws (☞ units 50 and 51). For example, the UK, as part of the EU, must comply with EU directives. UK law now protects most employees from working very long hours per week in response to EU legislation. As producers businesses are affected by laws relating to the way in which they work with other businesses, including competitors and suppliers. For example, contract laws seek to prevent businesses reneging on their payments to suppliers. A range of laws constrain the way in which businesses behave in relation to consumers and citizens. For example, a number of consumer laws (☞ unit 71) protect consumers against unscrupulous business practices.

The environment Governments are involved in a range of activities which affect the environment. With increasing public concern about its protection, governments have tried to regulate business activity to make sure it does not lead to a deterioration in the quality of the environment (☞ unit 70). There is a number of government policies designed to achieve this.

● Transport policy. Governments have taxed petrol and diesel and cancelled new road schemes to control the rate of growth of road transport. Public transport on buses and trains has been subsidised at a regional and local level, partly to encourage less use of cars. Charges have been made into London and on the M6 motorway to reduce traffic congestion. These can have both benefits and costs for businesses.

● Urban policy. Governments have spent to regenerate urban areas, particularly inner cities. One of the biggest urban schemes was the redevelopment of the London docklands with the creation of complexes such as Canary Wharf.

● Housing policy. The term 'green belt' describes areas of land, where the building of new houses is forbidden. The maintenance of green belt land is viewed by many as essential for the preservation of the environment.

Regional aid Regional policy aims to provide aid to businesses in different parts of the country. It has been used to support regions that have suffered from a decline in important industries and high levels of unemployment. It has included a range of measures to attract business to these areas, from UK government and EU grants, to the offering of 'tax breaks' for a limited period of time.

key terms

Aggregate demand - a measure of the level of demand in the economy as a whole.

Boom - the stage when an economy is at the peak of its activity.

Business cycle - a measure of the regular fluctuations in the level of economic activity.

Fiscal policy - a policy designed to manage the level of aggregate demand in the economy by changing government spending or taxation.

Gross Domestic Product (GDP) - like GNP, a measure of economic activity, but it does not include net property income from abroad.

Gross National Product (GNP) - a measure of the amount of income generated as a result of a country's economic activity.

Monetary policy - a policy designed to control the supply of money in the economy.

Recession - when income and output begin to fall in an economy.

Recovery - when growth begins to increase as an economy comes out of a slump or recession.

Slump - the lowest part of the business cycle.

Knowledge

1. What are the 4 main parts of the business cycle?
2. State 3 factors that might cause the business cycle.
3. Explain 5 effects of a boom on business.
4. State 4 government objectives.
5. Give an example of:
   (a) taxation on the price of a product;
   (b) taxation on income;
   (c) taxation on profits.
6. How might an increase in government spending affect a business producing hospital beds?
7. What effect would cutting interest rates have on business borrowing?

Case study   Signs of UK recovery?

Recovery or not? In December 2003 and January 2004 there was debate about the extent to which recovery had started in the UK economy, and even if there was likely to be recovery at all.

There were some encouraging signs that recovery was about to take place. Telecom equipment companies were enthusiastic about signs that big phone companies were starting to spend money again to upgrade their technologies and their stock. The share price of Marconi for example had risen by six per cent. Other areas buoyed by the prospect of a pick up in investment included media companies and music companies such as EMI.

On 8 January 2004 the Bank of England decided not to raise interest rates further. This followed the strongest demand for three years for exports in December 2003 according to the Confederation of British Industry (CBI). Export prospects had been boosted by the growth in the US since mid-2003. Whilst accepting that manufacturers were still struggling, the CBI argued that it was clear that conditions for industry were improving after the tough times since the collapse of the IT boom at the end of the Millennium. It pointed to annual growth of about 2 per cent. Doug Gooden, CBI head of economic analysis, said 'manufacturers are still facing a really tough uphill battle, with over a third saying order books remain below normal'.

Businesses reported stronger domestic demand also, with orders expected to feed through into the first increase in output in a year. However, manufacturers were unlikely to raise prices which had remained low due to competitive pressures in the recession periods of previous years.

The Organisation for Economic Cooperation and Development (OECD) suggested that recovery could be delayed unless interest rates were cut further. This would boost confidence among consumers and businesses. It forecast that any recovery would be slow to materialise.

The International Monetary Fund (IMF), however, cast doubt on growth predictions. Gordon Brown, the Chancellor of the Exchequer, had predicted growth of 3-3.5 per cent in 2004. The IMF suggested that it would be closer to 2.5 per cent. The Bank of England had a mixture of good and bad news. It predicted growth of just under 3 per cent and said that consumers were borrowing and spending again. However, it argued that many consumers were in debt and spending could be affected by changes in circumstances and levels of interest rates in future.

Source: adapted from news.bbc.co.uk, www.guardian.co.uk, uk.news.yahoo.com.

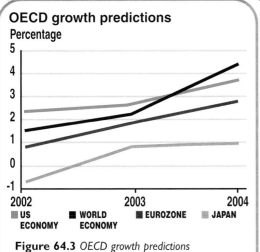

OECD growth predictions
Percentage

Figure 64.3 *OECD growth predictions*
Source: adapted from OECD.

(a) **Identify the conditions that UK businesses might have faced in recession periods mentioned in the article. (6 marks)**
(b) **Describe how changes in investment might bring about recovery using phone companies as an example. (6 marks)**
(c) **Explain two other factors that might have led to recovery in the UK economy. (8 marks)**
(d) **Examine how recovery might affect UK businesses. (10 marks)**
(e) **Discuss whether recovery was likely to take place. (10 marks)**

Interest rates

Businesses and people sometimes need to borrow money. A company might buy new machinery and not have enough funds in the business to pay for it. Consumers sometimes borrow to spend at Christmas or to take holidays and pay the money back later. INTEREST RATES are the cost or price of this borrowing. For example, if a business borrowed £10,000 at an interest rate of 5 per cent a year, assuming it did not pay off any of the loan it would be charged £500 in interest per year.

There are many different interest rates in the economy. Borrowing takes place in a number of ways. A business might have an overdraft facility at the bank and pay interest at 7-9 per cent a year. Interest rates on a mortgage to buy a house might be 6 per cent. Credit cards often charge higher rates, for example between 12-15 per cent.

Variations in interest rates

Interest rates change over time. Figure 65.1 shows changes in interest rates in the UK from 1990 to 2004. It shows that interest rates have been relatively stable over the period 1993-2003 and that interest rates after the year 2000 have been historically low.

What determines interest rates? In any market, such as the market for mortgages, interest rates are determined by the demand for and supply of money. Borrowers, such as businesses and consumers, will demand money and lenders, such as banks and other financial institutions, will supply it. If borrowers demand more money for mortgages, the interest rate (the price of borrowing) will rise, just like prices of goods rise when people demand more (☞ unit 61).

Many markets in the UK are influenced by the rate of interest set by the central bank in the UK - the Bank of England. The Bank of England has the power to control interest rates charged by banks such as HSBC, Abbey and NatWest to their customers. If the Bank of England increases interest rates, then the base rates of banks will follow. Other interest rates of banks will then follow the base rate. Banks charge higher rates of interest on short term borrowing than the base rate and pay lower rates on savings. They hope to make profit by earning more on loans than they pay on savings. Rates of interest on other forms of borrowing tend to follow changes in bank base rates so as to remain competitive, although there is no direct link.

Interest rates and consumer spending

Changes in interest rates can affect consumer spending in a number of ways.

● Higher interest rates increase the cost of borrowing to consumers. Consumers then tend to cut back on taking out loans and using overdrafts and credit cards. This can affect a wide variety of businesses, particularly those selling goods on credit, such as cars or electrical goods. It might also affect businesses selling 'luxury goods' such as jewellery or yachts. Businesses selling basic consumer goods might not be affected by small changes in interest rates.

● Higher interest rates lead to higher mortgage payments. This might affect businesses in two ways. Consumers with higher mortgage payments will have less money to spend on other goods. Also, higher payments mean that people may be less willing to take out a mortgage to buy property, affecting businesses involved in construction and houses for sale. Businesses which rent housing, however, might benefit, if people switch to renting property.

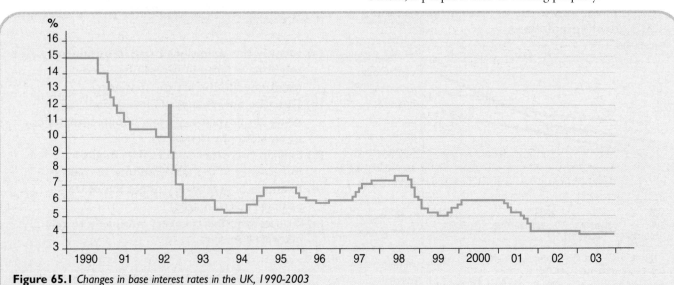

Figure 65.1 *Changes in base interest rates in the UK, 1990-2003*
Source: adapted from Bank of England.

Interest rates and business overheads

A change in interest rates will affect the overheads of a business. The interest businesses have to pay on their borrowing is an overhead cost for the business. So, for example, if interest rates fall from 10 per cent to 8 per cent, the cost to a business of borrowing £1,000 will fall from £100 to £80 a year. If interest rates rise, the overhead cost of the business will increase.

It may be possible for a business to obtain borrowing with fixed rates rather than variable rates of interest over a period. So if interest rates rise, its costs will not increase. The business would then have greater certainty about its cost payments. However, if interest rates fall, it may have to pay higher costs than other businesses borrowing on variable interest rates, whose interest rate payments would fall.

Interest rates and investment

Changes in interest rates can affect busines expenditure in investment in a number of ways. A business faced with higher interest rates has a number of possible choices.

● Stop new investment. Higher interest rates will lead to higher repayments on loans. So a business wanting to reduce average costs might decide not to invest in new machinery, for example, but find another less expensive method, such as reorganisation.

● Put off investment. A business might decide to delay investing until interest rates fall. It runs the risk, however, that the market may have changed and the investment might no longer be profitable.

● Saving. Higher interest rates encourage saving as savers gain more from the money saved. A business might decide to keep money in the bank at a secure steady interest rate rather than investing in a more risky venture.

● Paying off loans. Higher charges that result from interest rate increases might persuade a business to use retained profit to pay off outstanding loans. This should reduce payments in future and may lead to an increase in profit in the long term.

● Changing stock levels. Businesses keep stocks of raw materials to make other products and stocks of finished goods to sell to consumers and other businesses. Stocks are expensive to keep, so a rise in interest rates might lead a business to cut back on stocks, especially if it has borrowed to buy them. It might also decide that saving is a more profitable option.

Interest rates and the value of the pound

Interest rate changes can affect the exchange rate of a currency (☞ unit 68). The exchange rate is the rate at which the currency of one country can be exchanged for another,

such as the pound for the euro or the pound for the dollar. If interest rates rise, saving and investment in the UK becomes more attractive. Businesses and individuals outside the UK will buy pounds to save and invest in the UK. Demanding more pounds leads to a rise in the exchange rate. So:

● a rise in interest rates leads to a rise in the exchange rate;
● a fall in interest rates leads to a fall in the exchange rate.

The rise in exchange rates can affect UK businesses in a number of ways. For example, they might find it harder to sell abroad because prices are more expensive abroad. On the other hand they might benefit from buying supplies abroad because import prices fall. These effects are covered in more detail in unit 100. Those businesses that do not export or import from overseas will be relatively unaffected.

Taxation

TAXATION is the charges that the government makes on the activities, earnings and income of businesses and individuals.

In 2002 UK house prices were going through the roof. Close to £90 billion of new mortgage lending took place in the first half of the year. House purchases accounted for £50 billion of this, the rest being conversions and renovations.

The number of properties exchanged in April and May was up 18 per cent and people on average were paying 20 per cent more. It seemed surprising that the acceleration took place just at a time when the economy was stalling and there was an uncertain trading environment. The house boom was greatest in the South, with London house prices valued at on average five times London incomes. Nothing fundamental had happened in the UK economy in the last year. Inflation had remained stable, growth modest and employment growth much in line with what was expected. So the finger was pointed at low interest rates, particularly on short term affordability grounds.

Source: adapted from *The Guardian*, 22.7.2002.

(a) Explain the relationship between interest rates and the housing market.
(b) Examine how lower interest rates might affect businesses in the housing market.

The government uses the money raised by taxation to:
- pay for government spending on a wide variety of public sector activities (☞ unit 7) including transport, education, health, defence and housing;
- to affect factors in the economy such as inflation and unemployment (☞ units 66 and 67);
- to redistribute income, from those with higher incomes, to those who need it most;
- to influence patterns of consumer expenditure.

Taxes are sometimes classified into **direct** and **indirect** taxation. Direct taxes are taxes taken directly from the income of businesses or individuals, such as income tax. An indirect tax is a tax on a good or service, taken from income when it is used or spent, such as VAT.

Types of direct taxation

What are the main types of taxation in the UK?

Income tax This is a tax on the income or earnings of individuals. It includes charges made on the wages or salaries of employees and on the income of sole traders. It includes other earnings, such as the dividends paid to directors or limited companies. People do not pay tax on all their income. There are some allowances, such as a personal allowance on which people do not pay tax. After these allowances are taken into account, tax is charged on the remaining **taxable income**.

Income tax is a **progressive** tax. The more people earn the higher the rate they pay. In the UK in 2004 the personal allowance was £4,615. The lowest rate of tax was 10 per cent. This was chargeable on taxable income not exceeding £1,960. The basic rate on taxable income over this amount was 22 per cent. The highest rate, payable on taxable income over £30,500, was 40 per cent.

Other factors might also be taken into account when calculating income tax. For example, employees can claim a mileage allowance without tax for using company cars for business purposes. Certain gifts to charities by businesses are not liable for tax.

National Insurance contributions These are payable by both the employer and the employee. Different types of business organisation pay different rates of national insurance contribution. For example:
- a sole trader, where a person was self-employed, paid Class 2 contributions monthly or quarterly at a flat rate per week of £2 in 2004 plus Class 4 contributions based on profits (8 per cent on profit between £4,615 - £30,940 a year and 1 per cent on profit over £30,942 a year in 2004);
- for employees in a limited company, an employee in 2004 paid Class 1 contributions monthly or quarterly of 0 per cent on earnings below £89 a week, 11 per cent on earnings between £89-£585 a week, and 1 per cent on earnings over £595 a week. The employer paid no contributions on earnings below £89 a week and 12.8 per cent on the excess of earnings above £89 a week.

Corporation tax This is a tax on the profits of private and public limited companies. There are lower rates for small companies than for larger companies. Small companies were ranked as those with profits that did not exceed £300,000 in 2004.

A business can claim capital allowances. This is where it is able to claim allowances against certain types of spending, such as building hotels in enterprise zones or expenditure on research and development. It would not have to pay as much corporation tax if it could claim such allowances.

Capital gains tax This is a tax on the sales of capital assets. Capital gains usually involve the sale of shares, although they can involve non-business assets such as rental property owned by individuals. Individuals did not pay capital gains tax on the first £7,900 in 2004. They could also get taper relief on the sale of assets. The longer the shares were held, the lower the rate of tax charged.

Inheritance tax This is a tax on the transfer of money after death from one person to another. In 2004 transfers to a person's spouse, or to other bodies such as registered charities and political parties, incurred no tax. Transfers to other people, such as children, incurred 40 per cent tax, but only if the value was over £255,000.

Types of indirect tax

Value Added Tax (VAT) VAT is charged on goods or services which are made and bought in the UK. There were three rates of VAT in 2004:
- the standard rate of 17.5 per cent. This applies to most goods and services bought in the UK;
- the zero rate of 0 per cent. This applies to certain goods in the UK which are subject to VAT, but at a nil rate. Examples include food, books and children's clothing and footwear;
- the reduced rate of 5 per cent. This applies to a narrow category of products including womens' sanitary products, children's car seats and installation of energy saving items.

It is often argued that, within the standard rate band, VAT is a **regressive tax**. The more you earn the less you pay in tax. For example, someone paying 17.5 per cent tax on a good costing £10,000 would pay £1,750. This is 100 per cent of the income of someone earning £1,750. But it is only 1 per cent of the income of someone earning £175,000.

Customs duty This is a tax on goods and services imported into a country. CUSTOMS DUTIES (or tariffs, ☞ unit 68) are usually charged as a percentage of the value of the imported goods. They are often placed on imports of foreign businesses, to raise the price of their goods in an attempt to protect home businesses from competition. A problem, however, is that businesses importing supplies have to pay higher prices.

Excise duties These are taxes on the production and import of products such as alcohol, tobacco and minerals, oil and gas.

Other indirect taxes

● Landfill tax is charged on waste dumped in landfill sites in an attempt to encourage businesses to produce less waste and recycle products. In 2004 waste was taxed at £15 per tonne after 1st April.

● Air passenger duty is a departure tax on most air travel. There are different rates for different destinations.

● A climate change levy was introduced in 2001 as a charge on certain supplies of fuel for business. There are different charges for different types of fuel and exemptions for certain businesses, such as those carrying out energy saving measures.

● An aggregates levy was introduced in 2002 as a flat rate £1.60 per tonne charge on sand, gravel and crushed rock extracted in the UK or imported into the UK, although there are exemptions.

● Insurance premium tax was a 5 per cent charge in 2004 on all general insurance, such as cars and homes. Life assurance policies were exempt. A higher rate of 17.5 per cent was charged on specialist insurance such as travel insurance.

National non-domestic rates (NNDR) These are annual charges on the rateable value of business premises. They are sometimes known as business rates. In the UK in 2004 they were 44.4p per rateable value of business premises, although there were exemptions and reliefs, for example for empty properties. The rateable value is broadly the yearly rent that the property could be let out for.

Stamp duty This is a tax paid on the sale of land, property, leases and certain types of shares and securities.

Council tax This is a charge paid by residents of domestic housing in the UK to local authorities. The charge people pay is based on the council tax band in which the valuation officer places a dwelling. The bands are based on the size, location, layout and character of the property. The valuations are designed to show what the property would have been sold for on the open market, given certain assumptions. Different local authorities have different bands.

Effects of changes in taxation on business

How might changes in taxation affect businesses in the UK?

Consumer spending Changes in certain types of taxation are likely to increase the income consumers have left after tax. These include reductions in income tax rates, increases in personal allowances and an increase in the limits on which inheritance tax is paid or a reduction in the rate of inheritance tax. If consumers have more income left they might increase spending on the products of businesses. Increases in income tax, National Insurance contributions and council taxes are all likely to leave consumers with less income and could reduce spending on products.

Prices An increase in VAT or excise duty will raise the costs of a business. Businesses often pass this on to customers by raising the price of goods. An increase in customs duty will increase the price of goods being imported into a country.

Business costs, revenue and profits Increases in some taxes might raise the costs of business. For example, VAT will raise costs. A business might try to raise prices to cover this and maintain profit. However, higher prices can reduce sales and so profit could still be affected if revenue falls. Rises in corporation tax, business rates, employers' National Insurance contributions and landfill tax will all tend to reduce business profits. Reductions in taxes are likely to increase the profits of a business.

Business spending and investment Increases in costs and reduced profits mean that businesses have less retained profit (☞ unit 31). This can affect the ability of the business to pay its debts, buy stocks and meet other expenses. It can also affect whether it invests in new factories or machinery.

Shares Changes in capital gains tax and stamp duty might affect shareholding. For example, an increase in capital gains tax might deter shareholders or delay sales of shares.

Importing and exporting Increases in customs duties can affect businesses. For example, if the UK raised customs duties on imported products a UK business might benefit because as imports against which it competed would then have a higher price. However, UK businesses buying imported supplies would have to pay higher prices.

Business operations and employees Increases in National Insurance contributions of employers might deter employers from recruiting extra workers. Changes in taxation on company cars or mileage allowances might also changes how a business offers these benefits to employees.

Other effects Certain types of business might be affected by changes in tax. For example, an increase in landfill tax might encourage businesses to recycle. A rise in passenger duty could discourage holiday makers and reduce the demand for holidays.

Tax avoidance and evasion Increases in taxation often lead businesses to try to avoid paying the tax. For example, they might not hire workers to avoid higher National Insurance contributions or switch from buying imports to avoid customs duties. In some cases they might even try to evade the law, for example dumping waste in the countryside to avoid landfill taxes, which is illegal.

On 5 September 2003 JD Weatherspoon, the pub chain, announced a slowdown in its rapid expansion. In the financial year it opened only 45 new pubs, compared to 87 in the previous year. Some of its 638 pubs are converted garages, cinemas and railway offices. The company blamed an increase in bureaucracy and taxes for the slowdown. It argued that, although it saw possibilities for expansion, the uncertainty created by taxation meant that it was prudent to reduce the rate of growth.

The increase in fees and other regulatory costs seemed to come from the decision to hand over pub licences to local authorities. In addition, there were considerable increases in taxation, including excise duties, which had cost the business £2 million during that year.

The company had been diversifying to overcome lower consumer spending which had affected drink sales. It now makes around £13 million a year from sales of cappuccino. It also sells breakfast and children's food. In a further sign of a shift away from traditional drinks, the business also said that cocktails had been proving popular.

Source: adapted from *The Guardian*, 5.9.2003.

(a) Describe the changes in taxation that were affecting the business.
(b) Examine how the changes might affect the business in future.

Question 2

1. Why is interest charged?
2. State 4 business operations that changes in interest rates can affect.
3. If interest rates in the UK go down, what happens to the value of the pound?
4. What is the difference between a direct and an indirect tax?
5. State 6 types of tax in the UK.
6. Why is income tax progressive and VAT regressive?
7. State 3 taxes that might reduce company profits if they rise.

key terms

Customs duties - charges on the imports of goods into a country.
Interest rates - the charge or price of borrowing.
Taxation - the charges made by government on the activities, earnings and income of businesses and individuals.

Case study Belmont Cycles

Josh Belmont is a manufacturer of racing cycles in the UK. His business, Belmont Cycles, has been particularly successful at buying parts from abroad and then combining them in a unique way to produce lightweight and aerodynamic cycles. Josh is a sole trader and has a growing reputation in the market. In 2004 he expanded production from his small workshop in Leeds. He moved premises to a bigger site on an industrial estate just outside the city centre, encouraged by lower business rates. Josh was hoping to take on more workers, but noticed that there had been a change in employers' National Insurance contributions.

Part of the move involved refinancing the business. Josh was keen to get most of the finance from a fixed rate of interest bank loan. His bank offered him a loan over a number of

Table 65.1 *Changes in National Insurance contributions*

	2002/03	2003/04
Employers' National Insurance contributions		
Earnings £87-£595	9.3% on excess over £89	12.8% on excess over £89
Earnings over £595	12.8%	11.8%

Source: adapted from *The UK Pocket Tax Book*, PricewaterhouseCoopers.

years, using his building as collateral. However, he needed more than the bank was perpared to offer. So he had to borrow the rest at a variable rate of interest, which might change in future.

Josh had recently heard about possible increases in interest rates by the Bank of England. The interest rate in early 2004 was 3.75 per cent, but there was a lot of pressure on the Bank of England to raise this rate. This would determine rates of interest in other money markets and force them up as well. Josh was worried about the effect of a rise on his own business and his customers.

Most of Belmont's parts are brought in from Italy. This is part of the EU, with no trade restrictions. The euro had recently been worth 1.26 euros against the pound.

Josh is now considering buying products from the USA. The value of the pound against the dollar is strong. Between 2003 and 2004 it had risen from £1 = $1.6 to £1 = $1.8. This has made imports to the UK cheaper, but UK exports more expensive in the USA.

Josh has found some interesting new wheels which he hopes to incorporate into his designs. He has been assured that when the designs come out he will be able to sell them to US importers of British goods. But he has been worried about stories in the paper recently about US trade restrictions on EU imports. He is concerned that customs duties will raise the price and lower sales of his cycles in the USA.

Josh had also noticed a slowdown in spending, from both customers and businesses, and felt that indirect and direct taxation might have something to do with this.

Answer either A or B

A - Interest rates
(a) **What is meant by the following phrases which apply to Belmont Cycles?**
   (i) **Fixed and variable rates of interest. (4 marks)**
   (ii) **The decision by the Bank of England to raise interest rates. (4 marks)**
(b) **Explain how interest rates affected the choice of finance of the business. (8 marks)**
(c) **Examine how rises in interest rates in future might affect borrowing and investment by the business. (12 marks)**
(d) **Discuss the extent to which a possible rise in interest rates might affect:**
   (i) **the exchange rate; (4 marks)**
   (ii) **the imports and exports of the business. (8 marks)**

B - Taxation
(a) **What is meant by the following phrases which apply to Belmont Cycles?**
   (i) **Direct and indirect taxation. (4 marks)**
   (ii) **Customs duties will raise the price of cycles. (4 marks)**
(b) **Explain how business rates may have influenced the decision to move to new premises. (8 marks)**
(c) **Examine how the changes in Table 100.1 might affect:**
   (i) **the cost of the business; (4 marks)**
   (ii) **the operation of the business at the new location. (8 marks)**
(d) **Discuss the extent to which changes in taxation might have affected the consumer and business customers of Belmont. (12 marks)**

What is inflation?

INFLATION can be defined as a persistent tendency for prices to rise. It occurs when there is a general increase in the price level, not just if one business raises its prices. So, if inflation is 3 per cent for example, then prices are rising on average by 3 per cent over the period of a year.

To what extent is this a problem? Low levels of inflation, below 5 per cent, are likely to be considered acceptable in many countries. Governments, consumers and businesses do not suffer the difficulties of high inflation, such as rising costs, and gain benefits of some inflation, such as a fall in the value of repayments on borrowing. Rates of around 10 per cent or more, as experienced by the UK in the early 1990s, may lead to greater problems. HYPER-INFLATION, such as the inflation rate of 1,500 per cent in Tajikistan in 1995, can cause serious difficulties.

Governments may try to reduce the rate of inflation from 5 per cent to 2 per cent for example. This does not mean that prices are falling, just that the rate of inflation is slowing down. DEFLATION is a situation where average prices actually fall over a period. Governments also set target rates of inflation. They aim for rates that are lower than or the same as those of their main international competitors. The UK government in the early twenty-first century set target rates mainly around 2 per cent per annum.

The causes of inflation

What causes inflation? Certain arguments may be put forward.

Money Some believe that inflation is caused by increases in the MONEY SUPPLY. This is the total amount of money circulating in the economy. This view is often associated with the group of economists known as **monetarists**.

Supporters of this idea argue that any increase in the money supply which is not in line with growth in the output of the economy will lead to inflation. Take, for example, an increase in the money supply of 10 per cent. In the short term, consumer spending would increase, but the output of producers would not be able to expand as quickly. Instead, there would be an increase in prices. Supporters of this view argue strongly that it is important for governments to ensure that the rate of growth of the money supply is kept in line with the rate of growth of output or there will be inflation.

It has been suggested that the excessive inflation levels in some Eastern European and South American countries has been inflamed by governments simply printing money to cope with price rises. This has led to further price rises as the money supply has increased over and above any output rise. In the UK the independence of the Bank of England is said to be a factor which may have influenced the low levels of inflation in the late 1990s and early twenty first century.

Governments could no longer make the Bank increase the money supply before an election in order to gain public support.

Demand Too much spending or **demand** can lead to inflation. This is known as DEMAND-PULL INFLATION. The result is similar to that described under changes in the money supply, but the cause is different. Demand-pull inflation comes about when there is excessive spending in the economy. This expenditure leads to an increase in demand which cannot be matched by the level of supply. Because demand is greater than supply, prices rise. The increase in demand can be due to:
● a rise in consumer spending;
● firms investing in more machinery;
● government expenditure increasing;
● more exports being bought abroad.
Some economists argue that inflation in the UK at the end of the 1980s and early 1990s was caused by earlier tax cuts, leading to increases in consumer expenditure.

Increasing costs Another argument is that rising costs lead to inflation. This is known as COST-PUSH INFLATION, as rising costs force firms to push up their prices. What causes costs to increase?
● Rises in wages and salaries. There may be an increase in labour costs as workers and unions push for and receive an increase in their wages.
● Tax increases. Increases in indirect taxes, such as VAT (☞ unit 65), can raise the price of products. They can also increase the costs of production, which causes firms to raise their prices.
● Profits. A push by firms to raise profit levels, due to pressure from shareholders, can increase production costs.
● Imports. An increase in costs can be 'imported' from abroad (☞ unit 68). The prices of imported raw materials or semi-finished products, such as components, may rise. This could increase the price of home produced goods which use these in production. A rise in the price of imported finished goods can more directly lead to inflation, as it adds to the general level of prices. For example, a sudden fall in reserves of raw materials such as oil will force up the price. Businesses importing oil or using oil in their production process will have to pay higher costs.
Rises in wages or the price of imports are said to be examples of **supply shocks** because they affect the firms' costs and the supply of their products. It was argued that the high levels of inflation experienced by the UK in the 1970s and early 1980s was due to huge oil price rises. In the 1990s the UK had relatively low inflation rates. Some argued that one of the factors affecting this was the reduced power of trade

unions and their inability to negotiate high wage rises.

Expectations Some economists believe that employees expecting inflation to occur can actually be a cause of inflation. This is because workers pressing for a pay rise tend to build in an **anticipated** amount of inflation into their claim. For example, if they expect inflation to be four per cent, and want a two per cent pay rise, they will demand a six per cent pay increase. If awarded, this would give them a two per cent **real** increase in wages and a six per cent **money** increase. If this was the average for all businesses in the economy, they would be faced with a six per cent increase in their wage costs. This increase in costs may lead businesses to increase their prices, and inflation can occur. If expectations of inflation are reduced, wage costs may be kept down. It is also argued that increases in wages in line with increases in productivity do not lead to higher costs, and higher prices as a result.

Inflation is likely to fall following falling costs facing manufacturers and lower global demand for products. 'Small and medium sized manufacturers are facing extreme pressure from the global slowdown in demand' said a vice-chair of the Confederation of British Industry. The falling costs were accounted for by lower fuel prices arising out of the tumbling price of oil. In addition, many businesses were in the process of shedding labour leading to lower wage costs. 'Falling prices at the factory gate should spell lower prices in the shops. The rate of inflation should dip back down to 2.3 per cent' said one leading commentator.

Source: adapted from *The Guardian*, 14.8.2002.

(a) Using data from the article, identify two reasons why inflation was considered likely to fall.
(b) Explain whether you think deflation might occur following the events described in the article.

Question 1

Effects of inflation on business

Reducing inflation is one of the main economic objectives of UK governments (☞ unit 64). The UK government has had strong support from the Confederation of British Industry (CBI) and other business groups in following this approach. Why is inflation seen as such a problem? There is a number of effects that relatively high rates of inflation might have on business, and on consumer demand and confidence.

Increasing costs Inflation leads to an increase in business costs. Examples might be:
● increases in the cost of components or raw materials;
● increases in wages and salaries of employees to keep pace with inflation;
● increasing energy costs;

● rising 'service' costs, such as the cost of calling out technicians.
  If a business cannot pass on these costs to consumers as higher prices or 'absorb' the costs in greater productivity, profits can fall. Higher prices are likely to mean fewer sales. Whether this results in a fall in turnover depends on the response of consumers to a rise in price (☞ unit 18). Businesses may be able to raise the prices of essential products a great deal with little fall-off in sales.

Shoe leather costs During periods of price stability firms are likely to have good knowledge of the price that they will pay for various goods and services. Such purchases might include delivery vehicles, premises insurance, computer equipment and stationery. However, during periods of rising prices firms may be less able to recognise a 'reasonable' price. They may need to spend more time shopping around for the best price (hence the term shoe leather costs). The extra time spent on this can be extremely expensive for some small firms.

Menu costs This refers to the time and money which firms have to spend on changing their price lists. It is a problem for firms displaying their price either on the actual product or on its packaging. Some firms, such as those distributing their goods via vending machines, are particularly affected.

Wage negotiating When inflation is high, firms will be under strong pressure to upgrade wages and salaries in line with expected levels of inflation. As well as the increased wage costs there will be some administrative costs in these changes. Conflict between employees and employers can result from disagreements about the extent to which wages need to be raised to compensate for inflation.

Reduced purchasing power When prices are rising the REAL VALUE of money will fall. This is the value taking into account inflation. A consumer with £200 to spend will be able to buy far less if prices are increasing. So will a business aiming to purchase £20,000 worth of raw materials. There is said to be a fall in their **purchasing power**.

  In periods of inflation, sales of certain goods are particularly affected. Businesses that produce 'luxury' goods, such as designer footwear, are likely to suffer as consumers switch to more essential products. Producers of goods and services sold to groups that are badly hit by inflation may also lose sales. It is argued that fixed income groups, such as pensioners, are affected most because their earnings do not always keep pace with inflation.

  Businesses unable to increase their turnover in line with their costs will suffer similar effects. This may be the case, for example, with a local retailer with a geographically 'fixed' market, who is unable to raise prices for fear of losing customers to a local superstore. Profits will decline as costs, which are not covered by increased turnover, rise.

Borrowing and lending Inflation redistributes money from lenders to borrowers. A business that has borrowed £20,000 is likely to pay back far less in real terms over a ten year period if inflation is high. Those businesses that owe a large amount of money stand to gain in periods of high inflation as the value of their debts may be 'wiped out'. Businesses that have saved will lose out. Interest rates may fail to keep up with inflation, especially when inflation reaches levels of 10 per cent or more. So, if interest rates are 10 per cent and inflation is 20 per cent, the saver will lose 10 per cent of the real value of savings, but the borrower will find the value to be paid back falls 10 per cent a year.

Investment Views are divided as to the effects of inflation upon investment decisions. Some argue that, in the short term at least, it might increase the amount of investment undertaken by firms. This is because the real rate of interest (taking into account the rate of inflation) is often low during inflationary periods as inflation figures get close to, or exceed, the rate of interest. This makes investment using borrowed money relatively cheap.

Others believe that businesses are less likely to go ahead with investment projects. This is because inflation makes entrepreneurs less certain about the future and less willing to take risks.

Uncertainty Uncertainty may affect decisions other than investment that a business makes. Firms are often unwilling to enter into long term transactions in inflationary periods. Take, for example, a business ordering stocks of sheet metal in March to be delivered in June and paid for in August. Inflation of 24 per cent a year may mean that the price of the good increases by 12 per cent during this period. The firm supplying the sheet metal will receive the amount quoted in March when the payment is made in August. However, by August the value of this money will have declined as a result of the inflation.

Unemployment, growth and trade It is sometimes argued that inflation can actually cause unemployment and lower economic growth. The uncertainty that inflation creates in the minds of business people means they are less willing to take risks, invest in new ventures, expand production or hire workers. Also, if UK inflation rates are higher than those of competitors, UK products would be relatively more expensive in markets abroad, whilst foreign products would be relatively cheaper in the UK. An inability to compete on price in both domestic and foreign markets could mean the loss of many jobs. It could also result in a deterioration in the balance of payments (☞ unit 68) as the number of exports sold abroad falls and the number of imports coming into the country increases.

The value of assets The monetary value of assets increases in inflationary periods. Consumers who own antiques or scarce items may find their values soar. The money value of houses, factories, offices and machinery also rises. A business owning

an office can sell it for a higher price. Of course, it will have to pay a higher price for any other office it wants to buy.

A footloose business in an area of high demand may be able to sell a factory or a set of offices for a high price and move to an area where property is cheaper. This is true at any time, but in periods of inflation the gains to be made are larger because the difference between prices will be greater.

Measuring inflation

Inflation in the UK has been measured by the RETAIL PRICE INDEX. This is an **index** which is constructed to provide an accurate figure on the changes in the prices of goods and services each month. It is based upon a 'basket' of goods and services which is meant to represent the typical purchases of consumers throughout the UK. This basket of goods and services includes a range of items, such as foodstuffs, electrical items and petrol.

Index numbers can be used as indicators of changes and allow comparisons to be made. The Retail Price Index chooses a base year from which changes in prices can be calculated. Average prices are given a value of 100 in the base year. If the

---

Table 66.1 *Inflation in selected countries, 2003*

Percentage changes on previous 12 months

Country	
UK	2.1%
USA	1.6%
Japan	0.9%
Germany	1.3%
Czech Republic	0.6%
Hungary	5.3%
Turkey	45.2%
Zimbabwe	134.5%
Venezuela	31.2%
Ukraine	-1.2%
Switzerland	0.5%
Italy	2.4%
Spain	3.0%

Source: adapted from *The World Factbook*, 2003.

(a) Describe the UK's inflation rate relative to that of its international competitors during the period.
(b) Explain how inflation in the UK in 2003 may have affected the following UK businesses.
   (i) A small firm that considered investing in a new machine and had to borrow £20,000.
   (ii) A manufacturer of drinks machines for sports and leisure centres which had to buy parts from a variety of sources overseas.
   (iii) An exporter of men's suits to the USA.

index in the following year is 102, then on average prices may be said to have risen by 2 per cent. Table 66.3 shows the changes in the Retail Price Index.

The Retail Price Index (RPI) is a **weighted index** (☞ unit 13). This means that the importance attached to some goods and services included in the index is higher than for others. For example, petrol will tend to have a higher weighting in the index than soap. This is because petrol represents a higher proportion of the monthly expenditure of consumers than soap. The effect of this on the index is that a two per cent change in the price of petrol will have more impact upon the Retail Price Index than a two per cent rise in the price of soap.

The RPIX is another measure of inflation. It removes mortgage payments from the RPI figure, to take out any overemphasis of inflation when house prices are rising.

In 2003 the UK government announced that it would use a new price index as the main measure of inflation, called the CONSUMER PRICE INDEX (CPI). It is similar to the retail price index. But it is more sensitive to changes in household spending and allows better comparison with inflation in other countries. The main differences are that the CPI:

● excludes some housing items in the RPIX such as council tax, mortgage interest payments, house depreciation, buildings insurance, estate agents' fees and conveyancing fees;

● covers all private households, whereas the RPIX excludes the top 4 per cent by income and pensioner households who gain at least three quarters of their income from state benefits;

● includes the residents of institutional households such as student hostels and foreign visitors to the UK. So it covers some items that are not in the RPI, such as unit trust and stockbrokers' fees, university accommodation fees and foreign students' university tuition fees.

Also, different methods are used in the CPI and RPI to adjust prices for new cars and personal computers. Figure 98.1 shows how inflation would be measured by both the RPIX and the CPI over the period 1989-2003.

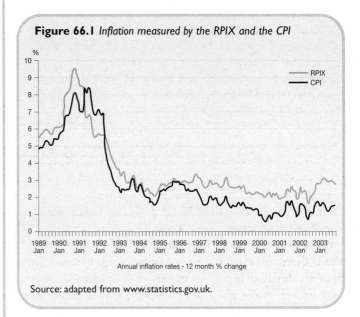

Figure 66.1 *Inflation measured by the RPIX and the CPI*

Annual inflation rates - 12 month % change

Source: adapted from www.statistics.gov.uk.

Table 66.2 *Percentage changes in retail prices on year earlier, 2002*

Food	3.6	Personal goods	2.5
Catering	4.1	and services	
Alcoholic drink	2.2	Motoring expenditure	-1.3
Tobacco	3.3	Fares and other	2.5
Housing	-1.4	travel costs	
Fuel and light	3.7	Leisure goods	-1.9
Household services	4.1		
Leisure services	6.7		
Clothing and footwear	-5.3		

Source: adapted from *Labour Market Trends*, Office for National Statistics.

(a) Identify the product with the: (i) largest percentage increase; (ii) smallest percentage increase; (ii) largest percentage decrease in prices in 2002.
(b) Suggest the possible effects on:
  (i) customers buying these products;
  (ii) businesses producing these products;
  (iii) other businesses.

Question 3

Knowledge ...Knowledge...Knowle...

1. How is inflation measured in the UK?
2. Describe the main causes of inflation.
3. What is imported inflation?
4. List 3 ways in which (a) a business and (b) consumers might be affected by inflation.
5. How might inflation lead to unemployment?
6. What is meant by the Consumer Price Index?

Table 66.3 *The Retail Price Index, Jan 1987 = 100*

1990	1991	1992	1993	1994	1995	1996	1997	1998	1999	2000	2001	2002	2003
126.2	133.8	138.5	140.7	144.1	149.1	152.7	157.5	162.9	165.4	170.3	173.3	176.2	181.3

Source: adapted from *Labour Market Trends*, Office for National Statistics.

key terms

Consumer Price Index - an indicator of changes in average prices of a range of goods typically bought by consumers in the UK. Currently used to measure inflation in the UK.

Cost-push inflation - inflation which occurs as a result of businesses facing increased costs, which are then passed on to consumers in the form of higher prices.

Deflation - a situation where prices are falling.

Demand-pull inflation - inflation which occurs as a result of excessive spending in the economy.

Hyper-inflation - a situation where inflation levels are very high.

Inflation - a continuing or persistent tendency for prices to rise.

Money supply - the total amount of money circulating in the economy.

Real value - any value which takes into account the rate of inflation.

Retail Price Index - an indicator of the changes in average prices of a range of goods typically bought by consumers in the UK.

Case study A spending spree?

Shoppers were snapping up everything from handbags to sofas at the Cribbs Causeway shopping centre on the outskirts of Bristol in 2003. The MetroCentre in Gateshead last Saturday enjoyed its busiest day in three years. Retailers from one end of the country to the other witnessed a wave of spending not seen since the heady days of the late 1980s. Official figures which showed retail sales up 6.9 per cent on the previous year came as no surprise to John Edwards, commercial director at Cribbs Causeway, a centre with 140 stores. 'Sales are very strong' he said. 'They are 13 per cent up so far. All our retailers tell us they are doing well, from Eissenger Klassiker and New Look through to Marks & Spencer and John Lewis.'

Some analysts of the market argue that the strength of the spending boom can be explained by retailers cutting prices as a consequence of ferocious competition. 'Its an endless cycle of sales and special offers and special events. The only winner at the moment is the consumer.' Others are concerned that this increased consumer spending might lead to higher inflation. This was what happened in the late 1980s as consumers embarked upon a debt crazed frenzy of spending. A UK based economist said it was easy to understand why consumers were on a spending spree. 'Money is cheap, and people are taking advantage of that. The conditions for borrowing are the best most people have seen for a generation.'

Source: adapted from *The Guardian*, 24.5.2003.

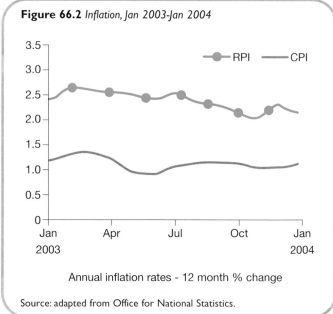

Figure 66.2 *Inflation, Jan 2003-Jan 2004*

Annual inflation rates - 12 month % change

Source: adapted from Office for National Statistics.

(a) **Describe the reasons for the spending spree highlighted in the article. (4 marks)**

(b) **Using data from the article, explain the possible causes of inflation. (6 marks)**

(c) **If inflation rises following the spending spree, examine how this might affect retailers such as those in the article. (10 marks)**

(d) **Discuss the extent to which the spending spree identified in the article might be expected to lead to a rise in inflation. (10 marks)**

What is unemployment?

UNEMPLOYMENT is concerned with people being out of work. It can measured as the **number** of people who are unemployed. So, for example, in the UK in October 2003, 1.47 million people were unemployed. Figure 67.1 illustrates the **rate of unemployment** in the UK between 1993 and 2002. This shows the number of people who are unemployed as a percentage of those who are either in employment or not in employment.

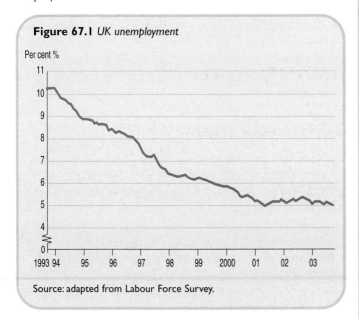

Figure 67.1 *UK unemployment*

Source: adapted from Labour Force Survey.

Types of unemployment

There is a number of different types of unemployment.

Seasonal unemployment Some workers are employed on a seasonal basis. In the UK construction, holiday and agricultural industries, workers are less in demand in winter because of the climate. Seasonal unemployment can therefore be high. In summer it may fall, as these workers are hired. It is difficult in practice for governments to 'solve' this type of unemployment, which may always occur. In producing unemployment statistics, governments often adjust the figures to allow for seasonal factors.

Search and frictional unemployment These two types of unemployment are very similar. FRICTIONAL UNEMPLOYMENT occurs when people are moving between jobs. Usually it only lasts for a short amount of time. For example, an electrician who had been working in the North East may have a few weeks 'off' before starting a new job in London. It is not seen as a serious problem by government. SEARCH UNEMPLOYMENT, however, can last longer. This type of unemployment occurs when people are searching for a new job. The greater the information on job opportunities, the lower search unemployment is likely to be.

Structural unemployment STRUCTURAL UNEMPLOYMENT is caused by changes in the structure of a country's economy which affect particular industries and occupations. Examples include the decline of the coal and steel industries in the second half of the twentieth century. Between 1963 and the mid-1990s almost half a million jobs were lost in the coal mining industry. This indicates the size of the problem in the UK. Because certain industries have traditionally been located in particular parts of the country, their decline can have a dramatic effect upon those regions. As a result, structural unemployment is closely linked with regional unemployment. It may also result from changes in demand for the goods and services produced by particular sectors of the economy. For example, there has been a decline in demand for natural fibres such as jute as a result of the development of synthetic products.

Technological unemployment This occurs when new technology replaces workers with machines. For example, new technology introduced to the newspaper industry has meant the loss of many print workers' jobs.

Cyclical or demand-deficient unemployment CYCLICAL UNEMPLOYMENT results from the cycles which occur in most economies. These ups and downs in economic activity over a number of years are known as the business cycle (☞ unit 64). In a recession, at the 'bottom' of a business cycle, unemployment results from a lack of demand. It is argued that demand is not high enough to employ all labour, machines, land, offices etc. in the economy.

Real wage unemployment The demand for workers by businesses and the supply of workers is influenced by the **real wage rate**. Relatively high real wages mean that workers will want to supply more labour than businesses want to employ. This results in unemployment. In other words, it is argued that workers 'price themselves' out of jobs. There are vacancies, but businesses will only be willing to pay wages which are lower than workers are prepared to accept.

Voluntary and involuntary unemployment Some suggest that unemployment can be voluntary or involuntary. Voluntary unemployment occurs when workers refuse to accept jobs at existing wage rates. Involuntary unemployment occurs when there are not enough jobs in the economy at existing wage rates. Economists sometimes talk about the **natural rate of unemployment**. This is the percentage of workers who are voluntarily unemployed.

In October, 2001 Britain's jobless rate rose for the first time in a year. The number unemployed increased by 4,300 to 951,000, government figures showed. Manufacturing firms, struggling with the slowdown in the global economy, had already laid off 123,000 employees in the three months leading up to this rise in unemployment.

This had the effect of leaving employment in the manufacturing sector at just 3.8 million, the lowest since records began. Part time workers, particularly women, bore the brunt of the job losses, with 68,000 female part time workers losing their jobs.

Source: adapted from *The Guardian*, 15.11.2001.

(a) Explain three types of unemployment that may occur in the manufacturing sector.
(b) What type of unemployment in the manufacturing sector is suggested in the article? Explain your answer.

Effects of unemployment on business

High levels of unemployment have a number of effects on businesses. The majority of the effects of unemployment are harmful for businesses. However, there are some businesses which may be unaffected by unemployment. A small minority may even benefit.

Demand The obvious effect of unemployment is that people are not earning income and are likely to have less to spend. Businesses will suffer a loss of demand for their products and reduced profits as a result. Producers of goods, such as clothing and household furniture, and providers of services, such as insurance and holidays, are all likely to suffer.

Organisation Unemployment can have a number of effects on the internal organisation of a business. It may mean that a firm can no longer afford to recruit new members of staff because of low demand for its products. New, often young, recruits to a firm will no longer be coming through. In addition, new posts which arise may be filled through retraining of existing staff rather than recruitment. This can lead to significant changes in the age profile of an organisation's employees.

Redundancies are also a common feature of a period of high unemployment. Whilst the work of some who are made redundant will not be replaced, the responsibilities and roles of others may be added to the job descriptions of those who remain with the firm. This can lead to increasing demands on existing employees.

During periods of high unemployment, some firms reorganise their internal structure. This may mean the loss of

a whole tier in the hierarchy or the changing of individual job descriptions. Businesses, such as IBM, have removed large numbers of middle managers in such restructuring exercises.

Payments Businesses may be faced with making redundancy payments to workers. These tend to vary between firms depending upon the average length of service of the employee.

The cost of any reorganisation caused by redundancies will also have to be borne by firms. Such costs may include lost productivity after a reorganisation as employees struggle to cope with new responsibilities.

Labour supply It may be easier for firms to recruit new employees during a period of high unemployment. This is because there is a larger pool of people to choose from, with more applicants for each available post. In addition, because of the increased competition for new jobs, people may be prepared to work for less money. In this way firms can lower their labour costs.

Output During periods of unemployment, many firms reduce their level of output to compensate for falling demand. This can lead to excess capacity and under-utilisation of capital equipment. In addition, falling levels of demand can interrupt the flow of production, causing production and stock control problems (☞ unit 57).

Government spending High levels of unemployment mean that government spending on social security will be high. Also, the government will lose revenue from tax and National Insurance contributions which people would have paid had they been in employment. To make up for this the government may borrow, increase taxation or reduce other items of spending.

Increased trade and reduced costs The services offered by some firms depend upon other firms going out of business. Firms specialising in receiverships and pawnbrokers may see an increase in the demand for their services. Firms also benefit from 'trading down', ie buying cheaper alternatives. Retailers and manufacturers selling goods aimed at lower income segments of the market tend to do well during periods of unemployment. Supermarkets, in particular, have benefited. It has been argued that this is because consumers spend more on home entertainment and less on going out during periods of high unemployment.

Social issues Research into unemployment has shown that it has a number of possible 'side effects'. These can have consequences for businesses. The suggested side effects include poverty and stress for those individuals, families and communities that have high levels of unemployment. They also include higher levels of vandalism and crime. This can lead to higher insurance premiums for businesses, disruption to businesses caused by crime and, in some cases, loss of custom and the need to relocate premises.

Measuring unemployment

How many people are unemployed? In the UK the main measure used as an indicator of unemployment in is the International Labour Force measure (ILO). This is based on a survey of people. To be unemployed, a person has to be out of work, have looked for work in the last four weeks and be able to start work in the next two weeks. It is a useful measure because it allows comparisons with unemployment rates in other countries, as other countries use this measure.

Another measure sometimes used only in the UK is the claimant count measure. This is based on the number of people claiming unemployment-related benefits, including jobseekers' allowance and National Insurance credits. People must declare that they are out of work and be capable of, available for and actively seeking work during the week the claim was made. A problems with this measure is that it excludes those who do not claim benefit and might be looking for work.

A certain number of people in the UK are said to be underemployed. They might not be seeking work for a variety reasons, including looking after children or because they have retired.

key terms

Cyclical unemployment - unemployment resulting from the ups and downs (cycles) which occur in most economies.
Frictional/search unemployment - unemployment caused by people moving from one job to another.
Structural unemployment - unemployment caused by changes in the structure of the economy.
Unemployment - the number of people looking for work who are unable to obtain a job.

In November 2002 the TUC highlighted a significant increase in the level of unemployment in London, making it Britain's most severely affected region. 3.5 per cent of manufacturing jobs in London were lost in the year to June. 23,000 service sector jobs were lost during the same period and more jobs were likely to go in finance and banking. The rate of unemployment in London was 7.5 per cent, almost 1 per cent higher than any other region, and compared to the national average of 5.3 per cent. London's total of 287,000 unemployed is more than the totals for Wales and Scotland combined, more than the entire Midlands and more than the North West and North East combined.

Mick Connolly, Regional Secretary for the TUC London Region said 'Unemployment is a personal tragedy and an economic waste. There are problems of unemployment throughout Britain ... but the media, many policy makers and some politicians seem blind to the level of unemployment in London. The government's own figures show the true extent of the problem ... Is it any wonder that a huge proportion of children in London are raised in poverty when nearly 300,000 workers who live in London are unemployed.'

Six London boroughs have unemployment levels of more than 6 per cent, as shown in Figure 67.2.

Source: adapted from www.brent.gov.uk.

(a) Examine the effects of unemployment in London boroughs on:
   (i)   businesses in the boroughs;
   (ii) people in the boroughs;
   (iii) local government.

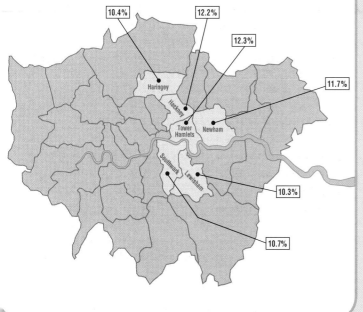

Figure 67.2 *Unemployment in London boroughs, 2002*

10.4% 12.2% 12.3% 11.7% 10.3% 10.7%

Haringey · Hackney · Tower Hamlets · Newham · Southwark · Lewisham

Question 2

1. What are the different types of unemployment?
2. Why is frictional unemployment not regarded as a problem by government?
3. What are the possible negative effects of unemployment on firms?
4. What are the possible positive effects of unemployment on firms?
5. State 2 methods of measuring unemployment.

Case study Unemployment in Manton, Nottinghamshire

In 1996 the coal mine at Manton in North Nottinghamshire was closed down. Manton was just one of a number of coal mines throughout the former mining areas of Britain that was closed down during the 1990s. This programme of pit closures resulted in thousands of miners losing their jobs. The effect was dramatic upon the former mining towns and villages and areas of the country, including south Wales, South Yorkshire, North Nottinghamshire, County Durham and parts of Scotland with large numbers of coal miners.

In Manton and surrounding areas the number of people registered as unemployed was close to 4,000 by the end of 1996. 'The community was dying on its feet' said Josie Potts whose husband lost his job when the mine closed.

By 2003 there was greater optimism in Manton amongst many. A number of new employers were moving to the area. B&Q's announcement of a 25 hectare distribution system would create 1,000 new jobs, for example. John Mann the MP for the area announced 'The transformation is so phenomenal. The number of unemployment claimants has fallen to 1,000'. He hopes that his constituency will be the first in the area to have full employment.

Not all are quite so impressed with developments in Manton and surrounding areas. Professor Steve Fothergill of the Coalfield Communities Campaign acknowledges that the number of unemployment claimants is lower, but thinks this may be obscuring a deeper problem. 'In many mining communities we have diverted huge numbers off job seekers' allowance, for example, onto other benefits, or even outside the benefits system altogether'.

Source: adapted from *The Guardian*, 6.12.2003.

(a) **Using an example, suggest the main type of unemployment referred to in the article. (4 marks)**

(b) **Explain the possible effects on the following businesses in the Manton area of the closure of the pit.**
   (i) A road haulage business.
   (ii) A restaurant.
   (iii) A garden centre. (14 marks)

(c) **Explain why the official unemployment figures might mask a deeper problem of unemployment in areas such as Manton. (10 marks)**

(d) **Assess the possible effects on businesses in the Manton area of B&Q's decision to build a distribution centre there. (12 marks)**

The balance of payments

Business transactions often take place across country borders. A UK manufacturer may buy components from the USA. Japanese businesses may use British insurance companies. A UK business may invest in a land reclamation project in a developing country.

All these transactions would be shown in a country's BALANCE OF PAYMENTS. It is a record of transactions between one country and the rest of the world. The balance of payments is usually divided into sections.

The current account The current account of the balance of payments is also divided into a number of sections.

- **Trade in goods.** Examples of traded goods might be computers, machine tools and chemicals. Goods which are manufactured in a country and sold abroad are called EXPORTS. Goods which are brought into a country from abroad are known as IMPORTS. An export from the UK, where goods are sold abroad, earns money for UK businesses. Money flows into the UK, so UK exports are recorded as **credits**. An import to the UK, where UK consumers or businesses buy goods from abroad, leads to an outflow of money from the UK. UK imports are recorded as **debits**. The difference between the value of exports and imports of goods is shown as TRADE IN GOODS on the balance of payments.
- **Trade in services.** Examples of traded services might be banking, shipping, travel and tourism, and insurance. Services which are sold abroad are exports and services bought from abroad are imports. Passenger tickets sold abroad for travel on a UK airline is an export of a service for the UK. The UK business earns money which flows into the UK. It appears as a credit. A UK business which insures with a foreign company is an example of an import of a service to the UK. The UK business spends abroad and money flows out of the UK. It appears as a debit. The difference between the value of exports and imports of goods is shown as TRADE IN SERVICES.
- **Income.** Income may be compensation paid to employees working abroad. Income sent home to the UK by a British computer programmer working in Saudi Arabia would appear as a credit under income on the UK accounts as money is entering the UK. Income may also be investment income. This is the interest, profit and dividends earned by companies abroad or foreign firms in a country. Profits sent to Japan made by a Japanese car firm in the UK would appear as a debit on the UK accounts.
- **Current transfers.** These include central government transfers. They also include gifts from individuals abroad to a country or gifts to foreign countries. For example, a payment to the EU by the UK government would be shown as a debit under current transfers on the UK current account, as money is leaving the UK.

The difference between the value of money entering a country (credits) and the value of money leaving a country (debits) for:
- trade in goods and services;
- income to/from abroad;
- transfers;
is called the CURRENT BALANCE. We can say that:

Current balance = sales of exports and services, income earned from abroad and transfers to a country *minus* purchases of imports and services, income going abroad and transfers from a country

Capital account This involves the transfer of ownership of assets, transfers of funds associated with the purchase and sale of assets and the cancellation of liabilities. Examples include transfers from the EU regional fund and the forgiveness of debt. This is a small part of the balance of payments account compared to the current and financial accounts.

Jobson plc is a UK based multinational business. It has plants in Singapore, the USA, the UK and Australia. It specialises in the manufacture and distribution of a wide variety of food and drink products. Below are some of its transactions over the past 12 months.
- Profits from plants in Singapore, Malaysia and Ireland taken back to the UK.
- Buying shares in a French drinks producing firm.
- Exporting £30 million of soft drinks to EU nations from its UK plant.
- Holding a conference for senior managers from all of its plants in Bermuda.
- Paying for a team of Japanese management consultants to help with the restructuring of its London headquarters.
- Buying new production machinery from Germany for its UK plant.
- Investing £50 million on upgrading production facilities in its USA, Singapore and Australian factories.

Explain which of the above would be shown as:
(a) exports of services;
(b) imports of services;
(c) exports of goods;
(d) imports of goods;
(e) transactions in liabilities;
(f) the purchase or sale of assets;
in the UK's balance of payments account.

Question 1

The financial account This covers the flow of money for transactions in **financial assets and liabilities**. For example, a foreign business may buy shares (an asset) in a UK company. Money would flow into the UK and would be shown as a credit on the financial account. Note that any dividend earned by the foreign business on the shares would be shown as a debit under investment income on the UK's current account as money is leaving the country. A transaction in liabilities on the UK accounts would be a UK business borrowing from a foreign bank. This would appear as a credit on the financial account, as money is flowing into the UK.

Balance of payments problems and business

The balance of payments must always 'balance'. Take a situation where a country has a **current account deficit**. This also means that outflows of money are greater than inflows to that country from trade in goods and services, income and transfers.

Where does the money come from to finance this deficit? The UK may, for example, borrow from foreign banks or sell its assets abroad to bring money back in. The Bank of England could sell some of the country's gold or foreign currency reserves. Whatever happens, the deficit on the current account would be made up by a surplus on the capital account and financial account. In practice, if the values do not actually balance a **balancing item** is added. This is a figure for errors and omissions. It is large or small enough so that the accounts always balance.

Although the accounts always balance, individual parts of the balance of payments may not. What if the current account deficit carried on for a long period? This could lead to a number of problems for the UK government and for UK business.

- The country as a whole will get more and more into debt. Other countries may refuse to lend more money, and may insist upon repayment of any debt. Third World and Eastern European countries have faced such problems over the past few decades.
- Loss of jobs. If consumers buy imports, they will not buy home produced goods or services. Thus opportunities for job creation are lost. Similarly, low levels of exports mean the demand by businesses for employees will be lower.
- UK businesses may become dependent on imports of components and raw materials. This may mean that costs are dependent upon the exchange rate value of the pound sterling. This is dealt with later in this unit. It may also make the UK economy more vulnerable to IMPORTED INFLATION (☞ unit 66).

Figure 68.1 shows the current account of the UK over the period 1980-2002. For most of the period the current balance was in deficit. This was because the UK tends to be a **net importer** of goods. In other words, it imports more goods than it exports. Although the UK exports a large amount of services (it is a **net exporter**), this is not enough to offset the deficit on the trade in goods (known as the **balance of trade**).

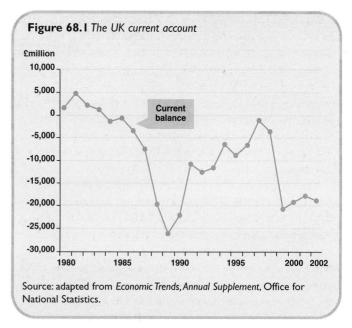

Figure 68.1 *The UK current account*

Source: adapted from *Economic Trends, Annual Supplement*, Office for National Statistics.

Exchange rates

An EXCHANGE RATE is the price of one country's currency in relation to that of another. So, for example, an exchange rate £1 = $2 means that one pound is worth two dollars. Alternatively, one dollar is worth 50 pence.

Exchange rates are determined on foreign exchange markets throughout the world. If an exchange rate is **freely floating,** then changes in the demand for or supply of a currency will result in a change in that country's exchange rate. For example, a fall in the demand for sterling will cause its value to fall. This is the same type of analysis that was used to show the effect of changes in the demand for and supply of goods on prices in unit 61. A **fixed** exchange rate system is where countries do not allow the values of their currencies to change against each other's.

If the value of a currency falls in relation to the value of another currency then the exchange rate is said to have DEPRECIATED. Under a system of fixed exchange rates the currency will be DEVALUED by the government or controlling organisation. If the value of the currency rises against that of another currency then it is said to have **appreciated** (or to have been revalued).

There is a number of factors that can affect the exchange rate of a currency.

The volume of exports An increase in exports by UK firms will mean that more pounds are required to buy these exports. This will result in an increase in the demand for sterling and cause the value of sterling to rise. A decrease in UK exports will have the opposite effect, resulting in a fall in the demand for sterling and a fall in its value.

The volume of imports An increase in imports coming into the UK will mean that more sterling has to be sold in order to purchase the foreign currencies needed to buy imports. This will cause an increase in the supply of sterling, leading to a fall in sterling's exchange rate. A decrease in imports will have the opposite effect, resulting in a fall in the supply of sterling and a rise in its value.

The level of interest rates A rise in interest rates in the UK will attract savings from abroad. This will raise the demand for sterling and thus its price. A fall in interest rates will have the opposite effect.

Speculation The short term price of a country's currency is mainly influenced by speculation. If dealers on foreign exchange markets expect the value of a currency to fall in the future, they may sell their reserves of that currency. This will cause the supply of that currency to increase and its price to fall. It has been argued that speculation led to the collapse in the price of the pound on the so-called 'Black Wednesday' in 1992 and to the collapse of the Russian rouble in 1998. If, however, speculators expect the value of a currency to rise in the future, then they will begin purchasing that currency leading to an increase in its value.

Government intervention Governments may intervene on foreign exchange markets. They may try to influence the price of either their own currency or that of another country. For example, the UK government may attempt to raise the value of the pound by purchasing it on foreign exchange markets. Governments may also raise interest rates in order to increase the value of the pound.

Investment and capital flows An inflow of funds for long-term investment in the UK will cause the demand, and therefore the price, of sterling to rise. Similarly an outflow of investment funds will cause the supply of sterling to rise and its price to fall, other factors remaining the same. Thus, French investment in a UK water bottling plant would cause a rise in the exchange rate.

Capital flows are largely determined by the rate of interest. Thus an increase in UK interest rates would lead to an inflow of funds into the UK and a rise in the value of sterling. Such inflows of funds following interest rate changes tend to be short term money moving from one of the world's financial centres to another in search of the highest rate of return.

Discuss the likely effects on the value of the pound against the Japanese yen of the following:
(a) increases in the number of UK residents visiting Japan;
(b) the yen coming under speculative selling pressure as an election comes nearer;
(c) an increase in UK aircraft sales to Japan;
(d) UK interest rates increased to 6 per cent whilst Japanese interest rates remain at 4 per cent.

Question 2

Exchange rates and business

The main reason why exchange rates are so important to businesses is because of their influence on the price of imports and exports. All but a very few small firms use at least some goods and services imported from abroad. Increasingly, large numbers of businesses are finding that they have to export their products in order to grow or survive. Thus the majority of firms are affected in some way by exchange rates.

The effect of falling exchange rates A fall in the exchange rate (a **depreciation** or **devaluation**) will affect the price of a business's exports and the price it pays for imports. Look at Table 68.1 which shows the effects of a fall in the value of the pound from £1 = $2 to £1 = $1.60. Note that if the value of a currency falls against another currency it becomes **weaker**. Less of another currency will be exchanged for one unit of that currency.

Table 68.1 *The effects of a fall in the value of the pound on the price of exports and imports*

	Exchange rate	UK price	USA price
Exported goods	£1 = $2	£10	$20
	£1 = $1.60	£10	$16
Imported goods	£1 = $2	£10	$20
	£1 = $1.60	£12.50	$20

At an exchange rate of £1 = $2, a book priced at £10 that is exported to the USA would cost Americans $20. If the value of the pound fell to £1 = $1.60, Americans would now be able to buy the same book for $16. So a fall in the exchange rate can make UK exports cheaper.

What about imports to the UK? A picture frame priced at $20 imported to the UK would cost £10 before the depreciation of the exchange rate. If the exchange rate fell to £1 = $1.60, the picture frame would now cost £12.50 ([$2÷$1.60]x£10) or ($20÷1.60). So a fall in the exchange rate can cause the price of imports to rise.

The overall effect should be beneficial for UK businesses. The price paid for UK exports should fall, allowing businesses to sell more in export markets. The price paid by UK businesses and consumers for imports should rise. This might encourage them to switch their purchases from foreign goods to UK products.

There are problems, however, for firms if exchange rates are falling.
● Rising import prices mean that the amount paid for any inputs, such as raw materials or components bought in from abroad, will rise.
● Rising import prices can lead to imported inflation and the

associated problems of this for businesses (☞ unit 66).

- Uncertainty over future prices of raw materials and components can result.
- Constant price changes may affect foreign demand for products as they are unsettling for customers.

The effect of rising exchange rates A rise in exchange rates means that a currency becomes **stronger** against another currency. So more of another currency will be exchanged for the unit of that currency. This is the opposite effect to devaluation. A rise in the exchange rate can cause the price of exports to rise and the price of imports to fall. For example, in Table 68.1 an increase in the exchange rate from £1=$1.60 to £1=$2 will cause the price of a £10 export to rise from $16 to $20 and the price of a $20 import to fall from £12.50 to £10.

The overall effect is likely to be negative. Not only will it become more difficult for UK firms to compete on price in export markets, but it will put pressure on them in UK markets, as they struggle to compete with lower priced imported goods. However, a rise in the exchange rate could allow UK businesses to buy cheaper imports from abroad.

The stability of exchange rates Unstable exchange rates can make it very difficult for firms to plan for the future. A rise in the exchange rate, for example, could turn a previously profitable export order into a loss maker. A devaluation, on the other hand, could mean that exports which looked unprofitable could now earn a profit for the firm.

In 2000 Ford announced that it was likely to axe car production at its Dagenham plant. This would lead to more than 3,000 workers being 'out in the cold'. One of the problems was the old style of the Fiesta. Ford had been overtaken in Europe by a number of manufacturers bringing out new models for the twenty first century. The old Ford Escort had been replaced by the Ford Focus, which was doing well. However, Ford suggested that it could not be successful on one car alone. Perhaps the biggest problem had been the rising value of the pound against the euro. Like all manufacturers with plants in the UK, Ford had a difficulty with the strength of the pound against the euro.

Source: adapted from *The Guardian*, 30.4.2000.

(a) Explain, using an example, what is meant by the rising value of the pound against the euro.
(b) Examine how this might have affected Ford.

Question3

How much are businesses affected?

Not all businesses are affected to the same extent by changes in exchange rates.

The response of consumers Some products have a strong brand identity. Even if their prices increase, consumers do not reduce the amount purchased by a great deal. Unit 18 refers to these products as having an **inelastic** demand. What effect will a fall in the value of the pound from £1=1.8 euros to £1=1.5 euros have on UK businesses exporting such goods?

A firm selling 1,000 books to Germany each month for 5 euros each at an exchange rate of £1 = 1.8 euros, would receive 5,000 euros (£2,777) in revenue. If the exchange rate fell to £1 = 1.5 euros, and the demand for books was price inelastic, then the business may be able to keep the price at 5 euros. At this new exchange rate the 5,000 euros would be worth £3,333 (5,000÷ 1.5). Thus, revenue would increase by £556.

Firms with products which are sensitive to price changes are likely to feel the impact of even minor exchange rate changes. If export prices rise the volume of sales will fall by a greater degree, and the overall revenue for exports will fall. If export prices fall, revenue should be greater because the increase in quantity sold is relatively greater than the fall in price.

The degree of control over prices Not all businesses have the same degree of control over the price at which their products are sold. Those with a high degree of control over their prices can adopt market based methods of pricing, such as customer value pricing (☞ unit 19). They might decide not to allow exchange rate changes to alter the price of their exports, although their sales revenue may change. For example, a business selling sportswear with a strong degree of brand loyalty amongst its customers might be unwilling to alter its price as a result of relatively small exchange rate fluctuations. This is because prices will have been carefully chosen to suit particular markets. In this case, only a large rise in the exchange rate, which threatened profits, would cause a pricing re-think.

The Reconstruction Company rebuilds cars such as Land Rovers and exports them to countries such as South Africa and Australia. It has exported 5 reconditioned vehicles for use on game reserves, selling each one for 120,000 rand. The exchange rate at the time was £1=10 rand.

(a) Calculate the earnings in rands and in pounds for the business.
(b) The exchange rate fell over the next year to £1=9.6 rand. The South African companies still needed vehicles and were not likely to find a supplier at this price and at short notice. The Reconstruction Company decided to keep its price the same in rand. It sells another 5 vehicles. Calculate the effect of this on the revenue of the business.

Question4

Importing components and raw materials The effect of a change in the exchange rate on firms that imported components or raw materials would depend on a number of factors. First, whether or not the firms from which they are importing decide to alter their prices. Second, whether or not any long term agreements on prices had been reached. Third, whether the firm had already bought foreign currency to pay for future imported components etc. A firm importing fabric from Hong Kong might want to buy a year's supply of Hong Kong dollars to make sure it was unaffected by changes in the exchange rate.

The single European market and the single European currency

In 1992 the single European market was created. This removed restrictions on trade between members of the European Union.

A further major step in European integration took place on January 1, 2002, when 12 European countries, including France, Germany, Ireland and Spain adopted a **single currency**, the euro. From January 1, 2002, euro notes and coins became the legal tender in these countries, replacing their national currencies. The UK decided to retain the pound as its currency and did not join.

The countries participating are known as the eurozone. The introduction of the euro has had a number of effects on businesses and consumers within the eurozone.

- Consumers and businesses can easily identify price differences between eurozone countries.
- There is no longer any need to change money from one currency into another within this area. This would reduce costs for individuals and businesses changing from one currency to another to buy goods and services within the eurozone.
- For businesses trading between eurozone countries there is none of the uncertainty associated with exchange rates changes. Thus businesses no longer, for example, experience a sudden change in exchange rates which might increase the price of imported goods and services.
- Businesses may incurred costs in retraining staff in the use

of the currency and in re-pricing products.
- Greater economic stability exists within the eurozone. There is some disagreement about this. Many argue that the introduction of a single interest rate across the eurozone will lead to lower inflation across the eurozone as a whole. This it is anticipated will be especially the case in countries such as Italy and Greece which have, in the past, been more prone to inflation.

Some people and groups within the UK are opposed to the single currency. They do not want control of economic policy to be from Europe. They argue that European policies that may suit Europe, such as high interest rates, may not be applicable to the UK at a particular time. UK businesses, they suggest, may suffer as a result.

key terms

Balance of payments - a record of the transactions between one country and the rest of the world over a given period of time.
Current balance - the difference between the value of money entering and leaving a country for trade in goods and services, income from abroad and transfers.
Devaluation/depreciation - a decline in the value of an exchange rate.
Exchange rate - the price of one currency in relation to another.
Exports - goods and services which leave the country and are sold to other countries.
Imports - goods and services which enter the country and are bought from other countries.
Imported inflation - a rise in prices, as a result of exchange rate changes, which raise the price of materials or components brought into a country.
Trade in goods - the difference between imports and exports of physical products.
Trade in services - the difference between the import and export of services.

Case study

Strong pound equals bargains in New York

Record numbers of Brits were heading to the US on weekend shopping trips in 2004. They were eager to cash in on the fact that the dollar had fallen to an eleven year low against the pound (also a rise in the strength of the pound's value against the dollar). In February 2004 the pound traded at £1 = $1.90, whereas in previous years it had been as low as £1 = $1.50. It was possible, for instance, to pay for a flight to the US, buy an Apple iMac desktop computer and still save on making the purchase at home. Ruby Briggs of North America Travel Services said 'America has come back into its own after the September 11 downturn. The number of people booking holidays has been huge. Bookings in January were 20 per cent up on last year. Shopping trips are particularly popular and we've seen a huge rise in the last few weeks'.

One of the biggest bargains was the iMac G4 desktop computer, which costs £999.99 in PC World in London but only £673.73 in the US. A pair of mens' Levi jeans could be bought in New York for £18.37 but in London the same pair cost £49.95. Sean Tipton of the Association of British Travel Agents said 'A combination of the weakness of the dollar and some of the cheapest flights that we've ever seen have meant a massive increase in the number of people travelling. Retail analyst, Richard Ratner, however warned that the British buyer must factor in all the costs. 'You have to consider the cost of going over there in the first place. And if it's an electrical item, make sure its compatible with UK voltage'.

Source: adapted from *The Daily Mirror*, 19.2.2004.

Table 68.2 *Savings in the US for UK buyers, based on an exchange rate of $1.90 = £1*

Product	Cost in London	Cost in New York (in pounds)	(in dollars)
Sony DSCVI digital camera	£440.99	£262.00	$497.80
Christian Dior mini aviator sunglasses	£120.00	£110.00	$209.00
Aveda 'Shakra' perfume 50ml	£40.00	£22.04	$41.88
Dido's 'Life for Rent' CD	£13.99	£9.94	$18.89
Men's Levi 501s	£49.95	£18.37	$34.90
Traditional Burberry handbag	£199.00	£171.00	$324.90
Gap women's combat trousers	£39.50	£30.44	$57.84
DVD 'Pirates of the Caribbean'	£15.99	£13.09	$24.87
Sony PlayStation 2	£139.00	£94.00	$17.86
Wonderbra	£25.00	£18.89	$35.89
iMac desktop computer	£1,000.00	£737.00	$1,400.30
Apple iPod	£399.00	£262.00	$497.80

(a) What is meant by (i) 'a rise in the value of the pound' and (ii) 'a British traveller must factor in all the costs'? (6 marks)

(b) Explain why, according to the article, New York retailers have benefited so much from the relatively weak dollar. (6 marks)

(c) Explain how the value of the exchange rate position in 2004 might affect the USA balance of payments. (8 marks)

(d) Calculate and explain the effect of a fall in the value of the pound from £1 = $1.90 to £1 = $1.50 on the sterling (pound) price of the following items.
  (i) A pair of mens' Levi 501s.
  (ii) A Sony DSCVI digital camera.
  (iii) A Sony PlayStation 2.
  (iv) A pair of Christian Dior mini aviator sunglasses. (10 marks)

(e) A UK business is seeking to expand exports to the USA in 2004. Assess whether this was an advisable strategy at the time the article was written. (10 marks)

What is economic growth?

ECONOMIC GROWTH is an indication of the change in the goods and services produced by an economy. One way an economy can tell if growth is taking place is to examine its GDP or GNP figures (☞ unit 64). These show how much money is flowing around the economy. A rise from one year to the next is usually an indication of growth. Growth is measured in **real** terms, in other words, it takes into account the rate of inflation (☞ unit 66).

If economic growth is taking place, there are likely to be favourable trading conditions for business. Many new businesses set up and continue to grow. In periods of growth, businesses may find a healthy demand for their products. Businesses will tend to suffer when growth is zero or even negative. Negative growth may be an indication of recession in an economy (☞ unit 64). This will have the opposite effect to a period of growth, with declining sales and many firms going out of business.

The growth rate of one country compared to others is also important. Figure 69.1 shows the growth rates in the UK compared to other countries over the period 1990-2001. The UK has performed relatively well against competitors in western and eastern europe, as well as Japan. However, it has lagged behind some countries in Asia and a little behind the USA.

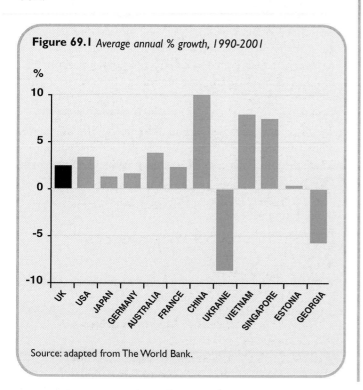

Figure 69.1 *Average annual % growth, 1990-2001*

Source: adapted from The World Bank.

The business cycle

Unit 96 explained how economies move through periods of 'up and downs' over time. This can be shown by the use of the **business cycle** or **trade cycle**. At the top of the cycle, in a boom, growth will be high. As output and income fall, the economy moves into recession. At the bottom of the cycle, in a trough, firms fail and unemployment is high. As the economy recovers, output and income start to rise again.

Figure 69.2 shows changes in GDP at constant prices since 1955 in the UK. The trends in the figures show that the performance of the UK economy has broadly been similar to the traditional business cycle (☞ unit 64). For example, the early 1990s saw a period of recession, with annual growth rates of minus 2 per cent or more at times. In the mid to late 1990s there was a recovery, with growth rates over 4 per cent. Annual growth rates slowed in the early twenty first century in the UK, as in many other countries. In 2002 it was estimated to be around 1.5 per cent.

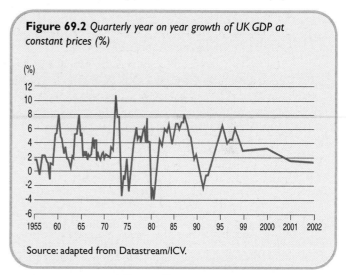

Figure 69.2 *Quarterly year on year growth of UK GDP at constant prices (%)*

Source: adapted from Datastream/ICV.

Factors affecting growth

There is a number of factors that can lead to economic growth.

Land Land includes all natural resources such as forests, lakes and oil and coal deposits, as well as land itself. It is possible for countries to experience economic growth through more effective exploitation of their natural resources. Saudi Arabia, for example, has generated the vast majority of its wealth from its oil reserves and the UK has benefited from North Sea oil.

Labour force/population Increasing the quantity of the labour force can contribute to economic growth.

Table 69.1 *Individual bankruptcies and company liquidations, 1989-2002*

	1989	1990	1991	1992	1993	1994	1995	1996	1997	1998	1999	2000	2001	2002
Bankruptcies	8,138	12,058	22,632	32,106	31,016	25,634	21,933	21,803	19,892	19,647	21,611	21,550	23,447	24,292
Total company liquidations	10,456	15,051	21,827	24,425	20,708	16,728	14,536	13,461	12,610	13,203	14,280	14,317	14,972	16,305

Source: adapted from *Annual Abstract of Statistics*, Office for National Statistics

(a) Describe the main trends taking place in the table.
(b) To what extent does the information suggest that there is a business cycle?

Question 1

● One relatively easy way of increasing the labour force is to encourage immigration. The success of the US economy has been partly attributed to the effects of immigration.
● Changes in the demography (☞ unit 63) of a country can be important. More young people will swell the size of the workforce, but an increase in the birth rate will create more dependants for a number of years. The UK is at present experiencing an ageing of its population, resulting in a relative decline in the number of people of working age.
● One of the biggest increases in the UK's workforce over the last thirty years has come about through the increasing participation of women in work. At any given time, there are usually large numbers of women willing to enter the workforce should suitable employment become available.

Whilst the quantity of labour in a country can be important, the quality of it tends to be especially significant in influencing growth rates. A well trained, well educated workforce, which is flexible and able to respond to change, can help to provide favourable trading conditions for businesses, leading to growth.

Investment and technology Economic growth requires an increase in the capital stock of the economy. This means the development of and investment in new technology (☞ unit 60) and the updating of capital equipment. Technological development also allows new products to be created. It is not just the quantity of investment in an economy which is important. Investment needs to be directed into growth industries whose products are likely to be in high demand in the future.

Government policy Governments can use a combination of fiscal, monetary, exchange rate and supply side policies to stimulate growth. The policies a government chooses will reflect its views about the operation of the economy. The choice of policy is important. Even if an economy has great natural resources, a well trained workforce and high levels of investment it may be held back by inappropriate government policy.

Competitive advantage Michael Porter has suggested that countries must have strategies that attempt to create a competitive advantage (☞ unit 5) in international trade. This, he suggests, can be done by building up the competitive

advantage of particular sectors of the economy, rather than attempting to compete in all sectors. For example, Singapore has been successful in achieving growth as a result of its trading policy despite a relatively weak agricultural sector.

The effects of economic growth on business

The majority of firms benefit from a growing economy. There are some, such as pawnbrokers and scrap-metal dealers who perhaps do better in recessions, but these tend to be exceptions. If a business is operating in a growing economy, experiencing economic growth rates of 3 per cent per annum or more, this is likely to have a number of effects upon it. Not all of them, however, are positive.

Sales revenue Consumer spending should be high during a period of economic growth. This will increase the demand for many firms' products and should lead to an increase in sales revenue. If a firm is able to keep its costs under control, this should also mean an increase in profits.

Expansion An increase in the demand for a firm's products generated by a sustained period of economic growth may lead to expansion. Some businesses are forced into expanding where they find that they cannot meet demand. Others plan their expansion well in advance. Expansion may involve some or all of the following:
● recruiting new staff;
● raising finance;
● increasing the size of premises;
● moving to new premises;
● purchasing more assets, for example, production facilities, machinery or office equipment;
● taking over competitors.

Security In a healthy business climate, a business is likely to feel more secure in its decisions. It will be able to order from suppliers with greater confidence. This may lead to a better and more effective relationship. Businesses should also be able to hire employees without concern about being forced to lay them off within a short period of time. This may result in a firm committing itself more to the workforce, for example, by investing in training programmes.

Planning for the future Economic growth should provide businesses with more confidence in planning for the future. Higher profit levels, for example, should help to provide investment funds for new projects. Year to year or even day to day survival is likely to become less of an issue as a firm seeks to consolidate its future position. However, confidence in planning for the future will hinge upon how long the business expects the growth to last. Due to the UK's past record of rapidly moving from boom to slump, there is evidence that many British businesses have not, in the past, regarded a period of economic growth as sufficient reason to undertake investment projects.

Increasing costs It is not unusual for high economic growth rates to be accompanied by rising costs. Land costs often rise during such periods. This was especially evident in the South East of England during the period 2000-2002, when property prices spiralled. Labour costs may also increase as employees and trade unions seek to benefit from the success of their business.

The effects of lack of growth on business

A lack of growth or negative growth in the economy can have a number of effects on business.

Changes in consumer demand Many firms will face a fall in the demand for their products. This is because the incomes of consumers tend to fall during such periods, forcing them into cutting back on spending. The effect of this is not spread evenly amongst firms. For some the impact can be dramatic, leading to redundancies and even closure. The construction industry is notoriously vulnerable to recessions. Producers of consumer goods tend to suffer less in a recession than producers of goods for industrial markets.

Confidence There tends to be a general lack of confidence amongst businesses during a recession. This can lead to investment projects being cancelled and orders being lost. Some businesses will be affected not only for the period of the recession itself, but also in the longer term. It may also lead to a loss of profitability and competitiveness.

Capthorn Ltd manufactures a variety of household products. It has seen a steady increase in turnover and profits in recent years. Faced with the challenges of a new millennium in the year 2000, it was considering expanding the business. However, it was likely to have to make a choice about which products to promote and in which areas to launch new products.

Table 69.2 *Individual consumption expenditure at current market prices*

£ million

	2000	2001	2002
Furniture, furnishings, carpets and coverings	13,758	14,934	17,897
Household textiles	4,465	4,677	5,317
Household appliances	4,948	6,054	5,859
Glassware, tableware and utensils	4,431	4,657	5,226
Tools and equipment for house and garden	2,722	2,960	3,154
Goods and services for household maintenance	5,343	5,587	5,824
All furnishings, household equipment and maintenance	**35,667**	**38,869**	**43,277**

Source: adapted from *Annual Abstract of Statistics*, Office for National Statistics.

(a) Discuss whether and how the business should expand in future.
(b) Explain the possible effects of the strategy you have advised.

Question 2

Effect on small firms Small firms tend to be especially vulnerable to recession. They often do not have the finance to withstand periods of negative cash flow (☞ unit 35) which occur during such times. Also, small firms tend to rely upon banks. This means that they may suffer as banks are reluctant to lend during recessions. Banks also tend to call in loans at short notice.

Possible benefits Those firms which survive during a recession may benefit from a reduction in competition, as their rivals go out of business. This should put them in a position to gain a greater share of the market, especially when the economy picks up again. The recession may also force businesses to become leaner and fitter operations. Government policies designed to bring an economy out of recession can be an advantage to many firms. For example, interest rates are often reduced to help bring a recession to an end.

Occasionally a slowdown helps to speed things up for a business. Great Universal Stores (GUS) consists of a range of businesses, including Burberry's, the coat manufacturer, Argos, the town centre catalogue company, the GUS catalogue company and Experian, the credit rating agency. It is this last, less well known, part of GUS that is responsible for over 40 per cent of the company's profits. Experian is involved in checking the credit ratings of hundreds of thousands of consumers applying to stores, car showrooms, mortgage businesses and others offering credit and loans.

Following much lower levels of economic growth in the US economy many had predicted serious difficulties for GUS. But a combination of factors has led to a revival in the business' fortunes despite the grim economic circumstances. New managers at Burberry and Argos performed minor miracles in making the businesses sharper with more sought after brands and identities. In addition, the slowdown in the US economy meant that business was booming for Experian. Because of difficulties in the US economy, car showrooms, stores and other credit providers were being far more careful about making credit available to consumers. Hence there were more credit checks and better profits for Experian and GUS.

Source: adapted from *The Guardian*, 12.4.2001.

(a) Describe the relationship between economic growth in the US and the performance of GUS.
(b) Explain how some businesses may be unaffected by or may perform better during periods of lower levels of economic growth.

Question 3

key terms

Economic growth - an indication of the change in the output or income of an economy. It is usually measured by a change in national income figures (GDP or GNP).

Knowledge

1. What does a business cycle show?
2. How might land contribute to economic growth?
3. In what ways might a firm be affected by demographic change?
4. How might a business benefit from economic growth?
5. What problems might economic growth cause for a business?
6. Why are small firms especially vulnerable to recession?

Case study *SkyTravel*

Sky Travel, a travel firm based in Bristol, was considering expanding the range of holidays which it would offer to the public in the next summer season. It already offered packages to traditional destinations such as the Greek Islands, the Costa del Sol and the Balearic Islands. It wished to expand into the long haul market, offering holidays to destinations previously out of the reach of mass tourism. Such destinations were likely to include India, Thailand and Bali.

A firm of economic consultants had been employed to provide the business with a report on future economic conditions. Before the consultants had presented the report, there had been concern expressed about the expansion plan by the firm's chief accountant, Errol Lee. He was worried about the building up of debt. He believed that economic conditions were such that it was unlikely sufficient revenue could be generated in the current year to finance expansionary plans.

Anne Doyle, the marketing director, who had been carefully researching the market for long haul flights, felt that consumer demand for long haul flights to some of these exotic locations might dry up just as quickly as it had initially grown. There was growing evidence of fickle behaviour amongst consumers of such holidays. In addition, concern about the link between sunbathing and skin cancer was leading to a trend towards taking holidays in countries with more moderate climates. The firm's personnel director, John Bryden, also expressed doubts about the extent to which staff currently employed in comfortable Mediterranean locations would cope if transferred to potentially much more difficult long haul destinations. He was particularly concerned about political unrest in Indonesia, of which Bali is a region, the sometimes dramatic changes in the Thai economy and possible terrorist activity.

At the next board meeting a number of these concerns were discussed, but the managing director, Chris Boughie, insisted that no decision could be made until the presentation by the economic consultants which was to take place the next day.

That evening, all directors watched the evening news in the comfort of their homes. The main stories were the redundancies to be made by several leading firms, rising unemployment and a large current account deficit on the balance of payments.

They arrived at work the next day in a gloomy mood. Erica Harper, a young economist working for the firm of

consultants, gave the presentation. 'It could be argued that the UK faces a prolonged period of low growth at the moment. Industrial output is down, unemployment is rising and there has been an upsurge in business failures. However, indicators suggest that growth will begin to increase after 2-3 years as government policies to stimulate growth begin to take effect. This should lead to much improved trading conditions as incomes begin to rise. Sky Travel should be aware that at least 70 per cent of its current and potential customers are unlikely to be influenced by current economic conditions and will continue to take holidays once, twice or even more times a year to destinations served by the business.'

(a) Identify the factors which may have influenced Sky Travel's decision to expand its business. (4 marks)

(b) Using evidence from the article, explain how low growth rates affected businesses in the economy at the time. (8 marks)

(c) Examine the factors that may act as a constraint on the decision of the business to expand. (10 marks)

(d) Explain why a percentage of the business's clients may not be affected by changes in the economic climate when making a decision to book holidays. (6 marks)

(e) Advise Sky Travel on whether it should go ahead with its expansion plans. (12 marks)

Business and social constraints

Businesses affect the societies in which they operate. A sole trader running a small grocery store may benefit local residents by opening for a few hours on a Sunday. On the other hand such a business may have negative effects. Canned drinks bought from the shop may be left in the street. Opening on a Sunday may lead to more traffic in the area. Decisions made by a multinational company can have a huge impact in many different countries. For example, it may decide to relocate its factory from one country to another. This is likely to lead to a fall in income and employment in the country that the company has left. The new location may gain from more jobs, the building of infrastructure, such as roads, and perhaps spending on health care and community projects.

These examples show that businesses do not operate in isolation. The decisions they make can affect a range of other groups and individuals. The businesses can be seen as part of the societies in which they operate. As a result, governments often pass laws and set regulations to control the conduct of businesses.

Such laws tend to set the legal minimum in terms of the way in which businesses behave. However, do businesses have any further responsibilities to society? Should businesses consider the implications of their decisions upon society and not just take into account whether these decisions help the business to achieve its objectives? For example, a cement factory may have emissions within legal limits. The local community might argue that the emissions cause health problems amongst children and the elderly in the area. Should the business try to reduce the emissions?

Some would argue that businesses are self-regulating. They do not need to be controlled by government. If they ignore the views of society, consumers will not buy their products. They will lose trade and perhaps go out of business. Others argue that, without external regulation, businesses may have negative effects upon society. People who are adversely affected by business activity may not be in a position to influence the business. The children and elderly people living near the cement factory may not buy cement. The young and old may not be able to exert any outside pressure by complaining to the management of the business.

Business and stakeholders

One way of considering the impact of businesses upon society is to view all of the groups affected by the behaviour of a business as **stakeholders** (☞ unit 3). The stakeholders in a business are likely to include customers, employees, shareholders, suppliers, government, local communities and businesses, financial institutions and other creditors.

Businesses have tended to be influenced mainly by customers, employees and shareholders. Increasingly, however, other groups are affecting business behaviour. For example, some businesses will only supply their products to other businesses that have an ethical or environmental policy. Some pension companies will not invest in businesses that sell arms. This suggests that businesses need to have a greater SOCIAL RESPONSIBILITY to groups beyond those immediately involved in the business.

Business ethics

The way in which businesses respond to issues such as the sale of arms or health risks from pollution may depend on their ETHICS. Ethics are the **values** and **beliefs** which influence how individuals, groups and societies behave. For example, an electricity generating business may be operating within legal emissions limits. However, it may feel that it has to change its production methods to reduce emissions even further because it believes businesses should work towards a cleaner environment.

In part the ethics of a business will depend upon the values of its employees. However, the ethical stance of the business is likely to be determined by the values of senior managers, directors and other important stakeholders. It will also be influenced by codes of conduct which may operate in the industry. The term ETHICAL is used to refer to businesses which explicitly recognise the importance of social responsibility and the need to consider the effects of its actions upon stakeholders. It is possible that a business following an ethical policy may:

● attract customers and employees who agree with its policy;
● have to change its operations to fit in with this policy, for

---

Cadbury is a business proud of its work in the community and has won many awards from within the business world for its work. However, in 2003 the company was criticised by a number of health groups for its Get Active campaign. Vouchers were available on its chocolate bars that could be used to provide more sports equipment for schools. Some felt that a business marketing products which are inherently unhealthy and in a climate of rising concerns about obesity in young people should not be engaging in marketing to schools. Others thought that schools needed all the help they could get in purchasing sports equipment and helping young people to lead more healthy lives.

Source: adapted from *The Observer*, 21.3.2004.

(a) Discuss to what extent businesses using vouchers to provide school equipment might be said to be acting in an ethical way.

Question 1

example approving certain suppliers;

- have to set a policy for all the business in areas such as recruitment and marketing.

Business and the environment

It is possible that the activities of business can have certain beneficial effects on the environment. For example, a new factory may be built in a derelict area. The new premises may be landscaped, improving the view. A grass area built might have a bench which could be used by pedestrians.

Businesses are becoming more and more aware of the need to consider the environment in their operations. Many critics of certain business activities suggest that they have a negative effect on the environment in the surrounding area. Some of the negative effects of business activity include:

- air pollution caused by the discharge of emissions into the atmosphere and traffic visiting retail outlets;
- water pollution as a result of the dumping of waste;
- congestion from employees going to work or consumers visiting retail outlets;
- noise from factories and traffic;
- destruction of natural habitats from the building of premises.

How might these effects be controlled?

- Laws can be passed which make it illegal for firms to pollute the environment. For example, various environmental protection acts and regulations set limits on the quantities of gas emissions.
- Increased fuel prices in the UK have been justified by

governments on the grounds that consumers should pay prices which accurately reflect the impact of car use on the environment. High taxes on petrol are designed to reduce car use. In 1996 the UK government introduced a **landfill tax**. This taxed businesses for dumping waste on a landfill site. It was designed to discourage waste and encourage recycling and reuse of materials.

- Firms could be forced by law to compensate those affected by business activities. For example, it is common for airports to provide grants for nearby housing to buy double glazing.
- Government could offer grants, tax allowances or subsidies to business to encourage the reduction of external costs. For example, a subsidy might be given to a business undertaking an environmentally friendly project, but not to another business with a project that could cause environmental damage. Subsidies may also be given by businesses, for example, to employees who share a car or cycle to work.
- Charging road users could be useful in reducing pollution and congestion. This method of control is used in European countries such as France and Italy. Similarly, vehicles entering city areas may be charged for travelling at certain times of the day.
- In the USA, pollution permits have been introduced. They allow businesses a certain amount of emissions. If a business reduces its emissions below a certain level it can save its allowance for later or even sell it to another firm.
- Businesses and government may work together to control

GREEN TYRES FOR YOUR VEHICLE

- ○ SAFE
- ○ GREAT VALUE FOR MONEY
- ○ ENVIRONMENTALLY FRIENDLY

The next time you change the tyres on your vehicle, it's worth considering the environmental benefits of quality British- manufactured retreaded tyres.

Every retread sold extends the tyre's natural life, thereby saving natural resources and helping reduce the scrap tyre mountain. In addition, each retreaded tyre requires **4.5 gallons** less oil than a new tyre.

For your nearest Green Tyre Dealer
www.greentyres.com

RETREAD MANUFACTURERS ASSOCIATION
2ND FLOOR, FEDERATION HOUSE,
STATION ROAD, STOKE-ON-TRENT,
STAFFORDSHIRE. ST4 2TJ
tel: 01782 417777 fax: 01782 417766
email: retreads@ukonline.co.uk

RETREADING IS RECYCLING

Enhance and Preserve your Environment the Green shop PRODUCTS FOR A SUSTAINABLE FUTURE

Quality Environmentally Friendly Interior Paints and Finishes

- Auro Natural Paint
- Green Paints
- Earthborn Clay Paints
- Lime Earth Paints
- OS Colour Wood Treatments
- Holkham Linseed Paint
- La Tienda Pigments
100's of other environmental products from solar torches to books and bodycare.

Go online or phone for a catalogue to see our full range

www.greenshop.co.uk
tel: 01452 770629

Look at the adverts.

(a) Explain how the businesses in these operations might be acting in the interests of the environment.

(b) Suggest how this might affect the businesses.

Question 2

their effects on the environment by sharing best practice, producing environmental codes of practice or developing waste strategies.

In many areas, businesses are becoming responsible for regulating their own behaviour. The ethics of a business can affect the extent to which it controls its impact on the environment. Some businesses have adopted their own stringent codes of practice and policies to control their activities. It is likely that attempts to control the effect on the environment by businesses will lead to:

● increased costs in the short term;
● the attraction of customers who agree with the policy of the business;
● a change in production methods.

Business and law

Governments often pass laws which are designed to control the conduct of businesses. Often governments will introduce laws when businesses have a record of failing to meet minimum standards or where it is anticipated that they will be unable to meet such standards. Laws act as a substitute for self regulation by businesses. The regulation of business activity by legislation falls into a number of categories.

● How businesses treat consumers in general and their customers in particular. Such laws attempt to ensure that consumers are not misled or customers are not treated unfairly by businesses. Unit 71 provides more details about consumer protection laws. Unit 21 provides information about restrictions on advertising.
● How businesses treat their employees. These laws are designed to protect the rights of employees and to ensure that they are treated fairly. Laws in this area include those relating to the terms and conditions of employees (☞ unit 48), equal opportunities (☞ unit 50) and the protection of employees in work (☞ unit 51).
● The ways in which businesses affect the wider communities within which they operate. For example, as explained earlier, legislation sets limits on the quantities of certain emissions which businesses are allowed to release into the atmosphere. The aim is to set limits on maximum amounts of pollution and control the harmful effects of businesses on the environment. Other laws governing business activity in this area include planning regulations which impose restrictions on where businesses may locate.
● Legislation which affects the information that businesses must maintain and produce. For example, Companies Acts (☞ unit 6) regulate the information that must be contained on company accounts. There are also restrictions on the information that can be kept about clients and the operation of computers (☞ unit 51).

Although laws can control the behaviour of businesses, there are some problems with this method of control. First, businesses can obey the 'letter of the law' rather than the 'spirit of the law'. This might mean, for example, a business adopting practices which are legal, but which do not greatly

reduce negative externalities. Second, legislation which only applies within national boundaries may not affect businesses in other countries. For example, legislation governing the behaviour of the UK or EU nuclear industry would have had no impact on the Chernobyl disaster in Eastern Europe. This led to radioactive materials being deposited in the UK and other Western European countries.

In 2004 UK business was bracing itself for the impact of EU regulation regarding working time. The EU Working Time Directive states that an employee should work only a 48 hour week. They should rest 11 consecutive hours per day and have a rest break when the day is longer than six hours, a minimum of one rest day per week and four weeks' holiday. Night working must not average out at more than eight hours at a stretch.

Previously the UK had negotiated an opt-out clause from the directive, so that UK businesses did not have to comply. However, within 18 months UK businesses that did not comply would face sanctions. These included fines for the company. Directors may also be taken to court if their company transgresses.

It was argued that the directive prevents exploitation of workers. Another benefit is the reduction in 'dead time'. It is suggested that 61 per cent of UK employees find themselves with dead time on their hands of around an hour a week. This is time they could have been spending better.

However, all companies and employees might not benefit. For example, a company that gets extra work might previously have asked its employees to work a little longer. Now it will have to employ another worker, who could be part time. This part time worker may not have the skills of the employee who previously would have worked overtime to do the job. A UK manufacturing business argued 'If you look at the sort of person we employ, which are semi-skilled individuals, they would tend to increase their earning capabilities through the provision of overtime or additional shifts. If their working time is restricted, they need to look at increasing their hourly rate to get them back to where they are currently in terms of take-home pay.'

Source: adapted from *The Guardian*, 25.3.2004.

(a) Why might legislation have been introduced on the length of the working week?
(b) Discuss whether such legislation is in the interests of (i) employees and (ii) businesses.

Question③

Business and technology

Technological innovations and developments influence the operation of businesses in a number of ways. For example, robots and computers have been increasingly used in the manufacture of goods and the provision of services. Computer based technologies have been used to store, retrieve and manipulate information. Generally it might be argued that the introduction of technology has improved the efficiency of businesses (☞ unit 60).

As well as affecting the ways in which businesses operate, such technologies can have an effect upon society.

● Many new technologies have reduced the need for businesses to employ so many people. This is because businesses have been able to reduce unit costs by replacing labour with new technology. For society as a whole this could be beneficial. The same level of income or more is being generated by fewer employees. The problem here is who benefits from the new technology. Consumers may benefit from relatively cheaper goods and services and increased quality. However, those who have lost their jobs may be faced with a dramatic loss of income and experience many of the problems associated with unemployment. Thus whilst new technologies can benefit some, others can be left worse off.

● The introduction of new labour saving technology should leave people with increased leisure time, as computers and other machines perform production and service tasks once carried out by workers. Increased leisure time would leave people with time to devote to activities such as sports and the arts and involve them undertaking less work. On the other hand, it could be argued that the increased use of new technologies has led to a surge of economic activity and to increases in working hours for many employees.

● New technologies have led to a significant increase in the choices available to consumers. A range of products has become available which were previously unheard of or out of the reach of consumers. So, for example, digital cameras, laptop computers and satellite television are now widely in use.

● Many believe that the introduction of new technologies, in particular information and communication technology, have enabled the economies of developed nations, such as the US and the UK, to continue growing. This has led to higher income levels amongst consumers and increased life expectancies associated with advances in medical technology. However, it should be noted that the increased incomes in the developed economies of the West have been far from equally shared. Many groups in society continue not to benefit from increased income and divisions between the rich and poor continue to widen.

Pressure groups

PRESSURE GROUPS are groups without the direct political power to achieve their aims, but whose aims lie within the sphere of politics. They usually attempt to influence local government, central government, businesses and the media. They aim to have their views taken into account when any decisions are made. Such influence can occur directly, through contact with politicians, local representatives and business people, or indirectly by influencing public opinion.

The use of pressure groups is one way in which

stakeholders can exert influence over those making decisions within a business. Pressure groups can represent stakeholders directly involved with the business, such as employees or shareholders. They can also represent those not directly involved in the business, such as local communities or consumer groups.

There are many different types of pressure group and many ways of classifying them. One way is to divide groups into those which have a single cause and those which have a number of different causes.

● Single cause groups include the Campaign for Nuclear Disarmament (CND), Survival International and the NSPCC. Such groups mainly try to promote one cause.

● Multi-cause groups include trade unions, Greenpeace and the Confederation of British Industry. Pressure groups falling into this category tend to campaign on a number of issues. Trade unions, for example, have campaigned on a variety of issues, including the rights of the unemployed and improving the pay and conditions of their members.

Over the last few decades there has been a huge increase in the number of pressure groups and in the scale of their activities. Inevitably this has brought them into much closer contact with businesses. As a result there are now a number of groups which focus their activities upon businesses in general or particular businesses and industries.

● Environmental groups such as Friends of the Earth campaign to prevent businesses from polluting the environment.

● Consumer groups, such as the Consumers' Association seek to protect the rights of consumers in general. Others include The Football Supporters' Federation and rail users' groups.

● Local community groups may, for example, seek to prevent particular business developments or influence the policies of individual firms which operate in their local area.

● Employee groups, such as trade unions and professional associations, try to influence firms on issues such as conditions of work and pay levels.

Pressure groups vary in size. Some, like a local group aiming to divert a by-pass, may be made up of a few local people. Others are national organisations such as Greenpeace or the Royal Society for the Protection of Birds, or international groups such as Amnesty International.

Factors influencing the success of pressure groups

The success of any group, no matter how large or small, will depend on a number of factors.

● Finance and organisational ability. A pressure group with large funds will be able to spend on well organised campaigns. This has been a tactic employed by trade unions and professional groups. A well financed pressure group may also be able to employ full time professional campaigners. Such people are likely to organise more effective campaigns than enthusiasts devoting some of their spare time to such an activity.

- Public sympathy. Capturing the imagination of the public will play an important role in the ability of a pressure group to succeed. The Campaign for Real Ale has been effective in this respect. Almost single handedly they caused a change in the types of beer available in public houses and in the brewing methods of the big brewing companies. As with many successful campaigns, CAMRA's ability to present a clear and simple message to the public was vital.

- Access to politicians. Pressure groups which have access to politicians are able to apply pressure for changes in the law. For example, the International League for the Protection of Horses persuaded the government to ban the export of live horses for human consumption within the EU. Their contacts with politicians were vital in this campaign. The process of applying pressure on politicians is known as lobbying. It has become dominated by skilled professional lobbyists, the fees of whom are out of the range of all but the wealthiest of groups.

- Reputation. Gaining a favourable reputation amongst politicians can be important. The British Medical Association, for example, has a good reputation amongst a variety of politicians and is therefore often consulted on a variety of health matters by the government.

The effects of pressure groups on business

There is a number of ways in which pressure groups can affect firms.

- Pressure groups often seek to influence the behaviour of members of the public about a particular product, business or industry. Friends of the Earth attempts to persuade the public to use cars less and public transport or bicycles more in order to reduce emissions into the atmosphere. This campaign, if successful, would have important implications for a wide range of firms involved in the transport industry.

- Political parties, through their representatives in Parliament, are able to pass laws which regulate the activities of businesses. Therefore it is not surprising that many pressure groups devote resources to lobbying politicians. An example of this is the attempt by the anti-smoking group, Action on Smoking and Health (ASH), to change the law so that all advertising of tobacco is made illegal.

In 2004 a controversial study by the RAC (Royal Automobile Club) Foundation suggested that Britain's busiest roads needed £20 billion of improvements over a ten year period to avert gridlock for millions of motorists. The RAC Foundation is an independent body, established in 1999 to carry out research into motoring issues and to take on the role of protecting the interests of the motorist. The Foundation carries out regular opinion surveys of RAC Members and has, in the course of its campaigning work, taken up many of the issues which they have raised.

The organisation claimed that drivers in Britain endure 'the worst conditions in Europe' and demanded greater government expenditure on widening schemes and bypasses. Edmund King, the foundation's executive director, said taking into account that roads account for 93 per cent of all journeys, '£20 billion over 10 years is very little. It's half what the motorist pays in tax every year'. The government pledged £7 billion in 2003 for roadbuilding. But the RAC said this was insufficient and published a wish-list of more than 30 additional schemes.

Environmentalists attacked the list as unnecessary. Steve Hounsham of the pressure group Transport 2000 said 'Roadbuilding on this scale is as old-fashioned and doomed as the dinosaurs. The future belongs to sustainable transport. The RAC should be supporting better public transport and better opportunities for walking and cycling.' Critics also accused the RAC of outdated 'predict and provide' thinking, which would just encourage more vehicles onto roads and damage the environment.

Source: adapted from *The Guardian*, 13.1.2004 and www.rac.co.uk.

(a) Using examples, explain why the groups in the article might be described as pressure groups.
(b) Examine the factors which may influence the success of the pressure groups in the article.
(c) Discuss how the success of the groups might affect:
  (i) road users;
  (ii) government.

Question 4

- The actions of pressure groups can reduce the sales of firms. This is often most successfully achieved when efforts are targeted at particular firms. Consumers are then called upon to boycott these firms.
- Firms can face increased costs as a result of the activities of pressure groups. This may involve new production processes or waste disposal methods. Firms may have to counteract any negative publicity from a pressure group. For example, many believe that the campaign to attract visitors to the Sellafield nuclear site was a result of the negative publicity from environmental groups.
- Businesses with a tarnished reputation as a result of pressure group activity may find it more difficult to recruit employees.

How might businesses react to pressure groups?

- By positively responding to the issues raised by pressure groups. It was argued that pressure from Greenpeace contributed to Shell's decision not to dump the Brent Spar oil platform in the North Sea in 1995. Instead it was dismantled and used to build a ferry quay in Norway. Similarly, local pressure groups have been successful in persuading some firms to change building plans and landscape nearby areas.
- Through promotions and public relations. Firms can attempt to counteract negative publicity through their own promotional and public relations work. For example, a number of oil companies which have been criticised for their impact upon the environment have sought to deal with this by promoting the 'greener' aspects of their industry, such as the availability of lead free petrol.

- A number of leading firms either lobby politicians themselves or pay for the services of professional lobbyists to represent their interests.
- Legal action. Where pressure groups make false allegations about a business, this can be dealt with by the legal system. For example, allegations by pressure groups that McDonald's were contributing to the destruction of the Amazonian rainforest were dealt with through legal action in the courts.

Knowledge

1. State 2 ways that a large business may affect the society in which it operates.
2. State 3 legal restrictions on the behaviour of businesses.
3. Why might the effect on society of a business's activities be self-regulating?
4. State 3 effects of ethical behaviour on a business.
5. How might a business be of benefit to the environment surrounding it?
6. State 5 problems caused by business activity to the environment.
7. State 3 ways in which the effect on the environment of business may be controlled.
8. What are the main types of pressure groups?
9. Give 3 reasons why a pressure group campaign may fail.
10. How can pressure groups affect the sales of a firm's product?

key terms

Ethics - the values and beliefs of individuals or groups.
Ethical behaviour - behaviour which is viewed as morally correct.
Pressure groups - groups of people without direct political power who seek to influence decision makers in politics, business and society.

Social responsibility - the responsibility that a business has towards those directly or indirectly affected by its activities.

Case study Toyota

The car is a machine that has changed the world. Consumers increasingly want the mobility, convenience and status that go with car ownership. But pressure groups such as Friends of the Earth constantly campaign for reductions in car emissions into the atmosphere.

It is estimated that today's world car population of 740 million will rise to 1.2 billion by 2020. Cars consume irreplaceable fuel (the United States Geological Survey believes that the world has between 30 and 50 years of oil left) and now account for 20 per cent of European CO_2 emissions, as shown in Figure 70.1. In addition, an estimated 2 million tonnes of car scrap materials go into landfill waste sites in Europe alone. So is a sustainable car industry possible?

Last year Toyota overtook Ford to become the second biggest vehicle manufacturer in the world with a 10.7 per cent market share. The Japanese company was also on target to hit its 15 per cent global share in the next decade. In 2003 it was the *Financial Times*' third most highly respected company after GE and Microsoft.

Toyota has recently launched its Primus range of cars. It is the first mass produced hybrid car, running on a combination of electricity and petrol. It is driven by electricity at low speed, when petrol is least efficient, and by a conventional petrol driven motor on the open road. By using the strengths of both, the combined technology improves fuel consumption figures and dramatically cuts low speed emissions. As a tribute to its cleanliness, the Primus is exempt from the London congestion charge.

Toyota argues that hybrid cars such as the Primus are the way forward. They have the advantage of being used with the existing car infrastructure and are acceptable to consumers because there is little fall-off in performance compared to more traditional cars. By March 2004, for example, consumers had bought more than half of the UK's allocation of 1,600 Toyota hybrid cars in 2004. No manufacturer can afford to ignore the new technology. Ford has just licensed it from Toyota and General Motors was due to produce a new range of hybrid sports utility and pick-up trucks.

Toyota suggests that its environmental credentials go even further than the car itself. The Toyota Production System (TPS) uses lean production techniques which minimise waste. The system operates on the principle that it is better to build in quality to cars than inspect them at the end. This 'pursuit of zero defects' has taken Toyota so far ahead of its rivals that it takes less time to build a Toyota Lexus than to correct faults on a car coming off a German car assembly line. In fact it is argued that if every car manufacturer followed Toyota's lead, then worldwide targets for pollution in agreements such as the Kyoto Protocol could be achieved far quicker or perhaps even raised.

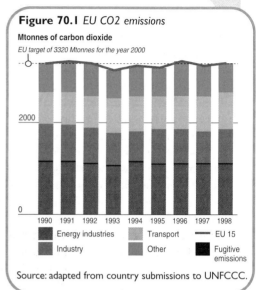

Figure 70.1 *EU CO2 emissions*

Mtonnes of carbon dioxide

EU target of 3320 Mtonnes for the year 2000

Legend: Energy industries, Industry, Transport, Other, EU 15, Fugitive emissions

Source: adapted from country submissions to UNFCCC.

In 2003, Toyota's UK plants at Burnaston in Derby and Deeside in Wales sent almost nothing to landfill tips, compared with 8.5 kilos per car in 2001. Over Europe, the Toyota group cut energy use by 19 per cent and used 6 per cent less water, while still increasing production.

Ultimately the company wants to produce a car that emits zero emissions over its lifetime. As Toyota President Fujo Cho says 'The expansion of automobile use will have a significant impact on the environment. In other words, there is no future for the automotive industry without the promotion of environmental technology. Toyota is convinced that only companies that succeed in this area will be acceptable to society'.

Source: adapted from *The Observer*, 21.3.2004.

(a) Using examples, identify the possible stakeholders in Toyota. **(6 marks)**

(b) Using evidence from the article, describe how car use may damage the environment. **(4 marks)**

(c) Explain how Toyota is acting in an ethical manner. **(10 marks)**

(d) Examine the reasons why Toyota might act as a socially responsible business. **(10 marks)**

(e) Discuss whether it is always in the interests of car companies to act in a socially responsible way. **(10 marks)**.

The growth of protection

At the beginning of the last century consumers and producers were seen as having equal responsibility. Indeed, consumers were expected to ensure that their purchases were satisfactory. This approach can be summarised by the expression caveat emptor, which means - 'let the buyer beware'.

Today, the relationship between consumers and businesses is viewed differently. Many see consumers as being at the mercy of powerful and well organised producers. This has led to a rise in interest about consumer affairs and increasing pressure on governments to pass legislation to protect consumers. Consumer magazines, such as *Which?*, and consumer television programmes, such as 'Watchdog', have lent pressure to this movement seeking to protect the rights of consumers.

There is a number of reasons why consumers may need protecting more than they did in the past.

- Globalisation of world markets. Goods and services from around the world can now easily be sold in countries other than their place of origin. Consumers in the UK might, for example, need protection from goods and services imported from abroad. These products might have been produced to standards which are lower than those imposed on UK and EU businesses. Safety standards of children's toys, for example, have been lower in goods produced in Asia in the past.
- The growth of the Internet. The Internet provides many opportunities for consumers. But it also leads to problems because it is largely unregulated. Goods and services may be purchased, but might not be delivered. Companies might advertise and be paid, but then close down. Financial information, such as credit card details, might be found and used against consumers' wishes. Companies might be able to 'spy' on consumers' buying activities and also send unwanted materials through e-mail.
- The increasing complexity of many goods and services. Technological advances, in particular, have increased the gap between the knowledge of consumers and producers about products. Few consumers have the ability to properly assess the quality of the technology which goes into everyday items such as televisions, microwave ovens or computers. Such ignorance might leave consumers at the mercy of producers.
- The environment within which businesses operate is becoming increasingly competitive. Some believe that this degree of competition encourages businesses to take advantage of consumers. This may be in the form of reductions in the level of service or the quality of goods offered, for example.
- The disposable income of many consumers has increased greatly over the last four to five decades. This means that

the average consumer purchases far greater quantities of goods and services than would have been the case in the past. It is argued that more protection needs to be offered to consumers as a result.

- Scientific advances have created a variety of materials that were not previously available. For example, genetically modified products have developed as a consequence of scientific advances in the production of foods. Consumers may need to be protected against any possible harmful effects of such scientific discoveries.

Consumer protection legislation

It could be argued that, in a number of areas, businesses cannot be relied upon to regulate themselves. These include their dealings with employees and other firms, as well as consumers. Governments in the past have found it necessary to regulate businesses, by passing laws which protect consumers from their activities. Some examples in the UK are shown below.

Weights and Measures Act, 1951, 1963 and 1985 These Acts are designed to prevent the sale of underweight or undervolume products. For example, they make it an offence to use false or unfair weighing equipment or to give short measures. All prepacked goods must have information about the net quantity of their contents. The Acts also give inspectors the power to test weighing and measuring equipment.

Trade Descriptions Act, 1968 This prohibits false or misleading descriptions of goods or services. For example, a pair of shoes which are described as made of leather cannot be made of plastic.

Unsolicited Goods and Services Act, 1971 This law seeks to prevent the practice of sending goods to consumers which they had not ordered, and then demanding payment. It states that unsolicited goods need not be paid for and that consumers can keep such goods after six months if the seller does not collect them. This was amended in 2001 to include electronic documents.

Consumer Credit Act, 1974 This aims to protect the rights of consumers when they purchase goods on credit, such as hire purchase or credit sale agreements. For example, it states that consumers must be given a copy of any credit agreements into which they enter. It also ensures that only licensed credit brokers can provide credit. There are many other offences listed which constitute a breaking of the law. These include credit firms sending representatives to people's homes to persuade them to take credit and credit agreements which have high interest rates.

Consumer Safety Act, 1978 This law was passed in order to prevent the sale of goods which might be harmful to consumers. It concentrates, in particular, upon safety matters relating to children's toys and electrical goods.

Sale of Goods Act, 1979 This law states that goods sold to consumers should meet three main conditions. First, that they are of merchantable quality which means that goods should not have any serious flaws or problems with them. Second, that they are fit for the purpose for which they were purchased. For example, paint which is sold to be used outdoors should not begin to peel or flake with the first outbreak of poor weather conditions. Third, that they are as described. Thus, an anorak described as waterproof should not leak in the rain.

Supply of Goods and Services Act, 1982 This seeks to protect users of services, ensuring services are of 'merchantable quality' and at 'reasonable rates'. For example, a holiday firm which booked clients into a four star hotel that turned out to be of lower quality would be in breach of the conditions. Breaches of this and the 1979 Act are subject to civil law. An injured person can sue for breach of the Act.

Consumer Protection Act, 1987 This law was introduced to bring Britain in line with other European Union nations. It ensures that firms are liable for any damage which their defective goods might cause to consumers. For example, a firm supplying defective electrical equipment would be liable for any injuries caused to consumers using that equipment. It also seeks to outlaw misleading pricing, such as exaggerated claims relating to price reductions on sale items. An example might be a statement that a good is '£2 less than the manufacturer's recommended price' when it isn't.

Food Safety Act, 1990 This law ensures that food is safe and does not mislead the consumer in the way it is presented. It is an offence to:
- sell food that does not comply with regulations, ie is unfit to eat or is contaminated;
- change food so that it becomes harmful;
- sell food that is not of the quality stated;
- describe food in a way that misleads.
Breaches of the Act are a criminal offence, punishable by a fine and/or a prison sentence.

Sale and Supply of Goods Act, 1994 This Act amends the Sale of Goods Act, 1979 and the Supply of Goods and Services Act, 1982 in favour of the buyer. For example, consumers now had a right to partial rejection. A buyer of a case of wine may accept ten bottles, but reject the two which do not match the description ordered.

Which UK and EU consumer protection legislation might the following contravene? Explain your answer.
- Winston Stanley buys a cotton tee shirt from a shop in Bath. When he takes it home, he discovers that it is made of polyester and cotton and has a small hole in its collar.
- Lena Hardman buys a 400 gramme box of chocolates, but later discovers there are only 250 grammes of chocolates in the box.
- A car dealer advertises that all of his cars have been approved by the AA. Irfan Patel, who has just bought a car from this dealer, rings up the AA and discovers that the car dealer has had no dealings with them.
- Bill Dean urgently requires £1,000 to pay a long overdue loan back to a friend. He goes to a credit agency and arranges a loan of £1,000 to be paid back over 12 months. His repayments on this loan will be £250 a month.
- Aaron Peters bought a can of lemonade. Before he drank it, the smell made him wary of the contents. It was found that the lemonade contained caustic soda.
- Silje Neilsen, who lives in Denmark, has recently bought a computer from a UK business over the Internet. When the computer arrived it had faulty parts. There was no contact address in the UK, but Silje found a telephone number via a friend in England. When she contacted the company she was told that she was not entitled to a refund because she did not live in the UK.

Question 1

Food Safety (General Food Hygiene) Regulations 1995 These list a whole series of regulations about the preparation and storage of food and equipment.

Food Labelling Regulations, 1996 These specify exactly what information should be included on food labels.

Financial Services and Markets Act, 2000 This set up the Financial Services Authority (FSA). The FSA is an independent body designed to develop confidence and regulate activities, promote public awareness, protect consumers and prevent crime in financial markets and exchanges. For example, it will only allow businesses to trade in financial markets if they meet criteria and it might investigate and prosecute businesses operating outside the rules.

Businesses that break these laws may be liable under **criminal** or **civil law**. Under criminal laws enforced by government, such as the Weights and Measures Acts, businesses can be prosecuted for breaking the law and, if found guilty, may be fined or imprisoned. Under civil law, such as the Sale and Supply of Goods Acts, a consumer or business may sue a business to gain compensation.

Consumer protection and the European Union

Increasingly the European Union is affecting legislation in member countries. The EU's aim is to harmonise (make the same) consumer laws. It is responsible for a series of directives which all EU nations implement as laws and regulations. Examples include:

- EU directive, Unfair Terms in Consumer Contracts, in April 1993, which led to the **Unfair Terms in Consumer Contracts Regulations, 1994** in the UK. This directive sought to prevent consumers being locked into unfair contracts which undermined their rights;
- the EU directive which led to **The General Product Safety Regulations, 1994** in the UK. These state that all products supplied to customers must be safe;
- EU directives 88/314 and 88/315 leading to the **Price Marking Order, 1991** which states that the selling price of goods must be indicated in writing;
- **Telecommunications (Data Protection and Privacy) Regulations, 1999** which prevent people and businesses from receiving unwanted direct marketing telephone calls or faxes;
- **Consumer Protection (Distance Selling) Regulations, 2000** which relate to sales over the Internet. They require a seller to provide information on the main characteristics of the goods, the price, including any taxes and delivery costs, payment arrangements, guarantees and where to address complaints about the goods;
- **Electronic Commerce (EC Directive) Regulations, 2002** which deal with the protection of consumers involved in e-commerce. For example, online selling and advertising is subject to UK legislation and online traders must give clear information about who they are and how to complete transactions;
- The **Sale and Supply of Goods to Consumers Regulations, 2002** provide minimum rights on faulty goods, such as rights to refunds, compensation and replacements. They are designed to encourage people to shop 'across borders', in other EU countries, knowing there is protection if something is wrong with goods they buy.

Effects of protection on business

The increase in the number of consumer laws and the concern about protecting consumers has a number of possible implications for firms.

- Increases in costs. Improving the safety of a good or ensuring that measuring equipment is more accurate can increase the costs of a firm. For example, an electrical firm producing table lamps may find that its product contravened legislation. The firm would have to change or improve the components used to make the lamps or re-design the lamp itself. Such changes would be likely to raise the firm's costs.

- Quality control. Many firms have needed to improve their quality control procedures as a result of legislation. For example, firms involved in bagging or packaging goods must ensure that the correct quantities are weighed out. Failure to do so could result in prosecution. In addition, businesses must be careful not to sell substandard or damaged products.
- Dealing with customer complaints. Many businesses now have a customer service or customer complaints department to deal with customers. These allow firms to deal with problems quickly and efficiently and to 'nip problems in the bud' - dealing with any problems before the customer turns to the legal system.
- Changes in business practice. Attempts to ensure that customers are treated fairly by a business may place pressure on it to become more market orientated (☞ unit 11). The firm would attempt to ensure that it is actually meeting the needs of those people it is attempting to serve. Such a change, for example, may lead to greater use of market research.

In December 2003 the UK government unveiled plans for revised consumer credit laws. They would include a regulation of 'loan sharks' who targeted the most vulnerable in society. These people often had to borrow large amounts, urgently and were charged high interest rates and extreme penalties for non-payment.

A new range of measures would be introduced. They included undercover officers to investigate loan companies and recover illegal profits. They would also make it easier for people to understand loans. The size of 'small print', stating the terms of agreements, was to be increased. And all businesses must present information in a standardised form, stating what people owe, how much they will pay, the length of the agreement, total charges, penalties and rights to cancel. The Office of Fair Trading (OFT) was given powers to make surprise raids on loan companies and to fine lenders acting against the law. It could also refuse to give a trading licence or vary the length of time for which the licence was granted.

Source: adapted from *The Independent*, 9.12.2003.

(a) Examine the implications of suggested changes to consumer credit legislation for:
  (i) consumers;
  (ii) businesses.

Monopolies and mergers

It is argued, by some, that competition between businesses benefits consumers. Such arguments have been one influence upon government's attempts to control monopolies and mergers.

In some cases just one business, a monopolist (☞ unit 62),

controls the market for a particular good or service although this is rare in the UK. Such market strength puts this firm in a position where it has the potential to exploit its consumers. It can also prevent other businesses from competing against it.

A LEGAL MONOPOLY in UK law is defined as any business which has over 25 per cent market share. An example may be Microsoft, in its production of operating systems for computers.

A merger is the joining together of two or more firms. Examples of mergers between well known companies in the UK in 2003 included:

- HSBC acquired Bank of Bermuda for £770 million, as part of a strategy to expand its private banking and fund administration operations;
- Warner Village, the chain of 36 cinemas, was acquired by SBC International Cinemas for £225 million, and the sites would be renamed as Vue;
- Selfridges, the department store group, accepted a £600 million takeover bid from the Wittington Canada private holding company;
- Holland & Barrett acquired Health & Diet Group from Royal Numico of the Netherlands for £7.5 million, gaining 49 GNC health food stores in the UK;
- Oasis Stores, the fashion retailer, was acquired by Baugur of Iceland for £152 million;
- Ryanair acquired the Buzz budget airline from KLM for £16 million;
- Gala, the operator of 166 bingo clubs and 28 casinos, was acquired by venture capital groups Cinven and Candover for £1.24 billion.

Some criticisms of monopolies and mergers for consumers and businesses include the following.

- They raise prices in order to make excess profits.
- They fix prices. When a small group of firms control the market for a product, it is believed that they may act in unison to fix prices at an artificially high level.
- They force competition out. It has been suggested that monopolists sometimes pursue pricing or promotional strategies designed to force competitors out of the market.
- They prevent new firms from entering markets.
- They carry out a range of practices to restrict competition.

Examples include putting pressure on retailers not to stock the goods of rival firms and attempting to prevent suppliers from doing business with new entrants to the market.

There are, however, a number of arguments which support the continued existence of monopolies.

- Because monopolies often operate on a large scale, they are able to benefit from economies of scale (☞ unit 56). The cost advantages from this can allow monopolies to set prices lower than would be the case if there were a number of firms competing, and still make profits.
- Monopolies can use their large profits to undertake research and development projects. Many of these projects, which result in technological and scientific breakthroughs,

could not be afforded by smaller firms.
- Monopolies are much better placed to survive in international markets. It is argued that this is only possible if a firm operates on a large scale.

Restrictive trade practices

Anti-competitive or RESTRICTIVE TRADE PRACTICES prevent competition between businesses. Examples of restrictive practices include the following.

- A business which is a dominant supplier in a particular market may set a minimum price for the re-sale of its products. Such firms may also seek to ensure that retailers stock their products alone. In return, retailers are often given exclusive rights to sell this product within a particular area.
- Firms forming agreements to fix prices and/or limit the supply of a product. Such agreements between firms are often referred to as COLLUSION.
- A dominant supplier requiring retailers to stock the full range of its product lines.

It is usually argued that consumers suffer as a result of these practices. For example, if two businesses join together to fix prices so that another business is forced to close, this will restrict consumers' choice. Such practices may benefit those businesses taking part, but will be against the interest of those that are faced with the restrictive practices.

Legislation in the UK

Certain legislation in the UK is designed to protect consumers from the problems created by monopolies, mergers and restrictive practices.

Fair Trading Act, 1973 This Act defined what constitutes a monopoly or merger in the UK. A monopoly is said to exist if a business has a 25 per cent share of the market or greater. A merger is said to exist if the combined total assets of businesses that joined together were greater than a certain value, ie £70 million in 2004. It also set up the **Office of Fair Trading (OFT)**. This was set up as a body to oversee all policy relating to competition and consumer protection. The current role of the OFT is discussed in the next section.

Competition Act, 1998 This Act:
- prohibits agreements, cartels or practices which prevent, restrict or distort competition;
- prohibits conduct which amounts to abuse of a dominant position;

although the government can grant exemptions. It also set up the **Competition Commission**. The current role of the Competition Commission is discussed later.

Enterprise Act, 2002 This Act replaced the provisions of the Fair Trading Act. Many of its new provisions were complementary to those of The Competition Act, which remained in force. The Act:

- set up the OFT as a corporate body in its own right;
- set up a Competition Appeals Tribunal (CAT) and stated how appeals could be made to it;
- made new provisions for merger controls, with decisions taken by the OFT and the Competition Commission. In most cases, mergers would be investigated on a 'competition test' (ie turnover over £70 million or 25 per cent of market share). Mergers would be prohibited or remedies required if there was a substantial lessening of competition as a result;
- allowed the OFT and ministers to refer investigations to the Competition Commission;
- outlined rules of investigations for the Competition Commission to decide if actions prevent, restrict or distort competition and how to take action to remedy the adverse effect on consumers;
- created a new criminal offence for individuals operating in certain cartels and investigation powers for the OFT. Cartel activities might involve price fixing, limiting supply, market sharing and bid-rigging;
- set out new competition provisions, for example disqualifying company directors who break competition law;
- outlined new procedures for enforcing consumer legislation, ie allowing the OFT to force businesses breaking the law to stop or be taken to court;
- set out rules for disclosing information by public authorities;
- changed insolvency law.

The Office of Fair Trading

The Office of Fair Trading (OFT) has an important role in promoting and protecting consumers' interests and ensuring that businesses in the UK are fair and competitive. It has a number of functions.

- Competition enforcement. The OFT enforces current legislation, stops cartels, damaging anti-competitive practices and abuses of dominant market positions, promotes a competitive culture, informs businesses about legislation, and works with the European Commission on cases.
- Consumer regulation enforcement. The OFT enforces current legislation and regulations, takes action against unfair traders, encourages codes of practice, gives consumers information to understand the law and works with bodies with enforcement powers.
- Markets and policies initiatives. The OFT can investigate markets and make public its findings. It might then recommend stronger enforcement, a change in regulations or an improvement in consumer awareness.

The OFT has the power to make market investigation references to the Competition Commission. To do this it must have reasonable grounds to suspect that features of the market prevent, restrict or distort competition. It must also publish its reasons. It also has the power to investigate

mergers where businesses have a combined turnover of £70 million (in 2004) or 25 per cent of the market. If it decides that the merger will lessen competition substantially, it can either refer the merger to the Competition Commission or ask the businesses to remedy the problems. There are exceptions, for example if the benefits of the restriction outweigh the adverse effects on consumers.

The Competition Commission

The Competition Commission (CC) also plays an important part in protecting consumers and ensuring businesses do not break consumer legislation. It is an independent body which carries out inquires into mergers and markets referred to it by

On 22 August 2003, the OFT asked the Competition Commission (CC) to investigate the proposed acquisition of five vessels and related assets of P&O by Stena. The vessels operated on the Liverpool to Dublin and Fleetwood to Larne routes. The acquisition would affect freight ferry services offered on these routes.

The CC undertook three months of investigations. These included two customer surveys and hearings with parties likely to be affected. In November 2003 the CC found provisionally that transfer would result in a substantial lessening of competition because it would:
- reduce the number of operators from four to three;
- more than double Stena's market share and make it far larger than its nearest rival;
- be likely to lead to price increases and inhibit price cutting on other routes.

The CC did not expect the reduction of competition to be offset by other factors, such as entry into this market by other operators.

Stena was given 21 days to respond. The CC was also considering remedies, which it would publish.

Source: adapted from The Competition Commission website.

(a) Describe the role of the CC in this situation.
(b) Examine the ways in which parties interested in the acquisition might be affected by the activities of the CC.

Question 3

the OFT, the Secretary of State or regulatory bodies.

The CC has around 50 part time members, appointed for eight years by the Secretary of State for Trade and Industry. They are appointed for their experience and ability. Members are supported by around 150 staff. The Chairperson of the Competition Commission usually appoints 4 or 5 members to undertake enquiries.

The Enterprise Act 2002 gave the CC powers to investigate mergers and carry out market investigations into anti-competitive practices referred to it. It will then determine whether or not:

● a merger has caused or may be expected to cause a lessening of competition;
● any feature of a market prevents, restricts or distorts competition.

It was also given enforcement powers. For example, if an adverse effect of competition is identified or a merger is found to reduce competition the CC can:

● prohibit a merger from taking place;
● impose remedies which the businesses involved must then agree to carry out.

The CC will take into account any possible benefits of mergers before deciding on remedies.

The Competition Commission has been criticised in the past for a number of reasons.

● It has no powers to investigate on its own, only referrals.
● Investigations have taken a long time to complete.
● The limited number of staff has restricted the number of investigations that can be carried out.
● Many findings have favoured businesses and not consumers.

The European Union

The European Community has rules to ensure free competition in member countries. The European Commission is responsible for applying these rules, working closely with national governments.

● Article 81 of the Treaty of Rome prohibits anti-competitive agreements which may affect trade between member states and which prevent, restrict or distort competition in the single market. The Commission can grant exemptions if there are benefits from the practices, such as improved efficiency or the promotion of research and development.
● Article 82 prohibits the abuse of a dominant position which may affect trade between member states.

In 2004 the EU was to introduce major changes to the 1990 EU Merger Regulations. These set out the EU merger control regime, including how mergers were referred to and investigated by the European Commission. The changes included:

● a revision of merger regulation, including a simplification in the system of referrals to the European Commission by member states for investigation and vice versa, and allowing the Commission to impose higher fines on businesses that do not provide required information for

investigations;
● setting guidelines on the appraisal of horizontal mergers, ie mergers between competitors;
● setting non-legislative measures to improve decision-making, to be contained in a set of 'best practices'.

Regulatory bodies

During the 1980s and 1990s, former state monopolies were sold off as part of the government's privatisation (☞ unit 7) programme. The aim was to increase efficiency in these firms by removing them from the public sector. However, the creation of private monopolies led to concern that these newly privatised firms would take advantage of their market position and exploit consumers. Regulatory bodies have been set up to regulate them as a result.

● Ofwat (the Office of Water Services). This was set up in 1989 to regulate the water and sewerage industry.
● Orr (the Office of the Rail Regulator). This was set up in 1993 to regulate the rail industry.
● Ofgem (the Office of Gas and Electricity Markets). This was set up in 1999 from the former regulatory bodies for the gas (Ofgas) and electricity (Offer) industries. It regulates the gas and electricity markets.
● Oftel (the Office of Telecommunications). This was set up to regulate the telecommunications industry. In 2003 it was replaced by Ofcom (the Office of Communications) which also took over the roles of the Broadcasting Standards Commission, the Independent Television Commission, the Radio Authority and the Radiocommunications Agency.

The regulatory bodies have many different powers, but perhaps two main functions.

● To operate a system of price controls. The regulatory authorities for water, gas and electricity and telecommunications have operated according to a Retail Price Index RPI (☞ unit 66) plus or minus formula. This allows the business to set its prices based on average rises in prices, which are then adjusted upwards or downwards. So if the regulator felt that prices needed to be controlled and reduced it is likely to set a RPI minus figure. For example, in 2001 and 2002 Oftel set price controls of RPI minus 4.5 per cent for BT. On the other hand Ofwat set Anglian Water's price limit at 2.5 per cent plus inflation in 2004-05.
● To help bring about the introduction of competition wherever this might be possible. In some respects, this is more difficult than implementing price controls. This is because telephone lines, gas pipelines, water pipes and the National Grid are examples of **natural monopolies**. If every house, factory and office were connected with a number of different water pipes or telephone lines from which to choose, the costs within these industries would rise significantly. It therefore makes sense for the regulated business to operate such services.

However, there is no reason why other businesses should

not be allowed to transmit their power, gas, telephone calls or water down the existing National Grid, gas pipeline network, telephone lines and water pipes. Indeed, this is the way in which competition has been introduced into these industries. A range of rail passenger businesses such as Virgin and First North Western are, for example, able to operate services on railways lines controlled by Railtrack.

Regulating other businesses

Other businesses are also controlled by regulatory bodies. The Financial Services Authority (FSA) is responsible for regulating the performance and behaviour of businesses operating in the financial services industry, such as insurance and pensions companies. This is an industry which has aroused suspicion in the past due to scandals regarding the mis-selling of pensions to consumers, for example. The FSA was set up as an independent non-government body but given statutory powers under the **Financial Services and Markets Act, 2000.**

It is the threat of government regulation which causes many industries to 'keep their own house in order' by establishing their own regulatory bodies. The Advertising Standards Authority is an example of a self-regulatory body for the advertising industry. The European Petroleum Industry Association (EUROPIA) regulates conduct by businesses operating in the European petroleum producing industry.

Knowledge ... Knowledge ... Knowle

1. What is meant by the term caveat emptor?
2. For what reasons might consumers need more protection today?
3. List 5 main consumer protection acts.
4. In what ways might businesses be affected by consumer protection legislation?
5. What are the possible advantages and disadvantages of monopolies?
6. How is a monopoly defined by UK law?
7. What is the role of the Competition Commission?
8. How does EU legislation affect monopolies and mergers?
9. What are the main bodies set up to regulate the former state monopolies?
10. State 2 other industries that are regulated.

key terms

Collusion - agreements between businesses designed to restrict competition.
Legal monopoly - in the UK, any business with over 25 per cent of the market.
Restrictive trade practices - any attempt by businesses to prevent competition.

A report by Ofcom, the telecommunications watchdog, in December 2003 suggested that BT had a dominant market position and a near monopoly in the UK wholesale broadband sector. BT's connections to 27.3 million UK homes and businesses are used by Internet service providers (ISP) to supply broadband services. Other telecom companies said that they are prevented from offering wholesale broadband to their own ISP customers because they cannot plug their networks into BT's local exchanges at an economic price and without problems in operation.

Ofcom proposed, in its report, that BT should allow other telecom companies to connect their networks into its system at a price below what BT charges ISP customers for its own wholesale broadband service. Ofcom argued that this would allow other telecom companies to compete against BT, leading to choice and value for the consumer.

Telecom rivals such as Energis, Cable & Wireless and Centrica were critical, arguing that the changes did not go far enough. The chief executive of Energis, said 'we still have one supplier, one product and one price'. He also argued that as Ofcom was directly involved in setting the price, this could lead to problems if BT felt that it was being made to sell its service too cheaply or if telecom companies felt that they were paying too much. An AOL spokesperson argued that although changes might take time, the proposals provided 'greater transparency, regulatory certainty and increased efficiency in the provision of wholesale

broadband services', which should lead to wider choice, product innovation and possibly lower prices for consumers.

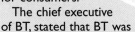

The chief executive of BT, stated that BT was 'strong, not dominant', pointing out that NTL and Telewest had as many customers as BT Wholesale. Broadband can also be accessed through cable systems as well as the BT network.

Source: adapted from *The Guardian*, 17.12.2003, news.zdnet.co.uk, 19.12.2003.

(a) Explain why Ofcom might have taken steps to regulate the activities of BT.
(b) Discuss whether the actions of Ofcom are likely to make markets more competitive and improve consumer choice.

Question 4

Case study *The AOL /Time Warner Merger*

In 2000 The European Commission approved the $130 plus billion merger between America Online (AOL) and Time Warner. It was suggested that Time Warner was looking to sell much of its music over the Internet in future.

The four month, in-depth investigation by the Commission was concerned with the detriment to music distribution and paid-for-content Internet access, such as music downloads. The Commission found that the merger satisfied its concerns. 'The Commission has a duty to prevent the creation of dominant positions' stated Mario Monti, one of the commissioners ruling on the case. 'In a music market already characterised by a high degree of consolidation, the danger, which has been averted, was ... that the resulting integrated company could have dominated on-line music distribution.' The Commission stated that broadband Internet access did not play a role in the decision as both companies did not have broadband infrastructure in Europe at the time.

Approval came only after AOL agreed to sever links with German company Bertelsmann, its 50/50 partner in AOL Europe. Without the break with Bertelsmann, AOL and Time Warner would have controlled the leading source of music publishing in Europe, as Bertelsmann Time Warner together owned a third of the European market in music publishing. 'Against this background, nothing would have prevented AOL from dominating the emerging market for Internet delivery, which includes both digital downloads and streaming' the Commission stated. Bertelsmann also agreed to end ties with AOL and Vivendi in Compuserve France. AOL and Time Warner agreed to make digital versions of their music compatible with all competing music software.

In a non-related action, Time

Warner had recently given up its proposed merger with EMI music, although observers argued that it might have been taken into account in the Commission's decision if it had gone ahead. An integrated EMI, AOL Time Warner would have had 25 per cent of the world's music market.

However, critics suggested that once European regulators have cleared such a deal it would be unlikely that they would exert much control on the activities of the business in future. One analyst argued that 'once its through ... there will be ... little upsets where the regulators will reprimand them for this and that' but on the whole the new business will be left to market forces. It was also suggested that the future for the business, might be a bit like the Microsoft-Netscape browser court case; 'It's all well and good them being fined, but Microsoft still has the market'.

In 2003 AOL Time Warner posted the largest annual loss in US history, $100 billion. In September 2003 the company was to revert to simply being known as Time Warner. The hoped for massive returns by distributing films and music over AOL's global Internet access had not materialised. This was blamed on the collapse of the Internet bubble and a clash of cultures between AOL and the more traditional approach of Time Warner.

Source: adapted from news.bbc.co.uk, 26.1.2000 and 18.9.2003, www.time.com, 31.1.2000, www.internetnews.com, 11.10.2000, www.nwfusion.com, 11.10.2000,

The main players

America Online (AOL)
The world's biggest Internet company. Activities include Internet provision and related services.

EMI
The UK music group. Its music acts include The Beatles, Robbie Williams, Radiohead and Norah Jones.

Bertelsmann
German media giant. Its Bertelsmann Music Group (BMG) owns 200 record labels. Other activities include magazines, books, film and tv, European online media store BOL.com and Internet auction site Andsold. It also owned 26 per cent of Lycos Europe at the time.

(a) What is meant by the terms:
   (i) 'dominant positions';
   (ii) 'a high degree of consolidation';
      in the article? (6 marks)
(b) Describe the role of the European Commission in the AOL/Time Warner merger. (8 marks)
(c) Examine reasons why the European Commission decided to investigate the proposed merger. (12 marks)
(d) Explain how the decision by the Commission affected interested parties in the merger. (12 marks)
(e) Discuss the extent to which the judgment prevented anti-competitive practices and protected consumers' interests. (12 marks)

Studying and assessment

Study skills are the skills that a student needs to plan, organise and carry out their work effectively. They also help a student to answer questions and carry out tasks which are designed to test their abilities. Units 72 and 73 are set out like a manual. They provide guidance and examples to help students when working in term time or when taking examinations. Examples are shown in italics. The units could be used:

● at the start of the course to get ideas on the best way to study;
● constantly throughout the course when studying;
● before examinations during revision preparation.

Action planning

Studying is more effective if there is a **plan** or **strategy**. An action plan can be formally written out, but it does not have to be. For any piece of work, it is important for a student to plan:

● how long it will take, bearing in mind any deadline;
● where the student will work;
● when the student will work;
● in what order tasks will be carried out;
● factors likely to affect the work, such as unforeseen occurrences.

A plan can be made for an individual piece of work, work over a term, coursework or project work, revision or an entire scheme of work. It is important for a student to develop a **routine** of work that is effective. It is also important for students to be **committed** to complete the plan. The table below shows a possible action plan that may be used for study, work or revision.

Title and nature of work	What needs to be done? What is the focus? How will it be judged?
Start and finish date	What is the deadline? How long will it take?
Collecting information	Where from? How can it be obtained? What help is needed? How long will it take? How will it be used?
Carry out the work	Where? When? How long? Who with? What order? Continuous or broken down? Help needed? What factors might affect the work? Possible changes?
Review	Did the plan work? Was the outcome successful? How could it have been done better? Was everything covered?

Time management

An important part of the action plan is planning how long to study or work. Certain factors must be considered when deciding how much time to take when studying.

When to start and when to finish There is a deadline for most pieces of work. This is the date by which it has to be completed. It is important to start early enough and to leave enough time to finish the work. Some people work faster than others. This will affect the time they allocate.

How long the work will take Some pieces of work will take longer than others. Short answer questions will perhaps take less time than an essay. A piece of coursework or project work may take months. So will revision. Some people work quicker than others, which may reduce the time taken.

How long to work The length of time spent on work can affect its quality.

● Spending a greater amount of time preparing and planning may improve a piece of work.
● The time spent writing may also improve work.
● Working for too long can be tiring and work may suffer. Sometimes it is better to take a short break.
● Some work, such as coursework and revision, can not be done all at once and must be broken up.
● It is useful to try to break up revision, by learning as you go along. There is likely to be too much to learn in one session at the end. Spreading the work also allows practice.

When to study This will depend on the time available. Some people have a free choice of time. They could work in free time in the day, at lunchtime, in the evening or at weekends. People with part time jobs or with great commitments may find it more difficult. They may have to work when they can. Sometimes there may be free time which could be usefully used, such as travelling to school or college on a bus or train. Students should also consider that it may not be useful to work:

● late at night because they are tired;
● after strenuous exercise because it may be difficult to concentrate;
● when they are doing lots of other things.

Where to study

It is important to consider where to work. Some students will work better in certain environments than others. Should you work at home or in a different place such as school, a library or another person's house? Issues to consider might be:

● the availability of materials. A library will have books you can use. It may also have a facility to find book titles, newspapers and magazines, perhaps on CD Rom, and access to the Iinternet. If you keep all your materials at home, it may be better to work there;

- ease of access. Working at home allows easy access to drinks and food. Some people may also want to take a break to watch television or do something else;
- comfortable or not? Working in a familiar environment, such as home, can make work easier. Other people prefer to work in a more 'academic' atmosphere;
- alone or in a group? Some people prefer to work alone. Others like to work with someone else, even if they are doing their own work. Sometimes group activities demand that people work together;
- silent or not? Some people prefer to work in silence as they concentrate better. Working in a library would allow this. Others prefer things to be happening around them.

Other learning considerations

There are other factors that students may want to take into consideration when working.

- Some people prefer to sit on a hard chair. Some prefer to be more comfortable and sit on a soft or relaxing chair.
- Some people like to listen to music whilst they are working. Others prefer silence.
- Some people prefer bright lighting so that everything is clear. Others work better in dimmed lighting.
- Some people prefer to carry out several tasks or activities at once. Others prefer to do one task and then move on to another.
- Some people prefer to eat or chew while they are working as it helps them to concentrate. Others don't.
- Some people learn better by moving around from time to time and some by standing up.

Learning and memory strategies

Different people learn in different ways. Some people learn and remember more easily when they hear something. Others prefer to see it written down and to read it. Some prefer a diagram or picture. Each of these styles of learning may be useful in different circumstances. If a student finds learning something difficult in one way, he or she might try another.

Written methods In many cases students will have to read information and take notes. This is often the most common form of learning on a course at advanced level.

A possible technique used to read information is to:

- choose a section of written material that you will read and quickly scan through it to get the overall idea;
- read the material more slowly;
- put the written material aside and recite the key ideas or points that you have read;
- check that you have covered the main points;
- if you have missed anything, re-read the information.

Often in work or for revision students have to condense large amounts of information into shorter note form. This makes it easier to remember. Steps to note taking may involve the following:

- reading the information and making sure that you understand it first;
- dividing up the information into topic headings and subheadings;
- making suitable notes that are clear and easy to read, and are in a logical order;
- underlining or highlighting important words or key phrases that will trigger memory of the point;
- using page references to the written material;
- leaving space for additions;
- creating an index for your notes, either using a card system or a computer package and updating the order.

Once you have a set of notes you can use the reading technique above to make sure you understand them or for revision.

Example

In 1999 The European Commission was poised to open an investigation into BP Amoco's proposed $26bn merger with Atlantic Richfield (Arco). EU sources said the merger, which would further tighten the oligopolistic structure of the oil market, had to be examined in the context of other anti-trust investigations involving the sector - notably the Exxon-Mobil project. Competition authorities in Brussels and the US were worried that these and other deals would enhance the power of a small number of oil companies in the exploration and production of oil and gas worldwide. If the two mergers went through, the top three oil majors - including the Anglo Dutch group Shell - would account for close to 50 per cent of crude oil production by publicly quoted western companies, bankers estimated.

EU officials had serious doubts about the BP Amoco-Arco merger. One problem involved the high joint share BP Amoco-Arco would have in pipeline transportation of natural gas in the UK sector of the North Sea. The potential blocks to the approval of Exxon-Mobil were greater. As well as its doubts about the global structure of the industry, Brussels identified numerous problems affecting Europe as a whole, as well as the EU member states. One was that the deal could harm competition in the onshore production and distribution of low calorific gas in the Netherlands and Germany, where the two companies jointly had a high market share. The Commission said that it was determined not to let the merger damage the consumer benefits expected to flow from the liberalisation of the European gas market.

Oil mergers
- *Possible investigation by European Commission of BP Amoco -Arco and Exxon-Mobil mergers.*
- *Concern that the mergers would increase oligopolistic nature of oil market. If mergers went through, BP Amoco-Arco, Exxon- Mobil and Shell would have nearly 50 per cent of crude oil production.*

(a) Mind maps

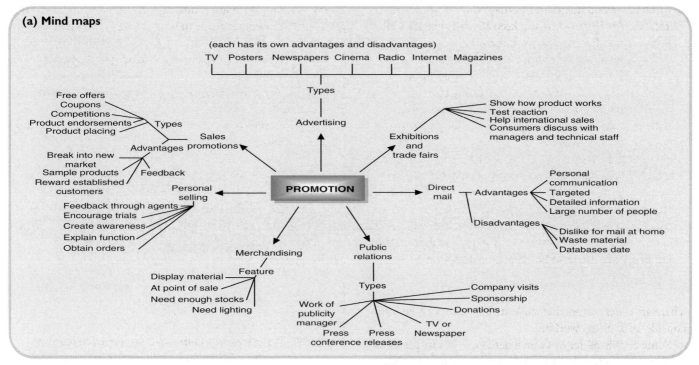

- *Problem of BP Amoco-Arco merger. Domination of natural gas pipelines.*
- *Problems of Exxon-Mobil merger. Harm to competition, transport of low calorific gas in Holland and Germany and possible benefits of market liberalisation (lower prices, better choice etc.)*

Oral methods It is sometimes easier to remember or understand something if you hear it. When you meet people do you remember their name? If so you may have a strong oral memory. Strategies for learning might include:

- answering questions asked by another person;
- making oral notes onto a tape recorder which are played back regularly;
- constantly repeating phrases or key words, perhaps in an order;
- make up a **mnemonic**, rhyme or phrase which can be repeated. For example, PEST analysis stands for the Political, Economic, Social and Technological factors that affect a business.

Pictorial/visual When you meet people do you remember their face? If so you may have a strong visual memory. Visual material can provide an instant 'picture' of information. Sometimes it is easier to see relationships by visual representation. Visual information may make use of some of the note taking techniques explained above. It may also make use of photographs. Examples of visual presentation include the following.

(a) Mind maps. *Promotion methods.*
(b) Family trees. *The sources of funds.*
(c) Flow diagrams. *The stages in the design process.*
(d) Horizontal family trees. *Herzberg's two-factor theory.*

(b) Family trees

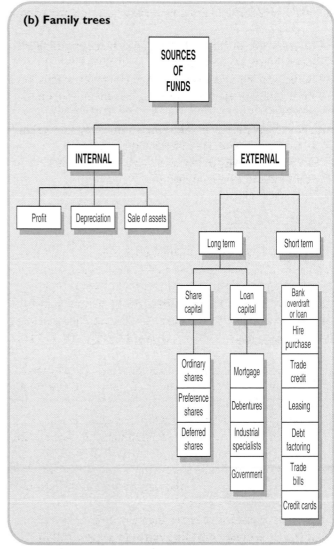

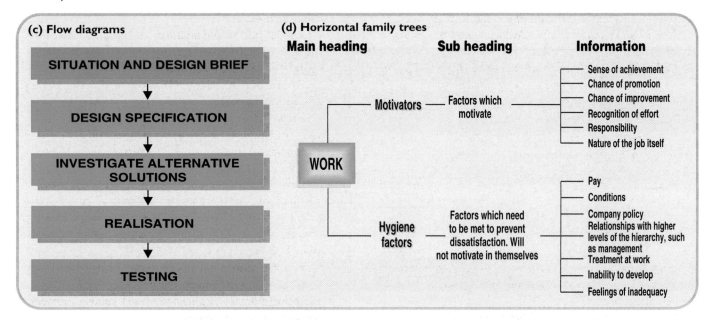

(c) Flow diagrams

(d) Horizontal family trees

(e) Block diagrams. *Calculating profit and loss.*
(f) Method of loci. This involves taking a room you know and imagining certain key words in parts of the room. *Types of integration.*

Learning by doing You may think that you know something or know how to do it. But you might only find out if you test yourself by doing something. It may be possible to test yourself by using:

- classroom or homework activities you have already completed earlier in the course;
- activities in textbooks or workbooks;
- applying ideas in a project or a piece of coursework;
- past examination questions;
- your own activities.

Key skills

Key skills allow a student to learn, select and apply important competences. Key skills at advanced level include

communication, application of number, information technology, working with others, improving own learning and performance, and problem solving. All of these skills can be developed by a student taking a course in Business Studies. Some examples of each key skill are shown below.

Communication

- Debates. *The extent to which business ethics should influence profit.*
- Role play. *An interview scenario or a meeting with a pressure group.*
- Group discussions. *How a business might promote a new product.*
- Interviews. *A one-to-one interview with a manager about a business problem.*
- Oral presentations. *The results of marketing research.*
- Passing information. *A memo to staff about reorganisation following the introduction of new technology.*
- Written analysis. *A report recommending action to solve*

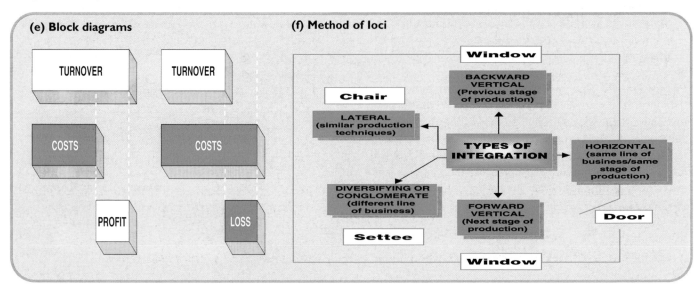

(e) Block diagrams

(f) Method of loci

problems identified in the profit and loss account and a balance sheet or a strategy to deal with entry into foreign markets.

- Written and visual presentations. *Producing a business plan or charts showing the market share of businesses in an industry.*
- Summarising information. *Producing a business organisational chart or a summary of performance from financial ratio data.*
- Written responses. *A letter to a dissatisfied customer.*
- Communication using technology. *An e-mail to the manager showing sales figures on a spreadsheet.*

Application of number
- Numerical calculations. *Calculating the depreciation of assets using different methods or calculating labour turnover.*
- Planning information. *Preparing information for a sales revenue budget.*
- Interpreting results. *Identifying gearing problems from ratios.*
- Numerical analysis. *Investment appraisal using various methods.*
- Graphical analysis. *Identifying stock problems from a chart.*
- Construction of graphs. *Constructing a break-even chart.*
- Construction of tables. *Constructing a balance sheet.*
- Collection and presentation of data. *Sales figures used to produce product life cycle diagrams or market research information showing customers' responses.*
- Forecasting. *Estimating future sales figures from a trend.*

Information technology
- Searching for information. *Finding information on a CD Rom or an Internet website.*
- Reviewing and selecting information. *Selecting appropriate information from the Internet to show accidents at work.*
- Written presentation and manipulation of information. *Writing a report using appropriate software on the impact on the business of the euro.*
- Visual presentation of information. *Illustrating the number of full time, part time and outworkers in a business as percentages in a pie chart.*
- Calculation using data. *Calculating cash flow using a spreadsheet.*
- Collection of data. *Marketing research information on a database.*
- Manipulation and management of data. *Updating stock figures over time on a spreadsheet to show stock balances.*
- Transfer of data. *Storing cost information on disk so that it can be used for financial calculations by someone else.*
- Communication technology. *Sending an e-mail containing ideas for a new product.*

Working with others
- Discussions. *To discuss possible effect on a business of lean production methods.*
- Group debates. *Should multinational businesses take their profits back to the 'home' country or spend it in foreign countries in which they operate?*
- Searching for information. *When dealing with a great deal of information such as changes in government legislation over a period.*
- Collecting information. *When dealing with a great deal of information such as the effects of government policy on a business over a year.*
- Summarising. *When a great deal of information has to be summarised, each group member could take one aspect. For example, when looking at changes in a business, summaries of marketing, production and approaches to human resources could be made.*
- Question practice and cross checking. *Using another person to ask questions or to check your answers.*
- Brainstorming. *Developing possible promotional methods using brainstorming sessions.*
- Using outside sources of information. *Discussing the effects of pedestrianisation of a town on a local retailer.*

Improving own learning performance
- Identifying areas to improve. *Knowledge, memory, time management, work and resource management, such as where to find information and what resources to use, interpreting questions, answering questions, working with others, the work environment, motivation.*
- Evaluating work. *Own evaluation, others' opinions, evaluation against criteria, past experience of problems.*
- Identifying methods of improvement. *More practice, changing the method of learning, identifying strengths and applying to other areas, reorganisation of environment such as changing the place or time of work, changing attitudes, changing resources.*
- Identifying help. *Resources, other people, self-help.*

Problem solving
- Identifying problems. *Identify the need to change operations or strategy as a result of variance analysis.*
- Identifying the possible solutions to a problem. *Identifying the different strategies that a business might use to effectively manage change.*
- Choosing solutions from alternatives. *Choosing the most effective advertising campaign using decision trees or the most effective method of work using critical path analysis.*
- Evaluating solutions. *Evaluate the reorganisation of a business to improve productivity using mean and standard deviation calculations.*
- Using IT. *Using spreadsheet calculations to solve problems by identifying the most cost effective or profitable solution.*
- Problem solving in students' own work. *Identifying and solving problems involved in coursework, such as collection of data, storage of data, presentation of data.*

Assessment criteria/objectives

It is possible to use a range of criteria when assessing the performance of students. This means that examiners or assessors want students to demonstrate a range of different skills. In order to be successful students must:
- understand the skills required by examiners or assessors;
- recognise the skill that is being assessed in a particular question;
- demonstrate all of the skills assessed by the examiner;
- practice skills before the examination.

The criteria used by examiners may fall into the following categories.

Knowledge Students have to demonstrate that they:
- understand business theories and concepts;
- recognise and understand business terms;
- interpret information given in a business context.

Students can recognise questions which test knowledge by looking at the command words in the question. Such words are explained in the section above. An example of a question assessing knowledge might be: *What is meant by best practice benchmarking?*

Application and understanding This assessment criterion requires students to apply theories and concepts in both familiar and unfamiliar situations. This might involve:
- using a business formula in appropriate circumstances, for example, calculating the current ratio for a business;
- using a theory to explain why a business has chosen a particular course of action, for example, using McGregor's Y theory to explain why a business has introduced quality circles;
- using a business theory to suggest a suitable course of action for a business, for example, suggesting a chainstore uses loyalty cards to increase repeat sales.

Questions requiring application can again be recognised by looking at the command word. An example of a question requiring application might be: *Explain why the business has cut its research and development budget.*

Analysis Students have to demonstrate that they can break down information and understand the implications of what they have been presented with. Students will encounter both qualitative and quantitative information and will need to:
- identify causes and effects and interrelationships, for example, recognise from a graph that sales are falling and could be a result of new competition in the market;
- break down information to identify specific causes or problems, for example, realise that a business is suffering

from inefficiency because according to the information staff motivation has fallen, equipment is worn and working practices are outdated;
- use appropriate techniques to analyse data, for example, use ratio analysis to assess the solvency of a business;
- use appropriate theories, business cases/practices to investigate the question, for example, use elasticity theory to show that raising price may be ineffective.

Questions requiring analysis can be recognised by looking at the command word. An example of a question requiring analysis might be: *Examine the factors which have influenced the firm's decision to close its Cardiff factory.*

Evaluation Evaluation involves making a judgment. Evaluation questions are often used to award the highest grades in examinations. Students might be expected to:
- show judgment in weighing up the relative importance of different points or sides of an argument, in order to reach a conclusion;
- comment on the reliability of information or evidence;
- distinguish between fact and opinion;
- distinguish between relevant and irrelevant information;
- draw conclusions from the evidence presented;
- show judgment on the wider issues and implications.

Questions requiring evaluation can be identified by looking at the command word. For example, *To what extent has the decision to delayer the business been successful?*

When evaluating it is often possible for a student to draw a number of different conclusions. Examiners may be less concerned with the particular conclusion drawn. Very often in business studies there is no 'right' answer. They are more interested in whether students have actually made a judgment and also the quality of their argument in support of the judgment.

Synthesis Opportunities to demonstrate this particular skill may be limited. Synthesis is required in long written answers such as essays, project work or report writing. It involves bringing together a wide range of information in a clear and meaningful way. In particular, students must:
- develop points and themes in a way which builds on previous material and ends with a rounded conclusion;
- produce an argument in a logical sequence;
- provide a clear summarised argument which draws on all the individual elements.

Examiners will tend to look for evidence of synthesis in essays and report writing questions. The sections below on essay writing and report writing will explain how students can demonstrate synthesis.

Quality of language Codes of Practice may require the assessment of candidates' quality of language wherever they are required to write in continuous prose. In these circumstances students are required to:

● avoid errors in grammar, punctuation and spelling;
● provide well structured arguments which are consistently relevant;
● write in sentences and paragraphs which follow on from one another smoothly and logically;
● express complex ideas clearly and fluently.

Command, directive or key words

When presented with a task or question as part of internally assessed work or externally assessed examinations:

● how do you know what the question is asking?
● how do you know what the assessor or examiner wants you to do?

In many forms of assessment certain **command, directive or key words** in a question will tell the student what is expected of them. Sometimes two or more words appear together in a question. They must all be taken into account when giving the answer.

Information and knowledge Certain command words are designed to find out what a student knows about the subject.

● Define - to state the exact meaning of a term or a phrase. *Define what is meant by marketing research.*
● Describe - to give an account or a portrayal of something. *Describe the hierarchy and span of control of the business.*
● Give - to write down or say something. Sometimes followed by 'an example' or 'an account of'. *Give an example of a private limited company.* May also be followed by 'reasons for' which may involve greater analysis.
● How - to present an account of something. *How has the business raised funds to buy new machinery?*
● Identify - to pick from a variety of information. *Identify three reasons for the merger.*
● Illustrate - to show clearly, often with the use of an example. *Illustrate the main methods used to promote the product.*
● Outline - to give a short description of the main aspects or features. *Outline the view of workers by management.*
● State - to write down or say something. Sometimes followed by what that 'something' should be. *State 3 features of an effective leader.*
● Summarise - to provide a brief account covering the main points. *Summarise the approach to quality at the business.*
● What - to clarify something. *What is meant by a stakeholder?*
● Which - to select from certain options or to indicate a choice. *Which location did the business find most suitable?*

Application and explanation Certain command words are designed to allow the student to apply knowledge to a given situation, to work out why something has happened and to give reasons for something that has happened.

● Account for - to give reasons for. *Account for the growth in part time workers over the period.*
● Analyse - to examine in detail, showing relationships, the importance of certain things and criticisms if applicable. *Analyse the approach to lean production of the organisation.*
● Apply - to bring knowledge to bear on a situation. Note that sometimes the word does not appear in the question. For example, 'Using examples from the article, explain how the business might promote its product' requires an application of knowledge to a particular situation. *Apply the Boston Matrix to the product mix of the company.*
● Calculate - to work out mathematically, usually numerically, but sometimes from a graph for example. *Calculate the return on net assets for the business.*
● Compare and contrast - to show the similarities and differences between two or more things. *Compare and contrast the approaches to recruitment of the two companies.*
● Distinguish - to show the differences between two or more things. *Distinguish between job and batch production.*
● Examine - to investigate closely to find out the 'truth' of the situation as if carrying out an inquiry. *Examine the factors that may have led to cash flow problems.*
● Explain - to make clear a concept, idea or viewpoint. It may involve giving an illustration of the meaning or examples. Note that it is sometimes followed by the word 'why' (see below). *Explain the pricing strategies used by the business.*
● Explore - to investigate or examine in detail, as explained above. *Explore the ways in which a business is affected by changes in interest rates.*
● Investigate - to carry out a detailed examination. *Investigate the factors that may have led the business to go into liquidation.*
● Suggest or give reasons for - to explain why, giving a justification. *Suggest reasons why the business chose to reduce its workforce.*
● Why - to present reasons for something. *Explain why labour turnover has increased.*

Evaluation Certain command words are designed to allow students to make a judgment or to evaluate a judgment that has taken place.

● Assess - an invitation to measure or place a value on the importance of something. *Assess whether the change to just in time manufacturing is likely to be successful.*
● Comment on - to give an opinion about the extent to which something has occurred. *Comment on the environmental policy of the organisation.*
● Criticise or critically analyse - to pass judgment on a debatable area. *Critically analyse the growing globalisation of business.*
● Determine - to settle, decide, or find out the nature of. *Determine the most suitable new location for the business.*
● Do you think - to comment on or give an opinion on the basis of evidence. *Do you think the decision of the business to expand was a suitable strategy in the circumstances?*

- Discuss - to consider a contentious statement or to review an area which might have two or more views. *Discuss whether the business should have introduced group decision making.*
- Evaluate - to make an appraisal of something and to find out how important it is. *Evaluate the strategy used by the business over the period.*
- To what extent (does/do) - to make a judgment or to measure. *To what extent has the change in corporate culture been successful?*

Levels of response

Examiners and assessors may award marks according to the levels of response demonstrated by the student in the answer. The higher the level of response the more marks are awarded to students. An example of different levels that might be identified is shown below.

Level 4 This is the most sophisticated of responses and attracts the most marks. At this level students must provide good evidence of the appropriate skill. Responses must be accurate, extensive, balanced and logical. For example, in evaluation, judgments must be well made and supported by logical arguments. Students must draw original conclusions from the evidence and show awareness of underlying and related themes or issues.

Level 3 At this level student responses are classified as good but with some weaknesses. For example, with regard to knowledge of the subject, to attain level 3 a student must demonstrate that his or her knowledge is satisfactory or better. However, there may be some weaknesses or perhaps the focus is too narrow.

Level 2 If students show that they have clearly used a particular skill, but evidence is limited and there are obvious weaknesses, the response may be classified as level 2. For example, a level 2 response in evaluation would mean that a student has made judgments but they are not well supported by arguments. The evidence will be generally too limited and often below average.

Level 1 This is the most basic of student responses. Some marks will be awarded if a student can demonstrate that they have at least tried to provide some evidence of a particular skill. For example, in analysis a level 1 response would involve some attempt at analysis of data, but lacking in insight and depth.

Level 0 There are no relevant points made and no application, analysis or evaluation.

This approach may be used by examiners when assessing performance in all of the above criteria, even quality of language. However, examiners do not expect students to offer level 4 responses in all of their answers. It depends on

the type of question being asked. For example, level 4 responses may only be required in essays, report writing questions and parts of structured questions in decision making case studies. Some examination questions may only require level 1 or level 2 responses. If this is the case, the answers required at level 1 and level 2 may be slightly different from the descriptions above. For example, a question which offers just 4 marks in an examination may require the responses described below.

- Level 2. Students must develop in detail at least one of the relevant factors identified and show some clarity in their explanation.
- Level 1. Students must identify at least one relevant factor and demonstrate some limited attempt at development.

The levels of response required are not normally shown on examination papers. However, students will understand that those questions which carry more marks will require higher levels of response.

Structured questions

The main features of structured questions are as follows.
- They contain several parts.
- The parts normally follow a sequence or pattern.
- Some of the parts may be linked in some way.
- They are generally accompanied by some data to provide students with a stimulus.
- The whole question may require students to demonstrate all skills covered by the assessment criteria, but only one part may be testing a particular skill.
- The parts of the question generally get more demanding as students work through it.
- Different parts may be assessed by different levels of response.
  Structured questions are broken down into 'parts'.

First part The first part of the structured question is usually the easiest. This may help students to 'settle' into a question and perhaps give them some confidence. The first part of a structured question:
- is usually designed to test knowledge of a business concept or business term;
- may require a student to perform a simple skill, eg a calculation;
- may require a student to give a straightforward explanation or definition;
- usually requires students to provide a basic level response.
- would carry only a few marks.

Examples
(a) Explain the term 'working capital'.
(a) Distinguish between job analysis and job evaluation.

Middle part The middle part of structured questions may vary. There is no set pattern and this gives examiners and assessors some flexibility when setting structured questions. However, the middle part of structured questions:

● may contain two or more parts;
● usually test knowledge, application, analysis and sometimes evaluation;
● may require students to perform simple or more difficult calculations;
● may require a mixture of straightforward explanation and more complex analysis;
● may carry more marks than the first part.

Examples
(b)(i) *Calculate the gross profit margin and the net profit margin for the business.*
   (ii) *Comment on your findings in (i).*
(b)(i) *Explain the meaning of the term price inelastic.*
   (ii) *To what extent is the concept of price elasticity helpful to a business?*
(c) *Analyse the possible reasons why increasing numbers of companies are introducing flexible working practices.*
(c) *Examine the possible implications of the data for:*
   (i) *employees;*
   (ii) *a large manufacturer planning to export for the first time.*

Final part This part of the question is usually the most demanding part. The final part of the structured question:

● will nearly always require a higher level response;
● will usually test knowledge, application, analysis and evaluation;
● will usually carry a higher mark allocation;
● may not be broken down into smaller parts.

Examples
(d) *Assess the view that business advertising practices should be more heavily regulated.*
(d) *Evaluate the non-financial factors which might influence the firm's decision to relocate its operations.*
(d) *Discuss the factors that have influenced the business to change its marketing strategy.*

Data response questions

Data response or case study questions are used to test student skills in unfamiliar circumstances. The key features of data response questions include:

● the provision of qualitative or quantitative data, or both, to provide a stimulus for students;
● hypothetical or real case study data;
● the use of structured questions;
● opportunities for students to demonstrate knowledge, application, analysis and evaluation.

Hints
● Always read the data at least twice.
● Use a felt pen to highlight important words, sentences or key numerical information.
● Read the structured questions very carefully, perhaps highlighting command words and other key terms.
● Some of your answers **must** be related to the data provided.
● Some of your answers **must** use ideas, concepts and theories not mentioned in the data.
● Answer the parts of the question in order.
● Allocate your time according to the number of marks offered for each part.
● Show all your working out when performing calculations.
● Always attempt all parts of the questions.
● **Do not** use bullet points when writing your answers.

Answering the first part The information below contains data from a case study question. The data is just a small extract from the question.

The directors are recommending a final dividend of 18p, making a full year dividend of 27p, an increase of 8 per cent over the previous year. The Directors will consider further limited reductions of dividend cover in the medium-term, allowing real dividend growth to be maintained.

(a) *Explain the term 'dividend cover'.*

● To begin with it is helpful to highlight the key words in the question and the key words in the data as shown above. This might help students to focus.
● To pick up all marks in this case it would be necessary to use a couple of sentences to explain the term and then give the formula which is used to calculate the dividend cover.
● The explanation needs to be crisp, clear and uncomplicated. Students need to demonstrate in their answer that they understand the term. The formula can be added at the end.
● A student could give a numerical illustration here. *For example, if a business made a total dividend payment of £300m and net profit for the year was £500m, dividend cover would be given by:*

$$\frac{Net\ profit}{Dividends} = \frac{£500m}{£300m} = 1.67\ times$$

Answering the middle part The data below is from another case study.

One of the things troubling Renton's is the accumulation of stock. Both stocks of raw materials and stocks of finished goods have been building up over recent years. The build up of finished goods is linked to poor sales performance.

However, there seems no real reason why stocks of raw materials should have grown. The suggestion made by the production manager to introduce Just-in-Time methods may be worth considering.

Renton's current assets and current liabilities 2000 - 2003

(£)

	2000	2001	2002	2003
Raw materials	21,000	22,900	26,600	34,200
Finished goods	31,300	36,800	42,300	49,600
Other current assets	42,300	41,200	44,900	43,800
Current liabilities	109,900	113,500	119,400	138,600

(b) (i) Use ratio analysis to show how the build up of stocks is causing liquidity problems for Renton's.
(ii) Analyse the advantages and disadvantages to Renton's of introducing just-in-time methods.

- Again the first step is to highlight the key words in the question as shown above.
- The question **cannot** be answered without reference to the data. The first part of the question requires students to analyse the data using a quantitative technique (ratio analysis)
- Students need to calculate the current ratio and/or the acid test ratio to comment on Renton's liquidity position.
- To earn all the marks in this question the student would need to perform the calculations correctly, interpret the results appropriately and draw a meaningful conclusion.
- In this case both the current ratios and the acid test ratios are below the 'ideal' range of 1.5:2 and 1:1 respectively. The acid test ratio is particularly low. This suggests that Renton's has liquidity problems.

The second part of this question requires more analysis.
- Again, begin by highlighting the key words in the question and data as above.
- Before writing the answer it is helpful to jot down a few key points for analysis, such as two advantages and two disadvantages of JIT. Advantages could be less money tied up in stock, more space for other activities or less waste stock. Disadvantages might be vulnerability to a break in supply, loss of flexibility in production or increased ordering and administration costs. These points are not likely to be in the case material. Students will have to bring in outside knowledge. There is nothing to be gained from identifying lots of advantages and disadvantages. The quality of application and analysis will generate marks for this question.
- Marks will be awarded for knowledge, application and analysis. Evaluation marks might also be awarded at this stage.

Answering the final part It is important that students leave enough time to answer this part properly as it usually carries high marks. The data below contains an extract from another case study.

It has been suggested that the economy will grow at around 3 per cent next year. Currently interest rates are relatively low and consumer confidence is buoyant. The use of credit cards to borrow money to finance spending is also likely to remain high.

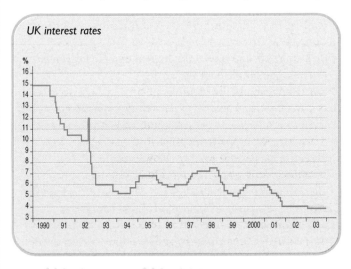

UK interest rates

(d) To what extent do external factors, such as those mentioned in the case, influence the performance of a business?

- Students will need to introduce a lot of their own material into their answer.
- Before writing, students should jot down a plan. A plan for this question might appear as follows.
  1. *Explain how external factors, eg interest rates, affect businesses.*
  2. *Identify 2 other factors which might affect businesses, eg consumer confidence, borrowing.*
  3. *Analyse the 2 factors.*
  4. *Evaluate, for example, by saying that external factors have a great influence because they are beyond the control of businesses. However, a good business will include their effect in its forecasting.*
- If the above plan is executed effectively the student will demonstrate all the skills required.
- Students should remember that it is not necessary to identify and list lots of factors. Listing is a low order skill and more marks are awarded for application, analysis and evaluation.

Decision making and problem solving case studies (unseen)

These are often in the form of extended case studies. They can be demanding and require a slightly different approach to

answering than shorter data response questions.
- The case material tends to be hypothetical but usually based on a real life situation.
- The case material tends to focus on a single business.
- The volume of material given is much greater.
- There tends to be some financial information in the case material.
- The case often emphasises analysis and evaluation skills.
- Many of the case questions require an integrated approach when answering. This means that students will need to embrace the full range of the specification in their answers. A single answer may need to address issues such as marketing, production, human resources, finance and external factors all at the same time.
- Questions set usually require students to make decisions or solve problems. For example, a question may require students to suggest a suitable future strategy for a business.
- One question will often require students to use a quantitative technique when answering.
- Examiners often want students to be critical.

Hints
- Skim read the case material to get a feel for the business, its people, its circumstances and its objectives (see section below on things to think about).
- Read again thoroughly highlighting key information.
- Look at the numerical information and analyse it briefly, without performing any calculations.
- Make brief notes on the key objectives and key themes.
- Read the questions highlighting command words and other key terms.
- Identify some business theories you might consider discussing in your answers. Questions will probably not request specific theories. The onus is on students to introduce relevant theories.
- Reread hints on answering data response questions above.

Issues to think about when planning answers
- People. Business is about people and your answers need to reflect this. Consider the age, family circumstances, the attitudes and personal interests of the people involved in the case material. What motivates them? What is their background? What are their objectives? What are their strengths and weaknesses? These are some of the people issues which students need to consider when shaping their answers.
- Situation. It is important to think about the context in which the business is set. Examples of issues to consider include the type of business organisation (Ltd, plc or sole trader), the prevailing culture, the type of industry, the nature of competition, the size, its financial position, its age, history and potential. It is often helpful to liken the case material to a business which actually exists in a similar context. However, this may not always be

possible.
- Objectives. Answers to questions are bound to be linked to what the business is trying to achieve in its given context. A business may be trying to survive following a recession, it may be trying to break into new markets, it may be trying to raise finance for a big investment project, it may be trying to change its culture or take over another business. It is often useful to consider, and distinguish between, short term and long term objectives.
- Theories. Students should introduce business theories into their answers. There may be little or no guidance as to what theories are required. Students need to be on the lookout for opportunities to introduce some business theory in every answer they write. For example, if a business is considering a price change, price elasticity theory could be introduced. If a business is merging with another, economies of scale may be discussed. If a business is downsizing the effect on staff might be discussed, in which case motivational theories such as Herzberg or Maslow might be applied.
- Be critical. Be prepared to challenge statements or claims made in a case study if relevant and applicable. Students with an enquiring and critical approach will be rewarded.

Example 1
Most of the structured questions in decision making/problem solving case studies usually require lengthy answers with analysis and evaluation. Therefore it is important to plan before writing an answer. Below is an extract from part of an extended case study. The case study is about Henshaws Ltd, a components manufacturer for the computer industry. It has faced difficulties in recent years due to escalating costs. It is considering ways of improving efficiency and reducing costs.

One option currently being considered by Henshaws Ltd is to outsource its marketing activities. The directors of the company have not been impressed with the performance of this department. Their expenditure has consistently exceeded their budget and they seem to get new business and then lose it. In addition, communications between the department and others in the organisation have not been good. Two of the four company directors have long claimed that the company's strength is manufacturing high quality components, although the other two directors argue that the company must avoid clinging to 'past glories' and move forward with the times. A number of marketing agencies have given presentations to the board of directors and a decision whether to outsource marketing is imminent.

(b) *Assess the likely advantages and disadvantages to Henshaws Ltd of outsourcing its marketing function.*

- To answer this question it is necessary to identify and

analyse 2 or 3 advantages, identify and analyse 2 or 3 disadvantages and then evaluate by making a judgment about whether Henshaws should outsource marketing or not.
- Although the question does not specifically ask for a judgment examiners are probably expecting one. This is because the mark allocation may be quite high.
- A plan should be drafted which might look like this:

Adv.	1. Costs fall
	2. More focus on manufacturing
	3. More effective marketing by specialists
Disadv.	1. Redundancies
	2. Loss of control of a vital function
	3. Long term marketing costs might rise.
Eval.	Yes - outsource because current marketing is expensive, ineffective and is causing problems. Henshaws will then be more focused and able to exploit its strengths.

- In the answer it is necessary to analyse the above advantages and disadvantages in detail explaining their relevance.
- In the evaluation some students may suggest that Henshaws should not outsource its marketing function. This does not matter. Examiners just want students to make a judgment and support it with a coherent and plausible argument. Remember that these case studies are decision making case studies and therefore a decision must be made!

Example 2

Some quantitative analysis is usually required in extended case studies. It may be quite complex and students often make the mistake of spending too long on this section. The data below contains an extract from an extended case study about a business which is considering a new investment. Arpan Shrinath & Co manufactures training shoes and Arpan is deciding which investment project to go ahead with.

Project 1. *Arpan has considered buying a large delivery van and undertaking his own distribution. At the moment he pays a local company to distribute training shoes to his customers. This has proved expensive and often ineffective.*

Project 2. *A new moulding machine has just been launched on the market by a German machine manufacturer. It is computer numerically controlled and would help to improve the quality of Arpan's products. It would also be more productive than his existing machine.*

Project 3. *Arpan is becoming increasingly concerned that his office staff are working in conditions which are too cramped. Staff frequently complain and he is aware of inefficiencies due to a lack of space. He is considering the construction of a purpose built annex to the factory where office staff can work more effectively.*

The table below shows the costs and expected returns for each of these projects over a 6 year period.

Expected returns								
	Cost	Year 1	Year 2	Year 3	Year 4	Year 5	Year 6	Total
Project 1	£15,000	£4,000	£4,000	£4,000	£4,000	£4,000	£4,000	£24,000
Project 2	£40,000	£12,000	£10,000	£10,000	£9,000	£9,000	£9,000	£59,000
Project 3	£30,000	£7,000	£7,000	£7,000	£7,000	£7,000	£7,000	£42,000

(c) Calculate the (i)payback; (ii)average rate of return for the 3 investment projects and decide which project is the most attractive. Take into account your results from the calculations and any other information you feel is appropriate.

- This question requires knowledge and understanding of investment appraisal techniques. Provided students have revised the quantitative techniques required they just need to apply the appropriate formulae.
- It is often helpful to produce calculations (or the results of calculations) in tables. One way in which the answers to the above question might be presented is:

	Project 1	Project 2	Project 3
Cost	£15,000	£40,000	£30,000
Total return	£24,000	£59,000	£42,000
Total profit	£9,000	£19,000	£12,000
Profit p.a.	£1,500	£3,167	£2,000
ARR	10%	7.9%	6.6%
Payback	3.75 years	3.88 years	4.29 years

- According to the calculations above project 1 appears the most attractive. It has the highest ARR and also the shortest payback period.
- There is likely to be other information in the case which will influence the decision here. For example, if customers are complaining about the quality of products, Arpan might decide to buy the new machine to improve quality, even though the projected financial returns are slightly lower.
- This question is likely to offer a high mark allocation. The calculations alone would not generate all the marks. Students must bring in other information from the case, use their own ideas and also evaluate.
- Some thought must be given to the setting out of numerical answers. Good presentation is important. Avoid deletions and sprawling calculations. Space answers generously and underline final answers.

Example 3

The final question in an extended case study often requires students to suggest a strategy or give an overall view. The question might also carry higher marks. A possible question might be:

(d) Taking the whole case into account, do you consider that the board of directors should discontinue production at the Newport factory?

- Again, planning is very important here. A lengthy answer is required with relevant points being identified, thorough analysis and evaluation. Students need to bring together a range of relevant points and make a decision.
- Timing is also crucial. Students must ensure that they leave sufficient time to plan and write the answer to this final, and important, question properly.
- Students may use some of the material generated in other answers in the case. But obviously repetition must be avoided.
- Again, it probably does not matter in this question whether students suggest that production is discontinued or not. Examiners want to see a well structured, logical argument with a meaningful conclusion drawn.
- Remember to consider the people, the situation, the objectives and to introduce theories.

Pre-seen case studies

A pre-seen case study is a method of assessment which involves giving students case study material before the day of the examination. This allows students to prepare more thoroughly for the examination by analysing the information and forming ideas in advance.

- Case study material may be issued a number of weeks before the day of the examination.
- The structured questions relating to the case study will not be known until the day of the examination.
- Additional information regarding the case may also be supplied within the question structure.
- The nature of the material provided in the case is likely to be the same as any other case study, but perhaps in more detail. Students should read the previous sections on data response and decision making questions.

Hints

- The general approach to pre-seen case studies is little different from those which are not pre-seen. The only important difference is that students have a great deal of time to study the data. Again, the hints in previous sections on answering data questions should be read.
- There is much more time to read the material so more time can be spent highlighting key words and terms. Students could also note theories, issues or themes which are relevant.
- Any words, terms or theories which are unfamiliar or

forgotten can be looked up in the text book. For example, if the case contains an extract from a balance sheet, it might be helpful to consult the balance sheet unit to reinforce understanding of balance sheet terms and structure.

- It is helpful to try and predict possible questions which the examiner might set. This will allow students to prepare answers.
- Try to identify trends, patterns and links in the data and account for them.
- Get help from friends and parents.
- When answering the questions in the examination it is very important to answer the ones set. Students should not try to reproduce their own 'model answers'.

Essay writing

An essay is an assessment method used to find out how students can respond in depth to an open question. It involves writing in continuous prose and provides an opportunity to explain something in detail.

- The quality of grammar, vocabulary, sentence construction and spelling is particularly important.
- A strong emphasis is usually placed on analysis, evaluation and synthesis.
- Essay questions may be integrated and synoptic. This means that students must consider the full range of the specification areas when writing answers. Essays based on one section of a specification or syllabus, such as marketing, may draw on all areas within it.
- The length will vary depending on the time allocated.
- They require a great deal of thought and planning before writing begins.
- The use of real world examples to illustrate points is essential.
- The use of diagrams, such as the Boston Matrix, is encouraged.
- There is rarely a 'right' answer. It is possible for two students to put forward opposing arguments and both be awarded high marks. It is the quality of the argument which is important, not the nature of it.

Planning

- Read the question very carefully.
- Highlight the command words and other key words to help provide focus.
- Planning could be in two stages. Stage one might involve a 2 or 3 minute session where students jot down an explosion of points and issues they think might be relevant.
- Stage two would then involve sorting points into an appropriate order and planning out a structure which will accommodate an argument.

Introduction

- It is common to begin with a short introduction where key

terms are defined and the question is put into context. Some general information may also be given. An introduction should be no more than a third of a side long, for example.

The main body
- When writing the main body of an answer it is important to follow the plan and write in detail, ensuring that evidence of analysis and evaluation is provided.
- It is vital to answer the question. It is better to write one side of relevant material than five sides of 'waffle'.
- Never use bullet points in essays.
- Never use subheadings in essays.
- Never write lists in essays. Extra marks are not awarded for identifying a large number of relevant points.
- Remember to include real world examples where appropriate.
- It is inadvisable to switch emphasis during the essay. It is best to stick to the plan.
- Diagrams, graphs and other illustrative material may be used but make sure it is clearly labelled and explained in the text.

Conclusion
- It is important to write a conclusion. It may be a statement which answers the question 'in a nutshell', drawing on the points analysed in the main body.
- Conclusions should not repeat material used elsewhere.
- The best conclusions are those which demonstrate evaluation and synthesis.
- Students are often required to make a judgment or give an opinion. Do not 'sit on the fence'.

Example
It has been argued that the productivity of UK businesses falls well behind that of its overseas rivals. Suggest possible reasons why this might be the case and examine the measures which might be taken by UK businesses to improve productivity?

- Essay questions can carry a relatively high number of marks.
- The words highlighted in the title are productivity, UK businesses, overseas rivals, suggest possible reasons, examine, measures and improve productivity.
- The following ideas may be suggested for the essay.
  Define productivity, labour, capital, Rover productivity poor, Nissan good, lack of investment, lack of funds, lack of R & D, dividends too high, too short termist. Standardisation, reengineering, kaizen, JIT, outsourcing, virtual companies, TQM, benchmarking, work study, culture, trade unions, weak management, quality circles, technology, training, labour flexibility, delayering, downsizing.

- The ideas generated may not be in any particular order. The focus in the above responses appears to be on production and ways of improving efficiency.
- Another 2 or 3 minutes spent planning might deliver the following essay structure.

Introduction
➤ *Define productivity - output in relation to inputs.*
➤ *An example of evidence which might support the statement is the low productivity of Rover compared with, say, Japanese car makers.*
➤ *Suggest that there is a number of approaches to improving productivity, some specific and some strategic.*

Main body
➤ *Analyse 3 possible reasons why productivity is lower in UK.*
➤ *Low investment, therefore inadequate and dated technology.*
➤ *Lack of R & D because the City wants higher dividends NOW.*
➤ *Trade unions may have resisted changes which might improve productivity.*
➤ *Explain that measures designed to improve efficiency might be specific or strategic.*
➤ *Analyse 3 specific measures - JIT, benchmarking and new technology.*
➤ *Analyse 3 strategic measures - kaizen, re-engineering and TQM.*

Conclusion
➤ *Argue that the statement is probably right for the reasons given. Evaluate by saying that one particular reason may be more important eg lack of investment.*
➤ *Argue that the methods employed to improve efficiency depend on the individual firms and their needs.*
➤ *Evaluate by suggesting that particular methods may be more suitable, if, for example, a business has dated machinery new technology may have a very significant impact on productivity.*
➤ *Argue that all measures will require cooperation of staff if they are to be successful.*

- When the essay is finished it is important to read through it and check for errors such as spelling, grammar and punctuation. However, avoid frantic crossing out at the last minute because this tends to have a negative effect on presentation.

Report writing

A business report is a formal method of communication. It is a written document designed to convey information in a concise but detailed way. A report is written in a structured way so that information is broken down into manageable parts. The end section of the report is very important. It will contain recommendations for action that a business should take.
- A report begins with a formal section showing who the report is for, who has written it, the date it was written and the title.
- A report is broken into a series of sections. Each section

might address a particular issue.

● Each new section should begin with a clear heading and each section could be numbered.

● Each section can be broken down into sub-sections, which again can be numbered. Each sub-section may be a single paragraph.

● Information should be written in sentences and not in note form. Sections will require application, analysis and evaluation.

● Numerical information such as tables, graphs and charts should be shown in an appendix. Similarly, calculations should be shown in an appendix.

● The conclusion is very important and should aim at bringing together points raised and analysed in previous sections. No new material should be introduced at this stage. A conclusion is often an action plan or a series of recommendations.

Features   Sometimes examiners require a report in a data response question. Students may be required to write reports based on a wide range of numerical data presented to them in tables or charts. It is this latter style which is the focus of attention here. It is sometimes called the numerical report. In a numerical report:

● information is presented in a number of tables or charts, perhaps 5 or 6 distinct pieces of data;

● the data will relate to a particular business and its market, there may also be some general economic data;

● students are required to interpret and analyse the data;

● some data may not be very helpful and should therefore be ignored, examiners deliberately give more information than is required to force students to be selective;

● the report question will normally be very specific and require students to make a decision, ie make recommendations;

● students are often allocated a role when writing the report;

● the structure of the report will often be indicated in the question.

Hints

● Read the introduction and become familiar with the type of business, its market and circumstances.

● Read the tables of data and begin to form views about what they show.

● Make brief notes and comments adjacent to tables and graphs relating to trends and patterns shown by the data.

● Decide whether any data is irrelevant.

● Try to spot links between the different tables of data.

● Start to plan the report structure by identifying some appropriate section headings, **but do not use a heading for each piece of data**. Identify 4 or 5 key issues.

● Identify the points to be raised in each section.

● Decide what your conclusions and recommendations will be. Remember that there is not likely to be a right or wrong answer, but you must make a judgment.

● Write the report using the structure outlined above and remembering that the student is playing a role.

● Remember to analyse and evaluate throughout, and also, that the conclusion requires synthesis.

Example

Moa Kuk Ltd is a family business which imports a wide range of oriental soft furnishings and household artifacts. The business has two large stores in London. The second store was opened two years ago and has very quickly returned a profit. Moa Kuk, the managing director, believes that the company could grow very quickly and become a successful franchising operation.

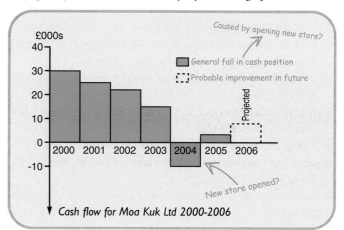

Cash flow for Moa Kuk Ltd 2000-2006

You are employed by a firm of business consultants. You have been asked to write a report to assess whether or not Moa Kuk should set up a franchising operation or grow independently.

● The question is likely to carry a relatively high number of marks.

● Begin to think of suitable section headings for the report structure. We only have an extract from a question here, but the limited information does provide some guidance for appropriate headings. For example:

  ➤ *The financial position of Moa Kuk Ltd*
  ➤ *The advantages of franchising*
  ➤ *The disadvantages of franchising*
  ➤ *Recommendations*

- Write brief notes by each data box. These are shown in the graph and the table.
- A plan can be drawn up for the first section.
  - ➤ *Cash flow has deteriorated over the period particularly in the last two years when the new store was opened.*
  - ➤ *The owners have not contributed any more capital to the business over the period.*
  - ➤ *The development of the business has been funded by increased borrowing.*
  - ➤ *Borrowing has increased steadily over the period making the company more highly geared.*
- A plan should be drawn up for the other sections in the answer. For example, the information may lead to a conclusion that: *Moa Kuk Ltd is not really in a financial position to fund independent growth. Therefore setting up a franchising operation may well be an effective strategy.*
- There will obviously be other points to consider based on other data which is not provided here.

Project/Coursework

A project or piece of coursework usually involves:

- extended research carried out over a period of time within a real business setting;
- the investigation of a problem or decision that the business is facing;
- the use of both qualitative and quantitative data and analysis in researching and analysing the problem or decision;
- the application of a range of business knowledge, skills and methods to the problem or decision;
- the identification of a number of feasible strategies that the business might pursue;
- evaluation of these strategies and making recommendations about which strategy should be pursued and why;
- the production of an extended report which presents the research and findings and use of a range of methods of presentation to enhance the quality of the report.

Unlike other elements of Business Studies examinations, this work is carried out over a period of time during the course. There will be a deadline by which time the project has to be completed, but it is largely the student's responsibility to set up and carry out the investigation and to produce the report by that deadline. The required length of the report is laid down by the awarding body.

Assessment The teacher is the first assessor for project work. He or she will mark the project as a whole and award marks based upon the assessment criteria set by the awarding body. This will vary between different examinations, but typically covers the following skills:

- the way the problem or decision has been explained and objectives for the project set;
- the use made of relevant business knowledge, ideas and concepts in tackling the problem;
- applying appropriate research methods;
- carrying out relevant analysis using both qualitative and quantitative information;
- evaluating evidence to draw conclusions and make recommendations;
- presentation of evidence in a structured way that shows a logical development of ideas;
- employing a good quality of language including spelling, punctuation and grammar.

There may then be some internal moderation of your teacher's marking by another teacher or lecturer in the school or college to check that all the teachers are marking in a consistent way. Finally a sample of projects will be sent to an external moderator, employed by the awarding body, who will check that the marking has been carried out to the criteria set by the examining body.

Hints

- Choose an organisation for your project with which you have contact, perhaps through family or friends and which will allow you access to the information you require. Your teacher may also have established initial contact with a number of organisations which will provide appropriate projects.
- Don't be too ambitious with your choice of problem. *How might Marks & Spencer improve its profitability?* would be too much of a challenge, whereas *How might Marks & Spencer's Wilmslow branch increase its sales of microwave meals?* might be a more realistic title.
- Produce a project/coursework action plan before you start your research - *what are your objectives? what information do you want to collect? what will be the sources of information? who do you want to talk to? when will you collect the information? what analysis will you carry out? when does the report have to be completed?*
- When carrying out your research within an organisation you will need to collect background information about the organisation as well as information specific to your project.
- Listen carefully and give yourself time each day to write up your notes - you will find that you will collect much more data than you will need, but you won't know which is relevant until you write up the project.
- When you analyse of the data, use the concepts and techniques that you have been learning in your lessons and explain in the project why you are using a particular technique as a means of analysis.
- Try to use both quantitative as well as qualitative analysis if the project lends itself to both.
- There are always alternative strategies for solving a problem - one alternative is always for an organisation to do nothing. You must present alternatives and evaluate

their strengths and weaknesses.
- Make your recommendations and relate these back to your project objectives. It does not matter if the organisation would not necessarily follow your advice; but your recommendation should be firmly backed by evidence from your analysis.
- There will always be more that you could have done, but keep to the time deadline and keep to the word limit.

Example
What is the feasibility of extending a 9-hole golf course to 18 holes?

This is an example of a project title that a student has negotiated with the local golf club where she plays as a junior member.

Objectives For this particular project the student, in discussion with the organisation, might set the following objectives:
- to identify the potential demand for an 18-hole course;
- to explore the local competition for the golf club;
- to examine the financial feasibility of building an 18-hole extension;
- to identify possible sources of finance for the extension to 18 holes;
- to make recommendations to the club on whether they should go ahead.

This is a piece of coursework that provides a reasonable problem for the student to tackle; it has scope for both qualitative and quantitative research and analysis and allows the student to make a clear choice at the end. By negotiating the objectives with the club, the student can hope to receive good access to the necessary people to talk to and the club's financial information. Access to accurate financial data is often the major constraint the students face when carrying out project research.

The scope of the project does not require the student to explore the legal background to expanding the golf course. This is a reasonable limitation that makes the project more manageable and the student would not be penalised for this provided the objectives and limitations of the project are made clear at the start.

Collecting information The student might plan to collect a range of data from primary and secondary sources. **Primary research** might include:
- a survey of existing members to establish their demand for an 18-hole course;
- a survey of potential members who might use the course if it had 18 holes;
- interviews with club officials who would be responsible for carrying out the extension;
- identifying the costs of building an extension;

- identifying the costs and availability of different sources of finance;
Secondary research might include:
- identification of the demand for golf through national statistics;
- identification of the location, size and facilities of other golf courses in the area;
- looking at the club's existing financial position through its published income and expenditure statements;
- looking at economic trends that might affect the future costs and revenue for a golf club;
- making use of any previous data that the club had collected if this problem had been considered previously.

Analysis Once the above research has taken place, the student would be in a position to carry out the following analyses of the information collected:
- a forecast of likely demand for the 18-hole course and thereby of the revenue that the club might generate;
- a forecast of the likely flow of expenditures on the project in order to set up and maintain the extended course;
- a cash flow for the project over the next 5/10 years;
- using the pay-back method or discounted cash flow method, an analysis of the financial benefits of the project when compared to other possible investments;
- a comparison of the costs and benefits of different sources of funding for the extension of the course.

Evaluation Before making his/her final recommendation, the student would need to consider the following questions, making use of evidence drawn from the information and analyses presented in the report.
- Does the decision to expand the course fit into the overall strategy of the club?
- On purely financial grounds, is the expansion a viable option? Are there better financial options for the club, eg leaving the money in a high interest bearing account?
- Can the club raise the necessary finance for the expansion? Would the costs of increased borrowing outweigh the benefits?
- How reliable are the forecasts of the demand and revenue figures and the cost and expenditure figures? How accurate is the research on demand? What might change to increase the cost estimates?
- What other external and internal factors would the club need to take into account before making a final decision?

This evaluation would help to provide the basis upon which the student is making their final recommendation as well as pointing forward to other areas that might be considered in a longer report. It should not be seen as a sign of weakness that the report writer asks such questions of their own work. It shows that he or she understands both the strengths and weaknesses of their final decision. It is important to remember that there is no correct answer in report or coursework writing.

Index

Investors in People 354-355
Invoice 15
ISO 9000 422
Issued share capital 231, 236
 defined 237
Issuing house 231
 defined 237

J

Jargon
 as barrier to communication 380
Job
 advertisement 333-334
 analysis 329
 defined 334
 centres 332
 descriptions 329-330
 defined 334
 design and redesign 308-309
 defined 313
 problems of 311-312
 enlargement 309
 defined 313
 enrichment 310
 defined 313
 evaluation 331
 defined 334
 full time 344
 part time 344
 permanent 344
 production 389-390
 defined 394
 rotation 309, 352
 defined 313
 satisfaction 296
 sharing 346
 temporary 344
Just-in-time manufacturing 397-398
 defined 401
 and stock rotation 415

K

Kaizen 396-397
 defined 401
 umbrella 396
Kanban 398
 defined 401
Kitemark 421, 422
Kruse and Weitzman 306

L

Labour
 as factor of production 2
 intensive 394
 defined 394
 productivity , 425
 quality 2
 turnover 324
 defined 327
Labour market 1, 5
 failure 351

 defined 357
Laissez-faire leadership 319
 defined 321
Land
 as factor of production 2
Landfill
 tax 471, 496
Late payment of commercial debts 264
Lateral
 communication 376
Law
 and business 496 (see also Legislation)
Law of multiples 405
Lead time 414
 defined 415
Leaders
 qualities of 318
Leadership 315-321
 autocratic 318-319
 defined 321
 democratic 319
 defined 321
 laissez-faire 319
 defined 321
 paternalistic 319
 defined 321
 qualities 318
 styles 318-321
 team based 319
Lean
 design 398
 defined 401
 production 396-400
 defined 401
Learning and skills councils 354
Lease 233
 defined 237
Leasehold 239
Leasing (see Lease)
Legal
 framework 3, 466
 identity 42
 monopoly 451, 504
 defined 507
Legislation
 advertising 153-154
 data protection 371
 consumer protection 501-504
 employment conditions 343-347
 equal opportunities 358-365
 health and safety 367-372
 monopolies and mergers 504-505
 restrictive trade practices 504-505
 and business activity 4
 and former state monopolies 506-507
Letters 377
Liabilities 223
 defined 228
 current 224
 defined 228
 long term 224
 defined 228

Licensing 15
LIFO 271-272
 defined 273
 and stock control 415
Limited
 companies 45
 defined 50
 profit and loss accounts 215-219
 liability 44
 defined 50
 liability partnership 45
 defined 50
 partnership 44
 defined 50
Line
 authority 285
 graph 81
 defined 84
Liquid asset 246
 defined 252
Liquidity
 defined 265
 crisis 262-263
 problems 261
 defined 265
 and uses of funds/of assets 241-242
 and profitability 261-263
Livewire 13
Loan capital 232
Loan guarantee scheme 14
Loans (see Bank loans and Loan capital)
Local authority services 53-54
Local business partnerships 13
Local government departments 54
Locke, E 312
Long list 337
 defined 341
Long run 198
 defined 202
 costs 198, 201
Long term liabilities 224
 defined 228
 and the balance sheet 236
Lorenz curve 82
 defined 84
Loss
 calculation 201
Loss leaders 141
 defined 143

M

M0 and M4 6
Magazines 377
Mail order catalogues 169
Make or buy decision 412
Management 315-321
 accounting 192
 defined 196
 by objectives 315-316
 defined 321
 and goal setting 312
 functions of 315

defined 454
control of former state 507
legal 451
legislation 451, 503-506
natural 55, 506
defined 59
pure 451
Mortgage 232
Motion study (see Work study)
Motivated 291
defined 298
Motivation theories 291-298
Motivators 296
defined 298
Multinational companies 47
Multiple shop organisations 167
Multi-media communication 379
Multi-stage sampling 97
Multiskilling 310-311
defined 313
and efficiency 427
Mutual organisations 48
defined 50

N

National Health Service 54
National Insurance contributions 16, 470
defined 16
National Minimum Wage Act 370
Nationalised Industries 55
defined 59
and privatisation 55
Natural monopolies 55, 506
defined 59
Natural rate of unemployment 479
Needs 4
defined 7
Maslow's hierarchy of 291-292
psychological 292
satisfaction of 292
self actualising 292
and the basic economic problem 67
Negative motivation 291
Net
assets 224
defined 228
book value 267
defined 273
cash flow 276
defined 281
current assets 228
defined 228
interest receivable 219
interest payable 219
migration 457
defined 460
present value 278-280
defined 281
profit 217
defined 221
Network Rail 53
New Deal 332, 354

New product development
and the product portfolio 127
New technology (see Technology)
Newspapers 377
Niche marketing 115
defined 116
Non-domestic rates (see Rates)
Non-durable goods 3
Non-excludability 52
Non-financial rewards 308-313
Non-operating income
and profit and loss account 217
Non-profit making organisations
and marketing mix 120
Non-rivalry 52
Non-verbal communication (see Written
communication)
Normal profit 215
Noticeboards 377

O

Objectives 27-34
defined 34
budgets 254
determinants of business 32-33
in the public sector 32
long term 32-33
managerial 30
SMART 27,316
defined 34
short term 32-33
and culture 32
Observation
in market research 96
Obsolete
assets 267
defined 273
Ofcom 153
Ofex 235
Offer 506
Offer for sale 231
Office of Fair Trading 505
Off-the-job training 352
Ofgas 506
Ofgem 506
Oftel 506
Ofwat 506
Ogive 81
Oligopoly 452
defined 454
On-the-job training 352
Online shopping 170
Open questions 95
Operating
lease 233
expenses (see Overheads)
profit 217
defined 221
Opportunity cost 67
defined 73
and zero based budgeting 256
Oral communication 378

Ordinary shares 232
Organisation 42
defined 50
behaviour modification 312
business 61-65
by area 63
by customer 64
by function 61-62
by process 64-65
by product or activity 62
charts 283-283
defined 289
formal 283-289
defined 41
structure 61-65
Organisational culture (see Corporate
culture)
Organic growth 404
defined 409
Orr 506
Outputs 1, 384
defined 387
Outsourcing
and efficiency 429
Overborrowing 262
Overdraft 232
Overheads 200, 216
defined 221
Overspecialisation 5
Overtime 300
Overtrading 262
defined 265
Own brands 167
defined 171
Owners 18
Ownership
forms of private 42-50

P

Packaging 160
Paging devices 378
Parallel bar chart 78
Parental Leave Directive 360
Part time job 344, 345-346
Part Time Workers Directive 346, 360
Partnership 44-45
defined 50
Act 44
deed of 44
limited 44
limited liability 45
Patent 12
defined 16
as an intangible asset 239
Pay
employer objectives for 301-302
employee objectives for 302
Payback period 276
defined 281
Payment
by results 300
defined 306